HEALTH LAW:

CASES, MATERIALS AND PROBLEMS

Abridged Sixth Edition

By

Barry R. Furrow

Professor of Law and Director, the Health Law Program,
Drexel University

Thomas L. Greaney

Chester A. Myers Professor of Law and
Director, Center for Health Law Studies,
Saint Louis University

Sandra H. Johnson

Professor Emeritus of Health Care Law and Ethics
Saint Louis University

Timothy Stoltzfus Jost

Robert L. Willett Family Professor of Law,
Washington and Lee University

Robert L. Schwartz

Henry Weihofen Professor of Law, and Professor of Pediatrics,
University of New Mexico

AMERICAN CASEBOOK SERIES®

Mat #40765887

American Casebook Series and West Group are trademarks registered in the U.S. Patent and Trademark Office.

© 2008 Thomson/West
    610 Opperman Drive
    St. Paul, MN 55123
    1–800–313–9378

Printed in the United States of America

ISBN: 978–0–314–19602–6

 *TEXT IS PRINTED ON 10% POST CONSUMER RECYCLED PAPER*

Preface

This abridged edition of the sixth edition of our Health Law casebook is new. It recognizes the increasing complicated teaching environment for health law, particularly the need for a concise health law casebook in schools other than law. The abridged edition continues to use the broad organization that health law teachers and students found so helpful in the last five editions. We have however trimmed material in the notes substantially and we have deleted some cases and sections of the primary casebook. Our goal has been to create a book better suited for schools that have curricular space for only one course, including medical schools and schools of public health.

Since we first published the first edition of our health law casebook, no part of the American landscape has changed more than the American health care system. The system has been stressed by demographic changes, buffeted by the winds of political change, and utterly transformed by social and economic developments. The formal structure of the business of health care was a small part of the subject of health law when we published our first edition; it is now the subject of entire graduate programs. The for-profit commercial sector of the health care economy sounded like a lamb twenty years ago; now it roars like a lion. Until a few years ago virtually no one attained elective office because of her position on issues related to health care; now opinion polls peg it as one of the most important issues in the 2008 election. Economic and political fortunes have been made (and lost) predicting the reactions of Americans to changes in our system for delivering health care. While the perspective that we must bring to the legal analysis of health care is far broader now than it was twenty years ago, the fundamental concerns on which that analysis is brought to bear are surprisingly unchanged. As was the case in 1987, we want to know what role the law might play in promoting the quality of health care, in organizing the delivery of health care, in assuring adequate control of the cost of health care, in promoting access to necessary health care, and in protecting the human rights of those who are provided care within the health care system.

We continue in this abridged edition to employ materials from a variety of sources. This book continues to contain the most significant and useful judicial opinions dealing with the issues of health law, drawn from the federal and state courts. The book also contains statutes, legislative history, administrative regulations, excerpts from contracts, consent forms, and a host of other kinds of materials designed to bring the subject of health law to life in the classroom. It also contains many classroom-tested problems that should be helpful in encouraging reflections on these materials.

This casebook is divided into an introduction and four major sections. Chapters 1 through 5 address ways in which the law can contribute to the promotion of the quality of health care. This part of the casebook includes coverage of governmental efforts to assure the quality of health care services, including the interaction between public and private quality initiatives, as well as analysis of medical malpractice law.

The second part of the text (chapters 6 through 9) addresses the issues of access to health care and control of health care costs. These chapters address both private and public financing mechanisms in the many varieties that have been formed and reformed over the past few years, including the Medicare and Medicaid and private health insurance. The continued evolution of managed care is examined, as is the emergence of the consumer-driven health care movement. This material also addresses legal obligations to provide medical services, and examines legal and policy issues in health care disparities.

The third part of the book (chapters 10 through 13) describes the role of the law in organizing the health care enterprise. This section of the casebook includes materials on different ways in which the business of health care delivery can be organized, materials describing the legal relationships among different players in the health care enterprise, including a chapter on tax and corporate law and another on health care fraud and government regulations of financial relationships among providers, and a clear, simple account of the application of antitrust law to health care.

Finally, the fourth major section of the text, (chapters 14 through 16) provides students with background on the role law plays in protecting the rights of patients in regard to reproductive decision making and decisions at the end of life. The casebook concludes with a brief introduction to the law of public health. All of these materials have been reviewed to assure that a wide range of perspectives leaven the authors' analysis of health law.

This abridged casebook, as with our large edition, is designed to be a teachable book. We are grateful for the many comments and helpful suggestions that health law teachers across the United States (and from elsewhere, too) have made to help us improve this new edition. We attempt to present all sides of policy issues, not to evangelize for any political, economic or social agenda of our own. It has been a splendid opportunity to work on this casebook, and we are especially pleased to have reached its twentieth anniversary. It has been a constant challenge to find a way to teach cutting edge issues influencing our health care system—at times before the courts or legislatures have given us much legal material for our casebook. Each time we have done a new edition, there have been developments that we find difficult to assess as to whether they will become more significant during the lifespan of the edition or are simply blips. It is always difficult to delete materials that required much labor and still remain quite relevant but that have been eclipsed in importance by others, and the length of each succeeding edition attests to our challenge. Finally, we don't write this casebook for our classes alone, but rather for yours as well. We enjoy teaching, and we hope that comes through to the students and teachers who use this book.

A large number of very well respected health law teachers have contributed a great deal to this and previous editions by making suggestions, reviewing problems, or encouraging our more thorough investigation of a wide range of health law subjects. We are especially grateful to Charles Baron, Eugene Basanta, David Bennahum, Robert Berenson, Kathleen Boozang, Arnold Celnicker,

Don Chalmers, Ellen Wright Clayton, Judith Daar, Dena Davis, Arthur Derse, Kelly Dineen, Ileana Dominguez-Urban, Stewart Duban, Margaret Farrell, David Frankford, Michael Gerhart, Joan McIver Gibson, Susan Goldberg, Jesse Goldner, Andrew Grubb, Art LaFrance, Diane Hoffmann, Jill Horwitz, Amy Jaeger, Eleanor Kinney, Thomasine Kushner, Pam Lambert, Theodore LeBlang, Antoinette Sedillo Lopez, Lawrence Singer, Joan Krause, Leslie Mansfield, Thomas Mayo, Maxwell Mehlman, Alan Meisel, Vicki Michel, Frances Miller, John Munich, David Orentlicher, Vernellia Randall, Ben Rich, Arnold Rosoff, Karen Rothenberg, Mark Rothstein, Sallie Sanford, Giles Scofield, Jeff Sconyers, Charity Scott, Ross Silverman, Loane Skene, George Smith, Sheila Taub, Michael Vitiello, Sidney Watson, Ellen Wertheimer, William Winslade and Susan M. Wolf for the benefit of their wisdom and experience.

We wish to thank those who provided support for our research and the preparation of the manuscript, including the Frances Lewis Law Center, the Robert L. Willett family, Carrie Snow, John Moore, Patrick Pedano, Yamini Laks, Mukta Agrawal, Maryellen Guinan, Ann Marter, Andrew Rusczek, Ann Marie Binns, Laura Spencer, Melanie Rankin, Melanie Riley, Katie Fink, Erik Lawson, Micah Jost, and Andrew Fairfield. We all have special appreciation for the exceptional work done by Mary Ann Jauer at St. Louis University, and for the tremendous publication assistance provided by Pamela Siege Herr and Louis Higgins of Thomson/Reuters. Finally, we wish to thank our deans, Roger Dennis, Jeffrey E. Lewis, Suellyn Scarnecchia, Leo Romero, and Rodney Smolla, and Department Chair Dr. James DuBois.

BARRY R. FURROW
THOMAS L. GREANEY
SANDRA H. JOHNSON
TIMOTHY S. JOST
ROBERT L. SCHWARTZ

July 2008

*

Acknowledgements

American College of Obstetrics and Gynecology Committee on Ethics, The Limits of Conscientious Refusal in Reproductive Medicine, 110 Obstetrics Genecology 1203 (2007). Reprinted with permission.

Annas, George J., A National Bill of Patients' Rights, 338 New England Journal of Medicine 695 (1998). Copyright 1998 George Annas. Reprinted with permission.

Austin, C.R., Human Embryos: Debate on Assisted Reproduction (1989). Copyright 1989, Oxford University Press. Reprinted by permission of Oxford University Press.

Battin, Margaret, The Least Worst Death, 13 Hastings Center Report (2) 13 (April 1983). Copyright 1983, The Hastings Center. Reprinted with permission of the Hastings Center. Reprinted with permission of the Hastings Center and the author.

Bernat, James, Charles Culver and Bernard Gert, Defining Death in Theory and Practice, 12 Hastings Center Report (1) 5 (February 1982). Copyright 1982, the Hastings Center. Reprinted with permission.

Capron, Alexander Morgan and Leon Kass, A Statutory Definition of the Standards for Determining Human Death: As Appraisal and a Proposal, 121 U. Pa. L. Rev. 87 (1972). Copyright 1972, the University of Pennsylvania Law Review. Reprinted with permission.

Council on Ethical and Judicial Affairs, American Medical Association, Current Opinion 2.035, Futility. Reprinted with permission of the American Medical Association.

Council on Ethical and Judicial Affairs, American Medical Association, Policy E-2.151, Frozen Pre-Embryos. Reprinted with permission of American Medical Association.

Council on Ethical and Judicial Affairs, The Use of Anencephalic Neonates as Organ Donors, 273 JAMA 1614 (1995). Copyright 1995, American Medical Association. All rights reserved. Reprinted with permission of American Medical Association.

Donabedian, Avedis, The Definition of Quality and Approaches to its Assessment, 1st ed., 4-6, 7, 13, 14, 27, 79-84, 102, 119 (Health Administration Press, Ann Arbor, MI, 1980). Reprinted from Avedis Donabedian, The Definition of Quality and Approaches to its Assessment, in Explorations in Quality Assessment and Monitoring, Volume 1. Copyright 1980. Reprinted with permission.

Ethics Committee of the American Society for Reproductive Medicine, Informing Offspring of Their Conception by Gamete Donation, 81 Fertilization and Sterilization 527 (2004). Reprinted with permission from Elsevier.

Fletcher, Joseph, Indicators of Humanhood, 2 Hastings Center Report (5) 1 (November 1972). Copyright 1972, the Hastings Center. Reprinted with permission of the Hastings Center.

Froedtert Hospital—Medical College of Wisconsin, Futility Policy, revised 2007. Reprinted with permission.

Gostin, Lawrence O., Public Health Law: Power, Duty, Restraint. Copyright 2000, University of California Press. Reprinted with permission of the University of California Press.

Hacker, Jacob S., and Theodore R. Marmor, How Not to Think About "Managed Care," 32 University of Michigan Journal of Law Reform 661 (1999). Copyright University of Michigan Journal of Law Reform. Used with permission.

Hager, Christie, The Massachusetts Health Care Plan. Copyright 2008, Christie Hager. Used with permission.

Hyman, David A., Regulating Managed Care: What's Wrong with a Patient Bill of Rights, 73 Southern California Law Review 221 (2000). Copyright 2000, Southern California Law Review. Reprinted with permission.

Jost, Timothy Stoltzfus, Why Can't We Do What They Do? National Health Reform Abroad, 32 Journal of Law, Medicine, and Ethics 432 (2004). Copyright 2004. Reprinted with permission of the American Society of Law, Medicine and Ethics.

Jost, Timothy S, and Mark A. Hall, The Role of State Regulation in Consumer-Driven Health Care, 31 American Journal of Law and Medicine 395 (2005). Copyright 2005. Reprinted with permission of the American Society of Law, Medicine and Ethics.

Leape, Lucian L., Error in Medicine, 272 JAMA 1851 (1994). Copyright 1994, American Medical Association. Reprinted with permission of the American Medical Association.

Levy, Barry, Twenty-First Century Challenges for Law and Public Health, 32 Ind. L. Rev. 1149 (1999). Copyright 1999, Indiana Law Review. Reprinted with permission of the Indiana Law Review.

Morreim, E Haavi, Redefining Quality by Reassigning Responsibility, 20 American Journal of Law and Medicine 79-104 (1994). Reprinted with permission of the American Society of Law, Medicine, and Ethics and Boston University School of Law.

National Conference of Commissioners on Uniform State Laws, Uniform Anatomical Gift Act. Copyright 1977, National Conference of Commissioners on Uniform State Laws. Reprinted with permission of National Conference of Commissioners on Uniform State Laws.

National Conference of Commissioners on Uniform State Laws, Uniform Determination Death Act. Copyright 1980, National Conference of Commissioners on Uniform State Laws. Reprinted with permission of National Conference of Commissioners on Uniform State Laws.

National Conference of Commissioners of Uniform State Laws, Uniform Health-Care Decisions Act. Copyright 1994, National Conference of Commissioners on Uniform State Laws. Reprinted with permission of National Conference of Commissioners on Uniform State Laws.

National Conference of Commissioners on Uniform State Laws, Uniform Parentage Act. Copyright 1973, 2000 and 2002, National Conference of Commissions on Uniform State Laws. Reprinted with permission of National Conference of Commissioners on Uniform State Laws.

National Conference of Commissioners on Uniform State Laws, Uniform Probate Code. Copyright, National Conference of Commissioners on Uniform State Laws. Reprinted with permission of National Conference of Commissioners on Uniform State Laws.

Neuman, Patricia, Medicare Advantage: Key Issues and Implications for Beneficiaries, (#7664), The Henry J. Kaiser Family Foundation (June 2007). This information was reprinted with permission from the Henry J. Kaiser Family Foundation. The Kaiser Family Foundation, based in Menlo Park, California, is a nonprofit, private operating foundation focusing on the major health care issues facing the nation and is not associated with Kaiser Permanente or Kaiser Industries.

Report of the Ad Hoc Committee of the Harvard Medical School to Examine the Definition of Brain Death: A Definition of Irreversible Coma, 205 JAMA 85 (August 1968). Copyright 1968, American Medical Association. Reprinted with permission of the American Medical Association.

Report of the Committee of Inquiry into Human Fertilisation and Embryology (Cmnd 9314) (1984). Copyright 1984, Her Majesty's Stationery Office. Crown copyright is produced with the permission of the Controller of Her Majesty's Stationery Office.

Roth, Loren, Alan Meisel and Charles Lidz, Tests of Competency to Consent to Treatment, 134 Am. J. Psychiatry 279 (1977). Copyright 1977. Reprinted with permission of the American Psychiatric Association.

Stone, Deborah, The Struggle for the Soul of Health Insurance, 18 Journal of Health Politics, Policy and Law 287 (1993), copyright Duke University Press, 1993. Reprinted with permission.

Ulrich, Lawrence P., Reproductive Rights of Genetic Disease, in J. Humber and R. Almeder, eds., Biomedical Ethics and the law. Copyright 1986. Reprinted with permission.

Veatch, Robert, Correspondence—What it Means to be Dead, 12 Hastings Center Report (5) 45 (October 1982). Copyright 1982, the Hastings Center. Reprinted with permission of the Hastings Center.

Wolf, Susan M., Gender, Feminism and Death: Physician Assisted Suicide and Euthanasia, in S.M. Wolf, ed., Feminism and Bioethics: Beyond Reproduction (1996). Copyright 1996, Oxford University Press. Reprinted by permission of Susan M. Wolf and Oxford University Press.

*

Summary of Contents

———

*

Table of Contents

Table of Cases

The principal cases are in bold type. Cases cited or discussed in the text are roman type. References are to pages. Cases cited in principal cases and within other quoted materials are not included.

*

HEALTH LAW:

CASES, MATERIALS AND PROBLEMS

Abridged Sixth Edition

*

Chapter 1

QUALITY CONTROL REGULATION: LICENSING OF HEALTH CARE PROFESSIONALS

The overarching concerns treated throughout this casebook—quality, cost, access, and choice—are at stake in the debate over whether the licensure and disciplinary system produces overall negative or positive outcomes for patients. Although this debate over professional licensure is an old one, it has been reenergized by changes in the health care system. Among these are a strong movement for alternative or complementary medicine; the growth of non-physician licensed health care professions; and fundamental changes in medical practice itself, including, for example, the movement to increase access to controlled substances for pain relief or the movement back toward midwifery for assistance in childbirth.

Perhaps the most significant change that challenges the conventional operation of state licensure and discipline is the development of more robust data banks formed from electronic patient medical records, pharmacy records, payment records, and other electronic health services information. The traditional rationale for health care quality regulation is the imperfect information available to consumers to make their own risk-benefit balance in selecting provider or treatment as well as limitations on the capacity of patients to evaluate the information that is available. As data becomes cheaper and more accessible—although not equally accessible across all patient populations—health care quality regulation will be challenged:

> One possible answer is that the health information revolution should prompt us to regulate less. A patient with access to information about individual providers' quality of care, for example, would have less need for state medical boards' assistance in rooting out poor quality providers.... A second possible answer is that the health information revolution should prompt us to regulate more. Information imperfections will persist forever, so regulation can at least potentially benefit some patients. Because information about quality is an input into the regulation process, and technological innovation has reduced the cost of such information, we can regulate more cheaply than we once could. Kristin Madison, Regulating Health Care Quality in an Information Age, 40 U.C. Davis L.Rev. 1577 (2007).

1

Professor Madison offers a third alternative to this either-or option. She argues that the less-or-more dichotomy doesn't entirely capture the reorientation of health care regulation that better information technology makes possible. She categorizes regulatory responses into three types: market-restricting interventions such as restrictive licensure; market-facilitating responses such as the mandates for report cards and increased disclosure of information (including disciplinary actions or malpractice settlements or patient satisfaction surveys or outcomes) to the public; and market-channeling efforts (such as certification) which influence provider behavior without restrictive governmental control mandates. See also, Timothy S. Jost, Oversight of the Quality of Medical Care: Regulation, Management or the Market, 37 Ariz. L. Rev. 825 (1995); William M. Sage, Regulating Through Information: Disclosure Laws and American Healthcare, 99 Colum. L. Rev. 1701 (1999).

A second focus in the critique of the operation of licensure boards goes to the structure of these boards. State law controls licensure of health care professionals under the state's police power. Licensing statutes govern entry into the licensed professions and disciplinary actions against licensed health care professionals. Licensure also regulates the scope of health care services that licensed professionals may provide and prohibits unlicensed persons from providing services reserved for the licensed professions. These statutes are implemented by boards that operate as state agencies but which generally are dominated by members of the licensed profession. Licensure in the U.S., thus, is often described as a system of professional self-regulation, even though the boards act as state agencies; usually include lay members; are governed by procedures and standards set in the state's licensing statute and administrative procedures act; and are subject to judicial review in both their adjudicatory and rulemaking decisions. Professional participation in licensure may further the public interest by bringing expertise to the evaluation of professionals' competency and behavior. Professional domination of licensure has been strongly criticized, however, as serving the interests of the professions at the expense of their competitors and of the public.

I. DISCIPLINE

IN RE WILLIAMS

Supreme Court of Ohio, 1991.
60 Ohio St.3d 85, 573 N.E.2d 638.

SYLLABUS BY THE COURT

* * *

... Between 1983 and 1986, Dr. Williams prescribed Biphetamine or Obetrol for fifty patients as part of a weight control treatment regimen. [Both drugs are controlled substances.]

On November 17, 1986, appellant, the Ohio State Medical Board ("board"), promulgated Ohio Adm.Code 4731–11–03(B), which prohibited the use of [drugs such as Biphetamine and Obetrol] for purposes of weight control. Dr. Williams ceased prescribing Biphetamine and Obetrol for weight control upon becoming aware of the rule.

By letter dated March 12, 1987, the board charged Dr. Williams with violating R.C. 4731.22(B)[2] by prescribing these stimulants without "reasonable care," and thereby failing to conform to minimal standards of medical practice. The crux of the board's charge was that Dr. Williams had departed from accepted standards of care by using these drugs as a long-term, rather than a short-term, treatment.

A hearing was held before a board examiner. The parties stipulated to the accuracy of the medical records of the patients in question, which detailed the use of Biphetamine and Obetrol for periods ranging from nearly seven months to several years. The board also introduced into evidence the Physician's Desk Reference entries for Biphetamine and Obetrol, which recommend that these drugs be used for only "a few weeks" in the treatment of obesity. The board presented no testimony or other evidence of the applicable standard of care.

Dr. Williams presented expert testimony from Dr. John P. Morgan, the director of the pharmacology program at the City University of New York Medical School, and Dr. Eljorn Don Nelson, an associate professor of clinical pharmacology at the University of Cincinnati College of Medicine. These experts stated that there are two schools of thought in the medical community concerning the use of stimulants for weight control. The so-called "majority" view holds that stimulants should only be used for short periods, if at all, in weight control programs. The "minority" view holds that the long-term use of stimulants is proper in the context of a supervised physician-patient relationship. Both experts testified that, though they themselves supported the "majority" view, Dr. Williams's application of the "minority" protocol was not substandard medical practice.

The hearing examiner found that Dr. Williams's practices violated R.C. 4731.22(B). The examiner recommended subjecting Dr. Williams to a three-year monitored probation period. The board modified the penalty, imposing a one-year suspension of Dr. Williams's license followed by a five-year probationary period, during which he would be unable to prescribe or dispense controlled substances.

Dr. Williams appealed to the Court of Common Pleas of Franklin County pursuant to R.C. 119.12. The court found that the board's order was ". . . not supported by reliable, probative and substantial evidence and . . . [was] not in accordance with law." The court of appeals affirmed.

HERBERT R. BROWN, JUSTICE.

In an appeal from an administrative agency, a reviewing court is bound to uphold the agency's order if it is ". . . supported by reliable, probative, and substantial evidence and is in accordance with law. . . ."[ ]. In the instant

---

2. R.C. 4731.22(B) provides in pertinent part:

"The board, pursuant to an adjudicatory hearing. . . . shall, to the extent permitted by law,. . . . [discipline] the holder of a certificate [to practice medicine] for one or more of the following reasons:

. . . .

"(2) Failure to use reasonable care, discrimination in the administration of drugs, or

failure to employ acceptable scientific methods in the selection of drugs or other modalities for treatment of disease;

"(3) Selling, prescribing, giving away, or administering drugs for other than legal and legitimate therapeutic purposes. . . .

. . . .

"(6) A departure from, or the failure to conform to, minimal standards of care. . . . [.]"

case, we must determine if the common pleas court erred by finding that the board's order was not supported by sufficient evidence. For the reasons, which follow, we conclude that it did not and affirm the judgment of the court below.

In its arguments to this court, the board contends that Arlen v. Ohio State Medical Bd. (1980), 61 Ohio St.2d 168, 15 O.O.3d 190, 399 N.E.2d 1251, is dispositive. In *Arlen*, the physician was disciplined because he had written prescriptions for controlled substances to a person who the physician knew was redistributing the drugs to others, a practice prohibited by R.C. 3719.06(A). The physician appealed on the ground that the board failed to present expert testimony that such prescribing practices fell below a reasonable standard of care.

We held that the board is not required in every case to present expert testimony on the acceptable standard of medical practice before it can find that a physician's conduct falls below this standard. We noted that the usual purpose of expert testimony is to assist the trier of facts in understanding "issues that require scientific or specialized knowledge or experience beyond the scope of common occurrences...."[ ] The board was then made up of ten (now twelve) persons, eight of whom are licensed physicians. [ ] Thus, a majority of board members are themselves experts in the medical field who already possess the specialized knowledge needed to determine the acceptable standard of general medical practice.

While the board need not, in every case, present expert testimony to support a charge against an accused physician, the charge must be supported by some reliable, probative and substantial evidence. It is here that the case against Dr. Williams fails, as it is very different from *Arlen*.

Arlen involved a physician who dispensed controlled substances in a manner that not only fell below the acceptable standard of medical practice, but also violated the applicable statute governing prescription and dispensing of these drugs. In contrast, Dr. Williams dispensed controlled substances in what was, at the time, a legally permitted manner, albeit one which was disfavored by many in the medical community. The only evidence in the record on this issue was the testimony of Dr. Williams's expert witnesses that his use of controlled substances in weight control programs did not fall below the acceptable standard of medical practice. While the board has broad discretion to resolve evidentiary conflicts [ ] and determine the weight to be given expert testimony [ ], it cannot convert its own disagreement with an expert's opinion into affirmative evidence of a contrary proposition where the issue is one on which medical experts are divided and there is no statute or rule governing the situation.

It should be noted, however, that where the General Assembly has prohibited a particular medical practice by statute, or where the board has done so through its rulemaking authority, the existence of a body of expert opinion supporting that practice would not excuse a violation. Thus, if Dr. Williams had continued to prescribe Biphetamine or Obetrol for weight control after the promulgation of Ohio Adm.Code 4731–11–03(B), this would be a violation of R.C. 4731.22(B)(3), and the existence of the "minority" view supporting the use of these substances for weight control would provide him no defense. Under those facts, *Arlen* would be dispositive. Here, however, there is insufficient evidence, expert or otherwise, to support the charges against Dr. Williams. Were the board's decision to be affirmed on the facts in this record, it would mean that a doctor would have no access to meaningful review of the board's decision. The board, though a majority of its members have special knowledge, is not entitled to exercise such unbridled discretion.

WRIGHT, JUSTICE, dissenting.

The message we send to the medical community's regulators with today's decision is one, I daresay, we would never countenance for their counterparts in the legal community. We are telling those charged with policing the medical profession that their expertise as to what constitutes the acceptable standard of medical practice is not enough to overcome the assertion that challenged conduct does not violate a state statute. * * *

HOOVER v. THE AGENCY FOR HEALTH CARE ADMINISTRATION

District Court of Appeal of Florida, 1996.
676 So.2d 1380.

JORGENSON, JUDGE.

Dr. Katherine Anne Hoover, a board-certified physician in internal medicine, appeals a final order of the Board of Medicine penalizing her and restricting her license to practice medicine in the State of Florida. We reverse because the board has once again engaged in the uniformly rejected practice of overzealously supplanting a hearing officer's valid findings of fact regarding a doctor's prescription practices with its own opinion in a case founded on a woefully inadequate quantum of evidence.

In March 1994, the Department of Business and Professional Regulation (predecessor in these proceedings to the Agency for Health Care Administration) filed an administrative complaint alleging that Dr. Hoover (1) inappropriately and excessively prescribed various . . . controlled substances to seven of her patients and (2) provided care of those patients that fell below that level of care, skill, and treatment which is recognized by a reasonably prudent similar physician as being acceptable under similar conditions and circumstances; in violation of sections 458.331(1)(q) and (t), Florida Statutes, respectively. All seven of the patients had been treated by Dr. Hoover for intractable pain arising from various non-cancerous diseases or ailments.

Dr. Hoover disputed the allegations of the administrative complaint and requested a formal hearing. * * *

The agency presented the testimony of two physicians as experts. Neither had examined any of the patients or their medical records. The sole basis for the opinions of the agency physicians was computer printouts from pharmacies in Key West where the doctor's patients had filled their prescriptions. These printouts indicated only the quantity of each drug filled for each patient, occasionally referring to a simplified diagnosis. Both of these physicians practiced internal medicine and neither specialized in the care of chronic pain. In fact, both doctors testified that they did not treat but referred their chronic pain patients to pain management clinics. The hearing officer found that this was a common practice among physicians—perhaps to avoid prosecutions like this case.[5] Both doctors "candidly testified that without being

_____
5. Referral to a pain management clinic was not an option for Dr. Hoover's indigent Key West resident patients.

provided with copies of the medical records for those patients they could not evaluate Respondent's diagnoses or what alternative modalities were attempted or what testing was done to support the use of the medication chosen by Respondent to treat those patients." Despite this paucity of evidence, lack of familiarity, and seeming lack of expertise, the agency's physicians testified at the hearing that the doctor had prescribed excessive, perhaps lethal amounts of narcotics, and had practiced below the standard of care.

Dr. Hoover testified in great detail concerning the condition of each of the patients, her diagnoses and courses of treatment, alternatives attempted, the patients' need for medication, the uniformly improved function of the patients with the amount of medication prescribed, and her frequency of writing prescriptions to allow her close monitoring of the patients. She presented corroborating physician testimony regarding the appropriateness of the particular medications and the amounts prescribed and her office-setting response to the patients' requests for relief from intractable pain.

Following post-hearing submissions, the hearing officer issued her recommended order finding that the agency had failed to meet its burden of proof on all charges. The hearing officer concluded, for instance, "Petitioner failed to provide its experts with adequate information to show the necessary similar conditions and circumstances upon which they could render opinions that showed clearly and convincingly that Respondent failed to meet the standard of care required of her in her treatment of the patients in question."

The agency filed exceptions to the recommended findings of fact and conclusions of law as to five of the seven patients. The board of medicine accepted all the agency's exceptions, amended the findings of fact in accordance with the agency's suggestions, and found the doctor in violation of sections 458.331(1)(q) and (t), Florida Statutes. The board imposed the penalty recommended by the agency: a reprimand, a $4,000 administrative fine, continuing medical education on prescribing abusable drugs, and two years probation. This appeal follows.

For each of the five patients, the hearing officer found the prescribing practices of Doctor Hoover to be appropriate. This was based upon (1) the doctor's testimony regarding the specific care given, (2) the corroborating testimony of her physician witness, and (3) the fact that the doctor's prescriptions did not exceed the federal guidelines for treatment of intractable pain in cancer patients, though none of the five patients were diagnosed as suffering from cancer.

The board rejected these findings as not based on competent substantial evidence. As particular reasons, the board adopted the arguments of the agency's exceptions to the recommended order that (1) the hearing officer's findings were erroneously based on irrelevant federal guidelines, and (2) the agency's physicians had testified that the doctor's prescription pattern was below the standard of care and outside the practice of medicine. * * *

First, the board mischaracterizes the hearing officer's reference to the federal guidelines. The board reasoned in its final order that "[t]he record reflects that the federal guidelines relied upon by the Hearing Officer for this finding were designed for cancer patients and [the five patients at issue were] not being treated for cancer." It is true, as the hearing officer noted,

"Respondent presented expert evidence that there is a set of guidelines which have been issued for the use of Schedule II controlled substances to treat intractable pain and that although those guidelines were established to guide physicians in treating cancer patients, those are the only guidelines available at this time. Utilizing those guidelines, because they exist, the amount of medication prescribed by Respondent to the patients in question was not excessive or inappropriate."

In so finding, however, the hearing officer did not, as the board suggests, rely solely upon the federal guidelines in its ruling that the doctor's prescribing practices were not excessive. Rather, the federal guidelines merely buttressed fact findings that were independently supported by the hearing officer's determination of the persuasiveness and credibility of the physician witnesses on each side. For example, though he admitted he had not even reviewed the federal guidelines, one of the agency physicians asserted that the amounts prescribed constituted a "tremendous number of pills" and that the doses involved would be lethal. That Dr. Hoover's prescriptions fell within the guidelines for chronic-pained cancer patients may properly be considered to refute this assertion. Such a use of the federal guidelines was relevant and reasonable.

Second, Dr. Hoover testified in great detail concerning her treatment of each patient, the patient's progress under the medication she prescribed, and that the treatment was within the standard of care and practice of medicine. The hearing officer, as arbiter of credibility, was entitled to believe what the doctor and her physician expert opined. [ ] The agency's witnesses' ultimate conclusions do not strip the hearing officer's reliance upon Dr. Hoover of its competence and substantiality. The hearing officer was entitled to give Dr. Hoover's testimony greater weight than that of the agency's witnesses, who did not examine these patients or regularly engage in the treatment of intractable pain.

* * *

Reversed.

Note: Federal Regulation of Prescribing Practices

Physician prescribing is also constricted by the Food and Drug Administration and the Drug Enforcement Administration, two powerful federal agencies. Congress did not intend that either the FDA or the DEA would engage in the regulation of the *legitimate* practice of medicine. The boundary between the agencies' statutory authority and the restraint on their regulation of medical practice is blurry, however, both because of inherent problems in drawing those boundaries as well as because of conflicts over appropriate health policy. See Lars Noah, Ambivalent Commitments to Federalism in Controlling the Practice of Medicine, 53 U. Kan. L. Rev. 149 (2004).

The FDA has the authority to approve and monitor the safety of drugs and devices; and this certainly makes the FDA an important gatekeeper of access to drugs. Once a drug is approved for prescribing, however, the FDA does not have the authority to restrict physicians in their prescribing of the drug for particular purposes. Thus, once a drug is approved for a particular purpose (e.g., for the treatment of a particular sort of cancer), a physician may prescribe the drug for other purposes (e.g., for the treatment of another type of cancer). Prescribing drugs for a different purpose, in a higher or lower dose, or for a different population (e.g., children) than those for which the FDA approved the medication is called "off-label" prescribing. Off-label prescribing is common and necessary in the practice of medicine and may be the standard of care in particular circumstances, although such prescribing raises issues of medical judgment, evidence-based medicine, and the relations between pharmaceutical firms and prescribing physicians. See, e.g., Sandra H. Johnson, Polluting Medical Judgment? False Assumptions in the Pursuit of False Claims Regarding Off-Label Prescribing, 9 Minn. J. L. Sci. Tech. 61 (2008).

The DEA more directly regulates the individual physician's prescribing practices through its authority under the Controlled Substances Act. 21 U.S.C. § 801. Under the CSA, the federal government governs the production and distribution of drugs that have the potential for abuse or addiction. Such drugs are categorized as controlled substances and placed on a "schedule" that rates a drug by its abuse potential from Schedule V (the lowest potential) to Schedules I and II (the highest potential). Schedule I drugs, including heroin and marijuana, are those that are believed to have a very high potential for abuse and no therapeutic benefit. Doctors may not prescribe Schedule I drugs. Schedule II medications have known therapeutic value and are available for prescribing.

Doctors must have a permit issued by the DEA to prescribe drugs on Schedules II through V. The DEA may revoke a permit or pursue criminal action against physicians whose prescription or distribution of these drugs falls outside of the DEA's view of legitimate medical practice. In recent years, DEA policies have conflicted directly with state health policy on several fronts.

One of the areas in dispute is the legalization of marijuana for medical use. At least eight states have enacted legislation to allow physicians or patients access to marijuana for the treatment of medical conditions. See, e.g., Cal. Health & Safety Code § 11362.5. The federal government has actively opposed such efforts by aggressively enforcing federal prohibitions under the CSA. In United States v. Oakland Cannabis Buyers' Cooperative, 532 U.S. 483, 121 S.Ct. 1711, 149 L.Ed.2d 722 (2001), the Supreme Court held that the CSA did not contain an implied "medical necessity" defense that would prevent the DEA from enforcing the prohibition on prescribing or using marijuana for medical purposes. Advocates then moved to a Constitutional challenge to the CSA. In Gonzales v. Raich, 545 U.S. 1, 125 S.Ct. 2195, 162 L.Ed.2d 1 (2005), the Supreme Court rejected the argument that the CSA exceeded the federal government's authority under the Commerce Clause. During the course of the litigation over federal authority in regard to marijuana, however, the Ninth Circuit held that physicians had a First Amendment right to discuss medical marijuana with their patients in the face of federal threats to prosecute doctors who did so. Conant v. Walters, 309 F.3d 629 (9th Cir. 2002), *cert. denied,* 540 U.S. 946, 124 S.Ct. 387, 157 L.Ed.2d 276 (2003).

Doctors treating patients in pain also confront an area of conflict between state and federal drug policy. At the time of the *Hoover* case, there was strong evidence that medical boards had not adjusted their standards to reflect medical evidence that supported the use of opioids for treatment over the long term and in higher doses than had been customary. In an attempt to balance legal risks, nearly half of the states enacted legislation generally referred to as "intractable pain treatment acts" which limit state agencies from taking action against physicians in certain circumstances. The Federation of State Medical Boards also adopted a model policy that specifically recognizes that opioids are essential to the treatment of pain and that state medical boards should be equally concerned about the neglect of pain as they are about prescribing abuse. FSMB, Model Policy for the Use of Controlled Substances for the Treatment of Pain (2004).

The DEA initially followed the pattern established in the states, but in 2004, the agency withdrew its support, signaling an enforcement policy that departed from that developed by the FSMB. The National Association of Attorneys General expressed concern that as state medical boards took steps to ensure access to pain treatment, the DEA was moving to criminalize physician prescribing, commenting that "the state and federal policies are diverging with respect to the relative emphasis on ensuring the availability of prescription pain medications to those who need them." Available at http://www.naag.org/news/pdf/so-20050119-prescription-pain-med.pdf. See Diane Hoffmann, Legitimate Prosecution or Unnecessary Persecution? The Investigation, Arrest, and Prosecution of Physicians for Opioid Prescribing, 1 St. L. U. J. Health L. & Pol'y ___ (2008); Symposium, Legal and Institutional Constraints on Effective Pain Relief, 24 J. L. Med. & Ethics (1997); Symposium, Legal and Regulatory Issues in Pain Management, 26 J. L. Med. & Ethics (1998); Symposium, Pain Management in the Emergency Department: Current Landscape and Agenda for Research, 33 J. L. Med. & Ethics (2005).

Notes and Questions

1. When the literature on health care regulation references "information failure" as a justification for licensure and discipline, it usually refers to the lack of information available to the patient or the limited capacity of the patient to use available information. Is that the only type of information problem we have in these first two cases? What evidence-based standards existed in the *Hoover* case, if any? Did access to increased health data (e.g., the computerized pharmacy records of her prescriptions) enhance or detract from regulatory decision making?

2. The Ohio State Medical Board promulgated an administrative rule, cited in *Williams*, requiring that physicians meet the majority standard of practice regarding the prescription of controlled substances. Should licensure boards establish standards of practice or practice guidelines that prefer one approach over another; or should they simply recognize the full range of medical practices, including minority views? Would your answer depend on whether the board was acting in a rulemaking or in an adjudicatory role? Do *Hoover* and *Williams* present special challenges because the medications may have a risk of use or diversion for nontherapeutic uses?

3. The rationale for physicians' dominance of the membership of state medical boards is that practitioners of the regulated profession are in the best position to judge the practices of their peers. What, then, is at the heart of the dispute over expert testimony in *Williams*? On what basis did the Florida court reject the testimony of the agency's experts in *Hoover*?

4. In 2006, 2,916 serious disciplinary actions were taken by state medical boards against physicians, with 0.318% of physicians being disciplined. States

varied widely in the rates of discipline. For a state-by-state ranking, see The Public Citizen, Ranking of State Medical Boards' Serious Disciplinary Actions, 2004–2006 available at www.citizen.org/publications. Is 0.318% of physicians too many or too few? How would you measure whether the number of disciplinary actions in your state was too many, too few, or just right? A study of disciplinary actions levied between 1994 and 2002 concludes that somewhere between 25% and 30% of actions were taken for incompetence or negligence or other quality concerns, but that it is hard to analyze the data accurately. Darren Grant & Kelly C. Alfred, Sanctions and Recidivism: An Evaluation of Physician Discipline by State Medical Boards, 32 J. Health Pol. Pol'y & L. 867 (2007). This study also found a high repeat rate among physicians disciplined. Of those physicians receiving a "medium or severe" sanction in one period (1994–1998), 20% were sanctioned at least once again in the second period (1999–2004).

5. If the boards must set priorities due to limited resources, what should those priorities be? Should they affirmatively seek outcomes data on individual physicians from hospitals and medical practice organizations and make it a priority to pursue doctors with poorer outcomes? How would the board's funding levels and staffing configuration influence its effectiveness in relation to this priority? For an excellent study of the operation of medical boards, see Randall R. Bovbjerg, et al., State Discipline of Physicians: Assessing State Medical Boards through Case Studies, U.S. Dept. of Health and Human Services (2006).

6. Following the lead of Massachusetts, most states have established publicly accessible web sites where they post physician profiles. The Massachusetts site posts background information on the physician (such as education, specialties, insurance plans) as well as malpractice claims paid, hospital credentialing actions, criminal convictions, and board disciplinary actions. Mass. Bd. of Reg. in Med., On–Line Physician Profile Site, http://profiles.massmedboard.org Should these sites expand to include complaints filed with the medical board? Malpractice suits filed? Deselection by health plans? If an open book on physicians is created, at what point could it replace the disciplinary system?

7. Congress established the National Practitioner Data Bank (NPDB) in part to create an effective system for preventing doctors with disciplinary history in one state from moving to another and practicing until detected, if ever. 42 U.S.C. §§ 11101–11152. State disciplinary and licensure boards are required to report certain disciplinary actions against physicians. Hospitals and other entities engaging in peer review processes are required to report adverse actions as well. Licensure boards have access to the Data Bank to check on licensees, and hospitals must check the Data Bank for physicians applying for staff privileges and periodically for physicians who hold staff privileges. The general public is not allowed access to the information in the Data Bank although there have been several proposals for allowing increased access.

8. The term telemedicine encompasses a wide range of activities—including online physician consultations with specialists, review of imaging by offsite radiologists, and continuing contact with a physician's patients through e-mail. These activities have generated volumes examining liability issues, the jurisdiction of dozens of regulatory bodies, credentialing, contract, and intellectual property issues, among other legal questions. See generally Symposium, E–Health: Perspective and Promise, 46 St. Louis U.L.J. 1 (2002); Archie A. Alexander, American Diagnostic Radiology Moves Offshore: Is this Field Riding the "Internet Wave" into a Regulatory Abyss?, 20 J. L. & Health 199 (2007). Telemedicine is oblivious to state boundaries. Medical licensure, however, is controlled by each state individually; and physicians, with few exceptions, must hold a license in each state

in which they practice. If the only contact between patient and doctor is via the Internet, has the doctor gone to the "out-of-state" patient or has the patient "come" to the doctor? Many states have adopted legislation specifically to regulate the practice of telemedicine. The state of Indiana, for example, permits physicians outside of Indiana to provide consultation services to Indiana physicians without any regulatory permit but otherwise requires an Indiana medical license for any physician who is "[p]roviding diagnostic or treatment services to a person in Indiana when [those services] are transmitted through electronic communications; and are on a regular, routine and non-episodic basis. . . ." Ind. Code Ann. § 25–22.5–1–1.1(a)(4). States are particularly concerned about Internet prescribing for controlled substances. A California statute, for example, provides for civil penalties of $25,000 per occurrence for prescribing over the Internet without a good faith physical exam. Cal. Bus. & Prof. Code § 2242.1.

Problem: Three Strikes and You're Out?

Medical boards report that disciplinary actions for substandard care or incompetency are the most difficult in terms of requirements of time, expert witnesses, legal representation, and expense. Although some studies point out the vagaries of the malpractice litigation system, studies are consistent on one point: the filing of a malpractice claim against a physician, even if no payment is made on the claim, is predictive of future malpractice claims. See, e.g., Randall R. Bovbjerg & Kenneth R. Petronis, The Relationship Between Physicians' Malpractice Claims History and Later Claims: Does the Past Predict the Future? 272 JAMA 1421(1994); Grant & Alfred, supra, note 4.

Some states are beginning to integrate malpractice actions into their disciplinary processes. Almost all states require that liability carriers report claims paid to the board, and some states require reporting of claims filed. State medical boards can access the NPDB, where 70% of the reports are of malpractice payouts. A study by Public Citizen, however, found that only 33% of doctors who had paid out on ten or more malpractice claims were disciplined in any way by their state boards. Public Citizen, The Great Medical Malpractice Hoax: NPDB Data Continue to Show Medical Liability System Produces Rational Outcomes, Jan. 2007, available at http://www.citizen.org/documents/NPDBReport_Final.pdf. State boards report that they received "far too many reports of malpractice payouts to investigate them all," and some boards don't even list these payouts as "complaints" against the defendant licensee. Randall R. Bovbjerg, et al., supra, note 5.

Assume that your state's licensure statute provides only that disciplinary action may be taken when a physician has engaged in:

> Any conduct or practice which is or might be harmful or dangerous to the mental or physical health of a patient or the public; or incompetency, gross negligence or repeated negligence in the performance of the functions or duties of any profession licensed or regulated by this chapter. For the purposes of this subdivision, "repeated negligence" means the failure, on more than one occasion, to use that degree of skill and learning ordinarily used under the same or similar circumstances by the member of the applicant's or licensee's profession.

Administrative agencies, such as state medical boards, have limited authority. One significant limitation is that an agency has only that authority delegated to it by the legislature in its enabling statute. Thus, any rulemaking by the agency must fall within its statutory authority. Does the medical board in this case have the authority to issue a rule or adopt a policy that it will sanction a doctor with final judgments of malpractice in three or more cases? A doctor with ten or more malpractice claims made? Should they do so; or should they hold a hearing to determine whether the doctor is incompetent or negligent?

II.   COMPLEMENTARY AND ALTERNATIVE MEDICINE (CAM)

CAM is a group of diverse medical and health care systems, practices, and products that are not presently considered to be part of conventional medicine as practiced by holders of M.D. or D.O. degrees and by their allied health practitioners. ... The list of what is considered to be CAM changes continually, as those therapies that are proven to be safe and effective become adopted into conventional health care and as new approaches to health care emerge.

CAM practices [fall] into four domains: Whole medical systems [including] homeopathy, naturopathy, Chinese medicine, and ayurveda ...; Mind-body medicine [including] meditation, prayer, mental healing, and therapies that use ... art, music, or dance ...; Biologically based practices [that] use substances found in nature, such as herbs, foods, and vitamins ...; Energy medicine [including] biofield therapies [such as] qi gong, reiki, and therapeutic touch ... and bioelectromagnetic-based therapies [such as] pulsed fields, magnetic fields, or alternating-current or direct-current fields.

"What is CAM?" National Institutes of Health, National Center for Complementary and Alternative Medicine (NCCAM), available at http://nccam.nih. gov/health/whatiscam/. See also, John Lunstroth, Voluntary Self–Regulation of Complementary and Alternative Medicine Practitioners, 70 Alb. L. Rev. 209 (2006); Michael H. Cohen, Complementary and Alternative Medicine: Legal Boundaries and Regulatory Perspectives (1998).

State professional licensure systems become involved in CAM in two ways. First, licensed doctors (or nurses, dentists, and so on) may utilize CAM therapies, integrating them within conventional medicine. This will attract the attention of the licensure board if the practice violates licensure standards for acceptable or appropriate treatment. See *McDonagh*, below. In addition, licensure boards may take action against CAM practitioners for violating the state's prohibition of the practice of medicine without a license. This second question is addressed in Section III of this Chapter.

STATE BOARD OF REGISTRATION FOR THE HEALING ARTS v. McDONAGH

123 S.W.3d 146 (Mo. 2003).

LAURA DENVIR STITH, JUDGE.

* * *

I.   FACTUAL AND PROCEDURAL BACKGROUND

The Board licensed Dr. McDonagh, D.O., as an osteopathic physician and surgeon in 1961. Soon after becoming licensed, he began employing alternative medical treatments in his family practice, including EDTA [ethylene diamine tetra-acetic acid] chelation therapy to treat atherosclerosis and other diseases. He also became certified by the American Board of Chelation Therapy, and has conducted research and written extensively on the use of this therapy.

A. Regulation of Chelation Therapy by the Board.

Chelation therapy has been approved by the federal Food and Drug Administration (FDA) only as a means for the removal of heavy metals from the body. However, non-FDA-approved, or "off-label," use of medications by physicians is not prohibited by the FDA and is generally accepted in the medical profession. [ ] Approximately 1,000 physicians in the United States engage in the off-label use of chelation therapy to treat atherosclerosis and other vascular conditions.[4] Of these 1,000 United States-based physicians, 750 belong to the American College for Advancement in Medicine (ACAM), which has 1,000 members worldwide and which endorsed chelation therapy as a valid course of treatment for occlusive vascular and degenerative diseases associated with aging.[5] To that end, ACAM developed a protocol, followed by Dr. McDonagh, for using chelation therapy to treat such diseases.

In 1989, the Board made an in-depth study of the efficacy of chelation therapy, but did not thereafter adopt any rules, regulations, or position papers on the use of this therapy. Then, in 1992 and 1994, two controlled studies were published that suggested that chelation therapy was ineffective in treating vascular disease. Dr. McDonagh disputes the validity of these studies. But, after the publication of the studies, the American Medical Association (AMA) adopted a position statement on chelation therapy, declaring that: "(1) [t]here is no scientific documentation that the use of chelation therapy is effective in the treatment of cardiovascular disease, atherosclerosis, rheumatoid arthritis, and cancer"; (2) chelation therapy proponents should conduct controlled studies and adhere to FDA research guidelines if they want the therapy to be accepted more broadly; and (3) "[t]he AMA believes that chelation therapy for atherosclerosis is an experimental process without proven efficacy." AMA, AMA Policy Compendium H–175 .994, H–175.997 (1994).

In spite of these developments, neither the FDA, the AMA, or the Board banned the use of chelation therapy to treat vascular disease, and Dr. McDonagh continued to prescribe and administer the therapy in his practice.

Effective October 30, 2001, the Board adopted a rule stating that chelation therapy was of no medical value but that it would not seek to discipline a

4. This practice, which began to emerge in the 1950s, involves the intravenous administration of a diluted solution containing EDTA, as well as various vitamins and minerals. Proponents contend EDTA "chelates"—or bonds—with substances that accumulate and block arteries, and, then, flushes these compounds from the body through the urine.

5. In 1999, the Federal Trade Commission and ACAM entered into a consent agreement under which ACAM agreed not to make any representations regarding EDTA chelation therapy's effectiveness as a treatment for atherosclerosis. *In re Am. Coll. for Advancement in Med.*, No. C–3882 (Fed. Trade Comm'n June 22, 1999) *at* http:// www.ftc.gov/os/1999/07/ 9623147c3881acam.do.htm. *See also* American College for Advancement in Medicine, 64 Fed. Reg. 12,338 (Fed. Trade Comm'n Mar. 12, 1999) (extension of public comment period on consent agreement).

physician for using it on a patient from whom appropriate informed consent is received:

(1) [T]he board declares the use of ethylinediaminetetracetic acid (EDTA) chelation on a patient is of no medical or osteopathic value except for those uses approved by the Food and Drug Administration (FDA) by federal regulation.

(2) The board shall not seek disciplinary action against a licensee based solely upon a non-approved use of EDTA chelation if the licensee has the patient sign the Informed Consent for EDTA Chelation Therapy form, included herein, before beginning the non-approved use of EDTA chelation on a patient. [CSR 150–2.165]

B. *Complaints Against Dr. McDonagh.*

In 1994, seven years prior to the adoption of CSR 150–2.165, and shortly after the two noted controlled studies, the Board filed a complaint against Dr. McDonagh arising out of two inquiries regarding his use of chelation therapy. This complaint was later dismissed without prejudice. In 1996, the Board filed a thirteen-count complaint alleging cause to discipline Dr. McDonagh's medical license for violating section 334.100 by, among other things: endangering the health of patients through the inappropriate provision of chelation therapy; misrepresenting the efficacy of this therapy for atherosclerosis and other diseases; conducting unnecessary testing and treatment in some instances, and insufficient testing and treatment in others; and failing to maintain adequate medical records.

Dr. McDonagh denied that his treatments endangered his patients, denied using inappropriate testing or treatment, and denied inadequate record keeping. He also denied making misrepresentations to patients, noting that, prior to receiving chelation therapy, his patients signed a consent form explaining the possible benefits and side effects of the treatment (very similar to that later approved in 4 CSR 150–2.165), and stating that the treatment was not approved by the FDA, the AMA, or other recognized medical organizations for the treatment of vascular disease. In addition to chelation therapy, Dr. McDonagh encouraged patients to follow a diet and exercise plan, and did not discourage patients from seeing other physicians, including specialists.

The AHC held a hearing in November 1997. The Board introduced expert testimony that the use of chelation therapy to treat vascular disease is not generally accepted in the field of treatment of vascular disease and does not meet the standard of care for treatment of vascular disease. Dr. McDonagh offered expert testimony that supported his off-label use of chelation therapy to treat vascular disease. * * * The AHC ultimately * * * found no evidence of harm from chelation therapy, rejected all thirteen counts, and found no cause to discipline Dr. McDonagh's medical license.

The circuit court affirmed the AHC's decision. The Board appealed. * * *

* * *

The Board * * * argues that, [McDonagh's expert evidence] was insufficient to counter the Board's allegations in various counts, and through expert and other evidence, that Dr. McDonagh's use of chelation therapy constituted "repeated negligence" as that term is used in section 334.100.2(5). That section defines "repeated negligence" as "the failure, on more than one occasion, to use that degree of skill and learning ordinarily used under the same or similar circumstances by the member[s] of the applicant's or licensee's profession."

The Board submits that, in order to counter the Board's experts, Dr. McDonagh's experts needed to testify as to whether he used the degree of skill and learning ordinarily used by members of his profession. But, while his experts testified that his treatment of his patients met "the standard of care," they never identified that standard of care. The Board argues that the standard of care he met must be the standard of care generally accepted in the profession, and this means that Dr. McDonagh is negligent if he treats his patients in a way other than the treatment generally offered by doctors in the field. And, given Dr. McDonagh's experts' admission that mainstream doctors generally do not use chelation therapy to treat vascular disease, the Board suggests, Dr. McDonagh's experts cannot have used the correct standard of care in giving their opinion that his treatment met the required standard.

Dr. McDonagh admits that his experts did not state by what standard of care they were evaluating his treatment of his patients, but argues, * * * the standard is that used by doctors who apply chelation therapy. In effect, he argues that, because he used the protocol approved by ACAM, he could not be found to be negligent and necessarily met the requisite standard of care.

Neither party's argument is correct. * * * The relevant standard of care for discipline for repeated negligence is necessarily that set out in the statute addressing that conduct, section 334.100.2(5). * * * As the issue here is the treatment of persons with vascular disease, the appropriate standard of care *is that used by doctors treating persons with vascular disease.*

Application of this standard does not merely require a determination of what treatment is most popular. Were that the only determinant of skill and learning, any physician who used a medicine for off-label purposes, or who pursued unconventional courses of treatment, could be found to have engaged in repeated negligence and be subject to discipline. * * *

Rather the statute requires only what it says—that Dr. McDonagh use that degree of skill and learning used by members of the profession in similar circumstances. By analogy, one doctor may use medicine to treat heart problems while another might chose to perform a by-pass and a third to perform angioplasty, yet all three may be applying the requisite degree of skill and learning. That they came to differing conclusions by applying that skill and learning does not make one negligent and one non-negligent.

So too, here, if Dr. McDonagh's treatment, including his use of a diet and exercise regimen, and the lack of evidence of harm from his approach, demonstrates the application of the degree of skill and learning ordinarily used by members of his profession, then it is not a basis for discipline under the statute, even if other doctors would apply these facts to reach a different result.

Because, in concluding that Dr. McDonagh did not violate section 334.100.2(5), the AHC relied on Dr. McDonagh's experts' testimony and because this testimony failed to establish whether the experts were using the legal standard of care for "repeated negligence" set out in section

334.100.2(5), this Court must reverse and remand. The circuit court should remand to the AHC for reconsideration * * * in light of the standard of care contained in section 334.100.2(5).

* * *

Wolff, J., concurring in part and dissenting in part.

* * *

The real question is: Is the healing arts board's use of section 334.100, which prescribes discipline for repeated acts of "negligence," an inappropriate use of the disciplinary process to impose the board's sense of orthodoxy?

Dr. McDonagh's use of chelation therapy to treat atherosclerosis and other vascular diseases may be unorthodox. None of the mainstream medical organizations endorse its use for vascular diseases. But, until 2001—after the acts the board complains of in this proceeding—there was no law or regulation regulating its use. * * *

* * *

The administrative hearing commission heard evidence for eight days on the board's complaint against Dr. McDonagh for his use of chelation therapy and related matters. The commission, in its 70 pages of findings of fact and conclusions of law, found no cause for discipline.

Specifically responding to the board's position that the use of chelation therapy is cause for discipline, the commission concluded: "It is not an unnecessary, harmful or dangerous treatment." The commission characterized McDonagh's conduct as "giving patients a treatment that has provided benefit to many patients, harms no one, and is given with informed consent and the information that this treatment may not work with all patients." The commission further stated, "[T]he evidence shows that patients are being helped. We cannot state that an entire treatment method that provides benefits to patients without harming them constitutes incompetent, inappropriate, grossly negligent, or negligent treatment. Nor can we say that this treatment is misconduct, unprofessional, or a danger to the public."

The commission, based on the record, does acknowledge that chelation therapy involves risks, as of course do other treatments for vascular disease, such as coronary artery surgery. The risks of chelation therapy are disclosed, according to the commission, in the informed consent form that Dr. McDonagh has used with all his patients. * * *

* * *

More to the point, when the board finally promulgated its rule that declares chelation therapy to be "of no medical or osteopathic value," the board's rule goes on to provide that the board "shall not seek disciplinary action against a licensee based solely upon a non-approved use of EDTA chelation if the licensee has the patient sign" the informed consent form that accompanies the regulation. [T]he consent form that Dr. McDonagh used for these patients—long before the consent form promulgated by the board—is very similar to the consent form accompanying the 2001 rule.

* * *

As to the board's claims heard in 1997 that are the subject of this appeal, it appears that the absence of a rule left the board to proceed against Dr. McDonagh under 334.100.2(5) for repeated acts of negligence. * * *

So is this off-label use of chelation therapy negligence? The real question—the answer to which is fatal to the board's position—is whether acts of negligence, as defined by this statute, can be cause for discipline if there is no showing that the physician's conduct "is or might be harmful or dangerous [meeting the statutory definition of negligence]." If there is no harm or danger, there is no cause for discipline under this section.

* * *

Physicians are afforded considerable leeway in the use of professional judgment to decide on appropriate treatments, especially when applying the negligence standard. * * * "Negligence" does not seem an appropriate concept where the physician has studied the problem and has made a treatment recommendation, even though that is not the prevailing view of the majority of the profession. The lack of general acceptance of a treatment does not necessarily constitute a breach of the standard of care. The use of negligence in licensing situations, in the absence of harm or danger, is particularly inappropriate.

One could argue that because chelation therapy is not accepted by mainstream medicine and is an off-label practice not approved by the FDA, it is therefore harmful and dangerous. If that were the board's position, the licensing statute would thwart advances in medical science. A dramatic example is the treatment of stomach ulcers, which were long thought to be caused by stress. In 1982, two Australians found the bacterium helicobacter pylori in the stomach linings of ulcer victims. Because helicobacter pylori is a bacterium, some physicians—a minority to be sure—began prescribing antibiotics to treat stomach ulcers as an infectious disease. The National Institutes of Health did not recognize antibiotic therapy until 1994; the FDA approved the first antibiotic for use in treating stomach ulcers in 1996; and the Centers for Disease Control began publicizing the treatment in 1997. Today's physicians accept as fact that most stomach ulcers are primarily caused by helicobacter pylori bacteria infection and not by stress. But, by the chronology of this discovery, if a physician in the late 1980s or early 1990s had treated ulcers with antibiotics, that treatment would have been "negligent" as the board in this case interprets that term because inappropriate use of antibiotics can be dangerous.

I do not mean to suggest that chelation therapy for vascular disease is of the same order as the use of antibiotics for treating stomach ulcers. In fact, I doubt it. But my point is that medicine is not readily regulated by a standard cookbook or set of rules. The board's position in publishing its 2001 rule on chelation therapy seems to recognize this point better than its position in this disciplinary action. If chelation therapy for vascular disease were dangerous, the board's rule that allows its use would be unconscionable.

* * *

Notes and Questions

1. Assume that you are on the Administrative Hearings Commission to which the Missouri Supreme Court remanded the *McDonagh* case. As you antici-

pated, the experts produced by the Board, none of whom practice chelation therapy, testify that it does not meet the standard of care and that no self-respecting M.D. or D.O. would use it, while McDonagh's experts testify that anecdotal evidence indicates that it benefits some patients with cardiovascular disease; that Dr. McDonagh meets the standard of care used by those who are willing to provide patients with chelation therapy; and that he uses ordinary medical tests to monitor his patients' progress with the therapy. Do you discipline McDonagh, or do you reject the Board's recommendation? Assume that among McDonagh's patients you find one who refused to undergo cardiac bypass surgery recommended by his cardiologist and who some months later died of a heart attack. What result now? Some are concerned that licensed health care professionals may defraud patients by misrepresenting the risks and benefits of the alternative treatment they prefer. How can the Board respond to that concern?

2.   If a medical board is not in a position to test the safety and effectiveness of particular treatments, can it instead rely upon prevailing practice in the medical community? See, In re Guess, 327 N.C. 46, 393 S.E.2d 833 (1990). In this case, Dr. Guess practiced family medicine but regularly incorporated homeopathic medical treatments into his care of his patients. The North Carolina medical board charged Guess with unprofessional conduct under a statute that defined such conduct as "any departure from ... the standards of acceptable and prevailing medical practice ... irrespective of whether or not a patient is injured thereby." The North Carolina Supreme Court held that Guess violated the statute even though no patient was harmed and that it was within the state's police power to enact a law that prohibited certain conduct based on a judgment that there was some inherent risk in allowing physicians to depart from prevailing standards. Why the difference in result between *Guess* and *McDonagh*? If the North Carolina statute had been in effect in Missouri, would the Board's discipline of McDonagh have been upheld? Which of these two approaches to nonconforming treatment better serves the public interest—North Carolina's or Missouri's?

3.   After the *Guess* decision, the North Carolina legislature amended the grounds for discipline to limit the section under which Dr. Guess was penalized:

> The Board shall not revoke the license of or deny a license to a person solely because of that person's practice of a therapy that is experimental, nontraditional, or that departs from acceptable and prevailing medical practices unless, by competent evidence, the Board can establish that the treatment has a safety risk greater than the prevailing treatment or that the treatment is generally ineffective. N.C. Gen. Stat. 90–14(a)(6).

How would the North Carolina Board prove the alternative treatment is less safe than prevailing practice where there may be little evidence that the current practice is safe? See, e.g., E. Haavi Morreim, A Dose of Our Own Medicine: Alternative Medicine, Conventional Medicine, and the Standards of Science, 31 J. L. Med. & Ethics 222 (2003); Julie Stone & Joan Matthews, Complementary Medicine and the Law (1996), arguing that while some alternative or complementary practices have a technological base and are subject to the same type of verification as allopathic medicine, other practices are not amenable to such testing; and, therefore, conventional quality-control regulation is inadequate.

4.   Some states have issued general guidance that addresses both conventional medicine and CAM. The Kentucky Board, for example, issued the following statement:

> Physicians may incorporate non-validated treatments if the research results are very promising, if the physician believes that a particular patient may benefit, if the risk of harm is very low, and if the physician adheres to the

conventions that govern the doctrine of informed consent for non-validated treatment. Available at http://www.state.ky.us/agencies/

How would Dr. McDonagh have fared under such a policy? Are these the appropriate standards for more conventional medical treatment decisions as well, including off-label prescribing?

5.   While licensed health care professionals are increasingly incorporating CAM into their standard medical and nursing practices, practitioners offering solely alternative health care services without conventional medical or nursing training or licensure are a very significant arm of the movement toward CAM. In fact, a dominant strain in the CAM movement would argue that only alternative providers can offer such services effectively and authentically. Some states license practitioners of particular CAM therapies. See, e.g., Ariz. Rev. Stat. § 32–1521 and Alaska Stat. § 08.45.030 (licensing naturopaths); Nev. Rev. Stat. § 630A.155 (licensing homeopaths); Cal. Bus. & Prof. Code § 4935 (licensing acupuncturists). Although medical licensure does not require specific license for specific specialties, some states require that licensed physicians who practice certain forms of CAM hold a separate state license or registration to do so. This seems particularly common with acupuncture. See, for example, Haw. Rev. Stat. § 436–E.

III.   UNLICENSED PROVIDERS

The state medical board has the primary responsibility for enforcing the prohibition against the unauthorized practice of medicine by unlicensed providers. This prohibition is enforced by criminal sanctions against the unlicensed practitioner and license revocation against any physician who aids and abets the unlicensed practitioner. The state medical practice acts prohibit anyone but licensed physicians and other licensed health care professionals practicing within the bounds of their own licensure from practicing medicine. The board responsible for licensure and discipline for nursing has parallel authority to pursue unlicensed practitioners charged with engaging in the practice of nursing. The issue of the scope of practice of licensed health care professionals is taken up in Section IV of this chapter. In this section, we focus on the practitioner who does not have a license.

STATE BOARD OF NURSING AND STATE BOARD OF HEALING ARTS v. RUEBKE

Supreme Court of Kansas, 1996.
259 Kan. 599, 913 P.2d 142.

LARSON, JUSTICE:

The State Board of Healing Arts (Healing Arts) and the State Board of Nursing (Nursing) appeal the trial court's denial of a temporary injunction by which the Boards had sought to stop E. Michelle Ruebke, a practicing lay midwife, from continuing her alleged practice of medicine and nursing.

* * *

FACTUAL BACKGROUND

* * *

The hearing on the temporary injunction revealed that Ruebke acts as a lay midwife comprehensively assisting pregnant women with prenatal care, delivery, and post-partum care. She is president of the Kansas Midwives Association and follows its promulgated standards, which include a risk screening assessment based upon family medical history; establishing prenatal care plans, including monthly visitations; examinations and assistance in birth; and post-partum care. She works with supervising physicians who are made aware of her mode of practice and who are available for consultation and perform many of the medical tests incident to pregnancy.

* * *

Dr. Debra L. Messamore, an obstetrician/gynecologist, testified she had reviewed the Kansas Midwives Association standards of care and opined those standards were similar to the assessments incident to her practice as an OB/GYN. Dr. Messamore concluded that in her judgment the prenatal assessments made by Ruebke were obstetrical diagnoses.

Dr. Messamore testified that the prescriptions Ruebke has women obtain from their physicians are used in obstetrics to produce uterine contractions. She further testified the Kansas Midwives Association standard of care relating to post-delivery conditions of the mother and baby involved obstetrical judgments. She reviewed the birth records of [one] birth and testified that obstetrical or medical judgments were reflected. [She admitted] that many procedures at issue could be performed by a nurse rather than a physician. * * * She also stated her opinion that so defined obstetrics as a branch of medicine or surgery.

Ginger Breedlove, a Kansas certified advanced registered nurse practitioner and nurse-midwife, testified on behalf of Nursing. She reviewed the records [of two births] and testified nursing functions were involved. She admitted she could not tell from the records who had engaged in certain practices and that taking notes, giving enemas, and administering oxygen is often done by people who are not nurses, although education, experience, and minimum competency are required.

* * * The court held that * * *, Ruebke's midwifery practices did not and were not intended to come within the healing arts act or the nursing act, and her activities fell within exceptions to the two acts even if the acts did apply and were constitutional.

The factual findings, highly summarized, were that Ruebke had not been shown to hold herself out as anything other than a lay midwife; has routinely used and consulted with supervising physicians; was not shown to administer any prescription drugs; was not shown to do any suturing or episiotomies, make cervical or vaginal lacerations, or diagnose blood type; and had engaged only in activities routinely and properly done by people who are not physicians.

REGULATORY HISTORY OF MIDWIFERY

One of the specific statutory provisions we deal with, K.S.A. 65–2802(a), defines the healing arts as follows:

The healing arts include any system, treatment, operation, diagnosis, prescription, or practice for the ascertainment, cure, relief, palliation, adjustment, or correction of any human disease, ailment, deformity, or injury, and includes specifically but not by way of limitation the practice of medicine and surgery; the practice of osteopathic medicine and surgery; and the practice of chiropractic.

K.S.A. 65–2869 specifically provides that for the purpose of the healing arts act, the following persons shall be deemed to be engaged in the practice of medicine and surgery:

(a) Persons who publicly profess to be physicians or surgeons, or publicly profess to assume the duties incident to the practice of medicine or surgery or any of their branches.

(b) Persons who prescribe, recommend or furnish medicine or drugs, or perform any surgical operation of whatever nature by the use of any surgical instrument, procedure, equipment or mechanical device for the diagnosis, cure or relief of any wounds, fractures, bodily injury, infirmity, disease, physical or mental illness or psychological disorder, of human beings.

* * *

[M]idwifery belonged to women from Biblical times through the Middle Ages. However, subsequent to the Middle Ages, women healers were often barred from universities and precluded from obtaining medical training or degrees. With the rise of barber-surgeon guilds, women were banned from using surgical instruments.

When midwives immigrated to America, they occupied positions of great prestige. Some communities licensed midwives and others did not. This continued until the end of the 19th century. In the 19th and 20th centuries, medical practice became more standardized. Economically and socially well-placed doctors pressed for more restrictive licensing laws and for penalties against those who violated them. [One commentator] suggests that licensure was a market control device; midwives were depriving new obstetricians of the opportunity for training; and elimination of midwifery would allow the science of obstetrics to grow into a mature medical specialty.

There is a notable absence of anything in the history of Kansas healing arts regulation illustrating any attempt to specifically target midwives. In 1870, the Kansas Legislature adopted its first restriction on the practice of medicine. * * *

[T]here can be little doubt that in 1870 Kansas, particularly in rural areas, there were not enough educated physicians available to deliver all of the children born in the state. In fact, until 1910 approximately 50 percent of births in this country were midwife assisted. [ ]

* * *

Although obstetricians held themselves out as a medical specialty in the United States as early as 1868, midwives were not seen as engaged in the practice of obstetrics, nor was obstetrics universally viewed as being a branch of medicine. In 1901, North Carolina recognized obstetricians as engaged in the practice of medicine but women midwives, as a separate discipline, were exempted from the licensure act. [ ] * * *

Although many states in the early 1900s passed laws relating to midwifery, Kansas has never expressly addressed the legality of the practice. In 1915

[ ] this court implied that a woman with considerable midwife experience was qualified to testify as an expert witness in a malpractice case against an osteopath for allegedly negligently delivering the plaintiff's child.

* * *

The 1978 Kansas Legislature created a new classification of nurses, Advanced Registered Nurse Practitioner (ARNP). [ ] One classification of ARNP is certified nurse midwives. Although the regulations permitting the practice of certified nurse midwives might be argued to show additional legislative intent to prohibit the practice of lay midwives, this argument has been rejected elsewhere. [ ]

In 1978, Kansas Attorney General opinion No. 78–164 suggested that the practice of midwifery is a violation of the healing arts act. * * * Although potentially persuasive, such an opinion is not binding on us.

Most probably in response to the 1978 Attorney General opinion, a 1978 legislative interim committee undertook a study of a proposal to recognize and regulate the practice of lay midwifery. However, the committee reached no conclusion.

* * *

A 1986 review of the laws of every state found that lay midwifery was specifically statutorily permitted, subject to licensing or regulation, in 25 jurisdictions. Twelve states, including Kansas, had no legislation governing or prohibiting lay midwifery directly or by direct implication. Several states recognized both lay and nurse midwives. Some issued new licensing only for nurse midwives, while others regulated and recognized both, often as separate professions, subject to separate standards and restrictions. [ ]

* * *

In April 1993, the Board of Healing Arts released Policy Statement No. 93–02, in which the Board stated it reaffirmed its previous position of August 18, 1984, that

[m]idwifery is the practice of medicine and surgery and any practice thereof by individuals not regulated by the Kansas State Board of Nursing or under the supervision of or by order of or referral from a licensed medical or osteopathic doctor constitutes the unlicensed practice of medicine and surgery.

* * *

This historical background brings us to the question of whether the healing arts act is unconstitutionally vague. * * *

* * *

We have held that the interpretation of a statute given by an administrative agency within its area of expertise is entitled to deference, although final construction of a statute always rests with courts. [ ] * * *

We do, of course, attempt wherever possible to construe a statute as constitutional [ ]. * * *

* * *

The definition of healing arts uses terms that have an ordinary, definite, and ascertainable meaning. The trial court's conclusion that "disease, ailment, deformity or injury" are not commonly used words with settled meanings cannot be justified.

* * *

* * * Although we hold the act not to be unconstitutionally vague, we also hold the definitional provisions do not cover midwifery. In their ordinary usage the terms in K.S.A. 65–2802(a) used to define healing arts clearly and unequivocally focus exclusively on pathologies (i.e., diseases) and abnormal human conditions (i.e., ailments, deformities, or injuries). Pregnancy and childbirth are neither pathologies nor abnormalities.

* * *

Healing Arts argues that the "practice of medicine" includes the practice of obstetrics. It reasons, in turn, that obstetrics includes the practices traditionally performed by midwives. From this, it concludes midwifery is the practice of medicine.

However, equating midwifery with obstetrics, and thus with the practice of medicine, ignores the historical reality, discussed above, that midwives and obstetricians coexisted for many years quite separately. From the time of our statehood, the relationship between obstetricians and midwives changed from that of harmonious coexistence, cooperation, and collaboration, to open market competition and hostility. [ ]

* * *

To even the most casual observer of the history of assistance to childbirth, it is clear that over the course of this century the medical profession has extended its reach so deeply into the area of birthing as to almost completely occupy the field. The introduction of medical advances to the childbirth process drew women to physicians to assist during the birth of their children. Yet, this widespread preference for physicians as birth attendants hardly mandates the conclusion that only physicians may assist with births.

* * * The fact that a person with medical training provides services in competition with someone with no medical degree does not transform the latter's practices into the practice of medicine.

* * *

Although we hold the practice of midwifery is not itself the practice of the healing arts under our statutory scheme, our conclusions should not be interpreted to mean that a midwife may engage in any activity whatsoever with regard to a pregnant woman merely by virtue of her pregnancy. * * *

* * * However, we need not decide the precise boundaries of what a midwife may do without engaging in the practice of the healing arts because, in the case before us, Ruebke was found to have worked under the supervision of physicians who were familiar with her practices and authorized her actions. Any of Ruebke's actions that were established at trial, which might otherwise have been the practice of the healing arts, were exempt from the healing arts act because she had worked under the supervision of such physicians.

K.S.A. 65–2872 exempts certain activities from the licensure requirements of the healing arts act. In relevant part it provides:

The practice of the healing arts shall not be construed to include the
following persons:

> (g) Persons whose professional services are performed under the supervi-
> sion or by order of or referral from a practitioner who is licensed
> under this act.

* * *

In light of the uncontested factual findings of the trial court, which were
supported by competent evidence in the record, we agree with the trial court
that the exception to the healing arts act recognized by K.S.A. 65–2872(g)
applies to any of Ruebke's midwifery activities which might otherwise be
considered the practice of the healing arts under K.S.A. 65–2802(a) and K.S.A.
65–2869.

* * *

As we have held, the legislature has never specifically acted with the
intent to restrict or regulate the traditional practice of lay midwifery. Nevertheless, Nursing argues such birth assistants must be licensed nurses before
they may render aid to pregnant women. In oral argument, Nursing conceded
much of its argument would be muted were we to hold, as we do above, that
the practice of midwifery is not the practice of the healing arts and thus not
part of a medical regimen.

* * *

The practice of nursing is defined [in the Kansas nurse practice act] by
reference to the practitioner's substantial specialized knowledge in areas of
the biological, physical, and behavioral sciences and educational preparation
within the field of the healing arts. Ruebke claims no specialized scientific
knowledge, but rather readily admits she has no formal education beyond
high school. Her assistance is valued not because it is the application of a firm
and rarified grasp of scientific theory, but because, like generations of midwives before, she has practical experience assisting in childbirth.

Moreover, "nursing" deals with "persons who are experiencing changes
in the normal health processes." As these words are commonly understood,
pregnancy and childbirth do not constitute changes in the normal health
process, but the continuation of it.

* * * As we have held, the practice of lay midwifery has, throughout the
history of the regulation of nursing, been separate and distinct from the
practice of the healing arts, to which nursing is so closely joined. While we
have no doubt of the legislature's power to place lay midwifery under the
authority of the State Board of Nursing, the legislature has not done so.

We find no legislative intent manifested in the language of the nursing
act clearly illustrating the purpose of including the historically separate
practice of midwifery within the practice of nursing. [ ] Assistance in childbirth rendered by one whose practical experience with birthing provides
comfort to the mother is not nursing under the nursing act, such that
licensure is required.

Affirmed in part and reversed in part.

Notes and Questions

1.   Courts have adopted many approaches to analyzing whether services provided in assistance at childbirth constitute the unauthorized practice of medicine. Some have examined individual actions that may be performed during childbirth. For example, in Leigh v. Board of Reg. in Nursing, 395 Mass. 670, 481 N.E.2d 1347 (1985), the court distinguished "ordinary assistance in the normal cases of childbirth" from that in which a lay midwife used "obstetrical instruments" and "printed prescriptions or formulas," and concluded that the former does not constitute the practice of medicine while the latter does. In People v. Jihan, 127 Ill.2d 379, 130 Ill.Dec. 422, 537 N.E.2d 751 (1989), the court distinguished "assisting" at birth from "delivering" the child. Statutes authorizing childbirth services by traditional midwives also set boundaries on their practice and may exclude, for example, use of any surgical instrument or assisting childbirth "by artificial or mechanical means." See, e.g., Minn. Stat. Ann. § 147D.03.

2.   *Ruebke* illustrates that lay midwifery confronts the unauthorized practice prohibitions of both nursing and medicine. In Sherman v. Cryns, 203 Ill.2d 264, 271 Ill.Dec. 881, 786 N.E.2d 139 (2003), the court held that the state had successfully established a prima facie case against a lay midwife for practicing nursing without a license. In *Cryns*, the court relied largely on the prenatal care in finding that Cryns had violated the nursing statute. The court distinguished its case from *Ruebke* on the basis of the breadth of the definition of professional nursing in the Illinois statute, which was quite similar to that of the statute in *Sermchief* in the next section. The Illinois statute specifically provided for licensure for certified nurse midwives but was silent on the question of lay midwifery.

3.   The court in *Ruebke* ultimately concludes that the midwife was operating within a common exception to the prohibition against the unauthorized practice of medicine by performing works delegated by a physician. But see, Marion OB/GYN v. State Med. Bd., 137 Ohio App.3d 522, 739 N.E.2d 15 (Ct. App. 2000), in which the court held that delivering infants was beyond the scope of practice allowed a physician assistant although state law allowed licensed nurses to practice midwifery. See the discussion of physician assistants in Section IV, below.

4.   The Kansas statute on certified nurse midwives describes substantial educational requirements. The court concluded, however, that formal education is unnecessary and that practical experience can be valued as highly. Should the legislature provide for minimal educational requirements for persons assisting in childbirth? Susan Corcoran, To Become a Midwife: Reducing Legal Barriers to Entry into the Midwifery Profession, 80 Wash. U.L.Q. 649 (2002); Sara K. Hayden, The Business of Birth: Obstacles Facing Low–Income Women in Choosing Midwifery Care After the Licensed Midwifery Practice Act of 1993, 19 Berkeley Women's L. J. 257 (2004). The North American Registry of Midwives provides certification for direct-entry or professional midwives. www.narm.org. Several states have incorporated certification by NARM within their standards for recognition of lay midwives. See, e.g., Minn. § 47D.01; Utah Code 1953 § 58–77–302.

5.   Claims of a constitutional right to choice of provider of health care services consistently fail even when made in the context of the woman's right to privacy in reproductive decision making, the lack of empirical evidence of better outcomes with commonly used obstetrical technology, and the substantial history

of conflict between medical and other approaches to childbirth. See Lisa C. Ikemoto, The Code of Perfect Pregnancy: At the Intersection of the Ideology of Motherhood, the Practice of Defaulting to Science, and the Interventionist Mindset of Law, 53 Ohio St. L. J. 1205 (1992); Amy F. Cohen, The Midwifery Stalemate and Childbirth Choice: Recognizing Mothers-to-Be as the Best Late Pregnancy Decisionmakers, 80 Ind. L. J. 849 (2005). Nor do claims that the unauthorized practice prohibitions violate the First Amendment rights of practitioners succeed. See, e.g., People v. Rogers, 249 Mich.App. 77, 641 N.W.2d 595 (Ct. App. 2001).

IV. SCOPE OF PRACTICE REGULATION

Licensed nonphysician health care providers cannot legally practice medicine, but practices that fall within their own licensure (for example, as a nurse or a physician assistant) are not considered the practice of medicine. So, for example, a nurse who is providing services authorized under the nurse practice act would not be practicing medicine while an unlicensed practitioner providing the same services would be guilty of the unauthorized practice of medicine or nursing. If a nurse engages in practices that exceed those authorized in the nurse practice act, however, that nurse would be guilty of exceeding the authorized scope of practice of the profession of nursing as well as violating the prohibition against the unauthorized practice of medicine.

The AMA and several other groups have formed the Scope of Practice Partnership (SOPP) as an advocacy group to influence the regulation of nonphysician health care providers, while a coalition of other health care professional associations, including the American Nurses Association, has formed the Coalition for Patients' Rights (CPR) to respond to the efforts of SOPP to limit their scope of practice. See James W. Hilliard, State Practice Acts of Licensed Health Professions: Scope of Practice, 8 DePaul J. Health Care L. 237 (2004).

SERMCHIEF v. GONZALES

Supreme Court of Missouri, 1983.
660 S.W.2d 683.

WELLIVER, JUDGE.

This is a petition for a declaratory judgment and injunction brought by two nurses and five physicians[6] employed by the East Missouri Action Agency (Agency) wherein the plaintiff-appellants ask the Court to declare that the practices of the Agency nurses are authorized under the nursing law of this state, § 335.016.8, RSMo 1978 and that such practices do not constitute the unauthorized practice of medicine under Chapter 334 relating to the Missouri State Board of Registration For the Healing Arts (Board). * * * The holding below was against appellants who make direct appeal to this Court alleging that the validity of the statutes is involved. [ ]. * * *

I

The facts are simple and for the most part undisputed. The Agency is a federally tax exempt Missouri not-for-profit corporation that maintains offices

---

6. The physicians are joined for the reason that they are charged with aiding and abetting the unauthorized practice of medicine by the nurses.

in Cape Girardeau (main office), Flat River, Ironton, and Fredericktown. The Agency provides medical services to the general public in fields of family planning, obstetrics and gynecology. The services are provided to an area that includes the counties of Bollinger, Cape Girardeau, Perry, St. Francis, Ste. Genevieve, Madison, Iron and Washington. Some thirty-five hundred persons utilized these services during the year prior to trial. The Agency is funded from federal grants, Medicaid reimbursements and patient fees. The programs are directed toward the lower income segment of the population. Similar programs exist both statewide and nationwide.

Appellant nurses Solari and Burgess are duly licensed professional nurses in Missouri pursuant to the provisions of Chapter 335 and are employed by the Agency. Both nurses have had post-graduate special training in the field of obstetrics and gynecology. Appellant physicians are also employees of the Agency and duly licensed to practice medicine (the healing arts) pursuant to Chapter 334. Respondents are the members and the executive secretary of the Missouri State Board of Registration for the Healing Arts (Board) * * *.

The services routinely provided by the nurses and complained of by the Board included, among others, the taking of history; breast and pelvic examinations; laboratory testing of Papanicolaou (PAP) smears, gonorrhea cultures, and blood serology; the providing of and giving of information about oral contraceptives, condoms, and intrauterine devices (IUD); the dispensing of certain designated medications; and counseling services and community education. If the nurses determined the possibility of a condition designated in the standing orders or protocols that would contraindicate the use of contraceptives until further examination and evaluation, they would refer the patients to one of the Agency physicians. No act by either nurse is alleged to have caused injury or damage to any person. All acts by the nurses were done pursuant to written standing orders and protocols signed by appellant physicians. The standing orders and protocols were directed to specifically named nurses and were not identical for all nurses.

The Board threatened to order the appellant nurses and physicians to show cause why the nurses should not be found guilty of the unauthorized practice of medicine and the physicians guilty of aiding and abetting such unauthorized practice. Appellants sought Court relief in this proceeding.

* * *

III

The statutes involved are:

It shall be unlawful for any person not now a registered physician within the meaning of the law to practice medicine or surgery in any of its departments, or to profess to cure and attempt to treat the sick and others afflicted with bodily or mental infirmities, or engage in the practice of midwifery in this state, except as herein provided.

Section 334.010.

This Chapter does not apply ... *to nurses licensed and lawfully practicing their profession within the provisions of chapter 335, RSMo;* ...

Section 334.155, RSMo Supp.1982 (emphasis added).

Definitions.—As used in sections 335.011 to 335.096, unless the context clearly requires otherwise, the following words and terms shall have the meanings indicated:

* * *

(8) "Professional nursing" is the performance for compensation of any act which requires substantial specialized education, judgment and skill based on knowledge and application of principles derived from the biological, physical, social and nursing sciences, including, but not limited to:

(a) Responsibility for the teaching of health care and the prevention of illness to the patient and his family; or

(b) Assessment, nursing diagnosis, nursing care, and counsel of persons who are ill, injured or experiencing alterations in normal health processes; or

(c) The administration of medications and treatments as prescribed by a person licensed in this state to prescribe such medications and treatments; or

(d) The coordination and assistance in the delivery of a plan of health care with all members of the health team; or

(e) The teaching and supervision of other persons in the performance of any of the foregoing.

Section 335.016.8(a)–(e).

At the time of enactment of the Nursing Practice Act of 1975, the following statutes were repealed:

2. A person practices professional nursing who for compensation or personal profit performs, *under the supervision and direction of a practitioner authorized to sign birth and death certificates,* any professional services requiring the application of principles of the biological, physical or social sciences and nursing skills in the care of the sick, in the prevention of disease or in the conservation of health.

Section 335.010.2, RSMo 1969 (emphasis added).

Nothing contained in this chapter shall be construed as conferring any authority on any person to practice medicine or osteopathy or to undertake the treatment or cure of disease.

Section 335.190, RSMo 1969.

The parties on both sides request that in construing these statutes we define and draw that thin and elusive line that separates the practice of medicine and the practice of professional nursing in modern day delivery of health services. A response to this invitation, in our opinion, would result in an avalanche of both medical and nursing malpractice suits alleging infringement of that line and would hinder rather than help with the delivery of health services to the general public. Our consideration will be limited to the narrow question of whether the acts of these nurses were permissible under § 335.016.8 or were prohibited by Chapter 334.

* * *

The legislature substantially revised the law affecting the nursing profession with enactment of the Nursing Practice Act of 1975. Perhaps the most significant feature of the Act was the redefinition of the term "professional nursing," which appears in § 335.016.8. Even a facile reading of that section reveals a manifest legislative desire to expand the scope of authorized nursing practices. Every witness at trial testified that the new definition of professional nursing is a broader definition than that in the former statute. A comparison with the prior definition vividly demonstrates this fact. Most apparent is the elimination of the requirement that a physician directly supervise nursing functions. Equally significant is the legislature's formulation of an open-ended definition of professional nursing. The earlier statute limited nursing practice to "services . . . in the care of the sick, in the prevention of disease or in the conservation of health." § 335.010.2, RSMo 1969. The 1975 Act not only describes a much broader spectrum of nursing functions, it qualifies this description with the phrase "including, but not limited to." We believe this phrase evidences an intent to avoid statutory constraints on the evolution of new functions for nurses delivering health services. Under § 335.016.8, a nurse may be permitted to assume responsibilities heretofore not considered to be within the field of professional nursing so long as those responsibilities are consistent with her or his "specialized education, judgment and skill based on knowledge and application of principles derived from the biological, physical, social and nursing sciences." § 335.016.8.

The acts of the nurses herein clearly fall within this legislative standard. All acts were performed pursuant to standing orders and protocols approved by physicians. Physician prepared standing orders and protocols for nurses and other paramedical personnel were so well established and accepted at the time of the adoption of the statute that the legislature could not have been unaware of the use of such practices. We see nothing in the statute purporting to limit or restrict their continued use.

Respondents made no challenge of the nurses' level of training or the degree of their skill. They challenge only the legal right of the nurses to undertake these acts. We believe the acts of the nurses are precisely the types of acts the legislature contemplated when it granted nurses the right to make assessments and nursing diagnoses. There can be no question that a nurse undertakes only a nursing diagnosis, as opposed to a medical diagnosis, when she or he finds or fails to find symptoms described by physicians in standing orders and protocols for the purpose of administering courses of treatment prescribed by the physician in such orders and protocols.

The Court believes that it is significant that while at least forty states have modernized and expanded their nursing practice laws during the past fifteen years neither counsel nor the Court have discovered any case challenging nurses' authority to act as the nurses herein acted.

* * * The hallmark of the professional is knowing the limits of one's professional knowledge. The nurse, either upon reaching the limit of her or his knowledge or upon reaching the limits prescribed for the nurse by the physician's standing orders and protocols, should refer the patient to the physician. There is no evidence that the assessments and diagnoses made by the nurses in this case exceeded such limits.

* * *

Having found that the nurses' acts were authorized by § 335.016.8, it follows that such acts do not constitute the unlawful practice of medicine for the reason that § 334.155 makes the provisions of Chapter 334 inapplicable "to nurses licensed and lawfully practicing their profession within the provisions of Chapter 335 RSMo."

This cause is reversed and remanded with instructions to enter judgment consistent with this opinion.

Notes and Questions

1.   Physician assistants and nurses have assumed different professional identities. Physician assistants are educated in a medical model of care and view themselves as practicing medicine through physician delegation of tasks under the supervision of physicians. Nurse practitioners or advanced practice nurses (including nurse midwives, nurse anesthetists, and other specialist nurse practitioners) view themselves as operating from a nursing model of health care and acting as independent practitioners who collaborate with physicians. Currently, organized medicine asserts that both physician assistants and nurse practitioners must be supervised by physicians, a position accepted by the American Academy of Physician Assistants, but rejected by the American Nurses Association.

Some advanced practice nursing statutes require that the nurse practitioner practice under the supervision of a physician, however. See e.g., Cal. Bus. & Prof. Code § 2746.5(b) (certificate authorizes nurse-midwife to practice nurse-midwifery "under the supervision of a licensed physician and surgeon who has current practice or training in obstetrics"); Cal. Bus. & Prof. Code § 2836.1(d), requiring physician supervision for the furnishing of drugs or devices by nurse practitioner. Others recognize advanced practice nursing in collaboration with licensed physicians. See e.g., Mo. Ann. Stat. § 334.104, enacted after *Sermchief*, authorizing collaborative practice arrangements in the form of written agreements, protocols or standing orders, but describing the prescriptive authority of the nurse practitioner as delegated.

2.   Authority to prescribe medication has been a major issue in debates over the appropriate scope of practice. See, e.g., Joy L. Delman, The Use and Misuse of Physician Extenders, 24 J. Legal Med. 249 (2003). Most states now authorize nurses to prescribe medications, at least under a doctor's supervision.

3.   Physician assistants first practiced under general delegation exceptions still included in medical practice acts. States vary in the standards and methods they use to assure that delegation to physician assistants is appropriate and supervision is adequate. Some states take an individualized approach and require the physician assistant or supervising physician to submit particular details about the specific position for review by an agency. See e.g., Md. Code Ann., Health Occ. § 15–302. Some limit the number of physician assistants a doctor may supervise. See e.g., Ohio Rev. Code Ann. § 4730.21. Other states simply define "supervision," with great variations among these statutes. See e.g., Mo. Ann. Stat. § 334.735(10), defining supervision as "control exercised over a physician assistant working within the same facility as the supervising physician sixty-six percent of the time a physician assistant provides patient care, except a physician assistant may make follow-up patient examinations in hospitals, nursing homes, patient homes, and correctional facilities, each such examination being reviewed, approved and signed by the supervising physician."

Problem: Retail Clinics

A national pharmacy chain wants to open health clinics in several of their stores in your state. These health clinics would be staffed by nurse practitioners or physician assistants and would handle non-emergency cases with referral relationships to hospitals and cooperative physicians in the area. The development of these retail clinics is generating some controversy, including conflict between your medical board and your board of nursing, both represented by you as the state's Attorney General.

Some states have engaged in negotiated rulemaking over such conflicts, and you have decided to give it a try. This would involve gathering stakeholders to engage in assisting the boards in developing rules or regulations applicable to the clinics. Who has a stake in regulatory standards applicable to the scope of practice of nursing or physician assistants in this setting such that they would be involved in the negotiation process? What positions do you expect to be taken by the stakeholders you have identified? Where does the public interest lie?

Chapter 2

QUALITY CONTROL REGULATION OF HEALTH CARE INSTITUTIONS

I. INTRODUCTION

Patient safety and well-being are directly dependent on the quality of health care institutions as much as on the quality of the individual patient's doctor or nurse or therapist. The range of institutional factors that can pose a danger to patients extends from building design, maintenance, and sanitation through health information technology and management; from fiscal soundness through the selection, training, and monitoring of the individuals directly providing care; from staffing levels through food service. The patient safety movement, in fact, focuses on the quality of systems within health care organizations rather than on the behaviors of individual caregivers standing alone.

A variety of public and private efforts influence the quality of health care facilities. For many consumer goods and services, the market plays a significant role in setting an acceptable level of quality. State and federal governments are making efforts to strengthen the influence of the market over the quality of health care facilities. Most of these efforts have focused on collecting and posting quality data to allow consumers to select among facilities and to encourage facilities to take action to improve their performance on reportable factors. Significant barriers to the working of the market, such as a persistent lack of relevant, timely, and accurate information on quality measures; inability to evaluate available information; and decision making processes that place the choice of facility in the hands of someone other than the patient, still diminish the impact of consumer choice in health care.

In the face of market failure, state and federal governments often use a "command-and-control" system of licensure or certification for many key health care organizations through which the government sets standards, monitors for compliance, and imposes sanctions for violations. The debate over whether the market or direct governmental regulation of performance is most effective in improving the quality of health care institutions has raged for decades. See, for example, Timothy S. Jost, Our Broken Health Care System and How to Fix It: An Essay On Health Law and Policy, 41 Wake Forest L. Rev. 537 (2006); Symposium, Who Pays? Who Benefits? Distributional Issues in Health Care, 69 Law & Contemp. Probs. 1 (2006).

State and federal governments are not the only players in the quality arena, of course. Private nonprofit organizations, for example, offer a voluntary accreditation process through which facilities can measure their compliance with standards accepted by their own segment of the industry. Facilities themselves also engage in internal quality assurance and quality improvement efforts, as a result of governmental mandate, accreditation standards, or risk of liability. In addition, private tort and related litigation raises the cost of poor quality in health care facilities. Finally, professionals working in health care facilities have ethical and legal obligations of their own to assure the quality of the organizations in which they care for patients. The question of the appropriate mix of quality control mechanisms does not produce a one-size-fits-all answer, however.

II. REGULATORY SYSTEMS

The materials in this chapter focus primarily on long-term care, a critically important and growing segment of our nation's health care sector. Nursing homes are subject to a high degree of public quality control regulation by both federal and state governments, especially as compared to hospitals, home health agencies, and other health care organizations. Enforcement of nursing home standards over the past three decades has created a revealing case study of the challenges of public quality control regulation. The contrast between nursing homes and hospitals also provides a framework for understanding the factors that determine under what circumstances particular forms of quality control efforts, e.g., market enhancing efforts as compared to licensure, are likely to be more or less effective.

A. DIFFERENCES BETWEEN HOSPITALS AND NURSING HOMES

Hospitals and nursing homes are quite distinctive organizations even though they both provide medical and nursing care for patients/residents. They differ in their patient population; their scope of services; the composition of their staffing; and other internal organizational characteristics. They are also subject to different external pressures.

Differences in Patient Population and Scope of Services

Part of what makes nursing homes unique in the health care system is their responsibility for the complete and total environment of their residents for a substantial length of time. Their involvement with the daily life of residents usually includes assistance in bathing, dressing, toileting, and eating. The majority of residents of a nursing home typically have resided in the facility for more than a year, but the average length of stay for persons entering nursing homes is only a few months. Only 11 in 1000 persons 65–74 years of age reside in nursing homes compared to 46 out of 1000 persons 75–84 and 192 out of 1000 persons 85 years of age or older. E. Kramarow et al., Health and Aging Chartbook. Health, United States (1999).

Nursing home residents typically bear multiple serious, chronic, and intractable medical conditions. Unlike hospital patients, nursing home residents are chronically rather than acutely ill. With the increasing utilization of home care and assisted living, however, the average nursing home patient is much sicker than those of the 1980s. Their physical frailty often requires rigorous and sophisticated care. Younger people who are severely disabled or mentally ill also reside in nursing homes; and regulations addressing their needs are attracting more enforcement effort as well.

The choice of nursing home is unlike the choice of other consumer goods or even the selection of a doctor or a hospital. The selection of a nursing home is typically made under duress, often upon discharge from an unexpected hospitalization; with uncertainty as to the individual's prognosis which influences, for example, whether the admission will be a short-stay rehabilitation admission or a longer term admission; and by an individual other than the patient/resident themselves with resultant persuasion or coercion even when the patient/resident is competent. See, e.g., Deborah Stone, Shopping for Long–Term Care, 23 Health Affairs 191 (2004). The ability of a resident to transfer from a facility providing unsatisfactory services is limited as well due to the physical and mental frailty of the resident. Furthermore, once serious considerations (such as level of care, proximity to family due to potential lengthy stay, and the nursing home's acceptance of Medicaid payments upon admission or once personal funds are exhausted) are accounted for, the remaining choice can be quite slim.

Differences in Organizational Structure

While hospitals in the United States grew as charitable institutions often under the direction of religious organizations, nursing homes developed originally as "mom-and-pop" enterprises, in which individuals boarded elderly persons in private homes. After the advent of Medicare and Medicaid, nursing homes attracted substantial activity from investors and were viewed primarily as real estate investments. Even today, most nursing homes are for-profit, while most hospitals are not-for-profit. National for-profit chains own a significant segment of the nursing home industry. In contrast to studies of the hospital industry, studies of nursing homes consistently find that nonprofit facilities offer higher quality care. M.P. Hilmer, Nursing Home Profit Status and Quality of Care: Is There Any Evidence of an Association?, 62 Med. Care Res. Rev. 139 (2005), reviewing studies published in 1990–2002. See also Charles Duhigg, At Many Homes, More Profit and Less Nursing, N.Y.Times 11 (Sept. 23, 2007), reporting on citations against investor-owned facilities.

Physicians are still largely absent from nursing homes, and professional nurses act primarily as administrators rather than direct care providers. Thus, the peer review oversight processes that are well-entrenched in hospitals are relatively new or absent in nursing homes. Further, hospitals have long subjected themselves to accreditation by the Joint Commission (formerly the Joint Commission on Accreditation of Healthcare Organizations, or JCA-HO), while private accreditation of nursing homes is not as well established or influential. See discussion in Section III, below.

In contrast to the typical hospital market, the demand for nursing home care exceeds available beds although demand may be ebbing somewhat in the face of more alternatives, such as assisted living facilities. Certificate of need programs in the majority of states restrict the number of nursing homes in a particular area on the theory that more beds will raise health care costs. Low supply and excess demand, however, have been associated with lower quality perhaps because of weak competition or because enforcement efforts are constrained by the lack of alternatives for continuing care of the residents. John V. Jacobi, Competition Law's Role in Health Care Quality, 11 Ann. Health L. 45 (2002); John A. Nyman, Prospective and "Cost–Plus" Medicaid Reimbursement, Excess Medicaid Demand, and the Quality of Nursing Home Care, 4 J. Health Econ. 237 (1985).

The Medicaid program paid for nearly half of nursing home care in the U.S. in 2002, while about 15% is paid for by Medicare, leaving approximately 36% paid out-of-pocket by residents or their families, a miniscule portion of which may be covered by long-term-care insurance. Cathy Cowan, et al., National Health Expenditures 2002, 25 Health Care Fin. Rev. 143 (2004). Because nursing home care consumes the bulk of the Medicaid dollar and Medicaid is the largest spending item in state budgets, Medicaid payment levels for nursing homes are contentious. Research on whether increases in payment levels improve the quality of nursing home care, however, has produced mixed results. See, e.g., David C. Grabowski, et al., Medicaid Payment and Risk–Adjusted Nursing Home Quality Measures, 23 Health Affairs 243 (2004), concluding that higher payment levels were associated with lower incidence of pressure sores and use of restraints but not with improvements in pain management; GAO, Nursing Homes: Quality of Care More Related to Staffing than Spending (2002); David C. Grabowski, Medicaid Reimbursement and the Quality of Nursing Home Care, 20 J. Health Econ. 549 (2001).

Differences in the Impact of Private Litigation over Quality

Hospitals are subject to frequent and substantial lawsuits for injuries to patients. In contrast, the characteristics of the nursing home population generally limit their ability to bring suit themselves for harms suffered as a result of poor care or abuse. Causation may be difficult to prove. Physical injuries in very frail elderly persons may be caused either by ordinary touching or by poor care or abuse. Mental impairment makes many nursing home residents poor witnesses. Limited remaining life spans and disabilities minimize legally recognizable damages. They do not suffer lost wages, and medical costs for treatment of injuries generally will be covered by Medicaid or Medicare.

The incidence and success of private lawsuits against these facilities have increased significantly in some regions of the country, however, particularly in Florida and Texas. Some cases have produced particularly large verdicts, but these are rare. In Muccianti v. Willow Creek Care Center, 108 Cal.App.4th 13, 133 Cal.Rptr.2d 1 (Ct. App. 2003), for example, the court specifically recognized that such litigation performs a public function regarding the quality of nursing home care. In *Muccianti*, the court rejected a post-verdict settlement in which the parties agreed to the payment of $1 million instead of the $5 million awarded by the jury. In rejecting the settlement, the court stated that "the public trust clearly could be undermined where a nursing facility has findings of negligence and willful misconduct expunged from the public record," and that "a court-ordered vacation of the judgment could well be interpreted as a judicial nullification of the jury's findings."

Although some of the awards against nursing homes have been spectacular, they may give a mistaken impression of liability risks for nursing homes.

See review of data in Michael L. Rustad, Heart of Stone: What Is Revealed About the Attitude of Compassionate Conservatives Toward Nursing Home Practices, Tort Reform, and Noneconomic Damages, 35 New Mex. L. Rev. 337 (2005). Even in states where private litigation has grown, the litigation is concentrated in just a few facilities. See, Toby S. Edelman, An Advocate's Response to Professor Sage, 9 J. Health Care L. & Pol'y 291 (2006), noting studies in Florida and the District of Columbia (where two facilities accounted for over half of the cases filed over an eight-year period and ten of D.C.'s 19 nursing homes had never had a suit filed against them). Increased frequency of litigation against nursing homes has raised concerns that such litigation might divert resources for care. Litigation successes in pursuing private remedies for negligence and abuse could make the risk of liability a new potent influence in improving the quality of care in nursing homes. Even with increased rates in some states, however, the risk of private litigation against nursing homes pales in comparison to that experienced by hospitals.

While many states enacted legislation some years ago to encourage nursing home patients to pursue private remedies as a means of enforcing regulatory standards, many states have since amended these statutes to make such litigation less viable by limiting damages and attorneys' fees or subjecting such claims to limitations included in general tort reform legislative packages. In an unusual provision in Florida, a plaintiff receiving an award of punitive damages is required to pay half to the Quality of Long–Term Care Facility Improvement Trust Fund. F.S.A. § 400.0238. Finally, nursing homes now frequently include binding arbitration clauses in admission agreements that preclude the award of punitive or exemplary damages to injured residents. While most courts have enforced these clauses unless the resident or legally authorized representative did not sign the agreement, a few decisions have concluded that particular clauses violated public policy by abrogating statutory remedies for nursing home residents. Florida appellate courts have disagreed on this question, for example. See, Fletcher v. Huntington Place Ltd. Partnership, 952 So.2d 1225 (Fla. App. 5th Dist. 2007) and Bland v. Health Care and Retirement Corp., 927 So.2d 252 (Fla. App. 2d Dist. 2006).

Notes and Questions

1.   Prepare a report card on the relative strengths and weaknesses of the various internal and external forces that influence the quality or the accountability of nursing homes as compared to hospitals. Grade each force according to its comparative strength. For general discussion, see Marshall Kapp, Quality of Care and Quality of Life in Nursing Facilities: What's Regulation Got To Do With It? 31 McGeorge L.Rev. 707 (2000); Jennifer Brady, Long–Term Care Under Fire: A Case for Rational Enforcement, 18 J. Contemp Health L. & Pol'y 1 (2001); Alexander D. Eremia, When Self–Regulation, Market Forces, and Private Legal Actions Fail: Appropriate Government Regulation and Oversight is Necessary to Ensure Minimum Standards of Quality in Long–Term Health Care, 11 Annals Health L. 93 (2002).

2.   Over the past several years, federal and state governments have increased mandates for the collection and disclosure of data concerning the performance of health care facilities, including both hospitals and nursing homes. The theory of these efforts is that they will create incentives for quality improvement by enhancing market choices by consumers (or proxy decision makers such as doctors

and discharge planners) and by better informing facilities themselves of their comparative performance. Does the theory apply equally well to hospitals and to nursing homes? David G. Stevenson, Is a Public Reporting Approach Appropriate for Nursing Home Care?, 31 J. Health Pol. Pol'y & L. 773 (2006); Dana Mukamel & William Spector, Quality Report Cards and Nursing Home Quality, 43 The Gerontologist 558 (2003). CMS implemented the Nursing Home Quality Initiative, a national effort aimed at improving care by sharing data with the public on quality in ten functional areas already provided to CMS by the facilities. The data is available at http://www.medicare.gov/NHCompare/home.asp. One of the key issues in report cards and other mandated report systems is the selection of the information that will be collected and posted. The GAO issued a report the day after the national rollout of the data in Nursing Home Compare saying that it was premature and that CMS had not done an effective evaluation of the usefulness of the pilot program it had conducted. GAO: Nursing Homes, Public Reporting of Quality Indicators Has Merit, but National Implementation is Premature, GAO 03–187 (2002). Consumers Union warns that persons searching for a nursing home should ignore the federal web site (in favor of the Nursing Home Quality Monitor database that CU produces, available at http://www.consumerreports.org/cro/health-fitness/nursing-home-guide/nursing-home-quality-monitor/0608–nursing-home-quality-monitor.htm), because the federal site provides only vague generalities about deficiencies. Consumer Reports (Sept. 2006). If you had to respond to the GAO or Consumers Union, how would you design a study to test the effectiveness of this initiative?

B. NURSING HOMES: LICENSURE AND MEDICARE/MEDICAID

Only nursing homes who wish to receive payment for services to Medicare or Medicaid beneficiaries must meet federal standards in order to be certified to enter into a provider agreement with those programs. Medicare and Medicaid standards apply to every resident in the facility, however, and not only to beneficiaries of those programs. If a nursing facility chooses not to participate in Medicare or Medicaid, it will be subject only to state licensure requirements. Realistically, however, most nursing homes cannot survive without Medicare payments, even though Medicare pays only a small portion of the nation's expenditures on institutional long-term care and offers very limited nursing home benefits.

The federal and state nursing home quality-control programs have engaged in a mutually influential relationship for decades. Until the late 1980s, the federal government largely deferred to the state licensure systems to monitor quality for Medicare and Medicaid. With federal nursing home reform in 1987 (the Nursing Home Reform Act in the Omnibus Budget Reconciliation Act of 1987), however, the federal government established standards and methods for the inspection and sanctions process to be used to enforce Medicare and Medicaid requirements, although it continued to rely on the states for on-site inspections. The new federal standards borrowed from a few states that had pioneered initiatives such as intermediate sanctions and, in turn, influenced other states to follow.

The history of nursing homes in the U.S. is characterized by a pattern of scandals, periodic waves of media coverage, and episodes of intense federal and state response. Nursing home abuses and quality failures are once again front-page news and the subject of government reports. See e.g., GAO, Continued Attention is Needed to Improve the Quality of Care in Small but Significant Share of Homes, GAO–07–794T (May 2007), reporting that serious and dangerous conditions persist in almost 20% of facilities and enforcement efforts suffer from data management problems in tracking violators, delays in imposing sanctions, inconsistencies in inspections and reports of violations, and inability to hire competent inspectors. See also GAO, Efforts to Strengthen Federal Enforcement Have Not Deterred Some Homes from Repeatedly Harming Residents, GAO 07–241 (Mar. 2006). These reports recognize that the number of nursing homes cited for deficiencies decreased between 1999–2005 but associate that decrease with less effective inspection and enforcement systems rather than improvements in quality. Consumers Union, in a study funded by the Commonwealth Fund, concluded that poor care is widespread and persistent. At the same time, the HHS reported that quality of care in nursing homes has improved. Nursing Home Quality Improves, HHS Says in Announcing Expanded Initiative, 14 Health L. Rep. 34 (2005).

The federal Centers for Medicare & Medicaid Services (CMS) has taken a number of steps to supplement federal-state enforcement of Medicaid/Medicare standards. In addition to making data on nursing homes available to the public (as discussed earlier), CMS has contracted with private Quality Improvement Organizations (QIOs) to provide consulting services to a particular subset of nursing homes that want to undertake internal efforts to improve quality. The GAO has reported that it is difficult to assess the impact of the QIO initiative because of the unreliability of the CMS's quality measurement data. GAO, Federal Actions Needed to Improve Targeting and Evaluation Assistance by Quality Improvement Organizations, GAO–07–373 (May 2007).

CMS is also considering revising payment systems to create more incentives for providing higher quality care. An Institute of Medicine study of pay-for-performance, however, recommended that implementation be delayed in the case of skilled nursing facilities as a group because of concerns over inadequate measures and data applicable to the short-stay, rehabilitative nursing home services paid for by Medicare. Institute of Medicine, Rewarding Provider Performance: Aligning Incentives in Medicare (2007). See also Jennifer L. Hilliard, The Nursing Home Quality Initiative, 26 J. Leg. Med. 41 (2005).

For a detailed analysis of the history of nursing home regulation as well as current controversies, see David A. Bohm, Striving for Quality Care in America's Nursing Homes: Tracing the History of Nursing Homes and the Effect of Recent Federal Government Initiatives to Ensure Quality Care in the Nursing Home Setting, 4 DePaul J. Health Care L. 317 (2001); Jennifer Brady, Long–Term Care Under Fire: A Case for Rational Enforcement, 18 J. Contemp. Health L. & Pol'y. 1 (2001); Symposium, The Crisis in Long Term Care, 4 J. Health Care L. & Pol'y 308 (2001). For a provocative comparative study of nursing home regulation, see John Braithwaite, et al., Regulating Aged Care: Ritualism and the New Pyramid (2007).

C. THE REGULATORY PROCESS

The regulatory process—whether licensure or Medicare/Medicaid certification–involves three functions: standard setting; inspection (known as the "survey" in nursing home regulation); and sanctions.

1. *Standard Setting*

AVEDIS DONABEDIAN, THE DEFINITION OF QUALITY AND APPROACHES TO ITS ASSESSMENT

Vol. 1 (1980) 79–84.

I have argued . . . that the most direct route to an assessment of the quality of care is an examination of that care. But there are * * * two other, less direct approaches to assessment: one of these is the assessment of "structure", and the other the assessment of "outcome."

By "structure" I mean the relatively stable characteristics of the providers of care, of the tools and resources they have at their disposal, and of the physical and organizational settings in which they work. The concept of structure includes the human, physical, and financial resources that are needed to provide medical care. The term embraces the number, distribution, and qualifications of professional personnel, and so, too, the number, size, equipment, and geographic disposition of hospitals and other facilities. [Donabedian goes on to include within structure the organization of financing and delivery, how doctors practice and how they are paid, staff organization, and how medical work is reviewed in institutions.] * * * The basic characteristics of structure are that it is relatively stable, that it functions to produce care or is a feature of the "environment" of care, and that it influences the kind of care that is provided.

* * * Structure, therefore, is relevant to quality in that it increases or decreases the probability of good performances. * * * But as a means for assessing the quality of care, structure is a rather blunt instrument; it can only indicate general tendencies.

* * *

I believe that good structure, that is, a sufficiency of resources and proper system design, is probably the most important means of protecting and promoting the quality of care. * * * As a source of accurate current information about quality, the assessment of structure is of a good deal less importance than the assessment of process or outcome.

* * *

The study of "outcomes" is the other of the indirect approaches that I have said could be used to assess the quality of care. [Outcome is] * * * a change in a patient's current and future health status that can be attributed to antecedent health care. * * * I shall include improvements of social and psychological function in addition to the more usual emphasis on the physical and physiological aspects of performance. By still another extension I shall add patient attitudes (including satisfaction), health-related knowledge acquired by the patient, and health-related behavioral change.

* * *

* * * [T]here are three major approaches to quality assessment: "structure," "process," and "outcome." This three-fold approach is possible because there is a fundamental functional relationship among the three elements, which can be shown schematically as follows:

Structure → Process → Outcome

This means that structural characteristics of the settings in which care takes place have a propensity to influence the process of care so that its quality is diminished or enhanced. Similarly, changes in the process of care, including variations in its quality, will influence the effect of care on health status, broadly defined.

IN RE THE ESTATE OF MICHAEL PATRICK SMITH v. HECKLER

United States Court of Appeals, Tenth Circuit, 1984.
747 F.2d 583.

McKay, Circuit Judge:

Plaintiffs, seeking relief under 42 U.S.C.A. § 1983, brought this class action on behalf of Medicaid recipients residing in nursing homes in Colorado. They alleged that the Secretary of Health and Human Services (Secretary) has a statutory duty under Title XIX of the Social Security Act, 42 U.S.C.A. §§ 1396–1396n (1982), commonly known as the Medicaid Act, to develop and implement a system of nursing home review and enforcement designed to ensure that Medicaid recipients residing in Medicaid-certified nursing homes actually receive the optimal medical and psychosocial care that they are entitled to under the Act. The plaintiffs contended that the enforcement system developed by the Secretary is "facility-oriented," not "patient-oriented" and thereby fails to meet the statutory mandate. The district court found that although a patient care or "patient-oriented" management system is feasible, the Secretary does not have a duty to introduce and require the use of such a system. [ ]

The primary issue on appeal is whether the trial court erred in finding that the Secretary does not have a statutory duty to develop and implement a system of nursing home review and enforcement, which focuses on and ensures high quality patient care. * * *

BACKGROUND

The factual background of this complex lawsuit is fully discussed in the district court's opinion. [ ] Briefly, plaintiffs instituted the lawsuit in an effort to improve the deplorable conditions at many nursing homes. They presented evidence of the lack of adequate medical care and of the widespread knowledge that care is inadequate. Indeed, the district court concluded that care and life in some nursing homes is so bad that the homes "could be characterized as orphanages for the aged." [ ]

* * *

THE MEDICAID ACT

An understanding of the Medicaid Act (the Act) is essential to understand plaintiffs' contentions. The purpose of the Act is to enable the federal government to assist states in providing medical assistance to "aged, blind or disabled individuals, whose income and resources are insufficient to meet the costs of necessary medical services, and ... rehabilitation and other services to help such ... individuals to attain or retain capabilities for independence or self care." 42 U.S.C.A. § 1396 (1982). To receive funding, a state must submit to the Secretary and have approved by the Secretary, a plan for medical assistance, which meets the requirements of 42 U.S.C.A. § 1396a(a).

* * * A state seeking plan approval must establish or designate a single state agency to administer or supervise administration of the state plan, 42 U.S.C.A. § 1396a(a)(5), and must provide reports and information as the Secretary may require. *Id.* § 1396a(a)(6). Further, the state agency is responsible for establishing and maintaining health standards for institutions where the recipients of the medical assistance under the plan receive care or services. *Id.* § 1396a(a)(9)(A). The plan must include descriptions of the standards and methods the state will use to assure that medical or remedial care services provided to the recipients "are of high quality." *Id.* § 1396a(a)(22)(D).

The state plan must also provide "for a regular program of medical review . . . of each patient's need for skilled nursing facility care . . ., a written plan of care, and, where applicable, a plan of rehabilitation prior to admission to a skilled nursing facility. . . ." *Id.* § 1396a(a)(26)(A). Further, the plan must provide for periodic inspections by medical review teams of:

> (i) the care being provided in such nursing facilities . . . to persons receiving assistance under the State plan; (ii) with respect to each of the patients receiving such care, the adequacy of the services available in particular nursing facilities . . . to meet the current health needs and promote the maximum physical well-being of patients receiving care in such facilities . . .; (iii) the necessity and desirability of continued placement of such patients in such nursing facilities . . .; and (iv) the feasibility of meeting their health care needs through alternative institutional or noninstitutional services. *Id.* § 1396a(a)(26)(B).

The state plan must provide that any skilled nursing facility receiving payment comply with 42 U.S.C.A. § 1395x(j), which defines "skilled nursing facility" and sets out standards for approval under a state plan. *Id.* § 1396a(a)(28). The key requirement for purposes of this lawsuit is that a skilled nursing facility must meet "such other conditions relating to the health and safety of individuals who are furnished services in such institution or relating to the physical facilities thereof as the Secretary may find necessary. . . ." *Id.* § 1395x(j)(15).

The state plan must provide for the appropriate state agency to establish a plan, consistent with regulations prescribed by the Secretary, for professional health personnel to review the appropriateness and quality of care and services furnished to Medicaid recipients. *Id.* § 1396a(a)(33)(A). The appropriate state agency must determine on an ongoing basis whether participating institutions meet the requirements for continued participation in the Medicaid program. *Id.* § 1396a(a)(33)(B). While the state has the initial responsibility for determining whether institutions are meeting the conditions of participation, section 1396a(a)(33)(B) gives the Secretary the authority to "look behind" the state's determination of facility compliance, and make an independent and binding determination of whether institutions meet the requirements for participation in the state Medicaid plan. Thus, the state is responsible for conducting the review of facilities to determine whether they comply with the state plan. In conducting the review, however, the states must use federal standards, forms, methods, and procedures. 42 C.F.R. § 431.610(f)(1) (1983). * * *

IMPLEMENTING REGULATIONS

Congress gave the Secretary a general mandate to promulgate rules and regulations necessary to the efficient administration of the functions with which the Secretary is charged by the Act. 42 U.S.C.A. § 1302 (1982). Pursuant to this mandate the Secretary has promulgated standards for the care to be provided by skilled nursing facilities and intermediate care facilities. See 42 C.F.R. § 442.200–.516 (1983). * * *

The Secretary has established a procedure for determining whether state plans comply with the standards set out in the regulations. This enforcement mechanism is known as the "survey/certification" inspection system. Under this system, the states conduct reviews of nursing homes pursuant to 42 U.S.C.A. § 1396a(a)(33). The Secretary then determines, on the basis of the survey results, whether the nursing home surveyed is eligible for certification and, thus, eligible for Medicaid funds. The states must use federal standards, forms, methods, and procedures in conducting the survey. 42 C.F.R. § 431.610(f)(1). At issue in this case is the form SSA–1569, [ ], which the Secretary requires the states to use to show that the nursing homes participating in Medicaid under an approved state plan meet the conditions of participation contained in the Act and the regulations. Plaintiffs contend that the form is "facility-oriented," in that it focuses on the theoretical capability of the facility to provide high quality care, rather than "patient-oriented," which would focus on the care actually provided. The district court found, with abundant support in the record, that the "facility-oriented" characterization is appropriate and that the Secretary has repeatedly admitted that the form is "facility-oriented." [ ]

THE PLAINTIFFS' CLAIMS

* * *

The plaintiffs do not challenge the substantive medical standards, or "conditions of participation," which have been adopted by the Secretary and which states must satisfy to have their plans approved. See 42 C.F.R. § 405.1101–.1137. Rather, plaintiffs challenge the enforcement mechanism the Secretary has established. The plaintiffs contend that the federal forms, form SSA–1569 in particular, which states are required to use, evaluate only the physical facilities and theoretical capability to render quality care. The surveys assess the care provided almost totally on the basis of the records, documentation, and written policies of the facility being reviewed. [ ] Further, out of the 541 questions contained in the Secretary's form SSA–1569 which must be answered by state survey and certification inspection teams, only 30 are "even marginally related to patient care or might require any patient observation. ..." [ ] Plaintiffs contend that the enforcement mechanism's focus on the facility, rather than on the care actually provided in the facility, results only in "paper compliance" with the substantive standards of the Act. Thus, plaintiffs contend, the Secretary has violated her statutory duty to assure that federal Medicaid monies are paid only to facilities, which meet the substantive standards of the Act—facilities which actually provide high quality medical, rehabilitative, and psychosocial care to resident Medicaid recipients.

THE DISTRICT COURT'S HOLDING

After hearing the evidence, the district court found the type of patient care management system advocated by plaintiffs clearly feasible and characterized the current enforcement system as "facility-oriented." [ ] However, the court concluded that the failure to implement and require the use of a "patient-oriented" system is not a violation of the Secretary's statutory duty. [ ] The essence of the district court's holding was that the State of Colorado, not the federal government, is responsible for developing and enforcing standards which would assure high quality care in nursing homes and, thus, the State of Colorado, not the federal government, should have been the defendant in this case. [ ]

* * *

THE SECRETARY'S DUTY

After carefully reviewing the statutory scheme of the Medicaid Act, the legislative history, and the district court's opinion, we conclude that the district court improperly defined the Secretary's duty under the statute. The federal government has more than a passive role in handing out money to the states. The district court erred in finding that the burden of enforcing the substantive provisions of the Medicaid Act is on the states. The Secretary of Health and Human Services has a duty to establish a system to adequately inform herself as to whether the facilities receiving federal money are satisfying the requirements of the Act, including providing high quality patient care. This duty to be adequately informed is not only a duty to be informed at the time a facility is originally certified, but is a duty of continued supervision.

Nothing in the Medicaid Act indicates that Congress intended the physical facilities to be the end product. Rather, the purpose of the Act is to provide medical assistance and rehabilitative services. 42 U.S.C.A. § 1396. The Act repeatedly focuses on the care to be provided, with facilities being only part of that care. For example, the Act provides that health standards are to be developed and maintained, *id.* § 1396a(a)(9)(A), and that states must inform the Secretary what methods they will use to assure high quality care. *Id.* § 1396a(a)(22). In addition to the "adequacy of the services available," the periodic inspections must address "the care being provided" in nursing facilities. *Id.* § 1396a(a)(26)(B). State plans must provide review of the "appropriateness and quality of care and services furnished," *id.* § 1396a(a)(33)(A), and do so on an ongoing basis. *Id.* § 1396a(a)(33)(B).

While the district court correctly noted that it is the state, which develops specific standards and actually conducts the inspection, there is nothing in the Act to indicate that the state function relieves the Secretary of all responsibility to ensure that the purposes of the Act are being accomplished. The Secretary, not the states, determines which facilities are eligible for federal funds. [ ] While participation in the program is voluntary, states who choose to participate must comply with federal statutory requirements. [ ] The inspections may be conducted by the states, but the Secretary approves or disapproves the state's plan for review. Further, the inspections must be made with federal forms, procedures, and methods.

It would be anomalous to hold that the Secretary has a duty to determine whether a state plan meets the standards of the Act while holding that the Secretary can certify facilities without informing herself as to whether the facilities actually perform the functions required by the state plan. The Secretary has a duty to ensure more than paper compliance. The federal responsibility is particularly evident in the "look behind" provision. 42 U.S.C.A. § 1396a(a)(33)(B) (1982). We do not read the Secretary's "look behind" authority as being "nothing more than permitted authority ... "as the district court found. Rather, we find that the purpose of that section is to assure that compliance is not merely facial, but substantive.

* * *

By enacting section 1302 Congress gave the Secretary authority to promulgate regulations to achieve the functions with which she is charged. The "look-behind" provision and its legislative history clearly show that Congress intended the Secretary to be responsible for assuring that federal Medicaid money is given only to those institutions that actually comply with Medicaid requirements. The Act's requirements include providing high quality medical care and rehabilitative services. In fact, the quality of the care provided to the aged is the focus of the Act. Being charged with this function, we must conclude that a failure to promulgate regulations that allow the Secretary to remain informed, on a continuing basis, as to whether facilities receiving federal money are meeting the requirements of the Act, is an abdication of the Secretary's duty. While the Medicaid Act is admittedly very complex and the Secretary has "exceptionally broad authority to prescribe standards for applying certain sections of the Act" [ ] the Secretary's authority cannot be interpreted so as to hold that that authority is merely permissive authority. The Secretary must insure that states comply with the congressional mandate to provide high quality medical care and rehabilitative services.

* * * Having determined that the purpose and the focus of the Act is to provide high quality medical care, we conclude that by promulgating a facility-oriented enforcement system the Secretary has failed to follow that focus and such failure is arbitrary and capricious. [ ]

Reversed and Remanded.

Notes and Questions

1. What explains the opposition of the federal government to patient-oriented standards in the *Smith* litigation? Should an administrative agency, as a matter of principle, simply resist all judicial mandates in standard setting? Do the courts have the expertise necessary for setting quality standards? After the *Smith* litigation, Congress commissioned the Institute of Medicine to conduct a study of nursing home regulation. See, Improving the Quality of Care in Nursing Homes (1986). The report significantly influenced the subsequent federal Nursing Home Reform Act, commonly referenced as OBRA 1987, which represented a comprehensive change in standards, surveillance methods, and enforcement and still provides the core of federal regulation of nursing homes.

2. Did the plaintiffs in *Smith* contest the standards as enacted in the statute? As promulgated in regulations? Would a challenge to the statute itself

likely be successful? On what basis would plaintiffs be able to challenge the regulations? Why would the survey forms themselves be of interest to attorneys representing facilities or residents? For similar litigation, see Rolland v. Patrick, 483 F.Supp.2d 107 (D. Mass. 2007), in which advocates challenged the state's standards for measuring mandated treatment for mentally retarded and developmentally disabled individuals in nursing homes.

3. The plaintiffs in *Smith* were concerned that federal standards at the time measured only the facility's "theoretical capability to render quality care." The CMS Nursing Home Quality Initiative (NHQI) identifies quality measurements (QMs) for nursing homes, using data collected in the Minimum Data Set (an instrument established in OBRA 1987 to require each facility to collect and report standardized data on each resident). For long-stay residents, the quality measurements are the percentage of residents with infections, pain, pressure sores (with residents allocated into low-risk and high-risk groups), physical restraints, and loss of ability in basic daily tasks. Data on these quality measures are posted on the Nursing Home Compare web site and may eventually be used for incentive-based payment programs. If you were an administrator of a nursing home and wanted to improve your performance on these outcome measures, you might increase or reorganize staff effort or other resources. Outcome measures at times create perverse incentives, however. For example, the measure of assistance in basic daily tasks excludes from the count patients who are terminally ill but does not exclude patients who have Alzheimer's disease or have suffered a stroke for whom natural progression may be increasing losses in self-care. Thus, the outcomes standards in the NHQI may encourage facilities to avoid admitting particular types of residents. Jennifer L. Hilliard, The Nursing Home Quality Initiative, 26 J. Legal. Med. 41 (2005); Katherine Berg, et al., Identification and Evaluation of Existing Nursing Home Quality Indicators, 23 Health Care Fin. Rev. 19 (2002); Steven Clauser & Arlene Bierman, Significance of Functional Status Data for Payment and Quality, 24 Health Care Fin. Rev. 1 (2003).

4. When the Secretary issued final regulations to implement a new survey system as ordered by the court in *Smith,* she refused to include the survey instrument itself in the regulations: "[T]he new forms and instructions are not set forth in these regulations, and any future changes will be implemented through general instructions, without further changes in these regulations. This allows flexibility to revise and improve the survey process as experience is gained." 51 Fed.Reg. 21550 (June 13, 1986). What else does this allow the agency to do? The federal district court rejected the final rules because they did not include the survey instruments or instructions and held the Secretary in contempt of court. Smith v. Bowen, 675 F.Supp. 586 (D.Colo. 1987). What was the judge's concern?

5. OBRA 1987 appears to have had a positive effect on several practices. For example, the use of physical restraints declined by 50%; inappropriate use of antipsychotic drugs declined at least 25%; the incidence of dehydration was reduced by 50%; the use of indwelling catheters by nearly 30%; and hospitalizations by 25%. Bruce C. Vladeck, The Past, Present and Future of Nursing Home Quality, 275 JAMA 425 (1996), reviewing the literature. But see, Catherine Hawes, et al., The OBRA–87 Nursing Home Regulations and Implementation of the Resident Assessment Instrument: Effects on Process Quality, 45 J. Am. Geriatrics Soc'y 977 (1997), discussing the difficulty of proving that changes in practices and outcomes were caused by the new regulations. Marshall Kapp, in an article that is quite skeptical about research indicating that the standards of OBRA 1987 have had a significant positive effect, notes that government studies of the quality of nursing home care reveal persistent problems in the quality of

care and the effectiveness of the regulatory system. Marshall B. Kapp, Quality of Care and Quality of Life in Nursing Facilities: What's Regulation Got To Do With It? 31 McGeorge L. Rev. 707 (2000).

6.   The court's opinion in *Smith* describes the allocation of authority in the federal-state Medicaid quality control program. Exactly which functions are allocated to the state and which to the federal government? Is the federal-state effort duplicative and inefficient? Should Congress consider requiring that nursing facilities receiving Medicaid or Medicare dollars merely be licensed by the state? What is the justification for the federal role in this situation? For further discussion of federal-state relations, see Senator Charles Grassley, The Resurrection of Nursing Home Reform: A Historical Account of the Recent Revival of the Quality of Care Standards for Long–Term Care Facilities Established in the Omnibus Reconciliation Act of 1987, 7 Elder L.J. 267 (1999); William Gromley & Christine Boccuti, HCFA and the States: Politics and Intergovernmental Leverage, 26 J. Health Pol. Pol'y and L. 557 (2001).

7.   Staff-to-resident and nurse-to-resident ratio is a structural standard that is receiving increasing support as a key indicator of quality in nursing homes and hospitals. See, e.g., GAO, Nursing Homes: Quality of Care More Related to Staffing than Spending (2002). An IOM report recommended increased nurse staffing levels in nursing homes and hospitals as essential to reducing hazards to patient care. Donald M. Steinwachs, Keeping Patients Safe: Transforming the Work Environment of Nurses (2003). The federal government and the states are responding to the evidence underlying these recommendations. See, Theresamarie Mantese, et al., Nurse Staffing, Legislative Alternatives and Health Care Policy, 9 DePaul J. Health Care L. 1171 (2006). A few states have established mandatory staffing ratios. See, e.g., Del. Code Ann. Tit. 16, § 1162; Cal. Health & Safety Code § 1276.5. CMS requires that nursing homes receiving Medicaid or Medicare post their daily resident count and their nurse (including RNs, LPNs, and CNAs) staffing numbers for each shift in a public place at the facility. 70 Fed. Reg. 62065 (Oct. 28, 2005). CMS also includes staffing data on its Nursing Home Compare web site.

8.   Federal standards aimed at reducing the use of physical and chemical restraints represented not only a regulatory change but a fundamental shift in the foundation of a customary practice. Prior to the mid 1980s, physically restraining a nursing home resident was viewed as protective of the patient in that it prevented falls. It was also believed that a nursing home would be liable for injuries due to falls if it did not restrain patients. Research in the field changed that view. See, for example, Julie A. Braun & Elizabeth A. Capezuti, The Legal and Medical Aspects of Physical Restraints and Bed Siderails and Their Relationship to Falls and Fall–Related Injuries in Nursing Homes, 4 DePaul J. of Health Care Law 1 (2000); Sandra H. Johnson, The Fear of Liability and the Use of Restraints in Nursing Homes, 18 Law, Med. & Health Care 263 (1990). The Department of Justice Civil Rights Division has approached the inappropriate use of physical and chemical restraints as a violation of the civil rights of residents of public nursing homes under the Civil Rights of Institutional Persons Act. 42 U.S.C. § 1997. See DOJ report at http://www.usdoj.gov/crt/split/cripa.htm.

Problem: Residents' Rights

Assume that you are the attorney for Pine Acres Nursing Home, located in an older section of the city. The administrator has approached you regarding problems with certain patients. One patient, Francis Scott, aged 88, has been a resident of the facility for a few months. Scott's mental and physical condition has been deteriorating slowly for several years and much more rapidly in the past six months. His family placed him in the nursing home because they wanted him to be safe. They were concerned because he had often left his apartment and become totally lost on the way back. Mr. Scott's family always promptly pays the monthly fee. Scott is angry about the placement, tends to be rude and insists on walking through the hallways and around the fenced-in grounds of the facility on his own. He has always been an early riser and likes to take his shower at the crack of dawn. He refuses to be assisted in showering by a nurses' aide. In addition, his friends from the neighborhood like to visit. They like to play pinochle when they come, and they usually bring a six-pack.

Another patient, Emma Kaitz, has fallen twice, apparently while trying to get out of bed. The staff is very concerned that she will be hurt. The physician who is medical director of the facility will write an order for restraints "as needed" for any resident upon the request of the director of nursing. Mrs. Kaitz's daughter is willing to try whatever the doctor advises. The staff have begun using "soft restraints" (cloth straps on her wrists) tied to the bedrails, but Mrs. Kaitz becomes agitated and cries. She says she feels like a dog when they tie her up. Other times they just use the bedrails alone. When she becomes agitated, she is given a sedative to help her relax, but it also tends to make her appear confused. To avoid the agitation as much as possible during the day, they have been able to position her wheelchair so that she can't get out by herself. She stops trying after a while and becomes so relaxed she nods off.

The administrator wants to know what he can do. What would you advise this administrator? Can he restrict the visiting hours for Mr. Scott? Can he require Mr. Scott to be assisted in the shower? Can Mr. Scott be transferred or discharged? Is the facility providing quality care for Mrs. Kaitz? How should an inspector treat Mr. Scott's and Mrs. Kaitz's complaints? What does your nursing home client expect of you here? What role should you play in regard to quality of care standards?

The text that follows includes excerpts from the Residents' Rights section of the Medicaid statute; the regulation on the use of physical restraints; and the interpretive guidelines on physical restraints provided to surveyors for the inspection of Medicaid facilities.

42 U.S.C.A. § 1396r

(b)(1) QUALITY OF LIFE.—

(A) IN GENERAL.—A nursing facility must care for its residents in such a manner and in such an environment as will promote maintenance or enhancement of the quality of life of each resident.

* * *

(c) REQUIREMENTS RELATING TO RESIDENTS' RIGHTS—

(1) GENERAL RIGHTS.—

(A) SPECIFIED RIGHTS.—A nursing facility must protect and promote the rights of each resident, including each of the following rights:

(i) FREE CHOICE.—The right to choose a personal attending physician, to be fully informed in advance about care and treatment that may affect the resident's well-being, and (except with respect to a resident adjudged incompetent) to participate in planning care and treatment or changes in care and treatment.

(ii) FREE FROM RESTRAINTS.—The right to be free from physical or mental abuse, corporal punishment, involuntary seclusion, and any physical or chemical restraints imposed for purposes of discipline or convenience and not required to treat the resident's medical symptoms. Restraints may only be imposed—

(I) to ensure the physical safety of the resident or other residents, and

(II) only upon the written order of a physician that specifies the duration and circumstances under which the restraints are to be used (except in emergency circumstances specified by the Secretary until such an order could reasonably be obtained).

(iii) PRIVACY.—The right to privacy with regard to accommodations, medical treatment, written and telephonic communications, visits, and meetings of family and of resident groups. [Does not require private rooms.]

(v) ACCOMMODATION OF NEEDS.—The right—

(I) to reside and receive services with reasonable accommodations of individual needs and preferences, except where the health or safety of the individual or other residents would be endangered, and

(II) to receive notice before the room or roommate of the resident in the facility is changed.

(viii) PARTICIPATION IN OTHER ACTIVITIES.—The right of the resident to participate in social, religious, and community activities that do not interfere with the rights of other residents in the facility.

* * *

(D) USE OF PSYCHOPHARMACOLOGIC DRUGS.

Psychopharmacologic drugs may be administered only on the orders of a physician and only as part of a plan (included in the written plan of care . . .) designed to eliminate or modify the symptoms for which the drugs are prescribed and only if, at least annually an independent, external consultant reviews the appropriateness of the drug plan of each resident receiving such drugs.

(2) TRANSFER AND DISCHARGE RIGHTS.—

(A) IN GENERAL.—A nursing facility must permit each resident to remain in the facility and must not transfer or discharge the resident from the facility unless—

(i) the transfer or discharge is necessary to meet the resident's welfare and the resident's welfare cannot be met in the facility;

(ii) the transfer or discharge is appropriate because the resident's health has improved sufficiently so the resident no longer needs the services provided by the facility;

(iii) the safety of individuals in the facility is endangered;

(iv) the health of individuals in the facility would otherwise be endangered;

(v) the resident has failed, after reasonable and appropriate notice, to pay . . . for a stay at the facility; or

(vi) the facility ceases to operate.

* * *

(B) PRE–TRANSFER AND PRE–DISCHARGE NOTICE.—

(i) IN GENERAL.—Before effecting a transfer or discharge of a resident, a nursing facility must—

(I) notify the resident (and, if known, an immediate family member of the resident or legal representative) of the transfer or discharge and the reasons therefore,

(II) record the reasons in the resident's clinical record * * * and

(III) include in the notice the items described in clause (iii). [concerning appeal of transfer]

(ii) TIMING OF NOTICE.—The notice under clause (i)(I) must be made at least 30 days in advance of the resident's transfer or discharge except—

(I) in a case described in clause (iii) or (iv) of subparagraph (A);

(II) in a case described in clause (ii) of subparagraph (A), where the resident's health improves sufficiently to allow a more immediate transfer or discharge;

(III) in a case described in clause (i) of subparagraph (A), where a more immediate transfer or discharge is necessitated by the resident's urgent medical needs; or

(IV) in a case where a resident has not resided in the facility for 30 days.

In the case of such exceptions, notice must be given as many days before the date of the transfer or discharge as is practicable. [The statute also requires the state to establish a hearing process for transfers and discharges contested by the resident or surrogate.]

(3) ACCESS AND VISITATION RIGHTS.—A nursing facility must—

(A) permit immediate access to any resident by any representative of the Secretary, by any representative of the State, by an ombudsman . . ., or by the resident's individual physician;

(B) permit immediate access to a resident, subject to the resident's right to deny or withdraw consent at any time, by immediate family or other relatives of the resident;

(C) permit immediate access to a resident, subject to reasonable restrictions and the resident's right to deny or withdraw consent at any time, by others who are visiting with the consent of the resident;

(D) permit reasonable access to a resident by any entity or individual that provides health, social, legal, or other services to the resident, subject to the resident's right to deny or withdraw consent at any time; and

(E) permit representatives of the State ombudsman . . ., with the permission of the resident (or the resident's legal representative) and consistent with State law, to examine a resident's clinical records.

(4) EQUAL ACCESS TO QUALITY CARE.—

A nursing facility must establish and maintain identical policies and practices regarding transfer, discharge and the provision of services ... for all individuals regardless of source of payment.

42 C.F.R. § 483.13(a)

Restraints. The resident has the right to be free from any physical or chemical restraints imposed for purposes of discipline or convenience, and not required to treat the resident's medical symptoms.

GUIDANCE TO SURVEYORS: § 483.13(a)

Medicare State Operations Manual, Appendix PP—Guidance to Surveyors—Long Term Care Facilities (Sept. 7, 2000), available at http://cms.hhs.gov/manuals/pm_trans/R20SOM.pdf.

Convenience is defined as any action taken by the facility to control a resident's behavior or manage a resident's behavior with a lesser amount of effort by the facility and not in the resident's best interest.

Restraints may not be used for staff convenience. However, if the resident needs emergency care, restraints may be used for brief periods to permit medical treatment to proceed unless the facility has a notice indicating that the resident has previously made a valid refusal of the treatment in question. If a resident's unanticipated violent or aggressive behavior places him/her or others in imminent danger, the resident does not have the right to refuse the use of restraints. In this situation, the use of restraints is a measure of last resort to protect the safety of the resident or others and must not extend beyond the immediate episode.

Physical Restraints are defined as any manual method or physical or mechanical device, material, or equipment attached or adjacent to the resident's body that the individual cannot remove easily which restricts freedom of movement or normal access to one's body.

"Physical restraints" include, but are not limited to, leg restraints, arm restraints, hand mitts, soft ties or vests, lap cushions, and lap trays the resident cannot remove easily. Also included as restraints are facility practices that meet the definition of a restraint, such as:

Using side rails that keep a resident from voluntarily getting out of bed;

Tucking in or using velcro to hold a sheet, fabric, or clothing tightly so that a resident's movement is restricted;

Using devices in conjunction with a chair, such as trays, tables, bars or belts, that the resident cannot remove easily, that prevent the resident from rising;

Placing a resident in a chair that prevents a resident from rising; and

Placing a chair or bed so close to a wall that the wall prevents the resident from rising out of the chair or voluntarily getting out of bed.

* * *

The same device may have the effect of restraining one individual but not another, depending on the individual resident's condition and circumstances.

For example, partial rails may assist one resident to enter and exit the bed independently while acting as a restraint for another ...

* * *

The resident's subjective symptoms may not be used as the sole basis for using a restraint. Before a resident is restrained, the facility must determine the presence of a specific medical symptom that would require the use of restraints, and how the use of restraints would treat the medical symptom, protect the resident's safety, and assist the resident in attaining or maintaining his or her highest practicable level of physical and psychosocial well-being. . . .

While there must be a physician's order reflecting the presence of a medical symptom, [CMS] will hold the facility ultimately accountable for the appropriateness of that determination. The physician's order alone is not sufficient to warrant the use of the restraint. . . .

In order for the resident to be fully informed, the facility must explain, in the context of the individual resident's condition and circumstances, the potential risks and benefits of all options under consideration including using a restraint, not using a restraint, and alternatives to restraint use. . . . In addition, the facility must also explain the potential negative outcomes of restraint use which include, but are not limited to, declines in the resident's physical functioning (e.g., ability to ambulate) and muscle condition, contractures, increased incidence of infections and development of pressure sores/ulcers, delirium, agitation, and incontinence. Moreover, restraint use may constitute an accident hazard. . . . Finally, residents who are restrained may face a loss of autonomy, dignity and self respect, and may show symptoms of withdrawal, depression, or reduced social contact. . . .

In the case of a resident who is incapable of making a decision, the legal surrogate or representative may exercise this right based on the same information that would have been provided to the resident. [ ] However, the legal surrogate or representative cannot give permission to use restraints for the sake of discipline or staff convenience or when the restraint is not necessary to treat the resident's medical symptoms. . . .

* * *

2. *Survey and Inspection*

An effective quality-control regulatory system requires an effective inspection process that, with an acceptable degree of accuracy, detects and documents violations of standards. Providers tend to believe that inspectors are overly aggressive; resident advocates, that they are too lax. Several studies have concluded that state and federal surveys seriously understate deficiencies, failing to cite for deficiencies or categorizing cited deficiencies as less serious than they are. See, e.g., GAO, Nursing Home Quality: Prevalence of Serious Problems, While Declining, Reinforces Importance of Enhanced Oversight, GAO–03–561 (July 2003), also noting that state inspections are "predictable in their timing, allowing homes to conceal problems;" GAO, Continued Attention is Needed to Improve Quality of Care in Small but Significant Share of Homes, GAO–07–794T (May 2007).

Surveyors may have difficulty with patient-focused and outcome-oriented survey techniques. In particular, researchers have reported that surveyors hesitate to cite facilities because they may be uncomfortable with the sophisticated level of assessment required for a citation on an outcome standard and may instead opt to cite the facility for less serious but more easily documented violations. What might steer surveyors toward "documentable" citations and away from problems on which there might be more room for disagreement?

Studies have concluded consistently that there is wide variation among the states in terms of the number of citations. Does this variation reflect the quality of facilities or of inspection processes? What role should the courts play in the question of surveyor discretion or inconsistency? Should the survey standards be more rigid?

Facilities that attack the survey process itself, as applied to the facility in a particular instance, are unlikely to succeed. In EPI Corp. v. Chater, 91 F.3d 143 (6th Cir. 1996), the court rejected claims that the survey team failed to follow appropriate procedures holding that the survey team had substantially complied with survey procedures; and that the plaintiff facility did not suffer substantial prejudice to its interests by the surveyors' failure to complete a particular form in advance of the exit conference. See also, Beverly California Corp. v. Shalala, 78 F.3d 403 (8th Cir. 1996). But see, Southern Health Facilities v. Somani, 1995 WL 765161 (Ohio Ct. App. 1995), reversing dismissal of facility's claim that the survey did not comply with federal and state rules in failing to conduct an exit conference.

What relationship should the surveyor establish with the facility? Is the surveyor a consultant or advisor? Should the surveyor offer suggestions for improvement? Should the surveyor commend the facility on noted improvements or other indicators of quality identified during the inspection? For a critique of the enforcement-oriented survey process, see John Braithwaite, et al., Regulating Aged Care: Ritualism and The New Pyramid (2007); Mary Kathleen Robbins, Nursing Home Reform: Objective Regulation or Subjective Decisions?, 11 Thomas Cooley L. Rev. 185 (1994).

3. Sanctions

The development of intermediate sanctions was a major effort among the states in the late 1970s and 1980s, and was adopted by the federal government in OBRA 1987. In Vencor Nursing Ctrs. v. Shalala, 63 F. Supp.2d 1 (D.D.C. 1999), the court described the rationale for intermediate sanctions:

> In enacting the enforcement provisions to the Medicare and Medicaid Acts, Congress expressly wished to expand the panoply of remedies available to HHS. [ ]. Committee reports noted with concern the "yo-yo" phenomenon in which noncomplying facilities temporarily correct their deficiencies before an on-site survey and then quickly lapse into noncompliance until the next review. [ ]. Presumably, the new version of the statute ameliorates this problem by giving HHS a set of intermediate sanctions to choose from rather than the extreme choices of termination or no sanction. There is no indication in the legislative history that Congress wished to limit HHS's ability to terminate a persistently non-compliant facility. [ ]. In fact, the recurring theme emerging from the

legislative history is that the new provisions would grant HHS remedial powers in addition to those already available. [ ].

An OIG report on CMS's implementation of mandatory statutory sanctions found that the agency failed to terminate the provider agreement in 30 out of 55 cases in which the facility remained out of compliance (on those specific citations) past the six-month deadline for reaching compliance or had an unabated condition that presented immediate jeopardy to the health and safety of the residents for more than 23 days. Nursing Home Enforcement: Application of Mandatory Remedies, OEI–06–03–00410 (May 2006). CMS also failed to deny payment for new admissions to 28% of the over 700 facilities that remained out of compliance for over 3 months after citation, as required by statute. CMS reported to the OIG that it did not intend to make any changes to its policies or practices:

> While the law requires that mandatory actions occur at specified times and under specific circumstances, it also contemplates that sanctions will be used to motivate improvements and lasting corrections. Where these expectations may be in conflict, we seek to resolve the conflict with the solution that best protects the well-being of the resident. Nursing Homes that Merit Punishment Not Terminated, Federal Review Finds, 15 Health L. Rep. 628 (2006).

Is this statement persuasive? Could a nursing home residents' advocacy group bring a *Smith v. Heckler* action against CMS for violation of the federal statute? See, California Advocates for Nursing Home Reform v. California Dept. of Health Services, 2006 WL 2829865 (Cal. Super. 2006), granting writ of mandamus on claim that Department failed to investigate complaints filed with the Department against nursing homes. See also Ineffective Enforcement Process Thwarts Efforts to Ban Poor Performers, Paper Finds, 13 Health L. Rep. 1237 (2004).

Among the reported judicial opinions reviewing sanctions under Medicare/Medicaid, it appears that the most frequently litigated questions are the determination of "immediate jeopardy," which triggers the most severe sanctions, and the appropriateness of the sanction chosen. In *Vencor,* supra, in which the facility contested termination of the provider agreement as inconsistent with the statute, the court describes the rationale for the deferential scope of review over the choice of sanctions:

> Broad deference is particularly warranted where the regulation "concerns a complex and highly technical regulatory program," like Medicare, "in which the identification and classification of relevant criteria necessarily require significant expertise and entail the exercise of judgment grounded in policy concerns."

What are the policy concerns in the choice of sanctions?

If a facility is cited for but then corrects a deficiency, should it still be penalized for that violation? One study concluded that the nursing home regulatory system relies extensively on correction and voluntary compliance rather than punishment even though the emphasis in OBRA was to use penalties as a deterrent. Still, the study concludes that the emphasis on surveillance in the U.S. system has led to more regimentation and inflexibility in U.S. nursing homes than in other countries with different systems, implying that quality of care and quality of life suffer. John Braithwaite, The Nursing Home Industry, 18 Crime & Justice 11 (1993). See also, Richard L. Peck, Does Europe Have the Answers?, 49 Nursing Homes 54 (June 2000); GAO, Nursing Homes: Efforts to Strengthen Federal Enforcement Have Not Deterred Some Homes from Repeatedly Harming Residents, GAO–07–241 (Mar. 2006). The OIG report, supra, noted that 23 of the 30 facilities that exceeded the statutory timeline for correction actually came into compliance 17 days after the statutory deadline. Would this prove that CMS's choice to forego termination was the right decision after all?

III. PRIVATE ACCREDITATION OF HEALTH CARE FACILITIES

Private accreditation is a nongovernmental, voluntary activity conducted by not-for-profit associations. The Joint Commission (formerly the Joint Commission on Accreditation of Healthcare Organizations or JCAHO), which offers accreditation programs for hospitals, nursing homes, home health, and other facilities, and the National Committee on Quality Assurance (NCQA), which accredits managed care plans and other providers, are two of the leading organizations in the accreditation of health care entities. You can review the scope of their activities and new developments through their websites at www.jointcommission.org and www.ncqa.org.

As a voluntary process, accreditation may be viewed as a private communicative device, providing the accredited health care entity merely with a seal of approval—a method for communicating in shorthand that it meets standards established by an external organization. See, Clark C. Havighurst, Foreword: The Place of Private Accrediting Among the Instruments of Government, 57 L. & Contemp. Probs. 1 (1994). In practice, however, there is a much closer marriage between some private accreditation programs and government regulation of health care facilities. This is especially true of the Joint Commission hospital accreditation program as virtually all U.S. hospitals with more than 25 beds are accredited by the Joint Commission. The Joint Commission's hospital accreditation program is the largest and most influential of its accreditation programs. In a survey identifying the most powerful influences on hospitals' adoption of patient safety initiatives, for example, hospital administrators reported that the Joint Commission was the key factor and that their patient safety programs were linked specifically to its patient safety standards and goals. Kelly J. Devers, et al., What is Driving Hospitals' Patient–Safety Efforts?, 23 Health Affairs 103 (2004).

Both state and federal governments rely to a great extent on accreditation in their hospital licensure and Medicare/Medicaid hospital certification programs. Most states have incorporated the Commission's accreditation standards, some explicitly, into their hospital licensure standards. Some have accepted accreditation in lieu of a state license. See e.g., Tex. Health & Safety Code § 222.024. Under the Medicare statute, Joint Commission-accredited hospitals are "deemed" to have met requirements for Medicare certification. 42 U.S.C. §§ 1395x(e), 1395bb. Although the Secretary retains a look-behind authority, the Joint Commission substitutes for the routine surveillance process.

Originally, the acceptance of accreditation by the Medicare program was designed to entice an adequate number of hospitals to participate in the then-new Medicare program. That original rationale has dissipated as hospitals have become much more dependent on Medicare payments. At the same time, the federal government's reliance on private accreditation as a substitute for routine government surveillance has expanded considerably beyond the original hospital setting and now extends to clinical laboratories and home health care, among others.

What might explain this extensive reliance on private organizations for public regulation? Some argue that private accreditation more effectively encourages voluntary compliance and avoids some of the prosecutorial environment of a government-conducted inspection program. Furthermore, and perhaps more pragmatically, deemed status allows the government to shift the cost of the inspection process because accredited facilities pay for the costs of accreditation, including the site visit.

How does the private accreditation process compare to public regulation? Private accreditation programs traditionally have engaged in practices that encourage voluntary subscription to the accreditation program. For example, accreditation programs often perform only announced site visits and keep negative evaluations confidential, at least until the accreditation status itself is reduced or not renewed. Standards established by accreditation programs, which are often dominated by professionals in the industry rather than consumer groups, may differ from those set by a process that arguably fosters broader public participation. With the Joint Commission, in particular, governance and policymaking are dominated by physician organization members such as the AMA.

The Joint Commission accreditation survey is explicitly consultative in nature. For example in regard to its survey of home health agencies, the Joint Commission states that "[a]n important characteristic of the Joint Commission survey process is on-site education and consultation conducted . . . throughout the survey as surveyors offer suggestions for approaches and strategies that may help your organization better meet the intent of the standards and . . . improve performance."

In recognizing deemed status for a particular accreditation program, the federal government typically requires that the program meet particular standards. For example, the recognition of deemed status for home health agencies includes the following requirements: release of survey reports to HHS routinely and to the public upon request; reporting of evidence of fraud and abuse; harmonization of Joint Commission standards with Medicare conditions of participation; and implementation of unannounced surveys utilizing federal methodology. CMS retains the right to inspect any facility certified through deemed status and will do validation and complaint surveys to monitor Joint Commission performance. 58 Fed. Reg. 35007 (June 30, 1993). Has the department adequately preserved its interests and authority? The GAO concluded that CMS lacks adequate information to monitor Joint Commission performance in hospital accreditation and lacks legal authority to take effective action if problems are detected. GAO, CMS Lacks Adequate Authority to Adequately Oversee Patient Safety in Hospitals, GAO–04–850 (July 2004). This study noted that "JCAHO's pre–2004 hospital accreditation process did not identify most of the hospitals found by state survey agencies in CMS' annual validation survey sample to have deficiencies in Medicare requirements." Joint Commission accreditation surveys had failed to identify 69% of Medicare deficiencies and 78% of the hospitals with deficiencies. The Joint Commission had been subjecting only a sample of 5% of its accredited organizations to unannounced surveys. In June, 2006, the American Nurses Association filed suit against HHS seeking a declaratory judgment that HHS' Delegation of Authority to the Joint Commission was unlawful in that Joint Commission standards regarding staffing are not equivalent to those required by the Medicare program and an order that HHS establish an effective system for determining that Joint Commission and HHS Medicare standards are equivalent. Nurses Association Lawsuit Latest Salvo in Campaign to Tackle Staffing Problems, 15 Health L. Rep. 1366 (2006).

The Joint Commission began performing its inspections on an unannounced basis in Spring, 2006. In addition, the Joint Commission has adopted several initiatives to focus its standards toward continuous quality improvement and toward medical error monitoring and patient safety. The "Sentinel Event" initiative, for example, encourages facilities to report errors and root cause analyses for the benefit of systemic change in areas such as wrong-site surgery and medication errors. Its "Shared Visions—New Pathways" initiative focuses on on-going compliance and self-assessment.

For a history of the Joint Commission and a broad review of legal issues related to private accreditation, see Timothy S. Jost, The Joint Commission on Accreditation of Hospitals: Private Regulation of Health Care and the Public Interest, 24 B.C.L.Rev. 835 (1983). For a discussion of the relation between private accreditation and public regulation, see Jody Freeman, The Private Role in Public Governance, 75 N.Y.U. L.Rev. 543 (2000); Symposium on Private Accreditation in the Regulatory State, 57 Law and Contemp. Prob.1 (1994); Gillian Metzger, Privatization as Delegation, 103 Col. L. Rev. 1367 (2003); Rand E. Rosenblatt, The Four Ages of Health Law, 14 Health Matrix 155 (2004); Louise G. Trubek, New Governance and Soft Law in Health Care Reform, 3 Ind. Health L. Rev. 139 (2006).

Chapter 3

THE PROFESSIONAL–PATIENT RELATIONSHIP

INTRODUCTION

The focus of legal duties and ethical analysis begins with the individual physician, who has primary responsibility for seeing the patient, diagnosing the problem, and prescribing the treatment. Health care today is however delivered in a variety of settings—hospitals, ambulatory care clinics, nursing homes, doctors' offices. And the institutional framework for such care, in terms of its financing, support, and obligations, may encompass medical staffs, managed care organizations, partnerships, and institutional employers.

Professional liability, discussed in Chapter 4, focuses upon a breach of duty of care owed by the physician to a particular patient. This chapter considers the formation of the physician-patient relationship and a range of other obligations that the law imposes on physicians and other health care professionals.

ESQUIVEL v. WATTERS
Court of Appeals of Kansas, 2007.
154 P.3d 1184.

Michelle and Jesse Esquivel, the parents of Jadon Esquivel, appeal the district court's entry of summary judgment in favor of Dr. Aaron T. Watters and the South Central Kansas Regional Medical Center (SCKRMC) in these survivor and wrongful death actions which arose from Jadon's death several weeks following his birth.

Upon learning she was pregnant, Michelle Esquivel obtained obstetric counseling from the Ark City Clinic. A clinic worker gave Michelle a certificate from SCKRMC for a free gender determination sonogram. Michelle went to SCKRMC for her free sonogram on November 15, 2001. Prior to the sonogram being performed, Michelle signed a document entitled "Consent to Procedure to Determine Sex of Unborn Baby." The consent form stated in relevant part:

> "2. The purpose of the procedure is to attempt to determine the sex of my unborn baby and I acknowledge there is no guarantee or assurance that an accurate determination can be made by this procedure.

57

"I further acknowledge that this procedure is not to determine any fetal abnormality or any other complication of pregnancy and is not considered a diagnostic examination for any medical purpose other than to attempt to determine the sex of my unborn baby.

"3. To induce Medical Center to perform this procedure the undersigned hereby waives and releases South Central Kansas Regional Medical Center, its officers, employees, agents, and affiliates from any and all claims, costs, liabilities, expenses, judgments, attorney fees, court costs, causes of action and compensation whatsoever arising out of the foregoing described procedure."

David Hazlett, an SCKRMC technician, performed the sonogram and noted that Michelle's baby's bowel was outside of his body, a condition known as gastroschisis. Hazlett did not inform Michelle of this irregularity because he is not a doctor and not qualified or licensed to make a medical diagnosis. Hazlett was unable to determine the baby's gender because of the gastroschisis. Nevertheless he took sonogram pictures which he sent to a radiologist at the Ark City Clinic. The radiologist refused to look at them because the sonogram was only for gender determination and not for diagnosis.

Hazlett also reported the irregularity to Watters, Michelle's obstetrician. Hazlett did not send any of the sonogram pictures to Watters. He sent no written report to Watters. Watters made no note of Hazlett's oral report in Michelle's medical chart. However, he directed his nurse to call Michelle. Watters' nurse made 11 attempts to contact Michelle by telephone over the next 10 days. On November 26, 2001, a man the nurse believed to be Jesse Esquivel answered the phone. The nurse told him to tell Michelle to call Watters' office. Michelle missed her prenatal appointment scheduled for that day. She next saw Watters on January 4, 2002. Since Watters had forgotten Hazlett's oral report of the abnormal sonogram and there was nothing in Michelle's chart to remind him, he failed to discuss it with her. When he saw Michelle again a month later, he again forgot to inform her of the abnormal sonogram.

On February 8, 2002, Michelle became ill and went to SCKRMC for treatment. Jadon was born by emergency caesarean section the next day. Neither Michelle nor Jesse nor the medical staff who delivered Jadon was aware that Jadon had gastroschisis until he was born.

Jadon was transferred to Wesley Medical Center (WMC) in Wichita on the day he was born. Dr. Phillip J. Knight performed surgery on Jadon that day. His examination of Jadon disclosed that almost all of Jadon's bowel had been dead for weeks prior to his birth. Since there was no hope that Jadon could survive without his bowel, Jadon was sent home with his parents on February 20, 2002, and placed on palliative care. Jadon died at home on March 3, 2002.

Michelle and Jesse commenced this action against Watters, the Ark City Clinic, and SCKRMC. The district court granted summary judgment to the Ark City Clinic, whose radiologist refused to examine Michelle's sonogram. That ruling is not a subject of this appeal.

The district court granted summary judgment in favor of Watters based upon the failure of plaintiffs to present expert testimony that Watters deviated from the applicable standard of care and the lack of proximate cause between Watters' failure to notify Michelle of the abnormal sonogram and Jadon's postnatal suffering and death. The court also granted summary judgment in favor of SCKRMC based upon its conclusions that SCKRMC did not owe Michelle and Jesse the duty upon which they based their claims, and their claims were barred by the release signed by Michelle before the sonogram.

Michelle and Jesse appeal the district court's entry of summary judgment in favor of Watters and SCKRMC.

* * *

[The court's discussion of the standard of care is omitted.]

1. Duty

The district court found that SCKRMC's undertaking was limited to performing a sonogram to determine the gender of Michelle's baby, which it did in a non-negligent manner. Thus, the court reasoned, having performed the sonogram in a careful manner, SCKRMC had no further duty to Michelle and was not obligated to inform her about anything other than Jadon's gender.

Our analysis of this essential element of Michelle and Jesse's causes of action is a rather disheartening exercise. As a society we expect of ourselves a certain level of looking out for the welfare of others. This is an attribute which society encourages rather than discourages. We would expect this urge to be particularly strong in the hearts of those who choose to enter the medical and health care community. However, the transition from a societal expectation to a legal duty is often determined by public policy considerations which are not within the purview of an intermediate appellate court such as ours. Consequently, we turn to the case law for guidance.

Whether a legal duty exists is a question of law over which this court exercises de novo review. [ ] In the context of a medical negligence claim, the existence of a doctor-patient relationship is crucial to the recognition of a legal duty. * * *. We recognize the distinction between a doctor-patient relationship which is fiduciary in nature, [ ] and a hospital-patient relationship which is not [ ]. Nevertheless, the doctor-patient cases are instructive.

Smith v. Welch [ ] involved an independent medical examination in a personal injury action. Welch, a neurologist, was retained by the defendant in the personal injury action to examine Smith. In the course of the examination Welch asked Smith inappropriate questions of a sexual nature and sexually battered her. Smith sued Welch for assault, battery, invasion of privacy, and related torts. The Supreme Court reversed the entry of summary judgment in Welch's favor, holding that when a physician is retained by the defendant in a personal injury action to provide an expert medical opinion on the plaintiff's condition, the traditional physician-patient relationship does not exist. Nevertheless, the physician performing the independent medical examination has a duty not to negligently injure the plaintiff being examined.[ ]

In Doss v. Manfredi,[ ] the plaintiff, who had been the plaintiff in a prior personal injury action and had been examined by the doctor selected by the defense, sued the examining doctor for performing a negligent evaluation. This court found no doctor-patient relationship, in accord with *Smith v.*

Welch. In doing so, the court cited with approval Ervin v. American Guardian Life Assur., [ ], in which plaintiff underwent an electrocardiogram at the request of the defendant in the course of applying for life insurance. The defendant's physician examined the EKG results which disclosed cardiac abnormalities that were not disclosed to the plaintiff. Less than a month later the plaintiff suffered a heart attack and died. The court in *Ervin* stated:

> "[T]he defendant physician in the instant case owed no duty to the plaintiff's decedent either to discover his heart problem or, having discovered it, to inform the decedent thereof. The defendant had been employed by American to advise the company whether the applicant was an insurable risk. He was not employed to make a diagnosis for the applicant or to treat the applicant for any condition which was discovered. Neither was there any evidence that the defendant, by giving the applicant advice or otherwise, had assumed a physician-patient relationship. In the absence of a physician-patient relationship between defendant and the applicant, the defendant physician did not owe a duty to the applicant to discover and disclose that the applicant was suffering from heart abnormalities."[ ]

In Clough v. Lively, [ ] which is cited by Michelle and Jesse, Lively lapsed into a coma and died shortly after being released from the hospital where he had undergone blood alcohol testing at the request of a police officer following his arrest for DUI. Nurse Clough, a hospital employee, drew the blood for the test. The court found that no patient-healthcare provider relationship existed between the parties and, thus, no duty to be breached.

In the case now before us, no patient-healthcare provider relationship existed between Michelle and SCKRMC. Webster's II New College Dictionary 1174 (2001), defines "treatment" as "medical application of remedies so as to effect a cure." SCKRMC did not undertake to advise Michelle regarding, or to treat Michelle for, any disease, illness, or medical condition. It undertook only to determine the gender of her baby. Thus, SCKRMC only owed Michelle the duty to perform the sonogram in a non-negligent manner, and no negligence in the performance of the sonogram is alleged. Summary judgment based upon the lack of a duty was appropriate.

[The court's discussion of the release and waiver in the consent form signed by the plaintiff is omitted.].

Affirmed.

Notes and Questions

1. Expert testimony in the case indicated that the standard of care would have required no different management of the pregnancy or the birth. In that case, what damage did the plaintiff suffer? How would you articulate her damage? How would early discovery of the condition have been beneficial to Michelle? Consider the time line of events—the free sonogram was performed on November 15, and the fetus was delivered by caesarean section on February 9, at 38 weeks, almost three months later.

Should the Ark City Clinic have been dismissed? Michelle went to the clinic for counseling, after all, and all their radiologist had to do was look at the sonogram to spot the problem with the fetus. And what is the relationship of the

Clinic to the hospital? Is this free coupon part of a marketing strategy to bring patients to the hospital?

2.   A physician-patient relationship is usually a prerequisite to a professional malpractice suit against a doctor, as the court in *Esquivel* observes. However, courts have disagreed about the nature of a duty to notify even in the absence of the physician-patient contract, as you saw in the cases cited in *Esquivel*.

3.   The court in *Esquivel* is troubled by the failures of health care providers in the case. How should the law recognize a higher, "fiduciary", duty on the part of health care providers to a person not yet a "contractual" patient, in a case such as this?

Once the physician-patient relationship is established, the law in fact imposes a higher level of duty on physicians. The language of fiduciary law is often used to describe special obligations that one person owes to another. See Restatement (Second) of Agency § 13 (1958). The general principle of loyalty owed by a fiduciary agent to a principal is described in the following terms: "Unless otherwise agreed, an agent is subject to a duty to his principal to act solely for the benefit of the principal in all matters connected with his agency." Id. § 387. Justice Cardozo writes : "Many forms of conduct permissible in a workaday world for those acting at arm's length, are forbidden to those bound by fiduciary ties. A trustee is held to something stricter than the morals of the market place. Not honesty alone, but the punctilio of an honor the most sensitive, is then the standard of behavior." Meinhard v. Salmon, 249 N.Y. 458, 164 N.E. 545, 546 (1928).

A fiduciary obligation in medicine means that the physician focuses exclusively on the patient's health; the patient assumes the doctor's single-minded devotion to him; and the doctor-patient relationship is expected to be free of conflict. One ethicist defines a health care fiduciary as "someone who commits to becoming and remaining scientifically and clinically competent, acts primarily to protect and promote the interests of the patient and keeps self-interest systematically secondary, and maintains and passes on medicine as a public trust for current and future physicians and patients." Laurence B. McCullough, A Primer on Bioethics (2nd Edition 2006).

4.   Trust has been proposed as a unifying theme in analyzing medical ethics, professionalism, and the doctor-patient relationship generally. In the words of Mark Hall, "[t]rust is the core, defining characteristic of the doctor-patient relationship—the 'glue' that holds the relationship together and makes it possible. Preserving, justifying, and enhancing trust is a prominent objective in health care law and public policy and is the fundamental goal of much of medical ethics." Mark Hall, Law, Medicine, and Trust, 55 Stan. L. Rev. 463, 470–71 (2002). For a contrary position, see M. Gregg Bloche, Trust and Betrayal in the Medical Marketplace, 55 Stan. L. Rev. 919 (2003).

I.   THE CONTRACT BETWEEN PATIENT AND PHYSICIAN

The physician-patient relationship can be considered initially as a contractual one. Physicians in private practice may contract for their services as they see fit, and retain substantial control over the extent of their contact with patients. Physicians may limit their specialty, their scope of practice, their geographic area, and the hours and conditions under which they will see patients. They have no obligation to offer services that a patient may require that are outside the physician's competence and training; or services outside the scope of the original physician-patient agreement, where the physician has limited the contract to a type of procedure, to an office visit, or to consultation only. They may transfer responsibility by referring patients to other specialists. They may refuse to enter into a contract with a patient, or to treat patients, even under emergency conditions. See discussion in Chapter Eight.

Physicians may also expressly contract with a patient for a specific result. Stewart v. Rudner, 349 Mich. 459, 84 N.W.2d 816, 822–23 (1957) (couple contracted with physician to have wife's child delivered by Caesarian section, as she had had two stillbirths and was worried about normal vaginal delivery; the court held that "a doctor and his patient * * * have the same general liberty to contract with respect to their relationship as other parties entering into consensual relationship with one another, and a breach thereof will give rise to a cause of action."). Courts will sometimes allow parol evidence to fill in the terms of these contracts, where the patient has signed other consent forms. Murray v. University of Penn. Hospital, 340 Pa.Super. 401, 490 A.2d 839 (1985) (court allowed parol evidence to show the existence of an oral agreement to guarantee the prevention of future pregnancies by a tubal ligation).

Once the physician-patient relationship has been created, physicians are subject to an obligation of "continuing attention." Ricks v. Budge, 91 Utah 307, 64 P.2d 208 (1937). Refusal to continue to treat a patient is abandonment, and it may also be malpractice. See, e.g., Tierney v. University of Michigan Regents, 257 Mich.App. 681, 669 N.W.2d 575 (2003)(treating gynecologist withdrew from treating plaintiff after she filed suit against another member of the medical group). Termination of the physician-patient relationship, once created, is subject in some jurisdictions to a "continuous treatment" rule to determine when the statute of limitations is tolled. Treatment obligations cease if the physician can do nothing more for the patient. See Jewson v. Mayo Clinic, 691 F.2d 405 (8th Cir.1982).

An express written contract is rarely drafted for specific physician-patient interactions. An implied contract is usually the basis of the relationship between a physician and a patient. A physician who talks with a patient by telephone may be held to have an implied contractual obligation to that patient. Bienz v. Central Suffolk Hospital, 163 A.D.2d 269, 557 N.Y.S.2d 139 (1990). Likewise, a physician, such as a pathologist, who renders services to a patient but has not contracted with him, is nonetheless bound by certain implied contractual obligations. When the physician evaluates information provided by a nurse and makes a medical decision as to a patient's status, a doctor-patient relationship may be established. Wheeler v. Yettie Kersting Memorial Hospital, 866 S.W.2d 32 (Tex.App.1993). Merely scheduling an appointment is not by itself sufficient to create a relationship. Jackson v. Isaac, 76 S.W.3d 177 (Tex.App. 2002).

When a physician treating a patient consults by telephone or otherwise with another physician, some courts are reluctant to find a doctor-patient relationship created by such a conversation. The concern is that such informal conferences will be deterred by the fear of liability. See Reynolds v. Decatur

Memorial Hosp., 277 Ill.App.3d 80, 214 Ill.Dec. 44, 49, 660 N.E.2d 235, 240 (1996) ("It would have a chilling effect upon practice of medicine. It would stifle communication, education and professional association, all to the detriment of the patient.") Others find a duty in such a consultation. See e.g. Diggs v. Arizona Cardiologists, Ltd., 198 Ariz. 198, 8 P.3d 386 (App. 2000), where just being the on-call physician is not sufficient in many states to create the physician-patient relationship. Prosise v. Foster, 261 Va. 417, 544 S.E.2d 331 (2001).

When a patient goes to a doctor's office with a particular problem, he is offering to enter into a contract with the physician. When the physician examines the patient, she accepts the offer and an implied contract is created. The physician is free to reject the offer and send the patient away, relieving herself of any duty to that patient.

A. PHYSICIANS IN INSTITUTIONS

Physicians who practice in institutions must provide health care within the limits of the health plan coverage or their employment contracts with the institution. In such a case, the contact between the physician and the patient is preceded by an express contract spelling out the details of the relationship. Physicians who are members of a hospital's medical staff have duties created by medical staff privilege bylaws; physicians who are part of health maintenance organizations have a duty to treat plan members as a result of their contractual obligation to the HMO. In these situations, the express contract is between the physician and the health plan, and the subscriber and the plan, with an implied contract between the subscriber and the treating physician.

A physician who has staff privileges at a hospital also agrees to abide by hospital bylaws and policies and has therefore agreed to a doctor-patient relationship with whomever comes into the hospital, according to most courts that have considered the issue. Physicians on call to treat emergency patients are under a duty to treat patients. See Noble v. Sartori, 799 S.W.2d 8 (Ky.1990); Hastings v. Baton Rouge Gen. Hosp., 498 So.2d 713 (La.1986). Texas requires some further affirmative step by the physician to establish the relationship. Merely volunteering to be "on call" at a hospital is not sufficient. Ortiz v. Shah, 905 S.W.2d 609, 611 (Tex.App.1995). See also Anderson v. Houser, 240 Ga.App. 613, 523 S.E.2d 342 (1999) (physician scheduled to be on call when patient admitted to emergency room, who never met or treated patient and was out of town during her hospitalization, owed no duty). However, the on-call physician owes a duty to foreseeable emergency room patients to provide reasonable notice to hospital personnel when he or she will not be able to respond to calls, and this duty exists independent of any physician-patient relationship. Oja v. Kin, 229 Mich.App. 184, 581 N.W.2d 739 (1998) (implied consent to doctor-patient relationship may be found only where the physician has done something such as participate in the patient's diagnosis and treatment). See also discussion of emergency care in Chapter Eight.

Physician contract obligations bind them to treat individual subscribers, and may extend to further obligations, such as completing a variety of benefit forms for a patient. If these forms are not properly and timely completed, and a patient suffers an economic detriment, courts have held that a suit for breach of contract will lie. Chew v. Meyer, 72 Md.App. 132, 527 A.2d 828 (1987).

Physicians who are part of managed care networks have a contractual relationship with the plan that requires them to treat subscribers. In Hand v. Tavera, 864 S.W.2d 678 (Ct.App. Texas 1993), the plaintiff went to the emergency room complaining of a headache. Dr. Tavera was the doctor responsible for authorizing admissions, and he sent Hand home and said he should be treated as an outpatient. Hand had a stroke. Dr. Tavera defended on the grounds that no physician-patient relationship existed. The court held that "[t]he contract between Humana and Southwest Medical Group (which employed Tavera) obligated its doctors to treat Humana enrollees as they would treat their other patients."

The court concluded that "the contracts in the record show that the Humana plan brought Hand and Tavera together just as surely as though they had met directly and entered the physician-patient relationship. Hand paid premiums to Humana to purchase medical care in advance of need; Humana met its obligation to Hand and its other enrollees by employing Tavera's group to treat them; and Tavera's medical group agreed to treat Humana enrollees in exchange for the fees received from Humana. In effect, Hand had paid in advance for the services of the Humana plan doctor on duty that night, who happened to be Tavera, and the physician-patient relationship existed. We hold that when the health-care plan's insured shows up at a participating hospital emergency room, and the plan's doctor on call is consulted about treatment or admission, there is a physician-patient relationship between the doctor and the insured."

The court also held that "when a patient who has enrolled in a prepaid medical plan goes to a hospital emergency room and the plan's designated doctor is consulted, the physician-patient relationship exists and the doctor owes the patient a duty of care."

B. EXCULPATORY CLAUSES

TUNKL v. REGENTS OF UNIV. OF CALIFORNIA

Supreme Court of California, 1963.
60 Cal.2d 92, 32 Cal.Rptr. 33, 383 P.2d 441.

TOBRINER, JUSTICE.

This case concerns the validity of a release from liability for future negligence imposed as a condition for admission to a charitable research hospital. For the reasons we hereinafter specify, we have concluded that an agreement between a hospital and an entering patient affects the public interest and that, in consequence, the exculpatory provision included within it must be invalid under Civil Code section 1668.

Hugo Tunkl brought this action to recover damages for personal injuries alleged to have resulted from the negligence of two physicians in the employ of the University of California Los Angeles Medical Center, a hospital operated and maintained by the Regents of the University of California as a nonprofit charitable institution. Mr. Tunkl died after suit was brought, and his surviving wife, as executrix, was substituted as plaintiff.

The University of California at Los Angeles Medical Center admitted Tunkl as a patient on June 11, 1956. The Regents maintain the hospital for the primary purpose of aiding and developing a program of research and education in the field of medicine; patients are selected and admitted if the study and treatment of their condition would tend to achieve these purposes. Upon his entry to the hospital, Tunkl signed a document setting forth certain "Conditions of Admission." The crucial condition number six reads as follows: "RELEASE: The hospital is a nonprofit, charitable institution. In consideration of the hospital and allied services to be rendered and the rates charged therefor, the patient or his legal representative agrees to and hereby releases The Regents of the University of California, and the hospital from any and all liability for the negligent or wrongful acts or omissions of its employees, if the hospital has used due care in selecting its employees."

Plaintiff stipulated that the hospital had selected its employees with due care. The trial court ordered that the issue of the validity of the exculpatory clause be first submitted to the jury and that, if the jury found that the provision did not bind plaintiff, a second jury try the issue of alleged malpractice. When, on the preliminary issue, the jury returned a verdict sustaining the validity of the executed release, the court entered judgment in favor of the Regents.[2] Plaintiff appeals from the judgment.

We shall first set out the basis for our prime ruling that the exculpatory provision of the hospital's contract fell under the proscription of Civil Code section 1668; we then dispose of two answering arguments of defendant.

We begin with the dictate of the relevant Civil Code section 1668. The section states: "All contracts which have for their object, directly or indirectly, to exempt anyone from responsibility for his own fraud, or willful injury to the person or property of another, or violation of law, whether willful or negligent, are against the policy of the law."

* * *

In one respect, as we have said, the decisions are uniform. The cases have consistently held that the exculpatory provision may stand only if it does not involve "the public interest."

* * *

If, then, the exculpatory clause which affects the public interest cannot stand, we must ascertain those factors or characteristics which constitute the public interest. * * *

* * * It concerns a business of a type generally thought suitable for public regulation. The party seeking exculpation is engaged in performing a service of great importance to the public, which is often a matter of practical necessity for some members of the public. The party holds himself out as willing to perform this service for any member of the public who seeks it, or at least for any member coming within certain established standards. As a result of the essential nature of the service, in the economic setting of the

---

2. Plaintiff at the time of signing the release was in great pain, under sedation, and probably unable to read. At trial plaintiff contended that the release was invalid, asserting that a release does not bind the releasor if at the time of its execution he suffered from so weak a mental condition that he was unable to comprehend the effect of his act. [ ]

transaction, the party invoking exculpation possesses a decisive advantage of bargaining strength against any member of the public who seeks his services. In exercising a superior bargaining power the party confronts the public with a standardized adhesion contract of exculpation, and makes no provision whereby a purchaser may pay additional reasonable fees and obtain protection against negligence. Finally, as a result of the transaction, the person or property of the purchaser is placed under the control of the seller, subject to the risk of carelessness by the seller or his agents.

* * *

In the light of the decisions, we think that the hospital-patient contract clearly falls within the category of agreements affecting the public interest. To meet that test, the agreement need only fulfill some of the characteristics above outlined; here, the relationship fulfills all of them. Thus the contract of exculpation involves an institution suitable for, and a subject of, public regulation. [ ] That the services of the hospital to those members of the public who are in special need of the particular skill of its staff and facilities constitute a practical and crucial necessity is hardly open to question.

The hospital, likewise, holds itself out as willing to perform its services for those members of the public who qualify for its research and training facilities. While it is true that the hospital is selective as to the patients it will accept, such selectivity does not negate its public aspect or the public interest in it. The hospital is selective only in the sense that it accepts from the public at large certain types of cases which qualify for the research and training in which it specializes. But the hospital does hold itself out to the public as an institution which performs such services for those members of the public who can qualify for them.

In insisting that the patient accept the provision of waiver in the contract, the hospital certainly exercises a decisive advantage in bargaining. The would-be patient is in no position to reject the proffered agreement, to bargain with the hospital, or in lieu of agreement to find another hospital. The admission room of a hospital contains no bargaining table where, as in a private business transaction, the parties can debate the terms of their contract. As a result, we cannot but conclude that the instant agreement manifested the characteristics of the so-called adhesion contract. Finally, when the patient signed the contract, he completely placed himself in the control of the hospital; he subjected himself to the risk of its carelessness.

* * *

We turn to a consideration of the * * * arguments urged by defendant to save the exemptive clause. Defendant contends that while the public interest may possibly invalidate the exculpatory provision as to the paying patient, it certainly cannot do so as to the charitable one. * * *

* * *

In substance defendant here asks us to modify our decision in *Malloy*, which removed the charitable immunity; defendant urges that otherwise the funds of the research hospital may be deflected from the real objective of the extension of medical knowledge to the payment of claims for alleged negligence. Since a research hospital necessarily entails surgery and treatment in which fixed standards of care may not yet be evolved, defendant says the hospital should in this situation be excused from such care. But the answer lies in the fact that possible plaintiffs must *prove negligence;* the standards of care will themselves reflect the research nature of the treatment; the hospital will not become an insurer or guarantor of the patient's recovery. To exempt the hospital completely from any standard of due care is to grant it immunity by the side-door method of a contractual clause exacted of the patient. We cannot reconcile that technique with the teaching of *Malloy.*

* * *

The judgment is reversed.

Notes and Questions

1.   Courts typically uphold waivers of the right to sue, if the waiver of negligence is clearly described, the activity is a voluntary one, the waiver freely given by a party who understands what he is giving up, and there is not a serious imbalance of bargaining power .. Courts view such waivers as a valid exercise of the freedom of contract. See generally Jaffe v. Pallotta Teamworks, 276 F. Supp.2d 102 (D.C.D.C. 2003)(upholding waiver by a runner in an AIDS charity event, a voluntary activity).

2.   The *Tunkl* context is a special case of a charitable teaching hospital. Why does the court view this context as special? In other health care situations other than emergencies, why shouldn't a patient be able to waive the right to sue in exchange for lower cost or free treatment? Is there something special about medical care in general, or Tunkl's situation in particular, that makes such a choice by a patient suspect? Do the court's arguments convince you as to the reasons for invalidating such attempts by health care institutions to limit their liability? Short of a complete waiver of a right to sue, how else might hospitals or doctors protect themselves? Can a patient be asked to waive the right to sue for punitive damages? Could the parties agree on liquidated damages? Could the parties agree that an action would be brought in the local state court? Could treatment be conditioned on the patient submitting any malpractice claim to an administrative body, or to arbitration?

California has continued to follow *Tunkl*'s analysis. Releases that the California courts now consider to affect the public interest include Gavin W. v. YMCA of Metropolitan Los Angeles, 106 Cal.App.4th 662, 131 Cal.Rptr.2d 168 (2003) (release of liability for negligence by provider of child care services); Health Net of California, Inc. v. Department of Health Services (2003) 113 Cal.App.4th 224, 6 Cal.Rptr.3d 235 (2003) (exculpatory clause related to managed health care for Medi–Cal beneficiaries).

One exception that has been found to be acceptable is an exculpatory agreement for treatments involving experimental procedures as the patient's last hope for survival. See Colton v. New York Hospital, 98 Misc.2d 957, 414 N.Y.S.2d 866 (1979).

C. PARTIAL LIMITATIONS ON THE RIGHT TO SUE

1. *Protecting Deeply Held Religious or Other Beliefs*

SHORTER v. DRURY

Supreme Court of Washington, 1985.
103 Wash.2d 645, 695 P.2d 116.

DOLLIVER, JUSTICE.

This is an appeal from a wrongful death medical malpractice action arising out of the bleeding death of a hospital patient who, for religious reasons, refused a blood transfusion. Plaintiff, the deceased's husband and personal representative, appeals the trial court's judgment on the verdict in which the jury reduced plaintiff's wrongful death damages by 75 percent based on an assumption of risk by the Shorters that Mrs. Shorter would die from bleeding. The defendant doctor appeals the judgment alleging that a plaintiff-signed hospital release form completely barred the wrongful death action. Alternatively, defendant asks that we affirm the trial court's judgment on the verdict. Defendant does not appeal the special verdict in which the jury found the defendant negligent.

The deceased, Doreen Shorter, was a Jehovah's Witness, as is her surviving husband, Elmer Shorter. Jehovah's Witnesses are prohibited by their religious doctrine from receiving blood transfusions.

Doreen Shorter became pregnant late in the summer of 1979. In October of 1979, she consulted with the defendant, Dr. Robert E. Drury, a family practitioner. Dr. Drury diagnosed Mrs. Shorter as having had a "missed abortion". A missed abortion occurs when the fetus dies and the uterus fails to discharge it.

When a fetus dies, it is medically prudent to evacuate the uterus in order to guard against infection. To cleanse the uterus, Dr. Shorter recommended a "dilation and curettage" (D and C). There are three alternative ways to perform this operation. The first is with a curette, a metal instrument which has a sharp-edged hoop on the end of it. The second, commonly used in an abortion, involves the use of a suction device. The third alternative is by use of vaginal suppositories containing prostaglandin, a chemical that causes artificial labor contractions. Dr. Drury chose to use curettes.

Although the D and C is a routine medical procedure there is a risk of bleeding. Each of the three principal methods for performing the D and C presented, to a varying degree, the risk of bleeding. The record below reflects that the curette method which Dr. Drury selected posed the highest degree of puncture-caused bleeding risk due to the sharpness of the instrument. The record also reflects, however, that no matter how the D and C is performed, there is always the possibility of blood loss.

Dr. Drury described the D and C procedure to Mr. and Mrs. Shorter. He advised her there was a possibility of bleeding and perforation of the uterus. Dr. Drury did not discuss any alternate methods in which the D and C may be performed. Examination of Mr. Shorter at trial revealed he was aware that the D and C posed the possibility, albeit remote, of internal bleeding.

The day before she was scheduled to receive the D and C from Dr. Drury, Mrs. Shorter sought a second opinion from Dr. Alan Ott. Mrs. Shorter advised Dr. Ott of Dr. Drury's intention to perform the D and C. She told Dr. Ott she was a Jehovah's Witness. Although he confirmed the D and C was the appropriate treatment, Dr. Ott did not discuss with Mrs. Shorter the particular method which should be used to perform it. He did, however, advise Mrs. Shorter that "she could certainly bleed during the procedure" and at trial confirmed she was aware of that possibility. Dr. Ott testified Mrs. Shorter responded to his warning by saying "she had faith in the Lord and that things would work out. * * * "

At approximately 6 a.m. on November 30, Mrs. Shorter was accompanied by her husband to Everett General Hospital. At the hospital the Shorters signed [a consent form that included the following language]: "I hereby release the hospital, its personnel, and the attending physician from any responsibility whatever for unfavorable reactions or any untoward results due to my refusal to permit the use of blood or its derivatives and I fully understand the possible consequences of such refusal on my part."

The operation did not go smoothly. Approximately 1 hour after surgery, Mrs. Shorter began to bleed internally and go into shock. Emergency exploratory surgery conducted by other surgeons revealed Dr. Drury had severely lacerated Mrs. Shorter's uterus when he was probing with the curette.

Mrs. Shorter began to bleed profusely. She continued to refuse to authorize a transfusion despite repeated warnings by the doctors she would likely die due to blood loss. Mrs. Shorter was coherent at the time she refused to accept blood. While the surgeons repaired Mrs. Shorter's perforated uterus and abdomen, Dr. Drury and several other doctors pleaded with Mr. Shorter to permit them to transfuse blood into Mrs. Shorter. He likewise refused. Mrs. Shorter bled to death. Doctors for both parties agreed a transfusion in substantial probability would have saved Doreen Shorter's life.

Mr. Shorter thereafter brought this wrongful death action alleging Dr. Drury's negligence proximately caused Mrs. Shorter's death; the complaint did not allege a survival cause of action. The release was admitted into evidence over plaintiff's objection. Plaintiff took exception to jury instructions numbered 13 and 13A which dealt with assumption of the risk.

The jury found Dr. Drury negligent and that his negligence was "a proximate cause of the death of Doreen Shorter". Damages were found to be $412,000. The jury determined, however, that Mr. and/or Mrs. Shorter "knowingly and voluntarily" assumed the risk of bleeding to death and attributed 75 percent of the fault for her death to her and her husband's refusal to authorize or accept a blood transfusion. Plaintiff was awarded judgment of $103,000. Both parties moved for judgment notwithstanding the verdict. The trial court denied both motions. Plaintiff appealed and defendant cross-appealed to the Court of Appeals, which certified the case pursuant to RCW 2.06.030(d).

The three issues before us concern the admissibility of the "Refusal to Permit Blood Transfusion" (refusal); whether assumption of the risk is a valid defense and if so, whether there is sufficient evidence for the jury to have found the risk was assumed by the Shorters; and whether the submission of the issue of assumption of the risk to the jury violated the free exercise clause of the First Amendment. The finding of negligence by Dr. Drury is not appealed by defendant.

I

Plaintiff argues the purpose of the refusal was only to release the defendant doctor from liability for not transfusing blood into Mrs. Shorter had she required blood during the course of a nonnegligently performed operation. He further asserts the refusal as it applies to the present case violates public policy since it would release Dr. Drury from the consequences of his negligence.

Defendant concedes a survival action filed on behalf of Mrs. Shorter for her negligently inflicted injuries would not be barred by the refusal since enforcement would violate public policy. Defendant argues, however, the refusal does not release the doctor for his negligence but only for the consequences arising out of Mrs. Shorter's voluntary refusal to accept blood, which in this case was death.

While the rule announced by this court is that contracts against liability for negligence are valid except in those cases where the public interest is involved [ ], the refusal does not address the negligence of Dr. Drury. This being so it cannot be considered as a release from liability for negligence. * * *

Plaintiff categorizes the refusal as an all or nothing instrument. He claims that if it is a release of liability for negligence it is void as against public policy and if it is a release of liability where a transfusion is required because of nonnegligent treatment then it is irrelevant. We have already stated the document cannot be considered as a release from liability for negligence. The document is more, however, than a simple declaration that the signer would refuse blood only if there was no negligence by Dr. Drury. * * *

We find the refusal to be valid. There was sufficient evidence for the jury to find it was not signed unwittingly but rather voluntarily. * * *

We also hold the release was not against public policy. We emphasize again the release did not exculpate Dr. Drury from his negligence in performing the surgery. Rather, it was an agreement that Mrs. Shorter should receive no blood or blood derivatives. The cases cited by defendant, Tunkl v. Regents of Univ. of Cal.; Colton v. New York Hosp., 98 Misc.2d 957, 414 N.Y.S.2d 866 (1979); Olson v. Molzen, 558 S.W.2d 429 (Tenn.1977), all refer to exculpatory clauses which release a physician or hospital from all liability for negligence. The Shorters specifically accepted the risk which might flow from a refusal to accept blood. Given the particular problems faced when a patient on religious grounds refuses to permit necessary or advisable blood transfusions, we believe the use of a release such as signed here is appropriate. [ ] Requiring physicians or hospitals to obtain a court order would be cumbersome and impractical. Furthermore, it might subject the hospital or physician to an action under 42 U.S.C. § 1983. [ ] The alternative of physicians or hospitals refusing to care for Jehovah's Witnesses is repugnant in a society which attempts to make medical care available to all its members.

We believe the procedure used here, the voluntary execution of a document protecting the physician and hospital and the patient is an appropriate alternative and not contrary to the public interest.

If the refusal is held valid, defendant asserts it acts as a complete bar to plaintiff's wrongful death claim. We disagree. While Mrs. Shorter accepted the consequences resulting from a refusal to receive a blood transfusion, she did not accept the consequences of Dr. Drury's negligence which was, as the jury found, a proximate cause of Mrs. Shorter's death. Defendant was not released from his negligence. We next consider the impact of the doctrine of assumption of the risk on this negligence.

II

[In Part II the court considered assumption of the risk as a defense.]

* * * Defendant argues, and we agree, that the Shorters could be found by the jury to have assumed the risk of death from an operation which had to be performed without blood transfusions and where blood could not be administered under any circumstances including where the doctor made what would otherwise have been correctable surgical mistake. The risk of death from a failure to receive a transfusion to which the Shorters exposed themselves was created by, and must be allocated to, the Shorters themselves.

* * *

III

[The court in Part III rejected the argument that the submission of the issue of assumption of the risk to the jury violated the free exercise clause of the First Amendment, since no state action was present.]

* * *

Affirmed.

Notes and Questions

1. Consider the relative risks of the different approaches to a missed abortion. Did the treating physician properly take into account the risk factors presented by a Jehovah's Witness patient? Is a religious or personal belief of this sort part of the presenting characteristics of a patient, requiring adjustment of the treatment approach?

2. Jehovah's Witnesses rarely sue physicians who respect their decisions not to receive blood. A decision to vitiate the partial release in *Shorter* might have discouraged surgeons from agreeing to treat Jehovah's Witnesses consistent with their religious beliefs.

The refusal by Jehovah's Witnesses to accept blood transfusions has its origins in their interpretation of the Bible. Their religious doctrine mandates that they "abstain from blood":

> A human is not to sustain his life with the blood of another creature. (Genesis 9:3, 4) When an animal's life is taken, the blood representing that life is to be "poured out," given back to the Life–Giver. (Leviticus 17:13, 14) And as decreed by the apostolic council, Christians are to "abstain from

blood," which applies to human blood as well as to animal blood. (Acts 15:28, 29.)

Jehovah's Witnesses and the Question of Blood 17 (1977).

Jehovah's Witnesses make no distinction between taking blood in by mouth and into the blood vessels, and treat the issue of blood as involving "the most fundamental principles on which they as Christians base their lives. Their relationship with their Creator and God is at stake." Id. at 19. The Jehovah's Witnesses have prepared brochures for health care professionals that explain these beliefs, stating that they will sign consent forms that relieve doctors of any responsibility for possible adverse consequences of blood refusal. There is also a split in the Church over the use of blood and blood products for medical reasons. See the website of the Associated Jehovah's Witnesses for Reform on Blood for an example of cards that reflect the Church's blood policies. http://www.ajwrb.org.

3.   How does the court support its allowance of the partial release? What does the court fear might happen to patients with particular religious beliefs? Can you think of any other methods by which a hospital or doctor might protect against the risk of lawsuits by patients who refuse certain kinds of medical interventions? Is the contract an adhesion contract, as were the contracts in *Tunkl* or *Porubianksy?*

4.   *Shorter* offers a defense of a partial waiver, under a special set of circumstances. The issue is important for two reasons. First, providers would like to limit their liability exposure in order to keep malpractice premiums under control. Second, economists and other reformers of the tort system advocate the use of contracts that allocate risk by agreement.

5.   Binding arbitration, virtually universal in agreements between stock brokers and customers, is being tried by physicians as they seek ways to avoid malpractice exposure. The Florida Medical Association, for example, has a program instructing physicians in their use. The goal is to help physicians reduce their liability risk. California has a binding arbitration provision in MICRA (Medical Injury Compensation Reform Act) and it is estimated that about 10% of medical malpractice disputes go to binding arbitration. The Florida standard provision reads:

> The patient agrees that any controversy, including any malpractice claim, arising out of or in any way relating to the diagnosis, treatment, or care of the patient by the undersigned physician ... shall be submitted to binding arbitration.... The patient further agrees that any controversy arising out of or in any way relating to the past diagnosis, treatment, or care of the patient by a provider of medical services, or the provider's agents or employees, shall likewise be submitted to binding arbitration.

See Tanya Albert, Patients In Liability Hot Spots Asked to Arbitrate, Not Litigate, AMA News 1 (February 10, 2003).

What objections might be raised to such forms of binding arbitration imposed by contract?

Several states have adopted contract approaches, such as elective arbitration contracts that allow the provider and the patient to change the forum for resolving the dispute. Similarly, living wills and durable powers of attorney allow a patient to control the extent of treatment, while protecting the treating doctor from liability for complying with the patient's refusal of treatment.

Some states do not mandate the reference of medical malpractice claims to arbitration, but instead authorize health care providers to include arbitration clauses in their contracts, so long as an agreement to arbitrate is not a condition of service. The patient must have a right to rescind within 90 days. See for example Colo. Rev. Stat. Ann. § 13–64–403 (West 1997). See generally Carol A. Crocca, Arbitration of Medical Malpractice Claims, 24 A.L.R.5th 1.

Problem: Arbitrating Disaster

Rhoda Cumin went to the Gladstone Clinic in Las Vegas, Nevada to get a prescription for an oral contraceptive. Her medical history put her at a higher risk of a stroke from use of birth control pills. She did not know this, but her medical records and history would have alerted an obstetrician to the risk. She obtained a prescription for the pills, and began taking them. Six months later she suffered a cerebral incident that left her partially paralyzed. Her lifetime medical expenses, including physical therapy, lost earning capacity, and pain suffering, could be as much as 10 million dollars.

Ms. Cumin has asked you to handle her suit against the clinic. Your investigation determines that the clinic was negligent in prescribing the contraceptive in light of Ms. Cumin's history. You file a negligence action. The clinic then moves to stay the lawsuit pending arbitration, and for a court order to compel arbitration. Its affidavit states that the clinic requires all patients to sign an arbitration agreement before receiving treatment. This agreement requires two things: first, it provides that all disputes must be submitted to binding arbitration and that the parties expressly waive their right to a trial. Second, it puts a cap on the patient's right to recover of $250,000. The clinic's standard procedure is to have the receptionist hand the patient the agreement along with two information sheets, informing her that any questions will be answered. The patient must sign the agreement before receiving treatment; the physician signs later. If the patient refuses to sign, the clinic refuses treatment. The agreement, signed by your client, is attached to the affidavit.

Ms. Cumin tells you that she does not remember either signing the agreement or having it explained to her, and you file an affidavit to that effect. Prepare a memorandum of law in support of your motion in opposition to arbitration.

Problem: Mediating Disaster

Rhoda Cumin suffered a cerebral incident as a result of her use of birth control pills (see previous problem). She was admitted to Gladstone Urban Hospital, a major teaching hospital in the State of Sympathy. At the time of admission, she was presented for her signature a mediation clause which stated:

> I agree that any claim which may arise out of the care provided to me by the physicians, nurses and other health care providers at the Gladstone Urban Hospital or any of its affiliates shall be governed by the law of the State of Sympathy. I also agree that before any lawsuit is filed for damages arising out of or related to the care provided to me, I must attempt to resolve any claim through mediation. Mediation is a process through which a neutral third person tries to help settle claims. I do not waive my right to file a lawsuit if the mediation process fails to resolve my claim. I further agree that any mediation or court proceeding must take place in the State of Sympathy. This agreement is binding on me and any individual or entity making claim on my behalf.

She signed the mediation clause. During the course of her treatment, she suffered a serious medical error during treatment for her stroke, which left her partially paralyzed. Gladstone is aware that this was a preventable adverse event, the result of a combination of surgical, charting, and nursing errors.

You represent Gladstone. How will you design mediation? What approach will you take to the mediation discussions? What goals do you have in mind on behalf of the Hospital?

2. Protecting Patient Choices About Health Care Costs: Consumer–Directed Health Plans

"Consumer-driven health care" (CDHC) has become the linchpin of current political debate over reforming the American health care system. In various forms, it requires insured patients to pay a major—or the entire—portion of their own medical costs out-of-pocket or from a designated savings account. Health benefit plans built around such a model would provide (1) consumer incentives to select more economical health care options, including self-care and no care, and (2) information and support to inform such selections. The most visible signs of this intensifying consumerism are the generously tax-sheltered "health savings accounts"(HSAs) authorized by recent federal legislation. HSAs can be used to pay for medical costs not covered by insurance if they are linked with catastrophic insurance policies that have annual deductibles in the range of $1000 to $10,000. A form of patient-cost sharing, consumer-directed health care requires patients to exert greater control over their spending decisions than before, and absorb more financial risk as a consequence. The merits and drawbacks of CDHCs are discussed in Chapter 7, *supra*. See generally Timothy Stoltzfus Jost, Health Care At Risk: A Critique of the Consumer–Driven Movement (2007).

From a patient choice/liability perspective, consumer-directed care will present difficult problems for the courts. Such care may present tiers of care explicitly, raising questions about a sliding scale for measuring physician practices, rather than monolithic standard of care. From a risk perspective, it will present the courts with patients who expressly consented by plan choices to forego certain levels of more expensive care. Whereas Mrs. Shorter refused transfusions for reasons of religious belief, the evolution of patient choice insurance models will force courts to consider patients who suffer health care costs or even death because they made the financial tradeoff in advance of the health care crisis. Patients certainly can check out of a hospital against medical advice, often to avoid the hospitals charges of their treatment, thereby assuming the risk of a bad outcome; Z.Y. Aliyu, Discharge Against Medical Advice: Sociodemographic, Clinical and Financial Perspectives, 56 Int'l J. Clin. Pract. 325 (2002). Malpractice doctrine allows assumption of risk as an affirmative defense, and informed refusal of recommended treatment is one form of express assumption of risk If a patient, rather than refusing treatment, opts for an alternative form of treatment that is less expensive, should the assumption of risk defense apply to protect the provider? Or should courts protect consumers in situations where they are vulnerable? See generally Mark A. Hall and Carl E. Schneider, Patients As Consumers: Courts, Contracts, and the New Medical Marketplace, 106 Mich. L. Rev. 643 (2008); Peter D. Jacobson and Michael R. Tunick, Consumer–Directed Health Care And The Courts: Let The Buyer (And Seller) Beware, 26 Health Affairs 704 (2007); Mark A. Hall, Paying For What You Get and Getting What you Pay For: Legal Responses to Consumer–Driven Healthcare, 69 Law & Contemp. Probs. 159 (2006); E. Haavi Morreim, High–Deductible Health Plans: New Twists on Old Challenges From Tort and Contract, 59 Vand. L. Rev. 1207 (2006).

Problem: Life Foregone

William Gaddis, a machinist, works for a small manufacturing company, *Machina*, that uses computerized machines to make specialty metal products to order. With only twenty employees, Machina has decided to offer a health reimbursement account (HRA) rather than traditional health insurance choices. The plan combines a a high-deductible insurance plan (HRA) with an employer-funded account (the HSA). The employer-funded account may be used to pay for covered health care services and is counted toward the deductible amount. The HRA has a $500 employer-funded account and a $1,500 deductible; this means that once the employer-funded account is depleted, the consumer must spend $1,000 out-of-pocket before insurance will begin sharing the costs of treatment. Unexpended funds from the employer funded account may be rolled over to the next year. The plan uses a debit card rather than asking employees to pay up front and file claims for reimbursement.

Gaddis begins to have headaches. He goes to his primary care doctor, who takes his history and suggests a course of aspirin. The headaches begin to worsen, and Gaddis goes back to the doctor. The doctor recommends a head MRI to look for the problem. The cost of the full head scan using the MRI will be around $1,000 at market rates and the radiologist who reads the scan will be another $800. Gaddis has already spent most of the $500 from Machina because of ear infections in his infant son; he is facing large oil bills for the winter and an escalating mortgage rate on his new house. He decides to stick with aspirin and forego the MRI for the time being. A week later, he dies from a posterior brain aneurysm that could have been detected by an MRI and surgically corrected. Does Gaddis have a claim against Machina? His physician?

II. INFORMED CONSENT: THE PHYSICIAN'S OBLIGATION

A. ORIGINS OF THE INFORMED CONSENT DOCTRINE

Informed consent has developed out of strong judicial deference toward individual autonomy, reflecting a belief that an individual has a right to be free from nonconsensual interference with his or her person, and a basic moral principle that it is wrong to force another to act against his or her will. This principle was articulated in the medical context by Justice Cardozo in Schloendorff v. Society of New York Hospital, 211 N.Y. 125, 105 N.E. 92 (1914): "Every human being of adult years and sound mind has a right to determine what shall be done with his own body * * *". Informed consent doctrine has guided medical decisionmaking by setting boundaries for the doctor-patient relationship and is one of the forces altering the attitudes of a new generation of doctors toward their patients. It has provided the starting point for federal regulations on human experimentation, and is now reflected in consent forms that health care institutions require all patients to sign upon admission and before various procedures are performed.

Professor Alexander Capron has argued that the doctrine can serve six salutary functions. It can:

1) protect individual autonomy;

2) protect the patient's status as a human being;

3) avoid fraud or duress;

4) encourage doctors to carefully consider their decisions;

5) foster rational decision-making by the patient; and

6) involve the public generally in medicine.

Alexander Capron, "Informed Consent in Catastrophic Disease Research and Treatment," 123 U.Penn.L.Rev. 340, 365–76 (1974).

Patient health outcomes may also improve following informed consent to medical treatment risks. Clinical evidence suggests involving the patient in the process may also improve overall physical and mental health. Brody et al. concluded that patients who were more actively involved in their health care had less discomfort, a reduction of symptoms, more improvement in their general medical conditions, a greater sense of control, less concern with the illness, and more satisfaction with their physician. David S. Brody et al., Patient Perception of Involvement in Medical Care: Relationship to Illness Attitudes and Outcomes, 4 J. Gen. Internal Med. 506, 510 (1989). See also James L. Bernat & Lynn M. Peterson, Patient–Centered Informed Consent in Surgical Practice, 141 Archives of Surgery 86, 87 (2006).

This section will examine how the doctrine developed and how it now functions as a litigation tool in American jurisdictions.

As you read the cases in this section, ask how far the courts have gone toward permitting patients to control treatment decisions that affect them. Consider also what a plaintiff must show to make out an informed consent case in various jurisdictions. Finally, ask if any other processes are likely to serve the purposes of informed consent more efficiently, and with less adverse effect on the doctor-patient relationship. Has the law improved the doctor-patient relationship?

B. THE LEGAL FRAMEWORK OF INFORMED CONSENT

1. *Negligence as a Basis for Recovery*

CANTERBURY v. SPENCE

United States Court of Appeals, District of Columbia Circuit, 1972.
464 F.2d 772.

SPOTTSWOOD W. ROBINSON, III, CIRCUIT JUDGE:

This appeal is from a judgment entered in the District Court on verdicts directed for the two appellees at the conclusion of plaintiff-appellant Canterbury's case in chief. His action sought damages for personal injuries allegedly sustained as a result of an operation negligently performed by appellee Spence, a negligent failure by Dr. Spence to disclose a risk of serious disability inherent in the operation, and negligent post-operative care by appellee Washington Hospital Center. On close examination of the record, we find evidence which required submission of these issues to the jury. We accordingly reverse the judgment as to each appellee and remand the case to the District Court for a new trial.

I

The record we review tells a depressing tale. A youth troubled only by back pain submitted to an operation without being informed of a risk of paralysis incidental thereto. A day after the operation he fell from his hospital bed after having been left without assistance while voiding. A few hours after the fall, the lower half of his body was paralyzed, and he had to be operated on again. Despite extensive medical care, he has never been what he was before. Instead of the back pain, even years later, he hobbled about on crutches, a victim of paralysis of the bowels and urinary incontinence. In a very real sense this lawsuit is an understandable search for reasons.

At the time of the events which gave rise to this litigation, appellant was nineteen years of age, a clerk-typist employed by the Federal Bureau of Investigation. In December, 1958, he began to experience severe pain between his shoulder blades. He consulted two general practitioners, but the medications they prescribed failed to eliminate the pain. Thereafter, appellant secured an appointment with Dr. Spence, who is a neurosurgeon.

Dr. Spence examined appellant in his office at some length but found nothing amiss. On Dr. Spence's advice appellant was x-rayed, but the films did not identify any abnormality. Dr. Spence then recommended that appellant undergo a myelogram—a procedure in which dye is injected into the spinal column and traced to find evidence of disease or other disorder—at the Washington Hospital Center.

Appellant entered the hospital on February 4, 1959. The myelogram revealed a "filling defect" in the region of the fourth thoracic vertebra. Since a myelogram often does no more than pinpoint the location of an aberration, surgery may be necessary to discover the cause. Dr. Spence told appellant that he would have to undergo a laminectomy—the excision of the posterior arch of the vertebra—to correct what he suspected was a ruptured disc. Appellant did not raise any objection to the proposed operation nor did he probe into its exact nature.

Appellant explained to Dr. Spence that his mother was a widow of slender financial means living in Cyclone, West Virginia, and that she could be reached through a neighbor's telephone. Appellant called his mother the day after the myelogram was performed and, failing to contact her, left Dr. Spence's telephone number with the neighbor. When Mrs. Canterbury returned the call, Dr. Spence told her that the surgery was occasioned by a suspected ruptured disc. Mrs. Canterbury then asked if the recommended operation was serious and Dr. Spence replied "not any more than any other operation." He added that he knew Mrs. Canterbury was not well off and that her presence in Washington would not be necessary. The testimony is contradictory as to whether during the course of the conversation Mrs. Canterbury expressed her consent to the operation. Appellant himself apparently did not converse again with Dr. Spence prior to the operation.

Dr. Spence performed the laminectomy on February 11 at the Washington Hospital Center. Mrs. Canterbury traveled to Washington, arriving on that date but after the operation was over, and signed a consent form at the hospital. The laminectomy revealed several anomalies: a spinal cord that was swollen and unable to pulsate, an accumulation of large tortuous and dilated veins, and a complete absence of epidural fat which normally surrounds the spine. A thin hypodermic needle was inserted into the spinal cord to aspirate any cysts which might have been present, but no fluid emerged. In suturing the wound, Dr. Spence attempted to relieve the pressure on the spinal cord by enlarging the dura—the outer protective wall of the spinal cord—at the area of swelling.

For approximately the first day after the operation appellant recuperated normally, but then suffered a fall and an almost immediate setback. Since there is some conflict as to precisely when or why appellant fell, we reconstruct the events from the evidence most favorable to him. Dr. Spence left orders that appellant was to remain in bed during the process of voiding. These orders were changed to direct that voiding be done out of bed, and the jury could find that the change was made by hospital personnel. Just prior to the fall, appellant summoned a nurse and was given a receptacle for use in voiding, but was then left unattended. Appellant testified that during the course of the endeavor he slipped off the side of the bed, and that there was no one to assist him, or side rail to prevent the fall.

Several hours later, appellant began to complain that he could not move his legs and that he was having trouble breathing; paralysis seems to have been virtually total from the waist down. Dr. Spence was notified on the night of February 12, and he rushed to the hospital. Mrs. Canterbury signed another consent form and appellant was again taken into the operating room. The surgical wound was reopened and Dr. Spence created a gusset to allow the spinal cord greater room in which to pulsate.

Appellant's control over his muscles improved somewhat after the second operation but he was unable to void properly. As a result of this condition, he came under the care of a urologist while still in the hospital. In April, following a cystoscopic examination, appellant was operated on for removal of bladder stones, and in May was released from the hospital. He reentered the hospital the following August for a 10–day period, apparently because of his urologic problems. For several years after his discharge he was under the care of several specialists, and at all times was under the care of a urologist. At the time of the trial in April, 1968, appellant required crutches to walk, still suffered from urinal incontinence and paralysis of the bowels, and wore a penile clamp.

In November, 1959 on Dr. Spence's recommendation, appellant was transferred by the F.B.I. to Miami where he could get more swimming and exercise. Appellant worked three years for the F.B.I. in Miami, Los Angeles and Houston, resigning finally in June, 1962. From then until the time of the trial, he held a number of jobs, but had constant trouble finding work because he needed to remain seated and close to a bathroom. The damages appellant claims include extensive pain and suffering, medical expenses, and loss of earnings.

II

* * *

At the close of appellant's case in chief, each defendant moved for a directed verdict and the trial judge granted both motions. The basis of the ruling, he explained, was that appellant had failed to produce any medical evidence indicating negligence on Dr. Spence's part in diagnosing appellant's malady or in performing the laminectomy; that there was no proof that Dr. Spence's treatment was responsible for appellant's disabilities; and that notwithstanding some evidence to show negligent post-operative care, an absence of medical testimony to show causality precluded submission of the case against the hospital to the jury. The judge did not allude specifically to the alleged breach of duty by Dr. Spence to divulge the possible consequences of the laminectomy.

We reverse. The testimony of appellant and his mother that Dr. Spence did not reveal the risk of paralysis from the laminectomy made out a prima facie case of violation of the physician's duty to disclose which Dr. Spence's explanation did not negate as a matter of law. * * *

III

* * *

* * * True consent to what happens to one's self is the informed exercise of a choice, and that entails an opportunity to evaluate knowledgeably the options available and the risks attendant upon each. The average patient has little or no understanding of the medical arts, and ordinarily has only his physician to whom he can look for enlightenment with which to reach an intelligent decision. From these almost axiomatic considerations springs the need, and in turn the requirement, of a reasonable divulgence by physician to patient to make such a decision possible.[3]

A physician is under a duty to treat his patient skillfully but proficiency in diagnosis and therapy is not the full measure of his responsibility. The cases demonstrate that the physician is under an obligation to communicate specific information to the patient when the exigencies of reasonable care call for it. Due care may require a physician perceiving symptoms of bodily abnormality to alert the patient to the condition. It may call upon the physician confronting an ailment which does not respond to his ministrations to inform the patient thereof. It may command the physician to instruct the

---

3. The doctrine that a consent effective as authority to form therapy can arise only from the patient's understanding of alternatives to and risks of the therapy is commonly denominated "informed consent." See, *e.g.,* Waltz & Scheuneman, Informed Consent to Therapy, 64 Nw.U.L.Rev. 628, 629 (1970). The same appellation is frequently assigned to the doctrine requiring physicians, as a matter of duty to patients, to communicate information as to such alternatives and risks. See, *e.g.,* Comment, Informed Consent in Medical Malpractice, 55 Calif.L.Rev. 1396 (1967). While we recognize the general utility of shorthand phrases in literary expositions, we caution that uncritical use of the "informed consent" label can be misleading. See, *e.g.,* Plante, An Analysis of "Informed Consent," 36 Ford.L.Rev. 639, 671–72 (1968).

In duty-to-disclose cases, the focus of attention is more properly upon the nature and content of the physician's divulgence than the patient's understanding or consent. Adequate disclosure and informed consent are, of course, two sides of the same coin—the former a *sine qua non* of the latter. But the vital inquiry on duty to disclose relates to the physician's performance of an obligation, while one of the difficulties with analysis in terms of "informed consent" is its tendency to imply that what is decisive is the degree of the patient's comprehension. As we later emphasize, the physician discharges the duty when he makes a reasonable effort to convey sufficient information although the patient, without fault of the physician, may not fully grasp it. See text *infra* at notes 82–89. Even though the factfinder may have occasion to draw an inference on the state of the patient's enlightenment, the factfinding process on performance of the duty ultimately reaches back to what the physician actually said or failed to say. And while the factual conclusion on adequacy of the revelation will vary as between patients—as, for example, between a lay patient and a physician-patient—the fluctuations are attributable to the kind of divulgence which may be reasonable under the circumstances.

patient as to any limitations to be presently observed for his own welfare, and as to any precautionary therapy he should seek in the future. It may oblige the physician to advise the patient of the need for or desirability of any alternative treatment promising greater benefit than that being pursued. Just as plainly, due care normally demands that the physician warn the patient of any risks to his well-being which contemplated therapy may involve.

The context in which the duty of risk-disclosure arises is invariably the occasion for decision as to whether a particular treatment procedure is to be undertaken. To the physician, whose training enables a self-satisfying evaluation, the answer may seem clear, but it is the prerogative of the patient, not the physician, to determine for himself the direction in which his interests seem to lie. To enable the patient to chart his course understandably, some familiarity with the therapeutic alternatives and their hazards becomes essential.

A reasonable revelation in these respects is not only a necessity but, as we see it, is as much a matter of the physician's duty. It is a duty to warn of the dangers lurking in the proposed treatment, and that is surely a facet of due care. It is, too, a duty to impart information which the patient has every right to expect. The patient's reliance upon the physician is a trust of the kind which traditionally has exacted obligations beyond those associated with arms-length transactions. His dependence upon the physician for information affecting his well-being, in terms of contemplated treatment, is well-nigh abject. As earlier noted, long before the instant litigation arose, courts had recognized that the physician had the responsibility of satisfying the vital informational needs of the patient. More recently, we ourselves have found "in the fiducial qualities of [the physician-patient] relationship the physician's duty to reveal to the patient that which in his best interests it is important that he should know." We now find, as a part of the physician's overall obligation to the patient, a similar duty of reasonable disclosure of the choices with respect to proposed therapy and the dangers inherently and potentially involved.

* * *

IV

Duty to disclose has gained recognition in a large number of American jurisdictions, but more largely on a different rationale. The majority of courts dealing with the problem have made the duty depend on whether it was the custom of physicians practicing in the community to make the particular disclosure to the patient. If so, the physician may be held liable for an unreasonable and injurious failure to divulge, but there can be no recovery unless the omission forsakes a practice prevalent in the profession. We agree that the physician's noncompliance with a professional custom to reveal, like any other departure from prevailing medical practice, may give rise to liability to the patient. We do not agree that the patient's cause of action is dependent upon the existence and nonperformance of a relevant professional tradition.

There are, in our view, formidable obstacles to acceptance of the notion that the physician's obligation to disclose is either germinated or limited by medical practice. To begin with, the reality of any discernible custom reflecting a professional concensus [sic] on communication of option and risk information to patients is open to serious doubt. We sense the danger that what in fact is no custom at all may be taken as an affirmative custom to maintain silence, and that physician-witnesses to the so-called custom may state merely their personal opinions as to what they or others would do under given conditions. We cannot gloss over the inconsistency between reliance on a general practice respecting divulgence and, on the other hand, realization that the myriad of variables among patients makes each case so different that its omission can rationally be justified only by the effect of its individual circumstances. Nor can we ignore the fact that to bind the disclosure obligation to medical usage is to arrogate the decision on revelation to the physician alone. Respect for the patient's right of self-determination on particular therapy demands a standard set by law for physicians rather than one which physicians may or may not impose upon themselves.

* * * The caliber of the performance exacted by the reasonable-care standard varies between the professional and non-professional worlds, and so also the role of professional custom. * * *

We have admonished, however, that "[t]he special medical standards are but adaptations of the general standard to a group who are required to act as reasonable men possessing their medical talents presumably would." There is, by the same token, no basis for operation of the special medical standard where the physician's activity does not bring his medical knowledge and skills peculiarly into play. And where the challenge to the physician's conduct is not to be gauged by the special standard, it follows that medical custom cannot furnish the test of its propriety, whatever its relevance under the proper test may be. The decision to unveil the patient's condition and the chances as to remediation, as we shall see, is ofttimes a non-medical judgment and, if so, is a decision outside the ambit of the special standard. Where that is the situation, professional custom hardly furnishes the legal criterion for measuring the physician's responsibility to reasonably inform his patient of the options and the hazards as to treatment.

The majority rule, moreover, is at war with our prior holdings that a showing of medical practice, however probative, does not fix the standard governing recovery for medical malpractice. Prevailing medical practice, we have maintained, has evidentiary value in determinations as to what the specific criteria measuring challenged professional conduct are and whether they have been met, but does not itself define the standard. That has been our position in treatment cases, where the physician's performance is ordinarily to be adjudicated by the special medical standard of due care. We see no logic in a different rule for nondisclosure cases, where the governing standard is much more largely divorced from professional considerations. And surely in nondisclosure cases the factfinder is not invariably functioning in an area of such technical complexity that it must be bound to medical custom as an inexorable application of the community standard of reasonable care.

Thus we distinguished, for purposes of duty to disclose, the special-and general-standard aspects of the physician-patient relationship. When medical judgment enters the picture and for that reason the special standard controls, prevailing medical practice must be given its just due. In all other instances, however, the general standard exacting ordinary care applies, and that standard is set by law. In sum, the physician's duty to disclose is governed by the same legal principles applicable to others in comparable situations, with modifications only to the extent that medical judgment enters the picture. We hold that the standard measuring performance of that duty by physicians, as by others, is conduct which is reasonable under the circumstances.

V

Once the circumstances give rise to a duty on the physician's part to inform his patient, the next inquiry is the scope of the disclosure the physician is legally obliged to make. The courts have frequently confronted this problem but no uniform standard defining the adequacy of the divulgence emerges from the decisions. Some have said "full" disclosure, a norm we are unwilling to adopt literally. It seems obviously prohibitive and unrealistic to expect physicians to discuss with their patients every risk of proposed treatment—no matter how small or remote—and generally unnecessary from the patient's viewpoint as well. Indeed, the cases speaking in terms of "full" disclosure appear to envision something less than total disclosure, leaving unanswered the question of just how much.

The larger number of courts, as might be expected, have applied tests framed with reference to prevailing fashion within the medical profession. Some have measured the disclosure by "good medical practice," others by what a reasonable practitioner would have bared under the circumstances, and still others by what medical custom in the community would demand. We have explored this rather considerable body of law but are unprepared to follow it. The duty to disclose, we have reasoned, arises from phenomena apart from medical custom and practice. The latter, we think, should no more establish the scope of the duty than its existence. Any definition of scope in terms purely of a professional standard is at odds with the patient's prerogative to decide on projected therapy himself. That prerogative, we have said, is at the very foundation of the duty to disclose, and both the patient's right to know and the physician's correlative obligation to tell him are diluted to the extent that its compass is dictated by the medical profession.

In our view, the patient's right of self-decision shapes the boundaries of the duty to reveal. That right can be effectively exercised only if the patient possesses enough information to enable an intelligent choice. The scope of the physician's communications to the patient, then, must be measured by the patient's need, and that need is the information material to the decision. Thus the test for determining whether a particular peril must be divulged is its materiality to the patient's decision: all risks potentially affecting the decision must be unmasked. And to safeguard the patient's interest in achieving his own determination on treatment, the law must itself set the standard for adequate disclosure.

Optimally for the patient, exposure of a risk would be mandatory whenever the patient would deem it significant to his decision, either singly or in combination with other risks. Such a requirement, however, would summon the physician to second-guess the patient, whose ideas on materiality could hardly be known to the physician. That would make an undue demand upon medical practitioners, whose conduct, like that of others, is to be measured in terms of reasonableness. Consonantly with orthodox negligence doctrine, the physician's liability for nondisclosure is to be determined on the basis of foresight, not hindsight; no less than any other aspect of negligence, the issue on nondisclosure must be approached from the viewpoint of the reasonableness of the physician's divulgence in terms of what he knows or should know to be the patient's informational needs. If, but only if, the fact-finder can say that the physician's communication was unreasonably inadequate is an imposition of liability legally or morally justified.

Of necessity, the content of the disclosure rests in the first instance with the physician. Ordinarily it is only he who is in position to identify particular dangers; always he must make a judgment, in terms of materiality, as to whether and to what extent revelation to the patient is called for. He cannot know with complete exactitude what the patient would consider important to his decision, but on the basis of his medical training and experience he can sense how the average, reasonable patient expectably would react. Indeed, with knowledge of, or ability to learn, his patient's background and current condition, he is in a position superior to that of most others—attorneys, for example—who are called upon to make judgments on pain of liability in damages for unreasonable miscalculation.

From these considerations we derive the breadth of the disclosure of risks legally to be required. The scope of the standard is not subjective as to either the physician or the patient; it remains objective with due regard for the patient's informational needs and with suitable leeway for the physician's situation. In broad outline, we agree that "[a] risk is thus material when a reasonable person, in what the physician knows or should know to be the patient's position, would be likely to attach significance to the risk or cluster of risks in deciding whether or not to forego the proposed therapy."

The topics importantly demanding a communication of information are the inherent and potential hazards of the proposed treatment, the alternatives to that treatment, if any, and the results likely if the patient remains untreated. The factors contributing significance to the dangerousness of a medical technique are, of course, the incidence of injury and the degree of the harm threatened. A very small chance of death or serious disablement may well be significant; a potential disability which dramatically outweighs the potential benefit of the therapy or the detriments of the existing malady may summon discussion with the patient.

There is no bright line separating the significant from the insignificant; the answer in any case must abide a rule of reason. Some dangers—infection, for example—are inherent in any operation; there is no obligation to communicate those of which persons of average sophistication are aware. Even more clearly, the physician bears no responsibility for discussion of hazards the patient has already discovered, or those having no apparent materiality to patients' decision on therapy. The disclosure doctrine, like others marking lines between permissible and impermissible behavior in medical practice, is in essence a requirement of conduct prudent under the circumstances. Whenever nondisclosure of particular risk information is open to debate by reasonable-minded men, the issue is for the finder of the facts.

Notes and Questions

1. Imagine you are a trial judge in the District Court of the District of Columbia circuit. What will you extract from *Canterbury* as a clear and precise

statement of the law of informed consent? How will you craft jury instructions on the evaluation of a physician's disclosure? Can you criticize Judge Robinson's logic? His statement of the standard?

2. A slight majority of courts has adopted the professional disclosure standard, measuring the duty to disclose by the standard of the reasonable medical practitioner similarly situated. Expert testimony is required to establish the content of a reasonable disclosure. The *Canterbury* rule, using the "reasonable patient" as the measure of the scope of disclosure, has won over several states in the last few years. Some states have adopted tort reform legislation that imposes the professional disclosure standard. See Eady v. Lansford, 351 Ark. 249, 92 S.W.3d 57 (2002); Walls v. Shreck, 265 Neb. 683, 658 N.W.2d 686 (2003). King and Moulton conclude that twenty five states have the physician-based standard, two a hybrid standard, and the rest a patient-based standard. Jaime Staples King and Benjamin Moulton, Rethinking Informed Consent: The Case for Shared Medical Decisionmaking, 32 Am. J. Law & Med. 429, 493–501 (2006)(Appendix).

The professional standard is justified by four arguments. First, it protects good medical practice—the primary duty of physicians is to advance their patients' best interests, and they should not have to concern themselves with the risk that an uninformed lay jury will later decide they acted improperly. Woolley v. Henderson, 418 A.2d 1123 (Me.1980). Second, a patient-oriented standard would force doctors to spend unnecessary time discussing every possible risk with their patients, thereby interfering with the flexibility that they need to decide on the best form of treatment. Third, only physicians can accurately evaluate the psychological and other impact that risk would have on particular patients. Fourth, malpractice costs are limited by keeping more cases away from the jury.

Jurisdictions that follow the professional standard ordinarily require the plaintiff to offer medical testimony to establish 1) that a reasonable medical practitioner in the same or similar community would make this disclosure, and 2) that the defendant did not comply with this community standard. Fuller v. Starnes, 268 Ark. 476, 597 S.W.2d 88 (1980). Expert testimony is essential, since determination of what information needs to be disclosed is viewed as a medical question.

3. Judge Robinson suggests that the *Canterbury* standard is nothing more than the uniform application of the negligence principle to medical practice. However, the negligence principle normally evaluates the conduct of a reasonable actor—not the expectations of a reasonable victim. The values served by the doctrine—patient autonomy and dignity—are unrelated to the values served by the doctrine of negligence. Informed consent really serves the values we otherwise identify with the doctrine of battery. It is ironic that a doctrine developed to foster and recognize individual choice should be measured by an objective standard.

4. The doctor must consider disclosure of a variety of factors:

a. *Diagnosis.* This includes the medical steps preceding diagnosis, including tests and their alternatives.

b. *Nature and purpose of the proposed treatment.*

c. *Risks of the treatment.* Risks that are remote can be omitted. The threshold of disclosure, as the *Canterbury* court suggests, varies with the product of the probability and the severity of the risk. Thus a five percent risk of lengthened recuperation might be ignored, while a one percent risk of paralysis, as in *Canterbury,* or an even smaller risk of death, should be disclosed. Cobbs v. Grant, 8 Cal.3d 229, 104 Cal.Rptr. 505, 502 P.2d 1 (1972). In Hartke v. McKelway, 707 F.2d 1544, 1549 (D.C.Cir.1983) the doctor performed a laparoscopic cauterization to prevent pregnancy of the plaintiff, who later became pregnant and had a healthy child. "In this case, the undisclosed risk was a .1% to .3% chance of subsequent pregnancy. For most people this risk would be considered very small, but this patient was in a particularly unusual position. In view of the very serious expected consequences of pregnancy for her—possibly including death—as well as the ready availability of ways to reduce the risk * * * a jury could conclude that a reasonable person in what Dr. McKelway knew to be plaintiff's position would be likely to attach significance to the risk here."

The difference between a temporary and permanent risk can be critical, and even mention in a consent form of the general risk, but characterized as temporary, will be insufficient to constitute full disclosure. See, e.g., Johnson v. Brandy, 1995 WL 29230 (Ohio App.1995)(risk of scalp numbness after scalp-reduction surgery for baldness not described as permanent risk, but only temporary; consent form held to be inadequate disclosure).

Where a drug or injectable substance is part of treatment, a patient is entitled to know whether that drug or substance has been tested or approved by Federal authorities such as the Food and Drug Administration. Gaston v. Hunter, 121 Ariz. 33, 588 P.2d 326 (App.1978) (investigational procedure must be disclosed); Retkwa v. Orentreich, 154 Misc.2d 164, 584 N.Y.S.2d 710 (N.Y.Sup. 1992) (patient entitled to information about FDA status of liquid injectable silicone).

d. *Treatment alternatives.* Doctors should disclose those alternatives that are generally acknowledged within the medical community as feasible, Martin v. Richards, 192 Wis.2d 156, 531 N.W.2d 70, 78 (1995), their risks and consequences, and their probability of success. Even if the alternative is more hazardous, some courts have held that it should be disclosed. Logan v. Greenwich Hospital Association, 191 Conn. 282, 465 A.2d 294 (1983).

A physician must disclose medical information even if the procedure is noninvasive, because forgoing aggressive treatments to observe a patient may entail significant risks. Martin v. Richards, 192 Wis.2d 156, 531 N.W.2d 70, 79 (1995) (physician failed to disclose to parents the risks of intracranial bleeding and the need for a CT scan or transfer to another facility in that case).

If the alternative is not a legitimate treatment option, it need not be disclosed to the patient. See Morris v. Ferriss, 669 So.2d 1316 (La.App. 4 Cir.1996) (physician did not have to advise patient that psychiatric treatment was an alternative treatment for epileptic partial complex seizures, since it was not accepted as feasible); Lienhard v. State, 431 N.W.2d 861 (Minn.1988) (managing pregnancy at home rather than in hospital not a choice between alternative methods of treatment; disclosure therefore not required).

e. *Consequences of patient refusal of tests or treatments.* How about offering a patient a test that may prevent a life-threatening outcome, and having the patient refuse the test? Must the doctor explain the consequences of such refusal? The California Supreme Court has held that "[i]f the physician knows or should know of a patient's unique concerns or lack of familiarity with medical procedures, this may expand the scope of required disclosure". Truman v. Thomas, 27 Cal.3d 285, 165 Cal.Rptr. 308, 611 P.2d 902 (1980). Mrs. Thomas, 29 years old, declined a Pap smear for financial and other personal reasons. The Court noted that the Pap smear was an accurate detector of cervical cancer, that the odds of Mrs. Truman having this cancer was low, but the failure to detect it at an early stage was death. The Court observed that '* * * even assuming such disclosure was not generally required, the circumstances in this case may establish that Dr. Thomas did have a duty to inform Mrs. Truman of the risks she was running by not undergoing a pap smear.' "

5. *Statutory Limits.* More than half of the states have enacted legislation dealing with informed consent, largely in response to various "malpractice crises" in their states. The statutes take a variety of forms, from specific to general, but they all share the common thread of moving the informed consent standard toward greater deference to medical judgment. Given the current state and national mood of legislative limitations on common law tort remedies, it may be expected that the common law of informed consent will continue to be affected by legislative action. A consent form, or other written documentation of the patient's verbal consent, is treated in many states as presumptively valid consent to the treatment at issue, with the burden on the patient to rebut the presumption. See West's Florida Statutes Ann. § 766.103(4); Official Code Georgia Ann. § 88–2906.1(b)(2); Idaho Code § 39–4305; Iowa Code Ann. § 147.137; LSA–R.S. 24, Tit. 40, § 1299.40.A; Maine Revised Statutes Ann. § 2905.2; Nevada Revised Statutes § 41A/110; North Carolina G.S., § 90–21.13(b); Ohio Revised Code § 2317.54; Vernon's Ann.Texas Revised Civil Statutes, Art. 4590i, § 6.06; Utah Code Ann. § 78–14–5(2)(e); West's Washington Revised Code Ann. § 7.70.060.

Note: Decision Aids and Informed Consent

John Wennberg and others have long argued for the use of decision aids to help patients decide whether or not to have procedures that Wennberg calls "preference-based", such as prostate surgery or treatments for heart disease. John E. Wennberg & Philip G. Peters, Unwanted Variations in the Quality of Health Care: Can the Law Help Medicine Provide a Remedy/Remedies?, 37 Wake Forest L. Rev. 925,925–941 (2002).

These tools may include DVDs that explain the clinical choices, brochures, and other methods of presenting useful information to patients. Decision Aids (DAs) are decision support tools that provide patients with detailed and specific information on options and outcomes, help them clarify their values, and guide them through the decision making process. DAs are superior to usual care interventions in improving knowledge and realistic expectations of the benefits and harms of options; reducing passivity in decision making; and lowering decisional conflict due to feeling uninformed. They also help patients with chronic diseases to feel socially supported and potentially improve their behavioral and clinical outcomes. See, e.g., Elie A Akl et al, A Decision Aid for COPD Patients Considering Inhaled Steroid Therapy: Development and Before and After Pilot Testing, http://www.biomedcentral.com/1472–6947/7/12. Another example is a benign prostatic hyperplasia videotape. See David R. Rovner et al., Decision Aids for Benign Prostatic Hyperplasia: Applicability across Race and Education 24 Med Decis. Making 359 (2004).

The process by which such decision aids are used by the provider and the patient has come to be called "shared medical decision-making". Shared decision-making is defined by King and Moulton as "a process in which the physician shares with the patient all relevant risk and benefit information on all treatment alternatives and the patient shares with the physician all relevant personal information that might make one treatment or side effect more or less tolerable than others. Then, both parties use this information to come to a mutual medical decision." Decision aids can be brochures, online tools, or DVDs; shared decisionmaking is intended for so called "preference" procedures where the patient has to balance the risks and benefits, such as prostate surgery for prostate cancer. Jaime Staples King and Benjamin Moulton, Rethinking Informed Consent: The Case for Shared Medical Decisionmaking, 32 Am. J. Law & Med. 429, 431 (2006). Numerous studies indicate that when decision aids (such as brochures, DVDs or online tools) are available to patients and they have the opportunity to participate in medical decision-making with their physician, the patient-physician dialogue improves, and patient well-being improves as well. See generally the website of the Foundation for Informed Medical Decisionmaking, http://www.fimdm.org

One state has already amended its informed consent statute to incorporate shared decisionmaking through such decision aids. Washington State by statute now creates a presumption of informed consent if a practitioner uses shared decisionmaking through decision aids. A patient decision aid is defined in (4) as:

> (4) * * *a written or online tool providing a balanced presentation of the condition and treatment options, benefits, and harms, including, if appropriate, a discussion of the limits of scientific knowledge about outcomes, that is certified by one or more national certifying organizations approved by the health care authority. In order to be an approved national certifying organization, an organization must use a rigorous evaluation process to assure that decision aids are competently developed, provide a balanced presentation of treatment options, benefits, and harms, and are efficacious at improving decision making.

The legislation requires the state Health Care Authority (HCA) to implement a shared decision-making demonstration project, to be conducted at one or more multi-specialty group practices. The demonstration project will incorporate decision aids into clinical practice to assess the effect of SDM on health care quality and cost.

III. INFORMED CONSENT: THE INSTITUTION'S OBLIGATION?

Consent forms are universally used in hospitals, where most health care is provided. Hospitals use them at several points in a patient's progress through the institution upon admission, when a generic form is signed; and before surgery or anesthesia, when more detailed forms may be offered. These forms operate as a legal surrogate for consent, sometimes memorializing an actual physician-patient discussion, sometimes not.

The legal responsibility for obtaining the patient's consent is the physician's, not the hospital's. The courts continue to hold that the hospital only assists in administering the process, typically through its nursing staff, but has no duty except under very narrow circumstances. Courts defer to the expertise of the treating physician. See, e.g., Foster v. Traul, 141 Idaho 890, 120 P.3d 278 (2005); Gotlin v. Lederman, 367 F.Supp.2d 349 (E.D.N.Y.2005). But see Magana v. Elie, 108 Ill.App.3d 1028, 64 Ill.Dec. 511, 439 N.E.2d 1319 (1982) (hospital has duty to obtain patient's informed consent); Rogers v. Samson, 276 F.3d 228 (6th Cir.2002) (hospital had a duty to obtain a patient's informed consent to the removal of his entire penis in order to prevent the progression of necrotizing fascitis throughout his groin area).

Consider the following language, taken from a standard hospital form:

Inpatient/Non–Surgical:

Consent to Medical and Surgical Procedures. The undersigned consents to the procedures which may be performed during this hospitalization or on an outpatient basis, including emergency treatment or procedures, or hospital services rendered to the patient under the general and special instructions of the patient's physician(s).

Surgical Patient:

Consent to Medical and Surgical Procedures. The undersigned consents to the procedures which may be performed during this hospitalization or on an outpatient basis, including emergency treatment or services, and which may include but are not limited to laboratory procedures, x-ray examination, anesthesia, medical or surgical treatment or procedures, or hospital services rendered to the patient under the general and special instructions of the patient's physician(s).

These are labeled "condition of admission" and to be signed by all patients entering a hospital. Are you impressed? They assume a conversation with the treating physician, and disclosure of risk, do they not? They do not say so explicitly, however.

Institutional responsibility to ensure that a patient's informed consent is obtained generally exists only in two limited areas: (1) documentation of patient consent for the record, and (2) experimental therapies. If a nurse fails to obtain a properly executed consent form and make it a part of the patient record, the hospital may be liable for this failure as a violation of its own internal procedures. See, e.g., Butler v. South Fulton Medical Center, Inc., 215 Ga.App. 809, 452 S.E.2d 768, 772 (1994). If a hospital participates in a study of an experimental procedure, it must ensure that the patient is properly informed of the risks of the procedure. See Kus v. Sherman Hospital, 268 Ill.App.3d 771, 206 Ill.Dec. 161, 644 N.E.2d 1214 (1995) (hospital was part of a research study on intraocular lens implantation; the court held that "... a hospital, as well as a physician, may be held liable for a patient's defective consent in a case involving experimental intraocular lenses ...").

Hospitals are asserting substantial control over the consent process, through standardized forms and through new processes for automated consent. The U.S. Department of Veterans Affairs has been implementing an automated informed consent application known as *iMedConsent* in its medical centers and many hospitals across the country are considering or implementing similar informed consent aids. See Robert Gatter, The Mysterious Survival of the Policy Against Informed Consent Liability for Hospitals, 81 Notre Dame L. Rev. 1203 (2006).

What might be the effect of imposing a duty on the hospital and its staff to ensure that patient consent is properly obtained by attending physicians? Might the hospital not work harder to make sure that consent is properly obtained? Or is deference to physicians too much a part of the hospital-physician relationship? Would it make any difference to the reality of patient consent? See Catherine Jones, Autonomy and Informed Consent in Medical Decisionmaking: Toward a New Self–Fulfilling Prophecy, 47 Wash. & Lee. L. Rev. 379, 429 (1990).

The law of informed consent is highly variable, and at the same time it lacks specificity as a guide to physicians. One commentator has proposed that explicit contracts between providers and patient groups might better serve the doctrine, allowing specific guidelines to be developed by agreement. This would allow the law to be tailor-made to the different settings in which risks arise, contextualizing consent. Contextualization would advance the aim of cost-effectiveness and would also be desirable in its own right. Each goal seeks to improve the informed consent dialogue, and the doctrine that regulates it, by tailoring the law's requirements more carefully to the different settings in which risks arise and are discussed, assessed, and acted upon. Peter H. Schuck, Rethinking Informed Consent, 103 Yale L.J. 899, 906 (1994).

A study by Charles W. Lidz et al., Informed Consent: A Study of Decisionmaking in Psychiatry 318, 326 (1985) concluded that informed consent forms were not important in the decisionmaking process: they were presented too late, were too complex, were unread by the patients before signed, and were treated by both staff and patients as simply a ritual for confirming a decision already made. There is little evidence since this study in 1985 that forms have improved in their drafting or their presentation to patients.

How can such forms be improved, so that they will facilitate doctor-patient conversation and risk disclosure? Try to redraft the language found above to properly facilitate an informed consent.

Is it time for the courts to move toward a duty on the hospital or other institution to properly administer informed consent and ensure patient understanding? What kinds of decision aids or other processes might you consider to achieve better patient comprehension of procedures they are facing in the hospital?

Problem: Automating Consent

Consider the automated consent process described at http://www.dialog medical.com/ic.htm.

The implementation of *iMedConsent* by the Veterans Health Administration is described in an information letter of February 22, 2007.

1. This Veterans Health Administration (VHA) Information Letter clarifies expectations for use of the iMedConsent™ software program and establishes guidelines for local customization of the consent forms in the iMedConsent™ library. Informed consent for treatments and procedures is essential to high quality patient care. Implementation of national standards for the informed consent process will help ensure that veterans across the country receive the information that they need before giving their consent to treatment.

2. Once implemented in a specialty, iMedConsent™ should be used to electronically generate, sign, and store consent forms for clinical treatments and procedures. If iMedConsent™ is unavailable due to a system failure, or if the patient is uncomfortable using the signature pad, consent may be obtained using a paper form (physicians should print the form in iMedConsent™ if possible).

3. At this time, paper forms should also be used to document consent in emergency situations, consent over the telephone, consent for employee health, and consent for research. The iMedConsent™ program may be modified to accommodate these processes in the future.

4. Clinicians will continue to be able to modify consent forms on a case-by-case basis to reflect each patient's medical condition. However, clinicians should

use their discretion appropriately. Risks, benefits, and alternatives disclosed on consent forms must be consistent with informed consent policy (see Handbook 1004.1, Informed Consent for Clinical Treatments and Procedures). It is not appropriate, for example, to delete this information and write "as discussed." Nor is it appropriate to add boilerplate risks that are not known to be associated with a particular procedure.

* * *

http://wwwl.va.gov/vhapublcations/ViewPublication.asp?pub_ID=1541

Assume that you are advising your local community hospital about the merits of such an automated process. What advantages do you see in implementing such a system? What are your legal concerns?

IV.   CONFIDENTIALITY AND DISCLOSURE IN THE PHYSICIAN–PATIENT RELATIONSHIP

A.   BREACHES OF CONFIDENCE

One of the most important obligations owed by a professional to a patient is the protection of confidences revealed by the patient to the professional. State courts have developed common law rules to protect these confidences. The Federal Medical Privacy Rules under HIPAA provide an elaborate protective framework for patient information. These state and federal obligations are discussed in this section.

HUMPHERS v. FIRST INTERSTATE BANK OF OREGON

Supreme Court of Oregon, In Banc, 1985.
298 Or. 706, 696 P.2d 527.

LINDE, JUSTICE.

We are called upon to decide whether plaintiff has stated a claim for damages in alleging that her former physician revealed her identity to a daughter whom she had given up for adoption.

In 1959, according to the complaint, plaintiff, then known as Ramona Elwess or by her maiden name, Ramona Jean Peek, gave birth to a daughter in St. Charles Medical Center in Bend, Oregon. She was unmarried at the time, and her physician, Dr. Harry E. Mackey, registered her in the hospital as "Mrs. Jean Smith." The next day, Ramona consented to the child's adoption by Leslie and Shirley Swarens of Bend, who named her Leslie Dawn. The hospital's medical records concerning the birth were sealed and marked to show that they were not public. Ramona subsequently remarried and raised a family. Only Ramona's mother and husband and Dr. Mackey knew about the daughter she had given up for adoption.

Twenty-one years later the daughter, now known as Dawn Kastning, wished to establish contact with her biological mother. Unable to gain access to the confidential court file of her adoption (though apparently able to locate the attending physician), Dawn sought out Dr. Mackey, and he agreed to assist in her quest. Dr. Mackey gave Dawn a letter which stated that he had registered Ramona Jean Peek at the hospital, that although he could not locate his medical records, he remembered administering diethylstilbestrol to her, and that the possible consequences of this medication made it important for Dawn to find her biological mother. The latter statements were untrue and made only to help Dawn to breach the confidentiality of the records concerning her birth and adoption. In 1982, hospital personnel, relying on Dr. Mackey's letter, allowed Dawn to make copies of plaintiff's medical records, which enabled her to locate plaintiff, now Ramona Humphers.

Ramona Humphers was not pleased. The unexpected development upset her and caused her emotional distress, worry, sleeplessness, humiliation, embarrassment, and inability to function normally. She sought damages from the estate of Dr. Mackey, who had died, by this action against defendant as the personal representative. After alleging the facts recounted above, her complaint pleads for relief on five different theories: First, that Dr. Mackey incurred liability for "outrageous conduct"; second, that his disclosure of a professional secret fell short of the care, skill and diligence employed by other physicians in the community and commanded by statute; third, that his disclosure wrongfully breached a confidential or privileged relationship; fourth, that his disclosure of confidential information was an "invasion of privacy" in the form of an "unauthorized intrusion upon plaintiff's seclusion, solitude, and private affairs;" and fifth, that his disclosures to Dawn Kastning breached a contractual obligation of secrecy. The circuit court granted defendant's motion to dismiss the complaint on the grounds that the facts fell short of each theory of relief and ordered entry of judgment for defendant. On appeal, the Court of Appeals affirmed the dismissal of the first, second, and fifth counts but reversed on the third, breach of a confidential relationship, and the fourth, invasion of privacy. [ ] We allowed review. We hold that if plaintiff has a claim, it arose from a breach by Dr. Mackey of a professional duty to keep plaintiff's secret rather than from a violation of plaintiff's privacy.

A physician's liability for disclosing confidential information about a patient is not a new problem. In common law jurisdictions it has been more discussed than litigated throughout much of this century. There are precedents for damage actions for unauthorized disclosure of facts conveyed in confidence, although we know of none involving the disclosure of an adoption. Because such claims are made against a variety of defendants besides physicians or other professional counselors, for instance against banks [ ], and because plaintiffs understandably plead alternative theories of recovery, the decisions do not always rest on a single theory.

Sometimes, defendant may have promised confidentiality expressly or by factual implication, in this case perhaps implied by registering a patient in the hospital under an assumed name. * * * [ ] A contract claim may be adequate where the breach of confidence causes financial loss, and it may gain a longer period of limitations; but contract law may deny damages for psychic or emotional injury not within the contemplation of the contracting parties, [ ] though perhaps this is no barrier when emotional security is the very object of the promised confidentiality. A contract claim is unavailable if the defendant physician was engaged by someone other than the plaintiff [ ] and it would be an awkward fiction at best if age, mental condition, or other circumstances prevent the patient from contracting; yet such a claim might be available to someone less interested than the patient, for instance her husband [ ].

Malpractice claims, based on negligence or statute, in contrast, may offer a plaintiff professional standards of conduct independent of the defendant's assent. * * * Finally, actions for intentional infliction of severe emotional distress fail when the defendant had no such intention or * * * when a defendant was not reckless or did not behave in a manner that a factfinder could find to transcend "the farthest reaches of socially tolerable behavior." [ ] Among these diverse precedents, we need only consider the counts of breach of confidential relationship and invasion of privacy on which the Court of Appeals allowed plaintiff to proceed. Plaintiff did not pursue her other theories * * * and we express no view whether the dismissal of those counts was correct.

PRIVACY

Although claims of a breach of privacy and of wrongful disclosure of confidential information may seem very similar in a case like the present, which involves the disclosure of an intimate personal secret, the two claims depend on different premises and cover different ground. Their common denominator is that both assert a right to control information, but they differ in important respects. Not every secret concerns personal or private information; commercial secrets are not personal, and governmental secrets are neither personal nor private. Secrecy involves intentional concealment. * * *

For our immediate purpose, the most important distinction is that only one who holds information in confidence can be charged with a breach of confidence. If an act qualifies as a tortious invasion of privacy, it theoretically could be committed by anyone. In the present case, Dr. Mackey's professional role is relevant to a claim that he breached a duty of confidentiality, but he could be charged with an invasion of plaintiff's privacy only if anyone else who told Dawn Kastning the facts of her birth without a special privilege to do so would be liable in tort for invading the privacy of her mother.

Whether "privacy" is a usable legal category has been much debated in other English-speaking jurisdictions as well as in this country, especially since its use in tort law, to claim the protection of government against intrusions by others, became entangled with its use in constitutional law, to claim protection against rather different intrusions by government. No concept in modern law has unleashed a comparable flood of commentary, its defenders arguing that "privacy" encompasses related interests of personality and autonomy, while its critics say that these interests are properly identified, evaluated, and protected below that exalted philosophical level. Indeed, at that level, a daughter's interest in her personal identity here confronts a mother's interest in guarding her own present identity by concealing their joint past. But recognition of an interest or value deserving protection states only half a case. Tort liability depends on the defendant's wrong as well as on the plaintiff's interest, or "right," unless some rule imposes strict liability. One's preferred seclusion or anonymity may be lost in many ways; the question remains who is legally bound to protect those interests at the risk of liability.

* * *

In this country, Dean William L. Prosser and his successors, noting that early debate was more "preoccupied with the question whether the right of privacy existed" than "what it would amount to if it did," concluded that invasion of privacy "is not one tort but a complex of four" * * * Prosser and Keeton, Torts 851, § 117 (5th ed. 1984). They identify the four kinds of claims grouped under the "privacy" tort as, first, appropriation of the plaintiff's name or likeness; second, unreasonable and offensive intrusion upon the seclusion of another; third, public disclosure of private facts; and fourth, publicity which places the plaintiff in a false light in the public eye. *Id.* at 851–66. [ ]

This court has not adopted all forms of the tort wholesale. * * *

* * *

* * * The Court of Appeals concluded that the complaint alleges a case of tortious intrusion upon plaintiff's seclusion, not by physical means such as uninvited entry, wiretapping, photography, or the like, but in the sense of an offensive prying into personal matters that plaintiff reasonably has sought to keep private. [ ] We do not believe that the theory fits this case.

Doubtless plaintiff's interest qualifies as a "privacy" interest. That does not require the judgment of a court or a jury; it is established by the statutes that close adoption records to inspection without a court order. [ ]. * * * But as already stated, to identify an interest deserving protection does not suffice to collect damages from anyone who causes injury to that interest. Dr. Mackey helped Dawn Kastning find her biological mother, but we are not prepared to assume that Ms. Kastning became liable for invasion of privacy in seeking her out. Nor, we think, would anyone who knew the facts without an obligation of secrecy commit a tort simply by telling them to Ms. Kastning.

Dr. Mackey himself did not approach plaintiff or pry into any personal facts that he did not know; indeed, if he had written or spoken to his former patient to tell her that her daughter was eager to find her, it would be hard to describe such a communication alone as an invasion of privacy. The point of the claim against Dr. Mackey is not that he pried into a confidence but that he failed to keep one. If Dr. Mackey incurred liability for that, it must result from an obligation of confidentiality beyond any general duty of people at large not to invade one another's privacy. We therefore turn to plaintiff's claim that Dr. Mackey was liable for a breach of confidence, the third count of the complaint.

BREACH OF CONFIDENCE

It takes less judicial innovation to recognize this claim than the Court of Appeals thought. A number of decisions have held that unauthorized and unprivileged disclosure of confidential information obtained in a confidential relationship can give rise to tort damages. [ ] * * *.

* * *

In the case of the medical profession, courts in fact have found sources of a nonconsensual duty of confidentiality. Some have thought such a duty toward the patient implicit in the patient's statutory privilege to exclude the doctor's testimony in litigation[ ]. More directly in point are legal duties imposed as a condition of engaging in the professional practice of medicine or other occupations.

[The court noted that medical licensing statutes and professional regulations have been used as sources of a duty.]

This strikes us as the right approach to a claim of liability outside obligations undertaken expressly or implied in fact in entering a contractual relationship. [ ] The contours of the asserted duty of confidentiality are determined by a legal source external to the tort claim itself.

* * *

Because the duty of confidentiality is determined by standards outside the tort claim for its breach, so are the defenses of privilege or justification. Physicians, like members of many ordinary confidential professions and occupations, also may be legally obliged to report medical information to others for the protection of the patient, of other individuals, or of the public. *See, e.g.,* ORS 418.750 (physician's duty to report child abuse); ORS 433.003, 434.020 (duty to report certain diseases). * * * Even without such a legal obligation, there may be a privilege to disclose information for the safety of individuals or important to the public in matters of public interest. [ ] Some cases have found a physician privileged in disclosing information to a patient's spouse, *Curry v. Corn,* 52 Misc.2d 1035, 277 N.Y.S.2d 470 (1966) or perhaps an intended spouse, *Berry v. Moench,* supra. In any event, defenses to a duty of confidentiality are determined in the same manner as the existence and scope of the duty itself. They necessarily will differ from one occupation to another and from time to time. A physician or other member of a regulated occupation is not to be held to a noncontractual duty of secrecy in a tort action when disclosure would not be a breach or would be privileged in direct enforcement of the underlying duty.

A physician's duty to keep medical and related information about a patient in confidence is beyond question. It is imposed by statute. ORS 677.190(5) provides for disqualifying or otherwise disciplining a physician for "wilfully or negligently divulging a professional secret." * * *

It is less obvious whether Dr. Mackey violated ORS 677.190(5) when he told Dawn Kastning what he knew of her birth. She was not, after all, a stranger to that proceeding. * * * If Ms. Kastning needed information about her natural mother for medical reasons, as Dr. Mackey pretended, the State Board of Medical Examiners likely would find the disclosure privileged against a charge under ORS 677.190(5); but the statement is alleged to have been a pretext designed to give her access to the hospital records. If only ORS 677.190(5) were involved, we do not know how the Board would judge a physician who assists at the birth of a child and decades later reveals to that person his or her parentage. But as already noted, other statutes specifically mandate the secrecy of adoption records. * * * Given these clear legal constraints, there is no privilege to disregard the professional duty imposed by ORS 677.190(5) solely in order to satisfy the curiosity of the person who was given up for adoption.

For these reasons, we agree with the Court of Appeals that plaintiff may proceed under her claim of breach of confidentiality in a confidential relationship. The decision of the Court of Appeals is reversed with respect to plaintiff's claim of invasion of privacy and affirmed with respect to her claim

of breach of confidence in a confidential relationship, and the case is remanded to the circuit court for further proceedings on that claim.

Notes and Questions

1. What harm was the plaintiff exposed to by the disclosure of her relationship to the plaintiff? Was the doctor's action a breach of medical ethics? Should he
have been sanctioned by the state medical licensing board?

2. Every time a person consults a medical professional, is admitted to a
health care institution, or receives a medical test, a medical record is created or an
entry is made in an existing record. Billions of such records exist in the United
States, most of which will be retained from 10 to 25 years. Many of these records
contain very personal information—revelations to psychotherapists or documentation of treatment for alcoholism or venereal disease, for example—the disclosure
of which could prove devastating to the patient. These records are now subject to
restrictions on use under the Medical Privacy Rules, section C, *infra*.

3. Who uses medical information? Professional and non-professional medical
staff must have access to records of patients in medical institutions for treatment
purposes. Consent to such access is commonly presumed. Third party payors are
the most common requestors of medical records outside the treatment setting.
Access to records also is sought routinely for a variety of medical evaluation and
support purposes. For example, in-house quality assurance committees, Joint
Commission accreditation inspection teams, and state institutional licensure reviewers all must review medical records to assess the quality of hospital care.
State public health laws require medical professionals and institutions to report a
variety of medical conditions and incidents: venereal disease, contagious diseases,
wounds inflicted by violence, poisonings, industrial accidents, abortions, and child
abuse.

Access to medical records is also sought for secondary, nonmedical, purposes.
Law enforcement agencies, for example, often seek access to medical information.
A moderate-size Chicago hospital reported that the FBI requested information
about patients as often as twice a month. Attorneys seek medical records to
establish disability, personal injury, or medical malpractice claims for their clients.
Though they most commonly will ask for records of their own clients, they may
also want to review records of other patients to establish a pattern of knowing
medical abuse by a physician or the culpability of a hospital for failing to supervise
a negligent practitioner. Life, health, disability and liability insurers often seek
medical information, as do employers and credit investigators. Disclosure of
information from medical records may occur without a formal request. Though
secondary users of medical information commonly receive information pursuant to
patient record releases, they have been known to seek and compile information
surreptitiously. These secondary disclosures of medical information are of great
import to patients, as disclosure can result in loss of employment or denial of
insurance or credit, or, at least, severe embarrassment. See generally the Preamble to the Medical Privacy Rules, *infra*.

4. What legal devices have traditionally protected the confidentiality of
medical information? The physician-patient privilege comes first to mind, but in
fact it plays a very limited role. First, and most important, it is only a testimonial
privilege, not a general obligation to maintain confidentiality: though it may
permit a doctor to refuse to disclose medical information in court, it does not
require the doctor to keep information from employers or insurers. Second, it is a
statutory privilege or one created through judicial rulemaking and does not exist

in all jurisdictions. According to the Privacy Protection Study Commission 43 states have some form of testimonial privilege, yet some of these are only applicable to psychiatrists. Third, as a privilege created by state statute, it does not apply in non-diversity federal court proceedings. Fourth, the privilege is in most states subject to many exceptions. In California, it is subject to twelve exceptions, including cases where the patient is a litigant, criminal proceedings, will contests, and physician licensure proceedings. State privilege statutes often cover physicians only, who today deliver only about 5% of health care. Finally, the privilege applies only to confidential disclosures made to a physician in the course of treatment and is easily waived.

5.   Several federal and state statutes protect the confidentiality of medical information. Most notable among these are amendments to the Drug Abuse and Treatment Acts and Comprehensive Alcohol Abuse and Alcoholism Prevention, Treatment, and Rehabilitation Act, 42 U.S.C.A. §§ 290dd–3, 390ee–3 (West 1982 & Supp.1986), and implementing regulations, 42 C.F.R. Part 2 (1985), which impose rigorous requirements on the disclosure of information from alcohol and drug abuse treatment programs. Some state statutes provide civil penalties for disclosure of confidential information. See Ill.Rev.Stat. ch. 91, § 815; West's Fla.Stat.Ann. § 395.018.

6.   State courts have imposed liability on doctors for violating a duty of confidentiality expressed or implied in state licensure or privilege statutes. Several common law theories have also been advanced to impose liability on professionals who disclose medical information. Two of these, invasion of privacy and breach of confidential relationship, are discussed in *Humphers*. See Berger v. Sonneland, 101 Wash.App. 141, 1 P.3d 1187 (2000) (allowing action for unauthorized disclosure of confidential information, including emotional distress damages.)

Where the doctor breaches a confidence in reporting a plaintiff's health problem to a third party, and the plaintiff arguably had an obligation to report directly, courts have refused to allow a suit for breach of confidentiality. See Alar v. Mercy Memorial Hospital, 208 Mich.App. 518, 529 N.W.2d 318 (1995) (psychiatrist informed Air Force Academy about suicide attempt of high school student who had been accepted to the Academy; the court held that there was no causal link between the defendant's disclosure and the harm suffered by plaintiff, since he had an independent obligation to inform.) Absent a compelling public interest or other justification, however, an action typically will be allowed for a physician's breach of the duty to maintain patient confidences. See McCormick v. England, 328 S.C. 627, 494 S.E.2d 431 (App.1997); Marek v. Ketyer, 733 A.2d 1268 (Pa.Super.1999).

7.   Medical records often play a pivotal role in medical malpractice cases. By the time a malpractice action comes to trial memories may have dimmed as to what actually occurred at the time negligence is alleged to have taken place, leaving the medical record as the most telling evidence. Medical records, if properly authenticated, will usually be admitted under the business records exception to the hearsay rule. Because either documentation of inadequate care or inadequate documentation of care may result in liability, physicians are sometimes tempted to destroy records or to alter them to reflect the care they wish in retrospect they had rendered. There is nothing wrong with correcting records, so long as corrections are made in such a way as to leave the previous entry clearly readable and the new entry clearly identified as a corrected entry. Conscious concealment, fabrication, or falsification of records may result in an inference of awareness of guilt, Pisel v. Stamford Hospital, 180 Conn. 314, 340, 430 A.2d 1, 15 (1980); Thor v. Boska, 38 Cal.App.3d 558, 113 Cal.Rptr. 296 (1974); or punitive

damages. It may also toll the statute of limitations. Finally, premature disposition of records could result in negligence liability, Fox v. Cohen, 84 Ill.App.3d 744, 40 Ill.Dec. 477, 406 N.E.2d 178 (1980).

Problem: The Hunt for Patient Records

Two partners of a law firm, Findem and Howe, got the idea of working with a hospital to determine whether unpaid medical bills could be submitted to the Social Security Administration for payment as reimbursable disability treatment. They proposed the idea to the President of the law firm, who was also a trustee of the Warner General Hospital Health System.

The hospital agreed to search patient records and provide four pieces of patient information: name, telephone number, age, and medical condition. The patient registration forms were then furnished to the firm. The hospital agreed to pay a contingency fee to the firm for claims paid by Social Security. Patients who were possible candidates were called by the firm, on behalf of the hospital, telling them that they might be entitled to Social Security benefits that would help them pay their hospital bills. Some of the patients came in to talk with firm lawyers. A total of twelve thousand patient records were examined as part of this enterprise.

A group of angry former patients of Warner General have come to you to see what rights they have for what they feel is a violation of their privacy rights. How will you proceed? What arguments can you make on their behalf?

B. FEDERAL MEDICAL PRIVACY STANDARDS

Concerns about the privacy of patient medical information have intensified with the growth of both electronic recordkeeping and the Internet. The federal government studied this problem for several years before developing a highly detailed set of standards for health care providers.

HERMAN v. KRATCHE

Ohio Court of Appeals, 2006.
2006 WL 3240680.

* * *

In March 2003, plaintiff worked for Nestle USA, Inc., located in Solon, Ohio. In March and April 2003, plaintiff received non-work related medical examinations and/or testing at the Clinic. After three appointments, the Clinic forwarded plaintiff's records and other private medical information to the Human Resources Department at Nestle.

Plaintiff received medical treatment from the Clinic on March 11, 2003. On that date, plaintiff was seen by Dr. Kratche for a physical examination. The written results of that examination were sent to Nestle.

Thomas Atkinson, Administrator for the Clinic's Solon Family Health Center, explained that the March 11th records were sent to Nestle for "workers' comp coverage." (Atkinson Dep. 21.) After plaintiff complained to defendants about her records being sent to Nestle, Atkinson acknowledged the error and changed the records designation for the March 11th visit. The designation was moved from a workers' compensation claim to "Ms. Herman's personal family account with her medical coverage." (Atkinson Dep. 31.) Defendant does not dispute that plaintiff had independent medical coverage under United Healthcare at all times relevant to this case.

Plaintiff returned to the Clinic on April 2, 2003 for a mammogram screening. The results and billing for that procedure were also designated as related to workers' compensation. The information was again forwarded to Nestle. Plaintiff returned to the Clinic for a diagnostic mammogram on April 10th. Again, those records were marked as workers' compensation and sent to Nestle. Atkinson acknowledged that all the records that were sent to Nestle from plaintiff's three visits in 2003 included protected private medical information that should never have been sent to Nestle. Plaintiff filed suit against defendants for unauthorized disclosure, invasion of privacy, and intentional infliction of emotional distress. Defendants filed a joint motion for summary judgment on all of plaintiff's claims. Without stating its reasons, the trial court granted defendants' motion.

* * *

I.   UNAUTHORIZED DISCLOSURE

One of plaintiff's claims here is that the Clinic is liable to her because it made an unauthorized disclosure of her personal health information to her employer.

"[I]n Ohio, an independent tort exists for the unauthorized, unprivileged disclosure to a third party of nonpublic medical information that a physician or hospital has learned within a physician-patient relationship." Biddle v. Warren Gen. Hosp.[ ]. An unauthorized disclosure under *Biddle* is "the tort of breach of confidence."[ ]. The only way to avoid liability for an unauthorized disclosure is for the hospital or other medical provider to obtain the patient's consent.[ ]

One of the first cases in Ohio to deal with the issue of an unauthorized disclosure by a physician is *Hammonds v. Aetna Cas. & Sur. Co. (N.D.* Ohio, 1965)[ ]. *Hammonds* explains the purpose of physician-patient confidentiality as follows:

> "A patient should be entitled to freely disclose his symptoms and condition to his doctor in order to receive proper treatment without fear that those facts may become public property. Only thus can the purpose of the relationship be fulfilled."[ ]

As is evident in *Biddle* [ ], a physician's breach of a patient's confidence in the form of an unauthorized disclosure of that patient's medical information is an independent tort separate and distinct from the tort of invading one's privacy.

Hammonds [ ] provides that an unauthorized patient disclosure by a physician or hospital constitutes a breach of their fiduciary duty.

> "A claim of breach of a fiduciary duty is basically a claim of negligence, albeit involving a higher standard of care. And in negligence actions, we have long held that 'one seeking recovery must show the existence of a duty on the part of the one sued not to subject the former to the injury complained of, a failure to observe such duty, and an injury resulting proximately therefrom.' "

[ ]

There is no dispute that the Clinic, as plaintiff's medical provider, held a fiduciary position with plaintiff as its patient and had a duty to keep plaintiff's medical information confidential. There is also no doubt that the Clinic breached that duty.

Plaintiff must next demonstrate that the Clinic's breach of its fiduciary duty was the proximate cause of her damages.[ ]

The Clinic argues that her employer was not a "third party," because it also held a duty of confidentiality to her. The Clinic concludes, therefore, that since no "third-party" read plaintiff's records and since the employer did not disclose the information contained in those records to anyone else, the Clinic is not the proximate cause of plaintiff's damages.

The tortious conduct of an unprivileged disclosure occurs the moment the nonpublic medical information is disclosed to an *unauthorized* third-party. The tortious conduct of the Clinic does not depend on what the duties of the third party are or what the third party subsequently does with that information. Any duties the third party may have had do not transform it into an "authorized" party. The key is whether the receiving party is "authorized" to receive the record.

Moreover, the Clinic is mistaken when it claims that no one at Nestle read plaintiff's records. To the contrary, the human resources person at Nestle returned these records to plaintiff because he had read enough of plaintiff's records to know that they did not have anything to do with plaintiff's employment and therefore returned the records to plaintiff.

For the foregoing reasons, we conclude that the Clinic had a fiduciary duty to plaintiff, and the Clinic breached that duty when it sent plaintiff's non-work-related medical records to Nestle. Moreover, as soon as Nestle opened the records, the Clinic became the proximate cause of plaintiff's harm. This part of the Clinic's argument fails.

In its motion for summary judgment, the Clinic further argues that it is not liable for its unauthorized disclosures because Nestle owed plaintiff the same duty of confidentiality under the Health Insurance Portability and Accountability Act of 1996[ ] ("HIPAA") as the Clinic did. The Clinic argues that since it and Nestle both occupy the same "circle of confidentiality" under HIPAA, the Clinic did not make an unauthorized disclosure.

In 1996, Congress enacted HIPAA. One of HIPAA's purposes is to protect the privacy of an individual's personal health information ("PHI"). [ ] Under HIPAA, "covered entities," including (1) health plans; (2) health care clearinghouses; and (3) health care providers, are required to follow specific regulations (45 CFR §§ 160–164) relating to the collection, use, or disclosure of an individual's personal health information. Generally, a covered entity may not disclose health information of persons without their consent.[ ][6]

"PHI" includes any information about an individual that "(1) is created or received by a health care provider, health plan, public health authority, employer, life insurer, school or university health care clearinghouse; and (2) relates to the past, present or future physical or mental health or condition of an individual; the provision of health care to an individual; or the past, present, or future payment for the provision of health care to an individual."[ ] As stated in *Smith:*

---

6. Under 45 C.F.R. § 164.501, "PHI," in part, includes information relating to an individual's past, present, or future physical or mental health or condition.

"The Privacy Rule prohibits covered entities from using or disclosing PHI in any form oral, written or electronic, except as permitted under the Privacy Rule.[ ] 'Use' and 'disclosure' are defined very broadly.[ ]. 'Use' includes an examination of PHI; 'disclosure' includes divulging or providing access to PHI. The Privacy Rule is also centered on the concept that, when using PHI or when requesting PHI from another covered entity, a covered entity must make reasonable efforts to limit PHI to the 'minimum necessary' to accomplish the intended purpose of the use, disclosure or request.[ ] In other words, even if a use or disclosure of PHI is permitted, covered entities must make reasonable efforts to disclose only the minimum necessary to achieve the purpose for which it is being used or disclosed. The 'minimum necessary' standard was implemented to prevent improper disclosure of PHI, yet to be flexible when a patient waives his or her privacy privilege for confidential medical information.

* * *

"[U]nder the HIPAA regulations as presently promulgated, only the minimum necessary amount of information consistent with the stated purpose is to be disclosed. Any further information, whether collateral or marginal, is prohibited."[ ]

The Clinic argues that since it and Nestle share the same duty of confidentiality, the Clinic could not have made an unauthorized disclosure. When Nestle received plaintiff's information from the Clinic, Nestle would be bound by its own duty of confidentiality to not disclose that medical information. According to the Clinic, "an employer receiving an employee's medical records is part of the same circle of confidentiality that encompasses the medical provider responsible for sending the records in the first place." (Defendants' motion for summary judgment, 9).

First, neither HIPAA nor the regulations that accompany it mention anything about a "circle of confidentiality." Second, because Nestle does not meet the definition of a "health plan," "healthcare clearinghouse," or "healthcare provider," we conclude Nestle is not a covered entity under HIPAA.[ ] Therefore, Nestle cannot possibly be "part of the same circle of confidentiality" as the Clinic.

The Clinic sent plaintiff's medical information to Nestle under the mistaken belief that her visits were related to workers' compensation claims from 1993 as a Nestle employee. HIPAA permits a covered entity to disclose an individual's personal health information to an employer for workers' compensation purposes without consent.[ ] However, when a covered entity makes a disclosure, it must be for a purpose stated under HIPAA and its regulations.[ ] The Clinic does not cite nor do we find any authority for an inadvertent disclosure under HIPAA.

The three cases the Clinic believes support its argument about a "circle of confidentiality" are not instructive in resolving this issue, since all three were decided years before the 1996 enactment of HIPAA. Accordingly, we have determined that HIPAA does not offer the Clinic any protection for the disclosures it made.

The Clinic additionally argues that plaintiff consented to having her medical information disclosed to Nestle. According to the Clinic, when plaintiff executed a consent form relating to its "Notice of Privacy Practices," she acknowledged that her medical information "for purposes of processing payment" would be sent to Nestle. The "Notice of Privacy Practices" provides in part as follows:

> "As described above, we will use your health information and disclose it outside CCHS for treatment, payment, health care operations, and when permitted or required by law. We will not use or disclose your health information for *other* reasons without your written authorization."

While the document authorizes the Clinic to release plaintiff's medical information for purposes of payment, that is not what occurred here. The Clinic does not dispute that plaintiff's bills should have been sent to United Healthcare for payment, not Nestle. There is nothing in the Clinic's notice document that authorized the release of plaintiff's medical information to the wrong payor, whether accidentally or not.

When it mistakenly forwarded plaintiff's personal health information to Nestle, the Clinic exceeded the scope of plaintiff's authorization. Accordingly, plaintiff did not consent to having her non-employment related medical information sent to Nestle.

II. INVASION OF PRIVACY

In its motion for summary judgment, the Clinic also argued that it did not tortiously invade plaintiff's privacy by disclosing her confidential medical information.

Ohio recognizes the tort of negligent invasion of the right of privacy.[ ] "An actionable invasion of the right of privacy is the unwarranted appropriation or exploitation of one's personality, the publicizing of one's private affairs with which the public has no legitimate concern, or the wrongful intrusion into one's private activities in such a manner as to outrage or cause mental suffering, shame or humiliation to a person of ordinary sensibilities."[ ].

In the case at bar, the Clinic generally argues that plaintiff has not proven that she suffered the type of damages required to prove an invasion of her privacy.

We have already determined that the Clinic made an unauthorized disclosure of plaintiff's personal health information to Nestle. When it mistakenly mailed plaintiff's information to Nestle, the Clinic wrongfully intruded into plaintiff's private life.

When plaintiff realized that people at Nestle learned of her medical diagnosis and were given access to her personal gynecological information, she was embarrassed, angry, and emotionally distraught, and she felt an on-going anxiety about her privacy.

From this record, there remain genuine issues of material fact as to whether a rational trier-of-fact would conclude that the Clinic's wrongful intrusion into plaintiff's private health information would cause a person of ordinary sensibilities outrage, mental suffering, shame, or humiliation. Accordingly, granting summary judgment to the Clinic was not appropriate.

III. INTENTIONAL INFLICTION OF EMOTIONAL DISTRESS

[The court rejected plaintiff's claim of the intentional infliction of emotional distress because of lack of evidence of "some guarantee of genuineness" of her injuries.]

For the foregoing reasons, we sustain plaintiff's sole assignment of error in part and overrule it in part. The trial court erred in granting the Clinic's motion for summary judgment on plaintiff's claims for unauthorized disclosure and invasion of privacy but correctly granted judgment in favor of defendants on plaintiff's claim for intentional infliction of emotional distress.

STANDARDS FOR PRIVACY OF INDIVIDUALLY IDENTIFIABLE HEALTH INFORMATION

Department of Health and Human Services Office of the Secretary.
45 CFR Parts 160 and 164.

This regulation has three major purposes: (1) To protect and enhance the rights of consumers by providing them access to their health information and controlling the inappropriate use of that information; (2) to improve the quality of health care in the U.S. by restoring trust in the health care system among consumers, health care professionals, and the multitude of organizations and individuals committed to the delivery of care; and (3) to improve the efficiency and effectiveness of health care delivery by creating a national framework for health privacy protection that builds on efforts by states, health systems, and individual organizations and individuals.

* * *

In enacting HIPAA, Congress recognized the fact that administrative simplification cannot succeed if we do not also protect the privacy and confidentiality of personal health information. The provision of high-quality health care requires the exchange of personal, often-sensitive information between an individual and a skilled practitioner. Vital to that interaction is the patient's ability to trust that the information shared will be protected and kept confidential. Yet many patients are concerned that their information is not protected. Among the factors adding to this concern are the growth of the number of organizations involved in the provision of care and the processing of claims, the growing use of electronic information technology, increased efforts to market health care and other products to consumers, and the increasing ability to collect highly sensitive information about a person's current and future health status as a result of advances in scientific research.

Rules requiring the protection of health privacy in the United States have been enacted primarily by the states. While virtually every state has enacted one or more laws to safeguard privacy, these laws vary significantly from state to state and typically apply to only part of the health care system. Many states have adopted laws that protect the health information relating to certain health conditions such as mental illness, communicable diseases, cancer, HIV/AIDS, and other stigmatized conditions. An examination of state health privacy laws and regulations, however, found that "state laws, with a few notable exceptions, do not extend comprehensive protections to people's medical records." Many state rules fail to provide such basic protections as ensuring a patient's legal right to see a copy of his or her medical record. See Health Privacy Project, "The State of Health Privacy: An Uneven Terrain," Institute for Health Care Research and Policy, Georgetown University (July 1999) (http://www.healthprivacy.org) (the "Georgetown Study").

Until now, virtually no federal rules existed to protect the privacy of health information and guarantee patient access to such information. This final rule establishes, for the first time, a set of basic national privacy standards and fair information practices that provides all Americans with a basic level of protection and peace of mind that is essential to their full participation in their care. The rule sets a floor of ground rules for health care providers, health plans, and health care clearinghouses to follow, in order to protect patients and encourage them to seek needed care. The rule seeks to balance the needs of the individual with the needs of the society. It creates a framework of protection that can be strengthened by both the federal government and by states as health information systems continue to evolve.

Need for a National Health Privacy Framework

The Importance of Privacy

Privacy is a fundamental right. As such, it must be viewed differently than any ordinary economic good. The costs and benefits of a regulation must, of course, be considered as a means of identifying and weighing options. At the same time, it is important not to lose sight of the inherent meaning of privacy: it speaks to our individual and collective freedom.

* * *

Increasing Public Concern About Loss of Privacy

Today, it is virtually impossible for any person to be truly "let alone." The average American is inundated with requests for information from potential employers, retail shops, telephone marketing firms, electronic marketers, banks, insurance companies, hospitals, physicians, health plans, and others. In a 1998 national survey, 88 percent of consumers said they were "concerned" by the amount of information being requested, including 55 percent who said they were "very concerned." See Privacy and American Business, 1998 Privacy Concerns & Consumer Choice Survey (http://www. pandab.org). These worries are not just theoretical. Consumers who use the Internet to make purchases or request "free" information often are asked for personal and financial information. Companies making such requests routinely promise to protect the confidentiality of that information. Yet several firms have tried to sell this information to other companies even after promising not to do so.

Americans' concern about the privacy of their health information is part of a broader anxiety about their lack of privacy in an array of areas. * * *

This growing concern stems from several trends, including the growing use of interconnected electronic media for business and personal activities, our increasing ability to know an individual's genetic make-up, and, in health care, the increasing complexity of the system. Each of these trends brings the potential for tremendous benefits to individuals and society generally. At the same time, each also brings new potential for invasions of our privacy.

Increasing Use of Interconnected Electronic Information Systems

Until recently, health information was recorded and maintained on paper and stored in the offices of community-based physicians, nurses, hospitals, and other health care professionals and institutions. In some ways, this imperfect system of record keeping created a false sense of privacy among patients, providers, and others. Patients' health information has never remained completely confidential. Until recently, however, a breach of confidentiality involved a physical exchange of paper records or a verbal exchange of information. Today, however, more and more health care providers, plans, and others are utilizing electronic means of storing and transmitting health information. * * *. The electronic information revolution is transforming the recording of health information so that the disclosure of information may require only a push of a button. In a matter of seconds, a person's most profoundly private information can be shared with hundreds, thousands, even millions of individuals and organizations at a time. While the majority of medical records still are in paper form, information from those records is often copied and transmitted through electronic means.

This ease of information collection, organization, retention, and exchange made possible by the advances in computer and other electronic technology affords many benefits to individuals and to the health care industry. Use of electronic information has helped to speed the delivery of effective care and the processing of billions of dollars worth of health care claims. Greater use of electronic data has also increased our ability to identify and treat those who are at risk for disease, conduct vital research, detect fraud and abuse, and measure and improve the quality of care delivered in the U.S. * * *.

At the same time, these advances have reduced or eliminated many of the financial and logistical obstacles that previously served to protect the confidentiality of health information and the privacy interests of individuals. And they have made our information available to many more people. The shift from paper to electronic records, with the accompanying greater flows of sensitive health information, thus strengthens the arguments for giving legal protection to the right to privacy in health information. In an earlier period where it was far more expensive to access and use medical records, the risk of harm to individuals was relatively low. In the potential near future, when technology makes it almost free to send lifetime medical records over the Internet, the risks may grow rapidly. It may become cost-effective, for instance, for companies to offer services that allow purchasers to obtain details of a person's physical and mental treatments. In addition to legitimate possible uses for such services, malicious or inquisitive persons may download medical records for purposes ranging from identity theft to embarrassment to prurient interest in the life of a celebrity or neighbor. The comments to the proposed privacy rule indicate that many persons believe that they have a right to live in society without having these details of their lives laid open to unknown and possibly hostile eyes. These technological changes, in short, may provide a reason for institutionalizing privacy protections in situations where the risk of harm did not previously justify writing such protections into law.

The growing level of trepidation about privacy in general, noted above, has tracked the rise in electronic information technology. Americans have embraced the use of the Internet and other forms of electronic information as a way to provide greater access to information, save time, and save money. * * *

Unless public fears are allayed, we will be unable to obtain the full benefits of electronic technologies. The absence of national standards for the confidentiality of health information has made the health care industry and the population in general uncomfortable about this primarily financially-driven expansion in the use of electronic data. Many plans, providers, and clearinghouses have taken steps to safeguard the privacy of individually identifiable health information. Yet they must currently rely on a patchwork of State laws and regulations that are incomplete and, at times, inconsistent. States have, to varying degrees, attempted to enhance confidentiality by establishing laws governing at least some aspects of medical record privacy. This approach, though a step in the right direction, is inadequate. These laws fail to provide a consistent or comprehensive legal foundation of health information privacy. For example, there is considerable variation among the states in the type of information protected and the scope of the protections provided. [ ]

Moreover, electronic health data is becoming increasingly "national"; as more information becomes available in electronic form, it can have value far beyond the immediate community where the patient resides. Neither private action nor state laws provide a sufficiently comprehensive and rigorous legal structure to allay public concerns, protect the right to privacy, and correct the market failures caused by the absence of privacy protections (see discussion below of market failure under section V.C). Hence, a national policy with consistent rules is necessary to encourage the increased and proper use of electronic information while also protecting the very real needs of patients to safeguard their privacy.

Advances in Genetic Sciences

Recently, scientists completed nearly a decade of work unlocking the mysteries of the human genome, creating tremendous new opportunities to identify and prevent many of the leading causes of death and disability in this country and around the world. Yet the absence of privacy protections for health information endanger these efforts by creating a barrier of distrust and suspicion among consumers. A 1995 national poll found that more than 85 percent of those surveyed were either "very concerned" or "somewhat concerned" that insurers and employers might gain access to and use genetic information. [ ] * * *

The Changing Health Care System

The number of entities who are maintaining and transmitting individually identifiable health information has increased significantly over the last 10 years. In addition, the rapid growth of integrated health care delivery systems requires greater use of integrated health information systems. The health care industry has been transformed from one that relied primarily on one-on-one interactions between patients and clinicians to a system of integrated health care delivery networks and managed care providers. Such a system requires the processing and collection of information about patients and plan enrollees (for example, in claims files or enrollment records), resulting in the creation of databases that can be easily transmitted. This dramatic change in the practice of medicine brings with it important prospects for the improvement of the quality of care and reducing the cost of that care. It also, however, means that increasing numbers of people have access to health information. And, as health plan functions are increasingly outsourced, a growing number of organizations not affiliated with our physicians or health plans also have access to health information.

* * *

Much of this sharing of information is done without the knowledge of the patient involved. While many of these functions are important for smooth functioning of the health care system, there are no rules governing how that information is used by secondary and tertiary users. For example, a pharmacy benefit manager could receive information to determine whether an insurance plan or HMO should cover a prescription, but then use the information to market other products to the same patient. Similarly, many of us obtain health insurance coverage though our employer and, in some instances, the employer itself acts as the insurer. In these cases, the employer will obtain identifiable health information about its employees as part of the legitimate health insurance functions such as claims processing, quality improvement, and fraud detection activities. At the same time, there is no comprehensive protection prohibiting the employer from using that information to make decisions about promotions or job retention.

* * *

Concerns about the lack of attention to information privacy in the health care industry are not merely theoretical. In the absence of a national legal framework of health privacy protections, consumers are increasingly vulnerable to the exposure of their personal health information. Disclosure of individually identifiable information can occur deliberately or accidentally and can occur within an organization or be the result of an external breach of security.
* * *

No matter how or why a disclosure of personal information is made, the harm to the individual is the same. In the face of industry evolution, the potential benefits of our changing health care system, and the real risks and occurrences of harm, protection of privacy must be built into the routine operations of our health care system.

Privacy Is Necessary To Secure Effective, High Quality Health Care

While privacy is one of the key values on which our society is built, it is more than an end in itself. It is also necessary for the effective delivery of health care, both to individuals and to populations. The market failures caused by the lack of effective privacy protections for health information are discussed below (see section V.C below). Here, we discuss how privacy is a necessary foundation for delivery of high quality health care. In short, the entire health care system is built upon the willingness of individuals to share the most intimate details of their lives with their health care providers.

The need for privacy of health information, in particular, has long been recognized as critical to the delivery of needed medical care. More than anything else, the relationship between a patient and a clinician is based on trust. The clinician must trust the patient to give full and truthful information about their health, symptoms, and medical history. The patient must trust the clinician to use that information to improve his or her health and to respect the need to keep such information private. In order to receive accurate and reliable diagnosis and treatment, patients must provide health care professionals with accurate, detailed information about their personal health, behavior, and other aspects of their lives. The provision of health information assists in the diagnosis of an illness or condition, in the development of a treatment plan, and in the evaluation of the effectiveness of that treatment. In the absence of full and accurate information, there is a serious risk that the treatment plan will be inappropriate to the patient's situation.

Patients also benefit from the disclosure of such information to the health plans that pay for and can help them gain access to needed care. Health plans and health care clearinghouses rely on the provision of such information to accurately and promptly process claims for payment and for other administrative functions that directly affect a patient's ability to receive needed care, the quality of that care, and the efficiency with which it is delivered.

Accurate medical records assist communities in identifying troubling public health trends and in evaluating the effectiveness of various public health efforts. Accurate information helps public and private payers make correct payments for care received and lower costs by identifying fraud. Accurate information provides scientists with data they need to conduct research. We cannot improve the quality of health care without information about which treatments work, and which do not.

Individuals cannot be expected to share the most intimate details of their lives unless they have confidence that such information will not be used or shared inappropriately. Privacy violations reduce consumers' trust in the health care system and institutions that serve them. Such a loss of faith can impede the quality of the health care they receive, and can harm the financial health of health care institutions.

Patients who are worried about the possible misuse of their information often take steps to protect their privacy. Recent studies show that a person who does not believe his privacy will be protected is much less likely to participate fully in the diagnosis and treatment of his medical condition. * * *

* * *

Breaches of Health Privacy Harm More Than Our Health Status

A breach of a person's health privacy can have significant implications well beyond the physical health of that person, including the loss of a job, alienation of family and friends, the loss of health insurance, and public humiliation. * * *

The answer to these concerns is not for consumers to withdraw from society and the health care system, but for society to establish a clear national legal framework for privacy. By spelling out what is and what is not an allowable use of a person's identifiable health information, such standards can help to restore and preserve trust in the health care system and the individuals and institutions that comprise that system. * * * The task of society and its government is to create a balance in which the individual's needs and rights are balanced against the needs and rights of society as a whole.

National standards for medical privacy must recognize the sometimes competing goals of improving individual and public health, advancing scientific knowledge, enforcing the laws of the land, and processing and paying claims for health care services. This need for balance has been recognized by many of the experts in this field. * * *

The Federal Response

There have been numerous federal initiatives aimed at protecting the privacy of especially sensitive personal information over the past several years—and several decades. While the rules below are likely the largest single federal initiative to protect privacy, they are by no means alone in the field. Rather, the rules arrive in the context of recent legislative activity to grapple with advances in technology, in addition to an already established body of law granting federal protections for personal privacy.

* * *

As described in more detail in the next section, Congress recognized the importance of protecting the privacy of health information by enacting the Health Insurance Portability and Accountability Act of 1996. The Act called on Congress to enact a medical privacy statute and asked the Secretary of Health and Human Services to provide Congress with recommendations for protecting the confidentiality of health care information. The Congress further recognized the importance of such standards by providing the Secretary with authority to promulgate regulations on health care privacy in the event that lawmakers were unable to act within the allotted three years.

Finally, it also is important for the U.S. to join the rest of the developed world in establishing basic medical privacy protections. In 1995, the European Union (EU) adopted a Data Privacy Directive requiring its 15 member states to adopt consistent privacy laws by October 1998. The EU urged all other nations to do the same or face the potential loss of access to information from EU countries.

* * *

Subpart E—Privacy of Individually Identifiable Health Information

§ 164.104   Applicability.

(a) Except as otherwise provided, the standards, requirements, and implementation specifications adopted under this part apply to the following entities:

(1) A health plan.

(2) A health care clearinghouse.

(3) A health care provider who transmits any health information in electronic form in connection with a transaction covered by this subchapter.

* * *

Subpart E—Privacy of Individually Identifiable Health Information

* * *

§ 164.501   Definitions.

As used in this subpart, the following terms have the following meanings:

* * *

Marketing means:

(1) To make a communication about a product or service that encourages recipients of the communication to purchase or use the product or service, unless the communication is made:

  (i) To describe a health-related product or service (or payment for such product or service) that is provided by, or included in a plan of benefits of, the covered entity making the communication, including communications about: the entities participating in a health care provider network or health plan network; replacement of, or enhancements to, a health plan; and health-related products or services available only to a health plan enrollee that add value to, but are not part of, a plan of benefits.

  (ii) For treatment of the individual; or

  (iii) For case management or care coordination for the individual, or to direct or recommend alternative treatments, therapies, health care providers, or settings of care to the individual.

(2) An arrangement between a covered entity and any other entity whereby the covered entity discloses protected health information to the other entity, in exchange for direct or indirect remuneration, for the other entity or its affiliate to make a communication about its own product or service that encourages recipients of the communication to purchase or use that product or service.

* * *

Protected health information means individually identifiable health information:

(1) Except as provided in paragraph (2) of this definition, that is:

  (i) Transmitted by electronic media;

  (ii) Maintained in any medium described in the definition of electronic media at § 162.103 of this subchapter; or

  (iii) Transmitted or maintained in any other form or medium.

* * *

Treatment means the provision, coordination, or management of health care and related services by one or more health care providers, including the coordination or management of health care by a health care provider with a third party; consultation between health care providers relating to a patient; or the referral of a patient for health care from one health care provider to another.

Use means, with respect to individually identifiable health information, the sharing, employment, application, utilization, examination, or analysis of such information within an entity that maintains such information.

§ 164.502   Uses and disclosures of protected health information: general rules.

(a) *Standard.* A covered entity may not use or disclose protected health information, except as permitted or required by this subpart or by subpart C of part 160 of this subchapter.

(1) Permitted uses and disclosures. A covered entity is permitted to use or disclose protected health information as follows:

(i) To the individual;

(ii) For treatment, payment, or health care operations, as permitted by and in compliance with Sec. 164.506;

(iii) Incident to a use or disclosure otherwise permitted or required by this subpart, provided that the covered entity has complied with the applicable requirements of Sec. 164.502(b), Sec. 164.514(d), and Sec. 164.530(c) with respect to such otherwise permitted or required use or disclosure;

(iv) Pursuant to and in compliance with an authorization that complies with § 164.508;

(v) Pursuant to an agreement under, or as otherwise permitted by, § 164.510; and

(vi) As permitted by and in compliance with this section, Sec. 164.512, or Sec. 164.514(e), (f), or (g).

(2) *Required Disclosures.* A covered entity is required to disclose protected health information:

(i) To an individual, when requested under, and as required by §§ 164.524 or 164.528; * * *

(b) *Standard: Minimum necessary.*

(1) *Minimum necessary applies.* When using or disclosing protected health information or when requesting protected health information from another covered entity, a covered entity must make reasonable efforts to limit protected health information to the minimum necessary to accomplish the intended purpose of the use, disclosure, or request.

(2) *Minimum necessary does not apply.*

This requirement does not apply to:

(i) Disclosures to or requests by a health care provider for treatment;

(ii) Uses or disclosures made to the individual, as permitted under paragraph (a)(1)(i) of this section or as required by paragraph (a)(2)(i) of this section;

(iii) Uses or disclosures made pursuant to an authorization under Sec. 164.508;

§ 164.506   Uses and disclosures to carry out treatment, payment, or health care operations.

(a) *Standard: Permitted uses and disclosures.* Except with respect to uses or disclosures that require an authorization under Sec. 164.508(a)(2) and (3), a covered entity may use or disclose protected health information for treatment, payment, or health care operations as set forth in paragraph (c) of this section, provided that such use or disclosure is consistent with other applicable requirements of this subpart.

(b) *Standard: Consent for uses and disclosures permitted.*

(1) A covered entity may obtain consent of the individual to use or disclose protected health information to carry out treatment, payment, or health care operations.

(2) Consent, under paragraph (b) of this section, shall not be effective to permit a use or disclosure of protected health information when an authorization, under Sec. 164.508, is required or when another condition must be met for such use or disclosure to be permissible under this subpart.

(c) *Implementation specifications: Treatment, payment, or health care operations.*

(1) A covered entity may use or disclose protected health information for its own treatment, payment, or health care operations.

(2) A covered entity may disclose protected health information for treatment activities of a health care provider.

(3) A covered entity may disclose protected health information to another covered entity or a health care provider for the payment activities of the entity that receives the information.

(4) A covered entity may disclose protected health information to another covered entity for health care operations activities of the entity that receives the information, if each entity either has or had a relationship with the individual who is the subject of the protected health information being requested, the protected health information pertains to such relationship, and the disclosure is:

(i) For a purpose listed in paragraph (1) or (2) of the definition of health care operations; or

(ii) For the purpose of health care fraud and abuse detection or compliance.

(5) A covered entity that participates in an organized health care arrangement may disclose protected health information about an individual to another covered entity that participates in the organized health care arrangement for any health care operations activities of the organized health care arrangement.

§ 164.508   Uses and disclosures for which an authorization is required.

(a) *Standard: Authorizations for uses and disclosures.*

(1) *Authorization required: General rule.* Except as otherwise permitted or required by this subchapter, a covered entity may not use or disclose protected health information without an authorization that is valid under this section. When a covered entity obtains or receives a valid

authorization for its use or disclosure of protected health information, such use or disclosure must be consistent with such authorization.

* * *

(3) *Authorization required: Marketing.*

(i) Notwithstanding any provision of this subpart, other than the transition provisions in Sec. 164.532, a covered entity must obtain an authorization for any use or disclosure of protected health information for marketing, except if the communication is in the form of:

(A) A face-to-face communication made by a covered entity to an individual; or

(B) A promotional gift of nominal value provided by the covered entity.

(ii) If the marketing involves direct or indirect remuneration to the covered entity from a third party, the authorization must state that such remuneration is involved.

* * *

§ 164.510 Uses and disclosures requiring an opportunity for the individual to agree or to object.

A covered entity may use or disclose protected health information, provided that the individual is informed in advance of the use or disclosure and has the opportunity to agree to or prohibit or restrict the use or disclosure, in accordance with the applicable requirements of this section. The covered entity may orally inform the individual of and obtain the individual's oral agreement or objection to a use or disclosure permitted by this section.

§ 164.512 Uses and disclosures for which consent, an authorization, or opportunity to agree or object is not required.

A covered entity may use or disclose protected health information without the written authorization of the individual as described in § 164.508, respectively, or the opportunity for the individual to agree or object as described in § 164.510, in the situations covered by this section, subject to the applicable requirements of this section. When the covered entity is required by this section to inform the individual of, or when the individual may agree to, a use or disclosure permitted by this section, the covered entity's information and the individual's agreement may be given orally.

(a) *Standard: Uses and disclosures required by law.*

(1) A covered entity may use or disclose protected health information to the extent that such use or disclosure is required by law and the use or disclosure complies with and is limited to the relevant requirements of such law.

(2) A covered entity must meet the requirements described in paragraph (c), (e), or (f) of this section for uses or disclosures required by law.

* * *

§ 164.514   Other requirements relating to uses and disclosures of protected health information.

(a) Standard: de-identification of protected health information. Health information that does not identify an individual and with respect to which there is no reasonable basis to believe that the information can be used to identify an individual is not individually identifiable health information.

(b) Implementation specifications: requirements for de-identification of protected health information. A covered entity may determine that health information is not individually identifiable health information only if:

(1) A person with appropriate knowledge of and experience with generally accepted statistical and scientific principles and methods for rendering information not individually identifiable:

(i) Applying such principles and methods, determines that the risk is very small that the information could be used, alone or in combination with other reasonably available information, by an anticipated recipient to identify an individual who is a subject of the information; and

(ii) Documents the methods and results of the analysis that justify such determination; * * *

* * *

(d)(1) Standard: minimum necessary requirements. In order to comply with § 164.502(b) and this section, a covered entity must meet the requirements of paragraphs (d)(2) through (d)(5) of this section with respect to a request for, and the use and disclosure of, protected health information.

* * *

(3) Implementation specification: Minimum necessary disclosures of protected health information.

(i) For any type of disclosure that it makes on a routine and recurring basis, a covered entity must implement policies and procedures (which may be standard protocols) that limit the protected health information disclosed to the amount reasonably necessary to achieve the purpose of the disclosure.

(ii) For all other disclosures, a covered entity must:

(A) Develop criteria designed to limit the protected health information disclosed to the information reasonably necessary to accomplish the purpose for which disclosure is sought; and

(B) Review requests for disclosure on an individual basis in accordance with such criteria.

* * *

§ 164.520   Notice of privacy practices for protected health information.

(a) *Standard: notice of privacy practices.*

(1) *Right to notice.* Except as provided by paragraph (a)(2) or (3) of this section, an individual has a right to adequate notice of the uses and disclosures of protected health information that may be made by the covered entity, and of the individual's rights and the covered entity's legal duties with respect to protected health information.

* * *

§ 164.522   Rights to request privacy protection for protected health information.

(a)(1) *Standard: Right of an individual to request restriction of uses and disclosures.*

(i) A covered entity must permit an individual to request that the covered entity restrict:

(A) Uses or disclosures of protected health information about the individual to carry out treatment, payment, or health care operations; and

(B) Disclosures permitted under s 164.510(b).

(i) A covered entity is not required to agree to a restriction.

(ii) A covered entity that agrees to a restriction under paragraph (a)(1)(i) of this section may not use or disclose protected health information in violation of such restriction, except that, if the individual who requested the restriction is in need of emergency treatment and the restricted protected health information is needed to provide the emergency treatment, the covered entity may use the restricted protected health information, or may disclose such information to a health care provider, to provide such treatment to the individual.

(iii) If restricted protected health information is disclosed to a health care provider for emergency treatment under paragraph (a)(1)(iii) of this section, the covered entity must request that such health care provider not further use or disclose the information.

(iv) A restriction agreed to by a covered entity under paragraph (a) of this section, is not effective under this subpart to prevent uses or disclosures permitted or required under ss 164.502(a)(2)(i), 164.510(a) or 164.512.

* * *

§ 164.524   Access of individuals to protected health information.

(a) *Standard: Access to protected health information.*

(1) *Right of access.* Except as otherwise provided in paragraph (a)(2) or (a)(3) of this section, an individual has a right of access to inspect and obtain a copy of protected health information about the individual in a designated record set, for as long as the protected health information is

maintained in the designated records [with exceptions for psychotherapy and other statutes enumerated] * * *

* * *

§ 164.526   Amendment of protected health information.

(a) *Standard: Right to amend.*

(1) *Right to amend.* An individual has the right to have a covered entity amend protected health information or a record about the individual in a designated record set for as long as the protected health information is maintained in the designated record set.

* * *

§ 164.528   Accounting of disclosures of protected health information.

(a) *Standard: Right to an accounting of disclosures of protected health information.*

(1) An individual has a right to receive an accounting of disclosures of protected health information made by a covered entity in the six years prior to the date on which the accounting is requested, except for disclosures:

(i) To carry out treatment, payment and health care operations as provided in § 164.506;

(ii) To individuals of protected health information about them as provided in § 164.502;

* * *

§ 164.530   Administrative requirements.

(a)(1) *Standard: Personnel designations.*

(i) A covered entity must designate a privacy official who is responsible for the development and implementation of the policies and procedures of the entity.

(ii) A covered entity must designate a contact person or office who is responsible for receiving complaints under this section and who is able to provide further information about matters covered by the notice required by § 164.520.

* * *

Notes and Questions

1.   Who is covered by the Medical Privacy Rules? What are "covered entities?" Notice that health care providers are covered only if they transmit patient information electronically. For a detailed analysis, see Janlori Goldman et al., The Health Insurance Portability and Accountability Act Privacy Rule and Patient Access to Medical Records, Health Privacy Project (2006).

2.   What does "minimum necessary" mean? The regulations stress that providers must undertake "reasonable efforts to limit protected health information to the minimum necessary to accomplish the intended purpose of the use,

disclosure or request." This requirement is backed up by the penalty provisions of HIPAA: each disclosure violation is a $100 fine, and a knowing violation imposes criminal penalties of a $50,000 fine and up to one year in prison. If information is provided or obtained under false pretenses, there is a $100,000 fine and up to five years in prison. If the wrongful sale, transfer or use of the information was for commercial advantage, there is a $250,000 fine and up to 10 years in prison. Hospital medical staff are worried that they will be jailed if they inadvertently release health care information to an unauthorized person.

The Office of Civil Rights (OCR) has reassured providers that they can discuss a patient's treatment among themselves. "Disclosures for treatment purposes (including requests for disclosures) between health care providers are explicitly exempted from the minimum necessary requirements."

Incidental uses and disclosures of individual identifiable health information are generally allowed when the covered entity has in place reasonable safeguards and "minimum necessary" policies and procedures to protect an individual's privacy. OCR confirmed that providers may have confidential conversations with other providers and patients even when there is a chance that they might be overheard. Nurses can speak over the phone with a patient or family member about the patient's condition. Providers may also discuss a patient's condition during training rounds at an academic medical institution.

3.   These rules fill a vacuum created by erratic state regulation and little federal regulation. Do they strike an appropriate balance between patient privacy and provider and insurer needs for information? Do they impose substantial new compliance costs on health care providers as a by-product of protecting privacy? Given the opacity of the law, many providers are unclear about the law, have failed to train their staff members to apply it properly, and are unrealistically afraid of the fines, even though no penalty has been imposed in four years. HIPAA allows voluntary disclosure and broad provider discretion. This often means that providers are defensive and arbitrary in what they think they can disclose. Examples of HIPAA overreaction include cancellation of birthday parties in nursing homes in New York and Arizona for fear that revealing a resident's birthdate would be a violation; refusal by ER nurses to call parents of sick students themselves. Jane Gross, Keeping Patients' Details Private, Even From Kin, New York Times, July 3, 2007.

Critics note that HIPAA standards create little more than a federal confidentiality code based around a regulatory compliance model rather than one that creates patient rights. Nicholas P. Terry and Leslie P. Francis, Ensuring the Privacy and Confidentiality of Electronic Health Records, 2007 Univ. Ill. Law. Rev. 681, 714 (2007). Terry and Francis note that the HIPAA standards focus on the process of patient consent to disclosure, not on limits to collection of data; lack any consent-to-disclosure restrictions; lack a true national standard, given the interplay between state and federal law; apply overbroad exceptions to consent such as public health; are too lax as to secondary uses of patient information; and fail to cover all medical data or users of data. The Government Accounting Office has issued a report criticizing HHS for its lack of progress in implementing the HIPAA privacy protections. See GAO, Health Information Technology: Early Efforts Initiated but Comprehensive Privacy Approach Needed for National Strategy (January 2007); Ilene N. Moore et al., Confidentiality and Privacy in Health Care From the Patient's Perspective: Does HIPAA Help? 17 Health Matrix 215 (2007).

4. The portions of the Medical Privacy Standards quoted above in a highly abbreviated form give some sense of the scope and detail of the rules. They have several laudatory goals. First and foremost, they aim to give consumers control over their own health information. Health providers must inform patients about how their information is being used and to whom it is disclosed. The rules create a "disclosure history" for individuals. Most important, the release of private health information is limited by a requirement of authorization under some circumstances. Some nonroutine disclosure requires specific patient authorization. Patients may access their own health files and request correction of potentially harmful errors.

Second, the rules set boundaries on medical record use and release. The amount of information to be disclosed is restricted to the "minimum necessary", in contrast to prevailing practice of releasing a patient's entire health record even if an entity needs very specific information.

Third, the rules attempt to ensure the security of personal health information. The rules are very specific in their mandates on providers and others who might access health information. They require privacy-conscious business practices, with internal procedures and privacy officers to protect the privacy of medical records. The rules create a whole new category of compliance officer within health care institutions as a result of the mandates in the rules.

Fourth, the rules create accountability for medical record use and release, with new criminal and civil penalties for improper use or disclosure.

Fifth, the rules attempt to balance public responsibility with privacy protections, requiring that information be disclosed only limited public purposes such as public health and research. They attempt to limit disclosure of information without sacrificing public safety.

5. The obvious benefits of computerized record keeping have propelled medical records to a central position in health care delivery. A standardized database of patient information has the potential to promote efficiency, further competition, and allow providers to better track patient outcomes. Only a computerized record, in spite of its confidentiality dimensions, can further such goals. The Medical Privacy Standards offer considerable protection to patients; they also require substantial expenditures by providers to achieve compliance with the complex requirements.

The Office of Civil Rights website provides useful information on HIPAA and its interpretation. See generally www.hhs.gov/ocr/hippa/.

For a useful site that critically addresses all aspects of HIPAA, see generally Health Privacy Project, http://www.healthprivacy.org.

6. One critic observes that HIPAA does not change much about information flow and protection in today's health care system, since it does not prohibit any disclosure routinely made today:

> To provide real privacy protections means changing many existing institutions so that they can function with less identifiable data. It also means fighting those institutions because none of them wants to change anything they do or to incur any cost or inconvenience in the interest of patient privacy. They all want to be left alone to carry out their activities—many perfectly reasonable and important—with as little disruption as possible. Indeed, many institutions want access to more identifiable health informa-

tion, centralized patient databases, and new health identifiers so that they can control costs, improve care, and prevent the spread of disease.

Robert Gellman, Health Privacy: The Way We Live Now, www.privacyrights.org

---

ACOSTA v. BYRUM ET AL.

North Carolina Court of Appeals, 2006.
638 S.E.2d 246.

Heather D. Acosta ("plaintiff") appeals from an order dismissing her complaint against David R. Faber, II, M.D. ("Dr. Faber") with prejudice. For the reasons stated herein, we reverse.

The issue in this case is whether the trial court properly dismissed plaintiff's complaint as to Dr. Faber. Plaintiff argues that the complaint stated a valid claim against Dr. Faber for negligent infliction of emotional distress.

On 12 May 2005, plaintiff filed an action alleging invasion of privacy and intentional infliction of emotional distress against Robin Byrum ("Byrum") and negligent infliction of emotional distress against Dr. Faber. Similar additional claims were made against two other defendants not associated with Psychiatric Associates of Eastern Carolina ("Psychiatric Associates").

Plaintiff was a patient of Psychiatric Associates, which is located in Ahoskie, North Carolina. She was also employed by Psychiatric Associates from September 2003 until early spring of 2004. Psychiatric Associates is owned by Dr. Faber, a citizen and resident of Alabama. Byrum was the office manager at Psychiatric Associates during the time period at issue. Plaintiff alleged that Byrum had severe personal animus towards plaintiff.

Plaintiff alleged that Dr. Faber improperly allowed Byrum to use his medical record access number. Numerous times between 31 December 2003 and 3 September 2004, Byrum used Dr. Faber's access code to retrieve plaintiff's confidential psychiatric and other medical and healthcare records. Byrum then provided information contained in those records to third parties without plaintiff's authorization or consent.

Plaintiff alleged in her complaint that by providing Byrum with his access code, Dr. Faber violated the rules and regulations established by University Health Systems, Roanoke Chowan Hospital, and the Health Insurance Portability and Accountability Act of 1996 ("HIPAA"). Plaintiff alleged that she experienced severe emotional distress, humiliation, and anguish from the exposure of her medical records to third parties. Plaintiff alleged that Dr. Faber knew or should have known that his negligence would cause severe emotional distress.

Responding to these claims, Dr. Faber filed a motion to dismiss pursuant to Rules 12(b)(2) and (6). After a hearing, the trial court granted Dr. Faber's motion to dismiss. Plaintiff appeals from that order.

* * *

[The court's discussion of the interlocutory appeal is omitted.]

II. SUFFICIENCY OF THE COMPLAINT

Plaintiff argues that the complaint should not have been dismissed because it sufficiently stated a claim for negligent infliction of emotional distress against Dr. Faber. We agree.

* * *

Plaintiff first contends she sufficiently alleged defendant's negligence. Plaintiff alleged that defendant negligently engaged in conduct by permitting Byrum to use his access code in violation of the rules and regulations of the University Health Systems, Roanoke Chowan Hospital, and HIPAA.

Plaintiff does not cite the exact rule or regulation of the University Health Systems, Roanoke Chowan Hospital, or HIPAA which allegedly establish Dr. Faber's duty to maintain privacy in her confidential medical records. She merely alleges that these rules provide the standard of care. * * *

Here, defendant has been placed on notice that plaintiff will use the rules and regulations of the University Health Systems, Roanoke Chowan Hospital, and HIPAA to establish the standard of care. Therefore, plaintiff has sufficiently pled the standard of care in her complaint. [The court further concludes that the pleadings sufficiently plead proximate cause and the negligent infliction of emotional distress.]

III. HIPAA VIOLATION

Plaintiff contends that no claim for an alleged HIPAA violation was made and therefore dismissal on the grounds that HIPAA does not grant an individual a private cause of action was improper. We agree.

In her complaint, plaintiff states that when Dr. Faber provided his medical access code to Byrum, Dr. Faber violated the rules and regulations established by HIPAA. This allegation does not state a cause of action under HIPAA. Rather, plaintiff cites to HIPAA as evidence of the appropriate standard of care, a necessary element of negligence. Since plaintiff made no HIPAA claim, HIPAA is inapplicable beyond providing evidence of the duty of care owed by Dr. Faber with regards to the privacy of plaintiff's medical records.

* * *

V. CONCLUSION

Plaintiff's complaint should not have been dismissed because plaintiff sufficiently stated a claim for negligent infliction of emotional distress against Dr. Faber, personal jurisdiction over Dr. Faber was proper, no HIPAA violation was alleged in the complaint, and Rule 9(j) is inapplicable. Accordingly, we reverse the decision of the trial court dismissing plaintiff's complaint against Dr. Faber.

Reversed.

Notes and Questions

1. *Herman* and *Acosta* represent two aspects of HIPAA litigation. First, is the party accused of breaching patient confidentiality a "covered entity"? Is so, that party may be protected by various HIPAA provisions.

Second, can HIPAA be used in civil litigation as a source of standard practice? As *Acosta* states, HIPAA creates a new standard of care for the handling of confidential patient information, and courts are likely to take notice of the standards and any violation of them in evaluating a negligence suit against a hospital or medical office. Could violations of Medical Privacy Standards constitute negligence per se? Some evidence of negligence? How do you predict the courts will approach the Standards?

2.   The HIPAA Privacy Standards do not give individuals the right to sue. A person must file a written complaint with the Secretary of Health and Human Services via the Office for Civil Rights. It is then within the Secretary's discretion to investigate the complaint. HHS may impose civil penalties ranging from $100 to $25,000. Criminal sanctions range from $50,000 to $250,000, with corresponding prison terms, enforced by the Department of Justice. However, according to the interim final rule addressing penalties, HHS "intends to seek and promote voluntary compliance" and "will seek to resolve matters by informal means whenever possible." Therefore enforcement "will be primarily complaint driven," and civil penalties will only be imposed if the violation was willful. Such penalties will not be imposed if the failure to comply was due to reasonable cause and is corrected within 30 days from when the covered entity knew or should have known of the failure to comply. The standard is even higher for imposing criminal penalties. §§ 160.306, 160.312 (a)(1), 160.304(b), 42 U.S.C § 1320 et seq., http://www.hhs.gov./news/facts/privacy.html.

Problem: *Leaking Patient Information*

1.   Dr. Jasmine is a dentist in sole practice. He submits his bills only by mail, not electronically, and he does not email his patients or use electronic media in any part of his business. He therefore does not give patients a Notice of Privacy Practices nor in any way indicate to patients what their rights are as to their dental history information. Jasmine sells his patient lists to various dental supply companies for their use in marketing. Has he violated HIPAA?

2.   Goldberg goes to the medical office laboratory for a series of tests, and her physician gives her a form indicating which tests have been ordered and tells her to take the form to the lab. When she arrives at the lab, she sees a sign-in sheet and a notice advising patients to deposit the form in the open basket that sits next to the sign-in sheet. The forms lie face-up in the basket, and they show a patient's name, address, birth date, social security number, and other demographic information, as well as the tests ordered. Is this a violation of HIPAA? If so, how can it be corrected?

3.   Dr. Newman, a psychiatrist, is having dinner out with colleagues when she is paged by her answering service with an urgent message to call one of her patients. She left her cell phone at home, so she borrows the phone of one of her dinner companions to return the patient's call. The borrowed cell phone automatically maintains a log of the outgoing phone number. Can a patient whose identity is thereby reviewed file a complaint against Dr. Newman?

4.   During a routine blood test, Frent chats with the lab technician, Gosford, about a new football game. Gosford responds by telling an amusing story about a well known sports figure who happened to have his blood test done on the previous day by Gosford. The technicians mentions the high level of steroids that the test revealed. Can the athlete sue Gosford? The laboratory? What are his options?

5. Gosford obtains her prescriptions for genital herpes treatment from CVS pharmacies in her area. One day she receives a mailing from a pharmaceutical company advertising their herpes treatment product. The mail has piled up with other pieces on the lobby of her apartment building, and her fellow tenants can easily see the description of the product, and her name on the flyer. What recourse does Gosford have?

6. Reconsider *Doe v. Medlantic Health Care Group, Inc., supra.* in light of HIPAA requirements and penalties. What if anything do the Medical Privacy Rules add to Doe's rights?

7. Reconsider **Problem: The Hunt for Patient Records** in light of HIPAA requirements and penalties. Did the hospital violate HIPAA? Did the law firm?

Chapter 4

LIABILITY OF HEALTH CARE
PROFESSIONALS

This chapter will examine the framework for a malpractice suit against health care professionals and the doctrinal and evidentiary dimensions of such litigation. As you read the chapter, think about the cases and materials on three levels. First, how is the plaintiff's case proved and how does the defendant counter it? Second, how does tort doctrine respond to different categories of medical error? And third, how does malpractice litigation affect medical practice and the cost and quality of medical care?

I. THE STANDARD OF CARE

HALL v. HILBUN

Supreme Court of Mississippi, 1985.
466 So.2d 856.

ROBERTSON, JUSTICE, for the Court:

I.

This matter is before the Court on Petition for Rehearing presenting primarily the question whether we should, as a necessary incident to a just adjudication of the case at bar, refine and elaborate upon our law regarding (a) the standard of care applicable to physicians in medical malpractice cases and (b) the matter of how expert witnesses may be qualified in such litigation.

* * *

When this matter was before the Court on direct appeal, we determined that the judgment below in favor of the surgeon, Dr. Glyn R. Hilbun, rendered following the granting of a motion for a directed verdict, had been correctly entered. * * *

For the reasons set forth below, we now regard that our original decision was incorrect. * * *

II.

Terry O. Hall was admitted to the Singing River Hospital in Jackson County, Mississippi, in the early morning hours of May 18, 1978, complaining of abdominal discomfort. Because he was of the opinion his patient had a surgical problem, Dr. R.D. Ward, her physician, requested Dr. Glyn R. Hilbun, a general surgeon, to enter the case for consultation. Examination suggested that the discomfort and illness were probably caused by an obstruction of the small bowel. Dr. Hilbun recommended an exploratory laparotomy [sic]. Consent being given, Dr. Hilbun performed the surgery about noon on May 20, 1978, with apparent success.

Following surgery Mrs. Hall was moved to a recovery room at 1:35 p.m., where Dr. Hilbun remained in attendance with her until about 2:50 p.m. At that time Mrs. Hall was alert and communicating with him. All vital signs were stable. Mrs. Hall was then moved to a private room where she expired some 14 hours later.

On May 19, 1980, Glenn Hall commenced this wrongful death action by the filing of his complaint * * *.

* * *

At trial Glenn Hall, plaintiff below and appellant here, described the fact of the surgery. He then testified that he remained with his wife in her hospital room from the time of her arrival from the recovery room at approximately 3:00 p.m. on May 20, 1978, until she ultimately expired at approximately 5:00 a.m. on the morning of May 21. Hall stated that his wife complained of pain at about 9:00 p.m. and was given morphine for relief, after which she fell asleep. Thereafter, Hall observed that his wife had difficulty in breathing which he reported to the nurses. He inquired if something was wrong and was told his wife was all right and that such breathing was not unusual following surgery. The labored breathing then subsided for an hour or more. Later, Mrs. Hall awakened and again complained of pain in her abdomen and requested a sedative, which was administered following which she fell asleep. Mrs. Hall experienced further difficulty in breathing, and her husband reported this, too. Again, a nurse told Hall that such was normal, that patients sometimes make a lot of noise after surgery.

After the nurse left the following occurred, according to Hall.

[A]t this time I followed her [the nurse] into the hall and walked in the hall a minute. Then I walked back into the room, and walked back out in the hall. Then I walked into the room again and I walked over to my wife and put my hand on her arm because she had stopped making that noise. Then I bent over and flipped the light on and got closer to her where I could see her, and it looked like she was having a real hard problem breathing and she was turning pale or a bluish color. And I went to screaming.

Dr. Hilbun was called and came to the hospital immediately only to find his patient had expired. The cause of the death of Terry O. Hall was subsequently determined to be adult respiratory distress syndrome (cardio-respiratory failure).

Dr. Hilbun was called as an adverse witness and gave testimony largely in accord with that above. * * *.

Dr. Hilbun stated the surgery was performed on a Saturday. Following the patient's removal to her room, he "went home and was on call that weekend for anything that might come up." Dr. Hilbun made no follow-up contacts with his patient, nor did he make any inquiry that evening regarding Mrs. Hall's post-operative progress. Moreover, he was *not* contacted by the nursing staff or others concerning Mrs. Hall's condition during the afternoon or evening of May 20 following surgery, or the early morning hours of May 21, although the exhibits introduced at trial disclose fluctuations in the vital signs late in the evening of May 20 and more so, in the early morning hours of May 21. Dr. Hilbun's next contact with his patient came when he was called by Glenn Hall about 4:55 or 5:00 that morning. By then it was too late.

* * *

The autopsy performed upon Mrs. Hall's body revealed the cause of death and, additionally, disclosed that a laparotomy [sic] sponge had been left in the patient's abdominal cavity. The evidence, however, without contradiction establishes that the sponge did not contribute to Mrs. Hall's death. Although the sponge may ultimately have caused illness, this possibility was foreclosed by the patient's untimely death.

Plaintiff's theory of the case centered around the post-operative care provided by Dr. Hilbun. Two areas of fault suggested were Dr. Hilbun's failure to make inquiry regarding his patient's post-operative course prior to his retiring on the night of May 20 and his alleged failure to give appropriate post-operative instructions to the hospital nursing staff.

When questioned at trial, Dr. Hilbun first stated that he had practiced for 16 years in the Singing River Hospital and was familiar with the routine of making surgical notes, i.e., a history of the surgery. He explained that the post-operative orders were noted on the record out of courtesy by Dr. Judy Fabian, the anesthesiologist on the case. He stated such orders were customarily approved by his signature or he would add or subtract from the record to reflect the exact situation.

[Dr. Hilbun testified as to the post-operative orders noted in the medical records as of May 20, 1978. Mrs. Hall had a nasogastric tube, an i.v., a catheter; she was receiving medications for pain, nausea, and infections.] His testimony continued:

Q.   Now after this surgery, while Mrs. Hall was in the recovery room did I understand you to say earlier that you checked on her there?

A.   When I got through operating on Mrs. Hall, with this major surgical procedure in an emergency situation—and I always do—I went to the recovery room with Mrs. Hall, stayed in the recovery room with Mrs. Hall, listened to her chest, took her vital signs, stayed there with her and discharged her to the floor. The only time I left the recovery room was to go into the waiting room and tell Mr. Hall. Mrs. Hall waked up, I talked to her, she said she was cold. She was completely alert.

* * *

Q.   Now, you went to the recovery room to see her because you were still her physician following her post-surgery?

A.   I was one of her physicians. I operated on her, and I go to the recovery room with everybody.

Q. Okay. You were the surgeon and you were concerned about the surgical procedures and how she was doing post-operatively, or either you are not concerned with your patients, how they do post-operatively?

A. As I said, I go to the recovery room with every one of my patients.

Q. Then you are still the doctor?

A. I was one of her physicians.

Q. Okay. And you customarily follow your patients following the surgery to see how they are doing as a result of the surgery, because you are the surgeon. Is that correct?

A. Yes.

* * *

Q. How long do you follow a patient like Terry Hall?

A. Until she leaves the hospital.

Q. Okay. So ever how long she is in the hospital, you are going to continue to see her?

A. As long as my services are needed.

Insofar as the record reflects, Dr. Hilbun gave the nursing staff no instructions regarding the post-operative monitoring and care of Mrs. Hall beyond those [summarized above]. Dr. Hilbun had no contact with Mrs. Hall after 3:00 p.m. on May 20. Fourteen hours later she was dead.

The plaintiff called Dr. S.O. Hoerr, a retired surgeon of Cleveland, Ohio, as an expert witness. The record reflects that Dr. Hoerr is a *cum laude* graduate of the Harvard Medical School, enjoys the respect of his peers, and has had many years of surgical practice. Through him the plaintiff sought to establish that there is a national standard of surgical practice and surgical care of patients in the United States to which all surgeons, including Dr. Hilbun, are obligated to adhere. Dr. Hoerr conceded that he did not know for a fact the standard of professional skill, including surgical skills and post-operative care, practiced by general surgeons in Pascagoula, Mississippi, but that he did know what the standard should have been.

* * * [T]he trial court ruled that Dr. Hoerr was not qualified to give an opinion as to whether Dr. Hilbun's post-operative regimen departed from the obligatory standard of care. * * *.

* * *

Parts of Dr. Hoerr's testimony excluded under the trial judge's ruling follow:

A. My opinion is that she [Mrs. Hall] did not receive the type of care that she should have received from the general surgical specialist and that he [Dr. Hilbun] was negligent in not following this patient; contacting, checking on the condition of his patient sometime in the evening of May 20th. *It is important in the post-operative care of patients to remember that very serious complications can follow abdominal operations, in particular in the first few hours after a surgical procedure.* And this can be inward bleeding; it can be an explosive development in an infection; or *it can be the development of a serious pulmonary complication, as it was in this patient. As a result of her condition, it is my opinion that he lost the opportunity to diagnose a condition, which in all probability could have been diagnosed at the time by an experienced general surgeon, one with expertise in thoracic surgery. And then appropriate treatment could have been undertaken to abort the complications and save her life.*

There are different ways that a surgeon can keep track of his patient—"follow her" as the expression goes—besides a bedside visit, which is the best way and which need not be very long at all, in which the vital signs are checked over. The surgeon gets a general impression of what's going on. He can delegate this responsibility to a competent physician, who need not be a surgeon but could be a knowledgeable family practitioner. He could call in and ask to speak to the registered nurse in charge of the patient and determine through her what the vital signs are, and if she is an experienced Registered Nurse what her evaluation of the patient is. *From my review of the record, none of these things took place, and there is no effort as far as I can see that Dr. Hilbun made any effort to find out what was going on with this patient during that period of time.* I might say or add an additional belief that I felt that the nursing responsibility which should have been exercised was not exercised, particularly at the 4:00 a.m. level when the pulse rate was recorded at 140 per minute without any effort as far as I can see to have any physician see the patient or to get in touch with the operating surgeon and so on.

There is an additional thing that Dr. Hilbun could have done if he felt that the nursing services might be spotty—sometimes good, sometimes bad. This is commonly done in Columbus, Ohio, in Ashtabula, Pascagoula, etcetera. *He could put limits on the degree in which the vital signs can vary, expressing the order that he should be called if they exceeded that.* Examples would be: Call me if the pulse rate goes over 110; call me if the temperature exceeds 101; call me if the blood pressure drops below 100. There is a simple way of spelling out for the nursing services what the limits of discretion belong to them and the point at which the doctor should be called.

* * *

Dr. Hilbun did not place any orders on the chart for the nurses to call him in the event of a change in the vital signs of Mrs. Hall. He normally made afternoon rounds between 4:00 and 5:00 p.m. but didn't recall whether he went by to see her before going home. Dr. Hilbun was on call at the hospital that weekend for anything which might come up. Subsequent to the operation and previous to Mrs. Hall's death, he was called about one other person on the same ward, one door down, twice during the night. He made no inquiry concerning Mrs. Hall, nor did he see or communicate with her.

Dr. Donald Dohn, of expertise unquestioned by plaintiff and with years of practical experience, gave testimony for the defendant. He had practiced on the staff at the Cleveland Clinic Foundation in Cleveland, Ohio, beginning in 1958. Fortuitously, he had moved to Pascagoula, Mississippi, about one month before the trial. Dr. Dohn stated he had practiced in the Singing River Hospital for a short time and there was a great difference in the standard of care in medical procedures in Cleveland, Ohio, and those in Pascagoula,

Mississippi. Although he had practiced three weeks in Pascagoula, he was still in the process of acquainting himself with the local conditions. He explained the differences as follows:

> Well, there are personnel differences. There are equipment differences. There are diagnostic differences. There are differences in staff responsibility and so on. For example, at the Cleveland Clinic on our service we had ten residents that we were training. They worked with us as our right hands. Here we have no staff. So it is up to us to do the things that our residents would have done there. There we had a team of five or six nurses and other personnel in the operating room to help us. Here we have nurses in the operating room, but there is no assigned team. You get the luck of the draw that day. I am finding out these things myself. Up there it is a big center; a thousand beds, and it is a regional center. We have tremendous advantages with technical systems, various types of x-ray equipment that is [sic] sophisticated. Also in terms of the intensive care unit, we had a Neurosurgical Intensive Care with people who were specially trained as a team to work there. From my standpoint personally, I seldom had to do much paperwork there as compared to what I have to do now. I have to dictate everything and take all my notes. So, as you can see, there is a difference.

Finally, he again stated the standard of care in Ohio and the standard of care in the Singing River Hospital are very different, although it is obvious to the careful reader of Dr. Dohn's testimony that in so doing he had reference to the differences in equipment, personnel and resources and not differences in the standards of skill, medical knowledge and general medical competence a physician could be expected to bring to bear upon the treatment of a patient.

At the conclusion of the plaintiff's case, defendant moved for a directed verdict on the obvious grounds that, the testimony of Drs. Hoerr and Sachs having been excluded, the Plaintiff had failed to present a legally sufficient quantum of evidence to establish a prima facie case. The Circuit Court granted the motion. * * *

III.

A. *General Considerations*

Medical malpractice is legal fault by a physician or surgeon. It arises from the failure of a physician to provide the quality of care required by law. When a physician undertakes to treat a patient, he takes on an obligation enforceable at law to use minimally sound medical judgment and render minimally competent care in the course of the services he provides. A physician does not guarantee recovery. If a patient sustains injury because of the physician's failure to perform the duty he has assumed under our law, the physician may be liable in damages. A competent physician is not liable *per se* for a mere error of judgment, mistaken diagnosis or the occurrence of an undesirable result.

The twin principles undergirding our stewardship of the law regulating professional liability of physicians have always been reason and fairness. For years in medical malpractice litigation we regarded as reasonable and fair what came to be known as the "locality rule" (but which has always consisted of at least two separate rules, one a rule of substantive law, the other a rule of evidence).

* * *

C. *The Physician's Duty of Care: A primary rule of substantive law*

1. *The Backdrop*

* * *

2. *The Inevitable Ascendency of National Standards*

* * *

We would have to put our heads in the sand to ignore the "nationalization" of medical education and training. Medical school admission standards are similar across the country. Curricula are substantially the same. Internship and residency programs for those entering medical specialties have substantially common components. Nationally uniform standards are enforced in the case of certification of specialists. Differences and changes in these areas occur temporally, not geographically.

Physicians are far more mobile than they once were. They frequently attend medical school in one state, do a residency in another, establish a practice in a third and after a period of time relocate to a fourth. All the while, they have ready access to professional and scientific journals and seminars for continuing medical education from across the country. Common sense and experience inform us that the laws of medicine do not vary from state to state in anything like the manner our public law does.

Medicine is a science, though its practice be an art (as distinguished from a business). Regarding the basic matter of the learning, skill and competence a physician may bring to bear in the treatment of a given patient, state lines are largely irrelevant. That a patient's temperature is 105 degrees means the same in New York as in Mississippi. Bones break and heal in Washington the same as in Florida, in Minnesota the same as in Texas. * * *

* * *

3. *The Competence–Based National Standard of Care: Herein of the Limited Role of Local Custom*

All of the above informs our understanding and articulation of the competence-based duty of care. Each physician may with reason and fairness be expected to possess or have reasonable access to such medical knowledge as is commonly possessed or reasonably available to minimally competent physicians in the same specialty or general field of practice throughout the United States, to have a realistic understanding of the limitations on his or her knowledge or competence, and, in general, to exercise minimally adequate medical judgment. Beyond that, each physician has a duty to have a practical working knowledge of the facilities, equipment, resources (including personnel in health related fields and their general level of knowledge and competence), and options (including what specialized services or facilities may be available in larger communities, e.g., Memphis, Birmingham, Jackson, New Orleans, etc.) reasonably available to him or her as well as the practical limitations on same.

In the care and treatment of each patient, each physician has a non-delegable duty to render professional services consistent with that objectively ascertained minimally acceptable level of competence he may be expected to apply given the qualifications and level of expertise he holds himself out as possessing and given the circumstances of the particular case. The professional services contemplated within this duty concern the entire caring process, including but not limited to examination, history, testing, diagnosis, course of treatment, medication, surgery, follow-up, after-care and the like.

* * *

Mention should be made in this context of the role of good medical judgment which, because medicine is not an exact science, must be brought to bear in diagnostic and treatment decisions daily. Some physicians are more reluctant to recommend radical surgery than are other equally competent physicians. There exist legitimate differences of opinion regarding medications to be employed in particular contexts. "Waiting periods" and their duration are the subject of bona fide medical controversy. What diagnostic tests should be performed is a matter of particularly heated debate in this era of ever-escalating health care costs. We must be vigilant that liability never be imposed upon a physician for the mere exercise of a bona fide medical judgment which turns out, with the benefit of 20–20 hindsight (a) to have been mistaken, and (b) to be contrary to what a qualified medical expert witness in the exercise of his good medical judgment would have done. We repeat: a physician may incur civil liability only when the quality of care he renders (including his judgment calls) falls below minimally acceptable levels.

Different medical judgments are made by physicians whose offices are across the street from one another. Comparable differences in medical judgment or opinion exist among physicians geographically separated by much greater distances, and in this sense local custom does and must continue to play a role within our law, albeit a limited one.

We recognize that customs vary within given medical communities and from one medical community to another. Conformity with established medical custom practiced by minimally competent physicians in a given area, while evidence of performance of the duty of care, may never be conclusive of such compliance. [ ] The content of the duty of care must be objectively determined by reference to the availability of medical and practical knowledge which would be brought to bear in the treatment of like or similar patients under like or similar circumstances by minimally competent physicians in the same field, given the facilities, resources and options available. The content of the duty of care may be informed by local medical custom but never subsumed by it.

* * *

4. The Resources–Based Caveat to the National Standard of Care

The duty of care, as it thus emerges from considerations of reason and fairness, when applied to the facts of the world of medical science and practice, takes two forms: (a) a duty to render a quality of care consonant with the level of medical and practical knowledge the physician may reasonably be expected to possess and the medical judgment he may be expected to exercise, and (b) a duty based upon the adept use of such medical facilities, services, equipment and options as are reasonably available. With respect to this second form of the duty, we regard that there remains a core of validity to the premises of the old locality rule.

* * *

A physician practicing in Noxubee County, for example, may hardly be faulted for failure to perform a CAT scan when the necessary facilities and equipment are not reasonably available. In contradistinction, objectively reasonable expectations regarding the physician's knowledge, skill, capacity for sound medical judgment and general competence are, consistent with his field of practice and the facts and circumstances in which the patient may be found, *the same everywhere.*

* * *

As a result of its resources-based component, the physician's non-delegable duty of care is this: given the circumstances of each patient, each physician has a duty to use his or her knowledge and therewith treat through maximum reasonable medical recovery, each patient, with such reasonable diligence, skill, competence, and prudence as are practiced by minimally competent physicians in the same specialty or general field of practice throughout the United States, who have available to them the same general facilities, services, equipment and options.

* * *

As we deal with general principles, gray areas necessarily exist. One involves the case where needed specialized facilities and equipment are not available locally but are reasonably accessible in major medical centers—New Orleans, Jackson, Memphis. Here as elsewhere the local physician is held to minimally acceptable standards. In determining whether the physician's actions comport with his duty of care, consideration must always be given to the time factor—is the physician confronted with what reasonably appears to be a medical emergency, or does it appear likely that the patient may be transferred to an appropriate medical center without substantial risk to the health or life of the patient? Consideration must also be given to the economic factors—are the proposed transferee facilities sufficiently superior to justify the trouble and expense of transfer? Further discussion of these factors should await proper cases.

D. *Who May Qualify As Expert Medical Witness In Malpractice Case: A rule of evidence*

As a general rule, if scientific, technical or other specialized knowledge will assist the trier of fact to understand the evidence or to determine a fact in issue, a witness qualified as an expert by knowledge, skill, experience, training or education (or a combination thereof), coupled with independence and lack of bias, may testify thereto in the form of an opinion or otherwise. Medical malpractice cases generally require expert witnesses to assist the trier of fact to understand the evidence.[ ]

Generally, where the expert lives or where he or she practices his or her profession has no relevance *per se* with respect to whether a person may be qualified and accepted by the court as an expert witness. There is no reason on principle why these factors should have *per se* relevance in medical malpractice cases.

* * *

In view of the refinements in the physician's duty of care * * * we hold that a qualified medical expert witness may without more express an opinion regarding the meaning and import of the duty of care * * *, given the peculiar circumstances of the case. Based on the information reasonably available to the physician, i.e., symptoms, history, test results, results of the doctor's own physical examination, x-rays, vital signs, etc., a qualified medical expert may express an opinion regarding the conclusions (possible diagnoses or areas for further examination and testing) minimally knowledgeable and competent physicians in the same specialty or general field of practice would draw, or actions (not tied to the availability of specialized facilities or equipment not generally available) they would take.

Before the witness may go further, he must be familiarized with the facilities, resources, services and options available. This may be done in any number of ways. The witness may prior to trial have visited the facilities, etc. He may have sat in the courtroom and listened as other witnesses described the facilities. He may have known and over the years interacted with physicians in the area. There are no doubt many other ways in which this could be done, but, significantly, we should allow the witness to be made familiar with the facilities (and customs) of the medical community in question via a properly predicated and phrased hypothetical question.

Once he has become informed of the facilities, etc. available to the defendant physician, the qualified medical expert witness may express an opinion what the care duty of the defendant physician was and whether the acts or omissions of the defendant physician were in compliance with, or fell substantially short of compliance with, that duty.

* * *

V. Disposition of the Case at Bar

[The court reversed and remanded for a new trial, on the grounds that the testimony of Drs. Hoerr and Sachs was improperly excluded, and with their testimony, the plaintiff might have survived the defense motion for a directed verdict.]

Notes and Questions

1. How did the court in *Hall v. Hilbun* view the customary practice of the defendant's medical specialty? Why did it adopt this position? How much of a burden is it for a defendant to rebut the plaintiff's evidence on customary practice? Could a plaintiff use the studies cited in Chapter 1 to support a position that the efficacy of a standard practice is not proven? How would a court react to such studies?

2. The medical profession sets standards of practice and the courts have historically enforced these standards in tort suits. Defendants trying to prove a standard of care normally present expert testimony describing the actual pattern of medical practice, without any reference to the effectiveness of that practice.

Most jurisdictions give professional medical standards conclusive weight, so that the trier of fact is not allowed to reject the practice as improper. See, e.g., Doe v. American Red Cross Blood Serv., 297 S.C. 430, 435, 377 S.E.2d 323, 326 (1989) (involving issue of blood bank failing to screening for HIV/AIDS at time when customary practice was not to screen).

A Mississippi jury instruction on the standard of care is:

A physician * * * is required to provide his patients with that same degree of care, skill and diligence which would be provided by a minimally competent, reasonably prudent physician in the same general field of practice, under the same or similar circumstances, and who has available to him the same general facilities, resources and options. Therefore, medical negligence or "malpractice" is defined as a physician's failure to provide a patient with that degree of care, skill and diligence which would be provided by a minimally competent, reasonably prudent physician in the same specialty when faced with the same or similar circumstances.

Beckwith v. Shah, 964 So.2d 552 (Miss.App.2007).

3. Why should conformity to customary practice be a conclusive shield for a health care professional? In tort litigation not involving professionals, courts are willing to reject customary practice if they find the practice dangerous or out of date. See Joseph King, In Search of a Standard of Care for the Medical Profession—the "Accepted Practice" Formula, 28 Vand.L.Rev. 1213, 1236 (1975). Critics such as King worry that standard practice may at times be little more than a routine into which physicians have drifted by default.

Customary practices are often little more than habitual practices lacking evidence of efficacy. As one physician has written, "In the past, medicine was based on what a bunch of gray-haired experts believed and, since now I have gray hair, I can count myself among them. Basically, based on what 'we' said medicine should be, 'we' determined how medical practice should occur. I call this 'Eminence–Based Medicine.' " Dan Mayer, "Evidence–Based Medicine," 36 New Eng. L. Rev. 601, 601 (2002).

4. The customary or accepted practice standard follows the general tort rule that physicians are measured against the standard of their profession, not merely the standard of a reasonable and prudent person. Medical practices are always evolving as new developments and scientific studies alter the customary practice. Such evolution in medical practices often creates tensions for the physician who believes that the customary practice is dangerous but the new standard has not yet been generally accepted. Courts have however been unwilling generally to allow a plaintiff to present evidence to attack a customary practice that the defendant physician complied with, except under rare circumstances. See, e.g., Burton v. Brooklyn Doctors Hospital, 88 A.D.2d 217, 452 N.Y.S.2d 875 (1982), where the plaintiff was exposed while in the hospital as a newborn to a prolonged liberal application of oxygen and developed retrolental fibroplasia (RFL) as a result. At the time of his birth, a "significant segment of the medical community continued to believe that the liberal administration of oxygen to prematures was important in preventing death or brain damage. Yet, a respected body of medical opinion believed that oxygen contributed to RLF." He was part of a study at the hospital examining various level of oxygen and the effects of its withdrawal or curtailment; the study found in 1954 that prolonged liberal use led to the development of RLF, and cutting off oxygen to premature infants after 48 hours decreased the incidence of RLF without increasing the risk of either death or brain damage. The court allowed a jury instruction to the effect that adherence to

acceptable practice is not a defense if the physician fails to use his best judgment. See also Toth v. Community Hospital at Glen Cove, 22 N.Y.2d 255, 292 N.Y.S.2d 440, 239 N.E.2d 368 (1968).

5. Courts expect the standard of care to follow available technology at the time the diagnosis or treatment was offered to the patient. Physicians who hold themselves out as having specialized knowledge will be held to the standard of specialists with those enhanced qualifications. See Zaverl v. Hanley, 64 P.3d 809 (Alaska 2003) (affirmative steps to present himself or herself to public as specialist is sufficient to elevate the standard).

6. *Hall* provides an excellent discussion of the locality rule. Most states have moved from the locality rule to a similar locality or a national standard, in part due to worries about a "conspiracy of silence" that unfairly limits the pool of available experts. Doctors do not like to testify against one another. As the court noted in Mulder v. Parke Davis & Co., 288 Minn. 332, 181 N.W.2d 882 (1970), "All too frequently, and perhaps understandably, practicing physicians are reluctant to testify against one another. Unfortunately, the medical profession has been slow to fashion machinery for making impartial and objective assessments of the performance of their fellow practitioners."

Legislatures enacting malpractice reform statutes on the other hand have often imposed modified locality rule tests in order to protect physicians from out-of-state witnesses for plaintiffs. See e.g. Henry v. Southeastern Ob–Gyn Associates, 142 N.C.App. 561, 543 S.E.2d 911 (2001) ("similar locality" test of N.C.Gen. Stat. S. 90–21.12 was intended to avoid the adoption of a national standard for health care providers).

The locality rule may have been displaced in many states by the national standard test, but many courts, like *Hall,* also allow evidence describing the practice limitations under which the defendant labors. *Hall*'s "resource component" allows the trier of fact to consider the facilities, staff and other equipment available to the practitioner in the institution, following the general rule that courts should take into account the locality, proximity of specialists and special facilities for diagnosis and treatment. See, e.g., Primus v. Galgano, 329 F.3d 236 (1st Cir. 2003) ("permissible to consider the medical resources available to the physician as one circumstance in determining the skill and care required"); Restatement (Second) of Torts, sec. 299A, Comment g. ("Allowance must be made also for the type of community in which the actor carries on his practice. A country doctor cannot be expected to have the equipment, facilities, experience, knowledge or opportunity to obtain it, afforded him by a large city.")

Note: Expert Testimony in Professional Liability Cases

The standard of practice in the defendant doctor's specialty or area of practice is normally established through the testimony of medical experts. *Hall* illustrates the burden that the plaintiff bears. In any jurisdiction, plaintiffs, to withstand a motion for a directed verdict, must 1) qualify their medical witnesses as experts; 2) satisfy the court that the expert's testimony will assist the trier of fact; and 3) have the witnesses testify based upon facts that support their expert opinions. The requirement that the expert be of the same specialty as the defendant typically governs the qualifying of the expert for testifying at trial. The standard of care may be based upon the expert's own practice and education. See Wallbank v. Rothenberg, M.D., 74 P.3d 413 (Colo.App. 2003) (personal practices of medical experts may be relevant to the standard of care).

Expert testimony is often based upon clinical literature, FDA statements, and other evidence of the standard of practice and of side-effects of treatments and drugs. Several sources of reliable and authoritative statements may be used by experts in professional liability cases, or relied upon by the trial judge as definitive.

a. *Practice guidelines or parameters.* Statements by medical societies as to good practice will provide a ready-made particularized standard that an expert can use as a benchmark against which to test a defendant's conduct. Some courts are becoming more demanding, requiring that an expert needs "published medical standards, manuals, or protocols" to support the expert opinion, rather than just the expert's own opinion or casual conversation with a few colleagues. Travers v. District of Columbia, 672 A.2d 566 (D.C.App.1996).

b. *Pharmaceutical package insert instructions and warnings.* Package inserts may be used to establish the standard of care for use of the particular drug. In Thompson v. Carter, 518 So.2d 609 (Miss.1987), the physician used Bactrim, a sulfonamide antibiotic, to treat the plaintiff's kidney infection. She developed Stevens Johnson Syndrome, a severe allergic reaction associated with use of Bactrim. The court allowed the admission of the package insert, holding that the package insert was prima facie proof of the proper method of use of Bactrim, an "authoritative published compilation by a pharmaceutical manufacturer." Accord, Garvey v. O'Donoghue, 530 A.2d 1141 (D.C.App.1987) (relevant evidence of the medical standard of care). But see Tarter v. Linn, 396 Pa.Super. 155, 578 A.2d 453 (1990) (sustaining trial court's refusal to allow plaintiff to establish the standard of care by introducing information on adverse drug reactions to the drug Diamox from the Physician's Desk Reference); Craft v. Peebles, 78 Hawai'i 287, 893 P.2d 138 (1995) ("some evidence"); Mozer v. Kerth, 224 Ill.App.3d 525, 166 Ill.Dec. 801, 586 N.E.2d 759 (1992) (while package insert may establish the standard of care, "plaintiff must still show by expert testimony that physician failed to follow explicit instructions of the manufacturer").

c. *Physicians Desk Reference(PDR).* The PDR is allowed by most courts as some evidence of the standard of care, if an expert witness relies on it. See, e.g., Morlino v. Medical Center, 152 N.J. 563, 706 A.2d 721 (1998), where a pregnant patient whose fetus died after she took an antibiotic brought action against prescribing physician, medical center, and obstetrician. The court held that Physicians' Desk Reference (PDR) entries alone did not establish standard of care, but the trier of fact can consider package inserts and parallel PDR references when they are supported by expert testimony. "When supported by expert testimony, PDR entries and package inserts may provide useful information of the standard of care. Physicians frequently rely on the PDR when making decisions concerning the administration and dosage of drugs."

The weight given to the PDR entries and contraindications listed may on occasion be held to be conclusive of the standard of care, in spite of defendant's experts testimony to the contrary. In Fournet v. Roule–Graham, 783 So.2d 439, 443 (La.App. 5 Cir. 2001), the defendant had prescribed a hormone drug Provera in spite of warnings in the PDR that it was contraindicated for patients with deep vein thrombosis. The defendant's OB/GYN witnesses testified that 70% of OB/GYNs nationwide would find no risk in this situation, contradicting the PDR. The court held that the PDR was an authoritative medical source, that it should not be ignored for any reason, and that "it may very well be the case that a majority of those OB/GYNs are simply unaware of this specific contraindication for Provera, or may simply ignore it."

Contra, see Swallow v. Emergency Medicine of Idaho, 138 Idaho 589, 67 P.3d 68 (2003), where the plaintiff alleged that an erroneously prescribed overdose of

Cipro, an antibiotic, caused his heart attack. The court held that information on Cipro's side effects in the Physician's Desk Reference and the FDA reports was inadmissible due to lack of "scientifically reliable proof that Cipro can cause such events."

d. *Judicial notice.* When the defendant physician's clinical decisions violate a clearly articulated practice within the specialty, courts are sometimes even willing to make a finding of per se negligence. See Deutsch v. Shein, 597 S.W.2d 141 (Ky.1980), where the defendant was negligent per se in ordering radiology and other tests on the pregnant plaintiff, injuring the fetus.

e. *Substantive use of a learned treatise.* At the common law, a treatise could be used only to impeach the opponent's experts during cross-examination. It could only undercut the expert's testimony, not build the plaintiff's case. The concern was hearsay, since the author of the treatise was not available for cross-examination as to statements contained in the treatise. Federal Rule of Evidence (FRE) 803(18) creates an exception to the hearsay rule, so that the learned treatise can be used for substantive purposes, so long as the treatise is accepted as reliable. Jacober v. St. Peter's Med. Ctr., 128 N.J. 475, 608 A.2d 304 (1992). An expert must be on the stand to explain and assist in the application of the treatise. Tart v. McGann, 697 F.2d 75 (2d Cir.1982). The treatise must be declared reliable by the trial court, after a motion by the moving lawyer to use the treatise substantively under FRE 803(18) or its state equivalent. Maggipinto v. Reichman, 481 F.Supp. 547 (E.D.Pa.1979).

f. *Expert reliance on research findings.* Experts in malpractice cases base their testimony on their knowledge, education and experience. They may also rely on outside studies in the research literature. On rare occasions, courts have allowed such research material into evidence in a malpractice suit. In Young v. Horton, 259 Mont. 34, 855 P.2d 502 (1993), the court allowed into evidence four medical journal articles that had concluded that a majority of patients forget that they gave informed consent to their doctors prior to surgery. The medical expert then testified based both on his experience with informed consent and on the articles' conclusions.

The admissibility of "novel" scientific evidence is often a thorny issue in environmental and toxic tort cases, although rarely in malpractice cases. The standard for evaluating such evidence had long been held to be established by the Court in Frye v. United States, 54 App.D.C. 46, 293 F. 1013 (1923), where the Supreme Court considered the polygraph test and its limitations. The Court held that expert opinion based on a scientific technique is inadmissible unless the technique is "generally accepted" as reliable in the relevant scientific community.

In Daubert v. Merrell Dow Pharmaceuticals, Inc., 509 U.S. 579, 113 S.Ct. 2786, 125 L.Ed.2d 469 (1993), the Court again considered the admissibility of scientific evidence, in this case epidemiological and other evidence of birth defects caused by mothers' ingestion of Bendectin. The Court rejected the *Frye* test of "general acceptability" as a threshold test of admissibility of novel scientific evidence, holding that the Federal Rules of Evidence, particularly Rule 702, make the trial judge the gatekeeper of such evidence, with the responsibility to assess the reliability of an expert's testimony, its relevance, and the underlying reasoning or methodology. Expert testimony must have a valid scientific connection to the issues in the case, and be based on "scientifically valid principles". The scientific evidence must pertain to scientific knowledge defined as falsifiable scientific theories capable of empirical testing.

The Supreme Court has extended the *Daubert* factors to all expert testimony, not just scientific testimony. In Kumho Tire v. Carmichael, 526 U.S. 137, 119 S.Ct. 1167, 143 L.Ed.2d 238 (1999), the Court held that *Daubert's* gatekeeping role for federal courts, requiring an inquiry into both relevance and reliability, applies not only to scientific testimony but to all expert testimony. The Court noted that this was a flexible test, not a checklist, and it is tied to the particular facts of the case. But "some of these factors may be helpful in evaluating the reliability even of experience-based expert testimony . . ." Id. At 1176. The use of the *Daubert* test is to "make certain that an expert, whether basing testimony upon professional studies or personal experience, employs in the courtroom the same level of intellectual rigor that characterizes the practice of an expert in the relevant field." Id. This would seem to impose a higher level of scrutiny on the typical malpractice expert, particularly in cases involving institutional liability, where the expert may testify about a system design in a hospital or a salary incentive system in a managed care system.

State courts have struggled with the applicability of the scientific evidence admissibility tests of *Frye*, *Daubert* and *Kumho* in medical malpractice cases. For example, in Drevenak v. Abendschein, 773 A.2d 396, 418–419 (D.C. 2001), the court held that *Frye* and *Daubert* apply only to a "novel scientific test or unique controversial methodology or technique"; where the issue is one of the exercise of clinical judgment based on scientific medical knowledge, reliability can be tested by several relevant factors: "the expert's training, board certification in the pertinent medical specialty, specialized medical experience, attendance at national seminars and meetings, familiarity with published specialized medical literature, and discussions with medical specialists form other geographical regions."

Courts have usually found that a qualified expert is reliable, without going into the underlying scientific qualities of the opinion. See, e.g. Potter ex rel. Potter v. Bowman, 2006 WL 3760267 (D.Colo.2006) ("the touchstone of reliability is 'whether the reasoning or methodology underlying the testimony is scientifically valid' ". * * * [t]he party proffering the expert opinion must demonstrate both that the expert has employed a method that is scientifically sound and that the opinion is "based on facts which enable [the expert] to express a reasonably accurate conclusion as opposed to conjecture or speculation." The court allowed all three of plaintiff's witnesses to testify). But see Carlen v. Minnesota Comprehensive Epilepsy Program, 2001 WL 1078633 (D. Minn. 2001) (rejecting expert testimony for failing to satisfy *Daubert* factors.). The court concluded that the expert's opinion on causation was not based on a proper differential diagnosis; while he reviewed several studies, there was no evidence as to the known or potential rate of error for his methodology of evaluating causation, or whether it was generally accepted within the medical community.

II.   CONTRIBUTORY FAULT OF THE PATIENT

Patients through their own mistakes or lifestyle often enhance, or even cause, their injuries. People don't take their doctor's advice; they fall off their diets, stop exercising, start smoking, or act in a variety of ways counterproductive to their health. Very few tort cases have raised a patient's lifestyle choice as a defense to a malpractice claim. Consider the following case.

OSTROWSKI v. AZZARA

Supreme Court of New Jersey, 1988.
111 N.J. 429, 545 A.2d 148.

O'HERN, J.

This case primarily concerns the legal significance of a medical malpractice claimant's pre-treatment health habits. Although the parties agreed that such habits should not be regarded as evidencing comparative fault for the medical injury at issue, we find that the instructions to the jury failed to draw the line clearly between the normal mitigation of damages expected of any claimant and the concepts of comparative fault that can preclude recovery in a fault-based system of tort reparation. Accordingly, we reverse the judgment below that disallowed any recovery to the diabetic plaintiff who had bypass surgery to correct a loss of circulation in a leg. The need for this bypass was found by the jury to have been proximately caused by the physician's neglect in performing an improper surgical procedure on the already weakened plaintiff.

I

As noted, the parties do not dispute that a physician must exercise the degree of care commensurate with the needs of the patient as she presents herself. This is but another way of saying that a defendant takes the plaintiff as she finds her. The question here, however, is much more subtle and complex. The complication arose from the plaintiff's seemingly routine need for care of an irritated toe. The plaintiff had long suffered from diabetes attributable, in unfortunate part perhaps, to her smoking and to her failure to adhere closely to her diet. Diabetic patients often have circulatory problems. For purposes of this appeal, we shall accept the general version of the events that led up to the operation as they are set forth in defendant-physician's brief.

On May 17, 1983, plaintiff, a heavy smoker and an insulin-dependent diabetic for twenty years, first consulted with defendant, Lynn Azzara, a doctor of podiatric medicine, a specialist in the care of feet. Plaintiff had been referred to Dr. Azzara by her internist whom she had last seen in November 1982. Dr. Azzara's notes indicated that plaintiff presented a sore left big toe, which had troubled her for approximately one month, and calluses. She told Dr. Azzara that she often suffered leg cramps that caused a tightening of the leg muscles or burning in her feet and legs after walking and while lying in bed. She had had hypertension (abnormally high blood pressure) for three years and was taking a diuretic for this condition.

Physical examination revealed redness in the plaintiff's big toe and elongated and incurvated toenails. Incurvated toenails are not ingrown; rather, they press against the skin. Diminished pulses on her foot indicated decreased blood supply to that area, as well as decreased circulation and impaired vascular status. Dr. Azzara made a diagnosis of onychomycosis (a fungous disease of the nails) and formulated a plan of treatment to debride (trim) the incurvated nail. Since plaintiff had informed her of a high blood sugar level, Dr. Azzara ordered a fasting blood sugar test and a urinalysis; she also noted that a vascular examination should be considered for the following week if plaintiff showed no improvement.

Plaintiff next saw Dr. Azzara three days later, on May 20, 1983. The results of the fasting blood sugar test indicated plaintiff's blood sugar was high, with a reading of 306. The urinalysis results also indicated plaintiff's blood sugar was above normal. At this second visit, Dr. Azzara concluded that plaintiff had peripheral vascular disease, poor circulation, and diabetes with a very high sugar elevation. She discussed these conclusions with plaintiff and explained the importance of better sugar maintenance. She also explained that a complication of peripheral vascular disease and diabetes is an increased risk of losing a limb if the diabetes is not controlled. The lack of blood flow can lead to decaying tissue. The parties disagree on whether Dr. Azzara told plaintiff she had to return to her internist to treat her blood sugar and circulation problems, or whether, as plaintiff indicates, Dr. Azzara merely suggested to plaintiff that she see her internist.

In any event, plaintiff came back to Dr. Azzara on May 31, 1983, and, according to the doctor, reported that she had seen her internist and that the internist had increased her insulin and told her to return to Dr. Azzara for further treatment because of her continuing complaints of discomfort about her toe. However, plaintiff had not seen the internist. Dr. Azzara contends that she believed plaintiff's representations. A finger-stick glucose test administered to measure plaintiff's non-fasting blood sugar yielded a reading of 175. A physical examination of the toe revealed redness and drainage from the distal medial (outside front) border of the nail, and the toenail was painful to the touch. Dr. Azzara's proposed course of treatment was to avulse, or remove, all or a portion of the toenail to facilitate drainage.

Dr. Azzara says that prior to performing the removal procedure she reviewed with Mrs. Ostrowski both the risks and complications of the procedure, including nonhealing and loss of limb, as well as the risks involved with not treating the toe. Plaintiff executed a consent form authorizing Dr. Azzara to perform a total removal of her left big toenail. The nail was cut out. (Defendant testified that she cut out only a portion of the nail, although her records showed a total removal.)

Two days later, plaintiff saw her internist. He saw her four additional times in order to check the progress of the toe. As of June 30, 1983, the internist felt the toe was much improved. While plaintiff was seeing the internist, she continued to see Dr. Azzara, or her associate, Dr. Bergman. During this period the toe was healing slowly, as Dr. Azzara said one would expect with a diabetic patient.

During the time plaintiff was being treated by her internist and by Dr. Azzara, she continued to smoke despite advice to the contrary. Her internist testified at the trial that smoking accelerates and aggravates peripheral vascular disease and that a diabetic patient with vascular disease can by smoking accelerate the severity of the vascular disease by as much as fifty percent. By mid-July, plaintiff's toe had become more painful and discolored.

At this point, all accord ceases. Plaintiff claims that it was the podiatrist's failure to consult with the patient's internist and defendant's failure to establish by vascular tests that the blood flow was sufficient to heal the wound, and to take less radical care, that left her with a non-healing, pre-gangrenous wound, that is, with decaying tissue. As a result, plaintiff had to undergo immediate bypass surgery to prevent the loss of the extremity. If left untreated, the pre-gangrenous toe condition resulting from the defendant's nail removal procedure would have spread, causing loss of the leg. The plaintiff's first bypass surgery did not arrest the condition, and she underwent two additional bypass surgeries which, in the opinion of her treating vascular surgeon, directly and proximately resulted from the unnecessary toenail removal procedure on May 31, 1983. In the third operation a vein from her right leg was transplanted to her left leg to increase the flow of blood to the toe.

At trial, defense counsel was permitted to show that during the pre-treatment period before May 17, 1983, the plaintiff had smoked cigarettes and had failed to maintain her weight, diet, and blood sugar at acceptable levels. The trial court allowed this evidence of the plaintiff's pre-treatment health habits to go to the jury on the issue of proximate cause. Defense counsel elicited admissions from plaintiff's internist and vascular surgeon that some doctors believe there is a relationship between poor self-care habits and increased vascular disease, perhaps by as much as fifty percent. But no medical expert for either side testified that the plaintiff's post-treatment health habits could have caused her need for bypass surgery six weeks after defendant's toenail removal. Nevertheless, plaintiff argues that defense counsel was permitted to interrogate the plaintiff extensively on her post-avulsion and post-bypass health habits, and that the court allowed such evidence of plaintiff's health habits during the six weeks after the operation to be considered as acts of comparative negligence that could bar recovery rather than reduce her damages. The jury found that the doctor had acted negligently in cutting out the plaintiff's toenail without adequate consideration of her condition, but found plaintiff's fault (fifty-one percent) to exceed that of the physician (forty-nine percent). She was therefore disallowed any recovery. On appeal the Appellate Division affirmed in an unreported decision. We granted certification to review plaintiff's claims.[ ] We are told that since the trial, the plaintiff's left leg has been amputated above the knee. This was foreseen, but not to a reasonable degree of medical probability at the time of trial.

II

Several strands of doctrine are interwoven in the resolution of this matter. The concepts of avoidable consequences, the particularly susceptible victim, aggravation of preexisting condition, comparative negligence, and proximate cause each play a part. It may be useful to unravel those strands of doctrine for separate consideration before considering them in the composite.

Comparative negligence is a legislative amelioration of the perceived harshness of the common-law doctrine of contributory negligence. * * *

Comparative negligence was intended to ameliorate the harshness of contributory negligence but should not blur its clarity. It was designed only to leave the door open to those plaintiffs whose fault was not greater than the defendant's, not to create an independent gate-keeping function. Comparative negligence, then, will qualify the doctrine of contributory negligence when that doctrine would otherwise be applicable as a limitation on recovery. * * *

* * * The doctrine [of avoidable consequences] proceeds on the theory that a plaintiff who has suffered an injury as the proximate result of a tort cannot recover for any portion of the harm that by the exercise of ordinary care he could have avoided.[ ] * * * Avoidable consequences, then, normally comes into action when the injured party's carelessness occurs *after* the defendant's legal wrong has been committed. Contributory negligence, however, comes into action when the injured party's carelessness occurs *before* defendant's wrong has been committed or concurrently with it.[ ]

A counterweight to the doctrine of avoidable consequences is the doctrine of the particularly susceptible victim. This doctrine is familiarly expressed in the maxim that "defendant 'must take plaintiff as he finds him.' "[ ] * * * It is ameliorated by the doctrine of aggravation of a preexisting condition. While it is not entirely possible to separate the doctrines of avoidable consequence and preexisting condition, perhaps the simplest way to distinguish them is to understand that the injured person's conduct is irrelevant to the consideration of the doctrine of aggravation of a preexisting condition. Negligence law generally calls for an apportionment of damages when a plaintiff's antecedent negligence is "found not to contribute in any way to the original accident or injury, but to be a substantial contributing factor in increasing the harm which ensues." *Restatement (Second) of Torts*, § 465 at 510–11, comment c. Courts recognize that a defendant whose acts aggravate a plaintiff's preexisting condition is liable only for the amount of harm actually caused by the negligence.[ ] * * *

Finally, underpinning all of this is that most fundamental of risk allocators in the tort reparation system, the doctrine of proximate cause. * * *

We have sometimes melded proximate cause with foreseeability of unreasonable risk. * * *

We have been candid in New Jersey to see this doctrine, not so much as an expression of the mechanics of causation, but as an expression of line-drawing by courts and juries, an instrument of "overall fairness and sound public policy."[ ] * * * [ ]

III

Each of these principles, then, has some application to this case.[34] Plaintiff obviously had a preexisting condition. It is alleged that she failed to minimize the damages that she might otherwise have sustained due to mistreatment. Such mistreatment may or may not have been the proximate cause of her ultimate condition.

But we must be careful in reassembling these strands of tort doctrine that none does double duty or obscures underlying threads. In particular, we must avoid the indiscriminate application of the doctrine of comparative negligence (with its fifty percent qualifier for recovery) when the doctrines of avoidable consequences or preexisting condition apply.

---

34. Each principle, however, has limitations based on other policy considerations. For example, the doctrine of avoidable consequences, although of logical application to some instances of professional malpractice, is neutralized by countervailing policy. Thus, a physician who performed a faulty tubal ligation cannot suggest that the eventual consequences of an unwanted pregnancy could have been avoided by termination of the fetus.[ ]

The doctrine of contributory negligence bars any recovery to the claimant whose negligent action or inaction *before* the defendant's wrongdoing has been completed has contributed to cause actual invasion of plaintiff's person or property. By contrast,

"[t]he doctrine of avoidable consequences comes into play at a later stage. Where the defendant has already committed an actionable wrong, whether tort or breach of contract, then this doctrine [avoidable consequences] limits the plaintiff's recovery by disallowing only those items of damages which could reasonably have been averted * * * [.]" "[C]ontributory negligence is to be asserted as a complete defense, whereas the doctrine of avoidable consequences is not considered a defense at all, but merely a rule of damages by which certain particular items of loss may be excluded from consideration * * *."

Hence, it would be the bitterest irony if the rule of comparative negligence, designed to ameliorate the harshness of contributory negligence, should serve to shut out any recovery to one who would otherwise have recovered under the law of contributory negligence. Put the other way, absent a comparative negligence act, it would have never been thought that "avoidable consequences" or "mitigation of damages" attributable to post-accident conduct of any claimant would have included a shutout of apportionable damages proximately caused by another's negligence. * * *

* * *

In this context of post-injury conduct by a claimant, given the understandable complexity of concurrent causation, expressing mitigation of damages as a percentage of fault which reduces plaintiff's damages may aid juries in their just apportionment of damages, provided that the jury understands that neither mitigation of damages nor avoidable consequences will bar the plaintiff from recovery if the defendant's conduct was a substantial factor without which the ultimate condition would not have arisen.

* * * In the field of professional health care, given the difficulty of apportionment, sound public policy requires that the professional bear the burden of demonstrating the proper segregation of damages in the aggravation context.[ ] The same policy should apply to mitigation of damages.[ ] Hence, overall fairness requires that juries evaluating apportionment of damages attributable in substantial part to a faulty medical procedure be given understandable guidance about the use of evidence of post-treatment patient fault that will assist them in making a just apportionment of damages and the burden of persuasion on the issues. This is consistent with our general view that a defendant bear the burden of proving the causal link between a plaintiff's unreasonable conduct and the extent of damages.[ ] Once that is established, it should be the "defendant who also has the burden of carving out that portion of the damages which is to be attributed to the plaintiff."[ ]

IV

As noted, in this case the parties agree on certain fundamentals. The pre-treatment health habits of a patient are not to be considered as evidence of fault that would have otherwise been pled in bar to a claim of injury due to the professional misconduct of a health professional. This conclusion bespeaks the doctrine of the particularly susceptible victim or recognition that whatever the wisdom or folly of our life-styles, society, through its laws, has not yet imposed a normative life-style on its members; and, finally, it may reflect in part an aspect of that policy judgment that health care professionals have a special responsibility with respect to diseased patients.[ ]

This does not mean, however, that the patient's poor health is irrelevant to the analysis of a claim for reparation. While the doctor may well take the patient as she found her, she cannot reverse the frames to make it appear that she was presented with a robust vascular condition; likewise, the physician cannot be expected to provide a guarantee against a cardiovascular incident. All that the law expects is that she not mistreat such a patient so as to become a proximate contributing cause to the ultimate vascular injury.

However, once the patient comes under the physician's care, the law can justly expect the patient to cooperate with the health care provider in their mutual interests. Thus, it is not unfair to expect a patient to help avoid the consequences of the condition for which the physician is treating her. * * *

Hence, we approve in this context of post-treatment conduct submission to the jury of the question whether the just mitigation or apportionment of damages may be expressed in terms of the patient's fault. If used, the numerical allocation of fault should be explained to the jury as a method of achieving the just apportionment of the damages based on their relative evaluation of each actor's contribution to the end result—that the allocation is but an aspect of the doctrine of avoidable consequences or of mitigation of damages. In this context, plaintiff should not recover more than she could have reasonably avoided, but the patient's fault will not be a bar to recovery except to the extent that her fault caused the damages.

An important caveat to that statement would be the qualification that implicitly flows from the fact that health care professionals bear the burden of proving that their mistreatment did not aggravate a preexisting condition: that the health care professional bear the burden of proving the damages that were avoidable.

Finally, before submitting the issue to the jury, a court should carefully scrutinize the evidence to see if there is a sound basis in the proofs for the assertion that the post-treatment conduct of the patient was indeed a significant cause of the increased damages. Given the short onset between the contraindicated surgery and the vascular incident here, plaintiff asserts that defendant did not present proof, to a reasonable degree of medical probability, that the plaintiff's post-treatment conduct was a proximate cause of the resultant condition. Plaintiff asserts that the only evidence given to support the defense's theory of proximate cause between plaintiff's post-treatment health habits and her damages was her internist's testimony regarding generalized studies showing that smoking increases vascular disease by fifty percent, and her vascular surgeon's testimony that some physicians believe there is a relationship among diabetes, smoking, and vascular impairment. Such testimony did not address with any degree of medical probability a relationship between her smoking or not between May 17, 1983, and the plaintiff's need for bypass surgery in July 1983. Defendant points to plaintiff's failure to consult with her internist as a cause of her injury, but the instruction to the jury gave no guidance on whether this was to be considered as conduct that concurrently or subsequently caused her injuries.[ ]

V

We acknowledge that it is difficult to parse through these principles and policies in the course of an extended appeal. We can well imagine that in the ebb and flow of trial the lines are not easily drawn. There are regrettably no easy answers to these questions.

* * *

[The court noted the factual complexities of the case, and concluded that "the instructions to the jury in this case did not adequately separate or define the concepts that were relevant to the disposition of the plaintiff's case." The case was remanded for a new trial.]

Notes and Questions

1. Do you advocate applying contributory negligence, or comparative negligence (depending upon the jurisdiction), to situations such as that of *Ostrowski*? Such cases raise fundamental questions about the limits of medicine and the role of patients in their own illnesses. Can a smoker easily stop? Is it fair to bar his recovery when his smoking is not a simple, easily abandoned, choice? See Sawka v. Prokopowycz, 104 Mich.App. 829, 306 N.W.2d 354 (1981), where the plaintiff sued the defendant for his failure to diagnose lung cancer. The court rejected the claim that the plaintiff's continued smoking and failure to return for further examination as instructed were contributory negligence.

In Shinholster v. Annapolis Hospital, 255 Mich.App. 339, 660 N.W.2d 361 (2003), the plaintiff suffered a stroke after a series of mini-strokes, and died. She had not regularly taken her blood pressure medication for at least a year before her symptoms began, and the defendant argued that this contributed to her fatal stroke. The court noted that "most jurisdictions that have considered the question have followed the rule that . . . the defendant may not argue that the plaintiff was comparatively negligent by creating the condition that caused him to seek treatment." Id. at 366.

See the reporters' note on Restatement Torts, 3d, Apportionment of Liability, § 7, comment m, p. 83:

> . . . the best explanation of pre-presentment negligence is that the consequences of the plaintiff's negligence—the medical condition requiring medical treatment—caused the very condition the defendant doctor undertook to treat so it would be unfair to allow the doctor to complain about that negligence.

Would you treat an overzealous jogger who had cardiac arrest while running in the same way as a chain smoking or obese sedentary patient? How much of your decision is based on your desire to punish the smoker or glutton for immoral or irresponsible behavior which may be virtually impossible to control? Blaming the victim, or scapegoating, is a frequent argument used by employers, insurers and the government to reduce obligations to insure, pay benefits, or, as in *Ostrowski*, to pay damages for patient injury. See Robert Schwartz, Life Style, Health Status, and Distributive Justice, 3 Health Matrix 195, 198 (1993) ("If all of those whose life style choices have health consequences were required to bear the full burden of those consequences, there would be few of us (and few diseases or injuries) that would not be implicated.")

2. A finding of contributory negligence was upheld in Ray v. Wagner, 286 Minn. 354, 176 N.W.2d 101, 104 (1970), where the physician performed a pap smear on the plaintiff, got back a positive test result, but was unable to reach the plaintiff by telephone for five months. The court noted:

> Ordinarily, a patient can rely on a doctor's informing her if the results of a test are positive. Here, however, plaintiff gave the doctor somewhat misleading information as to her status, she had no phone at the address where she lived, and she did not live at the address where she had a phone.

See also Harlow v. Chin, 405 Mass. 697, 545 N.E.2d 602 (1989) (plaintiff failed to return for further treatment when pain got worse; plaintiff held to be 13% comparatively negligent.)

3. Providers are expected to consider the needs and limitations of their patients. Bryant v. Calantone, 286 N.J.Super. 362, 669 A.2d 286 (A.D.1996). In Windisch v. Weiman, 161 A.D.2d 433, 555 N.Y.S.2d 731 (1990), the court held that the failure of a physician to properly follow-up a patient, resulting in a missed diagnosis of lung cancer, may provide the basis for imposing liability even when the patient is partially responsible for the delay in diagnosis.

4. A patient's lack of compliance with treatment instructions may be submitted to the jury under comparative negligence statutes for comparison with the malpractice of the treating physician. In Cox v. Lesko, 263 Kan. 805, 953 P.2d 1033 (1998), the physician performed shoulder surgery for traumatic posterior subluxation in the left shoulder. The plaintiff then missed most of her physical therapy sessions over several months, which were aimed to strengthen her muscles and increase her shoulder's range of motion. Her condition failed to improve. Plaintiff's lack of compliance with therapy instructions was properly submitted to the jury under the comparative negligence statute as fault to be compared with the malpractice of the physician who performed the surgery. See also Hall v. Carter, 825 A.2d 954 (D.C. C.A. 2003) (patient's continued smoking against medical advice was admissible; held that jury could consider whether physician had the last clear chance to avoid the harm).

5. Almost all American jurisdictions have adopted comparative fault, simplifying the issue by eliminating the harsh all-or-nothing effect of contributory negligence. Courts in comparative fault jurisdictions are likely to be more willing to allow evidence of plaintiffs' contributions to their injuries. See generally Victor Schwartz, Comparative Negligence (4th ed. 2002). The court in McIntyre v. Balentine, 833 S.W.2d 52 (Tenn.1992), lists only four states remaining without comparative fault: Alabama, Maryland, North Carolina, and Virginia.

6. Assumption of the risk. The doctrine of assumption of the risk is a viable defense even in many comparative fault jurisdictions. In Schneider v. Revici, 817 F.2d 987, 995 (2d Cir.1987), the Second Circuit considered whether a patient undergoing unconventional treatment for breast cancer after signing a consent form had waived all her rights to sue or assumed the risk of injury from the treatment. The court held that the consent form was not clear and unequivocal as a covenant not to sue, but that the doctrine of assumption of risk was available:

> * * * we see no reason why a patient should not be allowed to make an informed decision to go outside currently approved medical methods in search of an unconventional treatment. While a patient should be encouraged to exercise care for his own safety, we believe that an informed decision to avoid surgery and conventional chemotherapy is within the patient's right to "determine what shall be done with his own body,"[ ]

The court held that the jury could consider assumption of the risk as a total bar to recovery, based on the language of the signed consent form and the patient's general awareness of the risks of treatment.

Assumption of the risk is rarely argued except in cases of obvious defects of which the patient should have been aware, such as hazards in the hospital room. See, e.g., Charrin v. Methodist Hospital, 432 S.W.2d 572 (Tex.Civ.App.1968) (plaintiff tripped over television cord in hospital room; she knew it was there, having previously pointed it out to the staff.) The problem of assumption of the risk, in the sense of a conscious explicit assumption of medical risks, blends into the issues of informed consent and waivers of liability, discussed in Chapter 4, *infra.*

Problem: The Difficult Patient

Alice Frosty is profoundly obese and a diabetic. She is a smoker and drinks a bottle of gin a day. She works for the State as a disability counselor and her state health insurance coverage is excellent. She sees Dr. Wilson regularly. He has admonished her to stop smoking and cut down on her drinking, and to begin a program of exercise. He has also put her on hypertensive medications and on statins to control her cholesterol. He has also set up a series of monthly appointments with her to monitor her health.

Alice continues to smoke and drink. She fills her prescriptions and takes her medicine regularly for eight months, and then begins to cut back on the medications to save on her co-payment costs, cutting each pill in half. She also begins to miss her monthly appointments. Dr. Wilson has his nurse call her to remind her, but Alice never calls back. After six months of missed appointments, Alice has a heart attack and suffers major damage to her heart.

Can she sue Dr. Wilson?

III. DAMAGE INNOVATIONS

In the typical malpractice case, the available damages are the standard tort list: medical expenses, past and future; loss wages; diminished future earning capacity; loss of consortium; and noneconomic losses such as pain and suffering. In many health care settings, however, the alleged malpractice of the provider occurs to a patient who has a preexisting illness, such as a cancer patient. If the patient's chances of recovery are less than fifty percent, the old rule would deny recovery. The problem is one of both causation—did a provider's inaction increase the risk to the patient—and damage—exactly how should harm be quantified in such a situation.

HERSKOVITS v. GROUP HEALTH COOPERATIVE OF PUGET SOUND

Supreme Court of Washington, 1983.
99 Wash.2d 609, 664 P.2d 474.

DORE, JUSTICE.

This appeal raises the issue of whether an estate can maintain an action for professional negligence as a result of failure to timely diagnose lung cancer, where the estate can show probable reduction in statistical chance for survival but cannot show and/or prove that with timely diagnosis and treatment, decedent probably would have lived to normal life expectancy.

Both counsel advised that for the purpose of this appeal we are to *assume* that the respondent Group Health Cooperative of Puget Sound and Dr. William Spencer negligently failed to diagnose Herskovits' cancer on his first visit to the hospital and *proximately* caused a 14 percent reduction in his chances of survival. It is undisputed that Herskovits had less than a 50 percent chance of survival at all times herein.

The main issue we will address in this opinion is whether a patient, with less than a 50 percent chance of survival, has a cause of action against the hospital and its employees if they are negligent in diagnosing a lung cancer which reduces his chances of survival by 14 percent.

* * *

I

The complaint alleged that Herskovits came to Group Health Hospital in 1974 with complaints of pain and coughing. In early 1974, chest x-rays revealed infiltrate in the left lung. Rales and coughing were present. In mid-1974, there were chest pains and coughing, which became persistent and chronic by fall of 1974. A December 5, 1974 entry in the medical records confirms the cough problem. Plaintiff contends that Herskovits was treated thereafter only with cough medicine. No further effort or inquiry was made by Group Health concerning his symptoms, other than an occasional chest x-ray. In the early spring of 1975, Mr. and Mrs. Herskovits went south in the hope that the warm weather would help. Upon his return to the Seattle area with no improvement in his health, Herskovits visited Dr. Jonathan Ostrow on a private basis for another medical opinion. Within 3 weeks, Dr. Ostrow's evaluation and direction to Group Health led to the diagnosis of cancer. In July of 1975, Herskovits' lung was removed, but no radiation or chemotherapy treatments were instituted. Herskovits died 20 months later, on March 22, 1977, at the age of 60.

At hearing on the motion for summary judgment, plaintiff was unable to produce expert testimony that the delay in diagnosis "probably" or "more likely than not" caused her husband's death. The affidavit and deposition of plaintiff's expert witness, Dr. Jonathan Ostrow, construed in the most favorable light possible to plaintiff, indicated that had the diagnosis of lung cancer been made in December 1974, the patient's possibility of 5-year survival was 39 percent. At the time of initial diagnosis of cancer 6 months later, the possibility of a 5-year survival was reduced to 25 percent. Dr. Ostrow testified he felt a diagnosis perhaps could have been made as early as December 1974, or January 1975, about 6 months before the surgery to remove Mr. Herskovits' lung in June 1975.

Dr. Ostrow testified that if the tumor was a "stage 1" tumor in December 1974, Herskovits' chance of a 5-year survival would have been 39 percent. In June 1975, his chances of survival were 25 percent assuming the tumor had progressed to "stage 2". Thus, the delay in diagnosis may have reduced the chance of a 5-year survival by 14 percent.

Dr. William Spencer, the physician from Group Health Hospital who cared for the deceased Herskovits, testified that in his opinion, based upon a reasonable medical probability, earlier diagnosis of the lung cancer that afflicted Herskovits would not have prevented his death, nor would it have lengthened his life. He testified that nothing the doctors at Group Health could have done would have prevented Herskovits' death, as death within several years is a virtual certainty with this type of lung cancer regardless of how early the diagnosis is made.

Plaintiff contends that medical testimony of a reduction of chance of survival from 39 percent to 25 percent is sufficient evidence to allow the proximate cause issue to go to the jury. Defendant Group Health argues conversely that Washington law does not permit such testimony on the issue of medical causation and requires that medical testimony must be at least sufficiently definite to establish that the act complained of "probably" or "more likely than not" caused the subsequent disability. It is Group Health's contention that plaintiff must prove that Herskovits "probably" would have survived had the defendant not been allegedly negligent; that is, the plaintiff must prove there was at least a 51 percent chance of survival.

II

* * *

This court heretofore has not faced the issue of whether, under § 323(a), [of the Restatement (Second) of Torts (1965)] proof that the defendant's conduct increased the risk of death by decreasing the chances of survival is sufficient to take the issue of proximate cause to the jury. Some courts in other jurisdictions have allowed the proximate cause issue to go to the jury on this type of proof.[ ] These courts emphasized the fact that defendants' conduct deprived the decedents of a "significant" chance to survive or recover, rather than requiring proof that with absolute certainty the defendants' conduct caused the physical injury. The underlying reason is that it is not for the wrongdoer, who put the possibility of recovery beyond realization, to say afterward that the result was inevitable.[ ]

Other jurisdictions have rejected this approach, generally holding that unless the plaintiff is able to show that it was *more likely than not* that the harm was caused by the defendant's negligence, proof of a decreased chance of survival is not enough to take the proximate cause question to the jury.[ ] These courts have concluded that the defendant should not be liable where the decedent more than likely would have died anyway.

The ultimate question raised here is whether the relationship between the increased risk of harm and Herskovits' death is sufficient to hold Group Health responsible. Is a 36 percent (from 39 percent to 25 percent) reduction in the decedent's chance for survival sufficient evidence of causation to allow the jury to consider the possibility that the physician's failure to timely diagnose the illness was the proximate cause of his death? We answer in the affirmative. To decide otherwise would be a blanket release from liability for doctors and hospitals any time there was less than a 50 percent chance of survival, regardless of how flagrant the negligence.

III

[The court then discusses at length the case of *Hamil v. Bashline*, [481 Pa. 256, 392 A.2d 1280 (1978)], where the plaintiff's decedent, suffering from severe chest pains, was negligently treated in the emergency unit of the hospital. The wife, because of the lack of help, took her husband to a private physician's office, where he died. If the hospital had employed proper treatment, the decedent would have had a substantial chance of surviving the attack, stated by plaintiff's medical expert as a 75 percent chance of survival. The defendant's expert witness testified that the patient would have died regardless of any treatment provided by the defendant hospital.]

* * *

* * * In *Hamil* and the instant case, however, the defendant's act or omission failed in a *duty* to protect against harm from *another source*. Thus, as the *Hamil* court noted, the fact finder is put in the position of having to consider not only what *did* occur, but also what *might have* occurred.

* * *

The *Hamil* court held that once a plaintiff has demonstrated that the defendant's acts or omissions have increased the risk of harm to another, such evidence furnishes a basis for the jury to make a determination as to whether such increased risk was in turn a substantial factor in bringing about the resultant harm.

* * *

Under the *Hamil* decision, once a plaintiff has demonstrated that defendant's acts or omissions in a situation to which § 323(a) applies have increased the risk of harm to another, such evidence furnishes a basis for the fact finder to go further and find that such increased risk was in turn a substantial factor in bringing about the resultant harm. The necessary proximate cause will be established if the jury finds such cause. It is not necessary for a plaintiff to introduce evidence to establish that the negligence resulted in the injury or death, but simply that the negligence increased the *risk* of injury or death. The step from the increased risk to causation is one for the jury to make.

* * *

Where percentage probabilities and decreased probabilities are submitted into evidence, there is simply no danger of speculation on the part of the jury. More speculation is involved in requiring the medical expert to testify as to what would have happened had the defendant not been negligent.

Conclusion

* * * We reject Group Health's argument that plaintiffs *must show* that Herskovits "probably" would have had a 51 percent chance of survival if the hospital had not been negligent. We hold that medical testimony of a reduction of chance of survival from 39 percent to 25 percent is sufficient evidence to allow the proximate cause issue to go to the jury.

Causing reduction of the opportunity to recover (loss of chance) by one's negligence, however, does not necessitate a total recovery against the negligent party for all damages caused by the victim's death. Damages should be awarded to the injured party or his family based only on damages caused directly by premature death, such as lost earnings and additional medical expenses, etc.

We reverse the trial court and reinstate the cause of action.

PEARSON, J., concurring.

* * *

* * * I am persuaded * * * by the thoughtful discussion of a recent commentator. King, *Causation, Valuation, and Chance in Personal Injury Torts Involving Preexisting Conditions and Future Consequences,* 90 Yale L.J. 1353 (1981).

* * *

Under the all or nothing approach, typified by *Cooper v. Sisters of Charity of Cincinnati, Inc.,* 27 Ohio St.2d 242, 272 N.E.2d 97 (1971), a plaintiff who establishes that but for the defendant's negligence the decedent had a 51 percent chance of survival may maintain an action for that death. The defendant will be liable for all damages arising from the death, even though there was a 49 percent chance it would have occurred despite his negligence. On the other hand, a plaintiff who establishes that but for the defendant's negligence the decedent had a 49 percent chance of survival recovers nothing.

This all or nothing approach to recovery is criticized by King on several grounds, 90 Yale L.J. at 1376–78. First, the all or nothing approach is arbitrary. Second, it

> subverts the deterrence objectives of tort law by denying recovery for the effects of conduct that causes statistically demonstrable losses * * *. A failure to allocate the cost of these losses to their tortious sources * * * strikes at the integrity of the torts system of loss allocation.

90 Yale L.J. at 1377. Third, the all or nothing approach creates pressure to manipulate and distort other rules affecting causation and damages in an attempt to mitigate perceived injustices.[ ] Fourth, the all or nothing approach gives certain defendants the benefit of an uncertainty which, were it not for their tortious conduct, would not exist. * * * Finally, King argues that the loss of a less than even chance is a loss worthy of redress.

These reasons persuade me that the best resolution of the issue before us is to recognize the loss of a less than even chance as an actionable injury. Therefore, I would hold that plaintiff has established a prima facie issue of proximate cause by producing testimony that defendant probably caused a substantial reduction in Mr. Herskovits' chance of survival. * * *

Finally, it is necessary to consider the amount of damages recoverable in the event that a loss of a chance of recovery is established. Once again, King's discussion provides a useful illustration of the principles which should be applied.

> To illustrate, consider a patient who suffers a heart attack and dies as a result. Assume that the defendant-physician negligently misdiagnosed the patient's condition, but that the patient would have had only a 40% chance of survival even with a timely diagnosis and proper care. Regardless of whether it could be said that the defendant caused the decedent's death, he caused the loss of a chance, and that chance-interest should be completely redressed in its own right. Under the proposed rule, the plaintiff's compensation for the loss of the victim's chance of surviving

the heart attack would be 40% of the compensable value of the victim's life had he survived (including what his earning capacity would otherwise have been in the years following death). The value placed on the patient's life would reflect such factors as his age, health, and earning potential, including the fact that he had suffered the heart attack and the assumption that he had survived it. The 40% computation would be applied to that base figure.

(Footnote omitted.) 90 Yale L.J. at 1382.

I would remand to the trial court for proceedings consistent with this opinion.

Notes and Questions

1. How would damages be figured under the majority's approach? Under the Pearson/King theory? What is the relationship between causation and damages in these cases? The majority and Pearson opinions would effectively permit recovery but reduce damages as the causation link weakens. Is this a reasonable approach?

2. Judicial approaches to the loss of a chance can be grouped into four categories.

   a. *All or nothing*. The traditional rule allows the plaintiff no recovery unless survival was more likely than not. A less than 51% chance of survival receives nothing. Plaintiff who proves a chance of survival greater than 50% can receive judgment with no discount for the chance that the loss would have occurred without negligence. This award is based on the physical injury suffered and not the lost chance to avoid it. See Smith v. Parrott, 175 Vt. 375, 833 A.2d 843 (2003) (rejecting the doctrine due to "fundamental questions about its potential impact on not only the cost, but the very practice of medicine in Vermont; about its effect on causation standards to other professions and the principles—if any—which might justify its application to medicine but not other fields such as law, architecture, or accounting; and ultimately about the overall societal cots which may result from awarding damages to an entirely new class of plaintiffs who formerly had no claim under the common law in this state.")

   b. *Loss of an appreciable or substantial chance of recovery*. Jeanes v. Milner, 428 F.2d 598 (8th Cir.1970). This approach does not give proportional recovery based on the percentage of harm attributable to the defendant, instead manipulating the burden of proof rather than acknowledging the lost chance as the real injury. See Hicks v. United States, 368 F.2d 626 (4th Cir.1966). Defining "substantial possibility" has troubled some courts. Borgren v. United States, 716 F.Supp. 1378 (D.Kan.1989).

   c. *Increased risk of harm*. This approach, found in the Restatement (Second), Torts, section 323(a) and adopted by the majority in *Herskovits*, lowers causation requirements to allow causes of action for those who have a less than 50% chance of survival. Hamil v. Bashline, 481 Pa. 256, 392 A.2d 1280 (1978). Compensation is for the increased risk of harm rather than loss of a chance, and damage awards are not discounted for the percentage of harm caused by the physician, death is typically the compensable injury. Any percentage is enough to get to the jury. See Thompson v. Sun City Community Hospital, Inc., 141 Ariz. 597, 688 P.2d 605 (1984) (linking Restatement (Second), Torts, section 323A to the interest seen as "the chance itself"); Mayhue v. Sparkman, 653 N.E.2d 1384

(Ind.1995) (rejects lost chance but lightens plaintiff's burden of proving causation.)

d. *Compensation for the loss of a chance.* This looks at damages that include the value of the patient's life reduced in proportion to the lost chance. This approach was developed by Joseph King in his seminal article, Causation, Valuation and Chance in Personal Injury Torts Involving Pre-existing Conditions and Future Consequences, 90 Yale L.J. 1353 (1981). The approach requires a percentage probability test, with the value of the patient's life determined and damages decreased accordingly. This approach was considered in Pearson's concurring opinion in *Herskovits.* Iowa adopted the approach in DeBurkarte v. Louvar, 393 N.W.2d 131 (Iowa 1986). Ohio adopted it in Roberts v. Ohio Permanente Medical Group, Inc., 76 Ohio St.3d 483, 668 N.E.2d 480 (1996), and South Dakota in Jorgenson v. Vener, 616 N.W.2d 366 (S.D.2000).

Loss of a chance and increased risk are grounded in the same justifications of deterring negligent conduct and compensating for real harms that happen to fall below the fifty percent threshold of traditional tort doctrine. Increased risk allows recovery for harm that has not yet occurred, while loss of a chance requires the plaintiff to wait until the condition occurs and then sue. See generally United States v. Anderson, 669 A.2d 73 (Del.1995).

3. What problems do you foresee with the application of the "loss of a chance" doctrine to medical practice? Note that the evidence as to risk must be put in probabilistic form for the jury to consider. What about Judge Brachtenbach's concerns about the weight to be given statistical evidence? Would his concerns always prevent the use of statistics in litigation? Or can you offer some solutions to his problems? In Drew v. William W. Backus Hospital, 77 Conn.App. 645, 825 A.2d 810 (2003), the court rejected the testimony of the plaintiff's expert, who failed to apply general statistical data as to survival to the particular patient, so that the requirement of proof of a causal link was not satisfied.

4. *Ultimate outcome instructions.* Lost chance cases require calculations that assume a probability of loss and an ultimate outcome if the defendant's treatment had been faultless. One example of an "ultimate outcome" charge is found in the New Jersey Model Jury Charges (Civil) (4th ed.) § 5.36E (emphasis added):

> If you find that defendant has sustained his/her burden of proof, then you must determine based on the evidence what is the likelihood, on a percentage basis, that the plaintiff's ultimate injuries (*condition*) would have occurred even if defendant's treatment was proper. When you are determining the amount of damages to be awarded to the plaintiff, you should award the total amount of damage. Your award should not be reduced by your allocation of harm. The adjustment in damages which may be required will be performed by the Court.

See generally Fischer v. Canario, M.D., 143 N.J. 235, 670 A.2d 516, 524–526 (1996).

5. A judicial illustration of the calculation process for loss of a chance is found in McKellips v. St. Francis Hospital, Inc., 741 P.2d 467 (Okl.1987):

> "To illustrate the method in a case where the jury determines from the statistical findings combined with the specific facts relevant to the patient, the patient originally had a 40% chance of cure and the physician's negligence reduced the chance of cure to 25%, (40%–25%) 15% represents the patient's loss of survival. If the total amount of damages proved by the evidence is

$500,000, the damages caused by defendant is 15% x $500,000 or $75,000
* * *."

This has come to be called the percentage apportionment of damages method. A
detailed application of the percentage apportionment approach is found in Boody
v. United States, 706 F.Supp. 1458 (D.Kan.1989). See also Mays v. United States,
608 F.Supp. 1476 (D.Colo.1985).

6. Another judicial approach to these calculations is to treat the loss of a
chance as a wrong separate from wrongful death, and allow the jury to set a dollar
amount based on all the evidence, without mechanically applying a percentage to a
total damage award. See Smith v. State of Louisiana, 676 So.2d 543 (1996), where
the court held that

> * * * the method we adopt today in this decision, is for the factfinder—judge
> or jury—to focus on the chance of survival lost on account of malpractice as a
> distinct compensable injury and to value the lost chance as a lump sum award
> based on all the evidence in the record, as is done for any other item of
> general damages.

Another approach is simply to recognize the full survival or wrongful death
damages, without regard to the lost chance of survival. A variation is to refuse to
allow recovery for the loss of a chance, but allow recovery for unrelated damages
such as the reduced quality of life suffered, the need to undergo a more radical
intervention that otherwise necessary, and pain and suffering. Wickens v. Oakwood Healthcare Systems, 465 Mich. 53, 631 N.W.2d 686 (2001).

7. The classic article on the subject, cited in *Herskovitz*, is Joseph King,
Causation, Valuation and Chance in Personal Injury Torts Involving Preexisting
Conditions and Future Consequences, 90 Yale L.J. 1353 (1981).

Problem: The Patient's Choice?

Jane Rogers was a fair complected woman in her early thirties. She had
worked every summer during high school and college as a lifeguard at the beach.
While she was in graduate school, one of her sisters was diagnosed as having
melanoma, a deadly cancer that is often fatal if not detected and treated early.
Melanoma is more prevalent in people who have fair complexions, and prolonged
exposure to the sun over time, particularly severe sun burns, are a risk factor for
the cancer.

Ms. Roger's sister died. The family physician, Dr. James, told the family
members that they should all get a thorough physical to check for signs of skin
tumors that might be precancerous. Ms. Rogers went to the University Student
Clinic and requested a physical examination. She explained why she was worried.
Dr. Gillespie, an older physician who had retired from active practice and now
helped out part-time at the Clinic, examined her. He observed a nodule on her
upper back, but incorrectly diagnosed it as a birthmark. He told her not to worry.
She continued her lifeguarding and water safety instruction activities during the
summer to pay for her graduate education.

At a party one Friday night, Ms. Rogers met a young physician who was a
resident at the University hospital. She was wearing a shoulderless dress, and the
resident, Dr. Wunch, noted a mole on her shoulder. He recognized it as a
melanoma. He pointed it out to her, and told her that she really ought to get it
checked. He gave her his card, with his phone number, and said he would be glad
to set her up with an appointment with a good cancer specialist at the hospital.

Ms. Rogers called, made an appointment, and filled out the forms required by the University Hospital, but then missed her appointment. She never went back.

A year later, during a routine physical as part of an employment application, the examining physician found several large growths on Ms. Roger's back. She was diagnosed as having melanoma, which had spread into her blood and had metastasized into her lymph nodes. She was dead within a year.

What problems do you see with the suit by her estate against the available defendants?

Chapter 5

LIABILITY OF HEALTH CARE INSTITUTIONS

INTRODUCTION

The hospital is the classic health care "institution". Health care delivery also includes institutional forms such as managed care organizations that finance health care and contract with physicians to provide care, as well as ambulatory care facilities and physician offices. As more and more medicine is moved out of the hospital into less expensive settings, the liability of these institutional arrangements emerges as a new concern. Most caselaw is however still centered around hospitals, as the predominant form of delivery of high technology high risk care.

The modern hospital—with its operating theaters, stainless steel equipment, complex diagnostic tools, and its large staffs of nurses, doctors, and support personnel—has come to symbolize the delivery of medical care. It was not always so. For centuries, in Europe and in America, hospitals tended the sick and the insane but made no attempt to treat or cure. They were supported by the philanthropy of the wealthy and by religious groups. In the 1870s it could be said that only a small minority of doctors practiced in hospitals, and even they devoted only a small portion of their practice to such work. A person seeking medical care before 1900 did not consider hospitalization, since doctors made house calls and even operated in the home. By the late 1800s, however, developments in medical knowledge moved the hospital toward a central position in health care. The development of antiseptic and aseptic techniques reduced the previously substantial risk of infection within hospitals; the growing scientific content of medicine made hospitals a more attractive place for medical practice.

Therapeutic and diagnostic improvements became identified with hospital doctors. These doctors, the product of the modernization of medicine, discovered that the hospital was well suited to their practice needs. Control over the hospital began to shift from the trustees to the doctors during the early 1900s. As the hospital evolved, physicians became increasingly dependent upon hospital affiliation. By the 1970s, no doctor would consider practicing without the resources that a hospital offered, and 25 percent of active physicians practiced full-time in a hospital.

Today health care delivery has shifted again, from the hospital setting to outpatient settings for many kinds of surgery. The American hospital is moving from the hub of the health care delivery system to a satellite, but it continues to be central for emergency care and for highly complicated surgical and other procedures. For an excellent extended discussion of the history of the hospital, see Paul Starr, The Social Transformation of American Medicine (1982), particularly Chapter 4.

I. AGENCY LAW AND THE HOSPITAL

A. THE MEDICAL STAFF AND HOSPITAL GOVERNANCE

The hospital-physician relationship is an unusual one by corporate standards. A typical hospital may have several categories of practicing physicians, but the largest group is comprised of private physicians with staff privileges. Staff privileges include the right of the physicians to admit and discharge their private patients to the hospital and the right to use the hospital's facilities. See generally Chapter 12, *infra*.

These physicians are not typically employees of the hospital, but rather independent contractors. The hospital is therefore not easily targeted as a defendant in a malpractice suit. Only if the doctor whose negligence injured a patient is an employee could the hospital be reached through the doctrine of vicarious liability. The hospital was independently liable only if it were negligent in its administrative or housekeeping functions, for example causing a patient to slip and fall on a wet floor. Otherwise, the hospital was often immune from liability. This has changed as the courts have confronted the evolution of the modern hospital and expanded vicarious liability doctrine in the health care setting.

SCOTT v. SSM HEALTHCARE ST. LOUIS

Mo.App. E.D., 2002.
70 S.W.3d 560.

* * *

BACKGROUND

In 1994 Matthew Scott, then seventeen, sustained serious injuries as a result of a sinus infection that spread into his brain. Matthew was involved in a car accident and was taken to Hospital, where he was treated for minor injuries and released to his father. Two days later Matthew returned to Hospital's emergency room, complaining of a severe headache. Dr. Doumit was Hospital's emergency room physician who examined Matthew that day. Soon after Matthew arrived, a CT scan of his head was conducted. Dr. Richard Koch, a partner in RIC, read the CT film and concluded that the CT scan was normal. Matthew was diagnosed as having a mild concussion from the previous auto accident, was given medication for his headache and sent home.

The next day, Matthew's headache had not improved. His parents called Hospital three times and informed Dr. Doumit that Matthew was lethargic, nauseous and vomiting. Dr. Doumit told them that he was still exhibiting signs of a minor concussion, that he would probably improve within a few days, that they should continue to observe him, but that if they became very concerned about his condition they could bring him back to the emergency room.

Early the next morning, Matthew collapsed in the kitchen, unable to use the right side of his body. He was rushed by ambulance to Barnes Hospital in St. Peters, Missouri. A spinal tap and CT scan revealed an infection at the top of his brain, and his brain was swelling inside his skull. Matthew was taken to Barnes Hospital in St. Louis, where a number of surgeries were performed to remove infected brain tissue and portions of his skull. He remained in a coma for several weeks.

Eventually, after undergoing skull reconstructive surgery and an extensive program of rehabilitation, Matthew was able to achieve a considerable recovery. He also has sustained serious permanent injuries, however, including among others a significant degree of paralysis on the right side of his body, and the requirement of a permanent ventricular drainage tube in his brain.

Matthew and his mother filed this medical malpractice action against Hospital and others, alleging, *inter alia,* that the negligence of Dr. Doumit and Dr. Koch caused Matthew's injuries. Specifically, plaintiffs alleged that Dr. Koch had acted below the accepted standard of care in misreading the initial CT scan on September 24, and that Dr. Doumit had acted below the standard of care by failing to instruct Matthew's parents, when they called with their concerns, to bring him back to the emergency room. Plaintiffs' suit further alleged that at all relevant times Dr. Koch had been acting as an agent for Hospital, notwithstanding the fact that he was formally employed by RIC, which had contracted to provide radiology services at Hospital. Plaintiffs' action also named Dr. Koch and RIC as defendants. Before trial, plaintiffs settled their claims against Dr. Koch and RIC for the sum of $624,800 (hereinafter, "the Koch settlement"). The case then proceeded to trial against Hospital.

[The court first found that the evidence at trial supported the allegations of medical negligence by the treating physicians. The jury found for the plaintiffs, having found that Dr. Koch was the Hospital's agent.]

Discussion

1. *Sufficiency of Evidence on Issue of Dr. Koch's Agency*

In its first point on appeal, Hospital asserts that the trial court erred in denying its motions for directed verdict and for judgment notwithstanding the verdict on the issue of whether Dr. Koch was Hospital's agent. * * *

"An independent contractor is one who contracts with another to do something for him but is neither controlled by the other nor subject to the other's control with respect to his physical conduct in the performance of the undertaking."[ ] "As a general rule, a party who contracts with an independent contractor is not liable for the negligent acts of the independent contractor."[ ]. In contrast to the rule on independent contractors, the doctrine of *respondeat superior* imposes upon an employer vicarious liability for the negligent acts or omissions of his employee or agent that are committed within the scope of the employment or agency. [ ] "Generally, the relationship of principal-agent or employer-employee is a question of fact to be determined by the jury when, from the evidence adduced on the question, there may be a fair difference of opinion as to the existence of the relationship." [ ]

Two elements are required to establish an agency relationship: (1) the principal must consent, either expressly or impliedly, to the agent's acting on the principal's behalf, and (2) the agent must be subject to the principal's control.[ ] In the context of a hospital-physician relationship, the primary focus is on whether the hospital generally controlled, or had the right to control, the conduct of the doctor in his work performed at the hospital.[ ] Additionally, our courts have also cited with approval a list of ten factors set forth in the Restatement (Second) of Agency, § 220(2) (1958), as a helpful aid in "determining whether one acting for another is a servant or an independent contractor."[ ]

In the case at hand, Hospital cites a handful of facts from the record which, arguably, could support the conclusion that RIC and Dr. Koch were acting as independent contractors rather than as agents of Hospital. Among them are: the relationship between Dr. Koch and Hospital was based upon a written contract, in which RIC agreed to provide radiology services to Hospital; RIC was a partnership, of which Dr. Koch was a partner and signatory to the contract; Hospital did not employ or pay Dr. Koch (RIC did); Hospital did not directly set Dr. Koch's hours at the Hospital; and Hospital did not bill patients for the services of Dr. Koch or the other RIC radiologists.

However, a jury question is presented when the evidence is sufficiently conflicting that reasonable minds could differ as to whether agency existed.[ ] The following evidence, all of it from the contract and/or testimony in the record, supports finding a principal-agent relationship between Hospital and Dr. Koch: (1) Hospital establishes the medical standards for the provision of radiological services at Hospital; (2) Hospital determines the qualifications necessary for Dr. Koch; (3) Hospital has the right to require Dr. Koch to submit reports regarding radiological services rendered according to standards established by Hospital; (4) Hospital sets the prices for Dr. Koch's services, and those prices cannot be changed without prior approval of Hospital; (5) Hospital required that Dr. Koch be "an active member" of Hospital's medical staff; (6) Hospital required that Dr. Koch maintain liability insurance in specific amounts; (7) in the event that Dr. Koch fails to procure such insurance, Hospital has the right to procure it for him at his expense; (8) Hospital has the right to terminate Dr. Koch if dissatisfied with his performance; (9) Hospital provides all nurses and technicians for the radiology department; (10) Hospital owns and provides all of the office space for the radiology department, as well as providing all of the radiology equipment, films, supplies and fixtures; (11) Hospital decides what type of film, film boxes and view jackets will be used; (12) the contract between Hospital and RIC is of infinite duration; (13) RIC has provided the only radiologists working at Hospital for over 60 years; (14) RIC exclusively provides all of the radiologists for Hospital, including even the doctor who serves as the administrative director of the radiology department; and (15) the RIC radiologist who was the director of the radiology department testified that he considered himself and the other RIC radiologists at Hospital to in effect be "employees of the hospital."

Despite these facts, Hospital argues that the evidence at trial was insufficient to establish agency because there was nothing in the record to show that Hospital controlled Dr. Koch specifically "in the performance of the act at the heart of plaintiffs' claim—his alleged negligent reading of Matthew

Scott's CT scan." However, Missouri courts have long recognized that physicians must be free to exercise independent medical judgment; the mere fact that a physician retains such independent judgment will not preclude a court, in an otherwise proper case, from finding the existence of an employer-employee or principal-agent relationship between a hospital and physician.[ ] Courts in other states, as well, have strongly rejected the notion that such a relationship cannot be found merely because the hospital does not have the right to stand over the doctor's shoulder and dictate to him or her how to diagnose and treat patients. [ ]

In view of the foregoing principles of law, the evidence in this case and our standard of review, the trial court did not err in finding the evidence sufficient to present a jury question on the issue of Dr. Koch's agency. Point I is denied.

Notes and Questions

1. *Physicians as Employees.* The general definition of the term "servant" in the Restatement (Second) of Agency § 2(2) (1957) refers to a person whose work is "controlled or is subject to the right to control by the master." The Restatement's more specific definition of the term "servant" lists factors to be considered when distinguishing between servants and independent contractors, the first of which is "the extent of control" that one may exercise over the details of the work of the other. Id. The relevant factor for analyzing the hospital-physician relationship by agency tests is § 220(2)(a), which looks to "the extent of control which, by the agreement, the master may exercise over the details of the work." This becomes a fact-intensive analysis for the trier of fact.

Physicians need considerable autonomy in practice, given the complexity of their decisions and their relationship to particular patients. As a result, determining the degree of control necessary to create an employment relationship in a medical malpractice claim poses a unique set of difficulties. As the court writes in Lilly v. Fieldstone, 876 F.2d 857 (C.A. 10 Kan.), 1989. " * * * [i]t is uncontroverted that a physician must have discretion to care for a patient and may not surrender control over certain medical details. Therefore, the 'control' test is subject to a doctor's medical and ethical obligations. ... What we must do in the case of professionals is determine whether other evidence manifests an intent to make the professional an employee subject to other forms of control which are permissible. A myriad of doctors become employees by agreement without surrendering their professional responsibilities."

2. *The Medical Staff.* The medical staff is a self-governing body charged with overseeing the quality of care, treatment, and services delivered by practitioners who are credentialed and privileged through the medical staff process. The medical staff must credential and privilege all licensed independent practitioners. The self-governing organized medical staff creates and maintains a set of bylaws that defines its role within the context of a hospital setting and clearly delineates its responsibilities in the oversight of care, treatment, and services. It elects its own officers, and appoints its own committees.

The organized medical staff is intricately involved in carrying out, and in providing leadership in, all patient care functions conducted by practitioners privileged through the medical staff process. The medical staff oversees the quality of patient care, treatment, and services provided by practitioners privileged through the medical staff process; and it recommends practitioners for privileges to perform medical histories and physical examinations, The hospital governing body approves such privileges.

The organized medical staff is not simply another administrative component of the hospital, and is subject to only limited authority of the governing board of the hospital. While the hospital board must approve the staff's bylaws and can approve or disapprove particular staff actions, it cannot usually discipline individual physicians directly or appoint administrative officers to exercise direct authority. A hospital's medical staff is therefore a powerful body within the larger organization. See generally Clark C. Havighurst, Doctors and Hospitals: An Antitrust Perspective on Traditional Relationships, 1984 Duke L.J. 1071, 1084–92.

Ownership and control of physician services is therefore traditionally separate from the ownership and control of hospitals, and ownership and control of medical insurance is separate from both. The staff privilege model means that the hospitals and doctors have to engage in complicated transactions among themselves, and with insurers. From an economic perspective, this arrangement maximizes inefficiency rather than achieving the efficiencies of a single firm, to the detriment of quality as well as cost. Peter J. Hammer, Medical Antitrust Reform: Arrow, Coase, and the Changing Structure of the Firm, in the Privatization of Health Care Reform (Gregg M. Bloche, Ed. 2003).

3. What explains this curious structure, where two parallel systems exist side-by-side, with nurses and other allied health professionals operating as hospital employees subject to master-servant rules, and the medical staff operating relatively autonomously as independent contractors? The professional status and power of physicians? See generally Charles E. Rosenberg, The Care of Strangers: The Rise of America's Hospital System 66–68, 262–267 (1987).

II. INDEPENDENT CONTRACTORS AND VICARIOUS LIABILITY

Absent evidence of indicia of control sufficient to make a physician the employee of a hospital, courts have turned to traditional agency tests that evaluate situations in which health care institutions are vicariously liable for the negligence of their independent contractors.

BURLESS v. WEST VIRGINIA UNIVERSITY HOSPITALS, INC.

Supreme Court of West Virginia, 2004.
215 W.Va. 765, 601 S.E.2d 85.

DAVIS, JUSTICE:

In these two appeals from two orders of the Circuit Court of Monongalia County granting summary judgment to West Virginia University Hospitals (hereinafter referred to as "WVUH"), the Appellants ask this Court to rule that the circuit courts erred in finding that no actual or apparent agency relationship existed between physicians employed by the West Virginia University Board of Trustees (hereinafter referred to as "the BOT") and WVUH. We find no error in the circuit courts' rulings that no actual agency existed. However, we find that the courts erred in granting summary judgment on the issue of apparent agency. In reaching this conclusion, we find that for a hospital to be held liable for a physician's negligence under an apparent agency theory, a plaintiff must establish that: (1) the hospital either committed an act that would cause a reasonable person to believe that the physician in question was an agent of the hospital, or, by failing to take an action, created a circumstance that would allow a reasonable person to hold such a belief, and (2) the plaintiff relied on the apparent agency relationship.

I. FACTUAL PROCEDURAL HISTORY

Each of the two cases consolidated for purposes of this opinion involve a woman who gave birth to her child at WVUH under circumstances that she alleges resulted in severe birth defects to her child. The relevant facts of each case, as developed in the pleadings, depositions, affidavits, and exhibits, follow.

A. Jaclyn Burless

In July of 1998 Jaclyn Burless learned she was pregnant and sought prenatal care at the Cornerstone Care Clinic (hereinafter referred to as "the Cornerstone Clinic" or simply "the clinic") located in Greensboro, Pennsylvania. The Cornerstone Clinic was where Ms. Burless had routinely sought her primary medical care. Similarly, Ms. Burless elected to receive her prenatal care at the clinic. She received her prenatal care from Dr. Douglas Glover for approximately seven months.

In November, 1998, Dr. Glover sent Ms. Burless to WVUH for an ultrasound. At that time, Ms. Burless signed a WVUH consent form that stated: "I understand that the faculty physicians and resident physicians who provide treatment in the hospital are not employees of the hospital." Thereafter, in February of 1999 when she was at approximately 37 weeks of gestation, Ms. Burless experienced an elevated blood pressure and edema. On February 15, 1999, Dr. Glover advised Ms. Burless to report to the WVU Emergency Department for an evaluation. On February 17, 1999, Ms. Burless presented herself at the WVUH Emergency Department as instructed and, after an evaluation, was instructed to return to the High Risk Clinic, which is located on the WVUH premises, in two days with a urine sample for testing. Ms. Burless was also advised that she would receive the remainder of her prenatal care at the High Risk Clinic. She followed the instructions to return to the High Risk Clinic in two days. She was then instructed to return in one week for further evaluation. When she returned, on February 26, 1999, she was induced into labor at 7:50 p.m. Her labor was permitted to continue throughout the remainder of February 26 and until 4:00 p.m. on February 27. She alleges that during this time, doctors, residents, and nurses at WVUH noted variable decelerations in the fetal heart rate of her unborn daughter, Alexis Price. At 4:00 p.m. on February 27 the decision was made to deliver the baby via cesarean section, and such delivery was accomplished at 4:16 p.m. The child was born with an APGAR[2] score of two at one minute and six at five minutes. Soon after birth the child began to experience seizures and suffered

---

2. An APGAR Score is a newborn's first evaluation and serves as a predictive indicator of any potential problems. The infant is examined at one and five minutes after birth and ranked on a scale of zero to two on five characteristics: 1) skin color; 2) heart rate; 3) response to stimuli of inserting a catheter in the nose; 4) muscle tone; and 5) respiratory effort. Thus, the maximum score is 10 with most healthy newborns scoring an eight or nine. The five APGAR factors can be mnemonically summarized as *A*-ppearance, *P*-ulse, *G*-rimace, *A*-ctivity, *R*-espiration.[ ].

a stroke. Ms. Burless has alleged that the doctors and hospital were negligent, *inter alia,* in failing to monitor her labor and delivery, which negligence caused severe and permanent mental, neurological, and psychological injuries to the infant, Alexis Price.

Ms. Burless later filed a negligence action, claiming breaches of the standard of care in connection with the management of her labor, against the BOT as the physicians' employer, and claiming vicarious liability on the part of WVUH based upon a theory of apparent agency between WVUH and the physicians who provided the allegedly negligent care. WVUH moved for summary judgment asserting, in relevant part, that there was no apparent agency relationship between it and the doctors and residents who provided care to Ms. Burless. Finding no just cause for delay, pursuant to Rule 54(b) of the West Virginia Rules of Civil Procedure, the circuit court granted summary judgment to WVUH by final order entered December 11, 2002. The circuit court found that there was nothing in the record demonstrating the creation of an apparent agency relationship between the physicians who treated Ms. Burless and WVUH. Ms. Burless appealed the order and this Court granted her petition for appeal. For purposes of rendering our decision, we consolidated her case with a similar appeal filed by Ms. Melony Pritt.

B. Melony Pritt

Melony Pritt presented to the Emergency Department of WVUH on June 2, 1998, complaining of pain in her right lower abdomen. It was determined that she was nine weeks pregnant and had a left ovarian cyst. Ms. Pritt was released from the hospital on June 3 and was instructed to follow-up at the Obstetrics and Gynecology clinic at the Physicians Office Center (hereinafter "POC") for her prenatal care and monitoring of her ovarian cyst. When Ms. Pritt arrived for her first follow-up visit, she reported to the admissions clerk at WVUH and was assigned to Dr. Aparna Kamat, a second-year resident who was supervised in treating Ms. Pritt by Drs. Brita Boyd, Millard Simmons, and Leo Brancazio. Subsequent ultrasounds revealed the continued presence of the cyst. On September 4, Ms. Pritt saw Dr. Kamat at the POC and a left ovarian cystectomy using a laproscopic procedure was scheduled. On that same date, and during her visit with Dr. Kamat at the POC, Ms. Pritt signed an informed consent for the laparotomy and left ovarian cystectomy. This consent, and three other consent forms signed by Ms. Pritt during the course of her medical care, all contained the following statement: "I understand that the faculty physicians and resident physicians who provide treatment in the hospital are not employees of the hospital." The surgery was performed by Drs. Kamat and Boyd on September 8, 1998, when Ms. Pritt was estimated to be at about twenty-three-and-one-half weeks gestation. During the surgical procedure, the cyst broke open and yellow fluid leaked into the pelvic cavity. No irrigation was performed and no antibiotics were prescribed. Ms. Pritt was discharged from the hospital on September 10, 1998. On September 12, 1998, she presented to the Emergency Department at WVUH with severe abdominal pain. She was found to have a massive abdominal infection, which infection caused premature labor. Her son, Adam Pruitt, was born on September 13, 1998. Ms. Pritt contends that, due to his prematurity at birth, Adam has suffered severe permanent mental, neurological, and psychological injuries.

Ms. Pritt subsequently sued the BOT and WVUH claiming that injuries to herself and her son resulted from the negligence of the physicians in recommending and performing an elective laproscopic cystectomy procedure when she in only her twenty-third week of gestation. WVUH moved for summary judgment asserting the lack of any apparent agency relationship between it and the doctors and residents who provided care to Ms. Pritt. Finding no just cause for delay, pursuant to Rule 54(b), the circuit court granted summary judgment to WVUH by final order entered July 31, 2002. The circuit court found, *inter alia,* that Ms. Pritt's theory of apparent agency must fail because WVUH had not, through its actions or its conduct, held the physicians out to be its employees. Ms. Pritt appealed the order and this Court granted her petition for appeal. We consolidated her case with that of Ms. Burless for purposes of rendering our decision.

II.

[The court's discussion of the standard of review is omitted.]

III.

DISCUSSION

Ms. Burless and Ms. Pritt assert that the circuit courts erred both in finding no actual agency relationship between the doctors who treated them and WVUH, and in finding no apparent agency relationship. We address each of these assignments of error in turn.

A.   *Actual Agency*

[The court found no actual agency, since the hospital did not have "power of control" over the physicians who provided treatment to Ms. Burless and Ms. Pritt.]

B.   *Apparent Agency*

Ms. Burless and Ms. Pritt next assert that the circuit courts erred in finding no apparent agency relationship between the doctors who treated them and WVUH. Because we have explained in the previous section that we find no *actual* agency relationship in these cases, we have concluded that the doctors were, in fact, independent contractors. Our cases have recognized that, as a general rule, "[i]f [a physician] is found to be an independent contractor, then the hospital is not liable for his [or her] negligence."[ ]

As with most general rules, there are exceptions to the independent contractor rule. We have previously recognized that

One who by his acts or conduct has permitted another to act apparently or ostensibly as his agent, to the injury of a third person who has dealt with the apparent or ostensible agent in good faith and in the exercise of reasonable prudence, is estopped to deny the agency relationship.

[ ] In the instant cases, however, we are asked to determine the existence of an apparent agency relationship in the hospital/physician context. As explained in more detail below, modern hospitals and their relationships with the physicians who treat patients within their facilities are rather unique and

complex. Thus, instead of relying on a general rule for apparent agency such as those quoted above, we believe a more particular rule is in order.

In the hospital/physician context, this Court has heretofore established that even where a physician charged with negligence is an independent contractor, the hospital may nevertheless be found vicariously liable where the complained of treatment was provided in an emergency room.[ ] Although we have addressed using a theory of apparent agency to overcome the physician/independent contractor rule in the context of emergency room treatment, we have never expressly defined such a rule for use outside of the emergency room setting. We do so now.

1. Hospital/Physician Apparent Agency Outside the Emergency Room Setting. The public's confidence in the modern hospital's portrayal of itself as a full service provider of health care appears to be at the foundation of the national trend toward adopting a rule of apparent agency to find hospitals liable, under the appropriate circumstances, for the negligence of physicians providing services within its walls. As one court observed:

> In an often cited passage, a New York court explained: "The conception that the hospital does not undertake to treat the patient, does not undertake to act through its doctors and nurses, but undertakes instead simply to procure them to act upon their own responsibility, no longer reflects the fact. Present-day hospitals, as their manner of operation plainly demonstrates, do far more than furnish facilities for treatment. They regularly employ on a salary basis a large staff of physicians, nurses and interns, as well as administrative and manual workers, and they charge patients for medical care and treatment, collecting for such services, if necessary, by legal action. Certainly, *the person who avails himself of 'hospital facilities' expects that the hospital will attempt to cure him, not that its nurses or other employees will act on their own responsibility.*" . . . In light of this modern reality, the overwhelming majority of jurisdictions employed ostensible or apparent agency to impose liability on hospitals for the negligence of independent contractor physicians.

Mejia v. Community Hosp. of San Bernardino,[ ] (quoting Bing v. Thunig [ ] In fact), this Court has itself observed that

> "Modern hospitals have spent billions of dollars on marketing to nurture the image that they are full-care modern health facilities. Billboards, television commercials and newspaper advertisements tell the public to look to its local hospital for every manner of care, from the critical surgery and life-support required by a major accident to the minor tissue repairs resulting from a friendly game of softball. These efforts have helped bring the hospitals vastly increased revenue, a new role in daily health care and, ironically, a heightened exposure to lawsuits.[ ]"

[ ]

* * *

[ ] * * * [W]e now hold that for a hospital to be held liable for a physician's negligence under an apparent agency theory, a plaintiff must establish that: (1) the hospital either committed an act that would cause a reasonable person to believe that the physician in question was an agent of the hospital, or, by failing to take an action, created a circumstance that would allow a reasonable

person to hold such a belief, and (2) the plaintiff relied on the apparent agency relationship.

2. Hospital's Actions or Inactions. The first element of our test requires evidence that the hospital either committed an act that would cause a reasonable person to believe that the physician in question was an agent of the hospital, or, by failing to take an action, created a circumstance that would allow a reasonable person to hold such a belief. This portion of the test focuses on the acts of the hospital and is generally satisfied when "the hospital 'holds itself out' to the public as a provider of care."[ ] One court has explained that "[i]n order to prove this element, it is not necessary to show an express representation by the hospital.... Instead, a hospital is generally deemed to have held itself out as the provider of care, unless it gave the patient contrary notice."[ ]. The "contrary notice" referred to by the *Mejia* court generally manifests itself in the form of a disclaimer. As one court has acknowledged, "[a] hospital generally will be able to avoid liability by providing *meaningful written notice* to the patient, acknowledged at the time of admission."[ ]. It has been said that "[l]iability under apparent agency ... will not attach against a hospital where the patient knows, or reasonably should have known, that the treating physician was an independent contractor."[ ] Thus, a hospital's failure to provide a meaningful written notice may constitute "failing to take an action" and thereby allowing a reasonable person to believe that a particular doctor is an agent of the hospital. Conversely, absent other overt acts by the hospital indicating an employer/employee relationship, an unambiguous disclaimer by a hospital explaining the independent contractor status of physicians will generally suffice to immunize the hospital from being vicariously liable for physician conduct.[14]

Turning to the cases before us, the circuit courts in both cases relied on the disclaimers signed by Ms. Pritt & Ms. Burless in granting summary judgment in favor of WVUH. In addition, the circuit court considering Ms. Pritt's case summarily concluded that WVUH had not "held the physicians out to be its employees." We disagree with these conclusions.

The disclaimer that WVUH required both Ms. Pritt and Ms. Burless to sign stated: "I understand that the faculty physicians and resident physicians who provide treatment in the hospital are not employees of the hospital." WVUH contends that this "disclaimer" was sufficient to unequivocally inform Ms. Pritt and Ms. Burless that the physicians treating them were not employees of the hospital. We disagree.

We do not find the disclaimer language used by WVUH, which indicated that "faculty physicians and resident physicians who provide treatment in the hospital" are independent contractors, was sufficient to support a grant of summary judgment in their favor. The WVUH disclaimer provision presupposes that all patients can distinguish between "faculty physicians," "resident physicians" and any other type of physician having privileges at the hospital. In other words, for this disclaimer to be meaningful, a patient would literally have to inquire into the employment status of everyone treating him or her.

---

14. Of course, "we do not hold that the existence of an [unambiguous] independent contractor disclaimer ... is always dispositive on the issue [.]" [ ] A plaintiff may still be able to prove that, under the totality of the circumstances, an unambiguous disclaimer was insufficient to inform him or her of the employment status of a hospital's physicians.

Obviously, "[i]t would be absurd to require ... a patient ... to inquire of each person who treated him whether he is an employee of the hospital or an independent contractor."

Consequently, it was improper for the circuit court to grant summary judgment in favor of WVUH. Ms. Burless and Ms. Pritt have established a genuine question of material fact as to whether WVUH has either committed an act that would cause a reasonable person to believe that the physician in question was an agent of the hospital, or, by failing to take an action, created a circumstance that would allow a reasonable person to hold such a belief.

3. Reliance. The reliance prong of the apparent agency test is a subjective molehill. "Reliance ... is established when the plaintiff 'looks to' the hospital for services, rather than to an individual physician."[ ] It is "sometimes characterized as an inquiry as to whether 'the plaintiff acted in reliance upon the conduct of the hospital or its agent, consistent with ordinary care and prudence.'[ ] This factor 'simply focuses on the "patient's belief that the hospital or its employees were rendering health care." ' " "[ ] However, this portion of the test also requires consideration of the 'reasonableness of the patient's [subjective] belief that the hospital or its employees were rendering health care.' " "This ... determination is made by considering the totality of the circumstances, including ... any special knowledge the patient[/plaintiff] may have about the hospital's arrangements with its physicians."[ ]

Mrs. Pritt and Ms. Burless provided evidence indicating that they believed that the physicians treating them were employees of WVUH.

In the deposition testimony of Ms. Burless she stated her belief that the people treating her at the hospital were employees, as follows: "Q. Did anyone do anything to make you believe that they were employees of WVU Hospital? A. They were all wearing their coats and name tags and in the building, so, you know, you know they're—they work there, they're employees." In the affidavit submitted by Ms. Pritt in opposition to WVUH's motion for summary judgment, the following was stated:

2.   At the West Virginia University Hospitals, I was assigned doctors who treated me and consulted me through my prenatal care, surgery and delivery of my son Adam.

3.   Throughout all of my treatment and consultations, I believed that the doctors and nurses who treated me and spoke to me were employees of the West Virginia University Hospitals.

Ms. Burless and Ms. Pritt have also established a genuine question of material fact on the issue of their reliance on the apparent agency relationship between WVUH and their treating physicians. Consequently, on the issue of apparent agency, it is clear that summary judgment should not have been granted in favor of WVUH.

Notes and Questions

1.   Consider the nature of the modern hospital. Hospitals are big businesses, spending millions marketing themselves through "expensive advertising campaigns." Kashishian v. Port, 167 Wis.2d 24, 481 N.W.2d 277 (1992) (noting the substantial sums of money spent by U.S. hospitals on advertising in 1989, and the

fact the many people recall such advertising.) They provide a range of health services, and the public expects emergency care, radiological and other testing services, and other functions, as a result of hospitals' self-promotion. Hospitals do not actively inform the public about the various legal statuses of emergency room and other physicians. As the role and image of the hospital have evolved, judicial willingness to stretch agency exceptions has likewise followed suit, as *Burless* illustrates.

2. *Patient Reliance.* The patient in most cases relies on the reputation of the hospital, not any particular doctor, and for that reason selects that hospital. See e.g., White v. Methodist Hosp. South, 844 S.W.2d 642 (Tenn.App.1992). If the negligence results from emergency room care, most courts have held that a patient may justifiably rely on the physician as an agent unless the hospital explicitly disclaims an agency relationship. Ballard v. Advocate Health and Hospitals Corporations, 1999 WL 498702 (N.D.Ill. 1999). A promotional campaign or advertising can create such reliance. Clark v. Southview Hospital & Family Health Center, 68 Ohio St.3d 435, 628 N.E.2d 46 (1994) (promotional and marketing campaign stressed the emergency departments); Gragg v. Calandra, 297 Ill.App.3d 639, 231 Ill.Dec. 711, 696 N.E.2d 1282 (1998) (unless patient is put on notice of the independent status of the professionals in a hospital, he or see will reasonably assume they are employees).

What can a hospital do to avoid liability under the *Burless* court's analysis? Will explicit notice to the plaintiff at the time of admission be sufficient? How about a large sign in the admitting area of the hospital? A brochure handed to each patient? If the hospital advertises aggressively, will the reliance created by such advertising overwhelm all of the hospital's targeted attempts to inform patients about the intricacies of the physicians' employment relationships with the hospital?

To avoid liability, a hospital can try to avoid patient misunderstanding by its billing procedures, the letterhead used, signs, and other clues of the true nature of the relationship of the physician to the institution. Cantrell v. Northeast Georgia Medical Center, 235 Ga.App. 365, 508 S.E.2d 716 (1998) (sign over registration desk stated that the physicians in the emergency room were independent contracts; consent form repeated this.) The court is likely however to cut through these devices if the reliance on reputation by the patient is strong enough.

Explicit language in a patient consent form is the clearest way to put a patient on notice of the physician's legal status. A few states allow a clear statement in a consent form—that physicians in the hospital are independent contractors and not agents—to put a patient on notice. See, e.g., Roberts v. Galen of Virginia, Inc., 111 F.3d 405 (6th Cir. 1997) (statement in outpatient registration and authorization for medical treatment form stated that "physicians, residents, and medical students are independent practitioners and are not employees or agents of the hospital"; even though patient had neither read nor signed this, it is the action of the hospital that governs as to ostensible agency.)

3. *Nondelegable Duty Analysis.* Emergency room physicians are most often the source of vicarious liability claims against the contracting hospitals. In spite of various forms of notice as to the independent contractor status of emergency room physicians, many state courts have refused to allow the hospital to escape liability. The reasons typically given are based on the nature of patient reliance when entering a hospital for emergency care. As the court stated in Simmons v. Tuomey Regional Medical Center, 341 S.C. 32, 533 S.E.2d 312 (South Carolina, 2000), "[t]he point often made in the cases and commentary, either implicitly or

explicitly, is that expecting a patient in an emergency situation to debate or comprehend the meaning and extent of any representations by the hospital—which likely would be based on an opinion gradually formed over the years and not on any single representation—imposes an unfair and improper burden on the patient. Consequently, we believe the better solution, grounded primarily in public policy reasons we explain below, is to impose a nondelegable duty on hospitals.''(holding that a hospital owes a common law nondelegable duty to render competent service to its emergency room patients).

The nondelegable duty doctrine is similar to the "inherent function" test used by some courts to describe emergency room or radiology services. These courts refuse to allow the independent contractor defense in such cases. See, e.g., Beeck v. Tucson General Hospital, 18 Ariz.App. 165, 500 P.2d 1153 (1972)("The radiologist was employed by the hospital for an extended period of time (five years) to perform a service which was an inherent function of the hospital, a function without which the hospital could not properly achieve its purpose. All facilities and instrumentalities were provided by the hospital together with all administrative services for the radiology department.")

Other courts reach the same result by characterizing the duty of a hospital that uses physician independent contractors as a contractual or fiduciary duty to patients. See for example Pope v. Winter Park Healthcare Group, Ltd., 939 So.2d 185 (D.C. App.Florida, Fifth District, 2006).

4.   Anesthesia services may also be considered to create vicarious liability under the right set of facts. See Dragotta v. Southampton Hosp., 39 A.D.3d 697, 833 N.Y.S.2d 638 (N.Y.A.D. 2 Dept.,2007).

Problem: Creating a Shield

You represent Bowsman Hospital, a small rural hospital in Iowa. The hospital has until now relied on Dr. Francke for radiology services. It provides him with space, equipment and personnel for the radiology department, sends and collects bills on his behalf, and provides him with an office. It also pays him $300 a day in exchange for which Dr. Francke agrees to be at the hospital one day a week. Bowsman is one of several small hospitals in this part of Iowa that use Dr. Francke's services. Bowsman advertises in the local papers of several nearby communities. Its advertisements stress its ability to handle trauma injuries, common in farming areas. The ads say in part:

"Bowsman treats patient problems with big league medical talent. Our physicians and nurses have been trained for the special demands of farming accidents and injuries."

What advice can you give as to methods of shielding Bowsman from liability for the negligent acts of Dr. Francke? Must it insist that Dr. Francke operate his own outside laboratory? Or furnish his own equipment? Pay his own bills? Should the hospital hire its own radiologist?

The Chief Executive Officer asks you to develop guidelines to protect the hospital from liability for medical errors of the radiologist. Your research has uncovered the following cases.

Estates of Milliron v. Francke, 243 Mont. 200, 793 P.2d 824 (1990). The plaintiff was referred to the hospital and the radiologist who practiced there by his family physician, for evaluation of prostatis and uropathy. The radiologist used an intravenous pyelogram, to which the plaintiff had a reaction. The patient suffered brain damage. The hospital provided space, equipment and personnel for the radiology department, sent and collected bills on his behalf, and provided him with an office. The court granted summary judgment for the defendant on the ostensible agency claim. The court noted that this was a small hospital in a rural area, and the radiologist rotated between this and several other small hospitals. This was an ordinary practice in smaller communities in Montana.

> Providing these traveling physicians with offices at the hospital simply helps ensure that these smaller and more remote communities will be provided with adequate medical care and is not a sufficient factual basis to establish an agency relationship. Id. at 827.

Gregg v. National Medical Health Care Services, Inc., 145 Ariz. 51, 699 P.2d 925 (1985). Gregg went to the hospital's emergency room at 3 a.m. after having three episodes of crushing substernal chest pain accompanied by nausea and vomiting. The court noted that the hospital's right to control the physician was critical to its liability for the physician's acts, and held that the facts raised a jury question. The physician was paid $300 per week to commute from his office to the hospital clinic to act as a consultant. He was required to be at the hospital at least once a week.

III. HOSPITAL DIRECT LIABILITY

Patients may suffer injury in hospitals in many ways: they may fall out of bed because the bedrail is not raised; they may slip on the way to the bathroom; they may be given the wrong drug in their IV line; the MRI machine may not be working. If expert testimony is not needed, that is, if an ordinary person could evaluate the failure, then the case may not be considered malpractice but rather ordinary negligence. Negligence may have a different statute of limitations and may not be subject to restrictive legislative restrictions on malpractice recovery such as certificates of merit, caps on noneconomic loss, or other restrictions.

Most hospital cases will require expert testimony of some sort. If the case involves the standard of care applicable to a hospital rather than one of the medical staff physicians, then the courts will look at the standard applicable to hospitals of that type, and inquire into the professional judgment of providers or decisions of a hospital governing body, or the administration of the hospital. Such breaches of duty are considered malpractice, are subject to the rules pertaining to such cases, and require expert testimony.

A. NEGLIGENCE

WASHINGTON v. WASHINGTON HOSPITAL CENTER

District of Columbia Court of Appeals, 1990.
579 A.2d 177.

[The Court considered two issues: whether the testimony of the plaintiff's expert was sufficient to create a issue for the jury; and whether the hospital's failure to request a finding of liability of the settling defendants or to file a cross claim for contribution against any of the defendants defeated the hospital's claim for a pro rata reduction in the jury verdict. The discussion of the first issue follows.]

FARRELL, ASSOCIATE JUDGE:

This appeal and cross-appeal arise from a jury verdict in a medical malpractice action against the Washington Hospital Center (WHC or the hospital) in favor of LaVerne Alice Thompson, a woman who suffered permanent catastrophic brain injury from oxygen deprivation in the course of general anesthesia for elective surgery * * *

* * *

I. The Facts

On the morning of November 7, 1987, LaVerne Alice Thompson, a healthy 36–year–old woman, underwent elective surgery at the Washington Hospital Center for an abortion and tubal ligation, procedures requiring general anesthesia. At about 10:45 a.m., nurse-anesthetist Elizabeth Adland, under the supervision of Dr. Sheryl Walker, the physician anesthesiologist, inserted an endotracheal tube into Ms. Thompson's throat for the purpose of conveying oxygen to, and removing carbon dioxide from, the anesthetized patient. The tube, properly inserted, goes into the patient's trachea just above the lungs. Plaintiffs alleged that instead Nurse Adland inserted the tube into Thompson's esophagus, above the stomach. After inserting the tube, Nurse Adland "ventilated" or pumped air into the patient while Dr. Walker, by observing physical reactions—including watching the rise and fall of the patient's chest and listening for breath sounds equally on the patient's right and left sides—sought to determine if the tube had been properly inserted.

At about 10:50 a.m., while the surgery was underway, surgeon Nathan Bobrow noticed that Thompson's blood was abnormally dark, which indicated that her tissues were not receiving sufficient oxygen, and reported the condition to Nurse Adland, who checked Thompson's vital signs and found them stable. As Dr. Bobrow began the tubal ligation part of the operation, Thompson's heart rate dropped. She suffered a cardiac arrest and was resuscitated, but eventually the lack of oxygen caused catastrophic brain injuries. Plaintiffs' expert testified that Ms. Thompson remains in a persistent vegetative state and is totally incapacitated; her cardiac, respiratory and digestive functions are normal and she is not "brain dead," but, according to the expert, she is "essentially awake but unaware" of her surroundings. Her condition is unlikely to improve, though she is expected to live from ten to twenty years.

* * *

The plaintiffs alleged that Adland and Walker had placed the tube in Thompson's esophagus rather than her trachea, and that they and Dr. Bobrow had failed to detect the improper intubation in time to prevent the oxygen deprivation that caused Thompson's catastrophic brain injury. WHC, they alleged, was negligent in failing to provide the anesthesiologists with a device known variously as a capnograph or end-tidal carbon dioxide monitor which allows early detection of insufficient oxygen in time to prevent brain injury.

* * *

II.   WASHINGTON HOSPITAL CENTER'S CLAIMS ON CROSS-APPEAL

A.   Standard of Care

On its cross-appeal, WHC first asserts that the plaintiffs failed to carry their burden of establishing the standard of care and that the trial court therefore erred in refusing to grant its motion for judgment notwithstanding the verdict.

* * *

In a negligence action predicated on medical malpractice, the plaintiff must carry a tripartite burden, and establish: (1) the applicable standard of care; (2) a deviation from that standard by the defendant; and (3) a causal relationship between that deviation and the plaintiff's injury. [ ] * * *

Generally, the "standard of care" is "the course of action that a reasonably prudent [professional] with the defendant's specialty would have taken under the same or similar circumstances." [ ] With respect to institutions such as hospitals, this court has rejected the "locality" rule, which refers to the standard of conduct expected of other similarly situated members of the profession in the same locality or community, [ ] in favor of a national standard. [ ] Thus, the question for decision is whether the evidence as a whole, and reasonable inferences therefrom, would allow a reasonable juror to find that a reasonably prudent tertiary care hospital,[3] at the time of Ms. Thompson's injury in November 1987, and according to national standards, would have supplied a carbon dioxide monitor to a patient undergoing general anesthesia for elective surgery.

WHC argues that the plaintiffs' expert, Dr. Stephen Steen, failed to demonstrate an adequate factual basis for his opinion that WHC should have made available a carbon dioxide monitor. The purpose of expert opinion testimony is to avoid jury findings based on mere speculation or conjecture. [ ] The sufficiency of the foundation for those opinions should be measured with this purpose in mind. * * *

* * *

* * * [WHC] asserts that * * * Steen gave no testimony on the number of hospitals having end-tidal carbon dioxide monitors in place in 1987, and that he never referred to any written standards or authorities as the basis of his opinion. We conclude that Steen's opinion * * * was sufficient to create an issue for the jury.

Dr. Steen testified that by 1985, the carbon dioxide monitors were available in his hospital (Los Angeles County—University of Southern California Medical Center (USC)), and "in many other hospitals." In response to a question whether, by 1986, "standards of care" required carbon dioxide monitors in operating rooms, he replied, "I would think that by that time, they would be [required]." As plaintiffs concede, this opinion was based in part on his own personal experience at USC, which * * * cannot itself provide an adequate foundation for an expert opinion on a national standard of care. But Steen also drew support from "what I've read where [the monitors were]

---

3. Plaintiffs' expert defined a tertiary care hospital as "a hospital which has the facilities to conduct clinical care management of pa-   tients in nearly all aspects of medicine and surgery."

available in other hospitals." He referred to two such publications: The American Association of Anesthesiology (AAA) Standards for Basic Intra–Operative Monitoring, approved by the AAA House of Delegates on October 21, 1986, which "encouraged" the use of monitors, and an article entitled *Standards for Patient Monitoring During Anesthesia at Harvard Medical School,* published in August 1986 in the Journal of American Medical Association, which stated that as of July 1985 the monitors were in use at Harvard, and that "monitoring end-tidal carbon dioxide is an emerging standard and is strongly preferred."

WHC makes much of Steen's concession on cross-examination that the AAA Standards were recommendations, strongly encouraged but not mandatory, and that the Harvard publication spoke of an "emerging" standard. In its brief WHC asserts, without citation, that "[p]alpable indicia of widespread *mandated* practices are necessary to establish a standard of care" (emphasis added), and that at most the evidence spoke of "recommended" or "encouraged" practices, and "emerging" or "developing" standards as of 1986–87. A standard of due care, however, necessarily embodies what a *reasonably prudent* hospital would do, [ ] and hence care and foresight exceeding the minimum required by law or mandatory professional regulation may be necessary to meet that standard. It certainly cannot be said that the 1986 recommendations of a professional association (which had no power to issue or enforce mandatory requirements), or an article speaking of an "emerging" standard in 1986, have no bearing on an expert opinion as to what the standard of patient monitoring equipment was fully one year later when Ms. Thompson's surgery took place.

Nevertheless, we need not decide whether Dr. Steen's testimony was sufficiently grounded in fact or adequate data to establish the standard of care. The record contains other evidence from which, in combination with Dr. Steen's testimony, a reasonable juror could fairly conclude that monitors were required of prudent hospitals similar to WHC in late 1987. The evidence showed that at least four other teaching hospitals in the United States used the monitors by that time. In addition to Dr. Steen's testimony that USC supplied them and the article reflecting that Harvard University had them, plaintiffs introduced into evidence an article entitled *Anesthesia at Penn,* from a 1986 alumni newsletter of the Department of Anesthesia at the University of Pennsylvania, indicating that the monitors were then in use at that institution's hospital, and that they allowed "instant recognition of esophageal intubation and other airway problems. * * * "Moreover, WHC's expert anesthesiologist, Dr. John Tinker of the University of Iowa, testified that his hospital had installed carbon dioxide monitors in every operating room by early 1986, and that "by 1987, it is certainly true that many hospitals were in the process of converting" to carbon dioxide monitors.[5]

5. In its reply brief, WHC argues that the fact that four teaching hospitals used CO_2 monitors during the relevant time period is almost irrelevant. Institutions with significantly enhanced financial resources and/or government grants which accelerate their testing and implementation of new and improved technologies would naturally have available to them items which, inherently, were not yet required for the general populace of hospitals.

In fact, Dr. Steen, in voir dire examination on his qualification as an expert on the standard required of hospitals in WHC's position in regard to equipment, testified that his review of WHC's President's Report for 1986–87 led him to conclude that WHC was a teaching hospital. Counsel for the hospital could have identified

Perhaps most probative was the testimony of WHC's own Chairman of the Department of Anesthesiology, Dr. Dermot A. Murray, and documentary evidence associated with his procurement request for carbon dioxide monitors. In December 1986 or January 1987, Dr. Murray submitted a requisition form to the hospital for end-tidal carbon dioxide units to monitor the administration of anesthesia in each of the hospital's operating rooms, stating that if the monitors were not provided, the hospital would "fail to meet the national standard of care." The monitors were to be "fully operational" in July of 1987.[6] Attempting to meet this evidence, WHC points out that at trial

> Dr. Murray was *never asked to opine,* with a reasonable degree of medical certainty, that the applicable standard of care at the relevant time *required* the presence of CO_2 monitors. Indeed, his testimony was directly to the contrary. Moreover, the procurement process which he had initiated envisioned obtaining the equipment * * * over time, not even beginning until fiscal year 1988, a period ending June 30, 1988. [Emphasis by WHC.]

Dr. Murray opined that in November 1987 there was *no* standard of care relating to monitoring equipment. The jury heard this testimony and Dr. Murray's explanation of the procurement process, but apparently did not credit it, perhaps because the requisition form itself indicated that the equipment ordered was to be operational in July 1987, four months before Ms. Thompson's surgery, and not at some unspecified time in fiscal year 1988 as Dr. Murray testified at trial.

On the evidence recited above, a reasonable juror could find that the standard of care required WHC to supply monitors as of November 1987. The trial judge therefore did not err in denying the motion for judgment notwithstanding the verdict.

* * *

Notes and Questions

1. Does the plaintiff present sufficient evidence that the carbon dioxide monitor is now standard equipment for tertiary care hospitals? The court seems to say that expert testimony is not critical, that the evidence of use by other institutions is something a lay juror could evaluate even if expert testimony is deficient?

2. Is the Washington Hospital Center stuck in a zone of transition between older precautions and emerging technologies that improve patient care? Why did they not purchase such monitors earlier?

A companion device to the carbon dioxide monitor is the blood-monitoring pulse oximeter, which has become a mandatory device in hospital operating rooms. In 1984 no hospital had them; by 1990 all hospitals used oximeters in their

and probed fully before the jury any differences between WHC and the hospitals relied on to establish the standard of care. To the extent the record was not so developed, the jury could credit Steen's testimony that WHC was required to adhere to the standard applicable to teaching hospitals.

6. As supporting documentation for the requisition, Dr. Murray attached a copy of the Journal of the American Medical Association article on standards at Harvard University. The requisitions, with attachments, were exhibits admitted in evidence.

operating rooms. The device beeps when a patient's blood oxygen drops due to breathing problems or overuse of anesthesia. That warning can give a vital three or four minutes warning to physicians, allowing them to correct the problem before the patient suffers brain damage. These devices have so improved patient safety that malpractice insurers have lowered premiums for anesthesiologists.

The Joint Commission now requires hospitals to develop protocols for anesthesia care that mandate pulse oximetry equipment for measuring oxygen saturation. See Revisions to Anesthesia Care Standards Comprehensive Accreditation Manual for Hospitals Effective January 1, 2001 (Standards and Intents for Sedation and Anesthesia Care), *http://www.jointcommision.org*

3. A health care institution, whether hospital, nursing home, or clinic, is liable for negligence in maintaining its facilities, providing and maintaining medical equipment, hiring, supervising and retaining nurses and other staff, and failing to have in place procedures to protect patients. Basic negligence principles govern hospital liability for injuries caused by other sources than negligent acts of the medical staff. As *Washington* holds, hospitals are generally held to a national standard of care for hospitals in their treatment category. Reed v. Granbury Hospital Corporation, 117 S.W.3d 404 (2003); Richards v. Broadview Hts. Harborside Healthcare, 150 Ohio App.3d 537, 782 N.E.2d 609 (2002) (skilled nursing facility). They must provide a safe environment for diagnosis, treatment, and recovery of patients. Bellamy v. Appellate Department, 50 Cal.App.4th 797, 57 Cal.Rptr.2d 894 (5 Dist.1996).

a. Hospitals must have minimum facility and support systems to treat the range of problems and side effects that accompany procedures they offer. In Hernandez v. Smith, 552 F.2d 142 (5th Cir.1977), for example, an obstetrical clinic that lacked surgical facilities for caesarean sections was found liable for " * * * the failure to provide proper and safe instrumentalities for the treatment of ailments it undertakes to treat * * *." See also Valdez v. Lyman–Roberts Hosp., Inc., 638 S.W.2d 111 (Tex.App.1982).

b. Staffing must be adequate. Short staffing can be negligence. See Merritt v. Karcioglu, 668 So.2d 469 (La.App. 4th Cir.1996) (hospital ward understaffed in having only three critical care nurses for six patients). If existing staff can be juggled to cover a difficult patient, short staffing is no defense. See Horton v. Niagara Falls Memorial Medical Center, 51 A.D.2d 152, 380 N.Y.S.2d 116 (1976).

c. Equipment must be adequate for the services offered, although it need not be the state of the art. See Emory University v. Porter, 103 Ga.App. 752, 120 S.E.2d 668, 670 (1961); Lauro v. Travelers Ins. Co., 261 So.2d 261 (La.App.1972). If a device such as an expensive CT scanner has come into common use, however, a smaller and less affluent hospital can argue that it should be judged by the standards of similar hospitals with similar resources. This variable standard, reflecting resource differences between hospitals, would then protect a hospital in a situation where its budget does not allow purchase of some expensive devices. If an institution lacks a piece of equipment that has come to be recognized as essential, particularly for diagnosis, it may have a duty to transfer the patient to an institution that has the equipment. In Blake v. D.C. General Hospital (discussed in Maxwell Mehlman, Rationing Expensive Lifesaving Medical Treatments, 1985 Wisc.L.Rev. 239) the trial court allowed a case to go to the jury where the plaintiff's estate claimed that she died because of the hospital's lack of a CT scanner to diagnose her condition. The court found a duty to transfer in such circumstances.

d. A hospital and its contracting physicians may be liable for damages caused by inadequate or defective systems they develop and implement, particularly where emergency care is involved. On-call systems in smaller hospitals are a recurring issue in the caselaw. Delay in contacting physicians may be negligent, without the need for expert testimony. In Partin v. North Mississippi Medical Center, Inc., 929 So.2d 924 (Miss.Ct.App.2005), the plaintiff while in the hospital recovering from surgery became septic; the nurses failed to notify the on-call physician for more than twenty hours, and the patient died. The court observed:

" * * *[W]e are not fully convinced from the record that an expert would be required to demonstrate the negligence of NMMC in this case. The record reflects that the hospital failed or refused to contact the on-call doctor for roughly twenty hours, while Mrs. Partin's condition gradually and visibly worsened and while her family continued to plead with the hospital to contact the on-call doctor. By way of explanation (or lack thereof) for this twenty hour delay in contacting Dr. Gray, the hospital responds with the bald assertion that Partin put on nothing that would establish a fact issue. * * * [S]ummary judgment might just as well have been granted to Partin on the record before us.

See also Marks v. Mandel, 477 So.2d 1036 (Fla.App.1985) (failure of on-call system); Habuda v. Trustees of Rex Hospital, Inc., 3 N.C.App. 11, 164 S.E.2d 17 (1968)(hospital had inadequate rules for handling, storing, and administering medications); Herrington v. Hiller, 883 F.2d 411 (5th Cir.1989) (failure to provide for adequate 24–hour anesthesia service).

4. An institution's own internal rules and safety regulations for medical procedures must be followed, and a failure to follow them may be offered as evidence of a standard of care for the trier of fact to consider. They are material and relevant on the issue of quality of care, but are usually not sufficient by themselves to establish the degree of care owed. See Adams v. Family Planning Associates Medical Group, Inc., 315 Ill.App.3d 533, 248 Ill.Dec. 91, 733 N.E.2d 766 (2000) (internal policies and procedures of family planning clinic admissible as evidence of standard of care).

B. DUTIES TO TREAT PATIENTS

The relationship of the medical staff to the hospital insulates the hospital from liability, while giving physicians substantial autonomy in their treating decisions. What happens when the patient's insurance or other resources are exhausted but the staff physician believes that the standard of care requires continued hospitalization? Must the hospital accede to the doctor's request?

MUSE v. CHARTER HOSPITAL OF WINSTON–SALEM, INC.

Court of Appeals of North Carolina, 1995.
117 N.C.App. 468, 452 S.E.2d 589.

LEWIS, JUDGE.

This appeal arises from a judgment in favor of plaintiffs in an action for the wrongful death of Delbert Joseph Muse, III (hereinafter "Joe"). Joe was the son of Delbert Joseph Muse, Jr. (hereinafter "Mr. Muse") and Jane K. Muse (hereinafter "Mrs. Muse"), plaintiffs. The jury found that defendant Charter Hospital of Winston–Salem, Inc. (hereinafter "Charter Hospital" or "the hospital") was negligent in that, inter alia, it had a policy or practice which required physicians to discharge patients when their insurance expired and that this policy interfered with the exercise of the medical judgment of

Joe's treating physician, Dr. L. Jarrett Barnhill, Jr. The jury awarded plaintiffs compensatory damages of approximately $1,000,000. The jury found that Mr. and Mrs. Muse were contributorily negligent, but that Charter Hospital's conduct was willful or wanton, and awarded punitive damages of $2,000,000 against Charter Hospital. Further, the jury found that Charter Hospital was an instrumentality of defendant Charter Medical Corporation (hereinafter "Charter Medical") and awarded punitive damages of $4,000,000 against Charter Medical.

The facts on which this case arose may be summarized as follows. On 12 June 1986, Joe, who was sixteen years old at the time, was admitted to Charter Hospital for treatment related to his depression and suicidal thoughts. Joe's treatment team consisted of Dr. Barnhill, as treating physician, Fernando Garzon, as nursing therapist, and Betsey Willard, as social worker. During his hospitalization, Joe experienced auditory hallucinations, suicidal and homicidal thoughts, and major depression. Joe's insurance coverage was set to expire on 12 July 1986. As that date neared, Dr. Barnhill decided that a blood test was needed to determine the proper dosage of a drug he was administering to Joe. The blood test was scheduled for 13 July, the day after Joe's insurance was to expire. Dr. Barnhill requested that the hospital administrator allow Joe to stay at Charter Hospital two more days, until 14 July, with Mr. and Mrs. Muse signing a promissory note to pay for the two extra days. The test results did not come back from the lab until 15 July. Nevertheless, Joe was discharged on 14 July and was referred by Dr. Barnhill to the Guilford County Area Mental Health, Mental Retardation and Substance Abuse Authority (hereinafter "Mental Health Authority") for outpatient treatment. Plaintiffs' evidence tended to show that Joe's condition upon discharge was worse than when he entered the hospital. Defendants' evidence, however, tended to show that while his prognosis remained guarded, Joe's condition at discharge was improved. Upon his discharge, Joe went on a one-week family vacation. On 22 July he began outpatient treatment at the Mental Health Authority, where he was seen by Dr. David Slonaker, a clinical psychologist. Two days later, Joe again met with Dr. Slonaker. Joe failed to show up at his 30 July appointment, and the next day he took a fatal overdose of Desipramine, one of his prescribed drugs.

On appeal, defendants present numerous assignments of error. We find merit in one of defendants' arguments.

II.

Defendants next argue that the trial court submitted the case to the jury on an erroneous theory of hospital liability that does not exist under the law of North Carolina. As to the theory in question, the trial court instructed: "[A] hospital is under a duty not to have policies or practices which operate in a way that interferes with the ability of a physician to exercise his medical judgment. A violation of this duty would be negligence." The jury found that there existed "a policy or practice which required physicians to discharge patients when their insurance benefits expire and which interfered with the exercise of Dr. Barnhill's medical judgment." Defendants contend that this theory of liability does not fall within any theories previously accepted by our courts.

* * *

Our Supreme Court has recognized that hospitals in this state owe a duty of care to their patients. Id. In Burns v. Forsyth County Hospital Authority, Inc. [ ] this Court held that a hospital has a duty to the patient to obey the instructions of a doctor, absent the instructions being obviously negligent or dangerous. Another recognized duty is the duty to make a reasonable effort to monitor and oversee the treatment prescribed and administered by doctors practicing at the hospital. [ ] In light of these holdings, it seems axiomatic that the hospital has the duty not to institute policies or practices which interfere with the doctor's medical judgment. We hold that pursuant to the reasonable person standard, Charter Hospital had a duty not to institute a policy or practice which required that patients be discharged when their insurance expired and which interfered with the medical judgment of Dr. Barnhill.

III.

Defendants next argue that even if the theory of negligence submitted to the jury was proper, the jury's finding that Charter Hospital had such a practice was not supported by sufficient evidence. * * * We conclude that in the case at hand, the evidence was sufficient to go to the jury.

Plaintiffs' evidence included the testimony of Charter Hospital employees and outside experts. Fernando Garzon, Joe's nursing therapist at Charter Hospital, testified that the hospital had a policy of discharging patients when their insurance expired. Specifically, when the issue of insurance came up in treatment team meetings, plans were made to discharge the patient. When Dr. Barnhill and the other psychiatrists and therapists spoke of insurance, they seemed to lack autonomy. For example, Garzon testified, they would state, "So and so is to be discharged. We must do this." Finally, Garzon testified that when he returned from a vacation, and Joe was no longer at the hospital, he asked several employees why Joe had been discharged and they all responded that he was discharged because his insurance had expired. Jane Sims, a former staff member at the hospital, testified that several employees expressed alarm about Joe's impending discharge, and that a therapist explained that Joe could no longer stay at the hospital because his insurance had expired. Sims also testified that Dr. Barnhill had misgivings about discharging Joe, and that Dr. Barnhill's frustration was apparent to everyone. One of plaintiffs' experts testified that based on a study regarding the length of patient stays at Charter Hospital, it was his opinion that patients were discharged based on insurance, regardless of their medical condition. Other experts testified that based on Joe's serious condition on the date of discharge, the expiration of insurance coverage must have caused Dr. Barnhill to discharge Joe. The experts further testified as to the relevant standard of care, and concluded that Charter Hospital's practices were below the standard of care and caused Joe's death. We hold that this evidence was sufficient to go to the jury.

Defendants further argue that the evidence was insufficient to support the jury's finding that Charter Hospital engaged in conduct that was willful or wanton. An act is willful when it is done purposely and deliberately in violation of the law, or when it is done knowingly and of set purpose, or when the mere will has free play, without yielding to reason. [ ] * * * We conclude that the jury could have reasonably found from the above-stated evidence that

Charter Hospital acted knowingly and of set purpose, and with reckless indifference to the rights of others. Therefore, we hold that the finding of willful or wanton conduct on the part of Charter Hospital was supported by sufficient evidence.

* * *

For the reasons stated, we find no error in the judgment of the trial court, except for that part of the judgment awarding punitive damages, which is reversed and remanded for proceedings consistent with this opinion.

No error in part, reversed in part and remanded.

Notes and Questions

1. Should the *Muse* duty extend to all situations in which the physician and the hospital administration are in conflict? If the physician always prevails, then how does a hospital control its costs and its bad debts? Why does the court treat health care as special in this case? Surely a grocery store does not have to give us free groceries if we are short of cash as the checkout counter, nor does our landlord have to allow us to stay for free if we cannot cover our next month's rent. Is it simply the advantage of hindsight here that impels the court's imposition of such a duty on hospitals?

A provision in many hospital admissions forms states:

Legal Relationship Between Hospital and Physicians. All physicians and surgeons furnishing services to the patient, including the radiologist, pathologist, anesthesiologist, and the like, are not agents, servants, or employees of the above-named hospital, but are independent contractors, and as such are the agents, servants, or employees of the patient. The patient is under the care and supervision of his attending physician and it is the responsibility of the hospital and its nursing staff to carry out the instructions of such physician.

Could the *Muse* case have been brought as a breach of contract case by the plaintiff as third party beneficiary under the contract?

2. Consider the medical staff relationship under the bylaws. It is a shared power arrangement between the hospital and its medical staff, and the hospital has independent duties under Joint Commission accreditation and federal law to supervise quality within its walls. Insurance payment, whether private or governmental, will cover most hospital treatment. What is the hospital obligated to do in such situations? Offer free care? Or is this analogous to the duty of physicians to not abandon their patients? Does this case impose a corporate fiduciary duty on hospitals to treat high risk patients when their money runs out? Is it the equivalent of the EMTALA mandate that requires hospitals to treat all patients in their emergency rooms without regard to their ability to pay or their insurance status?

3. Does such a duty extend as well to managed care organizations, whose very design is premised on mechanisms for containing health care costs? What would happen to the underlying premises of cost control in managed care organizations, if the *Muse* doctrine were held to apply?

C. CORPORATE NEGLIGENCE

The courts' stretching of vicarious liability doctrine to sweep in doctors as conduits to hospital liability led inevitably to the direct imposition of corporate negligence liability on the hospital.

1. The Elements of Corporate Negligence

The next step was to hold the hospital directly liable for the failure of administrators and staff to properly monitor and supervise the delivery of health care within the hospital.

DARLING v. CHARLESTON COMMUNITY MEMORIAL HOSPITAL

Supreme Court of Illinois, 1965.
33 Ill.2d 326, 211 N.E.2d 253.

This action was brought on behalf of Dorrence Darling II, a minor (hereafter plaintiff), by his father and next friend, to recover damages for allegedly negligent medical and hospital treatment which necessitated the amputation of his right leg below the knee. The action was commenced against the Charleston Community Memorial Hospital and Dr. John R. Alexander, but prior to trial the action was dismissed as to Dr. Alexander, pursuant to a covenant not to sue. The jury returned a verdict against the hospital in the sum of $150,000. This amount was reduced by $40,000, the amount of the settlement with the doctor. The judgment in favor of the plaintiff in the sum of $110,000 was affirmed on appeal by the Appellate Court for the Fourth District, which granted a certificate of importance. 50 Ill.App.2d 253, 200 N.E.2d 149.

On November 5, 1960, the plaintiff, who was 18 years old, broke his leg while playing in a college football game. He was taken to the emergency room at the defendant hospital where Dr. Alexander, who was on emergency call that day, treated him. Dr. Alexander, with the assistance of hospital personnel, applied traction and placed the leg in a plaster cast. A heat cradle was applied to dry the cast. Not long after the application of the cast plaintiff was in great pain and his toes, which protruded from the cast, became swollen and dark in color. They eventually became cold and insensitive. On the evening of November 6, Dr. Alexander "notched" the cast around the toes, and on the afternoon of the next day he cut the cast approximately three inches up from the foot. On November 8 he split the sides of the cast with a Stryker saw; in the course of cutting the cast the plaintiff's leg was cut on both sides. Blood and other seepage were observed by the nurses and others, and there was a stench in the room, which one witness said was the worst he had smelled since World War II. The plaintiff remained in Charleston Hospital until November 19, when he was transferred to Barnes Hospital in St. Louis and placed under the care of Dr. Fred Reynolds, head of orthopedic surgery at Washington University School of Medicine and Barnes Hospital. Dr. Reynolds found that the fractured leg contained a considerable amount of dead tissue which in his opinion resulted from interference with the circulation of blood in the limb caused by swelling or hemorrhaging of the leg against the construction of the cast. Dr. Reynolds performed several operations in a futile attempt to save the leg but ultimately it had to be amputated eight inches below the knee.

The evidence before the jury is set forth at length in the opinion of the Appellate Court and need not be stated in detail here. The plaintiff contends that it established that the defendant was negligent in permitting Dr. Alexander to do orthopedic work of the kind required in this case, and not requiring him to review his operative procedures to bring them up to date; in failing, through its medical staff, to exercise adequate supervision over the case, especially since Dr. Alexander had been placed on emergency duty by the hospital, and in not requiring consultation, particularly after complications had developed. Plaintiff contends also that in a case which developed as this one did, it was the duty of the nurses to watch the protruding toes constantly for changes of color, temperature and movement, and to check circulation every ten to twenty minutes, whereas the proof showed that these things were done only a few times a day. Plaintiff argues that it was the duty of the hospital staff to see that these procedures were followed, and that either the nurses were derelict in failing to report developments in the case to the hospital administrator, he was derelict in bringing them to the attention of the medical staff, or the staff was negligent in failing to take action. Defendant is a licensed and accredited hospital, and the plaintiff contends that the licensing regulations, accreditation standards, and its own bylaws define the hospital's duty, and that an infraction of them imposes liability for the resulting injury.

* * *

The basic dispute, as posed by the parties, centers upon the duty that rested upon the defendant hospital. That dispute involves the effect to be given to evidence concerning the community standard of care and diligence, and also the effect to be given to hospital regulations adopted by the State Department of Public Health under the Hospital Licensing Act (Ill.Rev.Stat. 1963, chap. 111½, pars. 142–157.), to the Standards for Hospital Accreditation of the American Hospital Association, and to the bylaws of the defendant.

As has been seen, the defendant argues in this court that its duty is to be determined by the care customarily offered by hospitals generally in its community. Strictly speaking, the question is not one of duty, for " * * * in negligence cases, the duty is always the same, to conform to the legal standard of reasonable conduct in the light of the apparent risk. What the defendant must do, or must not do, is a question of the standard of conduct required to satisfy the duty." (Prosser on Torts, 3rd ed. at 331.) * * * Custom is relevant in determining the standard of care because it illustrates what is feasible, it suggests a body of knowledge of which the defendant should be aware, and it warns of the possibility of far-reaching consequences if a higher standard is required. [ ] But custom should never be conclusive.

In the present case the regulations, standards, and bylaws which the plaintiff introduced into evidence, performed much the same function as did evidence of custom. This evidence aided the jury in deciding what was feasible and what the defendant knew or should have known. It did not conclusively determine the standard of care and the jury was not instructed that it did.

"The conception that the hospital does not undertake to treat the patient, does not undertake to act through its doctors and nurses, but undertakes instead simply to procure them to act upon their own responsibility, no longer reflects the fact. Present-day hospitals, as their manner of operation plainly demonstrates, do far more than furnish facilities for treatment. They regularly employ on a salary basis a large staff of physicians, nurses and interns, as well as administrative and manual workers, and they charge patients for medical care and treatment, collecting for such services, if necessary, by legal action. Certainly, the person who avails himself of 'hospital facilities' expects that the hospital will attempt to cure him, not that its nurses or other employees will act on their own responsibility." (Fuld, J., in Bing v. Thunig (1957), 2 N.Y.2d 656, 163 N.Y.S.2d 3, 11, 143 N.E.2d 3, 8.) The Standards for Hospital Accreditation, the state licensing regulations and the defendant's bylaws demonstrate that the medical profession and other responsible authorities regard it as both desirable and feasible that a hospital assume certain responsibilities for the care of the patient.

* * * Therefore we need not analyze all of the issues submitted to the jury. Two of them were that the defendant had negligently: "5. Failed to have a sufficient number of trained nurses for bedside care of all patients at all times capable of recognizing the progressive gangrenous condition of the plaintiff's right leg, and of bringing the same to the attention of the hospital administration and to the medical staff so that adequate consultation could have been secured and such conditions rectified; * * * 7. Failed to require consultation with or examination by members of the hospital surgical staff skilled in such treatment; or to review the treatment rendered to the plaintiff and to require consultants to be called in as needed."

We believe that the jury verdict is supportable on either of these grounds. On the basis of the evidence before it the jury could reasonably have concluded that the nurses did not test for circulation in the leg as frequently as necessary, that skilled nurses would have promptly recognized the conditions that signalled a dangerous impairment of circulation in the plaintiff's leg, and would have known that the condition would become irreversible in a matter of hours. At that point it became the nurses' duty to inform the attending physician, and if he failed to act, to advise the hospital authorities so that appropriate action might be taken. As to consultation, there is no dispute that the hospital failed to review Dr. Alexander's work or require a consultation; the only issue is whether its failure to do so was negligence. On the evidence before it the jury could reasonably have found that it was.

[The remainder of the opinion, discussing expert testimony and damages, is omitted.]

Notes and Questions

1. Consider the issues submitted to the jury. It is alleged that both the nurses and the administrators were negligent in not taking steps to curtail Dr. Alexander's handling of the case. How can a nurse "blow the whistle" on a doctor without risking damage to her own career? See the section on labor law in health care institutions, Chapter 12, *infra*. How can a nurse exercise medical judgment in violation of Medical Practice statutes?

Nurses have independent obligations to care for patients. In Brandon HMA, Inc. v. Bradshaw, 809 So.2d 611 (Miss.2001), the plaintiff sued the hospital, alleging that while she was being treated for bacterial pneumonia she was negligently treated by the nursing staff leading to her permanent disability from brain damage. The staff failed to monitor her, report vital information to her doctor, and allowed her condition to deteriorate to a critical state before providing urgently needed care and life support. One nurse failed to take her vital signs on several visits to her room.

Nurses, as *Darling* indicates, have obligations to advocate for patients when care is substandard in a hospital. In Rowe v. Sisters of Pallottine Missionary

Society, 211 W.Va. 16, 560 S.E.2d 491 (2001), a 17 year old boy was admitted to the hospital ER after a motorcycle accident. He had severe pain in his left knee and numbness in his foot, and no pulse in his foot. He was discharged and told to make an appointment to see an orthopedist several days later, and come back to the hospital if the pain got worse. He got worse that night and was admitted to another hospital. He ended up with substantial impairment of his leg. The court held that the nurses had breached the standard of care by not adequately advocating his interests when he was discharged with unexplained and unaddressed symptoms.

In Jensen v. Archbishop Bergan Mercy Hospital, 236 Neb. 1, 459 N.W.2d 178, 183 (1990), the plaintiffs alleged that the nursing staff should have altered the attending physician's orders if they had reason to believe they were wrong. The court disagreed, holding that " * * * hospital staff members lack authority to alter or depart from an attending physician's order for a hospital patient and lack authority to determine what is a proper course of medical treatment for a hospitalized patient. The foregoing is recognition of the realities and practicalities inherent in the physician-hospital nurse relationship."

In Schoening v. Grays Harbor Community Hospital, 40 Wash.App. 331, 698 P.2d 593 (1985), the plaintiff was treated in the emergency room for an infection. The plaintiff's expert, in his affidavit, wrote that the hospital should have been aware of "obvious negligence." The court held that where the care by the attending physician is questionable and the patient's condition is deteriorating, the hospital staff should have continuously monitored and observed the patient and sought additional evaluations. The court held that a fact question was raised by the expert's affidavit as to the hospital's duty to intervene.

2. *Darling* disclosed the prevailing attitude of hospital administrators toward affiliated doctors, reflecting the earlier concept of the doctor as independent contractor. The hospital administrator was subjected to a prolonged cross-examination by the plaintiff's attorney exploring his obligations to evaluate doctor training and conduct. The administrator testified:

"As the Board's representative, I did nothing to see that Dr. Alexander reviewed his operating techniques for the handling of broken bones. So far as I know, Dr. Alexander may not have reviewed his operating techniques since he was first licensed to practice in 1928. No examinations were ever given. I never asked questions of the doctor about this matter. The governing board, neither through me nor through any other designated administrative representative, ever checked up on the ability of Dr. Alexander as compared by medical text books. I had access at the hospital to some good orthopedic books. * * * Other than buying these books, I never made any effort to see that Dr. Alexander, or any other physician admitted to practice more than thirty years ago, read them." Darling v. Charleston Community Memorial Hosp., 50 Ill.App.2d 253, 295, 200 N.E.2d 149, 171 (1964).

How can a hospital administrator devise procedures to trigger an alarm when a physician is incompetent? Must the administrator himself be an M.D.? Can you think of methods that would have avoided the *Darling* tragedy? Consider the ideas developed by Leape in Chapter 1. What systems might you implement to prevent such errors?

In Albain v. Flower Hospital, 50 Ohio St.3d 251, 553 N.E.2d 1038, 1046 (1990), the Ohio Supreme Court recognized a hospital's independent duty to exercise due care in granting staff privileges and retaining competent physicians, but qualified the duty. The Court held that an act of physician malpractice does not create a presumption that the hospital negligently granted staff privileges, and that a hospital is not expected "to constantly supervise and second-guess the activities of its physicians, beyond the duty to remove a known incompetent. Most hospital administrators are laypersons with no medical training at all." They added: " * * * the hospital is not an *insurer* of the skills of physicians to whom it has granted staff privileges."

3. Some states by statute have adopted corporate negligence for institutional providers. Florida, for example, has by statute incorporated "institutional liability" or "corporate negligence" in its regulation of hospitals. Hospitals and other providers will be liable for injuries caused by inadequacies in the internal programs that are mandated by the statute. West's Fla.Stat.Ann. § 768.60.

THOMPSON v. NASON HOSP.

Supreme Court of Pennsylvania, 1991.
527 Pa. 330, 591 A.2d 703.

ZAPPALA, JUSTICE.

Allocatur was granted to examine the novel issue of whether a theory of corporate liability with respect to hospitals should be recognized in this Commonwealth. For the reasons set forth below, we adopt today the theory of corporate liability as it relates to hospitals. * * *

     * * *

Considering this predicate to our analysis, we now turn to the record which contains the facts underlying this personal injury action. At approximately 7 a.m. on March 16, 1978, Appellee, Linda A. Thompson, was involved in an automobile accident with a school bus. Mrs. Thompson was transported by ambulance from the accident scene to Nason Hospital's emergency room where she was admitted with head and leg injuries. The hospital's emergency room personnel were advised by Appellee, Donald A. Thompson, that his wife was taking the drug Coumadin, that she had a permanent pacemaker, and that she took other heart medications.

Subsequent to Mrs. Thompson's admission to Nason Hospital, Dr. Edward D. Schultz, a general practitioner who enjoyed staff privileges at Nason Hospital, entered the hospital via the emergency room to make his rounds. Although Dr. Schultz was not assigned duty in the emergency room, an on-duty hospital nurse asked him to attend Mrs. Thompson due to a prior physician-patient relationship. Dr. Schultz examined Mrs. Thompson and diagnosed her as suffering from multiple injuries including extensive lacerations over her left eye and the back of her scalp, constricted pupils, enlarged heart with a Grade III micro-systolic murmur, a brain concussion and amnesia. X-rays that were taken revealed fractures of the right tibia and right heel.

Following Dr. Schultz's examination and diagnosis, Dr. Larry Jones, an ophthalmologist, sutured the lacerations over Mrs. Thompson's left eye. It was during that time that Dr. Schultz consulted with Dr. Rao concerning orthopedic repairs. Dr. Rao advised conservative therapy until her critical medical condition improved.

Dr. Schultz knew Mrs. Thompson was suffering from rheumatic heart and mitral valve disease and was on anticoagulant therapy. Because he had no specific training in establishing dosages for such therapy, Dr. Schultz called Dr. Marvin H. Meisner, a cardiologist who was treating Mrs. Thompson with an anticoagulant therapy. Although Dr. Meisner was unavailable, Dr. Schultz did speak with Dr. Meisner's associate Dr. Steven P. Draskoczy.

Mrs. Thompson had remained in the emergency room during this time. Her condition, however, showed no sign of improvement. Due to both the multiple trauma received in the accident and her pre-existing heart disease, Dr. Schultz, as attending physician, admitted her to Nason Hospital's intensive care unit at 11:20 a.m.

The next morning at 8:30 a.m., Dr. Mark Paris, a general surgeon on staff at Nason Hospital, examined Mrs. Thompson. He found that she was unable to move her left foot and toes. It was also noted by Dr. Paris that the patient had a positive Babinski—a neurological sign of an intracerebral problem. Twelve hours later, Dr. Schultz examined Mrs. Thompson and found more bleeding in her eye. He also indicated in the progress notes that the problem with her left leg was that it was neurological.

On March 18, 1978, the third day of her hospitalization, Dr. Larry Jones, the ophthalmologist who treated her in the emergency room, examined her in the intensive care unit. He indicated in the progress notes an "increased hematuria secondary to anticoagulation. Right eye now involved". Dr. Schultz also examined Mrs. Thompson that day and noted the decreased movement of her left leg was neurologic. Dr. Paris's progress note that date approved the withholding of Coumadin and the continued use of Heparin.

The following day, Mrs. Thompson had complete paralysis of the left side. Upon examination by Dr. Schultz he questioned whether she needed to be under the care of a neurologist or needed to be watched there. At 10:30 a.m. that day, Dr. Schultz transferred her to the Hershey Medical Center because of her progressive neurological problem.

Linda Thompson underwent tests at the Hershey Medical Center. The results of the tests revealed that she had a large intracerebral hematoma in the right frontal temporal and parietal lobes of the brain. She was subsequently discharged on April 1, 1978, without regaining the motor function of her left side.

* * * The complaint alleged inter alia that Mrs. Thompson's injuries were the direct and proximate result of the negligence of Nason Hospital acting through its agents, servants and employees in failing to adequately examine and treat her, in failing to follow its rules relative to consultations and in failing to monitor her conditions during treatment. * * *

* * *

The first issue Nason Hospital raised is whether the Superior Court erred in adopting a theory of corporate liability with respect to a hospital. This issue had not heretofore been determined by the Court. Nason Hospital contends that it had no duty to observe, supervise or control the actual treatment of Linda Thompson.

Hospitals in the past enjoyed absolute immunity from tort liability. [ ] The basis of that immunity was the perception that hospitals functioned as charitable organizations. [ ] However, hospitals have evolved into highly sophisticated corporations operating primarily on a fee-for-service basis. The corporate hospital of today has assumed the role of a comprehensive health center with responsibility for arranging and coordinating the total health care of its patients. As a result of this metamorphosis, hospital immunity was eliminated. [ ]

Not surprisingly, the by-product of eliminating hospital immunity has been the filing of malpractice actions against hospitals. Courts have recognized several bases on which hospitals may be subject to liability including respondeat superior, ostensible agency and corporate negligence. [ ]

The development of hospital liability in this Commonwealth mirrored that which occurred in other jurisdictions. * * * We now turn our attention to the theory of corporate liability with respect to the hospital, which was first recognized in this Commonwealth by the court below.

Corporate negligence is a doctrine under which the hospital is liable if it fails to uphold the proper standard of care owed the patient, which is to ensure the patient's safety and well-being while at the hospital. This theory of liability creates a nondelegable duty which the hospital owes directly to a patient. Therefore, an injured party does not have to rely on and establish the negligence of a third party.

The hospital's duties have been classified into four general areas: (1) a duty to use reasonable care in the maintenance of safe and adequate facilities and equipment—Candler General Hospital Inc. v. Purvis, 123 Ga.App. 334, 181 S.E.2d 77 (1971); (2) a duty to select and retain only competent physicians—Johnson v. Misericordia Community Hospital, 99 Wis.2d 708, 301 N.W.2d 156 (1981); (3) a duty to oversee all persons who practice medicine within its walls as to patient care—Darling v. Charleston Community Memorial Hospital, *supra*.; and (4) a duty to formulate, adopt and enforce adequate rules and policies to ensure quality care for the patients—Wood v. Samaritan Institution, 26 Cal.2d 847, 161 P.2d 556 (Cal. Ct. App.1945). [ ]

Other jurisdictions have embraced this doctrine of corporate negligence or corporate liability such as to warrant it being called an "emerging trend". [ ]

* * *

Today, we take a step beyond the hospital's duty of care delineated in Riddle in full recognition of the corporate hospital's role in the total health care of its patients. In so doing, we adopt as a theory of hospital liability the doctrine of corporate negligence or corporate liability under which the hospital is liable if it fails to uphold the proper standard of care owed its patient. In addition, we fully embrace the aforementioned four categories of the hospital's duties. It is important to note that for a hospital to be charged with negligence, it is necessary to show that the hospital had actual or constructive knowledge of the defect or procedures which created the harm. [ ] Furthermore, the hospital's negligence must have been a substantial factor in bringing about the harm to the injured party. [ ].

* * *

It is well established that a hospital staff member or employee has a duty to recognize and report abnormalities in the treatment and condition of its patients. [ ] If the attending physician fails to act after being informed of such abnormalities, it is then incumbent upon the hospital staff member or employee to so advise the hospital authorities so that appropriate action might be taken. [ ] When there is a failure to report changes in a patient's condition and/or to question a physician's order which is not in accord with standard medical practice and the patient is injured as a result, the hospital will be liable for such negligence. [ ]

A thorough review of the record of this case convinces us that there is a sufficient question of material fact presented as to whether Nason Hospital was negligent in supervising the quality of the medical care Mrs. Thompson received, such that the trial court could not have properly granted summary judgment on the issue of corporate liability.

The order of Superior Court is affirmed. Jurisdiction is relinquished.

Notes and Questions

1. What does *Thompson* add to *Darling*'s discussion of the scope of corporate negligence? As you think about the typical's hospital's complexity in both its administrative and operational structure, where do you think liability should best be focused? On its physicians? On the hospital? Joint liability? Or something different?

Thompson combines duties that can be found in isolation in the caselaw of other jurisdictions. Consider the nature of these hospital duties: (1) a duty to use reasonable care in the maintenance of safe and adequate facilities and equipment; (2) a duty to select and retain only competent physicians; (3) a duty to oversee all persons who practice medicine within its walls as to patient care; and (4) a duty to formulate, adopt and enforce adequate rules and policies to ensure quality care for the patients. Duty 2, Selection and Retention of Competent Doctors, is the core obligation of hospitals, and in many jurisdictions, it is what is meant by corporate negligence. Probably the most important function of a hospital is to select high quality physicians for its medical staff. We will discuss this duty in the next section.

2. Duty 1, Maintenance of Safe Facilities and Equipment, is really an extension of common law obligations of all institutions that invite the public onto their property. It encompasses slip-and-fall cases, and all forms of injury that patients and visitors might suffer while in the hospital.

3. Duty 3, Supervision of All Who Practice Medicine in the Hospital, encompasses staff physicians and all other health professionals, acknowledging that modern medicine is a "team" operation. Courts increasingly recognize the team nature of medical practice in hospitals, and liability follows from this recognition. In Hoffman v. East Jefferson General Hospital, 778 So.2d 33 (La. App. 5 Cir. 2000), the plaintiff underwent two surgical procedures: a hysteroscopy with endometrial ablation and, while under the anesthesia, a laparoscopic cholecystostomy. The first procedure was performed vaginally and the second was abdominal. Plaintiff suffered severe burns on her buttocks during the operation as the result of the use of a speculum that had been sterilized and was too hot. The hospital would sterilize the instruments and provide the means for cool down. It was the responsibility of hospital employees to communicate the status of the equipment— whether it was sufficiently cooled down—to the doctor, but that the final decision

as to when to use the equipment was the doctor's. The court found that "the use of an instrument before it is sufficiently cooled after sterilization is a breach of the standard of care both for hospital employees and the doctor performing the surgery. There is also testimony that it is the responsibility of all members of the surgical team, whether hospital employees or independent doctors, to make sure the instruments are cool."

Institutional complexity requires accountability—a person in charge—often the attending physician in situations where residents are part of the care. In Lownsbury v. VanBuren, 94 Ohio St.3d 231, 762 N.E.2d 354 (2002), the parents sued a teaching hospital's attending physician for the injury to their adopted daughter who was born with severe brain damage, and for the prenatal care provided to the biological mother by the residents. The physician as supervising physician had a duty to be familiar with the patient's condition and to review a contract stress test by the end of his scheduled working day and formulate a plan of management. The test revealed fetal distress.

4. *Nason*'s Duty 4, "to formulate, adopt and enforce adequate rules and policies to ensure quality care for the patients", moves well beyond monitoring staff, drawing our scrutiny to how the institution operates as a system, and allowing plaintiffs to search for negligence in the very design of the operating framework of the hospital. In Hook v. Auriemma, 2005 WL 3737318 (Pa. Com. Pl. 2005), the plaintiff argued that after a colon surgery, she manifested signs and symptoms consistent with an abdominal infection from a bowel perforation, but was not transferred to the intensive care unit. The court allowed the suit to proceed on Thompson's fourth duty.

Hospitals need strong policies to ensure coordination among providers as a patient undergoes complex procedures. In Jennison v. Providence St. Vincent Medical Center, 174 Or.App. 219, 25 P.3d 358 (C.A. Oregon 2001), the plaintiff sued the hospital and physicians after she suffered severe brain injury while recovering from surgery. The Court of Appeals held that evidence supported specification that hospital was negligent in failing to have policies and procedures controlling verification of placement and use of central venous lines in hospital's post anesthesia care unit. The court wrote:

> The hospital had no policy or procedure regarding the followup on central lines placed in the OR when a patient is transferred to the PACU. The call from radiology could potentially go to one of five different people, depending on whom the radiologist decides to call. Furthermore, no written documentation was required once one of those people received the call from radiology, thus precluding other people from knowing whether the call was ever actually made. Hospital's policy and procedure required verification, but it did not control what happened thereafter.

Expert testimony is required to establish a corporate negligence claim, unless it involves simple issues such as structural defects within the common knowledge and experience of the jury. See generally Neff v. Johnson Memorial Hospital, 93 Conn.App. 534, 889 A.2d 921 (Conn.App. 2006) (noting the complexity of the staff credentialing process, and holding that plaintiff needed an expert to determine what the standard of care was for a hospital in allowing a physician with three malpractice cases in his history to be recredentialed).

5. Corporate liability can extend beyond hospitals to professional associations. In Battaglia v. Alexander, 177 S.W.3d 893 (Tex. 2005), the Texas Supreme Court held that a professional association comprised of anesthesiologists had direct liability for medical malpractice as to the acts of their physician-principals

and the nurse anesthetist employed by the association, as well as vicarious liability. During outpatient arthroscopic surgery on a patient's shoulder at TOPS Surgical Specialty Hospital, the patient was deprived of oxygen for from ten to fourteen minutes. He died fourteen days later. The evidence was that the associations were negligent and careless in retaining the nurse, who had not been evaluated once during seventeen years with the associations. She was neither competent nor knowledgeable in physiology or anesthesia, she failed to recognize the clear warning signs of oxygen deprivation, that she had failed to set alarms on the monitoring equipment to give a warning, she misplaced an esophageal stethoscope in the patient's lungs rather than the esophagus, and inserted the endotracheal tube too deeply into his lungs.

The hospital settled before trial, but it is clear that they would have been liable for corporate negligence, just as the professional association was. So the tendrils of liability reach vertically through the integrated delivery system to all who agree by contract to provide care.

2. *Negligent Credentialing*

CARTER v. HUCKS–FOLLISS

North Carolina Court of Appeals, 1998.
131 N.C.App. 145, 505 S.E.2d 177.

GREENE, JUDGE.

Tommy and Tracy Carter (collectively, Plaintiffs) appeal from the granting of Moore Regional Hospital's (Defendant) motion for summary judgment entered 26 June 1997.

On 20 August 1993, Dr. Anthony Hucks–Folliss (Dr. Hucks–Folliss) performed neck surgery on plaintiff Tommy Carter at Defendant. Dr. Hucks–Folliss is a neurosurgeon on the medical staff of Defendant. He first was granted surgical privileges by Defendant in 1975, and has been reviewed every two years hence to renew those privileges. Though he has been on Defendant's staff for over twenty years, Dr. Hucks–Folliss never has been certified by the American Board of Neurological Surgery. Presently, Dr. Hucks–Folliss is ineligible for board certification because he has taken and failed the certification examination on three different occasions.

The credentialing and re-credentialing of physicians at Defendant is designed to comply with standards promulgated by the Joint Commission on Accreditation of Healthcare Organizations (JCAHO). In 1992, the time when Dr. Hucks–Folliss was last re-credentialed by Defendant prior to the neck surgery performed on Tommy Carter, the JCAHO provided that board certification "is an excellent benchmark and is [to be] considered when delineating clinical privileges."

On the application filed by Dr. Hucks–Folliss, seeking to renew his surgical privileges with Defendant, he specifically stated, in response to a question on the application, that he was not board certified. Dr. James Barnes (Dr. Barnes), one of Plaintiffs' experts, presented an affidavit wherein he states that Defendant "does not appear [to have] ever considered the fact that Dr. Hucks–Folliss was not board certified, or that he had failed board exams three times," when renewing Dr. Hucks–Folliss's surgical privileges. Jean Hill (Ms. Hill), the manager of Medical Staff Services for Defendant, stated in her deposition that board certification was not an issue in the re-credentialing of active staff physicians. There is no dispute that Dr. Hucks–Folliss was on active staff in 1992. Additionally, this record does not reveal any further inquiry by Defendant into Dr. Hucks–Folliss's board certification status (beyond the question on the application).

In the complaint, it is alleged that Defendant was negligent: (1) in granting clinical privileges to Dr. Hucks–Folliss; (2) in failing to ascertain whether Dr. Hucks–Folliss was qualified to perform neurological surgery; and (3) in failing to enforce the standards of the JCAHO. It is further alleged that as a proximate result of Defendant's negligence, Tommy Carter agreed to allow Dr. Hucks–Folliss to perform surgery on him in Defendant. As a consequence of that surgery, Tommy Carter sustained "serious, permanent and painful injuries to his person including quadraparesis, scarring and other disfigurement."

The issue is whether a genuine issue of fact is presented on this record as to the negligence of Defendant in re-credentialing Dr. Hucks–Folliss.

Hospitals owe a duty of care to its patients to ascertain that a physician is qualified to perform surgery before granting that physician the privilege of conducting surgery in that hospital.[ ] In determining whether a hospital, accredited by the JCAHO, has breached its duty of care in ascertaining the qualifications of the physician to practice in the hospital, it is appropriate to consider whether the hospital has complied with standards promulgated by the JCAHO. Failure to comply with these standards "is some evidence of negligence."[ ]

In this case, Defendant has agreed to be bound by the standards promulgated by JCAHO and those standards provided in part that board certification was a factor to be "considered" when determining hospital privileges. Defendant argues that the evidence reveals unequivocally that it "considered," in re-credentialing Dr. Hucks–Folliss, the fact that he was not board certified. It points to the application submitted by Dr. Hucks–Folliss, specifically stating that he was not board certified, to support this argument. We disagree. Although this evidence does reveal that Defendant was aware of Dr. Hucks–Folliss's lack of certification, it does not follow that his lack of certification was considered as a factor in the re-credentialing decision. In any event, there is evidence from Dr. Barnes and Ms. Hill that supports a finding that Defendant did not consider Dr. Hucks–Folliss's lack of certification, or his failure to pass the certification test on three occasions, in assessing his qualifications to practice medicine in the hospital. This evidence presents a genuine issue of material fact and thus precludes the issuance of a summary judgment.[ ]

We also reject the alternative argument of Defendant that summary judgment is proper because there is no evidence that any breach of duty (in failing to consider Dr. Hucks–Folliss's lack of board certification prior to re-credentialing) by it was a proximate cause of the injuries sustained by Tommy Carter. Genuine issues of material fact are raised on this point as well. [ ].

Reversed and remanded.

Notes and Questions

1. The court considers Joint Commission (formerly JCAHO) standards as an important source of duties with regard to hospital credentialing, and failure to comply "some evidence of negligence".

2. Probably the most important function of a hospital is to select high quality physicians for its medical staff. A typical hospital has several categories of practicing physicians. The largest category is comprised of private physicians with staff privileges. These privileges include the right of the physicians to admit and discharge their private patients to the hospital and the right to use the hospital's facilities. Hospitals will also have physicians in training present, including interns, residents, and externs. Hospitals will often also have full-time salaried physicians, including teaching hospital faculty, and physicians under contract with the hospital to provide services for an agreed upon price. The hospital's governing board retains the ultimate responsibility for the quality of care provided, but their responsibility is normally delegated to the hospital staff, and discharged in practice by medical staff review committees. The organization and function of these committees in accredited hospitals are described in publications of the Joint Commission.

3. The requirement of staff self-governance under Joint Commission standards maintains and reinforces this physician authority within hospitals. But courts have found that the chief executive officer of a hospital and the governing board have the "inherent authority to summarily suspend clinical privileges to prevent an imminent danger to patients". See Lo v. Provena Covenant Medical Center, 342 Ill.App.3d 975, 277 Ill.Dec. 521, 796 N.E.2d 607, 614 (4 Dist. 2003).

4. The process by which the medical staff is selected is of crucial importance. A hospital has an obligation to its patients to investigate the qualifications of medical staff applicants. The Wisconsin Supreme Court elaborated on this obligation in Johnson v. Misericordia Community Hospital, 99 Wis.2d 708, 301 N.W.2d 156 (1981).

> In summary, we hold that a hospital owes a duty to its patients to exercise reasonable care in the selection of its medical staff and in granting specialized privileges. The final appointing authority resides in the hospital's governing body, although it must rely on the medical staff and in particular the credentials committee (or committee of the whole) to investigate and evaluate an applicant's qualifications for the requested privileges. However, this delegation of the responsibility to investigate and evaluate the professional competence of applicants for clinical privileges does not relieve the governing body of its duty to appoint only qualified physicians and surgeons to its medical staff and periodically monitor and review their competency. The credentials committee (or committee of the whole) must investigate the qualifications of applicants. The facts of this case demonstrate that a hospital should, at a minimum, require completion of the application and verify the accuracy of the applicant's statements, especially in regard to his medical education, training and experience. Additionally, it should: (1) solicit information from the applicant's peers, including those not referenced in his application, who are knowledgeable about his education, training, experience, health, competence and ethical character; (2) determine if the applicant is currently licensed to practice in this state and if his licensure or registration has been or is currently being challenged; and (3) inquire whether the applicant has been involved in any adverse malpractice action and whether he has experienced a loss of medical organization membership or medical privileges or

membership at any other hospital. The investigating committee must also evaluate the information gained through its inquiries and make a reasonable judgment as to the approval or denial of each application for staff privileges. The hospital will be charged with gaining and evaluating the knowledge that would have been acquired had it exercised ordinary care in investigating its medical staff applicants and the hospital's failure to exercise that degree of care, skill and judgment that is exercised by the average hospital in approving an applicant's request for privileges is negligence. This is not to say that hospitals are *insurers* of the competence of their medical staff, for a hospital will not be negligent if it exercises the noted standard of care in selecting its staff. Id. 174–75.

5. Hospitals are expected to investigate adverse information with regard to possible appointments or reappointments of medical staff. See Elam v. College Park Hospital, 132 Cal.App.3d 332, 183 Cal.Rptr. 156 (1982); Purcell v. Zimbelman, 18 Ariz.App. 75, 500 P.2d 335 (1972); Oehler v. Humana Inc., 105 Nev. 348, 775 P.2d 1271 (1989). A hospital should also suspend or otherwise restrict the clinical privileges of staff physicians who are incompetent to handle certain procedures. The hospital must also have proper procedures developed to detect impostors. Insinga v. LaBella, 543 So.2d 209 (Fla.1989) (non physician fraudulently obtained an appointment to the medical staff, after having assumed the name of a deceased Italian physician; the court applied corporate negligence.)

6. Federal law requires that hospital bylaws reflect the hospital governing board's responsibility to ensure that "... the medical staff is accountable to the governing body for the quality of care provided to patients." 42 C.F.R. § 482.12(a)(5)(2001). States typically also mandate that the governing board is responsible for the competence of the medical staff. See for example Lo v. Provena Covenant Medical Center, 342 Ill.App.3d 975, 277 Ill.Dec. 521, 796 N.E.2d 607, 614 (4 Dist. 2003) (holding that the hospital has an "inherent right to summarily suspend the clinical privileges of a physician whose continued practice poses an immediate danger to patients").

7. Under the Health Care Quality Improvement Act of 1986 (HCQIA), hospitals must check a national database maintained under contract with the Department of Health and Human Services, before a new staff appointment is made. This National Practitioner Data Bank contains information on individual physicians who have been disciplined, had malpractice claims filed against them, or had privileges revoked or limited. If the hospital fails to check the registry, it is held constructively to have knowledge of any information it might have gotten from the inquiry. See discussion of staff privileges in Chapter 12, *infra*.

The Data Bank has been criticized by the Government Accounting Office as having unreliable and incomplete data. See U.S. Government Accounting Office, National Practitioner Data Bank: Major Improvements are Needed to Enhance Data Bank's Reliability, *http://www.gao.gov.* Some health policy researchers have even suggested that the Data Bank should be abolished. See William M. Sage et al., Bridging the Relational–Regulatory Gap: A Pragmatic Information Policy for Patient Safety and Medical Malpractice, 59 Vand. L. Rev. 1263, 1307 (2006).

8. *Liability of Boards of Directors of Hospitals.* Most American hospitals are incorporated as non-profits under Section 501(c)(3) of the Internal Revenue Code. As such, the duties of non-profit boards of directors have been limited by comparison to for-profit corporations. Compliance programs in the nonprofit healthcare context are usually for the purpose of detecting and preventing fraud in accordance with federal and state anti-fraud laws. Corporate negligence might

apply to boards of trustees of hospitals, however, under the right set of circumstances. See e.g. Zambino v. Hospital of the University of Pennsylvania, Slip Copy, 2006 WL 2788217 (E.D.Pa.2006). The court noted that Pennsylvania courts "... have extended the doctrine of corporate liability to other entities in limited circumstances, such as when the patient is constrained in his or her choice of medical care options by the entity sued, and the entity controls the patient's total health care. See Shannon v. McNulty, 718 A.2d 828 (Pa.Super.1998) (extending doctrine to an HMO that provided health care services similar to a hospital); *Fox v. Horn,* 2000 WL 49374 (E.D.Pa. January 21, 2000) (Buckwalter, J.) (applying doctrine to a company that contracted to provide physicians and medical services at a prison where the plaintiff was incarcerated)." The court concluded:

> The plaintiffs are entitled to develop a factual record to support the applicability of this theory of liability to the various hospital entities or affiliates they named as defendants. They may be able to show that the trustees, health system or urologic practice group are hospital entities, in which case, the defendants concede, plaintiffs may bring a corporate negligence claim against them.

The corporate negligence argument is based on the duty of a Board of Directors of a non-profit hospital not only to detect and prevent fraud, but to detect and prevent patient injury. It doesn't seem like such a stretch in an era of revelations about failures of patient safety. The traditional board fiduciary duties of care and obedience can arguably include responsibility of nonprofit hospital directors to ensure that the hospital promotes health. This new interpretation blends the oversight obligations stemming from the duty of care with the duty of obedience requiring obedience with the laws.

The reform of hospital corporate governance focuses on overcoming the lack of accountability that is frequently identified with the nonprofit sector. Nonprofit directors are subject to fewer lawsuits than for-profit directors largely because nonprofit corporations have no shareholders. Furthermore, hospital directors are well insulated from personal liability because of state shield laws. These protections minimize the effect of increased penalties as a means to change behavior in the nonprofit sector. With the application of some aspects of Sarbanes–Oxley principles through state law and federal action to non-profits as well as for-profit boards, the argument becomes increasingly attractive. Two provisions of Sarbanes–Oxley apply directly to non-profit entities: (1) the whistleblower provision, which says that an organization can't fire an employee for reporting illegal activities involving a federal issue, and (2) the document retention provision, which requires organizations to keep and maintain documents after they become aware of an investigation. States have passed laws encouraging non-profit accountability to varying degrees over the past few years.

See Sarah Kaput, Expanding the Scope of Fidicuary Duties to Fill a Gap in the Law: The Role of NonProfit Hospital Directors to Ensure Patient Safety, 38 J. Health L. 95 (2005); Russell Massaro, Investing in Patient Safety: An Ethical and Business Imperative, 56 Trustee 20, 23 (Jun. 2003).

Problem: Cascading Errors

Carolyn Gadner was driving when her car on the highway when another car driven by Bob Sneed passed her, sideswiped her, ran her off the road, and drove off. Gadner caught up with Sneed and forced him to stop. She got out of her vehicle and started to walk to his car when he drove away. While Gadner was walking back to her car, Charles Otis struck her with his vehicle. Gadner was transported to Bay Hospital, a small rural hospital, where Dr. Dick Samson, a second-year pediatric resident, was the attending emergency room physician. Upon arriving at Bay, Gadner's skin was cool and clammy and her blood pressure was 95/55, indicative of shock. Gadner received 200 cc's per hour of fluid and was x-rayed. She actively requested a transfer because of vaginal bleeding. Nurse Gilbert voiced her own concerns about the need for a transfer to the other nurses in the emergency room. Dr. Samson did not order one.

Bay is a rural hospital and is not equipped to handle multiple trauma patients like Gadner. Bay had no protocol or procedure for making transfers to larger hospitals. Bay breached its own credentialing procedures in hiring a physician who lacked the necessary training, expertise, or demonstrated competence to work the ER. Dr. Bay, the hospital's chief of staff, had screened Samson, who was not properly evaluated before he was hired. A second-year pediatric resident is not normally assigned to an ER setting, give his lack of experience.

The nurses failed to notice that Gadner was in shock and that this failure was substandard. After they initially noted that she arrived with cool and clammy skin and a blood pressure of 95/55, they did not advise Dr. Samson that the patient was likely in shock; they failed to place her on IV fluids, elevate her feet above her head and give oxygen as needed. Dr. Samson ordered the administration of 500 cc's of fluid per hour, but Gadner received only about 200 cc's per hour because the IV infiltrated, delivering the fluid to the surrounding tissue instead of the vein. The nursing staff normally would discover infiltration and correct it. Scanty nurses' notes revealed that vital signs were not taken regularly, depriving Dr. Samson of critical and ongoing information about Gadner's condition. Nurse Gilbert administered Valium and morphine to Gadner, following Dr. Samson's orders, a mixture of drugs counter-indicated for a patient with symptoms of shock. Nurse Gilbert did not notice or protest.

Three hours after arriving at Bay, Gadner "coded" and Dr. Samson tried unsuccessfully to revive her. After she coded, Dr. Samson attempted to use the laryngoscope, following standard practice, but the one provided was broken. He then ordered epinephrine, but there was none in the ER. An autopsy was performed, and Gadner died of treatable shock according to the coroner.

Consider the various theories of liability available to the plaintiff. Then develop a plan to improve the hospital from a patient safety perspective so that this kind of disaster will not happen again.

3.   *Peer Review Immunity and Corporate Negligence*

Credentialing decisions may be the central feature of corporate negligence claims, but such decisions are often the most difficult to prove. Virtually all American jurisdictions have peer review immunity statutes that block access to hospital decision making about physician problems that have been discovered.

LARSON v. WASEMILLER

Supreme Court of Minnesota, 2007.
738 N.W.2d 300.

OPINION

HANSON, JUSTICE.

Appellants Mary and Michael Larson commenced this medical malpractice claim against respondent Dr. James Wasemiller, Dr. Paul Wasemiller and the Dakota Clinic for negligence in connection with the performance of gastric bypass surgery on Mary Larson. The Larsons also joined respondent St. Francis Medical Center as a defendant, claiming, among other things, that St. Francis was negligent in granting surgery privileges to Dr. James Wasemiller. St. Francis then moved to dismiss for failure to state a claim. The district court denied the motion to dismiss, holding that Minnesota does recognize a claim for negligent credentialing, but certified two questions to the court of appeals. The court of appeals reversed the district court's denial of the motion to dismiss, holding that Minnesota does not recognize a common-law cause of action for negligent credentialing. [ ] We reverse and remand to the district court for further proceedings.

In April 2002, Dr. James Wasemiller, with the assistance of his brother, Dr. Paul Wasemiller, performed gastric bypass surgery on Mary Larson at St. Francis Medical Center in Breckenridge, Minnesota. Larson experienced complications following the surgery, and Dr. Paul Wasemiller performed a second surgery on April 12, 2002 to address the complications. On April 22, 2002, after being moved to a long-term care facility, Larson was transferred to MeritCare Hospital for emergency surgery. Larson remained hospitalized until June 28, 2002.

The Larsons claim that St. Francis was negligent in credentialing Dr. James P. Wasemiller. Credentialing decisions determine which physicians are granted hospital privileges and what specific procedures they can perform in the hospital. *See* Craig W. Dallon, Understanding Judicial Review of Hospitals' Physician Credentialing and Peer Review Decisions, 73 Temp. L.Rev. 597, 598 (2000). The granting of hospital privileges normally does not create an employment relationship with the hospital, but it allows physicians access to the hospital's facilities and imposes certain professional standards. [ ]. The decision to grant hospital privileges to a physician is made by the hospital's governing body based on the recommendations of the credentials committee. A credentials committee is a type of peer review committee. Minnesota, like most other states, has a peer review statute that provides for the confidentiality of peer review proceedings and grants some immunity to those involved in the credentialing process. [ ].

The district court noted that the majority of courts in other jurisdictions have recognized a duty on the part of hospitals to exercise reasonable care in granting privileges to physicians to practice medicine at the hospital. The court also noted that the existence of such a duty is objectively reasonable and consistent with public policy. The court therefore held that Minnesota "will and does recognize, at common law, a professional tort against hospitals and review organizations for negligent credentialing/privileging."

After denying St. Francis' motion to dismiss, the district court certified the following two questions to the court of appeals:

A.   Does the state of Minnesota recognize a common law cause of action of privileging of a physician against a hospital or other review organization?

B.   Does Minn.Stat. §§ 145.63–145.64 grant immunity from or otherwise limit liability of a hospital or other review organization for a claim of negligent credentialing/privileging of a physician?

* * *

A.   Does Minnesota's peer review statute create a cause of action for negligent credentialing?

We consider, first, whether the language of the peer review statute actually creates a cause of action for negligent credentialing. Section 145.63, subd. 1, provides that

> *No review organization and no person shall be liable for damages* or other relief in any action by reason of the performance of the review organization or person of any duty, function, or activity as a review organization or a member of a review committee or by reason of any recommendation or action of the review committee *when the person acts in the reasonable belief that the action or recommendation is warranted by facts known to the person or the review organization after reasonable efforts to ascertain the facts upon which the review organization's action or recommendation is made* * * *.

(emphasis added.) The legislature has the authority to create a cause of action for negligent credentialing. The question is whether section 145.63, subdivision 1, expresses an intent to do so.

Although stated in the negative, the language of this statute implies that a review organization shall be liable for granting privileges where the grant is not reasonably based on the facts that were known or that could have been known by reasonable efforts. This language could be read as evidencing the legislative intent to establish such a cause of action, whether or not one existed at common law.

We agree with the Larsons that the immunity provision of the peer review statute contemplates the existence of a cause of action for negligent credentialing—otherwise there would be no need for the legislature to address the standard of care applicable to such an action. But we are reluctant to conclude that the statute affirmatively creates such a cause of action because the standard of care is stated in the negative.

Ultimately, we need not determine whether the statute creates a cause of action because, at the very least, the statute does not negate or abrogate such a cause of action and this leaves us free to consider whether the cause of action exists at common law.

B.   Is there a common law cause of action for negligent credentialing?

In deciding whether to recognize a common law tort, this court looks to (1) whether the tort is inherent in, or the natural extension of, a well-established common law right, (2) whether the tort has been recognized in other common law states, (3) whether recognition of a cause of action will create tension with other applicable laws, and (4) whether such tension is outweighed by the importance of the additional protections that recognition of the claim would provide to injured persons. [ ] See Wal–Mart Stores, 582 N.W.2d at 234–36 (joining the majority of states that recognize the tort of invasion of privacy as inherent in property, contract and liberty rights, but declining to recognize the tort of false light because it would increase the tension between tort law and constitutional free speech guaranties).

    1.   Is the tort of negligent credentialing inherent in, or the natural extension of, a well-established common law right?

* * *

* * * [w]e have recognized that hospitals owe a duty of care directly to patients to protect them from harm by third persons. In *Sylvester v. Northwestern Hospital of Minneapolis*, we held that a hospital had a duty to protect a patient from another intoxicated patient. [ ]. We quoted from the Restatement of Torts § 320 (1934) as follows:

> One who * * * voluntarily takes the custody of another under circumstances such as to deprive the other of his normal power of self-protection or to subject him to association with persons likely to harm him, is under a duty of exercising reasonable care so to control the conduct of third persons as to prevent them from intentionally harming the other or so conducting themselves as to create an unreasonable risk of harm to him, if the actor,
>
> > (a) knows or has reason to know that he has the ability to control the conduct of the third persons, and
> >
> > (b) knows or should know of the necessity and opportunity for exercising such control.

* * *

Two other generally recognized common law torts also support recognition of the tort of negligent credentialing. The claim of negligent credentialing is analogous to a claim of negligent hiring of an employee, which has been recognized in Minnesota.[ ] *See also* Restatement (Second) of Agency § 213 (1958) ("A person conducting an activity through servants or other agents is subject to liability for harm resulting from his conduct if he is negligent or reckless * * * in the employment of improper persons or instrumentalities in work involving risk of harm to others * * *."). Some jurisdictions that recognize the tort of negligent credentialing do so as a natural extension of the tort of negligent hiring. [ ].

The tort of negligent credentialing is perhaps even more directly related to the tort of negligent selection of an independent contractor, which has been recognized in the Restatement of Torts to exist under certain circumstances. The Restatement (Second) of Torts § 411 (1965) provides that

> An employer is subject to liability for physical harm to third persons caused by his failure to exercise reasonable care to employ a competent and careful contractor
>
> > (a) to do work which will involve a risk of physical harm unless it is skillfully and carefully done, or
> >
> > (b) to perform any duty which the employer owes to third persons.

Although we have not specifically adopted this tort, we have frequently relied on the Restatement of Torts to guide our development of tort law in areas that we have not previously had an opportunity to address. [ ] Some of the courts that have recognized the tort of negligent credentialing do so as an application of the tort of negligent selection of an independent contractor.[ ].

Given our previous recognition of a hospital's duty of care to protect its patients from harm by third persons and of the analogous tort of negligent hiring, and given the general acceptance in the common law of the tort of negligent selection of an independent contractor, as recognized by the Restatement of Torts, we conclude that the tort of negligent credentialing is inherent in and the natural extension of well-established common law rights.

> *2.   Is the tort of negligent credentialing recognized as a common law tort by a majority of other common law states?*

At least 27 states recognize the tort of negligent credentialing, [ ] and at least three additional states recognize the broader theory of corporate negligence, even though they have not specifically identified negligent credentialing. In fact, only two courts that have considered the claim of negligent credentialing have outright rejected it.[5] The Larsons argue that this broad recognition of the claim evidences a national consensus that hospitals owe a common law duty to patients to exercise reasonable care when making privileging decision.

The decisions of other states that recognize the tort of negligent credentialing rely on various rationales, which essentially fall into the following groups.

Direct or Corporate Negligence

Some courts have recognized the tort of negligent credentialing as simply the application of broad common law principles of negligence. [ ]

In *Pedroza v. Bryant,* the Washington Supreme Court explained the policy reasons for adopting the theory of corporate negligence.

> The doctrine of corporate negligence reflects the public's perception of the modern hospital as a multifaceted health care facility responsible for the quality of medical care and treatment rendered. The community hospital has evolved into a corporate institution, assuming "the role of a comprehensive health center ultimately responsible for arranging and coordinating total health care."

* * *

Duty of Care for Patient Safety

Some courts have considered the tort of negligent credentialing to be an extension of previous decisions that hospitals have a duty to exercise ordinary care and attention for the safety of their patients. [ ]

Negligent Hiring

Some courts view the tort of negligent credentialing as the natural extension of the tort of negligent hiring. [ ]

---

5. See Svindland v. A.I. DuPont Hosp. for Children of Nemours Found., No. 05–0417, 2006 WL 3209953, * 3–4 (E.D.Pa. Nov.3, 2006) (holding that a claim of negligent credentialing is precluded by Delaware's peer review statute); McVay v. Rich, 255 Kan. 371, 874 P.2d 641, 645 (1994) (finding an express statutory bar to a claim of negligent credentialing). See also Gafner v. Down East Cmty. Hosp., 735 A.2d 969, 979 (Me.1999) (refusing to recognize a claim of corporate negligence for the hospital's failure to adopt policies controlling the actions of independent physicians).

Negligent Selection of Independent Contractors

Some courts have relied on the "well-established principle" that an employer must exercise reasonable care in the selection of a competent independent contractor, as outlined in Restatement (Second) of Torts § 411. [ ] In *Albain,* the court concluded that in a hospital setting, this rule "translates into a duty by the hospital only to grant and to continue staff privileges of the hospital to competent physicians."[ ] The court also noted that a physician's negligence does not automatically mean that the hospital is liable, rather, a plaintiff must demonstrate that but for the hospital's failure to exercise due care in granting staff privileges, the plaintiff would not have been injured. [ ].

Courts that have allowed claims for negligent credentialing have, either implicitly or explicitly, held that such claims are unrelated to the concept of derivative or vicarious liability. [ ]

We conclude that the tort of negligent credentialing is recognized as a common law tort by a substantial majority of the other common law states.

> 3. Would the tort of negligent credentialing conflict with Minnesota's peer review statute?

* * *

The Confidentiality Provision

The confidentiality provision of the peer review statute provides in part that

> [D]ata and information acquired by a review organization, in the exercise of its duties and functions, or by an individual or other entity acting at the direction of a review organization, shall be held in confidence, shall not be disclosed to anyone except to the extent necessary to carry out one or more of the purposes of the review organization, and shall not be subject to subpoena or discovery. No person described in section 145.63 shall disclose what transpired at a meeting of a review organization except to the extent necessary to carry out one or more of the purposes of a review organization. The proceedings and records of a review organization shall not be subject to discovery or introduction into evidence in any civil action against a professional arising out of the matter or matters which are the subject of consideration by the review organization.

[ ]. Credentialing committees are "review organizations" under the statutory definition. [ ]. Any unauthorized disclosure of the above information is a misdemeanor.[ ].

* * *

St. Francis' interpretation of the common law claim is too narrow because negligence could be shown on the basis of what was actually known or what *should have been known* at the time of the credentialing decision. [ ]. And Minnesota's confidentiality provision recognizes this broader concept, and addresses the problems of proof, by providing that

> [i]nformation, documents or records otherwise available from original sources shall not be immune from discovery or use in any civil action

merely because they were presented during proceedings of a review organization, nor shall any person who testified before a review organization or who is a member of it be prevented from testifying as to matters within the person's knowledge, but a witness cannot be asked about the witness' testimony before a review organization or opinions formed by the witness as a result of its hearings. [ ].

Thus, although section 145.64, subdivision 1 would prevent hospitals from disclosing the fact that certain information was considered by the credentials committee, it would not prevent hospitals from introducing the same information, as long as it could be obtained from original sources. In this respect, the confidentiality provision may provide a greater advantage to hospitals than to patients because a hospital knows what information it actually considered and why it granted privileges and it may emphasize the information that most strongly supports its decision. The difficulty of proof may fall most heavily on the patients because the effect of the statute is to preclude the discovery of what evidence was actually obtained by the hospital in the credentialing process, and the patients bear the burden of proof on negligence.

* * *

Although the confidentiality provision of Minnesota's peer review statute may make the proof of a common law negligent-credentialing claim more complicated, we conclude that it does not preclude such a claim.

The Limited Liability Provision

Minn.Stat. § 145.63, subd. 1 (2006) provides some immunity from liability, both for individual credentials committee members and hospitals, for claims brought by either a physician or a patient. Section 145.63, subdivision 1 provides that

No review organization and no person who is a member or employee, director, or officer of, who acts in an advisory capacity to, or who furnishes counsel or services to, a review organization shall be liable for damages or other relief in any action brought by a person or persons whose activities have been or are being scrutinized or reviewed by a review organization, by reason of the performance by the person of any duty, function, or activity of such review organization, unless the performance of such duty, function or activity was motivated by malice toward the person affected thereby. No review organization and no person shall be liable for damages or other relief in any action by reason of the performance of the review organization or person of any duty, function, or activity as a review organization or a member of a review committee or by reason of any recommendation or action of the review committee when the person acts in the reasonable belief that the action or recommendation is warranted by facts known to the person or the review organization after reasonable efforts to ascertain the facts upon which the review organization's action or recommendation is made.

* * *

Under the rules of statutory construction generally recognized by this court, a statute will not be construed to abrogate a common law right unless it does so expressly. [ ]. Although the plain language of the second sentence of section 145.63 does limit the liability of hospitals and credentials committees, it in no way indicates intent to immunize hospitals, or to abrogate a common law claim for negligent credentialing. In fact, read in conjunction with the evidentiary and discovery restrictions of section 145.64, the statutory scheme suggests that civil actions for credentialing decisions are indeed contemplated. If the legislature had intended to foreclose the possibility of a cause of action for negligent credentialing, it would not have addressed the standard of care applicable to such an action.

* * *

We conclude that the liability provisions of section 145.63 do not materially alter the common law standard of care and that, although the confidentiality provisions of section 145.64 present some obstacles in both proving and defending a claim of negligent credentialing, they do not preclude such a claim.

> 4. Do the policy considerations in favor of the tort of negligent credentialing outweigh any tension caused by conflict with the peer review statute?

The function of peer review is to provide critical analysis of the competence and performance of physicians and other health care providers in order to decrease incidents of malpractice and to improve quality of patient care. [ ] This court has held that the purpose of Minnesota's peer review statute is to promote the strong public interest in improving health care by granting certain protections to medical review organizations,[ ] and to encourage the medical profession to police its own activities with minimal judicial interference,[ ]. This court has also recognized that "the quality of patient care could be compromised if fellow professionals are reluctant to participate fully in peer review activities."[ ].

* * *

We recognize that a claim of negligent credentialing raises questions about the necessity of a bifurcated trial and the scope of the confidentiality and immunity provisions of the peer review statute. We likewise recognize that there is an issue about whether a patient must first prove negligence on the part of a physician before a hospital can be liable for negligently credentialing the physician. But, in part, these are questions of trial management that are best left to the trial judge. [ ] Further, they cannot be effectively addressed in the context of this Rule 12 motion.

We conclude that the policy considerations underlying the tort of negligent credentialing outweigh the policy considerations reflected in the peer review statute because the latter policy considerations are adequately addressed by the preclusion of access to the confidential peer review materials. We therefore hold that a claim of negligent credentialing does exist in Minnesota, and is not precluded by Minnesota's peer review statute. We reverse the answer of the court of appeals to the first certified question, answer that question in the affirmative, and remand to the district court for further proceedings consistent with this opinion.

The Larsons also challenge dicta in the court of appeals opinion, noting that the confidentiality provisions of the peer review statute may present due process issues in the trial of a negligent-credentialing claim. But because we have concluded that the confidentiality provisions of the peer review statute do not preclude the presentation of evidence in defense of a negligent-credentialing claim, we conclude that the confidentiality provision is not facially unconstitutional. We leave for another day the question of whether circumstances might arise that would render the provision unconstitutional as applied.

Reversed and remanded.

Notes and Questions

1. *Larsen* follows the majority view that a hospital can be negligent for a credentialing decision. The decision provides a careful overview of the law in other states and the rationale for a negligent credentialing decision. Will there be a negative effect on peer review activities in hospitals? What kinds of force align to promote strong peer review activities? What forces resist such review?

2. *Larsen* acknowledges the tension between peer review immunity statutes and corporate negligence theories. As the court noted, Delaware has concluded that a corporate negligence action may not exist in Delaware absent a showing of malice, in light of strong language of the statute and its interpretation by the Delaware courts. See Svindland v. A.I. DuPont Hosp. for Children of Nemours Foundation, 2006 WL 3209953 (E.D.Pa. 2006).

3. Florida, by Amendment 7 of the Florida constitution, appears to remove any immunity whatsoever, making relevant hospital committee decisions discoverable, although the work-product and attorney-client privileges still remain. Amendment 7 to the Florida constitution gives citizens injured by a health care provider full access to medical records of all providers. On November 2, 2004, the voters of Florida passed Amendment 7, which had been sponsored by the Academy of Florida Trial Lawyers. Amendment 7 created a constitutional right for persons to have access to records. Amendment 7 provides:

§ 25.   Patients' right to know about adverse medical incidents.

(a) In addition to any other similar rights provided herein or by general law, patients have a right to have access to any records made or received in the course of business by a health care facility or provider relating to any adverse medical incident.

* * *

The Florida Court of Appeals in Florida Hospital Waterman, Inc. v. Buster, 932 So.2d 344 (2006), held that " * * * Amendment 7 preempts the statutory privileges afforded health care providers regarding their self-policing procedures to the extent that such information is obtainable through a formal discovery request made by a patient or a patient's legal representative during the course of litigation."

4. *Hospital Committee Proceedings.* Plaintiffs in malpractice actions frequently seek discovery of the proceedings of hospital quality assurance committees, as the problem above illustrates. They may request production of a committee's minutes or reports, propound interrogatories about the committee process or outcome, or ask to depose committee members concerning committee deliberations. If the plaintiff is suing a health care professional whose work was reviewed

by the committee, the discovery may seek to confirm the negligence of the professional or to uncover additional evidence substantiating the plaintiff's claim. If the suit is against the hospital on a theory of corporate liability (i.e., claiming that the hospital itself was negligent in appointing or failing to supervise a professional), evidence of committee proceedings may prove vital to establishing the hospital's liability.

Statutes protecting committee proceedings from discovery are often subject to exceptions, either explicitly or through judicial interpretation. One common exception affords discovery to physicians challenging the results of committee action against them. Thus a physician whose staff privileges were revoked may discover information from the credentialing committee, Schulz v. Superior Court, 66 Cal.App.3d 440, 446, 136 Cal.Rptr. 67, 70 (1977). This seems to be required by notions of fair process.

5. *Hospital Incident Reports.* When a plaintiff seeks discovery of incident reports rather than committee proceedings, policy considerations are somewhat different. Hospitals have greater incentives to investigate untoward events than they have to carry on continuing quality review, and are less dependent on voluntary participation. The incident report would usually be more directly relevant to a single claim for malpractice than would general committee investigations. Possibly for these reasons, immunity statutes that protect committee proceedings less often protect incident reports, and courts have been less willing to immunize incident reports from discovery. On the other hand, since incident reports are more directly related to litigation of specific mishaps, two privileges can be asserted to protect them that would seldom apply to committee proceedings: the work product immunity and attorney client privilege.

The work product immunity protects materials prepared in anticipation of litigation. See Federal Rules of Civil Procedure 56. Courts look to the nature and purpose of incident reports. If they are regularly prepared and distributed for future loss prevention, they are not considered to be documents prepared in anticipation of litigation so as to invoke application of the work product exception to discovery. See St. Louis Little Rock Hospital, Inc. v. Gaertner, 682 S.W.2d 146, 150–51 (Mo.App.1984).

How would the result of data mining fit within this doctrine? The hospital may undertake a general search using data mining without a clear expectation of what if any problems they will find. The purpose is general adverse event detection and error reduction, and the results can hardly be argued to be prepared in anticipation of litigation.

6. *Attorney-client privilege.* This privilege protects communications, even if the attorney is not yet representing a client, provided that the communication was made between the client as an insured to his liability insuror during the course of an existing insured-insuror relationship. To be privileged, a communication between a client and his attorney, or between an insured and his insuror, must be within the context of the attorney-client relationship, with a purpose of securing legal advice from the client's attorney. The St. Luke Hospitals, Inc. v. Kopowski, 160 S.W.3d 771 (Kentucky 2005) (communications by two nurses about the post-delivery care of an infant who died at the hospital, to the officer in charge of risk management, who had conducted the interviews of the nurses at the direction of the hospital's attorney. Held protected by the privilege.)

Problem: Proctoring Peers

You have been asked by Hilldale Adventist Hospital to advise it on the implications of its use of proctors for assessing candidates for medical staff privileges. The hospital has used Dr. Hook, a surgeon certified by the American Board of Orthopedic Surgery, as a proctor during two different operations on the plaintiff at two different hospitals during the process of evaluation of Dr. Frank DiBianco for staff privileges. Dr. Hook had been asked to observe ten surgeries by Dr. DiBianco and then file a report. He observed an operation on the plaintiff during one of these observations. Two months later, he was again asked to proctor Dr. DiBianco at another hospital, and he again observed a procedure on the plaintiff. Prior to each procedure, Dr. Hook had reviewed the x-rays and discussed the operative plan, but he otherwise had taken no part in the care and treatment of the plaintiff. He did not participate in the operations, did not scrub in, and always observed from outside the "sterile field". He got no payment for his proctoring efforts, and he had never met the plaintiff nor had any other contact with her.

Can Hilldale be liable for its use of Dr. Hook as a proctor? Can Dr. Hook be directly liable for failing to stop negligent work by Dr. DiBianco?

Problem: The "Love" Surgeon

You have recently been contacted by Ms. Helen Brown as to the merits of a suit against Drs. Ruth and Blue, physicians on staff at St. Helen's Medical Center (SHMC). Ms. Brown had gone to Dr. Blue, a urologist, for bladder infections and difficulties she experienced voiding urine. Blue performed surgery upon Brown but her condition failed to improve. She began to complain of constant bladder pain and of pain during sexual relations with her husband. Blue then referred her to Dr. Ruth for "exploratory pelvic laparotomy with lysis" and "vaginoplasty."

Dr. Ruth met with Brown prior to surgery. He explained to Brown that the pain she experienced during sexual relations was caused by her husband's penis striking her bladder. Ruth explained that he and Dr. Blue would perform surgery to place her bladder upon a "pedestal," and that this procedure would correct her problems voiding urine and alleviate the pain she suffered during intercourse. Ruth also indicated that he would do some "cosmetic things" to improve Brown's sex life.

Ruth and Blue had staff privileges at St. Helen's Medical Center (SHMC). The hospital required that a form letter be given by Dr. Ruth to each of his patients prior to the surgical procedures he did to Ms. Brown. The form letter, which bears the SHMC letterhead, stated:

"Dear Patient:

"The Executive Committee of the Medical Staff of St. Elizabeth Medical Center wishes to inform you that the 'female coital area reconstruction' surgery you are about to undergo is:

"1. Not documented by ordinary standards of scientific reporting and publication.

"2. Not a generally accepted procedure.

"3. As yet not duplicated by other investigators.

"4. Detailed only in non-scientific literature.

"You should be informed that the Executive Committee of the Medical Staff considers the aforementioned procedure an unproven, non-standard practice of gynecology."

Drs. Ruth and Blue performed "vaginal reconstruction surgery" upon Brown at SHMC, purportedly to correct her painful bladder condition. The surgery actually performed upon Brown consisted of an exploratory pelvic laparotomy, vaginal reconstruction, circumcision of the clitoris and insertion of a urinary catheter. The vaginal reconstruction consisted of, among other things, a redirection and elongation of her vagina.

Brown has told you that after her "love surgery," she continued to suffer from bladder infections and developed problems with urinary incontinence. Her bladder infections after the surgery were more frequent than before. Following the surgery, Brown could not engage in sexual relations without extreme pain and difficulties. At some point, she also began to develop severe kidney problems. She underwent further surgery to correct her problems, with the final surgery removing her right kidney. She continued to suffer bladder infections, difficulties voiding, problems during sexual intercourse, and periods of urinary incontinence. She also developed bowel problems sometime during her treatment with Ruth and Blue. She was told by a gynecologist two months before she came to your office that the surgery performed upon her could not be corrected, and that Dr. Ruth "had cut away everything."

Consider any theories you might develop against the hospital in a malpractice action.

What if the process by which a hospital evaluates the credentials of a physician for staff privileges fails?

KADLEC MEDICAL CENTER v. LAKEVIEW ANESTHESIA ASSOCIATES

Eastern District of Louisiana, 2005.
2005 WL 1309153.

This lawsuit arises from statements or omissions made or omitted by defendants, LRMC, Louisiana Anesthesia Associates, L.L.C., and Doctors Dennis, Preau, Parr and Baldone, in professional reference letters or credentialing letters written on behalf of Dr. Robert Lee Berry. Dr. Berry practiced anesthesiology at LRMC in Covington, Louisiana from January, 1997, to March, 2001. During that time, Dr. Berry was an employee of Lakeview Anesthesia Associates, L.L.C. ("LAA") and, ultimately, he became a shareholder of LAA with defendants Drs. Dennis, Preau, Baldone, and Parr. Kadlec alleges that at some point during the year 2000, LRMC conducted an audit of Dr. Berry's narcotic medication records and discovered that he had failed to properly document withdrawals of the drug Demerol.

On March 13, 2001, Dr. Berry failed to respond to hospital pages during a 24–hour shift at LRMC. Kadlec alleges that hospital staff found Dr. Berry sleeping in a chair and that he "appeared to be sedated." Apparently in response to this incident and based on suspicions that Dr. Berry was diverting Demerol, LAA terminated Dr. Berry's employment effective that day. Dr. Berry's staff privileges at LRMC subsequently expired.

Following his termination from LAA, Dr. Berry sought employment through Staff Care, Inc., a temporary employment agency for medical professionals. Staff Care ultimately placed Dr. Berry at Kadlec Medical Center in Richland, Washington. Before Dr. Berry started practicing medicine in Washington, Kadlec sent a letter to LRMC requesting, among other things, (1) "evidence of current competence to perform the privileges requested" and (2) "a candid evaluation of [Dr. Berry's] training, continuing clinical performance, skill, and judgment, interpersonal skills and ability to perform the privileges requested." Kadlec included an "Appointment Reference Questionnaire" with the request for information. The questionnaire provided a fill-in-the-blank form which asked specific questions that the medical center wanted answered.

On October 26, 2001, in response to Kadlec's inquiry, LRMC sent Kadlec a brief letter which stated that Dr. Berry was on the active medical staff in the field of anesthesiology at LRMC from March 4, 1997 to September 4, 2001. The letter represented that such limited information was provided "due to the large volume of inquiries received in the office." LRMC admits that it did not answer any of the questions on the enclosed questionnaire, but says that this type of response was part of its standard business practice in responding to such inquiries.

Based in part on the information contained in the letter from LRMC and two other letters of recommendation written by Drs. Dennis and Preau, Kadlec retained Dr. Berry's services through Staff Care in late 2001. About a year later, Dr. Berry was the anesthesiologist for a tubal ligation surgery performed at Kadlec. The patient, Ms. Jones, suffered extensive brain damage and has remained in a non-responsive state since the surgery, allegedly due to Dr. Berry's gross negligence and the fact that he was impaired by drugs during the surgery.

The family of the injured patient sued Dr. Berry and Kadlec, as Dr. Berry's employer, in Washington for medical malpractice. Kadlec claims that during discovery in that case, it learned that LAA had terminated Dr. Berry "with cause" in 2001. Kaldec ultimately settled the medical malpractice lawsuit for $7.5 million. After the settlement, Kadlec filed this lawsuit against LRMC, LAA, and Drs. Dennis, Preau, Parr, and Baldone.

* * *

Plaintiffs, Kadlec Medical Center and Western Professional Insurance Company, assert claims against LRMC for intentional misrepresentation, negligent misrepresentation, strict responsibility misrepresentation, and negligence based on LRMC's alleged omission of material facts in a letter representing Dr. Berry's term of service at LRMC. When a federal court exercises diversity jurisdiction pursuant to 28 U.S.C. § 1332, the court must apply the substantive law of the forum state.[ ]

Accordingly, under Louisiana law, in order to prevail on a claim for negligent misrepresentation, a plaintiff must establish the following elements: 1) the defendant, in the course of its business or other matters in which it had a pecuniary interest, supplied false information; 2) the defendant had a legal duty to supply correct information to the plaintiff; 3) the defendant breached its duty, which can be breached by omission as well as by affirmative misrepresentation; and 4) the plaintiff suffered damages or pecuniary loss as a result of its justifiable reliance upon the omission or affirmative misrepresentation.[ ]. The elements of a claim for intentional misrepresentation are similar: 1) a misrepresentation of a material fact, 2) made with intent to deceive, and 3) causing justifiable reliance with resultant injury.[ ].

[The court relied on Section 552(1) of the Restatement (Second) of Torts:

> One who, in the course of his business, profession or employment, or in any other transaction in which he has a pecuniary interest, supplies false information for the guidance of others in their business transactions, is subject to liability for pecuniary loss caused to them by their justifiable reliance upon the information, if he fails to exercise reasonable care or competence in obtaining or communicating the information.

The court found adequate pecuniary interest. It noted that the defendant hospital LRMC omitted the information at issue because of a fear of liability to Dr. Berry for defamation and other causes of action based on disclosure. It also had a pecuniary interest in responding to credentialing inquiries, since a failure to respond would have create difficulty in recruiting and retaining physicians. The court noted that "[d]octors might want to avoid working at a medical facility which was unresponsive to requests for employment information, potentially foreclosing the possibility that those doctors could gain future employment elsewhere. Likewise, other health care providers could become unwilling to supply references to LRMC while their own inquiries went unanswered." The court also observed that the defendant might also have had a "pecuniary interest in avoiding public disclosure of information that Dr. Berry had been practicing medicine while impaired as such disclosure could have presented a risk of lawsuits by Dr. Berry's surgical patients." The court denied the defendant's request for summary judgment.]

Notes and Questions

1. The duty articulated in *Kadlec* does not give a remedy to third parties directly injured by a failure to warn, but it does create a fund for the hospital who ends up paying a judgment for injuries caused by a negligent physician in some situations.

The responsibility of a hospital for actions of either its staff physicians or employees is generally limited to acts occurring in the hospital while they are working. Failures to protect third parties outside the hospital are carefully limited to situations where others have specifically relied on statements and actions of the hospital. Pedroza v. Bryant, 101 Wash.2d 226, 677 P.2d 166 (1984). The *Tarasoff*-type of case, where a patient poses a risk of harm to others, may also impose liability on the institution as well as a treating physician, where the institution had a duty to notify a family member of the patient's discharge. See, e.g., Estate of Long v. Broadlawns Medical Center, 656 N.W.2d 71 (Iowa 2002) (noting both the relevance of *Tarasoff*'s analysis and the application of § 323 of the Restatement (Second) of Torts.)

2. In Douglass v. Salem Community Hospital, 153 Ohio App.3d 350, 794 N.E.2d 107 (2003), the hospital hired Wagner, a pedophile, as the assistant director of social services. It appears that in 1987, the police informed Western Reserve, his earlier hospital employer, that Wagner had been accused of exposing himself and molesting children and those accusations were being investigated at

that time. Wagner resigned his employment on the condition that Western Reserve would state to those conducting reference checks in the future that he had voluntarily resigned. He then later resigned from Salem Hospital. A boy who had received counseling was invited to spend the weekend with Wagner, and his mother checked with an employee of Salem whom she knew, Williams; Williams told her that Wagner "would be good". Wagner sexually assaulted the boy and his cousin at his house over the weekend.

The court accepted the plaintiff's argument that Restatement (Second) of Torts (1965), Section 323, negligent performance of an undertaking to render service, would apply in this situation of a failure to warn:

> One who undertakes, gratuitously or for consideration, to render services to another which he should recognize as necessary for the protection of the other's person or things, is subject to liability to the other for physical harm resulting from his failure to exercise reasonable care to perform his undertaking, if * * * (b) the harm is suffered because of the other's reliance upon the undertaking.

> The theory of recovery under Section 323(b) is that "when one undertakes a duty voluntarily, and another reasonably relies on that undertaking, the volunteer is required to exercise ordinary care in completing the duty." [ ] In other words, "[a] voluntary act, gratuitously undertaken, must be * * * performed with the exercise of due care under the circumstances." [ ] This theory of negligence does not require proof of a special relationship between the plaintiff and the defendant, or proof of somewhat overwhelming circumstances. This type of negligence follows the general rules for finding negligence, with the addition of one extra element of proof, that of reasonable reliance by the plaintiff on the actions of the defendant.

Why were the various institutions so hypercautious, when the harm threatened was criminal in nature? Is this level of defensiveness something the law should tolerate?

3. Can you make an argument that a hospital should be responsible, under some circumstances, for the negligent acts of physicians in their private practice, so long as they have staff privileges? What if the hospital is on notice of a long history of malpractice claims against one of its staff, resulting from negligence in that physician's private practice? If the physician has performed adequately while treating patients within the hospital, should the hospital have any further responsibility?

Consider the case of Copithorne v. Framingham Union Hospital, 401 Mass. 860, 520 N.E.2d 139 (1988). The plaintiff, Copithorne, was a technologist at Framingham Union Hospital who was drugged and sexually assaulted by a physician with staff privileges at the hospital. The Massachusetts Supreme Judicial Court imposed liability on the hospital. Helfant was a practicing neurosurgeon and a visiting staff member of the hospital, having been reappointed for seventeen years to the medical staff. The plaintiff Copithorne was a hospital employee. In the course of her employment, she injured her back, and, aware of Helfant's reputation within the hospital as a good neurosurgeon and a specialist in back injuries, she sought his professional assistance. In the course of treating her, Helfant made a house call to Copithorne's apartment, where he committed the drugging and rape for which he was convicted and which caused the injuries for which Copithorne seeks compensation. The hospital had actual notice, and " * * * owed a duty of care to Copithorne, as an employee who, in deciding to enter a doctor-patient relationship with Helfant, reasonably relied on Helfant's good standing and reputation within the hospital community, and that the hospital violated this duty by failing to take sufficient action in response to previous allegations of Helfant's wrongdoing.''

Are your encouraged by the action of the medical disciplinary board of the state, which did nothing? See criticisms of the state disciplinary process in Public Citizen Congress Watch, The Great Medical Malpractice Hoax: NPDB Data Continue to Show Medical Liability System Produces Rational Outcomes (January 2007), http://www.citizen.org/documents/NPDBReport_Final.pdf.

Problem: Referrals

You represent Chadds Hospital, a small nonprofit hospital that is trying to increase its patient count. One of the strategies it is contemplating is a physician referral service. The hospital plans to advertise, in local newspapers and on the radio, that individuals should call Chadds Hospital for the name of a doctor for specific problems. The referral service operator will then offer to make the appointment for the caller with the particular doctor, to be seen in his office practice. The draft of the advertising copy that the hospital marketing staff has prepared states: ''You can trust the high quality of these doctors because they are members of the medical staff of Chadds Hospital, and our doctors are the best.''

What is your advice to the hospital in light of the above cases? Do you foresee any legal risks in this marketing strategy?

Problem: The Birthing Center

You have been approached by Rosa Hernandez to handle a tort suit for damages for the death of her infant during delivery at the Hastings Birthing Center. Discovery reveals the following facts.

The death of the infant is attributable to the negligence of Dr. Jones, the physician who attended Ms. Hernandez at the Center during delivery. The death was caused in part by the infant's aspiration of meconium into the lungs. Although the Center is equipped to suction meconium and other material from a newborn's throat, it is not equipped to perform an intubation and attach the infant to a ventilator. To intubate the infant, it would have to be transferred to the hospital. Even if the infant had been transferred, it would probably have suffered brain damage due to oxygen deprivation before the procedure could have been undertaken.

Dr. Jones has a spotless record, but over the two weeks preceding the incident he had appeared at the hospital smelling of alcohol and evidencing other signs of intoxication. He was apparently having marital problems at the time. Nurses at the hospital had reported this behavior to their supervisor and had watched the physician's work very carefully, calling his attention to things he missed. The nurse supervisor had reported the situation to the head of OB/GYN, who said he would ''look into it''. Ms. Hernandez noticed the smell of liquor on Dr. Jones' breath during her labor, and was upset by his apparent intoxication. Dr. Jones has also dropped his malpractice insurance coverage, a fact of which the hospital is aware.

Further discovery has revealed that the nurse-midwife had observed that Dr. Jones' acts were questionable, but she had not intervened because she knew of his excellent reputation. She knew that doctors were resentful of the independence of nurse-midwives at the Center, and she believed she could ''compensate'' for his mistakes during the delivery. By the time she realized the extent of Dr. Jones' intoxication and took over the delivery, it was too late.

Your discovery reveals that there is a complicated relationship between the Birthing Center and the nearby Columbia Hospital. The hospital found that it had needed to increase its patient census, and that neonatology was one of its most profitable services. To increase its census in this area and to better serve the community, Columbia established the Hastings Birthing Center last year. The hospital receives a percentage of the profits of the Center.

The Center is located in a former convent one block from the hospital. The hospital owns the building and rents it to the Center. This particular birthing center, according to its promotional literature, offers "both a home-like setting for the delivery of your child and the security of the availability of back-up physicians and hospital care." The Center is separately incorporated and has its own Board of Directors. It is totally self-governing and is solely responsible for staff, provision of equipment, and policy.

The phone listing in the Yellow Pages describes the Hospital as a "cooperating hospital that will provide hospital care for mother and child if needed." Columbia has a contract with the Center requiring the Center to establish a screening program that will exclude high-risk patients and requiring that doctors attending patients at the Center have privileges at Columbia Hospital. The hospital allows the employees of the Center to participate in the hospital's group health and pension plans. Nurses from the hospital moonlight at the Center. When they do so, they receive a separate paycheck from the Center.

Although the Center's by-laws provide for a committee to review the qualifications of physicians who attend at the Center, it has in fact relied on the hospital's review of qualifications, since the hospital has a better opportunity to review credentials and performance. It is not clear that the hospital is aware of this; while it does notify the Center of the suspension, denial or revocation of privileges, it does not provide the Center with information used in investigations.

If you decide to litigate, should you sue both the Center and the hospital as well as Dr. Jones? Describe your theories, based on the information you have discovered to date, and consider what other facts you would like to know.

IV. TORT LIABILITY OF MANAGED CARE

Managed care organizations may also be defendants in liability suits, facing the same theories that hospitals face. "Managed care" is a phrase often used to describe organizational groupings that attempt to control the utilization of health care services through a variety of techniques, including prepayment by subscribers for services on a contract basis, use of physicians as "gatekeepers" for hospital and specialty services, and others. The groups cover a wide variety of plans—from plans that require little more than preauthorization of patient hospitalization, to staff model HMOs—that focus on utilization and price of services. The goal is reduction of health care costs and maximization of value to both patient and payer. A Managed Care Organization (MCO) is a reimbursement framework combined with a health care delivery system, an approach to the delivery of health care services that contrasts with "fee-for-service" medicine. Managed care is usually distinguished from traditional indemnity plans by the existence of a single entity responsible for integrating and coordinating the financing and delivery of services that were once scattered between providers and payers.

Managed care rapidly supplanted fee-for-service medicine. By 2006 fewer than 10 percent of employees in all firms were enrolled in conventional plans, with small firms as low as 4 percent. In 1980, in contrast, only five to ten percent of the workforce was enrolled in such plans. By 2006 employment based health insurance covered 155 million members. A shift has occurred however as to type of coverage, with Preferred Provider Plans (PPOs) now covering 60% of insured workers, and HMO plans covering 20%, Point Of Service (POS) plans 13%, and High Deductible Plans covering 4%. The shift away from the more intensively cost managed HMO model is apparent, as the tools of managed care—preapproval of specialists, capitation, and other features—has managed to alienate both providers and subscribers during those decades.

See Kaiser Family Foundation et al., Employer Benefits: 2006 Annual Survey (2006) particularly Exhibit 4.4. See also Debra A. Draper, Robert E. Hurley, Cara S. Lesser, and Bradley C. Strunk, The Changing Face of Managed Care, 21 Health Affairs 11 (2002).

Managed care plan liability is limited to a shrinking universe of plans. The Employee Retirement Income Security Act of 1974 (ERISA) preempts either explicitly or by U.S. Supreme Court interpretation the vast majority of managed care plans that are employment based and ERISA-qualified. See generally Ch. 8 for a full discussion of ERISA preemption. See also Ch. 7 for a discussion of state regulation of managed care. The following discussion is therefore applicable to managed care plans that fall in the shrinking category of non-ERISA qualified plans for which federal preemption is not a defense to the defendant, or to the increasingly limited range of theories that the Supreme Court has left open to plaintiffs in state courts.

A. VICARIOUS LIABILITY

Health maintenance organizations (HMOs) and Independent Practice Associations (IPAs) in theory face the same vicarious and corporate liability questions as hospitals, since they provide services through physicians, whether the physicians are salaried employees or independent contractors. These medical services can injure patients/subscribers, leading to a malpractice suit for such injuries.

Vicarious liability theories provided the first wave of successful litigation against managed care organizations.

PETROVICH v. SHARE HEALTH PLAN OF ILLINOIS, INC.

Supreme Court of Illinois, 1999.
188 Ill.2d 17, 241 Ill.Dec. 627, 719 N.E.2d 756.

JUSTICE BILANDIC delivered the opinion of the court:

The plaintiff brought this medical malpractice action against a physician and others for their alleged negligence in failing to diagnose her oral cancer in a timely manner. The plaintiff also named her health maintenance organization (HMO) as a defendant. The central issue here is whether the plaintiff's HMO may be held vicariously liable for the negligence of its independent-contractor physicians under agency law. The plaintiff contends that the HMO is vicariously liable under both the doctrines of apparent authority and implied authority.

* * *

FACTS

In 1989, plaintiff's employer, the Chicago Federation of Musicians, provided health care coverage to all of its employees by selecting Share and enrolling its employees therein. Share is an HMO and pays only for medical care that is obtained within its network of physicians. In order to qualify for benefits, a Share member must select from the network a primary care physician who will provide that member's overall care and authorize referrals when necessary. Share gives its members a list of participating physicians from which to choose. Share has about 500 primary care physicians covering Share's service area, which includes the counties of Cook, Du Page, Lake, McHenry and Will. Plaintiff selected Dr. Marie Kowalski from Share's list, and began seeing Dr. Kowalski as her primary care physician in August of 1989. Dr. Kowalski was employed at a satellite facility of Illinois Masonic Medical Center (Illinois Masonic), which had a contract with Share to provide medical services to Share members.

In September of 1990, plaintiff saw Dr. Kowalski because she was experiencing persistent pain in the right sides of her mouth, tongue, throat and face. Plaintiff also complained of a foul mucus in her mouth. Dr. Kowalski referred plaintiff to two other physicians who had contracts with Share: Dr. Slavick, a neurologist, and Dr. Friedman, an ear, nose and throat specialist.

Plaintiff informed Dr. Friedman of her pain. Dr. Friedman observed redness or marked erythema alongside plaintiff's gums on the right side of her mouth. He recommended that plaintiff have a magnetic resonance imaging (MRI) test or a computed tomography (CT) scan performed on the base of her skull. According to plaintiff's testimony at her evidence deposition, Dr. Kowalski informed her that Share would not allow new tests as recommended by Dr. Friedman. Plaintiff did not consult with Share about the test refusals because she was not aware of Share's grievance procedure. Dr. Kowalski gave Dr. Friedman a copy of an old MRI test result at that time. The record offers no further information about this old MRI test.

Nonetheless, Dr. Kowalski later ordered an updated MRI of plaintiff's brain, which was performed on October 31, 1990. Inconsistent with Dr. Friedman's directions, however, this MRI failed to image the right base of the tongue area where redness existed. Plaintiff and Dr. Kowalski discussed the results of this MRI test on November 19, 1990, during a follow-up visit. Plaintiff testified that Dr. Kowalski told her that the MRI revealed no abnormality.

Plaintiff's pain persisted. In April or May of 1991, Dr. Kowalski again referred plaintiff to Dr. Friedman. This was plaintiff's third visit to Dr. Friedman. Dr. Friedman examined plaintiff and observed that plaintiff's tongue was tender. Also, plaintiff reported that she had a foul odor in her mouth and was experiencing discomfort. On June 7, 1991, Dr. Friedman performed multiple biopsies on the right side of the base of plaintiff's tongue and surrounding tissues. The biopsy results revealed squamous cell carcinoma, a cancer, in the base of plaintiff's tongue and the surrounding tissues of the pharynx. Later that month, Dr. Friedman operated on plaintiff to remove the cancer. He removed part of the base of plaintiff's tongue, and portions of her palate, pharynx and jaw bone. After the surgery, plaintiff underwent radiation treatments and rehabilitation.

Plaintiff subsequently brought this medical malpractice action against Share, Dr. Kowalski and others. Dr. Friedman was not named a party defendant. Plaintiff's complaint, though, alleges that both Drs. Kowalski and Friedman were negligent in failing to diagnose plaintiff's cancer in a timely manner, and that Share is vicariously liable for their negligence under agency principles. Share filed a motion for summary judgment, arguing that it cannot be held liable for the negligence of Dr. Kowalski or Friedman because they were acting as independent contractors in their treatment of plaintiff, not as Share's agents. Plaintiff countered that Share is not entitled to summary judgment because Drs. Kowalski and Friedman were Share's agents. The parties submitted various depositions, affidavits and exhibits in support of their respective positions.

Share is a for-profit corporation. At all relevant times, Share was organized as an "independent practice association-model" HMO under the Illinois Health Maintenance Organization Act (Ill.Rev.Stat.1991, ch. 111 ½, par. 1401 et seq.). This means that Share is a financing entity that arranges and pays for health care by contracting with independent medical groups and practitioners. [ ] Share does not employ physicians directly, nor does it own, operate, maintain or supervise the offices where medical care is provided to its members. Rather, Share contracts with independent medical groups and physicians that have the facilities, equipment and professional skills necessary to render medical care. Physicians desiring to join Share's network are required to complete an application procedure and meet with Share's approval.

Share utilizes a method of compensation called "capitation" to pay its medical groups. Share also maintains a "quality assurance program." Share's capitation method of compensation and "quality assurance program" are more fully described later in this opinion.

Share provides a member handbook to each of its members, including plaintiff. The handbook states to its members that Share will provide "all your healthcare needs" and "comprehensive high quality services." The handbook also states that the primary care physician is "your health care manager" and "makes the decisions" about the member's care. The handbook further states that Share is a "good partner in sickness and in health." Unlike the master agreements and benefits contract discussed below, the member handbook which plaintiff received does not contain any provision that identifies Share physicians as independent contractors or nonemployees of Share. Rather, the handbook describes the physicians as "your Share physician," "Share physicians" and "our staff." Furthermore, Share refers to the physicians' offices as "Your Share physician's office" and states: "All of the Share staff and Medical Offices look forward to serving you * * *."

Plaintiff confirmed that she received the member handbook. Plaintiff did not read the handbook in its entirety, but read portions of it as she needed the information. She relied on the information contained in the handbook while Drs. Kowalski and Friedman treated her.

The record also contains a "Health Care Services Master Agreement," entered into by Share and Illinois Masonic. Dr. Kowalski is a signatory of this agreement. The agreement states, "It is understood and agreed that [Illinois Masonic] and [primary care physicians] are independent contractors and not employees or agents of SHARE." A separate agreement between Share and Dr. Friedman contains similar language. Plaintiff did not receive these agreements.

Share's primary care physicians, under their agreements with Share, are required to approve patients' medical requests and make referrals to specialists. These physicians use Share's standard referral forms to indicate their approval of the referral. Dr. Kowalski testified at an evidence deposition that she did not feel constrained by Share in making medical decisions regarding her patients, including whether to order tests or make referrals to specialists.

Another document in the record is Share's benefits contract. The benefits contract contains a subscriber certificate. The subscriber certificate sets forth a member's rights and obligations with respect to Share. Additionally, the subscriber certificate states that Share's physicians are independent contractors and that "SHARE Plan Providers and Enrolling Groups are not agents or employees of SHARE nor is SHARE or any employee of SHARE an agent or employee of SHARE Plan Providers or Enrolling Groups." The certificate elaborates: "The relationship between a SHARE Plan Provider and any Member is that of provider and patient. The SHARE Plan Physician is solely responsible for the medical services provided to any Member. The SHARE Plan Hospital is solely responsible for the Hospital services provided to any Member."

Plaintiff testified that she did not recall receiving the subscriber certificate. In response, Share stated that Share customarily provides members with this information. Share does not claim to know whether Share actually provided plaintiff with this information. Plaintiff acknowledged that she received a "whole stack" of information from Share upon her enrollment.

Plaintiff was not aware of the type of relationship that her physicians had with Share. At the time she received treatment, plaintiff believed that her physicians were employees of Share.

In the circuit court, Share argued that it was entitled to summary judgment because the independent-contractor provision in the benefits contract established, as a matter of law, that Drs. Kowalski and Friedman were not acting as Share's agents in their treatment of plaintiff. The circuit court agreed and entered summary judgment for Share.

The appellate court reversed, holding that a genuine issue of material fact is presented as to whether plaintiff's treating physicians are Share's apparent agents. 296 Ill.App.3d 849, 231 Ill.Dec. 364, 696 N.E.2d 356. The appellate court stated that a number of factors support plaintiff's apparent agency claim, including plaintiff's testimony, Share's member handbook, Share's quality assessment program and Share's capitation method of compensation. The appellate court therefore remanded the cause for trial. The appellate court did not address the theory of implied authority.

ANALYSIS

This appeal comes before us amidst great changes to the relationships among physicians, patients and those entities paying for medical care. Traditionally, physicians treated patients on demand, while insurers merely paid the physicians their fee for the services provided. Today, managed care organizations (MCOs) have stepped into the insurer's shoes, and often attempt to reduce the price and quantity of health care services provided to patients through a system of health care cost containment. MCOs may, for example, use prearranged fee structures for compensating physicians. MCOs may also use utilization-review procedures, which are procedures designed to determine whether the use and volume of particular health care services are appropriate. MCOs have developed in response to rapid increases in health care costs.

HMOs, i.e., health maintenance organizations, are a type of MCO. HMOs are subject to both state and federal laws. [ ] Under Illinois law, an HMO is defined as "any organization formed under the laws of this or another state to provide or arrange for one or more health care plans under a system which causes any part of the risk of health care delivery to be borne by the organization or its providers." Ill.Rev.Stat.1991, ch. 111 ½, par. 1402(9), now 215 ILCS 125/1–2(9) (West 1998). Because HMOs may differ in their structures and the cost-containment practices that they employ, a court must discern the nature of the organization before it, where relevant to the issues. As earlier noted, Share is organized as an independent practice association (IPA)-model HMO. IPA-model HMOs are financing entities that arrange and pay for health care by contracting with independent medical groups and practitioners. [ ]

This court has never addressed a question of whether an HMO may be held liable for medical malpractice. Share asserts that holding HMOs liable for medical malpractice will cause health care costs to increase and make health care inaccessible to large numbers of people. Share suggests that, with this consideration in mind, this court should impose only narrow, or limited, forms of liability on HMOs. We disagree with Share that the cost-containment role of HMOs entitles them to special consideration. The principle that organizations are accountable for their tortious actions and those of their agents is fundamental to our justice system. There is no exception to this principle for HMOs. Moreover, HMO accountability is essential to counterbalance the HMO goal of cost-containment. To the extent that HMOs are profit-making entities, accountability is also needed to counterbalance the inherent drive to achieve a large and ever-increasing profit margin. Market forces alone "are insufficient to cure the deleterious [e]ffects of managed care on the health care industry." Herdrich v. Pegram, 154 F.3d 362, 374–75 (7th Cir. 1998), cert. granted, 527 U.S. 1068, 120 S.Ct. 10, 144 L.Ed.2d 841 (1999). Courts, therefore, should not be hesitant to apply well-settled legal theories of liability to HMOs where the facts so warrant and where justice so requires.

Indeed, the national trend of courts is to hold HMOs accountable for medical malpractice under a variety of legal theories, including vicarious liability on the basis of apparent authority, vicarious liability on the basis of respondeat superior, direct corporate negligence, breach of contract and breach of warranty. [ ] * * * Share concedes that HMOs may be held liable for medical malpractice under these five theories.

This appeal concerns whether Share may be held vicariously liable under agency law for the negligence of its independent-contractor physicians. We must determine whether Share was properly awarded summary judgment on the ground that Drs. Kowalski and Friedman were not acting as Share's agents in their treatment of plaintiff. Plaintiff argues that Share is not entitled to summary judgment on this record. Plaintiff asserts that genuine issues of material fact exist as to whether Drs. Kowalski and Friedman were acting within Share's apparent authority, implied authority or both.

* * *

As a general rule, no vicarious liability exists for the actions of independent contractors. Vicarious liability may nevertheless be imposed for the actions of independent contractors where an agency relationship is established under either the doctrine of apparent authority [ ] or the doctrine of implied authority [ ].

I. APPARENT AUTHORITY

Apparent authority, also known as ostensible authority, has been a part of Illinois jurisprudence for more than 140 years. [ ] Under the doctrine, a principal will be bound not only by the authority that it actually gives to another, but also by the authority that it appears to give. [ ]. The doctrine functions like an estoppel. [ ]. Where the principal creates the appearance of authority, a court will not hear the principal's denials of agency to the prejudice of an innocent third party, who has been led to reasonably rely upon the agency and is harmed as a result.[ ]

* * *

We now hold that the apparent authority doctrine may also be used to impose vicarious liability on HMOs. * * * [ ]

To establish apparent authority against an HMO for physician malpractice, the patient must prove (1) that the HMO held itself out as the provider of health care, without informing the patient that the care is given by independent contractors, and (2) that the patient justifiably relied upon the conduct of the HMO by looking to the HMO to provide health care services, rather than to a specific physician. Apparent agency is a question of fact. [ ]

A. Holding Out

The element of "holding out" means that the HMO, or its agent, acted in a manner that would lead a reasonable person to conclude that the physician who was alleged to be negligent was an agent or employee of the HMO. [ ] Where the acts of the agent create the appearance of authority, a plaintiff must also prove that the HMO had knowledge of and acquiesced in those acts. [ ] The holding-out element does not require the HMO to make an express representation that the physician alleged to be negligent is its agent or employee. Rather, this element is met where the HMO holds itself out as the provider of health care without informing the patient that the care is given by independent contractors. [ ] Vicarious liability under the apparent authority doctrine will not attach, however, if the patient knew or should have known that the physician providing treatment is an independent contractor. [ ]

Here, Share contends that the independent-contractor provisions in the two master agreements and the benefits contract conclusively establish, as a matter of law, that Share did not hold out Drs. Kowalski and Friedman to be Share's agents. Although all three of these contracts clearly express that the physicians are independent contractors and not agents of Share, we disagree with Share's contention for the reasons explained below.

First, the two master agreements at issue are private contractual agreements between Share and Illinois Masonic, with Dr. Kowalski as a signatory, and between Share and Dr. Friedman. The record contains no indication that plaintiff knew or should have known of these private contractual agreements between Share and its physicians. Gilbert expressly rejected the notion that such private contractual agreements can control a claim of apparent agency. [ ] * * * We hold that this same rationale applies to private contractual agreements between physicians and an HMO. [ ] Because there is no dispute that the master agreements at bar were unknown to plaintiff, they cannot be used to defeat her apparent agency claim.

Share also relies on the benefits contract. Plaintiff was not a party or a signatory to this contract. The benefits contract contains a subscriber certificate, which states that Share physicians are independent contractors. Share claims that this language alone conclusively overcomes plaintiff's apparent agency claim. We do not agree.

Whether a person has notice of a physician's status as an independent contractor, or is put on notice by the circumstances, is a question of fact. [ ] In this case, plaintiff testified at her evidence deposition that she did not recall receiving the subscriber certificate. Share responded only that it customarily provides members with this information. Share has never claimed to know whether Share actually provided plaintiff with this information. Thus, a question of fact exists as to whether Share gave this information to plaintiff. If this information was not provided to plaintiff, it cannot be used to defeat her apparent agency claim.

* * *

Evidence in the record supports plaintiff's contentions that Share held itself out to its members as the provider of health care, and that plaintiff was not aware that her physicians were independent contractors. Notably, plaintiff stated that, at the time that she received treatment, plaintiff believed that Drs. Kowalski and Friedman were Share employees. Plaintiff was not aware of the type of relationship that her physicians had with Share.

Moreover, Share's member handbook contains evidence that Share held itself out to plaintiff as the provider of her health care. The handbook stated to Share members that Share will provide "all your healthcare needs" and "comprehensive high quality services." The handbook did not contain any provision that identified Share physicians as independent contractors or nonemployees of Share. Instead, the handbook referred to the physicians as "your Share physician," "Share physicians" and "our staff." Share also referred to the physicians' offices as "Your Share physician's office." The record shows that Share provided this handbook to each of its enrolled members, including plaintiff. Representations made in the handbook are thus directly attributable to Share and were intended by Share to be communicated to its members.

* * *

We hold that the above testimony by plaintiff and Share's member handbook support the conclusion that Share held itself out to plaintiff as the provider of her health care, without informing her that the care was actually provided by independent contractors. Therefore, a triable issue of fact exists as to the holding-out element. We need not resolve whether any other evidence in the record also supports plaintiff's claim. Our task here is to review whether Share is entitled to summary judgment on this element. We hold that Share is not.

B. *Justifiable Reliance*

A plaintiff must also prove the element of "justifiable reliance" to establish apparent authority against an HMO for physician malpractice. This means that the plaintiff acted in reliance upon the conduct of the HMO or its agent, consistent with ordinary care and prudence. [ ]

The element of justifiable reliance is met where the plaintiff relies upon the HMO to provide health care services, and does not rely upon a specific physician. This element is not met if the plaintiff selects his or her own personal physician and merely looks to the HMO as a conduit through which the plaintiff receives medical care. [ ]

Concerning the element of justifiable reliance in the hospital context, Gilbert explained that the critical distinction is whether the plaintiff sought care from the hospital itself or from a personal physician. * * *

This rationale applies even more forcefully in the context of an HMO that restricts its members to the HMO's chosen physicians. Accordingly, unless a person seeks care from a personal physician, that person is seeking care from the HMO itself. A person who seeks care from the HMO itself accepts that care in reliance upon the HMO's holding itself out as the provider of care.

Share maintains that plaintiff cannot establish the justifiable reliance element because she did not select Share. * * *

* * * We reject Share's argument. It is true that, where a person selects the HMO and does not rely upon a specific physician, then that person is relying upon the HMO to provide health care. This principle, derived directly from Gilbert, is set forth above. Equally true, however, is that where a person has no choice but to enroll with a single HMO and does not rely upon a specific physician, then that person is likewise relying upon the HMO to provide health care.

In the present case, the record discloses that plaintiff did not select Share. Plaintiff's employer selected Share for her. Plaintiff had no choice of health plans whatsoever. Once Share became plaintiff's health plan, Share required plaintiff to obtain her primary medical care from one of its primary care physicians. If plaintiff did not do so, Share did not cover plaintiff's medical costs. In accordance with Share's requirement, plaintiff selected Dr. Kowalski from a list of physicians that Share provided to her. Plaintiff had no prior relationship with Dr. Kowalski. As to Dr. Kowalski's selection of Dr. Friedman for plaintiff, Share required Dr. Kowalski to make referrals only to physicians approved by Share. Plaintiff had no prior relationship with Dr. Friedman. We hold that these facts are sufficient to raise the reasonable inference that plaintiff relied upon Share to provide her health care services.

Were we to conclude that plaintiff was not relying upon Share for health care, we would be denying the true nature of the relationship among plaintiff, her HMO and the physicians. Share, like many HMOs, contracted with plaintiff's employer to become plaintiff's sole provider of health care, to the exclusion of all other providers. Share then restricted plaintiff to its chosen physicians. Under these facts, plaintiff's reliance on Share as the provider of her health care is shown not only to be compelling, but literally compelled. Plaintiff's reliance upon Share was inherent in Share's method of operation.

* * *

In conclusion, as set forth above, plaintiff has presented sufficient evidence to support justifiable reliance, as well as a holding out by Share. Share, therefore, is not entitled to summary judgment against plaintiff's claim of apparent authority.

* * *

II.   IMPLIED AUTHORITY

Implied authority is actual authority, circumstantially proved. [ ] One context in which implied authority arises is where the facts and circumstances show that the defendant exerted sufficient control over the alleged agent so as to negate that person's status as an independent contractor, at least with respect to third parties. [ ] The cardinal consideration for determining the existence of implied authority is whether the alleged agent retains the right to control the manner of doing the work. [ ] Where a person's status as an independent contractor is negated, liability may result under the doctrine of respondeat superior.

Plaintiff contends that the facts and circumstances of this case show that Share exerted sufficient control over Drs. Kowalski and Friedman so as to negate their status as independent contractors. Share responds that the act of providing medical care is peculiarly within a physician's domain because it requires the exercise of independent medical judgment. Share thus maintains that, because it cannot control a physician's exercise of medical judgment, it cannot be subject to vicarious liability under the doctrine of implied authority.

* * *

We now address whether the implied authority doctrine may be used against HMOs to negate a physician's status as an independent contractor. Our appellate court in Raglin suggested that it can. [ ] Case law from other jurisdictions lends support to this view as well. [ ]

* * *

We do not find the above decisions rendered in the hospital context to be dispositive of whether an HMO may exert such control over its physicians so as to negate their status as independent contractors. We can readily discern that the relationships between physicians and HMOs are often much different than the traditional relationships between physicians and hospitals. * * *

Physicians, of course, should not allow the exercise of their medical judgment to be corrupted or controlled. Physicians have professional ethical, moral and legal obligations to provide appropriate medical care to their patients. These obligations on physicians, however, will not act to relieve an HMO of its own legal responsibilities. Where an HMO effectively controls a physician's exercise of medical judgment, and that judgment is exercised negligently, the HMO cannot be allowed to claim that the physician is solely responsible for the harm that results. In such a circumstance, both the physician and the HMO are liable for the harm that results. We therefore hold that the implied authority doctrine may be used against an HMO to negate a physician's status as an independent contractor. An implied agency exists where the facts and circumstances show that an HMO exerted such sufficient control over a participating physician so as to negate that physician's status as an independent contractor, at least with respect to third parties. [ ] No precise formula exists for deciding when a person's status as an independent contractor is negated. Rather, the determination of whether a person is an agent or an independent contractor rests upon the facts and circumstances of each case. [ ] As noted, the cardinal consideration is whether that person retains the right to control the manner of doing the work. [ ] * * *

With these established principles in mind, we turn to the present case. Plaintiff contends that her physicians' status as independent contractors should be negated. Plaintiff asserts that Share actively interfered with her physicians' medical decisionmaking by designing and executing its capitation method of compensation and "quality assurance" programs. Plaintiff also points to Share's referral system as evidence of control.

Plaintiff submits that Share's capitation method of compensating its medical groups is a form of control because it financially punishes physicians for ordering certain medical treatment. The record discloses that Share utilizes a method of compensation called "capitation."[ ]. Under capitation, Share prepays contracting medical groups a fixed amount of money for each member who enrolls with that group. In exchange, the medical groups agree to render health care to their enrolled Share members in accordance with the Share plan. Each medical group contracting with Share has its own capitation account. Deducted from that capitation account are the costs of any services provided by the primary care physician, the costs of medical procedures and tests, and the fees of all consulting physicians. The medical group then retains the surplus left in the capitation account. The costs for hospitalizations and other services are charged against a separate account. Reinsurance is provided for the capitation account and the separate account for certain high cost claims. Share pays Illinois Masonic in accordance with its capitation method of compensation. Dr. Kowalski testified that Illinois Masonic pays her the same salary every month. Plaintiff maintains that a reasonable inference to be drawn from Share's capitation method of compensation is that Share provides financial disincentives to its primary care physicians in order to discourage them from ordering the medical care that they deem appropriate. Plaintiff argues that this is an example of Share's influence and control over the medical judgment of its physicians.

Share counters that its capitation method of compensation cannot be used as evidence of control here because Dr. Kowalski is paid the same salary every month. We disagree with Share that this fact makes Share's capitation system irrelevant to our inquiry. Whether control was actually exercised is not dispositive in this context. Rather, the right to control the alleged agent is the proper query, even where that right is not exercised. [ ]

[The court rejects Share's "quality assurance program" as evidence of control, since it is done primarily to comply with state regulations of the Department of Public Health. The court however allows as evidence of control chart review by Share; control over referral to specialists; and use of primary care physicians as gatekeepers].

We conclude that plaintiff has presented adequate evidence to entitle her to a trial on the issue of implied authority. All the facts and circumstances before us, if proven at trial, raise the reasonable inference that Share exerted such sufficient control over Drs. Kowalski and Friedman so as to negate their status as independent contractors. As discussed above, plaintiff presents relevant evidence of Share's capitation method of compensation, Share's "quality assurance review," Share's referral system and Share's requirement that its primary care physicians act as gatekeepers for Share. These facts support plaintiff's argument that Share subjected its physicians to control over the manner in which they did their work. The facts surrounding treatment also support plaintiff's argument. According to plaintiff's evidence, Dr. Kowalski referred plaintiff to Dr. Friedman. Dr. Friedman evaluated plaintiff and recommended that plaintiff have either an MRI test or a CT scan performed on the base of her skull. Dr. Friedman, however, did not order the test that he recommended for plaintiff. Rather, he reported this information back to Dr. Kowalski in her role as plaintiff's primary care physician. Dr. Kowalski initially sent Dr. Friedman a copy of an old MRI test. Dr. Kowalski later ordered that an updated MRI be taken. In doing so, she directed that the MRI be taken of plaintiff's "brain." Hence, that MRI failed to image the base of plaintiff's skull as recommended by Dr. Friedman. Dr. Kowalski then reviewed the MRI test results herself and informed plaintiff that the results revealed no abnormality. From all the above facts and circumstances, a trier of fact could reasonably infer that Share promulgated such a system of control over its physicians that Share effectively negated the exercise of their independent medical judgment, to plaintiff's detriment.

We note that Dr. Kowalski testified at an evidence deposition that she did not feel constrained by Share in making medical decisions regarding her patients, including whether to order tests or make referrals to specialists. This testimony is not controlling at the summary judgment stage. The trier of fact is entitled to weigh all the conflicting evidence above against Dr. Kowalski's testimony.

In conclusion, plaintiff has presented adequate evidence to support a finding that Share exerted such sufficient control over its participating physicians so as to negate their status as independent contractors. Share, therefore, is not entitled to summary judgment against plaintiff's claim of implied authority.

* * *

CONCLUSION

An HMO may be held vicariously liable for the negligence of its independent-contractor physicians under both the doctrines of apparent authority and implied authority. Plaintiff here is entitled to a trial on both doctrines. The circuit court therefore erred in awarding summary judgment to Share. The appellate court's judgment, which reversed the circuit court's judgment and remanded the cause to the circuit court for further proceedings, is affirmed.

Affirmed.

PAGARIGAN v. AETNA U.S. HEALTHCARE OF CALIFORNIA, INC.

California Court of Appeal, 2005.
2005 WL 2742807.

In this case we consider the liability of an HMO which contracts out its health care responsibilities to various providers when one or more of those providers denies medically necessary services or commits malpractice in the delivery of those services. We conclude the HMO owes a duty to avoid contracting with deficient providers or negotiating contract terms which require or unduly encourage denials of service or below-standard performance by its providers. While appellants' complaint in its present form even with the amendments it tendered fails to adequately state a cause of action based on this theory, we find facts alleged which imply they may be able to do so if offered the chance. Accordingly, we allow appellants one more opportunity to file good faith amendments as to two of the nine proposed causes of action involving Aetna. * * *.

FACTS AND PROCEEDINGS BELOW

Appellants (and plaintiffs) are the children of an elderly woman, Johnnie Pagarigan (decedent) who died at a nursing home, allegedly as a result of elder abuse and malpractice. The respondents are the HMO which the decedent had joined and its parent corporation (collectively Aetna). Aetna, in turn, had contracted with a management organization, Greater Valley Management Services Organization, which contracted with medical groups Greater Valley Medical Group and Greater Valley Physician Association (collectively "Greater Valley") which contracted with Magnolia Gardens nursing home (owned and operated by Libby Care Center, Inc. and Longwood Management Corp.) and a physician, Dr. Buttleman, to care for decedent.

After their mother's death, and learning of what they saw as serious deficiencies in the care provided her by the physician and the nursing home, appellants sued all layers of this complex arrangement-including the HMO at the top, Aetna. They asserted ten causes of action as successors-in-interest to their mother (negligence, willful misconduct, elder abuse, constructive fraud, and fraud) and one for wrongful death. (This appeal, however, only involves the HMO and the trial court's action sustaining a demurrer and dismissing the complaint as to the HMO and its parent company.)

According to the allegations of this complaint, decedent was already on Medicare in 1995 when she enrolled in an Aetna HMO, Aetna Health Care of California, Inc., and remained a member of that HMO until her death in June 2000. In February of 2000, decedent suffered a debilitating stroke. As a member of the HMO, she was assigned to Magnolia Gardens and under the supervision of Dr. Buttleman. Allegedly, the deficient care she received at Magnolia Gardens caused her condition to deteriorate rapidly. In quick order she became malnourished and dehydrated, developed a huge pressure sore on her lower back and a severe infection and abscess at the site of the gastric tube insertion, and eventually her abdomen became protuberant and discolored.

Despite the critical nature of her condition, Dr. Buttleman delayed months before transferring decedent to an acute care hospital. By that time, it was too late for the hospital to cure her condition and she was sent home to die. In their brief but not in their complaint, appellants allege Aetna as well as Greater Valley requested the delay for economic reasons. As long as decedent remained at Magnolia Gardens the state's MediCal program reimbursed it for her medical care. But if and when she moved to an acute care hospital Aetna and its contracting parties would be financially responsible.

* * *

DISCUSSION

Before discussing the nine counts of the complaint implicating Aetna, we set the scene by providing some necessary background information about the health care industry and the specie of Health Maintenance Organization involved in this case. The core issue here is when, if ever, an HMO that contracts out its coverage decisions as well as its medical care responsibilities to health care providers like physician groups or to intermediary health management firms, or both, can be held liable when those contracting parties deny service or commit malpractice in the delivery of those services.

I.   BACKGROUND ON HMOS AND THEIR USE OF CAPITATION-BASED CONTRACTS TO ARRANGE FOR THE PROVISION OF HEALTH CARE TO THEIR MEMBERS THROUGH HEALTH CARE PROFESSIONALS AND INTERMEDIARIES

At the beginning, health insurance plans—and later Medicare and Medicaid funded plans—were primarily organized on a pure fee-for-service reimbursement basis. A pure fee-for-service health insurance plan employs no doctors and owns no hospitals. It merely pays the bills doctors and hospitals submit for the services they provide to patients from the insured population. Consequently, the insurer normally is not liable for malpractice the doctors whose bills they pay may commit. Moreover, only to the extent the health insurance company makes coverage decisions and refuses to pay for certain services a patient may require and a doctor or hospital stands ready to supply, may it be held liable if a court decides that denial was improper and caused injury or death to one of the plan's insureds.

In contrast, the classic form of HMO, such as the original Kaiser Permanente plan, employs its own doctors and operates its own hospitals. Thus, these HMOs are liable both for any improper denials of coverage and for any malpractice their patients experience.

Aetna calls its plan an HMO, but it is far from the classic model. Rather, in common with a classic fee-for-service health insurer, Aetna's plan employs no doctors and owns no hospitals. Consequently, it purports to avoid liability for any malpractice its insureds may suffer.

The shift in decision-making responsibility and financial risk is accomplished through what the industry calls a "capitation" arrangement. Aetna agrees to pay the management firm or provider a specified amount per year for each person its "HMO" has admitted into its "HMO" plan and then assigns to that firm or provider. The management firm or provider receives the same amount for a particular person whether that insured is so healthy he or she never incurs a single health-related expense the entire year as it receives for one who instead experiences a serious disease requiring hospitalization and a series of operations entailing hundreds of thousands of dollars in medical expenses over the year. Furthermore, if some patient's only chance for recovery is some expensive but experimental or otherwise problematical treatment, in theory at least it is not Aetna but the management firm or provider who must decide whether to offer-and pay for-that treatment. It also is that management firm or provider Aetna expects to bear the consequences should an insured or the insured's survivors successfully sue because the denial of some extraordinary or even ordinary treatment caused the insured serious injury or death.

* * *

II. STANDARD OF REVIEW

[The Court's discussion is omitted.]

III. APPELLANTS' PRESENT ALLEGATIONS FAIL TO STATE A VALID NEGLIGENCE CAUSE OF ACTION OR WRONGFUL DEATH CAUSE OF ACTION, ALTHOUGH IT IS POSSIBLE APPELLANTS COULD SUBMIT AMENDMENTS WHICH WOULD CURE THE DEFECTS IN THEIR PLEADINGS AS TO THESE CAUSES OF ACTION

In their first cause of action the Pagarigans essentially allege Aetna's negligent conduct caused decedent's injuries and ultimate death. Aetna responded and the trial court ruled Aetna owed no duties to decedent which it breached. Whatever happened to decedent at Magnolia Gardens nursing home was the responsibility of the nursing home staff and the supervising physician (Dr. Buttleman). Vicarious liability may extend to the owners and operators of the nursing home, but not to Aetna which was just the insurance company that paid the nursing home and physician to take care of decedent.

As their primary theory of liability, the Pagarigans focus on Aetna's role as a health management organization. They urge as such Aetna has "non-delegable" duties toward its enrollees for the quality of the care they receive from the health care providers Aetna contracts to provide that care. The Pagarigans find these "non-delegable" duties in the language of certain statutes. While we conclude Aetna is not directly responsible for its contractees' breaches of duties they owe the plan's enrollees, we also conclude Aetna owes its own duties to those enrollees. These include a duty of due care when choosing the providers who will supply health services to enrollees. They also include a duty to avoid executing contracts with those providers containing terms, especially low levels of capitation payments, which foreseeably require or unduly encourage below-standard care.

We find the above duties inherent in the common law and to require no statutory basis. But we also note the Legislature enacted Section 3428(a) which became effective shortly after Mrs. Pagarigan's treatment at Magnolia Gardens and confirmed the existence of such duties.

In other provisions, 3428 appears to exempt health insurance plans, such as Aetna, from liability for acts of malpractice committed by health care providers it contracts to care for its enrollees. "This section does not create any new or additional liability on the part of a health care service plan or managed care entity for harm caused that is attributable to the medical negligence of a treating physician or other treating health care provider."

But 3428(a) imposes a statutory duty on Aetna and like plans comparable to the common law duty this court finds to have existed before the Legislature acted—a duty of due care when arranging health care services for its enrollees. "A health care service plan or managed care entity . . . shall have a duty of ordinary care to arrange for the provision of medically necessary health care service to its subscribers and enrollees . . . and shall be liable for any and all harm legally caused by its failure to exercise that ordinary care . . ."

Such a duty of due care is not satisfied by contracting with just any old providers or on any terms whatsoever. To select a provider or to allow the selection of a provider the plan knows or should know is deficient or prone to malpractice is to violate that duty. Moreover, this breach of the plan's own specific duty toward its enrollees also constitutes a contributing cause when an enrollee suffers injury or death due to malpractice attributable in part to the plan's careless selection of the deficient provider organization.

A plan likewise breaches this duty when "arranging" services for its enrollees if it negotiates contract terms with a provider—or allows the negotiation of contract terms with such provider—that foreseeably enhance the likelihood the provider will offer below-standard services that will injure or kill a substantial number of the plan's enrollees. Although other terms may have this result, the most critical term is the level of the "capitation" payment. The plan breaches its duty of ordinary care in arranging services for its enrollees if the plan negotiates a per capita payment so low the plan knows or should know it will require the provider to furnish substandard services and/or deny medically necessary services in order to survive. And, once again this breach of the plan's own duty to its enrollees qualifies as a contributing cause of any injury or death an enrollee suffers at the hands of a provider attributable at least in part to the plan's serious underpayment to the provider for the services it is expected to supply.

Throughout their complaint, the Pagarigans repeat a refrain—Aetna creates economic incentives for providers to deny medically necessary services or to supply below-standard services. Aetna responds with its own refrain. What the Pagarigans are complaining about is the "capitation" system, which the Legislature has expressly endorsed. Thus, the Pagarigans cannot predicate a cause of action on economic incentives this legislatively-approved system may generate.

It is true economic analysis and anecdotal data both tell us a "capitation" system creates incentives to underinvest in health care services just as a "fee for service" approach creates incentives to overinvest. A provider maximizes profits by furnishing fewer services (and thus spending less) per capita if compensated on a "capitation" basis, but maximizes profits by furnishing more services (and billing more) per capita when compensated on a "fee for service" basis.

For this reason, the Pagarigans' repetitive allegations charging Aetna's providers had "conflicts of interest" in the sense of economic incentives to deny services, fail to make outside referrals, and the like, are not inaccurate. But Aetna also is correct in pointing out these incentives are inherent in the "capitation" compensation system both the federal and state governments have approved. Thus, as a general proposition, the ordinary incentives and "conflicts of interest" inherent in a "capitation" approach to health care financing cannot supply the foundation for a negligence cause of action against an HMO like Aetna.

But this does not mean Aetna cannot be held liable for breaches of due care in the way it carries out this "capitation" system. If the way it "arranges for the provision of medically necessary health care service to" enrollees generates economic incentives to deny services or furnish low quality care which are substantially stronger than those inherent in the "capitation" system, Aetna or any other HMO can be liable for this negligent conduct. Thus, for example, as discussed earlier, an HMO violates its duty of due care if it negotiates a "capitation" rate with a given provider which it knows or should know is so low the provider will have an undue economic incentive to deny medically necessary services or to deliver below-standard care. Likewise, as discussed above, an HMO can be liable where it chooses to arrange for the provision of services through a provider it knows or should know is seriously understaffed, poorly administered or otherwise likely to deny medically necessary services or deliver below-standard levels of care.[28]

The Pagarigans' complaint contains fragments of allegations which together approach, but do not quite state a valid cause of action claiming Aetna indeed violated its duty of due care in arranging medically necessary health care services by selecting—or allowing selection of—at least one deficient provider, Magnolia Gardens nursing home. In paragraph 15, it is alleged Aetna and Greater Valley contracted with the owners and operators of Magnolia Gardens "to provide long term care services to enrollees ... [in order to] satisfy Aetna's own obligation under a written agreement with Decedent and with Medicare, by which it had agreed to provide such long term care services to Decedent." In paragraph 25, the Pagarigans then allege, decedent "developed a very severe pressure sore ... because the [Magnolia Gardens] skilled nursing facility ... was *improperly administered* and their care operations were *inadequately funded*. Because of said *maladministration and inadequate funding,* there was insufficient staff to provide the care which Decedent required.... And when Decedent needed careful supervision of her 'G–Tube' and a prompt and proper response to the development of an infection, such care was not provided because such care was not available from an *undertrained and understaffed* nursing service." (Italics added.)

Missing from the above set of allegations, however, is an essential element—that Aetna *knew or should have known* Magnolia Gardens was

---

28. These duties and potential breaches of duty are akin to the "institutional negligence" cause of action the Illinois Supreme Court approved as a basis for holding an HMO liable for its provider's negligence in Jones v. Chicago HMO of Illinois [ ]. In that case the HMO breached its duty to arrange adequate care by allowing the assignment of too many patients to a small group of physicians. This closely resembles the action of contracting with or allowing patient assignments to an understaffed and underfunded medical provider such as a nursing home.

improperly administered and inadequately funded and inadequately staffed. Nor is it alleged Aetna had itself negotiated—or knew or should have known the capitation rate negotiated with Magnolia Gardens by an intermediary management company—was so low it meant Magnolia Gardens would be inadequately funded and staffed to care for Aetna insured patients. Nor is it alleged Aetna knew or should have known Magnolia Gardens had become inadequately funded and staffed to properly care for Aetna insured patients after entering into the contract to provide services to those patients.

It is one thing when an HMO negotiates a contract with a reasonably capable provider and at a reasonable capitation level and then sees that provider make an erroneous decision, deliberate or negligent, to deny some medically necessary service, or commit malpractice in delivering that service. That is not a violation of the HMO's own duty of due care in arranging the provision of services to its enrollees. But it is quite another thing when an HMO chooses to contract with a provider that is "improperly administered" with an "undertrained and understaffed" nursing corps or at a capitation level which supplies the provider "inadequate funding" to give the HMO's enrollees proper care.

We have no idea whether the Pagarigans in good faith will be able to allege—to say nothing of proving—Aetna knew or should have known it was choosing a "maladministered, understaffed, and undertrained" provider—or indeed if Magnolia Gardens skilled nursing facility fits that characterization. Nor is it clear they will be able to honestly allege and later demonstrate Aetna knew or should have known the capitation rate negotiated with Magnolia Gardens left the latter so underfunded the nursing home was destined to deny needed care and/or deliver inadequate care—or whether the capitation rate indeed was that low. But we are convinced appellants should be afforded the opportunity to determine whether they can file such amendments in good faith.

In their eleventh and final cause of action, the Pagarigans reallege many of the earlier allegations in the complaint, including the facts discussed above which bear on Aetna's own duties and negligence. The count then simply alleges: "As a result of the wrongful conduct of the Defendants [including Aetna] as alleged, Decedent died." This death, in turn, caused the Pagarigans to be "deprived of the care, comfort, society and love of the Decedent...." For the same reasons we concluded the Pagarigans should be offered another opportunity to state a valid negligence action against Aetna, we find they should be afforded the same opportunity to plead a valid wrongful death action against this HMO.

[The court's discussion of causes of action for elder abuse and negligent infliction of emotional distress, sections IV and V, are omitted.]

VI. APPELLANTS HAVE FAILED TO STATE A VALID CONSTRUCTIVE FRAUD CAUSE OF ACTION FOR AETNA'S ALLEGED FAILURE TO DISCLOSE TO DECEDENT AND OTHER ENROLLEES ITS CONTRACTS WITH PROVIDERS WERE BASED ON A "CAPITATION" PAYMENT SYSTEM

In their sixth cause of action, the Pagarigans allege defendants including Aetna were liable for constructive fraud because at the time they were making treatment decisions while decedent was at Magnolia Gardens they failed to disclose Aetna's financial arrangements with its provider organizations were based on a capitation basis. This capitation arrangement, the Pagarigans allege, created conflicts of interest Aetna (and the other defendants) were required to disclose to the Pagarigans.

Aetna responds it had no duty to disclose because a constructive fraud claim depends on the existence of a fiduciary relationship between Aetna and its enrollees. Because no fiduciary relationship exists between an insurer and its insured, Aetna further argues, it is not liable on a constructive fraud cause of action, even if it did fail to disclose it was paying its providers on a capitation basis.

We have some question whether an insurance company which chooses to operate an entity it labels a "health maintenance organization," as opposed to an insurance plan, can deny it has a fiduciary relationship with those who choose to become members of that health maintenance organization. We also have some question whether, assuming no fiduciary relationship, such an HMO at least owes a duty to reveal its financial relationships with entities providing health care to its members—especially when those arrangements affect the economic incentives influencing the behavior of those providers.

Nonetheless, we have no reason to inquire further into these concerns at this point, because the Pagarigans do not allege a failure to disclose at the time it would be reasonable to require Aetna to do so. Instead they object to the failure to disclose these financial arrangements only "at the time [the Magnolia Gardens owner and operator], Greater Valley and Buttleman considered treatment options, recommended treatment, and during the time they provided care and treatment to the Decedent." The Pagarigans did not allege Aetna failed to disclose its "capitation" arrangements earlier, especially in the various documents it provided decedent and other enrollees in its HMO when they were deciding to enroll. Accordingly, despite appellants' "last chance" amendments, we find the present allegations fall short of stating a viable cause of action against Aetna for constructive fraud.

[The court's discussion of the causes of action for fraudulent concealment and a Randi violation, section VII and VIII, are omitted.]

IX. FALSE REPRESENTATIONS IN AN HMO'S MARKETING MATERIALS CAN BE ACTIONABLE, BUT APPELLANTS' ALLEGATIONS ARE NOT SUFFICIENTLY SPECIFIC OR OF A NATURE TO STATE A VALID CAUSE OF ACTION UNDER THAT THEORY OF LIABILITY

In their ninth cause of action, again focused only on Aetna (and Does 1–5) the Pagarigans allege "fraud" based on misrepresentations and false promises the HMO allegedly included in its "marketing materials" aimed at prospective enrollees. The complaint describes the alleged misrepresentations and promises in the most general of terms, e.g., the care would include all benefits Medicare covers, would comply with state law, and the like. It then alleges "[s]aid representations and promises were, when made, false." And the motive? For economic reasons. Aetna, allegedly "had no intention of providing such care ... if the cost ... was higher than [that consistent with the] goals for the financial performance of AETNA's business operation ... even if ... reasonably ... necessary for ... good medical practice and even if ... required under the law."The complaint then alleges the purpose of the fraud was "tricking and inducing" decedent and others to enroll as members of the

Aetna HMO. Finally, it alleges decedent enrolled because she relied on the fraudulent marketing materials.

We find the trial court reached the correct result, sustaining a demurrer to this cause of action, but apparently for the wrong reason. The court appeared to rule it would be impossible to found a fraud claim on misrepresentations made in "marketing materials" issued by an HMO or other health provider. It found such representations are inherently merely generalized expressions of opinion and "puffery" on which no one is entitled to rely. In so ruling, the court appeared to rely heavily on Pulvers v. Kaiser Foundation Health Plan, Inc. In that case involving an HMO's marketing materials, Division Four held representations the plan "would provide 'high standards' of medical service" represent "generalized puffing" not amounting to a warranty of high quality service.

While we have no quarrel with that portion of the *Pulvers* opinion, we find it is a limited observation about certain types of representations commonly found in advertising, including HMO marketing materials. We do not read it to rule out the possibility of other misrepresentations an HMO's marketing materials might contain which would be actionable. Imagine, for instance, Aetna's marketing materials claimed this HMO employed its own physicians and owned its own hospitals and nursing homes—or would lead an average reader to gain that impression. Or perhaps those materials asserted Aetna's HMO provided certain specified services which it did not. Or what if the materials advised prospective enrollees Aetna did not pay its contracting providers on a capitation basis. Could such brazen lies be excused as "mere puffery"? Obviously not.

Indeed Medicare enrollees, like decedent, have been allowed to sue an HMO for misrepresentations in the plan's marketing materials. For example, in *Solorzano v. Superior Court,* Division One issued a writ overturning a judgment on the pleadings and allowing a lawsuit by Medicare recipients against an HMO for fraudulent representations in its marketing materials. The suit sought compensatory and punitive damages as well as injunctive relief.

The problem here for the Pagarigans is not the viability of their theory, but the manner of its execution. As is true of their other fraud-type counts, their present allegations lack both specificity and substance.

Ordinarily, plaintiffs must specifically plead the time, place and content of every misrepresentation they allege. The Pagarigans seek to excuse the lack of specificity because the marketing materials were part of a large scale advertising program and thus "the defendant must necessarily possess full information concerning the facts ..." Certainly, in such situations plaintiffs should not be required to identify each of the scores or hundreds or thousands of brochures, advertisements, broadcasts and the like they allege contain misrepresentations. But this does not mean they need not be specific about the *content* of the statements those plaintiffs deem to constitute fraud. Here, the Pagarigans describe the statements in only the most general of terms-far short of the specificity required in fraud actions.

The alleged misrepresentations also lack substance. They are not statements of fact but only vague promises. Indeed they are too vague and modest even to qualify as true "puffery"—instead merely claiming the HMO will adhere to California law, will provide what Medicare requires, and something more, etc. But although they fall short of "puffery" they clearly are akin to the sort of statements the *Pulvers* court found not to be actionable.

Notably, in these counts as amended, the Pagarigans never tender factual allegations supporting an inference Aetna's marketing materials even imply the Aetna HMO is a traditional HMO which employs or otherwise controls the physicians, hospitals, nursing homes, and other providers who will be supplying the enrollees' health care. As a result, they are in no position to claim the marketing materials create an "apparent agency" (or "ostensible agency") cause of action, as has been recognized in Illinois, Pennsylvania and other states. Nor do those allegations, at present, even imply the materials suggest the Aetna HMO does not pay its providers on a capitation basis, or state anything else that is both material and false.

* * *

The judgment is reversed and the cause remanded to the trial court with instructions to sustain the demurrer with leave to amend as to the first and eleventh causes of action in the Pagarigans' complaint and to sustain the demurrer without leave to amend as to the remaining counts against Aetna, and for further proceedings consistent with this opinion. Each side to bear its own costs on appeal.

Notes and Questions

1.   Does a subscriber to an IPA-style managed care organization look to it for care rather than solely to the individual physicians? In an IPA, there is no central office, staffed by salaried physicians; the subscriber instead goes to the individual offices of the primary care physicians or the specialists. What justifies extending ostensible agency doctrine to this arrangement?

Managed care advertising often holds out the plan in words such as "total care program", as "an entire health care system". A reliance by the subscriber on the managed care organization for their choice of physicians, and any holding out by the MCO as a provider, is sufficient. See McClellan v. Health Maintenance Organization of Pennsylvania, 413 Pa.Super. 128, 604 A.2d 1053 (1992) (ostensible agency based on advertisements by HMO claiming that it carefully screened in primary care physicians).

In *Petrovich*, the court allowed both an apparent authority claim and an implied authority claim. Implied authority required a court to find sufficient elements of plan control over a physician to reject the independent contractor defense. The court found that utilization review, limits on referrals to specialists and hospitals, and other financial constraints were sufficient to create implied authority.

2.   IPA-model HMOs that become "the institution", that "hold out" the independent contractor as an employee, and also restrict provider selection are vulnerable to ostensible agency arguments. Where the HMO exercises substantial control over the independent physicians by controlling the patients they must see and by paying on a per capita basis, an agency relationship has been found. See Dunn v. Praiss, 256 N.J.Super. 180, 606 A.2d 862 (App.Div.1992); Boyd v. Albert Einstein Medical Center, 377 Pa.Super. 609, 547 A.2d 1229 (1988).

3. The court in Decker v. Saini, 14 Employee Benefits Cas. 1556, 1991 WL 277590 (Mich.Cir.Ct.1991) observed that the application of vicarious liability has a powerful incentive effect on MCOs to select better physicians:

> As a matter of public policy, the Court notes that imposing vicarious liability on HMOs for the malpractice of their member physicians would strongly encourage them to select physicians with the best credentials. Otherwise, HMO's would have no such incentive and might be driven by economics to retain physicians with the least desirable credentials, for the lower prices.

4. Some courts have pushed the boundaries even further, using agency principles to reach consulting physicians chosen by physicians employed by the HMO. In *Schleier v. Kaiser Foundation Health Plan*, 876 F.2d 174 (D.C.Cir.1989), a staff model HMO was held vicariously liable for physician malpractice, not of its employee-physician, but of an independent consulting physician. The court found four grounds for holding the HMO vicariously liable: (1) the consultant physician had been engaged by an HMO-employed physician, (2) the HMO had the right to discharge the consultant, (3) services provided by the consultant were part of the regular business of the HMO, and (4) the HMO had some ability to control the consultant's behavior, since he answered to an HMO doctor, the plaintiff's primary care physician. This judicial willingness to impose respondeat superior liability for the negligence of a consulting, non-employee physician clearly applies to the IPA model HMOs and even PPOs.

5. The development of complex cost and quality controls, which strengthen the supervisory role of the MCO, together with use of the capitation method of physician compensation, has led courts to hold the IPA model HMO-physician relationship to respondeat superior liability. Even a plan-sponsored network risks exposure to ostensible agency arguments if a court can find that the plan sponsor has created an expectation on the part of patients that the plan will provide high-quality providers of care. If the plan restricts a member's choice of providers, as will be likely in most situations, the network providers look like "agents" of the sponsor. The alternative—disclaimers in a PPO directory or other subscriber material as to quality of care, reminders to patients that they are responsible for choosing their physicians—may provide a legal shield against ostensible agency arguments. Such disclaimers are, however, not very reassuring when marketing to subscribers of a network plan. Capitation has begun to fade as a tool of managed care in the face of physician resistance and subscriber anxiety. Use of fee-based service claims that doctors must submit for each procedure is becoming more common. See Leigh Page, Capitation At The Crossroads, 44 AMA News 17 (March 5, 2001).

6. A breach of contract suit can be brought against an MCO on the theory of a "contract" to provide quality health care. In *Williams v. HealthAmerica*, 41 Ohio App.3d 245, 535 N.E.2d 717 (1987), a subscriber sued an IPA model HMO, and her primary care physician, for injuries resulting from a delay in referring her to a specialist. The theory was that the physician and HMO failed to deliver quality health benefits as promised, i.e. the right to be referred to a specialist. The court upheld the breach of contract action against the primary care physician but recast the action against the HMO as a tort claim for breach of the duty to handle the plaintiff's claim in good faith.

MCO contracts and literature may also contain provisions to the effect that "quality" health care will be provided or that the organization will promote or enhance subscriber health. The *Share* literature contained such language. (See fn.29 in Pagarigan). Where such assurances are made in master contracts of HMO-physician agreements, subscribers may be able to bring a contract action under a third party beneficiary theory. In *Williams*, for example, the court suggested that the subscriber could be a third-party beneficiary of the HMO-physician contract that required the physician to "promote of the rights of enrollees as patients."

A claim for breach of an express contract or an implied contract may also be argued based on representations by an HMO as to quality of care. This would seem to overlap with a malpractice claim to the extent it is based on a contract to provide "adequate and qualified medical care in accordance with the generally accepted standards of the community". Natale v. Meia, 1998 WL 236089 (Sup.Ct. Conn., 1998)(defendant's motion to strike denied). Express promises, if proven, can give rise to a separate claim.

Health care providers are not held to guarantee a cure, based on general language. "Mere puffery", as the courts view it, is not the same as a warranty of a good result, and will not create a claim. Pulvers v. Kaiser Foundation Health Plan, Inc., 99 Cal.App.3d 560, 160 Cal.Rptr. 392 (1979)(breach of warranty claim rejected on grounds that a warranty of a good result was just "generalized puffing.") However, an assurance of high quality care in marketing materials and brochures might be treated by a court or jury as a promise that standards of quality will be met, leading to warranty liability.

MCOs also typically market themselves by describing the quality of the providers on the panel. An assertion of quality furnishes courts another reason to impose on the organization the duty to investigate the competency of participating physicians. Such assertions might even be viewed as a warranty that all panel members maintain a certain minimum competence.

7. Common law fraud or state consumer fraud statutes are another possible source of recovery. Representations in contracts and marketing brochures, or omissions of material information from these documents, inducing the patient to subscribe to the MCO or submit to a certain medical treatment, might be actionable. These theories are more demanding, however, often requiring proof of intentional misrepresentation and justifiable reliance.

Common law bad faith claims may be brought against non-ERISA managed car plans. Courts have held that a staff model HMO acts as an insurer when it refers a subscriber to an out-of-network provider, under the contract, and then denies reimbursement for that out-of-network care without reasonable grounds. This kind of non-medical, coverage-related decision is subject to a bad faith analysis. McEvoy v. Group Health Cooperative of Eau Claire, 213 Wis.2d 507, 570 N.W.2d 397 (1997) (allowing bad faith action against a non-ERISA HMO for a coverage denial). The managed care organization is liable for any damages from the breach, including damages. Such actions are not intended to be duplicative of malpractice actions. They require a showing "by clear, satisfactory, and convincing evidence that an HMO acted improperly, and that financial considerations were given unreasonable weight in the decision maker's cost-benefit analysis."ID at 405. The court in McEvoy noted that HMO subscribers are "in an inferior position for enforcing their contractual health care rights" (id. at 403.) Such actions are likely to be rare in light of the higher burden of proof required and ERISA preemption, but the question of what "unreasonable weight" means in considering the financial effects of treatment opens the door to more litigation. Pilot Life Insurance Co. v. Dedeaux, 481 U.S. 41, 107 S.Ct. 1549, 95 L.Ed.2d 39 (1987) held that actions such as bad faith sufficiently "relate to" employee benefits plans to fall within ERISA preemption.

B. DIRECT INSTITUTIONAL LIABILITY: CORPORATE NEGLI-GENCE

SHANNON v. McNULTY

Superior Court of Pennsylvania, 1998.
718 A.2d 828.

ORIE MELVIN, JUDGE:

Mario L. Shannon and his wife, Sheena Evans Shannon, in their own right and as co-administrators of the Estate of Evan Jon Shannon, appeal from an order entered in the Court of Common Pleas of Allegheny County denying their motion to remove a compulsory nonsuit. This appeal concerns the Shannons' claims of vicarious and corporate liability against HealthAmerica stemming from the premature delivery and subsequent death of their son. We reverse the order refusing to remove the compulsory nonsuit and remand for trial.

This medical malpractice action arises from the pre-natal care provided by appellees, Larry P. McNulty, M.D. and HealthAmerica, to Mrs. Shannon. The Shannons claimed Dr. McNulty was negligent for failing to timely diagnose and treat signs of pre-term labor, and HealthAmerica was vicariously liable for the negligence of its nursing staff in failing to respond to Mrs. Shannon's complaints by timely referring her to an appropriate physician or hospital for diagnosis and treatment of her pre-term labor. The Shannons also alleged HealthAmerica was corporately liable for its negligent supervision of Dr. McNulty's care and its lack of appropriate procedures and protocols when dispensing telephonic medical advice to subscribers.

[The trial court granted HealthAmerica's motion for compulsory nonsuit, and the Shannons appealed.]

* * *

[Thompson v. Nason Hospital, 527 Pa. 330, 591 A.2d 703 (Pa.1991), set out four corporate negligence duties:

> (1) Use of "reasonable care in the maintenance of safe and adequate facilities and equipment;"
>
> (2) Selection and retention of competent physicians;
>
> (3) Oversight of "all persons who practice medicine within its walls as to patient care;" and
>
> (4) Formulation, adoption and enforcement of "adequate rules and policies to ensure quality care for patients," including upholding "the proper standard of care owed its patient." Id. at 708.]

* * *

The evidence introduced by the Shannons may be summarized in relevant part as follows. Mrs. Shannon testified during the trial of this case that she was a subscriber of the HealthAmerica HMO when this child was conceived. It was Mrs. Shannon's first pregnancy. When she advised HealthAmerica she was pregnant in June 1992, they gave her a list of six doctors from which she could select an OB/GYN. She chose Dr. McNulty from the list. [ ] Her HealthAmerica membership card instructed her to contact either her physician or HealthAmerica in the event she had any medical questions or emergent medical conditions. The card contained the HealthAmerica emergency phone number, which was manned by registered nurses. [ ] She testified it was confusing trying to figure out when to call Dr. McNulty and when to call HealthAmerica because she was receiving treatment from both for various medical conditions related to her pregnancy, including asthma and reflux.[ ]

She saw Dr. McNulty monthly but also called the HealthAmerica phone line a number of times for advice and to schedule appointments with their in-house doctors. [ ] She called Dr. McNulty on October 2, 1992 with complaints of abdominal pain. The doctor saw her on October 5, 1992 and examined her for five minutes. He told Mrs. Shannon her abdominal pain was the result of a fibroid uterus, he prescribed rest and took her off of work for one week. He did no testing to confirm his diagnosis and did not advise her of the symptoms of pre-term labor. [ ]

She next called Dr. McNulty's office twice on October 7 and again on October 8 and October 9, 1992, because her abdominal pain was continuing, she had back pain, was constipated and she could not sleep. She asked Dr. McNulty during the October 8th call if she could be in pre-term labor because her symptoms were similar to those described in a reference book she had on labor. [ ] She told Dr. McNulty her pains were irregular and about ten minutes apart, but she had never been in labor so she did not know what it felt like. He told her he had just checked her on October 5th, and she was not in labor.[ ] The October 9th call was at least her fourth call to Dr. McNulty about her abdominal pain, and she testified that Dr. McNulty was becoming impatient with her. [ ]

On October 10th, she called HealthAmerica's emergency phone line and told them about her severe irregular abdominal pain, back pain, that her pain was worse at night, that she thought she may be in pre-term labor, and about her prior calls to Dr. McNulty. The triage nurse advised her to call Dr. McNulty again. [ ] Mrs. Shannon did not immediately call Dr. McNulty because she did not feel there was anything new she could tell him to get him to pay attention to her condition. She called the HealthAmerica triage line again on October 11, 1992, said her symptoms were getting worse and Dr. McNulty was not responding. The triage nurse again advised her to call Dr. McNulty. [ ] Mrs. Shannon called Dr. McNulty and told him about her worsening symptoms, her legs beginning to go numb, and she thought that she was in pre-term labor. He was again short with her and angry and insisted that she was not in pre-term labor.[ ]

On October 12, 1992, she again called the HealthAmerica phone service and told the nurse about her symptoms, severe back pain and back spasms, legs going numb, more regular abdominal pain, and Dr. McNulty was not responding to her complaints. One of HealthAmerica's in-house orthopedic physicians spoke with her on the phone and directed her to go to West Penn Hospital to get her back examined. [ ] She followed the doctor's advice and drove an hour from her house to West Penn, passing three hospitals on the way. At West Penn she was processed as having a back complaint because those were HealthAmerica's instructions, but she was taken to the obstetrics wing as a formality because she was over five (5) months pregnant. She delivered a one and one-half pound baby that night. He survived only two days and then died due to his severe prematurity. [ ]

The Shannons' expert, Stanley M. Warner, M.D., testified he had experience in a setting where patients would call triage nurses. Dr. Warner opined that HealthAmerica, through its triage nurses, deviated from the standard of care following the phone calls to the triage line on October 10, 11 and 12, 1992, by not immediately referring Mrs. Shannon to a physician or hospital for a cervical exam and fetal stress test. As with Dr. McNulty, these precautions would have led to her labor being detected and increased the baby's chance of survival. [ ] Dr. Warner further testified on cross examination that Mrs. Shannon turned to HealthAmerica's triage nurses for medical advice on these three occasions when she communicated her symptoms. She did not receive appropriate advice, and further, if HealthAmerica's triage nurses intended for the referrals back to Dr. McNulty to be their solution, they had a duty to follow up Mrs. Shannon's calls by calling Dr. McNulty to insure Mrs. Shannon was actually receiving the proper care from him.[ ]

Corporate Liability

[The court concludes that the third duty of *Thompson*, the duty to oversee all those who deliver care, is applicable.] * * *

Similarly, in the present case Dr. Warner, on direct examination, offered the following opinion when asked whether or not HealthAmerica deviated from the standard of care:

> I believe they did deviate from the standard of care. I believe on each occasion of the calls on October 10th, 11th, and October 12th, that Mrs. Shannon should have been referred to the hospital, and the hospital notified that this woman was probably in preterm labor and needed to be handled immediately. They did have the alternative of calling for a physician, if they wanted to, for him to agree with it, but basically she needed to be evaluated in a placd [sic] where there was a fetal monitor and somebody to do a pelvic examination to see what was happening with her.

[ ]. When asked whether this deviation increased the risk of harm Dr. Warner stated that "it did increase the risk of harm to the baby, and definitely decreased the chance of [the baby] being born healthy." Id., at 147.

[Dr. Warner further testified, in response to a series of hypothetical questions, that severe abdominal pain should have led the triage nurse either to call the doctor so he could instruct the patient to get to the hospital, or tell the patient to get to the hospital as soon as possible, and on each of the three days that Shannon called Health America, the standard of care dictated that she be sent to hospital to determine if she was in preterm labor.]

Viewing the evidence in the light most favorable to the Shannons as the non-moving party, our examination of the instant record leads us to the conclusion that the Shannons presented sufficient evidence to establish a prima facie case of corporate liability pursuant to the third duty set forth in Thompson, *supra*. However, due to the different entities involved, this determination does not end our inquiry. The Welsh case involved a suit against a hospital and thus Thompson was clearly applicable. Instantly, HealthAmerica, noting this Court's decision not to extend corporate liability under the facts in McClellan v. Health Maintenance Organization of Pennsylvania, 413 Pa.Super. 128, 604 A.2d 1053 (Pa.Super.1992), argues that the Thompson duties are inapplicable to a health maintenance organization. We disagree.

In adopting the doctrine of corporate liability the Thompson court recognized "the corporate hospital's role in the total health care of its patients." Thompson, at 708. Likewise, we recognize the central role played by HMOs in the total health care of its subscribers. A great deal of today's healthcare is channeled through HMOs with the subscribers being given little or no say so in the stewardship of their care. Specifically, while these providers do not practice medicine, they do involve themselves daily in decisions affecting their subscriber's medical care. These decisions may, among others, limit the length of hospital stays, restrict the use of specialists, prohibit or limit post hospital care, restrict access to therapy, or prevent rendering of emergency room care. While all of these efforts are for the laudatory purpose of containing health care costs, when decisions are made to limit a subscriber's access to treatment, that decision must pass the test of medical reasonableness. To hold otherwise would be to deny the true effect of the provider's actions, namely, dictating and directing the subscriber's medical care.

Where the HMO is providing health care services rather than merely providing money to pay for services their conduct should be subject to scrutiny. We see no reason why the duties applicable to hospitals should not be equally applied to an HMO when that HMO is performing the same or similar functions as a hospital. When a benefits provider, be it an insurer or a managed care organization, interjects itself into the rendering of medical decisions affecting a subscriber's care it must do so in a medically reasonable manner. Here, HealthAmerica provided a phone service for emergent care staffed by triage nurses. Hence, it was under a duty to oversee that the dispensing of advice by those nurses would be performed in a medically reasonable manner. Accordingly, we now make explicit that which was implicit in McClellan and find that HMOs may, under the right circumstances, be held corporately liable for a breach of any of the Thompson duties which causes harm to its subscribers.

[The court also held that HealthAmerican was vicariously liable for the negligent rendering of services by its triage nurses, under Section 323 of the Restatement (Second) of Torts.]

Notes and Questions

1. Consider the underlying failures of the system in *Shannon*. The treating physician was impatient and inattentive to warning signs, but it was the triage nurses staffing the phone lines who failed to properly direct Shannon to a physician or hospital. How should the system have been designed to avoid such an error? What would you suggest to avoid a repetition of this kind of disaster?

2. *Poor Plan Design.* Many of the ERISA preemption cases involve claims of negligent design of the managed care plan, including telephone call-in services staffed by nurses, as in *Shannon*. Other claims of negligent design and administration of the delivery of health care services have been allowed. See McDonald v. Damian, 56 F.Supp.2d 574 (E.D.Pa.1999) (claim for inadequacies in the delivery of medical services). The court in *Pappas v. Asbel* noted that contractual benefits

provided in "such a dilatory fashion that the patient was injured are intertwined with the provision of safe care," and would give rise to a negligent administration claim. 555 Pa. 342, 724 A.2d 889, 893 (1998). In *Pappas*, the issue was a delay in transporting the plaintiff to a specialty trauma unit for care. The delay was arguably caused by the utilization review process of the managed care organization, which did not allow transport to the best hospital unit in the area for spinal injuries. *Pappas* involves a delay induced by a plan determination as to out-of-network care and a benefits question as to which hospitals were available to U.S. Healthcare providers.

3. *Negligent Selection of Providers.* The managed care organization, like the hospital, has been held to owe its subscribers a duty to properly select its panel members. In *Harrell v. Total Health Care, Inc.,* 1989 WL 153066 (Mo.App.1989), affirmed, 781 S.W.2d 58 (Mo.1989), the court stated that an IPA model HMO owed a duty to its participants to investigate the competence of its panel members and to exclude physicians who posed a "foreseeable risk of harm." This logic also applies to PPOs, which control entry of physicians to the provider panel. While the merits of this claim were not reached, the case suggests that courts are willing to impose upon managed care organizations the duty to determine the competency of the providers on its panel.

The logic of a direct duty imposed on MCOs to properly select providers is even stronger for an MCO than for a hospital. In the hospital setting, the patient usually has selected the physician. He is then admitted to the hospital because his physician has admitting privileges at that hospital. By contrast, in a managed care program the patient has chosen the particular program, but not the physicians who are provided. The patient must use the physicians on the panel. The patient thus explicitly relies on the MCO for its selection of health care providers. The MCO's obligations for the patient's total care are more comprehensive than in the hospital setting. A plan sponsor that establishes provider networks and channels patients to those networks is likely to be liable for negligent selection. If, however, a plan sponsor uses a PPO sponsor as an intermediary to set up PPO networks, the chance of liability is less likely, although a court may still find a duty to properly select and monitor the sponsor.

A duty of proper selection will expose a managed care organization to liability both for failing to properly screen its physicians' competence, and also for failing to evaluate physicians for other problems. If the MCO selects a panel physician or dentist who has evidenced incompetence in her practice, it may risk liability. This is comparable to negligently granting staff privileges to an impaired physician with alcohol or other substance abuse problems, or one with sexual pathologies that might affect patients. See McClellan v. Health Maintenance Organization of Pennsylvania, 413 Pa.Super. 128, 604 A.2d 1053 (1992), where the court allowed a suit against HMO to proceed for negligence in selecting, retaining and evaluating primary care physician, misrepresenting the screening process for selecting its primary care physicians, and breach of contract.

4. *Failures to supervise and control staff.* Hospitals are required to supervise the medical care given to patients by staff physicians; to detect physician incompetence; and to take steps to correct problems upon learning of information raising concerns of patient risk. A hospital should also properly restrict the clinical privileges of staff physicians who are incompetent to handle certain procedures, or detect concealment by a staff doctor of medical errors.

Managed care organizations are likely to face similar duties to supervise. MCO liability for negligent control of its panel physicians derives from the same common law duty that underlies the negligent selection basis of liability as well as federal and state quality assurance regulations. As courts continue to characterize MCOs as health care providers, suits are likely to increase. Only PPOs with their reduced level of physician control might have an argument that liability should not be imposed for negligent supervision. However, statutes in some states require PPOs to implement quality assurance programs and others contemplate the use of such programs by PPOs. Iowa Code Ann. § 514.21; Ky. Rev. Stat. § 211.461; La. Stat. Ann.—Rev.Stat. § 22:2021; Me. Rev. Stat. Ann. tit. 24 § 2342 & tit. 24–A § 2771. The existence of such systems, with the PPOs having the right to remove a participating physician from the panel based on information generated by the quality assurance mechanism, imposes a duty to supervise. Managed care is likely to be forced to undertake both a duty to select with care and a duty to engage in continuous supervision.

5. Managed care organizations are motivated by goals of both quality and efficiency—the objective of cost sensitive health care. The style of practice in MCOs is different from fee-for-service practice, assuming a more conservative, less intensive level of intervention, specialist use, and hospitalization. Some courts have recognized that managed care plans should give providers leeway to practice a more conservative, cost-effective style. See, e.g., Harrell v. Total Health Care, Inc., 781 S.W.2d 58, 61 (Mo.1989)("People are concerned both about the cost and the unpredictability of medical expenses. A plan such as Total offered would allow a person to fix the cost of physicians' services.").

C. PHYSICIAN INCENTIVE SYSTEMS

Most managed care programs have three relevant features from a liability perspective. First, such programs select a restricted group of health care professionals who provide services to the program's participants. Second, such programs accept a fixed payment per subscriber, in exchange for provision of necessary care. This pressures managed care organizations to search for ways to minimize costs. Third, following from number two, managed care organizations use a variety of strategies to ensure cost effective care. Altering physician incentives is central to managed care, since physicians influence seventy percent of total health spending, while receiving only about twenty percent of each health care dollar. Such plans use utilization review techniques, incentives systems, and gatekeepers to control costs. Managed care organizations create a new set of relationships between payers, subscribers and providers. These new relationships create new liability risks. The subscriber typically pays a fee to the MCO rather than the provider, relinquishing control over treatment and choice of treating physician. The payor in turn shifts some of its financial risk to its approved providers, who must also accept certain controls over their practice.

Every medical decision is also a spending decision. Since physicians as agents for patients control a large percentage of the health care dollar, should we trust them to have unfettered freedom to spend the money of others and use others's resources? The record of health care cost inflation suggests that unfettered physician discretion is not desirable. Managed care organizations are institutional structures developed as a response to health care inflation, to better manage the cost of health care by reducing utilization of hospitalization, specialists and testing. See E. Haavi Morreim, Playing Doctor: Corporate Medical Practice and Medical Malpractice, 32 U.Mich.J.L.Ref. 939, 972–73 (1999).

The Supreme Court addressed the role of managed care design and incentives in Pegram v. Herdrich, In *Pegram*, the treating plan physician refused to order an ultrasound at a local hospital, instead making her wait eight additional days for an ultrasound to be performed at a Carle facility more than 50 miles away. Herdrich's appendix ruptured, causing peritonitis.

The U.S. Supreme Court rejected the reasoning of the Seventh Circuit. With regard to the incentive structure of managed care organizations, Justice Souter, writing for the Court, stated:

> Like other risk-bearing organizations, HMOs take steps to control costs. At the least, HMOs, like traditional insurers, will in some fashion make coverage determinations, scrutinizing requested services against the contractual provisions to make sure that a request for care falls within the scope of covered circumstances (pregnancy, for example), or that a given treatment falls within the scope of the care promised (surgery, for instance). They customarily issue general guidelines for their physicians about appropriate levels of care. See id., at 568–570. And they commonly require utilization review (in which specific treatment decisions are reviewed by a decisionmaker other than the treating physician) and approval in advance (precertification) for many types of care, keyed to standards of medical necessity or the reasonableness of the proposed treatment. [ ] These cost-controlling measures are commonly complemented by specific financial incentives to physicians, rewarding them for decreasing utilization of health-care services, and penalizing them for what may be found to be excessive treatment [ ]. Hence, in an HMO system, a physician's financial interest lies in providing less care, not more. The check on this influence (like that on the converse, fee-for-service incentive) is the professional obligation to provide covered services with a reasonable degree of skill and judgment in the patient's interest. [ ]

> The adequacy of professional obligation to counter financial self-interest has been challenged no matter what the form of medical organization. HMOs became popular because fee-for-service physicians were thought to be providing unnecessary or useless services; today, many doctors and other observers argue that HMOs often ignore the individual needs of a patient in order to improve the HMOs' bottom lines. See, e.g., 154 F.3d, at 375–378 (citing various critics of HMOs). In this case, for instance, one could argue that Pegram's decision to wait before getting an ultrasound for Herdrich, and her insistence that the ultrasound be done at a distant facility owned by Carle, reflected an interest in limiting the HMO's expenses, which blinded her to the need for immediate diagnosis and treatment.

The Court thus acknowledged a national health care policy to use managed care to constrain the rapid health care cost inflation so evidence by the 1970s.

Little evidence exists that HMO incentives have a detrimental effect on patient care. The argument about incentives assumes that physicians' sensitivity to financial incentives is so fine-tuned that they will vary the intensity of care they give to each patient. The alternative possibility is that professional norms, risk of malpractice suits, and the daily pressures of practice will be more powerful forces on physician behavior. This would mean that a physician will treat all patients in light of his sense of best practice as adopted to a particular locality. The evidence has not yet resolved this question of physician response to incentives. Some form of incentive for cost-conservation in health care is desirable, and the ongoing debate is over the extent to which payment incentives can strike the right balance. While incentives may create conflicts of interest, they also give physicians flexibility in their clinical decision-making. The alternative—administrative rules and review mechanisms for denying benefits—is both more inefficient and arguably more constraining of physician decision-making. This debate—incentives versus rules—is an ongoing one. Plaintiffs have nonetheless argued that payment systems can cause a reduction in the quality of care delivered by physicians in managed care organizations, an argument that *Pegram* finally rejected. Robert H. Miller and Harold S. Left, Does Managed Care Lead to Better or Worse Quality of Care? 16 Health Affairs 7, 18 (1997); David Orentlicher, Paying Physicians More to Do Less: Financial Incentives to Limit Care, 30 U.Rich. L.Rev. 155 (1996); Uwe E. Reinhardt, The Economist's Model of Physician Behavior, 281 J.A.M.A. 462, 464 (1999); Lawrence C. Baker, Association of Managed Care Market Share and Health Expenditures for Fee–For–Service Medicare Patients, 281 J.A.M.A. 432 (1999). See William M. Sage, Physicians As Advocates, 35 Houston L.Rev. 1529, 1620 (1999) (" . . . the use of financial incentives in managed care preserves professional autonomy and improves efficiency even if it compromises advocacy at the margin.")

The debate over the use of physician incentives to promote cost sensitive practice has abated, largely because managed care companies have decided, in the face of class action litigation and bad publicity, to restrict their use of some incentives. Aetna has announced that it will end the use of financial incentives to physicians that might have the effect of restricting member access to care. Aetna will limit the use of capitated fees, as well as the use of medical guidelines created by actuarial firms and used by some insurers to restrict reimbursement for care. See Milo Geyelin and Barbara Martinez, Aetna Weighs a Managed–Care Overhaul, Wall St. J. A3–10 (January 17, 2001).

Problem: Wanting the "Best"

Cheryl Faber, twenty years old and newly married, joined a managed care organization, Freedom Plus [the Plan], one of several choices offered by her employer, Primerica Bank. Cheryl had examined the literature for the various plan choices during her open enrollment period. She chose the Plan because its literature talked of a "high quality" program, with the "best doctors" in the area, and "no cost-cutting where subscriber health is concerned".

The Plan sets aside a certain amount of money each year for a "referral pool" and a "hospital/ancillary pool" for Plan physicians. The money in these pools is depleted with each referral to a specialist or hospitalization of a patient during the year. At the end of the year, any money left over in these pools is divided between the Plan and the individual physicians.

Cheryl went to her primary care physician in the Plan, Dr. Hanks, for her initial physical examination. Dr. Hanks found small lumps in her breasts, which he noted in the patient record as fibroid tumors. He talked briefly with Cheryl about the lumps, but stated that she shouldn't worry.

A year later Cheryl came back for another checkup. Dr. Hanks had left the Plan. It turned out Dr. Hanks had been the defendant in several malpractice suits filed against him in the five years he had worked for another HMO and he was terminated by that HMO. The Plan could have discovered this by accessing the National Practitioners Data Bank, or by calling up the previous employer.

Cheryl was then examined by another primary care physician, Dr. Wick. Dr. Wick was concerned about the lumps, and she prepared a referral to an oncologist, Dr. Scanem, who had recently joined the panel of specialists affiliated with the Plan. Cheryl went to Dr. Scanem, who ordered a biopsy and confirmed that the lumps were malignant Stage III cancer. Stage III cancers have about a 10% five year survival rate, Stage II a 40% five year survival, and Stage I almost 100% survival with prompt treatment.

Dr. Scanem recommended a treatment regime for Cheryl that included limited radical mastectomy and chemotherapy. He planned to use a new drug for breast cancers that had recently become available through a research protocol in which he was participating. This drug appeared to offer a slightly higher cure rate with young patients such as Cheryl with advanced breast cancer.

The Plan approved Dr. Scanem's recommendations, with the exception of the new drug. The Plan rejected his proposal for use of this drug, stating that it only reimbursed for chemotherapy using the standard drugs used generally by oncologists. The new drug was extremely expensive, and would have increased the cost of Cheryl's chemotherapy by about 200%. Dr. Scanem was angry about the refusal by the Plan to reimburse Cheryl's treatment in full, and told her so. He told her that there was nothing he could do about it, and so he said he would use the standard approach that most oncologists used. Cheryl was a very nervous patient, terrified of her cancer. Dr. Scanem was worried about upsetting her too much, given the other stresses created by the surgery and the side-effects from chemotherapy. She asked him what her chances were, and he said only that she had "a reasonable shot at beating it, with luck and prayer." He did not tell her anything more about the prognosis, nor did she ask.

Cheryl underwent the radical mastectomy and chemotherapy. Optimistic about her chances, Cheryl proceeded to get pregnant. She and her husband also bought a new house, assuming that she would recover and her salary would continue.

Cheryl's cancer proved to be too far advanced to respond to treatment. She died six months after the chemotherapy regime finished. Her fetus could not be saved, in spite of efforts by Plan obstetricians to do so. Her husband lost their new house since he could no longer afford the mortgage payments.

What advice will you give Mr. Faber about the merits of litigation against the Plan?

V. REFORMING THE TORT SYSTEM FOR MEDICAL INJURIES

Malpractice crises come and go in the United States, driven by an apparent insurance cycle of competitive entry in the market, following by rapid premium increases as the insurers' returns dropped. A new malpractice crisis resurfaced in 1999, precipitated by a rapid escalation in malpractice insurance premiums for most physicians and limited availability of coverage in some states—as carriers went bankrupt or left the malpractice line of insurance. A new round of legislative reform efforts, spearheaded by angry physician groups, has emerged from this latest "crisis", as physicians have faced increases in their insurance premiums and pockets of unavailability in some areas and for some specialties. The "crisis", following the cyclical pattern common to malpractice insurance, is again abating, but the outpouring of research and writing on the topic continues unabated.

The explanations for the current crises are as varied as their proponents. As David A. Hyman writes:

> Depending on one's perspective, there is too much medical malpractice litigation or not enough; contingent fee arrangements create an obscene form of bounty hunting or are absolutely necessary to ensure justice; physicians should not be second-guessed by those too dumb to avoid jury service or the jury system works just fine; and legislators who enact tort reform are protecting fat-cat doctors or have prudently restrained a tort system run amok.

David A. Hyman, Medical Malpractice and System Reform: Of Babies and Bathwater, 19 Health Aff. 258, 258 (2000).

A. MEDICAL PROGRESS AND OTHER CHANGES IN THE HEALTH CARE ENVIRONMENT

Malpractice suits require a plaintiff who suffers a medical injury at the hands of a health care provider. The hazards of health care are substantial. As we learned in Chapter 1, error rates in medicine are surprisingly high. As the Harvard Medical Practice study discovered in surveying medical iatrogenesis in New York hospitals, as many as four percent of hospitalized patients suffer an adverse medical event which results in disability or death. The Harvard Study projected that approximately one percent of all hospital patients suffer injury due to negligently provided care. Harvard Medical Practice Study, Patients, Doctors, and Lawyers: Medical Injury, Malpractice Litigation, and Patient Compensation in New York, Exec.Summ. 3–4 (1990). See Chapter 1 *infra*.

Medical progress has been one of the drivers of expanded tort liability; medicine has increased its power to treat and diagnose, and this power has created increased risks to patients along with it. William Sage writes: "[f]oremost, improvements in the clinical capabilities of medicine increase expectations of success, redefine success upwards, and foster the belief that failure is the result of negligence rather than misfortune. The first wave of malpractice suits in the late 19th century, involving nonunion of limb fractures, arose only because medical science had developed an alternative to amputation. Malpractice litigation has become as specialized as the medical care it attacks."

Sage notes medicine's increased power to diagnose and treat cancer, keep premature infants alive, and treat elderly patients who would not have survived surgery two decades ago. At the same time, rising health care costs also inflate the size of malpractice jury awards, since damages have increased as earnings and the costs of remedial treatment increased. See generally James C. Mohr, American Medical Malpractice Litigation in Historical Perspective, 283 JAMA 1731 (2000).

Second, industrialization in the health care industry has brought expanded liability, as Chapters 5 and 6 indicate. Health care is delivered in institutions and group practices. As a result, hospital actions are subject to increasingly intense scrutiny; long term care has become a new and growing target for malpractice litigation; managed care companies are less protected by ERISA preemption than a decade ago; even pharmacists are now exposed to substantial new risks. While malpractice crises historically have been driven by perceived litigation risks to physicians, this crisis includes increased exposure to malpractice suits by all the institutional players in the health care system.

Third, managed care and its cost containment mechanisms have had a strong effect on the system. Physicians are no longer able to pass increased malpractice premiums on to their patients or insurers, the result of tightened reimbursement by both private and public payers. At the same time, physicians have less time to talk to their patients, leaving an injured patient disgruntled and angry at the loss of personal relationship. Angry and injured patients are more likely to sue in such a situation.

Fourth, as a result of the above forces and others, the malpractice insurance market has become less profitable and less stable. See section B below.

Fifth, complexity in medicine—the combination of medical progress and industrialization—is producing more medical adverse events and errors. The Harvard Study discussed in Chapter 1, based on review of hospital records, may understate the problem. Lori Andrews conducted another study in a large Chicago area hospital, looking at the actual incidence of negligent events in hospital wards. She discovered that many injuries were not recorded on the records as required, especially when the main person responsible for the error was a senior physician. 17.7% of patients in her study experienced errors with a significant impact, many more than the 3.7% found in the Harvard Study. See Lori Andrews, Studying Medical Error *In Situ*: Implications for Malpractice Law and Policy, 54 DePaul L. Rev. 357 (2005).

See Medical Malpractice and the U.S. Health Care System (William M. Sage and Rogan Kersh, eds.2006); William M. Sage, Understanding the First Malpractice Crisis of the 21st Century, in The Health Law Handbook, 2003 Edition, Alice Gosfield, Editor. See also Marc S. Galanter, "Reading the Landscape of Disputes: What We Know and Don't Know (and Think We Know) About Our Allegedly Contentious and Litigious Society", 31 UCLA L.Rev. 4, 70–72 (1983); Michael Saks, In Search of the "Lawsuit Crisis", 14 Law, Medicine & Health Care 77 (1986); Kenneth Chesebro, Galileo's Retort: Peter Huber's Junk Scholarship, 42 Am. Univ. L. Rev. 1637 (1993).

For a review of the claims for the existence of a medical malpractice crisis justifying the imposition of limitations on the medical liability regime and interference in the structure of the market for medical liability insurance and a review of the counter claims, see, e.g., Tom Baker, The Medical Malpractice Myth (2005); Michelle M. Mello et al., The New Medical Malpractice Crisis, 348 New Eng. J. Med. 2281 (2003); Medical Malpractice and the U.S. Health Care System (William M. Sage & Rogan Kersh eds., 2006); Public Citizen Congress Watch, The Great Medical Malpractice Hoax: NPDB Data Continue to Show Medical Liability System Produces Rational Outcomes (January 2007), http://www.citizen.org/documents/NPDBŘeport_Final.pdf.

Review the cases in Chapters 4, 5, and 6. Consider the reasons for new theories such as the "loss of a chance" doctrine and hospital corporate negligence.

B.   THE NATURE OF THE INSURANCE INDUSTRY

Any serious analysis of the malpractice "crisis" begins (and some say it ends) with the insurance industry. The most visible manifestation of the malpractice crisis today, as in the 1970s and 1980s, has been rapid increases in premiums for malpractice insurance purchased by health care professionals and institutions. Insurance carriers have gone bankrupt or dropped out of the malpractice market, while others raised their malpractice premiums precipitously to compensate for investment losses. The insurance market has shrunk, rates have risen, and physicians and hospitals have felt the pinch. See generally Missouri Department of Insurance, Medical Malpractice Insurance In Missouri: The Current Difficulties in Perspective (2003).

Health care providers buy medical malpractice insurance to protect themselves from medical malpractice claims. Under the insurance contract, the insurance company agrees to accept financial responsibility for payment of any claims up to a specific level of coverage during a fixed period in return for a fee. The insurer investigates the claim and defends the health care provider. This insurance is sold by commercial insurance companies, health care provider owned companies, and joint underwriting associations. Some large hospitals also self-insure for medical malpractice losses rather than purchasing insurance, and a few physicians practice without insurance. Joint underwriting associations are nonprofit pooling arrangements created by state legislatures to provide medical malpractice insurance to health care providers in the states in which they are established.

Insurance rate setting uses actuarial techniques to set rates, to generate funds to cover (1) losses occurring during the period, (2) the administrative costs of running the company, and (3) an amount for unknown contingencies, which may become a profit if not used. The profit may be retained as capital surplus or returned to stockholders as dividends.

See generally U.S. GENERAL ACCOUNTING OFFICE, MEDICAL MALPRACTICE: NO AGREEMENT ON THE PROBLEMS OR SOLUTIONS 66–72 (1986), from which the above discussion was taken, describing the crises of the 1970s and mid–1980s.

The GAO has continued its study of the malpractice problem in a series of recent reports. In a more recent study, the GAO concluded:

> Based on available data, as well as our discussions with insurance industry participants, a variety of factors combined to explain the malpractice insurance cycle that produced several years of relatively stable premium rates in the 1990s followed by the severe premium rate increases of the past few years. To begin with, insurer losses anticipated in the late 1980s did not materialize as projected, so insurers went into the 1990s with reserves and premium rates that proved to be higher than the actual losses they would experience. At the same time, insurers began a

decade of high investment returns. This emerging profitability encouraged insurers to expand their market share, as both the downward adjustment of loss reserves and high investment returns increased insurers' income. As a result, insurers were generally able to keep premium rates flat or even reduce them, although the medical malpractice market as a whole continued to experience modestly increasing underlying losses throughout the decade. Finally, by the mid-to late 1990s, as excess reserves were exhausted and investment income fell below expectations, insurers' profitability declined. Regulators found that some insurers were insolvent, with insufficient reserves and capital to pay future claims. In 2001, one of the two largest medical malpractice insurers, which sold insurance in almost every state, determined that medical malpractice was a line of insurance that was too unpredictable to be profitable over the long term. Alternatively, some companies decided that, at a minimum, they needed to reduce their size and consolidate their markets. These actions, taken together, reduced the availability of medical malpractice insurance, at least in some states, further exacerbating the insurance crisis. As a result of all of these factors, insurers continuing to sell medical malpractice insurance requested and received large rate increases in many states. It remains to be seen whether these increases will, as occurred in the 1980s, be found to have exceeded those necessary to pay for future claims losses, thus contributing to the beginning of the next insurance cycle.

U.S. GENERAL ACCOUNTING OFFICE, MEDICAL MALPRACTICE INSURANCE: MULTIPLE FACTORS HAVE CONTRIBUTED TO INCREASED PREMIUM RATES (2003).

Notes and Questions

1. *The Flaws in the Malpractice Insurance Market.* The market for malpractice insurance fails to satisfy many of the economist's conditions for an ideal insurance market. The ideal market consists of a pooling by the insurer of a large number of homogeneous but independent random events. The auto accident insurance market is perhaps closest to fulfilling this condition. The large numbers of events involved make outcomes for the insurance pool actuarially predictable. Malpractice lacks these desirable qualities of "... large numbers, independence, and risk beyond the control of the insured." Patricia Danzon, Medical Malpractice: Theory, Evidence, and Public Policy 90 (1985) (hereafter Danzon). The pool of potential policyholders is small, as is the pool of claims, and a few states have most of the claims. The awards vary tremendously, with 50% of the dollars paid out on 3% of the claims. In small insurance programs, a single multimillion dollar claim can have a tremendous effect on total losses and therefore average loss per insured doctor.

Second, losses are not independent, since neither claims against an individual doctor nor against doctors as a group are independent; multiple claims against a doctor relate usually to some characteristic of his practice or his technique, and a lawyer can use knowledge gained in one suit in another. Claims and verdicts against doctors generally reflect social forces—shifts in jury attitudes and legal doctrine. Social and legal attitudes toward medicine recently have been in flux. Given the long tail, or time from medical intervention to the filing of a claim, the impact of these shifts is increased.

Finally, the problems of moral hazard and adverse selection distort the market. Moral hazard characterizes the effect of insurance in reducing an insured's incentives to prevent losses, since he is not financially responsible for losses. Adverse selection occurs when an insurer attracts policy holders of above-average risk, ending up with higher claim costs and lower profits as a result. This may have occurred because a competing insurer has attracted away lower risk policyholders through the use of lower rates and selective underwriting. Danzon at 91.

2. *Premium Increases and the Medical Rate of Inflation.* Causes of premium increases are disputed. Consumer groups such as Americans for Insurance Reform (AIR) contend that there is no malpractice "crisis" driven by rapid increases in frequency or severity of litigation. To the contrary, the AIR contends that malpractice insurer payouts, including all jury awards and settlements, track the rates of medical inflation. The cost of medical goods and services has increased faster than the Consumer Price Index, and this is reflected in malpractice settlements and payouts. There has been no explosion in insurance payouts over the past thirty years; to the contrary, payments (in constant dollars) have been stable and flat since the mid–1980s. Studies in some states have confirmed that all increases in award sizes are accounted for by medical inflation, wage inflation (for lost earnings) and the increase in severity of the injury to the patient. Missouri Department of Insurance, Medical Malpractice Insurance in Missouri: The Current Difficulties in Perspective 6 (February 2003).

3. *The Underwriting Cycle.* The malpractice crisis is more a product of the way the insurance industry does business than of changes in the frequency of medical malpractice litigation or the severity of judgments. The malpractice market is a "lumpy" market, prone to cycles of underpricing and catchup. What doctors and hospitals see as "sudden" price increases are actually deferred costs passed on when premiums no longer cover payments plus profit. Once premiums reach actuarially sound levels, profits rise, new insurers enter the market with lower rates, competitive pressures return, and the cycle starts all over again.

The cyclical nature of interest rates, as a measure of return on investments, plays a central role in insurers' pricing decisions. The insurance industry engages in cash-flow underwriting, in which insurers invest the premiums they collect in the bond market and to a lesser extent in the stock market. When interest rates and investment returns are high, insurance companies accept riskier exposures to acquire more investable premium and loss reserves. The insurance industry managed to be profitable from 1976 to 1984, and again during the 1990s. If underwriting and investment results are combined during these periods, investment gains more than offset losses. Malpractice insurance premiums charged by insurance companies do not relate to payouts, but rather rise and fall in concert with the state of the economy, reflecting gains and losses of invested reserves and the insurance industry's calculation of their rate of return on the investment "float" (the time between collecting premium dollars and paying out losses) provided by the physician premiums.

See AIR, Medical Malpractice Insurance: Stable Losses/Unstable Rates (October 10, 2002), www.insurance-reform.org/StableLosses.pdf.

4. *Price Wars.* Insurance carriers sometimes act like gasoline stations that enter into pricing wars to gain market share, inflicting wounds on themselves in an attempt to grab more of the market. Favorable operating results in the malpractice line of insurance led insurers to compete aggressively. New companies started up to capture some of the profitable malpractice market. The rate of return on investment income, that is, premiums invested in the bond and stock

markets, was high in the 1990s as the nation's economy boomed and the stock market increased dramatically in value. The overall performance of the market is thus a major factor in medical malpractice insurance. Companies sacrificed underwriting gains to attract more business and enhance their investment gains. In some cases the prices charged were far below good actuarial levels. If insurance premiums are priced low in competitive markets, carriers expect to generate investment income to offset underwriting losses. When return on investments decreases as a result of economic downturns, as has occurred starting in 2000 with the bursting of the stock market bubble, this underwriting strategy creates instability in the market, since losses have to be paid. If interest rates and investment yields drop, insurance companies must raise their premiums and drop some lines of insurance, in order to compete. See testimony of James Hurley, spokesman for the American Academy of Actuaries, testimony to the House Energy and Commerce Subcommittee on Health, www.actuary.org. See also Charles Kolodkin, Gallagher Healthcare Insurance Services, Medical Malpractice Insurance Trends? Chaos! (September 2001), at http://www.irmi.com/expert/articles/kolodkin001.asp.

One cause of this latest price war was due to accounting practices of one large carrier, St. Paul Company. An investigative report by the Wall Street Journal found that St. Paul, at that time with 20% of the national malpractice market, pulled out after a series of missteps in handling their reserves. In the 1980s they had set aside too much in reserve for claims. In the 1990s, using a new accounting strategy, they released $1.1 billion in reserves, which appeared in their income statements as profits. New carriers, responding to this perception of high profitability in the malpractice lines of coverage, moved aggressively to compete, forcing existing carriers to slash prices to compete. From 1995 to 2000, rates fell to such a low level that they could not cover claims, and with the drop of the stock market starting in 2000 many companies collapsed. St. Paul then stopped writing malpractice insurance, and that left physicians in many states with both a pricing and an access problem. Christopher Oster and Rachel Zimmerman, Insurers' Missteps Helped Provoke Malpractice "Crisis," Wall Street Journal, June 24, 2002.

This has happened before. The Government Accounting Office concluded of the insurance "crisis" of the early 1980s that "[t]he underwriting losses resulted, in part, from the industry's cash flow underwriting pricing strategy in which companies sacrificed underwriting gains in an attempt to attract more business and thereby enhance investment gains." Government Accounting Office, Insurance: Profitability of Medical Malpractice and General Liability Lines (1987).

5. *Premium Escalation.* Post 9/11, critics accused the insurance industry generally of price gouging in many lines of insurance, taking advantage of a changed political climate to raise premiums in all lines of insurance beyond what is actuarially justified. The malpractice lines may also be part of this pricing. See "Avoid Price Gouging, Consultant Warns," National Underwriter, January 14, 2002.

6. *Limitations on State Insurance Regulation.* Many states grant their insurance regulators limited authority to regulation medical malpractice insurance rates unless they are either excessive and the market is not competitive. States tend to rely on the marketplace to adjust rates instead of granting broader regulatory powers to their insurance commissioners. Some states are considering allowing their insurance departments to reject malpractice rate filings that do not meet acceptable standards. See, e.g., Missouri Department of Insurance, Medical Malpractice Insurance in Missouri: The Current Difficulties in Perspective 4 (February 2003).

7. Given the above materials, how would you approach reform of the insurance industry and its approach to malpractice insurance pricing and competition? Is wholesale reform needed? Or should means be found to assure coverage for physicians temporarily while waiting for the market to stabilize and premiums drop again?

C. IMPROVING INSURANCE AVAILABILITY

The response to the perceived "crisis" in malpractice litigation and insurance availability over the past thirty years has been twofold. First, the availability of insurance has been enhanced by a variety of changes in the structure of the insurance industry. Second, physicians have lobbied with substantial success at the state level for legislation to impede the ability of plaintiffs to bring tort suits and to restrict the size of awards.

Malpractice reform proposals can be evaluated by three overall standards. First, do the reforms improve the operation of the tort system for compensating victims of medical injuries? Second, will the reforms create incentives for the reduction of medical error and resulting injury to patients? Third, are changes likely to encourage insurers to make malpractice insurance more available and affordable? Institute of Medicine, Beyond Malpractice: Compensation for Medical Injuries 29–30 (1978). For a federal study that builds upon the Institute of Medicine report, see U.S. General Accounting Office (GAO), Medical Malpractice: No Agreement on the Problems or Solutions (1986). (hereafter GAO Malpractice Report). Can you think of other goals by which we should test tort reform? As you read through these materials, ask yourself if the various reforms are likely to promote or impede particular goals, and at what cost.

1. *New Sources of Insurance.* New sources of insurance were created in response to earlier crises, either by the states or by providers. Joint underwriting associations, reinsurance exchanges, hospital self-insurance programs, state funds, and provider owned insurance companies have sprung into being. Physician-owned companies now write as much as 60% of malpractice coverage nationally. Hospitals have begun to self-insure. Some states have adopted state programs, such as patient compensation funds, to limit doctor liability to individual patients.

2. *Claims–Made Policies.* Medical malpractice insurers changed in the late seventies to writing policies on a claims-made rather than an occurrence basis. Before 1975, most policies had been occurrence policies, covering claims made at any time as long as the insured doctor was covered during the time the medical accident giving rise to the claim occurred. The increase in the frequency and severity of claims in the mid–70s revealed the long tail problem of this kind of insurance. Insurers struggled to reliably predict their future losses and set premium prices, and often failed. Most insurers therefore have shifted to a claims-made policy, allowing them to use more recent claims experience to set premium prices and reserve requirements. The claims-made policy covers claims made during the year of the policy coverage, avoiding the predictability problem of the occurrence policy. Such policies arguably have allowed companies to continue to carry malpractice insurance lines, serving the goal of availability by keeping premium costs lower than they would otherwise have been.

3. *Stop–Gap State Coverage.* Self-insurance pools are also being considered by several states to provide a temporary fix for coverage until carriers reenter a state to offer coverage. See State Actions on Liability Crisis: From Self–Insurance to Damage Caps, 12 Health Law Reporter 247 (February 13, 2003).

4. *Hospital Provision of Coverage for Staff Physicians.* Some hospitals in states facing the highest premium escalation or coverage gaps in the insurance market in 2003 proposed to provide temporary assistance to staff physicians in obtain insurance. This could operate theoretically as an incentive for hospitals to better monitor their staff physicians to keep risks low.

5. *Selective Insurance Marketing.* Physician mutual companies, with physician-investors, have often ridden out the underwriting cycle with less distress than the commercial carriers. One example is Pennsylvania Healthcare Providers Insurance Exchange (PAHPIX), formed in 2002. It promises an intensive commitment to risk management, "looking for physicians who want to control their premium costs through a 'best practices' approach to clinical care." It promises not to seek temporary market share gains through lower prices. And it markets to physicians who will remain loyal through up and down markets: "We believe that the current crisis of availability is a result of under pricing the market. Our structure enables our members to benefit in the event our pricing exceeds what is needed to cover claims and expenses." The company wants to make the control of claims a daily task for covered physicians. The theory is that a malpractice carrier must manage risks as well as underwriting them, in order to control exposure. http://www.pahpix.com/risk.html.

6. *Hospital Complaint Profiling.* For hospitals, complaint profiling has been proposed, spotting litigation-prone staff physicians and intervening to retrain them to avoid risks. The Hickson study took six years worth of hospital patient advocacy files and concluded that unsolicited patient complaints about physicians are a highly reliable predictor of litigation-prone physicians. The study found that 9% of the physicians produced 50% of the complaints, and the study showed an 86% success rate in predicting physicians with multiple claims. The various explanations given for higher physician loss ratios, such as serving a litigation-prone population, treating higher-risk patients, and technical incompetence were not statistically significant. Only "connecting" to patients was significant. See Gerald B. Hickson et al., Patient Complaints and Malpractice Risk, 287 J.A.M.A. 2951 (2002). See also Nalini Ambady et al., Surgeons' Tone of Voice: A Clue To Malpractice History, 132 Surgery 5 (2002).

D. ALTERING THE LITIGATION PROCESS

Starting in the 1970s, states enacted tort reform legislation. The preamble to the California Medical Injury Compensation Reform Act, the current Holy Grail for tort reformers of the malpractice system, is typical of the legislative perceptions of the malpractice crisis:

> The Legislature finds and declares that there is a major health care crisis in the State of California attributable to skyrocketing malpractice premium costs and resulting in a potential breakdown of the health delivery system, severe hardships for the medically indigent, a denial of

access for the economically marginal, and depletion of physicians such as to substantially worsen the quality of health care available to citizens of this state.

Tort reform measures were intended by their proponents to reduce either the frequency of malpractice litigation or the size of the settlement or judgment. The goal was not to improve the lot of the injured patient, but instead to satisfy both the medical profession and the insurance industry.

These measures were designed to restrict the operation of the tort system in four ways: (1) affecting the filing of malpractice claims; (2) limiting the award recoverable by the plaintiff; (3) altering the plaintiff's burden of proof through changes in evidence rules and legal doctrine; (4) changing the role of the courts by substituting an alternative forum. These are characterized by Eleanor Kinney as "first generation" reforms. See generally Eleanor D. Kinney, Learning from Experience, Malpractice Reforms in the 1990s: Past Disappointments, Future Success?, 20 J. Health Pol. Pol'y & L. 99 (1995).

The most powerful reform in actually reducing the size of malpractice awards has been a dollar limit, or cap, on awards. Caps may take the form of a limit on the amount of recovery of general damages, typically pain and suffering; or a maximum recoverable per case, including all damages. Indiana has a $500,000 limit per claim; Nebraska $1 million; South Dakota a limit of $500,000 for general damages; and California $250,000 on recovery for non-economic damages, including pain and suffering. See David A. Hyman, Bernard Black, Charles Silver, and William M. Sage, Estimating the Effect of Damage Caps in Medical Malpractice Cases: Evidence From Texas, 1 J. Legal Analysis ___ (2008).

One reform proposal that has resurfaced in legislative discussions in some states has been to "schedule" pain and suffering awards, rather than capping them, to narrow the range of variability in jury awards. See Randall R. Bovbjerg, Frank Sloan, and James Blumstein, Valuing Life and Limb in Tort: Scheduling "Pain and Suffering," 83 Nw.Univ.L.Rev. 908 (1989).

Arbitration is often proposed as a way to solve the problems of the tort system. The expected advantages of arbitration include diminished complexity in fact-finding, lower cost, fairer results, greater access for smaller claims, and a reduced burden on the courts. See GAO Report at 139–40; American Arbitration Association, Arbitration—Alternative to Malpractice Suits, 5 (1975); Irving Ladimer, Joel Solomon, and Michael Mulvihill, Experience in Medical Malpractice Arbitration, 2 J.Legal Med. 443 (1981). No state requires compulsory arbitration. Like screening panels, the arbitration process uses a panel to resolve the dispute after an informal presentation of evidence. The panel typically consists of a doctor, a lawyer and a layperson or retired judge. The arbitration panel, however, uses members trained in dispute resolution and has the authority to make a final ruling as to both provider liability and damages. The process is initiated only when there is an agreement between the patient and the health care provider to arbitrate any claims.

Arbitration has distinct disadvantages from a consumer perspective. Lawyers can drive up the costs and length of arbitration to match litigation. Evidence is also emerging that the "repeat player" phenomenon means a much higher victory rate for employers and other institutional players who regularly engage in arbitration in contrast to one-shot players such as employees or consumers. In employment arbitration cases, one study found that the odds are 5–to–1 against the employee in a repeat-player case. Much of this imbalance may be due to the ability and incentive of repeat players to track the predisposition of arbitrators and bias the selection process in their favor. See Richard C. Reuben, The Lawyer Turns Peacemaker, 82 ABA Journ. 55, 61 (1996).

E. ALTERNATIVE APPROACHES TO COMPENSATION OF PATIENT INJURY

Second-generation reform proposals aim to eliminate or reduce some of these perceived flaws of the current system, without impairing consumer access to compensation. Such proposals can be categorized in light of several central attributes. They involve combining different reforms, choosing variables from a series of categories into a single package. The categories that are available include: (1) the compensable event, (2) the measure of compensation, (3) the payment mechanism, (4) the forum used to resolve disputes, and (5) the method of implementing the new rights and responsibilities. See generally Kenneth Abraham, Medical Liability Reform: A Conceptual Framework, 260 Journal of the American Medical Association 68–72 (1988).

Abraham summarizes the categories and reform choices in the following table:

Compensable Event	Measure of Compensation	Payment Mechanism	Forum for Resolution of Disputes	Method of Implementation
Fault Cause Loss	Full tort damages Full out-of-pocket losses Partial out-of- pocket losses Scheduled damages Lump-sum payment Periodic payment	First-party insurance Third-party insurance Taxation Hybrid Funding	Jury trial Expert review panels Bench trial Binding arbitration Administrative boards Insurance company decision	Legislation Mandatory reform Elective options Private contract

He concludes:

In sum, the possibilities for medical liability reform are no longer limited to tinkering with tort law by altering a few technical legal doctrines governing litigation. There is more to potential reform than merely making lawsuits more accurate, predictable, or cost efficient. Retaining the basic model of adversarial litigation is by no means the only available approach. A whole range of alternatives has developed, providing the reformer with a series of choices that must be made on the way to reform. No combination of reforms is without its problems, but no effort to adopt the most appropriate system of liability and compensation should ignore the variety of options that are available to deal with the concerns raised by the critics of reform.

1. *Alternative Dispute Resolution (ADR)*

Mandatory alternative dispute resolution has been proposed as an alternative to the tort system. The ADR decision is comparable to a jury verdict and could be overturned only if corruption, fraud, or undue influence is shown or new evidence unavailable at the ADR proceeding is presented. Judicial review of ADR decisions would be similar to review of adjudications by administrative agencies, limited to questions of whether the decision is sufficiently supported by the evidence or otherwise is in accord with the law. See Thomas Metzloff, Alternative Dispute Resolution Strategies in Medical Malpractice, 9 Alaska Law Review 429 (1992); Simpson, D., Compulsory Arbitration: An Instrument of Medical Malpractice Reform and a Step towards Reduced Health Care Costs? 17 Seton Hall Legislative Journal 457 (1993); U.S. Congress, Office of Technology Assessment, Impact of Medical Malpractice Tort Reform on Malpractice Costs (1993).

Mediation has also been proposed as an attractive alternative to litigation. See generally Edward A. Dauer, Leonard J. Marcus, and Susan M. C. Payne, Prometheus and the Litigators: A Mediation Odyssey, 21 J. Leg. Med. 159 (2000).

2. No–Fault Systems

a. Provider–Based Early Payment

Under this approach providers would voluntarily agree to identify and promptly compensate patients for avoidable injuries. Damages would be limited under most proposals. This approach was first proposed by Clark Havighurst and Lawrence Tancredi, and has been recommended in Institute of Medicine, Fostering Rapid Advances in Health Care: Learning from System Demonstrations 82 (2002).

Under the proposal, when the adverse outcome first occurred, the patient or provider would file the claim with the insurer, who would decide whether the injury was covered. If so, it would make prompt payment. Disputes would be resolved through the courts or arbitration. The plan as proposed would experience rate insurance premiums paid by providers, in order to create incentives for the providers to improve the quality of care, thereby reducing their exposure for the adverse outcomes listed. Provider experience under the plan would also be used to strengthen peer review within hospitals. See Clark Havighurst and Laurence Tancredi, "Medical Adversity Insurance"—A No–Fault Approach to Medical Malpractice and Quality Assurance, 51 Milbank Memorial Fund Quarterly 125 (1973); Clark Havighurst, "Medical Adversity Insurance—Has Its Time Come?", 1975 Duke L.J. 1254; Laurence Tancredi, Designing a No–Fault Alternative, 49 Law & Contemp. Probs. 277 (1986).

A variation on the Tancredi proposals is provided by Professor O'Connell, who has proposed a variety of elective no-fault options using a list of covered injuries and contract agreements between providers and patients. See Jeffrey O'Connell, No–Fault Insurance for Injuries Arising from Medical Treatment: A Proposal for Elective Coverage, 24 Emory L.J. 35 (1975).

Notes and Questions

1. What is gained by the Tancredi proposal? It takes certain adverse outcomes out of a fault-based system, and places them in a loss-based system, most likely in the hospital setting. What are the advantages of this approach from the physician's perspective? The hospital's? The patient's?

2. How should the panels set the level below which an adverse event is judged to be avoidable if good care is given? Should national data be used, with

this approach implemented on a national basis, perhaps through the Medicare program? Or should this be left state-by-state, or hospital-by-hospital? What approach do you prefer? Why?

b. Administrative Systems

Another proposal offered by the Institute of Medicine has been to legislate a state system loosely based on the Workers' Compensation model. Under this approach, providers would receive immunity from tort in exchange for "mandatory participation in a state-sponsored, administrative system established to provide compensation to patients who have suffered avoidable injuries." See Institute of Medicine, Fostering Rapid Advances in Health Care: Learning from System Demonstrations 82 (2002). The AMA developed an elaborate proposal in the late 1980s, but to date such state-administered systems have been limited to special categories of injuries, such as brain-damaged infants.

The State of Virginia has led the states in implementing a no-fault system for obstetric mishaps. The state enacted the "Birth–Related Neurological Injury Compensation Act", creating a compensation fund for neurologically damaged newborns. Virginia Code Ann. §§ 38.2–5000 to–5021; King v. Virginia Birth–Related Neurological Injury Compensation Program, 242 Va. 404, 410 S.E.2d 656 (1991). Only a handful of claims have qualified each year under the statute, and no claim has been filed. The definition is so narrow that only the most severe injuries are covered, and most of those eligible die as infants. Are the pressures toward participation by physician strong enough? If it is true that very few claims are being filed, what incentives exist for physicians to elect to participate? Can you suggest a redrafting of the eligibility provision to provide for better coverage?

See generally James Henderson, The Virginia Birth–Related Injury Compensation Act: Limited No–Fault Statutes as Solutions to the "Medical Malpractice Crisis", Institute of Medicine, Medical Professional Liability and the Delivery of Obstetrical Care: An Interdisciplinary Review (Vol. II) (1989); David G. Duff, Compensation for Neurologically Impaired Infants: Medical No–Fault In Virginia, 27 Harv.J.Legis. 391 (1990). For criticisms of the Virginia system, see Richard A. Epstein, Market and Regulatory Approaches to Medical Malpractice: The Virginia Obstetrical No–Fault Statute, in Institute of Medicine, Medical Professional Liability and the Delivery of Obstetrical Care: An Interdisciplinary Review (Vol. II), 115 (1989). Florida also adopted a no-fault system. See Florida State. Ann. § 408.02.

Notes and Questions

1. If you represent a hospital, what problems would you see in a offer system? Why should a provider come forward to inform a patient that he has suffered a compensable injury? What is in it for the provider in an uncertain case? Is the doctor in charge of the case likely to admit error, so that the hospital can present its offer to the patient? How can the hospital encourage staff doctors to come forward? How might legal rules improve the possibilities of disclosure of errors?

2. One of the primary goals in a no-fault system is to reduce the cost of insurance to providers. The California study in the 1970s estimated that a no-fault

system in California could increase malpractice premiums 300% higher than the tort system's insurance costs. California Medical and Hospital Associations, Report on the Medical Insurance Feasibility Study (1977). A critique of the Harvard New York study likewise concluded that the costs of a no-fault system could be greater than the present tort system, when the costs of many more claims and system administrative costs are combined. See Mehlman, Saying "No" to No–Fault: What the Harvard Malpractice Study Means for Medical Malpractice Reform (New York State Bar Association 1990).

From the insurance industry perspective, these proposals are worrisome, since there seems to be far more malpractice in the world than is ever detected or litigated. A no-fault system may set off an avalanche of litigation. For an account of such fears, see the comments of the Jerry Engelelter, government affairs officer for St. Paul's insurance, in Kleinfield, The Malpractice Crunch at St. Paul, The New York Times, Sunday, February 24, 1985 at p. 4F.

If a compensation system rewards many more claimants, particularly small ones, in an evenhanded and more rapid fashion than does the current tort system, it may well be an improvement. But it is unlikely to be a cheaper system. This suggests that we move directly to a social insurance scheme that moves financing out of the private insurance market and into the taxation structure of the government.

F. CONCLUSION

First-generation reforms are now in place in most states. Second-generation reforms, ranging from enterprise liability to contractual arbitration models, are far less likely to be adopted by either Congress or the states. The current push is to enact statutory caps on pain and suffering awards, using the California model as the solution to the problem. It remains to be seen whether broader innovations in malpractice compensation systems will be tried at either the federal or state levels. The vested interests are entrenched at this point, and serious system reform seems unlikely, particularly as the latest malpractice crisis abates as insurance costs drop for providers.

Problem: National Medical Error Disclosure and Compensation Act

Consider the proposal by Senators Hillary Clinton and Barack Obama. Review the ideas on patient safety in Chapter 1, and then analyze this bill and break down its approaches to improving patient safety using federal regulatory powers. Is this a significant improvement over the status quo? See *S.   1784. To amend the Public Health Service Act to promote a culture of safety within the health care system through the establishment of a National Medical Error Disclosure and Compensation Program* at www.govtrack.us/congress/billtext.xpd?bill=s 109–1784.

See also Hillary Rodham Clinton and Barack Obama, Making Patient Safety the Centerpiece of Medical Liability Reform, 354 New Eng.J.Med. 2205 (2006).

VI. PATIENT SAFETY REGULATION

We have thoroughly explored tort liability as both a quality control and compensation mechanism. The threat of a tort suit clearly puts pressure on providers, but most particularly institutions, to reduce the risks that their patients may suffer (and therefore reduce payouts and insurance costs).

Section V, looking at tort reform, makes it clear that the deterrence debate is ongoing, while many state legislatures continue to cut back on plaintiffs' ability to sue for malpractice through a variety of strategies.

The next step, to supplant tort litigation, is some form of patient safety regulation. The following section looks at several emerging ideas for improving patient safety, primarily in hospitals.

Regulation of medical errors or adverse events is risk regulation, aimed at improving patient safety when encountering drugs, hospital care, or other forms of medical treatments. The menu of patient safety approaches has rapidly increased since the IOM Report in 1999. The general strategies include legislative initiatives to force disclosure of hospital adverse events and "near misses" to patients along with an apology; publication of performance data about relative risks; "Pay For Performance" initiatives from corporate groups that have spread to Medicare payment; and legal tools ranging from warranties of performance by some providers to patients to improvements in tort liability rules of disclosure of physician performance. The field of Patient Safety is rapidly growing as a subspecialty within health law as a result of this burst of regulatory activity. See generally Barry Furrow, Regulating Patient Safety: Toward a Federal Model of Medical Error Reduction, 12 Widener L. Rev. 1 (2005).

A. ERROR TRACKING AND SYSTEM IMPROVEMENTS

The Institute of Medicine reports, beginning with **To Err Is Human**, focused attention on medical systems and the level of errors they produced. Hospitals and other providers were asked to respond by developing error tracking systems and strategies for improvement including disclosure of both errors and so-called "near misses", events that could have resulted in patient injury but were detected in time. This is not a new idea; as early as 1858 Florence Nightingale developed the use of statistical methodology to show the effects of unsanitary conditions in military field hospitals. Her approach laid the groundwork for standard statistical approaches for hospitals. Florence Nightingale, Notes on Matters affecting the Health, Efficiency and Hospital Administration of the British Army (1858). See also John Maindonald and Alice M. Richardson, This Passionate Study: A Dialogue with Florence Nightingale, 12 J. Stat. Ed. (2004), www.amstat.org/publications/jse/v12n1/maind onald.html.

The idea of systematically tracking errors in hospitals is also not new. The first systematic approach was developed by Dr. Ernest Codman, a Boston doctor who wanted hospitals and doctors to track their practices and evaluate outcomes of their patients, an ideal he developed around 1920. See Virgina A. Sharpe and Alan I. Faden, Medical Harm: Historical, Conceptual, and Ethical Dimensions of Iatrogenic Illness 31 (1998).

Reporting errors or adverse events is essential to system approaches, but it has been a concern for health care providers, who are afraid that disclosure of an error will come to plaintiff lawyers' attention. Voluntary reporting of mistakes has been argued to be the preferable approach to uncovering errors and correcting them. States that have mandatory reporting requirements for errors have found that underreporting is too often the norm. But the fact that underreporting occurs does not mean that performance cannot be improved.

The reasons for such poor performance are several. Mandatory systems lack support from physicians, who are worried about liability, damage to reputation, and the hassle factor of any reporting system. Brian Liang, Promoting Patient Safety Through Reducing Medical Error, 22 J.L.Med & Ethics 564 (2002); J. Rosenthal et al., Current State Programs Addressing Medical Errors: An Analysis of Mandatory Reporting and Other Initiatives (2001). Mandatory reporting is resisted by providers, even though it was recommended by the IOM report. A movement toward mandatory reporting models is observable, however. The Joint Commission Sentinel Events policy, the new CMS rules on hospital error, and the new Pennsylvania statute all require disclosure of errors.

1. *Sentinel Events and the Joint Commission*

The Joint Commission (formerly the Joint Commission on Accreditation of Healthcare Organizations) is a private accreditor, granted authority by federal and state governments to accredit hospitals. See Chapter 3, Section III *infra*. The Joint Commission Sentinel Event Policy has adopted the view of medical errors of the Institute of Medicine report **To Err is Human**. It requires reporting on two levels: first to Joint Commission of serious events, and second to patients.

A sentinel event is defined as "an unexpected occurrence involving death or severe physical or psychological injury, or the risk thereof," including unanticipated death or major loss of functioning unrelated to the patient's condition; patient suicide; wrong-side surgery; infant abduction/discharge to the wrong family; rape; and hemolytic transfusion reactions. Joint Commission, "Sentinel Event Policy and Procedures", online at www.JointCommi ssion.org.

Hospitals must report serious events to the Joint Commission, and if they do not and Joint Commission learns of the events from a third party, the hospital must conduct an analysis of the root cause or risk loss of accreditation. Loss of accreditation is rarely exercised, however. Sentinel Event Alert, Joint Commission on Accreditation of Healthcare Organizations, 2002, www. JointCommission.org/about+us/news+letters/sentinel+event+alert/index. htm.

The Joint Commission disclosure standard also requires that "[p]atients, and when appropriate, their families, are informed about the outcomes of care, including unanticipated outcomes." Joint Commission on Accreditation of Healthcare Organizations, Revisions to Joint Commission Standards in Support of Patient Safety and Medical/Health Care Error Reduction, at www. JointCommission.org/standard/fr_ptsafety.html (July 1, 2001)(JointCommis sion Revisions) at RI.1.2.2

The intent statement provides: "The responsible licensed independent practitioner or his or her designee clearly explains the outcomes of any treatments or procedures to the patient and, when appropriate, the family, whenever those outcomes differ significantly from the anticipated outcomes". Id.

Notes and Questions

1. The Joint Commission is a private accreditation organization, and its primary weapon for hospital improvement is the threat that accreditation will be revoked, or the hospital placed on the "Accreditation Watch List". Given the infrequency of revocation of hospital accreditation, how does the Joint Commission have a significant effect on hospital behavior?

2. Does the Joint Commission standard suffer from any infirmities? What does "significantly" mean? Is it self-defining? How might hospitals interpret it to reduce their disclosure obligations? Joint Commission indicates that they are the same as "sentinel events" or "reviewable sentinel events". A "sentinel event" is defined in Joint Commission standards as: " ... an unexpected occurrence involving death or serious physical or psychological injury, or the risk thereof. Serious injury specifically includes loss of limb or function. The phrase 'or the risk thereof' includes any process variation for which a recurrence would carry a significant chance of a serious adverse outcome." Joint Commission on Accreditation of Healthcare Organizations, Hospital Accreditation Standards 53 (2001)(Joint Commission Standards).

3. Where does the disclosure obligation repose? The intent statement specifies that "the responsible licensed independent practitioner or his or her designee" must clearly explain "the outcomes of any treatments or procedures." This practitioner is someone with clinical privileges, typically the patient's attending physician. Since the attending physician typically has the informed consent responsibility, he or she is the logical person to conduct such a conversation. But physicians are not subject to Joint Commission requirements. Are they therefore likely to resist such disclosures out of fear of liability, stigma, loss of hospital credentials, or other motivations? See, e.g. Nancy LeGros & Jason D. Pinkall, The New Joint Commission Patient Safety Standards and the Disclosure of Unanticipated Outcomes, 35 J. Health L. 189, 205 (2002).

2. *"Never" Events*

ELIMINATING SERIOUS, PREVENTABLE, AND COSTLY MEDICAL ERRORS—NEVER EVENTS

CMS Office of Public Affairs.
May 18, 2006.

OVERVIEW:

As part of its ongoing effort to pay for better care, not just more services and higher costs, the Centers for Medicare & Medicaid Services (CMS) today announced that it is investigating ways that Medicare can help to reduce or eliminate the occurrence of "never events"–serious and costly errors in the provision of health care services that should never happen. "Never events," like surgery on the wrong body part or mismatched blood transfusion, cause serious injury or death to beneficiaries, and result in increased costs to the Medicare program to treat the consequences of the error.

BACKGROUND:

According to the National Quality Forum (NQF), "never events" are errors in medical care that are clearly identifiable, preventable, and serious in their consequences for patients, and that indicate a real problem in the safety and credibility of a health care facility. The criteria for "never events" are listed in Appendix 1. Examples of "never events" include surgery on the wrong body part; foreign body left in a patient after surgery; mismatched blood transfusion; major medication error; severe "pressure ulcer" acquired in the hospital; and preventable post-operative deaths. * * *

* * *

Some states have enacted legislation requiring reporting of incidents on the NQF list. For example, in 2003, the Minnesota legislature, with strong support from the state hospital association, was the first to pass a statute requiring mandatory reporting of "never events". The Minnesota law requires hospitals to report the NQF's 27 "never events" to the Minnesota Hospital Association's web-based Patient Safety Registry. The law requires hospitals to investigate each event, report its underlying cause, and take corrective action to prevent similar events. In addition, the Minnesota Department of Health publishes an annual report and provides a forum for hospitals to share reported information across the state and to learn from one another.

During the first year of Minnesota's mandatory reporting program, 30 hospitals reported 99 events that resulted in 20 deaths and four serious disabilities. In the second year, 47 hospitals reported 106 events that resulted in 12 deaths and nine serious injuries. These included 53 surgical events, and 39 patient care management events. * * *

In 2004, New Jersey enacted a law requiring hospitals to report serious, preventable adverse events to the state and to patients' families, and Connecticut adopted a mix of 36 NQF and state-specific reportable events for hospitals and outpatient surgical facilities. An Illinois law passed in 2005 will require hospitals and ambulatory surgery centers to report 24 "never events" beginning in 2008. Several other states have considered or are currently considering never event reporting laws.

* * *

NEXT STEPS:

From its beginning, the Medicare program has generally paid for services under fee-for-service payment systems, without regard to quality, outcomes, or overall costs of care. In the past several years, CMS has been working with provider groups to identify quality standards that can be a basis for public reporting and payment.

Clearly, paying for "never events" is not consistent with the goals of these Medicare payment reforms. Reducing or eliminating payments for "never events" means more resources can be directed toward preventing these events rather than paying more when they occur. The Deficit Reduction Act represents a first step in this direction, allowing CMS, beginning in FY 2008, to begin to adjust payments for hospital-acquired infections. CMS is interested in working with our partners and Congress to build on this initial step to more broadly address the persistence of "never events."

In particular, CMS is reviewing its administrative authority to reduce payments for "never events," and to provide more reliable information to the public about when they occur. CMS will also work with Congress on further legislative steps to reduce or eliminate these payments. CMS intends to partner with hospitals and other healthcare organizations in these efforts.

Notes and Questions

1.   What regulatory weapon does CMS threaten for failures of hospitals to comply with their new rule? If you represent a hospital, what will you advise hospitals to do to achieve compliance and retain their Medicare status?

2.   This CMS position on "never events" and payment is a significant step toward "Pay for Performance". Tying Medicare payments to quality is a significant incentive for providers to reduce the levels of adverse events, but the CMS description of demonstration projects still suggests it is moving very slowly as it decides how to calibrate payment to quality.

3.   CMS has implemented a final rule that will deny payment where hospital "never events" occur. The rule implements a provision of the Deficit Reduction Act of 2005 (DRA) that takes the first steps toward preventing Medicare from giving hospitals higher payment for the additional costs of treating a patient who acquires a condition (including an infection) during a hospital stay. Already the feature of many state health care programs, the DRA requires hospitals to begin reporting secondary diagnoses that are present on the admission of patients, beginning with discharges on or after October 1, 2007. Beginning in FY 2009, cases with these conditions will not be paid at a higher rate unless they are present on admission. The rule identifies eight conditions, including three serious preventable events (sometimes called "never events") that meet the statutory criteria.

3.   *Disclosure of Errors to Patients*

The "never events" development in twenty odd states is a major step, forcing providers to disclose adverse outcomes on the list to the state department responsible, with the goal of improving their operations. It is more than just information disclosure. It allows for systematic recording and tracking of errors, for purpose of analysis of patterns of adverse events, feedback to hospitals, and in some states, information for consumers as to th e relative performance of hospitals and other providers.

Adverse event reporting is often coupled with disclosure of classes of bad outcomes to patients and their families. This disclosure idea developed as the result of a program begun by a Veterans Administration hospital, and has been adopted by the VA system. It served as the model for Pennsylvania's legislation creating the Patient Safety Authority.

DISCLOSURE OF ADVERSE EVENTS TO PATIENTS

VHA DIRECTIVE 2005–049.
October 27, 2005.

1.   WHAT ADVERSE EVENTS WARRANT DISCLOSURE?

a.   Patients and/or their representatives must be informed of the probable or definite occurrence of any adverse event that has resulted in, or is expected to result in, harm to the patient, including the following:

(1) Adverse events that have had or are expected to have a clinical effect on the patient that is perceptible to either the patient or the health

care team. For example, if a patient is mistakenly given a dose of furosemide (a diuretic that dramatically increases urine output), disclosure is required because a perceptible effect is expected to occur.

(2) Adverse events that necessitate a change in the patient's care. For example, a medication error that necessitates close observation, extra blood tests, extra hospital days, or follow-up visits that would otherwise not be required, or a surgical procedure that necessitates further (corrective) surgery.

(3) Adverse events with a known risk of serious future health consequences, even if the likelihood of that risk is extremely small. For example, accidental exposure of a patient to a toxin associated with a rare, but recognized serious long-term effect (e.g., HIV infection or increased incidence of cancer).

(4) Adverse events that require providing a treatment or procedure without the patient's consent. For example, if an adverse event occurs while a patient is under anesthesia, necessitating a deviation from the procedure the patient expected, the adverse event needs to be disclosed. Patients have a fundamental right to be informed about what is done to them and why.

* * *

2. WHEN SHOULD DISCLOSURE OF AN ADVERSE EVENT OCCUR?

Optimal timing of disclosure of adverse events varies with the specific circumstances of the case. * * *

3. HOW SHOULD ADVERSE EVENTS BE COMMUNICATED?

a. Disclosure of an adverse event needs to occur in an appropriate setting and be done face-to-face. The location needs to be a quiet, private place and adequate time needs to be set aside, with no interruptions.

b. In general, communication about the adverse event needs to be done through a clinical disclosure of adverse events, when one or more members of the clinical team provides preliminary factual information to the extent it is known, expresses concern for the patient's welfare, and reassures the patient or representative that steps are being taken to investigate the situation, remedy any injury, and prevent further harm. Social workers, chaplains, patient advocate, or other staff may be present to help the patient or representative cope with the news and to offer support, if needed. The patient's treating practitioner is responsible for determining who shall communicate this information.

c. Sometimes, given the nature, likelihood, and severity of injury, and the degree of risk for legal liability, there will be a need for institutional disclosure of adverse events either instead of, or in addition to, clinical disclosure. Institutional disclosure includes the following elements:

(1) Institutional Leaders (e.g., the Chief of Staff or facility Director) invite the patient or personal representative to meet for an Institutional Disclosure of Adverse Event Conference. Institutional leaders may only invite the representative if he or she is involved in the patient's care (and the patient does not object), or the representative is the personal repre-

sentative as outlined in VHA Handbook 1605.1. NOTE: The facility Risk Manager, treating physician, or other VHA personnel deemed appropriate, may be included in this conference at the discretion of facility leadership.

(2) Institutional disclosure of adverse events should not take place until organizational leaders, including, as appropriate, the facility Director, Chief of Staff, and members of the treatment team, have conferred with Regional Counsel and addressed what is to be communicated, by whom and how.

(3) Any request by a patient or personal representative to bring an attorney must be honored, but may influence whether providers will participate.

(4) The Risk Manager or organizational leaders need to engage in ongoing communication with the patient or personal representative to keep them apprised, as appropriate, of information that emerges from the investigation of the facts.

* * *

(5) Institutional disclosure of adverse events must include:

(a) An apology including a complete explanation of the facts.

(b) An outline of treatment options.

(c) Arrangements for a second opinion, additional monitoring, expediting clinical consultations, bereavement support, or whatever might be appropriate depending on the adverse event.

(d) Notification that the patient or representative has the option of obtaining outside legal advice for further guidance.

(e) After complete investigation of the facts, the patient or representative is to be given information about compensation under Title 38 United States Code (U.S.C.) Section 1151 and the Federal Tort Claims Act claims processes, including information about procedures available to request compensation and where and how to obtain assistance in filing forms. * * *

(f) If a patient or personal representative asks whether an investigation will be conducted and whether the patient or representative will be told of the results of an investigation, the patient or representative is to be informed that only the results of an administrative board of investigation (AIB) may be released.

Notes and Questions

1. Pennsylvania created a Patient Safety Authority that mandates reports to the Authority by hospitals of all "serious events". Fines may be levied for failures to report, and that statute provides for whistleblower protections among other things.

Pennsylvania also adopted a patient notification requirement:

A patient must be notified if he or she has been affected by a serious event. The statute provides:

308(b) Duty to notify patient.—A medical facility through an appropriate designee shall provide written notification to a patient affected by a serious event or, with the consent of the patient, to an available family member or designee, within seven days of the occurrence or discovery of a serious event. If the patient is unable to give consent, the notification shall be given to an adult member of the immediate family. If an adult member of the immediate family cannot be identified or located, notification shall be given to the closest adult family member. For unemancipated patients who are under 18 years of age, the parent or guardian shall be notified in accordance with this subsection. The notification requirements of this subsection shall not be subject to the provisions of section 311(a). Notification under this subsection shall not constitute an acknowledgment or admission of liability.

2. The patient notification requirements of the Joint Commission and the Veterans Administration raise the risk that patients will become aware of errors for the first time. Will the incidence of malpractice claims increase? Or will disclosure and an apology reduce litigation? The patient disclosure requirements of Joint Commission and the Pennsylvania statute have the potential to not only reduce medical errors but also the frequency of malpractice litigation, if done well. There is evidence that disclosure and apology is desired by patients, and it may even serve to reduce patient inclinations to sue for malpractice when they have experience a bad outcome. See Thomas H. Gallagher et al., Patients' and Physicians' Attitudes Regarding the Disclosure of Medical Errors, 289 J.A.M.A. 1001 (2003) (finding that patients are troubled by the unwillingness of physicians to discuss the cause and future prevention of medical errors).

The Sorry Works! Coalition has been heavily involved in promoting the benefits of an apology approach, www.sorryworks!.com.

Problem: Disclosing Errors

You represent St. Jude Hospital in Pennsylvania, which has implemented a new error management policy in light of the new Joint Commission, CMS, and Pennsylvania rules. How should the hospital handle the following medical misadventures?

1. Joseph Banes entered the hospital for surgery on a cervical disk to relieve his chronic back pain. During the surgery a nerve was severed at the base of his spine, causing severe pain and limitations in mobility in his left leg and foot. The injury is likely to be permanent. This is a rare risk of lower back surgery generally, but in this case the surgeon made a slip of the scalpel and cut the nerve. Your investigation reveals that the surgeon and the nurses in the operating room were aware of the surgical error. What steps should the hospital take to comply with Joint Commission sentinel event requirements? The CMS rules? The Pennsylvania MCare law requirements?

2. Sally Thomas, a 45 year old woman with a history of abdominal pain, was found lying on the floor of her home in severe pain. She was taken to the emergency room of St. Jude, admitted for diagnosis, and tested to determine the source of the problem. After several days of diagnostic uncertainty, the physicians considered an exploratory laparoscopy, suspecting an abnormality in her small intestine. Before surgery an anesthesiologist inserted a central venous catheter (central line) in Sally. She then underwent surgery, and her right fallopian tube and ovary were removed because of infection. She was taken to the Post Anesthesia Care Unit (PACU) with the central line still in place. A surgical resident who had assisted during the surgery wrote out post-operative orders. These orders included a portable chest x-ray to be taken in the PACU. The purpose of the chest

x-ray was to check the placement of the central line. The x-ray was completed by approximately 1:45 p.m. Sally continued to have pain, and was given pain medications. Finally the x-ray, taken four hours earlier, was checked and it revealed that the central line was inserted incorrectly, and the tip went into the pericardial sac of Thomas' heart. The doctors successfully resuscitated her. She recovered after a week in the hospital, narrowly escaping a cardiac tamponade, in which her heart would have been crushed by fluid pressure, leading to cardiac arrest. What steps do you advise the hospital to take?

3.   Wilhelm Gross entered St. Jude to have surgery on his left leg to repair an artery. The surgical team prepped Wilhelm, preparing his right leg for the procedure. Minutes before the surgeon was to make the first incision, nurse Jost noticed on the chart that the procedure was to be done on his left leg. The team then prepped the correct leg and the operation went smoothly. What reporting obligations does the hospital have?

B.   ABSORPTION OF LOSSES: "PAY FOR PERFORMANCE"

THOMAS H. LEE, PAY FOR PERFORMANCE, VERSION 2.0

357 NEJM 531 (2007).

Geisinger, an integrated healthcare delivery system in northeastern Pennsylvania, has begun a new "warranty" program. It promises that 40 key processes will be completed for every patient who undergoes elective CABG—even though several of the "benchmarks" are to be reached before or after hospitalization. And although Geisinger cannot guarantee good clinical outcomes, it charges a standard flat rate that covers care for related complications during the 90 days after surgery.

* * *

For patients who have surgery as part of this program, Geisinger will not charge for related care within 90 days. For example, there are no additional charges for treatment of sternal wound infections or heart failure due to a perioperative infarction, as long as patients receive their care at a Geisinger facility. On the other hand, the usual charges would apply to care for preexisting heart failure or unrelated problems, such as diverticulitis or a hip fracture.

* * *

The real question for Geisinger and for the rest of the health care system is whether this case rate approach might emerge as a new form of pay for performance. Many current models of pay for performance (involving, for example, quality-of-care measures for patients with diabetes) focus on populations of patients whose care is managed by primary care physicians. For most specialists and hospitals, existing incentive systems put only a modest amount of revenue at stake, and as would be expected, resulting changes in care have been modest as well. But the drumbeat is growing stronger for health care financing models that go beyond rewarding volume alone. Case rates and critical pathways are not foreign concepts at many hospitals—they just have not been married so explicitly before. Geisinger is actively working to extend this approach to other surgical procedures, and diseases treated on an outpatient basis, such as diabetes and hypertension, could be next. A reasonable guess is that models that work for organized delivery systems such as Geisinger will spread over time to the rest of U.S. health care. So this experiment bears watching.

Notes and Questions

1. Treatment costs induced by errors and adverse events are usually either covered by insurance or absorbed by patients, families, insurers, employers and state and private disability and income-support programs. This means that the adverse outcomes are externalized to other payors and not internalized by providers best able to reduce these hazards or prevent them. The added costs of a failed intervention caused either by error or by a failure to use an effective approach include added acute care costs, lost income, lost household production, and extra pain. As Leape and Berwick note,

> . . . [P]ayers often subsidize unsafe care quite well, although unknowingly. In most industries, defects cost money and generate warranty claims. In health care, perversely, under most forms of payment, health care professionals receive a premium for a defective product; physicians and hospitals can bill for the additional services that are needed when patients are injured by their mistakes.

Lucian L. Leape and Donald M. Berwick, Five Years After To Err Is Human: What Have We Learned? 293 JAMA 2384, 2388 (2005). Only tort suits have traditionally imposed these excess costs on the hospital or provider that was responsible for the patient's injury. Haavi Morreim, *Holding Health Care Accountable: Law and the New Medical Marketplace* (Oxford Univeersity Press 2001).

2. It costs money to generate and mine data, produce useful feedback and finally implement new quality measures. Computer software is needed, new personnel must be hired or retrained, and an institution would like to be able to recapture those costs from its payers or through greater efficiencies that increase its margins. But perverse incentives dominate, and poor care is reimbursed at the same level as high quality care. Use of market power through purchasing concentrations to increase consumer and purchaser knowledge about providers has been one attempted solution to poor quality care. The Leapfrog Group is the most visible current example of this manifestation. Leapfrog members are encouraged to refer patients to hospitals with the best survival odds, that staff intensive care units with doctors having credentials in critical care, and use error prevention software to prescribe medications. Leapfrog Initiatives to Drive Great Leaps in Patient Safety (2002c). Www.leapfroggroup.org/safety1.htm.

C. SHOPPING FOR QUALITY: INFORMATION FOR CONSUMERS

Will consumers pay for quality? Should employers as well as consumers shop on the basis of evidence of higher quality care? Can consumer choice be based on different levels of care, representing different levels of resources? The hope of consumer choice advocates is that the proliferation of information about quality will promote improvements in quality as consumer demand selects higher quality providers. There has also been a shift toward evaluating providers based on efficiency. See generally Arnold Milstein and Thomas H. Lee, Comparing Physicians on Efficiency, 357 N.E.J.M. 264 (2007).

The New York Cardiac Surgery reports appear to be effective: information about a surgeon's quality published in the reports influences provider selection by patients and referring physicians. Hospitals also take public reporting seriously, often changing their practices to improve their rank.

Critics note however that physicians and hospitals may seek to avoid sicker and more complicated patients in order to improve their ratings. This adverse selection is a real risk of public reporting.

A healthy skepticism toward consumer shopping is needed. Can we expect individual consumers to shop for their care on the basis of quality? A Rand review of health care report cards, provider profiles, and consumer reports concluded that few are influenced by this information: "consumers' choice of hospitals relied more on anecdotal press reports of adverse events than on the comparative assessments that were available." Is the public simply discounting this information, on the theory, so often probably true, that health information is usually aimed to sell a product? In a media environment full of advertising pretending to be scientific, and where medical journals get fooled, even the most intelligent laymen may not easily distinguish hype from information they need. It may also be that quality information—presented in terms of what a patient might reasonably expect—might create a new set of pressures on providers to guarantee their work. One recent study concluded that "... there is limited evidence that public report cards improve quality through this mechanism, and there is some evidence that they paradoxically reduce quality." R.M. Wserner and D.A. Asch, The Unintended Consequences of Publicly Reporting Quality Information, 293 J.A.M.A. 1239 (2005). See also Mark A. Hall and Carl E. Schneider, Patients as Consumers: Courts, Contracts, and the New Medical Marketplace, 106 Mich. L. Rev. 643 (2008).

It may be best for physicians to be the only audiences for such report cards to avoid the problem of adverse selection of higher risk patients, for example. Another study of hospital ratings found to the contrary that quality improvement can be stimulated by the publication of performance information. Dana B. Mukamel, et al., Quality Report Cards, Selection of Cardiac Surgeons, and Racial Disparities: A Study of the Publication of the New York State Cardiac Surgery Reports, 41 Inquiry 435, 443 (Winter 2004/2005).Z.G. Turi, The Big Chill–The Deleterious Effects of Public Reporting on Access to Health Care for the Sickest Patients, 45 J.Am.Coll.Cardiol 1766 (2005). Judith H. Hibbard, et al., Does Publicizing Hospital Performance Stimulate Quality Improvement Efforts? 22 Health Affairs 84 (2003).

Shopping by employers is not likely to fare much better. As employers face large and escalating premium increases over the next few years, it is likely to continue to be cost containment and not quality that is again the primary concern of purchasers. Employer purchasers—in 2003 only 6% of employers in small firms (<200 employees) and 24% of employers in large firms (200–5000 employees) were familiar with the HEDIS data (Health Plan Employer Data and Information Set), the national benchmark for measuring and comparing managed care plans. Less than 5% even thought quality was very important. And should we expect employers to make judgments about quality of care? Should they now have to play complex private contractual compliance games with providers to protect their workers? LeapFrog and other corporate quality groups hope so, but Gabel et al. note that only 3% of employers in small firms and only 18% in large firms were even aware of the LeapFrog Group's national quality effort. Leapfrog Initiatives to Drive Great Leaps in Patient Safety (2002). www.leapfroggroup.org/safety1.htm. Sheila Leatherman, et al, The Business Case for Quality: Case Studies and An Analysis, 22 Health Affairs 17, 25 (2003).

Informed consumerism is harder than it looks, and it may be that generating more information will have little effect on quality. Patients may not use the information, and employers are likely to disregard it. It provides a market driven ideological justification for shifting responsibility from government oversight to the forces of the market, although the consequences are that bad practices increase and patients suffer. Let the consumers suffer the consequences of their bad choices, the free marketeers argue. And the government agency is let off the hook for developing tough new rules to govern a complex health care system that will fight back, tooth and claw.

Chapter 6

ACCESS TO HEALTH CARE: THE OBLIGATION TO PROVIDE CARE

INTRODUCTION

This chapter sets out the legal obligations of doctors and hospitals to treat patients needing medical care. Among the cases you will read in this chapter are cases in which patients were refused medical treatment apparently because they couldn't pay; because of their race; or because of their particular medical condition.

Ability to Pay

In 2005, 43.6 million Americans (43.3 million under the age of 65) were uninsured: 9.3% of children and 19.8% of adults in the United States, percentages that were slightly increased over those of 2004 and significantly higher than those of a decade earlier. An additional 54.5 million individuals lacked health insurance for at least a part of that year; however, approximately three-fourths of those without insurance at the time of the survey (30.5 million individuals under the age of 65) had been uninsured for more than a year. CDC, Health Insurance Coverage: Early Release of Estimates from the National Health Interview Survey, 2006, available at, www.cdc.gov/nchs/data/nhis/earlyrelease/insur200706.pdf.

Even those who carry some form of health insurance may find themselves unable to pay for necessary care. Private health insurance plans frequently incorporate caps on coverage or high deductibles or co-pays that may exclude individuals or families from necessary health care.

Recent empirical work on the distribution of medical debt among individuals filing for bankruptcy indicates that inadequate funds to pay for the costs of illness reach families far above the poverty level. Furthermore, one-third of bankruptcy filers with significant medical debt had health insurance at the onset of illness but lost coverage at some point during their illness. Melissa B. Jacoby & Elizabeth Warren, 100 Nw. U. L. Rev. 535 (2006); Melissa B. Jacoby, et al., Rethinking the Debates Over Health Care Financing: Evidence From the Bankruptcy Courts, 76 N.Y.U.L.Rev. 375 (2001), concluding that "[n]early half of all bankruptcies involved a medical problem, and certain groups—particularly women heads of households and the elderly—were even more likely to report a health-related bankruptcy ... and about eighty percent [of filers] had some form of medical insurance."

Publicly funded health insurance programs in the U.S. are quite narrow. Only persons over the age of 65 (with some few interesting additions) qualify for Medicare; and only low-income individuals who fit into particular demographic groups (e.g., children, women with children, persons in nursing homes) qualify for Medicaid. In addition, particularly for individuals relying on Medicaid, access to medical care may be severely limited by the small number of physicians accepting payment from the program.

Race-based Disparities in Treatment

From the post-Civil War era through the mid–1960s, nearly the entire hospital industry was openly racially segregated. See David Barton Smith, Healthcare's Hidden Civil Rights Legacy, 48 St. Louis U. L.J. 37 (2003). Of course, continuing residential patterns originally established as a matter of *de jure* segregation in housing produce continuing *de facto* segregation in health care facilities. David Barton Smith, et al., Separate and Unequal: Racial Segregation and Disparities in Quality Across U.S. Nursing Homes, 26 Health Affairs 1448 (2007). The story of persistent racial disparities in access to quality health care is not captured entirely in the story of formal segregation, however.

Numerous studies have reported that African–Americans, for example, experience unequal health care, whether measured in terms of access to health care services or disparities in outcomes or health status. See, e.g., Institute of Medicine (IOM), Unequal Treatment: Confronting Racial and Ethnic Disparities in Health Care (Brian D. Smedley, et al., eds., 2002); Agency for Healthcare Research and Quality, National Health Care Disparities Report 2006, available at http://www.ahrq.gov/qual/nhdr06/nhdr06.htm.

One of the most influential early studies of health disparities documented that physicians' recommendations for cardiac catheterization depended entirely on the race and gender of the patient. In this study, doctors made treatment recommendations based on videotaped interviews of patients who all used the same script and presented the same symptoms but differed in race and gender. Kevin A. Schulman, et al., The Effect of Race and Sex on Physicians' Recommendations for Cardiac Catheterization, 340 NEJM 618 (1999). This and other studies expanded the focus on racial health disparities to include the quality of health care and clinical decisions. Louise G. Trubek & Maya Das, Achieving Equality: Healthcare Governance in Transition, 7 DePaul J. Health Care L. 245 (2004). The 2002 IOM study, supra, confirmed the clinical studies in finding serious "racial or ethnic differences in the quality of healthcare that are not due to access-related factors or clinical needs, preferences and appropriateness of intervention."

Nor does socioeconomic status explain the extent of racial health disparities in the U.S. While most empirical studies of race-based access problems are designed to exclude the impact of socioeconomic status, some argue that focusing solely on race without accounting for the interaction between race and class misses a critical part of the key for improving health status and health care access. See, e.g., Vernellia R. Randall, Racist Health Care: Reforming an Unjust Health Care System to Meet the Needs of African–Americans, 3 Health Matrix 127 (1993).

Access Barriers by Medical Condition

Payment systems often distinguish among their enrollees or beneficiaries on the basis of their medical condition. For example, the exclusion or severe restriction of mental health services by most private insurance plans results in inadequate access to treatment for such conditions. Furthermore, some treatable medical conditions are stigmatized. Although a good number of medical conditions are associated with social stigma, including chronic pain and mental illness, perhaps the classic presentation is the case of HIV/AIDS. One of the cases you will study in this chapter involves a patient with HIV/AIDS. This patient population that has encountered very significant barriers to treatment produced, only in part, by fears over the transmissibility of the disease.

I. COMMON LAW APPROACHES

The traditional legal principle governing the physician-patient relationship is that it is a voluntary and personal relationship which the physician may choose to enter or not. Only very limited legal obligations have emerged from common law doctrines, as you will see in the first set of cases below.

RICKS v. BUDGE

Supreme Court of Utah, 1937.
91 Utah 307, 64 P.2d 208.

EPHRAIM HANSON, JUSTICE.

This is an action for malpractice against the defendants who are physicians and surgeons at Logan, Utah, and are copartners doing business under the name and style of the "Budge Clinic." * * * [P]laintiff alleges that he was suffering from an infected right hand and was in immediate need of medical and surgical care and treatment, and there was danger of his dying unless he received such treatment; that defendants for the purpose of treating plaintiff sent him to the Budge Memorial Hospital [BMH] at Logan, Utah; that while at the hospital and while he was in need of medical and surgical treatment, defendants refused to treat or care for plaintiff and abandoned his case. * * *

* * *

[T]he evidence shows that when plaintiff left the hospital on March 15th, Dr. [S.M.] Budge advised him to continue the same treatment that had been given him at the hospital, and that if the finger showed any signs of getting worse at any time, plaintiff was to return at once to Dr. Budge for further treatment; that on the morning of March 17th, plaintiff telephoned Dr. Budge, and explained the condition of his hand; that he was told by the doctor to come to his office, and in pursuance of the doctor's request, plaintiff reported to the doctor's office at 2 p.m. of that day. Dr. Budge again examined the hand, and told plaintiff the hand was worse; he called in Dr. D.C. Budge, another of the defendants, who examined the hand, scraped it some, and indicated thereon where the hand should be opened. Dr. S.M. Budge said to plaintiff: "You have got to go back to the hospital." * * * Within a short time after the arrival of plaintiff, Dr. S.M. Budge arrived at the hospital. Plaintiff testified: "He [meaning Dr. S.M. Budge] came into my room and said, 'You are owing us. I am not going to touch you until that account is taken care of.'" (The account referred to was, according to plaintiff, of some years' standing and did not relate to any charge for services being then rendered.) Plaintiff testified that he did not know what to say to the doctor, but that he finally asked the doctor if he was going to take care of him, and the doctor replied: "No, I am not going to take care of you. I would not take you to the operating table and operate on you and keep you here thirty days, and then there is another $30.00 at the office, until your account is taken care of." Plaintiff replied: "If that is the idea, if you will furnish me a little help, I will try to move."

[A]fter being dressed, he left [BMH] to seek other treatment. At that time it was raining. He walked to the Cache Valley Hospital [CVH], a few blocks away, and there met Dr. Randall, who examined the hand. Dr. Randall testified that when the plaintiff arrived at [CVH], the hand was swollen with considerable fluid oozing from it; that the lower two-thirds of the forearm was red and swollen from the infection which extended up in the arm, and that there was some fluid also oozing from the back of the hand, and that plaintiff required immediate surgical attention; that immediately after the arrival of plaintiff at the hospital he made an incision through the fingers and through the palm of the hand along the tendons that led from the palm, followed those tendons as far as there was any bulging, opened it up thoroughly all the way to the base of the hand, and put drain tubes in. * * * About two weeks after the plaintiff entered [CVH], it became necessary to amputate the middle finger and remove about an inch of the metacarpal bone.

* * *

Defendants contend: (1) That there was no contract of employment between plaintiff and defendants and that defendants in the absence of a valid contract were not obligated to proceed with any treatment; and (2) that if there was such a contract, there was no evidence that the refusal of Dr. S.M. Budge to operate or take care of plaintiff resulted in any damage to plaintiff.

* * *

Under this evidence, it cannot be said that the relation of physician and patient did not exist on March 17th. It had not been terminated after its commencement on March 11th. When the plaintiff left the hospital on March 15th, he understood that he was to report to Dr. S.M. Budge if the occasion required and was so requested by the doctor. Plaintiff's return to the doctor's office was on the advice of the doctor. While at the doctor's office, both Dr. S.M. Budge and Dr. D.C. Budge examined plaintiff's hand and they ordered that he go at once to the hospital for further medical attention. That plaintiff was told by the doctor to come to the doctor's office and was there examined by him and directed to go to the hospital for further treatment would create the relationship of physician and patient. That the relationship existed at the time the plaintiff was sent to the hospital on March 17th cannot be seriously questioned.

We believe the law is well settled that a physician or surgeon, upon undertaking an operation or other case, is under the duty, in the absence of an agreement limiting the service, of continuing his attention, after the first operation or first treatment, so long as the case requires attention. The obligation of continuing attention can be terminated only by the cessation of the necessity which gave rise to the relationship, or by the discharge of the physician by the patient, or by the withdrawal from the case by the physician after giving the patient reasonable notice so as to enable the patient to secure other medical attention. A physician has the right to withdraw from a case, but if the case is such as to still require further medical or surgical attention, he must, before withdrawing from the case, give the patient sufficient notice so the patient can procure other medical attention if he desires.[ ]

* * *

We cannot say as a matter of law that plaintiff suffered no damages by reason of the refusal of Dr. S.M. Budge to further treat him. The evidence shows that from the time plaintiff left the office of the defendants up until the time that he arrived at [CVH] his hand continued to swell; that it was very painful; that when he left [BMH] he was in such condition that he did not know whether he was going to live or die. That both his mental and physical suffering must have been most acute cannot be questioned. While the law cannot measure with exactness such suffering and cannot determine with absolute certainty what damages, if any, plaintiff may be entitled to, still those are questions which a jury under proper instructions from the court must determine.

* * *

FOLLAND, JUSTICE (concurring in part, dissenting in part).

* * *

* * * The theory of plaintiff as evidenced in his complaint is that there was no continued relationship from the first employment but that a new relationship was entered into. He visited the clinic on March 17th; the Doctors Budge examined his hand and told him an immediate operation was necessary and for him to go to the hospital. I do not think a new contract was entered into at that time. There was no consideration for any implied promise that Dr. Budge or the Budge Clinic would assume the responsibility of another operation and the costs and expenses incident thereto. As soon as Dr. Budge reached the hospital he opened negotiations with the plaintiff which might have resulted in a contract, but before any contract arrangement was made the plaintiff decided to leave the hospital and seek attention elsewhere. As soon as he could dress himself he walked away. There is conflict in the evidence as to the conversation. Plaintiff testified in effect that Dr. Budge asked for something to be done about an old account. The doctor's testimony in effect was that he asked that some arrangement be made to take care of the doctor's bill and expenses for the ensuing operation and treatment at the hospital. The result, however, was negative. No arrangement was made. The plaintiff made no attempt whatsoever to suggest to the doctor any way by which either the old account might be taken care of or the expenses of the ensuing operation provided for. * * * Dr. Budge had a right to refuse to incur the obligation and responsibility incident to one or more operations and the treatment and attention which would be necessary. If it be assumed that the contract relationship of physician and patient existed prior to this conversation, either as resulting from the first employment or that there was an implied contract entered into at the clinic, yet Dr. Budge had the right with proper notice to discontinue the relationship. While plaintiff's condition was acute and needed immediate attention, he received such immediate attention at [CVH]. There was only a delay of an hour or two, and part of that delay is accounted for by reason of the fact that the doctor at [CVH] would not operate until some paper, which plaintiff says he did not read, was signed. Plaintiff said he could not sign it but that it was signed by his brother before the operation was performed. We are justified in believing that by means of this written obligation, provision was made for the expenses and fees about to be incurred. I am satisfied from my reading of the record that no injury or damage resulted from the delay occasioned by plaintiff leaving the Budge Hospital and going to [CVH]. He was not in such desperate condition but that he was able to walk the three or four blocks between the two hospitals. * * *

CHILDS v. WEIS

Court of Civil Appeals of Texas, 1969.
440 S.W.2d 104.

WILLIAMS, J.

On or about November 27, 1966 Daisy Childs, wife of J.C. Childs, a resident of Dallas County, was approximately seven months pregnant. On that date she was visiting in Lone Oak, Texas, and about two o'clock A.M. she presented herself to the Greenville Hospital emergency room. At that time she stated she was bleeding and had labor pains. She was examined by a nurse who identified herself as H. Beckham. According to Mrs. Childs, Nurse Beckham stated that she would call the doctor. She said the nurse returned and stated "that the Dr. said that I would have to go to my doctor in Dallas. I stated to Beckham that I'm not going to make it to Dallas. Beckham replied that yes, I would make it. She stated that I was just starting into labor and that I would make it. The weather was cold that night. About an hour after leaving the Greenville Hospital Authority I had the baby while in a car on the way to medical facilities in Sulphur Springs. The baby lived about 12 hours."

[Dr. Weis] said that he had never examined or treated Daisy Childs and in fact had never seen or spoken to either Daisy Childs or her husband, J.C. Childs, at any time in his life. He further stated that he had never at any time agreed or consented to the examination or treatment of either Daisy Childs or her husband. He said that on a day in November 1966 he recalled a telephone call received by him from a nurse in the emergency room at the Greenville Surgical Hospital; that the nurse told him that there was a negro girl in the emergency room having a "bloody show" and some "labor pains." He said the nurse advised him that this woman had been visiting in Lone Oak, and that her OB doctor lived in Garland, Texas, and that she also resided in Garland. The doctor said, "I told the nurse over the telephone to have the girl call her doctor in Garland and see what he wanted her to do. I knew nothing more about this incident until I was served with the citation and a copy of the petition in this lawsuit."

* * *

Since it is unquestionably the law that the relationship of physician and patient is dependent upon contract, either express or implied, a physician is not to be held liable for arbitrarily refusing to respond to a call of a person even urgently in need of medical or surgical assistance provided that the relation of physician and patient does not exist at the time the call is made or at the time the person presents himself for treatment.

* * *

Applying these principles of law to the factual situation here presented we find an entire absence of evidence of a contract, either express or implied, which would create the relationship of patient and physician as between Dr. Weis and Mrs. Childs. Dr. Weis, under these circumstances, was under no duty whatsoever to examine or treat Mrs. Childs. When advised by telephone that the lady was in the emergency room he did what seems to be a reasonable thing and inquired as to the identity of her doctor who had been treating her. Upon being told that the doctor was in Garland he stated that the patient should call the doctor and find out what should be done. This action on the part of Dr. Weis seems to be not only reasonable but within the bounds of professional ethics.

We cannot agree with appellant that Dr. Weis' statement to the nurse over the telephone amounted to an acceptance of the case and affirmative instructions which she was bound to follow. Rather than give instructions which could be construed to be in the nature of treatment, Dr. Weis told the nurse to have the woman call her physician in Garland and secure instructions from him.

The affidavit of Mrs. Childs would indicate that Nurse Beckham may not have relayed the exact words of Dr. Weis to Mrs. Childs. Instead, it would seem that Nurse Beckham told Mrs. Childs that the doctor said that she would "have to go" to her doctor in Dallas. Assuming this statement was made by Nurse Beckham, and further assuming that it contained the meaning as placed upon it by appellant, yet it is undisputed that such words were uttered by Nurse Beckham, and not by Dr. Weis. * * *

[The court affirmed summary judgment in favor of the defendant.]

Notes and Questions

1. Why did the doctor refuse to treat Mr. Ricks? Ms. Childs? Should the courts distinguish among such cases on the basis of the reason for the refusal? If the court were willing to make a distinction, how would you go about proving the basis for the refusal in each of these cases?

2. The principles in *Ricks* apply to hospitals. See, for example, New Biloxi Hospital, Inc. v. Frazier, 245 Miss. 185, 146 So.2d 882 (Miss. 1962), in which the court held a hospital liable for the death of a patient who remained untreated in the emergency room for over two hours and died twenty-five minutes after transfer to a Veterans Administration hospital. The court based its holding on the hospital's breach of the duty to exercise reasonable care once treatment had been "undertaken." The court described the scene in detail:

> Sam Frazier was a 42 year old Negro man, who had lost his left eye and his left arm, just below the elbow, during World War II. He and his wife had two young children.... [Mr. Frazier was brought to the ED after being shot.] The blast made two large holes in the upper arm and tore away the brachial artery.... Ambulance attendants carried him into the emergency room,

where one of the Hospital's nurses just looked at him and walked away. He was bleeding profusely at that time. There was blood all over the ambulance cot, and while waiting in the hospital, blood was streaming from his arm to the floor, forming a puddle with a diameter of 24–30 inches. After about twenty minutes, another Hospital nurse came, looked at Frazier and walked away. . . . Neither [the nurse] nor the doctor made any effort to stop the bleeding in any way. [The nurse] continued to come in and out of the emergency room on occasion, but simply looked at Frazier. He asked to see his little boy, and for water. His bleeding continued. . . . This summary of the evidence reflects that Frazier was permitted to bleed to death. . . .

See also Wilmington Gen. Hospital v. Manlove, 174 A.2d 135 (Del. 1961), holding that a hospital must provide emergency care to a person who relies on the presence of an emergency room in coming to the hospital. See Karen Rothenberg, Who Cares? The Evolution of the Legal Duty to Provide Emergency Care, 26 Hous.L.Rev. 21 (1989); Thomas Gionis, et al., The Intentional Tort of Patient Dumping: A New State Cause of Action to Address the Shortcomings of the Federal Emergency Medical Treatment and Active Labor Act, 52 Am. U.L. Rev. 173 (2002).

3.   The court may find that a doctor has a duty to treat a particular patient based on a contractual commitment to a third party. See, for example, Hiser v. Randolph, 126 Ariz. 608, 617 P.2d 774 (1980), holding that the physician had an obligation to treat the patient in the hospital under his on-call contract with the hospital. In *Hiser*, there was some evidence that the physician refused to treat the patient because she was the wife of an attorney, although the doctor claimed it was because he was not qualified to treat her condition.

Problem: Cheryl Hanachek

Cheryl Hanachek, a resident of Boston, discovered she was pregnant during an "action" called by the city's obstetricians in protest against increasing malpractice insurance premiums for physician childbirth services. Ms. Hanachek first called Dr. Cunetto, who had been her obstetrician for the birth of her first child two years earlier. Dr. Cunetto's receptionist informed Ms. Hanachek that Dr. Cunetto was not able to take any new patients because her practice was "full." In fact, Dr. Cunetto had limited her practice due to her patient load.

About two weeks later, Ms. Hanachek called Dr. Simms, who had been recommended by her friends. Dr. Simms' receptionist told Ms. Hanachek that Dr. Simms was not taking any new patients as his malpractice premiums were so high that he was even considering discontinuing his obstetrical practice. Ms. Hanachek reported to the receptionist that she was having infrequent minor cramping, and the receptionist told her that this was "nothing to worry about at this stage." Later that night Ms. Hanachek was admitted to the hospital on an emergency basis. Ms. Hanachek was in shock from blood loss due to a ruptured ectopic pregnancy. As a result of the rupture and other complications, Ms. Hanachek underwent a hysterectomy.

She has brought suit against Dr. Cunetto and Dr. Simms. If you were representing Ms. Hanachek, how would you proceed in arguing and proving your case?

II. STATUTORY EXCEPTIONS TO THE COMMON LAW

A. EMTALA

The federal Emergency Medical Treatment and Labor Act. 42 U.S.C.A. § 1395dd (EMTALA) was enacted in response to "patient dumping," a practice in which patients are discharged or are transferred from one hospital's emergency room to another's without necessary treatment.

EMTALA applies *only* to hospitals that accept payment from Medicare *and* operate an emergency department; however, EMTALA applies to all patients of such a hospital and not just to Medicare beneficiaries. EMTALA does not require a hospital to offer emergency room services, although some state statutes do and federal tax law strongly encourages tax-exempt hospitals to do so.

EMTALA specifically empowers patients to bring civil suits for damages against participating hospitals, but does not provide a private right of action against a treating physician. The Office of the Inspector General (OIG) of HHS enforces EMTALA against both hospitals and physicians. EMTALA litigation has burgeoned, while government enforcement has been less active. Administrative enforcement actions under EMTALA are few; monetary penalties are small; exclusion from Medicare is very rare; and there are regional differences in the number of complaints of EMTALA violations as well as the number of investigations and citations. Correction of violations rather than sanctions has been the primary goal of enforcement. GAO, Emergency Care: EMTALA Implementation and Enforcement Issues, GAO 01_747 (June 2001).

EMERGENCY MEDICAL TREATMENT AND LABOR ACT

42 U.S.C. § 1395dd.

(a) Medical screening requirement. In the case of a hospital that has a hospital emergency department, if any individual . . . comes to the emergency department and a request is made on the individual's behalf for examination or treatment for a medical condition, the hospital must provide for an appropriate medical screening examination within the capability of the hospital's emergency department, including ancillary services routinely available to the emergency department, to determine whether or not an emergency medical condition . . . exists.

(b) Necessary stabilizing treatment for emergency medical conditions and labor.

(1) In general. If any individual . . . comes to a hospital and the hospital determines that the individual has an emergency medical condition, the hospital must provide either—

(A) within the staff and facilities available at the hospital, for such further medical examination and such treatment as may be required to stabilize the medical condition, or

(B) for transfer of the individual to another medical facility in accordance with subsection (c).

(c) Restricting transfers until individual stabilized.

(1) Rule. If an individual at a hospital has an emergency medical condition which has not been stabilized ..., the hospital may not transfer the individual unless—

(A) (i) the individual (or a legally responsible person acting on the individual's behalf) after being informed of the hospital's obligations under this section and of the risk of transfer, in writing requests transfer to another medical facility,

(ii) a physician ... has signed a certification that[,] based upon the information available at the time of transfer, the medical benefits reasonably expected from the provision of appropriate medical treatment at another medical facility outweigh the increased risks to the individual and, in the case of labor, to the unborn child from effecting the transfer, or

(iii) [if no physician is available, another qualified person has signed the certificate] and

(B) the transfer is an appropriate transfer ... to that facility....

(2) Appropriate transfer. An appropriate transfer to a medical facility is a transfer—

(A) in which the transferring hospital provides the medical treatment within its capacity which minimizes the risks to the individual's health and, in the case of a woman in labor, the health of the unborn child;

(B) in which the receiving facility—

(i) has available space and qualified personnel for the treatment of the individual, and

(ii) has agreed to accept transfer of the individual and to provide appropriate medical treatment;

(C) in which the transferring hospital sends to the receiving facility all medical records ... related to the emergency condition for which the individual has presented, available at the time of the transfer ...; [and]

(D) in which the transfer is effected through qualified personnel and transportation equipment....

(d) Enforcement.

(1) Civil monetary penalties.

(A) A participating hospital that negligently violates a requirement of this section is subject to a civil money penalty of not more than $50,000 for each such violation....

(B) [A]ny physician who is responsible for the examination, treatment, or transfer of an individual in a participating hospital ... and who negligently violates a requirement of this section ... is subject to a civil money penalty of not more than $50,000 for each such violation and, if the violation is gross and flagrant or is repeated, to exclusion from participation in [Medicare and Medicaid]....

(2) Civil enforcement.

(A) Personal harm. Any individual who suffers personal harm as a direct result of a participating hospital's violation of a requirement of this section may, in a civil action against the participating hospital, obtain those damages available for personal injury under the law of the State in which the hospital is located, and such equitable relief as is appropriate.

(B) Financial loss to other medical facility. Any medical facility that suffers a financial loss as a direct result of a participating hospital's violation of a requirement of this section may, in a civil action against the participating hospital, obtain those damages available for financial loss, under the law of the State in which the hospital is located, and such equitable relief as is appropriate. . . .

(e) Definitions. In this section:

(1) The term "emergency medical condition" means—

(A) a medical condition manifesting itself by acute symptoms of sufficient severity (including severe pain) such that the absence of immediate medical attention could reasonably be expected to result in—

(i) placing the health of the individual (or, with respect to a pregnant woman, the health of the woman or her unborn child) in serious jeopardy,

(ii) serious impairment to bodily functions, or

(iii) serious dysfunction of any bodily organ or part; or

(B) with respect to a pregnant woman who is having contractions—

(i) that there is inadequate time to effect a safe transfer to another hospital before delivery, or

(ii) that transfer may pose a threat to the health or safety of the woman or the unborn child. . . .

* * *

(3) (A) The term "to stabilize" means . . . to provide such medical treatment of the condition as may be necessary to assure, within reasonable medical probability, that no material deterioration of the condition is likely to result from or occur during the transfer of the individual from a facility. . . .

(B) The term "stabilized" means . . . that no material deterioration of the condition is likely, within reasonable medical probability, to result from or occur during the transfer of the individual from a facility, or, with respect to an emergency medical condition described in paragraph (1)(B), that the woman has delivered (including the placenta). . . .

(h) No delay in examination or treatment. A participating hospital may not delay provision of an appropriate medical screening examination required under subsection (a) . . . or further medical examination and treatment required under subsection (b) . . . in order to inquire about the individual's method of payment or insurance status.

BABER v. HOSPITAL CORPORATION OF AMERICA

United States Court of Appeals, Fourth Circuit, 1992.
977 F.2d 872.

WILLIAMS, CIRCUIT JUDGE:

Barry Baber, Administrator of the Estate of Brenda Baber, instituted this suit against Dr. Richard Kline, Dr. Joseph Whelan, Raleigh General Hospital

(RGH), Beckley Appalachian Regional Hospital (BARH), and the parent corporations of both hospitals. Mr. Baber alleged that the Defendants violated the Emergency Medical Treatment and Active Labor Act (EMTALA)[ ]. The Defendants moved to dismiss the EMTALA claim under Rule 12(b)(6) of the Federal Rules of Civil Procedure. Because the parties submitted affidavits and depositions, the district court treated the motion as one for summary judgment. See Fed.R.Civ.P. 12(b).

* * *

Mr. Baber's complaint charged the various defendants with violating EMTALA in several ways. Specifically, Mr. Baber contends that Dr. Kline, RGH, and its parent corporation violated EMTALA by:

(a) failing to provide his sister with an "appropriate medical screening examination;"

(b) failing to stabilize his sister's "emergency medical condition;" and

(c) transferring his sister to BARH without first providing stabilizing treatment.

* * *

After reviewing the parties' submissions, the district court granted summary judgment for the Defendants. * * * Finding no error, we affirm.

* * *

* * * Brenda Baber, accompanied by her brother, Barry, sought treatment at RGH's emergency department at 10:40 p.m. on August 5, 1987. When she entered the hospital, Ms. Baber was nauseated, agitated, and thought she might be pregnant. She was also tremulous and did not appear to have orderly thought patterns. She had stopped taking her anti-psychosis medications, * * * and had been drinking heavily. Dr. Kline, the attending physician, described her behavior and condition in the RGH Encounter Record as follows: Patient refuses to remain on stretcher and cannot be restrained verbally despite repeated requests by staff and by me. Brother has not assisted either verbally or physically in keeping patient from pacing throughout the Emergency Room. Restraints would place patient and staff at risk by increasing her agitation.

In response to Ms. Baber's initial complaints, Dr. Kline examined her central nervous system, lungs, cardiovascular system, and abdomen. He also ordered several laboratory tests, including a pregnancy test.

While awaiting the results of her laboratory tests, Ms. Baber began pacing about the emergency department. In an effort to calm Ms. Baber, Dr. Kline gave her [several medications]. The medication did not immediately control her agitation. Mr. Baber described his sister as becoming restless, "worse and more disoriented after she was given the medication," and wandering around the emergency department.

While roaming in the emergency department around midnight, Ms. Baber * * * convulsed and fell, striking her head upon a table and lacerating her scalp. [S]he quickly regained consciousness and emergency department personnel carried her by stretcher to the suturing room, [where] Dr. Kline examined her again. He obtained a blood gas study, which did not reveal any oxygen deprivation or acidosis. Ms. Baber was verbal and could move her head, eyes, and limbs without discomfort. * * * Dr. Kline closed the one-inch laceration with a couple of sutures. Although she became calmer and drowsy after the wound was sutured, Ms. Baber was easily arousable and easily disturbed. Ms. Baber experienced some anxiety, disorientation, restlessness, and some speech problems, which Dr. Kline concluded were caused by her pre-existing psychiatric problems of psychosis with paranoia and alcohol withdrawal.

Dr. Kline discussed Ms. Baber's condition with Dr. Whelan, the psychiatrist who had treated Ms. Baber for two years. * * * Dr. Whelan concluded that Ms. Baber's hyperactive and uncontrollable behavior during her evening at RGH was compatible with her behavior during a relapse of her serious psychotic and chronic mental illness. Both Dr. Whelan and Dr. Kline were concerned about the seizure she had while at RGH's emergency department because it was the first one she had experienced. * * * They also agreed Ms. Baber needed further treatment * * * and decided to transfer her to the psychiatric unit at BARH because RGH did not have a psychiatric ward, and both doctors believed it would be beneficial for her to be treated in a familiar setting. The decision to transfer Ms. Baber was further supported by the doctors' belief that any tests to diagnose the cause of her initial seizure, such as a computerized tomography scan (CT scan), could be performed at BARH once her psychiatric condition was under control. The transfer to BARH was discussed with Mr. Baber who neither expressly consented nor objected. His only request was that his sister be x-rayed because of the blow to her head when she fell.

* * *

Because Dr. Kline did not conclude Ms. Baber had a serious head injury, he believed that she could be transferred safely to BARH where she would be under the observation of the BARH psychiatric staff personnel. At 1:35 a.m. on August 6, Ms. Baber was admitted directly to the psychiatric department of BARH upon Dr. Whelan's orders. She was not processed through BARH's emergency department. Although Ms. Baber was restrained and regularly checked every fifteen minutes by the nursing staff while at BARH, no physician gave her an extensive neurological examination upon her arrival. Mr. Baber unsuccessfully repeated his request for an x-ray.

At the 3:45 a.m. check, the nurse found Ms. Baber having a grand mal seizure. At Dr. Whelan's direction, the psychiatric unit staff transported her to BARH's emergency department. Upon arrival in the emergency department, her pupils were unresponsive, and hospital personnel began CPR. The emergency department physician ordered a CT scan, which was performed around 6:30 a.m. The CT report revealed a fractured skull and a right subdural hematoma. BARH personnel immediately transferred Ms. Baber back to RGH because that hospital had a neurosurgeon on staff, and BARH did not have the facility or staff to treat serious neurological problems. When RGH received Ms. Baber for treatment around 7 a.m., she was comatose. She died later that day, apparently as a result of an intracerebrovascular rupture.

The district court granted summary judgment for Dr. Kline and Dr. Whelan because it found that EMTALA does not give patients a private cause of action against their doctors. We review this finding de novo because the interpretation of a statute is a question of law.[ ] Because we hold EMTALA does not permit private suits for damages against the attending physicians, we affirm the district court's grant of summary judgment for Dr. Whelan and Dr. Kline.

* * *

Mr. Baber * * * alleges that RGH, acting through its agent, Dr. Kline, violated several provisions of EMTALA. These allegations can be summarized into two general complaints: (1) RGH failed to provide an appropriate medical screening to discover that Ms. Baber had an emergency medical condition as required by 42 U.S.C.A. § 1395dd(a); and (2) RGH transferred Ms. Baber before her emergency medical condition had been stabilized, and the appropriate paperwork was not completed to transfer a non-stable patient as required by 42 U.S.C.A. § 1395dd(b) & (c). Because we find that RGH did not violate any of these EMTALA provisions, we affirm the district court's grant of summary judgment to RGH.

Mr. Baber first claims that RGH failed to provide his sister with an "appropriate medical screening". He makes two arguments. First, he contends that a medical screening is only "appropriate" if it satisfies a national standard of care. In other words, Mr. Baber urges that we construe EMTALA as a national medical malpractice statute, albeit limited to whether the medical screening was appropriate to identify an emergency medical condition. We conclude instead that EMTALA only requires hospitals to apply their standard screening procedure for identification of an emergency medical condition uniformly to all patients and that Mr. Baber has failed to proffer sufficient evidence showing that RGH did not do so. Second, Mr. Baber contends that EMTALA requires hospitals to provide some medical screening. We agree, but conclude that he has failed to show no screening was provided to his sister.

* * *

While [the Act] requires a hospital's emergency department to provide an "appropriate medical screening examination," it does not define that term other than to state its purpose is to identify an "emergency medical condition."

* * *

[T]he goal of "an appropriate medical screening examination" is to determine whether a patient with acute or severe symptoms has a life threatening or serious medical condition. The plain language of the statute requires a hospital to develop a screening procedure[6] designed to identify such critical conditions that exist in symptomatic patients and to apply that screening procedure uniformly to all patients with similar complaints.

6. While a hospital emergency room may develop one general procedure for screening all patients, it may also tailor its screening procedure to the patient's complaints or exhibited symptoms. For example, it may have one screening procedure for a patient with a heart attack and another for women in labor. Under our interpretation of EMTALA, such varying screening procedures would not pose liability under EMTALA as long as all patients complaining of the same problem or exhibiting the same symptoms receive identical screening procedures. We also recognize that the hospital's screening procedure is not limited to personal observation and assessment but may include available ancillary services through departments such as radiology and laboratory.

[W]hile EMTALA requires a hospital emergency department to apply its standard screening examination uniformly, it does not guarantee that the emergency personnel will correctly diagnose a patient's condition as a result of this screening.[7] The statutory language clearly indicates that EMTALA does not impose on hospitals a national standard of care in screening patients. The screening requirement only requires a hospital to provide a screening examination that is "appropriate" and "within the capability of the hospital's emergency department," including "routinely available" ancillary services. 42 U.S.C.A. § 1395dd(a). This section establishes a standard, which will of necessity be individualized for each hospital, since hospital emergency departments have varying capabilities. Had Congress intended to require hospitals to provide a screening examination which comported with generally-accepted medical standards, it could have clearly specified a national standard. Nor do we believe Congress intended to create a negligence standard based on each hospital's capability. * * * EMTALA is no substitute for state law medical malpractice actions.

* * *

The Sixth Circuit has also held that an appropriate medical screening means "a screening that the hospital would have offered to any paying patient" or at least "not known by the provider to be insufficient or below their own standards."

* * *

Applying our interpretation of section (a) of EMTALA, we must next determine whether there is any genuine issue of material fact regarding whether RGH gave Ms. Baber a medical screening examination that differed from its standard screening procedure. Because Mr. Baber has offered no evidence of disparate treatment, we find that the district court did not err in granting summary judgment.

* * *

Mr. Baber does not allege that RGH's emergency department personnel treated Ms. Baber differently from its other patients. Instead, he merely claims Dr. Kline did not do enough accurately to diagnose her condition or treat her injury.[ ] The critical element of an EMTALA cause of action is not the adequacy of the screening examination but whether the screening examination that was performed deviated from the hospital's evaluation procedures that would have been performed on any patient in a similar condition.

* * *

7. Some commentators have criticized defining "appropriate" in terms of the hospital's medical screening standard because hospitals could theoretically avoid liability by providing very cursory and substandard screenings to all patients, which might enable the doctor to ignore a medical condition. See, e.g., Karen I. Treiger, Note, Preventing Patient Dumping: Sharpening COBRA's Fangs, 61 N.Y.U.L.Rev. 1186 (1986). Even though we do not believe it is likely that a hospital would endanger all of its patients by establishing such a cursory standard, theoretically it is possible. Our holding, however, does not foreclose the possibility that a future court faced with such a situation may decide that the hospital's standard was so low that it amounted to no "appropriate medical screening." We do not decide that question in this case because Ms. Baber's screening was not so substandard as to amount to no screening at all.

Dr. Kline testified that he performed a medical screening on Ms. Baber in accordance with standard procedures for examining patients with head injuries. He explained that generally, a patient is not scheduled for advanced tests such as a CT scan or x-rays unless the patient's signs and symptoms so warrant. While Ms. Baber did exhibit some of the signs and symptoms of patients who have severe head injuries, in Dr. Kline's medical judgment these signs were the result of her pre-existing psychiatric condition, not the result of her fall. He, therefore, determined that Ms. Baber's head injury was not serious and did not indicate the need at that time for a CT scan or x-rays. In his medical judgment, Ms. Baber's condition would be monitored adequately by the usual nursing checks performed every fifteen minutes by the psychiatric unit staff at BARH. Although Dr. Kline's assessment and judgment may have been erroneous and not within acceptable standards of medical care in West Virginia, he did perform a screening examination that was not so substandard as to amount to no examination. No testimony indicated that his procedure deviated from that which RGH would have provided to any other patient in Ms. Baber's condition.

* * *

The essence of Mr. Baber's argument is that the extent of the examination and treatment his sister received while at RGH was deficient. While Mr. Baber's testimony might be sufficient to survive a summary judgment motion in a medical malpractice case, it is clearly insufficient to survive a motion for summary judgment in an EMTALA case because at no point does Mr. Baber present any evidence that RGH deviated from its standard screening procedure in evaluating Ms. Baber's head injury. Therefore, the district court properly granted RGH summary judgment on the medical screening issue.

Mr. Baber also asserts that RGH inappropriately transferred his sister to BARH. EMTALA's transfer requirements do not apply unless the hospital actually determines that the patient suffers from an emergency medical condition. Accordingly, to recover for violations of EMTALA's transfer provisions, the plaintiff must present evidence that (1) the patient had an emergency medical condition; (2) the hospital actually knew of that condition; (3) the patient was not stabilized before being transferred; and (4) prior to transfer of an unstable patient, the transferring hospital did not obtain the proper consent or follow the appropriate certification and transfer procedures.

* * *

Mr. Baber argues that requiring a plaintiff to prove the hospital had actual knowledge of the patient's emergency medical condition would allow hospitals to circumvent the purpose of EMTALA by simply requiring their personnel to state in all hospital records that the patient did not suffer from an emergency medical condition. Because of this concern, Mr. Baber urges us to adopt a standard that would impose liability upon a hospital if it failed to provide stabilizing treatment prior to a transfer when the hospital knew or should have known that the patient suffered from an emergency medical condition.

The statute itself implicitly rejects this proposed standard. Section 1395dd(b)(1) states the stabilization requirement exists if "any individual ... comes to a hospital and the hospital determines that the individual has an emergency medical condition." Thus, the plain language of the statute dictates a standard requiring actual knowledge of the emergency medical condition by the hospital staff.

Mr. Baber failed to present any evidence that RGH had actual knowledge that Ms. Baber suffered from an emergency medical condition. Dr. Kline stated in his affidavit that Ms. Baber's condition was stable prior to transfer and that he did not believe she was suffering from an emergency medical condition. While Mr. Baber testified that he believed his sister suffered from an emergency medical condition at transfer, he did not present any evidence beyond his own belief that she actually had an emergency medical condition or that anyone at RGH knew that she suffered from an emergency medical condition. In addition, we note that Mr. Baber's testimony is not competent to prove his sister actually had an emergency medical condition since he is not qualified to diagnose a serious internal brain injury.

* * * [W]e hold that the district court correctly granted RGH summary judgment on Mr. Baber's claim that it transferred Ms. Baber in violation of EMTALA.

* * *

Therefore, the district court's judgment is affirmed.

Notes and Questions

1. Hospital emergency departments are severely strained, but EMTALA is not the culprit. In fact, emergency department overcrowding is attributable to a number of factors that do not relate to uncompensated care; and the rate of increase in patient volume in the ED predates EMTALA. Laura D. Hermer, The Scapegoat: EMTALA and Emergency Department Overcrowding, 14 J. L & Pol'y 695 (2006), arguing that EMTALA's unfunded mandate makes the poor and uninsured scapegoats for increased emergency department overcrowding. See also, Institute of Medicine, The Future of Emergency Care in the United States Health System–Report Brief (June 2006), summarizing three reports issued by the IOM and reporting that ED overcrowding relates to changes in the hospital industry and to patterns of care for insured as well as uninsured patients. As to the hospital industry, hospital closures (often a result of increased competitive pressures; consolidation in the industry; and closure of public hospitals) resulted in fewer emergency departments at the same time as the number of patient visits increased by 20,000,000 annually. In the same vein, hospitals reduced the number of inpatient beds in order to reduce costs; and this has resulted in longer waits for admission from the ED causing patients to occupy the ED unnecessarily. Staffing issues relating to nurse shortages mean that even existing in-patient beds may be unstaffed and unavailable. The lack of medical specialists willing to be on call for ED service also results in longer occupancy per patient in the ED. Finally, the IOM reports that insured patients actually are seeking non-emergent care more frequently in the ED for several reasons, including the practice of referring insured patients to the ED when care is needed outside of regular office hours or when tests or procedures cannot be done in the office.

2. *Baber* is typical of the majority of cases interpreting appropriate screening. How does the standard differ from that which would be used in a medical malpractice case? In contrast to the standard the courts have applied to the adequacy of medical screening, the standard generally applied to the question of whether the patient was discharged or transferred in an unstable condition is an

objective professional standard. How should plaintiff structure discovery to meet these two standards? What would be the role for expert testimony, if any? May the plaintiff simply choose to pursue an "unstable transfer or discharge" claim instead of an "inappropriate screening" claim?

3. The great majority of EMTALA claims are resolved through summary judgment, possibly reflecting judicial concerns that the Act is too broad. What is at stake for plaintiffs and defendants when federal courts resolve most EMTALA screening claims on summary judgment rather than submitting the case to the jury?

4. The Supreme Court has held that proof of improper motive is not required for a violation of the EMTALA requirement that the patient be *stabilized*. Roberts v. Galen of Va., Inc., 525 U.S. 249, 119 S.Ct. 685, 142 L.Ed.2d 648 (1999). The Court expressed no opinion as to whether proof of improper motive is essential for a claim of failure to provide an appropriate screening. Is it possible to distinguish the two provisions at issue? How are they different? The Circuits, except for the Sixth Circuit, in *Cleland v. Bronson Health Care Group*, 917 F.2d 266 (6th Cir. 1990), have almost uniformly held that EMTALA reaches beyond economically motivated decisions and that proof of motive is not required for either a screening or a stabilization claim. Could proof of improper motive be useful to the plaintiff in distinguishing negligent misdiagnosis from an EMTALA claim? How would you prove motive once the physician and hospital claim medical judgment as the basis for discharge or transfer?

Problem: Mrs. Miller

On May 21, Mrs. Nancy Miller, who was eight months pregnant, called her obstetrician, Dr. Jennifer Gibson, at 2:00 a.m. because she was experiencing severe pain which appeared to her to be labor contractions. Dr. Gibson advised Mrs. Miller to go to the emergency department of the local hospital and promised to meet her there shortly. Mrs. Miller was admitted to the emergency department of General Hospital at 2:30 a.m., and Dr. Gibson joined her there at 3:14 a.m. After examining Mrs. Miller, Dr. Gibson concluded that Mrs. Miller had begun labor and that, despite the fact that the pregnancy had not reached full-term, the labor should be continued to delivery. At that time, Dr. Gibson asked that the on-call anesthesiologist, Dr. Martig, see Mrs. Miller to discuss anesthesia during the delivery. At the same time, the procedure to admit Mrs. Miller to the hospital's maternity floor was begun. The nurse informed Mrs. Miller that there would be a short wait because there was no space available at that point.

Dr. Martig saw Mrs. Miller at 4:00 a.m. When asked, Dr. Martig informed Mrs. Miller that he was not qualified to and would not be able to perform an epidural (a spinal nerve-block anesthesia, often used in childbirth). Instead, he gave her Demerol and left the emergency department.

At 4:30 a.m., Mrs. Miller was admitted to the labor and delivery floor. At 4:45 a.m., the obstetrical nurse observed fetal distress and called Dr. Gibson. At 4:50 a.m., Dr. Gibson concluded that Mrs. Miller had a prolapsed umbilical cord and ordered an emergency caesarean section. The OB nurse paged Dr. Martig, but he could not be located. (Dr. Martig later stated that his pager had malfunctioned.) Because Dr. Martig could not be located, Dr. Gibson and a resident performed the C-section without an anesthetic and delivered the child healthy and alive. (These facts are based on Miller v. Martig, 754 N.E.2d 41 (Ind. Ct. App. 2001).)

Assume that Mrs. Miller has brought suit against the hospital and Dr. Martig. What federal and state claims might Mrs. Miller make? Assume that Dr. Martig has filed a motion for summary judgment on all claims. What result? In your discussion of this case, include consideration of the following regulations issued by HHS under EMTALA in September 2003:

42 C.F.R. § 489.24

(d)(2) . . . Application [of screening, stabilization and transfer obligations] to inpatients

(i) If a hospital has screened an individual . . . and found the individual to have an emergency medical condition, and admits that individual as an inpatient in good faith in order to stabilize the emergency medical condition, the hospital has satisfied its special responsibilities under this section with respect to that individual.

(ii) This section is not applicable to an inpatient who was admitted for elective (nonemergency) diagnosis or treatment.

[The language of section (i) was altered from that used in the proposed regulations. The earlier language had provided: "If a hospital admits an individual with an unstable emergency medical condition for stabilizing treatment, as an inpatient, and stabilizes that individual's emergency medical condition, the period of stability would be required to be documented by relevant clinical data in the individual's medical record, before the hospital has satisfied its special responsibilities under this section with respect to that individual. . . ." 67 Fed.Reg. 314045–01, 31496]

(j) Availability of on-call physicians.

(1) Each hospital must maintain an on-call list of physicians on its medical staff in a manner that best meets the needs of the hospital's patients who are receiving services required under this section in accordance with the resources available to the hospital, including the availability of on-call physicians.

(2) The hospital must have written policies and procedures in place—

(i) To respond to situations in which a particular specialty is not available or the on-call physician cannot respond because of circumstances beyond the physician's control. . . .

[The proposed regulations had not included the limiting phrase: "in accordance with the resources available to the hospital."]

B. THE AMERICANS WITH DISABILITIES ACT AND SECTION 504 OF THE REHABILITATION ACT

The Americans with Disabilities Act (ADA) prohibits discrimination against persons who have or are considered to have a "disability" as defined in the statute. The ADA extends an earlier federal statute (Section 504 of the Rehabilitation Act of 1973 (29 U.S.C. § 749)) which also prohibits discrimination against the disabled. The ADA and § 504 are quite similar in most respects, and courts have used cases under the Rehabilitation Act to assist in interpreting the later ADA. The Rehabilitation Act, however, is limited to programs and services receiving federal funding while the ADA applies to private programs and services as well, including hospitals and physician practices. Patients may bring claims against health care providers directly under both the ADA and the Rehabilitation Act. The federal government has enforcement authority as well.

BRAGDON v. ABBOTT

Supreme Court of the United States, 1998.
524 U.S. 624, 118 S.Ct. 2196, 141 L.Ed.2d 540.

KENNEDY, J., delivered the opinion of the Court, in which STEVENS, SOUTER, GINSBERG, and BREYER, JJ., joined. STEVENS, J., filed a concurring opinion. REHNQUIST, C.J., filed an opinion concurring in the judgment in part and dissenting in part, in which SCALIA and THOMAS, JJ., joined, and in Part II of which O'CONNOR, J., joined. O'CONNOR, J., filed an opinion concurring in the judgment in part and dissenting in part.

I

Respondent Sidney Abbott has been infected with HIV since 1986. When the incidents we recite occurred, her infection had not manifested its most serious symptoms. On September 16, 1994, she went to the office of petitioner Randon Bragdon in Bangor, Maine, for a dental appointment. She disclosed her HIV infection on the patient registration form. Petitioner completed a dental examination, discovered a cavity, and informed respondent of his policy against filling cavities of HIV-infected patients. He offered to perform the work at a hospital with no added fee for his services, though respondent would be responsible for the cost of using the hospital's facilities. Respondent declined.

* * *

* * * Notwithstanding the protection given respondent by the ADA's definition of disability, petitioner could have refused to treat her if her infectious condition "posed a direct threat to the health or safety of others."[ ] The ADA defines a direct threat to be "a significant risk to the health or safety of others that cannot be eliminated by a modification of policies, practices, procedures, or by the provision of auxiliary aids or services."[ ] * * *

The ADA's direct threat provision stems from the recognition in School Bd. of Nassau Cty. v. Arline[ ] of the importance of prohibiting discrimination against individuals with disabilities while protecting others from significant health and safety risks, resulting, for instance, from a contagious disease. In *Arline,* the Court reconciled these objectives by construing the Rehabilitation Act not to require the hiring of a person who posed "a significant risk of communicating an infectious disease to others."[ ] * * * [The ADA's] direct threat provision codifies *Arline.* Because few, if any, activities in life are risk free, *Arline* and the ADA do not ask whether a risk exists, but whether it is significant.[ ]

The existence, or nonexistence, of a significant risk must be determined from the standpoint of the person who refuses the treatment or accommodation, and the risk assessment must be based on medical or other objective evidence.[ ] As a health care professional, petitioner had the duty to assess the risk of infection based on the objective, scientific information available to him and others in his profession. His belief that a significant risk existed, even if maintained in good faith, would not relieve him from liability. To use the words of the question presented, petitioner receives no special deference simply because he is a health care professional. It is true that *Arline* reserved "the question whether courts should also defer to the reasonable medical judgments of private physicians on which an employer has relied."[ ] At most, this statement reserved the possibility that employers could consult with individual physicians as objective third-party experts. It did not suggest that an individual physician's state of mind could excuse discrimination without regard to the objective reasonableness of his actions.

* * * In assessing the reasonableness of petitioner's actions, the views of public health authorities, such as the U.S. Public Health Service, CDC, and the National Institutes of Health, are of special weight and authority.[ ] The views of these organizations are not conclusive, however. A health care professional who disagrees with the prevailing medical consensus may refute it by citing a credible scientific basis for deviating from the accepted norm.[ ]

[An] illustration of a correct application of the objective standard is the Court of Appeals' refusal to give weight to the petitioner's offer to treat respondent in a hospital.[ ] Petitioner testified that he believed hospitals had safety measures, such as air filtration, ultraviolet lights, and respirators, which would reduce the risk of HIV transmission.[ ] Petitioner made no showing, however, that any area hospital had these safeguards or even that he had hospital privileges.[ ] His expert also admitted the lack of any scientific basis for the conclusion that these measures would lower the risk of transmission.[ ] Petitioner failed to present any objective, medical evidence showing that treating respondent in a hospital would be safer or more efficient in preventing HIV transmission than treatment in a well-equipped dental office.

We are concerned, however, that the Court of Appeals [in granting summary judgment to Abbott] might have placed mistaken reliance upon two other sources. In ruling no triable issue of fact existed on this point, the Court of Appeals relied on the CDC Dentistry Guidelines and the 1991 American Dental Association Policy on HIV.[ ] This evidence is not definitive. * * * [T]he CDC Guidelines recommended certain universal precautions which, in CDC's view, "should reduce the risk of disease transmission in the dental environment."[ ] The Court of Appeals determined that, "[w]hile the guidelines do not state explicitly that no further risk-reduction measures are desirable or that routine dental care for HIV-positive individuals is safe, those two conclusions seem to be implicit in the guidelines' detailed delineation of procedures for office treatment of HIV-positive patients."[ ] In our view, the Guidelines do not necessarily contain implicit assumptions conclusive of the point to be decided. The Guidelines set out CDC's recommendation that the universal precautions are the best way to combat the risk of HIV transmission. They do not assess the level of risk.

Nor can we be certain, on this record, whether the 1991 American Dental Association Policy on HIV carries the weight the Court of Appeals attributed to it. The Policy does provide some evidence of the medical community's objective assessment of the risks posed by treating people infected with HIV in dental offices. It indicates:

"Current scientific and epidemiologic evidence indicates that there is little risk of transmission of infectious diseases through dental treatment if recommended infection control procedures are routinely followed. Patients with HIV infection may be safely treated in private dental offices when appropriate infection control procedures are employed. Such infection control procedures provide protection both for patients and dental personnel."[ ]

We note, however, that the Association is a professional organization, which, although a respected source of information on the dental profession, is not a public health authority. It is not clear the extent to which the Policy was based on the Association's assessment of dentists' ethical and professional duties in addition to its scientific assessment of the risk to which the ADA refers. Efforts to clarify dentists' ethical obligations and to encourage dentists to treat patients with HIV infection with compassion may be commendable, but the question under the statute is one of statistical likelihood, not professional responsibility. Without more information on the manner in which the American Dental Association formulated this Policy, we are unable to determine the Policy's value in evaluating whether petitioner's assessment of the risks was reasonable as a matter of law.

* * *

Notes and Questions

1. On remand, the Ninth Circuit upheld the District Court's grant of summary judgment in favor of the plaintiff:

> The [American Dental] Association's Council on Scientific Affairs, comprised of 17 dentists (most of whom hold advanced dentistry degrees), together with a staff of over 20 professional experts and consultants, drafted the Policy at issue here. By contrast, ethical policies are drafted by the Council on Ethics, a wholly separate body. [W]e think that the origins of the Policy satisfy any doubts regarding its scientific foundation.

> We next reconsider whether Dr. Bragdon offered sufficient proof of direct threat to create a genuine issue of material fact and thus avoid the entry of summary judgment.... The Supreme Court suggested that one such piece of evidence—the seven cases that the CDC considered "possible" HIV patient-to-dental worker transmissions—should be reexamined. Since an objective standard pertains here, the existence of the list of seven "possible" cases does not create a genuine issue of material fact as to direct threat.... Each piece of evidence to which [defendant directs] us is still "too speculative or too tangential (or, in some instances, both) to create a genuine issue of material fact." Abbott v. Bragdon, 163 F.3d 87 (1st Cir. 1998), cert. denied, 526 U.S. 1131, 119 S.Ct. 1805, 143 L.Ed.2d 1009 (1999).

2. The AMA Code of Ethics provides that "a physician may not ethically refuse to treat a patient whose condition is within the physician's current realm of competence solely because the patient is seropositive for HIV." Code of Ethics, E–9.131 HIV–Infected Patients and Physicians (1992). What is the significance of the AMA's use of the word "solely?" Many state legislatures have amended their medical practice acts to provide that discrimination against persons with HIV is grounds for disciplinary action, and usually this is the only antidiscrimination provision in the medical practice act. See e.g., Wis. Stat. § 252.14.

3. It may be difficult in a particular case to prove the reason for the refusal of treatment. In Lesley v. Hee Man Chie, 250 F.3d 47 (1st Cir. 2001), the District Court adopted the following standard:

> The case requires us to determine how far courts should defer to a doctor's judgment as to the best course of treatment for a disabled patient in the context of discriminatory denial of treatment claims. We hold that the doctor's judgment is to be given deference absent a showing by the plaintiff that the judgment lacked any reasonable medical basis.

How would you go about proving or defending against a claim that the medical judgment defense is a subterfuge? How does *Bragdon* deal with the question of medical judgment in its consideration of the direct threat issue?

Dr. Chie had been Ms. Lesley's OB/GYN for thirteen years when he discovered her HIV-positive status after testing as part of prenatal care. Lesley's pregnancy was high-risk before the diagnosis of HIV due to several factors. After making the diagnosis, Chie consulted with Lesley's psychiatrist and numerous community resources on the treatment of HIV and transmission reduction to the child and contacted the hospital and attempted to order a supply of AZT to administer during labor and delivery. Chie then recommended to Lesley that she obtain treatment at a nearby hospital that participated in NIH studies of treatment for HIV-positive women and infants and arranged for her enrollment in that protocol.

C. TITLE VI

U.S. hospitals and other health care facilities were segregated by law well into the late 1960s and by custom for some time thereafter. White-only hospitals refused admission to African–American citizens, and those white-dominated hospitals that did admit African Americans segregated them to separate units. Even publicly owned hospitals and hospitals funded by the federal government were segregated by race.

The post-World War II Hill–Burton program invested millions of federal tax dollars in the construction of hospitals across the country. The Hill–Burton legislation specifically institutionalized federally funded racial discrimination as it allowed federally funded hospitals to exclude African–Americans if other facilities were available. The segregated facilities available were hardly equal either by definition or in fact. See David Barton Smith, Health Care Divided: Race and Healing A Nation (1999). Not until 1963, did a federal Court of Appeals declare the "separate but equal" provision of the Hill–Burton Act unconstitutional. Simkins v. Moses H. Cone Mem'l Hosp., 323 F.2d 969 (4th Cir. 1963), cert. denied, 376 U.S. 938 (1964).

Title VI of the Civil Rights Act of 1964 (42 U.S.C.A. § 2000d *et seq.*) prohibits discrimination on the basis of race, color, or national origin by any program receiving federal financial assistance. With the advent of Medicare and Medicaid, enforcement of the nondiscrimination requirement of Title VI would have reached into most parts of the health care system from hospitals to physician offices to nursing homes. The implementation of Title VI, however, proved to be quite limited. First, the precursor of HHS declared that Title VI did not apply to physicians who received payment under Part B of Medicare, interpreting that program as a "contract of insurance" rather than payment of public funds. Second, hospitals could remain segregated *de facto* even while assuring the federal government that they did not discriminate if the physicians with admitting privileges refused to admit African Americans and if doctors who would admit more broadly were excluded from privileges. The Department originally threatened such hospitals, but then retreated. See David Barton Smith, Healthcare's Hidden Civil Rights Legacy, 48 St. Louis U. L.J. 37 (2003).

Finally, the U.S. Supreme Court decided a landmark case in 2001 restricting the ability of individuals to sue under Title VI. In Alexander v. Sandoval, 532 U.S. 275, 121 S.Ct. 1511, 149 L.Ed.2d 517 (2001), the Court held that only intentional discrimination is actionable through private suit under Title VI. The 5–4 majority held that only the federal government has the power to pursue a remedy for disparate impact claims.

For more on the issues raised by Title VI see Brietta R. Clark, Hospital Flight From Minority Communities: How Our Existing Civil Rights Framework Fosters Racial Inequality in Healthcare, 9 DePaul J. Health Care L. 1023 (2005); Sara Rosenbaum & Joel Teitelbaum, Civil Rights Enforcement in the Modern Healthcare System: Reinvigorating the Role of the Federal Government in the Aftermath of Alexander v. Sandoval, 3 Yale J. Health Pol'y, L. & Ethics 215 (2003). Title VI has been enforced by the federal government, even after *Sandoval*, as it applies to requiring interpreters for patients with limited English proficiency. Lisa Ikemoto, Racial Disparities in Health Care and Cultural Competency, 48 St. Louis U. L. J. 75 (2003); Leighton Ku & Glenn Flores, Pay Now or Pay Later: Providing Interpreter Services in Health Care, 24 Health Affairs 435 (2005).

Legal strategies for pursuing unequal treatment as a violation of law are following different paths at this point. Dayna Matthew, A New Strategy to Combat Racial Inequality in American Health Care Delivery, 9 DePaul J. Health Care L. 793 (2005); Sidney D. Watson, Equity Measures and Systems Reform as Tools for Reducing Racial and Ethnic Disparities in Health Care, The Commonwealth Fund (August 2005); Mary Crossley, Infected Judgment: Legal Responses to Physician Bias, 48 Vill. L. Rev. 195 (2003); Kevin Outterson, Tragedy and Remedy: Reparations for Disparities in Black Health, 9 DePaul J. Health Care L. 735 (2005).

Problem: Emmaus House

You are a volunteer attorney for a nonprofit organization that provides services to the homeless through a community center called Emmaus House. You and several other attorneys come to Emmaus House to offer legal services a couple of hours each week as part of a program organized by the local bar association. While you are there, the director of the center comes rushing into the cubicle where you are conducting interviews and tells you there is an emergency.

Mr. Jack Larkin, a homeless man who comes frequently to the center, is complaining of chest pains and shortness of breath. He has had these episodes before and, in fact, went to the public hospital very early this morning because of them. The doctor at the public hospital examined Mr. Larkin and concluded that he was not having a heart attack but rather was suffering from influenza. You and the director get Mr. Larkin into your car and take him to the nearest hospital which happens to be Eastbrook Memorial, a private hospital. Mr. Larkin is guided to a cubicle where the emergency room physician examines him. The doctor then tells you that they are going to transfer Mr. Larkin to the public hospital, twenty minutes away. What do you do?

Assume that Mr. Larkin is admitted to the public hospital but dies within the week. If you brought suit against Eastbrook, what would you have to prove? How would you structure discovery? Do you have a claim against the doctor?

Problem: What Kind of Care?

Elaine Osborne lives in Springfield. Ms. Osborne works in a minimum-wage job that provides no health insurance. As a woman with no dependent children, she would not qualify for Medicaid even if she met the income standards for eligibility. There is no public hospital in her city.

Ms. Osborne attended a free public health fair, and an evaluation by a volunteer medical student revealed a site suspicious for melanoma (cancer) on her face and some swelling of her lymph nodes. The student recommended that Ms. Osborne have a dermatologist do a biopsy as a follow up to the screening. Ms. Osborne went to the emergency department of each of the three local hospitals but was told that she was not in need of emergency care. Does Ms. Osborne have a claim against the hospitals or the medical student or the public health fair? She also called several doctors' offices but was told that they required insurance or payment in advance.

Eight months later, Ms. Osborne went to Westhaven Hospital complaining of pain and shortness of breath. She was admitted to Westhaven because it was suspected that she had had a heart attack. The emergency physicians eventually concluded, however, that her pain and shortness of breath were due to the spread of the cancer. Ms. Osborne was discharged from the hospital with a prescription for pain medication. Does she have a claim against Westhaven or the emergency physicians?

In your own community, where could Ms. Osborne go for treatment of the cancer? If Ms. Osborne had breast cancer rather than melanoma, she would probably qualify for Medicaid coverage for treatment of the cancer under the Breast and Cervical Cancer Prevention and Treatment Act of 2000, PL 106–354, which allowed states to add this particular group to their Medicaid programs. What, if anything, justifies the preferential status of breast/cervical cancer as compared to other medical conditions?

Chapter 7

PRIVATE HEALTH INSURANCE AND MANAGED CARE: STATE REGULATION AND LIABILITY

I. CONTRACT LIABILITY OF PRIVATE INSURERS AND MANAGED CARE ORGANIZATIONS

Insurance companies and insurance contracts have historically been governed primarily by state law, and states continue to have primary responsibility for regulating managed care. In the first instance, insurance and managed care contracts are governed by contract law, and the failure of an insurer or managed care plan to perform to the expectations of the insured may result in contract litigation in state court. Our discussion begins, therefore, with an examination of state insurance contract law.

LUBEZNIK v. HEALTHCHICAGO, INC.

Appellate Court of Illinois, 1994.
268 Ill.App.3d 953, 206 Ill.Dec. 9, 644 N.E.2d 777.

JUSTICE JOHNSON delivered the opinion of the court:

Plaintiff, Bonnie Lubeznik, filed this action in the Circuit Court of Cook County seeking a permanent injunction requiring defendant, HealthChicago, Inc., to pre-certify her for certain medical treatment. Following a hearing, the trial court granted the injunction. Defendant appeals, contending the trial court improperly (1) determined that the requested treatment was a covered benefit under plaintiff's insurance policy; * * *, and (4) granted the injunction.

We affirm.

The record reveals that in November 1988 plaintiff was diagnosed with Stage III ovarian cancer. At the time of her diagnosis, the cancer had spread through plaintiff's abdomen and liver and she had a 20 percent survival rate over the next five years. * * *

In June 1991, plaintiff was referred to Dr. Patrick Stiff, the director of the bone marrow treatment program at Loyola University Medical Center (hereinafter Loyola). Dr. Stiff sought to determine the prospect of treating plaintiff with high dose chemotherapy with autologous bone marrow transplant (hereinafter HDCT/ABMT). HDCT/ABMT is a procedure where bone marrow stem cells are removed from the patient's body and frozen in storage until after the patient has been treated with high dose chemotherapy. Following chemotherapy, which destroys the cancer, the marrow previously extracted is reinfused to proliferate and replace marrow destroyed by the chemotherapy. HDCT/ABMT had been a state of the art treatment for leukemia and Hodgkin's disease for many years. It began to be used in the late 1980's for women who were in the late stages of breast cancer.

* * *

On October 28, 1991, Dr. Stiff contacted defendant requesting that it pre-certify plaintiff for the HDCT/ABMT, i.e., agree in advance to pay for the treatment. Plaintiff's insurance policy required her to get pre-certified before receiving elective treatment, procedures and therapies. Dr. Wayne Mathy, defendant's medical director, received Dr. Stiff's pre-certification request and telephoned him shortly thereafter. During his conversation with Dr. Stiff, Dr. Mathy stated that the ABMT/HDCT was not a covered benefit under plaintiff's insurance policy because the treatment was considered experimental.

On October 31, 1991, plaintiff filed a two-count complaint against defendant * * *. In count one, plaintiff sought a mandatory injunction against defendant to pre-certify her for the HDCT/ABMT. * * *

Following a hearing, the trial court denied defendant's motion to dismiss and defendant filed its answer instanter. Thereafter, a hearing on the complaint was held at which Dr. Stiff testified that the HDCT/ABMT was an effective treatment for plaintiff given that all conventional treatment for her had been exhausted. He stated that he had performed 21 HDCT/ABMT procedures on patients with Stage III ovarian cancer and as a result, 75 percent of those patients were in complete remission.

During further testimony, Dr. Stiff opined that the HDCT/ABMT was not experimental and presented documents and literature in support of his testimony. * * *

Dr. Mathy testified at the hearing that his responsibilities as defendant's medical director included determining whether a requested medical treatment is covered under an insurance policy issued by defendant. He stated that after he received plaintiff's request for pre-certification, a member of defendant's benefit analysis staff contacted the National Institutes of Health, the National Cancer Institute, and Medicare seeking an assessment as to whether the requested treatment was experimental. According to Dr. Mathy, defendant determined that the HDCT/ABMT was experimental based on information received from those medical assessment bodies. * * *

During cross-examination, Dr. Mathy testified that he first learned on October 29, 1991, that Dr. Stiff was contemplating treating plaintiff with HDCT/ABMT. Dr. Mathy admitted that immediately upon learning of the proposed treatment, he decided that the HDCT/ABMT was experimental and that plaintiff's pre-certification request should be denied. Dr. Mathy stated that he did not consult with the National Institutes of Health or the National Cancer Institute before making the decision to deny plaintiff's request.

At the conclusion of the testimony, the parties presented final arguments to the trial court. Subsequently, the trial court issued an injunction against defendant ruling that the ABMT/HDCT is neither an experimental therapy for ovarian cancer, * * *. Defendant then filed this appeal.

Defendant initially argues that the trial court erroneously determined that the HDCT/ABMT procedure is a covered benefit under plaintiff's insurance policy. Defendant claims it supported its determination that the procedure is experimental with similar conclusions by appropriate medical technology boards as required by plaintiff's insurance contract. Plaintiff's insurance policy provides that "[e]xperimental medical, surgical, or other procedures as determined by the [Insurance] Plan in conjunction with appropriate medical technology assessment bodies," are excluded from coverage. Defendant contends that the trial court improperly disregarded the terms of the insurance contract, which, defendant argues, were clear and unambiguous.

At the outset, we note that coverage provisions in an insurance contract are to be liberally construed in favor of the insured to provide the broadest possible coverage.[ ] In determining whether a certain provision in an insurance contract is applicable, a trial court must first determine whether the specific provision is ambiguous.[ ] A provision which is clear or unambiguous, i.e., fairly admits but of one interpretation, must be applied as written.[ ] However, where a provision is ambiguous, its language must be construed in favor of the insured.[ ]

Moreover, where an insurer seeks to deny insurance coverage based on an exclusionary clause contained in an insurance policy, the clause must be clear and free from doubt.[ ] This is so because all doubts with respect to coverage are resolved in favor of the insured. * * *

After carefully reviewing the evidence, we cannot agree with defendant that the trial court improperly determined the HDCT/ABMT to be a covered benefit under plaintiff's insurance policy. First, we disagree with defendant that the exclusionary language was clear and unambiguous. We note that the plaintiff's insurance policy does not define the phrase "appropriate medical technology boards." The plain language of the policy does not indicate who will determine whether a certain medical board is appropriate. Further, the policy fails to outline any standards for determining how a medical board is deemed appropriate. Thus, the phrase, without more, gives rise to a genuine uncertainty about which medical boards are considered appropriate and how and by whom the determination is made.

Second, [the court concluded that the defendant's determination was not justified by a state statute on organ transplantation coverage].

Third, we must note that even if the exclusionary language did apply, defendant failed to follow the terms of the insurance policy. Plaintiff's insurance policy excludes from coverage medical and surgical procedures that are considered experimental by defendant "in conjunction with appropriate technology assessment bodies." At the hearing, Dr. Mathy testified that upon learning of plaintiff's pre-certification request, he had already determined that the HDCT/ABMT was experimental prior to receiving or reviewing any information from the medical assessment boards. Given our careful review of the evidence, including defendant's admitted disregard for the terms of the insurance policy, we hold that the trial court did not err in ruling that the requested treatment was a covered benefit under the policy.

* * *

Lastly, defendant claims that the trial court improperly granted the mandatory injunction because plaintiff failed to meet the requirements for an injunction to issue. An injunction may be granted only after the plaintiff establishes that (1) a lawful right exists; (2) irreparable injury will result if the injunction is not granted; and (3) his or her remedy at law is inadequate.[ ] * * *

* * *

At the hearing, Dr. Stiff testified that given the steady development of plaintiff's disease, it was imperative to begin the HDCT/ABMT treatment as quickly as possible. He opined that delaying the HDCT/ABMT any further might have rendered plaintiff ineligible for such treatment due to further development of the disease. Based on our understanding of Dr. Stiff's testimony, we do not believe, as defendant now posits, that plaintiff was not eligible for the treatment.

Moreover, Dr. Stiff further testified that the HDCT/ABMT was an effective treatment for plaintiff and offered her a "very high chance of a complete disappearance of her disease." In addition, when asked during direct examination to give a prognosis of plaintiff's condition, Dr. Stiff gave the following response:

> "[Plaintiff] has a fatal illness with a zero percent to one percent chance of being alive at five years, let alone alive and disease free."

Given the evidence presented at the hearing, including Dr. Stiff's testimony, we do not agree with defendant that plaintiff failed to show she would suffer irreparable harm without the treatment.[ ] Therefore, we hold that the trial court did not abuse its discretion in granting the requested injunctive relief.

* * *

Notes and Questions

1. Courts have traditionally viewed insurance contracts as adhesion contracts and interpreted them under the doctrine of *contra proferentem*. This has made it difficult for insurance companies to control their exposure to risk through general clauses that refuse payment for care that is not "medically necessary" or that is "experimental." Usually when such clauses are litigated, as in the principal case, the treating physician testifies that care is standard and is urgently necessary, while the insurer's medical director testifies that the care is experimental or unnecessary. What conflicts of interest does each face? Whom should the court believe? Are there more appropriate ways of resolving these disputes? What are the ramifications of these disputes for the cost of medical care?

2. Litigation challenging the refusal of insurance companies to cover ABMT provides a fascinating case study of the use of the courts to determine access to health care services, which is described in detail in Peter D. Jacobson and Stefanie A. Doebler, "We Were All Sold a Bill of Goods:" Litigating the Science of Breast Cancer Treatment, 52 Wayne L. Rev. 43 (2006). Nearly one hundred cases were

litigated from the late 1980s to the early 2000s by women with breast cancer seeking coverage of ABMT. Many insurers refused to cover the procedure, claiming that it was experimental. In most litigated cases, as in *Lubeznik*, the plaintiff's treating physician testified for the plaintiff, claiming that the procedure was not only standard treatment, but also necessary to save the plaintiff's life. The insurer's medical director (often supported by other expert witnesses), on the other hand, usually testified that the procedure was still experimental, and thus excluded by the language of the policy. Occasionally the insurer was also able to introduce into evidence a consent form signed by the insured acknowledging that the procedure was experimental. Plaintiffs won about half of these cases, with the other half going for the insurers. In 1993 a California jury awarded $89 million in damages against an insurer that had refused to cover ABMT, including $77 million of punitive damages. Fox v. HealthNet (No. 219692 [Cal. Super. Ct. Riverside Cty. December 28, 1993]). After that point, the focus of litigation and settlement negotiations turned from whether insurers had improperly denied the treatment to whether they had done so in bad faith, although defendants still continued to win cases. (Was the denial in *Lubeznik* in bad faith?) Coverage of the procedure also became much more common. In the year 2000, clinical trials of ABMT were finally published, demonstrating that in fact HDC/ABMT was not effective for treating breast cancer. By that time, however, 30,000 women had received ABMT at a cost of $3 billion. What can we learn from this about the nature of the development of medical knowledge? What can we learn about the nature of medical litigation? See also E. Haavi Morreim, From the Clinics to the Courts: The Role Evidence Should Play in Litigating Medical Care, 26 J. Health Pol., Pol'y & L. 409, 411–13 (2001); Karen Antman, *et al.*, High Dose Chemotherapy for Breast Cancer, 282 JAMA 1701 (1999).

3.   Another interesting empirical study of coverage disputes is described in Mark Hall, *et al.*, Judicial Protection of Managed Care Consumers: An Empirical Study of Insurance Coverage Disputes, 26 Seton Hall L. Rev. 1055 (1996). Professor Hall found that patients win coverage disputes over half of the time, and that the specificity of the language with which the insurer attempts to exclude coverage does not significantly affect its likelihood of winning. The issue of how medical necessity should be defined and who should determine it has become an important and controversial issue in managed care reform proposals. See Sara Rosenbaum, David M. Frankford, Brad More & Phyllis Borzi, Who Should Determine When Health Care is Medically Necessary? 340 JAMA 229 (1999) and the discussion of Utilization Controls in Section IV below. See also, regarding experimental treatment exclusions, J. Gregory Lahr, What is the Method to Their "Madness?" Experimental Treatment Exclusions in Health Insurance Policies, 13 J. Contemp. Health L. & Pol'y 613 (1997).

II.   TORT LIABILITY OF MANAGED CARE

Insurance and managed care coverage disputes present not only contract interpretation issues, but also issues of tort law. See Chapter 5, *infra*, for a full discussion of managed care tort liability.

III.   REGULATION OF PRIVATE HEALTH INSURANCE UNDER STATE LAW

A.   TRADITIONAL INSURANCE REGULATION

Historically, the states bore primary responsibility for regulating private health care finance, a role confirmed by Congress in the McCarran–Ferguson

Act of 1945. 15 U.S.C.A. §§ 1011–1015. In the next chapter we will consider the effect that the Employee Retirement Income Security Act of 1974 (ERISA) has had on state regulation. Although ERISA places some limits on the ability of the states to regulate employee benefit plans, the states still remain primarily responsible for regulating insurers who insure employee benefits plans as well as all health insurance plans not governed by ERISA, such as individual health insurance plans, group insurance plans covering church employees or employees of state and local government, no-fault auto insurance, uninsured motorist policies, and workers' compensation.

All states tax the premiums of commercial insurers and most tax Blue Cross/Blue Shield plan premiums (though some at a lower rate than commercial plans). States oversee the financial solvency of insurers by imposing minimal requirements for financial reserves and for allowable investments, and through requiring annual statements and conducting periodic examinations of insurers (usually on a triennial basis). Why might insurer insolvencies be of greater concern to government than bankruptcies in other sectors of the economy?

In most states, insurers must file policy forms with the state insurance regulatory agency. Some states allow a form to be used once it has been filed with the insurance agency (if it is not disapproved), while others require explicit approval of a policy form before it can be used. States also regulate insurance marketing and claims practices, including coordination of benefits where an insured is covered by more than one policy. (This is often the case in today's society with two-income and blended families.) State insurance commissions investigate consumer complaints and place insolvent companies into receivership. The National Association of Insurance Commissioners (NAIC) has issued model codes and regulations on many of these subjects, the wide adoption of which has brought about some uniformity among the states. See www.naic.org.

How do these traditional concerns of insurance regulation change in a managed care environment? Should health maintenance organizations be subject to the same solvency and reserve requirements as commercial insurers? Should provider-sponsored integrated delivery systems also be required to meet solvency and reserve requirements? Should independent practice associations, physician groups, and other provider entities that assume "downstream" risk from HMOs be subject to solvency requirements, or is it sufficient that the HMO agrees to assume the risk of solvency of such groups? (In the late 1990s hundreds of risk-bearing groups covering millions of patients became insolvent, see Brant S. Mittler and Andre Hampton, The Princess and the Pea: The Assurance of Voluntary Compliance Between the Texas Attorney General and Aetna's Texas HMOs and its Impact on Financial Risk Shifting by Managed Care, 83 F.U.L.Rev. 553 (2003)). Are marketing and claims practices more or less of a concern under managed care?

B. ATTEMPTS TO INCREASE ACCESS TO INSURANCE THROUGH REGULATION

States have not historically regulated the rates of commercial health insurers. Because the market for health insurance has been relatively competitive and because most insurance is sold to employers or large groups that have some bargaining power and expertise, rate regulation was not generally thought necessary. Rates and rate information are commonly filed with the insurance commissioner, and some states permit the commissioner to disapprove these filings if benefits do not bear a reasonable relationship to premiums charged. But most states have historically not set health insurance rates as such and have rarely intervened in insurer rate-setting processes. States have also not traditionally regulated underwriting practices, other than to attempt to assure that rates were not obviously discriminatory (e.g. treating different racial groups differently). Regulation of nonprofit Blue Cross and Blue Shield rates and underwriting, however, has been much more common because of a belief that the Blues have had a greater obligation to make their services readily available to the public at a fair rate in exchange for the favorable tax and regulatory treatment they have historically received. As many Blue plans have become for profit, this distinction has faded.

In recent years, however, states have increasingly regulated underwriting practices and premium rate-setting in an effort to assure equity of access to insurance. The number of uninsured in America has grown through most of the past decade, and at this writing over 47 million Americans are uninsured. Most of the uninsured are either employed or the dependents of employed persons. A major reason why so many employed persons are uninsured is that persons who are either self-employed or employed by small employers are far less likely to be insured, or even to have insurance available through their place of employment, than are employees of large businesses. Only about 45 percent of employers with fewer than 10 employees offer health insurance benefits, while nearly all employers with more than 200 do for their full-time employees. This is in part due to the fact that individual and small group insurance tends to be much more expensive than insurance covering large groups. This in turn is true because administrative, marketing, and underwriting costs are much higher for individual and small group coverage, and because insurers have to cover themselves against the greater risk of adverse selection inherent in insuring individuals and small groups. Although the growth in the number of the uninsured in recent years is attributable to increases in the number of employees declining insurance offered by their employers (usually because of high premium costs), as well as increases in the number of part-time or temporary workers not covered by employment-related insurance, the fact that small employers disproportionately do not offer their employees insurance is a key cause of lack of insurance in the United States.

For purposes of regulation, states usually distinguish between large groups, small groups, and individuals. While the boundaries vary from state to state (and can sometimes be manipulated by insurers), small groups are usually defined as groups with between 2 and 50 members, large groups with more than 50 members. The underwriting of insurance for large group plans is unregulated in most states. Most states, on the other hand, do regulate underwriting practices with respect to individuals. Every state has, moreover, adopted small group reforms during the past decade, which usually go further in limiting insurer discretion than reforms in individual insurance markets. These reforms were encouraged by the 1996 federal Health Insurance Portability and Accountability Act (HIPAA), which mandated the enactment of certain small group and individual reforms discussed in detail in the next chapter. Many of the reforms required by HIPAA, however, were already in place in numerous states before it went into effect, while many states have also adopted reforms going beyond HIPAA, thus HIPAA may have added little to state regulation in many states. Why might access to affordable insurance be less of a problem for large groups? Why might states be more willing to pass laws protecting small groups than individuals? What protections do small groups need?

COLONIAL LIFE INSURANCE COMPANY OF AMERICA v. CURIALE

Supreme Court, Appellate Division, Third Department, 1994.
205 A.D.2d 58, 617 N.Y.S.2d 377.

PETERS, JUSTICE.

* * *

Petitioner is a commercial insurance company which issues small group health insurance policies in this State. Petitioner challenged two regulations promulgated by respondent Superintendent of Insurance to implement chapter 501 of the Laws of 1992. Chapter 501 requires a commercial insurer doing business in this State to employ "community rating" and to offer "open enrollment"[2] for any insurance policies issued in this State. The underpinning of the new law was to spread the risk among more people and provide greater rate stability. The Superintendent was directed to promulgate regulations designed to protect insurers writing policies from claim fluctuations and "unexpected significant shifts in the number of persons insured"[ ]. Pursuant thereto, the Superintendent promulgated 11 NYCRR parts 360 and 361 which implemented what he deemed a statutory directive that insurers be required to share the risk of high-cost claims by establishing a pool system which compares the risk of insurers in seven regions of the State[ ]. After these comparisons were made, insurers with worse than average demographic factors would get money from regional pooling funds, while insurers with better than average factors would pay money into these pooling funds.

Petitioner commenced this proceeding seeking to have 11 NYCRR part 361 and two provisions of 11 NYCRR part 360 invalidated. Supreme Court [The trial court in New York] dismissed the petition to the extent that it challenged 11 NYCRR part 361, but granted the petition with respect to 11 NYCRR part 360. The parties have cross-appealed from the adverse portions of the court's judgment.

* * *

Petitioner contends that the pool system established by 11 NYCRR part 361 violates the intent of chapter 501 since the Legislature did not intend that (1) contributions to the system be mandatory, (2) contributions be based on existing policies, and (3) Empire Blue Cross and Blue Shield (hereinafter Empire) participate. * * *

The Superintendent established the pool system pursuant to Insurance Law § 3233 which provided that "the superintendent shall promulgate regu-

---

2. Open enrollment requires that any individual or small group applying for health in-   surance coverage must be accepted for any coverage offered by the insurer[ ].

lations to assure an orderly implementation and ongoing operation of the open enrollment and community rating required by [Insurance Law §§ 3231 and 4317] * * *. The regulations shall apply to all insurers and health maintenance organizations subject to community rating" (Insurance Law § 3233[a]). Based upon such language, there exists a clear expression by the Legislature that regulations shall be promulgated to further open enrollment which "shall include reinsurance or a pooling process involving insurer contributions to, or receipts from, a fund"[ ] and that those regulations "shall apply to all insurers and health maintenance organizations subject to community rating"[ ]. * * *

[The Court next held that the regulations were not improperly retroactive, and that Empire Blue Cross was properly included in the scheme].

Finally, petitioner contends that 11 NYCRR part 361 imposes an unconstitutional tax, gives State money to private organizations and takes property without just compensation. Our review indicates that the Legislature intended pool payments be mandatory and that those payments consist of the amounts necessary to permit sharing or equalization of the risk of high cost claims[ ]. Having chosen to require such payments, the Legislature could therefore delegate the responsibility to the Superintendent to collect such amounts[ ] We find that such pool contributions are a valid exercise of the Legislature's power to regulate[ ] and as the enactment intended to regulate rather than generate revenue it is not a tax[ ].

* * * We further agree with Supreme Court that there has not been an unconstitutional taking of what petitioner contends is its low-risk value of its book of business. We find, as did Supreme Court, that petitioner cannot support its contention that it has a constitutionally protected interest in maintaining a healthier than average risk pool[ ].

Supreme Court invalidated 11 NYCRR 360.4(c) and 360.3(a)(1)(ii), holding that they exceeded the scope of the authority delegated to the Superintendent by chapter 501. The Superintendent promulgated 11 NYCRR 360.4(c) in response to his understanding of the statutory directive contained in Insurance Law § 3231(b), which [regulation] reads as follows:

> Nothing herein shall prohibit the use of premium rate structures to establish different premium rates for individuals as opposed to family units or separate community rates for individuals as opposed to small groups. Individual proprietors and groups of two must be classified in the individual or small group rating category by the insurer.

Supreme Court held that this requirement exceeded the Superintendent's authority, determining that Insurance Law § 3231(b) applied only to the rating of policies and "does not provide authority for requiring insurers of small groups to extend coverage to individual proprietors and groups of two". Should the Superintendent's regulation be permitted to stand, [the trial court] reasoned, and we agree, that the definition of "small group" contained in Insurance Law § 3231(a) would be impermissibly expanded to now require small group insurers to cover individual proprietors and/or groups of two contrary to the clear and unambiguous language in the statute.[ ] * * *

As to 11 NYCRR 360.3(a)(1)(ii), we find that Supreme Court's findings should not be disturbed. Under Insurance Law § 4235(c)(1), if less than 50 percent of employees in a group do not agree to participate in a plan, the insurer does not have to offer coverage to the group. The Superintendent, however, promulgated 11 NYCRR part 360.3(a)(1)(ii) which provides as follows:

> [F]or purposes of determining said participation requirements, insurers must include as participating all eligible employees or members of the group covered under all the alternative health maintenance organization plans made available by the group.

Supreme Court properly invalidated the regulation since chapter 501 did not amend or change the minimum participation requirements set forth in Insurance Law § 4235(c)(1) and the Superintendent therefore exceeded his authority by redefining the calculation of participation levels[ ].

* * *

Notes and Questions

1. What is the purpose of laws requiring community rating and open enrollment? Why do these requirements in turn result in the need to create a pool to share risk among insurers? Why would commercial insurers object to including Blue Cross in this pool? Why are individual insureds not included in the small group pooling requirements? Why are insurers permitted to exclude from coverage groups in which fewer than 50 percent of the group members elect to be insured?

2. All states currently require insurers that sell in small group markets to offer coverage and guarantee renewal to any small group that requests it, regardless of the health status or claims experience of the group's members. Thirty-eight states had guaranteed issue and forty-three guaranteed renewal requirements before HIPAA, but HIPAA made these requirements universal. HIPAA also requires restrictions on preexisting conditions clauses (clauses that exclude coverage for conditions that existed prior to the inception of the insurance contract). Forty-five states had restricted preexisting conditions clauses for small group policies before HIPAA. A number of states continue to go beyond HIPAA in limiting preexisting conditions clauses, moreover, including three states that outlaw them altogether.

Although HIPAA does not address the level of insurance premiums, many states do. As of the end of 2006, 37 states limited the variation in premiums insurers charge to small groups, only allowing insurers to vary premiums because of claims experience, health status, or duration of coverage of the group within a specified range. Insurance rating limitations, for example, may allow the highest premiums charged by an insurer to be twice as high as the lowest premiums charged. Twelve states went further, requiring a form of community rating by prohibiting rating based on experience, health status, or duration of coverage. New York, the most restrictive of the states, even limited variance of premiums based on age. Seven states also had established mandatory reinsurance pools and 19 voluntary reinsurance pools, assuring that small group plans that end up carrying high risk groups can spread some of their risks to other insurers with more favorable risk experience. See Blue Cross Blue Shield Association, State Legislative Health Care and Insurance Issues: 2006 Survey of Plans (2007). What would you expect to be the effect of these laws?

3. Most of the states have also attempted to reform the individual insurance market. The most common individual market reform is guaranteed renewal,

required by HIPAA but adopted by twenty-one states before HIPAA. As of the end of 2006, thirty one states had adopted restrictions on preexisting conditions limitations covering persons beyond those who must be covered under HIPAA. Among other individual market reforms adopted by the states are 1) community rating requirements (8 states); 2) rating bands (i.e. requiring that the highest premiums charged not be more than a specified percentage higher than the lowest premiums charged) or other restrictions on rates (10 states); 3) provision for voluntary or mandatory participation in reinsurance pools (8 states); and 4) preexisting conditions limitations (31 states).

4. One issue that has seen a great deal of state legislative action in recent years has been insurance underwriting based on genetic information. All but a handful of states have adopted laws prohibiting insurers from establishing eligibility rules that take into account genetic information or from using genetic information for risk selection or classification. About half the states also prohibit insurers from requiring genetic tests or information. As this book goes to press, Congress has adopted the Genetic Information Nondiscrimination Act (GINA), which prohibits health insurers and plans from denying coverage or charging higher premiums to a healthy person based on that person's genetic predisposition to develop a disease in the future.

5. As a general rule, small groups get better insurance rates than individuals, and large groups better than small groups. One approach to making insurance more affordable, therefore, has been to promote "association health plans," (AHPs) which allow individuals or small business to band together to purchase insurance or to self-insure, thus limiting marketing, underwriting, and administrative costs. Legislation has been introduced into Congress each year in the recent past that would additionally permit association plans to be sold across state lines, regulated by the federal government or by a single state, and otherwise freeing these AHPs from state law underwriting requirements and coverage mandates. This legislation has received strong support from small businesses and insurers, who believe that it would reduce the cost of insurance. It has been opposed by consumer advocates, state insurance commissioners and Blue Cross and Blue Shield plans. Opponents claim that AHPs plans would attract lower risk insureds and thus destabilize state insurance markets. In particular, freeing AHPs from some state mandates, like required coverage of mental health or substance abuse treatment, would allow AHPs to attract less costly favorable risks, leaving other insurers with more costly groups and individuals. See, exploring these issues, Mila Kofman, *et al.*, Association Health Plans: What's All the Fuss About? 25(6) Health Affairs 1591, 1598 (2006); Mila Kofman, Association Health Plans: Loss of State Oversight Means Regulatory Vacuum and More Fraud (Georgetown Health Policy Institute 2005); Mark A. Hall, Elliot K. Wicks and Janice S. Lawlor, Health Marts, HIPCs, MEWAs, and AHPs: A Guide for the Perplexed, 20 Health Aff. (1), 142–53 (2001). See, discussing specifically one recent attempt to free nongroup health insurance from state regulation, Elizabeth A. Pendo, The Health Care Choice Act: The Individual Insurance Market and the Politics of "Choice," 29 W. New. Eng. L. Rev. 473 (2007).

6. Another focus of regulatory concern in recent years has been "post claims underwriting." The issue here is insurance companies accepting applications for insurance and then, often after collecting premiums for some time, canceling coverage after the insured files a substantial claim, asserting that the insured misrepresented health status on the original application. The California Department of Managed Health Care in March, 2007, fined California Blue Cross $1 million for this practice, which violates the Knox–Keene Health Care Service Plan Act. The Department alleged that Blue Cross had not shown that the applicants

had wilfully misrepresented their health status, and that the plans had failed to conduct an adequate pre-enrollment medical history investigation, or to conform to their own underwriting policies. See BNA Health Law Reporter, Mar. 29, 2007, 392.

7.   In the end, regulatory approaches seem to have done little toward making insurance available in small group and individual markets, although the reforms have certainly helped some individuals and firms that might otherwise not have been able to secure insurance. In part, their limited effect seems to be due to the endless creativity of insurers in evading regulation and limiting their risk. By manipulating coverage, imposing cost-sharing obligations, and marketing selectively, as well as by creating "association" plans or using other devices that allow small group or individual plans to masquerade as large group plans, insurers can still often control the risk to which they are exposed, allowing them to remain prosperous, but on the other hand, to continue to exclude high-risk individuals.

On the other hand, the disastrous effects of these reforms that many in the health insurance industry had predicted have also not materialized. Insurers have generally remained in business even in states that have adopted rigorous reforms, and markets have remained competitive, though individual reforms have had a more damaging effect on markets than small group reforms have had. To a considerable degree, however, the effects that small group reforms might have had on insurers or insureds have been masked by a dramatic growth of managed care in small group markets, which has held down increases in premiums that reforms might otherwise have caused.

Problem: Expanding Insurance Coverage

You are a state legislator and the chair of the legislative health and welfare committee. You have run on a platform calling for increased regulation to address the problem of the uninsured, which is quite serious in your state. You would like to make insurance coverage more attractive to small businesses, which often do not offer insurance to their employees in your state, and to self-employed individuals. What regulatory strategies will you consider? Are there non-regulatory strategies you might consider as well, such as tax credits or penalties or mandates? Whom will you invite to testify at hearings you will hold on this subject? What do you expect them to say at the hearings? Also reconsider this problem after you study the discussion of ERISA preemption of state reform efforts in Chapter 8.

IV. STATE REGULATION OF MANAGED CARE

A. INTRODUCTION

Managed Care Organizations (MCOs) differ from traditional health insurers, of course, insofar as they manage care. They do this through restricting members to the use of particular providers, reviewing the utilization of services, and creating incentives for limiting the cost of care. Some MCOs also attempt to oversee the quality of care their members receive. Terms commonly used to describe forms of managed care include:

   ● Health Maintenance Organizations (HMOs), which usually limit their members to an exclusive network of providers, permitting their members to go to non-network providers only in extraordinary circumstances, like medical emergencies. They have also historically emphasized preventive care, and usually use incentives such as capitation payments to direct the behavior of their professionals and providers. Some HMOs provide care through their own employees or the employees of affiliated foundations (staff model HMOs), while others contract with independent networks of providers to deliver care.

● Point-of-service plans (POSs) resemble HMOs, but allow their members to obtain services outside the network with additional cost-sharing (deductibles, coinsurance, or copayments), and often subject to gatekeeper controls.

● Preferred Provider Organizations (PPOs) are organized systems of health care providers who agree to provide services on a discounted basis to subscribers. PPO subscribers are not limited to preferred, in-plan, providers, but face financial disincentives, such as deductibles or larger copayment or coinsurance obligations, if they elect non-preferred providers. PPOs usually pay their providers on a fee-for-service basis, and often use utilization review controls for certain kinds of services, like hospital admissions.

● Finally, provider-sponsored-organizations (PSOs), also called, in their various guises, integrated delivery systems (IDSs), physician-hospital organizations (PHOs), and provider-sponsored networks (PSNs), are networks organized by providers that contract directly with employers or other purchasers of health benefits to provide their own services on a capitated basis.

Though managed care was generally welcomed at first as offering the potential both to restrain costs and to improve quality, beginning in the late 1990s a decided "backlash" against managed care gathered steam. See Alice A. Noble and Troyen A. Brennan, The Stages of Managed Care Regulation: Developing Better Rules, in John E. Billi and Gail B. Agrawal, The Challenge of Regulating Managed Care, 29 (2001). There was a general perception—encouraged by the media—that managed care controls had become excessive, threatening access to care. Almost every state has adopted some form of legislation, nearly 1000 statutes in all, during the last half of the 1990s. The following law, adopted in 2000 by Massachusetts, addresses most of the issues with which such legislation has been concerned.

MASSACHUSETTS GENERAL LAWS ANNOTATED: AN ACT RELATIVE TO MANAGED CARE PRACTICES IN THE INSURANCE INDUSTRY

* * *

Chapter 111, Section 217. (a) There is hereby established within the department [of public health] an office of patient protection. The office shall:

(2) establish a site on the internet and through other communication media in order to make managed care information collected by the office readily accessible to consumers. Said internet site shall, at a minimum, include (i) the health plan report card developed [by the state], (ii) a chart, prepared by the office, comparing the information obtained on premium revenue expended for health care services as provided pursuant to * * *, and (iii) [HEDIS data, see below];

(3) assist consumers with questions or concerns relating to managed care, including but not limited to exercising the grievance and appeals rights * * *;

* * *

(c) Each entity that compiles the health plan employer data and information set, [HEDIS] so-called, for the National Committee on Quality Assurance, or collects other information deemed by the entity as similar or equivalent thereto, shall * * * concurrently submit to the office of patient protection a copy thereof excluding, at the entity's option, proprietary financial data.

* * *

Chapter 176G: Section 5. (a) As used in this section, the following words shall have the following meanings:

* * *

"Emergency medical condition", a medical condition, whether physical or mental, manifesting itself by symptoms of sufficient severity, including severe pain, that the absence of prompt medical attention could reasonably be expected by a prudent layperson who possesses an average knowledge of health and medicine, to result in placing the health of a member or another person in serious jeopardy, serious impairment to body function, or serious dysfunction of any body organ or part, or, with respect to a pregnant woman, as further defined in [EMTALA, see Chapter 8].

"Stabilization for discharge", an emergency medical condition shall be deemed to be stabilized for purposes of discharging a member, * * *, when the attending physician has determined that, within reasonable clinical confidence, the member has reached the point where further care, including diagnostic work-up or treatment, or both, could be reasonably performed on an outpatient basis or a later scheduled inpatient basis if the member is given a reasonable plan for appropriate follow-up care and discharge instructions, * * *. Stabilization for discharge does not require final resolution of the emergency medical condition.

* * *

(b) A health maintenance organization shall cover emergency services provided to members for emergency medical conditions. After the member has been stabilized for discharge or transfer, the health maintenance organization or its designee may require a hospital emergency department to contact * * * the health maintenance organization * * * for authorization of post-stabilization services to be provided. * * * Such authorization shall be deemed granted if the health maintenance organization or its designee has not responded to said call within 30 minutes. Notwithstanding the foregoing provision, in the event the attending physician and * * * on-call physician do not agree on what constitutes appropriate medical treatment, the opinion of the attending physician shall prevail and such treatment shall be considered appropriate treatment for an emergency medical condition provided that such treatment is consistent with generally accepted principles of professional medical practice and a covered benefit under the member's evidence of coverage. * * *

* * *

(e) * * * No member shall in any way be discouraged from using the local pre-hospital emergency medical service system, the 911 telephone number, or the local equivalent, or be denied coverage for medical and transportation expenses incurred as a result of an emergency medical condition.

* * *

Chapter 176O: Health Insurance Consumer Protections.

Section 1. As used in this chapter, the following words shall have the following meanings:—

"Adverse determination", a determination, based upon a review of information provided by a carrier or its designated utilization review organization, to deny, reduce, modify, or terminate an admission, continued inpatient stay, or the availability of any other health care services, * * *.

* * *

"Grievance", any oral or written complaint submitted to the carrier which has been initiated by an insured, or on behalf of an insured with the consent of the insured, concerning any aspect or action of the carrier relative to the insured, including, but not limited to, review of adverse determinations regarding scope of coverage, denial of services, quality of care and administrative operations, * * *.

* * *

"Incentive plan", any compensation arrangement between a carrier and licensed health care professional or licensed health care provider group or organization that employs or utilizes services of one or more licensed health care professionals that may directly or indirectly have the effect of reducing or limiting services furnished to insureds of the organization.

* * *

"Medical necessity" or "medically necessary", health care services that are consistent with generally accepted principles of professional medical practice.

* * *

Section 4. A carrier * * * shall not refuse to contract with or compensate for covered services an otherwise eligible health care provider solely because such provider has in good faith communicated with or advocated on behalf of one or more of his prospective, current or former patients regarding the provisions, terms or requirements of the carrier's health benefit plans as they relate to the needs of such provider's patients, or communicated with one or more of his prospective, current or former patients with respect to the method by which such provider is compensated by the carrier for services provided to the patient. Nothing in this section shall be construed to preclude a * * * carrier from requiring a health * * * provider to hold confidential specific compensation terms.

Section 5. No contract between a carrier * * * and a health * * * care provider for the provision of services to insureds may require the health care provider to indemnify the carrier for any expenses and liabilities, including, without limitation, judgments, settlements, attorneys' fees, court costs and any associated charges, incurred in connection with any claim or action brought against the carrier based on the carrier's management decisions, utilization review provisions or other policies, guidelines or actions.

Section 6. (a) A carrier shall issue and deliver to at least one adult insured in each household residing in the commonwealth, upon enrollment, an evidence of coverage and any amendments thereto. Said evidence of coverage shall contain a clear, concise and complete statement of:

(1) the health care services and any other benefits which the insured is entitled to on a nondiscriminatory basis;

* * *

(3) the limitations on the scope of health care services and any other benefits to be provided, including an explanation of any deductible or copayment feature and all restrictions relating to preexisting condition exclusions;

(4) the locations where, and the manner in which, health care services and other benefits may be obtained;

(5) the criteria by which an insured may be disenrolled or denied enrollment and the involuntary disenrollment rate among insureds of the carrier;

(6) a description of the carrier's method for resolving insured complaints, including a description of the formal internal grievance process * * * and the external grievance process * * * for appealing decisions pursuant to said grievances, as required by this chapter;

* * *

(8) a summary description of the procedure, if any, for out-of-network referrals and any additional charge for utilizing out-of-network providers;

(9) a summary description of the utilization review procedures and quality assurance programs used by the carrier, including the toll-free telephone number to be established by the carrier that enables consumers to determine the status or outcome of utilization review decisions;

(10) a statement detailing what translator and interpretation services are available to assist insureds * * *;

(11) a list of prescription drugs excluded from any restricted formulary available to insureds under the health benefit plan * * *;

(12) a summary description of the procedures followed by the carrier in making decisions about the experimental or investigational nature of individual drugs, medical devices or treatments in clinical trials;

(13) a statement on how to obtain the report regarding grievances from the office of patient protection * * *;

(14) the toll-free telephone number, facsimile number, and internet site for the office of patient protection in the department of public health * * *;

* * *

Section 7. (a) A carrier shall provide to at least one adult insured in each household upon enrollment, and to a prospective insured upon request, the following information:

(1) a list of health care providers in the carrier's network, organized by specialty and by location and summarizing for each such provider the method

used to compensate or reimburse such provider; provided, however, that nothing in this clause shall be construed to require disclosure of the specific details of any financial arrangements between a carrier and a provider * * *;

(2) a statement that physician profiling information, so-called, may be available from the board of registration in medicine;

(3) a summary description of the process by which clinical guidelines and utilization review criteria are developed;

(4) the voluntary and involuntary disenrollment rate among insureds of the carrier;

* * *

(b) A carrier shall provide all of the information required under section 6 and subsection (a) of this section to the office of patient protection in the department of public health and, in addition, shall provide to said office the following information:

(1) a list of sources of independently published information assessing insured satisfaction and evaluating the quality of health care services offered by the carrier;

(2) the percentage of physicians who voluntarily and involuntarily terminated participation contracts with the carrier during the previous calendar year * * * and the three most common reasons for voluntary and involuntary physician disenrollment;

(3) the percentage of premium revenue expended by the carrier for health care services provided to insureds for the most recent year for which information is available; and

(4) a report detailing, for the previous calendar year, the total number of: (i) filed grievances, grievances that were approved internally, grievances that were denied internally, and grievances that were withdrawn before resolution; and (ii) external appeals pursued after exhausting the internal grievance process and the resolution of all such external appeals. The report shall identify for each such category, to the extent such information is available, the demographics of such insureds, which shall include, but need not be limited to, race, gender and age.

* * *

Section 10. (a) No contract between a carrier, * * * and a licensed health * * * care provider group shall contain any incentive plan that includes a specific payment made to a health * * * care professional as an inducement to reduce, delay or limit specific, necessary services covered by the * * * contract. Health * * * care professionals shall not profit from provision of covered services that are not necessary and appropriate. Carriers * * * shall not profit from denial or withholding of covered services that are necessary and appropriate. Nothing in this section shall prohibit contracts that contain incentive plans that involve general payments such as capitation payments or shared risk agreements that are made with respect to health * * * care providers or which are made with respect to groups of insureds if such contracts, which impose risk on such health * * * care providers for the costs of care, services and equipment provided or authorized by another * * * provider, comply with subsection (b).

(b) In order that patient care decisions are based on need and not on financial incentives, no carrier * * * shall enter into a new contract, revise the risk arrangements in an existing contract or, after July 1, 2001, revise the fee schedule in an existing contract with a health * * * care provider which imposes financial risk on such provider for the costs of care, services or equipment provided or authorized by another provider unless such contract includes specific provisions with respect to the following: (1) stop loss protection, (2) minimum patient population size for the provider group, and (3) identification of the health * * * care services for which the provider is at risk.

(c) A carrier or utilization review organization shall conduct an annual survey of insureds to assess satisfaction with access to specialist services, ancillary services, hospitalization services, durable medical equipment and other covered services. Said survey shall compare the actual satisfaction of insureds with projected measures of their satisfaction. Carriers that utilize incentive plans shall establish mechanisms for monitoring the satisfaction, quality of care and actual utilization compared with projected utilization of health care services of insureds.

* * *

Section 12. (a) Utilization review conducted by a carrier or a utilization review organization shall be conducted pursuant to a written plan, under the supervision of a physician and staffed by appropriately trained and qualified personnel, * * *.

A carrier or utilization review organization shall * * * conduct all utilization review activities pursuant to [written] criteria. The criteria shall be, to the maximum extent feasible, scientifically derived and evidence-based, and developed with the input of participating physicians, consistent with the development of medical necessity criteria * * *.

Adverse determinations rendered by a program of utilization review, or other denials of requests for health services, shall be made by a person licensed in the appropriate specialty related to such health service and, where applicable, by a provider in the same licensure category as the ordering provider.

(b) A carrier or utilization review organization shall make an initial determination regarding a proposed admission, procedure or service that requires such a determination within two working days of obtaining all necessary information. * * * In the case of a determination to approve an admission, procedure or service, the carrier or utilization review organization shall notify the provider rendering the service by telephone within 24 hours. * * * In the case of an adverse determination, the carrier or utilization review organization shall notify the provider rendering the service by telephone within 24 hours, * * *.

(c) A carrier or utilization review organization shall make a concurrent review determination within one working day of obtaining all necessary information. * * * The service shall be continued without liability to the insured until the insured has been notified of the determination.

(d) The written notification of an adverse determination shall include a substantive clinical justification therefor that is consistent with generally accepted principles of professional medical practice, and shall, at a minimum: (1) identify the specific information upon which the adverse determination was based; (2) discuss the insured's presenting symptoms or condition, diagnosis and treatment interventions and the specific reasons such medical evidence fails to meet the relevant medical review criteria; (3) specify any alternative treatment option offered by the carrier, if any; and (4) reference and include applicable clinical practice guidelines and review criteria.

(e) A carrier or utilization review organization shall give a provider treating an insured an opportunity to seek reconsideration of an adverse determination from a clinical peer reviewer in any case involving an initial determination or a concurrent review determination. Said reconsideration process shall occur within one working day of the receipt of the request and shall be conducted between the provider rendering the service and the clinical peer reviewer * * *. If the adverse determination is not reversed by the reconsideration process, the insured, or the provider on behalf of the insured, may pursue the grievance process * * *. The reconsideration process allowed herein shall not be a prerequisite to the formal internal grievance process or an expedited appeal required by section 13.

Section 13. (a) A carrier or utilization review organization shall maintain a formal internal grievance process that provides for adequate consideration and timely resolution of grievances, which shall include but not be limited to: * * * (2) the provision of a clear, concise and complete description of the carrier's formal internal grievance process and the procedures for obtaining external review * * *; (3) the carrier's toll-free telephone number for assisting insureds in resolving such grievances and the consumer assistance toll-free telephone number maintained by the office of patient protection; (4) a written acknowledgment of the receipt of a grievance within 15 days and a written resolution of each grievance within 30 days from receipt thereof; and (5) a procedure to accept grievances by telephone, in person, by mail, or by electronic means, * * *.

(b) The formal internal grievance process maintained by a carrier or utilization review organization shall provide for an expedited resolution of a grievance concerning a carrier's coverage or provision of immediate and urgently needed services. Said expedited resolution policy shall include, but not be limited to:

(i) a resolution before an insured's discharge from a hospital if the grievance is submitted by an insured who is an inpatient in a hospital;

(ii) provisions for the automatic reversal of decisions denying coverage for services * * *, pending the outcome of the appeals process, within 48 hours, * * *, of receipt of certification by said physician that, in the [treating] physician's opinion, the service * * * at issue in a grievance or appeal is medically necessary, that a denial of coverage for such services * * * would create a substantial risk of serious harm to the patient, and that the risk of that harm is so immediate that the provision of such services * * * should not await the outcome of the normal appeal or grievance process * * *;

(iii) a resolution within five days from the receipt of such grievance if submitted by an insured with a terminal illness.

* * *

(c) A grievance not properly acted on by the carrier within the time limits required by this section shall be deemed resolved in favor of the insured.

Section 14. (a) An insured who remains aggrieved by an adverse determination and has exhausted all remedies available from the formal internal grievance process * * *, may seek further review of the grievance by a review panel established by the office of patient protection * * *. The insured shall pay the first $25 of the cost of the review to said office which may waive the fee in cases of extreme financial hardship. The commonwealth shall assess the carrier for the remainder of the cost of the review * * *. The office of patient protection shall contract with at least three unrelated and objective review agencies * * *, and refer grievances to one of the review agencies on a random selection basis. The review agencies shall develop review panels appropriate for the given grievance, which shall include qualified clinical decision-makers experienced in the determination of medical necessity, utilization management protocols and grievance resolution, and shall not have any financial relationship with the carrier making the initial determination. The standard for review of a grievance by such a panel shall be the determination of whether the requested treatment or service is medically necessary, as defined herein, and a covered benefit under the policy or contract. * * * The panel shall send final written disposition of the grievance, and the reasons therefor, to the insured and the carrier within 60 days of receipt of the request for review, * * *.

(b) If a grievance is filed concerning the termination of ongoing coverage or treatment, the disputed coverage or treatment shall remain in effect through completion of the formal internal grievance process. An insured may apply to the external review panel to seek continued provision of health care services which are the subject of the grievance during the course of said external review upon a showing of substantial harm to the insured's health absent such continuation, or other good cause as determined by the panel.

(c) The decision of the review panel shall be binding. The superior court shall have jurisdiction to enforce the decision of the review panel.

* * *

(e) The grievance procedures authorized by this section shall be in addition to any other procedures that may be available to any insured pursuant to contract or law, and failure to pursue, exhaust or engage in the procedures described in this subsection shall not preclude the use of any other remedy provided by any contract or law.

* * *

Section 15. (a) A carrier that allows or requires the designation of a primary care physician shall notify an insured at least 30 days before the disenrollment of such insured's primary care physician and shall permit such insured to continue to be covered for health services, consistent with the terms of the evidence of coverage, by such primary care physician for at least 30 days after said physician is disenrolled, other than disenrollment for quality-related reasons or for fraud. * * *

(b) A carrier shall allow any female insured who is in her second or third trimester of pregnancy and whose provider in connection with her pregnancy is involuntarily disenrolled, * * * to continue treatment with said provider, consistent with the terms of the evidence of coverage, for the period up to and including the insured's first postpartum visit.

(c) A carrier shall allow any insured who is terminally ill and whose provider in connection with said illness is involuntarily disenrolled, * * *, consistent with the terms of the evidence of coverage, until the insured's death.

(d) A carrier shall provide coverage for health services for up to 30 days from the effective date of coverage to a new insured by a physician who is not a participating provider in the carrier's network if: (1) the insured's employer only offers the insured a choice of carriers in which said physician is not a participating provider, and (2) said physician is providing the insured with an ongoing course of treatment or is the insured's primary care physician. * * *

* * *

(f) A carrier that requires an insured to designate a primary care physician shall allow such a primary care physician to authorize a standing referral for specialty health care provided by a health care provider participating in such carrier's network when (1) the primary care physician determines that such referrals are appropriate, (2) the provider of specialty health care agrees to a treatment plan for the insured and provides the primary care physician with all necessary clinical and administrative information on a regular basis, and (3) the health care services to be provided are consistent with the terms of the evidence of coverage. * * *

(g) No carrier shall require an insured to obtain a referral or prior authorization from a primary care physician for the following specialty care provided by an obstetrician, gynecologist, certified nurse-midwife or family practitioner participating in such carrier's health care provider network: (1) annual preventive gynecologic health examinations, including any subsequent obstetric or gynecological services determined by such obstetrician, gynecologist, certified nurse-midwife or family practitioner to be medically necessary as a result of such examination; (2) maternity care; and (3) medically necessary evaluations and resultant health care services for acute or emergency gynecological conditions. * * *

(h) A carrier shall provide coverage of pediatric specialty care, including mental health care, by persons with recognized expertise in specialty pediatrics to insureds requiring such services.

(i) A carrier * * * shall provide health * * * care providers applying to be participating providers who are denied such status with a written reason or reasons for denial of such application.

(j) No carrier shall make a contract with a health care provider which includes a provision permitting termination without cause. A carrier shall provide a written statement to a provider of the reason or reasons for such provider's involuntary disenrollment.

(k) A carrier * * * shall provide insureds, upon request, interpreter and translation services related to administrative procedures.

Section 16. (a) The physician treating an insured, shall, consistent with generally accepted principles of professional medical practice and in consultation with the insured, make all clinical decisions regarding medical treatment to be provided to the insured, including the provision of durable medical equipment and hospital lengths of stay. Nothing in this section shall be construed as altering, affecting or modifying either the obligations of any third party or the terms and conditions of any agreement or contract between either the treating physician or the insured and any third party.

(b) A carrier shall be required to pay for health care services ordered by a treating physician if (1) the services are a covered benefit under the insured's health benefit plan; and (2) the services are medically necessary. A carrier may develop guidelines to be used in applying the standard of medical necessity, as defined herein. Any such medical necessity guidelines utilized by a carrier in making coverage determinations shall be: (i) developed with input from practicing physicians in the carrier's or utilization review organization's service area; (ii) developed in accordance with the standards adopted by national accreditation organizations; (iii) updated at least biennially or more often as new treatments, applications and technologies are adopted as generally accepted professional medical practice; and (iv) evidence-based, if practicable. In applying such guidelines, a carrier shall consider the individual health care needs of the insured.

* * *

Notes and Questions

What information about health plans must be provided under this legislation to consumers? Is this information that will be useful to consumers? How might they use it? What information is provided only to the regulator and not to consumers? Why? What information does the statute permit plans to conceal from consumers? Why does it permit this? Are the emergency access provisions (which also extend, under separate provisions, to commercial insurers, Blue Cross and Blue Shield plans, and preferred provider organizations) adequate to assure that members will be covered for true emergency care? Who might benefit from these provisions other than plan members? What is the concern that motivated the statute's prohibition against "gag clauses"(ch. 176O, § 4)? What exactly do the statute's limitations on incentives prohibit? Does this provide sufficient protection for consumers? Do the restrictions go too far? How many layers of internal and external review does this statute provide? Are all of these mechanisms necessary? Useful? Are the statute's time limits reasonable? How does the statute use the term "grievance"? What limitations does the statute impose on termination of provider contracts? What effect might these limitations have on health plans? How much discretion does this statute give physicians to decide what care is medically necessary? How much control does it give to MCOs (carriers)? What explains the choice of specialists to which members are given direct access? How great an impact will these requirements have on primary care gatekeeper plans? What protections does this statute afford providers? Might these protections also be of use to consumers? How much will this legislation cost health plans? Who will pay for these costs? How will these costs affect access to care?

Problems: Advising Under State Managed Care Law

Resolve the following problems under the Massachusetts statute reproduced above:

1) Sam Rogers has been feeling severe pain on the left side of his chest for the past two hours. It is Saturday, and his primary care physician is not available. He is reluctant to go to the emergency department at the local hospital, however, because he knows that emergency care is very expensive, and he has heard that managed care organizations sometimes refuse to pay for emergency department care when they later determine that it was not necessary. He does not know the exact terms of his own policy (and can't find it), but knows that the arrangement he is under is very restrictive. What should Sam do?

2) Mary Gomez found out several months ago that she has cancer. She discovered the cancer fairly late, and it is quite advanced. Through her own research on the web, however, she has learned of a new form of treatment that is still in clinical trials. She has found a specialist in her health plan that is willing to attempt the procedure. He is concerned, however, as to whether Mary's health plan will cover it. Under what circumstances can Mary's plan refuse to cover the procedure? She needs the procedure very quickly if she is to have it at all, so she also wants to know how quickly the plan must make a decision on her request? What avenues are open to Mary to appeal the decision if her plan denies coverage? To whom can she turn for help, if she needs it? Would your answer be different if she needed a prescription drug not covered by her health plans drug formulary instead of a medical procedure?

3) The Omega Health Plan has entered into a contract with the Springdale Medical Group to provide primary care services to its members. Under the terms of the arrangement, Springdale receives a fixed payment every month for each patient and is fully responsible for its own services and for any specialist services or medical tests that its doctors order for patients insured by Omega. Omega provides stop-loss coverage if specialist or test procedures for any member of Omega exceed $100,000 a year. Is this arrangement legal? Dr. Johnson, a physician affiliated with Springdale, is very unhappy with this arrangement, and has sent his patients who are insured with Omega a letter informing them of the arrangement and asking that they complain to Omega about it. Can Omega terminate Dr. Johnson's credentials as a plan provider?

4) Cindy Sparks has just changed jobs and become insured with the Red Sickle health plan. She is in her sixth month of pregnancy and is in treatment with Dr. Samuels. Dr. Samuels is not a network provider under Red Sickle. Can she remain in treatment with Dr. Samuels throughout the delivery? If she changes obstetricians, and her new obstetrician is subsequently terminated from plan participation, can she remain with him through the delivery?

5) Sue Shank has just begun working for a new employer. Her employer offers her a choice of four different HMOs. She would like to learn as much as she can about each of them before she chooses among them. What information is she entitled to under the law? How would she get access to it?

B. STATE LAW REGULATING MCO NETWORKS

Virtually all MCOs either limit their members to a particular network of providers or impose disincentives to discourage their members from "going out of network." As noted earlier, the type of limitations on access to providers imposed by an MCO has historically been seen as a defining characteristic of some forms of MCO, separating PPOs from HMOs from POSs.

Why might MCOs want to limit their members to particular providers? Of course, if the providers have agreed to deliver services to MCO members at a discount the answer is obvious, but more is at stake than this. MCOs are also interested in limiting participating professionals and providers to those who share their vision of cost and utilization control. They may additionally want to limit participating professionals and providers to those who offer high quality care, or at least to exclude providers who present clear quality problems. Finally, MCOs also often try to control access to specialists through gatekeeper arrangements to assure that the problems that can be handled more cheaply by primary care physicians are not passed on to specialists, in effect creating separate networks of primary care and specialist physicians.

The earliest response of the states to network limitations was to enact "free choice of provider" laws, which limited the ability of MCOs/insurers to build provider networks. Free choice laws prohibit MCOs from restricting their members to particular providers or, more often, limit the size of the cost-sharing obligations that MCOs can impose on their members who go out of plan. About 23 states currently have free choice of provider laws, though most antedate the mid–90s, and the vast majority apply only to pharmacies.

Another regulatory response to networks has been "any willing provider" (AWP) laws, which require MCO/insurers to accept into their network any provider who is willing to accept the terms offered by the MCO. Although the Supreme Court recently affirmed the ability of states to impose AWP laws on ERISA plans in Kentucky Association of Health Plans, Inc. v. Miller, 538 U.S. 329, 123 S.Ct. 1471, 155 L.Ed.2d 468 (2003), few have been adopted in recent years, and most of the laws on the books date from the mid–1990s or earlier. About 23 states have AWP statutes, though in most states these apply only to pharmacies.

More recent legislative efforts to limit the ability of MCOs to restrict access of their members to providers have been more modest in their reach. Some laws focus on network adequacy, requiring MCOs to maintain an acceptable ratio of providers to enrollees. Other states require MCOs to allow members to go out of network if network coverage is inadequate. Other states simply require plans to disclose their provider selection criteria.

Most recent legislation also focuses on narrower access issues, such as those found in section 15 of the Massachusetts law. A number of states have adopted laws guaranteeing MCO members access to particular specialists, such as gynecologists or pediatricians. Forty-two states currently require MCOs to allow women direct access to obstetrical and gynecological providers. Many states also require plans to allow specialists to serve as primary care providers, especially when a patient with a chronic condition is under the regular care of a specialist. A number of states require MCOs to offer "standing referrals" of persons with chronic conditions to specialists in lieu of requiring continual re-referrals from primary care physicians.

Also common are "continuity of care" requirements, which assure plan members continuing access to a particular health care provider for a period of time after the plan terminates the provider. Some continuity of care statutes permit new members to continue to see their previous, non-network, provider for a period of time if the patient has a serious condition or is pregnant. Thirty states now have continuity of care provisions, with transitional care periods lasting from 30 to 120 days.

Finally, a number of states have adopted laws that protect network providers. Almost forty states, for example, have adopted "prompt payment" laws that require insurers to pay "clean" provider claims (claims that are complete and not disputed) within periods ranging from 15 to 60 days. A smaller number of states require notices of disputed claims within similar periods. A number of states impose interest or fines for claims that are not paid promptly. A number of states have been quite aggressive in enforcing these laws. At least twelve states have adopted "due process" requirements, limiting the ability of MCOs to terminate providers from their networks or to deny providers access to their networks without permitting some form of appeal. Other statutes go further, prohibiting "without cause" terminations.

C. REGULATION OF UTILIZATION CONTROLS

Utilization review (UR) seems to be the approach to managing care that most irritates consumers and providers. UR refers to case-by-case evaluations conducted by insurers, purchasers, or UR contractors to determine the necessity and appropriateness (and sometimes the quality) of medical care. It is based on the knowledge that there are wide variations in the use of many medical services, and the belief that considered review of medical care by payers can eliminate wasteful and unnecessary care.

UR can take several forms. The oldest form is retrospective review, under which an insurer denies payment for care already provided, normally by judging it to be medically unnecessary, experimental, or cosmetic. Retrospective review is of limited value for containing costs since the cost of the care has already been incurred by the time the review takes place.

Contemporary UR programs stress prior or concurrent review and high-cost case management. Prior and concurrent review techniques include preadmission review (before elective hospital admissions); admission review (within 24 to 72 hours of emergency or urgent admissions); continued stay review (to assess length of stay and sometimes accompanied by discharge planning); preprocedure or preservice review (to review specific proposed procedures); and voluntary or mandatory second-opinions. High-cost case management addresses the small number (one to seven percent) of very expensive cases that account for most benefit plan costs. Case managers create individualized treatment plans for high-cost beneficiaries. Compliance with the plan is usually voluntary, but may be rewarded by the plan paying for services not otherwise covered by the insurer (such as home health or nursing home care), but less costly than covered alternatives. Disease management programs are similar but are designed to assure appropriate care for particular chronic or recurring medical conditions and often focus on self-care, prevention, and appropriate use of pharmaceuticals.

UR seems to reduce inpatient hospital use and costs. One of the best studies found that it reduced hospital admissions by 12.3 percent, inpatient days by 8 percent, and hospital expenditures by 11.9 percent. In particular, it reduced patient days by 34 percent and hospital expenditures by 30 percent for groups that had previously had high admission rates. Paul Feldstein, *et al.*, Private Cost Containment, 318 New Eng.J.Med. 1310 (1988). It is less clear that UR reduces total health care costs, however, since it often moves care from inpatient to outpatient settings, increasing outpatient costs as it reduces inpatient costs. Moreover, UR is most effective in the short run and has less effect on long-term cost increases. See, on UR generally, Institute of Medicine, Controlling Costs and Changing Patient Care?: The Role of Utilization Management (1989).

At the margins, utilization control blends into other care management strategies. Many MCOs have, for example, retreated from individual case review, instead keeping track of the practice patterns of particular physicians and using the information to decide which physicians to decertify from plan participation. Primary care gatekeeper systems, on the other hand, delegate UR decisions to primary care physicians, but motivate them to control utilization through the use of financial incentives.

UR decisions are basically coverage determinations—UR denies payment for experimental and medically unnecessary care because such care is not covered under the plan contract. UR decisions are also, however, medical treatment determinations, because in most instances they determine whether or not the insured will receive medical treatment. UR determinations can thus raise issues of medical practice regulation. Is the utilization review entity or its employees engaged in the unauthorized practice of medicine when it makes coverage decisions? Is a physician reviewer retained by a utilization review entity engaged in unauthorized practice of medicine if she reviews a case in a state in which she is not licensed? Might the acts of a utilization review entity violate a state's corporate practice of medicine statute or doctrine? Compare Murphy v. Board of Medical Examiners, 190 Ariz. 441, 949 P.2d 530 (Ct.App.1997) (utilization review physician practicing medicine); with Morris v. District of Columbia Board of Medicine, 701 A.2d 364 (D.C. 1997) (Blue Cross medical director not practicing medicine in particular UR situation). Thirty-two states have adopted statutes or regulations requiring that HMO medical directors meet specific requirements, usually to be a licensed physician in the state where they do reviews. See also, E. Haavi Morreim, Playing Doctor: Corporate Medical Practice and Medical Malpractice, 32 Mich. J. L. Ref. 939 (1999); J. Scott Andresen, Is Utilization Review the Practice of Medicine: Implications for Managed Care Administrators, 19 J. Legal Med. 431 (1998); John Blum, An Analysis of Legal Liability in Health Care Utilization Review and Case Management, 26 Hous.L.Rev. 191 (1989). Do these provisions protect patients or doctors?

UR has, as was noted above, become perhaps the most unpopular approach to managing care. While plans in fact infrequently deny coverage, coverage denial can have disastrous consequences for insureds. Also, the hassle involved in fulfilling UR requirements (the interminably busy fax, the voicemail messages that are never returned, the endless arguing with reviewers) undoubtedly deters physicians from offering or ordering services that would otherwise have been given.

A variety of regulatory strategies have been adopted for addressing utilization review issues. Every state has now adopted a law requiring MCOs to offer their members internal consumer grievance and appeal procedures (a requirement also imposed by ERISA for employee health benefit plans, see Chapter 8). These statutes often establish time frames for the appeals (again requiring expedited hearings for emergencies), specify who must decide the appeal (specifying, for example, the professional credentials of the decision maker, or requiring a decision maker not involved in the initial decision), and provide the format for the final decision (in writing, giving reasons, etc.).

Forty-four states also require external or independent reviews. Review statutes generally specify who may make the decision, usually an independent reviewer appointed or approved by the regulatory authority. Statutes again commonly provide time limits for proceedings. Most states provide that the external review decision is binding on the MCO, the remainder either explicitly state that it is non-binding or do not address the issue. See, on the resolution of grievances, appeals, and other disputes in managed care, Nan D. Hunter, Managed Process, Due Care: Structures of Accountability in Health Care, 6 Yale J. Health Pol'y, L. & Ethics 93 (2006); Carole Roan Gresenz and David M. Studdert, External Review of Coverage Denials by Managed Care Organizations in California, 2(3) Journal Empirical Legal Studies 449 (2005); Eleanor Kinney, Protecting American Health Care Consumers (2002); Gerard F. Anderson and Mark A. Hall, The Management of Conflict Over Health Insurance Coverage, in M. Gregg Bloche, ed., The Privatization of Health Care Reform (2003).

A key issue in UR decisions is the definition of medical necessity. About half of the states have adopted statutory definitions of medical necessity, though in some states the definition applies only to particular insurers (Medicaid, HMOs) or particular areas of care (mental health, long term care, inpatient care). A number of these statutes also require some level of deference to the decision of the treating physician on medical necessity issues.

With respect to some forms of care, state statutes have simply preempted coverage decisions by imposing mandates. Providers and consumer groups have for decades lobbied successfully for state insurance "mandates" that require insurance companies to provide certain benefits (mammography, mental health and substance abuse treatment); cover the services of certain providers (chiropractors, podiatrists); or cover certain insureds or dependents (newborn infants, laid-off employees). In recent years, however, state statutes mandating particular benefits have also often limited the reach of utilization controls.

Among the most common examples of this are emergency care mandates, which have been adopted in all but three states. (See chapter 176G, sec. 5, of the Massachusetts statute and Chapter 6 above discussing emergency care). A study of the effects of these laws found that many insurers were already applying a prudent layperson standard before these laws were adopted, and that the laws do not seem to have led to a significant increase in costs, although many MCOs reacted by raising copayments for emergency care. Mark A. Hall. The Impact and Enforcement of Prudent Layperson Laws, 43 Annals of Emergency Medicine 558 (2004).

Other statutes address length of stay issues, requiring at least 48 hours of hospitalization coverage for vaginal or 96 hours for Cesarean deliveries (the famous "drive through delivery" statutes of the mid–1990s) or hospitalization coverage for mastectomies. Still other statutes prohibit plans from denying access to particular benefits, such as off-formulary drugs (usually specifically for cancer or life-threatening diseases) or clinical trials. Popular benefit mandates in recent years include requirements of coverage for mental health care, cancer screenings, contraceptives, infertility treatment, osteoporosis prevention, newborn hearing treatments, and reconstructive surgery following mastectomy.

Finally, fourteen states have adopted laws providing for liability suits against plans for failure to exercise ordinary care in the provision of medical care. To the extent that UR decisions are in fact decisions with respect to plan provision of medical care, they would seem to be covered by these liability statutes. Though these statutes are not enforceable against ERISA plans (see Chapter 8), they do apply to non-ERISA insurers.

D. REGULATION OF PROVIDER INCENTIVES

The third strategy that MCOs have used to manage care is financial incentives for professionals and providers. The earliest form was capitation. Under capitation the provider gets paid a fixed fee for providing care for the MCO beneficiary for a fixed period of time. If the services the beneficiary receives cost more than this payment, the provider loses money; if the services cost less, the provider makes money. In other words, the provider becomes the true insurer—i.e. risk bearer—with respect to the patient.

A provider (e.g., a primary care physician) may be capitated for his, her, or its own services, but can also be paid on a capitated basis for other services the patient may need, such as specialist services, laboratory tests, hospitalization, or even drugs. Some of these services, however, cost far more than primary care services, and putting a single primary care physician, or even physician group, at risk for these services might in many instances impose unreasonable risks.

Instead, MCOs usually put the primary care provider only partially at risk. This is done through the use of bonuses or withholds. A pool is established either from money withheld from payments made directly to the physician (a withhold) or from funds provided in addition to regular payments (a bonus). Specified expenses—for specialists or hospitalization, for example—are paid out of this pool. Any money left over at the end of an accounting period (e.g., a year), is paid over to the physician. In addition, the physician may or may not be fully capitated for his or her own services.

Alternatively, the MCO can capitate physicians and hospitals separately, putting the hospital at risk for its expenses and physicians at risk for theirs. An HMO receives a premium, for example, and after subtracting its administrative costs and premiums, gives part to a hospital and part to a physician group, which may provide multispecialty services or might provide primary care and be at risk for paying specialists on a fee-for-service basis.

While incentives are an effective way to hold down costs, they can also result in underservice if the responses they elicit from providers are excessive. It is more difficult to regulate incentives, however, than it is to regulate network or utilization controls because it is more difficult to identify discrete unacceptable practices or to address these practices through enforcement procedures.

Thirty states in fact currently have statutes purporting to ban the use of financial incentives, usually prohibiting incentives that "deny, reduce, limit or delay medically necessary care." The statutes, however, usually go on, as does section 10 of the Massachusetts statute, to say that they are not intended to prohibit MCOs from using capitation payments or other risk-sharing arrangements. As MCOs would generally insist that their incentives are intended to deter unnecessary, rather than necessary care, these statutes have little effect on MCO incentive programs. More useful are statutes or regulations that more explicitly limit excessive incentives, restricting, for example, the proportion of a provider's income that can be put at risk or the size of the pool of patients or providers over which the risk is spread, or requiring stop-loss insurance.

A rather different regulatory approach is simply to require disclosure of financial incentives. Not surprisingly, there are problems with this approach as well. First, the vast majority of insured Americans receive their health coverage through their place of employment, and half of all employees are offered a choice of only one (33%) or two (17%) plans. Even employees offered a choice of two or more plans, of course, may not have much of a choice among incentive plan structures. Second, it is not at all clear how most plan members can use information about incentive plans structures, i.e. whether their understanding of health care finance and delivery is sophisticated enough to evaluate incentive structures. Finally, requiring disclosure imposes costs both on regulators, who need to devise a meaningful form of disclosure and police compliance, and on MCOs, which need to compile and disseminate the information.

Even if requiring plan disclosure to allow consumer choice is problematic, there may be other reasons for requiring disclosure. In a thoughtful article, William Sage identifies three other reasons why we might want to require MCOs and providers to disclose information. First, disclosure increases the likelihood that providers and MCOs will act as honest agents for their patients and members, while it facilitates the ability of patients and members to monitor fiduciary loyalty. Second, requiring collection and disclosure of particular kinds of performance-related information might increase incentives to direct practice in certain directions deemed to be socially important. Requiring disclosure of immunization rates, for example, may promote immunization programs. Finally, disclosure of more information might facilitate public deliberation and provider and MCO accountability. William M. Sage, Regulating Through Information: Disclosure Laws and American Health Care, 99 Columb. L. Rev. 1701 (1999). See also Tracy E. Miller & William M. Sage, Disclosing Physician Financial Incentives, 281 JAMA 1424 (1999).

Problem: Regulating Managed Care

You are the legal staff for the Health Committee of a state that adopted a managed care regulation statute identical to the Massachusetts statute. You are now considering repealing parts of the statute. Examine the statute again. Which of these provisions in the statute address provider networks? Whom do these provisions primarily benefit? What effect do these provisions have on the cost of coverage? To the extent that they increase costs, what effect might this have on access? Which of the provisions in the Massachusetts statute above address UR issues? Which of these provisions is likely to be most strongly supported by plan members? Which are most likely in fact to be of use to them? Which provisions also benefit providers? Which providers benefit from these provisions? Which provisions are likely to be opposed most strongly by managed care trade associations? Which of the requirements in the Massachusetts statute address plan incentive structures? How enforceable are these limitations? How useful are they to plan members? Which provisions, if any, address quality of care, and are they likely to be effective? Considering only the interest of the public, which provisions will you recommend keeping and which repealing?

V. WHAT FOLLOWS MANAGED CARE? CONSUMER–DIRECTED HEALTH CARE

If managed care is not the force it once was, what comes next? Many commentators have claimed that it will be consumer-driven health care. As broadly defined, CDHC could include a number of different approaches to health care organization and finance. It certainly includes the availability of more and better information on health care providers for consumers. It could include tiered networks, where insureds choose among a menu of coverage options, and receive access to different networks of providers based on the health plan they choose (paying more for access to the academic medical center, less for access to the community hospital). But most discussions of CDHC focus on health savings accounts (HSAs) coupled with high deductible health plans (HDHPs). The 2003 Medicare Modernization Act expanded federal tax subsidies for HSAs, making subsidies available to anyone who purchases a high-deductible health plan. The MMA, however, leaves consumer-driven health care largely unregulated, prescribing only minimum and maximum deductibles and maximum out-of-pocket limits for HDHPs and limiting tax-free expenditures from HSAs (prior to age 65) to "qualified medical expenses." As we have seen, the states have traditionally regulated health insurance and extensively regulated managed care. Do they have a role in regulating consumer-driven health care?

TIMOTHY S. JOST AND MARK A. HALL, THE ROLE OF STATE REGULATION IN CONSUMER–DRIVEN HEALTH CARE

31 American Journal of Law and Medicine 395 (2005).

[This article analyzes the findings of a survey of stakeholders examining state regulation of high deductible health plans (HDHPS) and health savings accounts (HSAs) in the spring of 2005].

Most public discussion of state regulatory issues affecting HSAs and HDHPs to date has centered around three issues, * * *. The first of these is * * * the problem of state mandates that bar high deductibles for particular services. * * * HSAs only qualify for tax subsidies under the [Medicare Modernization Act] if they are coupled with HDHPs that have minimum deductibles of at least $1000 for individuals, $2000 for families. [These amounts have subsequently been adjusted upwards for inflation]. * * *

At the time the MMA was adopted, a number of states mandated coverage of specific * * * health services * * * either without a deductible or with a low deductible. * * *

Most states quickly [repealed these laws]. * * * The states' responses were remarkably rapid and widespread. Without any specific federal requirement or threatened penalty, most were willing to set aside the particular public health or provider protection considerations that caused them to enact various benefits mandates in order to facilitate the federally-led consumer-driven market initiative.

* * *

[Discussion of the other two issues, whether an HMO can offer a HDHP and state tax subsidies for HSAs, is omitted.]

* * * As the states gain more experience with HSAs and HDHPs, they may well encounter a range of additional regulatory issues. Early recognition of these issues is important because it enables states to deal with them responsibly rather than waiting for a crisis to provoke precipitous or over-reactive action. Experiences from managed care regulation in the 1990s reveal that case-specific or crisis-driven regulation is often neither efficient nor effective.

First, how the health savings accounts are administered may raise several state regulatory issues. * * *

Under the MMA, HSAs may be administered by banks, insurance companies or "another person who demonstrates to the satisfaction of the Secretary [of the Treasury] that the manner in which such person will administer the trust will be consistent with the requirements of this section." * * * Most states, however, do not appear to have a regulatory mechanism that oversees insurers offering financial services. None of our interview sources could point to any actual regulatory requirements or consequences for insurers that administer their own HSAs, other than that the funds must be maintained in a separate account and must not be commingled with insurer funds that are at risk. If these funds are kept separate from the insurer's other funds, then they are not subject to, and do not affect, the insurer's solvency and reserve requirements.

The financial institutions, other than insurers, that the MMA authorizes to administer HSAs are familiar types of heavily regulated financial entities. Consumers who choose insurers to administer their HSAs will likely assume there is some similar oversight of financial services from insurers. The first time HSA holders (or providers who expect to be paid by HSAs) encounter major problems in getting an insurance administrator to honor checks or debit card transactions questions will undoubtedly surface about state regulatory oversight. Why did insurance regulators allow the problem to arise? Will state insurance guaranty funds cover the obligations of insolvent insurers under their HSAs, or only under their HDHPs? Do unfair claims practice laws cover HSA claims? We found little evidence in our interviews that insurers or insurance regulators were considering these issues.

A second issue HSAs raise is how state statutes and regulations that regulate managed care will apply to HSA transactions. * * *

All of the HDHP insurers with whom we spoke make their negotiated network discounts available to HSA holders. This is a great advantage to HSA owners, as it gives them the benefit of the considerable market power that insurers command for extracting discounts from providers. Insurers also use their standard claims processing systems, including medical necessity review, to determine when the policy deductible (and, ultimately, the out-of-pocket maximum) has been met for any particular subscriber. In general, only insured expenses can be counted against a deductible. If a subscriber with a $3,000 deductible receives an outpatient surgery costing $2,500, insurers are unlikely to credit the cost of the surgery fully against the deductible without determining whether the surgery was a covered expense, whether $2,500 was a reasonable charge, and whether the subscriber received pre-approval for the surgery if required under the policy. In short, even while spending their own money from HSAs, subscribers will be subject to some managed care controls to the extent that they attempt to claim these expenses against their insurance deductibles. * * *

This raises a host of questions, however. If an insurer refuses to credit the cost of the surgery fully against the deductible because it was not medically necessary, can the HSA holder appeal the decision under the state's claims review laws? If a network provider is treating an HSA holder and that provider's contract with the HDHP is terminated, must the provider continue to offer the HSA holder the HDHP negotiated discount for the period of time that a state's continuity of care statute requires the HDHP to cover services? Do state any-willing-provider statutes apply to HDHP networks for HSA-covered services as well as for HDHP funded services once the deductible is met? * * *

The answer to these questions in general is yes. Virtually all regulators and insurers we talked to assumed this to be the case, but this assumption has not yet been challenged or tested, as it might be if, for instance, a particular provider insisted it was not bound by the restraints in its managed care contract for services paid directly by patients through their HSAs. Even if the current understanding holds, it means that HDHPs will face no less of a restrictive regulatory environment than do conventional managed care plans. * * *

The interplay between the HSA and HDHP does not just raise questions as to how state managed care regulations apply; it also presents the very real potential for consumer misunderstanding and confusion. To understand clearly how MMA HSAs work when coupled with HDHPs, consumers first need to realize that HSAs are savings accounts, not insurance. * * * Next, consumers must appreciate that HSAs can pay for a broader range of qualified medical services than those covered by the HDHP. It is easy to imagine some consumers exhausting their HSAs on miscellaneous expenses that do not count toward the deductible at all and then facing the rude surprise of "catastrophic" medical expenses once a serious accident or illness strikes and learning that insurance coverage is still a long way off. * * * Added to this consumer burden are the already confusing distinctions between billed versus allowable charges, and in-network versus out-of-network providers, which bedevil all but the most expert readers of insurers' "explanation of benefits" forms. All of this is to say that HSA/HDHPs raise significant issues for consumer education and dispute resolution, and that these issues will likely reach the attention of state insurance regulators.

* * *

[Another] traditional focus of state insurance regulation has been improving access to health insurance for the uninsured by controlling insurer underwriting and rating practices primarily in the small group market, but also in the individual market in some states. * * *

A number of commentators have expressed a concern that HDHPs might further fragment insurers' risk pools by attracting mainly low-risk subscribers, leaving high-risk subscribers in separate risk pools with ever-increasing premiums for conventional insurance. HSAs and HDHPs are thought to be more attractive to low-risk subscribers because they are less likely to exhaust their high deductibles and therefore more likely to build up substantial savings in their accounts. Also, high-risk people are less likely in general to make any change in their health insurance, so at least initially any new type of policy, whatever kind it is, will tend to attract people who are healthier than average. HSA/HDHP advocates, on the other hand, argue that the flexibility available to HSA holders will be attractive to the chronically ill, as will be the absolute caps the MMA imposes on out-of-pocket expenses and lower premiums. * * *

* * *

Most of the regulators we interviewed felt that risk segmentation was not a pressing problem and that the rating issue just identified had not proven to be problematic. * * *

One reason this issue may not have emerged as a regulatory problem is that the major insurers may not be attempting to take advantage of any favorable risk selection. Several insurer representatives we spoke to said that PPO products are rated as a single risk pool in each market, adjusting only for deductible levels and other benefit differences, rather than pricing HSA plans as an entirely separate risk pool from other offerings. * * *

Another reason regulators may have refrained from scrutinizing rating practices for HDHPs is the growing disillusionment with traditional approaches to expanding access to coverage, which we detected in several quarters. Regulators seemed very sensitized to the "zero-sum" logic that, for every high risk subscriber whose rates are lowered by regulation, several lower risk subscribers must pay higher rates, which at the margin may deter some of them from purchasing any insurance. * * * Therefore, regulators appear willing to try approaches such as HSA/HDHPs that might make insurance dramatically more affordable for average purchasers. * * *

* * *

Overall, the states' initial response to the MMA has been quite remarkable. Most states have responded affirmatively to the latest federal legislation, despite its lack of explicit compulsion, by removing any regulatory barriers to qualified HDHPs. * * *

Perhaps the experience with managed care regulation has caused most states to lose their taste for insurance regulation; or perhaps the receptive regulatory response is explained by the newness of the HSA/HDHP product and thus the lack of experience with problems it might cause. Whatever the explanation, the new approach to federalism in insurance regulation evidenced by the MMA appears to have been very successful. At least for the moment, the lure of tax incentives has been sufficient to launch HSA/HDHPs successfully in most states without the need for either direct preemption of state law or the imposition of direct federal regulation of insurance, thus avoiding all of the friction and controversies that have accompanied these strategies under ERISA or HIPAA. * * *

* * *

Notes and Questions

1. Consumer-driven health plans include both HSA-based HDHPs and HDHPs paired with health reimbursement arrangements (HRAs). (An HRA is an account funded and held by an employer to cover employee health care expenses.) CDHC presents fascinating legal issues involving the physician-patient relationship. What cost information, for example, must a physician offer a patient who is paying for care out of her own health savings account to assure that the patient can give informed consent to a proposed treatment? If a physician recommends a particular procedure (or drug), and the patient declines it as too expensive, might the physician be liable for ensuing injury, or can the physician claim assumption of risk or comparative negligence, or even lack of proximate cause. Does a physician or hospital have any obligation to provide necessary treatment that a patient refuses to pay for? Must a physician or hospital contract with a patient beforehand for the patient to cover the cost of a procedure, or can the physician recover a reasonable charge. See Chapter 3 above and Timothy S. Jost, Health Care at Risk: A Critique of the Consumer Driven Movement, 150–65 (2007); Mark A. Hall and Carl E. Schneider, Patients as Consumers: Courts, Contracts, and the New Medical Marketplace, 106 Mich. L. Rev. 643 (2008); Haavi Morreim, High–Deductible Health Plans: New Twists on Old Challenges from Tort to Contract. Vanderbilt Law Review (2006).

2. See also, on the federal requirements for HSAs, David Pratt, Health and Wealthy and Dead: Health Savings Accounts, 19 St. Thomas L. Rev. 7 (2006); Richard L. Kaplan, Who's Afraid of Personal Responsibility? Health Savings Accounts and the Future of American Health Care, 36 McGeorge L. Rev. 534 (2005). See, discussing state regulation, Michele Melden, Guarding Against the High Risk of High Deductible Health Plans: A Proposal for Regulatory Protections, 18 Loy. Consumer L. Rev. 403 (2006). See generally, discussing the legal and policy issues raised by CDHC, Timothy S. Jost, Health Care at Risk: A Critique of the Consumer–Driven Movement (2007); The Promise and Peril of Ownership Society Health Care Policy, 80 Tul. L. Rev. 777 (2006); John Jacobi, After Managed Care: Gray Boxes, Tiers and Consumerism, 47 St. Louis U. L.J. 397 (2003).

Problems: Consumer–Driven Health Care

1. Return to problem 1 in the *Problems: Advising Under State Managed Care Law* at the end of section IV.A. above. Assume that Sam Rogers has a high deductible health plan with a $5000 deductible and 20 percent coinsurance requirement until an out-of-pocket maximum of $10,000 has been reached. He is not sure how much of his deductible he has met for this year, but has already exhausted the $300 his employer has deposited in his HSA. Assume further that his household income is $20,000 a year. How will this state of affairs affect the likelihood of him going to the emergency department to check out his chest pains? Is this a good or bad thing?

2.   Consider the facts of problem 2 above. Assume that Mary Gomez also has a $5000 deductible policy. She has only met $500 of the deductible but has $3000 in her HSA. Her health plan provides that only services that would be covered under the terms of the health plan count toward the deductible and that "experimental" treatment is not covered under the plan. How would Mary Gomez determine whether the proposed cancer treatment would count against her deductible? Does she have any route of appeal if she asks her plan and says no? Can she pay for the treatment out of her HSA?

3.   Review problem 4 above. Assume that Cindy Sparks was insured with a $3000 deductible, $5000 out-of-pocket maximum, health plan under her old job and is similarly insured under her new plan. Assume that she had a health reimbursement account with her old job that had a $5000 balance. The rules established by her previous employer provide that all funds left in an HRA upon resignation from the firm are forfeited. Does she have any recourse? Assume instead that she has $5000 in an HSA and the funds continue to be available. What advantages does this give Ms. Sparks over the situation she would be in with a traditional health plan? Assume that Doctor Samuels is not a network provider under her new employer's plan, or that he is, and is terminated by the plan before her delivery is due. Do either of these facts affect her situation in any way?

Chapter 8

REGULATION OF INSURANCE AND MANAGED CARE: THE FEDERAL ROLE

I. INTRODUCTION

Although regulation of health insurance has traditionally been the responsibility of the states, federal law has in recent years taken a more significant role. The most important federal statute affecting health insurance is the Employee Retirement Income Security Act of 1974, ERISA, which has already been alluded to several times in previous chapters. ERISA's primary role throughout the 1980s and 1990s was deregulatory, as its preemptive provisions repeatedly blocked state common law actions against health plans as well as state attempts at plan regulation. The Supreme Court seemed to relax its interpretation of ERISA preemption in the late 1990s, however, giving the states somewhat more flexibility for regulating insured health plans, although it has recently become clear that there are limits to this flexibility. Finally, ERISA itself provides employee health plan beneficiaries with a positive right to sue to recover denied benefits, while also imposing fiduciary obligations on plan fiduciaries. ERISA regulations also afford procedural rights to plan beneficiaries.

ERISA is not the only federal statute to affect health plans. The Americans with Disabilities Act places at least minimal constraints on the ability of employers and insurers to discriminate against the disabled in the provision of health insurance. The Health Insurance Portability and Accountability Act of 1996 (which amended ERISA, as well as other federal statutes) limits the use of preexisting condition clauses while prohibiting intragroup discrimination in coverage and rates. It also offers certain protections in the small group and individual insurance markets. The Consolidated Omnibus Budget Reconciliation Act of 1985 provides some protection for some who lose employee coverage. Finally, Congress has adopted in the past few years a handful of coverage mandates. These federal initiatives will be considered in this chapter.

II. THE EMPLOYEE RETIREMENT INCOME SECURITY ACT OF 1974 (ERISA)

A. ERISA PREEMPTION OF STATE HEALTH INSURANCE REGULATION

As noted in the introduction, the main effect of ERISA in recent decades has been deregulatory as ERISA has been interpreted as preempting a broad range of state laws. Section 514 of ERISA (codified as 29 U.S.C.A. § 1144) expressly preempts state regulatory statutes and common law claims that "relate to" employee benefit plans. Section 502 of ERISA (codified as 29 U.S.C.A. § 1132), has been interpreted by the Supreme Court as providing for exclusive federal court jurisdiction over and an exclusive federal cause of action for cases that could be brought as ERISA claims. Section 514, however, also explicitly exempts state regulation of insurance from preemption, while also prohibiting state regulation of self-insured plans. The text of these provisions follows:

29 U.S.C.A. § 1132 (Section 502)

A civil action may be brought—

(1) by a participant or beneficiary—

* * *

(B) to recover benefits due to him under the terms of his plan, to enforce his rights under the terms of the plan, or to clarify his rights to future benefits under the terms of the plan;

(2) by the Secretary, or by a participant, beneficiary or fiduciary for appropriate relief under section 1109 of this title [which imposes on plan fiduciaries the obligation to "make good" to a plan any losses resulting from a breach of fiduciary duties, and authorizes "other equitable or remedial relief" for breaches of fiduciary obligations];

(3) by a participant, beneficiary, or fiduciary (A) to enjoin any act or practice which violates any provision of this subchapter or the terms of the plan, or (B) to obtain other appropriate equitable relief (i) to redress such violations or (ii) to enforce any provisions of this subchapter or the terms of the plan;

* * *

29 U.S.C.A. § 1144 (Section 514)

(a) Except as provided in subsection (b) of this section, the provisions of this subchapter and subchapter III of this chapter shall supersede any and all State laws insofar as they may now or hereafter relate to any employee benefit plan * * *

(b) Construction and application

* * *

(2)(A) Except as provided in subparagraph (B), nothing in this subchapter shall be construed to exempt or relieve any person from any law of any State which regulates insurance, banking, or securities.

(B) Neither an employee benefit plan * * * nor any trust established under such a plan, shall be deemed to be an insurance company * * * or to be engaged in the business of insurance or banking for purposes of any law of any State purporting to regulate insurance companies, insurance contracts, banks, trust companies, or investment companies.

———————

The task of sorting out ERISA's complex preemption scheme has resulted in a tremendous volume of litigation, including, to date, over twenty Supreme Court decisions and hundreds of state and federal lower court decisions. In this subsection we will examine the effect of Section 502 and 514 preemption on state regulatory laws. In this context we will also consider the effect of Section 514's "savings clause," (§ 514(b)(2)(A)), which saves from preemption state laws "which regulate insurance," as well as § 514's "deemer" clause (§ 514(b)(2)(B)), which exempts self-insured ERISA plans from state insurance regulation. In the second subsection, we look at the effects of ERISA preemption on state health care reform efforts. In the third and final subsection of this section, we will consider the effect of ERISA preemption on state common law tort causes of action against managed care plans and insurers.

We begin with one of the most recent Supreme Court cases, which sets out the basic framework of ERISA preemption and debates the policies that ground it.

RUSH PRUDENTIAL HMO, INC., v. DEBRA C. MORAN, ET AL.

Supreme Court of the United States.
536 U.S. 355, 122 S.Ct. 2151, 153 L.Ed.2d 375 (2002).

JUSTICE SOUTER delivered the opinion of the Court.

* * *

Petitioner, Rush Prudential HMO, Inc., is a health maintenance organization (HMO) that contracts to provide medical services for employee welfare benefit plans covered by ERISA. Respondent Debra Moran is a beneficiary under one such plan, sponsored by her husband's employer. Rush's "Certificate of Group Coverage," issued to employees who participate in employer-sponsored plans, promises that Rush will provide them with "medically necessary" services. The terms of the certificate give Rush the "broadest possible discretion" to determine whether a medical service claimed by a beneficiary is covered under the certificate. * * *

As the certificate explains, Rush contracts with physicians "to arrange for or provide services and supplies for medical care and treatment" of covered persons. Each covered person selects a primary care physician from those under contract to Rush, while Rush will pay for medical services by an unaffiliated physician only if the services have been "authorized" both by the primary care physician and Rush's medical director.[ ]

In 1996, when Moran began to have pain and numbness in her right shoulder, Dr. Arthur LaMarre, her primary care physician, unsuccessfully administered "conservative" treatments such as physiotherapy. In October 1997, Dr. LaMarre recommended that Rush approve surgery by an unaffiliated specialist, Dr. Julia Terzis, who had developed an unconventional treatment for Moran's condition. Although Dr. LaMarre said that Moran would be "best served" by that procedure, Rush denied the request and, after Moran's internal appeals, affirmed the denial on the ground that the procedure was not "medically necessary."[ ] Rush instead proposed that Moran undergo standard surgery, performed by a physician affiliated with Rush.

In January 1998, Moran made a written demand for an independent medical review of her claim, as guaranteed by § 4–10 of Illinois's HMO Act,[ ] which provides:

> Each Health Maintenance Organization shall provide a mechanism for the timely review by a physician * * * who is unaffiliated with the Health Maintenance Organization, jointly selected by the patient ..., primary care physician and the Health Maintenance Organization in the event of a dispute between the primary care physician and the Health Maintenance Organization regarding the medical necessity of a covered service proposed by a primary care physician. In the event that the reviewing physician determines the covered service to be medically necessary, the Health Maintenance Organization shall provide the covered service. * * *

* * *

When Rush failed to provide the independent review, Moran sued in an Illinois state court to compel compliance with the state Act. Rush removed the suit to Federal District Court, arguing that the cause of action was "completely preempted" under ERISA.[ ]

While the suit was pending, Moran had surgery by Dr. Terzis at her own expense and submitted a $94,841.27 reimbursement claim to Rush. Rush treated the claim as a renewed request for benefits and began a new inquiry to determine coverage. The three doctors consulted by Rush said the surgery had been medically unnecessary.

Meanwhile, the federal court remanded the case back to state court on Moran's motion, concluding that because Moran's request for independent review under § 4–10 would not require interpretation of the terms of an ERISA plan, the claim was not "completely preempted" so as to permit removal * * * The state court enforced the state statute and ordered Rush to submit to review by an independent physician. * * * [The reviewer] decided that Dr. Terzis's treatment had been medically necessary, based on the definition of medical necessity in Rush's Certificate of Group Coverage, as well as his own medical judgment. Rush's medical director, however, refused to concede that the surgery had been medically necessary, and denied Moran's claim in January 1999.

Moran amended her complaint in state court to seek reimbursement for the surgery as "medically necessary" under Illinois's HMO Act, and Rush again removed to federal court, arguing that Moran's amended complaint stated a claim for ERISA benefits and was thus completely preempted by ERISA's civil enforcement provisions, 29 U.S.C. § 1132(a) [§ 502], * * * The District Court treated Moran's claim as a suit under ERISA, and denied the claim on the ground that ERISA preempted Illinois's independent review statute.

The Court of Appeals for the Seventh Circuit reversed. * * *

* * *

To "safeguar[d] ... the establishment, operation, and administration" of employee benefit plans, ERISA sets "minimum standards ... assuring the equitable character of such plans and their financial soundness,"[ ] and contains an express preemption provision that ERISA "shall supersede any and all State laws insofar as they may now or hereafter relate to any employee benefit plan. ..." § 1144(a)[§ 514(a)]. A saving clause then reclaims a substantial amount of ground with its provision that "nothing in this subchapter shall be construed to exempt or relieve any person from any law of any State which regulates insurance, banking, or securities." § 1144(b)(2)(A) [§ 514(b)(2)(A)]. The "unhelpful" drafting of these antiphonal clauses * * * occupies a substantial share of this Court's time. In trying to extrapolate congressional intent in a case like this, when congressional language seems simultaneously to preempt everything and hardly anything, we "have no choice" but to temper the assumption that " 'the ordinary meaning ... accurately expresses the legislative purpose,' "[ ] with the qualification " 'that the historic police powers of the States were not [meant] to be superseded by the Federal Act unless that was the clear and manifest purpose of Congress.' "[ ]

It is beyond serious dispute that under existing precedent § 4–10 of the Illinois HMO Act "relates to" employee benefit plans within the meaning of § 1144(a). * * * As a law that "relates to" ERISA plans under § 1144(a), § 4–10 is saved from preemption only if it also "regulates insurance" under § 1144(b)(2)(A). * * *

[The Court then proceeded to apply the savings clause analysis method that it had developed in earlier cases, concluding that the Illinois external review law was saved from preemption. As this analysis was superceded by the Court's decision in *Kentucky Association of Health Plans v. Miller*, described below, the discussion is omitted here. Ed.]

* * *

Given that § 4–10 regulates insurance, ERISA's mandate that "nothing in this subchapter shall be construed to exempt or relieve any person from any law of any State which regulates insurance," 29 U.S.C. § 1144(b)(2)(A), ostensibly forecloses preemption. [ ] Rush, however, does not give up. It argues for preemption anyway, emphasizing that the question is ultimately one of congressional intent, which sometimes is so clear that it overrides a statutory provision designed to save state law from being preempted. * * *

In ERISA law, we have recognized one example of this sort of overpowering federal policy in the civil enforcement provisions, 29 U.S.C. § 1132(a), *** In *Massachusetts Mut. Life Ins. Co. v. Russell*,[ ] we said those provisions amounted to an "interlocking, interrelated, and interdependent remedial scheme,"[ ] which *Pilot Life* described as "represent[ing] a careful balancing of the need for prompt and fair claims settlement procedures against the public interest in encouraging the formation of employee benefit plans"[ ]. So, we have held, the civil enforcement provisions are of such extraordinarily preemptive power that they override even the "well-pleaded complaint" rule for establishing the conditions under which a cause of action may be removed to a federal forum. *Metropolitan Life Ins. Co. v. Taylor*[ ].

Although we have yet to encounter a forced choice between the congressional policies of exclusively federal remedies and the "reservation of the business of insurance to the States,"[ ] we have anticipated such a conflict, with the state insurance regulation losing out if it allows plan participants "to obtain remedies . . . that Congress rejected in ERISA."

In *Pilot Life*, an ERISA plan participant who had been denied benefits sued in a state court on state tort and contract claims. He sought not merely damages for breach of contract, but also damages for emotional distress and punitive damages, both of which we had held unavailable under relevant ERISA provisions.[ ] We not only rejected the notion that these common-law contract claims "regulat[ed] insurance,"[ ] but went on to say that, regardless, Congress intended a "federal common law of rights and obligations" to develop under ERISA,[ ] without embellishment by independent state remedies.

Rush says that the day has come to turn dictum into holding by declaring that the state insurance regulation, § 4–10, is preempted for creating just the kind of "alternative remedy" we disparaged in *Pilot Life*. As Rush sees it, the independent review procedure is a form of binding arbitration that allows an ERISA beneficiary to submit claims to a new decisionmaker to examine Rush's determination *de novo,* supplanting judicial review under the "arbitrary and capricious" standard ordinarily applied when discretionary plan interpretations are challenged[ ]. * * *

We think, however, that Rush overstates the rule expressed in *Pilot Life*. * * *

* * *

[T]his case addresses a state regulatory scheme that provides no new cause of action under state law and authorizes no new form of ultimate relief. While independent review under § 4–10 may well settle the fate of a benefit claim under a particular contract, the state statute does not enlarge the claim beyond the benefits available in any action brought under § 1132(a). And although the reviewer's determination would presumably replace that of the HMO as to what is "medically necessary" under this contract, the relief ultimately available would still be what ERISA authorizes in a suit for benefits under § 1132(a). * * *

Rush still argues for going beyond *Pilot Life,* making the preemption issue here one of degree, whether the state procedural imposition interferes unreasonably with Congress's intention to provide a uniform federal regime of "rights and obligations" under ERISA. However, "[s]uch disuniformities . . . are the inevitable result of the congressional decision to 'save' local insurance regulation."[ ][11] Although we have recognized a limited exception from the saving clause for alternative causes of action and alternative remedies in the sense described above, we have never indicated that there might be additional justifications for qualifying the clause's application. * * *

To be sure, a State might provide for a type of "review" that would so resemble an adjudication as to fall within *Pilot Life's* categorical bar. Rush, and the dissent,[ ] contend that § 4–10 fills that bill by imposing an alternative scheme of arbitral adjudication at odds with the manifest congressional purpose to confine adjudication of disputes to the courts. * * *

In the classic sense, arbitration occurs when "parties in dispute choose a judge to render a final and binding decision on the merits of the controversy and on the basis of proofs presented by the parties."[ ] Arbitrators typically hold hearings at which parties may submit evidence and conduct cross-examinations.[ ]

Section 4–10 does resemble an arbitration provision, then, to the extent that the independent reviewer considers disputes about the meaning of the HMO contract and receives "evidence" in the form of medical records, statements from physicians, and the like. But this is as far as the resemblance to arbitration goes, for the other features of review under § 4–10 give the proceeding a different character, one not at all at odds with the policy behind § 1132(a). The Act does not give the independent reviewer a free-ranging power to construe contract terms, but instead, confines review to a single term: the phrase "medical necessity," used to define the services covered under the contract.[ ] This limitation, in turn, implicates a feature of HMO benefit determinations that we described in *Pegram v. Herdrich,*[ ] We explained that when an HMO guarantees medically necessary care, determinations of coverage "cannot be untangled from physicians' judgments about reasonable medical treatment."[ ] This is just how the Illinois Act operates; the independent examiner must be a physician with credentials similar to those of the primary care physician,[ ] and is expected to exercise independent medical judgment in deciding what medical necessity requires. * * *

Once this process is set in motion, it does not resemble either contract interpretation or evidentiary litigation before a neutral arbiter, as much as it looks like a practice (having nothing to do with arbitration) of obtaining another medical opinion. * * *

The practice of obtaining a second opinion, however, is far removed from any notion of an enforcement scheme, and once § 4–10 is seen as something akin to a mandate for second-opinion practice in order to ensure sound

11. Thus, we do not believe that the mere fact that state independent review laws are likely to entail different procedures will impose burdens on plan administration that would threaten the object of 29 U.S.C. § 1132(a); it is the HMO contracting with a plan, and not the plan itself, that will be subject to these regulations, and every HMO will have to establish procedures for conforming with the local laws, regardless of what this Court may think ERISA forbids. This means that there will be no special burden of compliance upon an ERISA plan beyond what the HMO has already provided for. And although the added compliance cost to the HMO may ultimately be passed on to the ERISA plan, we have said that such "indirect economic effect[s],"[ ], are not enough to preempt state regulation even outside the insurance context. We recognize, of course, that a State might enact an independent review requirement with procedures so elaborate, and burdens so onerous, that they might undermine § 1132(a). No such system is before us.

medical judgments, the preemption argument that arbitration under § 4–10 supplants judicial enforcement runs out of steam.

Next, Rush argues that § 4–10 clashes with a substantive rule intended to be preserved by the system of uniform enforcement, stressing a feature of judicial review highly prized by benefit plans: a deferential standard for reviewing benefit denials. Whereas *Firestone Tire & Rubber Co. v. Bruch*,[ ] recognized that an ERISA plan could be designed to grant "discretion" to a plan fiduciary, deserving deference from a court reviewing a discretionary judgment, § 4–10 provides that when a plan purchases medical services and insurance from an HMO, benefit denials are subject to apparently *de novo* review. If a plan should continue to balk at providing a service the reviewer has found medically necessary, the reviewer's determination could carry great weight in a subsequent suit for benefits under § 1132(a), depriving the plan of the judicial deference a fiduciary's medical judgment might have obtained if judicial review of the plan's decision had been immediate.[15]

Again, however, the significance of § 4–10 is not wholly captured by Rush's argument, which requires some perspective for evaluation. First, in determining whether state procedural requirements deprive plan administrators of any right to a uniform standard of review, it is worth recalling that ERISA itself provides nothing about the standard. It simply requires plans to afford a beneficiary some mechanism for internal review of a benefit denial, * * *.

Not only is there no ERISA provision directly providing a lenient standard for judicial review of benefit denials, but there is no requirement necessarily entailing such an effect even indirectly. When this Court dealt with the review standards on which the statute was silent, we held that a general or default rule of *de novo* review could be replaced by deferential review if the ERISA plan itself provided that the plan's benefit determinations were matters of high or unfettered discretion[ ]. Nothing in ERISA, however, requires that these kinds of decisions be so "discretionary" in the first place; whether they are is simply a matter of plan design or the drafting of an HMO contract. In this respect, then, § 4–10 prohibits designing an insurance contract so as to accord unfettered discretion to the insurer to interpret the contract's terms. As such, it does not implicate ERISA's enforcement scheme at all, and is no different from the types of substantive state regulation of insurance contracts we have in the past permitted to survive preemption, such as mandated-benefit statutes and statutes prohibiting the denial of claims solely on the ground of untimeliness.[ ] * * *

* * *

15. An issue implicated by this case but requiring no resolution is the degree to which a plan provision for unfettered discretion in benefit determinations guarantees truly deferential review. In *Firestone Tire* itself, we noted that review for abuse of discretion would home in on any conflict of interest on the plan fiduciary's part, if a conflict was plausibly raised. That last observation was underscored only two Terms ago in *Pegram v. Herdrich*,[ ] when we again noted the potential for conflict when an HMO makes decisions about appropriate treatment[ ]. It is a fair question just how deferential the review can be when the judicial eye is peeled for conflict of interest. Moreover, as we explained in *Pegram*, "it is at least questionable whether Congress would have had mixed eligibility decisions in mind when it provided that decisions administering a plan were fiduciary in nature."[ ] Our decision today does not require us to resolve these questions.

In deciding what to make of these facts and conclusions, it helps to go back to where we started and recall the ways States regulate insurance in looking out for the welfare of their citizens. Illinois has chosen to regulate insurance as one way to regulate the practice of medicine, which we have previously held to be permissible under ERISA[ ]. While the statute designed to do this undeniably eliminates whatever may have remained of a plan sponsor's option to minimize scrutiny of benefit denials, this effect of eliminating an insurer's autonomy to guarantee terms congenial to its own interests is the stuff of garden variety insurance regulation through the imposition of standard policy terms. * * * And any lingering doubt about the reasonableness of § 4–10 in affecting the application of § 1132(a) may be put to rest by recalling that regulating insurance tied to what is medically necessary is probably inseparable from enforcing the quintessentially state-law standards of reasonable medical care. See *Pegram v. Herdrich* [ ]. To the extent that benefits litigation in some federal courts may have to account for the effects of § 4–10, it would be an exaggeration to hold that the objectives of § 1132(a) are undermined. The savings clause is entitled to prevail here, and we affirm the judgment.

Justice Thomas, with whom The Chief Justice, Justice Scalia, and Justice Kennedy join, dissenting.

This Court has repeatedly recognized that ERISA's civil enforcement provision, § 502 of the Employee Retirement Income Security Act of 1974 (ERISA), 29 U.S.C. § 1132, provides the exclusive vehicle for actions asserting a claim for benefits under health plans governed by ERISA, and therefore that state laws that create additional remedies are pre-empted.[ ] Such exclusivity of remedies is necessary to further Congress' interest in establishing a uniform federal law of employee benefits so that employers are encouraged to provide benefits to their employees.[ ]

* * * Therefore, as the Court concedes,[ ] even a state law that "regulates insurance" may be pre-empted if it supplements the remedies provided by ERISA, despite ERISA's saving clause,[ ]. Today, however, the Court takes the unprecedented step of allowing respondent Debra Moran to short circuit ERISA's remedial scheme by allowing her claim for benefits to be determined in the first instance through an arbitral-like procedure provided under Illinois law, and by a decisionmaker other than a court.[ ] * * *

From the facts of this case one can readily understand why Moran sought recourse under § 4–10. * * *

In the course of its review, petitioner informed Moran that "there is no prevailing opinion within the appropriate specialty of the United States medical profession that the procedure proposed [by Moran] is safe and effective for its intended use and that the omission of the procedure would adversely affect [her] medical condition."[ ] Petitioner did agree to cover the standard treatment for Moran's ailment,[ ] concluding that peer-reviewed literature "demonstrates that [the standard surgery] is effective therapy in the treatment of [Moran's condition]."[ ]

Moran, however, was not satisfied with this option. * * * She invoked § 4–10 of the Illinois HMO Act, which requires HMOs to provide a mechanism for review by an independent physician when the patient's primary care physician and HMO disagree about the medical necessity of a treatment proposed by the primary care physician. * * *

Dr. A. Lee Dellon, an unaffiliated physician who served as the independent medical reviewer, concluded that the surgery for which petitioner denied coverage "was appropriate," that it was "the same type of surgery" he would have done, and that Moran "had all of the indications and therefore the medical necessity to carry out" the nonstandard surgery. * * * Under § 4–10, Dr. Dellon's determination conclusively established Moran's right to benefits under Illinois law.

* * *

Section 514(a)'s broad language provides that ERISA "shall supersede any and all State laws insofar as they ... relate to any employee benefit plan," except as provided in § 514(b). 29 U.S.C. § 1144(a). This language demonstrates "Congress's intent to establish the regulation of employee welfare benefit plans 'as exclusively a federal concern.' "[ ] It was intended to "ensure that plans and plan sponsors would be subject to a uniform body of benefits law" so as to "minimize the administrative and financial burden of complying with conflicting directives among States or between States and the Federal Government" and to prevent "the potential for conflict in substantive law ... requiring the tailoring of plans and employer conduct to the peculiarities of the law of each jurisdiction."[ ]

* * * [T]he Court until today had consistently held that state laws that seek to supplant or add to the exclusive remedies in § 502(a) of ERISA, 29 U.S.C. § 1132(a), are pre-empted because they conflict with Congress' objective that rights under ERISA plans are to be enforced under a uniform national system.[ ] The Court has explained that § 502(a) creates an "interlocking, interrelated, and interdependent remedial scheme," and that a beneficiary who claims that he was wrongfully denied benefits has "a panoply of remedial devices" at his disposal. * * *

* * *

Section 4–10 cannot be characterized as anything other than an alternative state-law remedy or vehicle for seeking benefits. In the first place, § 4–10 comes into play only if the HMO and the claimant dispute the claimant's entitlement to benefits; the purpose of the review is to determine whether a claimant is entitled to benefits. * * *

There is no question that arbitration constitutes an alternative remedy to litigation.[ ] Consequently, although a contractual agreement to arbitrate—which does not constitute a "State law" relating to "any employee benefit plan"—is outside § 514(a) of ERISA's pre-emptive scope, States may not circumvent ERISA preemption by mandating an alternative arbitral-like remedy as a plan term enforceable through an ERISA action.

To be sure, the majority is correct that § 4–10 does not mirror all procedural and evidentiary aspects of "common arbitration."[ ] But as a binding decision on the merits of the controversy the § 4–10 review resembles nothing so closely as arbitration. * * *

* * *

[I]t is troubling that the Court views the review under § 4–10 as nothing more than a practice "of obtaining a second [medical] opinion." * * * [W]hile a second medical opinion is nothing more than that—an opinion—a determination under § 4–10 is a conclusive determination with respect to the award of benefits. * * *

Section 4–10 constitutes an arbitral-like state remedy through which plan members may seek to resolve conclusively a disputed right to benefits. Some 40 other States have similar laws, though these vary as to applicability, procedures, standards, deadlines, and consequences of independent review. * * *

For the reasons noted by the Court, independent review provisions may sound very appealing. Efforts to expand the variety of remedies available to aggrieved beneficiaries beyond those set forth in ERISA are obviously designed to increase the chances that patients will be able to receive treatments they desire, and most of us are naturally sympathetic to those suffering from illness who seek further options. Nevertheless, the Court would do well to remember that no employer is required to provide any health benefit plan under ERISA and that the entire advent of managed care, and the genesis of HMOs, stemmed from spiraling health costs. To the extent that independent review provisions such as § 4–10 make it more likely that HMOs will have to subsidize beneficiaries' treatments of choice, they undermine the ability of HMOs to control costs, which, in turn, undermines the ability of employers to provide health care coverage for employees.

As a consequence, independent review provisions could create a disincentive to the formation of employee health benefit plans, a problem that Congress addressed by making ERISA's remedial scheme exclusive and uniform. While it may well be the case that the advantages of allowing States to implement independent review requirements as a supplement to the remedies currently provided under ERISA outweigh this drawback, this is a judgment that, pursuant to ERISA, must be made by Congress. I respectfully dissent.

Notes and Questions

1. ERISA only governs employee benefit plans, i.e. benefit plans established and maintained by employers to provide benefits to their employees. It does not reach health insurance purchased by individuals as individuals (including self-employed individuals) or health benefits not provided through employment-related group plans, such as uninsured motorist insurance policies or workers' compensation. Certain church and government-sponsored plans are also not covered. See Macro v. Independent Health Ass'n, Inc., 180 F. Supp.2d 427 (W.D.N.Y.2001). Finally, ERISA does not regulate group insurance offered by insurers to the employees of particular businesses without employer contributions or administrative involvement. See 29 C.F.R. § 2510.3–1(j); Taggart Corp. v. Life & Health Benefits Admin., Inc., 617 F.2d 1208 (5th Cir.1980), cert. denied, 450 U.S. 1030, 101 S.Ct. 1739, 68 L.Ed.2d 225 (1981). Nevertheless, ERISA does govern the vast majority of private health insurance provided in America, which is provided through employment-related group plans.

2. Part of the confusion inherent in ERISA preemption decisions is attributable to the fact that there are three distinct forms of ERISA preemption. One of these is express preemption based on § 514(a) (29 U.S.C. § 1144(a)). Section 514(a), reproduced above, provides that ERISA "supersedes" any state law that

"relates to" an employee benefits plan. Express 514(a) preemption, however, is subject to the "savings" clause, and thus does not reach state insurance regulation.

Just because a law is saved from 514(a) preemption, however, does not mean that it is not preempted, as the controversy in *Rush* illustrates. ERISA preemption can also be based on § 502(a) of ERISA (29 U.S.C. § 1132(a)) which provides for federal court jurisdiction over specified types of claims against ERISA plans. The Supreme Court has long held that ERISA plans may remove into federal court claims that were brought in state courts but that could have been brought under § 502(a) in federal court. Removal is permitted under the "complete preemption" exception to the well-pleaded complaint rule. The well-pleaded complaint rule normally limits removal of cases from state into federal court on the basis of federal question jurisdiction (under 28 U.S.C.A. § 1331) to cases in which federal claims are explicitly raised in the plaintiff's complaint. However, under the "complete preemption" exception to this rule (sometimes called "superpreemption") federal jurisdiction is permitted when Congress has so completely preempted an area of law that any claim within it is brought under federal law, and thus is removable to federal court. "Complete preemption" is, in reality, not a preemption doctrine, but rather a rule of federal jurisdiction.

Third, Section 502(a) also plays another role in ERISA jurisprudence, ousting state claims and remedies that would take the place of § 502 claims. The federal courts have interpreted this section to indicate a Congressional intent to preempt comprehensively the "field" of judicial oversight of employee benefits plans. Thus state tort, contract, and even statutory claims that could have been brought as claims for benefits or for breach of fiduciary duty under § 502(a) have been held to be preempted by § 502(a). As *Moran* demonstrates, § 502(a) preemption, like § 514(a) explicit preemption, is not comprehensive. In particular, ERISA does not necessarily preempt state court malpractice cases brought against managed care plans that provide as well as pay for health care, as we will see in subsection D. Also claims brought by persons who are not proper plaintiffs under § 502(a) or against persons who are not ERISA fiduciaries evade ERISA § 502(a) preemption. *Moran* also holds that external review procedures imposed by the states prior to the onset of litigation also may be exempt from § 502 preemption.

Section 502(a) and § 514(a) preemption are not, however, coextensive. Just because a lawsuit invokes a law that might be preempted as relating to an employee benefits claim does not mean that the claim could be brought under § 502(a), and is thus subject to "complete preemption." Not infrequently federal courts remand cases that could not have been brought as § 502(a) claims to state court for resolution of § 514(a) preemption issues. As we see below in *Aetna Health Insurance v. Davila*, moreover, laws that are saved from preemption by an exception to § 514(a), may still be preempted as inconsistent with § 502(a) field preemption.

3. Early cases interpreting § 514(a) read it very broadly. The Supreme Court's first consideration of § 514(a), Shaw v. Delta Air Lines, Inc., 463 U.S. 85, 103 S.Ct. 2890, 77 L.Ed.2d 490 (1983), adopted a very literal and liberal reading of "relates to" as including any provisions having a "connection with or reference to" a benefits plan. The Court rejected narrower readings of ERISA preemption that would have limited its reach to state laws that explicitly attempted to regulate ERISA plans or that dealt with subjects explicitly addressed by ERISA. For over a decade following *Shaw*, the Court applied the § 514(a) tests developed in *Shaw* expansively in a variety of contexts, almost always finding preemption when it found an ERISA plan to exist. The Court repeatedly expressed allegiance

to the opinion that ERISA § 514(a) preemption had a "broad scope" (Metropolitan Life v. Massachusetts, 471 U.S. 724, 739, 105 S.Ct. 2380, 85 L.Ed.2d 728 (1985)), and "an expansive sweep" (Pilot Life Ins. Co. v. Dedeaux, 481 U.S. 41, 47, 107 S.Ct. 1549, 95 L.Ed.2d 39 (1987)), and that it was "conspicuous for its breadth," (FMC Corp. v. Holliday, 498 U.S. 52, 58, 111 S.Ct. 403, 112 L.Ed.2d 356 (1990)).

Attending to these Supreme Court pronouncements, lower courts in the 1980s and 1990s held a wide range of state regulatory programs and common law claims that arguably "related to" the administration of an ERISA plan or imposed costs upon plans to be preempted. As the *Fiedler* case below demonstrates, the "connection with or reference to" test continues to sweep broadly. The Supreme Court finally recognized the limits of ERISA preemption, however, in New York State Conference of Blue Cross and Blue Shield Plans v. Travelers Ins. Co., 514 U.S. 645, 115 S.Ct. 1671, 131 L.Ed.2d 695 (1995). *Travelers* held that a New York law that required hospitals to charge different rates to insured, HMO, and self-insured plans was not preempted by § 514(a). Retreating from earlier expansive readings of ERISA preemption, the Court reaffirmed the principle applied in other areas of the law that Congress is generally presumed not to intend to preempt state law. 514 U.S. at 654. The Court proceeded to note that in cases involving traditional areas of state regulation, such as health care, congressional intent to preempt state law should not be presumed unless it was "clear and manifest." Id. at 655. Recognizing that the term "relate to" was not self-limiting, the Court turned for assistance in defining the term to the purpose of ERISA, which it defined as freeing benefit plans from conflicting state and local regulation. Id. at 656–57. Preemption was intended, the Court held, to affect state laws that operated directly on the structure or administration of ERISA plans, id. at 657–58, not laws that only indirectly raised the cost of various benefit options, id. at 658–64. Accordingly, the Court held that the challenged rate-setting law was not "related to" an ERISA plan, and thus not preempted.

The Court's post-*Travelers* preemption cases suggest that the Court in fact turned a corner in *Travelers*. It has rejected ERISA preemption in the majority of these cases, though it had almost never done so before *Travelers*. Post-*Travelers* lower court cases on the whole continued to apply ERISA preemption broadly, generally finding that state programs aimed at regulating insurance and managed care "relate to" ERISA plan. Some, however, have limited ERISA preemption. See, for example, Louisiana Health Service & Indemnity Co. v. Rapides Healthcare System, 461 F.3d 529 (5th Cir.2006), holding that a Louisiana statute that required insurance companies to honor all assignments of benefits by patients to hospitals did not have an impermissible connection with ERISA. See, reviewing comprehensively federal and state court cases applying ERISA to managed care regulation, Robert F. Rich, Christopher T. Erb, and Louis J. Gale, Judicial Interpretation of Managed Care Policy, 13 Elder L.J. 85 (2005).

4. As *Moran* notes, a state law that is otherwise preempted under § 514(a) is saved from preemption if it regulates insurance under the "savings clause" found in § 514(b)(2)(A) (29 U.S.C.A. § 1144(b)(2)(A)). In its early cases interpreting this clause, the Court read it conservatively, applying both a "common sense" test as well as the three part test developed in antitrust cases applying the McCarran–Ferguson Act for determining whether a law regulated "the business of insurance" to determine whether the savings clause applied. Metropolitan Life Ins. Co. v. Massachusetts, 471 U.S. 724, 740–44, 105 S.Ct. 2380, 85 L.Ed.2d 728 (1985), Pilot Life Ins. Co. v. Dedeaux, 481 U.S. 41, 107 S.Ct. 1549, 95 L.Ed.2d 39 (1987).

In Kentucky Association of Health Plans v. Miller, 538 U.S. 329, 123 S.Ct. 1471, 155 L.Ed.2d 468 (2003) the court abandoned its earlier precedents and crafted a new approach to interpreting the savings clause. This case involved the claim of an association of managed care plans that Kentucky's "any willing provider" law was preempted by ERISA. The Sixth Circuit had held that the regulatory provision was saved from preemption under ERISA's savings clause. In a brief and unanimous opinion written by Justice Scalia (who had dissented in *Moran*), the Court held that the law was saved from preemption, abandoning its previous savings clause jurisprudence. The Court acknowledged that use of the McCarran–Ferguson test had "misdirected attention, failed to provide clear guidance to lower federal courts, and * * * added little to relevant analysis." The Court also admitted that the McCarran–Ferguson tests had been developed for different purposes and interpreted different statutory language.

The Court concluded:

> Today we make a clean break from the McCarran–Ferguson factors and hold that for a state law to be deemed a 'law ... which regulates insurance' under § 1144(b)(2)(A), it must satisfy two requirements. First, the state law must be specifically directed toward entities engaged in insurance.[ ] Second, * * * the state law must substantially affect the risk pooling arrangement between the insurer and the insured. Kentucky's law satisfies each of these requirements. 123 S.Ct. at 1479.

Earlier in the opinion it had interpreted the "risk pooling" requirement as follows:

> We have never held that state laws must alter or control the actual terms of insurance policies to be deemed 'laws ... which regulat[e] insurance' under § 1144(b)(2)(A); it suffices that they substantially affect the risk pooling arrangement between insurer and insured. By expanding the number of providers from whom an insured may receive health services, AWP laws alter the scope of permissible bargains between insurers and insureds * * *. No longer may Kentucky insureds seek insurance from a closed network of health-care providers in exchange for a lower premium. The AWP prohibition substantially affects the type of risk pooling arrangements that insurers may offer. 123 S.Ct. at 1477–78.

Kentucky Association significantly clarifies, and expands, the coverage of ERISA's savings clause. Virtually any state law that requires insurers to provide particular benefits would seem to be covered. See Matthew O. Gatewood, The New Map: The Supreme Court's New Guide to Curing Thirty Years of Confusion in ERISA Savings Clause Analysis, 62 Wash. & Lee U. L. Rev. 643 (2005). What effect is this green light to state regulation of managed care and health insurance likely to have on the willingness of employers to offer health insurance plans to their workers? Might Justice Thomas' prediction on this matter prove true? See Haavi Morreim, ERISA Takes a Drubbing: Rush Prudential and Its Implications for Health Care, 38 Tort Trial and Ins. Practice J. 933 (2003). Ironically, this expansion of state regulatory authority comes at a time when many states have lost interest in more aggressive regulation of managed care.

5. As *Moran* acknowledges, even a statute saved from § 514(a) preemption by the savings clause may nevertheless, under *Pilot Life*, be preempted by § 502(a) if it provides a state remedy that takes the place of § 502(a). Aetna Health Inc. v. Davila, 542 U.S. 200, 124 S.Ct. 2488, 159 L.Ed.2d 312 (2004), reproduced below, applied this exception, holding that the Texas Health Care Liability Act, which allowed lawsuits against managed care companies for failing to exercise ordinary care in making coverage decisions, was preempted. Section 502 preemption is not limited to tort cases, but also extends to state statutes that

provide private actions for civil penalties to the extent that these cases could have been brought under § 502. See, for example, Prudential Insurance Co. v. National Park Medical Center, Inc., 413 F.3d 897 (8th Cir.2005), holding that the provisions of the Arkansas Patient Protection Act allowing private suits for injunctive relief, damages of at least $1,000, and attorney's fees were preempted by ERISA § 502 to the extent that they could have been brought under § 502. Thus an action to recover payment denied by a plan for the services of a provider who should have been qualified for payment under a state's "any willing provider" law would be preempted. In Hawaii Management Alliance Assoc. v. Insurance Comm'r, 106 Hawai'i 21, 100 P.3d 952 (2004), the Hawaiian Supreme Court held that Hawai'i's external review statute was preempted by ERISA because it provided a remedy alternative to § 502. Would any of the provisions of the Massachusetts managed care regulation statute in Chapter 7 be preempted under § 502?

6. ERISA's § 514(b)(2)(A) savings clause is subject to its own exception, the § 514(b)(2)(B) "deemer" clause. This subsection, reproduced above, provides that "neither an employee benefit * * * nor any trust established under such a plan, shall be deemed to be an insurance company or other insurer, * * * or to be engaged in the business of insurance * * * for purposes of any law of any State purporting to regulate insurance companies, [or] insurance contracts, * * *." 29 U.S.C.A. § 1144(b)(2)(B). In FMC Corporation v. Holliday, 498 U.S. 52, 111 S.Ct. 403, 112 L.Ed.2d 356 (1990), the Supreme Court interpreted this clause broadly to exempt self-funded ERISA plans entirely from state regulation and state law claims. None of the provisions of the Massachusetts managed care regulation statute in chapter 7, for example, would apply to self-insured ERISA plans.

The deemer clause offers a significant incentive for employers to become self-insured, as a self-insured plan can totally escape state regulation, and in particular, benefit mandates. Self-insurance, however, also has disadvantages—it imposes upon the employer the burden of administering the plan as well as open-ended liability for employee benefit claims made under the plan. To avoid these problems, self-insured employers often contract with third-party administrators to administer claims and with stop-loss insurers to limit their claims exposure. The courts have overwhelmingly held that employer plans remain self-insured even though they are reinsured through stop-loss plans, and have prohibited state regulation of stop-loss coverage for self-insured plans. See, e.g., Bill Gray Enterprises, Inc. Employee Health and Welfare Plan v. Gourley, 248 F.3d 206 (3rd Cir.2001) and Lincoln Mutual Casualty v. Lectron Products, Inc. 970 F.2d 206 (6th Cir.1992). Third-party administrators that administer self-insured plans are also protected from state insurance regulation. NGS American, Inc. v. Barnes, 805 F.Supp. 462, 473 (W.D.Texas 1992). Thus an employer who is willing to bear some risk can escape state regulation under the "deemer" clause, even though most of the risk of insuring the plan is borne by a stop-loss insurer and the burden of administering the plan is assumed by a third-party administrator. Can the states, however, impede this means of escape from state insurance regulation by prohibiting stop-loss insurers from selling policies that cover losses below a certain level, or requiring a specified level of self-insured coverage before a stop loss policy kicks in? See, arguing that such regulation is permitted under the savings clause, Russell Korobkin, The Battle Over Self–Insured Health Plans, or "One Good Loophole Deserves Another," 5 Yale J. Health Pol'y, L. & Ethics 89 (2005).

Problem: ERISA Preemption of State Managed Care Regulation

Two years ago, as part of a comprehensive managed care reform statute, your state adopted three new regulatory provisions. The first provides that all health insurance plans in your state, including all employee benefits plans that cover physician and hospital services, must cover all care that is "medically necessary." It defines "medically necessary" to include any care recommended by a plan member's treating physician that is recognized as "standard" by at least a "respectable minority" of physicians. The second provision establishes a state external review program to which any insured or plan member can appeal the decision of an insurer or benefit plan refusing coverage of a service as not "medically necessary" if internal plan remedies have been exhausted. A third statute provides a cause of action under state law that allows any plan member or insured who has been denied payment for services by a plan after those services have been decided by an external review entity to be medically necessary to sue the plan in state court for injunctive relief, and also for any consequential damages attributable to the plan's service denial.

An association of insurers and an association of self-insured ERISA plans have both sued in federal court asking that the court declare that all three provisions are preempted by and unenforceable under ERISA. At the same time, Joseph Ditka, who has health benefits through his employer covered by Health Star, Inc., a managed care organization, has sued the plan for damages he alleges that he suffered when Health Star refused to cover a procedure that his doctor recommended last year and that the state's external review program determined to be medically necessary. Who wins each claim, and why?

B. ERISA PREEMPTION AND STATE HEALTH CARE REFORM

Although *Moran* and *Miller* seemed to beat back the threat that ERISA had posed to state managed care regulation, ERISA preemption has recently reemerged on another front as a significant barrier to state health care reform. ERISA has long limited the ability of states to reform health care. A quarter of a century ago, Hawaii's mandate that employers provide health insurance to their employees was struck down as impermissibly interfering in the terms of employee benefit plans in violation of ERISA, Standard Oil Co. of California v. Agsalud, 633 F.2d 760 (CA9 1980), summarily aff'd, 454 U.S. 801, 102 S.Ct. 79, 70 L.Ed.2d 75 (1981). In 1983, Congress amended ERISA to exempt from preemption certain provisions of the Hawaii Act in place before the enactment of ERISA, but no other state has been afforded such an exemption. Recent attempts by other states to expand insurance coverage have tried to evade ERISA preemption, but the first ERISA challenge brought against such a statute was completely successful.

RETAIL INDUSTRY LEADERS ASSOCIATION v. FIEDLER

United States Court of Appeals, Fourth Circuit, 2007.
475 F.3d 180.

NIEMEYER, CIRCUIT JUDGE:

On January 12, 2006, the Maryland General Assembly enacted the Fair Share Health Care Fund Act, which requires employers with 10,000 or more Maryland employees to spend at least 8% of their total payrolls on employees' health insurance costs or pay the amount their spending falls short to the State of Maryland. Resulting from a nationwide campaign to force Wal–Mart Stores, Inc., to increase health insurance benefits for its 16,000 Maryland employees, the Act's minimum spending provision was crafted to cover just Wal–Mart. The Retail Industry Leaders Association, of which Wal–Mart is a member, brought suit against James D. Fielder, Jr., the Maryland Secretary of Labor, Licensing, and Regulation, to declare that the Act is preempted by the Employee Retirement Income Security Act of 1974 ("ERISA") and to enjoin the Act's enforcement. * * *

Because Maryland's Fair Share Health Care Fund Act effectively requires employers in Maryland covered by the Act to restructure their employee health insurance plans, it conflicts with ERISA's goal of permitting uniform nationwide administration of these plans. We conclude therefore that the Maryland Act is preempted by ERISA and accordingly affirm.

I

Before enactment of the Fair Share Health Care Fund Act ("Fair Share Act"), [ ] the Maryland General Assembly heard extensive testimony about the rising costs of the Maryland Medical Assistance Program (Medicaid and children's health programs). * * * The General Assembly also perceived that Wal–Mart Stores, Inc., a particularly large employer, provided its employees with a substandard level of healthcare benefits, forcing many Wal–Mart employees to depend on state-subsidized healthcare programs. Indeed, the Maryland Department of Legislative Services * * * prepared an analytical report of the proposed Fair Share Act for the General Assembly, that discussed only Wal–Mart's employee benefits practices. * * *

* * *

Some states claim many Wal–Mart employees end up on public health programs such as Medicaid. A survey by Georgia officials found that more than 10,000 children of Wal–Mart employees were enrolled in the state's children's health insurance program (CHIP) at a cost of nearly $10 million annually. Similarly, a North Carolina hospital found that 31% of 1,900 patients who said they were Wal–Mart employees were enrolled in Medicaid, and an additional 16% were uninsured.

* * *

According to the [New York] Times, Wal–Mart said that its employees are mostly insured, citing internal surveys showing that 90% of workers have health coverage, often through Medicare or family members' policies. Wal–Mart officials say the company provides health coverage to about 537,000, or 45% of its total workforce. As a matter of comparison, Costco Wholesale provides health insurance to 96% of eligible employees.

In response, the General Assembly enacted the Fair Share Act in January 2006, to become effective January 1, 2007. The Act applies to employers that have at least 10,000 employees in Maryland, * * * and imposes spending and reporting requirements on such employers. The core provision provides:

> An employer that is not organized as a nonprofit organization and does not spend up to 8% of the total wages paid to employees in the State on health insurance costs shall pay to the Secretary an amount equal to the difference between what the employer spends for health insurance costs and an amount equal to 8% of the total wages paid to employees in the State.

[ ] An employer that fails to make the required payment is subject to a civil penalty of $250,000.[ ]

The Act also requires a covered employer to submit an annual report on January 1 of each year to the Secretary, in which the employer must disclose: (1) how many employees it had for the prior year, (2) its "health insurance costs," and (3) the percentage of compensation it spent on "health insurance costs" for the "year immediately preceding the previous calendar year." * * *

Any payments collected * * * may be used only to support the Maryland Medical Assistance Program, which consists of Maryland's Medicaid and children's health programs.[ ]

The record discloses that only four employers have at least 10,000 employees in Maryland: * * * The parties agree that only Wal–Mart, who employs approximately 16,000 in Maryland, is currently subject to the Act's minimum spending requirements. Wal–Mart representatives testified that it spends about 7 to 8% of its total payroll on healthcare, falling short of the Act's 8% threshold.

The legislative record also makes clear that legislators and affected parties assumed that the Fair Share Act would force Wal–Mart to increase its spending on healthcare benefits rather than to pay monies to the State. * * *

* * *

III

* * *

A

ERISA establishes comprehensive federal regulation of employers' provision of benefits to their employees. It does not mandate that employers provide specific employee benefits but leaves them free, "for any reason at any time, to adopt, modify, or terminate welfare plans." * * *

* * *

The primary objective of ERISA was to "provide a uniform regulatory regime over employee benefit plans."[ ] To accomplish this objective, § 514(a) of ERISA broadly preempts "any and all State laws insofar as they may now or hereafter *relate to* any employee benefit plan" covered by ERISA.[ ] This preemption provision aims "to minimize the administrative and financial burden of complying with conflicting directives among States or between States and the Federal Government" and to reduce "the tailoring of plans and employer conduct to the peculiarities of the law of each jurisdiction."[ ]

The language of ERISA's preemption provision—covering all laws that "relate to" an ERISA plan—is "clearly expansive."[ ] The Supreme Court has focused judicial analysis by explaining that a state law "relates to" an ERISA plan "if it has a *connection with* or *reference to* such a plan."[ ] But even these terms, "taken to extend to the furthest stretch of [their] indeterminacy," would have preemption "never run its course."[ ] Accordingly, we do not rely on "uncritical literalism" but attempt to ascertain whether Congress would have expected the Fair Share Act to be preempted.[ ] To make this determination, we look "to the objectives of the ERISA statute" as well as "to the nature of the effect of the state law on ERISA plans,"[ ].

* * * States continue to enjoy wide latitude to regulate healthcare *providers*.[ ] And ERISA explicitly saves state regulations of *insurance companies* from preemption.[ ] But unlike laws that regulate healthcare providers and insurance companies, "state laws that mandate[ ] employee benefit structures or their administration" are preempted by ERISA.[ ]

* * *

In line with *Shaw,* [v. Delta Air Lines, Inc. 463 U.S. 85 (1983) courts have readily and routinely found preemption of state laws that act directly upon an employee benefit plan or effectively require it to establish a particular ERISA-governed benefit.[ ] Likewise, *Shaw* dictates that ERISA preempt state laws that directly regulate employers' contributions to or structuring of their plans.[ ]

A state law that directly regulates the structuring or administration of an ERISA plan is not saved by inclusion of a means for opting out of its requirements. * * * Additionally, a proliferation of laws like Washington's would have undermined ERISA's objective of sparing plan administrators the task of monitoring the laws of all 50 States and modifying their plan documents accordingly.[ ]

In sum, a state law has an impermissible "connection with" an ERISA plan if it directly regulates or effectively mandates some element of the structure or administration of employers' ERISA plans. On the other hand, a state law that creates only indirect economic incentives that affect but do not bind the choices of employers or their ERISA plans is generally not preempted.[ ] In deciding which of these principles is applicable, we assess the effect of a state law on the ability of ERISA plans to be administered uniformly nationwide.[ ] A state law is preempted also if it contains a "reference to" an ERISA plan, the alternative characterization referred to in *Shaw* for finding that it "relates to" an ERISA plan.[ ] The district court did not reach this issue because it found that preemption through the Fair Share Act's "connection with" ERISA plans. * * *

* * * At its heart, the Fair Share Act requires every employer of 10,000 or more Maryland employees to pay to the State an amount that equals the difference between what the employer spends on "health insurance costs" * * * and 8% of its payroll. * * *

In effect, the only rational choice employers have under the Fair Share Act is to structure their ERISA healthcare benefit plans so as to meet the minimum spending threshold. * * * Because the Fair Share Act effectively mandates that employers structure their employee healthcare plans to provide a certain level of benefits, the Act has an obvious "connection with" employee benefit plans and so is preempted by ERISA.

* * *

While the Secretary argues that the Fair Share Act is designed to collect funds for medical care under the Maryland Medical Assistance Program, the core provision of the Act aims at requiring covered employers to provide medical benefits to employees. The effect of this provision will force employers to structure their recordkeeping and healthcare benefit spending to comply with the Fair Share Act. Functioning in that manner, the Act would disrupt employers' uniform administration of employee benefit plans on a nationwide basis. * * *

This problem would not likely be confined to Maryland. As a result of similar efforts elsewhere to pressure Wal–Mart to increase its healthcare spending, other States and local governments have adopted or are considering healthcare spending mandates that would clash with the Fair Share Act. * * * If permitted to stand, these laws would force Wal–Mart to tailor its healthcare benefit plans to each specific State, and even to specific cities and counties. * * *

* * *

The Secretary argues that the Act is not mandatory and therefore does not, for preemption purposes, have a "connection with" employee benefit plans because it gives employers two options to avoid increasing benefits to employees. An employer can, under the Fair Share Act, (1) increase health-care spending on employees in ways that do not qualify as ERISA plans; or (2) refuse to increase benefits to employees and pay the State the amount by which the employer's spending falls short of 8%. Because employers have these choices, the Secretary argues, the Fair Share Act does not preclude Wal–Mart from continuing its uniform administration of ERISA plans nationwide. He maintains that the Fair Share Act is more akin to the laws upheld in *Travelers,* 514 U.S. at 658–59, 115 S.Ct. 1671, and *Dillingham,* 519 U.S. at 319, 117 S.Ct. 832, which merely created economic incentives that affected employers' choices while not effectively dictating their choice. This argument fails for several reasons.

First, the laws involved in *Travelers* and *Dillingham* are inapposite because they dealt with regulations that only *indirectly* regulated ERISA plans. * * *

* * *

In contrast to *Travelers* and *Dillingham,* the Fair Share Act *directly* regulates employers' structuring of their employee health benefit plans. * * *

Second, the choices given in the Fair Share Act, on which the Secretary relies to argue that the Act is not a mandate on employers, are not meaningful alternatives by which an employer can increase its healthcare spending to comply with the Fair Share Act without affecting its ERISA plans. * * *

In addition to on-site medical clinics, employers could, under the Fair Share Act, contribute to employees' Health Savings Accounts as a means of non-ERISA healthcare spending. Under federal tax law, eligible individuals may establish and make pretax contributions to a Health Savings Account and then use those monies to pay or reimburse medical expenses.[ ] Employers' contributions to employees' Health Savings Accounts qualify as healthcare spending for purposes of the Fair Share Act.[ ] This option of contributing to Health Savings Accounts, however, is available under only limited conditions, which undermine the impact of this option. For example, only if an individual is covered under a high deductible health plan and no other more comprehensive health plan is he eligible to establish a Health Savings Account. * * * In addition, for an employer's contribution to a Health Savings Account to be exempt from ERISA, the Health Savings Account must be established voluntarily by the employee. *See* U.S. Dep't of Labor, Employee Benefits Sec. Admin., Field Assistance Bulletin 2004–1. This would likely shrink further the potential for Health Savings Accounts contributions as many employees would not undertake to establish Health Savings Accounts.

* * * The undeniable fact is that the vast majority of any employer's healthcare spending occurs through ERISA plans. Thus, the primary subjects of the Fair Share Act are ERISA plans, and any attempt to comply with the Act would have direct effects on the employer's ERISA plans. * * *

Perhaps recognizing the insufficiency of a non-ERISA healthcare spending option, the Secretary relies most heavily on its argument that the Fair Share Act gives employers the choice of paying the State rather than altering their healthcare spending. * * * The Secretary contends that, in certain circumstances, it would be rational for an employer to choose to do so. * * * [I]ndeed, identifying the narrow conditions under which the Act would not force an employer to increase its spending on healthcare plans only reinforces the conclusion that the overwhelming effect of the Act is to mandate spending increases. This conclusion is further supported by the fact that Wal–Mart representatives averred that Wal–Mart would in fact increase healthcare spending rather than pay the State. *AFFIRMED.*

MICHAEL, CIRCUIT JUDGE, dissenting:

* * *

I respectfully dissent on the issue of ERISA preemption because the Act does not force a covered employer to make a choice that impacts an employee benefit plan. An employer can comply with the Act either by paying assessments into the special fund or by increasing spending on employee health insurance. The Act expresses no preference for one method of Medicaid support or the other. As a result, the Act is not preempted by ERISA.

* * *

Notes and Questions

1. What routes are open to a state that wants to engage employers in an attempt to expand insurance coverage? Clearly a direct mandate requiring employers to offer specified coverage to their employees is out of the question. On the other hand, state initiatives that offer tax credits to employers to expand coverage, create voluntary purchasing pools to enhance the purchasing power of small businesses, use Medicaid or State Children's Health Insurance Program funds to subsidize employment-based insurance for low-income workers, or require insurers to offer low cost insurance policies to small businesses should not be affected by ERISA because they do not impose any requirements on employers or on ERISA plans. The provisions of the Massachusetts plan that penalize employers who do not allow their employees to purchase health insurance with after-tax money through a § 125 cafeteria plan (which excludes from income taxation money that employees spend on health care) might survive an ERISA challenge, since § 125 plans are not technically benefit plans (because employers do not contribute to them) and thus should not be governed by ERISA. State tax-financed universal insurance programs funded through a payroll tax should also survive an ERISA challenge, although they would arguably affect the likelihood of

employers offering employee-benefit health plans. Finally, universal coverage systems based solely on an individual mandate should not implicate ERISA, because, again, they impose no obligations on employers.

The big question, however, is what, if anything, can be done to make a "pay-or-play" system pass ERISA muster after *Fiedler*. Several municipalities, including New York and San Francisco, have adopted pay-or-play ordinances. San Francisco's "pay-or-play" ordinance was struck down in 2007 under ERISA preemption. Golden Gate Restaurant Ass'n v. City and County of San Francisco, 535 F.Supp.2d 968 (N.D.Cal., December 26, 2007). As of this writing, the district court's judgment has been stayed by the Ninth Circuit Court of Appeals pending appeal. The Massachusetts "fair-share" assessment and "premiums" that Vermont imposes on employers to cover their uninsured workers would also seem vulnerable because they do impose obligations on employers. But the penalty imposed on Massachusetts employers who do not comply, $295 per employee, per year, is much smaller than that imposed by the Maryland law and will not compel employers to comply with the law who choose not to. Pay-or-play laws that are not focused on a particular employer, do not refer to ERISA plans, do not impose penalties substantial enough to force an employer to provide benefits, and do not require the employer to establish any particular kind of benefit plan may pass muster, but will almost certainly be challenged, and, if other courts follow the Fourth Circuit, may be difficult to defend. State laws that impose significant record-keeping obligations on employers will also face ERISA challenges, even if they do not require employer financial contributions, because they essentially require an employer to spend money for administrative costs. See, discussing these issues, Edward A. Zelinsky, The New Massachusetts Health Law: Preemption and Experimentation, 49 Wm. & Mary L. Rev. 229 (2007); Amy Monahan, Pay or Play Laws, ERISA Preemption, and Potential Lessons from Massachusetts, 55 Kansas Law Review 1203 (2007); Patricia A. Butler, ERISA Implications for State Health Care Access Initiatives: Impact of the Maryland "Fair Share Act" Court Decision, National Academy for State Health Policy (2006); and Patricia A. Butler, ERISA Update: Federal Court of Appeals Agrees ERISA Preempts Maryland's "Fair Share Act," National Academy for State Health Policy, 2007.

2. Does the fact that ERISA is a federal law that preempts state attempts to regulate employee benefit plans mean that federal legislation will be necessary to expand health care coverage to the uninsured? Or is the nation better off with a "laboratory of the states" approach to expanding health care coverage, even if the states have a quite limited range of approaches to expanding health care coverage, the most realistic of which are also very costly? Should Congress amend ERISA to allow states to adopt "pay-or-play" laws? What effects would this have on the national uniformity of employer obligations that seems to be an important value in ERISA jurisprudence?

C. ERISA PREEMPTION OF STATE TORT LITIGATION

Courts have struggled to determine the nature and extent of ERISA preemption in medical malpractice cases. Managed care plans as defendants are subject to the same theories of liability as hospitals—vicarious liability, corporate negligence, ordinary negligence. Vicarious liability has been allowed by most courts that have considered the question. See Chapter 5, Part IV. The Supreme Court however has severely limited the reach of state tort actions against ERISA-qualified health plans.

AETNA HEALTH INC. v. DAVILA

Supreme Court of the United States, 2004.
542 U.S. 200, 124 S.Ct. 2488, 159 L.Ed.2d 312.

JUSTICE THOMAS delivered the opinion of the Court.

In these consolidated cases, two individuals sued their respective health maintenance organizations (HMOs) for alleged failures to exercise ordinary care in the handling of coverage decisions, in violation of a duty imposed by the Texas Health Care Liability Act (THCLA)[ ]. We granted certiorari to decide whether the individuals' causes of action are completely pre-empted by the "interlocking, interrelated, and interdependent remedial scheme,"[ ] found at § 502(a) of the Employee Retirement Income Security Act of 1974 (ERISA)[ ]. We hold that the causes of action are completely pre-empted and hence removable from state to federal court. The Court of Appeals, having reached a contrary conclusion, is reversed.

I

A

Respondent Juan Davila is a participant, and respondent Ruby Calad is a beneficiary, in ERISA-regulated employee benefit plans. Their respective plan sponsors had entered into agreements with petitioners, Aetna Health Inc. and CIGNA HealthCare of Texas, Inc., to administer the plans. Under Davila's plan, for instance, Aetna reviews requests for coverage and pays providers, such as doctors, hospitals, and nursing homes, which perform covered services for members; under Calad's plan sponsor's agreement, CIGNA is responsible for plan benefits and coverage decisions.

Respondents both suffered injuries allegedly arising from Aetna's and CIGNA's decisions not to provide coverage for certain treatment and services recommended by respondents' treating physicians. Davila's treating physician prescribed Vioxx to remedy Davila's arthritis pain, but Aetna refused to pay for it. Davila did not appeal or contest this decision, nor did he purchase Vioxx with his own resources and seek reimbursement. Instead, Davila began taking Naprosyn, from which he allegedly suffered a severe reaction that required extensive treatment and hospitalization. Calad underwent surgery, and although her treating physician recommended an extended hospital stay, a CIGNA discharge nurse determined that Calad did not meet the plan's criteria for a continued hospital stay. CIGNA consequently denied coverage for the extended hospital stay. Calad experienced postsurgery complications forcing her to return to the hospital. She alleges that these complications would not have occurred had CIGNA approved coverage for a longer hospital stay.

Respondents brought separate suits in Texas state court against petitioners. Invoking THCLA § 88.002(a), respondents argued that petitioners' refusal to cover the requested services violated their "duty to exercise ordinary care when making health care treatment decisions," and that these refusals "proximately caused" their injuries. Ibid. Petitioners removed the cases to Federal District Courts, arguing that respondents' causes of action fit within the scope of, and were therefore completely pre-empted by, ERISA § 502(a). The respective District Courts agreed, and declined to remand the cases to state court. Because respondents refused to amend their complaints to bring explicit ERISA claims, the District Courts dismissed the complaints with prejudice.

B

Both Davila and Calad appealed the refusals to remand to state court. The United States Court of Appeals for the Fifth Circuit consolidated their cases with several others raising similar issues. The Court of Appeals recognized that state causes of action that "duplicat[e] or fal[l] within the scope of an ERISA § 502(a) remedy" are completely pre-empted and hence removable to federal court.[ ]. After examining the causes of action available under § 502(a), the Court of Appeals determined that respondents' claims could possibly fall under only two: § 502(a)(1)(B), which provides a cause of action for the recovery of wrongfully denied benefits, and § 502(a)(2), which allows suit against a plan fiduciary for breaches of fiduciary duty to the plan.

Analyzing § 502(a)(2) first, the Court of Appeals concluded that, under *Pegram v. Herdrich*,[ ], the decisions for which petitioners were being sued were "mixed eligibility and treatment decisions" and hence were not fiduciary in nature.[1] The Court of Appeals next determined that respondents' claims did not fall within § 502(a)(1)(B)'s scope. It found significant that respondents "assert tort claims," while § 502(a)(1)(B) "creates a cause of action for breach of contract,"[ ], and also that respondents "are not seeking reimbursement for benefits denied them," but rather request "tort damages" arising from "an external, statutorily imposed duty of 'ordinary care,' "[ ]. From *Rush Prudential HMO, Inc. v. Moran*,[ ], the Court of Appeals derived the principle that complete pre-emption is limited to situations in which "States ... duplicate the causes of action listed in ERISA § 502(a)," and concluded that "[b]ecause the THCLA does not provide an action for collecting benefits," it fell outside the scope of § 502(a)(1)(B). 307 F.3d, at 310–311.

II

A

Under the removal statute, "any civil action brought in a State court of which the district courts of the United States have original jurisdiction, may be removed by the defendant" to federal court.[ ] One category of cases of which district courts have original jurisdiction is "[f]ederal question" cases: cases "arising under the Constitution, laws, or treaties of the United States." § 1331. We face in these cases the issue whether respondents' causes of action arise under federal law.

Ordinarily, determining whether a particular case arises under federal law turns on the " 'well-pleaded complaint' "rule.[ ] The Court has explained that

> "whether a case is one arising under the Constitution or a law or treaty of the United States, in the sense of the jurisdictional statute[,] ... must be determined from what necessarily appears in the plaintiff's statement

---

1. In this Court, petitioners do not claim or argue that respondents' causes of action fall under ERISA § 502(a)(2). Because petitioners do not argue this point, and since we can resolve these cases entirely by reference to ERISA § 502(a)(1)(B), we do not address ERISA § 502(a)(2).

of his own claim in the bill or declaration, unaided by anything alleged in anticipation of avoidance of defenses which it is thought the defendant may interpose."[ ].

In particular, the existence of a federal defense normally does not create statutory "arising under" jurisdiction,[ ], and "a defendant may not [generally] remove a case to federal court unless the *plaintiff's* complaint establishes that the case 'arises under' federal law,"[ ]. There is an exception, however, to the well-pleaded complaint rule. "[W]hen a federal statute wholly displaces the state-law cause of action through complete pre-emption," the state claim can be removed.[ ] This is so because "[w]hen the federal statute completely pre-empts the state-law cause of action, a claim which comes within the scope of that cause of action, even if pleaded in terms of state law, is in reality based on federal law."[ ] ERISA is one of these statutes.

B

Congress enacted ERISA to "protect ... the interests of participants in employee benefit plans and their beneficiaries" by setting out substantive regulatory requirements for employee benefit plans and to "provid[e] for appropriate remedies, sanctions, and ready access to the Federal courts."[ ]. The purpose of ERISA is to provide a uniform regulatory regime over employee benefit plans. To this end, ERISA includes expansive pre-emption provisions, see ERISA § 514,[ ], which are intended to ensure that employee benefit plan regulation would be "exclusively a federal concern."[ ]

ERISA's "comprehensive legislative scheme" includes "an integrated system of procedures for enforcement."[ ] This integrated enforcement mechanism, ERISA § 502(a),[ ] is a distinctive feature of ERISA, and essential to accomplish Congress' purpose of creating a comprehensive statute for the regulation of employee benefit plans. As the Court said in *Pilot Life Ins. Co. v. Dedeaux,*[ ]:

> "[T]he detailed provisions of § 502(a) set forth a comprehensive civil enforcement scheme that represents a careful balancing of the need for prompt and fair claims settlement procedures against the public interest in encouraging the formation of employee benefit plans. The policy choices reflected in the inclusion of certain remedies and the exclusion of others under the federal scheme would be completely undermined if ERISA-plan participants and beneficiaries were free to obtain remedies under state law that Congress rejected in ERISA. 'The six carefully integrated civil enforcement provisions found in § 502(a) of the statute as finally enacted ... provide strong evidence that Congress did *not* intend to authorize other remedies that it simply forgot to incorporate expressly.' "[ ]

Therefore, any state-law cause of action that duplicates, supplements, or supplants the ERISA civil enforcement remedy conflicts with the clear congressional intent to make the ERISA remedy exclusive and is therefore pre-empted.[ ]

The pre-emptive force of ERISA § 502(a) is still stronger. In *Metropolitan Life Ins. Co. v. Taylor,*[ ] the Court determined that the similarity of the language used in the Labor Management Relations Act, 1947 (LMRA), and ERISA, combined with the "clear intention" of Congress "to make

§ 502(a)(1)(B) suits brought by participants or beneficiaries federal questions for the purposes of federal court jurisdiction in like manner as § 301 of the LMRA," established that ERISA § 502(a)(1)(B)'s pre-emptive force mirrored the pre-emptive force of LMRA § 301. Since LMRA § 301 converts state causes of action into federal ones for purposes of determining the propriety of removal,[ ] so too does ERISA § 502(a)(1)(B). Thus, the ERISA civil enforcement mechanism is one of those provisions with such "extraordinary pre-emptive power" that it "converts an ordinary state common law complaint into one stating a federal claim for purposes of the well-pleaded complaint rule."[ ] Hence, "causes of action within the scope of the civil enforcement provisions of § 502(a) [are] removable to federal court."[ ]

III

A

ERISA § 502(a)(1)(B) provides:

"A civil action may be brought—(1) by a participant or beneficiary—. . . (B) to recover benefits due to him under the terms of his plan, to enforce his rights under the terms of the plan, or to clarify his rights to future benefits under the terms of the plan."[ ]

This provision is relatively straightforward. If a participant or beneficiary believes that benefits promised to him under the terms of the plan are not provided, he can bring suit seeking provision of those benefits. A participant or beneficiary can also bring suit generically to "enforce his rights" under the plan, or to clarify any of his rights to future benefits. Any dispute over the precise terms of the plan is resolved by a court under a *de novo* review standard, unless the terms of the plan "giv[e] the administrator or fiduciary discretionary authority to determine eligibility for benefits or to construe the terms of the plan."[ ]

It follows that if an individual brings suit complaining of a denial of coverage for medical care, where the individual is entitled to such coverage only because of the terms of an ERISA-regulated employee benefit plan, and where no legal duty (state or federal) independent of ERISA or the plan terms is violated, then the suit falls "within the scope of" ERISA § 502(a)(1)(B)[ ]. In other words, if an individual, at some point in time, could have brought his claim under ERISA § 502(a)(1)(B), and where there is no other independent legal duty that is implicated by a defendant's actions, then the individual's cause of action is completely pre-empted by ERISA § 502(a)(1)(B).

To determine whether respondents' causes of action fall "within the scope" of ERISA § 502(a)(1)(B), we must examine respondents' complaints, the statute on which their claims are based (the THCLA), and the various plan documents. Davila alleges that Aetna provides health coverage under his employer's health benefits plan.[ ]. Davila also alleges that after his primary care physician prescribed Vioxx, Aetna refused to pay for it.[ ]. The only action complained of was Aetna's refusal to approve payment for Davila's Vioxx prescription. Further, the only relationship Aetna had with Davila was its partial administration of Davila's employer's benefit plan.[ ].

Similarly, Calad alleges that she receives, as her husband's beneficiary under an ERISA-regulated benefit plan, health coverage from CIGNA.[ ]. She alleges that she was informed by CIGNA, upon admittance into a hospital for major surgery, that she would be authorized to stay for only one day.[ ] She also alleges that CIGNA, acting through a discharge nurse, refused to authorize more than a single day despite the advice and recommendation of her treating physician.[ ] Calad contests only CIGNA's decision to refuse coverage for her hospital stay.[ ] And, as in Davila's case, the only connection between Calad and CIGNA is CIGNA's administration of portions of Calad's ERISA-regulated benefit plan.[ ].

It is clear, then, that respondents complain only about denials of coverage promised under the terms of ERISA-regulated employee benefit plans. Upon the denial of benefits, respondents could have paid for the treatment themselves and then sought reimbursement through a § 502(a)(1)(B) action, or sought a preliminary injunction,[ ].

Respondents contend, however, that the complained-of actions violate legal duties that arise independently of ERISA or the terms of the employee benefit plans at issue in these cases. Both respondents brought suit specifically under the THCLA, alleging that petitioners "controlled, influenced, participated in and made decisions which affected the quality of the diagnosis, care, and treatment provided" in a manner that violated "the duty of ordinary care set forth in §§ 88.001 and 88.002."[ ] Respondents contend that this duty of ordinary care is an independent legal duty. They analogize to this Court's decisions interpreting LMRA § 301,[ ] with particular focus on *Caterpillar Inc. v. Williams,* (suit for breach of individual employment contract, even if defendant's action also constituted a breach of an entirely separate collective-bargaining agreement, not pre-empted by LMRA § 301). Because this duty of ordinary care arises independently of any duty imposed by ERISA or the plan terms, the argument goes, any civil action to enforce this duty is not within the scope of the ERISA civil enforcement mechanism.

The duties imposed by the THCLA in the context of these cases, however, do not arise independently of ERISA or the plan terms. The THCLA does impose a duty on managed care entities to "exercise ordinary care when making health care treatment decisions," and makes them liable for damages proximately caused by failures to abide by that duty.[ ] However, if a managed care entity correctly concluded that, under the terms of the relevant plan, a particular treatment was not covered, the managed care entity's denial of coverage would not be a proximate cause of any injuries arising from the denial. Rather, the failure of the plan itself to cover the requested treatment would be the proximate cause.[3] More significantly, the THCLA clearly states that "[t]he standards in Subsections (a) and (b) create no obligation on the part of the health insurance carrier, health maintenance organization, or other managed care entity to provide to an insured or enrollee treatment which is not covered by the health care plan of the entity."[ ] Hence, a managed care entity could not be subject to liability under the THCLA if it denied coverage for any treatment not covered by the health care plan that it was administering.

3. To take a clear example, if the terms of the health care plan specifically exclude from coverage the cost of an appendectomy, then any injuries caused by the refusal to cover the appendectomy are properly attributed to the terms of the plan itself, not the managed care entity that applied those terms.

Thus, interpretation of the terms of respondents' benefit plans forms an essential part of their THCLA claim, and THCLA liability would exist here only because of petitioners' administration of ERISA-regulated benefit plans. Petitioners' potential liability under the THCLA in these cases, then, derives entirely from the particular rights and obligations established by the benefit plans. So, unlike the state-law claims in *Caterpillar, supra,* respondents' THCLA causes of action are not entirely independent of the federally regulated contract itself.[ ].

Hence, respondents bring suit only to rectify a wrongful denial of benefits promised under ERISA-regulated plans, and do not attempt to remedy any violation of a legal duty independent of ERISA. We hold that respondents' state causes of action fall "within the scope of" ERISA § 502(a)(1)(B),[ ] and are therefore completely pre-empted by ERISA § 502 and removable to federal district court.[4]

B

The Court of Appeals came to a contrary conclusion for several reasons, all of them erroneous. First, the Court of Appeals found significant that respondents "assert a tort claim for tort damages" rather than "a contract claim for contract damages," and that respondents "are not seeking reimbursement for benefits denied them."[ ] But, distinguishing between pre-empted and non-pre-empted claims based on the particular label affixed to them would "elevate form over substance and allow parties to evade" the pre-emptive scope of ERISA simply "by relabeling their contract claims as claims for tortious breach of contract." * * *[ ]. Nor can the mere fact that the state cause of action attempts to authorize remedies beyond those authorized by ERISA § 502(a) put the cause of action outside the scope of the ERISA civil enforcement mechanism. In *Pilot Life, Metropolitan Life,* and *Ingersoll-Rand,* the plaintiffs all brought state claims that were labeled either tort or tort-like.[ ] And, the plaintiffs in these three cases all sought remedies beyond those authorized under ERISA.[ ] And, in all these cases, the plaintiffs' claims were pre-empted. The limited remedies available under ERISA are an inherent part of the "careful balancing" between ensuring fair and prompt enforcement of rights under a plan and the encouragement of the creation of such plans.[ ].

Second, the Court of Appeals believed that "the wording of [respondents'] plans is immaterial" to their claims, as "they invoke an external, statutorily imposed duty of 'ordinary care.' "[ ] But as we have already discussed, the wording of the plans is certainly material to their state causes of action, and the duty of "ordinary care" that the THCLA creates is not external to their rights under their respective plans.

Ultimately, the Court of Appeals rested its decision on one line from *Rush Prudential.* * * * Nowhere in *Rush Prudential* did we suggest that the pre-

---

4. Respondents also argue that ERISA § 502(a) completely pre-empts a state cause of action only if the cause of action would be pre-empted under ERISA § 514(a); respondents then argue that their causes of action do not fall under the terms of § 514(a). But a state cause of action that provides an alternative remedy to those provided by the ERISA civil enforcement mechanism conflicts with Congress' clear intent to make the ERISA mechanism exclusive.[ ].

emptive force of ERISA § 502(a) is limited to the situation in which a state cause of action precisely duplicates a cause of action under ERISA § 502(a).

Nor would it be consistent with our precedent to conclude that only strictly duplicative state causes of action are pre-empted. Frequently, in order to receive exemplary damages on a state claim, a plaintiff must prove facts beyond the bare minimum necessary to establish entitlement to an award.[ ]. In order to recover for mental anguish, for instance, the plaintiffs in *Ingersoll-Rand* and *Metropolitan Life* would presumably have had to prove the existence of mental anguish; there is no such element in an ordinary suit brought under ERISA § 502(a)(1)(B).[ ] This did not save these state causes of action from pre-emption. Congress' intent to make the ERISA civil enforcement mechanism exclusive would be undermined if state causes of action that supplement the ERISA § 502(a) remedies were permitted, even if the elements of the state cause of action did not precisely duplicate the elements of an ERISA claim.

C

Respondents also argue—for the first time in their brief to this Court—that the THCLA is a law that regulates insurance, and hence that ERISA § 514(b)(2)(A) saves their causes of action from pre-emption (and thereby from complete pre-emption).[5] This argument is unavailing. The existence of a comprehensive remedial scheme can demonstrate an "overpowering federal policy" that determines the interpretation of a statutory provision designed to save state law from being pre-empted.[ ] ERISA's civil enforcement provision is one such example.[ ]

As this Court stated in *Pilot Life,* "our understanding of [§ 514(b)(2)(A)] must be informed by the legislative intent concerning the civil enforcement provisions provided by ERISA § 502(a).[ ]" The Court concluded that "[t]he policy choices reflected in the inclusion of certain remedies and the exclusion of others under the federal scheme would be completely undermined if ERISA-plan participants and beneficiaries were free to obtain remedies under state law that Congress rejected in ERISA."[ ] The Court then held, based on

> "the common-sense understanding of the saving clause, the McCarran–Ferguson Act factors defining the business of insurance, and, *most importantly,* the clear expression of congressional intent that ERISA's civil enforcement scheme be exclusive, ... that [the plaintiff's] state law suit asserting improper processing of a claim for benefits under an ERISA-regulated plan is not saved by § 514(b)(2)(A)."[ ]

Pilot Life's reasoning applies here with full force. Allowing respondents to proceed with their state-law suits would "pose an obstacle to the purposes and objectives of Congress."[ ] As this Court has recognized in both *Rush Prudential* and *Pilot Life,* ERISA § 514(b)(2)(A) must be interpreted in light of the congressional intent to create an exclusive federal remedy in ERISA § 502(a). Under ordinary principles of conflict pre-emption, then, even a state law that can arguably be characterized as "regulating insurance" will be pre-

---

5. ERISA § 514(b)(2)(A)[ ] reads, as relevant: "[N]othing in this subchapter shall be construed to exempt or relieve any person from any law of any State which regulates insurance, banking, or securities."

empted if it provides a separate vehicle to assert a claim for benefits outside of, or in addition to, ERISA's remedial scheme.

IV

Respondents, their *amici,* and some Courts of Appeals have relied heavily upon *Pegram v. Herdrich,*[ ], in arguing that ERISA does not pre-empt or completely pre-empt state suits such as respondents'. They contend that *Pegram* makes it clear that causes of action such as respondents' do not "relate to [an] employee benefit plan," ERISA § 514(a),[ ] and hence are not pre-empted.[ ]

Pegram cannot be read so broadly. In *Pegram,* the plaintiff sued her physician-owned-and-operated HMO (which provided medical coverage through plaintiff's employer pursuant to an ERISA-regulated benefit plan) and her treating physician, both for medical malpractice and for a breach of an ERISA fiduciary duty.[ ] The plaintiff's treating physician was also the person charged with administering plaintiff's benefits; it was she who decided whether certain treatments were covered.[ ] We reasoned that the physician's "eligibility decision and the treatment decision were inextricably mixed."[ ] We concluded that "Congress did not intend [the defendant HMO] or any other HMO to be treated as a fiduciary to the extent that it makes mixed eligibility decisions acting through its physicians."[ ]

A benefit determination under ERISA, though, is generally a fiduciary act.[ ] "At common law, fiduciary duties characteristically attach to decisions about managing assets and distributing property to beneficiaries."[ ] Hence, a benefit determination is part and parcel of the ordinary fiduciary responsibilities connected to the administration of a plan.[ ] The fact that a benefits determination is infused with medical judgments does not alter this result.

Pegram itself recognized this principle. *Pegram,* in highlighting its conclusion that "mixed eligibility decisions" were not fiduciary in nature, contrasted the operation of "[t]raditional trustees administer[ing] a medical trust" and "physicians through whom HMOs act."[ ] A traditional medical trust is administered by "paying out money to buy medical care, whereas physicians making mixed eligibility decisions consume the money as well."[ ] And, significantly, the Court stated that "[p]rivate trustees do not make treatment judgments."[ ] But a trustee managing a medical trust undoubtedly must make administrative decisions that require the exercise of medical judgment. Petitioners are not the employers of respondents' treating physicians and are therefore in a somewhat analogous position to that of a trustee for a traditional medical trust.

ERISA itself and its implementing regulations confirm this interpretation. ERISA defines a fiduciary as any person "to the extent ... he has any discretionary authority or discretionary responsibility in the administration of [an employee benefit] plan.[ ]. When administering employee benefit plans, HMOs must make discretionary decisions regarding eligibility for plan benefits, and, in this regard, must be treated as plan fiduciaries.[ ]" Also, ERISA § 503, which specifies minimum requirements for a plan's claim procedure, requires plans to "afford a reasonable opportunity to any participant whose claim for benefits has been denied for a full and fair review by the appropriate named fiduciary of the decision denying the claim."[ ] This strongly suggests that the ultimate decisionmaker in a plan regarding an award of benefits must be a fiduciary and must be acting as a fiduciary when determining a participant's or beneficiary's claim. The relevant regulations also establish extensive requirements to ensure full and fair review of benefit denials.[ ] These regulations, on their face, apply equally to health benefit plans and other plans, and do not draw distinctions between medical and nonmedical benefits determinations. Indeed, the regulations strongly imply that benefits determinations involving medical judgments are, just as much as any other benefits determinations, actions by plan fiduciaries.[ ] Classifying any entity with discretionary authority over benefits determinations as anything but a plan fiduciary would thus conflict with ERISA's statutory and regulatory scheme.

Since administrators making benefits determinations, even determinations based extensively on medical judgments, are ordinarily acting as plan fiduciaries, it was essential to *Pegram*'s conclusion that the decisions challenged there were truly "mixed eligibility and treatment decisions,"[ ], i.e., medical necessity decisions made by the plaintiff's treating physician *qua* treating physician and *qua* benefits administrator. Put another way, the reasoning of *Pegram* "only make[s] sense where the underlying negligence also plausibly constitutes medical maltreatment by a party who can be deemed to be a treating physician or such a physician's employer."[ ] Here, however, petitioners are neither respondents' treating physicians nor the employers of respondents' treating physicians. Petitioners' coverage decisions, then, are pure eligibility decisions, and *Pegram* is not implicated.

V

We hold that respondents' causes of action, brought to remedy only the denial of benefits under ERISA-regulated benefit plans, fall within the scope of, and are completely pre-empted by, ERISA § 502(a)(1)(B), and thus removable to federal district court. The judgment of the Court of Appeals is reversed, and the cases are remanded for further proceedings consistent with this opinion.[7]

It is so ordered.

[See Justice Ginsburg and Breyer's concurrence in the next section.]

Notes and Questions

1. What state law claims are left to plaintiff plan subscribers after *Davila*? Consider some of the language of *Davila*:

> "... [A]ny state-law cause of action that duplicates, supplements, or supplants the ERISA civil enforcement remedy conflicts with the clear congressional intent to make the ERISA remedy exclusive and is therefore preempted.

7. The United States, as *amicus*, suggests that some individuals in respondents' positions could possibly receive some form of "make-whole" relief under ERISA § 502(a)(3).[ ] However, after their respective District Courts denied their motions for remand, respondents had the opportunity to amend their complaints to bring expressly a claim under ERISA § 502(a). Respondents declined to do so; the District Courts therefore dismissed their complaints with prejudice.[ ] Respondents have thus chosen not to pursue any ERISA claim, including any claim arising under ERISA § 502(a)(3). The scope of this provision, then, is not before us, and we do not address it.

"It is clear, then, that respondents complain only about denials of coverage promised under the terms of ERISA-regulated employee benefit plans. Upon the denial of benefits, respondents could have paid for the treatment themselves and then sought reimbursement through a § 502(a)(1)(B) action, or sought a preliminary injunction."

"Hence, respondents bring suit only to rectify a wrongful denial of benefits promised under ERISA-regulated plans, and do not attempt to remedy any violation of a legal duty independent of ERISA."

"Congress' intent to make the ERISA civil enforcement mechanism exclusive would be undermined if state causes of action that supplement the ERISA § 502(a) remedies were permitted, even if the elements of the state cause of action did not precisely duplicate the elements of an ERISA claim."

" * * * [T]he reasoning of *Pegram* 'only make[s] sense where the underlying negligence also plausibly constitutes medical maltreatment by a party who can be deemed to be a treating physician or such a physician's employer.'[ ]. Here, however, petitioners are neither respondents' treating physicians nor the employers of respondents' treating physicians. Petitioners' coverage decisions, then, are pure eligibility decisions, and *Pegram* is not implicated."

Commentators have noted how restrictive *Davila* is. First, it allows tort actions for direct or vicarious liability only for physician owned and operated managed care plans. And these are a dying breed. The typical health plan today is an insurance vehicle that imposes coverage constraints on providers in its network, and would not be subject to tort liability. As Jost observes, ". . . [t]his will create yet another incentive for employers and managed care plans to move away from tighter staff model HMOs to preferred provider organizations (PPOs) and looser HMO or point-of-service (POS) arrangements." Second, *Davila* leaves a "regulatory vacuum" in which consumer have no remedies if they are injured as the result of health care provided through health plans. Third, *Davila* sharpens the framework for ERISA limits on plans, allowing internal and external claims review, with possible federal judicial review of coverage denials under 502. Fourth, *Davila* states that ERISA plan administrators are fiduciaries as to coverage decisions. *Pegram* however noted that such administrators may have mixed allegiances, balancing health plan financial and other interests. Fifth, the court dangles the possibility that broader damages might be allowed under ERISA itself.

See Timothy S. Jost, The Supreme Court Limits Lawsuits Against Managed Care Organizations, Health Affairs Web Exclusive 4–417 (11 August 2004). See also Theodore W. Ruger, The Supreme Court Federalizes Managed Care Liability, 32 J.L. Med. & Ethics 528, 529 (2004) (criticizing the current ERISA enforcement scheme as crabbed and penurious, failing to serve remedial goals of either tort or contract.). For a full discussion of litigation leading up to *Davila*, see generally Margaret Cyr–Provost, Aetna v. Davila: From Patient–Centered Care to Plan–Centered Care, A Signpost or the End of the Road? 6 Hous. J. Health L. & Pol'y 171 (2005); M.Gregg Bloche and David Studdert, A Quiet Revolution: Law as an Agent of Health System Change, 23 Health Affairs 2942 (2004). See also Peter Jacobson, Strangers in the Night (New York: Oxford, 2002).

2. What litigation theories remain after *Davila* and *Pegram*? Could a state legislature pass a statute subjecting all managed care plans to liability for negligent treatment decisions of their physicians? Would section 514 of ERISA preempt such a statute? Would it be a law regulating insurance, thereby saved from preemption? Or are all such escape holes plugged?

What about negligent plan design, either based on the incentives for paying physicians, or some other flaw in the design of the system? What about negligent selection of providers, the heart of most corporate negligence claims against hospitals?

a. *Negligent Plan Design.* Consider Smelik v. Mann Texas Dist. Ct. (224th Jud. Dist., Bexar Co. No. 03–CI–06936 2006), where a Texas jury awarded $7.4 million in actual damages to the family of an HMO participant who died from complications of acute renal failure. The jury found Humana liable for 35 percent of the $7.4 million in actual damages for negligence, but found no evidence that Humana committed fraud. The jury also determined that Humana's behavior was consistent with gross negligence, and the company stipulated to $1.6 million in punitive damages pursuant to an out-of-court agreement. Humana was found to be responsible for a total of $4.2 million.

Smelik is an attempt to escape from *Davila*'s restrictions, since the plaintiff argued that Humana was liable for "mismanaged managed care", or negligence in the coordination of medical care, rather than for a denial of medical care, as in *Davila*. Plaintiffs convinced the jury that Humana failed to follow its own utilization management policies, failing to refer Smelik to a kidney specialist or to its disease management program. Plaintiffs also established that Humana negligently approved payment for a combination of drugs considered dangerous for patients with kidney problems.

b. *Vicarious liability for physician negligence.* In Badal v. Hinsdale Memorial Hospital, 2007 WL 1424205 (N.D.Ill.2007), plaintiff's injured ankle was misdiagnosed by a plan physician as only a "sprain", and he suffered serious injury. The court analyzed ERISA preemption arguments, in light of *Davila*. The court noted that the plaintiff's claims under *Davila* were brought under THCLA, the Texas Health Care Liability Act, and its duties do not arise independently of ERISA or the plan terms. *Davila* was about wrongful denial of benefits. In *Badal,* by contrast, the plaintiff alleged that "[w]hile committing the above acts and omissions, Dr. Lofthouse failed to apply, use or exercise the standard of care ordinarily exercised by reasonably well qualified or competent medical doctors." ... The court noted that the plaintiff was not complaining of the wrongful denial of benefits, quoting the plaintiff: "Plaintiff is asking for damages for the injuries caused, and does not give one iota if it was covered under the plan, or whether it should in the future be covered under some plan[ ]. In short, whether or not it was a violation of ERISA is of no concern to plaintiff."

c. *Negligent Misrepresentation.* In McMurtry v. Wiseman, 445 F. Supp.2d 756 (2006) the U.S. District Court for the Western District of Kentucky held that negligent misrepresentations by an insurance broker that induced the plaintiff to buy disability insurance coverage were not ERISA preempted. The plaintiff claimed that the agent Botts' duty was independent of any duty related to ERISA, and that he, like any insurance agent, had a duty not to negligently misrepresent the terms of the policy and/or fraudulently induce the Plaintiff to purchase the coverage. The court quoted with approval the language of Morstein v. National Ins. Services, Inc., 93 F.3d 715, 723 (11th Cir.1996) "[a]llowing preemption of a fraud claim against an individual insurance agent will not serve Congress's purpose for ERISA. As we have discussed, Congress enacted ERISA to protect the interests of employees and other beneficiaries of employee benefit plans. To immunize insurance agents from personal liability for fraudulent misrepresentation regarding ERISA plans would not promote this objective."

The court held that the plaintiff's claims for "fraud and negligent misrepresentation did not arise directly from the plan, but rather from Botts' inducement to have the Plaintiff join the plan. The legal duty not to misrepresent the plan did not arise from the plan itself, but from an independent source of law; state tort law within Tennessee."

d. *Administrative/Clerical Errors.* In Duchesne–Baker v. Extendicare Health Services, Inc., 2004 WL 2414070 (E.D. La. Oct. 28, 2004), the district court concluded that while Aetna was a defendant in both this action and in *Davila* and each case was removed to federal court, there was no other similarity between these two cases. The court noted that *Davila* fell within the scope of ERISA Section 502(a)(1)(B) because an essential part of the plaintiffs' state law claim in *Davila* required an examination and interpretation of the relevant plan documents. By contrast, the allegation in *Duchesne-Baker* was that the insurance coverage was wrongly terminated due to a clerical error and Aetna failed to exercise due care to correct this error. Thus, the court concluded that, because the allegation did not involve improper processing of a benefit claim and did not otherwise seek enforcement of the plaintiff's rights under the plan or to clarify future right under the plan, the claim in Duchesne–Baker was distinguishable from Davila and, therefore, required remand back to the state court.

3. ERISA was interpreted by the federal courts in the first wave of litigation as totally preempting common law tort claims. See, e.g., Ricci v. Gooberman, 840 F.Supp. 316 (D.N.J.1993); It appeared from this caselaw that any managed care plan that was ERISA-qualified would receive virtually complete tort immunity.

The federal courts began to split, however, as to the limits of such preemption. The result was a litigation explosion against managed care as theories were imported from hospital liability caselaw, fiduciary law, and contract law to use against managed care organizations. Prihoda v. Shpritz, 914 F.Supp. 113 (D.Md. 1996) (ERISA does not preempt an action against physicians and an HMO for physicians' failure to diagnose a cancerous tumor, allowing a vicarious liability action to proceed). See also Independence HMO, Inc. v. Smith, 733 F.Supp. 983 (E.D.Pa.1990) (ERISA does not preempt medical malpractice-type claims brought against HMOs under a vicarious liability theory); Elsesser v. Hospital of the Philadelphia College of Osteopathic Medicine, 802 F.Supp. 1286 (E.D.Pa.1992) (same for a claim against an HMO for the HMO's negligence in selecting, retaining, and evaluating plaintiff's primary-care physician); Kearney v. U.S. Healthcare, Inc., 859 F.Supp. 182 (E.D.Pa.1994) (ERISA preempts plaintiff's direct negligence claim, but not its vicarious liability claim). See generally Barry Furrow, Managed Care Organizations and Patient Injury: Rethinking Liability, 31 Ga. L. Rev. 419 (1997).

Dukes v. U.S. Healthcare, Inc., 57 F.3d 350 (3d Cir.1995) was the watershed case that opened up a major crack in ERISA preemption of common law tort claims. In *Dukes*, the Third Circuit found that Congress intended in passing ERISA to insure that promised benefits would be available to plan participants, and that section 502 was "intended to provide each individual participant with a remedy in the event that promises made by the plan were not kept." The court was unwilling, however, to stretch the remedies of 502 to "control the quality of the benefits received by plan participants." The court concluded that " . . . [q]uality control of benefits, such as the health care benefits provided here, is a field traditionally occupied by state regulation and we interpret the silence of Congress as reflecting an intent that it remain such." The court developed the distinction between benefits to care under a plan and a right to good quality care, holding that " * * * patients enjoy the right to be free from medical malpractice regardless of whether or not their medical care is provided through an ERISA plan." Quality of care could be so poor that it is essentially a denial of benefits. Or the plan could describe a benefit in terms that are quality-based, such as a commitment that all x-rays will be analyzed by radiologists with a certain level of training. But absent either of these extremes, poor medical care—malpractice—is not a benefits issue under ERISA.

Theories of liability based on the organizational structure of health plans were used by most courts to determine what is preempted and what allowed under ERISA. While some meaningful functional distinctions can be made, the courts were not been consistent, and liability was often variable, depending on the court's attitude toward managed care. See Peter J. Hammer, Pegram v. Herdrich: On Peritonitis, Preemption, and the Elusive Goal of Managed Care Accountability, 26 J. Health Pol. Pol'y & L. 767, 768 n.2 (2001). The federal courts were often hostile to managed care plans, and struggled mightily to work around ERISA preemption and allow a common law tort action to go forward.

For an excellent overview of the interaction of ERISA preemption and MCO malpractice liability, see generally Gail B. Agrawal and Mark A. Hall, What If You Could Sue Your HMO? Managed Care Liability Beyond the ERISA Shield, 47 St. Louis U. L.J. 235 (2003). See also Wendy K. Mariner, Slouching Toward Managed Care Liability: Reflections on Doctrinal Boundaries, Paradigm Shifts, and Incremental Reform, 29 J.L. Med. & Ethics 253 (2001) (favoring enhanced liability); David Orentlicher, The Rise and Fall of Managed Care: A Predictable "Tragic Choices" Phenomenon, 47 St. Louis U. L.J. 411 (2003) (analyzing managed care as a device for concealing and avoiding tragic choices in a public forum).

D. CLAIMS AND APPEALS PROCEDURES UNDER ERISA

29 U.S.C.A. § 1133 (§ 503) provides:

In accordance with regulations of the Secretary, every employee benefit plan shall—

(1) provide adequate notice in writing to any participant or beneficiary whose claim for benefits under the plan has been denied, setting forth the specific reasons for such denial, written in a manner calculated to be understood by the participant, and

(2) afford a reasonable opportunity to any participant whose claim for benefits has been denied for a full and fair review by the appropriate named fiduciary of the decision denying the claim.

Rules implementing this statute are currently found at 29 C.F.R. § 2560.503–1.

The Rules require employee benefit plans to "establish and maintain reasonable procedures governing the filing of benefit claims, notification of benefit determinations, and appeal of adverse benefit determinations," and then provide that claims procedures will be considered reasonable only if they comply with specific requirements. Those provisions prohibit, for example, the requirement of the payment of a fee for the filing of an appeal or "the denial of a claim for failure to obtain a prior approval under circumstances that would make obtaining such prior approval impossible or where application of the prior approval process could seriously jeopardize the life or health of the claimant." The regulations prohibit plans from requiring a claimant to file more than two appeals prior to suing under § 502(a), though they do allow plans to interpose an additional opportunity for voluntary arbitration as long as the plan does not require it and any statutes of limitations are tolled while arbitration is pursued. The regulations preclude plans from imposing a requirement of arbitration which is binding and not reviewable under 502(a).

The regulations impose time limits for handling claims and appeals, including a maximum of seventy-two hours for processing "urgent care claims." Pre-service claims must be decided within fifteen days (thought the period can be extended by another fifteen days under certain circumstances) and post-service claims must be decided within thirty days (subject to one fifteen-day extension if necessary due to matters beyond the plan's control). A claim denial must explain the reason for the adverse decision, referencing the plan provision on which the denial is based. If the decision is based on a medical necessity or experimental treatment limitation, "either an explanation of the scientific or clinical judgment for the determination, applying the terms of the plan to the claimant's medical circumstances, or a statement that such explanation will be provided free of charge upon request" must be provided.

Group health plans must provide appeal procedures that "[p]rovide for a review that does not afford deference to the initial adverse benefit determination and that is conducted by an appropriate named fiduciary of the plan who is neither the individual who made the adverse benefit determination that is the subject of the appeal, nor the subordinate of such individual." The rules also provide time frames for appeals, seventy-two hours for urgent care claims, thirty days for pre-service claims (or fifteen days for each stage if two stage appeals are provided), and sixty days for post-service plans. The information that the plan must provide in an adverse appeal decision is similar to that which must be provided under an initial adverse decision.

The rules have their own provision for preemption of state law:

29 C.F.R. § 2560.503–1.

(k) Preemption of State law. (1) Nothing in this section shall be construed to supersede any provision of State law that regulates insurance, except to the extent that such law prevents the application of a requirement of this section.

(2)(i) For purposes of paragraph (k)(1) of this section, a State law regulating insurance shall not be considered to prevent the application of a requirement of this section merely because such State law establishes a review procedure to evaluate and resolve disputes involving adverse benefit determinations under group health plans so long as the review procedure is conducted by a person or entity other than the insurer, the plan, plan fiduciaries, the employer, or any employee or agent of any of the foregoing.

(ii) The State law [external review] procedures * * * [permitted under the regulations] are not part of the full and fair review required by section 503 of the Act. Claimants therefore need not exhaust such State law procedures prior to bringing suit under section 502(a) of the Act.

Finally, the rules also provide a sanction against plans that fail to follow them:

(*l*) In the case of the failure of a plan to establish or follow claims procedures consistent with the requirements of this section, a claimant shall be deemed to have exhausted the administrative remedies available under the plan and shall be entitled to pursue any available remedies to provide a reasonable claims procedure that would yield a decision on the merits of the claim.

Notes and Questions

1. As is discussed in the previous chapter, all states have adopted laws prescribing internal review procedures for health plans, and most require external reviews as well. Are these state law provisions enforceable under this regulation? In what respects does this regulation supplement state law for insured employee benefit plans? Return to the *Problems: Advising Under State Managed Care Law* in the previous chapter. How, if at all, do your resolutions of those problems change if the problem involves the same state law but an insured employee benefits plan? A self-insured plan?

2. Why does the regulation prohibit binding arbitration? Why does it limit plans to two stage appeals? The 1998 proposed regulations prohibited plan provisions that required claimants to submit claims to arbitration or to file more than one appeal. Can you see why these provisions proved quite controversial?

3. Though ERISA itself does not require a claimant to exhaust administrative remedies before pursuing judicial review, every circuit court of appeals has held that exhaustion is necessary. See, e.g. Amato v. Bernard, 618 F.2d 559, 566–68 (9th Cir.1980). Exhaustion is sometimes excused, however, where the claimant can establish futility or denial of meaningful access to plan remedies by a plan's failure to comply with ERISA requirements. See, e.g. Lee v. California Butchers' Pension Trust Fund, 154 F.3d 1075 (9th Cir.1998).

4. Section 502(a) of ERISA, reproduced at the beginning of this chapter, permits a plan participant or beneficiary to sue to "recover benefits due to him under the terms of the plan * * *" in federal or state court. 29 U.S.C.A. § 1132(a)(1). Although on its face this provision permits a suit against a plan for benefits denied, the courts have treated it instead as authorizing a review of the decision of the ERISA plan, i.e. the ERISA administrator is treated as an independent decisionmaker whose decision is subject to judicial review, much like an administrative agency, rather than as a defendant who has allegedly breached a contract. See Semien v. Life Insurance Co. of North America, 436 F.3d 805, 814 (7th Cir.2006); Jay Conison, Suits for Benefits Under ERISA, 54 U. Pitt. L. Rev. 1 (1992).

Firestone Tire & Rubber Co. v. Bruch, 489 U.S. 101, 109 S.Ct. 948, 103 L.Ed.2d 80 (1989), held that the courts should apply de novo review in reviewing ERISA plan decisions. In doing so the Court rejected the "arbitrary and capricious" standard of review generally applied in earlier lower federal court ERISA review cases. The Court went on to observe, however, that arbitrary and capricious review, rather than de novo review, would apply if "the benefit plan gives the administrator or fiduciary discretionary authority to determine eligibility for benefits or to construe the terms of the plan." 489 U.S. at 115, 109 S.Ct. at 957. The Court further stated, however, that if the plan administrator faced a conflict of interest, this should be taken into account in reviewing an administrator's decision.

As this book went to press, the Supreme Court decided MetLife v. Glenn, ___ U.S. ___, 128 S.Ct. 2343 (2008) partially resolving issues left open by *Firestone*. The Court decided that 1) insurers administering ERISA plans and self-insured plan administrators indeed have a conflict of interest, 2) their decisions are still entitled to deferential rather than de novo review, but 3) the conflict must be taken into account as a factor in reviewing a plan determination. The Court suggested that an important consideration in determining the weight to give these factors is the procedures that an administrator had in place to keep the conflict from biasing plan decisions. A vigorous dissent by Scalia and Thomas contended that a conflict was relevant only if the claimant could prove that it resulted in a biased plan determination.

5. Whether or not extracontractual damages can ever be available under ERISA is a question that has provoked considerable controversy. The answer seems to be no, though a good argument can be made that this is not the result Congress intended. In Massachusetts Mutual Life Insurance Co. v. Russell, 473 U.S. 134, 105 S.Ct. 3085, 87 L.Ed.2d 96 (1985), the Supreme Court held that ERISA does not authorize recovery of extracontractual damages by plan participants for breach of fiduciary duty. In Mertens v. Hewitt Associates, 508 U.S. 248, 113 S.Ct. 2063, 124 L.Ed.2d 161 (1993), the Court read provisions of ERISA permitting plan participants and beneficiaries "to obtain other appropriate equitable relief to redress such violations ..." (29 U.S.C.A. § 1132(a)(3)) to not authorize damage actions, as damages are not equitable in nature.

The effect of these cases is that an ERISA participant or beneficiary denied benefits can only recover the value of the claim itself and cannot recover damages caused by the claim denial. Punitive damages are also unavailable against plan administrators and fiduciaries under even the most egregious circumstances. What effect might the lack of this relief have on ERISA fiduciaries and administrators? To what extent might the fact that ERISA permits courts to award attorneys' fees in some cases ameliorate this effect? 29 U.S.C.A. § 1132(g). Would state tort cases against ERISA plan managed care organizations be necessary if more comprehensive remedies were available under ERISA? See, arguing that many of the problems that the courts have encountered in dealing with state claims against ERISA plans could have been avoided had the Court interpreted ERISA's remedial provisions to include broader remedies, John.H. Langbein, What ERISA Means by "Equitable": The Supreme Court's Trail of Error in Russell, Mertens and Great-West, 103 Columbia Law Review 1317 (2003).

Some members of the Court seem to be open to reconsidering this jurisprudence. In *Davila*, Justice Ginsberg, joined by Justice Breyer, suggested in concurrence that the Court should revisit the question:

> The Court today holds that the claims respondents asserted under Texas law are totally preempted by § 502(a) of [ ] ERISA [ ]. That decision is consistent with our governing case law on ERISA's preemptive scope. I therefore join the Court's opinion. But, with greater enthusiasm, as indicated by my dissenting opinion in Great–West Life & Annuity Ins. Co. v. Knudson,[ ], I also join "the rising judicial chorus urging that Congress and [this] Court revisit what is an unjust and increasingly tangled ERISA regime." DiFelice v. Aetna U.S. Healthcare, 346 F.3d 442, 453 (C.A.3 2003) (Becker, J., concurring).

Because the Court has coupled an encompassing interpretation of ERISA's preemptive force with a cramped construction of the "equitable relief" allowable under § 502(a)(3), a "regulatory vacuum" exists: "[V]irtually all state law remedies are preempted but very few federal substitutes are provided."[ ]

A series of the Court's decisions has yielded a host of situations in which persons adversely affected by ERISA-proscribed wrongdoing cannot gain make-whole relief. First, in Massachusetts Mut. Life Ins. Co. v. Russell,[ ], the Court stated, in dicta: "[T]here is a stark absence—in [ERISA] itself and in its legislative history—of any reference to an intention to authorize the recovery of extracontractual damages" for consequential injuries.[ ] Then, in Mertens v. Hewitt Associates,[ ], the Court held that § 502(a)(3)'s term "equitable relief" ... refer[s] to those categories of relief that were typically available in equity (such as injunction, mandamus, and restitution, but not compensatory damages).[ ] Most recently, in Great–West, the Court ruled that, as "§ 502(a)(3), by its terms, only allows for equitable relief," the provision excludes "the imposition of personal liability ... for a contractual obligation to pay money."[ ]

As the array of lower court cases and opinions documents,[ ] fresh consideration of the availability of consequential damages under § 502(a)(3) is plainly in order.[ ]

The Government notes a potential amelioration. Recognizing that "this Court has construed Section 502(a)(3) not to authorize an award of money damages against a non-fiduciary," the Government suggests that the Act, as currently written and interpreted, may "allo[w] at least some forms of 'make-whole' relief against a breaching fiduciary in light of the general availability of such relief in equity at the time of the divided bench." Brief for United States as Amicus Curiae[ ]. * * * "Congress ... intended ERISA to replicate the core principles of trust remedy law, including the make-whole standard of relief."[ ] I anticipate that Congress, or this Court, will one day so confirm.

Seven other justices, of course, were silent on this question, although remedies under ERISA were not at issue in the case. To date, attempts to obtain monetary relief in ERISA actions through traditional equitable remedies such as restitution or surcharge have failed. See Knieriem v. Group Health Plan, Inc. 434 F.3d 1058 (8th Cir.2006).

6. ERISA does not by its terms permit providers to sue plans to collect payments due them for providing services to beneficiaries. Courts have generally rejected the argument that providers are "beneficiaries" under ERISA plans. Pritt v. Blue Cross & Blue Shield of West Virginia, Inc., 699 F.Supp. 81 (S.D.W.Va. 1988). Providers have been more successful in asserting their rights as assignees of participants or beneficiaries, City of Hope Nat. Med. Ctr. v. HealthPlus, Inc., 156 F.3d 223 (1st Cir.1998); Hermann Hosp. v. MEBA Med. & Benefits Plan, 845 F.2d 1286 (5th Cir.1988), though a few courts have held that assignees have no standing to sue as they are not mentioned as protected parties within the statute. Other courts have upheld anti-assignment clauses in plan contracts.

Courts have split on whether providers can recover from insurers when the insurer leads the provider to believe that the insured or the service is covered, and then subsequently refuses payment and claims ERISA protection. Several courts have held that ERISA is intended to control relationships between employers and employees and should not preempt common law or statutory misrepresentation claims brought by providers. Transitional Hospitals Corp. v. Blue Cross & Blue Shield of Texas, Inc., 164 F.3d 952 (5th Cir.1999); Hospice of Metro Denver, Inc. v. Group Health Ins. of Okla., Inc., 944 F.2d 752 (10th Cir.1991). Other courts have held that misrepresentation claims are claims for benefits that are preempted by ERISA. Cromwell v. Equicor–Equitable HCA Corp., 944 F.2d 1272 (6th Cir.1991). Finally, several courts have allowed a provider to sue an ERISA plan on a contract or state statutory claim, stating that the claim was not preempted by ERISA because the provider had no standing to sue under ERISA. See Medical and Chirurgical Faculty v. Aetna U.S. Healthcare, Inc., 221 F.Supp.2d 618 (D.Md.2002), Foley v. Southwest Texas HMO, Inc., 226 F.Supp.2d 886 (E.D.Tex. 2002). See, generally, Scott C. Walton, Note, ERISA Preemption of Third–Party Provider Claims: A Coherent Misrepresentation of Coverage Exception, 88 Iowa L. Rev. 969 (2003).

III. FEDERAL INITIATIVES TO EXPAND PRIVATE INSURANCE COVERAGE: THE HEALTH INSURANCE PORTABILITY AND ACCOUNTABILITY ACT OF 1996 AND THE CONSOLIDATED OMNIBUS BUDGET RECONCILIATION ACT OF 1985

Although ERISA has done much to limit the rights that participants in employee benefit plans might otherwise have had under state law and ERISA's own remedial provisions do not completely fill the void left by preemption, federal law also provides privately-insured individuals some rights that they might not have had under state law. The most important of these are the rights to insurance portability and to freedom from discrimination on the basis of health status provided by the Health Insurance Portability and Accountability Act of 1996 (HIPAA) and the continuation of coverage benefits available under the Consolidated Omnibus Budget Reconciliation Act of 1985, commonly called "COBRA coverage".

HIPAA began as an attempt to enact the least controversial elements of the much more ambitious Clinton health insurance reform proposals of 1993 and 1994. In the end it became a lengthy "Christmas tree" bill addressing a hodge-podge of topics. HIPAA included, for example, major changes in the fraud and abuse laws and tax subsidies for medical savings accounts, discussed elsewhere in this book. It also provided tax incentives intended to encourage the purchase of long term care insurance and the availability of accelerated death benefits for the terminally and chronically ill, and encouraged the creation of state insurance pools to benefit high-risk individuals. In the past few years, HIPAA has been identified predominantly with its privacy provisions, which have provided the statutory underpinnings for far-reaching regulations issued by the Department of Health and Human Services. HIPAA was named, however, after the provisions it included amending ERISA, the Public Health Services Act, and the Internal Revenue Code to increase the portability and accessibility of health insurance, which were initially seen as its most important provisions. HIPAA does this in several ways.

First, HIPAA limits the use of preexisting conditions requirements. Preexisting conditions clauses are commonly used by insurers to limit adverse selection—the tendency of persons who are already ill disproportionately to seek out insurance. HIPAA provides that group health insurers can only impose a preexisting condition exclusion if the exclusion relates to a physical or mental condition for which medical advice, diagnosis, care, or treatment was recommended or received within the six-month period ending on the enrollment date. 29 U.S.C.A. §§ 1181(a)(1), 300gg(a)(1). A preexisting condition exclusion may only last for a maximum period of twelve months (or eighteen months in the case of a person who enrolls in a plan later than the time the plan is initially available to that person, unless the delay was based on the fact that the enrollee was covered under COBRA continuation coverage or as a dependent of another covered person) 29 U.S.C.A. §§ 1181(a)(2), 300gg(a)(2), (f)(1). Moreover, the period during which any such preexisting condition exclusion can be imposed must be reduced by the aggregate of the periods of time that the beneficiary had previously been enrolled under another private or public health plan, (called "creditable coverage" under HIPAA) provided that it has not been more than sixty-three days since coverage under the other policy ended. In other words, if a person who has been insured under a group health plan at one job for twelve months or more moves directly into another job, covered under a different plan, without being uninsured for more than two months between jobs, the new plan cannot impose a preexisting condition exclusion. Preexisting condition clauses cannot be imposed on the basis of a genetic predisposition to a particular condition. They also cannot ordinarily be imposed with respect to newborns, adopted children, or pregnant women.

HIPAA's preexisting conditions limitation was one of its most popular provisions. Why had preexisting conditions clauses been relatively common in insurance policies? What are the distributional effects of preexisting conditions clauses? Why might they be less important to insurers (or employer-financed health plans) in situations where applicants are merely changing insurers (usually incident to a change of jobs) rather than applying for insurance for the first time? Why might insurers and employers prefer a longer preexisting condition exclusion where employees who have previously declined offered insurance change their minds and request it? Why should coverage of pregnancy or of newborn or adopted children be specially excluded from preexisting condition exclusions? Preexisting conditions clauses were, prior to HIPAA, believed to have resulted in "job-lock" because employees could not change employers without losing coverage for "preexisting conditions." See GAO, Employer–Based Health Insurance, High Costs, Wide Variation Threaten System (1992). Does HIPAA adequately address this issue?

HIPAA also imposes several other requirements on ERISA plans. First, it prohibits group health plans from discriminating against individuals in determining eligibility to enroll or in setting premiums on the basis of health status-related characteristics of the insured individual or a dependent of the insured individual, including health status, medical conditions (including both physical and mental illnesses), claims experience, receipt of health care, medical history, genetic information, evidence of insurability (including conditions arising out of acts of domestic violence), or disability. 29 U.S.C.A § 1182(a) & (b).

HIPAA also requires insurers that sell insurance in the individual market to make insurance available to all applicants with 18 months or more of creditable coverage who have lost that coverage and exhausted COBRA coverage (see below) and who have not had a gap of more than sixty-three days between the end of their insurance coverage and their application for extension coverage. Insurers cannot impose preexisting conditions clauses on such individuals, 42 US.C.A. §§ 300gg–41. Insurers do not need to comply with the individual insurance mandate, however, in a state that makes available alternative means of coverage to uninsured individuals. All but seven of the states have chosen to adopt such alternative mechanisms for extending coverage to individuals, thus the federal rules apply in only twelve states. Twenty-eight of the alternative states are using a high-risk pool to provide coverage. Even in the states following the federal rule, there has been evidence of widespread ignorance of HIPAA protections and some indication that HIPAA has been circumvented by insurers who refuse to pay brokers commissions for selling it, delay processing of applications to cause a break in coverage in excess of the sixty-three days permitted by the statute, or suspend issuance of individual policies during the HIPAA implementation period. Even complying insurers have charged very high rates for HIPAA policies, sometimes exceeding 200 percent of the rates charged for non-HIPAA policies. See U.S.General Accounting Office, Health Insurance Standards: New Federal Law Creates Challenges for Consumers, Insurers, Regulators, GAO/HEHS–98–67 (Feb. 1998); U.S. General Accounting Office, Private Health Insurance: Progress and Challenges in Implementing 1996 Federal Standards, GAO/HEHS–99–100 (1999). HIPAA also requires insurers selling insurance in the individual market to renew coverage at the option of the insured at the expiration of a policy, except under certain circumstances as where the insured has failed to pay premiums. 42 U.S.C. 300gg–42.

Finally, HIPAA also requires insurance companies that sell insurance in the small group market to guarantee availability and renewability to all employers who apply for small group coverage, and to all individuals employed by such employers who opt for coverage on a timely basis. 42 U.S.C.A. §§ 300gg–11, 300gg–12. The legislation does not, however, regulate the rates that insurers may charge employers.

The HIPAA requirement of guaranteed issue to individuals supplements the earlier requirements of COBRA. COBRA applies to private employers and state and local government entities that employ twenty or more employees on a typical business day and that sponsor a group health plan. 29 U.S.C.A. § 1161. COBRA protects "qualified beneficiaries" whose group insurance is terminated because of a "qualifying event." Qualified beneficiaries include covered employees (or, in some circumstances, formerly covered employees) and their spouses and dependent children who were plan beneficiaries on the day before the qualifying event. 29 U.S.C.A. § 1167(3). Qualifying events entitling the employee or spouses and dependent children of an employee to continuation coverage include loss of coverage due to the death of the covered employee; termination of the employee's employment or reduction in hours (not caused by the employee's "gross misconduct"); divorce or legal separation of the covered employee from the employee's spouse; eligibility of the employee for Medicare; or the cessation of dependent child status under the health plan. 29 U.S.C.A. § 1163. Filing of bankruptcy proceedings by an employer is a qualifying event with respect to a retired employee (and the employee's previously covered spouse, dependent child, or surviving spouse) if the employee retired before the elimination of coverage and, with respect to the employee's spouse, dependent child, or surviving spouse, where the employer substantially eliminates coverage within one year of the bankruptcy filing. 29 U.S.C.A. § 1163(6).

Qualified beneficiaries are entitled upon the occurrence of a qualifying event to purchase continuation coverage for up to eighteen months where the qualifying event is termination of work or reduction in hours, or for up to thirty-six months for most other qualifying events. 29 U.S.C.A. § 1162(2). The right to continuation coverage may terminate before the end of the coverage period if the employer ceases to provide group health insurance to any employee; the qualified beneficiary fails to make a timely payment of the plan premium; the qualified beneficiary becomes covered under another group health plan that does not exclude or limit coverage for a preexisting condition; or the qualified beneficiary becomes eligible for Medicare. 29 U.S.C.A. § 1162(2)(B), (C), (D).

COBRA offers some enrollees a significant advantage over the individual insurance guarantees of the HIPAA—beneficiaries need only pay a premium which may not exceed 102 percent of the total cost of the plan for similarly situated beneficiaries who continued to be covered. 29 U.S.C.A. §§ 1162(3), 1164. Where the employer is self-insured, the employer may either make a reasonable estimate of plan cost for similarly situated beneficiaries on an actuarial basis or base the premium on the costs of the preceding determination period adjusted for inflation. 29 U.S.C.A. § 1164(2). Who pays for COBRA coverage: employers, insurers, employees or health insurance consumers? Under what circumstances would a person eligible for COBRA coverage be well advised to decline it and rather seek coverage in the nongroup market? Final regulations implementing COBRA, promulgated in 2001, are found at 26 C.F.R. §§ 59.4980B1–B10.

Notes and Questions

1.   Do the following situations involve preexisting condition exclusions subject to HIPAA's limitations? 1) The plan covers cosmetic surgery for accidental injuries, but only for those that occur while the beneficiary is covered by the plan. 2) The plan covers diabetes care without limitations, but imposes a $10,000 lifetime limit on expenditures if the beneficiary was diagnosed with diabetes before joining the plan. 3) Benefits under the plan for pregnancy are only available after a twelve month waiting period. See 26 C.F.R. § 54.9801–3.

2.   Congress for the first time in 1996 adopted limited benefit coverage mandates, including a "drive through delivery" bill requiring health plans to offer at least forty-eight hours of hospital coverage for vaginal deliveries, ninety-six hours for C–Sections; and a mental health parity law forbidding health plans from placing lifetime or annual limits on mental health coverage less generous than those placed on medical or surgical benefits. As this book goes to press, Congress is debating the terms under which mental health parity legislation will be extended. In 1998 Congress adopted the Women's Health and Cancer Rights Act, imposing a third mandate requiring health plans that cover mastectomies to also cover breast reconstruction surgery.

Does the drive through delivery bill address a real or imagined problem? If you were a lobbyist representing health plans, how strenuously would you argue against it? What would be your arguments? What are the likely effects of the mental health parity bill? Why is Congress beginning to impose coverage requirements on health plans? Why were these particular coverage requirements chosen?

Problem: Advising under HIPAA and COBRA

Martha Phillips has recently lost her job at Naturalway.com, a short-lived attempt to sell dietary supplements on the web. She was only with the company for ten months, most of its brief existence. She was covered during the ten month period by Naturalway's group health plan. Martha is experienced with web-based sales, and thinks she will soon be again employed. She is quite concerned, however, because she has chronic diabetes and needs to have health insurance coverage. She asks:

1) Does any federal law give her the right to insurance coverage? If so, what would be the terms of the coverage?

2) If she is able to find employment with health insurance coverage, as she hopes, can she be subjected to a preexisting conditions clause that will exclude coverage for her diabetes?

3) If she is able to find employment with health insurance coverage, can she be charged higher rates than other employees because of her diabetes?

Chapter 9

PUBLIC HEALTH CARE FINANCING PROGRAMS: MEDICARE AND MEDICAID

I. INTRODUCTION

Government provision or financing of health care has a long history in the United States. The first federal medical program was established in 1798 to provide care for sick seamen in the coastal trade. State hospitals for the mentally ill and local public hospitals were well established by the mid-nineteenth century.

Today, government at all levels finances a plethora of health care institutions and programs. In 2006, direct government health care financing programs accounted for $970.3 billion, 46 percent, of total national expenditures on personal health care. The federal government provides health care to millions of veterans in 1400 veterans' hospitals, clinics, and nursing facilities; 5.5 million members of the military and their dependents through the TRICARE program; 1.5 million Native Americans in over 600 facilities run by the Indian Health Service; disabled coal miners through the Black Lung program; and a variety of special groups through block grants to the states for maternal and child health, alcohol and drug abuse treatment, mental health, preventive health, and primary care. States provide health care both through traditional programs like state mental hospitals, state university hospitals, and workers' compensation, but also increasingly through a variety of newer programs intended to shore up the tattered safety net, including insurance pools for the high-risk uninsured, pharmaceutical benefit programs, and programs to provide health insurance for the poor uninsured. County and local governments operate local hospitals. Federal, state, and local governments provide comparatively generous health insurance programs for their own employees and less generous health care programs for their prisoners (the only Americans constitutionally entitled to government-funded health care). If one adds to the cost of direct government health care programs the cost of government employee health benefits and tax subsidies that support private health benefits, tax-financed health care spending in the United States amounts to sixty percent of total health care spending. See Steffie Woolhandler and David Himmelstein, Paying For National Health Insurance—And Not Getting It, Health Affairs, July/Aug. 2002, at 88, 91, 93.

By far the largest public health care programs, however, are the federal Medicare program and the state and federal Medicaid program, which respectively spent about $401.3 billion and $310.6 billion in 2006. This chapter focuses on these two programs, and does not discuss the State Children's Health Insurance Program (SCHIP), established in 1997 to provide health insurance for poor children.

For the past decade, the health care reform debate at the federal level has focused primarily on the future of Medicare and Medicaid. There are several reasons why this debate has focused on these programs and why it has been so passionate and contentious. First, Medicare and Medicaid policy have been driven by federal budget policy. Together the two programs consume over 20 percent of the federal budget. Moreover, if one excludes from consideration the costs of defense, Social Security, and the national debt—all of which are more or less protected from budget cuts at this time—Medicare and Medicaid consume over forty percent of what remains of the federal budget. Medicaid is also one of the largest, and fastest growing, items in state budgets. Congress is very aware of the cost of these programs.

Second, growth in the Medicare program threatens not only to continue to claim a large slice of the federal budget, but also ultimately to overwhelm the financing mechanisms that currently support it. The Part A trust fund (which funds the hospital insurance part of Medicare and is in turn funded by payroll taxes) is currently projected to go into deficit status in 2019. Part B expenditures (which cover the services of physicians and other professionals, as well as other non-institutional care), three quarters of which are covered by federal general revenue funds, are growing even faster than Part A expenditures. The financing of the program is projected to become even more problematic as a huge group of baby-boomers becomes eligible for Medicare in the first half the 21st century. By 2030, Medicare will be responsible for the health care of twenty-two percent of the American population, compared to fourteen percent today. By 2050, moreover, there will be 2.2 workers for every Medicare beneficiary compared to today's 3.8 to one ratio.

Third, debates about how to reform the programs touch repeatedly upon issues that divide policy makers sharply along ideological lines. Can costs be most effectively controlled through regulatory or market strategies? Should Medicare remain available to all beneficiaries equally, or should it be means tested in some way? Should the financing of health care services for the poor be a federal or state responsibility? Should poor persons have an entitlement to health care coverage, or should states have discretion to limit access? Or should the states simply receive block grants from the federal government for health care?

Finally, Medicare and Medicaid together insure about a quarter of the American population, including one of the most politically active segments of the American populace (the elderly). They also affect immediately the fortunes of most health care providers, who are invariably contributors to political campaigns. Politicians are acutely aware, therefore, of the existence and the exigencies of these programs.

To understand the debates raging around these programs, we must first understand how the programs work. Anyone designing or seeking to understand a public health care financing program must consider several basic questions.

First, who receives the program's benefits? Are the targeted recipients characterized by economic need, a particular disease, advanced age, disability, residence in a particular geographic jurisdiction, employment in a certain industry, or status as an enrollee and contributor to a social insurance fund? From these questions others follow: Who in fact receives most of the program's benefits? Whom does the program leave out? Why are some groups included and others excluded? Also, should beneficiaries receive an entitlement or should coverage otherwise be subject to governmental discretion?

Second, what benefits will be provided? Should the program stress institutional services such as hospitalization or nursing home care or non-institutional alternatives such as home health care, or should it encourage preventive care? Should the program be limited to services commonly covered by private insurance like hospital and physician care, or should it also cover services such as dental care and eyeglasses that private insurance covers less often because their use is more predictable and middle class insureds can afford to pay for them out of pocket? These services may be inaccessible to the poor unless the program covers them. Should the program cover medically controversial services, such as care provided by chiropractors or midwives? Should a public program cover socially controversial services such as abortion or treatment for erectile dysfunction? Should it cover services that provide relatively small marginal benefits at a very high cost, such as some organ transplants or some last ditch cancer therapies? Finally, how can the benefits package be kept up to date? In particular, how should it evaluate new technologies as they become available?

Third, how should the program provide or pay for benefits? Should it pay private professionals and institutions to deliver the services, as do Medicare and Medicaid, or should it deliver services itself directly, as does the Veterans' Administration and community health centers? Should it purchase services through "vendor payments" based on cost or charge, as Medicare used to, or through an administered price system, as Medicare does now for most services, or on a capitated basis through managed care plans, as Medicare does through parts C and D and most state Medicaid plans do for many recipients? Alternatively, should beneficiaries simply be given vouchers and be expected to purchase their own insurance in the private market? Should public health insurance programs be defined-contribution or defined-benefit programs? Should recipients be expected to share in the costs through coinsurance or deductibles?

Who should play what role in administering the program? Should the program be run by the federal, state, or local government? Should policy be set by the legislature or by an administrative agency (or by the courts)? Should payments to providers be administered by the government or by private contractors? Should program beneficiaries (or providers) have rights enforceable in court, or should the government retain unreviewable discretion in running the program? If rights are recognized, should these rights be enforceable in state or federal court, or perhaps only through administrative proceedings?

How should the program be financed? Through payroll taxes, income taxes, consumption taxes, or premiums? By state or federal taxes? Should taxes be earmarked (hypothecated) for health care, or should a program be funded through general revenue funds? If premiums play a role, should they be means tested?

This chapter will explore these issues with respect first to the Medicare and then to the Medicaid and SCHIP programs.

As you consider these major questions, keep in mind several other themes. First, notice the fragmentation and disconnectedness of our public health care financing programs. Unlike some other nations, we do not have a single public system creating a safety net for all of society, but rather a patchwork of programs, creating a variety of safety nets, some higher and some lower, many fairly tattered, and none catching everyone. Whom do the safety nets miss? What problems does this fragmented system create? What opportunities does it offer?

Second, notice who, other than covered populations of patients, benefits from federal and state programs. Consider which providers benefit most from public programs. Note the role Medicare and Medicaid have played in financing medical education or in subsidizing rural hospitals and safety net providers, such as inner city hospitals. Consider how providers position their operations to maximize their benefits from public programs, and how the mix of health care services in this country reflects the policies of these programs.

II. MEDICARE

A. ELIGIBILITY

Medicare covers nearly thirty-seven million elderly and 6.6 million disabled beneficiaries, one in seven Americans. Medicare eligibility is generally linked to that of the Social Security program, the other major social insurance program of the United States. Persons who are eligible for retirement benefits under Social Security are automatically eligible for Medicare upon reaching age 65. Spouses or former spouses who qualify for Social Security as dependents may also begin receiving Medicare at 65, as may former federal employees eligible for Civil Service Retirement and Railroad Retirement beneficiaries, 42 U.S.C.A. § 426(a).

Disabled persons who are eligible for Social Security or Railroad Retirement benefits may also receive Medicare, but only after they have been eligible for cash benefits for at least two years, 42 U.S.C.A. § 426(b). The number of disabled persons covered by Medicare is growing rapidly. Benefits are also available to persons who are eligible for Social Security, although not necessarily receiving it, and have end-stage renal (kidney) disease, who may receive Medicare benefits after a three-month waiting period, 42 U.S.C.A. § 426–1. About 350,000 Medicare beneficiaries are eligible for this reason.

Why is Medicare, a social insurance program, only available to the elderly and disabled? Why is it available to all members of these groups, regardless of their income or wealth? Is it a good idea to charge more for program benefits to those who have higher incomes, as does the Medicare Modernization Act which means-tests premiums for Part B? What effect does Medicare have on the workers who support it through their payroll taxes? What effect does it have on the children of Medicare recipients? What effect might it have on the children of Medicare recipients at the death of the recipient? The idea surfaces from time to time of extending Medicare to cover all of the uninsured. Why has this idea not been adopted?

Medicare has been generally successful in assuring broad and equitable access to health care for many who would probably otherwise be uninsured. Almost half of Medicare beneficiaries have incomes of 200 percent of the federal poverty level or less, and sixty percent of elderly Medicare beneficiaries receive at least half of their income from Social Security. When the program began only fifty-six percent of the elderly had hospital insurance and the poor and nonwhite elderly received substantially less medical care than did the wealthier or white elderly. While these disparities have been substantially reduced, problem still remain. In particular, there is a great deal of evidence that racial and ethnic minority Medicare beneficiaries have poorer health status than white beneficiaries, as well as evidence that they receive fewer common medical procedures. See Marian E. Gornick, Effects of Race and Income on Mortality and Use of Services Among Medicare Beneficiaries, 335 New Eng. J. Med. 791 (1996); A. Marshall McBean and Marian Gornick, Difference by Race of Procedures Performed in Hospitals for Medicare Beneficiaries, Health Care Fin. Rev., Summer 1994 at 77 (1994); Bruce C. Vladeck, Paul N. Van de Water, and June Eichner, eds., Strengthening Medicare's Role in Reducing Racial and Ethnic Health Disparities (2006), http://www.nasi.org/publications2763/publications_show.htm?doc_id=410031; Timothy Stoltzfus Jost, Racial and Ethnic Disparities in Medicare: What the Department of Health and Human Services and the Center for Medicare and Medicaid Services Can, and Should, Do, 1 DePaul J. Health Care L. 667 (2005).

B. BENEFITS

1. *Coverage*

The Medicare Hospital Insurance (HI) program, Part A, pays for hospital, nursing home, home health and hospice services. The Medicare Supplemental Medical Insurance (SMI) program, Part B, covers physicians' services and a variety of other items and services including outpatient hospital services, home health care, physical and occupational therapy, prosthetic devices, durable medical equipment, and ambulance services. Medicare covers only 90 days of hospital services in a single benefit period ("spell of illness"*). Each beneficiary also has an extra 60 "lifetime reserve" days of hospital coverage. A one time deductible, set at $1024 in 2008, must be paid each year before hospital coverage begins, and a daily copayment of $256 (in 2008) must be paid after the sixtieth day of hospital care, 42 U.S.C.A. § 1395e. Although the Medicare statute provides for coverage of up to 100 days of skilled nursing care, 42 U.S.C.A. § 1395d(a)(2), the nursing home benefit is intended to cover those recovering from an acute illness or injury and not to cover long term chronic care. Hospice benefits are provided on a limited basis, 42 U.S.C.A. § 1395d(a)(4). Physicians' services are provided subject to an annual deduct-

---

* A spell of illness begins when a patient is hospitalized, and continues until the patient has been out of a hospital or nursing home for at least 60 days. 42 U.S.C.A. § 1345x(a). Thus, a chronically ill person could remain indefinitely in a single spell of illness.

ible of $135 (for 2008) and a twenty percent coinsurance amount. In recent years, Medicare has added many preventive services, including prostate cancer screening; bone mass density measurement; diabetes self-management; mammography screening; glaucoma screening; pap smears; an initial physical examination; cardiovascular screening blood tests; diabetes screening tests; and hepatitis B, pneumococcal, and flu shots.

Leaving aside these preventive services, the Medicare benefits package still closely resembles the standard federal employee or Blue Cross/Blue Shield benefits package available in the mid–1960s when Medicare was established and is thus quite antiquated. It is very different, therefore, from standard benefit packages available today, which are likely to be managed care rather than fee-for-service based, have relatively low fixed-dollar copayments or percentage coinsurance requirements, have variable cost-sharing between in and out-of-plan providers, and have higher catastrophic coverage limits. Medicare's lack of out-of-pocket limits for beneficiary cost-sharing for Part B services and caps on the number of covered days of hospitalization are particularly problematic.

Medicare pays for about forty-nine percent of the health care received by the elderly in this country, while private sources (including both private insurance and out-of-pocket expenditures) pay for thirty percent, Medicaid for fifteen percent, and other sources for the rest. Many Medicare recipients purchase, or more commonly receive as a retirement benefit, Medicare Supplement (Medigap) insurance, which covers their cost-sharing obligations and some services not covered by Medicare. The average Medicare beneficiary spends nineteen percent of household income on medical expenses not covered by Medicare, but the average beneficiary below the poverty level pays thirty-five percent of household income for medical expenses. Medicare accounts for twenty-nine percent of the nation's expenditures for hospital care, twenty-one percent of physician expenditures, and thirty-eight percent of home health expenditures.

Beyond the broad political decisions of what categories of medical care Medicare will finance are the far more numerous decisions as to whether a particular item or service will be covered by Medicare at all or for a particular beneficiary. Decisions as to whether Medicare will finance new technologies are made at different levels.

A beneficiary in need of a noncovered item or service may request a national coverage determination (NCD). 42 U.S.C.A. § 1395ff(f)(4) & (5). CMS must act on the request within ninety days (although if CMS determines that the review will take longer than ninety days, it can simply say so and explain why). CMS also often reviews technologies in response to informal requests from technology manufacturers or from others. In making these decisions, CMS often consults with its Medicare Evidence Development Coverage Advisory Committee (MEDCAC), which consists of 120 health care experts. CMS also commissions extramural technology assessments to be used by the MEDCAC or by itself for evaluating technologies. The procedures followed by CMS in these decisions are described at 42 C.F.R. Part 426, and in Timothy S Jost, The Medicare Coverage Determination Process in the United States, in Timothy S. Jost, ed., Health Care Coverage Determinations: An International Comparative Study, 207 (2004). Technologies may also be evaluated by local

Medicare contractors, which make local coverage determinations (LCDs), valid only in the area covered by the contractor. LCDs are far more common than NCDs, as NCDs tend to be limited to more controversial and expensive technologies. These contractors are usually private insurers (such as Blue Cross plans) that process claims for Medicare so that private entities are essentially deciding what products and services Medicare covers. Manufacturers often attempt to get a technology covered by a number of contractors through LCDs before attempting to get an NCD. See Susan Bartlett Foote, The Impact of the Medicare Modernization Act's Contractor Reform on Fee-for-Service Medicare, 1 St. Louis U. J. Health L. & Pol'y 63 (2007); Susan Bartlett Foote, Focus on Locus: Evolution of Medicare's Local Coverage Policy, 22 Health Aff., July/Aug. 2003, at 137.

Not surprisingly, since there is a great deal of money involved, the Medicare coverage process is highly politicized, and CMS comes under tremendous pressure from the drug and device industry, professional and disease groups (which are often funded in part by industry), and Congress when it denies or threatens to deny coverage for a new technology. Medicare has taken steps to focus the process more on effectiveness review, and thus perhaps to depoliticize it. Under a new guidance issued in July of 2006, Medicare has two tracks for using coverage determinations to review effectiveness. First, it approves some technologies on a "coverage with appropriateness determination" or CAD basis, where additional information will be required at the time of use of the technology to assure clinical appropriateness. Second, some technologies are approved only for use in clinical trials on the "coverage with study participation" track, to further determine effectiveness. Through these processes, coverage is being used to drive research, which in turn can support more accurate coverage determinations process.

A beneficiary adversely affected by an NCD may seek review by the Departmental Appeals Board (DAB), subject to judicial review. 42 U.S.C.A. § 1395ff(f)(1). LCDs may be appealed to administrative law judges, and then further to the DAB. 42 U.S.C. § 1395ff(f)(2). Mediation is also available for disputes involving LCDs. The only persons with standing to appeal a coverage determination are Medicare beneficiaries who need or have received the items or services that are the subject of the coverage determination. 42 C.F.R. § 426.110(1). Contrary to the normal practice in Medicare appeals generally, moreover, a beneficiary appealing a coverage determination may not assign his or her rights to appeal to a provider. 42 C.F.R. § 426.320(b). CMS, however, will give public notice of each complaint, and allow "interested parties" to submit written or brief oral statements as amici. 42 C.F.R. §§ 426.510(f), 426.513. In actual practice, most coverage appeals are sponsored by manufacturers or providers with a stake in the particular technology, but the appeal has to be brought in the name of a particular beneficiary, who will be the identified party of interest in the case.

CMS rules also circumscribe the relief that ALJs may grant in reviewing LCDs or the DAB in reviewing NCDs. The DAB, for example, may not order CMS to add language to an NCD, order CMS to pay a specific claim, set a time limit for CMS to establish a new or revised NCD, or address how CMS implements an NCD. All an ALJ or the DAB can do is hold the determination to be invalid, at which point CMS will ask its contractors to readjudicate the claim without consideration of the LCD or NCD, and to review future claims without using the NCD. 42 C.F.R. §§ 426.455, 426.460, 426.555, 426.560.

In spite of these complex procedures, many coverage decisions in individual cases are in fact made less formally by Medicare's contractors, and are reviewable primarily through the general Medicare appeals process described below. Ultimately, whether any particular service is provided to any particular Medicare beneficiary will depend on the decision of a private Medicare contractor interpreting federal policy as mediated by Medicare regulations, manuals and manual transmittals, regional office instructions, NCDs and LCDs, rumor, and innuendo. This process is attended by a fair bit of inconsistency.

What categories of services should Medicare cover? Should its coverage be identical to employment-related benefit packages, or should it vary in some respects? What items might be more, or less, important to its beneficiary population than to working-age Americans? Should Medicare cover nursing home care—a benefit of obvious interest to the elderly—to a greater extent? Should Medicare take cost into account in setting coverage policy for new technologies? If so, what role should cost play in coverage determinations? Though "added value" is among the criteria that CMS proposed in 2000 for evaluating technologies, Medicare claims not to consider cost explicitly. Is the public interest served by having private "contractors" make many coverage decisions with few opportunities for appeal?

2. *Prescription Drugs*

At the time Medicare was created in 1965, private insurance policies did not generally cover outpatient prescription drugs. Prescription drugs were still relatively affordable and were not as an important part of the management of medical problems as they are today. Not surprisingly, therefore, Medicare did not include a drug benefit. Medicare was expanded briefly to cover prescription drugs by the 1988 Medicare Catastrophic Coverage Act, but the legislation proved intensely unpopular with higher-income beneficiaries who were charged higher premiums. It was repealed in 1989 before it could even be implemented. By the late 1990s, however, sharply escalating drug costs brought a Medicare prescription drug benefit back to the top of the political agenda. Pressure built on Congress to do something.

The national political leadership that took on the challenge of providing a Medicare drug benefit in the early 2000s, however, was very different from that which led the country in 1965 when the Medicare program was established. Whereas the presidency and both houses of Congress were held by Democrats in 1965, the presidency and both houses of Congress were held by Republicans in 2003. Whereas the inspiration for the Medicare program in 1965 had been the Social Security program and social insurance programs like it in other developed countries, the conservative leadership of the Republican Congress in 2003 was enamored with market approaches to providing health care coverage. The 2003 Congress had benefitted heavily from political contributions from drug manufacturers and from insurance and managed care companies, and thus was oriented toward a solution that would help rather than harm these interests. Any drug legislation adopted by Congress, therefore, had to meet several requirements.

First, the program had to be a voluntary program that beneficiaries could choose to join or not to join, like Part B. To encourage voluntary membership, however, the program would have to appeal to beneficiaries who had relatively low drug costs as well as to those with higher costs. Second, it had to be administered by private "prescription drug plans," rather than directly by the government. In particular, administered prices set by the Medicare program, which have been used in other parts of the Medicare program to hold down costs, were not acceptable to the drug companies and not acceptable to congressional leadership. Third, the cost of the program could not exceed $400 billion over ten years. This meant that Medicare beneficiaries would have to continue to bear a considerable share of total Medicare drug costs through cost-sharing obligations and premiums. Finally, the legislation had to provide some relief for the poor from these cost-sharing obligations. Medicare would not continue to be a social insurance program available to all on equal terms, but would become partially means tested.

As negotiations continued through the fall of 2003 between the House and Senate, other decisions were made. Medicare rather than Medicaid would cover the drug costs of beneficiaries eligible for both programs and employers who continued to provide drug benefits for their retirees would receive subsidies for doing so. In November of 2003, Congress, after an all-night session and by the narrowest of margins, adopted a Medicare drug benefit, signed into law by President Bush as Public Law 108–173.

This legislation created a voluntary Prescription Drug Benefit Program, establishing a new Part D of Medicare, which went into effect on January 1, 2006. All Medicare beneficiaries are eligible for the program. Beneficiaries who enroll in Part D pay a premium, the amount of which is basically set at twenty-six percent of the cost of the benefits provided (as calculated using a complex formula). The premiums vary from plan to plan relative to each plan's bid amount, and are increased if the beneficiary receives supplemental benefits. Those who chose not to join the program initially (or when they later become eligible for Medicare or lose drug coverage from some other source) are penalized by having to pay higher premiums. The vast majority of the cost of the program is borne by government, which pays not only three quarters of the premium cost, but also most of the cost of catastrophic coverage (and heavily subsidizes Medicare Advantage plans).

Drug benefits are provided by private Prescription Drug Plans (PDPs), by Medicare Advantage Medicare managed care plans, and by employers who offer drug coverage to employed or retired beneficiaries. Medicare Advantage plans usually offer drug coverage at much lower premiums than free-standing PDPs. The U.S. is divided up into thirty-four PDP regions, and PDPs submit bids to cover these regions. Plans are paid their bid price, adjusted to reflect the risk profile of their members. Each beneficiary must have a choice of at least two PDPs or of one PDP and one Medicare Advantage plan.

Free-standing risk-bearing drug plans did not exist at the time the legislation was adopted. To encourage the creation of such plans and to lure them into the Medicare market, the legislation transferred much of the risk for providing drug benefits to the Medicare program. Even "full-risk" plans in fact only bear risk within "risk corridors." Medicare also provides "reinsurance" at a level of eighty percent to plans for allowable costs of enrollees whose costs exceed the out-of-pocket threshold, described below.

The benefits offered by PDPs vary from plan to plan. "Standard prescription drug coverage" under the legislation is defined largely in terms of cost-sharing obligations. For 2008, "standard" coverage includes a $275 deductible and a twenty-five percent enrollee coinsurance obligation for the next $2235 in drug costs. This relatively generous coverage at the low end is intended to attract relatively healthy beneficiaries to the program. Once total expenditures reach $2510, however, the beneficiary hits the "doughnut hole" and receives no further coverage from the program until he or she has spent $4050 out of pocket (or until total drug costs, including both the beneficiary's and the program's payments, reach $5976.25). At this "out-of-pocket threshold" amount, stop-loss coverage kicks in, and the beneficiary is thereafter responsible for only five percent of further costs (or for a copayment of $2.25 to $5.60 if this is higher).

Though this is "standard coverage," almost ninety percent of plans offer instead "actuarially equivalent" coverage, which in most cases do not have a deductible and have tiered copayments (which differ by whether the beneficiary purchases a generic, preferred multiple source, or other drug) instead of coinsurance. Plans also offer "supplemental prescription coverage" in terms of reduced cost-sharing or access to additional drugs. In any event, plans pass on to the beneficiary the actual prices that they negotiate for drugs, including any discounts, concessions, rebates, or other remuneration, even in situations where no benefits are payable because of cost-sharing obligations.

The legislation provides a number of protections for PDP beneficiaries. PDP sponsors are required to permit the participation of any pharmacy that accepts a plan's terms and conditions, although PDPs may reduce cost-sharing obligations to encourage the use of in-network pharmacies. Plans must secure participation of enough pharmacies in their networks to meet "convenient access" requirements, and may not charge more for using community rather than mail-order pharmacies. PDPs may use formularies (lists of drugs covered by the plan), but a formulary must be based on scientific standards, and must include each therapeutic category and class of covered Part D drugs. Benefits may not be designed so as to discourage enrollment by particular categories of beneficiaries. PDPs must offer grievance and appeal procedures like those available in the Medicare Advantage program, including independent review. A beneficiary may gain access to drugs not included in the formulary or avoid increased cost-sharing for non-preferred drugs only if the prescribing physician determines that formulary or preferred drugs are not as effective for the beneficiary, cause adverse effects, or both. PDP sponsors must be licensed by their state or meet federal solvency requirements. See Geraldine Dallek, Consumer Protection Issues Raised by the Medicare Prescription Drug, Improvement, and Modernization Act of 2003, http://www.kff.org/medicare/upload/Consumer-Protection-Issues-Raised-by-the-Medicare-Prescription-Drug-Improvement-and-Modernization-Act-of-2003.pdf (2004); Vicki Gottlich, Beneficiary Challenges in Using the Medicare Part D Appeals Process to Obtain Medically Necessary Drugs http://www.kff.org/medicare/7557.cfm (2006); Vicki Gottlich, The Exceptions and Appeals Process: Issues and Concerns in Obtaining Coverage Under the Medicare Part D Prescription Drug Benefit, http://www.kff.org/medicare/7433.cfm (2005).

Because the high cost-sharing obligations imposed by the legislation would limit its value to low-income beneficiaries, the Act provides additional assistance for low-income beneficiaries. Persons who are eligible for Medicaid, or whose incomes fall below 135 percent of the poverty level and have resources in 2008 below $6,120 for an individual or $9,190 for a couple receive a subsidy that covers their premium, relieves them from any deductible, and limits their cost-sharing obligations up to the out-of-pocket threshold to $2.25 for generic or preferred multiple source drugs or $5.60 for other drugs. Dual eligibles (persons eligible for both Medicare and Medicaid) with incomes up to 100 percent of poverty level only have to pay $1.05 for generic or multiple source drugs and $3.10 for other drugs, and nursing home residents on Medicaid have no cost-sharing obligations. Persons with incomes between 135 percent and 150 percent of the poverty level and with up to $10,210 in resources for an individual or $20,410 for a couple benefit from a sliding scale premium subsidy, a $56 deductible, and cost-sharing up to the out-of-pocket threshold of $2.25 for generic or preferred multiple source drugs, and $5.60 for other drugs. As of 2007, about 3 to 4.7 million beneficiaries eligible for low income assistance were not receiving it.

The states are required to pay over to the Medicare program a "claw back" amount initially equal to ninety percent of what they would have spent to cover the dual eligibles under the Medicaid program. That amount will be reduced gradually to seventy-five percent after 2015. States may face marginally lower expenses than they would have faced had Medicaid continued to be responsible for these costs, but will have less control over spending.

What effect is this program likely to have on drug prices? PDPs negotiate with drug manufacturers over drug prices, but HHS is prohibited from interfering in these negotiations. Why did Congress choose this approach rather than an administrative price approach, as Medicare uses elsewhere? (The Democratic-controlled Congress elected in 2005 has sought to change this to permit government negotiations, as of this writing without success.) Who has more bargaining power, the federal government or prescription drug plans? Why might PDPs have considerable bargaining power, even though their market share is much less than that of the federal government? What can they do that the federal government cannot? Which approach is in the end more likely to lead to lower drug costs? What other effects might either approach have? What interest groups other than drug companies will benefit from the approach Congress initially chose? Who in particular among Medicare beneficiaries is most likely to benefit from this legislation; who will be least helped by it?

Early results of the prescription drug program were in many respects impressive, although the program remains controversial. Average premiums for 2006 were significantly below the levels initially estimated, and premiums remained low for 2007, although they rose in 2008, in some instances dramatically. Average premium rates are also deceptive, because they include the premiums of Medicare Advantage plans, which are heavily subsidized by Medicare and offer drug premiums much lower than stand-alone drug plans. In 2007, all states except Alaska had at least fifty plans available, and seventeen plans were available nationwide, although only two plans covered forty percent of beneficiaries nationally. By 2007, twenty-four million beneficiaries had Part D coverage, and almost ninety percent of beneficiaries, had some form of drug coverage, though four million beneficiaries remained without coverage. On the other hand, the costs of drugs used by seniors continued to increase significantly and the administrative costs of the program are very high.

See, describing the drug legislation, Richard L. Kaplan, The Medicare Drug Benefit: A Prescription for Confusion, 1 NAELA J. 165 (2005); Kaiser Family Foundation, Fact Sheet: The Prescription Drug Benefit (2008 and updated regularly); and other resources available at the Kaiser Family Foundation website, http://www.kff.org/medicare/rxdrugbenefit.cfm.

Problem: The Medicare Prescription Drug Benefit

Mary Belmont has just become eligible for Medicare and is trying to decide in which Medicare pharmacy benefit plan to enroll. Three options are available in her area. One PDP costs thirty dollars a month and offers the benefits of the standard benefit package, though its formulary does not cover two of the drugs she is currently using, and she would have to switch to drugs that the plan designates as therapeutically equivalent. The second PDP costs only twenty-five dollars a month, has no deductible, offers generic drug coverage in the donut hole and covers all of the drugs that she is currently using, but imposes an actuarially equivalent tiered copayment plan (i.e. it charges higher copays for brand name than generic drugs and even higher copays for non-preferred brand-name drugs) and would require her to pay fifty dollars each for a thirty day supply of two of her drugs. Her third option is a Medicare Advantage plan that covers drugs, and that also has a limited formulary, but that has a 200 dollar deductible for drugs and a tiered copayment formula with a maximum copayment of thirty-five dollars per prescription. To join the Medicare Advantage plan, however, she would have to leave her current primary care doctor, whom she has seen for ten years, because he is not part of the plan's network. The Medicare Advantage plan would only charge a twenty dollars a month premium for drug benefits. The first PDP plan also offers a supplementary drug plan at an additional thirty dollars a month that would reduce her cost-sharing obligations from twenty-five percent to twenty percent for the first $2,000 of coverage, and also cover certain over-the-counter drugs. Which plan should she choose? Should she be grateful for all of these choices?

C. PAYMENT FOR SERVICES

1. Medicare Prospective Payment Under Diagnosis–Related Groups

Congress established the diagnosis-related group (DRG) prospective payment system for hospitals in 1982. A DRG is a means of categorizing patients to reflect relative intensity of use of services. DRG-based payment treats hospitals as coordinating services to produce particular products, such as the diagnosis and treatment of heart attacks, ulcers, or tumors. The DRG system groups patients primarily by principal (admitting) diagnoses, which, together with other factors, are used to categorize patients. The purpose of this analysis is to yield groups of hospital patients, each covered by a distinct DRG, that more or less require the same quantity of medical resources. Once DRGs were defined, Medicare arrayed DRGs by relative intensity of resource consumption, with average resource use defined as a single unit. Thus, for 2007, DRG 75, surgery, major chest procedures, is weighted at 3.0340 (or over three times the average admission cost); DRG 59, tonsillectomy and/or adenoidectomy only on a patient over 17 years of age, at .6831 (a little more than two-thirds average cost).

To determine a hospital's actual payment for caring for a Medicare patient, the relative DRG weight assigned to that patient is first multiplied by standardized amounts for labor, non-labor, and capital costs. The standardized amounts in theory represent the cost to an efficient hospital of an average case. For FY 2007, the standardized amounts for hospitals that complied with performance disclosure requirements was $3,400.13 for labor costs, $1,478.10 for non-labor costs, and $427.38 for capital costs. These amount are multiplied by the DRG weight (e.g. .6831 for tonsillectomy) to achieve the basic DRG reimbursement amount per case.

This basic amount, however, is only the starting point for determining PPS hospital reimbursement. The sum of the product of the DRG weight and standardized amounts (or rather the sum of the products of the total DRG weights of all Medicare cases treated in the hospital during the payment period and the standardized amounts) is adjusted in several respects to determine a hospital's actual PPS payment. Because labor costs vary greatly throughout the country, the labor-related portion of the PPS payment is adjusted by an area wage index factor. PPS payments are further adjusted to recognize the cost of extraordinarily expensive cases, or "outliers." PPS payments are also enhanced to compensate teaching hospitals for the indirect costs of operating educational programs. CMS has also recently adopted a system of "severity adjusted" DRGS which take more account of co-morbidities and complications. Finally, PPS payments are increased or otherwise adjusted to benefit special categories of hospitals, such as disproportionate share hospitals (which serve large numbers of low-income patients, who presumably cost more to treat) or sole-community hospitals (which serve communities distant from other hospitals, and are protected by federal policy). These adjustments can be very important for hospitals in particular situations. Whereas straight unadjusted PPS payment accounts for 91 percent of Medicare payment for non-teaching hospitals, major urban teaching hospitals receive about 32 percent of their PPS payments from disproportionate share and indirect medical education cost adjustments.

A few categories of hospital costs continue to be reimbursed on a cost basis. The direct costs of medical education programs are reimbursed on a pass-through cost basis, as are hospital bad debts related to uncollectible Medicare deductible and coinsurance amounts and a few other miscellaneous expenses.

Any evaluation of DRG–PPS must certainly be mixed. PPS succeeded at its principal goal, limiting the escalation of Medicare expenditures for inpatient care. PPS also resulted in (or at least was accompanied by) a massive shift of care within hospitals from inpatient to outpatient settings or to long-term care units, often located within or owned by the same hospitals that had previously provided inpatient care. A great deal of surgery that used to be done on an inpatient basis, such as cataract surgery, is now done outpatient. PPS payment also encouraged hospitals to find ways to align their interests with those of their doctors, who in the end are responsible for admitting and discharging patients and ordering the tests and procedures that increase hospital costs. This led to many of the restructuring strategies discussed in chapter 11 and questionable incentive schemes discussed in chapter 12. There is also considerable evidence that there has been "DRG creep" over the years, as hospitals have moved to coding cases as more complicated and thus earned higher payment. In its latest rule, CMS has included a 2.4 percent rate reduction as a "behavioral offset" to acknowledge the likelihood that hospitals will inflate coding of case severity as CMS moves to severity-adjusted DRGs.

One apparent effect of DRG reimbursement has been the rise of specialty hospitals. There have always been a few hospitals that specialized in specific conditions, but within the last decade there has been a dramatic upswing in the number of hospitals specializing in cardiac, orthopedic, surgical and women's care. These hospitals are predominantly located in states that do not have health planning programs, and tend to be for profit. Most are owned at least to some extent by the physicians who refer to them. They are less likely to have emergency departments, they treat fewer Medicaid patients, and they derive a smaller share of their revenues from inpatient hospital services than general hospitals. These hospitals also tend to treat patients who are less severely ill than general hospitals, and are on average more profitable than general hospitals. Why would the DRG reimbursement system encourage the growth of such hospitals? See General Accounting Office, Specialty Hospitals: Geographic Location, Services Provided and Financial Performance. GAO–04–167 (2003). Specialty hospitals are further discussed in chapters 11. For good summaries of the literature on the effects of PPS, see the annual Medicare Payment Advisory Commission's Report to Congress on Medicare Payment Policy, filed every March. Earlier sources critiquing PPS and describing its effects include David Frankford, The Medicare DRGs: Efficiency and Organizational Rationality, 10 Yale J. Reg. 273 (1993); David Frankford, The Complexity of Medicare's Hospital Reimbursement System: Paradoxes of Averaging, 78 Iowa L. Rev. 517 (1993).

PPS does not seem to be making much business for lawyers. Most of the important issues PPS raises are not justiciable. Issues raised by PPS are either political questions, such as the standardized amount update level for any particular year, or technical questions, such as how a particular DRG should be weighted or which DRG should be assigned by a hospital to a particular admission. Congress has made it clear that it does not want the courts getting involved in these determinations:

42 U.S.C.A. § 1395ww(d)(7)

There shall be no administrative or judicial review under Section 1395oo of this title or otherwise of

(A) the determination of the requirement, or the proportional amount of any adjustment effected pursuant to subsection (e)(1) of this section [providing for updates in the standardized amount] * * *, and

(B) the establishment of diagnosis-related-groups, of the methodology for the classification of discharges within groups, and of the appropriate weighing of factors thereof * * *

Congress has established a tripartite dialogue among itself, CMS, and the Medicare Payment Advisory Commission (an independent advisory body established to advise Congress through the annual reports mentioned above and special reports), to determine these questions and has left no place for the courts. See Timothy Stoltzfus Jost, Governing Medicare, 51 Admin. L. Rev. 39 (1999); Eleanor Kinney, Making Hard Choices Under the Medicare Prospective Payment System: One Administrative Model for Allocating Resources under a Government Health Insurance Program, 19 Ind. L. Rev. 1151 (1986). Such Medicare provider payment litigation as continues under DRG–PPS consists primarily of fact-intensive disputes entailing particular providers, such as whether a hospital qualifies for special treatment under PPS as a disproportionate share hospital. See North Broward Hosp. Dist. v. Shalala, 172 F.3d 90 (D.C.Cir. 1999).

Insofar as PPS generates work for lawyers, it is primarily in the area of advising clients how to take advantage of PPS. Consider the following problem:

Problem: PPS

You are the in-house counsel for a large urban hospital that has a high percentage of Medicare patients. In recent years your hospital has either lost money or barely broken even. At the request of the hospital's CEO, you are serving on a committee considering how to improve the financial situation of the hospital, focusing particularly on your situation with respect to Medicare.

What strategies might be available for increasing your hospital's PPS revenues? Would changing your case-mix help? How might you achieve that? What opportunities might be available in terms of how discharges are coded? (Reconsider this question after you study Medicare fraud and abuse in chapter 14). What possibilities are available under Medicare prospective payment for increasing your Medicare payments that are not strictly tied to your case-mix? How does the teaching mission of your hospital affect your Medicare reimbursement? How might you go about increasing your Medicare reimbursement for non-inpatient services?

Alternatively, how might you go about lowering the cost of treating Medicare patients? In particular, what strategies can you use to create incentives for your doctors to reduce costs? (See chapters 11 and 12 for further discussion of these strategies.) Will cost reductions be accompanied by Medicare payment reductions?

2. Medicare Payment of Physicians

Medicare Part B payment for most services (including physician services) was based initially, at least in theory, on reimbursement of actual charges (minus deductibles and coinsurance). A number of concerns, however, including the rapid rise in the cost of physician services, increasing "balance-billing" to beneficiaries, and inequities in payments among medical specialties, led to consensus that payment reform was needed. In 1989 a political consensus came together around a package of reforms that were enacted by the Omnibus Budget Reconciliation Act of 1989 and codified at 42 U.S.C.A. 1395w–4(a) to (j).

At the heart of the payment reform was the creation of a physician fee schedule. As with Part A prospective payment, fees are determined by multiplying a weighted value (in this case representing a medical procedure rather than a diagnosis) times a conversion factor, which is adjusted to consider geographic variations in cost. Relative value units (RVUs) are assigned to procedures based on the CMS Common Procedure Coding System (HCPCS) and AMA Common Procedural Terminology (CPT) codes. The Relative Value Scale consists of three components: a physician work component, a practice expense component, and a malpractice component. Thus, for example, for CPT 45378, "diagnostic colonoscopy" under the proposed rule for 2008, the work RVU is 3.69; the practice expense RVU is 6.35 if the procedure is done in a physician's office; and the malpractice RVU is .30.

The physician work component is based on estimates of the relative time and intensity of physician work involved in delivering specified services. With respect to major surgeries, physician work is defined globally to include preoperative evaluation and consultation (inpatient or outpatient), beginning with the day before surgery, and post-operative care for a normal recovery from surgery for the ninety days following the surgery.

The practice expense component accounts for physician overhead, including rent and office expenses. The practice expense is based on resource use. Different practice expense RVUs are applied depending on whether the services are furnished in a facility (hospital, SNF or ASC) or in a physician's office. Malpractice expenses for particular services are separated out from other practice expenses, and are based on the malpractice expense resources required to furnish the service.

The RVUs are adjusted by a geographic practice cost index (GPCI) to recognize differences in cost in various parts of the country and then multiplied by a conversion factor to reach a final fee payment amount (of which Medicare pays eighty percent, the other twenty percent representing the beneficiary coinsurance obligation). While most practice expenses are fully adjusted for geographic variation, physician work is only adjusted for one quarter of the variation, which offers some incentive for physicians to work in rural areas. The RBRVS system also provides special bonuses for physicians working in health practitioner shortage areas and for physicians working in rural areas. Rates are also adjusted downward for physicians who are not participating providers (i.e., who do not accept assignment for the claims of all of their Medicare patients).

While the resource-based prices set by RBRVS addressed the problem of price inflation in physician payment, previous attempts to control prices through fee freezes had been defeated by providers simply increasing the volume of their services. To address this problem, the 1989 legislation established the Medicare Volume Performance Standard (MVPS), which represented Congress's attempt to create a global budget for physician expenditures. The volume performance adjustment in RBRVS failed to achieve its goal, and in the 1997 Balanced Budget Act Congress abandoned the MVPS in favor of a "sustainable growth rate," applicable to all specialties and based on growth in the real gross domestic product and increases in Medicare population and coverage. 42 U.S.C. § 1395w–4(f). Congress has repeatedly intervened, however, to provide physicians price increases above those indicated by this formula, assuring an increase in price even while the volume of services continues to increase.

Problem: Resource–Based Payment for Lawyers

It has recently become apparent to Congress that the high cost of legal services is having a substantial negative effect on the American economy and on our international competitive position. Congress also becomes concerned that there are gross and irrational disparities among the payments lawyers receive for legal services. Congress, therefore, proposes the adoption of a resource-based relative value schedule, limiting lawyers to the charges allowed by such a schedule (plus 15 percent where the client agrees). Adherence to the charges is enforced by criminal laws plus civil penalties ($5000 per infraction).

Legal services for representing corporations in corporate takeovers and tax and securities work and for representing individuals in estate planning, domestic relations, real estate transactions or criminal defense matters, will all be evaluated considering the (1) time, (2) mental effort and judgment, and (3) psychological stress involved in delivering each service.* Geographic variations in practice overhead will also be recognized in fee-setting, though historic geographical variations in payments for the work of lawyers will be recognized only to a very limited extent (i.e., a lawyer will be paid for his or her own work—as opposed to overhead—the same payment for similar work whether it is performed in Manhattan or in Peoria). No explicit recognition will be given in the fee schedule for experience, skill, or law school class standing of individual practitioners.

How might such a fee schedule affect access to legal services? The volume of legal services provided? The geographic and specialty distribution of lawyers? The quality of legal services? Innovation in developing new legal theories? Your plans after law school? How hard you study for the final in this class?

Where does the analogy between this problem and RBRVS break down? How, that is, does the market for physician services differ from the market for legal services?

3. Pay for Performance

Even though DRG–PPS and RB–RVS moved Medicare payment toward rewarding efficiency in service delivery, they still basically pay simply for providing a service and do little to recognize the quality of the service provided. In recent years, however, Medicare has begun to move towards paying for the quality of services with "pay for performance" or P4P programs. Medicare has already implemented two programs for hospital payment that link payment to quality measures–the Hospital Quality Initiative in which hospitals are given a small payment for reporting their performance on 10 quality measures, and the Premier Hospital Quality Incentive Demonstration, under which almost 300 hospitals are competing for incentive payments based on their performance with respect to thirty-four quality measures. Medicare has also begun to implement its first P4P project for physicians, the physician group practice demonstration project, in which ten large group practices will be able to earn performance-based payments by achieving quality and cost-saving goals. Two other physician P4P demonstration pro-

---

* These factors plus technical skill and physical effort are all considered in setting the physician RBRVS, see William Hsaio, et al., Estimating Physicians' Work for a Resource–Based Relative–Value Scale, 319 New Eng. J. Med. 835 (1988). Unless the additional physical exertion on the golf course consumed in soliciting corporate clients is considered, this latter factor does not seem relevant to legal services.

jects were authorized by the Medicare Modernization Act. Finally, CMS has announced that beginning in October, 2008 it will not pay hospitals for preventable errors.

On its face, P4P seems like a good idea. It hardly makes sense to reward nonperformance or poor performance. High quality care is something that Medicare should be prepared to pay for. Despite the obviousness of P4P, it has not been greeted universally with open arms. The main objections to P4P group into two general categories—technical or mechanical objections on the one hand, and philosophical or policy objections on the other.

An initial technical problem is what performance we want to pay for. This breaks down into a number of subsidiary questions. To begin, how many measures should be used? The answer to this seems to be enough to encourage a range of behavior, but not so many as to create an excessive burden on providers. Most programs seem to settle on one dozen to three dozen measures.

Not only is the number of indicators important, the specific indicators that are picked are obviously vital as well. First, and most important, they should be indicators that in fact correlate with high quality care across the board, if it is possible to identify such indicators. One of the most serious problems with P4P is that if it pays professionals and providers to do certain things, they will place a priority on doing those things, in all likelihood at the cost of doing other things. But the things for which providers are not paid (often because these things are difficult to measure) may in fact be the most important determinants of quality. On the other hand, providers can only be paid for performance that can be measured. This means that P4P programs must usually start with data that are already available, or can feasibly be assembled. The data most readily available are administrative data, such as claims data, which are already collected and reported. But these data were not collected to measure quality, but rather for other purposes, usually for payment. These data may overcount some activities but will almost certainly undercount others. The alternative is glean information for the particular purpose of quality reporting from medical records. But medical record abstraction is costly, in particular for the majority of providers who do not have electronic medical records.

Another question most often raised with respect to indicators is whether to look at structure, process, or outcome, using the typology established years ago by Avedis Donabedian. The advantages and disadvantages of each are discussed in Chapter One. Structure is easiest to measure but least predictive of quality. Process is usually more easily measured than outcome, but is only important if it leads to good outcomes. Before too much is paid for process performance, therefore, some certainty is needed that the processes being rewarded are in fact likely to result in the outcomes desired. Outcome measures, on the other hand, are often not feasible for use as quality indicators. Outcomes are often not fully known until long after a medical intervention takes place, and when they occur often are difficult to attribute to a particular medical intervention, particularly if the patient has been treated by a number of providers. Attributing success or failure in the treatment of patients with chronic diseases who are not receiving treatment from an integrated health care system is difficult, if not impossible. Moreover, humans are infinitely variable, and often respond in very different ways to the same interventions. It is not fair to hold providers accountable for results that they cannot influence or determine. It is tempting to rely on surrogate or intermediate outcomes when it is difficult to perceive and measure final outcomes, but these may not be sure markers of final outcomes.

Yet another consideration in measuring outcomes is sample size. If a provider treats only a few Medicare patients or only a few patients to which a particular indicator is relevant during a measurement period, the provider's outcomes may not establish any reliably measured pattern. Random variation may become the most important driver of outcome. Medical data privacy is another consideration that becomes particularly salient with small providers or sample sizes. Yet another problem for small providers may be lack of infrastructure to report necessary data. It is not accidental that Medicare's first P4P program for physicians involves large, technically sophisticated, group practices. Moving P4P to solo or small practices will be very challenging, both for Medicare and for the practices.

A final problem with using outcomes is that they only make sense if results are risk-adjusted. Obviously, outcomes are likely to be worse for patients who are in worse condition ab initio. The easiest way for a provider to achieve great outcomes, therefore, might be to avoid the sickest or most at risk patients. This might not be an entirely bad thing–there are probably many procedures being done today on patients who are not good candidates for them–but on the whole it is not a good idea to reward providers for avoiding high-risk patients.

Even more important, there is considerable evidence that severity of some medical conditions correlates with racial and ethnic or socio-economic status (SES). Providers may also fear, justifiably or otherwise, that some minorities or persons of lower SES may find it more difficult to comply with medical regimens. It is well established that racial and ethnic minorities already receive disproportionately less and worse care under Medicare, and it would be a great tragedy if our attempts to improve quality exasperated these disparities. See Lawrence P. Casalino and Arthur Elster, Will Pay-for-Performance And Quality Reporting Affect Health Care Disparities? Health Aff. Web Excl., April 10, 2007.

Once we determine what we want to measure and reward, we need to determine what benchmarks to use for measurement. One goal would be to shoot for six sigma quality, essentially perfection. For most services perfect outcomes are not a realistic expectation. Rather, realistic goals must be set for the best levels of achievement that can be hoped for. If levels are set too high, few will achieve them, and others may become discouraged and not even try. But if levels are set too low, all may achieve them, and the incentives may fail in their original purpose. P4P may end up rewarding mediocrity and simply adding cost to the system. Even benchmarks set relatively high may end up providing considerable rewards to already high-achieving providers who simply maintain the status quo.

Another major risk of paying for performance is that it is likely to have undesired effects on provider behavior. It is likely that the first result of paying for performance will be that it will improve reporting of whatever performance is paid for. Events that previously went unnoted will now be meticulously recorded and reported, because something now turns on them. This will be true not just for the actual indicators measured, but also for any other data that feeds into the P4P system, such as risk-adjustment factors. Of course, increased recording and reporting may be good thing, but it is far from costless and gathering and processing this additional information must be taken into account as one of the costs of P4P.

Not only will data be reported more frequently, however, it will also inevitably be manipulated. Of course, some reporting may be fraudulent, and once the false claims act and qui tam statute kick in and the HHS Office of Inspector General (OIG) and Department of Justice come down hard on a few violators, behavior may improve. Much reporting, however, will simply be creative rather than fraudulent, particularly once coding consultants get involved, and reporting will be difficult, and costly, to police. Not only is reporting subject to manipulation, however, so are patients. If performance is measured by, for example, length of time to discharge or to return to work, patients may be discharged or returned to work prematurely. Under a worst case scenario, infections or bed sores may not be noted, or perhaps even treated, if providers are rewarded for their absence.

These are some of the technical problems presented by P4P, but P4P also raises important policy, even philosophical questions, which must also be addressed. First, and most practically, P4P measures tend disproportionately to address underuse of services. Rewards are often directed, for example, at providing preventive services. As long as Medicare basically pays for services on a fee-for-service or per-admission basis, however, addressing underuse is going to result in increased costs for the entire system. A second cost consideration is that P4P may end up rewarding providers for behavior that does not in fact cause them to incur additional costs. Medicare may end up simply paying more for the same services it now gets (though hopefully of better quality). Better quality care may cost more, but it also may cost the same or even less. Given the limited funds available to Medicare, does it make sense to pay providers more if the increased funds simply go into additional profit?

Another fundamental issue that must be considered is the relationship between incentives and behavior. P4P is based on underlying rational choice assumptions that if Medicare can just get incentives right behavior will follow. The relationship between incentives and behavior is often, however, complex. An initial problem here is the incredibly complex nature of Medicare payment. DRG–PPS and RBRVS are trying to do a lot of things, from providing incentives for medical education, to serving rural areas, to recognizing the higher costs of institutions that provide services to the uninsured. Simply adding a small incremental payment for performance on top of the already large amounts Medicare is paying based on other considerations may not have much of an effect on performance. Of course, Medicare payment incentives must also be considered in the context of all of the other incentives providers face. The cost of compliance relative to its reward will be a key factor here. How much of a provider's practice is paid for by Medicare, as opposed to how much is paid for by other payers, could make an important difference. Noneconomic incentives affect behavior as well, and while these can be expected to reinforce P4P, this may not always be the case.

P4P explicitly highlights the problem of competency. If the standards Medicare comes up with for P4P are valid and realistic, but some providers are not reaching them, should Medicare beneficiaries be exposed to those providers? Why should Medicare continue to pay incompetent providers at all? Does it have an obligation to protect beneficiaries from them? Should tax dollars be used to purchase substandard care? Also, if providers who do not merit P4P disproportionately serve the poor or minorities, does Medicare have an obligation to get other providers to serve these populations?

There is also the problem of rewarding professionals to simply do what professionals ought to do. Should a doctor be paid significantly more for doing what the doctor would be doing anyway if the doctor were competent? Is payment, moreover, the most important motivation for professionals? And if so, should we focus on bonuses for good quality care or penalties for poor quality care (as in not paying for costs attributable to medical errors)? What should motivate health care professionals?

Indeed, one must wonder what P4P will do to the doctor-patient relationship. Many outcomes and processes depend on patient, and for that matter family, cooperation. What will happen to professional/patient relationship if a physician's payment depends on patient's behavior? Will doctors be discouraged from caring for noncompliant or difficult patient? But "compliance" is in one sense another way of describing patient preferences. Should a doctor be penalized if his or her patients strongly object to vaccinations? On the other hand, should patients also share in compensation if their behavior is key? Should we pay patients for having screening tests done or for receiving preventive services?

Moreover, paying hospitals for performance presumes that they are in turn capable of getting the professionals that practice within them to improve performance. What problems might hospitals face in creating incentives for those professionals? See William H. Thompson, Aligning Hospital and Physician Incentives in the Era of Pay-for-Performance, 3 Ind. Health L. Rev. 327 (2006).

Is P4P, after all, a good idea? See, arguing for P4P, Robert Berenson, Paying for Quality and Doing it Right, 60 Wash. & Lee L. Rev 1315 (2003), and taking a more negative view, Bruce Vladeck, If Paying for Quality is Such a Bad Idea, Why is Everyone for It? 60 Wash. & Lee L. Rev. 1345 (2003) and Michael Cannon, Pay for Performance: Is Medicare a Good Candidate? 7 Yale J. Health Pol'y, L. & Ethics 1 (2007). Finally, see, examining the theoretical basis of P4P, William M. Sage, Pay for Performance: Will it Work in Theory? 3 Ind. Health L. Rev. 305 (2006).

Problem: Pay for Performance

You are working for CMS and have been asked to design a pay-for-performance incentive program for Medicare. The system will redirect five percent of physician payments to reward high quality care. What measures of performance will you recommend, and how many of them? Will you focus on rewarding the absolute level of performance or improvement in performance from current levels? How will you assure that your system does not penalize physicians who care for high-risk patients or racial and ethnic minority patients? How will you assure that the data on which payment is based is accurate? How will you reduce the payments that physicians would otherwise receive to make sure that the program does not increase Medicare expenditures?

4. *Medicare Managed Care*

Samuel Johnson observed that remarriage evidences the triumph of hope over experience. The same can certainly be said of the Medicare Advantage program. Medicare Advantage (MA) is the name that Congress gave the former Medicare + Choice program in the Medicare Prescription Drug, Improvement, and Modernization Act of 2003 to give that failed program a fresh start. Congress evidently learned its own lessons from the failure of the Medicare + Choice program, and tried to respond to them in this legislation. These are:

1. *Medicare managed care cannot compete with traditional fee-for-service Medicare on a level playing field.* Unless Congress is willing to pay Medicare managed care plans at rates substantially in excess of the cost of traditional Medicare, private managed care plans will not join and stick with the program. Congress had raised rates for Medicare + Choice plans in 1999 and again in 2000, but plans kept leaving the program. The 2003 legislation lavishes money on Medicare managed care plans. Medicare payments for MA plans are established under a complex procedure that combines bidding and benchmark formulas, keyed to fee-for-service payments. They are too complex to explain here. See Mark Merlis, Medicare Advantage Payment Policy (2007), http://www.nhpf.org/pdfs_bp/BP_MAPaymentPolicy_09-24-07.pdf. The formulas, however assure that MA plans are paid at least as much as Medicare would have paid under the traditional Medicare program for a particular beneficiary, and often far more.

Other aspects of the Medicare law further guarantee MA plans rates of payment significantly greater than the costs of traditional Medicare for caring for the same beneficiaries. First, traditional Medicare, as noted above, is required to make some payments that are not directly linked to the cost of caring for Medicare beneficiaries, such as payments for direct and indirect medical education costs and disproportionate share hospital payments, or special payments to rural providers. MA rates are reduced to exclude direct medical education costs, but otherwise are not modified to reflect payments made by traditional Medicare for non-Medicare purposes, even though MA plans do not have to cover these costs when they make payments to providers. Second, although payments to MA plans are supposed to be risk-adjusted to take into account the fact that Medicare managed care beneficiaries are usually younger, healthier, and less expensive than beneficiaries who stay with traditional Medicare, risk adjustment is far from an exact science. In fact, MA plans have received payments substantially in excess of the cost of traditional Medicare because they draw a healthier population. In 2005, every plan in the country was paid more than its enrollees would have cost in traditional Medicare (12.4 percent more on average), for a total of $5.2 billion, $922 per enrollee. Brian Biles, et al., The Cost of Privatization: Extra Payments to Medicare Advantage Plans–Updated and Revised (Commonwealth Fund Issue Brief, Nov. 2006). The Medicare Payment Advisory Committee estimated in 2007 that leveling the playing field so that MA plans were paid the same amount per beneficiary as traditional Medicare paid would save the program $54 billion over five years, $149.1 billion over ten years. See also,

Robert A. Berenson & Melissa A. Goldstein, Will Medicare Wither on the Vine? How Congress Has Advantaged Medicare Advantage—And What's a Level Playing Field Anyway?, 1 St. Louis U. J. Health L. & Pol'y 5 (2007); GAO, Medicare Advantage: Increased Spending Relative to Medicare Fee-for-Service May Not Always Reduce Beneficiary Out-of-Pocket Costs, GAO-08-359 (Feb. 2008).

2. *Managed care plans will not serve large areas of the country unless they receive even greater incentives.* Prior to the MMA, Medicare managed care had never reached large parts of the country, particularly rural areas and areas where the low cost of traditional Medicare led to low Medicare managed care rates. The MMA, however, encouraged the creation of regional or national MA PPO plans to fill this gap, and offered them significant financial incentives.

Even more successful in reaching rural areas, however, have been "private fee-for-service" (PFFS) plans which were created by the 1997 Balanced Budget Act but were offered more favorable payment rates by the MMA, which essentially treats them as managed care plans. PFFS plans offer essentially the same benefits and free choice of provider as does traditional Medicare, but also may provide Part D drug benefits and catastrophic coverage. Medicare providers are not required to participate in PFFS plans, but if they accept PFFS beneficiaries, they cannot bill more than they would bill under traditional Medicare. Because PFFS plans offer essentially the same providers as traditional Medicare without managed care restrictions, and because they usually offer additional benefits to those offered by traditional Medicare, they have grown very quickly, 535 percent from December 2005 to February 2007. By early 2007, they covered 1.34 million beneficiaries, including many enrollees in rural areas. PFFS plans, however, were paid in 2006 119% of the local costs of traditional Medicare, making them far more profitable than other MA plans, even before adjusting for the fact that PFFS plans are probably attracting healthier beneficiaries. Unless one believes as a matter of faith that choice is in itself very valuable, it is hard to see what the added value was received for these extra payments. See Jonathan Blum, Ruth Brown, and Miryam Frieder, An Examination of Medicare Private Fee-for-Service Plans (Kaiser Family Foundation, March 2007).

3. *Medicare can be nudged towards managed competition, but not too quickly or overtly.* Under the scheme set out in the MMA, beginning in 2010, a "comparative cost adjustment" program will be implemented that for the following six years will expand direct competition between MA plans and traditional Medicare. The program will be implemented only in six sites where MA market penetration is at least twenty-five percent and at least two MA plans are available. In these areas, Part B premiums would be reduced or raised depending on whether traditional Medicare costs more or less than MA plans. Traditional Medicare will have to compete with a handicap, as it has to cover some costs MA plans do not. Traditional Medicare is likely also to be hindered in the competition by being burdened with more costly beneficiaries.

Direct competition between traditional Medicare and MA plans proved to be one of the most controversial provisions of the MMA. It should be noted, however, that Medicare managed care plans have always been in competition with traditional Medicare. The comparative adjustment project only raises the possibility that Medicare beneficiaries who stick with traditional Medicare may face increases in their Part B premiums, and not just the loss of additional benefits or lower premiums that they might gain by switching to

MA plans. The real problem, however, is the terms of the competition, which unfairly burden traditional Medicare and favor MA plans.

Indeed, the most striking feature of the Medicare Advantage program is the irony that the legislation should have acknowledged so openly—indeed embraced—the fact that Medicare managed care, which has long been looked to by market advocates as the salvation of the Medicare program, simply costs more than traditional Medicare.

4. *If they receive high enough subsidies, Medicare private plans can offer beneficiaries generous coverage, and therefore become very popular with beneficiaries.* Some of the excess payments will be kept by MA plans to cover their high expenses and as profits. But some must also, under existing law, be returned to beneficiaries in the form of enriched benefits or lower premiums or cost-sharing. This has allowed MA plans to lure many beneficiaries away from traditional Medicare by offering generous benefits at low premiums. In particular, MA plans offer drug benefits at much lower premiums than stand-alone PDP plans. As of April, 2007, 8.5 million beneficiaries were enrolled in MA plans, up from 5.3 million in 2003. The question remains, of course, why not use the extra money that MA pays for MA plans to make additional benefits available or to lower premiums for all Medicare beneficiaries?

If managed care does not save money, of what use is it? An analysis of the Medicare + Choice program by a distinguished study panel acknowledged that the program has not saved money for Medicare, but also concluded that:

> Access to coordinated care plans has allowed some beneficiaries to reduce significantly the burden of paperwork and improve their financial security. In addition, coordinated care plans have improved diagnosis of illness and reduced disparities related to race and income for preventive services.

The Report also contended that managed care has the potential to save money for Medicare, though this potential has not yet been realized. See Kathleen M. King and Mark Schlesinger, eds., Final Report of the Study Panel on Medicare and Markets–The Role of Private Health Plans in Medicare: Lessons from the Past, Looking to the Future (2003), available at http://www.nasi.org/publications2763/publications_show.htm?doc_id=197700.

Another argument made vociferously during the 2007 debate on cutting MA funding was that MA plans favor minorities and low income beneficiaries. See America's Health Insurance Plans, Low Income and Minority Beneficiaries in Medicare Advantage Plans (February 2007); Adam Atherly and Kenneth Thorpe, Value of Medicare Advantage to Low–Income and Minority Beneficiaries (Blue Cross and Blue Shield Ass'n, 2005). Indeed, during the 2007 MA subsidy debate, the NAACP and League of United Latin American Citizens opposed cuts. In fact, the data show that very low income beneficiaries overwhelmingly are covered by Medicaid and traditional Medicare, high income beneficiaries tend to have retiree coverage or traditional Medicare supplemented by Medigap, but that beneficiaries with low to middle incomes tend disproportionately to sign up for Medicare Advantage. This group includes many minority beneficiaries, but on balance minorities are as likely to enroll in Medicare Advantage as whites (though much more likely to receive Medicaid). The larger question, of course, is whether the high costs paid for MA are justified by whatever advantages it offers to minority beneficiaries.

Are there any other arguments for Medicare managed care? Are there other explanations as to why it has proved so popular with lawmakers?

D. ADMINISTRATION AND APPEALS

We have already discussed procedures that Medicare makes available for appealing national or local coverage determinations and managed care plan decisions. Most Medicare decisions, however, involve individual cases in which a Medicare contractor decides that care provided to a particular beneficiary in a particular instance is not covered. This Medicare appeals process was dramatically changed by sections 521 and 522 of the Medicare, Medicaid and State Children's Health Insurance Program Benefits Improvement and Protection Act of 2000, or BIPA (which amended 42 U.S.C.A. § 1395ff). These provisions of BIPA established a uniform appeals process for Part A and Part B. This five-step appeal process begins with the initial contractor determination. A beneficiary aggrieved by such a decision must request a redetermination by the contractor within 120 days (42 U.S.C.A. § 1395ff(a)(3)). A beneficiary dissatisfied with this redetermination may then request a reconsideration (42 U.S.C.A. § 1395ff(b)(1)(A)). This reconsideration is handled by a new group of twelve "qualified independent contractors" (QICs), private entities with which Medicare contracts to make these decisions. (42 U.S.C.A. § 1395ff(b)(2) & (c)). A beneficiary who remains dissatisfied may appeal to an Administrative Law Judge (ALJ) if the claim involves $100 or more, then to the Medicare Appeals Council (MAC) of the Departmental Appeals Board (DAB), and finally, if the claim involves $1000 or more, to the federal district court (42 U.S.C.A. § 1395ff (b) & (d)).

BIPA imposes time limits at every step of the review process, thirty days at the contractor and QIC level, ninety days at the ALJ and MAC level. (42 U.S.C.A. §§ 1395ff(a)(3)(C)(ii); (c)(3)(C), (d)). (The 2003 MMA extended the deadlines to sixty days at the contractor and QIC level). BIPA also provides for expedited (seventy-two hour) reconsideration where a provider plans to discharge a patient or to terminate services where the failure to provide the services is likely to put the beneficiary's health at significant risk. 42 U.S.C.A. §§ 1395ff(b)(1)(F); (c)(3)(C)(iii). Finally, BIPA provides for de novo, rather than appellate review at the MAC level. 42 U.S.C.A. § 1395ff(d)(2)(B). See, Andrew B. Wachler and Abby Pendleton, The New Medicare Appeals Process, 3 Health Law. 8 (2005).

One of the key changes that BIPA makes in the previous law is that it specifies the consequences of the failure of DHHS and its contractors to meet appellate deadlines. The provisions dealing with ALJ and MAC decisions follow:

42 U.S.C. § 1395ff (d)

(3) Consequences of failure to meet deadlines

(A) Hearing by administrative law judge—In the case of a failure by an administrative law judge to render a decision by the end of the period described in paragraph (1) [90 days], the party requesting the hearing may request a review by the Departmental Appeals Board [of which the MAC is a part] of the Department of Health and Human Services, notwithstanding any requirements for a hearing for purposes of the party's right to such a review.

(B) Departmental Appeals Board review—In the case of a failure by the Departmental Appeals Board to render a decision by the end of the period described in paragraph (2), [90 days] the party requesting the hearing may seek judicial review, notwithstanding any requirements for a hearing for purposes of the party's right to such judicial review.

How should the courts treat appellants who have skipped appellate steps because of these provisions? If no record has been developed below because the case has moved up at each level for failure to meet time deadlines, what would be the basis of judicial review? (The statute also provides for automatic advancement to the next level for failure to meet deadlines at the redetermination level). Should the court remand for failure to exhaust administrative remedies? Should it try the case itself? What opportunities does the new system offer to appellants who detect that one level of the review process is friendlier than others? What temptations does it create for reviewers under great time pressure (as it takes less time to rule for the appellant than to justify a decision against the appellants). If the courts remand to DHHS for the development of a record, what happens next? How should Congress have dealt with speeding up appeals? See Eleanor D. Kinney, Medicare Beneficiary Appeals Processes, in Eleanor D. Kinney, ed., Guide to Medicare Coverage Decision–Making and Appeals, 65 (2002). Interim rules to implement the BIPA appeals requirement were published at 70 Fed. Reg. 11420 (March 8, 2005).

The Medicare statute and regulations provide a variety of other procedures for administrative appeals and judicial review. Medicare eligibility determinations, for example, are made by the Social Security Administration and are subject to administrative review through SSA's three level reconsideration, administrative hearing, and Appeals Council procedures. A Part A provider dissatisfied with the amount of reimbursement may receive a hearing before a contractor hearing officer if the amount at issue is between $1,000 and $10,000. 42 C.F.R. § 405.1811. If the amount is $10,000 or more (or if smaller claims involving a common controversy can be aggregated in an amount of $50,000 or more), the provider can receive a hearing before the Medicare Provider Reimbursement Review Board (PRRB), 42 U.S.C.A. § 1395oo(a)(2), (b). If both the provider and Medicare contractor agree, these cases can be mediated. See Kathleen Scully–Hayes, Mediation and Medicare Part A Provider Appeals: A Useful Alternative, 5 J. Health Care L & Pol'y 356 (2002).

Medicare Advantage organizations must provide their beneficiaries with meaningful grievance resolution mechanisms. 42 U.S.C.A. § 1395w–22(f). They must explain their adverse coverage determinations in writing and must make initial determinations within thirty days for payment decisions, fourteen days for health care services requests, and seventy-two hours for requests for services where lack of the service could seriously jeopardize life or health. If a reconsideration is requested, it must be completed within thirty days if a health service is requested, and within seventy-two hours in emergencies. Coverage reconsideration may be appealed to an independent review organization under contract with CMS, and may ultimately be appealed to an administrative law judge if $100 or more is at stake, and to court if the amount in controversy is $1,000 or more. 42 U.S.C.A. § 1395w–22(g)(4) & (5).

In Grijalva v. Shalala, 152 F.3d 1115 (9th Cir.1998), certiorari granted and judgment vacated and case remanded, 526 U.S. 1096, 119 S.Ct. 1573, 143 L.Ed.2d 669 (1999), the Ninth Circuit held that notice and appeal provisions then in effect for Medicare managed care organizations violated the requirements of the Due Process Clause. The court held that the HMOs were making decisions for the Medicare program, and were thus "government actors" rather than private entities, and thus covered by the Constitution. The Supreme Court vacated and remanded the Ninth Circuit appeal for further consideration in light of the new managed care appeal procedures imposed by the BBA and implementing regulations. Significantly, however, the Court also required further consideration in light of its decision in American Manufacturers Mutual Insurance Co. v. Sullivan, 526 U.S. 40, 119 S.Ct. 977, 143 L.Ed.2d 130 (1999), which had held that the decisions of private insurers participating in a workers' compensation program were not state actors when they made medical necessity determinations, and thus not subject to the due process clause. The case was subsequently settled. Rules implementing the BBA and *Grijalva* were published at 68 Fed. Reg. 16652 (2003).

If the Supreme Court were ultimately to hold that Medicare managed care organizations are private actors not subject to constitutional constraints, the federal government would be effectively permitted to contract out its responsibilities under the Medicare program beyond constitutional control, although it would probably still have to provide some governmental means of review for managed care decisions. But is Medicare sufficiently different from state workers' compensation programs that the holding of *Sullivan* might not apply to managed care organizations to which Medicare contracts out its statutory responsibilities? See Healey v. Shalala, 2000 WL 303439 (D.Conn. 2000) (*Sullivan* does not support the argument that home health agencies providing Medicare benefits are not state actors). See also, Jennifer E. Gladieux, Medicare+Choice Appeal Procedures: Reconciling Due Process Rights and Cost Containment, 25 Am.J.L. & Med. 61 (1999); Jody Freeman, The Private Role in Public Governance, 75 N.Y.U. Law Rev. 543 (2000).

Problem: Administrative Appeals

You represent Viola Trettner who has been denied payment by her Medicare contractor for home health services she has received because the contractor believes that home health care was not medically necessary. How does she appeal the decision? Can she sue Medicare for the denial? You also represent Joseph Spencer who has been denied coverage for a new diagnostic procedure ordered by his doctor because a local coverage determination has rejected coverage for the procedure. How might the appeal procedures in Mr. Spencer's case differ from those pursued in Ms. Trettner's case?

III. MEDICAID

A. ELIGIBILITY

Problem: Medicaid Eligibility

Four generations of the Sawatsky family live together in two neighboring apartments. Stanislaus Sawatsky immigrated from Poland in the 1970s. He became a U.S. citizen ten years later and has worked for thirty years in construction. Work has been intermittent, however, and he has never been able to build up a nest egg. For the past year Stanislaus, now in his late 50s, has been unable to work because of his heart condition. He was recently awarded federal supplemental security assistance (SSI) because of his disability. His son, Peter, is married to Maria and lives next door to Stanislaus with his three children, aged 1, 5, and 7. Peter was recently laid off from his job in a trailer factory. Maria is currently pregnant and not employed outside the home. Finally, Stanislaus mother, Elzbieta, aged 83, has been living with Peter for a year now. She came to the U.S. from Poland last year on a tourist visa, and has not returned (even though the visa has expired). She fell yesterday and is in the hospital with a broken hip. No one in the family can afford to help pay her medical bills, and the hospital is saying she will need to be discharged to a nursing home. Who in this group, if anyone, is eligible for Medicaid? What sources of law would you consult to answer this question? What additional facts would you have to know to determine eligibility?

Medicaid eligibility is very complex. Medicaid is a state-administered program, and each state decides whom to cover and establishes its own eligibility requirements, although the discretion that the states have in determining eligibility is constrained by federal laws and regulations. Because Medicaid is a welfare program, eligibility is almost always related to economic need and virtually every Medicaid applicant must show that his or her income and resources fall below certain levels set by the states pursuant to broad federal guidelines.* Not every poor person is eligible for Medicaid, however. Rather Medicaid is intended to assist certain favored groups of the needy who are considered to be the "deserving" poor, though in recent years utilitarian considerations such as providing prenatal care or care for infants to avoid more expensive conditions later have arguably become as important as moral judgments in determining who should receive Medicaid. See Sandra Tanenbaum, Medicaid Eligibility Policy in the 1980s: Medical Utilitarianism and the "Deserving" Poor, 20 J. Health Pol., Pol'y & L. 933 (1995). The CCH Medicare and Medicaid Guide (an excellent source of legal information respecting these programs) identifies over three dozen discrete categories of the poor that must be covered by state Medicaid programs under current federal law, and about two dozen groups that may, but need not, be covered, 4 Medicare & Medicaid Guide (CCH), ¶¶ 14,231—14,247, 14,251.

Who are the "deserving" poor? Historically they were the aged, blind, and permanently and totally disabled, who were either eligible for assistance under the Federal Supplemental Security Income Program (SSI) or, if a state elected the "209(b)" option, persons who would have been eligible for state assistance under the eligibility requirements in effect in 1972 for the former state Aid to the Aged, Blind and Disabled program. They were also dependent children and their caretaker relatives who were eligible for assistance under the former federal/state Aid to Families with Dependent Children (AFDC) Program. These groups were known as the "categorically needy" and states that participate in the Medicaid program have generally been required to cover these groups. The deserving poor also included the "optional categorically needy," a variety of groups that states

---

* The only group eligible for Medicaid without regard to income or resources are women who have been screened through the Center for Disease Control and Prevention's early detection program and have been found to have breast or cervical cancer and who do not have private insurance or other health care coverage. This group was granted coverage by Breast and Cervical Cancer Prevention and Treatment Act of 2000, P.L. 106–354. This is an optional category, but most states now cover it.

may choose to cover, but who then must be provided the full scope of benefits offered the categorically needy. 42 C.F.R. § 435.201. Such groups include persons who would be eligible for Medicaid if institutionalized, but who are instead receiving services in the community. 42 C.F.R. § 436.217.

States have also long been permitted to cover a third group, the "medically needy" if they choose to do so. The medically needy are categorically-related (aged, disabled, blind, or families with dependent children) persons whose income exceeds the financial eligibility levels established by the states, but who incur regular medical expenses that, when deducted from their income, bring their net disposable income below the eligibility level for financial assistance. Thirty-five states plus the District of Columbia currently cover the medically needy. The medically needy are generally persons in need of expensive nursing home or hospital care. The medically needy program is effectively a catastrophic health insurance program for those who fall into the categories favored by the welfare system.

In recent years, the traditional categories of "worthy poor" have ceased to define Medicaid eligibility. Beginning with gradual Medicaid expansions in the mid–1980s, eligibility has become decoupled from welfare recipient status. This decoupling became complete for families with dependent children with the abolition of AFDC and creation of the Temporary Assistance for Needy Families (TANF) program by the Personal Responsibility and Work Opportunities Reconciliation Act (PRWORA) of 1996 (though for some groups Medicaid eligibility continues to be tied awkwardly to former AFDC eligibility).

Medicaid today covers primarily four groups. First, coverage of pregnant women has been extended: every state Medicaid program must cover all pregnant women in families with incomes of up to 133 percent of the poverty level, and states may cover pregnant women in families with incomes of up to 185 percent of poverty level. (The federal poverty level is $10,210 for an individual, $20,650 for a family of four for the year 2007.) States also have the flexibility to use "less restrictive" financial eligibility methodologies for pregnant women. Twenty-one states currently cover pregnant women with incomes of up to 200 percent of poverty or above, while sixteen more cover women with incomes of up to 185 percent of the level. This expansion is eminently pragmatic—expenditures on prenatal care are widely considered to be highly cost effective in avoiding future health care costs. In 2002, Medicaid paid for more than 1.6 million births, forty percent of the births in the United States, and in nine states paid for half or more of all births.

Second, Medicaid coverage has expanded to cover children. States must currently cover all children under age six with family incomes below 133 percent of the poverty level and children under age nineteen in families with incomes up to 100 percent of the poverty level. States have the option of offering more generous coverage. (States may also cover children at levels up to 200 percent of poverty or up to 150 percent of the state's Medicaid eligibility levels, whichever is higher, through the State Children's Health Insurance Program (SCHIP), which gives the states more flexibility and higher federal matching rates.) Several states now cover children in families with incomes at 200 percent of the poverty level or below, and three states up to 300 percent of the poverty level. States must also cover all children who would have been eligible for AFDC when that program was abolished in 1996 ("Section 1931 children") and, for a limited time, children whose parents are returning to work after leaving welfare ("Transitional Medical Assistance"). Medicaid covered twenty-eight million children in 2005, one quarter of the children in the United States, and many more are eligible for Medicaid but not covered, often because of bureaucratic barriers or poor outreach at the state level, but sometimes because they are covered as dependents on their parents employment-related policies. Almost half of Medicaid recipients (forty-nine percent in 2003) are children, but children are very cheap to cover, accounting for only eighteen percent of Medicaid expenditures. Medicaid also covers the parents of some of these children, but income eligibility levels for parents are set usually much lower, so that in many families the children are insured but not the parents.

Third, Medicaid has become a Medicare supplement policy for low-income elderly and disabled Medicare recipients, so-called "dual eligibles." Under amendments adopted in the late 1980s and early 1990s, Medicaid must today cover the Medicare premiums and cost-sharing obligations for "Qualified Medicare Beneficiaries," Medicare-eligible individuals whose income does not exceed 100 percent of the poverty level. It must also cover Medicare Part B premiums for "Specified Low–Income Medicare Beneficiaries," persons who would otherwise qualify as QMBs except that their income is between 100 percent and 120 percent of the federal poverty level. States also receive funds to cover all or part of the Part B premium for "qualifying individuals" above this level, but coverage is not an entitlement and is available on a first come, first served basis. Finally, Medicaid covers services for dual eligibles who are not covered by Medicare, of which nursing home care (a service only marginally covered by Medicare) is the most important. Dual eligibles tend to be in much worse health than other Medicaid recipients, and account for forty percent of Medicaid spending.

Fourth, Medicaid has become our most important program for providing medical care to disabled children and adults. Most are currently eligible because they are covered by the federal Supplemental Security Income (SSI) program. Many states provide home-and community-based care services to disabled persons under federal Medicaid waiver programs, which under certain circumstances permit the use of more liberal eligibility standards than those that normally govern Medicaid eligibility. The 1997 Balanced Budget Act and the Ticket to Work and Work Incentives Improvement Act of 1999 also permit states to cover working disabled persons whose income would otherwise have rendered them ineligible for Medicaid, or who would otherwise have lost eligibility coverage due to "medical improvement." Finally, the 2006 Family Opportunity Act authorizes states to allow families with incomes up to 300 percent of the poverty level to purchase Medicaid coverage for disabled children. The disabled are a very expensive group of Medicaid enrollees. Though they constitute fourteen percent of enrollees, they account for forty-two percent of expenditures.

Although Medicaid must cover certain populations, many of the categories described above are optional. Overall, approximately twenty-nine percent of Medicaid beneficiaries fall into optional categories. These recipients, however, account for sixty percent of Medicaid spending, since they tend disproportionately to include the elderly and disabled.

Medicaid by no means covers all of America's poor. Approximately fourteen percent of low-income children remain uninsured, although it is estimated that three quarters of uninsured children are eligible for Medicaid or SCHIP. Single adults who are under sixty-five and not disabled are ineligible under federal law, as are couples who do not have children living with them, except in a handful of states that cover some of them through Medicaid waivers. Financial eligibility levels for parents are very low in many states, and only about eighteen percent of adults whose income is between 100 and 200 percent of the poverty level are covered by Medicaid. Coverage also still varies significantly from state to state, both because states differ in their financial eligibility levels (and methodologies for determining eligibility) and because states make more or less generous choices with respect to coverage of optional categories or participation in waiver programs. A number of states have used Medicaid waivers or state funds to dramatically expand coverage of the uninsured, including adults not otherwise covered by Medicaid. Others, however, have maintained very restrictive eligibility requirements and fail to cover many of their residents for whom they could legally receive federal matching funds.

Medicaid coverage is limited to U.S. citizens and qualified aliens (except in emergency situations). Until 2006, an applicant could attest citizenship under penalty of perjury. Under the 2006 Deficit Reduction Act, however, a Medicaid applicant needs to prove citizenship, using a U.S. passport, certificate of citizenship or of naturalization, a valid driver's license in states that require proof of citizenship to get a license, or a combination of two specified documents (such as a birth certificate and voter registration card). SSI and Medicare recipients, as well as foster children and children receiving adoption assistance are exempt from these requirements. States can also used computerized matches of their data sources to determine eligibility.

Assume that you represent a Hurricane Katrina victim who was born and raised in Louisiana, but lost all of her household belongings in the flooding, including all identity papers. Your client does not summer in Europe, and has never had a passport. How does your client prove eligibility? Assume that you represent a hospital that is caring for a newborn baby, just born to an undocumented alien in your hospital, in the United States. How do you establish Medicaid eligibility for the child? (CMS took the position in an interim final rule in 2006 that infants born to undocumented aliens in the U.S. would not automatically qualify for Medicaid, even though children born on U.S. soil are U.S. citizens. In March of 2007 CMS abandoned this position.)

The best source of information on Medicaid eligibility and coverage is the website of the Kaiser Commission on Medicaid and the Uninsured, http://www.kff.org. One of the most comprehensive sources of information on Medicaid eligibility (and on all other Medicaid topics), is the Kaiser Commission's Medicaid Resource Book (2002). Another excellent general source on Medicaid law, including eligibility issues, is Jane Perkins and Sarah Somers, An Advocate's Guide to the Medicaid Program (National Health Law Program, 2001). For a thoughtful history of the politics of Medicaid eligibility decisions, see Colleen Grogan and Eric Patashnik, Between Welfare Medicine and Mainstream Entitlement: Medicaid at the Political Crossroads, 28 J. Health Pol., Pol'y & L. 821 (2002).

B. BENEFITS

Problem: Medicaid Benefits

Each member of the Sawatsky family needs medical services. Elzbieta is in the hospital and needs a hip replacement and a nursing home placement. Stanislaus needs to take regularly an expensive medication for his heart, and worries that he may need another bypass operation like the one he had last year. Peter badly needs some dental work. Maria, of course, needs prenatal care and will soon need maternity care. The teacher of the seven-year-old boy claims that he has attention deficit disorder, while the five year old needs glasses and the one year old has recurrent earaches. If the Sawatsky's are entitled to Medicaid, to what services are they entitled? What problems might they encounter in receiving covered services?

As is true with eligibility, the benefits provided by Medicaid programs vary from state to state. They will undoubtedly vary more under the provisions of the Deficit Reduction Act (DRA) adopted in 2006. This section describes the traditional law as well as DRA changes in that law.

The Medicaid statute identifies about three dozen categories of services that states may cover, but also permits under the final category coverage of "any other medical care, and any other type of remedial care recognized under State law, specified by the Secretary." 42 U.S.C.A. § 1396d(a)(28). At least one state has covered acupuncture under this category. Prior to 2006, states were required to provide the categorically needy with inpatient hospital services; outpatient hospital services and rural health clinic services; other laboratory and X-ray services; nursing facility services; rural health clinic (RHC) and federally-qualified health center (FQHC) services; early and periodic screening, diagnostic and treatment (EPSDT) services for children; family planning services and supplies; physicians' services; and nurse-midwife and other certified nurse practitioner services. 42 U.S.C.A. § 1396a(a)(10)(A).

States have had considerably more discretion in the benefits that they provide to the medically needy. There have been some limits to this discretion, however. States that elect to cover the medically needy must provide ambulatory services for children and prenatal and delivery services for pregnant women, 42 U.S.C.A. § 1396a(a)(10)(C)(iii)(II), and states that provide institutional services for any group must also cover ambulatory services, 42 U.S.C.A. § 1396a(a)(10)(C)(iii)(I). Moreover, if a state covers institutional care for the mentally ill or retarded, it must also provide them either the services it provides to the categorically needy or any seven services offered generally to Medicaid recipients, and if a state covers nursing facility services, it must also pay for home health services, 42 U.S.C.A. § 1396a(a)(10)(C)(iv). What policy considerations explain these requirements?

Some Medicaid services are aimed at specific population groups. The most prominent example of these is the EPSDT program, which requires not only that states provide screenings to diagnose physical or mental conditions in children, but also obligates states to provide treatment for identified conditions, whether or not the services required are otherwise included in its Medicaid plan. Much of the litigation challenging state Medicaid programs has involved the EPSTD program. See, e.g., Frew v. Hawkins, 540 U.S. 431, 124 S.Ct. 899, 157 L.Ed.2d 855 (2004); Oklahoma Chapter of the American Academy of Pediatrics v. Fogarty, 472 F.3d 1208 (10th Cir. 2007); Westside Mothers v. Olszewski, 454 F.3d 532 (6th Cir. 2006); Pediatric Specialty Care, Inc. v. Arkansas Department of Human Serv's, 293 F.3d 472 (8th Cir. 2002); Antrican v. Odom, 290 F.3d 178 (4th Cir. 2002). On the key role that EPSDT plays in child health, see, Sara Rosenbaum and Paul H. Wise, Crossing the Medicaid–Private Insurance Divide: The Case of EPSDT, 26 Health Aff.(2), 382 (2007). The Medicaid statute also requires coverage of certain categories of providers, such as nurse midwives and nurse practitioners.

Under the Medicaid law as it existed prior to 2006, a state's Medicaid plan was required to specify the "amount, duration, and scope" of each service that it provided for the categorically needy and each group of the medically needy. 42 C.F.R. § 440.230(a). Each service was required to be of sufficient amount, duration, and scope to achieve its purpose reasonably. 42 C.F.R. § 440.230(b). The Medicaid agency was not allowed to arbitrarily deny or reduce the amount, duration, or scope of a required service solely because of the diagnosis, type of illness, or condition. 42 C.F.R. § 440.230(c). States could refuse to cover specified optional categories of services (such as eyeglasses or dental care), but if they did cover a service, they could not simply decide to cover it for some medical diagnoses or conditions and not for others. Thus a state provision covering eyeglasses for individuals suffering from eye disease, but not for individuals with refractive error, was invalidated, White v. Beal, 555 F.2d 1146 (3d Cir.1977), as was a $50,000 cap on payment for hospital services which precluded coverage of $200,000 liver transplants, Montoya v. Johnston, 654 F.Supp. 511 (W.D.Tex.1987), and a state's refusal to cover sex reassignment surgery (which would fall within the general mandatory categories of hospital and physician services), Smith v. Rasmussen, 57 F.Supp.2d 736 (N.D.Iowa 1999). Although some courts have held that the benefits of a state Medicaid program are sufficient if they meet the needs of the Medicaid population of the state as a whole, DeSario v. Thomas (139 F.3d 80, 95 (2d Cir. 1998) cert. granted, judgment vacated on other grds, sub nom. Slekis v. Thomas, 525 U.S. 1098, 119 S.Ct. 864, 142 L.Ed.2d 767 (1999); Charleston Mem. Hosp. v. Conrad, 693 F.2d 324 (4th Cir. 1982)) most circuits have held that Medicaid must fund all medically necessary services within a covered category (see Hern v. Beye, 57 F.3d 906, 911 (10th Cir. 1995); Dexter v. Kirschner, 984 F.2d 979, 983 (9th Cir. 1992)), which seems also to be the position of CMS (T.L. v. Colorado Dept. of Health Care Pol'y and Fin., 42 P.3d 63, 66 (2002)).

The Deficit Reduction Act (DRA) of 2005 (actually adopted in 2006), dramatically changed these requirement for some groups of Medicaid recipients, allowing state Medicaid plans to ignore statutory requirements regarding mandatory and optional service coverage, state-wideness, freedom of choice, and comparability with respect to these groups. A number of groups remain subject to the preexisting laws governing benefits, including pregnant women with incomes below 133 percent of the poverty level, blind and disabled recipients, dually-eligible Medicare beneficiaries, most institutionalized recipients, the medically needy, parents receiving Temporary Assistance to Needy Families (TANF), and children in foster care. As to others, including mostly children, working parents, and pregnant women with incomes above 133 percent of FPL, states may, instead of complying with the prior law, provide coverage through "benchmark" or "benchmark equivalent" plans. Benchmark plans include the standard Blue Cross/Blue Shield PPO option under the Federal Employees Health Benefit Plan, the HMO plan with the largest commercial enrollment in state, any generally-available state employees plan (regardless of whether anyone actually enrolls in it) or any plan approved by HHS. These options are much like those which the states may offer under the SCHIP program. The DRA is unclear as to whether states have to provide EPSDT coverage beyond that provided by benchmark plans, though CMS has interpreted the statute to say that they do.

As of the spring of 2007, the four states that have established benchmark plans have chosen HHS approved coverage plans, i.e. set up plans for which they have themselves defined limited benefits. West Virginia, for example, is implementing a program that denies mental health counseling and other services and limits prescription drugs for recipients who do not sign a pledge to "do my best to stay healthy," "attend health improvement programs as directed," have routine checkups and screenings, keep appointments, take medicines as prescribed and go to emergency rooms only for real emergencies. Health care providers are expected under the West Virginia program to inform Medicaid if their patients are not complying with the pledge. Is such a program likely to improve recipient health? Is it likely to save money? What ethical issues does it pose for providers? See Judith Solomon, West Virginia's Medicaid Changes Unlikely to Reduce State Costs or Improve Beneficiaries' Health, available at http://www.cbpp.org/5–31–06health. htm(2006). See generally, describing the DRA, Sara Rosenbaum, Medicaid at Forty: Revisiting Structure and Meaning in a Post–Deficit Reduction Era, 9 J. Health Care L. & Pol'y 5 (2006). Were your state to adopt a DRA option, how would it affect your answer to the problem at the beginning of this section?

Notes and Questions

1. Who should make coverage decisions under the Medicaid program: the personal physicians of beneficiaries, low level state bureaucrats, national professional consensus groups, grass roots consensus panels? What should be the relationship between the federal and state governments in making coverage decisions? In particular, what role should the federal courts play?

2. The additional flexibility provided the states by the DRA for benefit coverage merely supplements the flexibility already provided under § 1115 of the Social Security Act which authorizes demonstration projects. Since the beginning of the Medicaid program, the federal government has under this provision permitted the states to deviate from federal Medicaid requirements to conduct "demonstration" projects (42 U.S.C. § 1315). In fact, many § 1115 waiver programs have not been true research projects, and indeed many have continued for years without effective review, in essence resulting in administrative waiver of statutory requirements. The DRA supplements § 1115 waiver authority, authorizing up to ten states to establish "health opportunity account" programs which provide high deductible plans coupled with health savings accounts for Medicaid recipients. But even prior to the DRA, CMS had authorized state programs that were very different from the traditional Medicaid model. Florida, for example, has received a § 1115 waiver to establish a "defined contribution" Medicaid program that pays flat, risk-adjusted amounts from which recipients can purchase private insurance. South Carolina has requested a waiver for a system of state-funded "personal health accounts" which beneficiaries may use to purchase private insurance or to purchase services directly from providers. What are the advantages and disadvantages of a defined contribution model for Medicaid? Health savings accounts were introduced in Chapter Seven. What additional considerations beyond those raised in that discussion affect the use of such accounts for Medicaid recipients?

3. A striking feature of the benefit packages provided by Medicaid traditionally is its emphasis on institutional care. In 2006, fifty-eight percent of Medicaid personal health expenditure payments went to hospitals and nursing homes (compared to about forty-four percent of personal health care expenditures in the U.S. generally). Medicaid pays for forty-three percent of the nursing home care provided in the United States, over six times the amount paid for by private insurance (which is primarily long-term care insurance, since most health insurance policies do not cover nursing home care). Eighty-five percent of Medicaid spending on long-term care is "optional," much of it for home and community-based services. Medicaid also pays for much of the care provided by intermediate care facilities for the mentally disabled. Most of the residents of nursing facilities and ICF–MRs are very debilitated, physically and mentally. Many of these people would not have survived in other periods in history or in other cultures. Medicaid is, in a very real sense, the cost that we pay as a society for valuing the lives of these persons.

While all state Medicaid programs cover some optional services, like intermediate care facility services and pharmaceuticals, some states do not cover other optional services, such as podiatry, dental care, eyeglasses, or dentures. All in all, sixty-five percent of Medicaid expenditures go for optional services. But when economic conditions or federal cutbacks have resulted in state Medicaid cutbacks, optional services are often the first to go. During the financial crises of the early 2000s, a number of states reduced dental and vision services, for example. Others restructured or limited their prescription drug coverage, in some instances capping the number of prescriptions a recipient could fill in a month. What explains the choice of services states cover under Medicaid or drop in lean times? Does Medicaid cover the services that are most vital to health or that are most cost-effective? Are covered services those that poor persons or elderly persons would themselves choose to have covered if they were purchasing insurance? Why does Medicaid cover some services for which private insurance is not generally purchased, such as nursing home care or birth control? What role might provider associations, their lawyers and lobbyists play in determining benefit coverage? Might services currently available under Medicaid mirror those covered by health programs previously financed by the states with their own money before federal matching funds became available (many of the residents of ICF–MRs were formerly in state mental institutions)?

In considering these questions, it is important to realize that Medicaid, like Medicare, does not just purchase services for its beneficiaries, but also plays a vital role in supporting the nation's health care infrastructure. Medicaid disproportionate share payments (i.e. payments to hospitals that provide a disproportionate amount of care to Medicaid and uninsured patients and are therefore unable to rely on private-pay patients to cross-subsidize the burden of caring for these patients) constitute almost six percent of Medicaid expenditures (although this money does not necessarily end up with the hospitals themselves, as will be explained later). Medicaid pays for much of the obstetric and pediatric care delivered in the United States, and plays a vital role in supporting teaching hospitals. Medicaid and Medicare (which also covers medical education costs) are largely responsible, therefore, for there being a safety net in the United States even for those not eligible for Medicaid itself.

C. PAYMENT FOR SERVICES

1. *Fee-for-Service Medicaid*

The original vision of the Medicaid program was that it would provide mainstream care for its recipients. In line with this dream, the Medicaid statute guaranteed recipients free choice of participating providers. 42 U.S.C.A. § 1396a(a)(23). With respect to access to physician services, however, this goal has always been more a dream than a reality. Physicians also have freedom to choose whether or not to participate in Medicaid. Medicaid physician fee schedules have been largely driven by state budget constraints, and low Medicaid fees have discouraged physician participation in the program. One recent study found that, on average, Medicaid only pays physicians about sixty-nine percent of Medicare rates, which are themselves well below private rates, although Medicaid fees in fact increased significantly in the late 1990s and early 2000s. Stephen Zuckerman, et al., Changes in Medicaid Fees, 1998–2003: Implications for Physician Participation, Health Aff., Web. Excl. June 23, 2004. Low payment levels, along with paperwork and billing hassles and possibly the characteristics of Medicaid recipients, have contributed to low physician participation in Medicaid. In 2001, only sixty-two percent of physicians, and (only 54 percent of primary care physicians) were accepting most or all new Medicaid patients.

Fee-for-service Medicaid recipients have also received a very distinctive sort of physician care. One study of pediatricians who treated a high volume of Medicaid patients in New York City, for example, found that ninety-one percent had attended medical schools outside the United States, only forty-two percent were board certified (compared to eighty-nine percent statewide), and only 49 percent had hospital admitting privileges. Gerry Fairbrother, et al., New York City Physicians Serving High Volumes of Medicaid Children, 32 Inquiry 345 (Fall 1995). When physicians are not readily available, Medicaid recipients have often had to rely on hospital outpatient clinics and emergency rooms for primary care.

Hospitals and nursing homes are more limited in their ability to refuse Medicaid patients. Many hospitals are obligated to serve Medicaid patients because of their tax-exempt status or because of lingering obligations under the Hill–Burton program. Many nursing homes also are not able to count on enough private pay business to permit them to decline Medicaid participation.

Prior to 1997 federal law required that the states pay hospitals and nursing homes "reasonable" rates, and many lawsuits were brought by providers challenging low state rates. The 1997 Balanced Budget Act repealed these provisions, but did not end litigation over Medicaid rates. Federal Medicaid law also requires payment rates to be "consistent with efficiency, economy, and quality of care and * * * sufficient to enlist enough providers so that care and services are available under the plan at least to the extent that such care and services are available to the general population in the geographic area." 42 U.S.C.A. § 1396a(a)(30). Several courts have held that this statute gives providers enforceable rights, Minnesota HomeCare Ass'n, Inc. v. Gomez, 108 F.3d 917 (8th Cir.1997); Methodist Hospitals, Inc. v. Sullivan, 91 F.3d 1026 (7th Cir.1996); Arkansas Medical Soc'y v. Reynolds, 6 F.3d 519 (8th Cir.1993); Visiting Nurse Ass'n of North Shore, Inc. v. Bullen, 93 F.3d 997 (1st Cir.1996). But more recent cases, postdating the repeal of the Boren Amendment have held that providers cannot sue to enforce this provision under § 1983. This seems to be part of a general trend, discussed below, toward limiting the enforceability of Medicaid requirements in federal court against the states. See Sanchez v. Johnson, 416 F.3d 1051 (9th Cir. 2005); Long Term Care Pharmacy Alliance v. Ferguson, 362 F.3d 50 (1st Cir.2004); Pennsylvania Pharmacists Ass'n v. Houstoun, 283 F.3d 531 (3d Cir.2002). See also Evergreen Presbyterian Ministries Inc. v. Hood, 235 F.3d 908 (5th Cir.2000) (beneficiaries have right to sue under equal access provision, but not providers). See Abigail Moncrieff, Payments to Medicaid Doctors: Interpreting the "Equal Access" Provision, 73 U. Chi. L. Rev. 673 (2006).

Problem: Representing Providers in Medicaid Litigation

You represent a hospital association in a state that has just cut Medicaid hospital payments by five percent to address a state budget crisis. Do you challenge the cut through litigation, or do you rather try lobbying or grass-roots organizing? Do you sue in federal or state court if you litigate? What evidence would you present if you litigate under § 1396a(a)(30) (and if the court lets your proceed under this section) arguing that the rates do not meet the standards set forth in that section? What arguments and evidence would you expect the state to present? Would your strategy be different if you represented a group of physicians and physician payments were at issue?

2. Medicaid Cost Sharing

As noted in chapter seven, one strategy for controlling health care utilization and cost favored by conservative advocates is increased cost-sharing by consumers. Whatever merits this strategy may offer in the private sector, it has very limited possibilities in the Medicaid program because of the poverty of Medicaid recipients. Until 2006, the law permitted only very nominal cost-sharing for Medicaid recipients, and prohibited cost sharing altogether for children, pregnant women with respect to pregnancy-related services, terminally ill individuals in hospice, and institutionalized recipients. Perhaps most importantly, the law prohibited Medicaid providers from denying services to recipients who could not afford a copayment.

The 2006 Deficit Reduction Act dramatically changed this. The DRA allows cost-sharing of up to ten percent of service cost for recipients with income of 100 to 150 percent of the poverty level, and up to twenty percent of the service cost for recipients with incomes above 150 percent of the poverty level, capped at five percent of total income. The DRA also allows states to charge premiums for recipients with incomes above 150 percent of the poverty level. Cost-sharing is still prohibited for the recipients listed above, as well as for emergency and family planning services. Special rules apply to non-preferred drugs and to non-emergency use of emergency rooms (see also chapter eight on emergency room use). States may allow participating providers to refuse services to recipients who do not pay cost-sharing obligations. What reasons can be given for imposing additional cost-sharing obligations on recipients? Do the general arguments for consumer-cost sharing reviewed in Chapter Seven apply to Medicaid recipients? What effect might cost sharing have on access to services for recipients? See Bill J. Wright, et al., The Impact of Increased Cost Sharing on Medicaid Enrollees, 24 Health Aff. (4) 1106 (2005); Leighton Ku & Victoria Wachino, The Effect of Increased Cost–Sharing in Medicaid: A Summary of Research Findings, http://www.cbpp.org/5–31–05health2.pdf (2005).

3. Medicaid Managed Care

Although the original vision of Medicaid was that recipients would have the same free choice of providers then enjoyed by the general population, Medicaid has in recent years, like private health insurance, moved dramatically in the direction of managed care. By 2006, 29.8 million Medicaid beneficiaries (sixty-five percent) were enrolled in managed care, compared to 2.7 million in 1991. In twenty-five states, over seventy percent of Medicaid recipients were enrolled in managed care, and in Tennessee and Missouri, 100 percent were enrolled.

This move to managed care has been driven by several factors. The most important, perhaps, has been the hope of saving money. Managed care seemed to have cut costs in the private sector, and it was hoped that it would work for Medicaid as well. Managed care advocates claimed that it might not only reduce the price of services, but that it would also reduce inappropriate use of expensive services like emergency room care. The move to managed care was also driven by the hope, however, that it would increase access by Medicaid recipients to providers and improve quality and coordination of care. A number of states, including Tennessee and Oregon, hoped further that savings from managed care might enable them to expand coverage to low income uninsured not otherwise eligible for Medicaid.

Attempts to move Medicaid recipients to managed care were thwarted for a time by federal requirements that guaranteed Medicaid recipients free choice of providers. In the late 1980s and 1990s, however, it became increasingly common for states to seek waivers under § 1915(b) of the Social Security Act (42 U.S.C.A. § 1396n(b)) which permitted CMS to waive the freedom of choice requirement, or under § 1115 (42 U.S.C.A. § 1315), which permits CMS to waive virtually all statutory requirements in the context of approved research and demonstration projects.

Arizona, which had previously refused to establish a Medicaid program, set up a statewide Medicaid managed care program under a § 1115 waiver in 1992. Arizona's program has matured over the years and has been regarded as one of the most successful Medicaid managed care programs. Tennessee launched its TennCare program under a § 1115 waiver in 1994, seeking both to control rapidly-growing Medicaid costs and to expand dramatically coverage to the uninsured. Tennessee's program got off to a rocky start, both because the program was implemented very quickly and because Tennessee had minimal experience with managed care before the program began. As the program has matured, it has enjoyed some success, but it has recently experienced difficulties and cutbacks. See, analyzing the TennCare program and the legal issues raised by managed care in great depth, James F. Blumstein and Frank A. Sloan, Health Care Reform Through Medicaid Managed Care: Tennessee (TennCare) as a Case Study and a Paradigm, 53 Vand. L. Rev. 125 (2000). See, also reporting on the early TennCare experience, Sidney Watson, Medicaid Physician Participation: Patients, Poverty, and Physician Self–Interest, 21 Am. J. L. & Med. 191 (1995).

The 1997 Balanced Budget Act amended the Medicaid statute to permit states to require recipients to enroll with Medicaid Managed Care (MMC) organizations or a primary care case manager. 42 U.S.C. § 1396u–2. States are not permitted, however, to require dual-eligible Medicare beneficiaries, Native Americans, or special needs children to enroll in managed care plans without federal permission. States must generally permit recipients a choice of two or more MMC plans, but this requirement is loosened in rural areas. 42 U.S.C.A. § 1396u–2(a)(3). Medicaid recipients who do not exercise their choice may be assigned by the State through a default enrollment process, and states may establish enrollment priorities for plans that are oversubscribed. 42 U.S.C.A. § 1396u–2(a)(4)(c) & (D). Recipients may terminate (or change) enrollment in an MMC organization for cause at any time, but may only do so without cause during the ninety day period following enrollment and once a year thereafter. 42 U.S.C.A. § 1396u–2(a)(4)(A). MMC plans are not permitted to discriminate on the basis of health status or need for health service in enrollment, reenrollment, or disenrollment of recipients. 42 U.S.C.A. § 1396b(m)(2)(A)(v).

Medicaid managed care plans are subject to many of the same consumer rights afforded private managed care members under state law described in chapter 7. See 42 U.S.C.A. §§ 1396b(m)(2)(A)(vii); 1396u–2(b)(2),(3) & (4); 1396u–2(c)(1). States must have available "intermediate sanctions" for dealing with MMC organizations that violate program requirements. 42 U.S.C.A.

§§ 1396u–2(e). In a number of instances, recipients have brought class actions against states for operating managed care programs in violation of federal requirements. See Michelle M. Mello, Policing Medicaid and Medicare Managed Care: The Role of Courts and Administrative Agencies, 27 J. Health Pol, Pol'y & L. 465 (2002).

Medicaid managed care has, not surprisingly, a mixed record. In particular, it has created problems in some instances for safety net providers, including public hospitals, academic medical centers, and federally qualified health centers, which have traditionally been heavily dependent on Medicaid for support. Commercial Medicaid managed care plans can refuse to contract with some safety net providers and may pay others less than traditional Medicaid has paid. On the other hand, in some communities, managed care organizations built around safety net providers are proving to be the most reliable managed care partners for Medicaid programs. Despite early commercial managed care plan interest in Medicaid managed care, Medicaid managed care is often very different from their normal lines of business. Medicaid recipients are needy and often plagued by chronic and expensive problems. Medicaid pays parsimoniously, but imposes demanding program requirements. In particular, it requires services that many commercial plans do not cover and coverage of populations that live in places where commercial plans do not have providers. Providers that contract with commercial plans, moreover, are often not eager to have Medicaid recipients in their waiting rooms. Increasingly, commercial plans have abandoned Medicaid, leaving the market to safety net plans or niche commercial plans that specialize in the Medicaid market. See Debra A Draper, Robert E Hurley, and Ashley C. Short, Medicaid Managed Care: The Last Bastion of the HMO? 23(2) Health Aff. 155 (2004); Robert E. Hurley and Stephen A. Somers, Medicaid and Managed Care: A Lasting Relationship, 22(1) Health Aff. 101 (2003);Sidney D. Watson, Commercialization of Medicaid, 45 St.Louis U.L.J. 53 (2001).

The states have generally found it relatively easy to move Medicaid-covered children and their families to MMC. This population is relatively healthy and their care inexpensive and predictable. It has proved more difficult to provide managed care for the disabled and elderly, which account for the vast majority of Medicaid costs. Disabled and elderly populations are very different than the population that is normally covered by commercial managed care. They are more expensive to cover, and present managed care organizations with greater risks. Managed care plans are not accustomed to covering chronic health care services like nursing home care or home health care that are rarely needed by beneficiaries of employment-related plans. Some states "carve out" these services and contract with separate managed care plans (like behavioral health plans) to cover them; other states simply cover them directly though fee-for-service payments. See, e.g., Kaiser Commission on Medicaid and the Uninsured, Medicaid's Disabled Population and Managed Care (2001); Sara Rosenbaum and David Rousseau, Medicaid at Thirty–Five, 45 St. Louis U. L.J. 7 (2001); Mary Crossley, Medicaid Managed Care and Disability Discrimination Issues, 54 Tenn. L. Rev. 419 (1998); S.A. Somers, et al, The Coverage of Chronic Populations under Medicaid Managed Care: An Essay on Emerging Challenges, 65 Tenn. L. Rev. 649 (1998); Robert N., Swidler, Special Needs Plans: Adapting Medicaid Managed Care for Persons with Serious Mental Illness or HIV/AIDS, 61 Alb.L.Rev. 1113 (1998).

In the end, managed care has arguably proved more successful in Medicaid than in Medicare. In most states managed care has not saved Medicaid programs a great deal of money, but neither has it added to program cost. Several studies show that it has decreased dependence of Medicaid recipients on emergency rooms, but most studies show that access to care has otherwise been unaffected. In some states, however, money has been saved and access and quality improved. The bottom line seems to be that in most states Medicaid was such a poor program before managed care that improvement was not difficult and was sometimes achieved. See Robert Hurley and Stephen Zuckerman, Medicaid Managed Care: State Flexibility in Action (2002).

D. PROGRAM ADMINISTRATION AND FINANCING: FEDERAL/STATE RELATIONSHIPS

Perhaps the most contentious of all of the controversial issues surrounding the Medicaid program has been the nature of the relationship between the federal and state governments in setting policy and administering the program. Particularly controversial has been the role of the federal courts in enforcing the rights that the program affords recipients and providers.

As of this writing in 2008, Medicaid is still a federal entitlement program administered and partially funded by the states. It is an entitlement program in the sense that the federal Medicaid statute and regulations create at least some rights under federal law enforceable against the states. The federal government also contributes a share of the Medicaid program's cost, known as Federal Financial Participation or FFP, which currently ranges from fifty percent to seventy-six percent.

The Medicaid program is also in a very real sense a state program. As should be clear by now, state legislatures and Medicaid agencies have significant discretion in deciding what groups to cover, which benefits to provide, how much to pay for benefits, and how to provide benefits. Nevertheless, states often consider the federal role in the Medicaid program as intrusive and oppressive.

Medicaid state programs are subject to federal oversight at several levels. States must submit a Medicaid state plan to CMS demonstrating that their programs conform with the federal statutes and regulations. If a state Medicaid program ceases to be in substantial compliance with federal requirements, CMS may, after a hearing, terminate federal funding to the state. Because this remedy is so drastic, CMS has rarely convened a hearing and has never terminated a state program. Additional statutory provisions permit HHS to disallow reimbursement claimed by the state where the services covered by the state (such as elective abortions) are not eligible for reimbursement, 42 C.F.R. §§ 457.204, 457.212. These provisions are used more frequently, and occasionally result in litigation between the federal government and the states. For an excellent review of the range of administrative law issues involved in the governance of the Medicaid Program, see Eleanor Kinney, Rule and Policy Making for the Medicaid Program: A Challenge to Federalism, 51 Ohio St.L.J. 855 (1990).

Perhaps most objectionable to the states, however, is the fact that the courts have for a quarter century permitted both recipients and providers a federal cause of action under 42 U.S.C.A. § 1983 to sue for violations of rights guaranteed by the Medicaid statute. See, e.g., Wilder v. Virginia Hosp. Ass'n, 496 U.S. 498, 110 S.Ct. 2510, 110 L.Ed.2d 455 (1990); Doe v. Chiles, 136 F.3d 709 (11th Cir.1998). The courts have also held that Medicaid recipients and providers can obtain injunctive relief against the states to compel compliance with the Medicaid statute, even though the Eleventh Amendment bars damage actions against the states for past violations of the Act. Edelman v. Jordan, 415 U.S. 651, 94 S.Ct. 1347, 39 L.Ed.2d 662 (1974).

The 2001 lower court decision in Westside Mothers v. Haveman, 133 F.Supp.2d 549 (E.D. Mich. 2001), sent shockwaves through the Medicaid advocacy community. It effectively held that Medicaid was no longer a federal entitlement (i.e. the rights of Medicaid recipients and, by extension, providers, were no longer enforceable in federal court under § 1983, and actions to enforce them prospectively were barred by the Eleventh Amendment). In 2002, the district court decision was reversed, in a Sixth Circuit opinion that thoroughly explores the legal nature of the Medicaid entitlement.

WESTSIDE MOTHERS v. HAVEMAN

United States Court of Appeals, Sixth Circuit, 2002.
289 F.3d 852.

MERRITT, Circuit Judge.

This suit filed under 42 U.S.C. § 1983 alleges that the state of Michigan has failed to provide services required by the Medicaid program. Plaintiffs, Westside Mothers, * * * allege that defendants James Haveman, director of the Michigan Department of Community Health,* * * did not provide the early and periodic screening, diagnosis, and treatment services mandated by the Medicaid Act and related laws.

* * *

At issue here is the federal requirement that participating states provide "early and periodic screening, diagnostic, and treatment services ... for individuals who are eligible under the plan and are under the age of 21." *Id.* § 1396d(a)(4)(B)[ ]. The required services include periodic physical examinations, immunizations, laboratory tests, health education, *see* 42 U.S.C. § 1396d(r)(1), eye examinations, eyeglasses, *see id.* § 1396d(r)(2), teeth maintenance, *see id.* § 1396d(r)(3), diagnosis and treatment of hearing disorders, and hearing aids, *see id.* § 1396d(r)(4).

In 1999, plaintiffs sued the named defendants under § 1983, which creates a cause of action against any person who under color of state law deprives an individual of "any right, privileges, or immunities secured by the Constitution and laws" of the United States. 42 U.S.C. § 1983. They alleged that the defendants had refused or failed to implement the Medicaid Act, its enabling regulations and its policy requirements, by (1) refusing to provide, and not requiring * * * HMOs [participating in the Medicaid program] to provide, the comprehensive examinations required by §§ 1396a(a)(43) and 1396d(r)(1) and 42 C.F.R. § 441.57; (2) not requiring participating HMOs to provide the necessary health care, diagnostic services, and treatment required by § 1396d(r)(5); (3) not effectively informing plaintiffs of the existence of the screening and treatment services, as required by § 1396a(a)(43); (4) failing to provide plaintiffs the transportation and scheduling help needed to take advantage of the screening and treatment services, as required by § 1396a(a)(43)(B) and 42 C.F.R. § 441.62; and (5) developing a Medicaid program which lacks the capacity to deliver to eligible children the care required by §§ 1396(a)(8), 1396a(a)(30)(A), and 1396u–2(b)(5).[ ]

Defendants moved to dismiss the plaintiffs and for dismissal of the suit. * * *

In March 2001 the district court granted defendants' motion to dismiss all remaining claims. *See Westside Mothers v. Haveman,* 133 F.Supp.2d 549, 553 (E.D.Mich.2001). In a detailed and far-reaching opinion, the district court held that Medicaid was only a contract between a state and the federal government, that spending-power programs such as Medicaid were not supreme law of the land, that the court lacked jurisdiction over the case because Michigan was the "real defendant and therefore possess[ed] sovereign immunity against suit," *id.,* that in this case *Ex parte Young* was unavailable to circumvent the state's sovereign immunity, and that even if it were available § 1983 does not create a cause of action available to plaintiffs to enforce the provisions in question.

This appeal followed. We reverse on all issues presented.

Analysis

A. Medicaid Contracts and the Spending Power

Much of the district court's decision rests on its initial determinations that the Medicaid program is only a contract between the state and federal government and that laws passed by Congress pursuant to its power under the Spending Clause are not "supreme law of the land." We address these in turn.

1. Whether Medicaid is only a contract.—The district court held that "the Medicaid program is a contract between Michigan and the Federal government." [ ] The program, it points out, is not mandatory; states choose whether to participate. [ ] If a state does choose to participate, Congress may then "condition receipt of federal moneys upon compliance by the recipient with federal statutory and administrative directives." [ ]

To characterize precisely the legal relationship formed between a state and the federal government when such a program is implemented, the district court turned to two Supreme Court opinions on related subjects. In *Pennhurst State School and Hosp. v. Halderman ("Pennhurst I"),* the Court described the Medicaid program as "much in the nature of a contract," and spoke of the " 'contract' "formed between the state and the federal government. [ ] * * *

Justice Scalia expanded on this contract analogy in his concurrence in *Blessing v. Freestone.* He maintained that the relationship was "in the nature of a contract" because:

> The state promises to provide certain services to private individuals, in exchange for which the Federal government promises to give the State funds. In contract law, when such an arrangement is made (A promises to pay B money, in exchange for which B promises to provide services to C), the person who receives the benefit of the exchange of promises between two others C is called a third-party beneficiary.

520 U.S. 329, 349, 117 S.Ct. 1353, 137 L.Ed.2d 569 (1997) (Scalia, J., concurring).

Drawing on above language, the district judge then concluded that the "Medicaid program is a contract between Michigan and the Federal government," [ ] * * * The only significant difference between Medicaid and an ordinary contract, he asserted, is "the sovereign status of the parties," which limits the available remedies each can seek against the other. [ ]

Contrary to this narrow characterization, the Court in *Pennhurst I* makes clear that it is using the term "contract" metaphorically, to illuminate certain aspects of the relationship formed between a state and the federal government in a program such as Medicaid. It does not say that Medicaid is *only* a contract. It describes the program as "much in the nature of" a contract, and places the term "contract" in quotation marks when using it alone. [ ] It did not limit the remedies to common law contract remedies or suggested that normal federal question doctrines do not apply. * * *

Binding precedent has put the issue to rest. The Supreme Court has held that the conditions imposed by the federal government pursuant to statute upon states participating in Medicaid and similar programs are not merely contract provisions; they are federal laws. In Bennett v. Kentucky Department of Education, Kentucky argued that a federal-state grant agreement "should be viewed in the same manner as a bilateral contract." 470 U.S. 656, 669, 105 S.Ct. 1544, 84 L.Ed.2d 590 (1985). The Court rejected this approach, holding that, "[u]nlike normal contractual undertakings, federal grant programs originate in and remain governed by statutory provisions expressing the judgment of Congress concerning desirable public policy." * * *

2. *Whether acts passed under the Spending Power are Supreme Law of the Land.*—After holding that Medicaid is only a contract to pay money enacted under the spending power, the district court then held that programs enacted pursuant to the Constitution's spending power are not the "supreme law of the land" and do not give rise to remedies invoked for the violation of federal statutes.[ ] Relying on its determination that Medicaid and similar programs are "contracts consensually entered into by the States with the Federal Government . . . ," the district court then reasons that they are "not statutory enactments by which States must automatically submit to federal prerogatives." [ ]. There are two ways to understand this passage. One is that the district court is merely following the logic of its previous finding, and holding that federal-state programs are not supreme law because they are only contracts. We have already rejected the line of reasoning that begins with the assumption that Medicaid is only a contract.

The district court may also be claiming that acts passed under the spending power are not supreme law because the spending power only gives Congress the power to set up these programs, not to force states to participate in them.* * * *South Dakota* [v. Dole] upholds the power of Congress to place conditions on a state's receipt of federal funds. 483 U.S. at 211–12, 107 S.Ct. 2793. *Pennhurst I* holds that if Congress wishes to impose obligations on states that choose to participate in volitional spending power programs, it must make the obligations explicit. 451 U.S. at 25, 101 S.Ct. 1531.

* * *

The district court acknowledges that "the Supreme Court has in the past held that federal-state cooperative programs enacted under the Spending Power fall within the ambit of the Supremacy Clause." [ ] It then states that in "recent years ... the Supreme Court has conducted a more searching analysis of the nature and extent of the Supremacy Clause," suggesting erroneously that its departure from precedent is dictated by recent Supreme Court jurisprudence. [ ] * * * The well-established principle that acts passed under Congress's spending power are supreme law has not been abandoned in recent decisions.

* * *

B. Whether the Suit is Barred Under Sovereign Immunity

The district court next held that the plaintiffs' suit is foreclosed by doctrines of sovereign immunity because Michigan is the "real party at interest" in the suit and plaintiffs cannot invoke any of the exceptions to sovereign immunity that would allow their suit. [ ]

As explained by the Supreme Court in many cases, sovereign immunity, though partially codified in the Eleventh Amendment, is a basic feature of our federal system. [ ] * * *

Under the doctrine developed in *Ex parte Young* and its progeny, a suit that claims that a state official's actions violate the constitution or federal law is not deemed a suit against the state, and so barred by sovereign immunity, so long as the state official is the named defendant and the relief sought is only equitable and prospective. [ ]

Of course, *Ex parte Young* is a "fiction" to the extent it sharply distinguishes between a state and an officer acting on behalf of the state, but it is a necessary fiction, required to maintain the balance of power between state and federal governments. "The availability of prospective relief of the sort awarded in *Ex parte Young* gives life to the Supremacy Clause."[ ] * * * On its surface this case fits squarely within *Ex parte Young*. Plaintiffs allege an ongoing violation of federal law, the Medicaid Act, and seek prospective equitable relief, an injunction ordering the named state officials henceforth to comply with the law.

The district court nonetheless held that *Ex parte Young* was inapplicable for four separate reasons. Two can be quickly dismissed. First, it held that plaintiffs could not invoke *Ex parte Young* because that doctrine can only be invoked to enforce federal laws that are supreme law of the land. [ ] Since we held above that spending clause enactments are supreme law of the land, they may be the basis for an *Ex parte Young* action. Second, the district court held *Ex parte Young* is unavailable because under this doctrine a court lacks "authority to compel state officers performing discretionary functions." [ ] This correctly states the holding in *Young,* but misunderstands what it means by "discretion." "An injunction to prevent [a state official] from doing that which he has no legal right to do is not an interference with the discretion of an officer." *Ex parte Young,* 209 U.S. at 159, 28 S.Ct. 441. Since the plaintiffs here claim that the defendants are acting unlawfully in refusing to implement mandatory elements of Medicaid's screening and treatment program, they seek only to prevent the defendants from doing "what [they] have no legal right to do," and their suit is permitted under *Ex parte Young.*

Third, the district court asserts that *Ex parte Young* is unavailable because the state "is the real party in interest when its officers act within their lawful authority." [ ] It has two reasons for finding Michigan the real party in interest. Its first reason follows from its finding that Medicaid is a contract. If Medicaid were only a contract, then this would be a suit seeking to compel a state to specific performance of a contract. Such suits are barred under a nineteenth century Supreme Court case, *In re Ayers,* 123 U.S. 443, 8 S.Ct. 164, 31 L.Ed. 216 (1887), which held that a "claim for injunctive relief against state officials under the Contracts Clause is barred by state sovereign immunity because the state [is] the real party at interest." [ ] We have already held that Medicaid is not merely a contract, but a federal statute. This suit seeks only to compel state officials to follow federal law, and thus is not barred by *Ayers.*

The district court also says erroneously that Michigan is the real party in interest because "[t]here is no personal, unlawful behavior attributed" to the defendants that plaintiffs seek to enjoin [ ]. In their initial complaint, plaintiffs make clear that they are suing the named defendants because of "their failure to provide children in Michigan ... with essential medical, dental, and mental health services *as required by federal law.*" [ ]

Finally, the district court refused to allow plaintiffs to proceed under *Young* because of the Supreme Court's holding in *Seminole Tribe* that "[w]here Congress has prescribed a detailed remedial scheme for the enforcement against a State of a statutorily created right, a court should hesitate before casting aside those limitations and permitting an action against a state officer based upon *Ex parte Young.*" [ ] The Medicaid Act allows the Secretary of Health and Human Services to reduce or cut off funding to states that do not comply with the program's requirements.[ ] This one provision, the district court held, was a detailed remedial scheme sufficient to make *Ex parte Young* unavailable. [ ]

We disagree. In *Seminole Tribe,* the Supreme Court found *Ex parte Young* was unavailable because Congress had established a *"carefully crafted and intricate* remedial scheme.... for the enforcement of a *particular* federal right." [ ] The scheme here, in contrast, simply allows the Secretary to reduce or cut off funds if a state's program does not meet federal requirements. *See* 42 U.S.C. § 1396c. This is not a detailed "remedial" scheme sufficient to show Congress's intent to preempt an action under *Ex parte Young.* [ ]

Plaintiffs seek only prospective injunctive relief from a federal court against state officials for those officials' alleged violations of federal law, and they may proceed under *Ex parte Young.*

C. Whether There is a Private Right of Action Under § 1983

Section 1983 imposes liability on anyone who under color of state law deprives a person of "rights, privileges, or immunities" secured by the laws or the constitution of the United States. 42 U.S.C. § 1983. The Supreme Court and this court have held that in some circumstances a provision of the Medicaid scheme can create a right privately enforceable against state officers through § 1983. *See Wilder* [ ].

In *Blessing*, the Supreme Court set down the framework for evaluating a claim that a statute creates a right privately enforceable against state officers through § 1983. [ ] A statute will be found to create an enforceable right if, after a particularized inquiry, the court concludes (1) the statutory section was intended to benefit the putative plaintiff, (2) it sets a binding obligation on a government unit, rather than merely expressing a congressional preference, and (3) the interests the plaintiff asserts are not so " 'vague and amorphous' that [their] enforcement would strain judicial competence." [ ] If these conditions are met, we presume the statute creates an enforceable right unless Congress has explicitly or implicitly foreclosed this.[ ] The district court erred when it did not apply this test to evaluate plaintiffs' claims.

We now apply this test. First, the provisions were clearly intended to benefit the putative plaintiffs, children who are eligible for the screening and treatment services. [ ] We have found no federal appellate cases to the contrary. Second, the provisions set a binding obligation on Michigan. They are couched in mandatory rather than precatory language, stating that Medicaid services *"shall* be furnished" to eligible children, 42 U.S.C. § 1396a(a)(8) (emphasis added), and that the screening and treatment provisions *"must* be provided," *id.* § 1396a(a)(10)(A). Third, the provisions are not so vague and amorphous as to defeat judicial enforcement, as the statute and regulations carefully detail the specific services to be provided. *See* 42 U.S.C. § 1396d®. Finally, Congress did not explicitly foreclose recourse to § 1983 in this instance, nor has it established any remedial scheme sufficiently comprehensive to supplant § 1983. [ ]

Plaintiffs have a cause of action under § 1983 for alleged noncompliance with the screening and treatment provisions of the Medicaid Act.

* * *

Notes

1. The debate over the nature of the Medicaid entitlement has focused since *Westside Mothers* on the enforceability of Medicaid rights under 42 U.S.C. § 1983, particularly after the Supreme Court again tightened the screws on § 1983 claims in Gonzaga University v. Doe, 536 U.S. 273, 122 S.Ct. 2268, 153 L.Ed.2d 309 (2002). In recent cases, the courts have been examining the Medicaid statute section by section, holding that some provisions offer enforceable rights to recipients (or perhaps to providers), while other sections are only statements of policy and do not create rights enforceable under § 1983. Even if provisions of the Medicaid statute are not enforceable as federal laws under § 1983, however, they may be enforceable under the Supremacy Clause. Few appellate cases discuss this issue, although the Supreme Court has allowed suits to be brought against the states under the Supremacy Clause in Medicaid litigation without expressly addressing the issues. See PhRMA v. Walsh, 538 U.S. 644, 123 S.Ct. 1855, 155 L.Ed.2d 889 (2003). What difference does it make for the nature of the Medicaid program whether or not a federal cause of action is available against the states? See, discussing these issues, Jane Perkins, Using Section 1983 to Enforce Federal Laws, Clearinghouse Review, March/April 2005 at 720; Lauren K. Saunders, Preemption as an Alternative to Section 1983, Clearinghouse Review, March/April 2005 at 704; Timothy Stoltzfus Jost, The Tenuous Nature of the Medicaid Entitlement, Health Affairs, Jan./Feb. 2003, at 145. Note that attorneys' fees are available under 42 U.S.C. § 1988 in 1983 actions.

2.   Federal Medicaid obligations are often enforced against the states through consent decrees. These often result in further litigation. In Frew v. Hawkins, 540 U.S. 431, 124 S.Ct. 899, 157 L.Ed.2d 855 (2004), the state of Texas had entered into a lengthy consent decree to settle litigation challenging the state's operation of the EPSDT program. The state later resisted enforcement of the decree, arguing successfully to the Fifth Circuit that "the Eleventh Amendment prevented enforcement of the decree unless the violation of the consent decree was also a statutory violation of the Medicaid Act that imposed a clear and binding obligation on the state." Frazar v. Gilbert, 300 F.3d 530, 543 (5th Cir.2002). The Supreme Court reversed unanimously. The Court held that "[t]he decree is a federal court order that springs from a federal dispute and furthers the objectives of federal law." 124 S.Ct. at 904. This order, the Court held, was agreed to by state officials, and under *Ex Parte Young,* was enforceable against them. "Federal courts," the Court stated, "are not reduced to approving consent decrees and hoping for compliance. Once entered, a consent decree may be enforced." 124 S.Ct. at 905. The Court did, however, acknowledge the importance of state sovereignty, and suggested that the state request modification of the decree if there was a change of fact or law justifying amendment. It also suggested that the federal courts should give the states "latitude and substantial discretion" in meeting their federal obligations. 124 S.Ct. at 906.

3.   While the states complain about federal oversight, the states have also proved quite adept at manipulating the program to serve their own ends. It has always been true that states that spend more on Medicaid can attract more federal matching funds and that federal funds flow disproportionately to a few states with generous programs. Over the past decade and a half, however, states have become even more creative in extracting federal financial participation (FFP).

One early means to this end was the use of provider donations or provider-specific taxes. The idea behind these exactions was that money could be taken from providers, passed through the Medicaid program where it would be matched by FFP, and paid back to the providers to enhance their payments, without any additional state money entering the system. This practice was accompanied by expanded state definitions of disproportionate share hospitals (DSH), which permitted the states to target reimbursement at certain hospitals from which it had extracted funds, or to public hospitals and nursing homes. In some states, DSH payments were in turn extracted by the state from public providers though intergovernmental transfers (IGTs), in some instances to be used for purposes unrelated to the Medicaid program. By 1995, thirty-four states were using provider taxes and donations, and DSH payments constituted eight percent of state Medicaid spending. DSH payments were one of the most significant factors causing growth in the Medicaid program in the late 1990s, and still constitute almost six percent of Medicaid costs. Legislation adopted by Congress in 1991 to curb these abuses was only partially successful.

In the late 1990s, the states adopted yet another revenue-maximizing practice, taking advantage of the fact that federal upper payment limits (UPLs) for hospitals were set on an aggregate basis for all hospitals. States stinted non-public hospitals so as to channel payments to public hospitals that significantly exceeded the cost of services, which were then channeled back to the states through IGTs. For example, a state with a fifty percent federal match could pay $6 million to a public hospital (including $3 million in state funds, $3 million in federal), then extract $4 million from the hospital through an IGT, leaving the hospital with $2 million and itself with $1 million, without spending any state money. Some states have also submitted excessive claims to the Medicaid program for school health services, thus using the Medicaid program as a means for financing their schools. State "creative financing" not only costs the federal government money, it also distorts the nature of the public debate about Medicaid by making the program appear to cost the states far more than it actually does. On the other hand, the states contend that DSH payments and IGTs are necessary to fund safety net facilities and programs. CMS has proposed a rule that would eliminate the use of IGTs but its implementation was blocked for a year by legislation adopted in 2007. An excellent description of these practices is found in the Kaiser Commission on Medicaid and the Uninsured's Medicaid Resource Book (2002), at 105–115.

Problem: Health Care Coverage for the Poor

Imagine that you are a member of the staff of a recently elected member of the House of Representatives who is very concerned about reforming the Medicaid program. You are working for this congresswoman because her ideological commitments mirror your own. She asks you to review the current Medicaid program and to come up with a proposal that would substantially improve the current program. Consider your response to her request in light of the following questions:

Whom should the program cover? What financial eligibility requirements should be imposed? What provisions should be made for family responsibility for individuals? Spousal impoverishment? Should eligibility be defined in terms of some definition of the worthy poor? How would you decide who is worthy and who is not?

What benefits should be afforded by the program? Should specific services be mandated, such as hearing aids, nurse midwife services, physical therapy, hospice? What mix of preventive, acute, and long-term care benefits should be covered? How should providers be paid? What role should managed care organizations play in providing care?

What should be the respective roles of the federal and state governments in administering the plan? What should be the respective roles of the legislative, executive, and judicial branches? Should recipients have any federally defined rights? Should providers have any rights? Should these rights be enforceable in federal or state court?

What interest groups do you expect to be most supportive of or opposed to your proposal? Would you expect that the members of any of these groups might be major contributors to your congresswoman? Do the members of these groups represent voting blocks important to your congresswoman?

Chapter 10

PROFESSIONAL RELATIONSHIPS IN HEALTH CARE ENTERPRISES

I. STAFF PRIVILEGES AND HOSPITAL–PHYSICIAN CONTRACTS

A physician or other health care professional may treat patients in a particular hospital only if the practitioner has "privileges" at that hospital. The hospital does not pay a fee or salary to a health care professional who only holds privileges and who has no other relationship (such as employment, a contract for services, or a joint business venture) with the hospital.

Hospital privileges include several distinct parts. Privileges may include admitting privileges for the authority to admit patients to the hospital and clinical privileges for the authority to use hospital facilities to treat patients, among other subsets of authority. The scope of an individual provider's clinical privileges must be delineated specifically by the hospital. A provider who is awarded privileges by the hospital is usually also a member of the hospital's medical staff and so is said to hold staff privileges.

The hospital medical staff historically has functioned as a relatively independent association within the hospital organization, operating within the hospital's by-laws but under its own medical staff by-laws as well. The medical staff as an entity traditionally has held substantial authority over the hospital's internal quality assurance system including the credentialing process through which physicians receive and maintain privileges. Only the hospital's governing board has legal authority to grant, deny, limit, or revoke privileges; but it is the hospital's medical staff that generally controls the credentialing process to that ultimate point.

There is, then, an inherent tension built into the common organizational structure of a hospital. This tension periodically erupts into spectacular conflicts that press on the unresolved ambiguity in this tripartite structure where authority is divided among the administration, the board of directors or trustees, and the medical staff. John D. Blum, Feng Shui and the Restructuring of the Hospital Corporation: A Call for Change in the Face of the Medical Error Epidemic, 14 Health Matrix 5 (2004), questioning the continuing viability of this "wobbly three-legged stool" structure.

The medical staff structure has allowed substantial physician control over access to hospital privileges for the purpose of assuring the quality of patient care through the staff's medical expertise and devotion to professional values. Most observers of the exercise of this control conclude that its purpose is not always fulfilled, however. Doctors sometimes have used access to privileges to achieve an advantage over competing physicians rather than solely for the benefit of the quality of care provided to patients.

More recent developments have pushed hospitals toward even greater administrative control of physician decisionmaking in general and staff privileges in particular. Greater emphasis on outcomes and patient safety raises the stakes for hospitals in regard to physician behavior, and greater consumer access to online information about physicians and hospitals raises the risk that such information will be used in litigation against the hospital. Cost containment mechanisms that place hospitals at financial risk for length of stay and utilization of resources per patient—decisions traditionally directed by the patient's doctor—also prodded hospitals to exert more control over physician practices. Because the positive and negative financial consequences of physician practices are experienced by the hospital, many facilities explicitly consider the financial impact of a doctor's treatment patterns in their privileges decisions. As physicians have more frequently become direct rivals of the hospitals in which they practice, some hospitals are taking this competition into account in their credentialing as well.

The staff privileges system has changed in several ways that reflect these pressures, as you will see in this chapter. For example, hospitals have shifted their relationships with physicians in some practice areas toward contract or employment relationships and away from the more independent traditional staff privileges relationships. Contracts for medical services are especially prevalent among the hospital-based practice areas such as radiology, anesthesiology, pathology, and emergency medicine as well as in some particular functions including hospitalists who oversee or manage the in-hospital care of patients admitted to the hospital by private physicians.

Generalizations about the relative power of hospitals and physicians are likely to be inaccurate in any particular circumstance. Each geographic market is different—including the extent of managed care coverage; the supply of physicians; and the degree of integration among facilities or among physicians. Each hospital is different in terms of its own relationships with managed care plans; its own dependence on physicians as the direct source of patients; and its own competitive position in the market for hospital and related services.

SOKOL v. AKRON GENERAL MEDICAL CENTER

United States Court of Appeals for the Sixth Circuit, 1999.
173 F.3d 1026.

NORRIS, CIRCUIT JUDGE.

Plaintiff is a cardiac surgeon on staff at Akron General. The Medical Council at Akron General received information in the mid–1990's indicating that plaintiff's patients had an excessively high mortality rate. Concerned about plaintiff's performance of coronary artery bypass surgery ("CABG"), the Medical Council created the CABG Surgery Quality Task Force in 1994 to conduct a review of the entire cardiac surgery program at Akron General. The Task Force hired Michael Pine, M.D., a former practicing cardiologist who performs statistical risk assessments for evaluating the performance of hospitals. At a presentation in 1994 attended by plaintiff, Dr. Pine identified plaintiff as having a mortality rate of 12.09%, a "high risk-adjusted rate." Risk adjustment analyzes the likelihood that a particular patient or group of patients will die, as compared to another patient or group of patients. Dr. Pine stated in a summary of his findings that the predicted mortality rate for plaintiff's CABG patients was 3.65%, and plaintiff's "high mortality rate was of great concern and warrants immediate action."

James Hodsden, M.D., Chief of Staff at Akron General, requested that the Medical Council consider plaintiff for possible corrective action. Pursuant to the Medical Staff Bylaws, the Medical Council forwarded the complaint to the chairman of plaintiff's department, who appointed an Ad Hoc Investigatory Committee to review plaintiff's CABG surgery performance. The Medical Staff Bylaws require the Investigatory Committee to interview the staff member being reviewed and provide the Medical Council with a record of the interview and a report. The Investigatory Committee met with plaintiff three times. At the first meeting, the Investigatory Committee identified the issues before it to include addressing questions raised by plaintiff about the Pine study and determining the cause of plaintiff's excessive mortality rate. At the second meeting, the Investigatory Committee examined the mortality rate of plaintiff's patients using the Society of Thoracic Surgeons ("STS") methodology. Under STS methodology, the Investigatory Committee, like Dr. Pine, determined that plaintiff's CABG risk-adjusted mortality rate was roughly three times higher than the predicted mortality rate. The Investigatory Committee discussed the results of this analysis with plaintiff at the meeting.

At the third meeting, the Investigatory Committee reviewed with plaintiff various records of his twenty-six CABG patients who died either during or around the time of surgery. The Investigatory Committee determined that one factor leading to the deaths of these patients was poor case selection, meaning plaintiff did not adequately screen out those patients for whom CABG surgery was too risky. The Investigatory Committee also found that the excessive number of deaths may have been due to insufficient myocardial protection, which led to heart attacks.

The Investigatory Committee ultimately reported to the Medical Council that plaintiff's mortality rate was excessively high and that the two principal causes for this high mortality rate were poor case selection and "improper myocardial protection." The Investigatory Committee recommended that all cases referred to plaintiff for CABG surgery undergo a separate evaluation by another cardiologist who could cancel surgery felt to be too risky. It also recommended that plaintiff not be permitted to do emergency surgery or serve on "cathlab standby" and that there be an ongoing review of his CABG patients by a committee reporting to the Medical Council. Finally, it recommended that a standardized myocardial protection protocol be developed, and that all cardiac surgeons should be required to comply with the protocol.

Plaintiff appeared before the Medical Council on November 21, 1996, and the Medical Council voted to implement the recommendations. Under the Akron General Medical Staff Bylaws, when the Medical Council makes a decision adverse to the clinical privileges of a staff member, the staff member must be given notice of the decision of the Medical Council, and the notice shall specify "what action was taken or proposed to be taken and the reasons for it." This notice allows the staff member to prepare for a hearing to review the Medical Council's decision....

Plaintiff and representatives from the Medical Council appeared before an Ad Hoc Hearing Committee on March 27, 1997. Plaintiff was represented by legal counsel, submitted exhibits, and testified on his own behalf. Dr. Gardner, a member of the Investigatory Committee, testified that although the Pine study and the STS methodology tended to underestimate the actual risk in some of plaintiff's cases, the Investigatory Committee concluded that the STS risk stratification tended to corroborate the Pine analysis. When asked about the Medical Council's determination that plaintiff engaged in poor case selection, Dr. Gardner had difficulty identifying specific cases that should not have had CABG surgery, yet he stated that "in the aggregate" there was poor case selection.

The Hearing Committee recommended that the Medical Council restore all plaintiff's CABG privileges. The Medical Council rejected the recommendation of the Hearing Committee and reaffirmed its original decision. In accordance with the Bylaws, plaintiff appealed the Medical Council's determination to the Executive Committee of the Board of Trustees of Akron General. This Committee affirmed the Medical Council's decision. Plaintiff then asked the district court for injunctive relief against Akron General.

* * *

Under Ohio law, private hospitals are accorded broad discretion in determining who will enjoy medical staff privileges at their facilities, and courts should not interfere with this discretion "unless the hospital has acted in an arbitrary, capricious or unreasonable manner or, in other words, has abused its discretion." [ ] However, hospitals must provide "procedural due process ... in adopting and applying" "reasonable, nondiscriminatory criteria for the privilege of practicing" surgery in the hospital. [ ]

A. INSUFFICIENT NOTICE

This appeal requires us to examine the extent of the procedural protections afforded plaintiff under Ohio law. In addition to an appeals process, "[f]air procedure requires meaningful notice of adverse actions and the grounds or reasons for such actions" when a hospital makes an adverse decision regarding medical staff privileges. [ ] Akron General's Medical Staff Bylaws require that notice of an adverse decision by the Medical Council state "what action was taken or proposed to be taken and the reasons for it" and thus do not contractually provide for a quality of notice exceeding that required by Ohio law.

The President of Akron General sent plaintiff a letter notifying him of the Medical Council's initial decision. The letter refers plaintiff to the minutes of the Medical Council's meeting which set out the reasons for the Council's decision. These minutes, provided to plaintiff, indicate that the findings and recommendations of the Investigatory Committee were presented. The Investigatory Committee found that "[t]he number and percentage of deaths in Dr. Sokol's population was excessively high compared to the published national statistics and other local surgeons." Two reasons for this high percentage were offered—poor case selection and problems with protecting against myocardial infarctions. * * *

According to the magistrate judge, the notice provided plaintiff was insufficient because [it failed] to provide Dr. Sokol with specific cases where he engaged in poor case selection and where he failed to provide appropriate myocardial protection.

The sort of notice demanded by the magistrate judge was not required by the circumstances of this case. Had Akron General restricted plaintiff's rights because the Medical Council determined that he had poor case selection or provided insufficient protections against myocardial infarctions, then perhaps specific patient charts should have been indicated, along with specific problems with each of those charts. However, Akron General had a more fundamental concern with plaintiff's performance: too many of his patients, in the aggregate, were dying, even after accounting for risk adjustment. Poor case selection and problems in preventing myocardial infarction were just two reasons suggested by the Investigatory Committee for the high mortality rate.

Plaintiff takes issue with the Pine study and the STS algorithm, claiming that they do not present an accurate picture of his performance as a surgeon because he is the "surgeon of last resort." In other words, so many of his patients die because so many of his patients are already at death's door. Perhaps plaintiff is correct about that. However, it is not for us to decide whether he has been inaccurately judged by the Investigatory Committee and the Medical Council. Instead, we are to determine whether plaintiff had sufficient notice of the charges against him to adequately present a defense before the Hearing Committee. He knew that the Medical Council's decision was based upon the results of the Pine study and the STS analysis, knew the identity of his patients and which ones had died, and had access to the autopsy reports and medical records of these patients. * * * Manifestly, he had notice and materials sufficient to demonstrate to the Hearing Committee's satisfaction that limiting his privileges was inappropriate.

It was well within Akron General's broad discretion to base its decision upon a statistical overview of a surgeon's cases. We are in no position to say that one sort of evidence of a surgeon's performance—a statistical overview—is medically or scientifically less accurate than another sort of evidence—the case-by-case study plaintiff suggests we require of Akron General.

B. ARBITRARY DECISION

The magistrate judge also ruled that the Medical Council's decision was arbitrary. She reasoned that because Akron General did not have a fixed mortality rate by which to judge its surgeons before it limited plaintiff's privileges, it was arbitrary to take action against him based upon his mortality rate. We cannot agree. Surely, if plaintiff's mortality rate were 100%, the Medical Council would not be arbitrary in limiting his medical staff privileges, despite not having an established mortality rate. The magistrate judge's reasoning would prevent the Medical Council from instituting corrective action unless there were a preexisting standard by which to judge its staff. It is true that surgeons must be judged by "nondiscriminatory criteria." [ ]. However, in this context, that means, for example, that if it came to the attention of the Medical Council that another surgeon had a mortality rate as high as plaintiff's, the latter surgeon's medical privileges would be similarly limited. * * *

On appeal, plaintiff argues that the Medical Council's decision was so wrong that it was arbitrary, capricious, or unreasonable. He points to evidence tending to show that the Medical Council's case against him was assailable. Indeed, the Hearing Committee recommended that plaintiff's full privileges be restored. But as the Ohio Supreme Court has recognized, "[t]he board of trustees of a private hospital has broad discretion in determining who shall be permitted to have staff privileges." [ ] The board of trustees will not have abused its discretion so long as its decision is supported by any evidence. Here, the Medical Council had both the Pine Study and the STS analysis. While it is conceivable that these are inaccurate measurements of plaintiff's performance, they are evidence that the hospital was entitled to rely upon, and accordingly, we are unable to say that Akron General abused its discretion in limiting plaintiff's privileges.

MERRITT, CIRCUIT JUDGE, dissenting.

* * *

The heart surgeon has been treated unfairly by his hospital. The Hearing Committee was the only group composed of experts independent of the hospital administration. * * * The Committee completely exonerated Dr. Sokol. No one has cited a single operation or a single instance in which Dr. Sokol has made a mistake, not one.

* * *

Notes and Questions

1. Are the public's interests well-served by statutory or common law requirements of minimum procedures for actions against a doctor's staff privileges, or do these efforts create an obstacle to the removal of incompetent physicians? The court in *Sokol* examines the fairness of the procedures used by the hospital. The basis for this requirement of fair process is not the constitutional doctrine of due process which is applicable to public hospitals (see, e.g., Patel v. Midland Mem. Hosp. & Med. Ctr., 298 F.3d 333 (5th Cir. 2007)); rather, it is the common law doctrine of "fundamental fairness" applied to private associations. The requirements of fundamental fairness have been established on a case-by-case basis, and so its minimum requirements are not always clear. Some states impose additional procedural requirements by statute. See e.g., N.Y. Public Health Law § 2801–b, which requires that the hospital provide a written statement of reasons and provides for review by the state's Public Health Council of any denial or diminution of privileges. The Health Care Quality Improvement Act, 42 U.S.C. § 11101, discussed below, also establishes minimum procedures for hospitals that desire HCQIA immunity.

2. In contrast to *Sokol*, the law in most states does not allow the courts to review the merits of privileges decisions at all. Instead, most states restrict judicial review to the question of whether the hospital followed its own by-laws; and for most of these states, the question is limited to compliance with the by-laws' procedural requirements only. See, e.g., Goldberg v. Rush Univ. Med. Ctr., 371 Ill.App.3d 597, 309 Ill.Dec. 197, 863 N.E.2d 829 (2007). A few states, like Ohio, also allow limited judicial review of the merits of staff privileges decisions. For example, California allows courts to review privileges decisions under a substan-

tial evidence standard. Gill v. Mercy Hosp., 199 Cal.App.3d 889, 245 Cal.Rptr. 304 (1988). (*Cf.* Sadler v. Dimensions Healthcare Corp., 378 Md. 509, 836 A.2d 655 (2003), holding that substantial evidence review is inappropriate.) What policy and practical considerations support broader and narrower judicial review? Why is the staff privileges system generally considered protective of physicians if judicial review is so limited in the majority of states?

3. The hospital relied on outcomes data for its actions regarding Dr. Sokol's privileges. Greater capacity for aggregating and analyzing patient data should mean that such actions will be increasing. Barry R. Furrow, Data Mining and Substandard Medical Practice: The Difference Between Privacy, Secrets and Hidden Defects, 51 Vill. L. Rev. 803 (2006), arguing that a hospital that fails to use available data effectively in peer review is negligent in credentialing. See, Unnamed Physician v. Board of Trustees of St. Agnes Med. Ctr., 93 Cal.App.4th 607, 113 Cal.Rptr.2d 309 (2001); Lo v. Provena Covenant Med. Ctr., 342 Ill.App.3d 975, 277 Ill.Dec. 521, 796 N.E.2d 607 (2003). See also Katherine Van Tassel, Hospital Peer Review Standards and Due Process: Moving From Tort Doctrine Toward Contract Principles Based on Clinical Practice Guidelines, 36 Seton Hall L. Rev. 1179 (2006), expressing concern about the quality of outcomes data.

4. The Joint Commission (formerly JCAHO) has had the most significant influence on credentialing procedures through its hospital accreditation standards. The Commission identified improvements in the staff privileges process as a special focus of accreditation in 2004 and it began implementing new criteria in 2007. These new criteria emphasize three central expectations: that privileging and re-privileging assess physician performance against several competencies including patient care, medical/clinical knowledge, interpersonal and communication skills, and professionalism, among others; that there be continuous evaluation of practitioners rather than annual or biennial reviews alone; and that a separate standardized process be established to flag practitioners when there are competency concerns, including a process for newly credentialed physicians.

Note: Immunity for Privileges Decisions

The federal Health Care Quality Improvement Act (HCQIA), 42 U.S.C. § 11101, affords hospitals complying with its requirements immunity from damages actions, except for civil rights claims. The HCQIA strikes the balance of interests in credentialing by providing immunity to hospitals (and other entities) only if their credentialing decisions meet substantive and procedural statutory standards. Several states have also enacted local variations on the HCQIA, as the Act does not override or preempt state laws which provide "incentives, immunities, or protection for those engaged in a professional review action that is in addition or greater than that provided" in the federal statute. 42 U.S.C. § 11115. See, e.g., Tex. Occ. Code Ann. § 160.010(a).

The HCQIA creates a presumption that the credentialing decision ("professional review action") complies with the standards of the Act. To rebut this presumption, the plaintiff must prove by a preponderance of the evidence that the health care entity did not act reasonably. Under the Act, the plaintiff must prove that the hospital: (1) did not act in the reasonable belief that the action was in furtherance of quality health care; (2) did not make a reasonable effort to obtain the facts of the matter; (3) did not afford the physician adequate notice and hearing procedures and such other procedures required by fairness under the circumstances; or (4) did not act in the reasonable belief that the action was warranted by the facts known after such reasonable effort to determine the facts and after meeting the Act's procedural requirements. For a case that clearly lays out the plaintiff's burden, see Van v. Anderson, 199 F.Supp.2d 550 (N.D. Tex. 2002).

In testing the "four reasonables," courts use an objective standard of reasonableness. Neither the ultimate accuracy of the hospital's conclusions nor direct evidence of improper motive or bad faith is considered relevant to the objective reasonableness of the hospital's actions. See Austin v. McNamara, 979 F.2d 728 (9th Cir. 1992), first establishing the objective standard so that immunity would be decided at an early stage of litigation. The courts have been supportive of adverse credentialing decisions, ordinarily resolving cases through summary judgment in favor of the hospital. In fact, physicians only rarely succeed in overturning the rebuttable presumption of immunity. One notable exception is Poliner v. Texas Health Systems, 2003 WL 22255677 (N.D. Tex.), which the court allowed to proceed to a jury trial with a resultant verdict of $366 million, later reduced by the court to $22,550,001.

Even with the courts' deferential interpretation of the HCQIA, however, the hospital that makes an adverse credentialing decision must engage in litigation testing whether the hospital complied with the Act. The likelihood that the litigation will be terminated with summary judgment is quite a significant advantage for the hospital, of course, but it doesn't completely remove the costs of litigation on the hospital's side. Unlike a motion to dismiss the claim, summary judgment requires significant discovery. Resolving HCQIA immunity claims on a motion to dismiss, however, is inappropriate as the Act requires some inquiry into the reasonableness of the hospital's actions in light of the facts of the particular case. See, e.g., Hilton v. Children's Hosp. San Diego, 107 Fed. Appx. 731 (9th Cir. 2004), reversing trial court's dismissal of physician's claims.

The HCQIA also established the National Practitioner Data Bank (NPDB). In order to earn the immunity available under the Act, hospitals must report certain adverse credentialing decisions to the NPDB and must check Data Bank records on the individual physician when considering an application for privileges and every two years for physicians who hold privileges at the hospital. The HCQIA provides hospitals limited immunity for their reports to the Data Bank, with the physician bearing the burden of proving that the hospital did not enjoy immunity.

The hospital's obligation to report to the NPDB extends to situations where the physician has resigned once an investigation into quality of care issues has begun but before an adverse action has been taken. This has created a small window where a physician may resign prior to the beginning of an "investigation." Some argue that this allows hospitals too great an opportunity to bypass reporting while enjoying immunity for activities that precede a final action. In any case, it is not entirely clear when the opportunity to resign without report has passed. See, e.g., Hooper v. Columbus Reg'l Healthcare System, 956 So.2d 1135 (Ala. 2006).

MATEO–WOODBURN v. FRESNO COMMUNITY HOSPITAL

Court of Appeal, Fifth District, 1990.
221 Cal.App.3d 1169, 270 Cal.Rptr. 894.

Brown, J.

* * *

Prior to August 1, 1985, and as early as 1970, the FCH department of anesthesiology operated as an open staff. The department was composed of anesthesiologists who were independently competing entrepreneurs with medical staff privileges in anesthesiology. Collectively, the anesthesiologists were responsible for scheduling themselves for the coverage of regularly scheduled, urgent and emergency surgeries.

[E]ach anesthesiologist was rotated, on a daily basis, through a first-pick, second-pick, etc., sequence whereby each anesthesiologist chose a particular operating room for that particular date. Usually no work was available for one or more anesthesiologists at the end of the rotation schedule. Once an anesthesiologist rotated through first-pick, he or she went to the end of the line. In scheduling themselves, the anesthesiologists established a system that permitted each anesthesiologist on a rotating basis to have the "pick" of the cases. This usually resulted in the "first-pick" physician taking what appeared to be the most lucrative cases available for that day.

The rotation system encouraged many inherent and chronic vices. For example, even though members of the department varied in their individual abilities, interests, skills, qualifications and experience, often "first-picks" were more consistent with economic advantage than with the individual abilities of the physician exercising his or her "first-pick" option. At times, anesthesiologists refused to provide care for government subsidized patients, allegedly due to economic motivations.

The department chairman had the authority to suggest to fellow physicians that they only take cases for which they were well qualified. However, the chairman was powerless to override the rotation system in order to enforce these recommendations.

Under the open-staff rotation system, anesthesiologists rotated into an "on call" position and handled emergencies arising during off hours. This led to situations where the "on-call" anesthesiologist was not qualified to handle a particular emergency and no formal mechanism was in place to ensure that alternative qualified anesthesiologists would become promptly available when needed. * * *

* * *

These chronic defects in the system led to delays in scheduling urgent cases because the first call anesthesiologists in charge of such scheduling at times refused to speak to each other. Often, anesthesiologists, without informing the nursing staff, left the hospital or made rounds while one or more of their patients were in post-anesthesia recovery. This situation caused delays as the nurses searched for the missing anesthesiologist.

The trial court found these conditions resulted in breaches of professional efficiency, severely affected the morale of the department and support staff, and impaired the safety and health of the patients. As a result of these conditions, the medical staff (not the board of trustees) initiated action resulting ultimately in the change from an "open" to a "closed" system. We recite the highlights of the processes through which this change took place.

* * *

[Mr.] Helzer, President and Chief Executive Officer of FCH, established an "Anesthesia Task Force" to study the proposed closure. In a subsequent memo to Helzer, dated April 6, 1984, the task force indicated it had considered four alternative methods of dealing with problems in the department of anesthesiology: (1) continuation of the status quo, i.e., independent practitioners with elected department chairman, (2) competitive groups of anesthesiologists with an elected department chairman, (3) an appointed director of anesthesia with independent practitioners and (4) an appointed director with subcontracted anesthesiologists, i.e., a closed staff.

The memo noted that under the third alternative—a director with independent practitioners—the director would have no power to determine who would work in the department of anesthesiology. "Any restriction or disciplinary action recommended by the director would need to go through the usual hospital staff procedure, which can be protracted." It was also noted in the memo that a director with subcontracted practitioners "would have the ability to direct their activities without following usual hospital staff procedures." The committee recommended a director with subcontracted practitioners.

[The board accepted the committee's recommendation and formed a search committee to recruit a director for the department.]

* * *

Mateo–Woodburn was offered the position of interim director on June 13, 1984, which position she accepted. Mateo–Woodburn was interviewed for the position of director on September 25, 1984. Hass was interviewed for the position on March 7, 1985.

At a special meeting of the board of trustees held on April 10, 1985, the anesthesia search committee recommended to the board that Hass be hired as director of the department of anesthesiology, and the recommendation was accepted by the board.

At the same April 10 meeting, the board authorized its executive committee to close the department of anesthesiology. On the same day, the executive committee met and ordered the department closed.

* * *

An agreement between FCH and the Hass corporation was entered into on June 7, 1985. On June 18, 1985, Helzer sent a letter to all members of the department of anesthesiology which states in relevant part:

* * *

"The Board of Trustees has now entered into an agreement with William H. Hass, M.D., a professional corporation, to provide anesthesiology services for all hospital patients effective July 1, 1985. The corporation will operate the Department of Anesthesia under the direction of a Medical Director who will schedule and assign all medical personnel. The corporation has appointed Dr. Hass as Medical Director, and the hospital has concurred with the appointment. The agreement grants to the corporation the exclusive right to provide anesthesia services to all hospital patients at all times."

"To provide the services called for by the agreement, it is contemplated that the Hass Corporation will enter into contractual arrangements with individual physician associates who must obtain Medical Staff membership and privileges as required by the staff bylaws. The negotiations with such associates are presently ongoing, and the hospital does not participate in them."

"Effective August 1, 1985, if you have not entered into an approved contractual agreement, with the Hass Corporation, you will not be permitted to engage in direct patient anesthesia care in this hospital. However, at your option, you may retain your staff membership and may render professional evaluation and assessment of a patient's medical condition at the express request of the attending physician."

The contract between the Hass corporation and FCH provided that the corporation was the exclusive provider of clinical anesthesiology services at the hospital; the corporation was required to provide an adequate number of qualified physicians for this purpose; physicians were to meet specific qualifications of licensure, medical staff membership and clinical privileges at FCH, and to have obtained at least board eligibility in anesthesiology; and the hospital had the right to review and approve the form of any contract between the corporation and any physician-associate prior to its execution.

Subject to the terms of the master contract between the Hass corporation and FCH, the corporation had the authority to select physicians with whom it would contract on terms chosen by the corporation subject to the approval of FCH. The contract offered to the anesthesiologists, among many other details, required that a contracting physician be a member of the hospital staff and be board certified or board eligible. The Hass corporation was contractually responsible for all scheduling, billing and collections. Under the contract, the corporation was to pay the contracting physician in accordance with a standard fee arrangement. The contracting physician was required to limit his or her professional practice to FCH except as otherwise approved by the FCH board of trustees.

[The contract also provided:] " . . . Provider shall not be entitled to any of the hearing rights provided in the Medical Staff Bylaws of the Hospital and Provider hereby waives any such hearing rights that Provider may have. However, the termination of this Agreement shall not affect Provider's Medical Staff membership or clinical privileges at the Hospital other than the privilege to provide anesthesiology services at the Hospital."

Seven of the thirteen anesthesiologists on rotation during July 1985 signed the contract. Of the six plaintiffs in this case, five refused to sign the contract offered to them. The sixth plaintiff, Dr. Woodburn, was not offered a contract but testified that he would not have signed it, had one been offered.

* * *

Some of the reasons given for refusal to sign the contract were: (1) the contract required the plaintiffs to give up their vested and fundamental rights to practice at FCH; (2) the 60–day termination clause contained no provisions for due process review; (3) the contract failed to specify amounts to be taken out of pooled income for administrative costs; (4) the contract required plaintiffs to change medical malpractice carriers; (5) the contract required plaintiffs to obtain permission to practice any place other than FCH; (6) the contract imposed an unreasonable control over plaintiffs' financial and professional lives; (7) the contract failed to provide tenure of employment. The Hass corporation refused to negotiate any of the terms of the contract with plaintiffs.

* * *

* * * Numerous cases recognize that the governing body of a hospital, private or public, may make a rational policy decision or adopt a rule of general application to the effect that a department under its jurisdiction shall be operated by the hospital itself through a contractual arrangement with one or more doctors to the exclusion of all other members of the medical staff except those who may be hired by the contracting doctor or doctors. * * *

* * *

[The position] of a staff doctor in an adjudicatory one-on-one setting, wherein the doctor's professional or ethical qualifications for staff privileges is in question, take[s] on a different quality and character when considered in light of a rational, justified policy decision by a hospital to reorganize the method of delivery of certain medical services, even though the structural change results in the exclusion of certain doctors from the operating rooms. If the justification is sufficient, the doctor's vested rights must give way to public and patient interest in improving the quality of medical services.

It is also noted, where a doctor loses or does not attain staff privileges because of professional inadequacy or misconduct, the professional reputation of that doctor is at stake. In that circumstance, his or her ability to become a member of the staff at other hospitals is severely impaired. On the other hand, a doctor's elimination by reason of a departmental reorganization and his failure to sign a contract does not reflect upon the doctor's professional qualifications and should not affect his opportunities to obtain other employment. The trial court correctly found the decision to close the department of anesthesiology and contract with Hass did not reflect upon the character, competency or qualifications of any particular anesthesiologist.

* * *

[I]f the hospital's policy decision to make the change is lawful, and we hold it is, then the terms of the contracts offered to the doctors was part of the administrative decision and will not be interfered with by this court unless those terms bear no rational relationship to the objects to be accomplished, i.e., if they are substantially irrational or they illegally discriminate among the various doctors.

Given the conditions existing under the open rotation method of delivering anesthesia services, including among others the lack of control of scheduling and the absence of proper discipline, we cannot say the terms of the contract were irrational, unreasonable or failed to bear a proper relationship to the object of correcting those conditions. Considered in this light, the terms are not arbitrary, capricious or irrational.

* * *

As to the contract provision which required waiver of hearing rights set forth in the staff bylaws, * * * those rights do not exist under the circumstances of a quasi-legislative reorganization of a department by the board of trustees. This quasi-legislative situation is to be distinguished from a quasi-judicial proceeding against an individual doctor grounded on unethical or unprofessional conduct or incompetency. Accordingly, the waiver did not further detract from or diminish plaintiffs' rights.

* * *

Plaintiffs contend the department of anesthesiology could not be reorganized without amending the bylaws of the medical staff in accordance with the procedure for amendment set forth therein. Closely allied to this argument is the assertion the hospital unlawfully delegated to Hass the medical staff's authority to make staff appointments.

* * * The hospital's action did not change the manner or procedure by which the medical staff passes upon the qualifications, competency or skills of particular doctors in accordance with medical staff bylaws. * * * In fact, plaintiffs remain members of the staff and the contract requires contracting anesthesiologists to be members of the staff. Moreover, it is clear the medical staff does not appoint medical staff members—it makes recommendations to the board of trustees who then makes the final medical staff membership decision. Hass was never given authority to appoint physicians to medical staff and never did so. Hass was merely hired to provide anesthesiology services to the hospital. His decision to contract with various anesthesiologists in order to provide those services was irrelevant to medical staff appointments except that all persons contracting with Hass were required to qualify as members of the medical staff.

We conclude the trial court's determination that the defendants' "actions were proper under the circumstance and that plaintiffs' Medical Staff privileges were not unlawfully terminated, modified or curtailed" is fully supported by the evidence and is legally correct.

Notes and Questions

1. *Mateo-Woodburn* considers two issues related to exclusive contracting. In addition to resolving the question of the procedural rights of the physician who held privileges prior to the institution of the exclusive contract, it reviews the termination provision in the exclusive contract itself. What contractual provision is made for termination of the contract and termination of staff privileges between Hass, P.C., and the anesthesiologists at Fresno Community Hospital? Would a contract clause that provides that termination of the contract will result automatically in termination of staff privileges without benefit of the by-laws' procedures (known as a "clean sweep" clause) be enforceable? See, for example, Madsen v. Audrain Health Care, 297 F.3d 694 (8th Cir. 2002) which, like most cases, upholds clean sweep agreements. Do the policy concerns underlying the procedural protections for credentialing decisions dissipate where there is a contract? Contracts such as those in *Mateo-Woodburn* allocate power and control differently than does the traditional staff privileges relationship. Which situation is more compatible with a goal of cost containment? With a goal of quality?

2. "Economic credentialing," at least as defined by the AMA, occurs when a hospital makes privileges decisions based on financial factors unrelated to quality. Traditionally, any local physician who presented credentials that sufficiently attested to their competency would be granted hospital privileges, unless the hospital operated as a "closed staff" hospital (such as a teaching hospital that required faculty status) or the credentialing process was corrupted by the medical staff's own economic interests. Economic credentialing signaled a major sea

change in the relationship between doctors and hospitals. James W. Marks & Jayme R. Matchinski, Conflicts Credentialing: Hospitals and the Use of Financial Considerations to Make Medical Staffing Decisions, 31 Wm. Mitchell L. Rev. 1009 (2005); Beverly Cohen, An Examination of the Right of Hospitals to Engage in Economic Credentialing, 77 Temp. L. Rev. 705 (2004). Of course, a single factor, such as overutilization of medical interventions, may relate both to cost and to quality. If cost control is a legitimate concern for hospitals, payers, and patients, one might argue that hospital efforts to monitor physician practices is beneficial; of course, others would be concerned that such controls threaten patients with inadequate diagnostic or medical care. For an excellent analysis, see John D. Blum, Beyond the ByLaws: Hospital–Physician Relationships, Economics, and Conflicting Agendas, 53 Buff. L. Rev. 459 (2005).

3. Exclusive contracting, as in *Mateo-Woodburn*, has sometimes been viewed as a form of economic credentialing as the hospital seeks the best deal in its contracting with physician groups and can exert more control over the group's practice patterns. As you saw in that case, however, exclusive contracting can have a quality justification. Even when hospitals have justified a contracting decision entirely on the basis of financial benefit, however, courts have accepted that reason standing alone as a legitimate ground for structuring the medical staff. See e.g., St. Mary's Hosp. of Athens, Inc. v. Radiology Prof'l Corp., 205 Ga.App. 121, 421 S.E.2d 731 (1992). But see, Ray v. St. John's Health Care Corp., 582 N.E.2d 464 (Ind. Ct. App.1991).

4. Courts often separate "staff privileges" from the privilege to admit and treat patients with the result that hospitals are not required to use procedures required for revocation of staff privileges when they have revoked or limited only the clinical privileges held by the physician. See, e.g., Plummer v. Community Gen'l Hosp. of Thomasville, Inc., 155 N.C.App. 574, 573 S.E.2d 596 (2002), holding that the hospital did not revoke privileges from a physician whose exclusive contract for anesthesiology had been terminated even though the hospital's entering an exclusive contract with another entity effectively foreclosed plaintiff from practicing anesthesiology at the hospital.

5. In *Mateo-Woodburn*, there was no implication of any performance or quality problems in any single physician's practice. If there had been, would the doctors have been entitled to a hearing? In Major v. Memorial Hosps. Assn., 71 Cal.App.4th 1380, 84 Cal.Rptr.2d 510 (1999), the court considered a case in which a hospital entered into an exclusive contract for anesthesiology after repeated scheduling problems, altercations among the doctors, and quality problems attributed specifically to the plaintiff doctors. The plaintiffs claimed that they were entitled to a hearing under *Mateo-Woodburn* because the revocation of their privileges required by the closing of the anesthesiology staff reflected on their personal character and competency and so required the by-laws' procedures. The court rejected this argument.

6. *Mateo-Woodburn* represents the majority view of cases considering a hospital's authority to restructure its medical staff without recourse to the hearings provisions of the medical staff by-laws. See, for example, Tenet Health Ltd. v. Zamora, 13 S.W.3d 464 (Tex.App.2000); Van Valkenburg v. Paracelsus Healthcare Corp., 606 N.W.2d 908 (N.D.2000). But see, Volcjak v. Washington County Hosp. Assn., 124 Md.App. 481, 723 A.2d 463 (1999).

MAHAN v. AVERA ST. LUKE'S

Supreme Court of South Dakota, 2001.
621 N.W.2d 150.

GILBERTSON, JUSTICE.

Orthopedic Surgery Specialists (OSS), a South Dakota corporation, and its individual physicians, commenced this action against Avera St. Lukes (ASL) alleging breach of contract. The trial court granted OSS' motion for summary judgment and entered a mandatory permanent injunction against ASL. ASL then filed this appeal. We reverse.

FACTS AND PROCEDURE

ASL is a private, nonprofit, general acute care hospital located in Aberdeen, South Dakota, organized under the nonprofit corporation laws of South Dakota. [Ed. Note: OSS opened a freestanding orthopedic surgery center, unrelated to the hospital, shortly before the hospital's decisions at issue in this case.]

ASL is part of Avera Health, a regional health care system sponsored by the Sisters of the Presentation of the Blessed Virgin Mary of Aberdeen, South Dakota. Since 1901, the Presentation Sisters have been fulfilling their mission statement "to respond to God's calling for a healing ministry ... by providing quality health services" to the Aberdeen community. ASL has expanded its mission beyond the Aberdeen community to become the only full-service hospital within a 90–mile radius of Aberdeen.

* * *

In mid-1996, ASL's neurosurgeon left Aberdeen. After his departure, the Board passed a resolution to recruit two neurosurgeons or two spine-trained orthopedic surgeons to fill the void. During the recruitment process, ASL learned that most neurosurgeon applicants would not be interested in coming to Aberdeen if there was already an orthopedic spine surgeon practicing in the area. This was due to the small size of the community and the probable need for the neurosurgeon to supplement his or her practice by performing back and spine surgeries. Back and spine surgeries are also performed by orthopedic spine surgeons and the applicants were doubtful whether Aberdeen could support the practice of both a neurosurgeon and an orthopedic spine surgeon.

ASL was successful in recruiting a neurosurgeon who arrived in December, 1996. Around this time, ASL learned that OSS, a group of Aberdeen orthopedic surgeons, had decided to build a day surgery center that would directly compete with ASL. During the first seven months that OSS' surgery center was open, ASL suffered a 1000 hour loss of operating room usage. In response to the loss of operating room income, ASL's Board passed two motions on June 26, 1997. The first motion closed ASL's medical staff with respect to physicians requesting privileges for three spinal procedures: (1) spinal fusions, (2) closed fractures of the spine and (3) laminectomies. The second motion closed ASL's medical staff to applicants for orthopedic surgery privileges except for two general orthopedic surgeons being recruited by ASL. The effect of "closing" the staff was to preclude any new physicians from applying for privileges to use hospital facilities for the named procedures. The

Board's decision did not affect those physicians that had already been granted hospital privileges, including the physician-members of OSS. In making its decision, the Board specifically determined that the staff closures were in the best interests of the Aberdeen community and the surrounding area.

In the summer of 1998, OSS recruited Dr. Mahan (Mahan), a spine-fellowship trained orthopedic surgeon engaged in the practice of orthopedic surgery. While OSS was recruiting Mahan, one of the OSS physicians advised Mahan that the staff at ASL had been closed to orthopedic surgery privileges. Despite this warning, Mahan began practicing with OSS. On at least two occasions, Mahan officially requested an application for staff privileges with ASL. These requests were denied due to the Board's decision on July 26, 1997.

In September of 1998, Mahan and OSS (Plaintiffs) commenced this action against ASL, challenging the Board's decision to close the staff. Plaintiffs claimed that the action was a breach of the medical/dental staff bylaws (Staff Bylaws) and sought a writ of mandamus and permanent injunction ordering ASL to consider Mahan's application for hospital privileges. Both parties submitted cross motions for summary judgment. After a hearing, the circuit court determined that ASL had breached the Staff Bylaws by closing the staff. In making its decision, the circuit court relied exclusively on the Staff Bylaws. The circuit court determined that the Board had delegated a significant amount of its power and authority concerning staff privileges to the medical staff. The circuit court reasoned that because of this delegation, the Board no longer had the power to initiate actions that affected the privileges of the medical staff. The circuit court concluded the Board had breached its contract with the medical staff when it closed the staff to the named procedures without first consulting the staff. Plaintiffs' request for a permanent injunction was granted, requiring ASL to consider Mahan's application for privileges. ASL appeals raising the following issues:

1. Whether the individual OSS physicians have standing to challenge the Board's decision.

2. Whether the Board's decision breached its contract with the Staff.

Analysis

1. Whether the individual OSS physicians have standing to challenge the Board's decision.

It is well settled in South Dakota that "a hospital's bylaws constitute a binding contract between the hospital and the hospital staff members." [ ] It is also well settled that when such bylaws are approved and accepted by the governing board they become an enforceable contract between the hospital and its physicians. [ ]

* * *

In regard to whether the OSS staff doctors suffered an injury, the circuit court found:

> "It is undisputed that the Board's decision resulted in an economic benefit for ASL and an economic hardship for these doctors in their private medical practice, OSS. It is also undisputed that the OSS staff doctors, through their medical corporation OSS, spent time and money to

recruit Mahan, only to end up with him unable to perform certain procedures because of his inability to obtain staff privileges at ASL. As a result, the OSS staff doctors have had to support Mahan while being unable to build their practice or increase their patient base as expected. Clearly [the OSS] [d]octors . . . have standing."

The circuit court properly found that the OSS staff doctors have standing to bring a cause of action for breach of contract.

2. Whether the Board's decision breached its contract with the Staff.

* * *

Pursuant to its authority, the Board of ASL has delegated certain powers associated with the appointment and review of medical personnel to its medical staff. These designated powers are manifested in the Staff Bylaws. Plaintiffs now claim that the Staff Bylaws trump the decision-making ability of the Board as to all decisions relating in any way to, or incidentally affecting, medical personnel issues. We do not agree.

The circuit court failed to give sufficient weight to the fact that the Staff Bylaws are derived from the Corporate Bylaws. Under Article XIV, section 14(u) of the Corporate Bylaws, any powers supposedly granted under the Staff Bylaws must originate from, and be authorized by, the Board pursuant to the Corporate Bylaws. Their legal relationship is similar to that between statutes and a constitution. They are not separate and equal sovereigns. * * *

Therefore, the medical staff has no authority over any corporate decisions unless specifically granted that power in the Corporate Bylaws or under the laws of the State of South Dakota. Plaintiffs have not alluded to any powers that arise under the statutory or common-law of South Dakota.

* * *

Under section 14(u), all that is designated to the medical staff is the responsibility to make recommendations to the Board regarding the professional competence of staff members and applicants. Article XVI, section 1(a) directs the Board to organize the staff under medical-dental bylaws, which must be approved by the Board before they become effective. Finally, article XVI, section 2(a) commands the Board to "assign to the medical-dental staff reasonable authority for ensuring appropriate professional care to the hospital's patients."

Clearly, under these explicit powers, the Board has the authority to make business decisions without first consulting the medical staff. Nowhere in the Corporate Bylaws is the staff explicitly authorized to make business decisions on behalf of the corporation. Plaintiffs instead rely on the Staff Bylaws as their source of authority to assume the Board's power. Yet, even within the Staff Bylaws, there is no explicit provision granting the medical staff control over personnel issues. Instead, the circuit court found that the actions of the Board violated "the spirit of the bylaws taken as a whole." Such reliance on the "spirit of the [Staff] bylaws" turns the corporate structure of ASL upside down, granting control over day to day hospital administration to a medical staff that is not legally accountable for the hospital's decisions, has no obligation to further the mission of the Presentation Sisters, and has unknown experience in running a hospital or meeting the medical needs of the community. * * *

When the Board made its decision to close the medical staff to the three procedures on June 26, 1997, it was acting within the powers granted it in the Corporate Bylaws. When making these decisions, the Board specifically determined that the staff closures were in the Aberdeen community's best interests, and were necessary to insure 24-hour neurosurgical coverage for the Aberdeen area. By preserving the profitable neurosurgical services at ASL, the Board also insured that other unprofitable services would continue to be offered in the Aberdeen area. When, as here, it is clear from the Corporate Bylaws that the Board has the authority to manage the corporation, that authority "would necessarily include decisions on how to operate individual departments in order to best serve the corporation's purposes. . . . The cost of such care and promotion of community health is vitally important to the community and a legitimate concern for the board." ASL cannot continue to offer unprofitable, yet essential services including the maternity ward, emergency room, pediatrics and critical care units, without the offsetting financial benefit of more profitable areas such as neurosurgery. The Board responded to the effect the OSS hospital would have on the economic viability of ASL's hospital and the health care needs of the entire Aberdeen community. These actions were within the power of the Board. It surely has the power to attempt to insure ASL's economic survival. As such, the courts should not interfere in the internal politics and decision making of a private, nonprofit hospital corporation when those decisions are made pursuant to its Corporate Bylaws.

* * *

* * * [M]erely because a decision of the Board affects the staff does not give the staff authority to overrule a valid business decision made by the Board. Allowing the staff this amount of administrative authority would effectively cripple the governing Board of ASL. ASL would cease to function in its current corporate form if its staff were given such power.

In its decision, the circuit court attempted to distinguish between this present situation and the situation wherein a hospital enters into an exclusive contract. We find this attempt to be unpersuasive. * * * Such exclusive contracts are common practice for most hospitals today, and have been almost universally found valid and enforceable, even if not explicitly provided for in corporate bylaws. [ ] * * *.

* * * There is no logical reason why ASL could close certain areas of its facility to all but a few physicians (via an exclusive contract), yet not be allowed to close its facilities to any new orthopedic surgeons performing certain, named procedures. In a sense, ASL has entered into an implied exclusive contract with all current orthopedic spine surgeons. The same implicit authority that allows the Board to enter into exclusive contracts allows it to close ASL's staff as was done here.

* * *

The Board's decision to close the hospital's facility for certain, named procedures was a reasonable administrative decision. It had determined that the closures were necessary to insure the continued viability of the hospital.

The Board must be allowed to make such reasonable, independent decisions if it is to continue to provide comprehensive medical services to the Aberdeen community. * * * Therefore, any allegations that ASL breached its implied duty of good faith must fail. * * *[8]

* * *

Because the actions of ASL's Board were permissible under the Corporate Bylaws and done in good faith, there has been no breach of the contract between the Board and the staff. Therefore, the circuit court's judgment is reversed.

Notes and Questions

1. "Conflicts credentialing," so called because of the apparent conflict of interest of a physician who is both a member of a hospital's medical staff and the owner of an entity that competes directly with the hospital, has escalated the controversy over economic credentialing. Although ambulatory surgery centers raise similar issues, specialty hospitals have been a lightening rod for conflicts between doctors and hospitals. The specialty hospital typically treats only a defined set of cases, such as neurosurgery or orthopedic surgery, which are profitable. Hospitals claim that specialty hospitals cherry pick the profitable procedures and patients, leaving the general hospital to satisfy all of the remaining needs, including meeting the community's needs for emergency care and charity care, without the ability to cross-subsidize. They also charge that the physician-entrepreneurs rely on the general hospital as a place to provide services to their less profitable cases. Payers are concerned about the self-referral aspect of physicians receiving payment as the owner of the facility to which they refer. Proponents of specialty hospitals argue that patients gain in lower cost, more efficient and more reliably scheduled services and that the specialty focus increases quality in terms of repetition and innovation. Studies of the impact and performance of specialty hospitals are quite mixed. See, GAO, Specialty Hospitals: Geographic Location, Services Provided, and Financial Performance, GAO–04–167 (Oct. 2003); MedPAC, Physician-owned Specialty Hospitals (Mar. 2005); Lawrence P. Casalino, et al., Focused Factories? Physician–Owned Specialty Facilities, 22 Health Affairs 56 (2003). For a complete discussion of the legal status of specialty hospitals including additional cases of conflicts credentialing, see Mike J. Wyatt, Leveling the Healing Field: Specialty Hospital Legal Reform as a Cure for an Ailing Health Care System, 46 Washburn L.J. 547 (2007); Anne S. Kimbol, The Debate Over Specialty Hospitals: How Physician–Hospital Relationships Have Reached a New Fault Line Over These "Focused Factories," 38 J. Health L. 633 (2005).

2. If hospitals are concerned about doctors taking unfair advantage of information gained as members of their medical staff or influencing the medical staff's decisions in a fashion that advantaged their competing enterprise, could the conflicts clause be more closely written to simply exclude such doctors from leadership positions in the hospital? David Argue, An Economic Model of Competition Between General Hospitals and Physician-owned Specialty Facilities, 20 Antitrust Health Care Chronicle 1 (2006); Elizabeth Weeks, The New Economic

8. How can a doctor who is a part owner of the for-profit OSS be expected to fulfill his or her duties towards his or her co-owners and in the same instance fulfill the duties towards the principal, ASL, who is a not-for-profit hospital? This does not imply ill-will on the part of the doctor, it simply faces fundamental medical issues such as at which institution does the doctor place his or her patients, OSS or ASL? We have often stated that an agent cannot serve two masters. This rule applies to medical professionals as well.

Credentialing: Protecting Hospitals from Competition by Medical Staff Members, 36 J. Health L. 247 (2003). In contrast to *Mahan*, the Arkansas Supreme Court affirmed a preliminary injunction against the exclusion of competing doctor-owners holding, in part, that the doctors were likely to succeed in their claims that the hospital intended that the exclusion of the doctor-owners interfere with their relationships with their patients and that the hospital's action violated the state deceptive trade practices statute (as an "unconscionable" act) thus making the principle of nonreview of privileges decisions in state law inapplicable. Baptist Health v. Murphy, 365 Ark. 115, 226 S.W.3d 800 (2006).

3. The imposition of conflicts prohibitions usually raises the ire of the hospital's medical staff and can spawn an acrimonious battle over whether the hospital has the authority to add a conflicts standard to the credentialing process without the agreement of the medical staff as an entity. These battles illustrate just how "wobbly" the three-legged stool can be. The most notorious of these disputes involved Community Memorial Hospital of San Buenaventura, California. Hospital, Doctors Settle Bitter Dispute Over Independence, Responsibility of Medical Staff, 13 Health L. Rep. 1253 (2004). The *Mahan* court viewed the medical staff as subordinate to the hospital. In contrast, the Buenaventura battle produced legislation that recognizes the medical staff as an independent entity to some extent. See James W. Marks & Jayme R. Matchinski, Conflicts Credentialing: Hospitals and the Use of Financial Considerations to Make Medical Staffing Decisions, 31 Wm. Mitchell L. Rev. 1009 (2005), discussing this case and legislation in detail.

Problem: Dr. Bennett and Onyx General Hospital

Onyx General Hospital (OGH) is a 300–bed hospital in Metropolis, a major city with six other hospitals. Several health insurance plans and major employers have negotiated substantial discounts with Metropolis hospitals for hospital services provided to their insureds or to their employees. The hospitals have actually been quite interested in such negotiations because the insurers and employers asking for the discounts control the choice of hospital for thousands of insured individuals in Metropolis. What the hospital might lose in the "discount," it hopes it will gain in having a relatively stable stream of patients.

OGH has been constrained in its negotiations for a number of reasons, however. For example, it has exclusive contracts for physician services in anesthesiology and radiology that are comparatively costly. The contracts are near the end of their terms, and OGH wants to renegotiate the terms of the contracts or replace the current physician groups with others more compatible with a cost-conscious and outcomes-oriented style of practice. The anesthesiology group, Physicians' Practice Group (PPG), has been responsive to the needs of the hospital relating to coverage and quality of anesthesia services; but a new group, General Anesthesiology Services (GAS), has approached OGH with much more favorable terms. Although the surgeons have been very happy with PPG, OGH believes that they will become equally satisfied with GAS. OGH has agreed to enter into an exclusive contract with GAS and has given PPG notice that their exclusive contract will not be renewed. The OGH–PPG contract provides for termination of the contract without cause.

Two of the three PPG anesthesiologists have already joined GAS, though at lower salaries than they enjoyed with PPG. GAS has refused to consider hiring Dr. Bennett, however. Dr. Bennett is considered somewhat difficult. He does not work well with the nurse anesthetists, and sometimes has conflicts with the surgeons. He has had two malpractice suits filed against him in the last few years; but both were dropped by the plaintiffs, one after the payment of a settlement and one without any payment. Other than these problems, his work has been of good quality, although he often tells patients that they should "just get tough" when they complain of post-operative pain.

Dr. Bennett's contract with PPG provides that PPG may terminate him "without cause with 60 days' notice," but is silent on the question of his privileges at OGH. The PPG contract with OGH states that the contract is exclusive and "only physician members of PPG may provide anesthesiology services at OGH." The original letter from OGH awarding Dr. Bennett staff privileges, including clinical privileges in anesthesiology, states: "Because you will be providing services at OGH under an exclusive contract, your clinical privileges will be automatically terminated upon termination of that contract." Each of the subsequent renewal letters contained the same statement. The medical staff was quite concerned a few years ago about automatic termination of privileges of physician administrators dismissed from their administrative positions and amended its by-laws to provide: "A physician member of the medical staff providing services to the hospital under contract will retain privileges even if that contract is terminated." The Board of Directors never approved this amendment and has essentially ignored it.

What should OGH do? Should it simply terminate Bennett's privileges without procedural review and for no cause? Or, should it follow the procedures in the by-laws? Should OGH proceed against Dr. Bennett on the basis of the quality of his work? If the medical staff by-laws provide that the hospital may revoke privileges of "any physician whose inability to work well with others jeopardizes patient care," would you recommend that they proceed under that clause? Are there any other alternatives? How might a court handle the case under each of these alternatives should Bennett sue? How would you redraft the termination provisions of these contracts for use with GAS?

OGH is facing another problem as well. Several of the surgeons with privileges at OGH are developing and will be co-owners of SportsMed, Inc., a 30–bed specialty hospital limited to diagnostic imaging, orthopedic surgery, and post-operative physical therapy. Originally, OGH approached the SportsMed developers with a proposal that it enter into a joint venture with the hospital. During those discussions, OGH let it be known that it may decide not to grant privileges to doctors recruited by SportsMed or to renew privileges for SportsMed doctors who already had privileges at OGH. SportsMed declined the offer, and OGH has since informed its medical staff that privileges at OGH would not be granted or renewed for doctors who practiced at SportsMed. Finally, it has informed both GAS and PPG that it will immediately terminate their exclusive contract at OGH if they provide services to SportsMed.

II.   EMPLOYMENT LAW AND HEALTH CARE PROFESSIONALS

Doctors, nurses, administrators, and in-house counsel working without an employment contract or under a contract that does not provide for a specific term of employment are subject to the doctrine of employment-at-will. Employees working under a collective bargaining agreement or under a contract with express provisions concerning length of employment or termination for just cause alone are not employees-at-will.

The common law at-will doctrine varies widely among the states, but generally provides that the employment relationship can be terminated without cause at the will of either the employer or the employee. The at-will doctrine allows a few exceptions, which in most states are relatively narrow.

The majority of nurses have long practiced as at-will employees. In contrast, doctors traditionally have practiced as owners of their own practices and have had the further protection of the staff privileges system for their economically necessary relationship with a hospital. Increasingly, however, doctors have become employees (often at-will employees) of group practices, HMOs, or hospitals. Some courts have borrowed from at-will doctrine in deciding cases of physician termination or delisting from health plans as well.

WRIGHT v. SHRINERS HOSPITAL
FOR CRIPPLED CHILDREN

Supreme Court of Massachusetts, 1992.
412 Mass. 469, 589 N.E.2d 1241.

O'CONNOR, JUSTICE.

In this case, which is here on direct appellate review, we consider the sufficiency of the evidence to warrant a jury's verdict of $100,000 in favor of the plaintiff, Anita Wright against her employer, the defendant Shriners Hospital for Crippled Children (Shriners Hospital), on Wright's claim that Shriners Hospital wrongfully terminated her at-will employment in violation of public policy. * * * We hold that the evidence was insufficient to warrant [the] verdict and that the trial judge should have allowed the defendants' motion for judgment notwithstanding the verdict. * * *

We summarize the evidence in the light most favorable to the plaintiff. [ ] Shriners Hospital hired Wright, a registered nurse, in 1976. Subsequently, she became assistant director of nursing, and she held that position until she was discharged in late February of 1987. At all times, she was an employee at will. Wright received excellent evaluations throughout her employment, including an evaluation in December, 1986, two months before her discharge. In June, 1986, a former assistant head nurse wrote a letter to the director of clinical affairs for the Shriners national headquarters detailing her concerns about the medical staff and administration at Shriners Hospital. Shriners Hospital is a separate corporation, but it is one of many Shriners facilities that are affiliated with the national headquarters. As a result of the letter, the national headquarters notified the defendant hospital administrator, Russo, that a survey team would visit Shriners Hospital in November, 1986. Russo was visibly upset. He spoke to the director of nursing about the letter and asked her: "Are you behind this? Is Anita Wright behind this?" The director of nursing denied that she was responsible for the letter. She did not address the question whether Wright was "behind" the letter.

The survey team visited the hospital in November and interviewed Wright and other employees. Wright told the survey team that there were communication problems between the medical and nursing staffs. She detailed problems with the assistant chief of staff and gave specific examples of patient care problems. The survey team reported Wright's comments to the assistant chief of staff.

Two members of the survey team prepared reports. In his report issued on December 22, 1986, Dr. Newton C. McCollough, director of medical affairs for the national organization, wrote: "The relationships between nursing administration, hospital administration, and chief of staff are much less than satisfactory, and significant friction exists both as regard nursing/administration relationships and nursing/medical staff relationships. Communication and problem solving efforts in this relationship are poor to nonexistent." A report issued on January 5, 1987, by Jack D. Hoard, executive administrator for the national Shriners organization, also documented the problematic relationship between the nursing and medical staff. Both reports recommended a follow-up site survey to determine the impact of this conflict on patient care. McCollough's report stated that during her interview, Wright had made severe criticisms of the medical staff and had expressed concern over a lack of consistent procedures and standards for patient care. Hoard's report stated that Wright discussed the breakdown in communication between the nursing staff and the attending medical staff, which she said was leading to deteriorating morale among nurses.

* * *

Upon reading the survey team's reports, Russo again became upset and told the director of nursing that it was the nursing department's fault that the team was making another visit. The survey team returned on February 18 and 19, 1987, specifically to review the problems between the medical and nursing staffs. On February 26, after consulting with the chairman and several officers of the board of governors of Shriners Hospital and with national corporate counsel, Russo ordered that Wright's employment be terminated for "patient care issues that had arisen as a result of the surveys."

Wright contends, and the defendants dispute, that the jury would have been warranted in finding that Shriners Hospital fired her from her employment at will in retaliation for her having criticized the hospital, specifically in regard to the quality of care rendered to patients, to the Shriners national headquarters survey team. Wright further asserts that such a retaliatory firing violates public policy and is therefore actionable. We hold that a termination of Wright's employment at will in reprisal for her critical remarks to the survey team would not have violated public policy. * * *

We begin with the general rule that "[e]mployment at will is terminable by either the employee or the employer without notice, for almost any reason or for no reason at all." [ ] We have recognized exceptions to that general rule, however, when employment is terminated contrary to a well-defined public policy. Thus, "[r]edress is available for employees who are terminated for asserting a legally guaranteed right (e.g., filing workers' compensation claim), for doing what the law requires (e.g., serving on a jury), or for refusing to do that which the law forbids (e.g., committing perjury)." [ ] * * *

The trial judge's view of the law was that public policy was violated if Shriners Hospital fired Wright in reprisal for her having criticized the hospital in interviews with the survey team. As is clear from his instructions to the jury, the judge's view was based in part on "the duty of doctors and nurses, found in their own code of ethics, to report on substantial patient care issues." We would hesitate to declare that the ethical code of a private professional organization can be a source of recognized public policy. * * *

It is also clear from his instructions that the judge's view was based in part on "various state laws of the commonwealth, requiring reports on patient abuse." The judge did not identify the State laws he had in mind. General Laws c. 119, § 51A (1990 ed.), requires nurses and others to make a report to the Department of Social Services concerning any child under eighteen years of age who they have reason to believe is suffering from physical or sexual abuse or neglect. Similarly, G.L. c. 19A, § 15(a) (1990 ed.), requires nurses and others who have reasonable cause to believe that an elderly person is suffering from abuse to report it to the Department of Elder Affairs. Subsection (d) of that provision provides that no employer or supervisor may discharge an employee for filing a report. Finally, G.L. c. 111, § 72G (1990 ed.), requires nurses and others to report to the Department of Public Health (department) when they have reason to believe that any patient or resident of a facility licensed by the department is being abused, mistreated, or neglected and provides a remedy of treble damages, costs, and attorney's fees for any employee who is discharged in retaliation for having made such a report. None of these statutes applies to Wright's situation, however, and we are unaware of any statute that does. Also, we are unaware of any statute that clearly expresses a legislative policy to encourage nurses to make the type of internal report involved in this case. In fact, Wright testified that she did not consider the patient care that caused her concern to be abuse, neglect, or mistreatment warranting a report to the department, nor did she feel that there was an issue of physician incompetence warranting a report to the board of registration in medicine as required by G.L. c. 112, § 5F (1990 ed.).

Wright urges us to recognize a regulation promulgated by the Board of Registration in Nursing as a source of public policy sufficient to create an exception to the general rule regarding termination of at-will employment. Title 244 Code Mass.Regs. § 3.02(3)(f) (1986) describes the responsibilities and functions of a registered nurse, including the responsibility to "collaborate, communicate and cooperate as appropriate with other health care providers to ensure quality and continuity of care." Even if that regulation called for Wright to report perceived problems or inadequacies to the survey team, a doubtful proposition, we have never held that a regulation governing a particular profession is a source of well-defined public policy sufficient to modify the general at-will employment rule, and we decline to do so now. Furthermore, as we have noted above, Wright's report was an internal matter, and "[i]nternal matters," we have previously said, "could not be the basis of a public policy exception to the at-will rule."

* * *

We reverse the judgments for the plaintiff and remand to the Superior Court for the entry of judgments for the defendants.

Liacos, Chief Justice (dissenting).

I disagree with the court's conclusion that a hospital employer violates no public policy when it fires an employee for alerting supervisors to matters detracting from good patient care. The court has construed far too narrowly the public policy exception to the doctrine of employment at will. Moreover, in demanding a statutory basis for public policy, the court has relinquished to the Legislature its role in shaping the common law. I dissent.

* * *

Given the public interest in good patient care, it must be the public policy of the Commonwealth to protect, if not encourage, hospital employees who perceive and report detriments to patient care. Only when problems are identified can they be adequately addressed; an employee's failure to report perceived detriments to patient care may allow the problems to persist. A hospital employer therefore violates public policy when it fires an employee for trying to improve the quality of patient care. That an employer may deter other employees from reporting problems (for fear of losing their jobs) inhibits the provision of good patient care and offends the public interest.

* * * The plaintiff was not terminated for contributing to the hospital's problems, nor for refusing to accept her supervisor's method of addressing the problems; she was fired for reporting the problems to appropriate accreditation authorities. Such a termination offends the public interest and is actionable. I dissent.

Notes and Questions

1. *Wright* represents the majority view concerning the scope of the public policy exception to employment-at-will. Most courts employ a narrow concept of public policy and exclude, for example, professional codes of conduct as a legitimate basis for an exception to at-will employment. For example, in Warthen v. Toms River Community Mem. Hosp., 199 N.J.Super. 18, 488 A.2d 229 (1985), the court rejected the nurse's claim of wrongful discharge under the public policy exception where a nurse refused to dialyze a patient who had twice suffered heart attacks and severe internal hemorrhaging during dialysis. Warthen based her legal claim on a provision of the American Nurses Association Code for Nurses allowing nurses to refuse to provide treatment that was contrary to the nurse's personal beliefs so long as the patient would not be abandoned. The court held as a matter of law that the Code did not state public policy, but rather was beneficial only to the nursing profession and the individual nurse. See also, Jaynes v. Centura Health Corp. 148 P.3d 241 (Colo. Ct. App. 2006), rejecting the ANA code as a basis for the public policy exception. In the unusual case of risk to a specific patient, at least one court in a state with a narrow public policy exception allowed a wrongful discharge claim to survive. Kirk v. Mercy Hosp. Tri–County, 851 S.W.2d 617 (Mo.App.1993). In *Kirk*, the nurse had asked her supervisor repeatedly about a patient admitted with life-threatening toxic shock syndrome for whom no antibiotics had been ordered. The nurse alleged that she had been told to document the situation and "stay out of it." The patient died, and the nurse suggested to the family that they obtain the patient's medical record. See also, LoPresti v. Rutland Reg. Health Services, 177 Vt. 316, 865 A.2d 1102 (2004), reversing summary judgment against physician claiming that his termination was a result of his refusal to refer patients to substandard physician co-employees; Deerman v. Beverly California Corp., 135 N.C.App. 1, 518 S.E.2d 804 (1999). For a very informative treatise on employment-at-will case law and relevant statutes, see Frank J. Cavico & Nancy M. Cavico, Employment-at-Will, Public Policy, and the Nursing Profession, 8 Quinnipiac Health J. 161 (2005).

2. The federal government and many states have whistleblower statutes that protect employees who report wrongdoing to government agencies in specific circumstances. These statutes typically are drafted narrowly and have been interpreted by the courts quite strictly. See e.g., United States ex rel. Howard v. Life Care Ctrs. of America, 2005 WL 2674939 (E.D. Tenn. 2005); Hays v. Beverly Enterprises, 766 F.Supp. 350 (W.D.Pa.1991); Minnesota Assn. of Nurse Anesthetists v. Unity Hosp., 59 F.3d 80 (8th Cir. 1995). As detailed in *Wright*, some state

abuse reporting statutes may provide some protection to reporters. Several states also have statutes that provide limited protection for physicians in advocating for patients. See discussion in Note below.

Note on Managed Care Contracting

Contracts with managed care and other health plans are essential to the practice of physicians and other some health care professionals. For this reason, "deselection," "decapitation," "delisting"—all used to describe termination of the contract with the plan or managed care organization—have a very serious impact on the professional's ability to practice. Patients could suffer adverse consequences as well if physicians are penalized for engaging in quality care or for protecting their patients. At a minimum, patients experience discontinuity of care if their physician is terminated from their insurance plan. On the other hand, patients benefit if the plan does a good job in excluding those who provide substandard care or whose care is unnecessarily intensive and imposes unnecessary risks and costs upon patients, either directly or indirectly.

In considering claims of wrongful discharge from health plans, courts have looked to two strains of law in health care—the staff privileges system with its emphasis on procedural protections (unless the physician holds privileges subject to a clean sweep clause) and employment-at-will (with its quite narrow grounds for wrongful discharge).

State courts considering claims by doctors charging that their termination was wrongful have reached different results. See, e.g., Mayer v. Pierce County Med. Bureau, 80 Wash.App. 416, 909 P.2d 1323 (1995), holding that no-cause termination of a doctor from the preferred provider program of the health plan did not violate common law when his membership in the plan itself remained intact; Grossman v. Columbine Med. Group, 12 P.3d 269 (Colo. Ct. App. 1999, as modified Jan. 14, 2000), holding that public policy supports no-cause termination clause agreed upon by physician in managed care contract; Harper v. Healthsource New Hampshire, 140 N.H. 770, 674 A.2d 962 (1996), prohibiting bad faith termination of physician.

In one of the more well-known cases, Potvin v. Metropolitan Life Ins. Co., 22 Cal.4th 1060, 95 Cal.Rptr.2d 496, 997 P.2d 1153 (2000), the California Supreme Court overturned the appellate court's holding that Dr. Potvin was entitled to common-law "fair procedure" prior to termination from the plan. The state Supreme Court, instead, held that the physician would not be entitled to procedure prior to termination unless certain circumstances existed. The plan would have to provide pretermination procedure "only when the insurer possesses power so substantial that the [termination] impairs the ability of an ordinary, competent physician to practice medicine or a medical specialty in a particular geographic area, thereby affecting an important substantial economic interest." In a footnote, the court notes, however, that its holding does not apply to employer-employee relationships.

A good number of state legislatures entered the fray and enacted legislation that aimed at providing doctors some level of economic security in their relations with managed care. Most of this legislation addresses only those situations in which the doctor is terminated for "advocating" on behalf of a patient. These statutes may not apply in the employment-at-will context, however. See Eusterman v. Northwest Permanente, P.C., 204 Or.App. 224, 129 P.3d 213 (2006). Thus, a doctor working as an employee of an HMO would not be protected by the statute and would have to rely on employment-at-will while a doctor working under contract with an HMO would be protected by the statute (and by the contract terms on termination, if any).

The dispute over whether this type of legislation protects or harms patients by effectively dismantling managed care still persists. Virginia Gray, et al., The Political Management of Managed Care: Explaining Variations in State Health Maintenance Organization Regulations, 32 J. Health Pol. Pol'y & L. 457 (2007); Mitesh S. Patel, et al., The Impact of the Adoption of Gag Laws on Trust in the Patient-Physician Relationship, 32 J. Health Pol. Pol'y & L. 819 (2007); Robert F. Rich & Christopher T. Erb, The Two Faces of Managed Care Regulation & Policymaking, 16 Stan. L. & Pol'y Rev. 233 (2005).

Note on the National Labor Relations Act

The beginning of the 21st century has seen a surge in unionization in the health care field, including unionization of doctors and nurses. In fact, a group of health law experts included labor law in its "Top Ten for 2007," noting that "[u]nion campaigns and initiatives will make labor and employment a big issue as workers seek to expose inequities and alleged quality of care deficiencies." 16 Health L. Rep. 5 (2007).

Union organizing among nurses has provided a platform for advocacy on staffing issues in hospitals and nursing homes. See, e.g., SEIU Contract with Allegheny Hospital Provides Specific Nurse-to-Patient Ratios, 15 Health L. Rep. 1110 (2006). California nurse unions were instrumental in the passage and implementation of legislation establishing minimum nursing staff ratios for particular hospital services. California Governor Drops Appeal in Fight Over Hospital Staffing Ratios, 14 Health L. Rep. 1489 (2005). Staffing ratios are associated closely with quality of care. GAO, Nursing Homes: Quality of Care More Related to Staffing than Spending (2002); Donald M. Steinwachs, Keeping Patients Safe: Transforming the Work Environment of Nurses, Institute of Medicine (2003), recommending increased nurse staffing levels in nursing homes and hospitals as essential to reducing hazards to patient care. Advocacy on staffing by the nurse unions is self-interested as well.

Doctors also have engaged in collective action, especially in connection with managed care relationships. In 1999, the American Medical Association created a union to represent doctors. Physicians for Responsible Negotiation, the AMA union, currently represents doctors at several sites. In order to be covered by the NLRA, however, workers must be employees, and not independent contractors, as understood in the common law.

The health care professions traditionally resisted unionization stridently as an indicator of a lack of professionalism. What explains the turnaround? Are the factors that have changed the profession's view of unions the same for nurses as for doctors? See, generally, Marion Crain, The Transformation of the Professional Workforce, 79 Chi.-Kent L. Rev. 543 (2004).

In contrast to the doctrine of at-will employment discussed in the previous section, the National Labor Relations Act offers significant protections to workers who fall within its coverage.

One of the most significant protections that the NLRA provides to qualified workers is protection from adverse job actions (such as termination, demotion, or salary action) by the employer in response to covered employees' acting in concert over the terms and conditions of employment. Terms and conditions of employment include the expected areas of wages and salary, staffing, job security, discipline, union organization, promotion paths, hours, assignments, and other working conditions. It has also been held to include employee complaints and resistance to hospital reorganizations and preparation of reports prepared by more than one employee concerning the quality of care at a hospital and even concerns about hospital billing practices for their effects on the patients with whom the employees work. Thus, the NLRA can provide protection in areas in which employment-at-will does not.

An employee need not be a member of a recognized or even informal union in order to have the benefit of this protection. An employee, however, is not covered by the Act if he or she is a "supervisor." The application of this term, as used in the NLRA, has been a serious problem in the health care industry. After many years of battles among the National Labor Relations Board, the Supreme Court, and the Circuit Courts of Appeal over the appropriate interpretation of the statutory definition of the term, the Board issued decisions in 2006 that may resolve that issue, at least for the moment. In Oakwood Healthcare, Inc., 348 NLRB No. 37 (2006) and Golden Crest, 348 NLRB No. 39 (2006), the Board acquiesced in the definition that the Supreme Court had sought to impose many years earlier.

Prior to *Oakwood* and *Golden Crest*, the Board had applied a very narrow concept of supervisor to health care professionals. The Board's view at that time recognized that most health care professionals are inherently engaged in supervisory functions over the persons who assist them in their work. The Board's position was that a broader definition of supervisor would exclude almost every health care professional from the scope of the Act, a result that Congress could not have intended when they acted to bring the health care workplace within the coverage of the NLRA in 1974.

In *Oakwood* and *Golden Crest*, however, the Board adopted a narrow definition. Under this definition, an employee (such as an RN or an LPN) who assigns or "responsibly directs," using his or her independent judgment, other employees (such as nurse aides and nurse techs) and who is evaluated and faces real consequences based on his or her performance of the supervisory function is a supervisor. It is still too early to tell whether these decisions will thwart the union movement in health care. Early ALJ decisions reviewing pending cases under this new standard have not produced uniform results. In addition, some unions in health care have been able to negotiate contracts with employers who agree not to challenge the supervisory status of some groups of employees.

Note on Discrimination Law

Discrimination cases arise in the health care setting as they do in any workplace. For most issues, the health care workplace does not present unique issues for the application of state and federal law protecting individuals against employment discrimination on account of age (the Age Discrimination in Employment Act, 29 U.S.C. § 621), disability (the Americans with Disabilities Act, 42 U.S.C. § 12101, and the Rehabilitation Act, 29 U.S.C. § 701), gender, national origin, religion, or race (Title VII of the Civil Rights Act of 1964, 42 U.S.C. § 2000e).

In the area of disability discrimination, however, the issue of risk to patients has been a special concern. An employee claiming under one of the federal disability statutes must prove that he or she can perform the essential functions of the job either with or without accommodation for his or her disability. If the employee poses a "direct threat" to the employee's or others' health and safety, which cannot be eliminated through a reasonable accommodation, the employee is not qualified for the job and has no claim. In dealing with communicable diseases, the cases under the federal disability statutes require a number of inquiries. Has the employer made a reasonable accommodation, for example, in the form of job assignment, adjustment of duties, or provision of protective equipment, that would allow the disabled employee to perform the job safely? Or, is the job assignment or adjustment made by the employer itself discriminatory in excluding the employee from work he or she is capable of doing? Much of the litigation concerning "direct threat" has arisen in the context of HIV infection:

> To prevail under his Americans with Disabilities Act claim, [plaintiff William Mauro] must show that he is "otherwise qualified" for the job at issue. [ ] A person is "otherwise qualified" if he or she can perform the essential functions of the job in question. [ ] A disabled individual, however, is not "qualified" for a specific employment position if he or she poses a "direct threat" to the health or safety of others which cannot be eliminated by a reasonable accommodation. [ ]

> The "direct threat" standard applied in the Americans with Disabilities Act is based on the same standard as "significant risk" applied by the Rehabilitation Act. [ ]. Our analysis under both Acts thus merges into one question: Did Mauro's activities as a surgical technician at Borgess pose a direct threat or significant risk to the health or safety of others?

> [School Bd. of Nassau Cty. v. Arline, 480 U.S. 273, 107 S.Ct. 1123, 94 L.Ed.2d 307 (1987)] laid down four factors to consider in this analysis: (a) the nature of the risk (how the disease is transmitted), (b) the duration of the risk (how long is the carrier infectious), (c) the severity of the risk (what is the potential harm to third parties) and (d) the probabilities the disease will be transmitted and will cause varying degrees of harm. [ ]

> To show that one is "otherwise qualified," neither Act requires the elimination of all risk posed by a person with a contagious disease. In Arline the Supreme Court determined that a person with an infectious disease "who poses a significant risk of communicating an infectious disease to others in the workplace," is not otherwise qualified to perform his or her job. [ ] If the risk is not significant, however, the person is qualified to perform the job. The EEOC guidelines provide further insight:

>> An employer ... is not permitted to deny an employment opportunity to an individual with a disability merely because of a slightly increased risk. The risk can only be considered when it poses a significant risk, i.e. high probability, of substantial harm; a speculative or remote risk is insufficient. [ ]

* * *

The parties agree that the first three factors of the Arline test: the nature, duration, and severity of the risk, all indicate that Mauro posed a significant risk to others. Mauro argues, however, that because the probability of transmission, the fourth factor of Arline, was so slight, it overwhelmed the first three factors and created a genuine issue of material fact.

In determining whether Mauro posed a significant risk or a direct threat in the performance of the essential functions of his job as a surgical technician, Arline, instructs that courts should defer to the "reasonable medical judgments of public health officials." [ ] The Centers for Disease Control is such a body of public health officials. [ ] The Centers for Disease Control has released a report discussing its recommendations regarding HIV-positive health care workers. [ ]

The Report states that the risk of transmission of HIV from an infected health care worker to a patient is very small, and therefore recommends allowing most HIV-positive health care workers to continue performing most surgical procedures, provided that the workers follow safety precautions outlined in the Report. [ ] The Report, however, differentiates a limited category of invasive procedures, which it labels exposure-prone procedures, from general invasive procedures. [ ] General invasive procedures cover a wide range of procedures from insertion of an intravenous line to most types of surgery. [ ] Exposure-prone procedures, however, involve those that pose a greater risk of percutaneous (skin-piercing) injury. Though the Centers for Disease Control did not specifically identify which types of procedures were to be labeled exposure-prone, it supplies a general definition: "Characteristics of exposure-prone procedures include digital palpation of a needle tip in a body cavity or the simultaneous presence of the [health care worker's] fingers and a needle or other sharp instrument or object in a poorly visualized or highly confined anatomic site." [ ] The Report advises that individual health care institutions take measures to identify which procedures performed in their hospital should be labeled exposure-prone and recommends that HIV-infected health care workers should not perform exposure-prone procedures unless they have sought counsel from an expert review panel and have been advised under what circumstances they may continue to perform these procedures. The Report further recommends that those health care workers who engage in exposure-prone procedures notify prospective patients of their condition.

We must defer to the medical judgment expressed in the Report of the Centers for Disease Control in evaluating the district court's ruling on whether Mauro posed a direct threat in the essential functions of his job.

* * *

Mauro explained that during his training, discussion had occurred indicating that nicks and cuts were always a possibility for a surgical technician. In fact, the record included two incident reports involving Mauro. One report indicated that Mauro had sliced his right index finger while removing a knife blade from a handle on June 25, 1991, and another report indicated that he had scratched his hand with the sharp end of a dirty needle while threading it on June 8, 1990.

* * *

We conclude that the district court did not err in determining that Mauro's continued employment as a surgical technician posed a direct threat to the health and safety of others.

* * *

Estate of Mauro v. Borgess Medical Center, 137 F.3d 398 (6th Cir.1998).

Mauro is typical of cases that have considered claims by health care workers performing surgical functions. See e.g., Doe v. University of Maryland Med. System Corp., 50 F.3d 1261 (4th Cir. 1995). In decisions involving nonsurgical health care jobs, the courts have often rejected claims of unacceptable risk, viewing those risks as speculative or hypothetical. Doe v. Attorney General, 62 F.3d 1424 (9th Cir. 1995).

Risk assessment is a critical function in the ADA's direct-threat defense. See Sarah R. Christie, AIDS, Employment, and the Direct Threat Defense: The Burden of Proof and the Circuit Court Split, 76 Fordham L. Rev. 235 (2007); Manju Gupta, Occupational Risk: The Outrageous Reaction to HIV Positive Public Safety and Health Care Employees in the Workplace, 19 J. L. & Health 39 (2004–2005); Sidney D. Watson, Eliminating Fear Through Comparative Risk: Docs, AIDS and the Anti–Discrimination Ideal, 40 Buffalo L. Rev. 739 (1992); Mary Anne Bobinski, Risk and Rationality: The Centers for Disease Control and the Regulation of HIV–Infected Workers, 36 St. Louis U.L.J. 213 (1991).

As of 2003, the CDC reported 57 documented cases of occupational transmission of the virus to health care workers. Of these, twenty-six workers developed AIDS. There were an additional 139 HIV-positive health care workers who reported no risk factors for HIV and who reported workplace exposure to the virus but who tested negative after the exposure. Worker Health Chartbook 2004. NIOSH Publication No. 2004–146. Surveillance indicates that the route of exposure makes a difference in whether the individual will become infected with the virus. The risk after needlestick or cut exposure to HIV-infected blood is 0.3% (99.7% of those who are exposed in that way do not become infected) and exposure of the mouth, eyes, or nose to HIV-infected blood is 0.1%. Post-exposure prophylactic treatment does bring its own health risks, and so it is not recommended for the lowest-risk exposures (as defined by route of exposure and HIV status of patient). See, CDC, Updated U.S. Public Health Service Guidelines for the Management of Occupational Exposures to HIV and Recommendations for Postexposure Prophylaxis, MMWR, September 30, 2005. In contrast, the risk of transmission of hepatitis C from needlestick is 1.8%. CDC, Exposure to Blood (2003). Because needlesticks present the greatest risk of transmission for HIV and other bloodborne pathogens, there are several regulatory efforts to set prevention standards, including efforts to engineer safety devices to avoid needlesticks.

There have been only six patients infected with HIV, and these are all reported from a single dentist before 1990. Studies conducted on 22,000 patients treated by 63 HIV-positive health care providers found no evidence of transmission from the providers. Are Patients in a Health Care Setting at Risk of Getting HIV?, available at www.cdc.gov/hiv/pubs/faq/faq29.htm.

The most common bloodborne infection in the U.S. is hepatitis C, and it is estimated that 3.9 million people in the U.S. have been infected. Of persons infected with hepatitis C, 70% will develop chronic liver disease with a death rate of approximately 3%. The virus is responsible for forty percent of all chronic liver disease which is the tenth leading cause of death in adults. It is most commonly transmitted by people who do not feel ill and, therefore, do not know that they are infected. The CDC has not made recommendations restricting the duties of health care workers infected with hepatitis C, and health care workers are only tested after they are exposed to blood or body fluids of patients. CDC, Recommendations for Prevention and Control of Hepatitis C Virus Infection and HCV–Related Chronic Disease, MMWR 1998. See also, Viral Hepatitis Transmission in Ambulatory Health Care Settings (Dec. 2006), http://www.cdc.gov/ncidod/diseases/hepatitis/spotlights/ambulatory.htm.

Health care workers with a wide variety of disabilities have brought claims under § 504 and the ADA. These cases can raise similar issues of accommodation and patient risk as do the HIV cases. For an overview, see Laura F. Rothstein, Health Care Professionals With Mental and Physical Impairments: Developments in Disability Discrimination Law, 41 St. Louis U.L.J. 973 (1997).

Chapter 11

THE STRUCTURE OF THE HEALTH CARE ENTERPRISE

I. INTRODUCTION

In 1978, Waldo, a 35 year old graphic artist, visited his family physician, Doctor Goodscalpel, complaining of gas, bloating and irregularity. Doctor Goodscalpel, a solo practitioner, took a brief history and ordered blood tests, urinalysis and various chemistry tests, all of which were performed at Llama Labs. Llama Labs was an outpatient facility organized as a corporation, the shares of which were owned by Dr. Goodscalpel and two other physicians. On a subsequent office visit several weeks later, Dr. Goodscalpel performed a rigid sigmoidoscopy and ordered x-rays for an upper GI which were done at the Midstate Hospital. Midstate was a small community hospital from which Dr. Goodscalpel leased his office and at which he maintained staff privileges.

The results of these tests led Dr. Goodscalpel to recommend that Waldo consult a specialist, Dr. Jones, a gastroenterologist, who was a member of Practice Group, a professional corporation located in an adjacent town. Dr. Jones admitted Waldo as an inpatient and performed a colonoscopy at Mt. St. Hilda Hospital, a not-for-profit teaching hospital controlled by the Order of Caramel Fellowship, a religious denomination that operates 20 hospitals nationwide. Unfortunately, during this procedure Waldo suffered a perforated colon and required additional surgery which was performed by Dr. Smith, whom Waldo met the night before the surgery and Dr. Mack, a resident studying at Mt. St. Hilda.

The bill for these services ran four pages and included over 150 separate services, items and supplies. Waldo's not-for-profit health insurance company, Red Flag, paid each provider separately for their services, although Waldo was responsible for nominal co-payments and in some cases, for the "balance billing" where the billed charges of the provider exceeded Red Flag's "maximum allowable charges."

Waldo's encounter with the health care system brought him into contact with a number of different kinds of health care providers doing business in a variety of organizational structures. Arrangements of this kind were not unusual a few years ago and persist even today in many communities. What kinds of problems and inefficiencies do you see arising from this "system" of delivery of services? What are its advantages? As a "consumer" of health services, was Waldo well-served in this episode? For example, how were choices made and on what basis?

This chapter will explore the legal issues posed by many of these business and institutional arrangements. It will also analyze the trend toward integration that has created many new organizational structures designed to unite the various providers of care. These new arrangements, it will be seen, are still in their formative stages and entail a host of legal issues for the modern health law practitioner.

II. FORMS OF BUSINESS ENTERPRISES AND THEIR LEGAL CONSEQUENCES

A. GOVERNANCE AND FIDUCIARY DUTIES IN BUSINESS ASSOCIATIONS

The governance of corporations is shared by three groups: shareholders (or members in the case of some not-for-profits), the board of directors, and officers. In practice, particularly in large corporations, the officers have almost complete control over the business affairs of the corporation. This separation of ownership and control in the for-profit corporate setting may give rise to the exploitation of shareholders. It also poses problems in not-for-profit corporations as boards may not faithfully or diligently pursue the entity's charitable purposes. To deal with this problem, the common law imposes fiduciary duties on those who govern the corporation, essentially obligating directors and officers to act in its best interests.

STERN v. LUCY WEBB HAYES NATIONAL TRAINING SCHOOL FOR DEACONESSES AND MISSIONARIES

United States District Court, District of Columbia, 1974.
381 F.Supp. 1003.

Gesell, District Judge.

This is a class action which was tried to the Court without a jury. Plaintiffs were certified as a class under Rule 23(b)(2) of the Federal Rules of Civil Procedure and represent patients of Sibley Memorial Hospital, a District of Columbia non-profit charitable corporation organized under D.C.Code s 29–1001 et seq. They challenge various aspects of the Hospital's fiscal management. The amended complaint named as defendants nine members of the Hospital's Board of Trustees, six financial institutions, and the Hospital itself. Four trustees and one financial institution were dropped by plaintiffs prior to trial, and the Court dismissed the complaint as to the remaining financial institutions at the close of plaintiffs' case.

* * *

The two principal contentions in the complaint are that the defendant trustees conspired to enrich themselves and certain financial institutions with which they were affiliated by favoring those institutions in financial dealings with the Hospital, and that they breached their fiduciary duties of care and loyalty in the management of Sibley's funds. The defendant financial institutions are said to have joined in the alleged conspiracy and to have knowingly benefited from the alleged breaches of duty. The Hospital is named as a nominal defendant for the purpose of facilitating relief.

I. CORPORATE HISTORY

The Lucy Webb Hayes National Training School for Deaconesses and Missionaries was established in 1891 by the Methodist Women's Home Missionary Society for the purpose, in part, of providing health care services to the poor of the Washington area. The School was incorporated under the laws of the District of Columbia as a charitable, benevolent and educational institution by instrument dated August 8, 1894. During the following year, the School built the Sibley Memorial Hospital on North Capitol Street to facilitate its charitable work. Over the years, operation of the Hospital has become the School's principal concern, so that the two institutions have been referred to synonymously by all parties and will be so treated in this Opinion.

* * *

Under the ... by-laws, the Board was to consist of from 25 to 35 trustees, who were to meet at least twice each year. Between such meetings, an Executive Committee was to represent the Board, and was authorized, inter alia, to open checking and savings accounts, approve the Hospital budget, renew mortgages, and enter into contracts. A Finance Committee was created to review the budget and to report regularly on the amount of cash available for investment. Management of those investments was to be supervised by an Investment Committee, which was to work closely with the Finance Committee in such matters.

In fact, management of the Hospital from the early 1950's until 1968 was handled almost exclusively by two trustee officers: Dr. Orem, the Hospital Administrator, and Mr. Ernst, the Treasurer. Unlike most of their fellow trustees, to whom membership on the Sibley Board was a charitable service incidental to their principal vocations, Orem and Ernst were continuously involved on almost a daily basis in the affairs of Sibley. They dominated the Board and its Executive Committee, which routinely accepted their recommendations and ratified their actions. Even more significantly, neither the Finance Committee nor the Investment Committee ever met or conducted business from the date of their creation until 1971, three years after the death of Dr. Orem. As a result, budgetary and investment decisions during this period, like most other management decisions affecting the Hospital's finances, were handled by Orem and Ernst, receiving only cursory supervision from the Executive Committee and the full Board.

Dr. Orem's death on April 5, 1968, obliged some of the other trustees to play a more active role in running the Hospital. The Executive Committee, and particularly defendant Stacy Reed (as Chairman of the Board, President of the Hospital, and ex officio member of the Executive Committee), became more deeply involved in the day-to-day management of the Hospital while efforts were made to find a new Administrator. The man who was eventually selected for that office, Dr. Jarvis, had little managerial experience and his performance was not entirely satisfactory. Mr. Ernst still made most of the financial and investment decisions for Sibley, but his actions and failures to act came slowly under increasing scrutiny by several of the other trustees, particularly after a series of disagreements between Ernst and the Hospital Comptroller which led to the discharge of the latter early in 1971.

Prompted by these difficulties, Mr. Reed decided to activate the Finance and Investment Committee in the Fall of 1971. However, as Chairman of the Finance Committee and member of the Investment Committee as well as Treasurer, Mr. Ernst continued to exercise dominant control over investment decisions and, on several occasions, discouraged and flatly refused to respond to inquiries by other trustees into such matters. It has only been since the death of Mr. Ernst on October 30, 1972, that the other trustees appear to have assumed an identifiable supervisory role over investment policy and Hospital fiscal management in general.

Against this background, the basic claims will be examined.

II. CONSPIRACY

Plaintiffs first contend that the five defendant trustees and the five defendant financial institutions were involved in a conspiracy to enrich themselves at the expense of the Hospital. They point to the fact that each named trustee held positions of responsibility with one or more of the defendant institutions as evidence that the trustees had both motive and opportunity to carry out such a conspiracy.

* * *

Plaintiffs further contend that the defendants accomplished the alleged conspiracy by arranging to have Sibley maintain unnecessarily large amounts of money on deposit with the defendant banks and savings and loan associations, drawing inadequate or no interest. [T]he Hospital in fact maintained much of its liquid assets in savings and checking accounts rather than in Treasury bonds or investment securities, at least until the investment review instituted by Mr. Reed late in 1971. In that year, for example, more than one-third of the nearly four million dollars available for investment was deposited in checking accounts, as compared to only about $135,000 in securities and $311,000 in Treasury bills.

* * *

It is also undisputed that most of these funds were deposited in the defendant financial institutions. A single checking account, drawing no interest whatever and maintained alternately at Riggs National Bank and Security National Bank, usually contained more than $250,000 and on one occasion grew to nearly $1,000,000.

Defendants were able to offer no adequate justification for this utilization of the Hospital's liquid assets. By the same token, however, plaintiffs failed to establish that it was [the] result of a conscious direction on the part of the named defendants.

* * *

[The court concluded that plaintiffs failed to establish a conspiracy between the trustees and the financial institutions or among the members of each group.]

III. BREACH OF DUTY

Plaintiffs' second contention is that, even if the facts do not establish a conspiracy, they do reveal serious breaches of duty on the part of the defendant trustees and the knowing acceptance of benefits from those breaches by the defendant banks and savings and loan associations.

A. *The Trustees*

Basically, the trustees are charged with mismanagement, nonmanagement and self-dealing. * * * [T]he modern trend is to apply corporate rather than trust principles in determining the liability of the directors of charitable corporations, because their functions are virtually indistinguishable from those of their "pure" corporate counterparts.

1. *Mismanagement*

Both trustees and corporate directors are liable for losses occasioned by their negligent mismanagement of investments. However, the degree of care required appears to differ in many jurisdictions. A trustee is uniformly held to a high standard of care and will be held liable for simple negligence, while a director must often have committed "gross negligence" or otherwise be guilty of more than mere mistakes of judgment.

This distinction may amount to little more than a recognition of the fact that corporate directors have many areas of responsibility, while the traditional trustee is often charged only with the management of the trust funds and can therefore be expected to devote more time and expertise to that task. Since the board members of most large charitable corporations fall within the corporate rather than the trust model, being charged with the operation of ongoing businesses, it has been said that they should only be held to the less stringent corporate standard of care. Beard v. Achenbach Mem. Hosp. Ass'n, 170 F.2d 859, 862 (10th Cir.1948). More specifically, directors of charitable corporations are required to exercise ordinary and reasonable care in the performance of their duties, exhibiting honesty and good faith. Beard v. Achenbach Mem. Hosp. Ass'n, *supra*, at 862.

2. *Nonmanagement*

Plaintiffs allege that the individual defendants failed to supervise the management of Hospital investments or even to attend meetings of the committees charged with such supervision. Trustees are particularly vulnerable to such a charge, because they not only have an affirmative duty to "maximize the trust income by prudent investment," Blankenship v. Boyle, 329 F.Supp. 1089, 1096 (D.D.C. 1971), but they may not delegate that duty, even to a committee of their fellow trustees. Restatement (Second) of Trusts § 171, at 375 (1959). A corporate director, on the other hand, may delegate his investment responsibility to fellow directors, corporate officers, or even outsiders, but he must continue to exercise general supervision over the activities of his delegates. Once again, the rule for charitable corporations is closer to the traditional corporate rule: directors should at least be permitted to delegate investment decisions to a committee of board members, so long as all directors assume the responsibility for supervising such committees by periodically scrutinizing their work.

Total abdication of the supervisory role, however, is improper even under traditional corporate principles. A director who fails to acquire the information necessary to supervise investment policy or consistently fails even to attend the meetings at which such policies are considered has violated his fiduciary duty to the corporation. While a director is, of course, permitted to rely upon the expertise of those to whom he has delegated investment responsibility, such reliance is a tool for interpreting the delegate's reports, not an excuse for dispensing with or ignoring such reports. A director whose failure to supervise permits negligent mismanagement by others to go unchecked has committed an independent wrong against the corporation; he is not merely an accessory under an attenuated theory of respondent [sic] superior or constructive notice.

3. *Self-dealing*

Under District of Columbia Law, neither trustees nor corporate directors are absolutely barred from placing funds under their control into a bank having an interlocking directorship with their own institution. In both cases, however, such transactions will be subjected to the closest scrutiny to determine whether or not the duty of loyalty has been violated. A deliberate conspiracy among trustees or Board members to enrich the interlocking bank at the expense of the trust or corporation would, for example, constitute such a breach and render the conspirators liable for any losses. In the absence of clear evidence of wrongdoing, however, the courts appear to have used different standards to determine whether or not relief is appropriate, depending again on the legal relationship involved. Trustees may be found guilty of a breach of trust even for mere negligence in the maintenance of accounts in banks with which they are associated, while corporate directors are generally only required to show "entire fairness" to the corporation and "full disclosure" of the potential conflict of interest to the Board.

Most courts apply the less stringent corporate rule to charitable corporations in this area as well. It is, however, occasionally added that a director should not only disclose his interlocking responsibilities but also refrain from voting on or otherwise influencing a corporate decision to transact business with a company in which he has a significant interest or control.

Although defendants have argued against the imposition of even these limitations on self-dealing by the Sibley trustees, the Hospital Board recently adopted a new by-law, based upon guidelines issued by the American Hospital Association, which essentially imposes the modified corporate rule. * * *

* * *

Having surveyed the authorities as outlined above and weighed the briefs, arguments and evidence submitted by counsel, the Court holds that a director or so-called trustee of a charitable hospital organized under the Non–Profit Corporation Act of the District of Columbia [ ] is in default of his fiduciary duty to manage the fiscal and investment affairs of the hospital if it has been shown by a preponderance of the evidence that:

(1) while assigned to a particular committee of the Board having general financial or investment responsibility under the by-laws of the corporation, he has failed to use due diligence in supervising the actions of those

officers, employees or outside experts to whom the responsibility for making day-to-day financial or investment decisions has been delegated; or

(2) he knowingly permitted the hospital to enter into a business transaction with himself or with any corporation, partnership or association in which he then had a substantial interest or held a position as trustee, director, general manager or principal officer without having previously informed the persons charged with approving that transaction of his interest or position and of any significant reasons, unknown to or not fully appreciated by such persons, why the transaction might not be in the best interests of the hospital; or

(3) except as required by the preceding paragraph, he actively participated in or voted in favor of a decision by the Board or any committee or subcommittee thereof to transact business with himself or with any corporation, partnership or association in which he then had a substantial interest or held a position as trustee, director, general manager or principal officer; or

(4) he otherwise failed to perform his duties honestly, in good faith, and with a reasonable amount of diligence and care.

Applying these standards to the facts in the record, the Court finds that each of the defendant trustees has breached his fiduciary duty to supervise the management of Sibley's investments. All except Mr. Jones were duly and repeatedly elected to the Investment Committee without ever bothering to object when no meetings were called for more than ten years. Mr. Jones was a member of the equally inactive Finance Committee, the failure of which to report on the existence of investable funds was cited by several other defendants as a reason for not convening the Investment Committee. In addition, Reed, Jones and Smith were, for varying periods of time, also members of the Executive Committee, which was charged with acquiring at least enough information to vote intelligently on the opening of new bank accounts. By their own testimony, it is clear that they failed to do so. And all of the individual defendants ignored the investment sections of the yearly audits which were made available to them as members of the Board. In short, these men have in the past failed to exercise even the most cursory supervision over the handling of Hospital funds and failed to establish and carry out a defined policy.

The record is unclear on the degree to which full disclosure preceded the frequent self-dealing which occurred during the period under consideration. It is reasonable to assume that the Board was generally aware of the various bank affiliations of the defendant trustees, but there is no indication that these conflicting interests were brought home to the relevant committees when they voted to approve particular transactions. Similarly, while plaintiffs have shown no active misrepresentation on defendants' part, they have established instances in which an interested trustee failed to alert the responsible officials to better terms known to be available elsewhere.

It is clear that all of the defendant trustees have, at one time or another, affirmatively approved self-dealing transactions. Most of these incidents were of relatively minor significance.

* * *

That the Hospital has suffered no measurable injury from many of these transactions—including the mortgage and the investment contract—and that the excessive deposits which were the real source of harm were caused primarily by the uniform failure to supervise rather than the occasional self-dealing vote are both facts that the Court must take into account in fashioning relief, but they do not alter the principle that the trustee of a charitable hospital should always avoid active participation in a transaction in which he or a corporation with which he is associated has a significant interest.

* * *

IV. RELIEF

* * *

[The Court ordered by injunction (1) that the appropriate committees and officers of the Hospital present to the full Board a written policy statement governing investments and the use of idle cash in the Hospital's bank accounts and other funds, (2) the establishment of a procedure for the periodic reexamination of existing investments and other financial arrangements to insure compliance with Board policies, and (3) that each trustee fully disclose his affiliation with financial institutions doing business with the Hospital. Declining to remove defendant trustees from the Board or to impose personal liability on directors, Judge Gesell offered the following guidance.]

The management of a non-profit charitable hospital imposes a severe obligation upon its trustees. A hospital such as Sibley is not closely regulated by any public authority, it has no responsibility to file financial reports, and its Board is self-perpetuating. The interests of its patients are funneled primarily through large group insurers who pay the patients' bills, and the patients lack meaningful participation in the Hospital's affairs. It is obvious that, in due course, new trustees must come to the Board of this Hospital, some of whom will be affiliated with banks, savings and loan associations and other financial institutions. The tendency of representatives of such institutions is often to seek business in return for advice and assistance rendered as trustees. It must be made absolutely clear that Board membership carries no right to preferential treatment in the placement or handling of the Hospital's investments and business accounts. The Hospital would be well advised to restrict membership on its Board to the representatives of financial institutions which have no substantial business relationship with the Hospital. The best way to avoid potential conflicts of interest and to be assured of objective advice is to avoid the possibility of such conflicts at the time new trustees are selected.

As an additional safeguard, the Court will require that each newly-elected trustee read this Opinion and the attached Order. [The Court also required public disclosure of all business dealings between the hospital and any financial institution with which any officer or trustee of the hospital is affiliated and that the hospital make summaries of all such dealings available on request to all patients.]

IN RE CAREMARK INTERNATIONAL
INC. DERIVATIVE LITIGATION

Court of Chancery of Delaware, 1996.
698 A.2d 959.

ALLEN, CHANCELLOR.

Pending is a motion ... to approve as fair and reasonable a proposed settlement of a consolidated derivative action on behalf of Caremark International, Inc. ("Caremark"). The suit involves claims that the members of Caremark's board of directors (the "Board") breached their fiduciary duty of care to Caremark in connection with alleged violations by Caremark employees of federal and state laws and regulations applicable to health care providers. As a result of the alleged violations, Caremark was subject to an extensive four year investigation by the United States Department of Health and Human Services and the Department of Justice. In 1994 Caremark was charged in an indictment with multiple felonies. It thereafter entered into a number of agreements with the Department of Justice and others. Those agreements included a plea agreement in which Caremark pleaded guilty to a single felony of mail fraud and agreed to pay civil and criminal fines. Subsequently, Caremark agreed to make reimbursements to various private and public parties. In all, the payments that Caremark has been required to make total approximately $250 million.

This suit was filed in 1994, purporting to seek on behalf of the company recovery of these losses from the individual defendants who constitute the board of directors of Caremark. The parties now propose that it be settled.

* * *

The ultimate issue then is whether the proposed settlement appears to be fair to the corporation and its absent shareholders.

* * *

Legally, evaluation of the central claim made entails consideration of the legal standard governing a board of directors' obligation to supervise or monitor corporate performance. For the reasons set forth below I conclude, in light of the discovery record, that there is a very low probability that it would be determined that the directors of Caremark breached any duty to appropriately monitor and supervise the enterprise. Indeed the record tends to show an active consideration by Caremark management and its Board of the Caremark structures and programs that ultimately led to the company's indictment and to the large financial losses incurred in the settlement of those claims. It does not tend to show knowing or intentional violation of law. Neither the fact that the Board, although advised by lawyers and accountants, did not accurately predict the severe consequences to the company that would ultimately follow from the deployment by the company of the strategies and practices that ultimately led to this liability, nor the scale of the liability, gives rise to an inference of breach of any duty imposed by corporation law upon the directors of Caremark.

[As part of its patient care business, which accounted for the majority of its revenues, Caremark provided alternative site health care services, including infusion therapy, growth hormone therapy, HIV/AIDS-related treatments and hemophilia therapy. Caremark's managed care services included prescription drug programs and the operation of multi-specialty group practices and it employed over 7,000 employees in ninety branch operations. It had a decentralized management structure but began to centralize operations in 1991 to increase supervision over branch operations. Caremark had taken a number of steps to assure compliance with the antikickback provisions of the Medicare fraud and abuse law discussed in Chapter 14. As early as 1989, Caremark's predecessor issued an internal "Guide to Contractual Relationships" ("Guide"), which was reviewed and updated, annually, to govern its employees in entering into contracts with physicians and hospitals. Caremark claimed there was uncertainty concerning the interpretation of federal antikickback laws because of the scarcity of court decisions and the "limited guidance" afforded by HHS "safe harbor" regulations. After the federal government had commenced its investigation, Caremark announced that it would no longer pay management fees to physicians for services to Medicare and Medicaid patients and required its regional officers to approve each contractual relationship it entered into with a physician. Caremark also established an internal audit plan designed to assure compliance with its business and ethics policies. Although a report by Price Waterhouse, its outside auditor, concluded that there were no material weaknesses in Caremark's control structure, the Board's ethics committee adopted a new internal audit charter, and took various other steps throughout to assure compliance with its policies.

In August and September, 1994, two federal grand juries indicted Caremark and individuals for violations of the anti-kickback laws, charging among other things that Caremark had made payments to a physician under "the guise of research grants . . . and consulting agreements" so he would prescribe Protropin, a Caremark-manufactured drug. Plaintiff shareholders filed this derivative suit claiming Caremark directors breached their duty of care by failing adequately to supervise Caremark employees or institute corrective measures thereby exposing the company to liability. In September, 1994, Caremark publicly announced that as of January 1, 1995, it would terminate all remaining financial relationships with physicians in its home infusion, hemophilia, and growth hormone lines of business.]

B. Directors' Duties To Monitor Corporate Operations

The complaint charges the director defendants with breach of their duty of attention or care in connection with the on-going operation of the corporation's business. The claim is that the directors allowed a situation to develop and continue which exposed the corporation to enormous legal liability and that in so doing they violated a duty to be active monitors of corporate performance. The complaint thus does not charge either director self-dealing or the more difficult loyalty-type problems arising from cases of suspect director motivation, such as entrenchment or sale of control contexts. The theory here advanced is possibly the most difficult theory in corporation law upon which a plaintiff might hope to win a judgment. * * *

1. Potential liability for directorial decisions: Director liability for a breach of the duty to exercise appropriate attention may, in theory, arise in two distinct contexts. First, such liability may be said to follow from a board

decision that results in a loss because that decision was ill advised or "negligent". Second, liability to the corporation for a loss may be said to arise from an unconsidered failure of the board to act in circumstances in which due attention would, arguably, have prevented the loss. The first class of cases will typically be subject to review under the director-protective business judgment rule, assuming the decision made was the product of a process that was either deliberately considered in good faith or was otherwise rational. What should be understood, but may not widely be understood by courts or commentators who are not often required to face such questions, is that compliance with a director's duty of care can never appropriately be judicially determined by reference to the content of the board decision that leads to a corporate loss, apart from consideration of the good faith or rationality of the process employed. That is, whether a judge or jury considering the matter after the fact, believes a decision substantively wrong, or degrees of wrong extending through "stupid" to "egregious" or "irrational", provides no ground for director liability, so long as the court determines that the process employed was either rational or employed in a good faith effort to advance corporate interests. To employ a different rule—one that permitted an "objective" evaluation of the decision—would expose directors to substantive second guessing by ill-equipped judges or juries, which would, in the long-run, be injurious to investor interests.[1] Thus, the business judgment rule is process oriented and informed by a deep respect for all good faith board decisions.

2. Liability for failure to monitor: The second class of cases in which director liability for inattention is theoretically possible entail circumstances in which a loss eventuates not from a decision but, from unconsidered inaction. Most of the decisions that a corporation, acting through its human agents, makes are, of course, not the subject of director attention. Legally, the board itself will be required only to authorize the most significant corporate acts or transactions: mergers, changes in capital structure, fundamental changes in business, appointment and compensation of the CEO, etc. As the facts of this case graphically demonstrate, ordinary business decisions that are made by officers and employees deeper in the interior of the organization can, however, vitally affect the welfare of the corporation and its ability to achieve its various strategic and financial goals.

Modernly this question has been given special importance by an increasing tendency, especially under federal law, to employ the criminal law to assure corporate compliance with external legal requirements, including environmental, financial, employee and product safety as well as assorted other health and safety regulations. In 1991, pursuant to the Sentencing Reform Act of 1984, the United States Sentencing Commission adopted Organizational Sentencing Guidelines which impact importantly on the prospective effect these criminal sanctions might have on business corporations. The Guidelines

---

1. The vocabulary of negligence while often employed, is not well-suited to judicial review of board attentiveness, especially if one attempts to look to the substance of the decision as any evidence of possible "negligence." * * * It is doubtful that we want business men and women to be encouraged to make decisions as hypothetical persons of ordinary judgment and prudence might. The corporate form gets its utility in large part from its ability to allow diversified investors to accept greater investment risk. If those in charge of the corporation are to be adjudged personally liable for losses on the basis of a substantive judgment based upon what persons of ordinary or average judgment and average risk assessment talent regard as "prudent," "sensible" or even "rational", such persons will have a strong incentive at the margin to authorize less risky investment projects.

set forth a uniform sentencing structure for organizations to be sentenced for violation of federal criminal statutes and provide for penalties that equal or often massively exceed those previously imposed on corporations. The Guidelines offer powerful incentives for corporations today to have in place compliance programs to detect violations of law, promptly to report violations to appropriate public officials when discovered, and to take prompt, voluntary remedial efforts.

* * *

[I]t would, in my opinion, be a mistake to conclude that our Supreme Court's [prior statements regarding directors' duty to monitor] means that corporate boards may satisfy their obligation to be reasonably informed concerning the corporation, without assuring themselves that information and reporting systems exist in the organization that are reasonably designed to provide to senior management and to the board itself timely, accurate information sufficient to allow management and the board, each within its scope, to reach informed judgments concerning both the corporation's compliance with law and its business performance.

Obviously the level of detail that is appropriate for such an information system is a question of business judgment. And obviously too, no rationally designed information and reporting system will remove the possibility that the corporation will violate laws or regulations, or that senior officers or directors may nevertheless sometimes be misled or otherwise fail reasonably to detect acts material to the corporation's compliance with the law. But it is important that the board exercise a good faith judgment that the corporation's information and reporting system is in concept and design adequate to assure the board that appropriate information will come to its attention in a timely manner as a matter of ordinary operations, so that it may satisfy its responsibility.

Thus, I am of the view that a director's obligation includes a duty to attempt in good faith to assure that a corporate information and reporting system, which the board concludes is adequate, exists, and that failure to do so under some circumstances may, in theory at least, render a director liable for losses caused by non-compliance with applicable legal standards.

* * *

[The Court went on to find that the Caremark directors had not breached their duty of care because, first, there was no evidence they knew of the violations of the law and they reasonably relied on expert reports that their company's practices, although "contestable," were lawful. Second, applying a test of whether there was a "sustained or systematic failure ... to exercise reasonable oversight," it found no actionable failure to monitor. The court concluded that the corporate oversight systems described above constituted a "good faith effort to be informed of relevant facts."]

Notes and Questions

1. Section 8.30 of The Revised Model Nonprofit Corporation Act adopts the corporate standard for the members of the board ("trustees") of not-for-profits, as do many state statutes. What arguments support a stricter standard for not-for-profit corporations? For one case applying a trust standard, see Lynch v. John M.

Redfield Foundation, 9 Cal.App.3d 293, 88 Cal.Rptr. 86 (1970). See generally Daniel L. Kurtz, Board Liability: Guide for Nonprofit Directors 22 (1988). Might a shifting standard of care apply, depending on the nature of the decision and how important that decision is to the organization's core functions or the community benefits it was designed to supply? See James J. Fishman & Stephen Schwarz, Nonprofit Organizations, 225–6 (2d. ed. 2000); 1 Furrow, et al., Health Law § 5–15—5–16 (2d ed. 2000). See also discussion of IRC § 501(c)(3) requirements *infra* this chapter. Thoughtful discussions of the issue of fiduciary duties in nonprofit charities can be found in American Law Institute, Principles of the Law of Nonprofit Organizations, Tentative Draft No. 1 (March 19, 2007) and James Fishman, Improving Charitable Accountability, 62 Md. L. Rev. 218 (2003).

2. In the case of for-profit corporations, the business judgment rule has come to pose an almost impermeable shield protecting directors and officers charged with breaches of the duty of care in connection with business decisions that prove to be unwise or imprudent. As long as the director has made a business judgment that is informed, in good faith and free of conflicts of interest, that judgment will not be subject to attack, even if the decision would not meet the simple negligence standard applicable to the "ordinarily prudent person." See Charles Hansen, The ALI Corporate Governance Project: Of the Duty of Care and the Business Judgment Rule, 41 Bus. Law. 1237 (1986). Should the business judgment rule apply with equal force to not-for-profit corporations? See Beard v. Achenbach Mem. Hosp. Association, 170 F.2d 859, 862 (10th Cir.1948) (business judgment rationale used to uphold hospital's payment of questionable retroactive "incentive bonuses"). Does the absence of shareholders or a public market for the stock make a difference? Are directors of not-for-profit boards more or less likely to be vigilant and savvy businesspersons than their for-profit counterparts? As Evelyn Brody has noted, because of the "pervasive challenge" posed by the "financially generous supporter who has little interest in participating in governance," many recommend adopting structural arrangements such as "strong executive committees and advisory boards." ALI Principles of the Law of Nonprofit Organizations, Reporter's memorandum at xxxv. See also 1 Furrow et al., Health Law § 5–15a (2d ed. 2000); Michael Peregrine, Revisiting the Duty of Care of the Nonprofit Director, 36 J. Health L. 183 (2003). For the view that the decision in the Sibley Hospital case typified the tendency of courts to be more receptive to duty of care complaints where the transaction is tainted by duty-of-loyalty implications, see Evelyn Brody, The Limits of Charity Fiduciary Law, 57 Md. L. Rev. 1400, 1442 (1998) ("One wonders whether Judge Gesell would have found any duty-of-care breach—or, more important, even granted standing to the plaintiff patients—had the funds been deposited at banks where the hospitals' directors were not also directors."). On the fiduciary duties of boards in health care institutions generally, see Naomi Ono, Boards of Directors Under Fire: An Examination of Nonprofit Board Duties in the Health Care Environment, 7 Annals Health L. 107 (1998); Peggy Sasso, Comment, Searching for Trust in the Not–For–Profit Boardroom: Looking Beyond the Duty of Obedience to Ensure Accountability, 50 UCLA L.Rev. 1485 (2003); Denise Ping Lee, Note, The Business Judgment Rule: Should it Protect Nonprofit Directors? 103 Colum. L.Rev. 925 (2003).

Does the standard established by the Chancellor in approving the settlement of the Caremark litigation give directors and senior officers of large, far-flung corporate enterprises sufficient incentives to ensure that their employees comply with the law? What factors mitigate against imposing a simple negligence standard with regard to the duty to monitor? Are the interests of the Caremark shareholders advanced by this holding? What role, if any, should the public interest in compliance with the anti-kickback laws play?

3. *Executive Compensation in Nonprofit Healthcare Organizations.* Consider also the increasingly controversial issue of executive compensation for nonprofit managers. Should the business judgment rule protect directors who pay little attention to the details of sometimes extravagant compensation packages they award to top executives? In the for-profit sector, the rule has shielded boards that have been extremely lax in their oversight of executive pay, although an emerging "good faith" requirement may give courts some additional elbowroom to review egregious abuses in this area. See In re Walt Disney Co. Derivative Litigation, 906 A.2d 27 (Del. Supr. 2006); Sarah H. Duggin & Stephan M. Goldman, Restoring Trust in Corporate Directors: The Disney Standard and the "New" Good Faith, 56 Am. U. L. Rev. 211 (2006).

A GAO survey of the 65 largest nonprofit hospital systems found that most hospitals had in place an executive compensation committee or entire board with the primary responsibility of approving executives' compensation packages and a conflict of interest policy and processes that reviewed comparable market data of total compensation and benefits. However, almost 40% had no written criteria for the selection of compensation committee members and did not require that compensation consultants be free of conflicts of interest; furthermore, 16% allowed the CEO or other top executives to be a voting member of an Executive Compensation body. Kimberly Brooks, et al., General Accountability Office, Survey of Nonprofit Health Systems Executive Compensation Policies (June 2006), www.gao.gov/new.items/d06907r.pdf., George Anning, et al., AHLA Corporate Governance Task Force, Corporate Governance Implications of Nonprofit Executive Compensation (June 2007). Should the executive compensation practices of nonprofit hospitals be held to a different standard than for profit entities? For that matter, should executives be paid less than their counterparts in the private sector? If your answer is yes to these questions, is scrutiny of approval practices of boards using fiduciary duties an efficient way of assuring the best results? Note that we will revisit this issue later in the chapter in the discussion of federal tax policies. In addition, some commentators and courts also recognize a "duty of obedience" which obligates directors to see to it that nonprofit corporations comply with legal obligations and adhere at all times to their corporate purposes or mission. This duty is discussed in the following section of this chapter.

4. The duty of loyalty applies to a variety of transactions in which directors or officers acting in their corporate capacity serve their own interests at the expense of those of the corporation. Self-dealing, taking of corporate opportunities, and acting in competition with the corporation may violate this duty. See, e.g. Gilbert v. McLeod Infirmary, 219 S.C. 174, 64 S.E.2d 524 (1951) (sale of property by hospital to trustees void where board members participated in the approval of the transaction and the hospital did not seek other buyers); Delaware Open MRI Radiology Associates v. Kessler, 898 A.2d 290 (Del. Ch. 2006) (directors representing majority shareholders of radiology group voting to "squeeze out" minority's ownership via merger constitutes conflict of interest and subjects transaction to judicial review of fairness of procedure and of buyout price). However, directors owe fiduciary duties only to their corporations, not to individual shareholders. Hence a professional corporation's termination of the contract of a physician shareholder-employee will not implicate the duty of loyalty. Berman v. Physical Medicine Associates, 225 F.3d 429 (4th Cir. 2000). State attorneys general have frequently advanced claims based on breaches of the duty of loyalty in cases involving conflicts of interest such as a hospital entering into an emergency room

contract with a physician group owned by the chairman of its board; loans from a hospital to a physician serving on the board; and the hiring of architectural firms and employment agencies in which trustees have an interest. See Michael W. Peregrine, The Nonprofit Board's Duty of Loyalty in an "Integrated" World, 29 J. Health L. 211 (1996).

Most state statutes governing nonprofit and for-profit corporations make it relatively easy to resolve such conflicts of interest. (Can you explain the policy underlying this?) For example, most allow a majority of disinterested directors, shareholders or members in the case of not-for-profit corporations to validate in advance interested transactions provided there is full disclosure of all material facts about the transaction, and the approving directors reasonably believe the transaction is fair to the corporation. See, e.g., Revised Model Business Corp. Act. §§ 8.60 et seq.; Revised Model Nonprofit Corporations Act (RMNCA) § 8.30. Cf. ALI Tentative Draft §§ 310 & 330 (describing board member's general obligation under duty of loyalty to "act in a manner that he or she reasonably believes to be in the best interests of the charity, in light of its stated purposes" but subject to obligation "to handle appropriately" conflicts of interests e.g., by seeking approvals of disinterested members of the board). Conflicting interests involving not-for-profit corporations may also be resolved if the transaction was "fair" at the time it was entered into (i.e. it "carries the earmarks of an arms-length transaction"). RMNCA § 8.30(a), § 8.30 cmt. 2(a). Otherwise they may be approved before or after the transaction by the state attorney general, § 8.30(b)(2)(i), or a court of proper jurisdiction § 8.30(b)(2)(ii).

The obligation of fiduciaries to make full disclosures in self-dealing transactions is illustrated by Boston Children's Heart Foundation, Inc. v. Nadal–Ginard, 73 F.3d 429 (1st Cir.1996). The case involved the activities of a physician, Dr. Nadal–Ginard, who was president and a member of the board of Boston Children's Heart Foundation ("BCHF"), a non-profit corporation established to conduct the clinical and research activities of the cardiology department at Boston Children's Hospital. The defendant was also chairman of the cardiology department at the hospital and a member of the faculty of Harvard Medical School. Conflicting interest problems arose in connection with Dr. Nadal–Ginard's activities on behalf of the Howard Hughes Medical Institute ("Institute"), which provided him substantial compensation for directing the activities of the Institute's Laboratory of Cellular and Molecular Cardiology at Boston Children's Hospital. In his capacity as president of BCHF, Dr. Nadal–Ginard was empowered to set his own salary and determine other compensation-related matters. In so doing, however, Dr. Nadal–Ginard failed to disclose to the BCHF board that BCHF was paying him for much of the same work for which he was receiving substantial compensation from the Institute. The First Circuit concluded that Dr. Nadal–Girard's actions setting his own compensation at BCHF constituted self-dealing and required full disclosure of all material information regarding his salary and compensation determinations. Despite the fact that the BCHF by-laws granted Dr. Nadal–Ginard exclusive authority to set his own salary, the Court found that he had not acted in good faith in failing to make full disclosures, specifically in failing to inform the BCHF board of his compensation from the Institute. 73 F.3d at 434. It further held the information regarding his compensation arrangements with the Institute was material because, had BCHF been armed with the information, it may have concluded that he was over-compensated. In so holding, the First Circuit rejected the defendant's claim that no breach occurred because the salary was fair and reasonable, as the failure to act in good faith was sufficient to establish the breach regardless of the reasonableness of the salary. Id. For an analysis of the implications of fiduciary duties and other legal obligations for physicians serving on hospital boards, see Michael Peregrine, Structuring Physician Membership on the Hospital Governing Board, 31 J. Health L. 133 (1998).

5. *Sarbanes Oxley for Nonprofits?* Enacted in 2002 in response to multiple corporate financial scandals such as Enron, the federal Sarbanes–Oxley law is one of the most important securities laws adopted in the United States since the Great Depression. Sarbanes–Oxley Act of 2002, Pub. L. No. 107–204, 116 Stat. 745 (codified in sections of 11, 15, 18, 28 and 29 U.S.C.). Although corporate governance has historically been the province of state law, many provisions of Sarbanes–Oxley impose highly specific requirements on publicly traded corporations, such as mandating they have an audit committee comprised of independent directors (and that at least one member of that committee be a financial expert); requiring that the corporation's president and treasurer attest to the accuracy of financial information and the soundness of the methodology used to generate that information; prohibiting personal loans to directors; prohibiting public accounting firm that performing audit services from providing consulting services; and requiring or encouraging disclosures of various kinds.

Importantly, while Sarbanes–Oxley for the most part does not apply to nonprofit corporations, a number of states have adopted or are considering adopting statutes that would apply similar requirements upon nonprofits. See Kansas Stat. Ann. § 17–1763(b)(15) (Supp. 2005) (requiring that larger nonprofits' audit and annual financial statement be signed by two officers); Cal. Corp. Gov't Code § 12586(e)(2) (West 2005) (large nonprofits must establish audit committee with independent members); Maine Nonprofit Corporation Act, 13–B M.R.S.A § 715 (requiring that nonprofits keep records of accounts and minutes of proceedings available for inspection by any officer, director, or voting member of the nonprofit corporation). See Lumen N. Mulligan, What's Good for the Goose is Not Good for the Gander: Sarbanes–Oxley–Style Nonprofit Reforms, 105 Mich. L. Rev. 1981 (2007). What factors militate in favor or against applying such rules to nonprofit hospitals and other health care institutions such as insurers or clinics? Are disclosure-based reforms likely to have a positive influence on how nonprofits are managed? Might there be risks in "corporatizing" the way nonprofits are run and how directors perceive their ethical obligations? See Nicole Gilkeson, For–Profit Scandal in the Non–Profit World: Should States force Sarbanes–Oxley Provisions onto Nonprofit Corporations?, 95 Geo. L.J. 831 (questioning the normative bases for SOX-style reforms on nonprofits); Dana Brakman Reiser, Enron.org: Why Sarbanes–Oxley Will not Ensure Comprehensive Nonprofit Accountability, 38 U.C. Davis L. Rev. 205; Jane Heath, Who's Minding the Nonprofit Store: Does Sarbanes–Oxley Have Anything to Offer Nonprofits?, 38 U.S.F. L. Rev. 781; Glen T. Troyer et al., Governance Issues for Nonprofit Healthcare Organizations and the Implications of the Sarbanes–Oxley Act, 1 Ind. Health L. Rev. 175; Wendy K. Szymanski, An Allegory of Good (and Bad) Governance: Applying the Sarbanes–Oxley Act to Nonprofit Organizations., 2003 Utah L. Rev. 1303. See also Henry B. Hansmann, Reforming Nonprofit Corporation Law, 129 U. Pa. L. Rev. 497 (1981) (arguing for strict prohibition for self dealing by directors of "commercial" nonprofits such as hospitals).

Many nonprofit hospitals have voluntarily adopted some of the Sarbanes reforms. This trend may have been accelerated by the endorsement of certain elements of Sarbanes–Oxley by the major bond rating agencies. Finding a relationship between corporate accountability and credit worthiness, these entities consider adoption of certain "best practices" in their evaluations of the credit profile of nonprofit institutions. See e.g. Fitch Ratings, Special Report (Aug. 9, 2005); Michael W. Peregrine & James R. Schwartz, Key Nonprofit Corporate Law developments in 2005, 15 No.4 Health L. Rep. 116 (BNA) (2006) (rating agencies' emphasis on Sarbanes–Oxley compliance based on both support for basic principles of law and belief that regulatory bodies will compel adoption in the future). Others weighing in include The Panel on the Non Profit Sector, see Principles for Good Governance and Ethical Practice—A Guide for Charities and Foundations, and the IRS, which has set forth its own list of recommended practices and taken other actions affecting corporate governance in nonprofit organizations, see *infra*.

6. *Charitable Trust Law*. States almost uniformly apply nonprofit corporate fiduciary standards to evaluate the actions of nonprofit corporate boards and find that they should not be treated as trusts for donations or other property they hold. See Revised Model Nonprofit Corporation Act, Comment to 2.02 (drafters' intent that nonprofit statute not be treated as charitable trust); Health Midwest v. Kline, 2003 WL 328845 (Kan. Dist. Ct. 2003) (applying corporate standard in conversion transaction). Nevertheless, charitable trust law may in some cases govern the responsibilities of boards of charitable corporations. For example, gifts to a nonprofit corporation for a specific purpose or with an express declaration of intent may create a charitable trust and establish stricter fiduciary duties associated with trust law. See, e.g. St. Joseph's Hospital v. Bennett, 281 N.Y. 115, 22 N.E.2d 305 (1939). Less clear however are circumstances in which a constructive or implied trust may exist. See discussion of Banner Health System litigation and other conversion cases in the following section. Some commentators accuse attorney generals of attempting to import stricter trust fiduciary standards to cases involving the conduct of directors of nonprofit corporations. See Peregrine and Schwartz, *supra*.

7.   State Attorneys General around the country have been active in challenging decisions of board members and officers of nonprofit health care organizations under various legal theories including breaches of fiduciary duties. See, e.g., Nathan Littauer Hospital Ass'n v. Spitzer, 287 A.D.2d 202, 734 N.Y.S.2d 671 (App. Div. 2001) (challenge to affiliation between two hospitals involving substantial changes to corporate purposes; restatement of purposes and required compliance with Religious Directives for Catholic Health Care Facilities do not constitute change of magnitude sufficient to require judicial review under New York law). These cases arise in a variety of contexts including change of control transactions, allegations of self-dealing and waste of charitable assets by insiders, and bankruptcies. In many of these cases the attorney general must balance her responsibility to protect the public interest in the operation of public charities against the need to give managers the flexibility they need to operate efficiently in the market. See Michael W. Peregrine & James R. Schwartz, The Application of Nonprofit Corporation Law to Health Care Organizations (2002). The following cases illustrate the twin responsibilities of state attorneys general.

AHERF. Before Enron, there was AHERF. The collapse of the Allegheny Health, Education, and Research Foundation (AHERF) was the nation's largest failure of a nonprofit health care corporation. Under the dominant leadership of its Chief Executive Officer, Sherif Abdelhak, AHERF grew rapidly, borrowed heavily, and collapsed precipitously. The many causes for AHERF's failure include poor business strategy, misleading and perhaps fraudulent accounting practices and financing arrangements, over-expansion, and unwise physician acquisitions. But the over-arching problem was the structure and performance of its governance system. The complex AHERF organization was governed by a parent board consisting of no less than thirty-five members. Ten other boards, having little overlapping membership, governed fifty-five corporations; each board was general-ly unaware of what other parts of the system were doing. Directors were chosen and dominated by Mr. Abdelhak and board meetings were, according to one analysis, "scripted affairs, intentionally staged to limit oversight and participation by board members ... Members received one thousand page briefing books and had little time to read them." See Lawton R. Burns et al., The Fall of the House of AHERF: The Allegheny Bankruptcy, 19 Health Affs. 7 (Jan/Feb 2000). Although the AHERF boards consisted of top-notch executives, all were extremely busy and unable to perform a broad oversight responsibility over the organization. In addition, the bylaws permitted many key decisions to be made by Mr. Abdelhak. Id. Over sixty lawsuits were filed, most alleging breaches of the duty of care and duty of loyalty by directors. A global settlement of almost all of the civil lawsuits ended with recovery by the Pennsylvania Attorney General of up to $35 million for losses to charitable endowment funds (the Attorney General had claimed restricted endowment funds had been diverted to system operation in violation of charitable trust law as well as other violations of state law). Criminal prosecutions also resulted in confinement for Mr. Abdelhak. See Editorial, AHERF Whimper, Pittsburgh Post–Gazette, Sept. 8, 2002, available at: www.post-gazette.com/forum/20020908edsharif0908p1.asp; Anatomy of a Bankruptcy (six part series published Jan. 17–Jan. 24, 1999) collected at www.post-gazette/com/aherf. The Attorney General's prosecution and its resulting recovery (which was funded primarily from director and officer insurance) stressed the role of nonprofit directors to safeguard assets and their responsibilities for effective oversight.

Allina and HealthPartners. Investigations by the Attorney General of Minne-sota of two large nonprofit entities, Allina Health System (a large IDS that also operated an insurance plan, Medica) and HealthPartners (a large health insurer) revealed patterns of what he termed "lavish" and "wasteful" expenditures, conflicts of interest, lax oversight and other abuses. Pursuant to a Memorandum of Understanding, Allina agreed to spin off Medica with a new board selected by the Attorney General and adopt policies regarding expense reimbursement, execu-tive compensation and other matters. Finding questionable expenditures for travel, consulting and compensation by HealthPartners and concluding that its board "did little to exercise independent judgment concerning the lavish activities of management," the Attorney General petitioned a court to appoint two new members to its board. The court declined to add new board members but agreed to appoint one of the individuals selected by the Attorney General as a special administrator with powers to make recommendations and report suspected abus-es. Does the power of the Attorney General in these cases to personally select members of the board of nonprofit organizations blur the line between public and private institutions?

Problem: The Catch–22 of Divided Loyalty

As a result of changes in federal reimbursement policies and antikickback laws and because of persistently high maintenance costs, Corsica Medical Group, LLC (CMG) has concluded that it is impractical for it to continue to own the lithotripter it uses in its outpatient clinic. As part of negotiations with Pianosa Community Hospital regarding a joint venture to operate outpatient facilities, CMG has offered to sell its lithotripter to the hospital. Dr. Daneka is a member of CMG and also serves on the board of directors of Pianosa Community Hospital. What advice would you give to CMG regarding its proposed transaction? What information should the Pianosa Community Hospital board review before making its decision?

Note on Certificate of Need Regulation

Many states require that local facilities obtain a certificate of need (CON) prior to undertaking construction or renovation of facilities, purchasing major equipment, or offering new health services. Operating under the mandates of state statutory schemes, health planning agencies require that health care facilities demonstrate the "need" for such improvements or purchases and meet other financial and regulatory requirements. CON regulation is often criticized for inhibiting competition and innovation by requiring that providers satisfy regulatory requirements that are often vague, subjective, and conflicting. Moreover, the process of demonstrating need, financial feasibility, and quality of service may entail lengthy and costly administrative proceedings. At the same time CON laws provide the states one of the few mechanisms by which they can control the supply and location of health care resources.

State CON regulation was spawned by the 1974 National Health Planning and Resources Development Act, 42 U.S.C. §§ 300k–300t, Pub. L. No. 93–641 (1974) which conditioned eligibility for a variety of healthcare funding programs on adoption of state plans for allocating healthcare resources and CON laws to help implement those plans. As originally conceived, adoption of CON laws and CON proceedings would reduce healthcare costs by reducing wasteful duplication of facilities while also improving access by rationalizing the allocation of service providers. Although 49 states eventually adopted CON laws, the repeal of NHPRD in 1987 prompted many states to alter or eliminate their certificate of need statutes. As a result, today there is a wide array of statutory schemes. States vary considerably in the kinds of facilities subject to CON regulation (e.g., hospitals, skilled nursing facilities, intermediate care facilities, and ambulatory surgical facilities), the capital thresholds at which the law applies, and the standards used to determine need.

Most commentary is highly critical of CON regulation, arguing that it posed obstacles to efficient reorganization of healthcare markets, invited obstructionist behavior and was incompatible with the evolution of competitive health care markets. See e.g., Patrick J. McGinley, Beyond Health Care Reform: Reconsidering Certificate of Need Laws in a "Managed Competition" System, 23 Fla., St. U. L. Rev. 141, 167–68 (1995) ("Certificate of need laws shelter health care providers from the price-cutting demands of health care alliances.") Lauretta H. Wolfson, State Regulation of Health Facility Planning: The Economic Theory and Political Realities of Certificate of Need, 4 DePaul J. Health Care L. 261, 310 (1997). ("The process of obtaining a CON has become an enterprise in itself, becoming so lucrative that it attracts many politicians and former politicians who successfully use their influence to weight the process for those who employ their services.") Other studies question whether CON achieved its purposes of lowering costs and allocating services more equitably. See e.g., Morrissey and Shafeldt, J. Reg. Econ. 187 (1991).

Another difficulty with CON statutes lies in their drafting. In many cases, the approach is to set forth a "laundry list" of numerous factors, many of which are vague and thus invite subjective determinations. For example, West Virginia's statute contains twenty-two criteria for assessing need; a twenty-third allows the regulators to utilize any additional criteria it sees fit in determining need. For an excellent analysis see Randall Bovjberg, Problems and Prospects for Health Planning: The Importance of Incentives, Standards and Procedures in Certificate of Need, 1978 Utah L. Rev. 83. Cases involving CON disputes raise a variety of issues, e.g., the tension between quantitative standards based on need for additional beds or sophisticated equipment and qualitative standards. See e.g., Department Health and Rehabilitative Services v. Johnson and Johnson Home Health Care, 447 So.2d 361 (Fla. Ct. App. 1984); the existence of anticompetitive conspiracies to deny a CON, see e.g., Hospital Building Co. v. Trustees of Rex Hosp., 791 F.2d 288 (4th Cir. 1986).

As noted, CON laws were widely regarded as out of step with the development of competitive health care markets. Can you make a case for maintaining or strengthening CON laws as part of a health care reform plan? We will revisit the role of CON regulation in several contexts such as its effect on the development of specialty hospitals and its importance in planning joint ventures and integrated systems.

Note on Limited Liability for Investors

An important objective for many investors is limited liability, i.e., the guarantee that they will not be personally liable for the acts or debts of the business except to the extent of their investment. Limited liability is a key characteristic of corporations, limited partnerships, limited liability companies and limited liability partnerships. Although it is not a common occurrence, courts have been willing to disregard the corporate form, or "pierce the corporate veil," and hold shareholders personally liable in certain circumstances. The jurisprudence on piercing is somewhat incoherent, with courts remarkably prone to rely on labels or characterizations of relationships (like "alter ego," "instrumentality" or "sham") or mechanically recite piercing factors (such as the failure to follow corporate formalities, the absence of adequate capitalization, or the commingling of personal and corporate assets) without explaining why it is appropriate to upset the parties' expectation of limited liability. Although piercing is rarely allowed, egregious facts, coupled with severe undercapitalization bordering on fraud, may occasionally justify disregard of the corporate entity. See, e.g., Autrey v. 22 Texas Services Inc., 79 F.Supp.2d 735 (S.D. Tex. 2000) (triable issues found in wrongful death action against severely undercapitalized corporation that owned forty nine nursing homes).

In cases involving hospital systems with multiple corporate entities, courts are usually reluctant to pierce the corporate veil even where the parent exercises extensive control over the subsidiary and its name is prominently displayed in the advertising, signs and literature of the subsidiary hospital. See, e.g., Humana, Inc. v. Kissun, 221 Ga.App. 64, 471 S.E.2d 514 (1996); see also, Ritter v. BJC Barnes Jewish Christian Health Systems, 987 S.W.2d 377 (Mo. Ct. App. 1999) (refusing to hold parent entity liable on agency, veil-piercing, vicarious liability or apparent authority theories despite extensive control over subsidiary hospital's operations). However, where regulatory evasion is possible, piercing might be available. In United States v. Pisani, 646 F.2d 83 (3d Cir. 1981), the government sought to recover Medicare overpayments made to a corporation owned by a single physician/shareholder. The Third Circuit pierced the corporate veil, holding the physician personally liable despite the absence of fraud. Although some of the traditional factors militating in favor of disregard of the corporate entity were also present, the court stressed the clear legislative purpose embodied in the Medicare law that providers may only be reimbursed for the reasonable costs of their services. This purpose would be easily circumvented if providers could freely submit inflated cost reports, pocket the money through distributions or repayment of loans from a corporation and avoid personal liability. In other cases, courts have pierced the corporate veil despite the absence of any traditional factors where failure to do so would allow providers to avoid the strong statutory objective of preventing abuse of the Medicare and Medicaid program. United States v. Normandy House

Nursing Home, Inc., 428 F.Supp. 421 (D. Mass. 1977); see also United States v. Arrow Medical Equip. Co., 1990 WL 210601 (E.D. Pa. 1990). On the other hand multiple corporate entities can effectively shield business operations from regulatory sanctions. See Joseph E. Casson & Julia McMillen, Protecting Nursing Home Companies: Limiting Liability Through Corporate Restructuring, 36 J. Health L. 577 (2003) (multi-corporate form enables nursing home chains to limit licensure revocation and Medicare sanctions to individual entities). See also, Charles Duhigg, Inquiries at Investor–Owned Nursing Homes, N.Y. Times (Oct. 24 2007) (Investigative report by the New York Times charging that private equity firms that have acquired thousands of nursing homes had shielded themselves from regulatory oversight and liability actions by employing complicated corporate structures has prompted Congressional investigations).

Many professional corporations statutes provide for: (1) limited liability for shareholders as to the ordinary business obligations of the corporation (e.g., business debts, negligence unassociated with professional services, bankruptcy); (2) unlimited liability as to the shareholder's own professional negligence and the negligence of those under her direct supervision and control; and (3) limited liability (or capped joint and several liability) for the negligent acts of other shareholders or other employees not under their supervision or control. See, e.g., Kan. Stat. Ann. § 17–2715 (Supp. 1994); 1995 Me. Legis. Serv. H. P. 231 (West). What policies justify these differences? Are they still valid in an era of greater integration among practitioners operating in business entities? What arrangements might you advise for a professional corporation that anticipates purchasing expensive assets like an MRI or valuable interests in real estate? Are there arrangements that might also help allocate capital expenditures in a multi-specialty practice where not every physician will be using the MRI?

Problem: Hope Springs Eternal

Hope Springs Eternal Health System, a not-for-profit hospital system headquartered in Hope Springs, Kansas operates three acute care hospitals in Kansas and one in New Budapest, Missouri. Two of its four hospitals (one in Kansas and one in Missouri) have lost money over the last two years and both are operating as a drain on the System's overall finances. One of the hospitals losing money, Western Missouri Hope (WMH), located in rural New Budapest, is the only hospital in its small town and its emergency room there operates at a large loss. The articles of incorporation, drafted upon WMH's formation during the Great Depression, describe as its purpose "to operate a hospital and other facilities to best serve the health needs of the deserving in New Budapest."

WMH enjoys strong community support and receives substantial local donations, and volunteer services have kept it afloat for many years. The System's CEO is concerned about newspaper reports that Milo Minderbender, president and chairman of the board of WMH, has attended several expensive seminars in Las Vegas and San Francisco to learn from national experts about correcting the problems of distressed hospitals. The local newspaper in New Budapest has also gathered data showing that Minderbender's salary ranks in the top 1% of all hospital executives running comparable rural hospitals. Further, the paper has discovered that despite the considerable poverty in New Budapest, WMH Hospital provides less charity care than any other Missouri hospital located in similar economically deprived communities.

Without telling the System Board, the System's CEO hired a consultant to make recommendations regarding the future of WMH. The consultant's study confirmed the dire financial status of WMH, but explored only the option of closing the hospital. The consultant has made several recommendations which the CEO wants to put before the Board at its next meeting. She would like your advice on the legal risks associated with each proposal.

- Close the hospital in New Budapest and form a limited liability company with a group of local physicians to own and operate an ambulatory surgery center, leasing the old hospital facility to this joint venture. The hospital system will own 51% of the joint venture. According to the consultant, the venture should be sufficiently profitable to offset the losses of the other System hospital losing money and contribute to the capital needs of its other hospitals.

- Stop accepting patients who are insured by MissouriCares, a State-run insurance program for the working poor. MissouriCares, which is not affiliated with Medicaid or SCHIP, sets its reimbursement rates for hospitals at levels lower than Medicaid and fails to cover WMH's costs of service to its beneficiaries. The consultant believes this move might shake up state policy makers and get them to reconsider their rate structure for both Medicaid and MissouriCares.

- Award a large consulting contract to Dr. Homer Green, a senior board member of WMH who has just sold his medical practice in New Budapest. It is hoped that his strong professional and personal contacts in the medical community will be instrumental in obtaining the joint venture agreement with the physicians and facilitating the transition from operating a hospital to partnering with physicians to run an ambulatory surgery center.

B. PROFESSIONALISM AND THE CORPORATE PRACTICE OF MEDICINE DOCTRINE

BERLIN v. SARAH BUSH LINCOLN HEALTH CENTER

Supreme Court of Illinois, 1997.
179 Ill.2d 1, 227 Ill.Dec. 769, 688 N.E.2d 106.

JUSTICE NICKELS delivered the opinion of the court:

Plaintiff, Richard Berlin, Jr., M.D., filed a complaint for declaratory judgment and a motion for summary judgment seeking to have a restrictive covenant contained in an employment agreement with defendant, Sara[sic] Bush Lincoln Health Center (the Health Center), declared unenforceable. The circuit court of Coles County, finding the entire employment agreement unenforceable, granted summary judgment in favor of Dr. Berlin. The circuit court reasoned that the Health Center, as a nonprofit corporation employing a physician, was practicing medicine in violation of the prohibition on the corporate practice of medicine. A divided appellate court affirmed, and this court granted the Health Center's petition for leave to appeal.

The central issue involved in this appeal is whether the "corporate practice doctrine" prohibits corporations, which are licensed hospitals from employing physicians to provide medical services. We find the doctrine inapplicable to licensed hospitals and accordingly reverse.

BACKGROUND

The facts are not in dispute. The Health Center is a nonprofit corporation duly licensed under the Hospital Licensing Act to operate a hospital. In December 1992, Dr. Berlin and the Health Center entered into a written agreement whereby the Health Center employed Dr. Berlin to practice medicine for the hospital for five years. The agreement provided that Dr. Berlin could terminate the employment relationship for any reason prior to the end of the five-year term by furnishing the Health Center with 180 days advance written notice of such termination. The agreement also contained a restrictive covenant, which prohibited Dr. Berlin from competing with the hospital by providing health services within a 50–mile radius of the Health Center for two years after the end of the employment agreement.

On February 4, 1994, Dr. Berlin informed the Health Center by letter that he was resigning effective February 7, 1994, and accepting employment with the Carle Clinic Association. After his resignation, Dr. Berlin immediately began working at a Carle Clinic facility located approximately one mile from the Health Center. Shortly thereafter, the Health Center sought a preliminary injunction to prohibit Dr. Berlin from practicing at the Carle Clinic based on the restrictive covenant contained in the aforesaid employment agreement.

* * *

Hospital Employment of Physicians

The Health Center and its supporting amici curiae contend that no judicial determination exists which prohibits hospitals from employing physicians. In support of this contention, the Health Center argues that this court has acknowledged the legitimacy of such employment practices in past decisions. See, e.g., Gilbert v. Sycamore Municipal Hospital, 156 Ill.2d 511, 190 Ill.Dec. 758, 622 N.E.2d 788 (1993); Darling v. Charleston Community Memorial Hospital, 33 Ill.2d 326, 211 N.E.2d 253 (1965). In the alternative, the Health Center contends that if a judicial prohibition on hospital employment of physicians does exist, it should be overruled. In support of this contention, the Health Center argues that the public policies behind such a prohibition are inapplicable to licensed hospitals, particularly nonprofit hospitals.

The Health Center also contends that there is no statutory prohibition on the corporate employment of physicians. The Health Center notes that no statute has ever expressly stated that physicians cannot be employed by corporations. To the contrary, the Health Center argues that other legislative actions recognize that hospitals can indeed employ physicians.

Dr. Berlin and supporting amici curiae contend that this court, in People ex rel. Kerner v. United Medical Service, Inc. adopted the corporate practice of medicine doctrine, which prohibits corporations from employing physicians. Dr. Berlin concludes that the Health Center, as a nonprofit corporation, is prohibited by the Kerner rule from entering into employment agreements with physicians.

Dr. Berlin also disputes the Health Center's contention that public policy supports creating an exception to the Kerner rule for hospitals. He argues that, because no legislative enactment subsequent to the Kerner case expressly grants hospitals the authority to employ physicians, the legislature has ratified the corporate practice of medicine doctrine as the public policy of Illinois. At this point, a review of the corporate practice of medicine doctrine is appropriate.

Corporate Practice of Medicine Doctrine

The corporate practice of medicine doctrine prohibits corporations from providing professional medical services. Although a few states have codified the doctrine, the prohibition is primarily inferred from state medical licensure acts, which regulate the profession of medicine and forbid its practice by unlicensed individuals. See A. Rosoff, The Business of Medicine: Problems with the Corporate Practice Doctrine, 17 Cumb. L. Rev. 485, 490 (1987). The rationale behind the doctrine is that a corporation cannot be licensed to practice medicine because only a human being can sustain the education, training, and character screening, which are prerequisites to receiving a professional license. Since a corporation cannot receive a medical license, it follows that a corporation cannot legally practice the profession.

The rationale of the doctrine concludes that the employment of physicians by corporations is illegal because the acts of the physicians are attributable to the corporate employer, which cannot obtain a medical license. The prohibition on the corporate employment of physicians is invariably supported by several public policy arguments, which espouse the dangers of lay control over professional judgment, the division of the physician's loyalty between his patient and his profitmaking employer, and the commercialization of the profession.

Application of Doctrine in Illinois

This court first encountered the corporate practice doctrine in Dr. Allison, Dentist, Inc. v. Allison, 360 Ill. 638, 196 N.E. 799 (1935). In Allison, the plaintiff corporation owned and operated a dental practice. When defendant, a dentist formerly employed by plaintiff, opened a dental office across the street from plaintiff's location, plaintiff brought an action to enforce a restrictive covenant contained in defendant's employment contract. Defendant's motion to dismiss the action was granted on the grounds that plaintiff was practicing dentistry in violation of the Dental Practice Act. In affirming the judgment of the lower court, this court stated:

"To practice a profession requires something more than the financial ability to hire competent persons to do the actual work. It can be done only by a duly qualified human being, and to qualify something more than mere knowledge or skill is essential. The qualifications include personal characteristics, such as honesty, guided by an upright conscience and a sense of loyalty to clients or patients, even to the extent of sacrificing pecuniary profit, if necessary. These requirements are spoken of generically as that good moral character which is a pre-requisite to the licensing of any professional man. No corporation can qualify." [The Court next discussed cases finding the corporate practice doctrine barred corporations from operating dental clinics employing dentists and prevented a medical clinic providing medical services through licensed physicians.]

* * *

Prior to the instant action, apparently no Illinois court has applied the corporate practice of medicine rule set out in People ex rel. Kerner v. United Medical Service, Inc., or specifically addressed the issue of whether licensed hospitals are prohibited from employing physicians. We therefore look to other jurisdictions with reference to the application of the corporate practice of medicine doctrine to hospitals.

APPLICABILITY OF DOCTRINE TO HOSPITALS IN OTHER JURISDICTIONS

Although the corporate practice of medicine doctrine has long been recognized by a number of jurisdictions, the important role hospitals serve in the health care field has also been increasingly recognized. Accordingly, numerous jurisdictions have recognized either judicial or statutory exceptions to the corporate practice of medicine doctrine which allow hospitals to employ physicians and other health care professionals. See, e.g., Cal. Bus. & Prof. Code § 2400 (West 1990) (exception for charitable hospitals).... A review of this authority reveals that there are primarily three approaches utilized in determining that the corporate practice of medicine doctrine is inapplicable to hospitals.

First, some states refused to adopt the corporate practice of medicine doctrine altogether when initially interpreting their respective medical practice act. These states generally determined that a hospital corporation that employs a physician is not practicing medicine, but rather is merely making medical treatment available. See, e.g., State ex rel. Sager v. Lewin, 128 Mo. App. 149, 155, 106 S.W. 581, 583 (1907) ("[H]ospitals are maintained by private corporations, incorporated for the purpose of furnishing medical and surgical treatment to the sick and wounded. These corporations do not practice medicine but they receive patients and employ physicians and surgeons to give them treatment")....

Under the second approach, the courts of some jurisdictions determined that the corporate practice doctrine is inapplicable to nonprofit hospitals and health associations. These courts reasoned that the public policy arguments supporting the corporate practice doctrine do not apply to physicians employed by charitable institutions. See, e.g., Group Health Ass'n v. Moor, 24 F.Supp. 445, 446 (D.D.C. 1938) (actions of nonprofit association which contracts with licensed physicians to provide medical treatment to its members in no way commercializes medicine and is not the practice of medicine), aff'd, 107 F.2d 239 (D.C.Cir.1939)....

In the third approach, the courts of several states have determined that the corporate practice doctrine is not applicable to hospitals, which employ physicians because hospitals are authorized by other laws to provide medical treatment to patients....

We find the rationale of the latter two approaches persuasive. We decline to apply the corporate practice of medicine doctrine to licensed hospitals. The instant cause is distinguishable from Kerner, Allison, and Winberry. None of those cases specifically involved the employment of physicians by a hospital. More important, none of those cases involved a corporation licensed to provide health care services to the general public.

The corporate practice of medicine doctrine set forth in Kerner was not an interpretation of the plain language of the Medical Practice Act. The Medical Practice Act contains no express prohibition on the corporate employment of physicians.[5] Rather, the corporate practice of medicine doctrine was inferred from the general policies behind the Medical Practice Act. Such a prohibition is entirely appropriate to a general corporation possessing no licensed authority to offer medical services to the public, such as the appellant in Kerner. However, when a corporation has been sanctioned by the laws of this state to operate a hospital, such a prohibition is inapplicable.

The legislative enactments pertaining to hospitals provide ample support for this conclusion. For example, the Hospital Licensing Act defines "hospital" as:

> "any institution, place, building, or agency, public or private, whether organized for profit or not, devoted primarily to the maintenance and operation of facilities for the diagnosis and treatment or care of * * * persons admitted for overnight stay or longer in order to obtain medical, including obstetric, psychiatric and nursing, care of illness, disease, injury, infirmity, or deformity." (Emphasis added.) 210 ILCS 85/3 (West Supp.1995).

[The Court cites other statutes that require hospitals to furnish services.]

The foregoing statutes clearly authorize, and at times mandate, licensed hospital corporations to provide medical services. We believe that the authority to employ duly-licensed physicians for that purpose is reasonably implied from these legislative enactments. We further see no justification for distinguishing between nonprofit and for-profit hospitals in this regard. The authorities and duties of licensed hospitals are conferred equally upon both entities.

In addition, we find the public policy concerns, which support the corporate practice doctrine inapplicable to a licensed hospital in the modern health care industry. The concern for lay control over professional judgment is alleviated in a licensed hospital, where generally a separate professional medical staff is responsible for the quality of medical services rendered in the facility.[6]

Furthermore, we believe that extensive changes in the health care industry since the time of the Kerner decision, including the emergence of corporate health maintenance organizations, have greatly altered the concern over the commercialization of health care. In addition, such concerns are relieved when a licensed hospital is the physician's employer. Hospitals have an independent duty to provide for the patient's health and welfare. [Citations to Darling and other cases omitted].

We find particularly appropriate the statement of the Kansas Supreme Court that "[i]t would be incongruous to conclude that the legislature intended a hospital to accomplish what it is licensed to do without utilizing physicians as independent contractors or employees. * * * To conclude that a hospital must do so without employing physicians is not only illogical but

---

5. In contrast, the Dental Practice Act, applied by this court in [the dental clinic and Allison cases], expressly prohibited a corporation from furnishing dentists and owning and operating a dental office.

6. Moreover, in the instant case, the employment agreement expressly provided that the Health Center had no control or direction over Dr. Berlin's medical judgment and practice, other than that control exercised by the professional medical staff. Dr. Berlin has never contended that the Health Center's lay management attempted to control his practice of medicine.

ignores reality." St. Francis Regional Med. Center v. Weiss, 254 Kan. 728, 745, 869 P.2d 606, 618 (1994). Accordingly, we conclude that a duly-licensed hospital possesses legislative authority to practice medicine by means of its staff of licensed physicians and is excepted from the operation of the corporate practice of medicine doctrine.

Consequently, the employment agreement between the Health Center and Dr. Berlin is not unenforceable merely because the Health Center is a corporate entity.

* * *

Notes and Questions

1. Consider the following rationale for the corporate practice of medicine doctrine offered by the Illinois Supreme Court:

> [T]he practice of a profession is subject to licensing and regulation and is not subject to commercialization or exploitation. To practice a profession . . . requires something more than the financial ability to hire competent persons to do the actual work. It can be done only by a duly qualified human being, and to qualify something more than mere knowledge or skill is essential . . . No corporation can qualify.

People v. United Medical Service, 362 Ill. 442, 200 N.E. 157, 163 (1936). Can you articulate the specific concerns that underlie the court's statement? Are the sources of the doctrine statutory or do they emanate from general public policy principles? If the latter, what are those principles and are they still valid today? For a decidedly negative assessment of the doctrine, see Mark A. Hall, Institutional Control of Physician Behavior: Legal Barriers to Health Care Cost Containment, 137 U. Pa. L. Rev. 431, 509–518 (1988)("puzzling doctrine . . . clouded with confused reasoning and . . . founded on an astounding series of logical fallacies"). See also Arnold J. Rosoff, The Business of Medicine: Problems with the Corporate Practice Doctrine, 17 Cumb. L. Rev. 485 (1986–87).

2. Does the corporate practice of medicine doctrine apply to nonphysicians and complementary and alternative medicine? The answer depends on whether the services in question implicate the policy concerns underlying the doctrine. If one construes the doctrine to apply to "healing" professions, it might reach many forms of CAM. However, courts, attorneys general and legislatures have tended to require that the healing practice in question must involve significant training and education, and that the practitioner exercise independent professional judgment. Thus, because massage therapy requires no training or licensure under Minnesota law, the Minnesota Supreme Court found the corporate practice doctrine inapplicable. Isles Wellness, Inc. v. Progressive Northern Insurance, 703 N.W.2d 513 (Minn. 2005). Likewise, because physical therapy services required an order of referral from a physician or certain other licensed practitioners, and in some cases periodic review of the treatment provided by the physical therapist, the court concluded that "the public policy concerns regarding a conflict of interest between the health care provider and the lay person or entity are lessened" and again declined to apply the CPM doctrine. Id. at 523. However, the court went on to find that the doctrine did apply to the practice of chiropractic because that profession requires extensive training and is provided without supervision by other professionals, whereas physical therapists direct patients under the order of referral or periodic review of other specified health care providers. Id. at 524. Does this mean that all contracts entered into by the corporation violating the CPM doctrine are automatically void? After remand and appeal, the Minnesota Supreme Court said

"no." Noting that the corporation did not knowingly violate the law by practicing chiropractic under lay ownership and "the lack of clarity regarding the applicability of the corporate practice of medicine doctrine to chiropractors before this court's decision," the court declined to void the contracts entered into with insurance companies by the corporation. Isles Wellness, Inc. v. Progressive Northern Insurance, 725 N.W.2d 90, 95 (Minn. 2006).

3. The question of whether the holding in *Berlin* should be extended to other nonprofit health care organizations was addressed by the Illinois Supreme Court in Carter–Shields v. Alton Health Institute, 201 Ill.2d 441, 268 Ill.Dec. 25, 777 N.E.2d 948 (2002). The case involved a physician seeking to avoid application of a non-competition agreement she had signed with the Alton Health Institute, Inc. (AHI). AHI was a nonprofit corporation fifty-percent owned by St. Anthony's Health Systems, also a nonprofit corporation. Although not licensed as a hospital, St. Anthony's controlled two licensed hospitals in the area. The remaining fifty percent of AHI was owned by a partnership composed primarily of physician groups. The Court strongly reaffirmed the corporate practice of medicine doctrine, stating "the exercise of control or influence over the medical decision making of a physician by a lay, unlicensed corporation results in a division of the physician's loyalty between the often divergent interests of the corporation and the patient." Id. at 957. It declined to extend its holding in *Berlin*, characterizing that decision as "carving out a narrow exception for an entity, such as a hospital, that must meet certain professional criteria established by the legislature." Id. Although AHI was a charitable nonprofit health care organization, it lacked a legislatively-determined role and was not subject to comparable regulatory oversight. The court also refused to view federal Medicare regulations governing kickbacks and conflicts of interests as sufficient to invoke the *Berlin* exception.

4. As noted above, commentators have been highly critical of the corporate practice of medicine doctrine. Can it be argued that the doctrine can help rectify the problems associated with risk sharing and managed care? Does it help restore the fiduciary ties between patient and physician that have been eroded by managed care? For an affirmative answer, see Andre Hampton, Resurrection of the Prohibition on the Corporate Practice of Medicine: Teaching Old Dogma New Tricks, 66 U. Cin. L. Rev. 489 (1998).

5. Early on, concerns about "corporate medical practice" focused on corporations contracting with physicians to provide medical care for their employees for a fixed salary or corporations that marketed physicians' services to the public. The AMA considered the corporate practice of medicine the "commercialization" of medicine, and believed that it would increase physician workload, decrease the quality of patient care, and would introduce lay control over the practice of medicine that would interfere with the physician-patient relationship. The AMA promulgated ethical guidelines that restricted or prohibited the corporate practice of medicine. The prohibition against corporate medical practice was enforced by the courts, using statutory prohibitions against the practice of medicine by unlicensed individuals. See Jeffrey F. Chase–Lubitz, The Corporate Practice of Medicine Doctrine: An Anachronism in the Modern Health Care Industry, 40 Vand. L. Rev. 445 (1987). What does it matter that a doctor is employed by a partnership of doctors or a professional corporation rather than by a lay person or business entity controlled by non-physicians? Should the state eliminate corporate practice prohibitions and pursue quality concerns directly through quality-control regulation or malpractice litigation?

6. In states recognizing the corporate practice of medicine doctrine, what is the relationship between that doctrine's prohibitions and other statutes permit-

ting physicians to organize their practice under a professional corporation form? In Pediatric Neurosurgery v. Russell, 44 P.3d 1063 (Colo. 2002), the Supreme Court of Colorado held that the state's professional corporation statute did not abolish the corporate practice of medicine doctrine but carved out an exception allowing corporations to practice medicine while prohibiting them from doing anything that violates medical standards of conduct. The court went on to conclude that principles of respondeat superior would apply and a professional corporation could be held vicariously liable for the torts of its employee doctors acting in the course of their employment.

7. Although (by one estimate) as many as 37 states have statutory or common law prohibitions on the corporate practice of medicine and only 13 states either reject the doctrine or have no authority establishing it, in many states relevant precedent is quite old and in some cases widely ignored. See Adam M. Freiman, Comment, The Abandonment of the Antiquated Corporate Practice of Medicine Doctrine: Injecting a Dose of Efficiency into the Modern Health Care Environment, 47 Emory L.J. 697, 712–13 (1998). How should an attorney counsel a client as to the legal risks and propriety of undertaking actions that violate old precedent, which is likely to be overturned if ever challenged? See Norman P. Jeddeloh, Physician Contract Audits: A Hospital Management Tool, 21 J. Health & Hosp. L. 105 (1988) ("Obviously, in modern practice the rule against physician employment is honored mainly in the breach. That does not mean that these traditional prohibitions cannot again serve as a basis for hospital liability. . . . Therefore, it is usually best, whenever possible, to establish true independent contractor arrangements or retain physicians through a separate corporation.") For an insightful analysis of the dangers of ignoring this latent doctrine, see Rosoff, *supra*.

III.   INTEGRATION AND NEW ORGANIZATIONAL STRUCTURES

WHERE'S WALDO—PART II

The year is 1996 and Waldo, now 53 years old, visits Dr. Goodscalpel for a routine check-up. Doctor Goodscalpel, who has joined a 10–doctor partnership called Medical Associates, recommends a PSA screening test. He sends Waldo down the hall to MedServices, an outpatient for-profit corporation owned by a subsidiary of the Llama Hilda Foundation. Llama Hilda is a not-for-profit corporation that now controls Mt. St. Hilda Hospital and numerous other entities providing health and administrative services. Unfortunately, the lab tests come back positive and Dr. Goodscalpel refers Waldo to a surgeon, Dr. Mack, who has joined Doctors Inc., a large (50 doctor) multi-specialist group organized as a professional corporation. Doctors Inc. and Medical Associates both are co-owners, along with Mt. St. Hilda Hospital, of a physician-hospital organization (PHO), an entity that negotiates contracts with insurance companies and supplies billing and other services to the medical groups.

After receiving prior approval from the PHO utilization manager, Dr. Mack sends Waldo to the Radiology Center for an MRI. The Radiology Center, an outpatient facility on Mt. St. Hilda's campus, is a joint venture organized as a corporation. Fifty percent of its stock is owned by Llama Hilda Foundation, and the other 50 percent is owned by a partnership comprised of 5 radiologists. After getting the MRI report back from the consulting radiologists, Dr. Mack recommends surgery to be performed at Mt. St. Hilda.

Waldo has joined BlueStaff's new managed care plan, CarePlan, which provides coverage only if he visits participating providers. Although Waldo had wanted Dr. Immel, an internationally known anesthesiologist who teaches at a local medical school, to assist in the operation, Dr. Immel was not a CarePlan participating provider and did not have staff privileges at Mt. St. Hilda hospital. Instead, Mt. St. Hilda has an exclusive contract with GasAssociates, a professional group organized as a limited liability company controlled by its anesthesiologist-owners. The anesthesia was furnished by a CRNA under the supervision of an anesthesiologist.

Most of the providers furnishing services to Waldo were paid on a pre-paid capitated basis. Waldo was responsible for a small co-payment on certain services.

Comparing Waldo's recent episode of care to his experience in 1978 (set forth at the beginning of this chapter), what changes have occurred in terms of provider coordination and control of their activities? How do the organizational structures to which the physicians and hospitals belong accommodate the changed environment? How have the economic incentives facing the providers changed? Is Waldo, the "consumer," better off under managed care?

A. THE STRUCTURE OF THE MODERN HEALTH CARE ENTERPRISE

Organizational arrangements for the delivery of health services have undergone dramatic changes over the last forty years. As depicted in the Where's Waldo I episode, for many years health care services were delivered primarily by doctors working in solo practice or as members of small groups usually practicing the same specialty, and by non-profit hospitals operating independently or as part of relatively simple systems that shared a few administrative or operational services. This began to change with the advent of managed care in the 1980's as hospitals adopted more complex organizational structures and entered into joint ventures and alliances with other hospitals and with their physicians. Prompted by developments in health care financing and the possibility of health care reform, physicians, hospitals and other providers began to reorganize their business enterprises and contractual relationships. In particular, they developed so-called "integrated delivery systems" via physician practice acquisitions and mergers, and establishing physician hospital organizations, joint ventures and other organizations that enhanced inter-provider linkages in order to meet the demands of capitated payments and the requirements of managed care. With the "backlash" against managed care at the end of the 1990's and increasing concerns about patient safety and quality of care, a new era began and organizational structures began to change once again. Physicians and hospitals "disintegrated," with many organizations disbanding and hospitals selling back to physicians' their practices. Looser networks of physicians and alliances became more prominent, while administrators focused on means of improving the flow of information both internally and to consumers. See Cara S. Lesser et al., The End of an Era: What Became of the "Managed Care Revolution?" 38 Health Serv. Research 337 (2003).

The health care organizations discussed in this section are business entities (e.g., corporations, LLCs, partnerships or contractual joint ventures) that link providers "horizontally" and "vertically" or on both levels. That is, physicians may combine horizontally with other physicians to form group practices, IPAs, PPOs, or other networks. Likewise, hospitals may merge or establish joint ventures and alliances with other hospitals. Hospitals and physicians have also integrated vertically by creating various kinds of integrated delivery systems, which bring together complementary provider services at several levels. Some of these organizations only loosely link hospitals and physicians and are primarily devices to facilitate joint contracting with payers. Other forms of vertical integration more fully bind hospitals and physicians by having them share both financial risk and control. In these forms, physicians and hospitals may co-own and co-manage services or enterprises; the hospital may undertake administrative or management services for physicians; the hospital may purchase the physician practices, with the physicians becoming employees of or independent contractors for the organization; or the physicians may control the enterprise with hospitals assuming a contracting relationship. Vertical integration may also include the insurance component, as provider systems may integrate into insurance or insurers may integrate into delivery through HMOs or joint ventures with providers. The following excerpt from the Physician Payment Review Commission [predecessor to Medicare Payment Advisory Commission, MEDPAC,] describes many of the organizational models, and how they enhance integration.

PHYSICIAN PAYMENT REVIEW COMMISSION, ANNUAL REPORT TO CONGRESS

(1995).

* * *

INTEGRATING ORGANIZATIONS

Defining the new integrating organizations is not an easy task. Health care organizations are in flux as markets move toward more intensive management of care. A definition that describes the typical organization today might be obsolete two years from now as the typical style of practice changes. Consequently there are no agreed-upon standard definitions, and these definitions should be taken as approximate only.

* * *

Independent Practice Association

The independent practice association (IPA) is typically a physician-organized entity that contracts with payers on behalf of its member physicians. The typical IPA negotiates contracts with insurers and pays physicians on a fee-for-service basis with a withhold. Physicians may maintain significant business outside the IPA, join multiple IPAs, retain ownership of their own practices, and typically continue in their traditional style of practice. Physicians usually invest a modest fee (a few thousand dollars) to join the IPA. IPAs may also undertake a variety of additional roles, including utilization review, and practice management functions such as billing and group purchasing, resulting in greater centralization and standardization of medical practice.

* * *

Physician–Hospital Organization

The physician-hospital organization [PHO] contracts with payers on behalf of the hospital and its affiliated physicians. The organization is responsible for negotiating health plan contracts, and in some cases, conducting utilization review, credentialing, and quality assurance. The PHO may centralize some aspects of administrative services or encourage use of shared facilities for coordination of clinical care.

The typical PHO is a hospital-sponsored organization that centers around a single hospital and its medical staff. PHOs may also form as joint ventures between hospitals and existing physician organizations such as a large multispecialty medical group or an IPA. PHOs are further divided into open PHOs, which are open to all members of the hospital's staff, and closed PHOs, where the PHO chooses some physicians and excludes others.

As with the IPA, the typical PHO accounts for only a modest share of the physician's (or the hospital's) business. Physicians retain their own practices, and their relationship to payers other than those with whom the PHO negotiates is unchanged. As with IPAs, the PHO can move toward greater centralized control over practice management and medical practice.

* * *

Group Practice

A medical group practice is defined as "the provision of health care services by three or more physicians who are formally organized as a legal entity in which business and clinical facilities, records, and personnel are shared. Income from medical services provided by the group are treated as receipts of the group and are distributed according to some prearranged plan."

The group practice is a well-established form of organization and one of the few organizational types for which good data are available. In 1991, physicians were split almost equally among three practice settings: group practice, solo or two-physician practice, or other patient care such as hospital-based practice.

* * *

Group Practice Without Walls

A group practice without walls (GPWW) refers to physicians in physically independent facilities who form a single legal entity to centralize the business aspects of their organization. In the typical case, the GPWW is organized by a strong, centralized clinic that adds individual physicians or small groups in satellite offices. In some cases, the GPWW is financially identical to a traditional group practice: It owns the assets of the individual practices and physicians share ownership of the GPWW, making it a unified business organization for the decentralized delivery of care. In other cases, physicians retain ownership of their own practices but enter into agreements for administrative and marketing functions. The GPWW may itself own certain ancillary services such as laboratory services.

Management Services Organization

The management services organization provides administrative and practice management services to physicians. An MSO may typically be owned by a hospital, hospitals, or investors. Large group practices may also establish MSOs as a way of capitalizing on their organizational skill by selling management services to otherwise unorganized physician groups.

MSOs can provide a very wide variety of services. Smaller and not-for-profit MSOs may limit operations to selling to physicians various administrative support services, such as billing, group purchasing, and various aspects of office administration. In other cases, hospital-owned MSOs are the vehicle through which hospitals purchase physician practices outright, leaving the physician either as an employee of the hospital or as an independent contractor with the physical assets of the practice owned by the hospital. Large, for-profit MSOs typically purchase the assets of physician practices outright, install office managers and other personnel, hire the physician through a professional services contract, and negotiate contracts with managed-care plans, all in exchange for a share of gross receipts typically based on the physicians' current practice expenses.

* * *

Hospital–Owned Medical Practice

In addition to the purchase of a medical practice through an MSO, hospitals can directly purchase medical practices, typically as part of their outpatient department.

* * *

Integrated Delivery System

Finally, a number of functionally similar organizations are built around hospitals and physicians linked in exclusive arrangements. In these integrated delivery systems (IDSs), a hospital or hospitals and large multispecialty group practices form an organization for the delivery of care, with all physician revenues coming through the organization.[7] These include foundation model, staff model, and equity model IDSs.

The main difference among these organizations is in the legal formalities of who works for whom and in the professional autonomy of the affiliated physicians. In a typical foundation model system, the hospital establishes a not-for-profit foundation that purchases the assets of an existing physician group, signing an exclusive professional services contract with the physician corporation. Payers pay the foundation, which then pays the physicians' professional corporation.[8] In a staff model system, physicians work directly for the system without the intervening not-for-profit foundation and professional corporation. In an equity model system, physicians own a part of the system and share significantly in its financial success or failure.

---

7. While some researchers would call these integrated delivery systems a form of PHO, most reserve the term PHO for those organizations where only a small fraction of the physicians' revenues come through the organization.

8. The presence of the foundation model system is due in part to state laws prohibiting the corporate practice of medicine, and the need for arms-length financial agreements between for-profit and not-for-profit entities.

Notes

1. *Integration: Objectives.* The integrating organizations described above bring together in various combinations physicians, hospitals and other providers that had previously operated independently. In counseling in this area, it is obviously critical to have a firm understanding of the different objectives of the various parties. For example, physicians typically are looking for a structure that will assist them in the contracting process by providing capital, information systems, administrative support, patient referrals and access to a competitively strong network. At the same time, physicians want some assurance that their incomes will not erode and that they will have a substantial voice in the governance of the new organization. Hospitals are eager to assure themselves of an adequate flow of patients to fill their beds and outpatient facilities and a cadre of physicians committed to their organization. At the same time, hospitals are reluctant to give up control of the organizational structure of the enterprise (after all, they usually supply the lion's share of the financial investment), although shared control is sometimes attempted.

2. *Organizational Structures for Physician Integration.* Physicians face a choice of a number of structural and contractual organizations in which to conduct their practices. The most complete form of organization is the formation of a Fully Integrated Medical Group (FIMGs), which usually take the form of professional corporations or unincorporated entities such as LLCs and typically entails considerable operational integration. A tightly integrated FIMG, for example, might entail: centralized governance that controls all aspects of the group's business; formal quality control and utilization management programs; FIMG responsibility for entering into managed care contracts; and income allocation systems that rely on achievement of the group rather than individual performance. These groups may be formed among members of a single specialty or kind of practice (single specialty groups) or among practitioners of multiple specialties (multi-specialty groups). Less complete integration is available through several kinds of physician organizations. Partially Integrated Medical Groups (PIMGs) or Group Practices Without Walls (GPWWs) entail physicians operating as a single legal entity (e.g. a professional corporation) with common management, staff and administrative services. However, physicians in PIMGs may maintain their practice locations and employment relationships with certain staff; they also retain autonomy in many respects, such as participation in managed care contracts and purchasing and other business decisions. Costs and profits are frequently allocated on an individualized or "cost center" basis.

Finally, physicians may join entities which are essentially contracting entities that enable them to offer a single network to payers, with perhaps some integration through common utilization controls. The Preferred Provider Organization, for example, which is typically a joint venture, usually entails contractual agreements to deliver care to a defined group of patients at discounted fee-for-service rates and to submit to certain controls on utilization or membership restrictions based on quality and utilization criteria. Similarly, physicians may join Independent Practice Associations (IPAs), which also involve only limited operational integration of physician practices through billing services and utilization review. Although IPA members sometimes agree to accept distributions of capitated revenues, which create incentives to alter practice styles, neither IPAs nor PPOs typically have controls over physician behavior and the percentage of each physician's revenues from the IPA is often not sufficient to cause significant changes in the way he or she provides care.

3. *Organizational Structures for Physician–Hospital Integration.* As described by the Physician Payment Review Commission above, physicians and hospitals desiring to achieve some degree of integration can choose from several organizational models: e.g., the MSO, the PHO or the staff, equity or foundation model (fully integrated) IDS. The PHO is in most respects the least structurally integrated and least complex form. Its primary purpose is to negotiate and administer managed care contracts for its providers, and may even do so on a capitated basis; in which case the PHO is regarded as a provider of care. However, PHOs typically provide fewer services for physician practices than do the other forms and do not significantly alter the clinical practice patterns of providers. MSOs also provide contracting services as well as many of the "back-room" functions necessary to operate physician offices, including billing, claims processing, ancillary services and many of the credentialing and utilization control services needed for contracting. In the more comprehensive form, MSOs may acquire physician practices outright or supply "turnkey" operations by purchasing and leasing equipment and office space and hiring staff for physicians. Finally, fully integrated systems, including the foundation model IDS, are entities that bring together ownership of an organization that supplies all types of health services and coordinates case management and the flow of information. This may be done through foundations or clinics that acquire physician practices or through "equity models" that enable physicians to acquire an ownership interest in the system.

4.   Through most of the 1990's, integration between hospitals and physicians grew rapidly, with most large hospital systems developing PHOs and acquiring physician practices. Many health industry experts confidently predicted that the new integrating organizations such as PHOs and MSOs were really transitional vehicles that would serve to "acclimate" hospitals and physicians to the new environment created by managed care. By this account, after becoming accustomed to cooperating with each other, most providers would ultimately wind up in more fully integrated organizations that entail employment relationships and asset purchases. However, predictions of an inevitable progression toward integration proved erroneous. Mark Pauly and Lawton Burns described it as follows:

> During the 1990's many hospitals pursued twin strategies of vertical and horizontal integration. Each type of integration assumed multiple forms. Vertical combination included acquisition of primary care physicians, strategic alliances with physicians in [PHOs and MSOs, and the development of HMOs]. Horizontal combinations included the formation of Multi-hospital systems mergers, and strategic alliances with neighboring hospitals to form local networks . . .

> While the form of integration varied across hospitals and markets, their economic performance, after a decade of experience, was genuinely uniform: Nothing worked.

Lawton R. Burns & Mark V. Pauly, Integrated Delivery Networks: A Detour on the Road to Integrated Health Care? 21 Health Aff. 128 (July/Aug. 2002). Some large for-profit health systems that aggressively acquired or networked with physicians were spectacularly unsuccessful and several publicly traded physician practice management companies, once the darlings of Wall Street, also went into bankruptcy. The picture was no brighter in the nonprofit sector. Acquisitions of physician practices have imposed a monumental drain on the budgets of nonprofit hospitals; 80 percent of all physician practices acquired by hospitals lost money, by some estimates at a rate of nearly $50,000–100,000 per year per physician. Finally, countless large IPAs and group practices have been forced to disband for financial reasons. For accounts and analyses of these developments, see James Robinson,

The Future of Managed Care, 18 Health Aff. 7 (March/April 1999); Thomas Bodenheimer, The American Health Care System—Physicians and the Changing Medical Marketplace, 340 New Eng. J. Med. (Feb. 18, 1999).

What explains these seismic shifts in organizational structures? Examining both the *ex ante* justifications for integration and the performance of various systems in recent years, Burns and Pauly conclude that the integration phenomenon was built on faulty premises such as the inevitable spread of capitation payment and the ability of hospitals to "partner" with physicians and achieve economic savings, and that most participants ignored obstacles to realizing significant economies of scale and developing an appropriate regulatory infrastructure. Burns & Pauly, *supra*.

B. THE NEW LANDSCAPE FOR HEATH CARE ORGANIZATIONS

WHERE'S WALDO—PART III

It is the year 2008 and Waldo, now 62 years old, has developed diabetes and high blood pressure, both of which are treated with expensive drugs and require regular exams and tests. Responding to complaints from employees about the HMO options previously offered, Waldo's employer has decided to switch to consumer directed health care and now offers only two plans. CarePlan is a PPO with an annual deductible of $1,000, maximum out of pocket liability of $5,000, and tiered co-pays for doctors, hospitals and outpatient care and tests. The tier in which each participating physician is placed determines the insured's co-pay responsibility. CarePlan sets tiers according to various performance criteria and the terms of its contract with the provider, such as utilization history and quality indicators. Waldo's primary care physician and endocrinologist are Tier One Doctors for Care Plan (co-pay of 10%) and his cardiologist is a Tier 4 doctor (co-pay of 40%). Alternatively, Waldo may choose HealthSaver, a health savings account plan which features a tax-preferred health savings account and catastrophic coverage under a PPO plan. This plan has a large deductible ($2000) and allows him to put both his monthly contribution and his employer's contribution into a Health Savings Account. Waldo hopes to retire when he reaches the age of 68. Unfortunately, after the passage of the Medicare Prescription Drug Improvement and Modernization Act of 2003, his employer dropped health coverage for retirees. In addition, CarePlan does not participate in Medicare Advantage. Waldo is concerned about both insurance coverage and maintaining his relationships with his long time internist, Dr. Goodscalpel, his endocrinologist, Dr. Douce, and his cardiologist, Dr. Coeur–Casse. Using what you've learned in this chapter and chapters 8, 9 and 10, what advice would you give to Waldo to help him evaluate his options?

1. *Health Financing and Physician Practice Arrangements*

The choice of organizational structures by physicians is highly responsive to changes in health care financing. Payment systems create financial incentives that affect how physicians organize their business relationships and how they interact with other providers in delivering care. The ways in which the new payment landscape have influenced physicians are discussed below.

Fee for Service Payment. As managed care payment grew, physicians began to join larger physician groups. This trend has continued but not to the degree or in the manner once predicted. Although the proportion of physicians in solo and two-physician practices has decreased significantly in recent years (from 40.7 percent in 1996–97 to 32.5 percent in 2004–05), physicians are not moving to multispecialty practices. The proportion of physicians in multispecialty practices decreased from 30.9 percent to 27.5 percent between 1998 and 2005, while the proportion of single specialty practices has grown considerably. Allison Liebhaber & Joy M. Grossman, Physicians Moving to Mid–Sized, Single Specialty Practice, Center for Studying Health System Change, Tracking Report No. 18 (August, 2007), http://www.hschange.org/CONTENT/941/. Is the trend toward practice in single specialty groups a good thing? What legal and policy issues are raised by these developments? Some studies suggest that large, multispecialty practices, which combine primary care physicians and a range of specialists in the same practice, offer the organizational structure with the greatest potential to provide consistently high-quality care. Francis J. Crosson, The Delivery System Matters, 24 No. 6 Health Affairs 1543 (November/December 2005). See also Lawrence Casalino et al., Benefits of and Barriers to Large Group Medical Practice in the United States, 163 Archives Internal Med. 1958 (September 2003).

> Consider also the following analysis:

> Most of the growth so far has been in mid-sized practices, which, although better equipped than solo and two-physician practices, do not yet approach the capabilities envisioned by quality improvement leaders. Moreover, increased consolidation in single-specialty practices raises the potential in some markets that certain specialties can drive up prices in negotiation with health plans. Some market observers are concerned that if physicians are aggregating into larger practices to provide profitable procedures and ancillary services, the greater ability of physicians to legally self-refer patients under exceptions to self-referral laws could lead to overuse of certain services, further driving up costs of care. At the same time, some benefits to society may be lost from the movement out of smaller practices and away from practice ownership. For example, [some] research shows that physicians in smaller practices with an ownership stake are substantially more likely to provide charity care than physicians in larger practices or non-owners.

Center for Studying Health System Change, *supra*.

Notice how the shift away from capitation and risk sharing financing influences physicians' choice of practice arrangements. While capitation encouraged the formation of multi-specialty groups and integrated delivery systems to facilitate cost-benefit trade offs among providers and services, fee-for-service reimbursement creates very different incentives. Under this form of payment, physicians have incentives to provide the most profitable procedures and ancillary services, with procedure- and service-intensive specialties benefiting more than other specialists and primary care physicians. Physicians in such specialties found they could form large single-specialty practices that could aggregate capital to invest in equipment and facilities to provide their services without having to redistribute income to primary care physicians—as is traditionally the case in multispecialty groups. See Center for Studying Health System Change, Tracking Report 18 *supra*. Furthermore, the decline in the use of gatekeepers and restrictions on referral have also helped fuel the movement toward single specialty practice and away from multi-specialty practice. Can you see why that may be the case? What role should antitrust policy play in monitoring these developments?

Pay for Performance. Pay for performance (P4P) initiatives by private health plans have also had an effect on the structure of delivery arrangements. Although most health plans have instituted some form of P4P, or have plans under development, their scope varies widely. Some P4P initiatives involve focused pilot programs targeting particular diseases, such as diabetes or mellitus, while others involve comprehensive efforts directed at the broader measures of performance of primary care physicians, specialists, and hospitals. In addition, "performance" may be gauged by a variety of criteria, e.g., provision of specified treatments, conformance to practice protocols, health outcomes, adoption of technology and information systems, and patient satisfaction. See also discussion of P4P under Medicare *supra* Chapter 11.

Designing and implementing P4P arrangements may be problematic in some cases. While payers and employers may want performance measures closely tied to outcomes, providers argue that they should be held to account only for those outcomes they are in a position to influence through changes in their medical practice. In markets in which physicians practice in small unintegrated practices and make referrals to independent specialists and facilities, it may not be possible to target individual physicians for the outcomes they are responsible for. See Michael F. Cannon, Pay–For–Performance: Is Medicare a Good Candidate?, 7 Yale J. Health Pol'y L. & Ethics 1 (2007). Likewise hospitals may not be fully accountable for outcomes where they can exercise little control over the choices made by the physicians who practice in their facilities. In addition, both physicians and hospitals argue they should not be held accountable for outcomes resulting from patients' choices stemming from their health insurance benefit design. For example, a patient might decline to seek preventive or follow up care because of large out-of-pocket costs in her plan. On the other side of the equation, in markets where there are dominant hospitals or specialty groups, it may be difficult to secure cooperation from providers, as they have little economic incentive to cooperate with plans hoping to institute performance based reimbursement. Thus while P4P might seem to create incentives pushing providers toward adopting more integrated structures, many factors may undermine the opportunity for P4P arrangements to get started. See Sally Trude et al., Health Plan Pay–For–Performance Strategies, 12 Am. J. Managed Care 537 (2006).

Consumer-Directed Health Care

As discussed in Chapter 9, the movement toward consumer directed health care (CDHC) has altered many of the contracting arrangements facing providers. It is true of course that CDHC has much in common with managed care. Both models rely on markets and competition among providers to produce the optimal mix of quality and cost. Further, both assume that providers will respond to competition by creating organizational arrangements that optimize cost and quality controls and promote innovation. At the same time, however, the two models differ fundamentally with respect to who should make choices and what kind of infrastructure is needed to promote efficient outcomes. As a general matter, rather than rely on intermediary organizations such as integrated health plans, group practices, or employers to assist in comparing cost and quality of providers, CDHC vests consumers—aided by enhanced information-supplying tools—with responsibility to make choices that serve their particular needs and drive providers to offers care at a low cost and high quality. See Regina Herzlinger, Market Driven Health Care: Who Wins, Who Loses in the Transformation of America's Largest Service Industry (1997); Michael Porter, Redefining Competition in Health Care, 82 Harv. Bus. Rev. 64 (2004). For a comprehensive critique of CDHC, see Timothy Stoltzfus Jost, Health Care at Risk: A Critique of the Consumer–Driven Movement (2007). The difference between these paradigms has important implications for the structure of provider organizations. Rather than viewing large physician and hospital organizations as efficient and aiding patients by coordinating care, CDHC proponents views them as bureaucratic and emphasize the benefits of smaller physician practices, single specialty hospitals and illness-focused delivery systems. See James C. Robinson, Managed Consumerism in Health Care, 24 No. 6 Health Aff. 1478, 1480 (Nov./Dec. 2005). Physicians and hospitals may also change their practices radically to accommodate patients who are willing to pay a set fee for extensive service offerings, especially preventive care; assured and prompt access and greater amenities. See Frank Pasquale, The Three Faces of Retainer Care: Crafting a Tailored Regulatory Response, 7 Yale J. Health Pol'y, L. & Ethics 39 (2007), Sandra Carnahan, Concierge Medicine: Legal and Ethical Issues, 35 J. L. Med & Ethics 211 (2007).

2. *The Specialty Hospital Phenomenon*

An important recent development in health care organization has been the emergence of physician-owned "specialty hospitals." These facilities (also referred to as "carve-out" or "boutique" hospitals) are hospitals that only provide care for certain conditions or perform only specified procedures. See United States General Accounting Office ("GAO") Specialty Hospitals: Geographic Location, Services Provided, and Financial Performance, GAO–04–167 (Washington D.C.: Oct. 2003). Most physician specialty hospitals are owned by the specialty physicians who practice in them or by for-profit specialty chains. Typically these hospitals concentrate their service in one of several profitable areas of medicine or illness such as heart care, surgery and orthopedics. A number of factors have contributed to the rapid growth of these facilities: generous reimbursement rates for certain hospital and facility-based services, such as cardiology; stagnant physician incomes for specialist physicians practicing in these fields; the declining effectiveness of certificate of need laws in limiting development of new facilities; and increased convenience for patients and doctors able to obtain care in different geographic location than older community hospitals. For physicians owning or investing in such hospitals, these hospitals are dreams come true. They can exercise greater control over the quality and conditions of practice in the facility; and with increased specialization and familiarity with staff, outcomes may improve and medical error can be reduced. Further, physician investors in specialty hospitals share in the facility fee paid by insurers for their services, thus enhancing their incomes considerably. With patients usually willing to "follow their doctor," the financial risk of the doctors' investment is often minimal.

For hospitals, the picture is rather less rosy. Community hospitals argue that specialty hospitals threaten their viability and do not compete on a level playing field. Not only are the most profitable services pulled out of the general purpose hospital, but it is left with EMTALA obligations and must bear regulatory costs that the specialty hospital does not. See Doctor Owned Specialty Hospitals Spur Investor Interest, Capital Hill Worries, 12 Health L. Rep. (BNA), April 17, 2003, at 623 (cardiac and orthopedic services carved out of general hospitals earn profit margins of 20 to 30 percent making the investment in such facilities lucrative to investors, while losing such services can be drastic for a hospital's bottom line); Boom in Specialty Hospitals Signals Payment Discrepancies, 57 Health Care Fin. Mgmt. 20 (2003) (cardiology services alone can account for 25% or hospital stays and 35% or more of community hospital revenues). In addition, there is the risk that specialty hospitals will "cherry pick" healthier patients, either because their doctors are admitting their costlier, sicker patients to the community hospital or because the staff privileging process will segment the market. See United States General Accounting Office, Specialty Hospitals: Information on National Market Share, Physician Ownership, and Patients Served, GAO–03–683R (Washington D.C.: April 2003) (specialty hospitals treated a lower percentage of severely ill patients than did general community hospitals). But see Allan Dobson, Randy Haught & Namarata Sen, Specialty Heart Hospital: A Comparative Study, 1 Am Heart Hosp. J. 21, 21 (2003) (specialty hospital sponsored study showing that specialty heart hospitals have a higher-case mix severity than patients at general community hospitals). See also, Newt Gingrich, A Health Threat We're Not Treating: Don't Let Doctors Rig the Market for Specialty Hospitals, Wash Post (Nov. 12, 2005) at A25 ("It's just human nature for [doctors with financial interest in hospitals] to increase their own income by the simple act of giving the specialty hospital . . . all the easy and inexpensive cases while sending very risky and expensive cases to the larger community hospital").

The physician-owned specialty hospital phenomenon has produced a torrent of studies and a number of legislative and regulatory responses. As part of the Medicare Modernization Act of 2003, Pub. L. No. 108–173, § 507 (2003). Congress imposed an eighteen month moratorium on physician referrals to cardiac, orthopedic or surgical specialty hospitals in which the physician had an ownership or investment interest, and requiring studies by HHS and MedPAC of the issue. CMS effectively extended the moratorium into 2006 through administrative actions suspending processing of Medicare enrollment applications submitted by specialty hospitals and Congress extended the suspension in the Deficit Reduction Act of 2005. A complex and sometimes contentious dialogue involving Congress, CMS, and MedPAC produced a number of studies and recommendations as to future courses of action in this area. Particularly influential have been reports mandated by Congress, MedPAC and CMS. See MedPAC, Report to the Congress: Physician–Owned Specialty Hospitals (March 2005); Michael Leavitt, Study of Physician Owned Specialty Hospitals (May, 2005), http://www.cms.hhs.gov/MLNProducts/Downloads/RTC–StudyoFPhysOwnedSpecHosp.pdf. The MedPAC report found that specialty hospitals tended to treat more profitable patients, captured most of their patients from community hospitals, and earned returns far in excess of the average margin of community hospitals in their market though they showed no appreciable improvements in efficiency. However MedPAC also found no evidence that specialty hospitals had a significant impact on the financial performance of community hospitals with which they competed. MedPac Report *supra*. The CMS report, which focused on six markets, found that specialty hospitals received Medicare referrals primarily from physician owners, that the care received at cardiac specialty hospitals was good or better than that received at competitor hospitals, and that community hospitals treated more severely ill patients. See also, Jeffrey Stensland & Ariel Winter, Do Physician–Owned Hospitals Increase Utilization 25 No.1 Health Aff. 119 (Jan./Feb. 2006) (markets with specialty hospitals have small increase in number of cardiac surgeries, but no increase in treating healthier patients). The Federal Trade Commission has weighed in on the competitive implications of physician-owned specialty hospitals and ambulatory surgical centers, observing that they may provide a needed source of competition in many markets and serve to "enhance quality of care, lower prices and improve access." The FTC emphasized the need for other reforms such as eliminating certificate of need regulation and refining payment rates to avoid cross subsidization among services as the preferred means of eliminating artificial incentives for these facilities. Prepared Statement of the Federal Trade Commission before the Senate Subcommittee on Federal Financial Mangement, Government Information and International Security (May 24, 2005) available at www.ftc.gove/os/2005/05/052405newentryintohopsitalcomp.pdf. Finally, because specialty hospitals lack the capability to deal with complications and emergency conditions, legislators have also raised concerns about patient safety. See Grassley Baucus Ask Specialty Hospitals About Patient Safety After 911 Calls (Press release, Aug. 2007) http://grassley.senate.gov/public (Senators reacting to an investigative report that specialty hospital made 911 calls to transfer 150 patients to community hospitals for emergency care).

The reason these arrangements are allowed in the first place, and not treated as illegal "self referral" arrangements under the federal Stark law, is that there is an exception for "whole hospital" joint ventures. (See Chapter 12 *infra*). Critics of physician owned specialty hospitals have introduced legislation to remove this exception and thereby effectively ban those entities from receiving referrals from their investor physicians. Since specialty hospitals have developed predominantly in those states lacking certificate of need laws (60% of all such hospitals are located in four states, Texas, Kansas, Oklahoma and South Dakota), some believe stronger state legislation is warranted. Some states have attempted to outlaw physician ownership of hospitals in which they practice, or mandate that specialty hospitals provide emergency services. See, e.g., S.B. 828, Gen. Assem., Reg. Sess. (Cal. 2003) available at www.leginfo.ca.gov/pub/bill/sen/sb_0801–0850/sb_828_bill_20030626_amended_asm.pdf; S.B. 1341, 145th Gen Assem., 2d. Reg. Sess. (Az. 2002). Those who believe specialty hospitals provide a potentially valuable source of competition and innovation support efforts to remove financial incentives in DRG and other payment systems that reward physicians for self referrals and harm community hospitals. CMS appears to have taken the position that its recently-adopted refinements to the prospective payment system together with requiring disclosure of hospital ownership information to patients will solve the problem. United States Department of Health and Human Services, Final Report to Congress and Strategic and Implementing Plan Required under Section 5006 of the Deficit Reduction Act of 2005, (August 2006), http://www.cms.hhs.gov/PhysicianSelfReferral/06a_DRA_Reports.asp See also, Physician–Owned Specialty Hospitals: Profits Before Patients?: Hearing Before the Sen. Finance Comm., 109th Cong. 15 (2006) (statement of Mark McClellan, Administrator, Centers for Medicare and Medicaid Services) (stating that CMS has "proposed the most important reforms in the Diagnosis–Related Group payment system for hospitals since this system was created more than 20 years ago").

Problem: Making Policy Choices Under Uncertainty

You have just been designated by the new director of CMS to take a fresh look at the specialty hospital issue. How would you go about deciding what to do about physician-owned specialty hospitals? What would you define as the key policy issues? What empirical or other proof would you need to make a determination about whether to take action? What steps, legislative and regulatory, might be on the table and what are their risks and benefits?

Review Problem: Organizing All Saints Health Care

All Saints Health Care Enterprise, a not-for-profit religiously affiliated corporation, operates two hospitals, St. Timothy's and St. Patrick's, in River City. River City and the surrounding metropolitan area are served by 20 acute care hospitals and 3000 physicians. Like most markets, managed care has begun to make serious inroads in River City. As a result of the growth of managed care contracting, employers and insurers are insisting that hospitals and physicians assume financial risk through capitation or other means. A notable byproduct of these changes has been a sharp increase in the demand for primary care physicians and a surplus of specialists.

Two rivals have begun to form integrated systems. Madison Hospital, a large teaching hospital, has recently acquired five other hospitals and has developed a PHO, signing up as co-owners some 300 physicians who have staff privileges at these hospitals. Jefferson Medical Enterprises, a for-profit entity, owns three hospitals in the market and has formed an IPA-style HMO.

St. Timothy's Hospital, located in downtown River City, has 250 physicians with staff privileges, including 150 family practitioners and a large proportion of specialists practicing obstetrics and pediatric health specialties. A core group of 100 doctors, mostly in solo practice, concentrate their admissions at St. Timothy's. A relatively large proportion of these physicians are over 45 years old and many of the older doctors are amenable to selling their practices. Most of the remaining doctors, however, are fiercely independent and highly suspicious of managed care contract proposals being offered by insurance companies. There is a widespread consensus that St. Timothy's needs to recruit additional doctors to maintain its viability.

St. Patrick's, located in an affluent suburb adjacent to River City, has a much heavier proportion of specialists on its staff and offers a wide range of sophisticated services. Five group practices, including two large multispecialty groups, supply a large percentage of St. Patrick's inpatient and outpatient business.

Assuming you represent All Saints, what model or models of integrating organizations would you recommend that it consider forming? What form of business organization should each adopt and how should control be allocated between the hospital and physicians? What governance arrangements would you recommend to avoid conflicts and deadlocks in the future?

What advice would you give if you represented one of the multispecialty physician groups practicing at St. Patrick's? Suppose some of the independent All Saints physicians not currently in a group practice wanted to organize some form of entity before affiliating with the All Saints system. Explain the advantages and disadvantages of the organizational forms they might adopt.

IV. TAX–EXEMPT HEALTH CARE ORGANIZATIONS

INTRODUCTION

A. CHARITABLE PURPOSES: HOSPITALS

UTAH COUNTY v. INTERMOUNTAIN HEALTH CARE, INC.

Supreme Court of Utah, 1985.
709 P.2d 265.

DURHAM, JUSTICE:

Utah County seeks review of a decision of the Utah State Tax Commission reversing a ruling of the Utah County Board of Equalization. The Tax Commission exempted Utah Valley Hospital, owned and operated by Intermountain Health Care (IHC), and American Fork Hospital, leased and operated by IHC, from *ad valorem* property taxes. At issue is whether such a tax exemption is constitutionally permissible. We hold that, on the facts in this record, it is not, and we reverse.

IHC is a nonprofit corporation that owns and operates or leases and operates twenty-one hospitals throughout the intermountain area, including Utah Valley Hospital and American Fork Hospital. IHC also owns other subsidiaries, including at least one for-profit entity. It is supervised by a board of trustees who serve without pay. It has no stock, and no dividends or pecuniary profits are paid to its trustees or incorporators. Upon dissolution of the corporation, no part of its assets can inure to the benefit of any private person.

* * *

* * * These [tax] exemptions confer an indirect subsidy and are usually justified as the *quid pro quo* for charitable entities undertaking functions and services that the state would otherwise be required to perform. A concurrent rationale, used by some courts, is the assertion that the exemptions are granted not only because charitable entities relieve government of a burden, but also because their activities enhance beneficial community values or goals. Under this theory, the benefits received by the community are believed to offset the revenue lost by reason of the exemption.

* * *

An entity may be granted a charitable tax exemption for its property under the Utah Constitution only if it meets the definition of a "charity" or if its property is used exclusively for "charitable" purposes. Essential to this definition is the element of gift to the community.

* * * A gift to the community can be identified either by a substantial imbalance in the exchange between the charity and the recipient of its services or in the lessening of a government burden through the charity's operation.

* * *

Given the complexities of institutional organization, financing, and impact on modern community life, there are a number of factors which must be weighed in determining whether a particular institution is in fact using its property "exclusively for * * * charitable purposes." Utah Const. art. XIII, § 2 (1895, amended 1982). These factors are: (1) whether the stated purpose of the entity is to provide a significant service to others without immediate expectation of material reward; (2) whether the entity is supported, and to what extent, by donations and gifts; (3) whether the recipients of the "charity" are required to pay for the assistance received, in whole or in part; (4) whether the income received from all sources (gifts, donations, and payment from recipients) produces a "profit" to the entity in the sense that the income exceeds operating and long-term maintenance expenses; (5) whether the beneficiaries of the "charity" are restricted or unrestricted and, if restricted, whether the restriction bears a reasonable relationship to the entity's charitable objectives; and (6) whether dividends or some other form of financial benefit, or assets upon dissolution, are available to private interests, and whether the entity is organized and operated so that any commercial activities are subordinate or incidental to charitable ones. * * *

Because the "care of the sick" has traditionally been an activity regarded as charitable in American law, and because the dissenting opinions rely upon decisions from other jurisdictions that in turn incorporate unexamined assumptions about the fundamental nature of hospital-based medical care, we deem it important to scrutinize the contemporary social and economic context of such care. We are convinced that traditional assumptions bear little relationship to the economics of the medical-industrial complex of the 1980's. Nonprofit hospitals were traditionally treated as tax-exempt charitable institutions because, until late in the 19th century, they were true charities providing custodial care for those who were both sick and poor. The hospitals' income was derived largely or entirely from voluntary charitable donations, not government subsidies, taxes, or patient fees.[9] The function and status of hospitals began to change in the late 19th century; the transformation was substantially completed by the 1920's. "From charities, dependent on voluntary gifts, [hospitals] developed into market institutions financed increasingly out of payments from patients." The transformation was multidimensional: hospitals were redefined from social welfare to medical treatment institutions; their charitable foundation was replaced by a business basis; and their orientation shifted to "professionals and their patients," away from "patrons and the poor."

* * *

9. Paul Starr, *The Social Transformation of American Medicine* at 150 (1982). "Voluntary" hospitals, like public hospitals (which evolved from almshouses for the dependent poor), performed a "welfare" function rather than a medical or curing function: the poor were housed in large wards, largely cared for themselves, and often were not expected to recover. *See id.* at 145, 149, 160. Early voluntary hospitals had paternalistic, communal social structures in which patients entered at the sufferance of their benefactors, "had the moral status of children," and received more moralistic and religious help than medical treatment. *Id.* at 149, 158. * * *

[Ed. note: The opinion relies on Starr's book extensively. Further citations have been omitted.]

Also of considerable significance to our review is the increasing irrelevance of the distinction between nonprofit and for-profit hospitals for purposes of discovering the element of charity in their operations. The literature indicates that two models, described below, appear to describe a large number of nonprofit hospitals as they function today.

(1) The "physicians' cooperative" model describes nonprofit hospitals that operate primarily for the benefit of the participating physicians. Physicians, pursuant to this model, enjoy power and high income through their direct or indirect control over the nonprofit hospitals to which they bring their patients. * * * A minor variation of the above theory is the argument that many nonprofit hospitals operate as "shelters" within which physicians operate profitable businesses, such as laboratories. [ ]

(2) The "polycorporate enterprise" model describes the increasing number of nonprofit hospital chains. Here, power is largely in the hands of administrators, not physicians. Through the creation of holding companies, nonprofit hospitals have grown into large groups of medical enterprises, containing both for-profit and nonprofit corporate entities. Nonprofit corporations can own for-profit corporations without losing their federal nonprofit tax status as long as the profits of the for-profit corporations are used to further the nonprofit purposes of the parent organization.

* * *

* * * Dramatic advances in medical knowledge and technology have resulted in an equally dramatic rise in the cost of medical services. At the same time, elaborate and comprehensive organizations of third-party payers have evolved. Most recently, perhaps as a further evolutionary response to the unceasing rise in the cost of medical services, the provision of such services has become a highly competitive business.

* * *

The stated purpose of IHC regarding the operation of both hospitals clearly meets at least part of the first criterion we have articulated for determining the existence of a charitable use. Its articles of incorporation identify as "corporate purposes," among other things, the provision of "care and treatment of the sick, afflicted, infirm, aged or injured within and/or without the State of Utah." The same section prevents any "part of the net earnings of this Corporation" to inure to the private benefit of any individual. Furthermore, under another section, the assets of the corporation upon dissolution likewise may not be distributed to benefit any private interest.

The second factor we examine is whether the hospitals are supported, and to what extent, by donations and gifts. * * * [W]e have examined the testimony and exhibits in evidence on this question. The latter demonstrate that current operating expenses for both hospitals are covered almost entirely by revenue from patient charges. * * * The evidence was that both hospitals charge rates for their services comparable to rates being charged by other similar entities, and no showing was made that the donations identified resulted in charges to patients below prevailing market rates.

* * *

One of the most significant of the factors to be considered in review of a claimed exemption is the third we identified: whether the recipients of the services of an entity are required to pay for that assistance, in whole or in part. The Tax Commission in this case found as follows:

> The policy of [IHC's hospitals] is to collect hospital charges from patients whenever it is reasonable and possible to do so; however, no person in need of medical attention is denied care solely on the basis of a lack of funds.

The record also shows that neither of the hospitals in this case demonstrated any substantial imbalance between the value of the services it provides and the payments it receives apart from any gifts, donations, or endowments. The record shows that the vast majority of the services provided by these two hospitals are paid for by government programs, private insurance companies, or the individuals receiving care.

* * *

Between 1978 and 1980, the value of the services given away as charity by these two hospitals constituted less than one percent of their gross revenues. Furthermore, the record also shows that such free service as did exist was deliberately not advertised out of fear of a "deluge of people" trying to take advantage of it. Instead, every effort was made to recover payment for services rendered. * * *

The defendants argue that the great expense of modern hospital care and the universal availability of insurance and government health care subsidies make the idea of a hospital solely supported by philanthropy an anachronism. We believe this argument itself exposes the weakness in the defendants' position. It is precisely because such a vast system of third-party payers has developed to meet the expense of modern hospital care that the historical distinction between for-profit and nonprofit hospitals has eroded. * * *

The fourth question we consider is whether the income received from all sources by these IHC hospitals is in excess of their operating and maintenance expenses. Because the vast majority of their services are paid for, the nonprofit hospitals in this case accumulate capital as do their profit-seeking counterparts.

* * *

A large portion of the profits of most for-profit entities is used for capital improvements and new, updated equipment, and the defendant hospitals here similarly expend their revenues in excess of operational expenses. There can be no doubt, in reviewing the references in the record by members of IHC's administrative staff, that the IHC system, as well as the two hospitals in question, has consistently generated sufficient funds in excess of operating costs to contribute to rapid and extensive growth, building, competitive employee and professional salaries and benefits, and a very sophisticated management structure. While it is true that no financial benefits or profits are available to private interests in the form of stockholder distributions or ownership advantages, the user *entity* in this case clearly generates substantial "profits" in the sense of income that exceeds expenses.

* * *

On the question of benefits to private interests, certainly it appears that no individuals who are employed by or administer the defendants receive any distribution of assets or income, and some, such as IHC's board of trustees members, volunteer their services. We have noted, however, that IHC owns a for-profit entity, as well as nonprofit subsidiaries, and there is in addition the consideration that numerous forms of private commercial enterprise, such as pharmacies, laboratories, and contracts for medical services, are conducted as a necessary part of the defendants' hospital operations. The burden being on the taxpayer to demonstrate eligibility for the exemption, the inadequacies in the record on these questions cannot be remedied by speculation in the defendants' favor. * * *

Neither can we find on this record that the burdens of government are substantially lessened as a result of the defendants' provision of services. The record indicates that Utah County budgets approximately $50,000 annually for the payment of hospital care for indigents. Furthermore, the evidence described two instances within a three-month period where, after a Utah County official had declined to authorize payment for a person in the emergency room, Utah Valley Hospital refused to admit the injured person on the basis of that person's inability to pay. The county official was told in these instances to either authorize payment or to "come and get" the person. Such behavior on the hospital's part is inconsistent with its argument that it functions to relieve government of a burden. Likewise, as we have pointed out, there has been no showing that the tax exemption is a significant factor in permitting these defendants to operate, thereby arguably relieving government of the burden of establishing its own medical care providers. In fact, government is already carrying a substantial share of the operating expenses of defendants, in the form of third-party payments pursuant to "entitlement" programs such as Medicare and Medicaid.

* * *

We reverse the Tax Commission's grant of an *ad valorem* property tax exemption to defendants as being unconstitutional.

* * *

STEWART, JUSTICE (dissenting):

* * *

III.   DEFINITION OF CHARITY
* * *

The legal concept of charity does not require, as the majority apparently requires, that a hospital incur a deficit to qualify as a charitable institution. Charitable hospitals need not be self-liquidating.

* * *

It is true that the hospitals in this case receive substantial revenues from third-party payors and patients, but there is not a shred of evidence in this record, much less a finding by the Tax Commission, that one cent of the revenues is used for any purpose other than furthering the charitable purposes of providing hospital services to the sick and infirm. On the contrary, the Tax Commission's findings affirmatively establish that no person has profited from the revenues produced at either Utah Valley or American Fork Hospitals other than patients. Under time-honored legal principles, both hospitals qualify as charitable institutions.

IV. UTAH VALLEY HOSPITAL'S AND AMERICAN FORK
HOSPITAL'S GIFTS TO THE COMMUNITY

* * *

A. *Direct Patient Subsidies*

* * *

During the years 1978–80, Utah Valley Hospital rendered wholly free services to indigents in the amount of $200,000, and in each of those years the amount increased substantially over the preceding year. During the same period, the hospital subsidized services rendered to Medicare, Medicaid, and worker's compensation patients in the amount of $3,174,024. The corresponding figures for American Fork Hospital were $39,906 in indigent care and $421,306 for subsidization of Medicare, Medicaid, and worker's compensation benefits.

However, the value of the charity extended to indigents is in fact greater than the amounts stated. The cost of the charity extended to patients who are first identified as charity patients *after* admission rather than *at* admission is charged to the "bad debts" account, along with traditional uncollectible accounts or bad debts, instead of being charged to charity.

* * *

In sum, the *direct* cost of patient charity given away by Utah Valley Hospital for the period in question is in excess of $3,374,024, but less than $4,942,779 (which includes bad debts). The *direct* cost of the charity given away by American Fork Hospital is in excess of $461,212, but less than $639,024 (which includes bad debts). * * * Unlike for-profit hospitals, Utah Valley and American Fork have a policy against turning away indigent patients. Therefore, that portion of the hospitals' bad debts which is attributable to indigency is bona fide charity since the charges would have been initially made to the charity account had the patient's indigency been discovered at admission. Those charges are not just ordinary business bad debts experienced by all commercial enterprises, as the majority would have it.

* * *

B. *Capital Subsidies and Gifts*

The most glaring lapse in the majority opinion, in my view, is its flat-out refusal to recognize that there would be no Utah Valley Hospital—at all—if it had not been given lock, stock, and barrel to IHC by the Church of Jesus Christ of Latter–Day Saints, which initially built the hospital. American Fork Hospital apparently was initially erected by taxpayers' money. At the City's request, IHC took over the operation of the hospital as a lessee of American Fork City to relieve the City of a governmental burden. It follows that all patients at both hospitals, whether indigent, part-paying, or fully paying patients, are direct beneficiaries of large monetary investments in land, buildings, and medical equipment. * * *

In addition to the "gift to the community" of the actual physical facilities, each and every patient benefits from the fact that IHC is a nonprofit corporation whose hospitals make no profit on the value of the assets dedicated to hospital care. The majority's effort to portray IHC hospitals as if they were operated as for-profit entities has no substance in the record whatsoever. A for-profit hospital, unlike a nonprofit hospital, must necessarily price its services to make a profit on its investment if it is to stay in business. The surplus that Utah Valley and American Fork budget for is not by any means the equivalent of profit, as the majority wrongly suggests. * * *

Furthermore, the majority inaccurately asserts that Utah Valley charges rates comparable to other similar entities. The evidence is to the contrary. Utah Valley Hospital, with its 385 beds and expensive, sophisticated acute care equipment, charges rates comparable to the rates charged by Payson Hospital, a small for-profit hospital that renders inexpensive types of services. * * * In addition, there are no "prevailing market rates" for tertiary care hospitals, if by that term the majority means prevailing rates of competitive for-profit hospitals. There is no for-profit tertiary care hospital in the entire state of Utah; all tertiary care hospitals are non-profit institutions. In fact, there is no other tertiary care hospital, whether nonprofit or for-profit, in the immense, sparsely populated area served by the Utah Valley Hospital, which extends from Utah County to the Nevada–Arizona border. Indeed, the facts strongly suggest that a for-profit tertiary care hospital could not survive in the geographical market area served by Utah Valley. * * *

V. TAX EXEMPT STATUS OF NON-PROFIT HOSPITALS UNDER THE MAJORITY OPINION

The record also demonstrates that the primary care hospital and the tertiary care hospital involved in this case relieve a significant governmental burden, one of the two alternative tests for determining whether a nonprofit hospital qualifies to be treated as a charitable institution. * * * In the wide-open spaces of the West, where small communities are widely separated, the profit motive has not been sufficient to provide the needed impetus for the building of community hospitals (except in rare instances). Nor has it resulted in the construction of tertiary care hospitals in the more populous parts of the state.

The majority's argument is that no government burden is relieved by providing hospital service to those who can pay for it on a for-profit basis. The argument misses the mark for two reasons. First, the alternatives are not for-profit or nonprofit hospitals. The alternatives are nonprofit hospital care or no hospital care at all, at least within the relevant geographical markets. Second, the charitable status of a hospital does not turn on whether it provides care for patients who can pay. The basic policy is not to tax the sick and infirm irrespective of ability to pay. A county provides many services to rich and poor alike without charging the rich for those services. Parks and playgrounds are but examples. Providing medical services may not be manda-tory for counties or cities, but if they do, they most certainly promote the public health, safety, morals, and welfare in a most fundamental way. Surely cities and counties would, as a practical matter, be compelled to provide hospital services if the nonprofit hospitals in this state did not exist.

* * *

VI.   DIFFERENCES BETWEEN FOR-PROFIT AND NONPROFIT HOSPITALS

* * *

[A] for-profit hospital's investment decisions as to what markets or communities to enter and what kinds of equipment to invest in are made from a basically different motive than a nonprofit hospital's. The decisions of a for-profit hospital corporation must be based upon careful calculations as to the rate of return that may be expected on invested capital. If the rate of return is not sufficient, the investment is not made. Whether the surplus is reinvested in part or paid out to investors in dividends in whole or in part, the investor receives personal monetary benefit either in the increased value of his stock or in dividends.

Nonprofit hospitals must, of course, be concerned with generating sufficient revenue to maintain themselves, but they are not concerned with earning a return on their investment for the benefit of stockholders. Their purposes are altruistic. Any surplus must be used in a manner that aggrandizes no one, such as for the lowering of rates, the acquisition of new equipment, or the improvement of facilities.

* * *

IHC's Board of Trustees considers itself a trustee of the health care facilities for the public. "[W]e see ourselves as owned by the community since the corporation owns itself and in effect the church gave the hospitals to the communities, and we're entrusted with the running of the hospitals. We see them as in effect owned by the communities."

* * *

Notes and Questions

1.   The Intermountain Health Care opinion provides a useful history of the nonprofit hospital in America. How have changing practices, technologies, and payment systems affected those institutions? How do those factors influence the obligation to provide charity care? Should charity care be provided this way or through direct governmental expenditures? Critics of exemption point to the lack of oversight and control that occurs when care is financed publicly through foregone revenue, and that benefits awarded through the tax system are not subject to budgetary discipline as they are not reported as budget outlays. See Harry G. Gourevitch, Congressional Research Service, Tax Aspects of Health Care Reform: The Tax Treatment of Health Care Providers, 94 Tax Notes Today 94–90 (May 16, 1994).

2.   A series of articles in the Wall Street Journal in 2003 inaugurated an intense debate about the charitable behavior of hospitals, leading federal and state tax officials to closely examine the practices of tax exempt hospitals, including unfair billing and collection practices, excessive executive compensation and participation in for profit ventures. See Lucette Lagnado, Full Price: A Young Woman, an Appendectomy, and a \$19,000 Debt, Wall St. J. (Mar. 17, 2003); Nancy M. Kane, Tax–Exempt Hospitals: What is Their Charitable Responsibility and

How Should it Be Defined and Reported? 51 St. Louis U. L.J. 459 (2007). Many states have also begun to look at whether the law should delineate more precisely the community benefits expected of hospitals that enjoy exemption from state taxes. While several states have had in place for many years legislation aimed at reducing the disparity between the amount of benefit provided by tax exempt hospitals and the amount of foregone state and local taxes, new reform proposals are proliferating. See, Peyton M. Sturges, Review of Community Benefit Standard Exposes Concerns About Other Approaches, 15 No. 38 Health L. Rep. 1093 (BNA) (Sept. 2006). See also, Jill R. Horwitz, Does Nonprofit Ownership Matter?, 24 Yale J. on Reg. 139 (Winter 2007). Some states have adopted a "process" approach, requiring tax exempt hospitals to adopt a mission statement, undertake community needs assessments, engage with their communities in planning, and report the amount of community benefit provided. Laws in other states require nonprofit hospitals to account for and report their community benefits. For example, California established a presumption that hospitals earning less than a ten percent surplus or making an appropriate showing concerning their use of profits are entitled to the welfare property tax exemption. Cal. Rev. & Tax'n Code § 214 (a)(1). See also Ind. Code Ann. § 16–21–6–6 et seq. (1997)(reporting and assessment requirements); N.Y. Public Health Law § 2803–1 (same).

A few states have adopted a more "prescriptive" approach, requiring hospitals to make specified minimum expenditures on community benefits. See, e.g. Pa. Cons. Stat. Ann. Sec. 371–85 (setting forth five statutory standards including providing uncompensated goods or services equal to at least 5% of costs or maintaining an open admissions policy and providing uncompensated goods or services equal to at least 75% of net operating income but not less than 3% of total operating expenses; also allowing payments in lieu of taxes). For an analysis of Pennsylvania's actions regarding community benefits, see T.J. Sullivan and Karen McAfee, To Shiver or Not to Shiver, 28 Exempt Organization Tax Review 471 (June 2000). The Attorney General of Illinois proposed, and subsequently withdrew, legislation that would have required each tax exempt hospital in the state to furnish charity care to any uninsured resident earning less than 150 percent of the poverty level and to furnish aggregate charity care in an amount equal to eight percent of its total operating costs; "charity care" was defined as the marginal cost of providing care and bad debt losses did not count. See Lawmakers Shelve Plan to Quantify Charity Care for Tax–Exempt Hospitals, 15 No. 13 Health L. Rep. 373 (BNA) (March 30, 2006). What arguments do you think were levied against this proposal?

3. State taxing authorities have also been increasingly willing to seek revocation of exempt status for failure to meet statutory standards of charitable conduct and purpose. In a decision that generated considerable alarm among nonprofits, the Illinois Department of Revenue revoked the property tax exemption of Provena Covenant Medical Center. Michael Bologna & Peyton M. Sturges, Illinois Department of Revenue Director Says Provena Covenant Hospital Taxable, 15 No. 39 Health L. Rep. 1129 (BNA) (2006). The decision stressed that the total charges that Provena had waived from patients unable to pay represented less than 1% of its revenues, based on the costs of those services; had "outsourced" the provision of many services such as pharmacy, clinical labs and MRI/CT services to for-profit entities; had used flat discount rates to gauge payment due from individuals in low income rather than assessing their ability to pay the amount otherwise due; and had referred patients with unpaid balances to collection agencies, a practice the decision characterized as "lacking in the warmth and spontaneity indicative of a charitable impulse." Id. at 1131. An Illinois Circuit Court issued a bench ruling summarily reversing the Department's

decision and restoring Provena's property tax exemption. The hospital had argued that reliance on quantitative factors was unprecedented and inconsistent with state law. Do the other factors mentioned by the court provide convincing evidence that the hospital property was not used exclusively (defined to mean "primarily") for charitable purposes? See also City of Washington v. Board of Assessment, 550 Pa. 175, 704 A.2d 120 (1997) (applying five-part test governing hospitals' purposes and sufficiency of efforts to serve charitable ends). In contrast to *Intermountain* and the Pennsylvania actions, see Callaway Community Hospital Association v. Craighead, 759 S.W.2d 253 (Mo. Ct. App. 1988) (granting state tax exemption for a hospital that transferred indigent patients and viewing transfers as within individual physicians' and not hospital's control); see also Rideout Hospital Foundation, Inc. v. County of Yuba, 8 Cal.App.4th 214, 10 Cal.Rptr.2d 141 (1992) (upholding tax exemption to hospital with surplus revenue in excess of 10%).

4. Whether the amount of charity care provided by tax-exempt hospitals justifies the benefit of the tax exemption is hotly disputed. Studies comparing the value of tax exemptions for hospitals to the amount of charity care (measured in terms of costs, not charges) find that most hospitals could not justify their exemption on the basis of charity care alone. See Cong. Budget Office, Nonprofit Hospitals and the Provision of Community Benefits (Dec. 2006) http://www.cbo. gov/ftpdocs/76xx/doc7695/12–06–Nonprofit.pdf; David Walker, Nonprofit, For–Profit, and Government Hospitals: Uncompensated Care and Other Community Benefits, U.S. Government Accountability Office (2006) http://www.gao.gov/new. items/d05743t.pdf (little difference in uncompensated care burden shouldered by nonprofit and investor owned hospitals; government hospitals provide much greater proportion than either); cf. Michael Morrissey, et al., Do Nonprofit Hospitals Pay Their Way?, 15 Health Aff. 132 (1996) (hospitals failing to provide uncompensated care in excess of tax subsidy constitute only a small subset of all hospitals in California). Benchmarking the appropriate level of community benefits as the sum of those benefits provided by for profit hospitals plus the profits earned by those hospitals, another economic study concludes that nonprofit hospitals as a group are either underproviding community benefits or providing benefits that cannot be measured. Sean Nicholson et al., Measuring Community Benefits Provided by For–Profit and Nonprofit Hospitals, 19 Health Affairs 168 (2000). See also Uwe E. Reinhardt, The Economics of For–Profit and Not–For–Profit Hospitals, 19 Health Affairs 178 (Nov./Dec. 2000).

What problems does *Intermountain Health Care* raise in relation to defining, evaluating and measuring charity care? For example, what should count as charity care? See David Burda, Stop Playing Politics With Charity, Mod. Healthcare (June 5, 2006) at 20 (describing disagreement between the Catholic Hospital Association and American Hospital Association about whether bad debt expenses and Medicare shortfalls should be considered community benefits); see generally, M. Gregg Bloche, Health Policy Below the Waterline: Medical Care and the Charitable Exemption, 80 Minn. L. Rev. 299 (1995). Are there other "community benefits" besides charity care that should be taken into account? Consider for example the empirical research conducted by Professor Jill Horwitz which shows that nonprofit hospitals are more likely than for-profits to offer unprofitable services needed by poor and uninsured patients though less so than government-controlled hospitals. Jill R. Horwitz, Why We Need the Independent Sector: The Behavior, Law and Ethics of Not–For–Profit Hospitals, 50 UCLA L. Rev. 1345 (2003). Making Profits and Providing Care: Comparing Nonprofit, For–Profit and Government Hospitals, 24 Health Aff. 790 (May/June 2005). See also Jack Needleman, The Role of Nonprofits in Health Care, 26 J. Health Pol., Pol'y & L. 1113 (2002) (noting that nonprofits may have stronger "commitment to place" and be more likely to engage in "trustworthy behavior"); Mark Schlesinger & Bradford H. Gray, How Nonprofits Matter in American Medicine and What to Do About It, 25 No. 4 Health Aff. 287 (June 20, 2006) (finding nonprofits less aggressive in marking up prices, less likely to make misleading claims and acting as "incubators of innovation"). Mark A. Hall and John D. Colombo offer another rationale: subsidization is appropriate for those organizations capable of attracting a substantial level of donative support in the face of market imperfections. The Charitable Status of Nonprofit Hospitals: Toward a Donative Theory of Tax Exemption, 66 Wash. L. Rev. 307 (1991). What implications does this research have for legislative proposals regarding the obligations of exempt hospitals? For attorneys general reviewing conversions of nonprofit hospitals?

5.   In over seventy lawsuits filed against hundreds of hospitals, renowned plaintiffs' attorney Richard Scruggs charged that hospitals' failure to provide "mutually affordable medical care" violates a host of laws, including federal and state tax exemption standards, the Emergency Medical Treatment and Active Labor Act (EMTALA), charitable trust law, state consumer protection law, and implied contractual obligations to uninsured patients not to bill more than a fair and reasonable charge. The relief requested in these cases includes injunctions requiring hospitals to change their billing and collection practices, and imposing a constructive trust on hospitals savings from tax exempt status, profits, and assets, so as to assure the availability of affordable medical care. Courts have dismissed almost all of these claims on standing and substantive grounds. See e.g. Sabeta v. Baptist Hosp. of Miami, Inc., 410 F.Supp.2d 1224 (S.D. Fla. 2005) (holding that the hospital did not enter into an express or implied "charitable trust" to provide mutually affordable medical care to its uninsured patients by virtue of federal tax exempt status and that patients did not have an implied private right of action under Internal Revenue Code based on the hospital's federal tax exempt status). Despite their lack of success in court, these cases seem to have focused the attention of regulators, legislatures, and the public on the quantity of charity care provided nonprofit hospitals and their billing and collection practices.

Federal Tax Exemption: Charitable Purpose under Section 501(c)(3)

Exemption from federal taxation plays a more prominent role in the affairs of tax exempt hospitals than does state tax exemption. This is not necessarily because more money is at stake—the loss of state and local property tax exemptions may be more costly to a nonprofit hospital that has small or no earnings subject to income taxation—but because federal tax law reaches into many aspects of hospitals operations, including governance, relationships with other providers, and charity care policies. Of course Federal tax exempt status carries with it significant benefits. Besides exemption from liability for corporate income tax, it permits the organization to enjoy exemption from federal unemployment taxes, preferred postal rates and various other benefits respecting pensions and special treatment under various regulatory laws. Second, only donations to charitable organizations exempt under 501(c)(3) are deductible to donors under IRC Section 170. Third, only charitable organizations can issue tax exempt bonds, an important source of financing for nonprofit hospitals. IRC § 145. Finally, state property, sales and other tax exemptions (which as a matter of practical economics may be far more important than federal income exemption to many hospitals) often—but not always—follow federal standards.

Section 501(c)(3) of the Internal Revenue Code exempts from federal income tax entities "organized and operated exclusively for religious, charitable, scientific, testing for public safety, literary, or educational purposes, or to foster . . . amateur sports competition . . . or for the prevention of cruelty to animals." An organization must meet three important requirements to qualify for tax exempt status:

(1) no part of its net earnings may inure to the benefit of any private shareholder or individual;

(2) no substantial part of its activities may consist of certain activities aimed at influencing legislation; and

(3) it may not participate or intervene in any political campaign on behalf of any candidate for public office.

26 U.S.C.A. § 501(c)(3). Is there an internal logic to these requirements? Does the view that foregoing taxes on charitable and other organizations amounts to a "subsidy" help explain these provisions?

To qualify for § 501(c)(3) status, a health care facility must meet both an "organizational test," which requires that the hospital's constitutive documents, such as the corporate articles of incorporation, limit its activities to exempt purposes, and an "operational test," which requires that the hospital be operated primarily for exempt purposes, including "charitable," "educational," or "religious" purposes. Most hospitals must qualify as charities as healthcare is not specifically listed among exempt purposes. The definition of charitable purposes under the Code has been quite controversial, with the Internal Revenue Service attempting to adjust the definition to meet changes in the modern health care sector while the statute remained unchanged. Unfortunately, the federal tax authorities have not been clear or consistent in explaining when the provision of health care services are charitable. As a practical matter, few hospitals have failed to satisfy the flexible—some say overly flexible—standard that has evolved. However, as you read subsequent sections in this chapter, notice that the IRS and courts have, especially in recent years, been far less lenient with other kinds of health care entities.

The confused trail of the exemption standard for hospitals begins with a 1956 Revenue Ruling that required a tax-exempt hospital to be operated "to the extent of its financial ability for those not able to pay for the services rendered." Rev. Ruling 56–185. In 1958, the Tax Court upheld the denial of exempt status for a hospital that devoted between 2% and 5% of its revenue to care for the indigent (Lorain Avenue Clinic v. Commissioner, 31 T.C. 141). Thus one can identify in the early history of IRS analysis of the issue a direct link between exempt status and the provision of a specified quantum of free care for the poor. A pivotal turning point, however, occurred in 1969 when an IRS Revenue Ruling adopted a "community benefit" standard, under which the provision of charity care was no longer the sine qua non for charitable status as long as the hospital "promot[ed] health for the general benefit of the community." The Ruling went on to suggest that the existence of a community board, an open emergency room treating indigent patients free of charge, an open medical staff and treatment of government-insured patients would provide adequate evidence the entity was serving charitable purposes. The Service illustrated its position by describing a hospital that operated an emergency room that was open to all regardless of ability to pay and whose care for the indigent was not otherwise described, which it stated met the Revenue Ruling's standards for exemption. This remarkable shift was not the product of an informed analysis of the benefits of nonprofit health care, nor did it involve legislative action. Instead it appears it was the result of the erroneous assumption of IRS staff attorneys that the recently-enacted Medicaid statute would obviate the need for charity care and that a new justification was therefore needed to preserve the dominant nonprofit hospital sector. See generally, Daniel M. Fox & Daniel C. Schaffer, Tax Administration as Health Policy: Hospitals, The

Internal Revenue Service and the Courts, 16 J. Health Pol., Pol'y & L. 251 (1991)(describing political and legal issues involved in Rev. Ruling 69–545). The link to the provision of charity care under federal law was further diluted by a 1983 Revenue Ruling, in which a hospital that did not even operate an emergency room and usually referred indigent patients to another hospital was described as qualifying for tax-exempt status. The illustrative hospital did not operate an ER because the state health planning agency had concluded that the emergency room was not needed in the area, as other nearby hospitals had adequate emergency services. Rev. Rul. 83–157. Thus, for almost forty years federal tax exempt status has not been tied to the provision of charity care, or for that matter to doing anything terribly differently than for profit hospitals. For academic criticism of the standard and a thoughtful proposal to shift the IRS's focus to the question of whether an exempt hospital increases access to health services, see John D. Colombo, The Role of Access in Charitable Tax Exemption, 82 Washington U. L.Q. 343 (2004).

The intensifying scrutiny of nonprofit hospitals described earlier in this chapter appears to have awoken politicians and the IRS to the shortcomings of the community benefit standard. The Senate Finance Committee and House Ways and Means Committee have been particularly active, holding hearings on the issue in 2006 and pressing the IRS and GAO to survey and report on the provision of charity care by tax exempt hospitals. Charitable Care and Community Benefits at Nonprofit Hospitals: Hearing Before the Comm. on Finance, 109th Cong. (2006) (statement of Charles Grassley, Chairman). See also Nonprofit Hospitals and the Provision of Community Benefits, *supra* (study of five states finding that nonprofit hospitals as a group provide more charity care than for-profits; the amount of uncompensated care varied widely; and nonprofits provided care to fewer Medicaid-covered patients as a percentage of their overall patient population); IRS Interim Report (July 19, 2007) (finding wide variation in the definitions used by exempt entities to report charity care to the IRS) available at www.irs.gov/pub/irs-tege/eo_interim_hospital_report_072007.pdf. As this book was going to press, the minority staff of the Senate Finance Committee released a discussion draft of policy recommendations which proposed that hospitals must attain a minimum five percent charity care (measured by Medicare or Medicaid reimbursement rates or other actual rates and not including bad debt) and meet certain other requirements in order to retain 501(c)(3) status. Senate Finance Committee Minority Staff, Tax–Exempt Hospitals: Discussion Draft (July, 2007) www.senate.gov/?finance/press/Gpress2007/prg07/19/07a. The staff's wide ranging proposals also included placing restrictions on conversions, imposing requirements on joint ventures between nonprofit and for-profit hospitals, limiting charges billed to the uninsured, and curtailing unfair billing and collection practices.

Perhaps the most important outcome thus far of this flurry of activity has been the issuance by the IRS of a redesigned Form 990—the annual information return that most exempt hospitals file annually. Modeled to some extend on SEC disclosure forms, the new Form 990 would work revolutionary change in to the reporting requirements for nonprofit entities. Of particular relevance to the issues discussed in this chapter, the form creates a new Schedule H which requires each exempt organization to submit a Community Benefit Report that includes cost based data for community benefits including charity care and Medicaid, a description of its charity care policy, a statement of how it assess community needs and detailed information about billing and debt collection practices. Discussion Draft, www.irs.gov/charities/index.html. See Gerald M. Griffith et al., IRS Mandates Heightened Transparency in Redesigned Form 990, 11 Health Law. News 8 (Aug. 2007).

What factors might have prompted policymakers' rather sudden interest in the standard for tax exempt status applicable to hospitals? While it is impossible to predict whether legislation will be passed or IRS will amend the standard on its own, what would you recommend? Is the move toward greater disclosure and transparency enough? Are there pitfalls in attempting to define, quantify and prescribe the obligations of charitable institutions? In answering these questions, return to the underlying issue of why the law prefers (and subsidizes) a nonprofit sector. See Bloche, *supra*; Gabriel O. Aitsebaomo, The Nonprofit Hospital: A Call for New National Guidance Requiring Minimum Annual Charity Care to Qualify for Federal Tax Exemption, 26 Campbell L. Rev. 75 (2004); Jack E. Karns, Justifying the Nonprofit Hospital Tax Exemption in a Competitive Market Environment, 13 Widener L.J. 383 (2004).

Problem: St. Andrew's Medical Center

St. Andrew's Medical Center is a 750–bed not-for-profit hospital in a metropolitan area. It offers residency programs in internal medicine, obstetrics, surgery and several other areas. St. Andrew's is facing an uncertain financial future, and its Board of Directors is concerned about serious cutbacks in federal funds for graduate medical education, further reductions in health care reimbursement and its own inability to raise enough capital for modernization through retained earnings and donations. The Board is hesitant to increase the facility's substantial debt to make capital improvements in its 40–year–old physical plant. It also finds that it provides a significant amount of charity care each year in part because of its self-identified institutional mission and in part because it is one of only three hospitals in the area. The other two hospitals are a for-profit, 250–bed hospital operated by Americare, Inc., which is an investor-owned multi-facility system, and a municipal hospital, which regularly operates at 98% capacity and is often unable to receive transfers from St. Andrew's.

St. Andrew's has been approached by Health Care Enterprises (HCE), a for-profit corporation that owns eighty-five hospitals in thirty states and is interested in acquiring St. Andrew's. HCE has made an initial offer of $100 million for St. Andrew's, which would include the acquisition of all assets of St. Andrew's, including the name itself. The Board is very interested in the offer but is concerned that the provision of charity care continue at St. Andrew's and that HCE conform with the mission of St. Andrew's as a religiously affiliated hospital. For the Board, this latter concern relates, in part, to their interest in having St. Andrew's not offer abortion or assisted suicide services and in assuring an adequate pastoral care program.

HCE has suggested to St. Andrew's that St. Andrew's place $75 million (the amount of purchase money remaining after St. Andrew's pays off outstanding debts) into an endowment for a new St. Andrew's Foundation. The income from this endowment would then be paid to HCE for charity care and the medical education program at St. Andrew's. HCE has also suggested that it is itself also willing to provide "appropriate" charity care and adhere to the "traditional mission of St. Andrew's." HCE has suggested that it would agree to a buy-back provision in the sales agreement through which St. Andrew's could repurchase the hospital at a price to be agreed upon at the time of purchase should HCE fail to perform on either item.

The community is generally quite upset about the proposal. Many have charged that St. Andrew's is abandoning the community and that HCE is simply seeking to build a reputation by owning a teaching hospital and to "corner the market" by eliminating the only not-for-profit hospital in the metropolitan area.

The Board has not attempted to solicit other offers. However, one of its members had a casual conversation with the Chair and CEO of St. Olaf's Hospital, another nonprofit charitable hospital, who indicated that it would be interested in buying St. Andrew's but could pay no more than $80 million.

The Board meeting to decide whether St. Andrew's will be sold to HCE is tomorrow morning. You are a member of the Board. What will you recommend? If the transfer is approved, how would you draft the agreement between St. Andrew's and HCE? For example, how would you draft a contract with enforceable standards for conformance with the religious mission? For "appropriate charity care"? How should the buy-back provision be structured? Will the hospital still be called "St. Andrew's"?

For excellent analyses of issues relating to religious affiliation see, Kathleen M. Boozang, Deciding The Fate of Religious Hospitals in The Emerging Health Care Market, 31 Hous. L. Rev. 1429 (1995); Lawrence E. Singer & Elizabeth Johnson Lantz, The Coming Millennium: Enduring Issues Confronting Catholic Health Care, 8 Annals Health L. 299 (1999).

As discussed earlier, conversions and sales of not-for-profit, tax-exempt entities to for-profit providers have been quite controversial. The Internal Revenue Service's authority in these situations is limited and the rules have not been interpreted to restrict conversions as long an entity remains properly organized as a nonprofit entity and continues to pursue an exempt purpose. However, the Internal Revenue Service has the authority to prevent private inurement, which may help ensure an adequate purchase price. See Section C *infra* and Anclote Psychiatric Ctr., Inc. v. Commissioner, T.C. Memo 1998–273, aff'd 190 F.3d 541 (11th Cir. 1999). With the enactment of intermediate sanctions authority, discussed *infra*, the IRS now has greater flexibility and capacity to monitor conflicts of interest; however, it still lacks legal authority to require advanced approval except for joint ventures between for-profit and nonprofit organizations. Consequently, regulation of conversions has been governed principally by state common law and statutes. See generally, IRS Should Oversee Sales of Nonprofit Hospitals, Organization Asserts, 95 Tax Notes Today 111–46 (June 8, 1995).

B. JOINT VENTURES BETWEEN TAX–EXEMPT AND FOR–PROFIT ORGANIZATIONS

Tax-exempt organizations may engage in business activities jointly with for-profit organizations; may own for-profit organizations; and may themselves directly engage in non-tax-exempt activities. An exempt organization's participation in a joint venture with a for-profit entity will not affect its tax exempt status provided the purpose of its involvement in the ventures is in furtherance of its exempt purpose. Section 501(c)(3) requires that the exempt entity be organized and operated "exclusively" for exempt purposes, but the Internal Revenue Code regulations interpret that standard as requiring that exempt organizations engage "primarily in activities that accomplish one or more ... exempt purposes" and further state that the exempt organization violates this standard if "more than an insubstantial" amount of its activities are not in furtherance of exempt purposes. 26 C.F.R. § 1.501(c)(3)–1(c)(1). Thus, § 501(c)(3) organizations may engage in trade or business unrelated to their exempt purposes, though income from such unrelated business is taxable and not tax-exempt.

GENERAL COUNSEL MEMORANDUM

39862.
(Dec. 2, 1991).

[The Service reviews a physician-hospital agreement in which the hospital sold its future net income from certain departments to entities that were owned by physicians who admitted and treated patients at the hospital. For example, obstetricians who treated patients at the hospital could invest in the hospital's OB department with the return on investment being a proportionate share of the net income of that department. Thus, the physician practicing in the department would experience financial gain or loss depending on the department's financial performance.]

The [net income stream] joint venture arrangements ... are just one variety of an increasingly common type of competitive behavior engaged in by hospitals in response to significant changes in their operating environment. Many medical and surgical procedures once requiring inpatient care, still the exclusive province of hospitals, now are performed on an outpatient basis, where every private physician is a potential competitor. The marked shift in governmental policy from regulatory cost controls to competition has fundamentally changed the way all hospitals, for-profit and not, do business.

A driving force behind the new hospital operating environment was the federal Medicare Program's 1983 shift from cost-based reimbursement for covered inpatient hospital services to fixed, per-case, prospective payments. This change to a diagnosis-related prospective payment system ("PPS") dramatically altered hospital financial incentives. PPS severed the link between longer hospital stays with more services provided each patient and higher reimbursement. It substituted strong incentives to control the costs of each individual inpatient's care while attracting a greater number of admissions. Medicare policies are highly influential; the program accounts for nearly 40% of the average hospital's revenues.

The need to increase admission volume was accompanied by a perceived need to influence physician treatment decisions which, by and large, were unaffected by the change to PPS. Hospitals realized that, in addition to attracting more patients, they needed to control utilization of ancillary hospital services, discharge Medicare beneficiaries as quickly as is medically appropriate, and operate more efficiently. Traditionally, physicians treating their private patients at a hospital had enjoyed nearly complete independence of professional judgement. Since they are paid separately by Medicare and other third party payers on the basis of billed charges, they still have an incentive to render more services to each patient over a longer period in order to enhance their own earnings. Once hospital and physician economic incentives diverged, hospitals began seeking ways to stimulate loyalty among members of their medical staffs and to encourage or reward physician behaviors deemed desirable.

* * *

... Here, there appears to be little accomplished that directly furthers the hospitals' charitable purposes of promoting health. No expansion of health care resources results; no new provider is created. No improvement in treatment modalities or reduction in cost is foreseeable. We have to look very carefully for any reason why a hospital would want to engage in this sort of arrangement.

* * *

Assuming, arguendo, that [a hospital engaged in the transaction because it had] a pressing need for an advance of cash, we could examine this type of transaction strictly as a financing mechanism. . . . [W]e do not believe it would be proper under most circumstances for a charitable organization to borrow funds under an agreement, even with an outside commercial lender, where the organization would pay as interest a stated percentage of its earnings. . . . In any event, we do not believe these transactions were undertaken to raise needed cash.

Whether admitted or not, we believe the hospitals engaged in these ventures largely as a means to retain and reward members of their medical staffs; to attract their admissions and referrals; and to pre-empt the physicians from investing in or creating a competing provider [of outpatient services].

* * *

. . . In our view, there are a fixed number of individuals in a community legitimately needing hospital services at any one time. Paying doctors to steer patients to one particular hospital merely to improve its efficiency seems distant from a mission of providing needed care. We question whether the Service should ever recognize enhancing a hospital's market share vis-a-vis other providers, in and of itself, as furthering a charitable purpose. In many cases, doing so might hamper another charitable hospital's ability to promote the health of the same community.

* * *

Notes and Questions

1. Evaluate the economic incentives created by the proposed arrangement. How would a physician gain by making such an investment? Why would a hospital sell a share of its income? Isn't the potential improvement in the hospital's competitive position in the community or enhancement of its efficiency a community benefit? Compare these arrangements to "gainsharing" arrangements discussed in the next chapter which allow staff physicians to share in the savings arising from process improvement initiatives or other cost-effective methods which are attributable in part to the physician's efforts. What distinguishes gainsharing arrangements from the sale of revenue stream at issue in GCM 39862? See Stacey L. Murphy & Edward J. Buchholz, Internal Revenue Service Approval of Two Gainsharing Programs—The Rulings and Their Implications, 32 J. Health L. 381 (1999).

2. Unrelated trade or business is that which an exempt organization regularly carries on "the conduct of which is not substantially related (aside from the need of such organization for income or funds or the use it makes of the profits derived)" to its exempt purpose and is taxable as "unrelated business taxable income" (UBTI). 26 CFR § 1.513–1(a). Services that contribute to patient recovery and convenience are "related" to the exempt purposes of the health care organization and income from these activities is not taxable. Generally, services

provided to non-hospital patients are taxable unless they fall within certain narrow exceptions relating to (1) whether the services to non-patients are otherwise available in the community or (2) whether the services to non-patients contribute to the achievement of other exempt purposes, such as medical education. Thus sales of pharmaceuticals to individuals who are not hospital patients are taxable, with limited exceptions made for situations in which there are no local alternatives. See Hi–Plains Hosp. v. U.S., 670 F.2d 528 (5th Cir. 1982). See also Private Letter Ruling 8125007 (undated), in which the Service decided that sophisticated lab services, not otherwise available and provided by an exempt hospital to industry for employee examinations, did not produce UBTI. The PLR concluded, however, that the provision of ordinary lab services performed for non-hospital patients of private physicians may do so. This may lead to rather confusing results. A hospital's revenues from providing MRI services to patients of another hospital or to outpatients served by its staff physicians might well be UBTI, though the revenues from the same services to admitted patients would not. Likewise income from management or administrative services sold by a tax-exempt hospital to physicians in private practices could certainly be considered UBTI. If the hospital purchased the physician practices, would the provision of these services to the hospital-owned practices produce taxable income? On the issue of gift shops, parking facilities and cafeterias on hospital campuses, the law carves out an exception to taxable income by excluding business "carried on by the organization primarily for the convenience of its .. members, patients or employees." I.R.C. § 513(a) (2006).

3.   In evaluating the permissibility of joint ventures between for-profit and exempt entities, the IRS has long used a two-prong "close scrutiny" test. That test requires (1) that the exempt organization's participation in the venture serves a charitable purpose and (2) that the structure of the venture permits the exempt organization to act exclusively in furtherance of its charitable purpose and whether the arrangement impermissibly benefits for profit persons. See Housing Pioneers, Inc. v. Commissioner, T.C. Memo 1993–120 (March 29, 1993), 65 T.C.M. 2191, aff'd 49 F.3d 1395 (9th Cir. 1995), amended, 58 F.3d 401 (9th Cir. 1995). Consider how the following Revenue Ruling and cases alter that test.

REVENUE RULING 98–15

1998–12 I.R.B. 6.

[In this Revenue Ruling, the IRS provides the following examples to illustrate whether an organization that operates an acute care hospital constitutes an organization whose principal purpose is providing charitable hospital care when it forms a limited liability company (LLC) with a for-profit corporation and then contributes its hospital and all of its related operating assets to the LLC, which then operates the hospital.]

Situation 1

A is a nonprofit corporation that owns and operates an acute care hospital. A has been recognized as exempt from federal income tax ... as an organization described in § 501(c)(3).... B is a for-profit corporation that owns and operates a number of hospitals.

A concludes that it could better serve its community if it obtained additional funding. B is interested in providing financing for A's hospital, provided it earns a reasonable rate of return. A and B form a limited liability company, C. A contributes all of its operating assets, including its hospital to C. B also contributes assets to C. In return, A and B receive ownership interests in C proportional and equal in value to their respective contributions.

C's Articles of Organization and Operating Agreement ("governing documents") provide that C is to be managed by a governing board consisting of three individuals chosen by A and two individuals chosen by B. A intends to appoint community leaders who have experience with hospital matters, but who are not on the hospital staff and do not otherwise engage in business transactions with the hospital.

The governing documents further provide that they may only be amended with the approval of both owners and that a majority of three board members must approve certain major decisions relating to C's operation including decisions relating to any of the following topics:

A. C's annual capital and operating budgets;

B. Distributions of C's earnings;

C. Selection of key executives;

D. Acquisition or disposition of health care facilities;

E. Contracts in excess of $x per year;

F. Changes to the types of services offered by the hospital; and

G. Renewal or termination of management agreements.

The governing documents require that C operate any hospital it owns in a manner that furthers charitable purposes by promoting health for a broad cross section of its community. The governing documents explicitly provide that the duty of the members of the governing board to operate C in a manner that furthers charitable purposes by promoting health for a broad cross section of the community overrides any duty they may have to operate C for the financial benefit of its owners. Accordingly, in the event of a conflict between operation in accordance with the community benefit standard and any duty to maximize profits, the members of the governing board are to satisfy the community benefit standard without regard to the consequences for maximizing profitability.

The governing documents further provide that all returns of capital and distributions of earnings made to owners of C shall be proportional to their ownership interests in C. The terms of the governing documents are legal, binding, and enforceable under applicable state law.

C enters into a management agreement with a management company that is unrelated to A or B to provide day-to-day management services to C. The management agreement is for a five-year period, and the agreement is renewable for additional five-year periods by mutual consent. The management company will be paid a management fee for its services based on C's gross revenues. The terms and conditions of the management agreement, including the fee structure and the contract term, are reasonable and comparable to what other management firms receive for similar services at similarly situated hospitals. C may terminate the agreement for cause.

None of the officers, directors, or key employees of A who were involved in making the decision to form C were promised employment or any other inducement by C or B and their related entities if the transaction were approved. None of A's officers, directors, or key employees have any interest, including any interest through attribution determined in accordance with the principles of § 318, in B or any of its related entities.

Pursuant to § 301.7701–3(b) of the Procedure and Administrative Regulations, C will be treated as a partnership for federal income tax purposes.

A intends to use any distributions it receives from C to fund grants to support activities that promote the health of A's community and to help the indigent obtain health care. Substantially all of A's grantmaking will be funded by distributions from C. A's projected grantmaking program and its participation as an owner of C will constitute A's only activities.

Situation 2

D is a nonprofit corporation that owns and operates an acute care hospital. D has been recognized as exempt from federal income tax ... as an organization described in § 501(c)(3).... E is a for-profit hospital corporation that owns and operates a number of hospitals and provides management services to several hospitals that it does not own.

D concludes that it could better serve its community if it obtained additional funding. E is interested in providing financing for D's hospital, provided it earns a reasonable rate of return. D and E form a limited liability company, F. D contributes all of its operating assets, including its hospital to F. E also contributes assets to F. In return, D and E receive ownership interests proportional and equal in value to their respective contributions.

F's Articles of Organization and Operating Agreement ("governing documents") provide that F is to be managed by a governing board consisting of three individuals chosen by D and three individuals chosen by E. D intends to appoint community leaders who have experience with hospital matters, but who are not on the hospital staff and do not otherwise engage in business transactions with the hospital.

The governing documents further provide that they may only be amended with the approval of both owners and that a majority of board members must approve certain major decisions relating to F's operation, including decisions relating to any of the following topics:

A. F's annual capital and operating budgets;

B. Distributions of F's earnings over a required minimum level of distributions set forth in the Operating Agreement;

C. Unusually large contracts; and

D. Selection of key executives.

F's governing documents provide that F's purpose is to construct, develop, own, manage, operate, and take other action in connection with operating the health care facilities it owns and engage in other health care-related activities. The governing documents further provide that all returns of capital and distributions of earnings made to owners of F shall be proportional to their ownership interests in F.

F enters into a management agreement with a wholly-owned subsidiary of E to provide day-to-day management services to F. The management agreement is for a five-year period, and the agreement is renewable for additional five-year periods at the discretion of E's subsidiary. F may terminate the agreement only for cause. E's subsidiary will be paid a management fee for its services based on gross revenues. The terms and conditions of the management agreement, including the fee structure and the contract term other than the renewal terms, are reasonable and comparable to what other management firms receive for similar services at similarly situated hospitals.

As part of the agreement to form F, D agrees to approve the selection of two individuals to serve as F's chief executive officer and chief financial officer. These individuals have previously worked for E in hospital management and have business expertise. They will work with the management company to oversee F's day-to-day management. Their compensation is comparable to what comparable executives are paid at similarly situated hospitals.

Pursuant to § 301.7701–3(b). F will be treated as a partnership for federal income tax purposes.

D intends to use any distributions it receives from F to fund grants to support activities that promote the health of D's community and to help the indigent obtain health care. Substantially all of D's grantmaking will be funded by distributions from F. D's projected grantmaking program and its participation as an owner of F will constitute D's only activities.

ANALYSIS

A § 501(c)(3) organization may form and participate in a partnership, including an LLC treated as a partnership for federal income tax purposes, and meet the operational test if participation in the partnership furthers a charitable purpose, and the partnership arrangement permits the exempt organization to act exclusively in furtherance of its exempt purpose and only incidentally for the benefit of the for-profit partners. Similarly, a § 501(c)(3) organization may enter into a management contract with a private party giving that party authority to conduct activities on behalf of the organization and direct the use of the organization's assets provided that the organization retains ultimate authority over the assets and activities being managed and the terms and conditions of the contract are reasonable, including reasonable compensation and a reasonable term. However, if a private party is allowed to control or use the non-profit organization's activities or assets for the benefit of the private party, and the benefit is not incidental to the accomplishment of exempt purposes, the organization will fail to be organized and operated exclusively for exempt purposes.

Situation 1

After A and B form C, and A contributes all of its operating assets to C, A's activities will consist of the health care services it provides through C and any grantmaking activities it can conduct using income distributed to C. A will receive an interest in C equal in value to the assets it contributes to C, and A's and B's returns from C will be proportional to their respective investments in C. The governing documents of C commit C to providing health care services for the benefit of the community as a whole and to give charitable purposes priority over maximizing profits for C's owners. Furthermore, through A's appointment of members of the community familiar with the hospital to C's board, the board's structure, which gives A's appointees voting control, and the specifically enumerated powers of the board over changes in activities, disposition of assets, and renewal of the management agreement. A can ensure that the assets it owns through C and the activities it conducts through C are used primarily to further exempt purposes. Thus, A can ensure that the benefit to B and other private parties, like the management company, will be incidental to the accomplishment of charitable purposes. Additionally, the terms and conditions of the management contract, including the terms for renewal and termination are reasonable. Finally, A's grants are intended to support education and research and give resources to help provide health care to the indigent. All of these facts and circumstances establish that, when A participates in forming C and contributes all of its operating assets to C, and C operates in accordance with its governing documents, A will be furthering charitable purposes and continue to be operated exclusively for exempt purposes.

* * *

Situation 2

When D and E form F, and D contributes its assets to F, D will be engaged in activities that consist of the health care services it provides through F and any grantmaking activities it can conduct using income distributed by F. However, unlike A, D will not be engaging primarily in activities that further an exempt purpose.... In the absence of a binding obligation in F's governing documents for F to serve charitable purposes or otherwise provide its services to the community as a whole, F will be able to deny care to segments of the community, such as the indigent. Because D will share control of F with E, D will not be able to initiate programs within F to serve new health needs within the community without the agreement of at least one governing board member appointed by E. As a business enterprise, E will not necessarily give priority to the health needs of the community over the consequences for F's profits. The primary source of information for board members appointed by D will be the chief executives, who have a prior relationship with E and the management company, which is a subsidiary of E. The management company itself will have broad discretion over F's activities and assets that may not always be under the board's supervision. For example, the management company is permitted to enter into all but "unusually large" contracts without board approval. The management company may also unilaterally renew the management agreement. Based on all these facts and circumstances, D cannot establish that the activities it conducts through F further exempt purposes. "[I]n order for an organization to qualify for exemption under § 501(c)(3) the organization must 'establish' that it is neither organized nor operated for the 'benefit of private interests.' "[ ] Consequently, the benefit to E resulting from the activities D conducts through F will not be incidental to the furtherance of an exempt purpose. Thus, D will fail the operational test when it forms F, contributes its operating assets to F, and then serves as an owner to F.

Notes and Questions

1. Some recommended changes for the hospital in Situation 2 to retain its § 501(c)(3) status include shortening the management term to five years, requiring a 24–hour emergency room at one or more of the LLC hospitals, and adopting a list of reserved powers similar to those in Situation 1. See Gerald M. Griffith,

Revenue Ruling 98–15: Dimming the Future of All Nonprofit Joint Ventures?, 31 J. Health L. 71, 88 (1998). How do these relate to the criteria for tax exemption discussed earlier? What other changes would you recommend? Why?

2. Although eagerly awaited, the guidance offered by Revenue Ruling 98–15 has met with criticism for what it does not address. See Robert C. Louthian, III, IRS Provides Whole Hospital Joint Venture Guidance in Revenue Ruling 98–15, 7 Health L. Rep., Mar. 19, 1998, at 477. Many feel that the ruling's "polar opposite" situations do not help to clarify the many gray areas experienced in joint ventures. What situations would still be left unanswered by the ruling?

REDLANDS SURGICAL SERVICES v. COMMISSIONER OF INTERNAL REVENUE

United States Tax Court, 1999.
113 T.C. 47, aff'd per curiam 242 F.3d 904 (2001).

THORNTON, J.

[Petitioner Redlands Surgical Services is a nonprofit member corporation whose sole member is RHS Corp. (RHS), a nonprofit public benefit corporation that is also parent of tax-exempt Redlands Community Hospital. Surgical Care Affiliates Inc. (SCA), a for-profit, publicly held corporation that owns and manages 40 ambulatory surgical centers, owns two for-profit subsidiaries: Redlands–Centers and Redlands Management.

Petitioner entered into two partnerships relevant to this proceeding: (1) the Redlands Ambulatory Surgery Center Partnership (the General Partnership) with Redlands Centers as co-partner; and (2) the Inland Surgery Center Limited Partnership (Inland or the Operating Partnership) of which the General Partnership is the general partner and 32 physicians from Redlands Hospital's medical staff are limited partners. The Operating Partnership owned the Surgery Center, an ambulatory surgical center located two blocks away from Redlands Hospital. The IRS denied Petitioner's Application for Recognition of Exemption stating, "Basically all you have done is invest in a for-profit entity, Inland, and transfer the profits from this investment to your parent."]

OPINION

I. The Parties' Positions

Respondent contends that petitioner is not operated exclusively for charitable purposes because it operates for the benefit of private parties and fails to benefit a broad cross-section of the community. In support of its position, respondent contends that the partnership agreements and related management contract are structured to give for-profit interests control over the Surgery Center. Respondent contends that both before and after the General Partnership acquired an ownership interest in it, the Surgery Center was a successful profit-making business that never held itself out as a charity and never operated as a charitable health-care provider.

Petitioner argues that it meets the operational test under section 501(c)(3) because its activities with regard to the Surgery Center further its purpose of promoting health for the benefit of the Redlands community, by providing access to an ambulatory surgery center for all members of the community based upon medical need rather than ability to pay, and by integrating the outpatient services of Redlands Hospital and the Surgery Center. Petitioner argues that its dealings with the for-profit partners have been at arm's length, and that its influence over the activities of the Surgery Center has been sufficient to further its charitable goals. Petitioner further contends that it qualifies for exemption because it is organized and operated to perform services that are integral to the exempt purposes of RHS, its tax-exempt parent, and Redlands Hospital, its tax-exempt affiliate.

II. Applicable Legal Principles

* * *

B. Promotion of Health as a Charitable Purpose

* * *

The promotion of health for the benefit of the community is a charitable purpose. . . . As applied to determinations of qualification for tax exemption, the definition of the term "charitable" has not been static. [ ] Suffice it to say that, in recognition of changes in the health-care industry, the standard no longer requires that "the care of indigent patients be the primary concern of the charitable hospital, as distinguished from the care of paying patients". Sound Health Association v. Commissioner, *supra* at 180. Rather, the standard reflects "a policy of insuring that adequate health care services are actually delivered to those in the community who need them." [ ] Under this standard, health-care providers must meet a flexible community benefit test based upon a variety of indicia, one of which may be whether the organization provides free care to indigents. * * * To benefit the community, a charity must serve a sufficiently large and indefinite class; as a corollary to this rule, private interests must not benefit to any substantial degree.

[Discussion of the proscription against private benefit omitted. The issue is discussed later in this chapter.]

* * *

III. Petitioner's Claim to Exemption on a "Stand–Alone" Basis

Applying the principles described above, we next consider whether petitioner has established that respondent improperly denied it tax-exempt status as a section 501(c)(3) organization.

A. The Relevance of Control—The Parties' Positions

Respondent asserts that petitioner has ceded effective control over its sole activity—participating as a co-general partner with for-profit parties in the partnerships that own and operate the Surgery Center—to the for-profit partners and the for-profit management company that is an affiliate of petitioner's co-general partner. Respondent asserts that this arrangement is indicative of a substantial nonexempt purpose, whereby petitioner impermissibly benefits private interests.

Without conceding that private parties control its activities, petitioner challenges the premise that the ability to control its activities determines its purposes. Petitioner argues that under the operational test, "the critical issue in determining whether an organization's purposes are noncharitable is not whether a for profit or not for profit entity has control. Rather, the critical issue is the sort of conduct in which the organization is actually engaged."

* * *

We disagree with petitioner's thesis. It is patently clear that the Operating Partnership, whatever charitable benefits it may produce, is not operated "in an exclusively charitable manner". As stated by Justice Cardozo (then Justice of the New York Court of Appeals), in describing one of the "ancient principles" of charitable trusts, "It is only when income may be applied to the profit of the founders that business has a beginning and charity an end." Butterworth v. Keeler, 219 N.Y. 446, 449–450, 114 N.E. 803, 804 (1916). The Operating Partnership's income is, of course, applied to the profit of petitioner's co-general partner and the numerous limited partners. . . . It is no answer to say that none of petitioner's income from this activity was applied to private interests, for the activity is indivisible, and no discrete part of the Operating Partnership's income-producing activities is severable from those activities that produce income to be applied to the other partners' profit.

Taken to its logical conclusion, petitioner's thesis would suggest that an organization whose main activity is passive participation in a for-profit health-service enterprise could thereby be deemed to be operating exclusively for charitable purposes. Such a conclusion, however, would be contrary to well-established principles of charitable trust law . . . .

Clearly, there is something in common between the structure of petitioner's sole activity and the nature of petitioner's purposes in engaging in it. An organization's purposes may be inferred from its manner of operations; its "activities provide a useful indicia of the organization's purpose or purposes." [ ] The binding commitments that petitioner has entered into and that govern its participation in the partnerships are indicative of petitioner's purposes. To the extent that petitioner cedes control over its sole activity to for-profit parties having an independent economic interest in the same activity and having no obligation to put charitable purposes ahead of profit-making objectives, petitioner cannot be assured that the partnerships will in fact be operated in furtherance of charitable purposes. In such a circumstance, we are led to the conclusion that petitioner is not operated exclusively for charitable purposes.

Based on the totality of factors described below, we conclude that petitioner has in fact ceded effective control of the partnerships' and the Surgery Center's activities to for-profit parties, conferring on them significant private benefits, and therefore is not operated exclusively for charitable purposes within the meaning of section 501(c)(3).

B. Indicia of For–Profit Control Over the Partnerships' Activities

1. No Charitable Obligation

Nothing in the General Partnership agreement, or in any of the other binding commitments relating to the operation of the Surgery Center, establishes any obligation that charitable purposes be put ahead of economic objectives in the Surgery Center's operations. . . .

After the General Partnership acquired its 61–percent interest, the Operating Partnership—which had long operated as a successful for-profit enterprise and never held itself out as a charity—never changed its organizing documents to acknowledge a charitable purpose. . . .

2. Petitioner's Lack of Formal Control

a. Managing Directors

Under the General Partnership agreement, control over all matters other than medical standards and policies is nominally divided equally between petitioner and SCA Centers, each appointing two representatives to serve as managing directors. (As discussed *infra*, matters of medical standards and policies are determined by the Medical Advisory Group, half of whom are chosen by the General Partnership's managing directors.) Consequently, petitioner may exert influence by blocking actions proposed to be taken by the managing directors, but it cannot initiate action without the consent of at least one of SCA Center's appointees to the managing directors. . . .

The administrative record shows that petitioner has successfully blocked various proposals to expand the scope of activities performed at the Surgery Center. Petitioner's ability to veto expansion of the scope of the Surgery Center's activities, however, does not establish that petitioner has effective control over the manner in which the Surgery Center conducts activities within its predesignated sphere of operations. Nor does it tend to indicate that the Surgery Center is not operated to maximize profits with regard to those activities. . . .

In sum, the composition of the managing directorship evidences a lack of majority control by petitioner whereby it might assure that the Surgery Center is operated for charitable purposes.[ ] Consequently, we look to the binding commitments made between petitioner and the other parties to ascertain whether other specific powers or rights conferred upon petitioner might mitigate or compensate for its lack of majority control.

b. Arbitration Process

[The court notes that although the General Partnership agreement provides for an arbitration process in the event that the managing directors of the General Partnership deadlock, the ground rules for the arbitration process are minimal and provide petitioner no assurance that charitable objectives will govern the outcome and the arbitrators are not required to take into account any charitable or community benefit objective. It concludes that the arbitration process does not significantly mitigate petitioner's lack of majority control.]

c. The Management Contract

[The court observes that the management contract between the Operating Partnership and SCA Management confers broad powers on SCA Management to enter into contracts, to negotiate with third-party payers and state and federal agencies, and to set patient charges. The court also notes that, as a practical matter, the Operating Partnership is locked into the management agreement with SCA Management for at least 15 years.]

[N]either the General Partnership agreement, the Operating Partnership agreement, nor the management contract itself requires that SCA Management be guided by any charitable or community benefit, goal, policy, or objective. Rather, the management contract simply requires SCA Management to render services as necessary and in the best interest of the Operating Partnership, "subject to the policies established by [the Operating Partnership], which policies shall be consistent with applicable state and Federal law."

* * *

Respondent asserts, and we agree, that this long-term management contract with an affiliate of SCA Centers is a salient indicator of petitioner's surrender of effective control over the Surgery Center's operations to SCA affiliates, whereby the affiliates were given the ability and incentive to operate the Surgery Center so as to maximize profits. This surrender of effective control reflects adversely on petitioner's own charitable purposes in contracting to have its sole activity managed in this fashion.

d.   Medical Advisory Group

The Operating Partnership agreement delegates authority for making decisions about care and treatment of patients and other medical matters to the Operating Partnership's Medical Advisory Group. This group was inactive before the General Partnership became involved with the Operating Partnership, but there is no evidence to show what role, if any, petitioner played in reconstituting the Medical Advisory Group. * * *

e.   Termination of Quality Assurance Activities

As required by the General Partnership agreement, on April 30, 1990, SCA Management entered into a quality assurance agreement with RHS. The term of the quality assurance agreement was conditioned on maintenance of a specified level of surgery activity in the Surgery Center. Petitioner concedes that the quality assurance agreement terminated after the first year. Although the agreement required the parties to negotiate a new quality assurance agreement in the event of such a termination, there is no evidence in the record that such negotiations ever occurred.

The termination of the quality assurance agreement vividly evidences petitioner's lack of effective control over vital aspects of the Surgery Center's operations. * * * The record does not reflect that petitioner performed any quality assurance work. Likewise, the record is silent as to how petitioner, in the absence of any operable quality assurance agreement, purports to assure itself that these vital functions will be discharged consistently with charitable objectives.

3.   Lack of Informal Control

The administrative record provides no basis for concluding that, in the absence of formal control, petitioner possesses significant informal control by which it exercises its influence with regard to the Surgery Center's activities. Nothing in the administrative record suggests that petitioner commands allegiance or loyalty of the SCA affiliates or of the limited partners to cause them to put charitable objectives ahead of their own economic objectives. Indeed, until April 1992, petitioner was in a debtor relationship to SCA.

* * *

a. Provision for Indigent Patients

Petitioner concedes that as of December 31, 1993, Medi–Cal patients accounted for only 0.8 percent of total procedures performed at the Surgery Center. Petitioner argues that the type of services which the Service Center offers is not the type of services typically sought by low-income individuals. Petitioner notes that Redlands Hospital has negotiated certain provider agreements that designate the Surgery Center as a subcontractor to provide outpatient services for Medi–Cal patients, and that Redlands Hospital has caused the Surgery Center to increase its number of managed care contracts. Petitioner suggests that these efforts demonstrate petitioner's influence over the operations of the Surgery Center and evidence petitioner's charitable purposes.

We do not find petitioner's arguments convincing. The facts remain that the Surgery Center provides no free care to indigents and only negligible coverage for Medi–Cal patients. * * *

b. Coordination of Activities of Redlands Hospital and the Surgery Center

* * *

Although there may be cooperation between the Surgery Center and Redlands Hospital, nothing in the record suggests that these various cooperative activities are more than incidental to the for-profit orientation of the Surgery Center's activities. [ ]

C. Competitive Restrictions and Market Advantages

By entering into the General Partnership agreement, RHS (petitioner's parent corporation and predecessor in interest in the General Partnership) not only acquired an interest in the Surgery Center, but also restricted its future ability to provide outpatient services at Redlands Hospital or elsewhere without the approval of its for-profit partner. Paragraph 16 of the General Partnership agreement, *supra*, prohibits the co-general partners and their affiliates from owning, managing, or developing another freestanding outpatient surgery center within 20 miles of the Surgery Center, without the other partner's consent. Moreover, Redlands Hospital may not "expand or promote its present outpatient surgery program within the Hospital." In fact, outpatient surgeries performed at Redlands Hospital decreased about 17 percent from 1990 to 1995, while those performed at the Surgery Center increased.

. . . Consequently, RHS effectively restricted its own ability to assess and service community needs for outpatient services until the year 2020. It is difficult to conceive of a significant charitable purpose that would be furthered by such a restriction.

* * *

Viewed in its totality, the administrative record is clear that SCA and petitioner derive mutual economic benefits from the General Partnership agreement. By borrowing necessary up-front capital from SCA, RHS (petitioner's predecessor in interest in the General Partnership), overcame a capital barrier to gain entry into a profitable and growing market niche. By forming a partnership with RHS, SCA Centers was able to benefit from the established relationship between Redlands Hospital and the limited partner physicians to acquire its interest in the Surgery Center at a bargain price.

By virtue of this arrangement, petitioner and SCA Centers realized further mutual benefits by eliminating sources of potential competition for patients, as is evidenced by the restrictions on either party's providing future outpatient services outside the Surgery Center, and by Redlands Hospital's agreeing not to expand or promote its existing outpatient surgery facility at the hospital. In light of the statement in the record that it is typical for national chains such as SCA to "shadow-price" hospitals in charging for services at outpatient surgery centers, it seems most likely that one purpose and effect of the containment and contraction of Redlands Hospital's outpatient surgery activities is to eliminate a competitive constraint for setting Surgery Center fees (a matter delegated to SCA Management under the management contract, excluding charges for physicians' services).

* * *

There is no per se proscription against a nonprofit organization's entering into contracts with private parties to further its charitable purposes on mutually beneficial terms, so long as the nonprofit organization does not thereby impermissibly serve private interests. [ ] In the instant case, however, RHS relied on the established relationship between Redlands Hospital and Redlands physicians to enable RHS and SCA affiliates jointly to gain foothold, on favorable terms, in the Redlands ambulatory surgery market. Then, by virtue of their effective control over the Surgery Center, the SCA affiliates have been enabled to operate it as a profit-making business, with significantly reduced competitive pressures from Redlands Hospital, and largely unfettered by charitable objectives that might conflict with purely commercial objectives. [ ]

D. Conclusion

Based on all the facts and circumstances, we hold that petitioner has not established that it operates exclusively for exempt purposes within the meaning of section 501(c)(3). In reaching this holding, we do not view any one factor as crucial, but we have considered these factors in their totality: The lack of any express or implied obligation of the for-profit interests involved in petitioner's sole activity to put charitable objectives ahead of noncharitable objectives; petitioner's lack of voting control over the General Partnership; petitioner's lack of other formal or informal control sufficient to ensure furtherance of charitable purposes; the long-term contract giving SCA Management control over day-to-day operations as well as a profit-maximizing incentive; and the market advantages and competitive benefits secured by the SCA affiliates as the result of this arrangement with petitioner. Taken in their totality, these factors compel the conclusion that by ceding effective control over its operations to for-profit parties, petitioner impermissibly serves private interests.

[The Court goes on to reject petitioner's argument that it qualifies for exemption under the integral part doctrine.]

Notes and Questions

1. In an important affirmation of the analysis contained in Rev. Ruling 98–15, the Court of Appeals for the Fifth Circuit followed the *Redlands* Court's insistence on the centrality of control in evaluating a whole hospital joint venture. St. David's Health Care System v. United States, 349 F.3d 232 (5th Cir. 2003). St. David's Health Care System, a tax exempt entity operating an acute care hospital, entered into a limited partnership with HCA Inc. pursuant to which HCA would operate and manage the hospital in a whole hospital joint venture arrangement. The IRS subsequently revoked St. David's tax-exempt status retroactive to the partnership's formation finding that it was no longer engaged in activities that primarily furthered its charitable purpose. The court squarely rejected the hospital's contention, which the district court had endorsed, that the pivotal question was one of function, not control, i.e. exempt organizations that engage in activities via the joint venture that further their charitable purposes should retain their exempt status. Instead the court stressed that the operational test under 501(c)(3) focuses on the purpose rather than the nature of an organization's activities. Thus, even though the court had "no doubt that St. David's via the partnership provides important medical services to the community," it found the hospital "cannot qualify for tax exempt status under 501(c)(3) if its activities under the partnership substantially further the private, profit-seeking interests of HCA." Where private parties or for-profit entities have either "formal or effective control," a presumption attaches "that the organization furthers the profit seeking motivations of those private individuals or entities." While remanding the case to the district court to determine whether control was effectively ceded to HCA, the court was openly skeptical of the claim that various protective measures were sufficient to save the day for St. David's. It questioned, for example, whether St. David's ability to appoint half the members of the board, its right to unilaterally remove the venture's CEO, assurances in the management services agreement that St. David's exempt status would not be endangered, and its right to compel dissolution, sufficed to establish control. Although on remand a jury held that St. David's should retain its exempt status, the IRS adheres to the view that the Fifth Circuit opinion "provided the proper framework for judging joint ventures between non-profits and for-profits ... [i.e.] a non-profit must have effective control in the joint venture." Fred Sokeld, IRS official Unfazed by Jury Decision in Joint Venture Case, 2004 Tax Notes Today 50 (May 12, 2004).

2. The succinct verdict of the commentators after Revenue Ruling 98–15 and the Tax Court's decision in *Redlands* is that "control is king." (This view was strongly reinforced by the *St. David's* decision). Why should that be so? Can you make an argument based on the language and history of the tax code that control should not be the ultimate touchstone for exemption? Can you imagine a compelling set of circumstances in which exemption is warranted even though the exempt organization lacked control over a partnership with a for-profit entity?

3. *Ancillary Joint Ventures.* The implications of *Redlands* & *St. David's* for "ancillary joint ventures" is somewhat uncertain. The IRS has approved dozens of such joint ventures involving medical office buildings, imaging centers, ambulatory surgical centers, treatment centers, physical therapy centers, hospital home care services, and nursing homes. See, e.g., Private Letter Ruling 200206058 (Nov. 16, 2001) (L.L.C. formed by hospital and physicians to provide new medical service); Private Letter Ruling 9517029 (acute care hospital and psychiatric hospital L.L.C. joint venture between an exempt university subsidiary and a for-profit company); 9645018 (outpatient dialysis service L.L.C. joint venture among an exempt hospital, an unrelated exempt health care system, and nephrologists).

Private Letter Ruling 200118054 (Feb. 7, 2001) (proposed joint venture L.L.C. formed between a tax-exempt affiliate of a health care system and a group of local physicians); 200117043 (Jan. 30, 2001) (proposed joint venture between two tax-exempt health care entities). Note an important distinction between ancillary joint ventures and the whole hospital ventures involved in Revenue Ruling 98–15: in the former, the exempt hospital retains its separate existence, is subject to the community benefit standard, and often is contributing only a fraction of its assets. See Nicholas A. Mirkay, Relinguish Control! Why the IRS Should Change its Stance on Exempt Organizations in Ancillary Joint Ventures, 6 Nev. L. J. 21, 50 (2005). Whether the IRS is ready to move off the control standard for such ventures remains unclear. In a notable ruling the IRS approved an L.L.C. joint venture between a tax exempt university offering seminars to teachers to improve their skills and a for-profit entity that conducted interactive video training programs. Rev. Rul. 2004–51. Membership in the L.L.C. was divided equally between the for-profit and the university, but the latter retained "exclusive right to approve curriculum, training materials and instructors and determine standards" for the seminars. Noting that the venture did not constitute a substantial part of the University's activities, the IRS ruled that its participation in the venture would not jeopardize its exempt status. The fact that the ruling cited *St. David's* and Rev. Ruling 98–15, but did not explicitly apply those precedents or invoke the "control" standard and permitted a 50–50 venture to go forward has been interpreted by some to suggest that the test may be loosened in the future. See Mirkay supra at 57–59. But see id. at 59 (quoting IRS official reminding tax bar that Revenue Ruling 98–15 is "still on the books").

What alternative approaches might be applied to ancillary joint ventures? Professor John Colombo has proposed a framework that would employ the principles of UBIT to analyze distinct scenarios under which exempt organizations may engage in joint undertakings that involve businesses not in furtherance of their charitable purpose without losing their exempt status. See John D. Colombo, Commercial Activity and Charitable Tax Exemption, 44 Wm. & Mary L. Rev. 487 (2002). Others have proposed a bright-line quantitative rule that would also employ a UBIT analysis, but would impose a quantitative safe harbor (e.g. use of less than fifteen percent of the exempt organization's assets in the ancillary joint venture). Michael Sanders, Joint Ventures Involving Tax–Exempt Organizations For an excellent critique and proposed synthesis of these proposals see Mirkay, Relinquish Control supra at 70–72.

C. INUREMENT, PRIVATE BENEFIT AND EXCESS BENEFIT TRANSACTIONS: RELATIONSHIPS BETWEEN PHYSICIANS AND TAX–EXEMPT HEALTH CARE ORGANIZATIONS

Physicians and hospitals are highly interdependent both clinically and financially. In the language of economics, they jointly produce the end services provided to patients. As you have seen in the previous sections, hospitals may establish joint ventures with physicians for ancillary services both inside and outside the hospital or to provide care through free standing entities. Hospitals are motivated by both the desire to more efficiently use these resources and to cement their relationships with the physicians and thus assure themselves a steady flow of patients. For similar reasons hospitals and integrated delivery system also have frequently purchased physician practices or recruited physicians to establish a private practice in their geographic area, usually supplying some form of financial support provided to entice the doctor to relocate or open a practice.

These relationships between physicians and tax-exempt organizations raise issues for the tax-exempt provider. Several of these have been explored in the earlier sections of this chapter: IRS limitations on control in joint ventures; standards for unrelated trade or business income; and the achievement and protection of its charitable purposes.

In addition, the exempt organization must comply with three other major legal constraints on relationships between non-exempt (which includes physicians) and tax-exempt health care organizations. These are the proscriptions against private benefit and against private inurement (both of which flow from the language of Section 501(c)(3)) and the new statutory sanctions against excess benefit transactions (codified in IRC Section 4958). However, it appears that the excess benefit statute, which is discussed at the end of this section, will be the predominant tool for future enforcement by the IRS.

1. *Joint Ventures With Physicians*

GENERAL COUNSEL MEMORANDUM

39862 (Dec. 2, 1991).

[The Service reviews a physician-hospital agreement in which the hospital sold its future net income from certain departments to entities owned by physicians who admitted and treated patients at the hospital. Other excerpts from the GCM are included in the previous section on Joint Ventures.]

I. SALE OF THE REVENUE STREAM FROM A HOSPITAL ACTIVITY ALLOWS
NET PROFITS TO INURE TO THE BENEFIT OF PHYSICIAN–INVESTORS

* * *

[Editors' Note: At the time of this GCM, the IRS took the position that all physician members of the medical staffs of hospitals—including those not employed by the hospital—have a such a close working relationship with and a private interest in the exempt hospital so as to be subject to the prohibition against inurement, which applies only to "insiders." The GCM stressed physicians' close professional working relationship with the hospitals, that "they largely control the flow of patients to and from the hospital and patients' utilization of hospital services while there", the binding effect of the medical staff bylaws, and that some may serve other roles at the hospital, such as that of part-time employee, department head, Board member, etc. As discussed in Section F, *infra*, the Service does not take the position that staff physician are "disqualified persons" with regard to application of the Excess Benefit statute, which will govern most inurement-type questions in the future. Whether it would adhere to the position taken in this GCM in future inurement cases involving staff member doctors is uncertain].

Even though medical staff physicians are subject to the inurement proscription, that does not mean there can be no economic dealings between them and the hospitals. The inurement proscription does not prevent the payment of reasonable compensation for goods or services. It is aimed at preventing dividend-like distributions of charitable assets or expenditures to benefit a private interest. This Office has stated "inurement is likely to arise where the financial benefit represents a transfer of the organization's financial resources to an individual solely by virtue of the individual's relationship with the organization, and without regard to the accomplishment of exempt purposes." ... [ ]

* * *

Whether admitted or not, we believe the hospitals engaged in these ventures largely as a means to retain and reward members of their medical staffs; to attract their admissions and referrals; and to pre-empt the physicians from investing in or creating a competing provider.... Giving (or selling) medical staff physicians a proprietary interest in the net profits of a hospital under these circumstances creates a result that is indistinguishable from paying dividends on stock. Profit distributions are made to persons having a personal and private interest in the activities of the organization and are made out of the net earnings of the organization. Thus, the arrangements confer a benefit which violates the inurement proscription of section 501(c)(3).

* * *

II. SALE OF THE REVENUE STREAM FROM A HOSPITAL ACTIVITY BENEFITS PRIVATE INTERESTS MORE THAN INCIDENTALLY

[A] key principle in the law of tax exempt organizations is that an entity is not organized and operated exclusively for exempt purposes unless it serves a public rather than a private interest. Thus, in order to be exempt, an organization must establish that it is not organized or operated for the benefit of private interests such as designated individuals, the creator or his family, shareholders of the organization, or persons controlled, directly or indirectly, by such private interests. [ ] However, this private benefit prohibition applies to all kinds of persons and groups, not just to those "insiders" subject to the more strict inurement proscription.

* * *

In our view, some private benefit is present in all typical hospital-physician relationships. Physicians generally use hospital facilities at no cost to themselves to provide services to private patients for which they earn a fee. The private benefit accruing to the physicians generally can be considered incidental to the overwhelming public benefit resulting from having the combined resources of the hospital and its professional staff available to serve the public. Though the private benefit is compounded in the case of certain specialists, such as heart transplant surgeons, who depend heavily on highly specialized hospital facilities, that fact alone will not make the private benefit more than incidental.

In contrast, the private benefits conferred on the physician-investors by the instant revenue stream joint ventures are direct and substantial, not incidental. If for any reason these benefits should be found not to constitute inurement, they nonetheless exceed the bounds of prohibited private benefit. Whether viewed as giving the physicians a substantial share in the profits of the hospital or simply as allowing them an extremely profitable investment, the arrangements confer a significant benefit on them. Against this, we must balance the public benefit achieved by the hospitals in entering into the arrangements. The public benefit expected to result from these transactions— enhanced hospital financial health or greater efficiency achieved through improved utilization of their facilities—bears only the most tenuous relationship to the hospitals' charitable purposes of promoting the health of their communities. Obtaining referrals or avoiding new competition may improve the competitive position of an individual hospital, but that is not necessarily the same as benefiting its community.

* * *

2. *Physician Recruitment*

REVENUE RULING 97–21

1997–18 I.R.B. 8.

* * *

Situation 1

Hospital A is located in County V, a rural area, and is the only hospital within a 100 mile radius. County V has been designated by the U.S. Public Health Service as a Health Professional Shortage Area for primary medical care professionals (a category that includes obstetricians and gynecologists). Physician M recently completed an ob/gyn residency and is not on Hospital A's medical staff. Hospital A recruits Physician M to establish and maintain a full-time private ob/gyn practice in its service area and become a member of its medical staff. Hospital A provides Physician M a recruitment incentive package pursuant to a written agreement negotiated at arm's-length. The agreement is in accordance with guidelines for physician recruitment that Hospital A's Board of Directors establishes, monitors, and reviews regularly to ensure that recruiting practices are consistent with Hospital A's exempt purposes. The agreement was approved by the committee appointed by Hospital A's Board of Directors to approve contracts with hospital medical staff. Hospital A does not provide any recruiting incentives to Physician M other than those set forth in the written agreement.

In accordance with the agreement, Hospital A pays Physician M a signing bonus, Physician M's professional liability insurance premium for a limited period, provides office space in a building owned by Hospital A for a limited number of years at a below market rent (after which the rental will be at fair market value), and guarantees Physician M's mortgage on a residence in County V. Hospital A also lends Physician M practice start-up financial assistance pursuant to an agreement that is properly documented and bears reasonable terms.

Situation 2

Hospital B is located in an economically depressed inner-city area of City W. Hospital B has conducted a community needs assessment that indicates both a shortage of pediatricians in Hospital B's service area and difficulties Medicaid patients are having obtaining pediatric services. Physician N is a pediatrician currently practicing outside of Hospital B's service area and is not on Hospital B's medical staff. Hospital B recruits Physician N to relocate to City W, establish and maintain a full-time pediatric practice in Hospital B's service area, become a member of Hospital B's medical staff, and treat a reasonable number of Medicaid patients. Hospital B offers Physician N a recruitment incentive package pursuant to a written agreement negotiated at arm's-length and approved by Hospital B's Board of Directors. Hospital B does not provide any recruiting incentives to Physician N other than those set forth in the written agreement.

Under the agreement, Hospital B reimburses Physician N for moving expenses as defined in § 217(b), reimburses Physician N for professional liability "tail" coverage for Physician N's former practice, and guarantees Physician N's private practice income for a limited number of years. The private practice income guarantee, which is properly documented, provides that Hospital B will make up the difference to the extent Physician N practices full-time in its service area and the private practice does not generate a certain level of net income (after reasonable expenses of the practice). The amount guaranteed falls within the range reflected in regional or national surveys regarding income earned by physicians in the same specialty.

Situation 3

Hospital C is located in an economically depressed inner city area of City X. Hospital C has conducted a community needs assessment that indicates indigent patients are having difficulty getting access to care because of a shortage of obstetricians in Hospital C's service area willing to treat Medicaid and charity care patients. Hospital C recruits Physician O, an obstetrician who is currently a member of Hospital C's medical staff, to provide these services and enters into a written agreement with Physician O. The agreement is in accordance with guidelines for physician recruitment that Hospital C's Board of Directors establishes, monitors, and reviews regularly to ensure that recruiting practices are consistent with Hospital C's exempt purpose. The agreement was approved by the officer designated by Hospital C's Board of Directors to enter into contracts with hospital medical staff. Hospital C does not provide any recruiting incentives to Physician O other than those set forth in the written agreement. Pursuant to the agreement, Hospital C agrees to reimburse Physician O for the cost of one year's professional liability insurance in return for an agreement by Physician O to treat a reasonable number of Medicaid and charity care patients for that year.

Situation 4

Hospital D is located in City Y, a medium to large size metropolitan area. Hospital D requires a minimum of four diagnostic radiologists to ensure adequate coverage and a high quality of care for its radiology department. Two of the four diagnostic radiologists currently providing coverage for Hospital D are relocating to other areas. Hospital D initiates a search for diagnostic radiologists and determines that one of the two most qualified candidates is Physician P.

Physician P currently is practicing in City Y as a member of the medical staff of Hospital E (which is also located in City Y). As a diagnostic radiologist, Physician P provides services for patients receiving care at Hospital E, but does not refer patients to Hospital E or any other hospital in City Y. Physician P is not on Hospital D's medical staff. Hospital D recruits Physician P to join its medical staff and to provide coverage for its radiology department. Hospital D offers Physician P a recruitment incentive package pursuant to a written agreement, negotiated at arm's-length and approved by Hospital D's

Board of Directors. Hospital D does not provide any recruiting incentives to Physician P other than those set forth in the written agreement.

Pursuant to the agreement, Hospital D guarantees Physician P's private practice income for the first few years that Physician P is a member of its medical staff and provides coverage for its radiology department. The private practice income guarantee, which is properly documented, provides that Hospital D will make up the difference to Physician P to the extent the private practice does not generate a certain level of net income (after reasonable expenses of the practice). The net income amount guaranteed falls within the range reflected in regional or national surveys regarding income earned by physicians in the same specialty.

* * *

ANALYSIS

When a § 501(c)(3) hospital recruits a physician for its medical staff who is to perform services for or on behalf of the organization, the organization meets the operational test by showing that, taking into account all of the benefits provided the physician by the organization, the organization is paying reasonable compensation for the services the physician is providing in return. A somewhat different analysis must be applied when a § 501(c)(3) hospital recruits a physician for its medical staff to provide services to members of the surrounding community but not necessarily for or on behalf of the organization. In these cases, a violation will result from a failure to comply with the [requirements that] ... the organization ... not engage in substantial activities that do not further the hospital's exempt purposes or that do not bear a reasonable [or]in activities that result in inurement of the hospital's net earnings to a private shareholder or individual; [or] engage in substantial activities that cause the hospital to be operated for the benefit of a private interest rather than public; [or]engage in substantial unlawful activities.

Situation 1

... Hospital A has objective evidence demonstrating a need for obstetricians and gynecologists in its service area and has engaged in physician recruitment activity bearing a reasonable relationship to promoting and protecting the health of the community ... [The hospital's payments and loans] .. are reasonably related to causing Physician M to become a member of Hospital A's medical staff and to establish and maintain a full-time private ob/gyn practice in Hospital A's service area....

Situation 2

Like Hospital A in Situation 1, Hospital B has objective evidence demonstrating a need for pediatricians in its service area and has engaged in physician recruitment activity bearing a reasonable relationship to promoting and protecting the health of the community [and the incentives provided] are reasonably related to causing Physician N to become a member of Hospital B's medical staff ...

Situation 3

In accordance with the standards for exemption. ...Hospital C admits and treats Medicaid patients on a non-discriminatory basis. Hospital C has identified a shortage of obstetricians willing to treat Medicaid patients. The payment of Physician O's professional liability insurance premiums in return for Physician O's agreement to treat a reasonable number of Medicaid and charity care patients is reasonably related to the accomplishment of Hospital C's exempt purposes. Because the amount paid by Hospital C is reasonable and any private benefit to Physician O is outweighed by the public purpose served by the agreement, the recruitment activity described is consistent with the requirements for exemption as an organization described in § 501(c)(3).

Situation 4

Hospital D has objective evidence demonstrating a need for diagnostic radiologists to provide coverage for its radiology department so that it can promote the health of the community. The provision of a reasonable private practice income guarantee as a recruitment incentive that is conditioned upon Physician P obtaining medical staff privileges and providing coverage for the radiology department is reasonably related to the accomplishment of the charitable purposes served by the hospital. A significant fact in determining that the community benefit provided by the activity outweighs the private benefit provided to Physician P is the determination by the Board of Directors of Hospital D that it needs additional diagnostic radiologists to provide adequate coverage and to ensure a high quality of medical care. . . .

Notes and Questions

1. Note the key differences between private inurement and private benefit. The former is akin to a per se rule, requiring revocation or denial of exempt status, with no de minimis exception. Moreover, it applies only to "insiders," defined as private shareholders or individuals having a personal and private interest in or opportunity to influence the activities of the organization from the inside. Treas. Reg. § 1.50(a)–1(c). The private benefit limitation applies to transactions with "outsiders" to the exempt organization and entails a broader inquiry, weighing private benefits against community benefits. See Sonora Community Hosp. v. Commissioner, 46 T.C. 519 (1966). What goals of the two proscriptions explain the different approaches? What factors did the Service take into account in evaluating each of the scenarios in Rev. Ruling 97–21? Why did the balance tip against the hospital in GCM 39862? Who is considered an insider for inurement purposes? Might a prominent donor and fundraiser for a tax exempt hospital qualify even if she holds no formal office with the hospital? An influential consultant under contract to give management advice?

2. The core of the analysis of private benefit and private inurement is the relationship between what the exempt organization pays and the value, to its achievement of its exempt purposes, of what it receives. Might not-for-profit entities behave differently than for-profits in acquiring physician practices, recruiting physicians or structuring physician compensation and investment? Do a tax-exempt hospital's relationships with physicians require more careful scrutiny than its contracts with third party vendors? The IRS's view that staff physicians were in a position to influence administrators of tax exempt hospitals led to treating them as "insiders" for inurement purposes, a position that it may no longer adhere to. See Charles F. Kaiser and Amy Henchey, Valuation of Medical Practices, CPE Technical Instruction Program Textbook, 95 Tax Notes Today 168–69 (Aug. 28, 1995)(arms-length negotiation would ordinarily produce a purchase price that equates to fair market value in other transactions, but that in the purchase of practices by hospitals from physicians, especially those currently on the staff of the hospital, this assumption may not be valid). Compare the

prohibition on private inurement to the approach to insider transactions contained in the Intermediate Sanctions on Excess Benefits law discussed in the next section of this chapter.

3. The requirement that the § 501(c)(3) organization pay no more than fair market value for the physician practice or for physician compensation or for services received in a joint venture is a clear and understandable goal. It is hard to monitor, however, in the absence of functioning markets. The valuation of physician practices in particular presents substantial problems. Appraisal of the future income potential of the practice itself is particularly difficult and subject to differences among professional appraisers. Furthermore, although the IRS wants to assure that the § 501(c)(3) organization pays for no more than it receives in value, the Medicare and Medicaid programs prohibit payment for the value of future referrals by the doctors to the hospital. Thus, the parties might lean toward inflating the value of certain intangibles or certain allowable items (such as copy expenses for patient records) to bear the value of the referrals to the hospital. Does GCM 39862 indicate that the Service does not consider future referrals a value received? What issues arise when a system decides to divest itself of unprofitable physician practices and decides to sell the practices back to the physicians at a much lower price than it originally paid?

4. Inurement and private benefit issues frequently arise in a variety of other contexts, such as joint ventures involving hospitals and physicians. For example, in the *Redlands* case, reproduced earlier in this chapter, the Tax Court dealt with private benefit arising out of the arrangement:

> There is no per se proscription against a nonprofit organization's entering into contracts with private parties to further its charitable purposes on mutually beneficial terms, so long as the nonprofit organization does not thereby impermissibly serve private interests. [ ] In the instant case, however, RHS relied on the established relationship between Redlands Hospital and Redlands physicians to enable RHS and SCA affiliates jointly to gain foothold, on favorable terms, in the Redlands ambulatory surgery market. Then, by virtue of their effective control over the Surgery Center, the SCA affiliates have been enabled to operate it as a profit-making business, with significantly reduced competitive pressures from Redlands Hospital, and largely unfettered by charitable objectives that might conflict with purely commercial objectives. The net result to the SCA affiliates is a nonincidental "advantage; profit; fruit; privilege; gain; [or] interest" that constitutes a prohibited private benefit. See American Campaign Academy v. Commissioner, 92 T.C. 1053, 1065 (1989).

See also Anclote Psychiatric Ctr., Inc. v. Commissioner, T.C. Memo 1998–273, aff'd 190 F.3d 541 (11th Cir. 1999)(upholding IRS revocation of converting hospital's exemption based on inurement where sale of its assets to for profit entity owned by its former board members was for consideration less than fair market value).

5. Many other issues raised in the purchase of physician practices, physician recruitment and hospital-physician joint ventures are covered elsewhere in this text. For example, issues of self-referral and fraud and abuse are discussed in Chapter 14; antitrust concerns are covered in Chapter 15; and physician contracts are discussed in Chapter 12.

D. EXCESS BENEFIT TRANSACTIONS: PROTECTING HOSPITALS AND OTHER TAX EXEMPT ORGANIZATIONS FROM EXPLOITATION BY INSIDERS

In 1996 Congress adopted the Taxpayer Bill of Rights II (26 U.S.C.A. § 4958), an important new law designed to clarify the obligations of insiders in exempt organizations and to provide an alternative sanction for violations. The basic concept of the law is straightforward: it imposes an excise tax on insiders ("disqualified persons") engaged in "excess benefit transactions." But, as we've seen, nothing in tax law is simple. In January 2002, following four years of comment and revision, the Department of the Treasury issued final regulations which supply guidance concerning the numerous new concepts contained in § 4958. 26 C.F.R. § 53.4958–1—53.4958–8. Some key terminology and concepts must be mastered to apply the supposedly simple, "bright line" approach of the statute.

Scope. Congress intended § 4958 to be the exclusive sanction unless the conduct arises to such an extreme level (evidenced by the size and scope of the excess benefit and the organization's efforts to prevent the conduct) that the tax exempt organization can no longer be regarded as "charitable" and hence revocation is the appropriate sanction.

Excess Benefit Transactions. The statute defines an "excess benefit transaction" (EBT) as any transaction in which an economic benefit is provided by a tax exempt organization directly or indirectly to or for the use of a "disqualified person" where the value of the economic benefit provided by the organization exceeds the value of the consideration (including the performance of services) received for providing the benefit. 26 U.S.C.A. § 4958(c)(1). The core prohibited transactions are those in which the disqualified person engages in a *non-fair market transaction*, such as a bargain sale or loan; *unreasonable compensation arrangements*; or proscribed *revenue sharing arrangements*. The revenue sharing provisions have been reserved for future rulemakings which will give additional guidance as to the scope of permissible arrangements. The regulations give some additional guidance, such as indicating that compensation is reasonable only if its an amount that ordinarily would be paid for like services by like enterprises under like circumstances existing at the time the contract was made. Treas. Reg. 534958–4(b)(3). Further, compensation includes all forms of deferred income if earned and vested and fringe benefits (even if not taxable); however, payments must be intended as compensation by the tax exempt entity. Treas. Reg. 534958–4(c).

Disqualified Persons. "Disqualified persons" (DQPs) include "any person who was, at any time during the 5–year period ending on the date of such transaction, in a position to exercise substantial influence over the affairs of the organization, a member of the family of [such] an individual and, a 35–percent controlled entity [an entity in which such persons own more than 35% of the combined voting power if a corporation or of the profits interest if a partnership or of the beneficial interest of a trust or estate]." I.R.C. 4958(f)(1)(A).

Among those included in the category of DQPs are: officers, directors, and their close relatives. However, the detailed regulations make clear that persons with titles are not to be so regarded if their position is honorary or they have no powers or ability to exercise substantial influence. Treas. Reg. 534958–3(c). On the other hand, those with "substantial influence" are covered regardless of whether they hold a formal position with the exempt organization.

An important issue for hospitals has been whether staff physicians will automatically be considered to have substantial influence. Although the IRS had previously indicated that they would be considered "insiders" for inurement purposes, it has reversed its position for excess benefit analysis, as the following excerpts from the regulations indicate.

> Example 10. U is a large acute-care hospital that is an applicable tax-exempt organization for purposes of section 4958. U employs X as a radiologist. X gives instructions to staff with respect to the radiology work X conducts, but X does not supervise other U employees or manage any substantial part of U's operations. X's compensation is primarily in the form of a fixed salary. In addition, X is eligible to receive an incentive award based on revenues of the radiology department. X's compensation is greater than the amount referenced for a highly compensated employee in section 414(q)(1)(B)(i) in the year benefits are provided. X is not related to any other disqualified person of U. X does not serve on U's governing body or as an officer of U. Although U participates in a provider-sponsored organization [ ] X does not have a material financial interest in that organization. X does not receive compensation primarily based on revenues derived from activities of U that X controls. X does not participate in any management decisions affecting either U as a whole or a discrete segment of U that represents a substantial portion of its activities, assets, income, or expenses. Under these facts and circumstances, X does not have substantial influence over the affairs of U, and therefore X is not a disqualified person with respect to U.

> Example 11. W is a cardiologist and head of the cardiology department of the same hospital U described in Example 10. The cardiology department is a major source of patients admitted to U and consequently represents a substantial portion of U's income, as compared to U as a whole. W does not serve on U's governing board or as an officer of U. W does not have a material financial interest in the provider-sponsored organization (as defined in section 1855(e) of the Social Security Act) in which U participates. W receives a salary and retirement and welfare benefits fixed by a three-year renewable employment contract with U. W's compensation is greater than the amount referenced for a highly compensated employee in section 414(q)(1)(B)(i) in the year benefits are provided. As department head, W manages the cardiology department and has authority to allocate the budget for that department, which includes authority to distribute incentive bonuses among cardiologists according to criteria that W has authority to set. W's management of a discrete segment of U that represents a substantial portion of its income and activities (as compared to U as a whole) places W in a position to exercise substantial influence over the affairs of U. Under these facts and circumstances, W is a disqualified person with respect to U.

Treas. Reg. 534958–3(g), Examples 10 and 11. What generalizable principles emerge from these examples that can be applied in other factual settings?

Organization Managers. Importantly, besides imposing penalties on the individuals receiving the benefits (see below), the act also levies a separate excise tax of 10 per cent on "organization managers," whose participation in the transaction was knowing, willful and not due to reasonable cause. The regulations define organization managers to include directors, trustees or officers and administrators with delegated or regularly exercised administrative powers, but not independent contractors such as lawyers and account-ants, investment advisors or middle managers with power to make recommen-dations but not to implement decisions. See Treas. Reg. 534958–3(d)(2)(i). Where the organizational manager makes full disclosure of all facts to a professional advisor and relies on that advisor's reasoned, written legal opinion, no penalty will be imposed; the advisor may be a lawyer, accountant or independent valuation firm with expertise. Treas. Reg. 534958–1(d)(4)(iii).

Rebuttable Presumption of Reasonableness. A key element of the interme-diate sanctions statutory scheme is a rebuttable presumption of reasonable-ness applicable to compensation arrangements and transfers of property with a disqualified person where specified procedural steps are followed. To qualify for the presumption, the terms of the transaction must be approved by a board of directors or committee thereof composed entirely of individuals who have no conflicts of interest with respect to the transaction and who have obtained and relied upon appropriate comparability data prior to making their determination and have adequately documented the basis for the determina-tion. See Treas. Reg. 534958–6. The IRS may rebut the presumption with evidence that the compensation was not reasonable or the transfer was not at fair market value, such as by contesting the validity of comparables. The regulations give detailed instructions on standards for comparability determi-nations and give some relief for small organizations as to the data that must be used. Id. In its first advisory on compensation, the IRS found reliance by an independent board on a five-year old consultant report and the board's failure to separately evaluate compensation to comparable CEOs and consul-tants inadequate to establish the rebuttable presumption under Section 4958. Internal Revenue Service, Technical Advice Memorandum 200244028 (June 21, 2002).

Penalties and "Correction". Sanctions, in the form of an initial tax of 25 per cent of the excess benefit, are imposed on individuals who benefited from the transaction; the excess benefit is calculated as the amount by which a transaction differs from fair market value. Disqualified persons are subject to an additional tax of 200 per cent of the excess benefit unless the transaction is "corrected" promptly (generally meaning that the disqualified person must undo the transaction and compensate the exempt organization for any losses caused by the transaction). Notably, no sanctions are imposed on the exempt organization (however, as described above, organizational managers who knowingly and willfully participate are subject to a 10 per cent tax). Abate-ment of penalties is possible where the violation is due to reasonable cause and not willful neglect. In the notorious Bishop Estate case, one of the first uses of § 4958, the IRS imposed sanctions against the trustees of an estate in Hawaii who paid themselves exorbitant salaries for its management. See Carolyn D. Wright, IRS Assesses Intermediate Sanctions Against Bishop Estate Incumbent Trustees, 2001 Tax Notes Today 405 (January 5, 2001).

Caracci v. Commissioner, *Caracci v. Commissioner*, 118 T.C. 379 (2002), rev'd 456 F.3d 444 (5th Cir. 2006), the Tax Court took on for the first time the task of applying the intermediate sanctions provisions to a health care organization and, in a major setback, was reversed by the Fifth Circuit. The Caracci family had operated their tax-exempt home health businesses, known as the Sta–Home Health Agency, very much as a family business. Family members were the sole members of the board of each of the tax exempt entities and also held all key employment positions. For these services, the Caracci family paid themselves what the tax court characterized as "executive level" compensation. After experiencing operating losses for three years, and facing the prospect that Medicare, the principal payer for Sta–Home patients, would shift from cost reimbursement to prospective payment, the Caracci's undertook to convert the entities to for-profit status by selling their assets to three closely held corporations which were controlled and operated by the Caracci family. Concluding that the corporations paid inadequate consideration for the assets of the tax exempt entities, the Service asserted that the transaction resulted in an excess benefit transaction under § 4958. In a 71–page opinion the Tax Court upheld the IRS's assessment of excise taxes but rejected revocation of the Sta–Home entities' tax exempt status. It also concluded that the total excess benefit to the disqualified persons was approximately $5 million.

The Fifth Circuit's reversal contained a blistering criticism of the IRS's valuation analysis. It emphasized the lack of qualifications of the IRS's appraiser and his lack of direct exposure to the specific circumstances of the home healthcare market in Mississippi. Although the Caracci's tax advisor rendered an opinion at the time of the transaction and the family later obtained an appraisal from an expert appraiser with greater experience, the Tax Court had sided with the Internal Revenue Service. Indeed, the Sta–Home entities had lost money and had a negative cash flow, but the Tax court found value in the entities' intangible assets. For an analysis of *Caracci* and its implications for future disputes over valuation, authored by the taxpayers' expert witness, see Allen D. Hahn, Caracci and the Valuation of Exempt Organizations, 40 J. Health L. 267 (2007)(valuation models and reliance on comparables must be sensitive to the characteristics of the exempt organization and the regulatory policies affecting reimbursement).

Problems: Excess Benefit Transactions

1. Analyze whether the excess benefit law would apply in the following situations:

- Expenditures by a tax exempt hospital to recruit an obstetrician, currently practicing at a nearby hospital, to relocate his office nearby and obtain staff privileges. The expenditures (free rent, moving allowances, malpractice insurance subsidies) exceed payments customarily made and there is no documentation of a community shortage of obstetricians.

- Payment by a tax exempt hospital to certain Department Chairs, a fixed percentage of all revenues of the department.

- C, a tax exempt hospital, contracts with Y, a management company, which will provide a wide range of services for a management fee of 7% of C's adjusted gross revenues, as specifically defined in the contract. Y will also receive payments for any expenses it incurs including legal, consulting or accounting throughout the term of the contract.

2. Larry Levy, CEO of Exempt Hospital (EH) has received an offer from a for-profit system in another state that will pay him $2.2 million per year; provide him with a loan of $1 million; and give a performance bonus of $500,000 per year if he meets revenue targets. This package amounts to 50% more than EH currently pays him. It is believed to be in line with compensation at for-profit

systems but is about 20% more than comparable nonprofit hospital systems pay. What should the Board of EH do and why?

3. EH currently pays Dr. Brady, an independent staff physician who serves as its Department Chair of Oncology (with responsibility for hiring staff, supervising credentialing, and handling administrative duties of hospital but no role in budgetary matters), a sum of $1000 per month. Dr. Brady has requested a new compensation arrangement pursuant to which EH would pay him an additional $1000 for each new patient he or any member of the staff admits to EH who incurs total bills greater than $10,000. The EH Board approved this arrangement after a short briefing from its CEO who stressed that EH would have to shut down its oncology department if they didn't accede to Dr Brady's demand. What excess benefit tax liability and for whom? What steps should the parties take?

Review Problem: St. Andrew's Medical Center, Part Two

The Board of tax-exempt St. Andrew's voted against selling the hospital to for-profit Health Care Enterprises. Instead, it has chosen to follow an aggressive strategic plan to achieve the following objectives:

To develop closer working relationships with compatible health care institutions in our region in order to create a comprehensive system of health care delivery that will allow St. Andrew's to better respond to the needs of the purchasers of health care and the patients themselves;

To establish more effective collaborative and mutually beneficial relationships with the physicians who currently hold privileges at St. Andrew's and to develop new alliances with physicians who do not currently admit patients to St. Andrew's;

To develop new, more efficient and more accessible forms of delivery for our services.

St. Andrew's has served primarily an urban and suburban population, but its home city is actually located in a rural state. There is a very small for-profit, free-standing hospital called Parkdale Hospital, located about 50 miles southwest of St. Andrew's. It was originally established by the lead mining company located in that town, but is now owned by a group of three physicians. The physicians are finding the hospital management business terribly trying these days as they do not have the capital that is needed to renovate and improve Parkdale; and St. Anthony's sees Parkdale as a very low-cost facility that has a strong patient census for its size and that, most importantly, can "feed" St. Andrew's those patients who need a higher level of care. St. Andrew's has proposed a number of arrangements that might serve the interests of both Parkdale and St. Andrew's. St. Andrew's has asked you to advise them on the tax implications in light of St. Andrew's § 501(c)(3) status. If you see problems in the transactions, describe how you would remedy them to allow the transaction to go forward and achieve its essential purposes.

1. St. Andrew's has offered Parkdale a Management Services Agreement, in which St. Andrew's agrees to manage and administer Parkdale, providing it with all administrative services, including personnel management, financial planning, quality assurance and so on. The agreement would include a base price of approximately $150,000 per year plus 1% of Parkdale's net revenues. In coming to the price, St. Andrew's did consider its hope that the relationship with Parkdale will develop over time.

2. Alternatively, St. Andrew's has proposed that Parkdale and St. Andrew's establish a new entity called Rural Healthcare Partners. Partners would be structured as a limited partnership, with Parkdale and St. Andrew's as general partners and the three physician-owners of Parkdale as limited partners. St. Andrew's will provide 80% of the capital for the entity. Parkdale and St. Andrew's will share equally in decision making through a management committee. Profits will be distributed in proportion to the contribution to capital, although it is understood that any excess of revenue over expenses will be re-invested in Partners during its first years. Much of it will be passed through to Parkdale for essential improvements. It is not clear exactly what Partners will do eventually. It is being established now as a vehicle for the development of future joint ventures between St. Andrew's and Parkdale. It will begin by doing physician recruitment for Parkdale, and perhaps later for rural hospitals outside of the area, and providing public relations for the Parkdale–St. Andrew's affiliation.

3. Dr. Simpson is a member of St. Andrew's board with strong professional and personal contacts in the medical community in and around Parkdale Hospital. He was instrumental in originating the contacts which gave rise to the discussions resulting in the preceding proposals. St. Andrew's plans to reward Dr. Simpson with a one year consulting contract for a sum of $100,000 for his past and future liaison efforts with Parkdale.

4. Recently, twenty obstetricians/gynecologists in the suburban area near St. Andrew's have formed an organization through which they operate as an entity even though they still practice in their own offices. Although these doctors currently admit patients both to St. Andrew's and to the other private hospital in town, they have been approached with an offer by the other hospital, Memorial, which is owned by a for-profit organization. Memorial Hospital has offered the entity below-market-value space in the doctors' office building attached to the hospital; free administrative services in the management of their practices including free use of the hospital's management information system; and the opportunity to become limited partners in the "Birthing Center," a special area which will be developed on the OB floor at the hospital and which will be the subject of an intense media campaign. The doctors will receive a proportionate share of the net revenue of the Center. In exchange, the doctors would agree to take any patient who wishes to receive OB/GYN services at Memorial as long as they have the requisite skills to care for the patient and as long as the patient has the ability to pay. Memorial has several contracts with health maintenance organizations for hospital services to their enrollees, and this arrangement between the OBs and Memorial would require the physicians to contract with and take patients covered by those HMOs. The physicians will not become employees of the HMO. A large number of the physicians' patients are located near the suburban Memorial Hospital, and fewer are located in the more urban area in which St. Andrew's is located, so the attraction to Memorial is strong despite the doctors' distrust of its for-profit structure.

Although obstetrics is not a very "profitable" service for St. Andrew's, OB patients are highly desirable to a hospital because they represent a potential stream of patients from the family. St. Andrew's wants to maintain active OB and neonatal services and requires a minimum number of patients to do so. There are a few OBs who are not members of this new entity, but they tend to be older and tend to practice in less desirable geographic areas, though no one spot in town is more than twenty minutes away from any other spot.

St. Andrew's plans to match Memorial's offer. In addition, it intends to further strengthen its ties to Parkdale by offering the physicians a generous income guarantee if they will establish an office near Parkdale where there is only one OB practicing part time. St. Andrew's will also require that the physicians agree to provide back-up services and consultation for high-risk pregnancies referred to it by Parkdale. The doctors will also be paid for any services they actually provide under this arrangement.

Chapter 12

FRAUD AND ABUSE

Health care providers are subject to a large body of law governing their financial arrangements with each other and with payors. These state and federal laws cover many practices that amount to fraud, bribery, or stealing. In addition, they prohibit many contractual relationships, investments, and marketing and recruitment practices that are perfectly legal in other businesses. As will be seen, these laws are well-intentioned: they seek to rectify a number of serious flaws in the health care financing system, save the government money, and prevent conflicts of interest that taint the physician-patient relationship. Indeed, they have been used to bring to justice a large number of providers, including some major corporate entities, that have engaged in systematic fraud. Unfortunately, the particular statutes (and the regulations, cases and interpretative rulings and guidelines they have spawned) are also bewilderingly complicated and have generated confusion and cynicism in the health care industry. Further, some aspects of these laws may prove anachronistic under evolving payment systems. Nevertheless, they continue to have a profound impact on the health care industry and generate an enormous amount of work for health care lawyers designing organizational structures that must comply with their strictures.

I. FALSE CLAIMS

According to some estimates, Medicare and Medicaid fraud and abuse costs federal and state governments tens of billions of dollars per year. The Centers for Medicare & Medicaid Services (CMS) estimated that in 2005 Medicare overpaid $9.8 billion in fee-for-service payments, a sum that amounts to over four per cent of its fee-for-service reimbursement. Centers for Medicare & Medicaid Services, Improper Medicare FFS Payments Long Report for November 2006. Much of this problem undoubtedly can be traced to the structure and complexities of Medicare and Medicaid payment systems which give incentives and opportunities to engage in fraud or to "game the system" to maximize reimbursement. See Alice G. Gosfield, Medicare and Medicaid Fraud and Abuse § 1:2 (2007). The term "fraud and abuse" is a broad one, covering a large number of activities ranging from negligent or careless practices that result in overbilling, to "self-referral arrangements" that are seen as improperly enriching providers and encouraging overutilization, to outright fraudulent schemes to bill for services never rendered. Indeed, the "fraud" aspects of "fraud and abuse" prosecutions have involved overtly criminal schemes, sometimes with elements of racketeering and the involvement of organized crime. Recently federal prosecutors have sought to expand the reach of the anti-fraud laws to reach deficiencies in quality of care or products and the provision of misleading information by providers. This section deals with the law of false claims, which is designed to protect the government from paying for goods or services that have not been provided or were not provided in accordance with government regulations. Specific problems addressed by the law include: provider charges or claims for unreasonable costs, services not rendered, services provided by unlicensed or unapproved personnel, excessive or unnecessary care, and services not in compliance with CMS regulations, cost reports or other requirements.

A. GOVERNMENTAL ENFORCEMENT

UNITED STATES v. KRIZEK

United States District Court, District of Columbia, 1994.
859 F.Supp. 5.

SPORKIN, DISTRICT JUDGE.

MEMORANDUM OPINION AND ORDER

On January 11, 1993, the United States filed this civil suit against George O. Krizek, M.D. and Blanka H. Krizek under the False Claims Act, 31 U.S.C. §§ 3729–3731, and at common law. The government brought the action against the Krizeks alleging false billing for Medicare and Medicaid patients. The five counts include claims for (1) "Knowingly Presenting a False or Fraudulent Claim", 31 U.S.C. § 3729(a)(1); (2) "Knowingly Presenting a False or Fraudulent Record", 31 U.S.C. § 3729(a)(2); (3) "Conspiracy to Defraud the Government"; (4) "Payment under Mistake of Fact"; and (5) "Unjust Enrichment". In its claim for relief, the government asks for triple the alleged actual damages of $245,392 and civil penalties of $10,000 for each of the 8,002 allegedly false reimbursement claims pursuant to 31 U.S.C. § 3729.

The government alleges two types of misconduct related to the submission of bills to Medicare and Medicaid. The first category of misconduct relates to the use of billing codes found in the American Medical Association's "Current Procedural Terminology" ("CPT"), a manual that lists terms and codes for reporting procedures performed by physicians. The government alleges that Dr. Krizek "up-coded" the bills for a large percentage of his patients by submitting bills coded for a service with a higher level of reimbursement than that which Dr. Krizek provided. As a second type of misconduct, the government alleges Dr. Krizek "performed services that should not have been performed at all in that they were not medically necessary." []

Given the large number of claims, and the acknowledged difficulty of determining the "medical necessity" of 8,002 reimbursement claims, it was decided that this case should initially be tried on the basis of seven patients and two hundred claims that the government believed to be representative of Dr. Krizek's improper coding and treatment practices. [] It was agreed by the parties that a determination of liability on Dr. Krizek's coding practices would be equally applicable to all 8,002 claims in the complaint. A three week bench trial ensued.

Findings of Fact

Dr. Krizek is a psychiatrist. Dr. Krizek's wife, Blanka Krizek was responsible for overseeing Dr. Krizek's billing operation for a part of the period in question. Dr. Krizek's Washington, D.C. psychiatric practice consists in large part in the treatment of Medicare and Medicaid patients. Much of Doctor Krizek's work involves the provision of psychotherapy and other psychiatric care to patients at the Washington Hospital Center.

Under the Medicare and Medicaid systems, claims for reimbursement are submitted on documents known as Health Care Financing Administration ("HCFA") 1500 Forms. These forms are supposed to contain the patient's identifying information, the provider's Medicaid or Medicare identification number, and a description of the provided procedures for which reimbursement is sought. These procedures are identified by a standard, uniform code number as set out in the American Medical Association's "Current Procedural Terminology" ("CPT") manual, a book that lists the terms and codes for reporting procedures performed by physicians.

* * *

The government in its complaint alleges both improper billing for services provided and the provision of medically unnecessary services. The latter of these two claims will be addressed first.

Medical Necessity

The record discloses that Dr. Krizek is a capable and competent physician. * * * The trial testimony of Dr. Krizek, his colleagues at the Washington Hospital Center, as well as the testimony of a former patient, established that Dr. Krizek was providing valuable medical and psychiatric care during the period covered by the complaint. The testimony was undisputed that Dr. Krizek worked long hours on behalf of his patients, most of whom were elderly and poor.

Many of Dr. Krizek's patients were afflicted with horribly severe psychiatric disorders and often suffered simultaneously from other serious medical conditions.* * *

The government takes issue with Dr. Krizek's method of treatment of his patients, arguing that some patients should have been discharged from the hospital sooner, and that others suffered from conditions which could not be ameliorated through psychotherapy sessions, or that the length of the psychotherapy sessions should have been abbreviated. The government's expert witness's opinions on this subject came from a cold review of Dr. Krizek's notes for each patient. The government witness did not examine or interview any of the patients, or speak with any other doctors or nurses who had actually served these patients to learn whether the course of treatment prescribed by Dr. Krizek exceeded that which was medically necessary.

Dr. Krizek testified credibly and persuasively as to the basis for the course of treatment for each of the representative patients. The medical necessity of treating Dr. Krizek's patients through psychotherapy and hospitalization was confirmed via the testimony of other defense witnesses. The Court credits Dr. Krizek's testimony on this question as well as his interpretation of his own notes regarding the seriousness of each patients' condition and the medical necessity for the procedures and length of hospital stay required. The Court finds that the government was unable to prove that Dr. Krizek rendered services that were medically unnecessary.

Improper Billing

On the question of improper billing or "up-coding," the government contends that for approximately 24 percent of the bills submitted, Dr. Krizek used the CPT Code for a 45–50 minute psychotherapy session (CPT Code 90844) when he should have billed for a 20–30 minute session (CPT Code 90843). The government also contends that for at least 33 percent of his patients, Dr. Krizek billed for a full 45–50 minute psychotherapy session, again by using CPT code 90844, when he should have billed for a "minimal psychotherapy" session (CPT 90862). These two latter procedures are reimbursed at a lower level than 90844, the 45–50 minute psychotherapy session, which the government has referred to as "the Cadillac" of psychiatric reimbursement codes.

The primary thrust of the government's case revolves around the question whether Dr. Krizek's use of the 90844 CPT code was appropriate. For the most part, the government does not allege that Dr. Krizek did not see the patients for whom he submitted bills. Instead, the government posits that the services provided during his visits either did not fall within the accepted definition of "individual medical psychotherapy" or, if the services provided *did* fit within this definition, the reimbursable service provided was not as extensive as that which was billed for. In sum, the government claims that whenever Dr. Krizek would see a patient, regardless of whether he simply checked a chart, spoke with nurses, or merely prescribed additional medication, his wife or his employee, a Mrs. Anderson, would, on the vast majority of occasions, submit a bill for CPT code 90844—45–50 minutes of individual psychotherapy.

[Documents sent to providers by Pennsylvania Blue Shield, the Medicare carrier for Dr. Krizek's area, explained the services in the 90800 series of codes as involving "[i]ndividual medical psychotherapy by a physician, with continuing medical diagnostic evaluation, and drug management when indicated, including insight oriented, behavior modifying or supportive psychotherapy" for specified periods of time.]

* * *

The government's witnesses testified that as initially conceived, the definition of the CPT codes is designed to incorporate the extra time spent in its level of reimbursement. It was expected by the authors of the codes that for a 45–50 minute 90844 session a doctor would spend additional time away from the patient reviewing or dictating records, speaking with nurses, or prescribing medication. The government's witnesses testified that the reimbursement rate for 90844 took into account the fact that on a 45–50 minute session the doctor would likely spend twenty additional minutes away from the patient. As such, the doctor is limited to billing for time actually spent "face-to-face" with the patient.

Dr. and Mrs. Krizek freely admit that when a 90844 code bill was submitted on the doctor's behalf, it did not always reflect 45–50 minutes of face-to-face psychotherapy with the patient. Instead, the 45–50 minutes billed captured generally the total amount of time spent on the patient's case, including the "face-to-face" psychotherapy session, discussions with medical staff about the patient's treatment/progress, medication management, and other related services. Dr. Krizek referred to this as "bundling" of services, all of which, Dr. and Mrs. Krizek testified, they reasonably believed were reimbursable under the 90844 "individual medical psychotherapy" code.

Defendant's witnesses testified that it was a common and proper practice among psychiatrists nationally, and in the Washington, D.C. area, to "bundle" a variety of services, including prescription management, review of the patient file, consultations with nurses or the patients' relatives into a bill for individual psychotherapy, whether or not these services took place literally in view of the patient. Under the defense theory, if a doctor spent 20 minutes in a session with a patient and ten minutes before that in a different room discussing the patient's symptoms with a nurse, and fifteen minutes afterwards outlining a course of treatment to the medical staff, it would be entirely appropriate, under their reading and interpretation of the CPT, to bill the 45 minutes spent on that patients' care by using CPT code 90844.

The testimony of the defense witnesses on this point was credible and persuasive. * * * The CPT codes which the government insists require face-to-face rendition of services never used the term "face-to-face" in its code description during the time period covered by this litigation. The relevant language describing the code is ambiguous.

The Court finds that the government's position on this issue is not rational and has been applied in an unfair manner to the medical community, which for the most part is made up of honorable and dedicated professionals. One government witness testified that a 15 minute telephone call made to a consulting physician in the patient's presence would be reimbursable, while if the doctor needed to go outside the patient's room to use the telephone—in order to make the *same* telephone call—the time would not be reimbursable. * * *

The Court will not impose False Claims Act liability based on such a strained interpretation of the CPT codes. The government's theory of liability is plainly unfair and unjustified. Medical doctors should be appropriately reimbursed for services legitimately provided. They should be given clear guidance as to what services are reimbursable. The system should be fair. The system cannot be so arbitrary, so perverse, as to subject a doctor whose annual income during the relevant period averaged between $100,000 and $120,000, to potential liability in excess of 80 million dollars[1] because telephone calls were made in one room rather than another.

---

1. The government alleges in the complaint that overbills amounted to $245,392 during the six-year period covered by the lawsuit. Trebling this damage amount, and adding the $10,000 statutory maximum penalty requested by the government for each of the 8,002 alleged false claims, results in a total potential liability under the complaint of more than $80,750,000. Dr. Krizek is not public enemy number one. He is at worst, a psychiatrist with

The Court finds that Doctor Krizek did not submit false claims when he submitted a bill under CPT Code 90844 after spending 45–50 minutes working on a patient's case, even though not all of that time was spent in direct face-to-face contact with the patient. * * * The Court finds that the defendants' "bundled" services interpretation of the CPT code 90844 is not inconsistent with the plain, common-sense reading of the "description of services" listed by Pennsylvania Blue Shield in its published Procedure Terminology Manual.

Billing Irregularities

While Dr. Krizek was a dedicated and competent doctor and cannot be faulted for his interpretation of the 90844 code, his billing practices, or at a minimum his oversight of his wife's and Mrs. Anderson's billing system, was seriously deficient. Dr. Krizek knew little or nothing of the details of how the bills were submitted by his wife and Mrs. Anderson. * * *

The basic method of billing by Mrs. Krizek and Mrs. Anderson was to determine which patients Dr. Krizek had seen, and then to assume what had taken place was a 50–minute psychotherapy session, unless told specifically by Dr. Krizek that the visit was for a shorter duration. Mrs. Krizek frequently made this assumption without any input from her husband. Mrs. Krizek acknowledged at trial that she never made any specific effort to determine exactly how much time was spent with each patient. Mrs. Krizek felt it was fair and appropriate to use the 90844 code as a rough approximation of the time spent, because on some days, an examination would last up to two hours and Mrs. Krizek would still bill 90844.

Mrs. Anderson also would prepare and submit claims to Medicare/Medicaid with no input from Dr. Krizek. Routinely, Mrs. Anderson would simply contact the hospital to determine what patients were admitted to various psychiatrists' services, and would then prepare and submit claims to Medicare/Medicaid without communicating with Dr. or Mrs. Krizek about the claims she was submitting and certifying on Dr. Krizek's behalf. * * *

The net result of this system, or more accurately "nonsystem," of billing was that on a number of occasions, Mrs. Krizek and Mrs. Anderson submitted bills for 45–50 minute psychotherapy sessions on Dr. Krizek's behalf when Dr. Krizek could not have spent the requisite time providing services, face-to-face, or otherwise. * * * The defendants do not deny that these unsubstantiated reimbursement claims occurred or that billing practices which led to such inaccurate billings continued through March of 1992.

While the Court does not find that Dr. Krizek submitted bills for patients he did not see, the Court does find that because of Mrs. Krizek's and Mrs. Anderson's presumption that whenever Dr. Krizek saw a patient he worked at least 45 minutes on the matter, bills were improperly submitted for time that was not spent providing patient services. Again, the defendants admit this occurred. []

a small practice who keeps poor records. For the government to sue for more than eighty million dollars in damages against an elderly doctor and his wife is unseemly and not justified. During this period, a psychiatrist in most instances would be reimbursed between $48 and $60 for a 45–50 minute session and $40 or less for a 20–30 minute session. This is hardly enough for any professional to get rich.

At the conclusion of the trial, both parties agreed that an appropriate bench-mark for excessive billing would be the equivalent of twelve 90844 submissions (or nine patient-service hours) in a single service day. [] Considering the difficulty of reviewing all Dr. Krizek's patient records over a seven-year period, Dr. Wilson's testimony as to having submitted as many as twelve 90844 submissions in a single day, and giving full credence to unrefuted testimony that Dr. Krizek worked very long hours, the Court believes this to be a fair and reasonably accurate assessment of the time Dr. Krizek actually spent providing patient services. *See Bigelow v. RKO Radio Pictures, Inc.*, 327 U.S. 251, 264, 66 S.Ct. 574, 579, 90 L.Ed. 652 (1946) (permitting factfinder to make "just and reasonable estimate of damage based on relevant data" where more precise computation is not possible). Dr. and Mrs. Krizek will therefore be presumed liable for bills submitted in excess of the equivalent of twelve 90844 submissions in a single day.

Nature of Liability

While the parties have agreed as to the presumptive number of excess submissions for which Dr. and Mrs. Krizek may be found liable, they do not agree on the character of the liability. The government submits that the Krizeks should be held liable under the False Claims Act, 31 U.S.C. § 3729, *et seq*. By contrast, defendants posit that while the United States may be entitled to reimbursement for any unjust enrichment attributable to the excess billings, the Krizeks' conduct with regard to submission of excess bills to Medicare/Medicaid was at most negligent, and not "knowing" within the definition of the statute. In their defense, defendants emphasize the "Ma and Pa" nature of Dr. Krizek's medical practice, the fact that Mrs. Krizek did attend some Medicare billing seminars in an effort to educate herself, and the fact that Mrs. Krizek consulted hospital records and relied on information provided by her husband in preparing bills.

By its terms, the False Claims Act provides, *inter alia*, that: Any person who—

(1) knowingly presents, or causes to be presented, to [the Government] . . . a false or fraudulent claim for payment or approval;

(2) knowingly makes, uses, or causes to be made or used, a false record or statement to get a false or fraudulent claim paid or approved by the Government;

(3) conspires to defraud the Government by getting a false or fraudulent claim allowed or paid;

* * *

is liable to the United States Government for a civil penalty of not less than $5,000.00 and not more than $10,000.00, plus three times the amount of damages which the Government sustains because of the act of that person. * * *

31 U.S.C. § 3729(a). The mental state required to find liability under the False Claims Act is also defined by the statute:

For the purposes of this section, the terms "knowing" and "knowingly" mean that a person, with respect to information—

(1) has actual knowledge of the information;

(2) acts in deliberate ignorance of the truth or falsity of the information; or

(3) acts in reckless disregard of the truth or falsity of the information, and no proof of specific intent is required.

31 U.S.C. § 3729(b). The provision allowing for a finding of liability without proof of specific intent to defraud was a feature of the 1986 amendments to the Act.

* * *

The Court finds that, at times, Dr. Krizek was submitting claims for 90844 when he did not provide patient services for the requisite 45 minutes. The testimony makes clear that these submissions were made by Mrs. Krizek or Mrs. Anderson with little, if any, factual basis. Mrs. Krizek made no effort to establish how much time Dr. Krizek spent on a particular matter. Mrs. Krizek and Mrs. Anderson simply presumed that 45–50 minutes had been spent. There was no justification for making that assumption. In addition, Dr. Krizek failed utterly in supervising these agents in their submissions of claims on his behalf. As a result of his failure to supervise, Dr. Krizek received reimbursement for services which he did not provide.

These were not "mistakes" nor merely negligent conduct. Under the statutory definition of "knowing" conduct, the Court is compelled to conclude that the defendants acted with reckless disregard as to the truth or falsity of the submissions. As such, they will be deemed to have violated the False Claims Act.

Conclusion

Dr. Krizek must be held accountable for his billing system along with those who carried it out. Dr. Krizek was not justified in seeing patients and later not verifying the claims submitted for the services provided to these patients. Doctors must be held strictly accountable for requests filed for insurance reimbursement.

The Court believes that the Krizeks' billing practices must be corrected before they are permitted to further participate in the Medicare or Medicaid programs. Therefore an injunction will issue, enjoining the defendants from participating in these systems until such time as they can show the Court that they can abide by the relevant rules.

The Court also will hold the defendants liable under the False Claims Act on those days where claims were submitted in excess of the equivalent of twelve (12) 90844 claims (nine patient-treatment hours) in a single day and where the defendants cannot establish that Dr. Krizek legitimately devoted the claimed amount of time to patient care on the day in question. The government also will be entitled to introduce proof that the defendants submitted incorrect bills when Dr. Krizek submitted bills for less than nine (9) hours in a single day. The assessment of the amount of overpayment and penalty will await these future proceedings.

Other Observations

While the Court does not discount the seriousness of the Krizeks' conduct here, this case demonstrates several flaws in this country's government health insurance program. The government was right in bringing this action, because it could not countenance the reckless nature of the reimbursement systems in this case. While we are in an age of computers, this does not mean that we can blindly allow coding systems to determine the amount of reimbursement without the physician being accountable for honestly and correctly submitting proper information, whether by code or otherwise.

Nonetheless, the Court found rather troubling some of the government's procedures that control reimbursements paid to providers of services. Here are some of these practices:

1) The government makes no distinction in reimbursement as to the status or professional attainment or education of the provider. Thus, a nontechnical person rendering a coded service will be reimbursed the same amount as a board-certified physician.

2) The sums that the Medicare and Medicaid systems reimburse physicians for services rendered seem to be so far below the norm for charges reimbursed by non-governmental insurance carriers. Indeed, the amount could hardly support a medical practice. As the evidence shows in this case, Board certified physicians in most instances were paid at a rate less than $60 per hour and less than $35 per 1/2 hour. The government must certainly review these charges because if providers are not adequately compensated, they may not provide the level of care that our elderly and underprivileged citizens require. What is more, the best physicians will simply not come into the system or will refuse to take on senior citizens or the poor as patients.

3) The unrealistic billing concept of requiring doctors to bill only for face-to-face time is not consistent with effective use of a doctor's time or with the provision of good medical services. Doctors must be able to study, research, and discuss a patient's case and be reimbursed for such time.

4) When Medicare dictates that a physician must report each service rendered as a separate code item, the physician is entitled to believe that he will be reimbursed for each of the services rendered. In actuality, the system pays for only one of the multitude of services provided. If this were done by a private sector entity, it would be considered deceitful. Because the government engages in such a deceitful practice does not make it right.

These are the lessons learned by this Court during this case. Hopefully, HCFA will reexamine its reimbursement practices to see what, if any, changes should be made.

UNITED STATES v. KRIZEK

United States Court of Appeals, District of Columbia Circuit, 1997.
111 F.3d 934.

SENTELLE, CIRCUIT JUDGE.

This appeal arises from a civil suit brought by the government against a psychiatrist and his wife under the civil False Claims Act ("FCA"), 31 U.S.C. §§ 3729–3731, and under the common law. The District Court found defendants liable for knowingly submitting false claims and entered judgment against defendants for $168,105.39. The government appealed, and the defendants filed a cross-appeal. We hold that the District Court erred and remand for further proceedings.

[The Court held that the district court erred in changing its benchmark for a presumptively false claim from 9 hours billed in any given day to 24 hours because it did not afford the government the opportunity to introduce additional evidence. It also agreed with the Krizeks cross-appeal that the District Court erroneously treated each CPT code as a separate "claim" for purposes of computing civil penalties instead of treating the government form 1500 which contained multiple codes as the "claim."

The court questioned the fairness of the government's definition of claim because it "permitted it to seek an astronomical $81 million worth of damages for alleged actual damages of $245,392."

* * *

[W]e turn now to the question whether, in considering the sample, the District Court applied the appropriate level of scienter. The FCA imposes liability on an individual who "knowingly presents" a "false or fraudulent claim." 31 U.S.C. § 3729(a). A person acts "knowingly" if he:

(1) has actual knowledge of the information;

(2) acts in deliberate ignorance of the truth or falsity of the information; or

(3) acts in reckless disregard of the truth or falsity of the information,

and no proof of specific intent to defraud is required.

31 U.S.C. § 3729(b). The Krizeks assert that the District Court impermissibly applied the FCA by permitting an aggravated form of gross negligence, "gross negligence-plus," to satisfy the Act's scienter requirement.

In Saba v. Compagnie Nationale Air France, 78 F.3d 664 (D.C.Cir. 1996), we considered whether reckless disregard was the equivalent of willful misconduct for purposes of the Warsaw Convention. We noted that reckless disregard lies on a continuum between gross negligence and intentional harm. In some cases, recklessness serves as a proxy for forbidden intent. Such cases require a showing that the defendant engaged in an act known to cause or likely to cause the injury. Use of reckless disregard as a substitute for the forbidden intent prevents the defendant from "deliberately blind[ing] himself to the consequences of his tortuous action." Id. at 668. In another category of cases, we noted, reckless disregard is "simply a linear extension of gross negligence, a palpable failure to meet the appropriate standard of care." Id. In Saba, we determined that in the context of the Warsaw Convention, a showing of willful misconduct might be made by establishing reckless disregard such that the subjective intent of the defendant could be inferred.

The question, therefore, is whether "reckless disregard" in this context is properly equated with willful misconduct or with aggravated gross negligence. In determining that gross negligence-plus was sufficient, the District Court cited legislative history equating reckless disregard with gross negligence. A sponsor of the 1986 amendments to the FCA stated,

Subsection 3 of Section 3729(c) uses the term "reckless disregard of the truth or falsity of the information" which is no different than and has the same meaning as a gross negligence standard that has been applied in other cases. While the Act was not intended to apply to mere negligence, it is intended to apply in situations that could be considered gross negligence where the submitted claims to the Government are prepared in such a sloppy or unsupervised fashion that resulted in overcharges to the Government. The Act is also intended not to permit artful defense counsel to require some form of intent as an essential ingredient of proof. This section is intended to reach the "ostrich-with-his-head-in-the-sand" problem where government contractors hide behind the fact they were not personally aware that such overcharges may have occurred. This is not a new standard but clarifies what has always been the standard of knowledge required.

132 Cong. Rec. H9382–03 (daily ed. Oct. 7, 1986) (statement of Rep. Berman).

While we are not inclined to view isolated statements in the legislative history as dispositive, we agree with the thrust of this statement that the best reading of the Act defines reckless disregard as an extension of gross negligence. Section 3729(b)(2) of the Act provides liability for false statements made with deliberate ignorance. If the reckless disregard standard of section 3729(b)(3) served merely as a substitute for willful misconduct—to prevent the defendant from "deliberately blind[ing] himself to the consequences of his tortuous action"—section (b)(3) would be redundant since section (b)(2) already covers such struthious conduct. Moreover, as the statute explicitly states that specific intent is not required, it is logical to conclude that reckless disregard in this context is not a "lesser form of intent," [ ] but an extreme version of ordinary negligence.

We are unpersuaded by the Krizeks' citation to the rule of lenity to support their reading of the Act. Even assuming that the FCA is penal, the rule of lenity is invoked only when the statutory language is ambiguous. Because we find no ambiguity in the statute's scienter requirement, we hold that the rule of lenity is inapplicable.

We are also unpersuaded by the Krizeks' argument that their conduct did not rise to the level of reckless disregard. The District Court cited a number of factors supporting its conclusion: Mrs. Krizek completed the submissions with little or no factual basis; she made no effort to establish how much time Dr. Krizek spent with any particular patient; and Dr. Krizek "failed utterly" to review bills submitted on his behalf. Most tellingly, there were a number of days within the seven-patient sample when even the shoddiest record keeping would have revealed that false submissions were being made—those days on which the Krizeks' billing approached twenty-four hours in a single day. On August 31, 1985, for instance, the Krizeks requested reimbursement for patient treatment using the 90844 code thirty times and the 90843 code once, indicating patient treatment of over 22 hours. Outside the seven-patient sample the Krizeks billed for more than twenty-four hours in a single day on three separate occasions. These factors amply support the District Court's determination that the Krizeks acted with reckless disregard.

Finally, we note that Dr. Krizek is no less liable than his wife for these false submissions. As noted, an FCA violation may be established without reference to the subjective intent of the defendant. Dr. Krizek delegated to his wife authority to submit claims on his behalf. In failing "utterly" to review the false submissions, he acted with reckless disregard.

* * *

Notes and Questions

1. Exactly what conduct by Dr. Krizek did the government charge violated the False Claims Act? For what conduct and on what basis was he exonerated by the district court? Did the court's liability finding rest on the actions of Dr. Krizek or those of his subordinates?

2. The United States introduced expert evidence that the CPT codes 90843 and 90844 (individual psychotherapy) envisioned face-to-face therapy with the patient for the entire time for which the service was billed (either 25 or 50 minutes). The Krizeks admitted they received reimbursement for time spent other than in face-to-face therapy, and introduced evidence from other physicians that "bundling" was common practice in obtaining reimbursement for private payors. What was the legal basis for absolving Dr. Krizek of liability for "upcoding"?

3. What hurdles does the government face in proving that services provided by a physician were not "medically necessary?" Do the patient's medical records and the physician's notes supply persuasive evidence on this issue? What reform efforts would assist the government in proving a knowing violation of the law? Does requiring providers to sign a certification attesting that they have reviewed each claim, that the service was medically necessary, and that the service was actually provided resolve all problems? See U.S. ex rel. Mikes v. Straus, the next case in this chapter. How do electronic claims submissions affect the proof problem?

4. Does the opinion of the Court of Appeals in *Krizek* clarify the boundary between reckless disregard and willful misconduct? Between reckless disregard and gross negligence? What evidence did it rely upon to reach its conclusion that the Krizeks had run afoul of that standard? Can you explain at what point evidence of shoddy record keeping and submission of implausible claims would constitute "reckless disregard" under the False Claims Act?

5. Following the Court of Appeals' determination that each 1500 Form constituted a "claim," the district court faced on remand the question of how many of the multiple forms, which taken together exceeded 24 hours in a single day, constituted separate "claims." Absent proof as to which specific claims were submitted beyond the 24-hour limit, the district court chose to count only the number of days (three) exceeding the 24-hour benchmark rather than the total number of claims exceeding that benchmark (eleven). United States v. Krizek, 7 F.Supp. 2d 56 (D.D.C. 1998). Judge Sporken voiced continued frustration with the government's case: "The Government's pursuit of Dr. Krizek is reminiscent of Inspector Javert's quest to capture Jean Valjean in Victor Hugo's Les Miserables . . . [T]here comes a point when a civilized society must say enough is enough." Id. at 60. Evaluate this and Judge Sporkin's "other observations." Do they betray a judicial sympathy toward medical professionals that is not customarily afforded to other defendants charged with violating statutory directives? Are they persuasive? Has the government brought this criticism on itself by "piling on," i.e., using all the weapons in its arsenal? The Krizek case became a cause celebre for some in the provider community who felt the government was overreaching in its prosecution of false claims against providers. Mrs. Krizek testified before a congressional committee relating her views on the case and the government's conduct. Adminis-

trative Crimes and Quasi Crimes: Hearing Before the Subcomm. on Commercial and Admin. Law of the H. Comm. on the Judiciary, 105th Cong. (1998), available at http://commdocs.house.gov/committees/judiciary/hju59925.000/hju59925_0. HTM.

6. How should the "reckless disregard" standard be applied in practice? Consider the following situations:

A defendant continues to submit claims despite having had similar claims rejected in the past by the Medicare carrier and receiving explicit warnings that such claims would not be reimbursed in the future. The defendant is able to point to advice by a consultant that, notwithstanding the above, his billing was proper. See United States v. Lorenzo, 768 F.Supp. 1127 (E.D. Pa. 1991).

A defendant who is charged with improperly billing Medicare for services asserts that the HCFA Provider Handbook (which sets forth general billing guidelines for physician services) contains no specific instructions concerning the services that the government claims were improperly billed. In addition, the defendant sought to clarify his obligations by making inquiries through the Freedom of Information Act to HCFA. However, language in HCFA's Carrier Manual suggests that the billing may be improper. Expert testimony establishes that physicians are generally familiar with the provisions of the Carrier Manual, but it dictates whether carriers should pay claims and is not intended to guide the physician's decision to submit a claim for reimbursement. Finally, in internal discussions with other defendants, the doctor stated his concern that the billings were "on uncertain ground." See United States ex rel. Swafford v. Borgess Medical Center, 98 F. Supp. 2d 822 (W.D. Mich. 2000). But see In re Cardiac Devices Qui Tam Litig., 221 F.R.D. 318, 340 (D. Conn. 2004) (government's allegations that hospital's billing for procedures involving non-FDA approved cardiac devices in contravention of payment policy set forth in the Hospital Manual provided to all hospitals by HHS sufficiently pleaded scienter under FCA).

A nursing home bills Medicaid for skilled nursing care services rendered to a patient who had entered into a continuing care contract with that facility under which he had no responsibility to pay for skilled nursing care services if he ever needed them. The nursing home administrator assumed that the patient's prior payments under the contract were implied payments for subsequent skilled nursing services and therefore he could legally bill Medicaid. Medicaid regulations make it clear he could not. The administrator never sought a legal opinion as to whether the home could bill Medicaid under such a theory even though it was a significant potential source of revenue for his facility. See United States ex rel. Quirk v. Madonna Towers, Inc., 278 F.3d 765 (8th Cir. 2002).

7. What steps would you advise a provider client to take to guard against false billing? What internal safeguards, billing practices or supervision should the provider implement?

B. QUI TAM ACTIONS

31 U.S.C. § 3730. Civil actions for false claims

* * *

(b) Actions by private persons.—(1) A person may bring a civil action for a violation of [the False Claims Act] for the person and for the United States Government. The action shall be brought in the name of the Government.

The action may be dismissed only if the court and the Attorney General give written consent to the dismissal and their reasons for consenting.

(2) A copy of the complaint and written disclosure of substantially all material evidence and information the person possesses shall be served on the Government * * * The complaint shall be filed in camera, shall remain under seal for at least 60 days, and shall not be served on the defendant until the court so orders. The Government may elect to intervene and proceed with the action within 60 days after it receives both the complaint and the material evidence and information.

* * *

(4) Before the expiration of the 60–day period or any extensions obtained under paragraph (3), the Government shall—

(A) proceed with the action, in which case the action shall be conducted by the Government; or

(B) notify the court that it declines to take over the action, in which case the person bringing the action shall have the right to conduct the action.

* * *

(c) Rights of the parties to qui tam actions.—(1) If the Government proceeds with the action, it shall have the primary responsibility for prosecuting the action, and shall not be bound by an act of the person bringing the action. Such person shall have the right to continue as a party to the action, subject to the limitations set forth in paragraph (2).

* * *

(d) Award to qui tam plaintiff. If the Government proceeds with an action brought by a person under subsection (b), such person [shall receive between 15 and 25 percent of the proceeds of the action or settlement of the claim, depending on the extent to which the person contributed to the prosecution, plus attorneys' fees and costs. If the government does not proceed the person may receive between 25 and 30 percent plus attorneys' fees and costs. If the action was brought by a person who planned and initiated the violation of the statutes, the court may reduce the person's share of proceeds and if the person is convicted of a crime for his or her role that person may not share any proceeds.]

(e) Certain actions barred.

* * *

(3) In no event may a person bring an action under subsection (b) which is based upon allegations or transactions which are the subject of a civil suit or an administrative civil money penalty proceeding in which the Government is already a party.

(4)(A) No court shall have jurisdiction over an action under this section based upon the public disclosure of allegations or transactions in a criminal, civil, or administrative hearing, in a congressional, administrative, or Government Accounting Office report, hearing, audit, or investigation, or from the news media, unless the action is brought by the Attorney General or the person bringing the action is an original source of the information.

(B) For purposes of this paragraph, "original source" means an individual who has direct and independent knowledge of the information on which the allegations are based and has voluntarily provided the information to the Government before filing an action under this section which is based on the information.

* * *

(h) Any employee who is discharged, demoted, suspended, threatened, harassed, or in any other manner discriminated against in the terms and conditions of employment by his or her employer because of lawful acts done by the employee on behalf of the employee or others in furtherance of an action under this section, including investigation for, initiation of, testimony for, or assistance in an action filed or to be filed under this section, shall be entitled to all relief necessary to make the employee whole. Such relief shall include reinstatement with the same seniority status such employee would have had but for the discrimination, 2 times the amount of back pay, interest on the back pay, and compensation for any special damages sustained as a result of the discrimination, including litigation costs and reasonable attorneys' fees. An employee may bring an action in the appropriate district court of the United States for the relief provided in this subsection.

Notes and Questions

1. What advice would you have given to a hypothetical assistant working for Mrs. and Dr. Krizek in United States v. Krizek, supra, if she had approached you for legal advice before any investigation had begun of her employer? How would you have handled discussions with the U.S. Attorney's Office concerning her involvement in the matter? Could she continue to perform her job responsibilities for Dr. Krizek if she became a whistleblower or would it be necessary for her to quit? Before advising her, you may want to consult Luckey v. Baxter Healthcare Corp., 183 F.3d 730 (7th Cir. 1999), discussed in the preceding section of this chapter. In a portion of the opinion not reprinted above, Judge Easterbrook rejected the relator's claim for whistleblower protection under § 3730(h). Baxter had fired Ms. Luckey before her qui tam suit was unsealed and the court concluded that Baxter was not aware of the pending action. The court rejected the claim that because the employer knew of her strongly-held feelings about its testing practices, it should have been on notice of the possibility of her "assistance in" a suit. Likewise, despite Luckey's statements to co-workers that she planned to "shut down" the lab and "get rid" of her supervisors, the court concluded that Baxter was not prohibited from firing her: "Sabre-rattling is not protected conduct. Only investigation, testimony, and litigation are protected, and none of these led to Luckey's firing." 183 F.3d at 733.

2. If you represented Dr. Krizek and the matter went to trial, how would you seek to impeach the testimony of the assistant who became a qui tam relator? As a lawyer for the Department of Justice (assuming it has entered and taken over the lawsuit), how would you insulate against this cross-examination or mitigate it? Suppose instead that it is Mrs. Krizek who decided to become the qui tam "relator." Would your advice change? What information would you need to elicit before advising her?

3. The constitutionality of the qui tam statute has come under attack on several grounds. In Vermont Agency of Natural Resources v. United States ex rel.

Stevens, 529 U.S. 765, 120 S.Ct. 1858, 146 L.Ed.2d 836 (2000), the Supreme Court laid one question to rest, holding that, as partial assignees of the claim of the United States, qui tam relators satisfy the "case or controversy" requirements of Article III. In *Vermont Agency* the Supreme Court also held that states and state entities could not be subject to qui tam liability. 529 U.S. at 727–28. See Donald v. University of California Bd. of Regents, 329 F.3d 1040 (9th Cir. 2003) (denying share of settlement to relator who filed qui tam action regarding state university teaching hospital's billing practices). However, case law establishing that state employees and states may be qui tam relators remains undisturbed. See United States ex rel. Wisconsin v. Dean, 729 F.2d 1100 (7th Cir. 1984); United States ex rel. Fine v. Chevron, U.S.A., Inc., 72 F.3d 740 (9th Cir. 1995). See also Dorthea Beane, Are Government Employees Proper Qui Tam Plaintiffs?, 14 J. Leg. Med. 279 (1993); Gosfield, *supra*, § 5:13. Should a discharged employee who has signed an agreement with her employer releasing the employer of all claims and agreeing not to sue be able to pursue a qui tam action? What public policy arguments can be raised in favor of and against allowing such an action to proceed?

4. Qui tam actions have become the principle means by which the government uncovers fraud as over 80 percent of all government false claims actions are initiated by whistleblowers. Recoveries in cases involving health care fraud were $1.2 billion in 2003, $474 million in 2004 and $906 million in 2005. Taxpayers Against Fraud, Qui Tam Statistics, available at www.taf.org/fcastatistics2006.pdf. Although the Department of Justice declines to intervene in most qui tam actions and the large majority of those in which it does not intervene are unsuccessful, most of the largest health care fraud cases in recent years have been the result of qui tam actions. In recent years, over 60 percent of all qui tam actions involved the health care industry, with the pharmaceutical industry drawing particular attention. Financial Impacts of Waste, Fraud, and Abuse in Pharmaceutical Pricing: Hearing Before the H. Comm. On Oversight, 110th Cong. (2007) (testimony of Lewis Morris, Chief Counsel to the Inspector General of HHS, and James Moorman, President of Taxpayers Against Fraud) (2006 FCA recoveries involving pharmautical industry total $4 billion; $60 billion in additional potential liability in pending cases), available at http://oversight.house.gov/story.asp?ID=1168. For the view that "privatization" of public law enforcement through the qui tam statute creates incentives to over-enforce the False Claims Act, see Dana Bowen Matthew, The Moral Hazard Problem with Privatization of Public Enforcement: The Case of Pharmaceutical Fraud, 40 Mich. J.L. Ref. 281 (2007). Does the fact that the government has on several occasions obtained large settlements from corporations only to later fail to obtain criminal convictions against individuals responsible for the alleged fraud suggest that incentives under the FCA are out of kilter? See id. at 309–17 (discussing the TAP litigation and other pharmaceutical industry settlements under the FCA).

What is the justification for qui tam actions? Do they advance legitimate law enforcement objectives? Might they create undesirable incentives that poison the employer-employee relationship? In evaluating the effectiveness of the qui tam law in enhancing the deterrent effect of the FCA, consider the need to assure that damages are set at levels that take into account the likelihood of detection and the total social costs imposed by the violator. See Gary Becker, Crime and Punishment: An Economic Approach, 76 J. Pol. Econ. 169 (1968); Robert Lande, Optimal Sanctions for Antitrust Violations, 50 U. Chi. L. Rev. 652 (1983).

II. MEDICARE AND MEDICAID FRAUD AND ABUSE

A. THE STATUTE: 42 U.S.C. § 1320A–7B

* * *

(b) Illegal remunerations

(1) Whoever knowingly and willfully solicits or receives any remuneration (including any kickback, bribe, or rebate) directly or indirectly, overtly or covertly, in cash or in kind—

(A) in return for referring an individual to a person for the furnishing or arranging for the furnishing of any item or service for which payment may be made in whole or in part under a Federal health care program, or

(B) in return for purchasing, leasing, ordering, or arranging for or recommending purchasing, leasing, or ordering any good, facility, service, or item for which payment may be made in whole or in part under a Federal health care program,

shall be guilty of a felony and upon conviction thereof, shall be fined not more than $25,000 or imprisoned for not more than five years, or both.

(2) Whoever knowingly and willfully offers or pays any remuneration (including any kickback, bribe or rebate) directly or indirectly, overtly or covertly, in cash or in kind to any person to induce such person—

(A) to refer an individual to a person for the furnishing or arranging for the furnishing of any item or service for which payment may be made in whole or in part under a Federal health care program, or

(B) to purchase, lease, order, or arrange for or recommend purchasing, leasing, or ordering any good, facility, service, or item for which payment may be made in whole or in part under a Federal health care program,

shall be guilty of a felony and upon conviction thereof shall be fined not more than $25,000 or imprisoned for not more than five years, or both.

* * *

[Subsection (c) prohibits knowing and willful false statements or representations of material facts with respect to the conditions or operation of any entity in order to qualify such an entity for Medicare or Medicaid certification. Subsection (d) prohibits knowingly and willfully charging patients for Medicaid services where such charges are not otherwise permitted.]

(f) "Federal health care program" defined

For purposes of this section, the term "Federal health care program" means—

(1) any plan or program that provides health benefits, whether directly, through insurance, or otherwise, which is funded directly, in whole or in part, by the United States Government [other than the federal employees health benefit program]; or

(2) any State health care program, as defined in section 1320a–7(h) of this title.

B. PROBLEMS: ADVISING UNDER THE FRAUD AND ABUSE LAWS

Do any of the following transactions violate the fraud and abuse laws? Is there anything else wrong with them from a legal, ethical, or public policy perspective?

1.   Starkville Community Hospital is located in a rural area in a distant corner of a large mid-western state. Recently, Dr. McPherson, the hospital's only obstetrician, announced his retirement. Few new physicians have settled in Starkville in recent years, and the community and hospital are very concerned about the loss of obstetric services. The hospital has decided, therefore, to implement a plan to attract a new obstetrician. It is offering to provide any board-certified obstetrician who will settle in Starkville and obtain privileges at Starkville Memorial the following for the first two years the physician is on staff at the hospital: (1) a guaranteed annual income of $110,000, (2) free malpractice insurance through the hospital's self-insurance plan, and (3) free rent in the hospital's medical practice building. The new obstetrician would not be required to refer patients to Starkville Community, though the closest alternative hospital is 60 miles away. The obstetrician would also be expected to assume some administrative duties in exchange for the compensation package Starkville is offering. Starkville Community is currently engaged in negotiations with a young doctor who has just finished her residency and appears likely to accept this offer. There is a potential problem, however. Dr. Waxman, who came to Starkville two years ago and is the hospital's only cardiologist, has threatened that he will leave unless he gets the same terms.

2.   Dr. Ness, a successful ophthalmologist, advertises in the weekly suburban shopping newspaper, offering free cataract examinations for senior citizens. He in fact does not charge those who respond to the offer for the Medicare deductible or co-insurance amounts, but bills Medicare for the maximum charge allowable for the service.

3.   Managed care organizations are insisting that Samaritan Hospital offer wider geographic coverage in order to bid on contracts. A market study reveals that Samaritan is receiving few admissions from Arlington, a rapidly growing affluent suburb eight miles to the northwest. To remedy this problem, Samaritan has formed an MSO and has entered into negotiations to purchase the Arlington Family Practice Center, a successful group practice containing five board-certified family practitioners. The MSO has offered a generous price for the practice, which would be renamed Samaritan–Arlington Family Practice Center and its doctors would become salaried employees of the MSO entity. They would thereafter be required to admit patients only at Samaritan and to refer only to specialists who have privileges at Samaritan. The five doctors, who are weary of the administrative hassles of private practice, are eager to sell.

4.   MegaPharma, a leading pharmaceutical manufacturer, plans to roll out several new drugs next year. Once it receives approval from the FDA, it plans to market these drugs aggressively to physicians. MegaPharma's mar-

keting director intends to have her "detailers"—representatives who visit doctors' offices to market pharmaceutical products and explain their benefits—upgrade the quality of lunches they supply to the doctors and staff when they visit, offer large amounts of free samples, and give each doctor a souvenir IPOD inscribed with the MegaPharma logo and the names of the new drugs. In addition, MegaPharma will offer a $5000 honorarium and free travel to 50 physician "opinion leaders" from around the country to attend an annual educational seminar it sponsors. MegaPharma also hopes that many physicians will prescribe pezophine, one of its new drugs, for a use not approved by the FDA. (Such "off-label" prescribing is not in itself illegal, but FDA law forbids the manufacturer from marketing or advertising for that purpose). MegaPharma plans to offer honoraria to academics who have produced research about the off-label uses of pezophine and who themselves prescribe pezophine for off-label uses; it will offer honoraria for any talk or paper published regardless of whether other sources are also funding the academics' work.

5. Twenty-three small rural hospitals in a mid-western state have entered into a contract with a group-purchasing agent to purchase medical equipment and supplies for them. The agent will take advantage of volume discounts and of careful market research to significantly lower the cost of supplies and equipment purchased for the hospitals. The agent obtains, on average, a 5% rebate from suppliers for all goods it purchases.

6. Intermodal Health System, an integrated delivery system, has suffered losses averaging $100,000 per year per doctor on the physician practices it acquired five years ago. It has developed a plan to terminate the contracts of half of the physicians it now employs. Pursuant to their employment contract, each physician will receive a severance fee of $50,000. Intermodal will also waive covenants not to compete contained in contracts with terminated physicians. In addition, Intermodal plans to offer to its "most valued" terminated physicians lease agreements to continue to occupy the medical office space owned by an Intermodal subsidiary.

C. TREATMENT OF REFERRAL FEES UNDER FRAUD AND ABUSE LAWS

Sharing the profits of collective economic activity is common throughout the economy generally. Landlords rent commercial properties under percentage leases, agents sell goods and services produced by others on commission, merchants grant discounts to those who use their services or encourage others to do so. Such activity has, however, long been frowned upon as it relates to health care. It is widely believed that patients lack the knowledge and information (or even the legal right, in the case of prescription drugs) to make health care decisions for themselves (choosing appropriate drugs or specialists, for example). Therefore, providers have a fiduciary obligation to recommend goods and services for patients considering only the patient's medical needs and not the provider's own economic interest. With the advent of government financing of health care, this concern has been supplemented by another: that financial rewards to providers for patient referrals might drive up program costs by encouraging the provision of unnecessary or inordinately expensive medical care.

For these reasons, the fraud and abuse statutes reproduced above prohibit paying or receiving any remuneration (directly or indirectly, overtly or covertly) for referring, purchasing, or ordering goods, facilities, items or services paid for by Medicare or Medicaid. Interpreted broadly, however, these provisions seem to proscribe a wide variety of transactions that might encourage competition or efficient production of health care. Indeed, many of the arrangements undertaken in connection with forming or operating PHOs, MSOs or integrated delivery systems discussed in Chapter 11 might, under a literal reading of the fraud and abuse statute, be felonies under the federal law. Considerable attention has been focused recently on the question of whether the statute and the judicial and administrative interpretations thereof successfully distinguish beneficial and detrimental conduct in the current market environment.

UNITED STATES v. GREBER

United States Court of Appeals, Third Circuit, 1985.
760 F.2d 68, cert. denied, 474 U.S. 988, 106 S.Ct. 396, 88 L.Ed.2d 348.

WEIS, CIRCUIT JUDGE.

In this appeal, defendant argues that payments made to a physician for professional services in connection with tests performed by a laboratory cannot be the basis of Medicare fraud. We do not agree and hold that if one purpose of the payment was to induce future referrals, the Medicare statute has been violated. * * *

After a jury trial, defendant was convicted on 20 of 23 counts in an indictment charging violations of the mail fraud, Medicare fraud, and false statement statutes. Post-trial motions were denied, and defendant has appealed.

Defendant is an osteopathic physician who is board certified in cardiology. In addition to hospital staff and teaching positions, he was the president of Cardio–Med, Inc., an organization which he formed. The company provides physicians with diagnostic services, one of which uses a Holter-monitor. This device, worn for approximately 24 hours, records the patient's cardiac activity on a tape. A computer operated by a cardiac technician scans the tape, and the data is later correlated with an activity diary the patient maintains while wearing the monitor.

Cardio–Med billed Medicare for the monitor service and, when payment was received, forwarded a portion to the referring physician. The government charged that the referral fee was 40 percent of the Medicare payment, not to exceed $65 per patient.

Based on Cardio–Med's billing practices, counts 18–23 of the indictment charged defendant with having tendered remuneration or kickbacks to the referring physicians in violation of 42 U.S.C. § 1395nn(b)(2)(B) (1982).

* * *

The proof as to the Medicare fraud counts (18–23) was that defendant had paid a Dr. Avallone and other physicians "interpretation fees" for the doctors' initial consultation services, as well as for explaining the test results to the patients. There was evidence that physicians received "interpretation fees" even though defendant had actually evaluated the monitoring data.

Moreover, the fixed percentage paid to the referring physician was more than Medicare allowed for such services.

The government also introduced testimony defendant had given in an earlier civil proceeding. In that case, he had testified that "... if the doctor didn't get his consulting fee, he wouldn't be using our service. So the doctor got a consulting fee." In addition, defendant told physicians at a hospital that the Board of Censors of the Philadelphia County Medical Society had said the referral fee was legitimate if the physician shared the responsibility for the report. Actually, the Society had stated that there should be separate bills because "for the monitor company to offer payment for the physicians ... is not considered to be the method of choice."

The evidence as to mail fraud was that defendant repeatedly ordered monitors for his own patients even though use of the device was not medically indicated. As a prerequisite for payment, Medicare requires that the service be medically indicated.

The Department of Health and Human Services had promulgated a rule providing that it would pay for Holter-monitoring only if it was in operation for eight hours or more. Defendant routinely certified that the temporal condition had been met, although in fact it had not.

* * *

I. MEDICARE FRAUD

The Medicare fraud statute was amended by P. L. 95–142, 91 Stat. 1183 (1977). Congress, concerned with the growing problem of fraud and abuse in the system, wished to strengthen the penalties to enhance the deterrent effect of the statute. To achieve this purpose, the crime was upgraded from a misdemeanor to a felony.

Another aim of the amendments was to address the complaints of the United States Attorneys who were responsible for prosecuting fraud cases. They informed Congress that the language of the predecessor statute was "unclear and needed clarification." H. Rep. No. 393, Part II, 95th Cong., 1st Sess. 53, *reprinted in* 1977 U.S. CODE CONG. & AD. NEWS 3039, 3055.

A particular concern was the practice of giving "kickbacks" to encourage the referral of work. Testimony before the Congressional committee was that "physicians often determine which laboratories would do the test work for their medicaid patients by the amount of the kickbacks and rebates offered by the laboratory.... Kickbacks take a number of forms including cash, long-term credit arrangements, gifts, supplies and equipment, and the furnishing of business machines." Id. at 3048–3049.

To remedy the deficiencies in the statute and achieve more certainty, the present version of 42 U.S.C. § 1395nn(b)(2) was enacted. It provides:

"whoever knowingly and willfully offers or pays any remuneration (including any kickback, bribe or rebate) directly or indirectly, overtly or covertly in cash or in kind to induce such person—

(B) to purchase, lease, order, or arrange for or recommend purchasing ... or ordering any ... service or item for which payment may be made ... under this title, shall be guilty of a felony."

The district judge instructed the jury that the government was required to prove that Cardio–Med paid to Dr. Avallone some part of the amount received from Medicare; that defendant caused Cardio–Med to make the payment; and did so knowingly and willfully as well as with the intent to induce Dr. Avallone to use Cardio–Med's services for patients covered by Medicare. The judge further charged that even if the physician interpreting the test did so as a consultant to Cardio–Med, that fact was immaterial if a purpose of the fee was to induce the ordering of services from Cardio–Med.

Defendant contends that the charge was erroneous. He insists that absent a showing that the only purpose behind the fee was to improperly induce future services, compensating a physician for services actually rendered could not be a violation of the statute.

The government argues that Congress intended to combat financial incentives to physicians for ordering particular services patients did not require.

The language and purpose of the statute support the government's view. Even if the physician performs some service for the money received, the potential for unnecessary drain on the Medicare system remains. The statute is aimed at the inducement factor.

The text refers to "any remuneration." That includes not only sums for which no actual service was performed but also those amounts for which some professional time was expended. "Remunerates" is defined as "to pay an equivalent for service." Webster Third New International Dictionary (1966). By including such items as kickbacks and bribes, the statute expands "remuneration" to cover situations where no service is performed. That a particular payment was a remuneration (which implies that a service was rendered) rather than a kickback, does not foreclose the possibility that a violation nevertheless could exist.

In United States v. Hancock, 604 F.2d 999 (7th Cir.1979), the court applied the term "kickback" found in the predecessor statute to payments made to chiropractors by laboratories which performed blood tests. The chiropractors contended that the amounts they received were legitimate handling fees for their services in obtaining, packaging, and delivering the specimens to the laboratories and then interpreting the results. The court rejected that contention and noted, "The potential for increased costs to the Medicare–Medicaid system and misapplication of federal funds is plain, where payments for the exercise of such judgments are added to the legitimate cost of the transaction.... [T]hese are among the evils Congress sought to prevent by enacting the kickback statutes...." Id. at 1001.

Hancock strongly supports the government's position here, because the statute in that case did not contain the word "remuneration." The court nevertheless held that "kickback" sufficiently described the defendants' criminal activity. By adding "remuneration" to the statute in the 1977 amendment, Congress sought to make it clear that even if the transaction was not considered to be a "kickback" for which no service had been rendered, payment nevertheless violated the Act.

We are aware that in United States v. Porter, 591 F.2d 1048 (5th Cir.1979), the Court of Appeals for the Fifth Circuit took a more narrow view of "kickback" than did the court in *Hancock*. *Porter's* interpretation of the predecessor statute which did not include "remuneration" is neither binding nor persuasive. We agree with the Court of Appeals for the Sixth Circuit, which adopted the interpretation of "kickback" used in *Hancock* and rejected that of the *Porter* case. United States v. Tapert, 625 F.2d 111 (6th Cir. 1980).

We conclude that the more expansive reading is consistent with the impetus for the 1977 amendments and therefore hold that the district court correctly instructed the jury. If the payments were intended to induce the physician to use Cardio–Med's services, the statute was violated, even if the payments were also intended to compensate for professional services.

A review of the record also convinces us that there was sufficient evidence to sustain the jury's verdict.

* * *

Having carefully reviewed all of the defendant's allegations, we find no reversible error. Accordingly, the judgment of the district court will be affirmed.

Notes and Questions

1. What is controversial about the *Greber* decision? What kinds of salutary or benign practices might it affect?

2. Other courts dealing with arrangements that have multiple purposes have generally followed *Greber's* holding that the purpose to induce referrals need not be the dominant or sole purpose of the scheme in order to fall within the anti-kickback law's prohibition. See, e.g., United States v. McClatchey, 217 F.3d 823, 834–35 (10th Cir. 2000). However, several decisions have introduced variations on that theme. For example, one court has required proof of a "material purpose" to obtain money for the referral of services to support a conviction under the statute. United States v. Kats, 871 F.2d 105, 108 (9th Cir. 1989). Another, more demanding approach holds that proof that a "primary purpose" of the payment was to induce future referrals is required. United States v. Bay State Ambulance and Hosp. Rental Serv., 874 F.2d 20, 30 (1st Cir. 1989). Not surprisingly, the OIG has chosen to follow the *Greber* standard. 42 C.F.R. § 1001.951(a)(2)(i) (exclusion applies "irrespective of whether the individual or entity may be able to prove that the remuneration was also intended for some other purpose ... "). For criticism of *Greber*, see Eugene E. Elder, The Hypocrisy of the One Purpose Test in the Anti–Kickback Enforcement Law, 11 Medicare Rep. (BNA) 802 (July 28, 2000).

3. What purposes does the anti-kickback legislation serve? Does it advance or impede the provision of quality medical services? What economic or efficiency arguments might be made in support of the law? Can it be argued that the law sweeps too broadly given the dynamics of today's market? At the time the legislation was passed, providers were almost uniformly paid on a cost-based, fee-for-service basis. With much of the private sector comprised of managed care or capitated provider payments, should a less restrictive rule be devised? See James Blumstein, The Fraud and Abuse Statute in an Evolving Health Care Marketplace: Life in the Health Care Speakeasy, 22 Am. J. L. & Med. 205 (1996). For the regulatory response to this problem, see the statutory exception applicable to risk-sharing arrangements, discussed *infra*.

4. With the defendant's intent to obtain referrals in exchange for remuneration as the central issue in most criminal prosecutions under the anti-kickback

statute, courts often must evaluate circumstantial evidence regarding defendant's mental state. The widely noted *McClatchey* case, United States v. McClatchey, 217 F.3d 823 (10th Cir. 2000), involved the appeal from conviction under the act by Dennis McClatchey, Chief Operating Officer of Baptist Medical Center. McClatchey oversaw negotiations with doctors Robert and Ronald LaHue who were principals in Blue Valley Medical Group, a medical practice providing care to nursing home patients. Prior contracts between Baptist and the LaHues had provided for payment of $75,000 per year to the doctors for serving as co-directors of gerontology services at Baptist; however, the LaHues performed almost no services and circumstances strongly suggested that the payments were made in return for their providing patient referrals to Baptist. 217 F.3d at 828–30. The evidence at trial showed that McClatchy directed negotiations which resulted in a revised contract that was legal and that McClatchy sought and received legal advice throughout the process. Weighing competing inferences regarding defendant's intent, the Tenth Circuit upheld a jury verdict convicting McClatchy. The court found that his knowledge that the LaHues had not performed substantial services under prior contracts, that the hospital staff did not want the LaHues' services, and that McClatchey stressed the importance of maximizing admissions from BVMG patients constituted sufficient evidence to sustain the jury's findings. Id. at 830. Concerning McClatchey's reliance on counsel, the court held as follows:

> McClatchey also argues that his actions throughout the negotiation process cannot give rise to an inference of his criminal intent because they were entirely directed and controlled by legal counsel. McGrath [a subordinate directly involved in the negotiations with the LaHues] testified however, that he and McClatchey told the lawyers what services to include in the contracts, not visa versa. Thus, the jury could reasonably attribute to McClatchey and McGrath both the decision to remove a minimum hour provision from the contract after the LaHues objected to such a requirement and the inculpatory inference of intent that can be drawn therefrom. Moreover, it was not the attorneys but McClatchey, Anderson, and McGrath who made the important decision to negotiate a new contract rather than ending Baptist's relationship with BVMG. Finally, McClatchey did not always heed the attorneys' advice. . . . The evidence, therefore, permitted the jury to reasonably reject McClatchey's good faith reliance on counsel defense and instead find he harbored the specific intent to violate the Act.

Id. at 830–31. The advice of counsel "defense" in this context really amounts to a claim that the government did not establish that the defendant "knowingly and willfully" engaged in unlawful kickback activities. To avail oneself of this defense, however, the defendant must establish that he disclosed all relevant facts to his attorneys and that he relied in good faith on that advice and acted in strict accordance with it. See Gosfield, *supra*, § 2:67. What problems do you foresee for a defendant wanting to invoke this defense at trial? The district court acquitted two attorneys indicted for their role in the scheme finding they did not cover up fraud with sham agreements, had "attempted to advise their clients to engage in legal transactions," and relied on clients' representations as to their conduct. See Osteopathy, Former Hospital Executives Convicted by Kansas Jury in Bribery Scheme, 8 Health L. Rep. (Apr. 18, 1999). What implications do these holdings have for attorney-client communications? The government also named several prominent attorneys as unindicted co-conspirators. Joan Burgess Killgore, Comment: Surgery with a Meat Cleaver: The Criminal Indictment of Health Care Attorneys in United States v. Anderson, 43 St. Louis U. L.J. 1215 (1999). A court subsequently held that the government had violated the due process rights of these individuals by identifying them in a pre-trial motion.

5. *Greber* dealt with the issue of whether defendant's evidence of purpose satisfied the statutory standard that remuneration be given or received "in return for" an item or service reimbursable under Medicare or Medicaid. A second and distinct *mens rea* requirement concerns whether defendant knew that the transaction was unlawful. In Hanlester Network v. Shalala, 51 F.3d 1390 (9th Cir. 1995), the Ninth Circuit held that the statute's "knowing and willful" language requires the government to prove not only that the defendant intentionally engaged in conduct prohibited by the statute, but that the defendant did so with the knowledge that his conduct violated the law. Under this standard, the government must show not only that the defendant intentionally entered into a referral arrangement later determined to violate the statute, but also that when the defendant entered into the arrangement, or while the defendant benefited from it, he or she knew the arrangement violated the dictates of the anti-kickback law.

D. STATUTORY EXCEPTIONS, SAFE HARBORS AND FRAUD ALERTS

The fraud and abuse statute contains several common sense exceptions. For example, discounts or reductions in price obtained by providers of services, literally proscribed by the language of the statute, are permitted if properly disclosed and reflected in the claimed costs or charges of the provider. Likewise, amounts paid by employers to employees and rebates obtained by group purchasing organizations are exempted under specified circumstances. (The employment exception is discussed in Note 2 following U.S. v. Starks, supra.) The Health Insurance Portability and Accountability Act of 1996 added an important new exception for "risk-sharing" arrangements. As described below, this exception is designed to answer criticisms that the law unreasonably deters arrangements such as capitated payments that foster delivery of cost-effective care and pose no substantial risk of overutilization, the key concern of the anti-kickback rules.

In addition to these statutory exceptions, the Secretary of HHS, acting pursuant to Congressional directive, has promulgated so-called "Safe Harbor" regulations to describe conduct that is not criminal under the fraud and abuse laws. This is a somewhat unusual provision in that it permits an administrative agency to designate conduct otherwise illegal under federal law as not subject to prosecution by the Justice Department. 42 C.F.R. § 1001.952. The total number of safe harbors now stands at twenty-five. Among the more important of the safe harbors are the following:

Rental, Personal Services, and Management Contracts

Three safe harbors for space and equipment rentals and for personal services and management contracts have very similar standards. Leases for space or equipment must be in writing and signed by the parties; must identify the space or equipment covered; must specify when and for how long space or equipment will be used and the precise rental charge for each use if the lease is not for full time use; and must be for at least one year. The amount of rent must be set in advance, must not take into account the volume and value of any referrals or business generated, and, most importantly, must reflect the fair market value of the space or equipment. Fair market value is defined as the value of the property for "general commercial purposes," or "the value of the equipment when obtained from a manufacturer or professional distributor," and cannot take into account the proximity or convenience of the equipment or space to the referral course. The requirements for personal services or management contracts are nearly identical to the rental provisions.

Personal Services and Management Contracts

This provision excepts payments made by a principal to an agent as compensation for the agent's services for written agency agreements of at least one year, provided the agreement specifies and covers all the services that the agent provides during that period. The aggregate compensation for the services must be set in advance, consistent with fair market value in an arms-length transaction, and not take into account the volume or values of any referrals or business otherwise generated between the parties. An agent is defined as any person other than an employee of the principal who has an agreement to perform services for or on behalf of the principal.

Sale of Practice

A limited safe harbor exists to protect sales of practices by retiring physicians. The sale must be completed within one year from the date of the agreement, after which the selling practitioner must no longer be in a professional position to refer Medicare or Medicaid patients or otherwise generate business for the purchasing practitioner. Sale options are not permitted unless they are completely performed within a year. The increasingly common practice of hospitals and MSOs purchasing the practices of physicians who thereafter are retained on staff is explicitly not protected by this rule, though a separate safe harbor for physician recruitment currently under consideration may protect some of these activities, and buying out a physician for a flat payment and then later employing the physician may be permissible.

Practitioner Recruitment

A practitioner recruitment safe harbor protects recruitment efforts by hospitals and entities located in government-specified health professional shortage areas (HPSAs). It permits payments or other exchanges to induce practitioners relocating from a different geographic area or new practitioners (in practice within their current specialty for less than one year) provided nine conditions are met. Among those conditions are that the agreement be in writing; that at least 75 per cent of the business of the relocated practice come from new patients; that at least 75 per cent of the new practice revenue be generated from the HPSA or other defined underserved areas; that the practitioner not be barred from establishing staff privileges with or referring to other entities; and that benefits and amendments to the contract may not be based on the value or volume of practitioners' referrals.

Safe Harbor for Price Reductions Offered to
Eligible Managed Care Organizations

After a lengthy negotiated rulemaking process, the OIG announced two interim final rules to implement the statutory exception governing certain Eligible Managed Care Organizations (EMCOs). The two safe harbors apply to (1) financial arrangements between managed care entities paid by a federal health care program on a capitated basis and individuals or entities agreeing to provide to the manage care entity items or services under a written agreement and (2) financial agreements that, through a risk sharing arrangement, place individuals or entities at "substantial financial risk" for the cost or utilization of the items or services which they are obligated to provide. Recognizing that EMCOs having risk contracts which operate on a capitated rather than fee-for-service basis present little risk of overutilization and increased health program costs, the safe harbor protects price reductions (and other exchanges or remunerations) between eligible MCOs and individuals and entities. The second part of the price reduction safe harbor regulation addresses financial arrangements (subcontracts) between first tier contractors and other individuals or entities, known as downstream contractors.

Referral Agreements for Specialty Services

This safe harbor is designed to reduce any untoward effects that the anti-kickback laws may have on continuity of care and patient access to specialists. It protects any exchange of value among individuals and entities if one provider agrees to refer a patient to another provider for the rendering of a specialty service in exchange for an agreement by the other party to refer that patient back at a later time, as long as neither party may pay the other for the referral, although members of the same group practice may share revenues of the group practice.

Ambulatory Surgery Centers

This safe harbor provides a detailed regulatory scheme that protects returns on an investment interest, such as dividend or interest income, in four kinds of Ambulatory Surgery Centers (ASCs): surgeon-owned ASCs, single-specialty ASCs, multi-specialty ASCs, and hospital/physician ASCs. It does not apply to an ASC located on a hospital's premises that shares operating or recovery room space with the hospital for treatment of the hospital's inpatients or outpatients. Advisory Opinion 03–05, set forth following this note, deals with this Safe Harbor.

Investment Interests

This complex safe harbor provides that there is no violation for returns on "investment interests" including both equity and debt interests in corporations, partnerships and other entities held directly or indirectly through family members or other indirect ownership vehicles. It covers, first, investments in large, publicly-traded entities registered with the SEC and having $50 million in net tangible assets. The investment must also be obtained on terms equally available to the public, the entity must market items and services in the same way to investors and non-investors, and must comply with other requirements. Second, certain investments in small entities are permitted provided no more than 40 percent of the value of the investment interests in each class of investment is held by persons who are in a position to make or influence referrals to, furnish items or services to, or otherwise generate business for the entity. Moreover, no more than 40 percent of the gross revenue of the entity may come from referrals, items or services from investors. A number of other requirements apply including several that are different for active investors and passive investors. The 1999 amendments to this safe harbor allow for higher investment percentages in medically underserved areas. The importance of this safe harbor is limited by the fact that it does not shelter arrangements covered by the Stark Law (discussed in the next section of this chapter) which applies different standards to investments. However, for services not covered by Stark, the safe harbor has continuing importance.

Group Practices

A safe harbor shelters payments (such as dividend or interest income) received in return for investment interests in group practices. 42 C.F.R. § 1001.952(p). It covers business arrangements having centralized decision-making, pooled expenses and revenues, and profit distribution systems "not based on satellite offices operating substantially as if they were separate enterprises or profit centers." Modeled on the Stark exception, it adopts that statute's definition of "group practice" and provides that income from ancillary services must meet the Stark definition of "in-office ancillary services."

Electronic Health Records Arrangements and Electronic Prescribing

Two safe harbors adopted in 2006 establish conditions under which hospitals and certain other entities may (1) donate to physicians interoperable electronic health records (EHR), software, information technology, and training services and (2) provide physicians with hardware, software, or information technology and training services necessary and used solely for electronic prescribing. Substantially identical standards were adopted as exceptions to the Stark Law discussed in the next section.

The electronic prescribing safe harbor covers items and services that are necessary and used solely to transmit and receive electronic prescription information and requires that donated technology comply with standards adopted by the Secretary of HHS. Protected donors and recipients are: (1) hospitals to members of their medical staffs; (2) group practices to physician members; (3) Prescription Drug Plan sponsors and Medicare Advantage organizations to network pharmacist and pharmacies, and prescribing health care professionals. There is no limit on the value of donations but donors may not select recipients using any method that takes into account the volume or value of referrals from the recipient or other business generated between the parties.

The EHR safe harbor protects arrangements involving electronic health records software or information technology and training services necessary and used predominately to create, maintain, transmit, or receive electronic health records. While neither hardware nor software with a core functionality other than electronic health records is covered, software packages may include functions related to patient administration such as clinical support. Protected donors are individuals and entities that provide covered services to any Federal health care program and health plans. Donors may not select recipients using any method that takes into account directly the volume or value of referrals from the recipient or other business between the parties and while there is no limit on the aggregate value of technology that may qualify for safe harbor protection, recipients must pay 15 percent of the donor's cost for the donated technology.

A wide variety of other arrangements are covered by safe harbors, including subsidies for obstetrical malpractice insurance subsidies, and waivers of copayments and deductibles for inpatient hospital care and group purchasing organizations. Many of these safe harbors are narrowly drawn and afford only limited protection despite sometimes broader coverage sometimes implied by their titles. Moreover, safe harbor protection requires compliance with every requirement of all applicable safe harbors and the OIG has refused to adopt a standard of "substantial compliance" or to declaim intention to pursue "technical" or de minimis violations. See 56 Fed. Reg. 35,953, 35,957 (July 29, 1991). At the same time however, the safe harbors are not standards; conduct falling outside their boundaries may still pass muster under the intent-based statutory standard.

Note on Gainsharing and the Anti–Kickback Laws

An area of continuing controversy involving fraud and abuse laws has been hospital "gainsharing" programs. Broadly defined, the term refers to "an arrangement in which a hospital gives physicians a share of any reduction in the hospital's costs attributable in part to the physicians' efforts." Hearing on Gainsharing Before the Subcomm. on Health of the H. Comm. on Ways and Means, 109th Cong. (2005) (testimony of Lewis Morris, Chief Counsel to the Inspector General, U.S. Dep't of Health and Human Services)[hereinafter Morris Testimony], available at http://waysandmeans.house.gov/hearings.asp?formmode= view & id=3828. Some gainsharing practices are narrowly-targeted, such as those giving physicians a financial incentive to reduce the use of specific medical devices and supplies, to switch to specific products that are less expensive, or to adopt specific clinical practices or protocols that reduce costs. More comprehensive—and legally problematic—arrangements include those that offer the physician payments to reduce total average costs per case below target amounts. Of special concern for the government have been "black box" gainsharing arrangements that give physicians money for overall cost savings without knowing what specific actions physicians are taking to generate those savings. See Office of Inspector General, Dep't Health & Human Services, Special Advisory Bulletin: Gainsharing Arrangements and CMPs for Hospital Payments to Physicians to Reduce or Limit Services to Beneficiaries (July 1999), available at http://oig.hhs.gov/fraud/docs/ alertsandbulletins/gainsh.htm.

It can readily be seen that gainsharing arrangements may help align physician incentives with those of a hospital and thereby promote hospital cost reductions. Indeed, as discussed in Chapter 11, prospective payment under Medicare provides a strong impetus for hospitals to find a way to induce independent physicians to adopt practices that reduce costs. See Richard Saver, Squandering the Gain: Gainsharing and the Continuing Dilemma of Physician Financial Incentives, 98 Nw. U.L. Rev. 145, 146 (2003). At the same time, such payments may encourage physicians to use a particular provider, implicating concerns that underlie the anti-kickback law and the Stark Law (discussed in the next section of this chapter). Finally, gainsharing arrangements may serve as an inducement to deny services that are medically necessary. This risk is directly addressed by the Civil Monetary Penalty Law (CMP), 42 U.S.C. § 1320a–7a(b), which prohibits a hospital from "knowingly making a payment, directly or indirectly, to a physician as an inducement to reduce or limit items or services" furnished to Medicare or Medicaid beneficiaries under a physician's direct care.

The Office of Inspector General has been extremely wary of gainsharing arrangements, but has recently issued a series of favorable advisory opinions in which it indicated it would not challenge certain carefully-tailored proposals. Office of Inspector General, Dep't Health & Human Services, Advisory Opinions

05–01 through 05–06 (2005), available at http://oig.hhs.gov/fraud/advisoryopinions/ opinions.html. Notably, the OIG's General Counsel has cautioned that despite these rulings, "absent a change in law, it is not currently possible for gainsharing arrangements to be structured without implicating the fraud and abuse laws." Morris Testimony, supra. In each letter the OIG stressed the significance of safeguards and characteristics of the arrangement that alleviated its concerns. Three important factors guide the OIG's analysis: accountability, quality controls and safeguards against payments for referrals. To ensure accountability, OIG favors transparent arrangements that "clearly and separately identify the actions that will result in cost savings," thus permitting both objective reviews by the government (and by the malpractice system) and a more complete understanding by patients and their doctors. Morris Testimony, supra. To ensure that quality of care is not impaired, the OIG deems it important to have qualified, outside, independent parties "perform a medical expert review of each cost-savings measure to assess the potential impact on patient care" and to establish baseline thresholds based on historic data that set limits on reductions of service so they do not impair patient safety. Where product standardization incentives are involved, the OIG looks favorably on assurances that individual physicians will still have available the same selection of devices and can make a case-by-case determination of the most appropriate device for the patient.

Finally, the OIG's advisory opinions insist on certain safeguards to prevent gainsharing from being used to reward or induce patient referrals. Consider the following limitations on how payments are calculated and distributed to physicians contained in the advisory opinions:

- Limiting participation to physicians already on the hospital's medical staff;
- Limiting the amount, duration, and scope of the payments;
- Distributing the gainsharing profits on a per capita basis to all physicians in a single-specialty group practice;
- Basing cost sharing payments on all surgeries, regardless of payor, with procedures not being disproportionately performed on Medicare or Medicaid patients.

What policies of the anti-kickback law does each safeguard serve and how does it do so?

While many support steps to legalize gainsharing on a wider scale, there is still considerable uncertainty about the circumstances in which gainsharing should be permitted and what regulations are needed to assure quality and avoid the risks inherent in payment for referrals. The DRA 2005 mandated that HHS establish a qualified gainsharing demonstration program under which the Secretary shall approve up to six demonstration projects to test and evaluate methodologies and arrangements between hospitals and physicians. See DRA 5007 Medicare Hospital Gainsharing Solicitation, http://www:cms.hhs.gov/DemoProjectsEval Rpts/downloads/DRA 5007 Solicitation.pdf. What information would you recommend be gathered to determine whether new regulations governing gainsharing arrangements are needed?

Problem: Sorting It Out

When you have completed your analysis of the problems at the beginning of this section, reconstruct the arrangements there presented to accomplish as substantially as possible the legitimate goals of the parties to the transaction without offending the fraud and abuse laws.

Next, consider the following problems affecting the formation of integrating organizations discussed in Chapter 11. For each of the scenarios below, explain how the anti-kickback law and any relevant safe harbor might apply and what steps should be taken to reduce legal risks.

- A hospital-controlled MSO provides staff, administrative services and equipment rentals to member physicians at "cost" or at levels below the fees it charges to non-members.

- An Integrated Delivery System purchases the tangible assets and patient records of a physician practice and pays on a five-year installment arrangement. The physicians work as employees at the hospital.

- A hospital-controlled MSO leases office space to its member physicians pursuant to a signed, written agreement for a five-year term. The lease terms reflect the fair market value of the leased space. In each of the first three years, the MSO has lost money.

- A PHO is jointly owned (50–50 equity split) by a hospital and its physicians. The hospital contributes 80% of the PHO's capital.

III.   THE STARK LAW: A TRANSACTIONAL APPROACH TO SELF–REFERRALS

An alternative approach to dealing with fraud and abuse is to list and describe exhaustively transactions that are alternatively legitimate or illegitimate under the law. The Ethics in Patient Referrals Act (commonly referred to as the Stark Law in recognition of the legislation's principal sponsor, Rep. Fortney "Pete" Stark) does just that with respect to physician referrals for certain Medicare-financed services in which the physician (or immediate family member) has a financial interest. Besides making it illegal for physicians to make such referrals, Stark also prohibits any billings for services provided pursuant to illegal referrals. As originally enacted, Stark only applied to referrals for clinical laboratory services. Its reach was significantly expanded by the 1993 Omnibus Budget Reconciliation Act. As a result Stark now applies to services paid for by Medicaid as well as by Medicare and covers eleven "designated health services" (DHS): clinical laboratory services; physical therapy services; occupational therapy services; radiology, including MRI, CAT and ultrasound services; radiation therapy services and supplies; durable medical equipment and supplies; parenteral and enteral nutrients, equipment, and supplies; prosthetics, orthotics, and prosthetic devices; home health services and supplies; outpatient prescription drugs; and inpatient and outpatient hospital services. No payment can be made by Medicare or Medicaid for referrals for such services where the referring physician or member of his family has a financial interest. Any amounts billed in violation of the section must be refunded. Any person knowingly billing or failing to make a refund in violation of the prohibition is subject to a civil fine of $15,000 per item billed and to exclusion.

The Stark legislation responded to increasing evidence that "self-referrals" had become quite common, and quite costly. An OIG study issued in 1989 found that of 2690 physicians who responded to its study, 12 percent had ownership interests and 8 percent had compensation arrangements with businesses to which they referred patients. Office of Inspector General, Financial Arrangements Between Physicians and Health Care Businesses: Report to Congress (1989). It further determined that nationally 25 percent of independent clinical laboratories (ICLs), 27 percent of independent laboratories, and 8 percent of durable medical equipment suppliers were owned at least in part by referring physicians. Beneficiaries treated by physicians who owned or invested in ICLs received 45 percent more clinical laboratory services and 34 percent more services directly from ICLs than beneficiaries in general, resulting in $28 million in additional costs to the Medicare program. Do studies finding high rates of self-referral patterns establish that the additional services provided were unnecessary? Is strong and consistent empirical evidence of higher utilization among self-referring physicians sufficient to justify legislative decisions to broadly proscribe the practice?

Note that, subject to the exceptions discussed below, Stark adopts a "bright line" test. Unlike Medicare fraud and abuse laws, there is no requirement that the conduct involve the knowing and willful receipt of a kickback: if no exception applies, the law has been violated. However, as we will see, CMS has promulgated numerous exceptions and the Federal Register contains hundreds of pages of detailed regulations and commentary purporting to clarify or simplify compliance with the law.

A. SCOPE OF THE PROHIBITION

Stark I and II prohibit physicians who have (or whose immediate family member has) a "financial relationship" with a provider of designated health services from making "referrals" of Medicare or Medicaid patients to such providers for purposes of receiving any of the eleven "designated health services." The key terms are defined in 42 U.S.C. § 1395nn as follows:

(a) Prohibitions of certain referrals

* * *

(2) Financial relationship specified

For purposes of this section, a financial relationship of a physician (or an immediate family member of such physician) with an entity specified in this paragraph is—

(A) except as provided in subsections (c) and (d) of this section, an ownership or investment interest in the entity, or

(B) except as provided in subsection (e) of this section, a compensation arrangement (as defined in subsection (h)(1) of this section) between the physician (or an immediate family member of such physician) and the entity.

An ownership or investment interest described in subparagraph (A) may be through equity, debt, or other means and includes an interest in an entity that holds an ownership or investment interest in any entity providing the designated health service.

* * *

(h) Definitions and special rules

For purposes of this section:

(1) Compensation arrangement; remuneration

(A) The term "compensation arrangement" means any arrangement involving any remuneration between a physician (or an immediate family member of such physician) and an entity other than an arrangement involving only remuneration described in subparagraph (C).

(B) The term "remuneration" includes any remuneration, directly or indirectly, overtly or covertly, in cash or in kind.

* * *

(5) Referral; referring physician

(A) Physicians' services

Except as provided in subparagraph (C), in the case of an item or service for which payment may be made under part B of this subchapter, the request by a physician for the item or service, including the request by a physician for a consultation with another physician (and any test or procedure ordered by, or to be performed by (or under the supervision of) that other physician), constitutes a "referral" by a "referring physician."

* * *

(6) Designated health services

The term "designated health services" means any of the following items or services:

(A) Clinical laboratory services.

(B) Physical therapy services.

(C) Occupational therapy services.

(D) Radiology services, including magnetic resonance imaging, computerized axial tomography scans, and ultrasound services.

(E) Radiation therapy services and supplies.

(F) Durable medical equipment and supplies.

(G) Parenteral and enteral nutrients, equipment, and supplies.

(H) Prosthetics, orthotics, and prosthetic devices and supplies.

(I) Home health services.

(J) Outpatient prescription drugs.

(K) Inpatient and outpatient hospital services.

Notes and Questions

1. Note several things about these provisions. First, recall that the principal problem identified by academic studies that led to the enactment of Stark I was excessive and perhaps inappropriate referrals by physicians to entities in which they had an ownership interest. Why did Congress extend the law's reach beyond "ownership and investment interests?" Was this a necessary or wise policy choice? Second, Stark II reaches arrangements in which the flow of money is reversed from the normal self-referral pattern, i.e., the physician pays the entity for services provided. Why should such arrangements be outlawed? Third, consider the broad sweep of the term "referral" as used in the Act. Suppose Dr. Gillespe requests a consultation from Dr. Demento who in turn orders a lab test and physical therapy for the patient. For what referrals is Dr. Gillespe responsible?

2. Complying with the Stark law may pose problems for integrated organizations. Consider a joint venture PHO entity which is owned by staff physicians and

a hospital in which the PHO will negotiate and administer managed care contracts for the physicians and the hospital. Assume the physicians have been given 50 percent ownership in the entity even though the bulk of the start-up costs were paid by the hospital. Do the physicians have an ownership or investment interest in the hospital? Is there a compensation arrangement? The answer is that no ownership or investment interest is present because the participating physicians have an ownership interest in the PHO, not the hospital to which they refer, and the PHO has no ownership interest in the hospital. A compensation arrangement may well exist because physicians may receive an indirect form of remuneration when, after an HMO contract is secured by the PHO, they begin to refer patients to the hospital. While conceivably certain exceptions might apply, the arrangement is obviously risky. See Leonard C. Homer, How New Federal Laws Prohibiting Physician Self–Referrals Affect Integrated Delivery Systems, 11 HealthSpan 21 (Apr. 1994).

3. Strong criticisms have been lodged against Stark. Organized medicine argues that the law is too complex and needlessly duplicative of other laws affecting self-referrals. Moreover, opponents assert that the law goes far beyond prohibiting physician ownership of facilities and invites governmental "micromanagement" of evolving network structures. Even Representative Stark has asked the Institute of Medicine to study ways to improve and simplify the statute. Medicare: Stark Asks Institute of Medicine to Form Working Group on Self–Referral Laws, Health Care Daily (BNA) (July 28, 1998). On the other side, the law has been defended as a pragmatic legislative choice that avoids the pitfalls of case-by-case litigation over issues of intent or reasonableness while unambiguously barring the most risk-prone referrals and permitting the most efficiency-enhancing arrangements. One proposal, vetoed by President Clinton in 1995, would have eliminated the law's ban on "compensation arrangements." Would confining Stark Law's coverage to ownership and investment interests capture the most problematic relationships, or as Representative Stark has opined, would it create a "loophole you can drive an Armored Division through?"

B. EXCEPTIONS

The Stark anti-referral law is an example of what is sometimes called an "exceptions bill." It sweepingly prohibits self-referrals but then legitimizes a large number of specific arrangements. Stark's exceptions are of three kinds: (1) those applicable to ownership or investment financial relationships; (2) those applicable to compensation arrangements; and (3) generic exceptions that apply to all financial arrangements.

Many of the exceptions cover self-referral arrangements that pose little risk of abuse. For example, the statute rules out liability where referring physicians' incentives are controlled in some way, as with prepaid health plans; or where other circumstances reduce the risk of excess utilization, such as where the physician is an employee of the entity to which the referral is made, has a personal services contract or a space or equipment rental that meets commercial reasonableness tests or engages in isolated, one-time transactions with the entity. One notable exception, the "whole hospital exception," 42 U.S.C. 1395nn(e)d(3) which allows referring physicians who are "authorized to provide services at a hospital" to invest in that hospital, (but not "in a subdivision" thereof), gave ruse to the specialty hospital phenomenon discussed in Chapter 13. Perhaps the most important category, however, involves situations in which the physician is part of a group practice that is directly involved in providing the service. These latter provisos, the ancillary services and group practice exceptions, which do not necessarily involve circumstances that reduce the threat of overutilization, seem primarily designed to encourage the integration of practice among physicians.

Problem: Space and Equipment Rentals, Physician Recruitment

The Stark Law covers much of the same conduct as the bribe and kickback prohibition, but the legislation has its own exceptions that are worded somewhat differently. How does your analysis of problems 1 and 4 at pages ___ change under the exceptions reproduced below?

42 U.S.C. § 1395nn.

(e) Exceptions relating to other compensation arrangements

The following shall not be considered to be a compensation arrangement described in subsection (a)(2)(B) of this section:

(1) Rental of office space; rental of equipment

(A) Office space

Payments made by a lessee to a lessor for the use of premises if—

(i) the lease is set out in writing, signed by the parties, and specifies the premises covered by the lease,

(ii) the space rented or leased does not exceed that which is reasonable and necessary for the legitimate business purposes of the lease or rental and is used exclusively by the lessee when being used by the lessee, * * *

(iii) the lease provides for a term of rental or lease for at least 1 year,

(iv) the rental charges over the term of the lease are set in advance, are consistent with fair market value, and are not determined in a manner that takes into account the volume or value of any referrals or other business generated between the parties,

(v) the lease would be commercially reasonable even if no referrals were made between the parties, and

(vi) the lease meets such other requirements as the Secretary may impose by regulation as needed to protect against program or patient abuse.

* * *

(3) Personal service arrangements

[Certain personal service contracts are permitted if they meet certain conditions, including the condition that compensation not be related to the volume or value of referrals.]

* * *

(5) Physician recruitment

In the case of remuneration which is provided by a hospital to a physician to induce the physician to relocate to the geographic area served by the hospital in order to be a member of the medical staff of the hospital, if—

(A) the physician is not required to refer patients to the hospital,

(B) the amount of the remuneration under the arrangement is not determined in a manner that takes into account (directly or indirectly) the volume or value of any referrals by the referring physician, and

(C) the arrangement meets such other requirements as the Secretary may impose by regulation as needed to protect against program or patient abuse.

Note on Fair Market Value

The meaning of "fair market value" is often critical for determining the legality of business arrangements under both Stark and the Anti–Kickback law. For example, in United States ex rel. Goodstein v. McLaren Regional Med. Ctr., 202 F. Supp. 2d 671 (E.D. Mich. 2002), a qui tam action in which the government intervened, the issue was whether the defendant medical center had paid physicians illegal remuneration disguised as a lease agreement for the office building owned by the physicians' limited liability company. Because the physician defendants referred Medicare patients to the medical center and operated their practice out of the leased offices, and the payments allegedly violated both Stark and the anti-kickback statutes, the government asserted that false claims were involved. The court rejected the contention that the amount of rent paid was excessive, concluding that the lease agreement was an arms length transaction and that the lease rate set forth in the agreement was consistent with fair market value. Id. at 675. The court reasoned that defendants' expert testimony was sufficiently grounded on facts or data, was a product of reliable principles and methods, and reliably applied those principles to the facts in evidence. Id. at 679. Despite the fact that their appraisals were prepared in response to litigation, defendants won the "battle of experts" because of defects in the government's case, including the failure of its witnesses to consider certain comparables and their inconsistent application of valuation methodology. Moreover, the court held that the lease rate was not determined in a manner that took into account the value of potential patient referrals. Id. at 686. Do you find this holding controversial in view of the fact that the medical center had insisted on non-compete provisions and retained the right to vacate the leased space if the physician group ever moved out of the building (which the government had claimed "could have deprived [the medical center] of capturing a 'steady flow' of patient referrals)"? What if an arrangement satisfies the fair market value test, but the arrangement was nevertheless "influenced by the value or volume of referrals," e.g., a hospital chooses to enter into a lease with physicians at FMV, but decided to do so because it would result in referrals. For a discussion of this aspect of McClaran, see David M. Deaton, What is "Safe" about the Government's Recent Interpretation of the Anti–Kickback Statute Safe Harbors? ... And Since When Was Stark an Intent–Based Statute?, 36 J. Health L. 549 (2003).

In the context of hospitals acquiring physician practices, the future revenue stream from referrals by the acquired physicians is almost invariably an important factor for a hospital deciding whether it will buy the practice. Yet the anti-kickback law squarely prohibits any excess payment that could be considered "remuneration" for such referrals. Hence, it is necessary to separate out the value of referrals before ascertaining the fair market value of the practice. In United States ex rel. Obert–Hong v. Advocate Health Care, 211 F. Supp. 2d 1045, 1049 n.2 (N.D. Ill. 2002), a district court acknowledged the difficulty in doing so:

> We note that fair market value here may differ from traditional economic valuation formulae. Normally, we would expect the acquisition price to account for potential revenues from future referrals. Because the Anti–Kickback Act prohibits any inducement for those referrals, however, they

must be excluded from any calculation of fair value here. See 42 C.F.R. §§ 1001.952(b) and (c). There is, nonetheless, some value that would be considered fair and would comply with the statute.

The court went on to find the complaint failed to allege any facts such as what assets were acquired, their purported value, or the amount actually paid, from which it could draw such an inference that the hospital's payment exceeded fair market value. Id. at 1049. What, then, is the value of the practice to the hospital?

The court also rejected the claim that the requirement (in their employment contracts) that the doctors selling their practices refer their patients to defendant hospitals was, by definition, an inducement. It noted that both "[t]he Stark and Anti–Kickback statutes are designed to remove economic incentives from medical referrals, not to regulate typical hospital-physician employment relationships . . . [and] [b]oth statutes explicitly include employee exceptions." Id. at 1050.

Problem: Group Practices

Drs. Chung, Snyder, Williams, Mendez, Patel, and Jones each operate independent solo practices. All have offices within a three square mile area, but none share offices with each other. Several years ago, they formed a joint venture to provide a variety of laboratory services to their patients. Their attorney has now informed them that their joint venture violates the prohibitions of the Stark legislation. He has suggested that they consider forming a group practice to operate the laboratory. What steps must they take to form a group practice that will permit them to operate a laboratory together under the relevant language of revised 42 U.S.C. § 1395nn?

42 U.S.C. § 1395nn:

(b) General exceptions to both ownership and compensation arrangement prohibitions

[The self-referral prohibitions] of this section shall not apply in the following cases:

(1) Physicians' services

In the case of physicians' services * * * provided personally by (or under the personal supervision of) another physician in the same group practice (as defined in subsection (h)(4) of this section) as the referring physician.

(2) In-office ancillary services

In the case of services (other than durable medical equipment (excluding infusion pumps) and parenteral and enteral nutrients, equipment, and supplies)—

(A) that are furnished—

(i) personally by the referring physician, personally by a physician who is a member of the same group practice as the referring physician, or personally by individuals who are directly supervised by the physician or by another physician in the group practice, and

(ii)(I) in a building in which the referring physician (or another physician who is a member of the same group practice) furnishes physicians' services unrelated to the furnishing of designated health services, or

(II) in the case of a referring physician who is a member of a group practice, in another building which is used by the group practice—

(aa) for the provision of some or all of the group's clinical laboratory services, or (bb) for the centralized provision of the group's designated health services (other than clinical laboratory services), unless the Secretary determines other terms and conditions under which the provision of such services does not present a risk of program or patient abuse, and

(B) that are billed by the physician performing or supervising the services, by a group practice of which such physician is a member under a billing number assigned to the group practice, or by an entity that is wholly owned by such physician or such group practice, * * *

* * *

(h)(4)

(A) Definition of group practice

The term "group practice" means a group of 2 or more physicians legally organized as a partnership, professional corporation, foundation, not-for-profit corporation, faculty practice plan, or similar association—

(i) in which each physician who is a member of the group provides substantially the full range of services which the physician routinely provides, including medical care, consultation, diagnosis, or treatment, through the joint use of shared office space, facilities, equipment and personnel,

(ii) for which substantially all of the services of the physicians who are members of the group are provided through the group and are billed under a billing number assigned to the group and amounts so received are treated as receipts of the group,

(iii) in which the overhead expenses of and the income from the practice are distributed in accordance with methods previously determined,

(iv) except as provided in subparagraph (B)(i), in which no physician who is a member of the group directly or indirectly receives compensation based on the volume or value of referrals by the physician,

(v) in which members of the group personally conduct no less than 75 percent of the physician-patient encounters of the group practice, and

(vi) which meets such other standards as the Secretary may impose by regulation.

(B) Special rules

(i) Profits and productivity bonuses

A physician in a group practice may be paid a share of overall profits of the group, or a productivity bonus based on services personally performed or services incident to such personally performed services, so long as the share or bonus is not determined in any manner which is directly related to the volume or value of referrals by such physician.

Note on Stark Regulations

Complex as the statute might seem, it is only the beginning. Practitioners must master hundreds of pages of detailed regulations and commentary that interpret and explain the law. The first wave of regulations came in 1995, a full six years after the passage of Stark I, with the issuance of the final rule governing physician self-referrals under that Act. 60 Fed. Reg. 41,914 (Aug. 14,

1995)(codified at 42 C.F.R. § 411.350). To give one important example, one section clarifies the requirement in the "group practices" exception that "substantially all" of the services of the physicians in the group be provided through the group and that these services be billed under a billing number assigned to the group so that amounts so received are treated as receipts of the group. 42 U.S.C. § 1395nn(h)(A)(ii). The Stark I regulations fix the "substantially all" requirement at 75 percent of all patient care services, as measured by time spent (rather than the dollar value of physician services provided) and as an average for all of the group members during a specific 12–month period. Notably, time spent on physician care services includes time devoted to consultation, diagnosis or "any tasks performed ... that address the medical needs of specific patients." The regulations also define group members as "physicians, partners and full-time and part-time physician contractors and employees during the time they furnish services to patients of the group practice...." 42 C.F.R. § 411.351. Why might these provisions be important to physicians?

In March 2004, CMS published its Stark II "Phase II Regulations" which interpreted many statutory provisions, clarified some of the provisions of the "Phase I Regulations" issued in 2001, and added some new exceptions to the law. 69 Fed. Reg. 15,932 (Mar. 26, 2004). A summary of the changes is found in Sonnenschein Nath & Rosenthal, Stark II, Phase II—Highlights and Preliminary Analysis, 13 Health Law Rep. (BNA) 481 (Apr. 1, 2004). Among the more important provisions are those that define or explain a host of terms including the meaning of "fair market value," "referral," "indirect financial relationship," and, the most vexing of technical terms, "to." Critically important is what falls within the definition of certain designated health services, e.g., are PET scans within the statutory definition of "radiology services, including [MRI and CAT] scans and ultrasound services?" Can CMS include it by adopting a regulation?

Exceptions. The Phase I Regulations added six new exceptions governing compensation arrangements and five new all-purpose exceptions. Phase II added six more compensation exceptions and one all-purpose exception, while deleting one all-purpose exception and clarifying some of the 16 exceptions that preceded Phase I. Among the more important are exceptions for: non-monetary compensation to physicians up to a maximum of $300 per year; incidental benefits, such as free parking, for members of a hospital's medical staff; charitable donations by physicians; compliance training given by a hospital to its medical staff; hospital purchases of medical malpractice insurance for OB–GYNs practicing in a physician shortage area; DHS furnished by academic medical providers (subject to many requirements); risk sharing arrangements involving compensation between managed care organizations or IPAs and physicians furnishing services to enrollees in a plan; free or reduced fee services extended as professional courtesy to members of a physician's office staff; arrangements that have "unavoidably and temporarily fallen out of compliance" with an exception; physician recruitment payments permitted for physicians' "relocation" (defined in the regulations); and isolated transactions, defined now to permit certain installment payments. See Sonnenschein, supra. More recently exceptions have been added allowing entities furnishing DHAs to provide hardware or software used solely for electronic prescription systems and for interoperable electronic health records. These exceptions closely parallel the safeharbors established under the antikickback law described supra at pp. 560–64. Do these exceptions seem justified? Do they undermine the overarching purposes of the Stark law or are they pragmatic accommodations?

On August 27, 2007, CMS posted the third phase of the final Stark II regulation (Phase III). Though lengthy and replete with detailed prescriptions, the

Phase III regulations made relatively few major changes to Phase II and do not create any new exceptions. In the preamble to the final rule, CMS emphasized that it continues to interpret the self-referral prohibition narrowly and the exceptions broadly. Only two of the many modifications—an expanded "stand in the shoes" provision for purposes of applying the rule describing direct and indirect compensation arrangements and a modified physician recruitment exception—are viewed as major changes. The first rule provides that a physician is deemed to stand in the shoes of his or her "physician organization" and have the same compensation arrangements with the same parties and on the same terms as does the physician organization. Phase III changes in the physician recruitment rules revise the definition of "geographic area served by the hospital" and add a special optional rule for rural hospitals that expands the geographic area into which a rural hospital may recruit a physician. See also 42 C.F.R. § 411.357(e)(4)(iii), 42 C.F.R. § 411.357(e)(4)(vi) (loosening rules affecting recruitment to rural areas and allowing physician practices to impose practice restrictions on a recruited physician such as reasonable liquidated damages provisions and nonsolicitation clauses as long as they do not unreasonably restrict the recruited physician's ability to practice medicine in the geographic area served by the hospital).

In-Office Ancillary Services. Perhaps the most significant and controversial exception for physicians allows them to benefit from referrals for ancillary services when they are furnished in an office of the referring physician or his or her group. 42 C.F.R. § 411.355(b). As illustrated by the problem preceding this section, this exception allows DHS to be furnished to patients in the same building where the referring physicians provide their regular medical services, or, in the case of a group practice, in a centralized building provided certain conditions are met. On July 2, 2007, as one of several contemplated and potentially far-reaching changes to the Stark regulations, CMS evidenced its frustration with what it regards as abuses of this exception. Although not proposing specific changes to the in-office ancillary services exception, the announcement signaled that it may in the future attempt to curtail use of this and other exceptions that have permitted a "migration of sophisticated and expensive imaging or other equipment to physician offices" that was not intended by the law or the drafters of the exception. 72 Fed. Reg. 38,122, 38,181 (July 12, 2007). Explaining that the purpose of the in-office exception was to allow a limited range of services to be provided in physicians' offices when "necessary to the diagnosis or treatment of the medical condition that brought the patient to the physicians' office," CMS asked for comments on ways to ensure that the DHS qualifying for the exception are truly ancillary to the physician's core medical office practice and are not provided as part of a separate business enterprise. The Agency gave the following illustration of a problematic arrangement that "appears to be nothing more than enterprises established for the self-referral of DHS":

> [A] group practice provides pathology services furnished in a centralized building that is not physically close to any of the other group's other offices, and in some cases, the technical component of such services is furnished by laboratory technologists who are employed by an entity unrelated to the group. The professional component of the pathology services may be furnished to contractor pathologists who have virtually no relationship to the group practice.

72 Fed. Reg. at 38,181. Further, even when ancillary services are furnished in the same building as the group practice's office, CMS apparently is concerned that there may be little interaction between the physicians who are treating the patients and the staff who provide the ancillary services.

A closer examination of the regulations governing this exception reveals how CMS's fine-tuned distinctions defining the scope of the exception allow considerable leeway for physicians to self-refer. To qualify for the exception, the services must be provided either in a "centralized building" used by a group practice to furnish DHS or in the "same building" in which the referring physician (or his or her group) furnishes physician services "unrelated to the furnishing of DHS." CMS has been wary of the potential that the prospect of lucrative ancillary services will prompt physicians to abuse this exception. By way of illustration, the regulations describe a group practice that leases space at an imaging center away from their practice office, provides physician services there one day a week, and then provides imaging services for the rest of the week with no involvement or presence of the group physicians. 69 Fed. Reg. 16,054, 16,072 (Mar. 26, 2004). Consequently, CMS has set very specific limits on what constitutes the "same building" under this exception.

The Phase II regulations specify three situations as the exclusive circumstances that will satisfy the test:

- Where the office is open to patients at least 35 hours per week and is regularly used by the referring physician or group to practice medicine and the referring physician or group provide physician services for at least 30 hours per week (including "some" services that are non-DHS).

- Where the office is open to patients at least 8 hours per week and regularly used by the referring physician or group to practice medicine and furnish physician services for at least 6 hours per week. However, services provided by the referring physician's group practice do not count toward the 6–hour requirement, and the building must be one in which the patient receiving the DHS usually sees the referring physician or a member of his group for physician services.

- Where the office is open to patients at least 8 hours per week and regularly used by the physician or group to practice medicine and furnish physician services for at least 6 hours per week. Under this provision the referring physician must be present and order the DHS in connection with the patient's visit or the physician must be present when the DHS is furnished.

Is there a logic to these detailed rules? Why should there be an exception for in-office ancillary services in the first place? Can you explain to Doctors Chung, et al. (in the problem on p. 572) what options they have if they want to offer ancillary services? What factors will likely influence their decision on which option to choose?

The Stark Law issues also arise in physician joint ventures and contractual arrangements with hospitals. CMS has expressed concern about abuse of exceptions permitting some of these arrangements, and has also announced proposed rules aimed at dealing with areas of concern involving a number of arcane (but potentially lucrative) arrangements, such as "per click" leases, percentage compensation arrangements and "under arrangements" joint ventures. 72 Fed. Reg. at 38,182–83. As hospitals elicit the assistance of their physician staffs in improving quality and efficiency, payments for those services may pose Stark Law problems. The following problem deals with an important exception designed to permit such arrangements.

Problem: Medical Directors

Facing declining admissions and rampant administrative inefficiency, Jeff Lewis, the CEO of Alta Bonita Central Hospital ("ABC") decided to create six new medical directorship positions effective January 1, 2007. Medical directors are typically independent staff physicians who enter into contracts with hospitals to perform certain administrative functions such as assisting in the development and implementation of standards of care, ensuring compliance with JCAHO standards and those of other regulatory bodies, providing consultations on high risk cases, and participating in the work of various hospital committees. The following chart indicates the specialty and number of referrals to ABC for each of its six medical directors for 2006, the year preceding their appointments, and for 2007.

Physician	Specialty	2007 Referrals	2006 Referrals
Dr. Singh	Orthopaedics	80	68
Dr. Kaur	Nephrology/Dialysis	78	46
Dr. LaCombe	OB/GYN	40	38
Dr. Hicks	Cardiology	62	46
Dr. Russell	Surgery	45	45
Dr. Anderson	Geriatrics	50	27

These physicians were all among the top ten referring physicians at ABC, collectively accounting for 65% of the hospital's admissions before they became medical directors. The agreements delineated specific requirements that each medical director was to fulfill, including a requirement that he or she work 16 hours per month and document the number of "actual hours" worked, and specified a monthly stipend. Doctors LaCombe, Hicks and Russell were given stipends of $1500 per month and Doctors Singh, Kaur and Anderson were paid $2500 per month

Recently, the new outside counsel for ABC conducted a compliance audit and found the following in the reporting records of the doctors. Dr. Russell reported 4 hours in March 2007, 3 hours in April 2007, 0 hours in May 2007, and 0 hours in June 2007. Dr. Russell turned in these timesheets in December 2007. Dr. Hicks turned in her timesheets for April, May, June, July, and August 2007 in September 2007, reporting on each timesheet 8 hours of work. Regardless of when the timesheets were turned in or how they were filled out (hours worked, duties completed), all the medical directors were paid their full monthly stipend at the end of every month.

What issues are raised under the Stark Law by the way ABC established its medical directorships and the way it has implemented its agreements? Using the following exception and guidance, how should ABC have proceeded in contracting with its medical directors?

The Personal Services arrangements exception to compensation arrangements, 42 USC § 1395nn(e)(3)(A), provides:

Remuneration from an entity under an arrangement (including remuneration for specific physicians' services furnished to a nonprofit blood center), if—

> (i) the arrangement is set out in writing, signed by the parties, and specifies the services covered by the arrangement,

> (ii) the arrangement covers all of the services to be furnished by the physician (or an immediate family member of such physician) to the entity,

> (iii) the aggregate services contracted for do not exceed those that are reasonable and necessary for the legitimate business purposes of the arrangement,

> (iv) the term of the arrangement is for at least 1 year.

    (v) the compensation to be paid over the term of each arrangement is set in advance, does not exceed fair market value, and except in the case of a physician incentive plan, is not determined in a manner that takes into account the volume or value of any referrals or other business generated between the parties,

    (vi) the services to be performed under the arrangement do not involve the counseling or promotion or a business arrangement or other activity that violates any State or Federal law, and

    (vii) the arrangement meets such other requirements as the Secretary may impose by regulation as needed to protect against program or patient abuse.

42 C.F.R. § 411.351 provides in pertinent part:

Fair market value means the value in arm's-length transactions, consistent with the general market value. "General market value" means the price that an asset would bring as the result of bona fide bargaining between well-informed buyers and sellers who are not otherwise in a position to generate business for the other party; or the compensation that would be included in a service agreement as the result of bona fide bargaining between well-informed parties to the agreement who are not otherwise in a position to generate business for the other party, on the date of acquisition of the asset or at the time of the service agreement. Usually, the fair market price is the price at which bona fide sales have been consummated for assets of like type, quality, and quantity in a particular market at the time of acquisition, or the compensation that as been included in bona fide service agreements with comparable terms at the time of the agreement, where the price or compensation has not been determined in any manner that takes into account the volume or value of anticipated or actual referrals.

    The Phase III Regulations, *supra* state:

    Nothing precludes parties from calculating fair market value using any commercially reasonable methodology that is appropriate under the circumstances and otherwise fits the definition [in the Act] and § 411.351. Ultimately, fair market value is determined based on facts and circumstances. The appropriate method will depend on the nature of the transaction, its location, and other factors. Because the statute covers a broad range of transactions, we cannot comment definitively on particular valuation methodologies.

Chapter 13

ANTITRUST

INTRODUCTION

Antitrust law has played a pivotal role in the development of institutional and professional arrangements in health care. Following the Supreme Court's decision in Goldfarb v. Virginia State Bar, 421 U.S. 773, 95 S.Ct. 2004, 44 L.Ed.2d 572 (1975), which held that "learned professions" were not implicitly exempt from the antitrust laws and found the Sherman Act's interstate commerce requirement satisfied with regard to legal services, extensive antitrust litigation spurred significant changes in the health care industry. Most importantly, cases following *Goldfarb* helped remove a series of private restraints of trade that had long inhibited competition. Antitrust enforcement has come to assume a somewhat different, albeit equally important, focus in today's market. The law has emerged as a powerful overseer of institutional and professional arrangements and ideally helps assure the evolution of market structures that will preserve the benefits of a competitive marketplace.

At the same time, however, applying antitrust law to the health care industry entails some special problems. In particular, the peculiarities and distortions of health care markets often necessitate a sophisticated analysis in order to reach economically sound results. A host of questions arise: What place is there for defenses related to the quality of health care in a statutory regime designed to leave such issues to the market? Does the behavior of not-for-profit health care providers conform to traditional economic assumptions about competitors? If not, should they somehow be treated differently? What impact do the widespread interventions by state and federal government have on the application of federal antitrust law? Do "market failures" in health care, particularly imperfect information, suggest more restrained approaches to applying antitrust law? Perspectives on these and other questions underlying antitrust's role are found in a number of academic writings. See, e.g. Peter J. Hammer & William M. Sage, Antitrust, Health Care Quality, and the Courts, 102 Colum. L. Rev. 545 (2002) (empirical study of case law finding "no cogent theory of nonprice competition has been developed to guide courts" and that decisions "divorce quality from competition rather than factoring it into a competitive mix"); Thomas L. Greaney, Chicago's Procrustean Bed: Applying Antitrust Law in Health Care 71 Antitrust L.J. 857 (2004) (courts' pervasive neglect of market failures in health care antitrust cases systematically biases outcomes); Thomas Rice, The Economics of Health Care

Reconsidered (1998) (questioning whether market forces will produce efficient or socially desirable outcomes); Sara Rosenbaum, A Dose of Reality: Assessing the Federal Trade Commission/Department of Justice Report in an Uninsured, Underserved, and Vulnerable Population Context, 31 J. Health Pol. Pol'y & L. 657 (2006).

The Statutory Framework

The principal antitrust statutes are notable for their highly generalized proscriptions. Rather than specifying activities that it deemed harmful to competition, Congress vested the federal courts with the power to create a common law of antitrust. This chapter will not deal with all of the antitrust laws applicable to the health care industry. The following introduction summarizes portions of the three principal federal statutes: the Sherman Act, the Federal Trade Commission Act, and the Clayton Act. It should be noted that most states have enacted antitrust statutes that are identical to or closely track these federal laws.

Sherman Act § 1: Restraints of Trade

Section One of the Sherman Act prohibits "every contract, combination . . . or conspiracy in restraint of trade." 15 U.S.C. § 1. This broad proscription establishes two substantive elements for finding a violation: an agreement and conduct that restrains trade. The concept of an agreement—the conventional shorthand for Section One's "contract, combination or conspiracy" language—limits the law's reach to concerted activities, i.e., those that are a result of a "meeting of the minds" of two or more independent persons or entities. The second requirement of Section One, that the agreement restrain trade, has generated extensive analysis by the courts. Recognizing that all commercial agreements restrain trade, the Supreme Court has narrowed the inquiry to condemn only "unreasonable restraints" and has developed presumptive ("per se") rules to simplify judicial inquiries in particular circumstances. Among the restraints of trade that are reached by Section One are: price fixing (the setting of prices or terms of sale cooperatively by two or more businesses that do not involve sharing substantial risk in a common business enterprise); market division (allocating product lines, customers, or territories between competitors); exclusive dealing (requiring that a person deal exclusively with an enterprise so that competitors are foreclosed or otherwise disadvantaged in the marketplace); group boycotts (competitors collectively refusing to deal, usually taking the form of denying a rival an input or something it needs to compete in the marketplace); and tying arrangements (a firm with market power selling one product on the condition that the buyer buy a second product from it).

Sherman Act § 2: Monopolization and Attempted Monopolization

Section Two of the Sherman Act prohibits monopolization, attempted monopolization, and conspiracies to monopolize. 15 U.S.C. § 2. Unlike Section One, it is primarily directed at unilateral conduct. Monopolization entails two elements: the possession of monopoly power, defined as the power to control market prices or exclude competition, and the willful acquisition or maintenance of that power as distinguished from growth or development as a consequence of a superior product, business acumen, or historic accident.

Clayton Act § 7: Mergers and Acquisitions

Section Seven of the Clayton Act prohibits mergers and acquisitions where the effect may be "substantially to lessen competition" or "to tend to create a monopoly." 15 U.S.C. § 18. To test the legality of a proposed merger or acquisition, courts emphasize market share and concentration data but also take other factors into consideration to determine whether a merger makes it more likely than not that the merged firm will exercise market power.

Federal Trade Commission Act § 5: Unfair Methods of Competition

Section Five of the Federal Trade Commission Act prohibits "unfair methods of competition" (which the courts have interpreted to include all violations of the Sherman Act and Clayton Act), and "unfair or deceptive acts or practices." 15 U.S.C. § 45(a)(1). The Act empowers the FTC to enforce the provisions of the Sherman Act in civil suits, as well as by administrative procedures. Although the FTC Act covers only the activities of a corporation "organized to carry on business for its own profit or that of its members," courts have found that non profit associations whose activities provide substantial economic benefit to their members are within the FTC's jurisdiction.

Defenses and Exemptions

There are numerous statutory and judicially-crafted defenses to antitrust liability, several of which are of particular importance to health care antitrust litigation. The state action doctrine exempts from antitrust liability actions taken pursuant to a clearly expressed state policy to restrict free competition, where the challenged conduct is under the active control and supervision of the state. The high degree of state regulation of health care has spawned state action defenses in staff privileges cases, for example, when state law authorizes public hospitals to undertake mergers that lessen competition and supervises their conduct. The McCarran–Ferguson Act generally exempts the "business of insurance" from antitrust enforcement to the extent that the particular insurance activities are regulated by state law. 15 U.S.C. § 1011. (This should not be taken to mean, however, that "insurance companies" are exempt from antitrust scrutiny). The Noerr–Pennington doctrine protects the exercise of the First Amendment right to petition the government, so long as the "petitioning" is not merely a "sham" to cover anti-competitive behavior. This defense is relevant to lobbying efforts on health care issues and to participation in administrative proceedings, such as certificate-of-need applications, each of which may lead to an outcome that lessens competition. The most recent statutory defense relevant to health care is the Health Care Quality Improvement Act, 42 U.S.C. §§ 11101–11152, enacted by Congress in 1986, which grants limited immunity for peer review activities.

Interpretive Principles

The Law's Exclusive Focus on Competitive Concerns

There has long been widespread agreement in the case law that antitrust inquiries should focus exclusively on competitive effects and should not take into account purported non-economic benefits of collective activities such as advancing social policies or even protecting public safety. See National Society of Professional Engineers v. United States, 435 U.S. 679, 98 S.Ct. 1355, 55 L.Ed.2d 637 (1978) (rejecting as a matter of law a professional society's safety justifications for its ban on competitive bidding). This self-imposed boundary is based on the judiciary's skepticism about its competence to balance disparate social policies and the judgment that such concerns are more appropriately addressed to the legislature. Importantly, then, under Section One of the Sherman Act, courts will not consider justifications other than those asserting that a practice, on balance, promotes competition. As discussed *infra* in Section IA2, this constraint is in obvious tension with justifications by professionals that their collective activities have the purpose of advancing the quality of patient care.

An important corollary to the foregoing is the often-repeated maxim that antitrust law seeks to "protect competition, not competitors." Brown Shoe Co. v. United States, 370 U.S. 294, 82 S.Ct. 1502, 8 L.Ed.2d 510 (1962). This tenet serves to emphasize the distinction between harm to competitors who lose out in the competitive struggle due to chance or their own inadequacies and harm resulting from the impermissible conduct of rivals. Only the latter are cognizable under the federal antitrust laws. Courts have fashioned rules regarding standing and antitrust injury for private plaintiffs as well as substantive doctrines that serve to preserve this distinction. See e.g., Todorov v. DCH Healthcare Authority, 921 F.2d 1438 (11th Cir. 1991); see generally, 2 Barry R. Furrow, et al., Health Law § 14–3 (2d ed. 2000).

Per Se Rules and The Rule of Reason

Traditionally, judicial analyses of conduct under Section One of the Sherman Act have employed two approaches to testing the "reasonableness" of restraints. Some activities, such as price fixing, market allocations, and certain group boycotts have been considered so likely to harm competition that they are deemed illegal "per se." That is, if a plaintiff can prove that the defendant's conduct fits within one of these categories, the inquiry ends; the agreement itself constitutes a violation of the statute. In effect, then, the per se categorization establishes a conclusive presumption of illegality.

Activities not falling within the per se rubric are subject to broader examination under the rule of reason. Under this form of analysis, defendants escape liability if they prove that the pro-competitive benefits of the challenged activity outweigh any anticompetitive effects so that competition, the singular policy concern of the statute, is strengthened rather than restrained. In theory, courts undertaking a full-blown rule of reason analysis will balance competitive harms against competitive benefits. For example, if a large number of hospitals collectively assembled and shared information about the utilization practices of physicians on their staffs, a court might balance the potential collusive harm resulting from lessened inter-hospital competition against the market-wide competitive benefits of dispensing such information—assuming the information was shared with payors.

In practice, however, such balancing is rarely done. Courts usually truncate the process in one of several ways. For example, they may find that an alleged restraint has no possibility of harming competition where the colluding parties lack "market power." As a proxy for market power, which is defined as the ability profitably to raise price (or reduce quality or output), courts estimate the market shares of the colluding parties and examine other market conditions. (A firm's market share is the ratio of its volume of business in a market to that of all of its competitors.) Doing this, of course, requires that the factfinder define the dimensions of the geographic and product markets—determinations that require the exercise of considerable judgment. Even where a party has a high market share and there are relatively few competitors, however, market power still may be lacking. For example, the colluding parties may be unable to raise price because entry by others is easy or because buyers would quickly detect such an increase and cease dealing with the parties.

Indeed, in recent years, a series of Supreme Court decisions have shifted antitrust analyses away from a rigid per se/rule of reason dichotomy, treating the approaches instead as "complementary" and essentially establishing a continuum of levels of scrutiny. See California Dental Association v. FTC *infra* Section B1, this chapter. Thus, the modern approach allows courts to undertake threshold examinations of purported justifications and competitive effects before characterizing the conduct as governed by the per se rule. By the same token, courts may need only a "quick look" to condemn conduct under the rule of reason; they may dispense with prolonged factual inquiries when the truncated review reveals that purported efficiency benefits are lacking or an anticompetitive effect is obvious.

I. CARTELS AND PROFESSIONALISM

A. CLASSIC CARTELS

IN RE MICHIGAN STATE MEDICAL SOCIETY

101 F.T.C. 191 (1983).

OPINION OF THE COMMISSION

BY CLANTON, COMMISSIONER:

I. INTRODUCTION

This case involves allegations that direct competitors, acting through a professional association, conspired to restrain trade by organizing boycotts and tampering with the fees received from third party insurers of their services. Of particular antitrust significance is the fact that the competitors are medical doctors practicing in Michigan, the association is the Michigan State Medical Society ["MSMS"], and the insurers are Blue Cross and Blue Shield of Michigan ("BCBSM") and Michigan Medicaid.

More specifically, the complaint in this matter charges, and the administrative law judge found, that the medical society unlawfully conspired with its members to influence third-party reimbursement policies in the following ways: by seeking to negotiate collective agreements with insurers; by agreeing to use coercive measures like proxy solicitation and group boycotts; and by actually making coercive threats to third party payers. . . .

* * *

Becoming frustrated in its negotiations with BCBSM on [issues regarding reimbursement], MSMS authorized its first proxy solicitation. Reacting to what it perceived to be the recalcitrant attitude of Blue Shield on the subjects of regionalization of fees and physician profiles, coupled with what appears to be a total lack of willingness to cooperate with MSMS in the development of a uniform claim form or even consider the use of the CPT procedural code, the Negotiating Committee recommended that the House of Delegates urge MSMS members to write letters to BCBSM withdrawing from participation but mail them to the Negotiating Committee to be held as "proxies." The House of Delegates authorized the committee to collect the proxies, but to use them only at the discretion of the Council, with prior notice to the members who submitted them, "if a negotiating impasse develops with Michigan Blue Cross/Blue Shield."

* * *

Each member of MSMS was urged by letter to resist "so-called cost-containment programs that in effect reduce reimbursement to physicians or place the responsibility for the reduction of costs solely on the practicing physician." The letter, from the Council chairman, referred pointedly to the fact that a threshold percentage of physicians must formally participate in order for BCBSM to operate under its enabling legislation. It enclosed two blank "powers of attorney," one for BCBSM and one for Medicaid, empowering the Negotiating Committee to cancel the signer's participation in either program if such action was deemed warranted by the Council. These powers of attorney were revocable at any time. . . .

As a result of this response, [a] dispute over radiologists' and pathologists' reimbursement was resolved in MSMS' favor with the status quo being preserved and BCBSM withdrawing its proposal. [ ] As explained below, these proxies also played a role in MSMS' dealings with Medicaid.

[In response to additional efforts by BCBSM to reduce utilization of physician services, the leadership of MSMS advised members to react to new reimbursement policies by writing letters threatening departicipation or actually withdrawing from participation. In addition, MSMS representatives protested cuts of approximately 11% in physician reimbursement under the Medicaid program by "waving" the departicipation proxies during meetings with the Governor and Medicaid officials. Although evidence suggested that physician participants in the Medicaid program fell off markedly after the MSMS collective action, the Commission did not find that state officials had been coerced by these actions.]

* * *

Conspiracy Allegations

The threshold issue here is whether MSMS' importunings with BCBSM and the Medicaid program amounted to conspiratorial conduct of the kind alleged in the complaint or simply represented nonbinding expressions of views and policy, as argued by respondent. . . . As discussed previously, the evidence quite clearly reveals that MSMS members, acting through their House of Delegates, agreed in 1976 to establish a Division of Negotiations for the purpose of working out differences with third party payers. The Division was specifically empowered, *inter alia*, to coordinate all negotiating activities of MSMS, collect "non-participation" proxies and obtain a negotiated participation agreement with third party payers that would obviate the need for physician non-participation. It also was specifically contemplated by MSMS that the Division of Negotiations would obtain authorization of all members to serve as their "exclusive bargaining agent." The debate in the House of Delegates clearly indicated that, although the Division would not negotiate specific fees, it would have authority to negotiate the manner by which fees or reimbursement levels would be established. [ ]

Thus, at the outset we find that the very creation of the Division of Negotiations reveals a collective purpose on the part of MSMS and its members to go beyond the point of giving advice to third party payers; in fact, it reveals a purpose to organize and empower a full-fledged representative to negotiate and resolve controversies surrounding physician profiles, screens and other similar matters. [ ] There is, in fact, considerable additional evidence that the Negotiating Division not only had the authority to reach understandings with third party payers but also utilized that authority (acting as agent for its members) in soliciting, collecting and threatening to exercise physician departicipation proxies, as well as in other negotiations with third party payers.

* * *

Turning to the boycott issue, the law is clear that the definition of that term is not limited to situations where the target of the concerted refusal to deal is another competitor or potential competitor. As the Supreme Court indicated, . . . a concerted refusal to deal may be characterized as an unlawful group boycott where the target is a customer or supplier of the combining parties. . . . In the instant case, the alleged boycott involves concerted threats by MSMS and its members to refrain from participating in BCBSM and Medicaid unless the latter modified their reimbursement policies. Although BCBSM and Medicaid—the targets of the boycott—are not in competitive relationships with MSMS, that fact alone does not preclude a finding of a boycott.

Respondent, however, argues that the proxies were not exercised and, in the case of the departicipation letter campaign, that there was no adverse effect on BCBSM. As to the latter contention, MSMS points out that more physicians signed up to participate in BCBSM during the relevant period than withdrew from the program as a result of the campaign. The success [or] failure of a group boycott or price-fixing agreement, however, is irrelevant to the question of either its existence or its legality. Whether or not the action succeeds, "[i]t is the concerted activity for a common purpose that constitutes the violation." . . . Furthermore, an agreement among competitors affecting price does not have to be successful in order to be condemned.

It is the "contract, combination . . . or conspiracy in restraint of trade or commerce" which § 1 of the [Sherman] Act strikes down, whether the concerted activity be wholly nascent or abortive on the one hand, or successful on the other. [ ] Moreover, even if less than all members of an organization or association agree to participate, that fact does not negate the presence of a conspiracy or combination as to those who do participate. [ ]

As for the collection of proxies that were never exercised, the law does not require that a competitor actually refuse to deal before a boycott can be found or liability established. Rather, the threat to refuse to deal may suffice to constitute the offense. [ ] The evidence indicates that the threat implicit in the collection of departicipation proxies and the attendant publicity can be as effective as the actual execution of the threatened action. Indeed, it may be assumed that parties to a concerted refusal to deal hope that the announcement of the intended action will be sufficient to produce the desired response. That appears to be precisely what happened here, and there are contemporaneous testimonials by MSMS officials confirming the success of that strategy. For example, Dr. Crandall suggested that MSMS' "waving the proxies in the face of the legislature" persuaded the state attorney general that if he sued MSMS the state would have "orchestrated the demise of the entire Michigan Medicaid program." Also, as noted above, the Negotiations Division credited the members' response to the proxy solicitation with the favorable outcome of the dispute between the radiologists and BCBSM. And, as further evidence, there is the fact that MSMS reached a formal agreement with BCBSM which included the implementation of a statewide screen.

* * *

B. Legality of the Concerted Action

* * *

[I]t would appear that respondent's conduct approaches the kind of behavior that previously has been classified as per se illegal. Nevertheless, since this conduct does not involve direct fee setting, we are not prepared to declare it per se illegal at this juncture and close the door on all asserted pro-competitive justifications.

To briefly recap, respondent has offered the following justifications for its behavior: (1) the practices had no effect on fee levels and, in any event, BCBSM and Medicaid took independent action to correct the perceived problems; (2) MSMS simply sought to insure that physicians were treated fairly especially in view of BCBSM's bargaining power; (3) the actions were, in part, an effort to counter BCBSM's violations of its charter and Michigan law in connection with its modified participation program; and (4) MSMS was striving to correct abuses of the Medicaid system and the poor perpetrated by "Medicaid mills."

With respect to respondent's first contention, MSMS claims that the conduct never led to uniform fees or prevented individual physicians from deciding whether to participate in BCBSM or Medicaid. We believe that these arguments miss the point with respect to the likely competitive effects of the restrictive practices. Where horizontal arrangements so closely relate to prices or fees as they do here, a less elaborate analysis of competitive effects is required. [ ] The collective actions under scrutiny clearly interfere with the rights of physicians to compete independently on the terms of insurance coverage offered by BCBSM and Medicaid. Moreover, the joint arrangements directly hamper the ability of third party payers to compete freely for the patronage of individual physicians and other physician business entities. . . .

* * *

On the question of whether the proposed policies of BCBSM and Medicaid were fair to physicians, respondent would apparently have us become enmeshed in weighing the comparative equities of the different parties to these transactions. In fact, considerable portions of the record are devoted to an assessment of the relative merits of MSMS' bargaining position. For us to consider whether the terms offered by the third party payers were fair or reasonable would lead us into the kind of regulatory posture that the courts have long rejected.... It would be analogous to the Commission serving as a quasi-public utility agency concerned with balancing interests unrelated to antitrust concerns. We believe that it is undesirable and inappropriate for us to step in and attempt to determine which party had the better case in these dealings. [The Commission found that the objective of correcting violations of law cannot justify a group boycott because alternative means of seeking redress were available.]

* * *

Respondent also suggests that its activities were motivated by concern for the welfare of its members' patients, especially in the case of Medicaid where, it is alleged, reductions in reimbursement levels might lead to lower physician participation rates and force low-income patients to seek less reputable providers (the so-called Medicaid mills). We concluded there that the relationship between such reimbursement mechanisms and health care quality was simply too tenuous, from a competitive perspective, to justify the broad restrictions imposed.... While we are not addressing ethical standards in this case, many of the quality and patient welfare arguments asserted here have a ring similar to those advanced in [*In re AMA*, discussed *infra*, in which the FTC rejected a ban on advertising justified by defendants as protecting informed consumer choice and a prohibition on contract-based reimbursement which defendants claimed resulted in harm to the public and inferior quality of medical service]. Even in the case of Medicaid reductions, where an argument might be made that arbitrary cuts could be counter-productive by impairing physicians' economic incentives to treat the poor, it is difficult to see how concerted agreements and refusals to deal can be sanctioned as a means of fighting proposed payment cutbacks. While granting MSMS' laudable concerns about the effects of physician withdrawal from Medicaid, we observe that respondent clearly had public forums available to it to correct perceived mistakes made by the state legislature or the administrators of Medicaid; it could have expressed its views in ways that fell well short of organized boycott threats.

Finally, we find no suggestion among MSMS' justifications that the concerted behavior here enhanced competition in any market by injecting new elements or forms of competition, reducing entry barriers, or facilitating or broadening consumer choice. The price-related practices in question here are not ancillary to some broader pro-competitive purpose, such as a joint venture, an integration of activities, or an offer of a new product or service....

* * *

In fact, we believe there are less anti-competitive ways of providing such information to insurers. The order that we would impose upon respondent allows it to provide information and views to insurers on behalf of its members, so long as the Society does not attempt to extract agreements, through coercion or otherwise, from third party payers on reimbursement issues. In allowing respondent to engage in non-binding, non-coercive discussions with health insurers, we have attempted to strike a proper balance between the need for insurers to have efficient access to the views of large groups of providers and the need to prevent competitors from banding together in ways that involve the unreasonable exercise of collective market power.

Notes and Questions

1. Does a decision by competing physicians to deal collectively in their negotiations with third party payers constitute price fixing? If so, why didn't the FTC treat this as a per se offense?

2. Consider the justifications offered by the Michigan State Medical Society physicians for their actions. Do any meet the requirement discussed in the introduction to this chapter that justifications must concern pro-competitive benefits arising from the restraint? Could collective negotiations be viewed as a market-improving step if they corrected market imperfections? Did they here? See Thomas E. Kauper, The Role of Quality of Health Care Considerations in Antitrust Analysis, 51 L. & Contemp. Probs. 273 (Spring, 1988); Thomas L. Greaney, Quality of Care and Market Failure Defenses in Antitrust Health Care Litigation, 21 Conn. L. Rev. 605, 650–52 (1989).

3. Boycotts traditionally have been subject to per se analysis, although the Supreme Court has cautioned in recent years that only certain collective refusals to deal will be summarily condemned. In Northwest Wholesale Stationers, Inc. v. Pacific Stationery, 472 U.S. 284, 105 S.Ct. 2613, 86 L.Ed.2d 202 (1985), the Court noted somewhat elliptically that, in order to merit per se treatment, some of the following factors must be present: (1) cutting off access to a supply, facility, or market necessary to enable the boycotted firms to compete; (2) market power in the boycotting firms; and (3) no plausible efficiency justifications. Only a few years later, however, the Court applied the per se rule to a boycott by lawyers serving as court-appointed counsel for indigent defendants and strongly defended presumptive treatment as administratively efficient and as a means of discouraging individuals from attempting inherently dangerous conduct. FTC v. Superior Court Trial Lawyers Ass'n, 493 U.S. 411, 110 S.Ct. 768, 107 L.Ed.2d 851 (1990). While the exact boundaries of the doctrine remain murky, plausible pro-competitive justifications for collective refusals to deal will remove conduct from per se classification. Lower courts have readily applied rule of reason analysis to alleged boycotts where, for example, providers were excluded from an IPA based on valid cost containment objectives. Hassan v. Independent Practice Associates, P.C., 698 F.Supp. 679 (E.D. Mich. 1988); Hahn v. Oregon Physicians' Service, 868 F.2d 1022 (9th Cir.1988).

4. The federal agencies have successfully challenged scores of provider cartels that engaged in a wide variety of practices designed to raise prices, thwart competition from other providers, or stymie cost containment efforts of managed care organizations. For example, the FTC entered into a consent decree with Montana Associated Physicians, Inc. (MAPI), an organization of 115 physicians practicing in over 30 independent physician practices and constituting 43% of all the physicians in Billings, Montana. In re Montana Associated Physicians, Inc. and Billings Physician Hospital Alliance, Inc., FTC Docket No. C–3704, 62 Fed. Reg. 11,201 (1997). According to the FTC's complaint, physicians formed MAPI to present a "united front" when dealing with managed care plans in an attempt to "resist competitive pressures to discount fees" and forestall entry of HMOs and PPOs into the area. Individual members of MAPI told HMOs that they would negotiate only through their organization, and no individual MAPI member contracted with HMOs. See also United States v. North Dakota Hospital Associa-

tion, 640 F.Supp. 1028 (D.N.D. 1986) (hospitals' joint refusal to extend discounts in bidding for contracts); American Medical Association, 94 F.T.C. 701 (1979) (final order and opinion), aff'd, 638 F.2d 443 (2d Cir. 1980), aff'd by an equally divided court, 455 U.S. 676, 102 S.Ct. 1744, 71 L.Ed.2d 546 (1982) (ethical rules barring salaried employment, working for "inadequate compensation," and affiliating with non-physicians); Medical Staff of Holy Cross Hospital, 114 F.T.C. 555 (1991) (consent order) (conspiracy by medical staff to obstruct development of Cleveland Clinic's multi-specialty group practice by denying staff privileges to clinic doctors). Collective bargaining undertaken by "sham" networks or purported physician unions are discussed *infra*.

   5.   In a very few instances, criminal charges have been filed against providers who have engaged in price fixing or price-affecting boycotts. In United States v. Alston, 974 F.2d 1206 (9th Cir. 1992), the Justice Department had indicted a group of dentists who allegedly conspired to fix co-payment fees received from insurers. The Ninth Circuit affirmed a jury verdict based on circumstantial evidence of meetings, discussions of mutual dissatisfaction and parallel conduct that the dentist entered into a price fixing conspiracy; however, the court upheld a motion for a new trial based on the contention that defendants lacked the necessary *mens rea* because they believed the payor had proposed the revised fee schedule. *Alston* was the first federal criminal prosecution involving health care providers since American Medical Ass'n v. United States, 130 F.2d 233 (D.C.Cir. 1942), aff'd, 317 U.S. 519, 63 S.Ct. 326, 87 L.Ed. 434 (1943), in which the AMA and an affiliated society were convicted of violating the Sherman Act by engaging in a variety of efforts to suppress HMOs. These efforts included expulsion from the medical society and the circulation of "white lists" to encourage boycotts of those doctors cooperating with HMOs. As will be discussed, in recent years the FTC has uncovered numerous cartelizing schemes by physicians organizing "sham" networks or undertaking other strategies to insulate themselves from competition fostered by managed care. However, no criminal charges have been brought by the Department of Justice. We have seen no similar reluctance by DOJ to bring criminal charges in cases involving anti-kickback schemes. What may explain the different treatment? See Thomas L. Greaney, Thirty Years of Solicitude: Antitrust Law and Physician Cartels, 7 Hous. J. Health L. & Pol. 101 (2007) (discussing the political, bureaucratic, and doctrinal forces making DOJ reluctant to pursue criminal enforcement in antitrust health care cases).

B.   COLLECTIVE ACTIVITIES WITH JUSTIFICATIONS

CALIFORNIA DENTAL ASSOCIATION v. FEDERAL TRADE COMMISSION

Supreme Court of the United States, 1999.
526 U.S. 756, 119 S.Ct. 1604, 143 L.Ed.2d 935.

JUSTICE SOUTER delivered the opinion of the Court.

   There are two issues in this case: whether the jurisdiction of the Federal Trade Commission extends to the California Dental Association (CDA), a nonprofit professional association, and whether a "quick look" sufficed to justify finding that certain advertising restrictions adopted by the CDA violated the antitrust laws. We hold that the Commission's jurisdiction under the Federal Trade Commission Act (FTC Act) extends to an association that, like the CDA, provides substantial economic benefit to its for-profit members, but that where, as here, any anticompetitive effects of given restraints are far from intuitively obvious, the rule of reason demands a more thorough enquiry into the consequences of those restraints than the Court of Appeals performed.

I

[Petitioner CDA, a nonprofit association of local dental societies to which about three-quarters of the State's dentists belong, provides desirable insurance and preferential financing arrangements for its members and engages in lobbying, litigation, marketing, and public relations for members' benefit. Members agree to abide by the CDA's Code of Ethics, which, *inter alia*, prohibits false or misleading advertising. The CDA has issued interpretive advisory opinions and guidelines relating to advertising. The FTC claimed that in applying its guidelines so as to restrict two types of truthful, nondeceptive advertising (price advertising, particularly discounted fees, and advertising relating to the quality of dental services), the CDA violated § 5 of the FTC Act. In its administrative proceedings, the Commission held that the advertising restrictions violated the Act under an abbreviated rule-of-reason analysis. In affirming, the Ninth Circuit sustained the Commission's jurisdiction and concluded that an abbreviated or "quick look" rule of reason analysis was proper in this case.]

The dentists who belong to the CDA ... agree to abide by a Code of Ethics (Code) including the following § 10:

"Although any dentist may advertise, no dentist shall advertise or solicit patients in any form of communication in a manner that is false or misleading in any material respect. In order to properly serve the public, dentists should represent themselves in a manner that contributes to the esteem of the public. Dentists should not misrepresent their training and competence in any way that would be false or misleading in any material respect."

The CDA has issued a number of advisory opinions interpreting this section, and through separate advertising guidelines intended to help members comply with the Code and with state law the CDA has advised its dentists of disclosures they must make under state law when engaging in discount advertising.[1]

Responsibility for enforcing the Code rests in the first instance with the local dental societies, to which applicants for CDA membership must submit copies of their own advertisements and those of their employers or referral services to assure compliance with the Code. The local societies also actively seek information about potential Code violations by applicants or CDA members. Applicants who refuse to withdraw or revise objectionable advertisements may be denied membership; and members who, after a hearing, remain

---

1. The disclosures include:

1. The dollar amount of the nondiscounted fee for the service[.]

2. Either the dollar amount of the discount fee or the percentage of the discount for the specific service[.]

3. The length of time that the discount will be offered[.]

4. Verifiable fees[.]

5. [The identity of] [s]pecific groups who qualify for the discount or any other terms and conditions or restrictions for qualifying for the discount. Id., at 724.

similarly recalcitrant are subject to censure, suspension, or expulsion from the CDA. [ ]

* * *

II

[The Court interpreted the FTC Act, which gives the Commission authority over a "corporatio[n]" that is "organized to carry on business for its own profit or that of its members," 15 U.S.C. §§ 44, 45(a)(2), as conferring jurisdiction over nonprofit associations whose activities provide substantial economic benefits to their for-profit members. The Court declined to predicate FTC jurisdiction on a showing that a supporting organization devoted itself entirely to its members' profits or that its activities focused on raising members' bottom lines.]

III

The Court of Appeals treated as distinct questions the sufficiency of the analysis of anticompetitive effects and the substantiality of the evidence supporting the Commission's conclusions. Because we decide that the Court of Appeals erred when it held as a matter of law that quick-look analysis was appropriate (with the consequence that the Commission's abbreviated analysis and conclusion were sustainable), we do not reach the question of the substantiality of the evidence supporting the Commission's conclusion.[2]

In National Collegiate Athletic Assn. v. Board of Regents of Univ. of Okla.[ ] we held that a "naked restraint on price and output requires some competitive justification even in the absence of a detailed market analysis." [ ]. Elsewhere, we held that "no elaborate industry analysis is required to demonstrate the anticompetitive character of" horizontal agreements among competitors to refuse to discuss prices. [ ] In each of these cases, which have formed the basis for what has come to be called abbreviated or "quick-look" analysis under the rule of reason, an observer with even a rudimentary understanding of economics could conclude that the arrangements in question would have an anticompetitive effect on customers and markets.... As in such cases, quick-look analysis carries the day when the great likelihood of anticompetitive effects can easily be ascertained....

The case before us, however, fails to present a situation in which the likelihood of anticompetitive effects is comparably obvious. Even on Justice Breyer's view that bars on truthful and verifiable price and quality advertising are prima facie anticompetitive, and place the burden of procompetitive justification on those who agree to adopt them, the very issue at the threshold of this case is whether professional price and quality advertising is sufficiently verifiable in theory and in fact to fall within such a general rule. Ultimately our disagreement with Justice Breyer turns on our different responses to this issue. Whereas he accepts, as the Ninth Circuit seems to have done, that the restrictions here were like restrictions on advertisement of price and quality generally, it seems to us that the CDA's advertising restrictions might

2. We leave to the Court of Appeals the question whether on remand it can effectively assess the Commission's decision for substantial evidence on the record, or whether it must remand to the Commission for a more extensive rule-of-reason analysis on the basis of an enhanced record.

plausibly be thought to have a net procompetitive effect, or possibly no effect at all on competition. The restrictions on both discount and nondiscount advertising are, at least on their face, designed to avoid false or deceptive advertising[3] in a market characterized by striking disparities between the information available to the professional and the patient.[4] [] In a market for professional services, in which advertising is relatively rare and the comparability of service packages not easily established, the difficulty for customers or potential competitors to get and verify information about the price and availability of services magnifies the dangers to competition associated with misleading advertising. What is more, the quality of professional services tends to resist either calibration or monitoring by individual patients or clients, partly because of the specialized knowledge required to evaluate the services, and partly because of the difficulty in determining whether, and the degree to which, an outcome is attributable to the quality of services (like a poor job of tooth-filling) or to something else (like a very tough walnut). See Leland, Quacks, Lemons, and Licensing: A Theory of Minimum Quality Standards, 87 J. Pol. Econ. 1328, 1330 (1979); 1 B. Furrow, T. Greaney, S. Johnson, T. Jost, & R. Schwartz, Health Law § 3–1, p. 86 (1995) (describing the common view that "the lay public is incapable of adequately evaluating the quality of medical services"). Patients' attachments to particular professionals, the rationality of which is difficult to assess, complicate the picture even further. [] The existence of such significant challenges to informed decisionmaking by the customer for professional services immediately suggests that advertising restrictions arguably protecting patients from misleading or irrelevant advertising call for more than cursory treatment as obviously comparable to classic horizontal agreements to limit output or price competition.

[The Court of Appeals] brushe[d] over the professional context and describe[d] no anticompetitive effects. Assuming that the record in fact supports the conclusion that the CDA disclosure rules essentially bar advertisement of across-the-board discounts, it does not obviously follow that such a ban would have a net anticompetitive effect here. Whether advertisements that announced discounts for, say, first-time customers, would be less effective at conveying information relevant to competition if they listed the original and discounted prices for checkups, X-rays, and fillings, than they would be if they simply specified a percentage discount across the board, seems to us a question susceptible to empirical but not a priori analysis.... Put another way, the CDA's rule appears to reflect the prediction that any costs to competition associated with the elimination of across-the-board advertising will be outweighed by gains to consumer information (and hence competition) created by discount advertising that is exact, accurate, and more easily verifiable (at least by regulators). As a matter of economics this view

3. That false or misleading advertising has an anticompetitive effect, as that term is customarily used, has been long established. []

4. "The fact that a restraint operates upon a profession as distinguished from a business is, of course, relevant in determining whether that particular restraint violates the Sherman Act. It would be unrealistic to view the practice of professions as interchangeable with other business activities, and automatically to apply to the professions antitrust concepts which originated in other areas. The public service aspect, and other features of the professions, may require that a particular practice, which could properly be viewed as a violation of the Sherman Act in another context, be treated differently." Goldfarb v. Virginia State Bar, 421 U.S. 773, 788–789, n. 17, 95 S.Ct. 2004, 44 L.Ed.2d 572 (1975).

may or may not be correct, but it is not implausible, and neither a court nor the Commission may initially dismiss it as presumptively wrong.[5]

* * *

The Court of Appeals was comparably tolerant in accepting the sufficiency of abbreviated rule-of-reason analysis as to the nonprice advertising restrictions. The court began with the argument that "[t]hese restrictions are in effect a form of output limitation, as they restrict the supply of information about individual dentists' services." Although this sentence does indeed appear as cited, it is puzzling, given that the relevant output for antitrust purposes here is presumably not information or advertising, but dental services themselves. The question is not whether the universe of possible advertisements has been limited (as assuredly it has), but whether the limitation on advertisements obviously tends to limit the total delivery of dental services. The court came closest to addressing this latter question when it went on to assert that limiting advertisements regarding quality and safety "prevents dentists from fully describing the package of services they offer," adding that "[t]he restrictions may also affect output more directly, as quality and comfort advertising may induce some customers to obtain non-emergency care when they might not otherwise do so," ibid. This suggestion about output is also puzzling. If quality advertising actually induces some patients to obtain more care than they would in its absence, then restricting such advertising would reduce the demand for dental services, not the supply; and it is of course the producers' supply of a good in relation to demand that is normally relevant in determining whether a producer-imposed output limitation has the anticompetitive effect of artificially raising prices.[6] ...

Although the Court of Appeals acknowledged the CDA's view that "claims about quality are inherently unverifiable and therefore misleading," it responded that this concern "does not justify banning all quality claims without regard to whether they are, in fact, false or misleading." As a result, the court said, "the restriction is a sufficiently naked restraint on output to justify quick look analysis." The court assumed, in these words, that some dental quality claims may escape justifiable censure, because they are both verifiable and true. But its implicit assumption fails to explain why it gave no

---

5. Justice Breyer suggests that our analysis is "of limited relevance," because "the basic question is whether this ... theoretically redeeming virtue in fact offsets the restrictions' anticompetitive effects in this case." He thinks that the Commission and the Court of Appeals "adequately answered that question," but the absence of any empirical evidence on this point indicates that the question was not answered, merely avoided by implicit burden-shifting of the kind accepted by Justice Breyer. The point is that before a theoretical claim of anticompetitive effects can justify shifting to a defendant the burden to show empirical evidence of pro-competitive effects, as quick-look analysis in effect requires, there must be some indication that the court making the decision has properly identified the theoretical basis for the anti-competitive effects and considered whether the effects actually are anticompetitive. Where, as here, the circumstances of the restriction are

somewhat complex, assumption alone will not do.

6. Justice Breyer wonders if we "mea[n] this statement as an argument against the anticompetitive tendencies that flow from an agreement not to advertise service quality." But as the preceding sentence shows, we intend simply to question the logic of the Court of Appeals's suggestion that the restrictions are anticompetitive because they somehow "affect output," presumably with the intent to raise prices by limiting supply while demand remains constant. We do not mean to deny that an agreement not to advertise service quality might have anticompetitive effects. We merely mean that, absent further analysis of the kind Justice Breyer undertakes, it is not possible to conclude that the net effect of this particular restriction is anticompetitive.

weight to the countervailing, and at least equally plausible, suggestion that restricting difficult-to-verify claims about quality or patient comfort would have a procompetitive effect by preventing misleading or false claims that distort the market. It is, indeed, entirely possible to understand the CDA's restrictions on unverifiable quality and comfort advertising as nothing more than a procompetitive ban on puffery. . . .

The point is not that the CDA's restrictions necessarily have the procompetitive effect claimed by the CDA; it is possible that banning quality claims might have no effect at all on competitiveness if, for example, many dentists made very much the same sort of claims. And it is also of course possible that the restrictions might in the final analysis be anticompetitive. The point, rather, is that the plausibility of competing claims about the effects of the professional advertising restrictions rules out the indulgently abbreviated review to which the Commission's order was treated. The obvious anticompetitive effect that triggers abbreviated analysis has not been shown.

In light of our focus on the adequacy of the Court of Appeals's analysis, Justice Breyer's thorough-going, de novo antitrust analysis contains much to impress on its own merits but little to demonstrate the sufficiency of the Court of Appeals's review. The obligation to give a more deliberate look than a quick one does not arise at the door of this Court and should not be satisfied here in the first instance. Had the Court of Appeals engaged in a painstaking discussion in a league with Justice Breyer's (compare his 14 pages with the Ninth Circuit's 8), and had it confronted the comparability of these restrictions to bars on clearly verifiable advertising, its reasoning might have sufficed to justify its conclusion. Certainly Justice Breyer's treatment of the antitrust issues here is no "quick look." Lingering is more like it, and indeed Justice Breyer, not surprisingly, stops short of endorsing the Court of Appeals's discussion as adequate to the task at hand.

Saying here that the Court of Appeals's conclusion at least required a more extended examination of the possible factual underpinnings than it received is not, of course, necessarily to call for the fullest market analysis. Although we have said that a challenge to a "naked restraint on price and output" need not be supported by "a detailed market analysis" in order to "requir[e] some competitive justification," . . . The truth is that our categories of analysis of anticompetitive effect are less fixed than terms like "per se," "quick look," and "rule of reason" tend to make them appear. We have recognized, for example, that "there is often no bright line separating per se from Rule of Reason analysis," since "considerable inquiry into market conditions" may be required before the application of any so-called "per se" condemnation is justified. As the circumstances here demonstrate, there is generally no categorical line to be drawn between restraints that give rise to an intuitively obvious inference of anticompetitive effect and those that call for more detailed treatment. What is required, rather, is an enquiry meet for the case, looking to the circumstances, details, and logic of a restraint. The object is to see whether the experience of the market has been so clear, or necessarily will be, that a confident conclusion about the principal tendency of a restriction will follow from a quick (or at least quicker) look, in place of a more sedulous one. And of course what we see may vary over time, if rule-of-reason analyses in case after case reach identical conclusions. For now, at least, a less quick look was required for the initial assessment of the tendency of these professional advertising restrictions. Because the Court of Appeals did not scrutinize the assumption of relative anticompetitive tendencies, we vacate the judgment and remand the case for a fuller consideration of the issue.

It is so ordered.

JUSTICE BREYER, with whom JUSTICE STEVENS, JUSTICE KENNEDY, and JUSTICE GINSBURG join, concurring in part and dissenting in part.

I ... agree that in a "rule of reason" antitrust case "the quality of proof required should vary with the circumstances," that "[w]hat is required ... is an enquiry meet for the case," and that the object is a "confident conclusion about the principal tendency of a restriction." But I do not agree that the Court has properly applied those unobjectionable principles here. In my view, a traditional application of the rule of reason to the facts as found by the Commission requires affirming the Commission—just as the Court of Appeals did below.

* * *

I

The Commission's conclusion is lawful if its "factual findings," insofar as they are supported by "substantial evidence," "make out a violation of Sherman Act § 1." [ ] To determine whether that is so, I would not simply ask whether the restraints at issue are anticompetitive overall. Rather, like the Court of Appeals (and the Commission), I would break that question down into four classical, subsidiary antitrust questions: (1) What is the specific restraint at issue? (2) What are its likely anticompetitive effects? (3) Are there offsetting procompetitive justifications? (4) Do the parties have sufficient market power to make a difference?

* * *

A

The most important question is the first: What are the specific restraints at issue? [ ] Those restraints do not include merely the agreement to which the California Dental Association's (Dental Association or Association) ethical rule literally refers, namely, a promise to refrain from advertising that is " 'false or misleading in any material respect.' "[ ] Instead, the Commission found a set of restraints arising out of the way the Dental Association implemented this innocent-sounding ethical rule in practice, through advisory opinions, guidelines, enforcement policies, and review of membership applications. As implemented, the ethical rule reached beyond its nominal target, to prevent truthful and nondeceptive advertising. In particular, the Commission determined that the rule, in practice:

(1) "precluded advertising that characterized a dentist's fees as being low, reasonable, or affordable,"

(2) "precluded advertising ... of across the board discounts," and

(3) "prohibit[ed] all quality claims."

Whether the Dental Association's basic rule as implemented actually restrained the truthful and nondeceptive advertising of low prices, across-the-board discounts, and quality service are questions of fact. The Administrative Law Judge (ALJ) and the Commission may have found those questions difficult ones. But both the ALJ and the Commission ultimately found against the Dental Association in respect to these facts. And the question for us— whether those agency findings are supported by substantial evidence, is not difficult.

The Court of Appeals referred explicitly to some of the evidence that it found adequate to support the Commission's conclusions. It pointed out, for example, that the Dental Association's "advisory opinions and guidelines indicate that . . . descriptions of prices as 'reasonable' or 'low' do not comply" with the Association's rule; that in "numerous cases" the Association "advised members of objections to special offers, senior citizen discounts, and new patient discounts, apparently without regard to their truth"; and that one advisory opinion "expressly states that claims as to the quality of services are inherently likely to be false or misleading," all "without any particular consideration of whether" such statements were "true or false." [ ]

The Commission itself had before it far more evidence. It referred to instances in which the Association, without regard for the truthfulness of the statements at issue, recommended denial of membership to dentists wishing to advertise, for example, "reasonable fees quoted in advance," "major savings," or "making teeth cleaning . . . inexpensive." It referred to testimony that "across-the-board discount advertising in literal compliance with the requirements 'would probably take two pages in the telephone book' and '[n]obody is going to really advertise in that fashion.' "And it pointed to many instances in which the Dental Association suppressed such advertising claims as "we guarantee all dental work for 1 year," "latest in cosmetic dentistry," and "gentle dentistry in a caring environment."

* * *

B

Do each of the three restrictions mentioned have "the potential for genuine adverse effects on competition"? I should have thought that the anticompetitive tendencies of the three restrictions were obvious. An agreement not to advertise that a fee is reasonable, that service is inexpensive, or that a customer will receive a discount makes it more difficult for a dentist to inform customers that he charges a lower price. If the customer does not know about a lower price, he will find it more difficult to buy lower price service. That fact, in turn, makes it less likely that a dentist will obtain more customers by offering lower prices. And that likelihood means that dentists will prove less likely to offer lower prices. . . .

The restrictions on the advertising of service quality also have serious anticompetitive tendencies. . . . [I]t is rather late in the day for anyone to deny the significant anticompetitive tendencies of an agreement that restricts competition in any legitimate respect, let alone one that inhibits customers from learning about the quality of a dentist's service.

Nor did the Commission rely solely on the unobjectionable proposition that a restriction on the ability of dentists to advertise on quality is likely to limit their incentive to compete on quality. Rather, the Commission pointed to record evidence affirmatively establishing that quality-based competition is important to dental consumers in California. [The dissent goes on to summarize evidence that advertising concerning quality will bring in more patients and that restrictions adversely affected dentists who advertise.]

C

We must also ask whether, despite their anticompetitive tendencies, these restrictions might be justified by other procompetitive tendencies or redeeming virtues. [ ] This is a closer question—at least in theory. The Dental Association argues that the three relevant restrictions are inextricably tied to a legitimate Association effort to restrict false or misleading advertising. The Association, the argument goes, had to prevent dentists from engaging in the kind of truthful, nondeceptive advertising that it banned in order effectively to stop dentists from making unverifiable claims about price or service quality, which claims would mislead the consumer.

The problem with this or any similar argument is an empirical one. Notwithstanding its theoretical plausibility, the record does not bear out such a claim. The Commission, which is expert in the area of false and misleading advertising, was uncertain whether petitioner had even made the claim. It characterized petitioner's efficiencies argument as rooted in the (unproved) factual assertion that its ethical rule "challenges only advertising that is false or misleading." Regardless, the Court of Appeals wrote, in respect to the price restrictions, that "the record provides no evidence that the rule has in fact led to increased disclosure and transparency of dental pricing." With respect to quality advertising, the Commission stressed that the Association "offered no convincing argument, let alone evidence, that consumers of dental services have been, or are likely to be, harmed by the broad categories of advertising it restricts." Nor did the Court of Appeals think that the Association's unsubstantiated contention that "claims about quality are inherently unverifiable and therefore misleading" could "justify banning all quality claims without regard to whether they are, in fact, false or misleading."

With one exception, my own review of the record reveals no significant evidentiary support for the proposition that the Association's members must agree to ban truthful price and quality advertising in order to stop untruthful claims. The one exception is the obvious fact that one can stop untruthful advertising if one prohibits all advertising. But since the Association made virtually no effort to sift the false from the true, [ ] that fact does not make out a valid antitrust defense. [ ]

In the usual Sherman Act § 1 case, the defendant bears the burden of establishing a procompetitive justification. [ ] And the Court of Appeals was correct when it concluded that no such justification had been established here.

D

I shall assume that the Commission must prove one additional circumstance, namely, that the Association's restraints would likely have made a real difference in the marketplace. The Commission, disagreeing with the ALJ on this single point, found that the Association did possess enough market power to make a difference.... These facts, in the Court of Appeals' view, were sufficient to show "enough market power to harm competition through [the Association's] standard setting in the area of advertising." []

II

In the Court's view, the legal analysis conducted by the Court of Appeals was insufficient, and the Court remands the case for a more thorough application of the rule of reason. But in what way did the Court of Appeals fail? I find the Court's answers to this question unsatisfactory—when one divides the overall Sherman Act question into its traditional component parts and adheres to traditional judicial practice for allocating the burdens of persuasion in an antitrust case.

* * *

The upshot, in my view, is that the Court of Appeals, applying ordinary antitrust principles, reached an unexceptional conclusion. It is the same legal conclusion that this Court itself reached in *Indiana Federation*—a much closer case than this one. There the Court found that an agreement by dentists not to submit dental X rays to insurers violated the rule of reason. The anticompetitive tendency of that agreement was to reduce competition among dentists in respect to their willingness to submit X rays to insurers, [ ]—a matter in respect to which consumers are relatively indifferent, as compared to advertising of price discounts and service quality, the matters at issue here. The redeeming virtue in Indiana Federation was the alleged undesirability of having insurers consider a range of matters when deciding whether treatment was justified—a virtue no less plausible, and no less proved, than the virtue offered here. The "power" of the dentists to enforce their agreement was no greater than that at issue here (control of 75% to 90% of the relevant markets). It is difficult to see how the two cases can be reconciled.

* * *

Notes and Questions

1. On remand, the Ninth Circuit ordered dismissal finding the FTC had failed to show that the CDA's restrictions had a net anticompetitive effect and that the evidence of anticompetitive intent was ambiguous. 224 F.3d 942 (9th Cir. 2000). While acknowledging that the Supreme Court had not mandated a full blown rule of reason inquiry, the Ninth Circuit "opt[ed] for a particularly searching rule of reason inquiry in light of the plausibility and strength of the procompetitive justifications" supplied by expert testimony that advertising restrictions tend to protect the public from false or misleading information or unscrupulous providers. In view of the Supreme Court's decision and the Ninth Circuit's prior findings, do you find this approach surprising? If you do, you are in good company; see Stephen Calkins, California Dental Association: Not a Quick Look but Not the Full Monty, 67 Antitrust L.J. 495 (2000); William J. Kolasky, California Dental Association v. FTC: The New Antitrust Empiricism, 14 Antitrust 68 (Fall 1999). Equally controversial was the Ninth Circuit's decision not to remand to the FTC for further proceedings. The Court concluded that the FTC had ample opportunity to present evidence under a rule of reason theory but had failed to do so.

In finding the FTC's proof of net anticompetitive effect wanting, the Ninth Circuit parsed a number of economic studies advanced by the Commission in support of the proposition that restrictions on advertising tend to raise prices and do not materially improve quality of services. Ultimately it declined to rely on empirical studies which dealt with complete bans on advertising (in contrast to the partial restrictions imposed by the CDA) or with professions other than dentistry, such as optometry or law. How exacting should a court's proof requirements be when dealing with empirical economic evidence? Does the expertise of the FTC as an administrative agency charged with combating misleading advertising supply a basis for decreasing the role of the courts as arbiters of competing economic studies? For a useful survey of the evidence concerning the effects of advertising, concluding that evidence not in the record before the Supreme Court "overwhelmingly demonstrates that the fears of the CDA majority [were] unjustified," see Timothy J. Muris, The Rule of Reason After California Dental, 68 Antitrust L.J. 527 (2000). See also Viazis v. American Association of Orthodontists, 314 F.3d 758 (5th Cir. 2002) (applying *California Dental* and concluding that orthodontist suspended for violating association's advertising rules had failed to proffer "relevant data").

2. In FTC v. Indiana Federation of Dentists, 476 U.S. 447, 106 S.Ct. 2009, 90 L.Ed.2d 445 (1986), the FTC examined an agreement among dentists to refuse to submit x-rays used for diagnosis and treatment of patients to insurers. Insurers required x-rays to carry out review of the necessity of treatment pursuant to dental insurance plans limiting payment to the "least expensive set adequate treatment." While not employing the per se rule, the Court adopted the form of analysis described in CDA as a "quick look."

> Application of the Rule of Reason to these facts is not a matter of any great difficulty. The Federation's policy takes the form of a horizontal agreement among the participating dentists to withhold from their customers a particular service that they desire—the forwarding of x-rays to insurance companies along with claim forms. "While this is not price fixing as such, no elaborate industry analysis is required to demonstrate the anti-competitive character of such an agreement." . . . A refusal to compete with respect to the package of services offered to customers, no less than a refusal to compete with respect to the price term of an agreement, impairs the ability of the market to advance social welfare by ensuring the provision of desired goods and services to consumers at a price approximating the marginal cost of providing them.

Id. at 459. Is there a significant difference between the conduct in *California Dental* and *Indiana Federation of Dentists*? Didn't both cases involve actions by a sizable majority of dentists to withhold information from purchasers on the grounds that they could not adequately evaluate it? Note the absence of direct proof of the restraint's effect on consumers in either case. Has the Court changed the requirements for "quick look" evaluations? What does *California Dental* suggest about the way courts should evaluate restrictions involving professionals in the future? Are the problems associated with asymmetry of information so pronounced in health care markets that professionals should be free from antitrust scrutiny? See Marina Lao, Comment: The Rule of Reason and Horizontal Restraints Involving Professionals, 68 Antitrust L.J. 499 (2000). For an insightful analysis of how antitrust might evaluate restraints of trade that improve overall welfare by overcoming market imperfections, see Peter J. Hammer, Antitrust Beyond Competition: Market Failures, Total Welfare, and the Challenge of Intramarket Second–Best Tradeoffs, 98 Mich. L. Rev. 849 (2000).

Problem: Quick Stop Clinics

Drug World, a pharmacy chain operating a large number of retail pharmacies in the upper Midwest, has announced plans to open 24–Hour "Quick Stop Clinics" at all its locations. The clinics will be staffed by RNs and PAs depending on state licensure and scope of practice laws. These providers will perform routine exams, take cultures, and prescribe medications within the scope of practice permitted under state law. Each clinic will enter into referral agreements with one or more local hospitals to assure direct access to physicians when the need presents. Good Samaritan Hospital (GSH) has entered into such an arrangement with a local Quick Stop Clinic. Under their partnership agreement, all doctors providing back up to Quick Stop RNs will have admitting privileges at GSH, and the clinics will be able to "streamline" a patient's journey to a specialist or through the emergency room at GSH, when medically appropriate.

A number of doctors holding staff privileges at GSH became quite upset when they got wind of this agreement. The group, though small (fewer than 5% of all doctors with privileges at the hospital), includes both primary care physicians who are concerned about losing current patients to the doctors to whom the clinic refers and several prominent specialists who feel they will lose established lines of referrals from primary care physicians. Some doctors believe that patients will come to them in worse shape, with missed diagnoses, and inadequate follow up. They have posted a notice at the hospital calling for an emergency meeting to discuss options to counter GSH's plan. The doctors intend to propose three possible courses of action, asking colleagues to:

- Agree that no doctors will serve as a supervisory physician to Quick Stop Clinic RNs or PAs or or accept referrals from the Clinic;

- Sign a letter to GSH adminstrators announcing plans to change their admitting practices so as to reduce the number of patients they admit to GSH; or

- Send a letter to all GSH physicians supplying academic studies and historical evidence of potential risks to patients from receiving care from nonphysicians under arrangements such as are proposed.

The CEO of GSH has approached you for advice on the legality of each action contemplated by the staff physicians. She says she wants to fight them vigorously and that she is willing to consider filing an antitrust lawsuit, complaining to the Department of Justice, terminating the staff privileges of the ringleaders of the group, or undertaking any other steps you recommend.

II.   MERGERS AND ACQUISITIONS

HOSPITAL CORPORATION OF AMERICA

106 F.T.C. 361 (1985).

CALVANI, COMM'R.

I.   INTRODUCTION TO THE CASE

A.   *The Acquisitions*

In August 1981, Respondent Hospital Corporation of America ("HCA"), the largest proprietary hospital chain in the United States, acquired Hospital Affiliates International ("HAI") in a stock transaction valued at approximately $650 million. [ ] At the time of the acquisition, HAI owned or leased 57 hospitals and managed 78 hospitals nationwide. Prior to its acquisition by HCA, HAI owned or managed five acute care hospitals in the general area of Chattanooga, Tennessee, and HCA acquired ownership or management of these hospitals through the transaction. Some four months later HCA acquired yet another hospital corporation, Health Care Corporation ("HCC"), in a stock transaction valued at approximately $30 million. At the time of the acquisition, HCC owned a single acute care hospital in Chattanooga. These two transactions provide the genesis for the instant case.

As a result of the HCA–HAI acquisition, Respondent increased its hospital operations in Chattanooga and its suburbs from ownership of one acute care hospital to ownership or management of four of the area's eleven acute care hospitals. Within the six-county Chattanooga Metropolitan Statistical Area ("Chattanooga MSA"), HCA changed its position from owner of one hospital to owner or manager of six of fourteen acute care hospitals. With the acquisition of HCC, HCA obtained yet another acute care hospital in Chattanooga. Thus, HCA became owner or manager of five of the eleven acute care hospitals within the Chattanooga urban area and seven of the fourteen in the Chattanooga MSA.

* * * Administrative Law Judge Parker found that the acquisitions violated Section 7 of the Clayton Act and Section 5 of the Federal Trade Commission Act, and ordered HCA to divest two of the hospitals of which it had acquired ownership. Judge Parker also ordered that HCA provide prior notification to the Commission of certain of its future hospital acquisitions. HCA appeals the Initial Decision on several grounds; Complaint Counsel appeal certain of Judge Parker's findings as well.

* * * We affirm Judge Parker's finding of liability and modify his opinion only as stated below.

* * *

III. THE PRODUCT MARKET

An acquisition violates Section 7 of the Clayton Act "where in any line of commerce in any section of the country, the effect of such acquisition may be substantially to lessen competition, or to tend to create a monopoly." 15 U.S.C. Sec. 18 (1982). Accordingly, we now turn to the definition of the relevant "line of commerce" or "product market" in which to measure the likely competitive effects of these acquisitions. In measuring likely competitive effects, we seek to define a product or group of products sufficiently distinct that buyers could not defeat an attempted exercise of market power on the part of sellers of those products by shifting purchases to still different products. Sellers might exercise market power by raising prices, limiting output or lowering quality. * * *

Complaint Counsel argued below that the product market [ ] was properly defined as the provision of acute inpatient hospital services and emergency hospital services provided to the critically ill. [ ] This definition would exclude non-hospital providers of outpatient services, e.g., free standing emergency centers, as well as non-hospital providers of inpatient services, e.g., nursing homes, from the product market. It would also exclude the outpatient business of hospitals, except for that provided to the critically ill in the emergency room. The rationale for excluding outpatient care is that inpatient services are the reason for being of acute care hospitals; inpatient services are needed by and consumed by patients in combination and therefore can be offered only by acute care hospitals. Inpatients in almost all cases will purchase a range of services and not just one test or procedure; they will typically consume a "cluster" of services involving 24–hour nursing, the services of specialized laboratory and X-ray equipment, the services of equipment needed to monitor vital functions or intervene in crises, and so forth. An acutely ill patient must be in a setting in which all of these various services can be provided together. * * * According to this reasoning, outpatient services are not an integral part of this "cluster of services" offered by acute care hospitals, and therefore must be excluded.

Respondent, on the other hand, urged that the market be defined to include outpatient care as well as inpatient care. Respondent's expert witness, Dr. Jeffrey E. Harris, testified that outpatient care is growing rapidly for hospitals, as well as for free-standing facilities such as emergency care and one-day surgery centers, which compete with hospitals for outpatients. Moreover, because of substantial changes in medical technology, there are a growing number of procedures that can be provided on an outpatient basis that previously could have been done on only an inpatient basis.

Judge Parker agreed that the market should include outpatient services provided by hospitals but excluded outpatient services provided by non-hospital providers, holding that only hospitals can provide the "unique combination" of services which the acute care patient needs. He defined the relevant product market to be the cluster of services offered by acute care hospitals, including outpatient as well as inpatient care, "since acute care hospitals compete with each other in offering both kinds of care and since . . . acute care outpatient facilities feed patients to the inpatient facilities."

Neither HCA nor Complaint Counsel appeal Judge Parker's product market definition.[ ] Accordingly, for purposes of this proceeding only, we accept Judge Parker's finding on this issue. [ ]

However, we do note that Judge Parker's definition does not necessarily provide a very happy medium between the two competing positions; the evidence in this case tended to show *both* that free-standing outpatient facilities compete with hospitals for many outpatients and that hospitals offer and inpatients consume a cluster of services that bears little relation to outpatient care. If so, it may be that defining the cluster of hospital inpatient services as a separate market better reflects competitive reality in this case. * * * Certainly, it is clear that anti-competitive behavior by hospital firms could significantly lessen competition for hospital inpatients that could not be defeated by competition from non-hospital outpatient providers. Our analysis will hence proceed with primary reference to the cluster of services provided to inpatients.

IV. THE GEOGRAPHIC MARKET

* * * Because we are concerned only with an area in which competition could be harmed, the relevant geographic market must be broad enough that buyers would be unable to switch to alternative sellers in sufficient numbers to defeat an exercise of market power by firms in the area. * * * If an exercise of market power could be defeated by the entry of products produced in another area, both areas should be considered part of the same geographic market for Section 7 purposes, since competition could not be harmed in the

smaller area. That is, the geographic market should determine not only the firms that constrain competitors' actions by currently selling to the same customers, but also those that would be a constraint because of their ability to sell to those customers should price or quality in the area change. * * *

* * *

HCA would have us adopt Hamilton County, Tennessee, together with Walker, Dade and Catoosa counties in Georgia, the "Chattanooga urban area," as the relevant geographic market. HCA predicates its conclusion largely on an analysis of evidence concerning physician admitting patterns.

* * * With few exceptions, every physician who admitted to Chattanooga urban area hospitals admitted exclusively to other hospitals in the Chattanooga urban area. Conversely, physicians admitting and treating patients at hospitals outside the Chattanooga urban area rarely admitted and treated patients at hospitals in the Chattanooga urban area.

* * *

Additionally, the weight of the evidence concerning patient origin suggests that patients admitted to Chattanooga urban area hospitals who live outside of the Chattanooga urban area are, with few exceptions, in need of specialized care and treatment unavailable in their own communities. * * * Hospitals in outlying communities do not always provide quite the same product that the urban area hospitals provide such patients, and therefore patient inflows are not necessarily indicative of the willingness of patients to leave their home areas for services that are available in those areas. Judge Parker agreed with HCA that the Chattanooga urban area is the relevant geographic market in this case. [ ]

On appeal, Complaint Counsel agree that the Chattanooga urban area is an appropriate geographic area in which to assess the competitive effects of these acquisitions. However, they claim that a much more appropriate geographic market is the federally designated Metropolitan Statistical Area that includes Chattanooga. In effect, Complaint Counsel would have us add the Tennessee counties of Marion and Sequatchie to the market proffered by HCA and adopted by Judge Parker. By adding this area, three additional hospitals—South Pittsburgh Municipal Hospital, Sequatchie General Hospital, and Whitwell Community Hospital—would be included in the relevant market. Both South Pittsburgh and Sequatchie were acquired by HCA from HAI, and Complaint Counsel seek divestiture by HCA of its long-term lease arrangement with South Pittsburgh. [ ]

* * *

* * * Geopolitical designations such as "MSA" may reflect a host of considerations that do not concern the issue of competition between hospitals. * * * Nor do we find any evidence that MSA designations were ever intended to reflect an economic market for purposes of Section 7. We do not here conclude that an MSA will never accurately reflect the relevant geographic market in a hospital merger case. But where, as here, the MSA designation excludes important sources of potential competition, it must be rejected. * * *

* * *

V. The Effect on Competition

A. *The Effect of HCA–Managed Hospitals*

One of the major dimensions of HCA's purchase of HAI was the acquisition of some 75 to 80 hospital management contracts. * * * Two of these were management contracts HAI had with two hospitals in the Chattanooga urban area—Downtown General Hospital and Red Bank Community Hospital. * * * HCA argues, and Judge Parker agreed, that Downtown General and Red Bank hospitals should be treated as entities completely separate from HCA, incapable of being significantly influenced by HCA in its role as administrator. * * *

We conclude that treating the two managed hospitals as entities completely independent of HCA is contrary to the overwhelming weight of the evidence in this case. As manager, HCA controls the competitive variables needed for successful coordination with the activities of HCA-owned hospitals in Chattanooga. Moreover, as manager it knows the competitive posture of managed hospitals so well that the likelihood of any anti-competitive behavior HCA wished to engage in is greatly increased.

* * *

Indeed, the very reason that a management firm is hired, as reflected in the management contracts, is to direct the competitive operations of the managed hospital. The evidence shows clearly that management recommendations, including proposed rate increases, are almost invariably followed by the boards of directors of Downtown General and Red Bank. * * *

* * *

* * * The evidence compels us to consider the market shares of Downtown General and Red Bank as part of HCA's market share in considering the effect on competition in this case. [ ] Even were the evidence not as compelling, we would consider HCA's management of the two hospitals to greatly enhance the likelihood of collusion in this market. [ ]

* * *

B. *The Nature of Competition Among Chattanooga Hospitals*

Traditionally, hospitals have competed for patients in three general ways: first, by competing for physicians to admit their patients; second, by competing directly for patients on the basis of amenities and comfort of surroundings; and third, by competing to a limited degree on the basis of price. The first two constitute "non-price" or "quality" competition, and by far have been in the past the most important of the three.

[The court explains that although nonprice competition has been the primary form of rivalry among hospitals, price competition is growing in the hospital industry and Chattanooga hospitals are now "far more likely to present themselves to insurers, employers and employee groups as less costly than their competitors as one method of attracting business."]

. . . We do not here conclude that price has been the prime arena in which hospitals in Chattanooga compete. However, we do think it clear that even though rates are not constantly adjusted due to a changing price structure, they have been periodically set with some reference to what the market will bear in face of the prices of other hospitals.

It is clear that Section 7 protects whatever price competition exists in a market, however limited. * * *

* * *

C.   Respondent's Market Share and Concentration in the Chattanooga Urban Area

Three ways to measure a hospital's share of the acute care hospital services market are by using: (1) bed capacity; (2) inpatient days; and (3) net revenues. Bed capacity and inpatient days measure a hospital's position with regard to the cluster of inpatient services, the heart of hospital care. Net revenues, on the other hand, account for both inpatient and outpatient services.

Naturally, because of their proposed market definitions, Complaint Counsel advocate use of inpatient measures, while HCA urges net revenues as the preferable measure since it accounts for outpatient services. We conclude, however, that the three measures are so similar in this case that they yield the same result whatever measure is used.

* * *

[The court concludes that HCA's market share increased significantly and that it considered "an increase in concentration in an already concentrated market to be of serious competitive concern, all other things being equal."]

[A]ll other things being equal, an increase in market concentration through a reduction in the absolute number of competitive actors makes interdependent behavior more likely. * * * These acquisitions decreased the number of independent firms in the market from 9 to 7. [ ] The costs of coordination or of policing any collusive agreement are less with fewer participants, and the elimination of competitive forces in this market facilitates joint anti-competitive behavior.

In sum, evidence of the increased concentration caused by these acquisitions points toward a finding of likely harm to competition, all other things being equal. [ ] HCA's acquisitions have made an already highly concentrated market more conducive to collusion by eliminating two of the healthiest sources of competition in the market and increasing concentration substantially. But all other things are not equal in this market, and statistical evidence is not the end of our inquiry. In the absence of barriers to entry, an exercise of market power can be defeated or deterred by the entry or potential entry of new firms regardless of the structure of the existing market. * * * We now turn to the issue of entry barriers and conclude that they confirm and even magnify the inference to be drawn from the concentration evidence in this case.

D.   Barriers to Entry

* * *

* * * [T]here is hardly free entry into the acute care hospital industry in either Tennessee or Georgia. Indeed, the CON [certificate of need] laws at

issue here create a classic "barrier to entry" under every definition of that term. In *Echlin Manufacturing Co.,* we defined a "barrier to entry" to include "additional long-run costs that must be incurred by an entrant relative to the long-run costs faced by incumbent firms." * * * We explained that "[t]he rationale underlying this definition is that low-cost incumbent firms can keep prices above the competitive level as long as those prices remain below the level that would provide an incentive to higher-cost potential entrants."

If a potential entrant desires to build a new hospital in Chattanooga, he must incur all the costs in time and money associated with obtaining a CON. The cost of starting a new hospital includes not only the start-up costs that any firm would incur to enter the market but also the costs of surviving the administrative process. Incumbents in this market, however, did not incur such costs during initial construction. They have only had to incur those costs for additions made to bed capacity since the enactment of the CON laws a decade ago. [ ] Incumbents thus have a long run cost advantage over potential entrants. The result is that market power could be exercised by incumbents without attracting attempts at entry as long as supracompetitive profits are not high enough for a potential entrant to justify incurring all the ordinary costs of starting a hospital *plus* the significant costs of obtaining a CON.

The evidence is clear that those costs are significant in this market. We agree with Judge Parker that because incumbent hospitals can oppose new entry, even an unsuccessful opposition to a CON application may delay its disposition by several years. * * *

Thus the CON process provides existing hospitals in the Chattanooga urban area ample opportunity to significantly forestall the entry of a new hospital or the expansion of an existing hospital within the area. Indeed, the evidence shows that existing hospitals frequently oppose CON applications when they feel competitively threatened. * * *

* * *

In sum, it is not merely the costs of obtaining a CON that a potential entrant faces, but the significant risk of being denied entry once those costs have been incurred. This risk, which incumbents did not have to face when building their hospitals, in effect raises the costs of entry a significantly greater amount. As a result, many potential entrants may decide not to even attempt entry. Indeed, the evidence shows that CON regulation has had a deterrent effect in the Chattanooga market.

* * *

E. The Nature and Likelihood of Anti-competitive Behavior in the Chattanooga Hospital Market

1. The Nature of Anti-competitive Behavior

* * *

Some of the most likely forms of collusion between hospitals would involve collective resistance to emerging cost containment pressures from third-party payors and alternative providers. For example, joint refusals to deal with HMOs or PPOs may occur, or perhaps joint refusals to deal on the most favorable terms. Conspiracies to boycott certain insurance companies that are generating price competition may occur. Utilization review programs may also be resisted. Hospitals could concertedly refuse to provide the information desired by third-party payors—information that would otherwise be provided as hospitals vie to attract the business of those payors and their subscribers. The result of any such boycott would be to raise prices, reduce quality of services or both. [ ]

* * *

Quality competition itself might also be restricted. For example, the group of hospitals in a relevant market might agree to staff their wards with fewer nurses yet continue to maintain current rates for inpatient services. Patients would be harmed by the resulting drop in quality of services without any compensating reduction in price of services. Colluding hospitals in the market, however, would profit from their agreement by cutting costs without cutting revenues. Again, hospitals could accomplish anti-competitive ends not only by fixing staff-patient ratios but by agreeing on wages or benefits to be paid certain personnel—for example, laboratory technicians. Indeed, wage and salary surveys are common in this market. The result would be the same—to hold the cost of inputs down with probable harm to the quality of output of health care services. [ ] Hospitals could also agree not to compete for each other's personnel or medical staff. Indeed, some Chattanooga urban area hospital firms have already engaged in such behavior.

Moreover, under certificate of need legislation, the addition of new services and purchases of certain kinds of new equipment require a demonstration of need for the expenditure, and the existence of need is determined in part by the facilities already provided in the community. It would thus be to the advantage of competing hospitals to enter into agreements among themselves as to which competitor will apply for which service or for which piece of equipment. * * * Such market division by private agreement would save hospitals the expense of applying for numerous CONs but may harm the quality of care that would be available to patients were CON approval sought independently by each hospital with reference to its own merits and expertise.

Concerted opposition to the CON application of a potential new entrant is yet another manner in which Chattanooga hospitals could successfully collude. * * *

Anti-competitive pricing behavior could also take several forms. For example, hospitals could work out agreements with respect to pricing formulas. * * * Hospitals could also successfully collude with respect to price by agreeing not to give discounts to businesses, insurers and other group purchasers such as HMOs and PPOs. * * *

In sum, we conclude that hospitals compete in a myriad of ways that could be restricted anti-competitively through collusion. [ ] Thus, it appears that a merger analysis in this case need be no different than in any other case; market share and concentration figures, evidence of entry barriers and other market evidence taken together appear to yield as accurate a picture of competitive conditions as they do in other settings. Nevertheless, although HCA concedes that many of the above described forms of collusion *could* occur, the heart of HCA's case is that collusion in this market is inherently unlikely, and to that contention we now turn.

2. *The Likelihood of Anti-competitive Behavior*

Section 7 of the Clayton Act prohibits acquisitions that may have the effect of substantially lessening competition or tending to create a monopoly. Because Section 7 applies to "incipient" violations, actual anti-competitive effects need not be shown; an acquisition is unlawful if such an effect is reasonably probable. * * *

The small absolute number of competitors in this market, the high concentration and the extremely high entry barriers indicate a market in which anti-competitive behavior is reasonably probable after the acquisitions. The fact that industry members recognize the enormity of entry barriers makes collusion even more probable. In addition, hospital markets have certain features that evidence a likelihood of collusion or other anti-competitive behavior when they become highly concentrated.

First, price elasticity of demand for hospital services is very low, which makes anti-competitive behavior extremely profitable and hence attractive. * * * Second, because consumers of hospital services cannot arbitrage or resell them as is often possible with goods, discrimination among different groups of consumers is possible. That is, collusion may be directed at a certain group or certain groups of consumers, such as a particular insurance company, without the necessity of anti-competitive behavior toward other groups. Third, the traditions of limited price competition and disapproval of advertising provide an incentive for future anti-competitive restrictions of those activities. Fourth, and in the same vein, the advent of incentives to resist new cost containment pressures may create a substantial danger of hospital collusion to meet pressures. Fifth, the hospital industry has a tradition of cooperative problem solving which makes collusive conduct in the future more likely. Hospitals have historically participated in voluntary health planning in a coordinated manner, and along with other professional organizations, such as medical societies, have participated in developing joint solutions to industry problems.

* * * The most convincing evidence of the facility with which such collusion could occur is a blatant market allocation agreement executed in 1981 between Red Bank Community Hospital and HCC. The parties actually *signed a contract* under which Red Bank agreed that for a period of three years it would not "file any application for a Certificate of Need for psychiatric facilities or nursing home facilities." Moreover, the parties agreed that they would not compete for each other's personnel and medical staff during that time period, and that they would not oppose each other's CON applications in certain areas. Such an overt agreement to refrain from competition at the very least demonstrates the predisposition of some firms in the market to collude when it is in their interest; at worst it shows a callous disregard for the antitrust laws. [ ]

* * *

Furthermore, a basis for collusion is provided by the exchanges of rate, salary and other competitively sensitive information that occur in this market. * * *

* * *

* * * It is true that the undisputed evidence shows that more vigorous competition, including more direct price competition, is emerging in the health care industry, but it is a fallacy to conclude that growing competition in health care markets means that these acquisitions pose no threat to that competition. In fact, it is just that emerging competition that must be protected from mergers that facilitate the suppression of such competition. * * *

a. *Non-profit Hospitals and the Likelihood of Collusion*

HCA contends that the most fundamental difference between hospitals in Chattanooga is that several of the hospitals are "non-profit" institutions. Economic theory presumes that businesses in an industry are profit-maximizers and that output will be restricted in pursuit of profits. Non-profit hospitals, the argument goes, have no incentive to maximize profits, rather, they seek to maximize "output" or the number of patients treated. HCA contends that non-profit hospitals may have other goals as well, such as providing the most sophisticated and highest quality care possible, or pursuing religious or governmental goals. In short, HCA argues that collusion would not occur because the "for-profit" and "non-profit" competitors have no common goal.

We disagree that non-profit hospitals have no incentive to collude with each other or with proprietary hospitals to achieve anti-competitive ends. First, we note that non-profit status of market participants is no guarantee of competitive behavior. * * *

* * *

In addition, administrators of non-profit hospitals may seek to maximize their personal benefits and comfort through what would otherwise be known as profit-seeking activity. * * *

* * *

[T]wo major non-profit hospitals, Erlanger and Tri–County, have a tremendous incentive to participate in price collusion. Erlanger has sole responsibility for unreimbursed indigent care in Hamilton County. * * * Because it must subsidize unreimbursed care out of the rates charged to paying customers, Erlanger cannot compete effectively through price cutting. Erlanger's rates are 50 dollars per day *or 10%* higher than they would be if such cross-subsidization between paying and non-paying patients were not necessary. Because it cannot price below a level that covers the direct costs it incurs for indigent care, Erlanger would in fact benefit from a decrease in price competition through interdependent behavior. The same analysis applies to Tri–County, which must provide care for indigent residents of Walker, Dade and Catoosa counties in Georgia, and shift costs from non-paying to paying patients. * * *

* * *

b. *Purported Obstacles to Successful Coordination*

... HCA argues that even if hospitals in Chattanooga were inclined to collude, the administrators of those hospitals would find it difficult to reach anti-competitive agreements or understandings, or to sustain them if they ever were reached. This is so because the ideal market circumstances for collusion are not present, i.e. where manufacturers are selling "some simple, relatively homogeneous good, well characterized by a single price." HCA contends that hospital services are heterogeneous and influenced by a variety of complicating factors. Hospitals provide a large number of varied medical tests and treatments and each patient receives unpredictable personalized service the extent of which is determined by physicians. Moreover, HCA claims costs and demand vary between hospitals. And because the dominant avenues of competition relate to the quality of medical care and patient amenities, hospitals would have to agree on a whole host of things to eliminate competition in a manner sufficient to earn monopoly returns, it is alleged.

* * *

HCA's analysis of the likelihood of collusion distorts competitive reality. HCA would have us believe that the world of possible collusion is limited to complicated formulae concerning every aspect of hospital competition—that market power can only be exercised with respect to the entire cluster of services that constitutes the acute care hospital market through a conspiracy fixing the overall quantity or quality of treatment running to each patient in the market. Rather than focus on the likely avenues of collusion among hospitals, HCA assumes into existence a world in which collusion is infeasible.

* * *

HCA offers an additional reason why the acquisitions allegedly create no risk that Chattanooga hospitals will collude to eliminate price competition, arguing that price collusion is unlikely because of the role of Blue Cross in this market. * * *

We cannot accept HCA's claims that Blue Cross has both the omniscience and market power to halt successful collusion by Chattanooga hospitals. First, under the current Blue Cross charge approval system, collusion could be difficult to detect. If all the hospital firms in Chattanooga attempt to raise prices a similar amount in the review process, coordinated pricing could be overlooked; there is no *a priori* reason why Blue Cross would consider this to be the result of collusion rather than a rise in costs. * * *

Furthermore, even if detected, we do not think such collusion could be easily deterred by Blue Cross. HCA ignores the fact that Blue Cross has a contract not only with participating hospitals but also with its subscribers. Blue Cross must serve its subscribers in the Chattanooga area, and HCA does not explain how Blue Cross could reject a concerted effort by the hospitals there even if it wanted to; certainly, Blue Cross could not ask its subscribers to all go to Knoxville for hospital care if Chattanooga urban area hospitals colluded. * * *

* * *

VII. Conclusion

We hold that HCA's acquisitions of HAI and HCC may substantially lessen competition in the Chattanooga urban area acute care hospital market in violation of Section 7 of the Clayton Act and Section 5 of the Federal Trade Commission Act.

Notes and Questions

1. The Seventh Circuit reviewed and upheld the decision of the Federal Trade Commission in Hospital Corporation of America v. FTC, 807 F.2d 1381 (7th Cir. 1986). Calling the FTC's decision a "model of lucidity," Judge Posner reviewed the Commission's analysis of the merger:

> When an economic approach is taken in a section 7 case, the ultimate issue is whether the challenged acquisition is likely to facilitate collusion. In this perspective the acquisition of a competitor has no economic significance in itself; the worry is that it may enable the acquiring firm to cooperate (or cooperate better) with other leading competitors on reducing or limiting output, thereby pushing up the market price. *Hospital Corporation* calls the issue whether an acquisition is likely to have such an effect "economic," which of course it is. But for purposes of judicial review, as we have said, it is a factual issue subject to the substantial evidence rule.

Judge Posner discussed HCA's arguments that collusion is unlikely because of the heterogeneity of hospital markets, the rapid technological and economic change experienced by the hospital industry, and the size of third party payers. He concluded: "Most of these facts do detract from a conclusion that collusion in this market is a serious danger, but it was for the Commission—it is not for us—to determine their weight." This analysis is directed at the risk of "coordinated effects" resulting from a merger—that is, an enhancement of the ability of the merged entity to exercise market power by acting in coordination with others competitors in a market. Compare this kind of harm with the "unilateral effects" analysis in the Evanston Hospital case *infra*. For an explication of the overall methodology followed by the federal enforcement agencies in evaluating mergers see U.S. Department of Justice and Federal Trade Commission, Merger Guidelines (1992), 57 Fed. Reg. 41552 (Sept. 10, 1992).

2. Note that the enforcement agencies, affirmed by the courts, have identified as the relevant product market in hospital merger cases a "cluster market" consisting of most inpatient services and some outpatient services for which there are no practical alternatives. A factor complicating product market definition is the fact that the numerous services in the "cluster" have widely differing geographic market dimensions. For some sophisticated tertiary care services like organ transplants, the geographic market is certainly regional or perhaps national, while the markets for emergency care and many routine acute care services are obviously very local. Almost all litigated hospital merger cases have settled on a product market definition that encompasses primary and secondary services, but excludes tertiary care which has a wider geographic market but usually does not impact the competitive dynamics among local hospitals. Might it be better to refine the analysis further by delineating those portions of the product market which are predominantly local and not subject to substitution by distant hospitals? Should each DRG be a separate product market? See, FTC v. Butterworth Health Corp., 946 F.Supp. 1285 (W.D.Mich. 1996).

Antitrust enforcement has reached mergers involving numerous other segments of the health care industry besides hospitals. For example, state and federal enforcers have challenged mergers of physician groups (Maine v. Cardiovascular & Thoracic Assocs., P.A., 1992–2 Trade Cas. (CCH) ¶ 69,985 1992 WL 503594 (Maine Sup. Ct., Kennebec Cnty., 1992) (consent decree); Maine v. Mid Coast Anesthesia, P.A., 1991–2) Trade Cas. (CCH) ¶ 69,683 (Maine Sup. Ct., Kennebec Cty., 1992) (consent decree), and Letter from Charles F. Rule, Assistant Attorney General, Antitrust Division, to William L. Trombetta (Aug. 28, 1987) (Business Review Letter to Danbury Surgical Associates); rehabilitation hospitals (Healthsouth Rehabilitation Corp., 60 Fed. Reg. 5,401–01 (Dept. of Justice, 1994) (consent order); hospitals providing inpatient psychiatric care (Charter Medical and National Medical Enterprises, 59 Fed. Reg. 60,804–01 (Dept. of Justice, 1994)); skilled nursing facilities (United States v. Beverly Enterprises, 1984–1 Trade Cas. (CCH) ¶ 66,052 (M.D. Ga. 1984) (consent decree); retail pharmacy services (THC Corp., 59 Fed. Reg. 46,438 (Dept. of Justice, 1994); HMOs (In the Matter of Harvard Community Health Plan, Inc. and Pilgrim Health Care, Inc., No. 95–0331 (Suffolk Superior Ct. Mass. 1995)); and an "innovation market" in gene therapy techniques (Ciba–Geigy Ltd., 62 Fed. Reg. 409 (1997) (consent decree). See also FTC v. Cardinal Health, Inc., 12 F. Supp. 2d 34 (D.D.C. 1998) (enjoining two mergers involving wholesale drug distributors and rejecting defendants' argument that the relevant market should include self-distribution by large pharmaceutical chains that purchased and warehoused their own pharmaceuticals directly from manufacturers). Market definition poses difficult questions in these cases. For example, how would you go about determining the geographic market for skilled nursing home services? Who is the "buyer" of these services?

FEDERAL TRADE COMMISSION v. TENET HEALTH CARE CORPORATION

United States Court of Appeals Eighth Circuit, 1999.
186 F.3d 1045

Beam, Circuit Judge.

Tenet Healthcare and Poplar Bluff Physicians Group, Inc., doing business as Doctors' Regional Medical Center (collectively, Tenet) appeal the district court's order enjoining the merger of two hospitals in Poplar Bluff, Missouri. After a five-day hearing, the district court granted a motion for a preliminary injunction filed by the Federal Trade Commission (FTC) and the State of Missouri. The district court found a substantial likelihood that the merger would substantially lessen competition between acute care hospitals in Poplar Bluff, Missouri, in violation of section 7 of the Clayton Act, 15 U.S.C. § 18. We reverse.

I. Background

* * *

Tenet Healthcare Corporation owns Lucy Lee Hospital in Poplar Bluff, a general acute care hospital that provides primary and secondary care services 201 licensed beds ... and operates ten outpatient clinics in the surrounding counties. Doctors' Regional Medical Center in Poplar Bluff is presently owned by a group of physicians, ... has 230 licensed beds ... and also operates several rural health clinics in the area. Though profitable, both hospitals are underutilized and have had problems attracting specialists to the area. Tenet recently entered into an agreement to purchase Doctors' Regional which it will operate as a long-term care facility, consolidating inpatient services of the two hospitals at Lucy Lee. It plans to employ more specialists at the merged facility and to offer higher quality care in a comprehensive, integrated delivery system that would include some tertiary care.

* * *

The evidence adduced at the hearing shows that Lucy Lee and Doctors' Regional are the only two hospitals in Poplar Bluff, other than a Veteran's Hospital. The combined service area of these hospitals covers eight counties and an approximate fifty-mile radius from Poplar Bluff.*

Market participants, specifically, employers, healthplans and network providers testified that they had negotiated substantial discounts and favorable per diem rates with either or both Lucy Lee and Doctors' Regional as a result of "playing the two hospitals off each other." These managed care organizations and employers testified that if the merged entity were to raise its prices by 10 percent, the health plans would have no choice but to simply pay the increased price. They testified that they perceive it is essential for the plans to include a Poplar Bluff hospital in their benefit packages because their enrollees would not travel to other towns for primary and secondary inpatient treatment. They stated that their employees and subscribers find it convenient to use a Poplar Bluff hospital; are loyal to their physicians in Poplar Bluff and would not be amenable to a health benefit plan that did not include a Poplar Bluff hospital.

The evidence shows that patient choice of hospitals is determined by many variables, including patient/physician loyalty, perceptions of quality, geographic proximity and, most importantly or determinatively, access to hospitals through an insurance plan. Managed care organizations have been able to influence or change patient behavior with financial incentives in other healthcare markets. This practice is known as "steering." Representatives of Poplar Bluff managed care entities testified, however, that they did not believe such efforts would be successful in the Poplar Bluff market. They testified it would be unlikely that they could steer their subscribers to another hospital, or could exclude the merged Poplar Bluff entity in the event of a price increase, in spite of the fact that such tactics had been successful in other markets. They did not regard the Cape Girardeau hospitals as an alternative to Poplar Bluff hospitals because the Cape Girardeau hospitals were more costly. Witnesses conceded, however, that employees had been successfully "steered" to other area hospitals in the past. Several employers testified that they could successfully steer their employees to Missouri Delta Hospital in Sikeston, Missouri. The representative of one large employer testified that the large employers could prevent price increases through negotiation based on their market power and that the merged entity would provide better quality healthcare.

Lucy Lee and Doctors' Regional obtain ninety percent of their patients from zip codes within a fifty-mile radius of Poplar Bluff. In eleven of the top twelve zip codes, however, significant patient admissions-ranging from 22% to 70%-were to hospitals other than those in Poplar Bluff. There is no dispute that Poplar Bluff residents travel to St. Louis, Memphis, and Jonesboro for tertiary care. The evidence also shows, however, that significant numbers of patients in the Poplar Bluff service area travel to other towns for primary and secondary treatment that is also available in Poplar Bluff.

* * *

---

* A "service area" is generally defined as the area from which a hospital derives ninety per-cent of its inpatients.

II. DISCUSSION

* * *

A geographic market is the area in which consumers can practically turn for alternative sources of the product and in which the antitrust defendants face competition. Market share must be established in a well-defined market. [ ] A properly defined geographic market includes potential suppliers who can readily offer consumers a suitable alternative to the defendant's services. [ ] Determination of the relevant geographic market is highly fact sensitive. [ ] The proper market definition can be determined only after a factual inquiry into the commercial realities faced by consumers.

The government has the burden of proving the relevant geographic market. [ ] To meet this burden, the FTC must present evidence on the critical question of where consumers of hospital services could practicably turn for alternative services should the merger be consummated and prices become anticompetitive. [ ] This evidence must address where consumers could practicably go, not on where they actually go. [ ] *Bathke,* 64 F.3d at 346 (articulating the test as the distance "customers will travel in order to avoid doing business at [the entity that has raised prices]" rather than the distance customers would travel absent a price increase); [ ].

The FTC proposes a relevant geographic market that essentially matches its service area: a fifty-mile radius from downtown Poplar Bluff. It is from this service area that the two hospitals obtain ninety percent of their patients. A service area, however, is not necessarily a merging firm's geographic market for purposes of antitrust analysis.

* * *

The question before us is whether the FTC provided sufficient evidence that the proposed merger will result in the merged entity possessing market power within the relevant geographic market. Because we conclude that the FTC produced insufficient evidence of a well-defined relevant geographic market, we find that it did not show that the merged entity will possess such market power.

The district court found that statistical evidence did not establish either the geographic market proposed by the FTC or the market proposed by Tenet. It nonetheless found, relying on anecdotal evidence, that the merger would likely be anticompetitive. Our review of the record convinces us that the district court erred in several respects. The evidence in this case falls short of establishing a relevant geographic market that excludes the Sikeston or Cape Girardeau areas. The evidence shows that hospitals in either or both of these towns, as well as rural hospitals throughout the area, are practical alternatives for many Poplar Bluff consumers.

In adopting the FTC's position, the district court improperly discounted the fact that over twenty-two percent of people in the most important zip codes already use hospitals outside the FTC's proposed market for treatment that is offered at Poplar Bluff hospitals. The district court also failed to fully credit the significance of the consumers who live outside Poplar Bluff, particularly those patients within the FTC's proposed geographic market who actually live or work closer to a hospital outside that geographic market than to either of the Poplar Bluff hospitals. If patients use hospitals outside the service area, those hospitals can act as a check on the exercise of market power by the hospitals within the service area. [ ] The FTC's contention that the merged hospitals would have eighty-four percent of the market for inpatient primary and secondary services within a contrived market area that stops just short of including a regional hospital (Missouri Delta in Sikeston) that is closer to many patients than the Poplar Bluff hospitals, strikes us as absurd. The proximity of many patients to hospitals in other towns, coupled with the compelling and essentially unrefuted evidence that the switch to another provider by a small percentage of patients would constrain a price increase, shows that the FTC's proposed market is too narrow.

We question the district court's reliance on the testimony of managed care payers, in the face of contrary evidence, that these for-profit entities would unhesitatingly accept a price increase rather than steer their subscribers to hospitals in Sikeston or Cape Girardeau. Without necessarily being disingenuous or self-serving or both, the testimony is at least contrary to the payers' economic interests and thus is suspect.* In spite of their testimony to the contrary, the evidence shows that large, sophisticated third-party buyers can do resist price increases, especially where consolidation results in cost savings to the merging entities. The testimony of the market participants spoke to current competitor perceptions and consumer habits and failed to show where consumers could practicably go for inpatient hospital services.

The district court rejected the Cape Girardeau hospitals as practicable alternatives because they were more costly. In so doing, it underestimated the impact of nonprice competitive factors, such as quality. The evidence shows that one reason for the significant amount of migration from the Poplar Bluff hospitals to either Sikeston, Cape Girardeau, or St. Louis is the actual or perceived difference in quality of care. The apparent willingness of Poplar Bluff residents to travel for better quality care must be considered. As the district court noted, healthcare decisions are based on factors other than price. It is for that reason that, although they are less expensive, HMOs are not always an employer's or individual's choice in healthcare services. *See* Blue Cross and Blue Shield United of Wisconsin v. Marshfield Clinic, 65 F.3d 1406, 1412, 1410 (7th Cir. 1995) (Posner, J.) (noting "[g]enerally you must pay more for higher quality" and "the HMO's incentive is to keep you healthy if it can but if you get very sick, and are unlikely to recover to a healthy state involving few medical expenses, to let you die as quickly and cheaply as possible."). Thus, the fact that Cape Girardeau hospitals are higher priced than Poplar Bluff hospitals does not necessarily mean they are not competitors. [ ] The district court placed an inordinate emphasis on price competition without considering the impact of a corresponding reduction in quality.

We further find that although Tenet's efficiencies defense may have been properly rejected by the district court, the district court should nonetheless have considered evidence of enhanced efficiency in the context of the competitive effects of the merger. The evidence shows that a hospital that is larger and more efficient than Lucy Lee or Doctors' Regional will provide better medical care than either of those hospitals could separately. The merged

---

* We add that, in making this observation, we do not question the district court's assessment of the credibility of these witnesses. Although the witnesses may have testified truthfully as to their present intentions, market participants are not always in the best opinion to assess the market long term. [ ]

entity will be able to attract more highly qualified physicians and specialists and to offer integrated delivery and some tertiary care. [ ] The evidence shows that the merged entity may well enhance competition in the greater Southeast Missouri area.

In assessing the "commercial realities" faced by consumers, the district court did not ... consider the impact of the entry of managed care into the Cape Girardeau market. The evidence shows that managed care has reduced prices in Poplar Bluff and in other markets. A similar downward pressure on prices is now being felt in Cape Girardeau, with the recent entry of managed care into that market. The district court also relied on the seemingly outdated assumption of doctor-patient loyalty that is not supported by the record. The evidence shows, and the district court acknowledged, that the issue of access to a provider through an insurance plan is determinative of patient choice. Essentially, the evidence shows that patients will choose whatever doctors or hospitals are covered by their health plan. Undeniably, although many patients might prefer to be loyal to their doctors, it is, unfortunately, a luxury they can no longer afford.... As much as many patients long for the days of old-fashioned and local, if expensive and inefficient, healthcare, recent trends in healthcare management have made the old healthcare model obsolete.

The reality of the situation in our changing healthcare environment may be that Poplar Bluff cannot support two high-quality hospitals. Third-party payers have reaped the benefit of a price war in a small corner of the market for healthcare services in Southeastern Missouri, at the arguable cost of quality to their subscribers. Antitrust laws simply do not protect that benefit when the evidence shows that there are other practical alternatives for healthcare in the area. We are mindful that competition is the driving force behind our free enterprise system and that, unless barriers have been erected to constrain the normal operation of the market, "a court ought to exercise extreme caution because judicial intervention in a competitive situation can itself upset the balance of market forces, bringing about the very ills the antitrust laws were meant to prevent." [] This appears to have even more force in an industry, such as healthcare, experiencing significant and profound changes. Under the circumstances presented in this case, the FTC has not shown a likelihood of success on the merits of its section 7 complaint and we find the district court erred in granting injunctive relief.

Notes and Questions

1. The geographic market determination turns on the question of where customers could practicably turn in the event that prices were increased as a result of enhanced market power (or in the terminology of the Merger Guidelines, there was a "small but significant increase in price"). In the context of hospital mergers, patient origin data (usually compiled using the zip code of the residence of each patient) has traditionally been used to calculate the inflow and outflow of patients to hospitals from a geographic region. This data, however, is at best a starting point for analysis, as the Eighth Circuit points out. Courts must ask where buyers (patients) or their health plans or employers would turn in the event of a price increase resulting from the merger. What evidence did the FTC and the State of Missouri rely on to answer this question? Do you agree with the reasons supplied by the court to dispute the government's analysis? Given the speculative nature of the question, what evidence would you regard as most

reliable? Does the fact that some individuals are willing to travel some distance to receive hospital services necessarily imply that others will also do so if prices are increased? For the view of economists branding these assumptions as fallacious because individuals have highly heterogeneous preferences regarding traveling for hospitals care based on the availability of family support, their place of employment, convenience, and because hospitals are highly differentiated in their services, amenities, reputations, and so forth, see Cory Capps et al., The Silent Majority Fallacy of the Elzinga Hogarty Criteria: A Critique and New Approach to Analyzing Hospital Mergers. Natl'l Bureau of Econ. Research, Working Paper No. 8216, 2001. See also, Kenneth Danger & H.E. Frech, Critical Thinking about "Critical Loss" in Antitrust, 46 Antitrust L. Bull. 339 (2001); James Langenfeld & W. Li, Critical Loss Analysis in Evaluating Mergers, 46 Antitrust Bull. 299 (2001). But see Barry Harris & Joseph J. Simon, Focusing Market Definition: How Much Substitution is Enough?, 12 Research L. & Econ. 207 (1989).

2.   The government lost seven consecutive hospital merger cases in the 1990s, most on the issue of whether the government had correctly defined the geographic market. See e.g., FTC v. Freeman Hospital, 69 F.3d 260 (8th Cir. 1995); California v. Sutter Health System, 84 F. Supp. 2d 1057 (N.D.Cal. 2000). See Thomas L. Greaney, Chicago's Procrustean Bed, *supra* (analyzing cases and noting courts' failures to acknowledge market failures and product differentiation as cause of overestimating size of hospital markets). Does the court's opinion in *Tenet* suggest a hostility toward managed care or skepticism about the benefits of hospital competition in general? See id. (suggesting that the "managed care backlash" may have subtlety influence courts in certain antitrust cases).

Responding to their lack of success in court, the FTC and DOJ produced a lengthy report on competition policy in health care, and conducted retrospective studies of the impact of horizontal hospital mergers in selected markets around the country, including some that were the subject of unsuccessful litigation by the government. See FTC & Department of Justice, Dose of Competition *supra*. The FTC ultimately brought an administrative complaint challenging one already consummated merger, between the Evanston Northwestern Healthcare Corporation and Highland Park Hospital, which is discussed in the following section.

3.   *Overcoming the Presumption of Illegality: Nonprofit Status and Other Factors.* If the government establishes a prima facie case of illegality based on market share and market concentration data, defendants may overcome that presumption by showing that the merger is not likely to have anticompetitive effects. They may do this by proving that market conditions or special characteristics of the merging firms make it unlikely that they will exercise market power after the merger is consummated. See Merger Guidelines, § 2; 2 Furrow, et al., Health Law § 14–58. A number of courts have refused to find that the not-for-profit status of the merging hospitals constitutes sufficient grounds to rebut the government's prima facie case. See, e.g., U.S. v. Rockford Memorial Corp., 898 F.2d 1278 (7th Cir. 1990) A district court closely examined the issue with novel results in FTC v. Butterworth Health Corporation and Blodgett Memorial Medical Center, 946 F.Supp. 1285 (W.D.Mich. 1996), aff'd 121 F.3d 708 (6th Cir. 1997). The court found that not-for-profit hospitals do not operate in the same manner as profit-maximizing businesses, especially when their boards of directors are comprised of community business leaders who have a direct stake in maintaining high quality, low cost hospitals.

Do you agree that such hospitals are, as the court suggested, more likely to behave in the interests of their consumers (akin to "consumer cooperatives") rather than acting as profit maximizers? What assumptions does this finding make about the role of board members in directing the affairs of a hospital? What limits are placed on them by their fiduciary duties as board members? In this connection, the *Butterworth* court also relied on a number of voluntary "community commitments" made by the merging hospitals, including a freeze on prices or charges, commitments to limit profit margins, and promises to serve the medically needy. Do such assurances provide a sufficient guarantee that the parties will not exercise market power? See FTC & Dept. of Justice, A Dose of Competition, ch. 4 at 33 ("nonprofit status should not be considered as a factor in predicting whether a hospital merger is likely to be anticompetitive"); Barak K. Richman, Antitrust and Nonprofit Hospital Mergers: A Return to Basics, ___ U. Penn L. Rev. ___ (criticizing courts' analysis of nonprofit status and arguing the issue has diverted attention from the core concerns of antitrust merger doctrine); Thomas L. Greaney, Antitrust and Hospital Mergers: Does the Nonprofit Form Affect Competitive Substance? 31 J. Health Pol. Pol'y & L. 511 (2006) (rejecting FTC/DOJ preemptive approach and suggesting that systematic differences between nonprofit and for-profit hospital behavior may warrant consideration in some cases).

4. Other factors sometimes advanced to rebut the presumption of illegality include the financial weakness of one of the merging firms and the relative strength of buyers in the market. Entities claiming protection under the "failing firm" defense face high proof burdens, see Merger Guidelines § 5.1, but the defense was successfully asserted in California v. Sutter Health System, 84 F. Supp. 2d 1057 (N.D.Cal. 2000). In FTC v. Cardinal Health, Inc., 12 F. Supp.2d 34 (D.C. 1998), the court carefully analyzed the defendants' rebuttal claims that ease of entry into the wholesale drug distribution market should obviate competitive concerns. The court found that, despite a few examples of successful entry by new drug wholesalers, the defendants had failed to demonstrate that significant and effective entry was likely given various barriers that had impeded or slowed new competitors' effectiveness in the market. The court also rejected the defendants' claim that powerful buyers would likely counteract the defendants' market power.

IN THE MATTER OF EVANSTON NORTHWESTERN HEALTHCARE CORP.

Federal Trade Commission, August 6, 2007.

OPINION OF THE COMMISSION

I. INTRODUCTION

In 2000, Evanston Northwestern Healthcare Corporation ("Evanston") merged with Highland Park Hospital ("Highland Park"). Prior to the merger, Evanston owned Evanston Hospital and Glenbrook Hospital.

The Commission issued an administrative complaint challenging Evanston's acquisition of Highland Park under Section 7 of the Clayton Act four years after the transaction closed. Given that the merger was consummated well before the Commission commenced this case, we were able to examine not only pre-merger evidence, but also evidence about what happened after the merger.

There is no dispute that ENH substantially raised its prices shortly after the merging parties consummated the transaction. There is disagreement about the cause of those price increases, however. Complaint counsel maintains that the merger eliminated significant competition between Evanston and Highland Park, which allowed ENH to exercise market power against health care insurance companies. Respondent argues that, during the due diligence process for the merger, ENH obtained information about Highland Park's prices that showed that Evanston had been charging rates that were below competitive levels for a number of years. Respondent contends that most of ENH's merger-related price increases simply reflect its efforts to raise Evanston Hospital's prices to competitive rates. Respondent also maintains that some portion of the merger-related price increases reflects increased demand for Highland Park's services due to post-merger improvements at the hospital.

Chief Administrative Law Judge Stephen J. McGuire ("ALJ") found in his Initial Decision that the transaction violated Section 7 of the Clayton Act and ordered ENH to divest Highland Park. We affirm the ALJ's decision that the transaction violated Section 7 of the Clayton Act. Considered as a whole, the evidence demonstrates that the transaction enabled the merged firm to exercise market power and that the resulting anticompetitive effects were not offset by merger-specific efficiencies. The record shows that senior officials at Evanston and Highland Park anticipated that the merger would give them greater leverage to raise prices, that the merged firm did raise its prices immediately and substantially after completion of the transaction, and that the same senior officials attributed the price increases in part to increased bargaining leverage produced by the merger.

The econometric analyses performed by both complaint counsel's and respondent's economists also strongly support the conclusion that the merger gave the combined entity the ability to raise prices through the exercise of market power. The economists determined that there were substantial merger-coincident price increases and ran regressions using different data sets and a variety of control groups that ruled out the most likely competitively-benign explanations for substantial portions of these increases. The record does not support respondent's position that the merger-coincident price increases reflect ENH's attempts to correct a multi-year failure by Evanston's senior officials to charge market rates to many of its customers, or increased demand for Highland Park's services due to post-merger improvements.

We do not agree with the ALJ, however, that a divestiture is warranted. The potentially high costs inherent in the separation of hospitals that have functioned as a merged entity for seven years instead warrant a remedy that restores the lost competition through injunctive relief.

* * *

Notes and Questions

1. In challenging a merger that had been completed over six years prior to its final decision in the case, the FTC faced both challenges and opportunities. On the plus side, the Commission could look at the actual outcome of the merger, examining whether the anticompetitive effects associated with a facially anticompetitive acquisition actually occurred. On the other hand, it was forced to deal with the difficult dilemmas concerning relief: would it be feasible to insist on "structural relief" (i.e. order divestiture of Highland Hospital)? If not, what alternative remedy would restore the competitive conditions the market enjoyed before the merger? To the surprise of many, the Commission's order required the hospital to "establish separate and independent negotiating teams—one of Evanston and Glenbrook Hospitals and another for Highland Park." The FTC explained its remedy as follows:

While not ideal, this remedy will allow MCOs to negotiate separately again for these competing hospitals, thus re-injecting competition between them for the business of MCOs....[In future cases involving consummated mergers], where it is relatively clear that the unwinding of a hospital merger would be unlikely to involve substantial costs, all else being equal, the Commission would likely select divestiture as the remedy.

With the FTC having conceded that the hospitals have significantly merged operations, what benefit will separate negotiations serve? For example, will the two hospitals be able to "compete" on the basis of cost, service or reputation? In view of the remedy adopted, was *Evanston* a Pyrrhic victory for the Commission or a strategic move designed to reverse the course of hospital merger doctrine?

2. Note the following differences between the theories advanced by the FTC in *Evanston* and those employed in prior litigation.

- The FTC rejected patient origin data as a useful tool in defining the relevant geographic market. Instead it relied on the actual effects in the market place to prove the existence of a market.

- The FTC's theory of harm to competition from the merger rested on "unilateral effects" analysis. That is, the two merging hospitals were able to raise prices because each was the next best alternative of the other in the eyes of a significant number of patients and thus were able to raise prices after the merger without regard to the actions of other area hospitals.

- Although the majority of the Commission found it unnecessary to address the theory, complaint counsel alleged, and two commissioners agreed, that it would not be necessary to prove a geographic market in the case because anticompetitive effect was established independently.

3. The principal basis on which the FTC relied to find proof of harm to competition was its economic analysis of post-merger price increases by Evanston Hospital. Underlying the econometrics presented by experts are some common-sense factors that must be accounted for before one can attribute the price increases to enhanced market power resulting from the merger. What factors do you think were considered to test whether price actually increased? Remember that nonprice variables affecting costs may influence the price of any product or service. See Peter J. Hammer, Competition and Quality as Dynamic Processes in the Balkans of American Health Care, J. Health Pol. Pol'y & L. 473 (2006).

In fact, experts for both sides *agreed* that the ENH had significantly increased the prices of one of the hospitals it previously owned, Evanston Hospital, after its acquisition of Highland Park Hospital. Given this fact, what factors might explain that increase *other than* the exercise of market power? Defendants advanced one unprecedented explanation for the price increases: the "learning about demand" defense. They claimed that ENH raised price at only at Evanston Hospital and did so there only because it discovered through the merger that it was underpricing its services. It learned that the acquired hospital, Highland Park, a somewhat less sophisticated hospital than Evanston Hospital, had been receiving higher reimbursement from third party payers in the area. The FTC rejected this explanation on several grounds; for example, after the merger, ENH terminated the executive responsible for managed care contracting at Highland, and retained his counterpart from Evanston Hospital.

Although the Commission relied heavily on the economic evidence regarding price increases, it noted a number of pre- and post-acquisition internal documents that supported its theory. Several of these documents indicated that ENH thought that Highland Park was its chief competitor and that after the merger it would be easier to increase prices. Other documents suggested that managed care entities played Evanston Hospital and Highland Park off against each other. The Commission also examined the testimony of managed care executives which to some degree supported its theory of unilateral effects, but also provided some evidence that the merging hospitals faced competitive pressures from a number of other area hospitals. (Note that the Evanston hospitals are located in a small, affluent and densely populated area less than 20 miles from Chicago). Does the FTC's discounting of this testimony conflict with its insistence in *Tenet* and other cases that factfinders should credit the views of third party payors with respect to geographic market definition? Did the FTC even need to rely on testimony other than that of the economists?

Problem: Evaluating A Hospital Merger in Your Community

Suppose the largest and third largest hospitals (or hospital systems) in your community proposed to merge. What will the key issues be? What facts would you gather in seeking to defend this transaction against antitrust challenge? What testimony from payors, employers, expert witnesses, or parties to the transaction would be helpful?

Chapter 14

REPRODUCTION AND BIRTH

I. INTRODUCTION

The rights, obligations, privileges, and relationships previously described in this book are generally rights, obligations, privileges, and relationships of people. But who ought to be recognized as a person, subject to the principles that apply to persons, and not to human limbs, individual cells, hair pieces, animals, disembodied souls, state legislatures or other entities? While a fertilized ovum is life in some form, so is a single still-functioning liver cell taken from the body of a person who died yesterday. Is there a difference in these two entities? When does a person, entitled to formal legal respect as such, come into existence? When does one who is so defined go out of existence? The obvious answers—at the point of life and at the point of death—are fraught with ambiguities that can be resolved only through an analysis of medicine, philosophy, law, social history, anthropology, theology and other disciplines which seek to answer the basic questions of human existence. Physicians and lawyers have been deeply involved in determining when life begins and when it ends, and it is therefore appropriate to consider these issues in this text. The first portion of this chapter deals with the definition of human life; the definition of death is taken up in the next chapter.

Physicians and lawyers have also been deeply involved in facilitating and defining new forms of procreation, and in determining the role that society ought to play in limiting and facilitating reproduction. Issues surrounding contraception, genetic screening and manipulation, sterilization, abortion, the social allocation of the cost of failed reproduction, and potential fetal-maternal conflicts have all been addressed by law-makers, in either a judicial or legislative forum. In addition, forms of facilitating reproduction such as artificial insemination, *in vitro* fertilization, ovum transfer, surrogacy and cloning have also been addressed in the law. The second portion of this chapter examines the interdisciplinary debate that has given rise to legal intervention that may result in limiting or facilitating reproduction.

Problem: Death During Pregnancy

Ms. Baggins was carrying a fetus in the twenty-fifth week of gestation when the automobile she was driving was struck by a truck racing away from a convenience store and pursued by a city police car. The driver of the truck, who was unlicensed and highly intoxicated, was attempting to escape after committing an armed robbery at the convenience store when the collision occurred. The truck struck the driver's door of Ms. Baggins's car and flung her through the passenger window onto the ground about thirty feet from the car. The chasing police officer arrested the intoxicated driver, who was subsequently charged with armed robbery, driving while intoxicated, and driving without a license. The police officer did not call for medical help for Ms. Baggins, and no ambulance came for her until a passing motorist called the fire department. The ambulance arrived to find her unconscious.

When Ms. Baggins arrived at the hospital, physicians immediately provided her cardiopulmonary support. An examination revealed that the fetus she was carrying had suffered serious cranial injuries which could result in severe brain dysfunction if the child were born alive. Tests done about 24 hours after Ms. Baggins's admission to the hospital indicated no spontaneous activity in any part of her brain. Physicians have determined that maintaining Ms. Baggins on the cardiopulmonary support systems would provide the only chance for the fetus to be born alive.

Ms. Baggins was widowed in the fifth month of her pregnancy, two months ago. Her only living relatives are her two sisters, whom she despises. In fact, to avoid the possibility that they might inherit some of her wealth, last month she executed a will leaving all of her property to "my children, and, if I have none at the time of my death, to the National Abortion Rights League and the American Eugenics Society."

What actions should the hospital staff take in this case? Should Ms. Baggins be maintained on cardiopulmonary support, or should she be removed? For further discussion of brain death, see Chapter 15.

Consider the medical, social, political and legal (both civil and criminal) consequences of your actions as you read this chapter.

II. WHEN DOES HUMAN LIFE BECOME A "PERSON"?

This society has had difficulty defining who is a "person." In part, this arises out of the different and inconsistent purposes for which we seek a definition. The "person" from whom we wish to harvest a kidney for transplantation may be defined differently from the "person" who is protected by the Fourteenth Amendment, federal civil rights laws, and various other federal and state laws. Even when the purpose of the definition is settled—as when we seek to know who is a person able to bring an action under state tort law—there is no consensus on when the status of "personhood" first attaches. The most obvious definition of personhood is a recursive one: a human being (and, thus, a "person") is the reproductive product of other human beings. Even if we accept this "human stock" definition of person, however, the inquiry remains open. Does that human stock become a person, for tort law or other purposes, upon conception? Upon quickening? Upon viability? Upon birth? A year after birth? Upon physical maturity?

The definition of "person" is not limited to various stages in the development of human stock. "Personhood" could commence upon ensoulment, upon the development of self concept, upon the development of a sense of personal history, or upon the ability to communicate through language. The resolution of the question appears to require a resort to first principles.

In the vast majority of cases, it is not difficult to distinguish a person from something else. You are easily distinguishable from your arms, your dog, your insurance company and your gold bust of Elvis, as close as you may feel to each of them. The most difficult questions tend to arise at the very beginning and at the very end of human life. Just as you may be able to identify the fact that you were in love, but not be able to identify exactly when it began, or the moment when it ended, the beginnings and the endings of "personhood" are the fuzzy portions.

There are limits to what may reasonably be considered a "person," even when we limit our consideration to human stock. Few suggest that anything independent of the unified sperm and ovum, or its consequences, ought to be considered a person, although advances in cloning and cellular manipulation may challenge this assumption. A great many religious groups consider "personhood" to attach at conception. Aristotle viewed the development of the person as a three stage process, going from vegetable (at conception), to animal (in utero), to rational (sometime after birth). For many centuries, Christian theology fixed the point of "immediate animation" when the fetus was "ensouled" as forty days after conception for males and eighty days after conception for females. St. Thomas Aquinas determined that the ensoulment took place at the time of quickening, usually fourteen to eighteen weeks after conception, and his determination had a very substantial effect on the development of the common law in England and in this country. Recently some philosophers have suggested that "personhood," at least to the extent that it includes a right to life, depends on attributes that are not likely to be developed until sometime after birth. For example, Michael Tooley, a philosopher, defends infanticide on the grounds that it is indistinguishable from abortion and that neither constitutes the improper killing of a human being because there can be no human being until the being possesses a concept of itself as a continuing subject of experiences and other mental states, and recognizes that it is such a continuing entity. Professor Tooley suggests that this occurs sometime after birth, perhaps many weeks after birth. M. Tooley, *Abortion and Infanticide* (1983).

One thoughtful and oft-cited set of attributes of personhood has been developed by Joseph Fletcher, a bioethicist. Consider his fifteen criteria, described below, and determine whether some or all of them can be used to properly define who is your colleague in personhood and who is not. Consider whether the fact that many of these criteria disqualify fetuses, newborns, and the seriously developmentally disabled affects their acceptability as standards. Further, does the fact that some animal or some man-made machine might eventually fulfill all of these criteria cause you to doubt their validity? What are the consequences of our failure to define as a person a clone, a highly intelligent and communicative ape, a robot, or a manufactured cell that can be brought to term in an artificial womb, with regard to our conceptions of "democracy" and "slavery," for example?

A. THE ATTRIBUTES OF PERSONHOOD

JOSEPH FLETCHER, "HUMANNESS," IN HUMANHOOD: ESSAYS IN BIOMEDICAL ETHICS

12–16 (1979).

Synthetic concepts such as human and man and person require operational terms, spelling out the which and what and when. Only in that way can we get down to cases—to normative decisions. There are always some people who prefer to be visceral and affective in their moral choices, with no desire to have any rationale for what they do. But ethics is precisely the business of rational, critical reflection (encephalic and not merely visceral) about the problems of the moral agent—in biology and medicine as much as in law, government, education, or anything else.

To that end, then, for the purposes of biomedical ethics, I now turn to a *profile of man* in concrete and discrete terms.* * * There is time only to itemize the inventory, not to enlarge upon it, but I have fifteen positive propositions. Let me set them out, in no rank order at all, and as hardly more than a list of criteria or indicators, by simple title.

1. Minimum Intelligence

Mere biological life, before minimal intelligence is achieved or after it is lost irretrievably, is without personal status.

2. Self-awareness

* * *

3. Self–control

If an individual is not only not controllable by others (unless by force) but not controllable by the individual himself or herself, a low level of life is reached about on a par with that of a paramecium. * * *

4. A Sense of Time

* * *

5. A Sense of Futurity

How "truly human" is any man who cannot realize there is a time yet to come as well as the present? Subhuman animals do not look forward in time; they live only on what we might call visceral strivings, appetites. Philosophical anthropologies (one recalls that of William Temple, the Archbishop of Canterbury, for instance) commonly emphasize purposiveness as a key to humanness. Chesterton once remarked that we would never ask a puppy what manner of dog it wanted to be when it grows up. * * *

6. A Sense of the Past

* * *

7. The Capability to Relate to Others

Interpersonal relationships, of the sexual-romantic and friendship kind, are of the greatest importance for the fullness of what we idealize as being truly personal. * * *

8. Concern for Others

Some people may be skeptical about our capacity to care about others (what in Christian ethics is often distinguished from romance and friendship as "neighbor love" or "neighbor concern"). * * * But whether concern for others is disinterested or inspired by enlightened self-interest, it seems plain that a conscious extra-ego orientation is a trait of the species. * * *

9. Communication

Utter alienation or disconnection from others, if it is irreparable, is dehumanization. * * *

10. Control of Existence

It is of the nature of man that he is not helplessly subject to the blind workings of physical or physiological nature. He has only finite knowledge, freedom, and initiative, but what he has of it is real and effective. * * *

11. Curiosity

To be without affect, sunk in *anomie,* is to be not a person. Indifference is inhuman. Man is a learner and a knower as well as a tool maker and user. * * *

12. Change and Changeability

To the extent that an individual is unchangeable or opposed to change, he denies the creativity of personal beings. It means not only the fact of biological and physiological change, which goes on as a condition of life, but the capacity and disposition for changing one's mind and conduct as well. Biologically, human beings are developmental: birth, life, health, and death are processes, not events, and are to be understood progressively, not episodically. All human existence is on a continuum, a matter of becoming. * * *

13. Balance of Rationality and Feeling

* * * As human beings we are not coldly rational or cerebral, nor are we merely creatures of feeling and intuition. It is a matter of being both, in different combinations from one individual to another. * * *

14. Idiosyncrasy

The human being is idiomorphous, a distinctive individual. * * * To be a person is to have an identity, to be recognizable and callable by name.

15. Neocortical Function

In a way, this is the cardinal indicator, the one all the others are hinged upon. Before cerebration is in play, or with its end, in the absence of the synthesizing function of the cerebral cortex, the person is nonexistent. Such individuals are objects but not subjects. This is so no matter how many other spontaneous or artificially supported functions persist in the heart, lungs, neurologic and vascular systems. Such noncerebral processes are not personal. * * * But what is definitive in determining death is the loss of cerebration, not just of any or all brain function. Personal reality depends on cerebration and to be dead "humanly" speaking is to be excerebral, no matter how long the body remains alive.

Notes and Questions

1. Which attributes does Fletcher consider to be necessary for personhood? Are any sufficient? Would you add any others to his list? Is there any underlying principle that describes the fifteen attributes selected by Fletcher? Are they all really a subset of the first?

2. Some commentators have concluded that the real consensus requirement of personhood is the capacity for conscious experience. Do you think that it is a necessary attribute? A sufficient attribute? Does it encompass many—or all—of the attributes described by Fletcher? For a good discussion of this issue, see Ben Rich, Postmodern Personhood: A Matter of Consciousness, 11 Bioethics (3) 207 (1997).

3. Which attributes of personhood, if any, does Ms. Baggins possess? Which attributes does her fetus possess?

4. Fletcher commenced a serious debate over whether the persons protected by law ought to be defined in terms of attributes we wish to protect or in terms of the human stock from which the person is created. Both forms of definition may be valuable for different purposes. We provide some rights to people because they possess many or all of the attributes that distinguish human beings. The right to make medical decisions, based on the autonomy of individuals, is not accorded to those without some "minimum intelligence." On the other hand, we provide minimally adequate housing, food, medical care, and other necessities for those of human stock, even when they do not meet some of Fletcher's criteria, and even when we do not provide those same benefits to others, (e.g., animals) who fail the same criteria. In the end, the Fletcher propositions may be useful in determining some of the rights of persons and the "human stock" definition may be helpful in determining others. Just as property is often described as a bundle of rights, it may turn out that "personhood" is a bundle of attributes that need to be separated out and individually analyzed.

5. As we saw earlier, even the adoption of a "human stock" definition does not answer the question of when that human stock becomes a person. What is the attribute of the human stock that makes it a person—genetic uniqueness? Responsiveness? The potential to be born? The appearance of a human being? Consider the following list of the alternative medical points of personhood.

C.R. AUSTIN, WHEN DOES A PERSON'S LIFE REALLY BEGIN? IN HUMAN EMBRYOS: THE DEBATE ON ASSISTED REPRODUCTION 22–31 (1989)

* * * Probably most people who were asked this question would answer "at fertilization" (or "conception"). Certainly, several interesting and unusual things happen then—it is really the most *obvious* event to pick—but for biologists the preceding and succeeding cellular processes are *equally* impor-

tant. Nevertheless, "fertilization" continues to be the cry of many religious bodies and indeed also of the august World Medical Association, who, in 1949, adopted the Geneva Convention Code of Medical Ethics, which contains the clause: "I will maintain the utmost respect for human life from the time of conception." So we do need to look more closely at this choice, for a generally acceptable "beginning" for human life would be a great help in reaching ethical and legal consensus.

In the first place human *life,* as such, obviously begins before fertilization, since the egg or oocyte is alive before sperm entry, as were innumerable antecedent cells, back through the origin of species into the mists of time. A more practical starting point would be that of the life of the human *individual,* so it is individuality that we should be looking for, at least as one of the essential criteria. Now the earliest antecedents of the eggs, as of sperm, are the primordial germ cells, which can be seen as a group of distinctive little entities migrating through the tissues of the early embryo. When they first become recognizable, they number only about a dozen or two, but they multiply fast and soon achieve large numbers, reaching a peak of 7–10 million about 6 months after conception. Then, despite continued active cell division, there is a dramatic decline in the cell population, which has tempted people to suggest that some sort of "selection of the fittest" occurs, but there is no good evidence in support of this idea; nor is there any good reason to look for individuality in that mercurial population. In due course, the primordial germ cells, while still undergoing cell divisions, settle down in the tissues of the future ovary, change subtly in their characteristics, and thus become oogonia; and then, soon after birth, *cell division ceases,* the cells develop large nuclei and are now recognizable as primary oocytes. From now on, there are steady cell losses but no further cell divisions * * *; it is the same entity that was a primary oocyte, becomes a fertilized egg, and then develops as an embryo. The primary oocytes are very unusual cells, for they have the capacity to live for much longer than most other body cells; the *same* oocytes can be seen in the ovaries of women approaching the menopause—cells that have lived for about 40 years or longer. And it is with the emergence of the primary oocytes that we can hail the start of *individuality*. Then, in those oocytes that are about to be ovulated, the first meiotic division takes place—another important step, for the "shuffling" of genes that occurs at that point bestows *genetic uniqueness* on the oocyte. So both individuality and genetic uniqueness are established before sperm penetration and fertilization; these processes have distinctly different actions—providing the stimulus that initiates cleavage and contributing to biparental inheritance. Thus, the preferred choice for the start of the human individual should surely be the formation of the primary oocyte, but there is certainly no unanimity on this score.

Passing over now the popularity of fertilization, for many people it is instead the emergence of the embryonic disc and primitive streak that most appeals as the stage in which to identify the start of "personhood" (one or more persons, in view of the imminent possibility of twinning), and there is much to support this opinion. Here, for the first time, are structures that are designed to have a different destiny than *all the rest of the embryo*—they represent the primordium of the fetus, and the developmental patterns of embryo and fetus progressively diverge from this stage onwards. An additional point is that this new emergence is not inevitable, for in around one in two-thousand pregnancies the embryo grows, often to quite a large size, but there is no fetus; the clinical conditions are known as blighted ovum, dropsical ovum, hydatidiform mole, etc. Evidence suggests that hydatidiform mole is attributable to fertilization of a faulty egg, the embryo developing only under the influence of the sperm chromosomes.

At the time of appearance of the embryonic disc, and shortly beforehand, the process of implantation is occurring, and this is considered by many to have special significance in relation to embryonic potential—so far as we know, implantation cannot occur once the development of the embryo has passed the stage when interaction with * * * the uterus normally takes place.

But despite all that has been said, there are still many folk who remain unconvinced—is the being at this stage sufficiently "human" to qualify as the start of a person? After all, the disc is just a collection of similar cells, virtually undifferentiated, poorly delineated from its surroundings, about a fifth of a millimetre long, non-sentient, and without the power of movement. It is in no way a "body" and it does not bear the faintest resemblance to a human being—*and* the soul cannot enter yet, for the disc may yet divide in the process of twinning, and the soul being unique is indivisible. Also, it is argued that we should be looking for some spark of personality, and a moral philosopher has proposed that some sort of responsiveness is an essential feature.

One of the earliest succeeding changes in the direction of humanness could be the development of the heart primordium, and soon after that the beginnings of a circulatory system; the first contractions of the heart muscle occur possibly as early as day 21, with a simple tubular heart at that stage, and in the fourth week a functional circulation begins. With the heart beats we have the first movements initiated within the embryo (?fetus) and thus in a way the first real "sign of life." The conceptus is now about 6 mm long. During the fifth and sixth weeks, nerve fibres grow out from the spinal cord and make contact with muscles, so that at this time or soon afterwards, a mechanical or electrical stimulus might elicit a muscle twitch; this is important for it would be the first indication of sentient existence—of "responsiveness." At this stage, too, the embryo could possibly feel pain. But, still, some would find cause to demur: only an expert could tell that this embryo/fetus, now 12–13 mm in length, with branchial arches (corresponding to the "gill-slits" in non-mammalian embryos), stubby limbs, and a prominent tail, is human. A marginally more acceptable applicant is the fetus at 7½ weeks, when the hands and feet can be seen to have fingers and toes, and thereafter physical resemblance steadily improves; also at this time, a special gene on the Y-chromosome (the "testis-determining factor" or TDF) is switched on, and the fetuses that have this chromosome, the males, proceed thenceforward to develop *as* males, distinguishable from females.

At about 12 weeks, electrical activity can be detected in the brain of the fetus, which could signal the dawn of consciousness. Here, we would seem to have a very logical stage marking the *start* of a person, for the cessation of electrical activity in the brain ("brain death") is accepted in both medical and legal circles as marking the *termination* of a person—as an indication that life no longer exists in victims of accidents or in patients with terminal illnesses. Around the fourth or fifth month of pregnancy, the mother first experiences movements of the fetus ("quickening"), which were regarded by St. Thomas Aquinas as the first indication of life, for he believed that life was distinguished by two features, knowledge and movement; moreover, it would seem logical that the fetus would move when the *animus* (life or soul) took up residence.[1] * * *

At about 24 weeks, the fetus reaches a state in which it can commonly survive outside the maternal body, with assistance. * * * Just which stage marks the start of a person's life is a matter of personal opinion. Much of the foregoing argumentation may seem to some people difficult to comprehend, especially if they have not had formal training in biology, and to others may even seem irrelevant, in view of the firm line taken by many church authorities. But it really is important that we should try to reach a consensus on just when a person's life should be held to begin, for the decision does have important practical consequences—it directly affects the rights of other embryos, of fetuses, and of people.

B. LEGAL RECOGNITION OF THE BEGINNING OF HUMAN LIFE

The law is increasingly forced to confront the question of when rights and privileges of persons attach to fetuses and young children. While children have always been treated differently from adults in the law, those fundamental common law and Constitutional rights that uniformly extend to both competent and incompetent adults also have been extended to children from the time of birth. Courts have had greater difficulty determining which rights, if any, attach to a fetus.

The trend over the past thirty years has been for states to expand the common law rights of the fetus and to recognize that the fetus can be an independent victim for purposes of the criminal law. For example, most states now permit a tort action to be filed by an estate of a stillborn child. Just twenty years ago, the vast majority of states required that the child be born alive before any right to sue would attach. Similarly, many states now extend the protection of their homicide law to fetuses; several years ago that extension was very unusual. The extent of any Constitutional protection of fetuses is far less certain.

1. *Constitutional Recognition*

While the Supreme Court has never formally determined when a fetus becomes a "person" for constitutional purposes, it has not been able to completely avoid that question despite its several attempts to finesse it. Indeed, some commentators thought that the matter was finally resolved in the watershed case of Roe v. Wade, 410 U.S. 113, 93 S.Ct. 705, 35 L.Ed.2d 147 (1973), in which the Supreme Court was called upon to determine whether a fetus was a person for purposes of the protections of the Fourteenth Amendment. While *Roe v. Wade* will be considered in some greater detail below, it is significant to know that the Court held that the term "person," at least as that term appears in the Fourteenth Amendment, was not intended to encompass the fetus. After reviewing over 2,000 years of the history of abortion the Court addressed the question directly:

1. The modern equivalent would be at about day 21, when the heart begins to beat.

The appellee and certain amici argue that the fetus is a "person" within the language and meaning of the Fourteenth Amendment. In support of this, they outline at length and in detail the well-known facts of fetal development. If this suggestion of personhood is established, the appellant's case, of course, collapses, for the fetus' right to life is then guaranteed specifically by the Amendment. The appellant conceded as much on reargument. On the other hand, the appellee conceded on reargument that no case could be cited that holds that a fetus is a person within the meaning of the Fourteenth Amendment.

The Constitution does not define "person" in so many words. Section 1 of the Fourteenth Amendment contains three references to "person." The first, in defining "citizens," speaks of "persons born or naturalized in the United States." The word also appears both in the Due Process Clause and in the Equal Protection Clause. "Person" is used in other places in the Constitution: in the listing of qualifications for Representatives and Senators, Art I, § 2, cl 2, and § 3, cl 3; in the Apportionment Clause, Art I, § 2, cl 3;[2] in the Migration and Importation provision, Art I, § 9, cl 1; in the Emolument Clause, Art I, § 9, cl 8; in the Electors provisions, Art II, § 1, cl 2, and the superseded cl 3; in the provision outlining qualifications for the office of President, Art II, § 1, cl 5; in the Extradition provisions, Art IV, § 2, cl 2, and the superseded Fugitive Slave Clause 3; and in the Fifth, Twelfth, and Twenty-second Amendments, as well as in §§ 2 and 3 of the Fourteenth Amendment. But in nearly all these instances, the use of the word is such that it has application only postnatally. None indicates, with any assurance, that it has any possible prenatal application.[3]

* * *

All this, together with our observation * * * that throughout the major portion of the 19th century prevailing legal abortion practices were far freer than they are today, persuades us that the word "person," as used in the Fourteenth Amendment, does not include the unborn. * * * 410 U.S. at 156–157, 93 S.Ct. at 728–729.

The Supreme Court recognized that there were protectable interests beyond those specified in the Constitution and determined:

[W]e do not agree that, by adopting one theory of life, Texas may override the rights of the pregnant woman that are at stake. We repeat,

2. We are not aware that in the taking of any census under this clause, a fetus has ever been counted.

3. When Texas urges that a fetus is entitled to Fourteenth Amendment protection as a person, it faces a dilemma. Neither in Texas nor in any other State are all abortions prohibited. Despite broad proscription, an exception always exists. The exception contained in Art 1196, for an abortion procured or attempted by medical advice for the purpose of saving the life of the mother, is typical. But if the fetus is a person who is not to be deprived of life without due process of law, and if the mother's condition is the sole determinant, does not the

Texas exception appear to be out of line with the Amendment's command?

There are other inconsistencies between Fourteenth Amendment status and the typical abortion statute. It has already been pointed out[ ] that in Texas the woman is not a principal or an accomplice with respect to an abortion upon her. If the fetus is a person, why is the woman not a principal or an accomplice? Further, the penalty for criminal abortion specified by Art 1195 is significantly less than the maximum penalty for murder prescribed by Art 1257 of the Texas Penal Code. If the fetus is a person, may the penalties be different?

however, that the state does have an important and legitimate interest in preserving and protecting the health of the pregnant woman * * *, and that it has still *another* important and legitimate interest in protecting the potentiality of human life. 410 U.S. at 162, 93 S.Ct. at 731.

Thus, a state may be able to define and protect rights in the fetus, but these are not the Fourteenth Amendment rights of "persons."

Of course, the continued viability of *Roe v. Wade* itself has been called into question continually since 1973. See section II, below. In Webster v. Reproductive Health Services, 492 U.S. 490, 109 S.Ct. 3040, 106 L.Ed.2d 410 (1989), the Supreme Court reviewed a Missouri statute that restricted the availability of abortions in several ways. In addition, that statute included a preamble that defined personhood:

1. The general assembly of this state finds that:

(1) the life of each human being begins at conception;

(2) unborn children have protectable interests in life, health, and well being; * * *

2. * * * the laws of this state shall be interpreted and construed to acknowledge on behalf of the unborn child at every stage of development, all the rights, privileges, and immunities available to other persons, citizens, and residents of this state, subject only to the Constitution of the United States, and decisional interpretations thereof. * * *

3. As used in this section, the term "unborn children" or "unborn child" shall include all unborn child or children or the offspring of human beings from the moment of conception until birth at every stage of biological development. * * *

Vernon's Ann.Mo.Stat. § 1.205. This preamble was attacked on the grounds that it was beyond the Constitutional authority of the state legislature to define personhood, at least to the extent that the definition extended personhood to pre-viable fetuses. The Supreme Court sidestepped that question by concluding that the preamble was nothing more than a state value judgment favoring childbirth over abortion, and that such a value judgment was clearly within the authority of the legislature. For a vigorous discussion of why the Constitution should be read to treat all "human beings" as "persons" from the moment of conception, partly based on religious principles, see Charles Lugosi, Respecting Human Life in 21st Century America: A Moral Perspective to Extend Civil Rights to the Unborn from Creation to Natural Death, 48 St. Louis U. L. J. 425 (2004).

There are two separate Constitutional issues that surround the definition of person. First, is there a definition of "person" for purposes of the Constitution? Second, do the substantive provisions of the Constitution put any limit on the way that *states* may define "person" for any other purpose? Could each state define "person" differently for Constitutional purposes? States effectively did so before the Thirteenth Amendment, of course. Could the definition of "person" for Constitutional purposes be different from that definition for other purposes?

2. *Statutory Recognition*

Justice Blackmun pointed out in *Roe v. Wade* that courts have generally considered killing a fetus to be substantially different from killing a person who was born alive. This is reflected in the different penalties that usually attach to feticide and other forms of homicide and the fact that feticide itself has been distinguished from murder or manslaughter in most jurisdictions. Over the past several years, however, some states have made the penalties for feticide commensurate with the penalties for homicide, and several have promulgated new homicide statutes that explicitly include fetuses as those whose death may give rise to homicide prosecutions. Most commonly, these statutes seek to impose the homicide penalty on one who kills an "unborn child," although the California statute provides:

> Murder is the unlawful killing of a human being, *or a fetus,* with malice aforethought.

Cal. Penal Code Sec. 187(a). The words "or a fetus" were added to the statute in 1970 in reaction to a California Supreme Court decision, Keeler v. Superior Court, 2 Cal.3d 619, 87 Cal.Rptr. 481, 470 P.2d 617 (1970), which defined "human being" as a person born alive.

The statutes which do not distinguish between viable and nonviable fetal victims of a homicide have been unsuccessfully attacked on due process and equal protection grounds in at least three states. The due process attack is two pronged. First, criminal defendants argue that the statutes violate their due process rights because they apply even when the perpetrator (and, for that matter, the pregnant woman) do not know of the existence of the pregnancy. As the Minnesota court said in rejecting such an argument, though, "[t]he fair warning rule has never been understood to excuse criminal liability simply because the defendant's victim proves not to be the victim the defendant had in mind." State v. Merrill, 450 N.W.2d 318, 323 (Minn.1990). Second, defendants argue that terms like "unborn child" are unconstitutionally vague because it is uncertain when a conceptus, embryo or fetus becomes an "unborn child." As an Illinois appellate court pointed out, the statute "only requires proof that whatever the entity within the mother's womb is called, it had life, and, because of the acts of the defendant, it no longer does." People v. Ford, 221 Ill.App.3d 354, 163 Ill.Dec. 766, 581 N.E.2d 1189, 1200 (1991).

The defendants' equal protection argument is based in the failure of the statutes to distinguish between viable and nonviable fetuses. Defendants have argued that the state makes an improper distinction when it treats some who end the life of a nonviable fetus as murderers, while others, including the pregnant woman herself and her doctor, who are protected by the Constitutionally recognized right to an abortion, are not treated as murderers. This argument has also failed. See State v. Merrill, *supra,* and People v. Ford, *supra*.

The California statute was upheld and applied to both nonviable and viable fetuses by a divided court in People v. Davis, 7 Cal.4th 797, 30 Cal.Rptr.2d 50, 872 P.2d 591 (1994), where the Court found that the history of applying the statute only when the victim was a viable fetus required that it be applied to cases where the victims were nonviable fetuses only prospectively, and not to the case before it. The dissent argued that the majority's application of the statute to nonviable fetuses "will make our murder law unique in the nation in its severity: it appears that in no other state is it a capital offense to cause the death of a nonviable and invisible fetus that the actor neither knew nor had reason to know existed." 30 Cal.Rptr.2d at 79, 872 P.2d at 620. For an excellent survey of the way state laws dealt with feticide, an account of those that criminalize only the killing of a viable fetus and those that also criminalize the killing of a nonviable fetus, and a survey of punishments imposed on those whose acts result in the death of a fetus, see People v. Davis, 30 Cal.Rptr.2d at 79–83, 872 P.2d at 621–623 (Mosk, J. dissenting).

In State v. Merrill, *supra*, the majority distinguished human life from "personhood," and determined that the feticide statute was designed to protect human life, not persons. Could the legislature also protect other forms of human life—human blood cells, for example—in the same way that it has decided to protect "nonperson" human life in this case, or is the potential personhood of the embryo fundamental to the majority's decision that the statute's protection of human life is constitutional?

Do you agree with the decisions in *Merrill*, *Ford* and *Davis*? Whose interests were really at stake in those cases? To what extent should these courts depend upon the interests of the pregnant woman, and to what extent should the courts depend on the interests of the embryo or fetus in deciding these cases?

In her dissent in the *Merrill* case, Justice Wahl argues that Roe v. Wade forbids a state from treating a nonviable fetus like a person, at least for purposes of the criminal law. How strong is that argument? For purposes of the homicide law, is there any reason to draw a line between a viable and a nonviable fetus if the mother of each intends to carry the fetus in utero to term? If not, why have so many states decided to criminalize only the killing of a viable fetus? Might it be that at the point of viability the fact of pregnancy is likely to be obvious to the assailant? Are any purposes of the criminal law served by application of a feticide statute to a case (like the *Merrill* case) in which neither the pregnant woman nor the assailant knew of the pregnancy?

The Supreme Court of South Carolina found a woman guilty of "child abuse resulting in death" of her stillborn child as a consequence of her prenatal use of cocaine. State v. McKnight, 352 S.C. 635, 576 S.E.2d 168 (2003). Could the court apply the same criminal statute if the cocaine use resulted in the termination of the mother's pregnancy after the fetus was viable? What if the fetus was not yet viable? What if the illegal drug use resulted in a fertilized ovum not properly implanting in the mother's uterus? Would the 20–year sentence handed down in this case constitute cruel and unusual punishment in any of these cases?

In Michigan the question of the status of the fetus for purposes of the criminal law arose in very different circumstances. Jaclyn Kurr was convicted of voluntary manslaughter when she knifed to death the father of the 17–week fetuses (twins) that she was carrying. In the midst of a fight over cocaine use, the father, who had a history of violently attacking Ms. Kurr, came at her and punched her twice in the stomach. She told him not to hit her any more because she was "carrying his babies." As he came at her again, she stabbed him. Although Michigan law recognizes that one may use deadly force in defense of another, the trial court refused her request for an instruction on "defense of others" on the grounds that the fetus was nonviable, and thus could not be an "other" for purposes of Michigan law.

The Michigan Court of Appeal reversed and held that "an individual may indeed defend a fetus from such an assault and may use deadly force if she honestly and reasonably believes the fetus to be in imminent danger of death or great bodily harm." People v. Kurr, 253 Mich.App. 317, 654 N.W.2d 651, 656 (2002). The court based its decision on the state policy of fetal protection that was explicit in Michigan's 1998 Fetal Protection Act.

> We conclude that in this state, the defense should also extend to the protection of a fetus, viable or nonviable, from an assault against the mother, and we base this conclusion primarily on the fetal protection act adopted by the Legislature in 1998. * * *
>
> *The plain language of these provisions shows the Legislature's conclusion that fetuses are worthy of protection as living entities as a matter of public policy.* * * * Moreover, in enacting the fetal protection act, the Legislature did not distinguish between fetuses that are viable, or capable of surviving outside the womb, and those that are nonviable. In fact, the Legislature used the term "embryo" as well as the term "fetus" [in the relevant statutory sections.] * * *. This definition clearly encompasses nonviable fetuses. Moreover, the legislative analysis of the act indicates that, in passing the act, the Legislature was clearly determined to provide criminal penalties for harm caused to nonviable fetuses during assaults or negligent acts against pregnant women.[ ]
>
> Because the act reflects a public policy to protect even an embryo from unlawful assaultive or negligent conduct, we conclude that the defense of others concept does extend to the protection of a nonviable fetus from an assault against the mother. We emphasize, however, that the defense is available *solely* in the context of an assault against the mother. Indeed, the Legislature has *not* extended the protection of the criminal laws to embryos existing outside a woman's body, i.e., frozen embryos stored for future use, and we therefore *do not* extend the applicability of the defense of others theory to situations involving these embryos.

People v. Kurr, 654 N.W.2d at 654 (italics in original).

The question of the statutory recognition of the fetus as a person has also arisen in litigation over whether state statutes allow for the appointment of a guardian (or a guardian ad litem) for a fetus. For a sense of the deep symbolism attached to such an appointment by all sides in the debate, see Wixstrom v. Department Children & Fam. Servs. (In re J.D.S.), 864 So.2d 534 (Fla.App.2004), reprinted below.

3. Common Law Recognition

The debate over the common law recognition of the personhood of the fetus has been waged primarily over whether a fetus may recover under state wrongful death and survival statutes. Until recently courts were divided over whether such actions would be permitted only if the decedent were born alive, or whether such actions would be permitted if the decedent had reached the point of viability, even though the decedent was not born alive. In Amadio v. Levin, 509 Pa. 199, 501 A.2d 1085 (1985), the court listed the five reasons courts had traditionally articulated for limiting such actions to children born alive:

> First, the Court surmised that the real objective of such a lawsuit was to compensate the parents of the deceased child for their emotional distress, and that since parents already had the ability in their own right to institute such an action, it would only be duplication to permit parents to file a second action on behalf of the estate of the child.
>
> Second, because wrongful death actions are derivative, and since the Court refused to acknowledge that a stillborn child was an individual under the wrongful death or survival statutes, it was concluded that the Acts were not intended to provide for recovery by the estate of a stillborn child.
>
> Third, extending causes of actions to the estates of stillborn children was felt to increase problems of causation and damages.
>
> Fourth, the prior cases arose out of an era when most jurisdictions did not permit the filing of such actions. * * *
>
> Fifth, it was reasoned that since only children born alive may take property by descent under our Intestate Laws, the Court assumed that the Legislature had already limited the creation of causes of actions to those instances where the existence or estate of a child was recognized by the laws of intestacy.

That court rejected those five arguments and determined that the live birth requirement was an arbitrary line that served no purpose of the wrongful death and survival statute:

> Today's holding merely makes it clear that the recovery afforded the estate of a stillborn is no different than the recovery afforded the estate of a child that dies within seconds of its release from its mother's womb. In view of the current attitude throughout our sister states to let the representatives of the stillborn's estate prove their losses, it would be illogical to continue to deny that such claims could be established, when we permit them for the child that survives birth for an instant.

Others more influenced by the arguments over abortion urged that such actions should be recognized for another reason: the fetus is, they argued, a full human being entitled to all protections accorded to all other human beings. Those who opposed recovery on behalf of fetuses who were not born alive argued that there was no genuine loss that was being compensated in such cases, and that the real reason for permitting the recovery was to allow plaintiffs a greater chance at a larger recovery—i.e., a pro-plaintiff bias.

Many courts now distinguish between a viable and a pre-viable fetus for purposes of recovery under wrongful death and survival statutes. If a fetus becomes a "person" for purposes of commencing a tort action only upon viability, the court must address several questions when it hears a tort action commenced on behalf of a fetus. First, what is the legally relevant moment when the fetus must be viable for that fetus to possess a cause of action—is it the time of the injury or the time of the tortious action? Second, when is a fetus viable as a general matter? Is this a matter of law or fact? Third, was the plaintiff-fetus viable at the legally relevant time in the instant case?

All of these questions were before the court upon a motion for summary judgment in In re Air Crash Disaster at Detroit Metropolitan Airport on August 16, 1987, 737 F.Supp. 427 (E.D.Mich.1989), an action brought on behalf of the fetus of a flight attendant killed in an air crash. The District Court determined that Michigan law would permit recovery on behalf of the fetus only if the fetus were "viable at the time of the injury." Further, the court rejected evidence that fetuses could be viable as early as twenty weeks, and adopted the "generally accepted *Roe [v. Wade]* proposition that viability occurs at twenty-four weeks." Finally, the court concluded:

> [The plaintiff] submits a sonogram report from July 13, 1987, which concludes that the "[e]stimated gestational age is 15.8 +/− 2 weeks." The fatal accident involving Northwest Flight 255 occurred five weeks later. Therefore, on the date of the accident the * * * fetus was 20.8 weeks old +/− 2 weeks. Therefore, the fetus was, at most, 22.8 weeks old. * * *
>
> Thus, the subject fetus in this case was nonviable as a matter of law [and has no cause of action under Michigan law].

The *Rademacher* case also discusses the irony in allowing the estate of a fetus to recover damages even if the tortious act was committed at a time when the mother could have chosen to abort the fetus. The court suggests that while a mother's interest in terminating a pregnancy may outweigh a state's interest in maintaining the life of a pre-viable fetus, a third party's interest does not overcome both the state's and the mother's interest in continuing the pregnancy. Is this distinction sound? Is there any place for abortion jurisprudence in analyzing the propriety of tort liability for the death of a fetus?

In fact, is there any reason to draw the line for recovery at viability? Why not just permit a wrongful death recovery on behalf of a fetus of any gestational age, from the moment of conception? While this was generally uncharted territory before the 1990s, in the middle of that decade three states suddenly recognized such a cause of action. In Wiersma v. Maple Leaf Farms, 543 N.W.2d 787 (S.D.1996), the South Dakota court, in response to a certified question, announced that the wrongful death statute permitted an action on behalf of a first trimester fetus who was alleged to have been miscarried as a result of salmonella in a frozen dinner consumed by the decedent-fetus's mother. The court treated the case as a simple one of statutory construction: the statute allowed actions on behalf of an "unborn child," and that term was unqualified. The dissent argued that such a term was necessarily ambiguous, and thus it needed to be interpreted. As the dissenting justice pointed out, "The heart of the issue, in my opinion, is whether an action for wrongful death can stand where no sustainable life exists at the time of the negligent act." 543 N.W.2d at 794. Shortly before the South Dakota court rendered its opinion, courts in West Virginia and Missouri had allowed similar actions on behalf of nonviable fetuses. See Connor v. Monkem Co., 898 S.W.2d 89 (Mo.1995) and Farley v. Sartin, 195 W.Va. 671, 466 S.E.2d 522 (W.Va.1995).

Such actions are now permitted in other states as well, although at least two states permit wrongful death actions on behalf of non-viable fetuses only after quickening. Arizona has refused to allow a frozen eight cell pre-embryo that was never implanted in any body to be the decedent for purposes of a wrongful death action. Jeter v. Mayo Clinic Arizona, 211 Ariz. 386, 121 P.3d 1256 (2005). Should extra-corporeal pre-embryos be treated differently from womb-bound non-viable fetuses for purposes of wrongful death actions? Why or why not?

In New York and Maryland, at least, because a fetus is not a legal person, it is considered a part of the mother for tort law purposes. Thus, an injury to the fetus may be compensable as an injury to the mother. See Smith v. Borello, 370 Md. 227, 804 A.2d 1151 (2002) and Johnson v. Verrilli, 134 Misc.2d 582, 511 N.Y.S.2d 1008 (N.Y.Super.1987), modified, 139 A.D.2d 497, 526 N.Y.S.2d 600 (1988).

Consider the Baggins problem on pages 622–623. Would the estate of Ms. Baggins or the estate of her fetus have a tort action against a police department that negligently failed to seek medical assistance for her? Suppose Ms. Baggins is declared dead and then gives birth to a child who lives for two days. Should Ms. Baggins's estate be distributed to the beneficiaries listed in her will, or might her sisters be able to argue successfully that her child inherited her estate, and that under the state's probate code they were the heirs of that child? Would your answer be different if Ms. Baggins were declared dead and the fetus were subsequently stillborn? What if Ms. Baggins died before the fetus were even viable? Should any of these distinctions make a legal difference?

For a thoughtful general analysis of these questions, looking to legislative definitions of death for suggestions as to how legislatures may define the beginning of life, see Kirsten Smolensky, Defining Life from the Perspective of Death: An Introduction to the Forced Symmetry Approach, 2006 U. Chi. Legal F. 41 (2006).

III. MEDICAL INTERVENTION IN REPRODUCTION

The law has been invoked regularly to order the relationships of private individuals and to constrain government to its appropriate role with regard to the limitation of reproduction. The law has also been engaged to regulate medical interventions designed to facilitate reproduction, such as artificial insemination, ovum and embryo transfer, in vitro fertilization, and surrogacy. While the propriety of legal intervention in these matters will undoubtedly remain a matter of dispute, the sexual nature of the issues, as well as their novelty and moral complexity, is likely to cause society to maintain a high interest in regulating them. This section of this chapter is not intended to be a comprehensive analysis of all of these questions; many related issues are discussed elsewhere in this text or in other courses. It is the purpose of this section of this chapter to provide structure to those issues surrounding procreation and reproduction that are likely to be of special concern to attorneys representing health care professionals, institutions and their patients.

A. LIMITING REPRODUCTION

1. *Government Prohibitions on Reproduction*

Is there a role for the government in prohibiting reproduction, at least in some circumstances? To control population growth, as China has attempted to do? To serve political, economic, or environmental goals? For eugenic purposes? Dr. Joseph Fletcher has argued that there is a moral obligation to prevent the birth of genetically diseased or defective children, and a failure to carry out that obligation to those children "who would suffer grievously if conceived or born * * * would be tantamount to rejecting the whole notion of preventive medicine, sanitation, environmental protection law, and all the other ways in which we express our obligation to the unborn." Consider the following argument and determine whether it is strong enough to overcome the potential abuses inherent in allowing the government to determine who can reproduce, and under what circumstances.

> My fundamental commitment is that survival of the human species is a good and that it is a good of such importance and value that it can be accredited as a right. From this I deduce that individuals and social units have the concomitant obligation to pursue courses of actions that will foster and protect the right of the species' survival. Among these acknowledged and traditional courses of action is general health care. One segment of that health care involves the protection of the population from the transmission of identifiable, seriously deleterious genes and from debilitating and costly (in terms of natural, economic and human resources) genetic disease which can neither be cured nor treated with any preservation of the quality of life and relative independence of the afflicted. Because individual human rights are negotiable according to their historical context, and because there is legal precedent for restricting the exercise of reproductive rights, those who are at high risk for passing on clearly identifiable and severely deleterious genes and debilitating genetic disease should not be allowed to exercise their reproductive prerogative.

E. Ulrich, Reproductive Rights and Genetic Disease, in J. Humber and R. Almender, Biomedical Ethics and the Law, 351, 360 (1976).

Of course, manipulation of the gene pool is not the only reason governments seek to regulate procreation. Because of the theological, ethical, and social values related to sexual conduct and its consequences, governments have often regulated techniques designed to limit reproduction. In the United States, legislatures and courts have often considered the propriety of contraception, sterilization, and abortion. Because these issues are considered in detail in constitutional law courses, they are only briefly addressed here.

2. *Contraception*

Historical and religious reasons explain why some states made the use of contraceptives a crime. The question of the propriety of those statutes reached the Supreme Court in Griswold v. Connecticut, 381 U.S. 479, 85 S.Ct. 1678, 14 L.Ed.2d 510 (1965). An official of the Planned Parenthood League of Connecticut and a Yale physician were charged with aiding and abetting "the use of a drug, medicinal article, or instrument for the purpose of preventing conception," a crime under Connecticut law, by providing contraceptives to a married couple. The Supreme Court reversed their conviction. Justice Douglas, writing for the Court, concluded:

> [S]pecific guarantees in the Bill of Rights have penumbras, formed by emanations from those guarantees that helped give them life and substance. Various guarantees create zones of privacy. The rights of association contained in the penumbra of the first amendment is one * * * the third amendment in its prohibition against the quartering of soldiers "in any house" in time of peace without the consent of the owner is another facet of that privacy. The fourth amendment explicitly affirms the right of the people to be secure in their persons, houses, papers, and effects against unreasonable searches and seizures. The fifth amendment in its self-incrimination clause enables the citizen to create a zone of privacy which government may not force him to surrender to his detriment. The ninth amendment provides "the enumeration in the constitution of certain rights will not be construed to deny or disparage others retained by the people."

> The present case * * * concerns a relationship lying within the zone of privacy created by several fundamental constitutional guarantees * * *.

> We deal with a right of privacy older than the Bill of Rights—older than our political parties, older than our school system. Marriage is a coming together for better or worse, hopefully enduring, and intimate to the degree of being sacred. It is an association that promotes a way of life, not causes; a harmony in living, not political faith; a bilateral loyalty, not commercial or social projects. Yet it is an association for as noble a purpose as any involved in our prior decisions.

381 U.S. at 484, 85 S.Ct. at 1681. Although a majority concurred in Justice Douglas's opinion, Chief Justice Warren and Justices Brennan and Goldberg based their determination on the Ninth Amendment. Justice Harlan based his concurrence entirely on the due process clause of the Fourteenth Amendment. Separately, Justice White concurred in the judgment and based his determination on the Fourteenth Amendment. Justices Black and Stewart dissented. Justice Black wrote:

> There is no single one of the graphic and eloquent strictures and criticisms fired at the policy of this Connecticut law either by the court's opinion or by those of my concurring brethren to which I cannot subscribe—except their conclusion that the evil qualities they see in the law make it unconstitutional. * * *

> I like my privacy as well as the next one, but I am nevertheless compelled to admit the government has a right to invade it unless prohibited by some specific constitutional provision. For these reasons, I cannot agree with the court's judgment and the reasons it gives for holding this Connecticut law unconstitutional.

381 U.S. at 510, 85 S.Ct. at 1696. The *Griswold* case left open the question of whether this new right of privacy extended only to married couples or to single people as well. It also left open the question of whether it extended only

to decisions related to procreation or whether it extended to all health care decisions. The first of these questions was answered in 1972 when the Court determined that a law that allowed married people, but not unmarried people, to have access to contraceptives violated the equal protection clause of the Fourteenth Amendment because there could be no rational basis for distinguishing between married and unmarried people in permitting access to contraceptives. The Court suggested that "if the right of privacy means anything, it is the right of the individual, married or single, to be free from unwarranted government intrusion into matters so fundamentally affecting a person as a decision whether to bear a child." Eisenstadt v. Baird, 405 U.S. 438, 453, 92 S.Ct. 1029, 1038, 31 L.Ed.2d 349 (1972). In Carey v. Population Services International, 431 U.S. 678, 97 S.Ct. 2010, 52 L.Ed.2d 675 (1977), the Supreme Court confirmed that since *Griswold* declared it unconstitutional for a state to deny contraceptives to married couples, and *Eisenstadt* declared it unconstitutional for a state to distinguish between married couples and unmarried people in controlling access to contraceptives, a state was without authority to ban the distribution of contraceptives to any adult.

May a state still limit access to contraceptives for minors? Should different kinds of contraceptives be regulated in different ways? Could a state require that condoms be available only through a face-to-face encounter with a pharmacist? In the mid–2000s many state health and education officials became concerned over federally funded "abstinence only" programs that provided middle and high school students with sex education programs that did not even mention most forms of contraception. By early 2008 more than a dozen states had decided to turn down millions of dollars of federal money because of the apparent failure of these programs in limiting teen pregnancy, which was already far more common in the United States than in most of the developed world. See Jennifer Medina, New York Just Says No to Abstinence Funding, New York Times, September 21, 2007. For a report suggesting that there is little evidence to support this multi-million dollar program, see Government Accountability Office, Abstinence Education: Efforts to Assess the Accuracy and Effectiveness of Federally Funded Programs, Report GAO–07–87 (October 3, 2006). Does federal funding of these programs, which are strongly supported by religious groups, pose any legal issue? Does it make a difference that even those who advocate teaching about contraception agree that abstinence is the most healthy choice for individual teens? Should public entities be involved in encouraging or discouraging contraceptive use?

Note: The Blurry Distinction Between Contraception and Abortion— Plan B (The "Morning After" Pill) and Mifepristone (RU–486)

Are some "contraceptives" that work by making implantation difficult (like the "morning after pill") really contraceptives, subject to very limited government regulation, or are they agents of abortion, subject to far greater restriction and regulation (and, perhaps, prohibition)? In addition, there is some question about how to treat medications that are recognized as nonsurgical abortifacients, like the drug Mifepristone.

If contraception refers to any process designed to prevent a pregnancy, and abortion refers to any process designed to end an established pregnancy, then the point at which the process of contraception becomes the process of abortion is at the commencement of the pregnancy. There is some ambiguity, however, about when the pregnancy begins, just as there is some ambiguity about when "conception" takes place. While standard medical texts equate conception with implantation, some states legislatures have provided that conception occurs at the moment of fertilization, some days before implantation. See Webster v. Reproductive Health Services, 492 U.S. at 561, (Stevens, J., concurring in part and dissenting in part).

When does the pregnancy begin? Does the fact that a large number of fertilized eggs—perhaps 50%—never implant, suggest that pregnancy does not begin until implantation? Is the fact that cells of the fertilized ovum are identical for about three days, and then begin to separate into differentiated cells that will become the placenta, on one hand, and cells that will become the embryo and fetus, on the other, relevant?

If there is to be a legal difference between contraception and abortion, the courts will have to determine when "conception" takes place and when a pregnancy begins. As Justice Stevens points out, some forms of what we now consider contraception are really devices designed to stop the fertilized egg from implanting in the uterus, not devices designed for avoiding fertilization of the egg in the first place.

> An intrauterine device, commonly called an IUD "works primarily by preventing a fertilized egg from implanting"; other contraceptive methods that may prevent implantation include "morning-after pills," high-dose estrogen pills taken after intercourse, particularly in cases of rape, and mifepristone (also known as RU 486), a pill that works "during the indeterminate period between contraception and abortion," low level estrogen "combined" pills—a version of the ordinary, daily ingested birth control pill—also may prevent the fertilized egg from reaching the uterine wall and implanting[ ].

Webster, 492 U.S. at 563, 109 S.Ct. at 3081 (Stevens, J., concurring in part and dissenting in part). If the law recognizes a distinction between contraception and abortion, should the law also be required to define that point at which contraception becomes abortion? Justice Stevens suggests that we must depend upon a medical definition of pregnancy, because any alternative would constitute the legal adoption of a theological position and thus be a violation of the establishment clause of the First Amendment. Do you agree? Can you develop a coherent legal argument that the state may regulate abortion in any way it sees fit, but *may not* prohibit a woman's choice to stop a fertilized ovum from reaching her uterus and implanting?

The issue has become higher profile since the FDA approved non-prescription access to the "morning after pill," the emergency contraceptive Plan B, for those over 18 in 2006. In 1999 an FDA advisory panel had recommended that the drug be made available over the counter for all purchasers, but objections (arguably political and arguably medical) caused the FDA to delay approval until 2003 and then require a prescription for this medication. After a threat by some members of the Senate to withhold confirmation of a newly appointed FDA Commissioner in 2006, Plan B was made available over the counter for persons over 18. Those under 18 were still required to provide a prescription, and those over 18 were required to prove their age before they could make a purchase. As a consequence, an adult seeking Plan B is required to have a face-to-face encounter with a pharmacist to get the medication. As a matter of policy, does it make any sense to treat those under 18 any differently than those over 18?

Problem: When a Pharmacist Chooses Not to Dispense Emergency Contraception

Carrie Snow is a pharmacist in the small town of Carver in the state of Baxley. She has worked for many years in a DRUGCO pharmacy, where she is now the assistant pharmacy manager. The local DRUGCO pharmacy is owned by the DRUGCO Pharmacy Corporation, with headquarters in New York. Although the Carver DRUGCO employs several pharmacists, Carrie frequently works alone because Carver is in a rural area of the state.

Unlike all of her fellow Carver DRUGCO pharmacists, Snow is concerned about the moral propriety of the emergency contraceptive, Plan B, which DRUGCO stocks at all of its pharmacies. Plan B is a concentrated form of the ingredient in ordinary birth control pills; it requires two doses of medication twelve hours apart. It reduces the chance of pregnancy by almost 90% if the first dose is taken within 72 hours of sexual intercourse. Carrie's moral problem with Plan B arises out of the several different ways in which Plan B works: it can delay the release of an ovum from the ovary, prevent fertilization of the ovum, block the implantation of the fertilized ovum in the uterus, make it more difficult for the sperm to make it to the fallopian tube, or, most worrisome, dislodge an implanted fertilized ovum. Given the time at which it is used—before implantation would have occurred—dislodging a fertilized ovum would happen very rarely if at all, unless the woman were already pregnant before she engaged in the intercourse that caused her to seek Plan B. For that reason, some physicians will recommend or perform pregnancy tests before prescribing (for minors) or recommending (for adults) Plan B. Snow has no idea whether such a test has been done on those coming into her pharmacy seeking Plan B. Snow's moral concern that there is a small chance Plan B will result in an abortion is exacerbated by her religiously based doubt about the propriety of any artificial form of contraception and her politically based concern about the moral decay of a society that depends upon this form of medication. After a great deal of consideration, Snow has concluded that she should not dispense Plan B under any circumstances because it would violate her own personal beliefs to do so.

Two years ago the State of Baxley passed a statute entitled, "The Health Care Providers' Right of Conscience," which provides:

> Every individual possesses a fundamental right to exercise that person's religious belief and conscience. No individual health care provider or health care facility may be mandated to perform specific services if that provider or facility objects to doing so for reason of conscience or religion. Any person who chooses not to provide such treatment may not be discriminated against in employment or disadvantaged in terms of professional privileges, or in any other way, as a result of the choice. This provision shall not be construed so that a patient is denied timely access to any health service.

Baxley Stat. Sec. 14–238. The Baxley State Board of Pharmacy also regulates the conduct of pharmacists and has the authority to create rules for the dispensing, distribution, wholesaling, and manufacture of drugs and devices and the practice of pharmacy for the protection and promotion of the public health, safety and welfare. After reviewing the statute, they issued "duty to dispense" regulations that state the following:

> (1) Pharmacies have a duty to deliver lawfully prescribed drugs or devices to patients and to distribute drugs and devices approved by the U.S. Food and Drug Administration for restricted distribution by pharmacies, or provide a

therapeutically equivalent drug or device in a timely manner consistent with reasonable expectations for filling the prescription.

(2) A pharmacist may refuse to dispense a prescription because of his or her religious or moral views only if the pharmacist works simultaneously with another pharmacist who does dispense the medication in place of the pharmacist who has a conscientious objection to doing so.

(3) A pharmacist who refuses to dispense a prescription because of his or her religious or moral views is not in violation of this regulation if that pharmacist refers the patient to another pharmacist within a reasonable distance who has confirmed by telephone or through an electronic form of communication that the prescribed medication in stock and that it will be dispensed immediately upon the receipt of the prescription.

Code Baxley Reg. 12.1632.

In a letter directed to the Pharmacy Board, the Baxley State Human Rights Commission, which is authorized to enforce antidiscrimination laws in the state, offered its opinion on the subject of the right of conscience and access to Plan B:

It is the position of the HRC that allowing pharmacists to discriminate, based on their personal religious beliefs, against women and others trying to fill lawful prescriptions would be discriminatory, unlawful, and against good public policy and the public interest. It is also HRC's position that allowing a practice of 'refuse and refer' as a means of addressing this issue, allows and perpetuates discriminatory behavior.

Jane Wishner, who also lives in Carver, Baxley, is concerned that women in her community may not have access to Plan B pills because Snow will not dispense them. She is concerned that because DRUGO is the only pharmacy in Carver and Snow is sometimes the only pharmacist on duty for eight hour shifts, a woman seeking Plan B will not have the ability to get the pills quickly, thus reducing their effectiveness. If a woman in Carver had to travel four hours to the next closest pharmacy or wait until another pharmacist who will dispense the medication is on duty at the Carver DRUGCO, she might not get the treatment she needs in time for it to be effective if at all. Although Wishner has not used Plan B, she says that she may wish to do so in the future.

Wishner has aired her concerns on television news shows which have caught the attention of the CEO of DRUGCO in New York. He is concerned as to what possible legal effect Carrie's refusal to dispense emergency contraceptives will have on the DRUGCO Corporation. He is not sure whether DRUGCO should support his assistant manager's decision not to dispense the medication, require his employee to dispense the medication, or attempt to schedule Carrie only when there is some other pharmacist who will dispense Plan B on duty. The last alternative will lead to extra expense for the corporation, and it is unacceptable to Carrie because it will make it impossible for her to work the more lucrative graveyard shift, when only one pharmacist is on duty.

Because of your reputation as the leading health lawyer in Baxley, all of the principals have sought to have you advise them. Your office assistant has phone messages from (1) Carrie Snow, who wants you to get "some kind of court order that says she doesn't have to dispense Plan B," (2) Jane Wishner, who wants you to get "some kind of court order that will assure that women in Carver get Plan B when they need it," and (3) the DRUGCO corporate office, which wants you to advise them on what limitations the law imposes on any policy they develop to apply in this case.

Whom will you choose to represent? Why? Are your own moral considerations relevant when you choose your client? Are those moral considerations any different for you, as a lawyer, choosing a client than they should be for a pharmacist or another health care provider choosing a patient?

Is Carrie Snow entitled to injective or other relief? Is Jane Wishner? Should DRUGCO be able to obtain a declaratory judgment, if that is permitted under state law? If the state were to sanction Carrie Snow for not dispensing the medication, would that violate her First Amendment free exercise rights? If a woman were to be denied the medication on religious or moral grounds, would she have been the subject of discrimination based on her religious beliefs? On her gender? If Carrie Snow diligently exercised a policy of "refuse and refer," described in section (3) of the regulation above, when it came to Plan B, would that meet all legal requirements? If Carrie Snow or Jane Wishner were to bring an action, should the other be able to intervene? Could DRUGCO intervene in this lawsuit in order to determine their legal responsibilities?

See Stormans, Inc. v. Selecky, 524 F.Supp.2d 1245 (W.D.Wa.2007), Vandersand v. Wal–Mart Stores, 525 F.Supp.2d 1052 (C.D.Ill.2007) and Menges v. Blagojevich, 451 F.Supp.2d 992 (C.D.Ill.2006). For a more academic discussion, see Ryan Lawrence and Farr Curlin, Clash of Definitions: Controversies About Conscience in Medicine, 7 Am. J. Bioethics (12) 10 (2007). That issue of that journal also includes eleven commentaries focusing on this issue. See also Farr A. Curlin, Ryan E. Lawrence, Marshall H. Chin, and John D. Lantos, Religion, Conscience and Controversial Clinical Practice, 356 N.E.J.Med. 593 (2007), and R. Alta Charo, The Celestial Fire of Conscience–Refusing to Deliver Medical Care, 352 N.E.J.Med. 2471 (2005).

The American College of Obstetrics and Gynecology ethics opinion on this issue provides:

1. In the provision of reproductive services, the patient's well-being must be paramount. Any conscientious refusal that conflicts with a patient's well-being should be accommodated only if the primary duty to the patient can be fulfilled.

* * *

2. Where conscience implores physicians to deviate from standard practices, including abortion, sterilization and provision of contraceptives, they must provide potential patients with accurate and prior notice of their personal moral commitments. * * *

4. Physicians and other health care professionals have the duty to refer patients in a timely manner to other providers if they do not feel that they can in conscience provide the standard reproductive services that their patients request.

* * *

6. In resource poor areas, access to safe and legal reproductive services should be maintained. * * *

American College of Obstetrics and Gynecology Committee on Ethics, The Limits of Conscientious Refusal in Reproductive Medicine, 110 Obstetrics Gynecology 1203 (2007).

3. *Abortion*

The right to privacy discussed (and perhaps invented) in *Griswold* found its most significant articulation in Roe v. Wade, 410 U.S. 113, 93 S.Ct. 705, 35 L.Ed.2d 147 (1973), the original abortion case. Imagine Justice Blackmun writing this opinion, going through medicine and history texts hoping to find out just when a person protected by the Fourteenth Amendment really did come into existence. Justice Blackmun, who had been counsel to the Mayo Clinic earlier in his legal career, was keenly aware of the medical consequences of his determination. A comparison of Justice Blackmun's approach to this problem and Justice Douglas's approach, which is discussed in note 1, following *Roe*, suggests that Justice Blackmun viewed abortion as a medical problem, while Justice Douglas viewed it as a personal issue. In any case, *Roe v. Wade* clearly recognized a Constitutionally based right of privacy which extended to personal procreative decisions. Further, this right was based on the due process clause of the Fourteenth Amendment, not the penumbras and emanations that formed the unstable foundation for *Griswold*. While *Roe* was increasingly narrowed during the 1980s, and while its death was often predicted, in 1992 the Court concluded that "the essential holding of *Roe v. Wade* should be retained and once again reaffirmed." *Planned Parenthood of Southeastern Pennsylvania v. Casey*, 505 U.S. 833, 112 S.Ct. 2791, 120 L.Ed.2d 674 (1992). In 2007 the Supreme Court "assume[d] * * * the principles [of *Roe* and *Casey*] for the purpose of this opinion," although it was not clear that those principles continued to command the respect of the majority of the Court. *Gonzales v. Carhart*, ___ U.S. ___, 127 S.Ct. 1610, 167 L.Ed.2d 480 (2007). But what is the "essential holding" of *Roe* that was retained in *Casey* and "assumed" in *Carhart*?

ROE v. WADE

Supreme Court of the United States, 1973.
410 U.S. 113, 93 S.Ct. 705, 35 L.Ed.2d 147.

MR. JUSTICE BLACKMUN delivered the opinion of the Court.

* * *

We forthwith acknowledge our awareness of the sensitive and emotional nature of the abortion controversy, of the vigorous opposing views, even among physicians, and of the deep and seemingly absolute convictions that the subject inspires. One's philosophy, one's experiences, one's exposure to the raw edges of human existence, one's religious training, one's attitudes toward life and family and their values, and the moral standards one establishes and seeks to observe, are all likely to influence and to color one's thinking and conclusions about abortion.

In addition, population growth, pollution, poverty, and racial overtones tend to complicate and not to simplify the problem.

Our task, of course, is to resolve the issue by constitutional measurement, free of emotion and of predilection. We seek earnestly to do this, and, because we do, we have inquired into, and in this opinion place some emphasis upon, medical and medical-legal history and what that history reveals about man's attitudes toward the abortion procedure over the centuries. We bear in mind, too, Mr. Justice Holmes' admonition in his now-vindicated dissent in Lochner v. New York[ ]:

[The Constitution] is made for people of fundamentally differing views, and the accident of our finding certain opinions natural and familiar or novel and even shocking ought not to conclude our judgment upon the question whether statutes embodying them conflict with the Constitution of the United States.

* * *

The principal thrust of appellant's attack on the Texas statutes is that they improperly invade a right, said to be possessed by the pregnant woman, to choose to terminate her pregnancy. Appellant would discover this right in the concept of personal "liberty" embodied in the Fourteenth Amendment's Due Process Clause; or in personal, marital, familial, and sexual privacy said to be protected by the Bill of Rights or its penumbras,[ ]; or among those rights reserved to the people by the Ninth Amendment[ ]. Before addressing this claim, we feel it desirable briefly to survey, in several aspects, the history of abortion, for such insight as that history may afford us, and then to examine the state purposes and interests behind the criminal abortion laws.

VI

It perhaps is not generally appreciated that the restrictive criminal abortion laws in effect in a majority of States today are of relatively recent vintage. Those laws, generally proscribing abortion or its attempt at any time during pregnancy except when necessary to preserve the pregnant woman's life, are not of ancient or even of common-law origin. Instead, they derive from statutory changes effected, for the most part, in the latter half of the 19th century.

[The Court then reviewed, in great detail, ancient attitudes, the Hippocratic Oath, the common law, English statutory law, American Law, the position of the American Medical Association, the position of the American Public Health Association, and the position of the American Bar Association.]

VII

Three reasons have been advanced to explain historically the enactment of criminal abortion laws in the 19th century and to justify their continued existence.

[The first, Victorian sexual morality, is dismissed as an anachronism.]

A second reason is concerned with abortion as a medical procedure. When most criminal abortion laws were first enacted, the procedure was a hazardous one for the woman. * * * Thus, it has been argued that a State's real concern in enacting a criminal abortion law was to protect the pregnant woman, that is, to restrain her from submitting to a procedure that placed her life in serious jeopardy.

Modern medical techniques have altered this situation. Appellants and various amici refer to medical data indicating that abortion in early pregnancy, this is, prior to the end of the first trimester, although not without its risk, is now relatively safe. Mortality rates for women undergoing early abortions, where the procedure is legal, appear to be as low as or lower than the rates for normal childbirth. Consequently, any interest of the State in protecting the woman from an inherently hazardous procedure, except when it would be equally dangerous for her to forgo it, has largely disappeared. Of course, important state interests in the area of health and medical standards do remain. The State has a legitimate interest in seeing to it that abortion, like any other medical procedure, is performed under circumstances that assure maximum safety for the patient. * * *

The third reason is the State's interest—some phrase it in terms of duty—in protecting prenatal life.

* * *

It is with these interests, and the weight to be attached to them, that this case is concerned.

VIII

The Constitution does not explicitly mention any right of privacy. In a line of decisions, however, going back perhaps as far as[ ] 1891 the Court has recognized that a right of personal privacy, or a guarantee of certain areas or zones of privacy, does exist under the Constitution. In varying contexts, the Court or individual Justices have, indeed, found at least the roots of that right in the First Amendment,[ ] in the Fourth and Fifth Amendments,[ ] in the penumbras of the Bill of Rights, Griswold v. Connecticut,[ ] the Ninth Amendment,[ ] or in the concept of liberty guaranteed by the first section of the Fourteenth Amendment.[ ] These decisions make it clear that only personal rights that can be deemed "fundamental" or "implicit in the concept of ordered liberty,"[ ] are included in this guarantee of personal privacy. They also make it clear that the right has some extension to activities relating to marriage,[ ] family relationships,[ ] and child rearing and education[ ].

This right of privacy, whether it be founded in the Fourteenth Amendment's concept of personal liberty and restrictions upon state action, as we feel it is, or, as the District Court determined, in the Ninth Amendment's reservation of rights to the people, is broad enough to encompass a woman's decision whether or not to terminate her pregnancy. The detriment that the State would impose upon the pregnant woman by denying this choice altogether is apparent. Specific and direct harm medically diagnosable even in early pregnancy may be involved. Maternity, or additional offspring, may force upon the woman a distressful life and future. Psychological harm may be imminent. Mental and physical health may be taxed by child care. There is also the distress, for all concerned, associated with the unwanted child, and there is the problem of bringing a child into a family already unable, psychologically and otherwise, to care for it. In other cases, as in this one, the additional difficulties and continuing stigma of unwed motherhood may be involved. All these are factors the woman and her responsible physician necessarily will consider in consultation.

On the basis of elements such as these, appellant and some amici argue that the woman's right is absolute and that she is entitled to terminate her pregnancy at whatever time, in whatever way, and for whatever reason she alone chooses. With this we do not agree. * * * [A] State may properly assert important interests in safeguarding health, in maintaining medical standards, and in protecting potential life. At some point in pregnancy, these respective interests become sufficiently compelling to sustain regulation of the factors that govern the abortion decision.

* * *

X

* * *

With respect to the State's important and legitimate interest in the health of the mother, the "compelling" point, in the light of present medical knowledge, is at approximately the end of the first trimester. This is so because of the now-established medical fact * * * that until the end of the first trimester mortality in abortion may be less than mortality in normal childbirth. It follows that, from and after this point, a State may regulate the abortion procedure to the extent that the regulation reasonably relates to the preservation and protection of maternal health. * * *

This means, on the other hand, that, for the period of pregnancy prior to this "compelling" point, the attending physician, in consultation with his patient, is free to determine, without regulation by the State, that, in his medical judgment, the patient's pregnancy should be terminated. If that decision is reached, the judgment may be effectuated by an abortion free of interference by the State.

With respect to the State's important and legitimate interest in potential life, the "compelling" point is at viability. This is so because the fetus then presumably has the capability of meaningful life outside the mother's womb. State regulation protective of fetal life after viability thus has both logical and biological justifications. If the State is interested in protecting fetal life after viability, it may go so far as to proscribe abortion during that period, except when it is necessary to preserve the life or health of the mother.

* * *

XI

To summarize and to repeat:

1. A state criminal abortion statute of the current Texas type, that excepts from criminality only a *lifesaving* procedure on behalf of the mother, without regard to pregnancy stage and without recognition of the other interests involved, is violative of the Due Process Clause of the Fourteenth Amendment.

(a) For the stage prior to approximately the end of the first trimester, the abortion decision and its effectuation must be left to the medical judgment of the pregnant woman's attending physician.

(b) For the stage subsequent to approximately the end of the first trimester, the State, in promoting its interest in the health of the mother, may, if it chooses, regulate the abortion procedure in ways that are reasonably related to maternal health.

(c) For the stage subsequent to viability, the State in promoting its interest in the potentiality of human life may, if it chooses, regulate, and even proscribe, abortion except where it is necessary, in appropriate medical judgment, for the preservation of the life or health of the mother.

* * *

Notes and Questions

1. Justice Blackmun's Fourteenth Amendment analysis is not the only way that the Court could have reached this result. Justice Douglas, concurring, would have depended on the Ninth Amendment, as did the District Court. His approach would have recognized a far broader right of privacy:

> The Ninth Amendment obviously does not create federally enforceable rights. It merely says, "The enumeration in the Constitution, of certain rights, shall not be construed to deny or disparage others retained by the people." But a catalogue of these rights includes customary, traditional, and time-honored rights, amenities, privileges, and immunities that come within the sweep of "the Blessings of Liberty" mentioned in the preamble to the Constitution. Many of them, in my view, come within the meaning of the term "liberty" as used in the Fourteenth Amendment.

> *First is the autonomous control over the development and expression of one's intellect, interests, tastes, and personality.*

> *Second is freedom of choice in the basic decisions of one's life respecting marriage, divorce, procreation, contraception, and the education and upbringing of children.*

> *Third is the freedom to care for one's health and person, freedom from bodily restraint or compulsion, freedom to walk, stroll, or loaf.*

Consider how the subsequent history of abortion legislation and litigation might have been different had this less medical, much broader, definition of the right been accepted by the Court in 1973.

2. The Court's opinion was vigorously criticized and stirred into action political forces opposed to abortion. They have encouraged state legislatures to seek creative ways to discourage abortions without running afoul of the requirements of *Roe v. Wade.* The Supreme Court at first resisted attempts to limit the underlying rights recognized in 1973, although the number of justices supporting that decision declined over time. *Roe* was reaffirmed more than a dozen times in its first decade, but by 1986 the 7–2 majority was down to 5–4, Thornburgh v. American College of Obstetricians and Gynecologists, 476 U.S. 747, 106 S.Ct. 2169, 90 L.Ed.2d 779 (1986), and by 1989 the Court appeared to be evenly divided, with Justice O'Connor unwilling to confront the issue. Webster v. Reproductive Health Services, 492 U.S. 490, 109 S.Ct. 3040, 106 L.Ed.2d 410 (1989). The two most important cases reinterpreting *Roe*—Planned Parenthood of Southeastern Pennsylvania v. Casey, 505 U.S. 833, 112 S.Ct. 2791, 120 L.Ed.2d 674 (1992) and Gonzales v. Carhart, ___ U.S. ___, 127 S.Ct. 1610, 167 L.Ed.2d 480 (2007), are reprinted below.

3. Government funding for abortions has been limited and the restrictions on the use of government funds for abortions have generally been upheld by the courts. In 1977, the Supreme Court upheld state statutes and Medicaid plans that refused to fund nontherapeutic abortions as well as a city's determination that its hospitals would not provide nontherapeutic abortions. Beal v. Doe, 432 U.S. 438, 97 S.Ct. 2366, 53 L.Ed.2d 464 (1977); Maher v. Roe, 432 U.S. 464, 97 S.Ct. 2376, 53 L.Ed.2d 484 (1977); Poelker v. Doe, 432 U.S. 519, 97 S.Ct. 2391, 53 L.Ed.2d 528 (1977). Three years later in Harris v. McRae, 448 U.S. 297, 100 S.Ct. 2671, 65 L.Ed.2d 784 (1980), the Supreme Court upheld the Hyde Amendment, which

provided that federal funds could not be used for virtually any abortion. Some states have continued to provide entirely state-funded Medicaid abortions. Simat Corp. v. Arizona Health Care Cost Containment System, 203 Ariz. 454, 56 P.3d 28 (2002)(reviewing, in detail, the state court decisions that have considered this issue). A handful of states have passed legislation requiring insurers to charge a separate and identifiable premium if a health insurance policy will cover abortion procedures.

4. There were two legal lines of attack on the Supreme Court's decision in *Roe v. Wade*. The first argued that the Supreme Court had returned to the unhappy Lochnerian days of substantive due process, during which the Court acted as if it were free to make social policy without regard to legal or constitutional restrictions. Of course, the authors of the Fourteenth Amendment were not confronted with abortion as a political and social issue, and the intent of the framers with regard to this particular question is not likely to be helpful in resolving this issue. While the Fourteenth Amendment has been broadly interpreted, *Roe v. Wade* and the subsequent abortion cases are among the few examples of the application of a "right to privacy" that arise out of that amendment. The Supreme Court has refused to extend this right of privacy to other areas, even within the health care system. See United States v. Rutherford, 442 U.S. 544, 99 S.Ct. 2470, 61 L.Ed.2d 68 (1979) (no privacy right to use an unproven cancer drug). In the first right to die case considered by the Court, none of the Justices even used the word "privacy" to describe the underlying constitutional right; instead they depended upon the apparently more limited "liberty interest" explicitly mentioned in the Fourteenth Amendment. Cruzan v. Director, Missouri Dept. of Health, 497 U.S. 261, 110 S.Ct. 2841, 111 L.Ed.2d 224 (1990). See Chapter 15. In 1986 the Supreme Court explicitly rejected the application of the right of privacy to protect those engaging in homosexual conduct in Bowers v. Hardwick, 478 U.S. 186, 106 S.Ct. 2841, 92 L.Ed.2d 140 (1986), and, in a strictly legal, conceptual sense, *Roe v. Wade* appeared to be a derelict on the waters of the law.

The vitality of the doctrine of substantive due process was suddenly revived when the Court overturned *Bowers* in 2003. In Lawrence v. Texas, 539 U.S. 558, 123 S.Ct. 2472, 156 L.Ed.2d 508 (2003) the Court announced that those who engaged in gay and lesbian sex are protected from criminal action by the state of Texas by the right of privacy, which itself is firmly rooted in the Due Process Clause of the Fifth and Fourteenth Amendments. Does the fact that the opinion was written by Justice Kennedy, who also wrote the 2007 opinion in *Gonzales v. Carhart*, below, suggest that the substantive due process right defined in Lawrence is not broad enough to encompass decisions relating to abortion?

The second line of attack on *Roe v. Wade* focused on the opinion's scientific foundation. *Roe v. Wade* made two kinds of distinctions. First, it identified that point at which it became more dangerous to abort than to bear the child; second, it identified that point at which the fetus was viable. The court identified those points as occurring at the end of the first and second trimesters. As the science of obstetrics improved and safer techniques of abortion developed, the first point moved back, closer to the time of delivery, and the second point moved forward, closer to the time of conception. It is now quite safe to have an abortion long after the end of the first trimester, and a fetus may be viable before the end of the second trimester. Should the Supreme Court stick to its scientifically justifiable points (the point of increased danger and the point of viability), which would create an ambiguity because it changes with the latest medical developments, or should it stick with the arbitrary first and second trimester timelines, which are easy to apply, even though they are no longer supported by science? The Court attempted to answer this question in City of Akron v. Akron Center for Reproductive Health, Inc., 462 U.S. 416, 103 S.Ct. 2481, 76 L.Ed.2d 687 (1983), and finally reconsidered the trimester division altogether in 1992.

PLANNED PARENTHOOD OF SOUTHEASTERN PENNSYLVANIA v. CASEY

Supreme Court of the United States, 1992.
505 U.S. 833, 112 S.Ct. 2791, 120 L.Ed.2d 674.

JUSTICE O'CONNOR, JUSTICE KENNEDY, and JUSTICE SOUTER announced the judgment of the Court and delivered the opinion of the Court with respect to Parts I, II, III, V–A, V–C, and VI, an opinion with respect to Part V–E, in which JUSTICE STEVENS joins, and an opinion with respect to Parts IV, V–B, and V–D.

I.

Liberty finds no refuge in a jurisprudence of doubt. Yet 19 years after our holding that the Constitution protects a woman's right to terminate her pregnancy in its early stages,[ ] that definition of liberty is still questioned. * * *

At issue in these cases are five provisions of the Pennsylvania Abortion Control Act of 1982. * * * The Act requires that a woman seeking an abortion give her informed consent prior to the abortion procedure, and specifies that she be provided with certain information at least 24 hours before the abortion is performed.[ ] For a minor to obtain an abortion, the Act requires the informed consent of one of her parents, but provides for a judicial bypass option if the minor does not wish to or cannot obtain a parent's consent.[ ] Another provision of the Act requires that, unless certain exceptions apply, a married woman seeking an abortion must sign a statement indicating that she has notified her husband of her intended abortion.[ ] The Act exempts compliance with these three requirements in the event of a "medical emergency," which is defined in the Act.[ ] In addition to the above provisions regulating the performance of abortions, the Act imposes certain reporting requirements on facilities that provide abortion services.[ ]

* * *

After considering the fundamental constitutional questions resolved by *Roe*, principles of institutional integrity, and the rule of stare decisis, we are led to conclude this: the essential holding of *Roe v. Wade* should be retained and once again reaffirmed.

It must be stated at the outset and with clarity that *Roe's* essential holding, the holding we reaffirm, has three parts. First is a recognition of the right of the woman to choose to have an abortion before viability and to obtain it without undue interference from the State. Before viability, the State's interests are not strong enough to support a prohibition of abortion or the imposition of a substantial obstacle to the woman's effective right to elect the procedure. Second is a confirmation of the State's power to restrict abortions after fetal viability, if the law contains exceptions for pregnancies which endanger a woman's life or health. And third is the principle that the State has legitimate interests from the outset of the pregnancy in protecting the health of the woman and the life of the fetus that may become a child. These principles do not contradict one another; and we adhere to each.

II.

* * *

Men and women of good conscience can disagree, and we suppose some always shall disagree, about the profound moral and spiritual implications of terminating a pregnancy, even in its earliest stage. Some of us as individuals find abortion offensive to our most basic principles of morality, but that cannot control our decision. Our obligation is to define the liberty of all, not to mandate our own moral code. The underlying constitutional issue is whether the State can resolve these philosophic questions in such a definitive way that a woman lacks all choice in the matter, except perhaps in those rare circumstances in which the pregnancy is itself a danger to her own life or health, or is the result of rape or incest. * * * Abortion is a unique act. It is an act fraught with consequences for others: for the woman who must live with the implications of her decision; for the persons who perform and assist in the procedure; for the spouse, family, and society which must confront the knowledge that these procedures exist, procedures some deem nothing short of an act of violence against innocent human life; and, depending on one's beliefs, for the life or potential life that is aborted. Though abortion is conduct, it does not follow that the State is entitled to proscribe it in all instances. That is because the liberty of the woman is at stake in a sense unique to the human condition and so unique to the law. The mother who carries a child to full term is subject to anxieties, to physical constraints, to pain that only she must bear. That these sacrifices have from the beginning of the human race been endured by woman with a pride that ennobles her in the eyes of others and gives to the infant a bond of love cannot alone be grounds for the State to insist she make the sacrifice. Her suffering is too intimate and personal for the State to insist, without more, upon its own vision of the woman's role, however dominant that vision has been in the course of our history and our culture. The destiny of the woman must be shaped to a large extent on her own conception of her spiritual imperatives and her place in society.

* * *

While we appreciate the weight of the arguments made on behalf of the State in the case before us, arguments which in their ultimate formulation conclude that *Roe* should be overruled, the reservations any of us may have in reaffirming the central holding of *Roe* are outweighed by the explication of individual liberty we have given combined with the force of stare decisis. We turn now to that doctrine.

III.

A.

[In this section, the court discussed the conditions under which it is appropriate for the Court to reverse its own precedent.]

So in this case we may inquire whether *Roe's* central rule has been found unworkable; whether the rule's limitation on state power could be removed without serious inequity to those who have relied upon it or significant damage to the stability of the society governed by the rule in question; whether the law's growth in the intervening years has left *Roe's* central rule a doctrinal anachronism discounted by society; and whether *Roe's* premises of fact have so far changed in the ensuing two decades as to render its central holding somehow irrelevant or unjustifiable in dealing with the issue it addressed.

* * *

The sum of the precedential inquiry to this point shows *Roe's* underpinnings unweakened in any way affecting its central holding. While it has engendered disapproval, it has not been unworkable. An entire generation has come of age free to assume *Roe's* concept of liberty in defining the capacity of women to act in society, and to make reproductive decisions; no erosion of principle going to liberty or personal autonomy has left *Roe's* central holding a doctrinal remnant; *Roe* portends no developments at odds with other precedent for the analysis of personal liberty; and no changes of fact have rendered viability more or less appropriate as the point at which the balance of interests tips. Within the bounds of normal stare decisis analysis, then, and subject to the considerations on which it customarily turns, the stronger argument is for affirming *Roe's* central holding, with whatever degree of personal reluctance any of us may have, not for overruling it.

B.

[The Court next distinguished the rule in the abortion cases from the rules in *Lochner* and the "separate but equal" cases, two areas in which the Supreme Court did reverse its well settled precedents this century. The Court also explained that it should not expend its political capital and put the public respect for the Court and its processes at risk by reversing *Roe*.]

IV.

From what we have said so far it follows that it is a constitutional liberty of the woman to have some freedom to terminate her pregnancy. We conclude that the basic decision in *Roe* was based on a constitutional analysis which we cannot now repudiate. The woman's liberty is not so unlimited, however, that from the outset the State cannot show its concern for the life of the unborn, and at a later point in fetal development the State's interest in life has sufficient force so that the right of the woman to terminate the pregnancy can be restricted.

* * *

We conclude the line should be drawn at viability, so that before that time the woman has a right to choose to terminate her pregnancy. We adhere to this principle for two reasons. First, as we have said, is the doctrine of stare decisis. * * *

The second reason is that the concept of viability, as we noted in *Roe,* is the time at which there is a realistic possibility of maintaining and nourishing a life outside the womb, so that the independent existence of the second life can in reason and all fairness be the object of state protection that now overrides the rights of the woman. * * *

The woman's right to terminate her pregnancy before viability is the most central principle of *Roe v. Wade*. It is a rule of law and a component of liberty we cannot renounce.

* * *

Yet it must be remembered that *Roe v. Wade* speaks with clarity in establishing not only the woman's liberty but also the State's "important and legitimate interest in potential life."[ ] That portion of the decision in *Roe* has been given too little acknowledgment and implementation by the Court in its subsequent cases. Those cases decided that any regulation touching upon the abortion decision must survive strict scrutiny, to be sustained only if drawn in narrow terms to further a compelling state interest.[ ] Not all of the cases decided under that formulation can be reconciled with the holding in *Roe* itself that the State has legitimate interests in the health of the woman and in protecting the potential life within her. In resolving this tension, we choose to rely upon *Roe,* as against the later cases.

* * *

We reject the trimester framework, which we do not consider to be part of the essential holding of *Roe*.[ ] Measures aimed at ensuring that a woman's choice contemplates the consequences for the fetus do not necessarily interfere with the right recognized in *Roe*, although those measures have been found to be inconsistent with the rigid trimester framework announced in that case. A logical reading of the central holding in *Roe* itself, and a necessary reconciliation of the liberty of the woman and the interest of the State in promoting prenatal life, require, in our view, that we abandon the trimester framework as a rigid prohibition on all previability regulation aimed at the protection of fetal life.

* * *

The fact that a law which serves a valid purpose, one not designed to strike at the right itself, has the incidental effect of making it more difficult or more expensive to procure an abortion cannot be enough to invalidate it. Only where state regulation imposes an undue burden on a woman's ability to make this decision does the power of the State reach into the heart of the liberty protected by the Due Process Clause.

* * *

Not all burdens on the right to decide whether to terminate a pregnancy will be undue. In our view, the undue burden standard is the appropriate means of reconciling the State's interest with the woman's constitutionally protected liberty.

* * *

A finding of an undue burden is a shorthand for the conclusion that a state regulation has the purpose or effect of placing a substantial obstacle in the path of a woman seeking an abortion of a nonviable fetus. A statute with this purpose is invalid because the means chosen by the State to further the interest in potential life must be calculated to inform the woman's free choice, not hinder it. And a statute which, while furthering the interest in potential life or some other valid state interest, has the effect of placing a substantial obstacle in the path of a woman's choice cannot be considered a permissible means of serving its legitimate ends. * * *

Some guiding principles should emerge. What is at stake is the woman's right to make the ultimate decision, not a right to be insulated from all others in doing so. Regulations which do no more than create a structural mechanism by which the State, or the parent or guardian of a minor, may express profound respect for the life of the unborn are permitted, if they are not a substantial obstacle to the woman's exercise of the right to choose.[ ]

[The Justices then summarized their new undue burden test:]

(a) To protect the central right recognized by *Roe v. Wade* while at the same time accommodating the State's profound interest in potential life, we will employ the undue burden analysis as explained in this opinion. An undue burden exists, and therefore a provision of law is invalid, if its purpose or effect is to place a substantial obstacle in the path of a woman seeking an abortion before the fetus attains viability.

(b) We reject the rigid trimester framework of *Roe v. Wade*. To promote the State's profound interest in potential life, throughout pregnancy the State may take measures to ensure that the woman's choice is informed, and measures designed to advance this interest will not be invalidated as long as their purpose is to persuade the woman to choose childbirth over abortion. These measures must not be an undue burden on the right.

(c) As with any medical procedure, the State may enact regulations to further the health or safety of a woman seeking an abortion. Unnecessary health regulations that have the purpose or effect of presenting a substantial obstacle to a woman seeking an abortion impose an undue burden on the right.

(d) Our adoption of the undue burden analysis does not disturb the central holding of *Roe v. Wade*, and we reaffirm that holding. Regardless of whether exceptions are made for particular circumstances, a State may not prohibit any woman from making the ultimate decision to terminate her pregnancy before viability.

(e) We also reaffirm *Roe's* holding that "subsequent to viability, the State in promoting its interest in the potentiality of human life may, if it chooses, regulate, and even proscribe, abortion except where it is necessary, in appropriate medical judgment, for the preservation of the life or health of the mother."[ ]

* * *

V.

* * *

A.

Because it is central to the operation of various other requirements, we begin with the statute's definition of medical emergency. Under the statute, a medical emergency is "that condition which, on the basis of the physician's good faith clinical judgment, so complicates the medical condition of a pregnant woman as to necessitate the immediate abortion of her pregnancy to avert her death or for which a delay will create serious risk of substantial and irreversible impairment of a major bodily function."[ ]

Petitioners argue that the definition is too narrow, contending that it forecloses the possibility of an immediate abortion despite some significant health risks.

[The Justices accepted the Court of Appeals interpretation of the statute, which assured that "abortion regulation would not in any way pose a significant threat to the life or health of a woman," and determined that the definition imposed no undue burden on a woman's right to an abortion.]

B.

We next consider the informed consent requirement.[ ] Except in a medical emergency, the statute requires that at least 24 hours before performing an abortion a physician inform the woman of the nature of the procedure, the health risks of the abortion and of childbirth, and the "probable gestational age of the unborn child." The physician or a qualified nonphysician must inform the woman of the availability of printed materials published by the State describing the fetus and providing information about medical assistance for childbirth, information about child support from the father, and a list of agencies which provide adoption and other services as alternatives to abortion. An abortion may not be performed unless the woman certifies in writing that she has been informed of the availability of these printed materials and has been provided them if she chooses to view them.

* * *

If the information the State requires to be made available to the woman is truthful and not misleading, the requirement may be permissible. [The Court then rejects the argument that the physician's first amendment speech rights trump the state-mandated obligation to provide patients with identified truthful information.]

* * *

The Pennsylvania statute also requires us to reconsider the holding[ ] that the State may not require that a physician, as opposed to a qualified assistant, provide information relevant to a woman's informed consent.[ ] * * * Our cases reflect the fact that the Constitution gives the States broad latitude to decide that particular functions may be performed only by licensed professionals, even if an objective assessment might suggest that those same tasks could be performed by others.[ ] Thus, we uphold the provision as a reasonable means to insure that the woman's consent is informed.

Our analysis of Pennsylvania's 24–hour waiting period between the provision of the information deemed necessary to informed consent and the performance of an abortion under the undue burden standard requires us to reconsider the premise behind the decision in *Akron I* invalidating a parallel requirement. In *Akron I* we said: "Nor are we convinced that the State's legitimate concern that the woman's decision be informed is reasonably served by requiring a 24–hour delay as a matter of course."[ ] We consider that conclusion to be wrong. The idea that important decisions will be more informed and deliberate if they follow some period of reflection does not strike us as unreasonable, particularly where the statute directs that important information become part of the background of the decision.

* * *

C.

Pennsylvania's abortion law provides, except in cases of medical emergency, that no physician shall perform an abortion on a married woman without receiving a signed statement from the woman that she has notified her spouse that she is about to undergo an abortion.

* * *

This information and the District Court's findings reinforce what common sense would suggest. In well-functioning marriages, spouses discuss important intimate decisions such as whether to bear a child. But there are millions of women in this country who are the victims of regular physical and psychological abuse at the hands of their husbands. Should these women become pregnant, they may have very good reasons for not wishing to inform their husbands of their decision to obtain an abortion. Many may have justifiable fears of physical abuse, but may be no less fearful of the consequences of reporting prior abuse to the Commonwealth of Pennsylvania. Many may have a reasonable fear that notifying their husbands will provoke further instances of child abuse; these women are not exempt from [the] notification requirement. Many may fear devastating forms of psychological abuse from their husbands, including verbal harassment, threats of future violence, the destruction of possessions, physical confinement to the home, the withdrawal of financial support, or the disclosure of the abortion to family and friends. * * *

The spousal notification requirement is thus likely to prevent a significant number of women from obtaining an abortion. It does not merely make abortions a little more difficult or expensive to obtain; for many women, it will impose a substantial obstacle. We must not blind ourselves to the fact that the significant number of women who fear for their safety and the safety of their children are likely to be deterred from procuring an abortion as surely as if the Commonwealth had outlawed abortion in all cases.

Respondents attempt to avoid the conclusion that [the spousal notification provision] is invalid by pointing out that it imposes almost no burden at all for the vast majority of women seeking abortions. * * * Respondents argue that since some of [the 20% of women who seek abortions who are married] will be able to notify their husbands without adverse consequences or will qualify for one of the exceptions, the statute affects fewer than one percent of women seeking abortions. For this reason, it is asserted, the statute cannot be invalid on its face.[ ] We disagree with respondents' basic method of analysis.

The analysis does not end with the one percent of women upon whom the statute operates; it begins there. Legislation is measured for consistency with the Constitution by its impact on those whose conduct it affects. * * * [A]s we have said, [the Act's] real target is narrower even than the class of women seeking abortions * * *: it is married women seeking abortions who do not wish to notify their husbands of their intentions and who do not qualify for one of the statutory exceptions to the notice requirement. The unfortunate yet persisting conditions * * * will mean that in a large fraction of the cases * * *, [the statute] will operate as a substantial obstacle to a woman's choice to undergo an abortion. It is an undue burden, and therefore invalid.

* * *

[The spousal notification provision] embodies a view of marriage consonant with the common-law status of married women but repugnant to our present understanding of marriage and of the nature of the rights secured by the Constitution. Women do not lose their constitutionally protected liberty when they marry. * * *

D.

* * *

Our cases establish, and we reaffirm today, that a State may require a minor seeking an abortion to obtain the consent of a parent or guardian, provided that there is an adequate judicial bypass procedure.[ ] Under these precedents, in our view, the [Pennsylvania] one-parent consent requirement and judicial bypass procedure are constitutional.

* * *

E.

[The Justices upheld all of the record keeping and reporting requirements of the statute, except for that provision requiring the reporting of a married woman's reason for failure to give notice to her husband.]

VI.

Our Constitution is a covenant running from the first generation of Americans to us and then to future generations. It is a coherent succession. Each generation must learn anew that the Constitution's written terms embody ideas and aspirations that must survive more ages than one. We accept our responsibility not to retreat from interpreting the full meaning of the covenant in light of all of our precedents. We invoke it once again to define the freedom guaranteed by the Constitution's own promise, the promise of liberty.

* * *

[In addition to those parts of the statute found unconstitutional in the three-justice opinion, Justice Stevens would find unconstitutional the requirement that the doctor deliver state-produced materials to a woman seeking an abortion, the counseling requirements, and the 24–hour-waiting requirement. His concurring and dissenting opinion is omitted. Justice Blackman's opinion, concurring in the judgment in part and dissenting in part, is also omitted.]

CHIEF JUSTICE REHNQUIST, with whom JUSTICE WHITE, JUSTICE SCALIA, and JUSTICE THOMAS join, concurring in the judgment in part and dissenting in part.

The joint opinion, following its newly-minted variation on stare decisis, retains the outer shell of *Roe v. Wade*,[ ] but beats a wholesale retreat from the substance of that case. We believe that *Roe* was wrongly decided, and that it can and should be overruled consistently with our traditional approach to stare decisis in constitutional cases.

* * *

The end result of the joint opinion's paeans of praise for legitimacy is the enunciation of a brand new standard for evaluating state regulation of a woman's right to abortion—the "undue burden" standard. As indicated above, *Roe v. Wade* adopted a "fundamental right" standard under which state regulations could survive only if they met the requirement of "strict scrutiny." While we disagree with that standard, it at least had a recognized basis in constitutional law at the time *Roe* was decided. The same cannot be said for the "undue burden" standard, which is created largely out of whole cloth by the authors of the joint opinion. It is a standard which even today does not command the support of a majority of this Court. And it will not, we believe, result in the sort of "simple limitation," easily applied, which the joint opinion anticipates.[ ] In sum, it is a standard which is not built to last.

In evaluating abortion regulations under that standard, judges will have to decide whether they place a "substantial obstacle" in the path of a woman seeking an abortion.[ ] In that this standard is based even more on a judge's subjective determinations than was the trimester framework, the standard will do nothing to prevent "judges from roaming at large in the constitutional field" guided only by their personal views.[ ]

* * *

The sum of the joint opinion's labors in the name of stare decisis and "legitimacy" is this: *Roe v. Wade* stands as a sort of judicial Potemkin Village, which may be pointed out to passers by as a monument to the importance of adhering to precedent. But behind the facade, an entirely new method of analysis, without any roots in constitutional law, is imported to decide the constitutionality of state laws regulating abortion. Neither stare decisis nor "legitimacy" are truly served by such an effort.

* * *

Justice Scalia, with whom the Chief Justice, Justice White, and Justice Thomas join, concurring in the judgment in part and dissenting in part.

* * *

The States may, if they wish, permit abortion-on-demand, but the Constitution does not require them to do so. The permissibility of abortion, and the limitations upon it, are to be resolved like most important questions in our democracy: by citizens trying to persuade one another and then voting. As the Court acknowledges, "where reasonable people disagree the government can adopt one position or the other." [ ] The Court is correct in adding the qualification that this "assumes a state of affairs in which the choice does not intrude upon a protected liberty,"[ ]—but the crucial part of that qualification is the penultimate word. A State's choice between two positions on which reasonable people can disagree is constitutional even when (as is often the case) it intrudes upon a "liberty" in the absolute sense. Laws against bigamy, for example—which entire societies of reasonable people disagree with— intrude upon men and women's liberty to marry and live with one another.

But bigamy happens not to be a liberty specially "protected" by the Constitution.

That is, quite simply, the issue in this case: not whether the power of a woman to abort her unborn child is a "liberty" in the absolute sense; or even whether it is a liberty of great importance to many women. Of course it is both. The issue is whether it is a liberty protected by the Constitution of the United States. I am sure it is not. I reach that conclusion not because of anything so exalted as my views concerning the "concept of existence, of meaning, of the universe, and of the mystery of human life." [ ] I reach it for the same reason I reach the conclusion that bigamy is not constitutionally protected—because of two simple facts: (1) the Constitution says absolutely nothing about it, and (2) the longstanding traditions of American society have permitted it to be legally proscribed.

* * *

I am certainly not in a good position to dispute that the Court has saved the "central holding" of *Roe*, since to do that effectively I would have to know what the Court has saved, which in turn would require me to understand (as I do not) what the "undue burden" test means. * * * I thought I might note, however, that the following portions of *Roe* have not been saved:

- Under *Roe*, requiring that a woman seeking an abortion be provided truthful information about abortion before giving informed written consent is unconstitutional, if the information is designed to influence her choice[ ]. Under the joint opinion's "undue burden" regime (as applied today, at least) such a requirement is constitutional[ ].

- Under *Roe,* requiring that information be provided by a doctor, rather than by nonphysician counselors, is unconstitutional[ ]. Under the "undue burden" regime (as applied today, at least) it is not[ ].

- Under *Roe*, requiring a 24–hour waiting period between the time the woman gives her informed consent and the time of the abortion is unconstitutional. Under the "undue burden" regime (as applied today, at least) it is not[ ].

- Under *Roe*, requiring detailed reports that include demographic data about each woman who seeks an abortion and various information about each abortion is unconstitutional[ ]. Under the "undue burden" regime (as applied today, at least) it generally is not[ ].

* * *

GONZALES v. CARHART

Supreme Court of the United States, 2007.
__ U.S. __, 127 S.Ct. 1610, 167 L.Ed.2d 480.

JUSTICE KENNEDY delivered the opinion of the Court.

These cases require us to consider the validity of the Partial–Birth Abortion Ban Act of 2003 (Act),[ ] a federal statute regulating abortion procedures. * * * We conclude the Act should be sustained against the objections lodged by the broad, facial attack brought against it.

* * *

I

A

[The Medical Procedure]

The Act proscribes a particular manner of ending fetal life, so it is necessary here[ ] to discuss abortion procedures in some detail. * * *

Abortion methods vary depending to some extent on the preferences of the physician and, of course, on the term of the pregnancy and the resulting stage of the unborn child's development. Between 85 and 90 percent of the approximately 1.3 million abortions performed each year in the United States take place in the first three months of pregnancy, which is to say in the first trimester.[ ] The most common first-trimester abortion method is vacuum aspiration (otherwise known as suction curettage) in which the physician vacuums out the embryonic tissue. Early in this trimester an alternative is to use medication, such as mifepristone (commonly known as RU–486), to terminate the pregnancy.[ ] The Act does not regulate these procedures.

Of the remaining abortions that take place each year, most occur in the second trimester. The surgical procedure referred to as "dilation and evacuation" or "D & E" is the usual abortion method in this trimester.[ ] Although individual techniques for performing D & E differ, the general steps are the same.

A doctor must first dilate the cervix at least to the extent needed to insert surgical instruments into the uterus and to maneuver them to evacuate the fetus.[ ] The steps taken to cause dilation differ by physician and gestational age of the fetus. * * *

After sufficient dilation the surgical operation can commence. The woman is placed under general anesthesia or conscious sedation. The doctor, often guided by ultrasound, inserts grasping forceps through the woman's cervix and into the uterus to grab the fetus. The doctor grips a fetal part with the forceps and pulls it back through the cervix and vagina, continuing to pull even after meeting resistance from the cervix. The friction causes the fetus to tear apart. For example, a leg might be ripped off the fetus as it is pulled through the cervix and out of the woman. The process of evacuating the fetus piece by piece continues until it has been completely removed. A doctor may make 10 to 15 passes with the forceps to evacuate the fetus in its entirety, though sometimes removal is completed with fewer passes. Once the fetus has been evacuated, the placenta and any remaining fetal material are suctioned or scraped out of the uterus. The doctor examines the different parts to ensure the entire fetal body has been removed.[ ]

Some doctors, especially later in the second trimester, may kill the fetus a day or two before performing the surgical evacuation. They inject digoxin or potassium chloride into the fetus, the umbilical cord, or the amniotic fluid. Fetal demise may cause contractions and make greater dilation possible. Once dead, moreover, the fetus' body will soften, and its removal will be easier. * * *

The abortion procedure that was the impetus for the numerous bans on "partial-birth abortion," including the Act, is a variation of this standard D & E.[ ] The medical community has not reached unanimity on the appropriate name for this D & E variation. It has been referred to as "intact D & E," "dilation and extraction" (D & X), and "intact D & X."[ ] For discussion purposes this D & E variation will be referred to as intact D & E. The main difference between the two procedures is that in intact D & E a doctor extracts the fetus intact or largely intact with only a few passes. There are no comprehensive statistics indicating what percentage of all D & Es are performed in this manner.

Intact D & E, like regular D & E, begins with dilation of the cervix. Sufficient dilation is essential for the procedure. * * * In an intact D & E procedure the doctor extracts the fetus in a way conducive to pulling out its entire body, instead of ripping it apart. * * *

Intact D & E gained public notoriety when, in 1992, Dr. Martin Haskell gave a presentation describing his method of performing the operation.[ ] In the usual intact D & E the fetus' head lodges in the cervix, and dilation is insufficient to allow it to pass.[ ] Haskell explained the next step as follows:

> " 'At this point, the right-handed surgeon slides the fingers of the left [hand] along the back of the fetus and "hooks" the shoulders of the fetus with the index and ring fingers (palm down).

> " 'While maintaining this tension, lifting the cervix and applying traction to the shoulders with the fingers of the left hand, the surgeon takes a pair of blunt curved Metzenbaum scissors in the right hand. He carefully advances the tip, curved down, along the spine and under his middle finger until he feels it contact the base of the skull under the tip of his middle finger.

> " 'The surgeon then forces the scissors into the base of the skull or into the foramen magnum. Having safely entered the skull, he spreads the scissors to enlarge the opening.

> " 'The surgeon removes the scissors and introduces a suction catheter into this hole and evacuates the skull contents. With the catheter still in place, he applies traction to the fetus, removing it completely from the patient.' "[ ]

This is an abortion doctor's clinical description. Here is another description from a nurse who witnessed the same method performed on a 26–week fetus and who testified before the Senate Judiciary Committee:

> " 'Dr. Haskell went in with forceps and grabbed the baby's legs and pulled them down into the birth canal. Then he delivered the baby's body and the arms—everything but the head. The doctor kept the head right inside the uterus....

> " 'The baby's little fingers were clasping and unclasping, and his little feet were kicking. Then the doctor stuck the scissors in the back of his head, and the baby's arms jerked out, like a startle reaction, like a flinch, like a baby does when he thinks he is going to fall.

> " 'The doctor opened up the scissors, stuck a high-powered suction tube into the opening, and sucked the baby's brains out. Now the baby went completely limp....

" 'He cut the umbilical cord and delivered the placenta. He threw the baby in a pan, along with the placenta and the instruments he had just used.' "[ ]

[JUSTICE KENNEDY next describes other varieties of this procedure in equally vivid terms.]

* * *

D & E and intact D & E are not the only second-trimester abortion methods. * * *

B

[The Statute]

After Dr. Haskell's procedure received public attention, with ensuing and increasing public concern, bans on " 'partial birth abortion' " proliferated. By the time of the *Stenberg* decision [finding Nebraska's statutory partial birth abortion ban to be unconstitutional in 2003], about 30 States had enacted bans designed to prohibit the procedure.[ ]. In 1996, Congress also acted to ban partial-birth abortion. President Clinton vetoed the congressional legislation, and the Senate failed to override the veto. Congress approved another bill banning the procedure in 1997, but President Clinton again vetoed it. In 2003, after this Court's decision in *Stenberg*, Congress passed the Act at issue here.[ ] President Bush signed the Act into law. It was to take effect the following day.[ ]

The Act responded to *Stenberg* in two ways. First, Congress made factual findings. Congress determined that this Court in *Stenberg* "was required to accept the very questionable findings issued by the district court judge,"[ ], but that Congress was "not bound to accept the same factual findings,"[ ]. Congress found, among other things, that "[a] moral, medical, and ethical consensus exists that the practice of performing a partial-birth abortion . . . is a gruesome and inhumane procedure that is never medically necessary and should be prohibited."[ ]

Second, and more relevant here, the Act's language differs from that of the Nebraska statute struck down in *Stenberg*.[ ] The operative provisions of the Act provide in relevant part:

"(a) Any physician who, in or affecting interstate or foreign commerce, knowingly performs a partial-birth abortion and thereby kills a human fetus shall be fined under this title or imprisoned not more than 2 years, or both. This subsection does not apply to a partial-birth abortion that is necessary to save the life of a mother whose life is endangered by a physical disorder, physical illness, or physical injury, including a life-endangering physical condition caused by or arising from the pregnancy itself. * * *

"(b) As used in this section—

"(1) the term 'partial-birth abortion' means an abortion in which the person performing the abortion—

"(A) deliberately and intentionally vaginally delivers a living fetus until, in the case of a head-first presentation, the entire fetal head is outside the body of the mother, or, in the case of breech presentation, any part of the fetal trunk past the navel is outside the body of the mother, for the purpose of performing an overt act that the person knows will kill the partially delivered living fetus; and

"(B) performs the overt act, other than completion of delivery, that kills the partially delivered living fetus;

* * *

"(e) A woman upon whom a partial-birth abortion is performed may not be prosecuted under this section, for a conspiracy to violate this section, * * *.

The Act also includes a provision authorizing civil actions [for damages following a "Partial Birth Abortion"] that is not of relevance here.[ ]

* * *

II

[The Holding in *Casey*]

The principles set forth in the joint opinion in *Casey*,[ ] did not find support from all those who join the instant opinion.[ ] Whatever one's views concerning the *Casey* joint opinion, it is evident a premise central to its conclusion—that the government has a legitimate and substantial interest in preserving and promoting fetal life—would be repudiated were the Court now to affirm the judgments of the Courts of Appeals. *Casey* involved a challenge to *Roe* v. *Wade*[ ]. [One of the three essential principles of *Roe* that was upheld in Casey was] the principle that the State has legitimate interests from the outset of the pregnancy in protecting the health of the woman and the life of the fetus that may become a child. * * * [W]e must determine whether the Act furthers the legitimate interest of the Government in protecting the life of the fetus that may become a child.

To implement its holding, *Casey* rejected both *Roe*'s rigid trimester framework and the interpretation of *Roe* that considered all previability regulations of abortion unwarranted. * * *

We assume the following principles for the purposes of this opinion. Before viability, a State "may not prohibit any woman from making the ultimate decision to terminate her pregnancy."[ ] It also may not impose upon this right an undue burden, which exists if a regulation's "purpose or effect is to place a substantial obstacle in the path of a woman seeking an abortion before the fetus attains viability."[ ] On the other hand, "regulations which do no more than create a structural mechanism by which the State, or the parent or guardian of a minor, may express profound respect for the life of the unborn are permitted, if they are not a substantial obstacle to the woman's exercise of the right to choose."[ ] *Casey*, in short, struck a balance. The balance was central to its holding. We now apply its standard to the cases at bar.

III

We begin with a determination of the Act's operation and effect. A straightforward reading of the Act's text demonstrates its purpose and the scope of its provisions: It regulates and proscribes, with exceptions or qualifications to be discussed, performing the intact D & E procedure.

Respondents agree the Act encompasses intact D & E, but they contend its additional reach is both unclear and excessive. Respondents assert that, at the least, the Act is void for vagueness because its scope is indefinite. In the alternative, respondents argue the Act's text proscribes all D & Es. Because D & E is the most common second-trimester abortion method, respondents suggest the Act imposes an undue burden. In this litigation the Attorney General does not dispute that the Act would impose an undue burden if it covered standard D & E.

We conclude that the Act is not void for vagueness, does not impose an undue burden from any overbreadth, and is not invalid on its face.

A

[Interpreting the Statute]

The Act punishes "knowingly performing" a "partial-birth abortion."[ ] It defines the unlawful abortion in explicit terms.[ ]

First, the person performing the abortion must "vaginally deliver a living fetus."[ ] The Act does not restrict an abortion procedure involving the delivery of an expired fetus. The Act, furthermore, is inapplicable to abortions that do not involve vaginal delivery (for instance, hysterotomy or hysterectomy). The Act does apply both previability and postviability because, by common understanding and scientific terminology, a fetus is a living organism while within the womb, whether or not it is viable outside the womb. * * *

Second, the Act's definition of partial-birth abortion requires the fetus to be delivered "until, in the case of a head-first presentation, the entire fetal head is outside the body of the mother, or, in the case of breech presentation, any part of the fetal trunk past the navel is outside the body of the mother." * * *

Third, to fall within the Act, a doctor must perform an "overt act, other than completion of delivery, that kills the partially delivered living fetus."[ ] For purposes of criminal liability, the overt act causing the fetus' death must be separate from delivery. And the overt act must occur after the delivery to an anatomical landmark. This is because the Act proscribes killing "the partially delivered" fetus, which, when read in context, refers to a fetus that has been delivered to an anatomical landmark.[ ]

Fourth, the Act contains scienter requirements concerning all the actions involved in the prohibited abortion. To begin with, the physician must have "deliberately and intentionally" delivered the fetus to one of the Act's anatomical landmarks. * * * In addition, the fetus must have been delivered "for the purpose of performing an overt act that the [doctor] knows will kill [it]." * * *

B

[Vagueness]

Respondents contend the language described above is indeterminate, and they thus argue the Act is unconstitutionally vague on its face. "As generally stated, the void-for-vagueness doctrine requires that a penal statute define the criminal offense with sufficient definiteness that ordinary people can understand what conduct is prohibited and in a manner that does not encourage arbitrary and discriminatory enforcement."[ ] The Act satisfies both requirements.

* * * Unlike the statutory language in *Stenberg* that prohibited the delivery of a " 'substantial portion' " of the fetus—where a doctor might question how much of the fetus is a substantial portion—the Act defines the line between potentially criminal conduct on the one hand and lawful abortion on the other.[ ]

* * *

C

[Undue Burden]

We next determine whether the Act imposes an undue burden, as a facial matter, because its restrictions on second-trimester abortions are too broad. A review of the statutory text discloses the limits of its reach. The Act prohibits intact D & E; and, notwithstanding respondents' arguments, it does not prohibit the D & E procedure in which the fetus is removed in parts.

* * *

A comparison of the Act with the Nebraska statute struck down in *Stenberg* confirms this point. The statute in *Stenberg* prohibited " 'deliberately and intentionally delivering into the vagina a living unborn child, or a substantial portion thereof, for the purpose of performing a procedure that the person performing such procedure knows will kill the unborn child and does kill the unborn child.' "[ ]. The Court concluded that this statute encompassed D & E because "D & E will often involve a physician pulling a 'substantial portion' of a still living fetus, say, an arm or leg, into the vagina prior to the death of the fetus." * * *

Congress, it is apparent, responded to these concerns because the Act departs in material ways from the statute in *Stenberg*. It adopts the phrase "delivers a living fetus,"[ ] instead of " 'delivering . . . a living unborn child, or a substantial portion thereof,' "[ ]. The Act's language, unlike the statute in *Stenberg*, expresses the usual meaning of "deliver" when used in connection with "fetus," namely, extraction of an entire fetus rather than removal of fetal pieces. * * *

The identification of specific anatomical landmarks to which the fetus must be partially delivered also differentiates the Act from the statute at issue in *Stenberg*. * * *

By adding an overt-act requirement Congress sought further to meet the Court's objections to the state statute considered in *Stenberg*. * * * The fatal overt act must occur after delivery to an anatomical landmark, and it must be something "other than [the] completion of delivery."[ ] This distinction matters because, unlike intact D & E, standard D & E does not involve a delivery followed by a fatal act.

The canon of constitutional avoidance, finally, extinguishes any lingering doubt as to whether the Act covers the prototypical D & E procedure. " 'The elementary rule is that every reasonable construction must be resorted to, in order to save a statute from unconstitutionality.' "[ ] It is true this longstanding maxim of statutory interpretation has, in the past, fallen by the wayside when the Court confronted a statute regulating abortion. * * * *Casey* put this novel statutory approach to rest. * * *

* * *

IV

[Substantial Obstacle]

Under the principles accepted as controlling here, the Act, as we have interpreted it, would be unconstitutional "if its purpose or effect is to place a substantial obstacle in the path of a woman seeking an abortion before the fetus attains viability." *Casey*,[ ] The abortions affected by the Act's regulations take place both previability and postviability; so the quoted language and the undue burden analysis it relies upon are applicable. The question is whether the Act, measured by its text in this facial attack, imposes a substantial obstacle to late-term, but previability, abortions. The Act does not on its face impose a substantial obstacle, and we reject this further facial challenge to its validity.

A

[Congressional Purpose]

The Act's purposes are set forth in recitals preceding its operative provisions. A description of the prohibited abortion procedure demonstrates the rationale for the congressional enactment. The Act proscribes a method of abortion in which a fetus is killed just inches before completion of the birth process. Congress stated as follows: "Implicitly approving such a brutal and inhumane procedure by choosing not to prohibit it will further coarsen society to the humanity of not only newborns, but all vulnerable and innocent human life, making it increasingly difficult to protect such life."[ ] The Act expresses respect for the dignity of human life. Congress was concerned, furthermore, with the effects on the medical community and on its reputation caused by the practice of partial-birth abortion. * * *

There can be no doubt the government "has an interest in protecting the integrity and ethics of the medical profession." *Washington* v. *Glucksberg*,[ ] [reprinted in Chapter 15, below]. Under our precedents, it is clear the State has a significant role to play in regulating the medical profession.

Casey reaffirmed these governmental objectives. The government may use its voice and its regulatory authority to show its profound respect for the life within the woman. * * * The three premises of *Casey* must coexist.[ ] The third premise, that the State, from the inception of the pregnancy, maintains its own regulatory interest in protecting the life of the fetus that may become a child, cannot be set at naught by interpreting *Casey*'s requirement of a health exception so it becomes tantamount to allowing a doctor to choose the abortion method he or she might prefer. Where it has a rational basis to act, and it does not impose an undue burden, the State may use its regulatory power to bar certain procedures and substitute others, all in furtherance of its legitimate interests in regulating the medical profession in order to promote respect for life, including life of the unborn.

* * * The Court has in the past confirmed the validity of drawing boundaries to prevent certain practices that extinguish life and are close to actions that are condemned. *Glucksberg* found reasonable the State's "fear that permitting assisted suicide will start it down the path to voluntary and perhaps even involuntary euthanasia."[ ]

Respect for human life finds an ultimate expression in the bond of love the mother has for her child. The Act recognizes this reality as well. Whether to have an abortion requires a difficult and painful moral decision.[ ] While we find no reliable data to measure the phenomenon, it seems unexceptionable to conclude some women come to regret their choice to abort the infant life they once created and sustained.[ ] Severe depression and loss of esteem can follow.[ ]

In a decision so fraught with emotional consequence some doctors may prefer not to disclose precise details of the means that will be used, confining themselves to the required statement of risks the procedure entails. From one standpoint this ought not to be surprising. Any number of patients facing imminent surgical procedures would prefer not to hear all details, lest the usual anxiety preceding invasive medical procedures become the more intense. This is likely the case with the abortion procedures here in issue.[ ]

It is, however, precisely this lack of information concerning the way in which the fetus will be killed that is of legitimate concern to the State.[ ] The State has an interest in ensuring so grave a choice is well informed. It is self-evident that a mother who comes to regret her choice to abort must struggle with grief more anguished and sorrow more profound when she learns, only after the event, what she once did not know: that she allowed a doctor to pierce the skull and vacuum the fast-developing brain of her unborn child, a child assuming the human form.

* * *

It is objected that the standard D & E is in some respects as brutal, if not more, than the intact D & E, so that the legislation accomplishes little. * * * It was reasonable for Congress to think that partial-birth abortion, more than standard D & E, "undermines the public's perception of the appropriate role of a physician during the delivery process, and perverts a process during which life is brought into the world." * * * In sum, we reject the contention that the congressional purpose of the Act was "to place a substantial obstacle in the path of a woman seeking an abortion."[ ]

B

[Protecting the Health of the Mother]

The Act's furtherance of legitimate government interests bears upon, but does not resolve, the next question: whether the Act has the effect of imposing an unconstitutional burden on the abortion right because it does not allow use of the barred procedure where " 'necessary, in appropriate medical judgment, for [the] preservation of the ... health of the mother.' "[ ] The prohibition in the Act would be unconstitutional, under precedents we here assume to be controlling, if it "subjected [women] to significant health risks." * * * Here, by contrast, whether the Act creates significant health risks for women has been a contested factual question. The evidence presented in the trial courts and before Congress demonstrates both sides have medical support for their position.

* * *

The question becomes whether the Act can stand when this medical uncertainty persists. The Court's precedents instruct that the Act can survive this facial attack. The Court has given state and federal legislatures wide discretion to pass legislation in areas where there is medical and scientific uncertainty.

* * *

In reaching the conclusion the Act does not require a health exception we reject certain arguments made by the parties on both sides of these cases. On the one hand, the Attorney General urges us to uphold the Act on the basis of the congressional findings alone.[ ] Although we review congressional factfinding under a deferential standard, we do not in the circumstances here place dispositive weight on Congress' findings. The Court retains an independent constitutional duty to review factual findings where constitutional rights are at stake.[ ]

As respondents have noted, and the District Courts recognized, some recitations in the Act are factually incorrect. * * * Uncritical deference to Congress' factual findings in these cases is inappropriate.

On the other hand, relying on the Court's opinion in *Stenberg*, respondents contend that an abortion regulation must contain a health exception "if 'substantial medical authority supports the proposition that banning a particular procedure could endanger women's health.' " * * * *Stenberg* has been interpreted to leave no margin of error for legislatures to act in the face of medical uncertainty.[ ]

A zero tolerance policy would strike down legitimate abortion regulations, like the present one, if some part of the medical community were disinclined to follow the proscription. This is too exacting a standard to impose on the legislative power, exercised in this instance under the Commerce Clause, to regulate the medical profession. Considerations of marginal safety, including the balance of risks, are within the legislative competence when the regulation is rational and in pursuit of legitimate ends. * * * The Act is not invalid on its face where there is uncertainty over whether the barred procedure is ever necessary to preserve a woman's health, given the availability of other abortion procedures that are considered to be safe alternatives.

V

[Propriety of a Facial Attack on the Statute]

The considerations we have discussed support our further determination that these facial attacks should not have been entertained in the first instance. In these circumstances the proper means to consider exceptions is by as-applied challenge. * * * This is the proper manner to protect the health of the woman if it can be shown that in discrete and well-defined instances a particular condition has or is likely to occur in which the procedure prohibited by the Act must be used. In an as-applied challenge the nature of the medical risk can be better quantified and balanced than in a facial attack.

* * *

As the previous sections of this opinion explain, respondents have not demonstrated that the Act would be unconstitutional in a large fraction of relevant cases. * * *

The Act is open to a proper as-applied challenge in a discrete case. * * * No as-applied challenge need be brought if the prohibition in the Act threatens a woman's life because the Act already contains a life exception.[ ]

* * *

JUSTICE THOMAS, with whom JUSTICE SCALIA joins, concurring.

I join the Court's opinion because it accurately applies current jurisprudence, including Casey,[ ]. I write separately to reiterate my view that the Court's abortion jurisprudence, including Casey and Roe[ ] has no basis in the Constitution.[ ] I also note that whether the Act constitutes a permissible exercise of Congress' power under the Commerce Clause is not before the Court. The parties did not raise or brief that issue; it is outside the question presented; and the lower courts did not address it.[ ]

JUSTICE GINSBURG, with whom JUSTICE STEVENS, JUSTICE SOUTER, and JUSTICE BREYER join, dissenting.

* * *

In reaffirming Roe, the Casey Court described the centrality of "the decision whether to bear ... a child,"[ ] to a woman's "dignity and autonomy," her "personhood" and "destiny," her "conception of ... her place in society."[ ] Of signal importance here, the Casey Court stated with unmistakable clarity that state regulation of access to abortion procedures, even after viability, must protect "the health of the woman."[ ]

Seven years ago, in Stenberg,[ ] the Court invalidated a Nebraska statute criminalizing the performance of a medical procedure that, in the political arena, has been dubbed "partial-birth abortion." With fidelity to the Roe-Casey line of precedent, the Court held the Nebraska statute unconstitutional in part because it lacked the requisite protection for the preservation of a woman's health.[ ]

Today's decision is alarming. It refuses to take Casey and Stenberg seriously. It tolerates, indeed applauds, federal intervention to ban nationwide a procedure found necessary and proper in certain cases by the American College of Obstetricians and Gynecologists (ACOG). It blurs the line, firmly drawn in Casey, between previability and postviability abortions. And, for the first time since Roe, the Court blesses a prohibition with no exception safeguarding a woman's health.

I dissent from the Court's disposition. Retreating from prior rulings that abortion restrictions cannot be imposed absent an exception safeguarding a woman's health, the Court upholds an Act that surely would not survive under the close scrutiny that previously attended state-decreed limitations on a woman's reproductive choices.

I

A

As *Casey* comprehended, at stake in cases challenging abortion restrictions is a woman's "control over her [own] destiny." * * * Women, it is now acknowledged, have the talent, capacity, and right "to participate equally in the economic and social life of the Nation."[ ] Their ability to realize their full potential, the Court recognized, is intimately connected to "their ability to control their reproductive lives."[ ] Thus, legal challenges to undue restrictions on abortion procedures do not seek to vindicate some generalized notion of privacy; rather, they center on a woman's autonomy to determine her life's course, and thus to enjoy equal citizenship stature.[ ]

In keeping with this comprehension of the right to reproductive choice, the Court has consistently required that laws regulating abortion, at any stage of pregnancy and in all cases, safeguard a woman's health.[ ]

We have thus ruled that a State must avoid subjecting women to health risks not only where the pregnancy itself creates danger, but also where state regulation forces women to resort to less safe methods of abortion. * * *

In *Stenberg*, we expressly held that a statute banning intact D & E was unconstitutional in part because it lacked a health exception.[ ] We noted that there existed a "division of medical opinion" about the relative safety of intact D & E,[ ], but we made clear that as long as "substantial medical authority supports the proposition that banning a particular abortion procedure could endanger women's health," a health exception is required.[ ] We explained:

> "The word 'necessary' in *Casey*'s phrase 'necessary, in appropriate medical judgment, for the preservation of the life or health of the [pregnant woman],' cannot refer to an absolute necessity or to absolute proof. Medical treatments and procedures are often considered appropriate (or inappropriate) in light of estimated comparative health risks (and health benefits) in particular cases. Neither can that phrase require unanimity of medical opinion. Doctors often differ in their estimation of comparative health risks and appropriate treatment. And *Casey*'s words 'appropriate medical judgment' must embody the judicial need to tolerate responsible differences of medical opinion...."[ ]

Thus, we reasoned, division in medical opinion "at most means uncertainty, a factor that signals the presence of risk, not its absence."[ ] "[A] statute that altogether forbids [intact D & E] ... consequently must contain a health exception."[ ]

B

In 2003, a few years after our ruling in *Stenberg*, Congress passed the Partial–Birth Abortion Ban Act—without an exception for women's health.[ ] The congressional findings on which the Partial–Birth Abortion Ban Act rests do not withstand inspection, as the lower courts have determined and this Court is obliged to concede.

* * *

C

* * *

During the District Court trials, "numerous" "extraordinarily accomplished" and "very experienced" medical experts explained that, in certain circumstances and for certain women, intact D & E is safer than alternative procedures and necessary to protect women's health.[ ]

According to the expert testimony plaintiffs introduced, the safety advantages of intact D & E are marked for women with certain medical conditions, * * *. Further, plaintiffs' experts testified that intact D & E is significantly safer for women with certain pregnancy-related conditions, such as placenta previa and accreta, and for women carrying fetuses with certain abnormalities, such as severe hydrocephalus.[ ]

Intact D & E, plaintiffs' experts explained, provides safety benefits over D & E by dismemberment for several reasons [which Justice Ginsburg lists and describes]. * * *

* * *

Nevertheless, despite the District Courts' appraisal of the weight of the evidence, and in undisguised conflict with *Stenberg*, the Court asserts that the Partial–Birth Abortion Ban Act can survive "when … medical uncertainty persists."[ ] This assertion is bewildering.

* * *

II

A

The Court offers flimsy and transparent justifications for upholding a nationwide ban on intact D & E *sans* any exception to safeguard a women's health. Today's ruling, the Court declares, advances "a premise central to [*Casey*'s] conclusion"—i.e., the Government's "legitimate and substantial interest in preserving and promoting fetal life."[ ] But the Act scarcely furthers that interest: The law saves not a single fetus from destruction, for it targets only a *method* of performing abortion.[ ] And surely the statute was not designed to protect the lives or health of pregnant women.[ ]

* * *

Ultimately, the Court admits that "moral concerns" are at work, concerns that could yield prohibitions on any abortion.[ ] Notably, the concerns expressed are untethered to any ground genuinely serving the Government's interest in preserving life. By allowing such concerns to carry the day and case, overriding fundamental rights, the Court dishonors our precedent.[ ]

Revealing in this regard, the Court invokes an antiabortion shibboleth for which it concededly has no reliable evidence: Women who have abortions come to regret their choices, and consequently suffer from "severe depression and loss of esteem."[ ] Because of women's fragile emotional state and because of the "bond of love the mother has for her child," the Court worries, doctors may withhold information about the nature of the intact D & E procedure.[ ] The solution the Court approves, then, is *not* to require doctors to inform women, accurately and adequately, of the different procedures and their attendant risks.[ ] Instead, the Court deprives women of the right to make an autonomous choice, even at the expense of their safety.

This way of thinking reflects ancient notions about women's place in the family and under the Constitution—ideas that have long since been discredited. * * *

Though today's majority may regard women's feelings on the matter as "self-evident,"[ ] this Court has repeatedly confirmed that "the destiny of the woman must be shaped . . . on her own conception of her spiritual imperatives and her place in society." *Casey*[ ].

B

* * *

The Court's hostility to the right *Roe* and *Casey* secured is not concealed. Throughout, the opinion refers to obstetrician-gynecologists and surgeons who perform abortions not by the titles of their medical specialties, but by the pejorative label "abortion doctor."[ ] A fetus is described as an "unborn child," and as a "baby,"[ ]; second-trimester, previability abortions are referred to as "late-term,"[ ]; and the reasoned medical judgments of highly trained doctors are dismissed as "preferences" motivated by "mere convenience,"[ ]. Instead of the heightened scrutiny we have previously applied, the Court determines that a "rational" ground is enough to uphold the Act,[ ]. And, most troubling, *Casey*'s principles, confirming the continuing vitality of "the essential holding of *Roe*," are merely "assumed" for the moment,[ ], rather than "retained" or "reaffirmed," *Casey*[ ].

III

A

The Court further confuses our jurisprudence when it declares that "facial attacks" are not permissible in "these circumstances," i.e., where medical uncertainty exists. * * *

Without attempting to distinguish *Stenberg* and earlier decisions, the majority asserts that the Act survives review because respondents have not shown that the ban on intact D & E would be unconstitutional "in a large fraction of relevant cases."[ ] But *Casey* makes clear that, in determining whether any restriction poses an undue burden on a "large fraction" of women, the relevant class is *not* "all women," nor "all pregnant women," nor even all women "seeking abortions."[ ]. Rather, a provision restricting access to abortion, "must be judged by reference to those [women] for whom it is an actual rather than an irrelevant restriction,"[ ] Thus the absence of a health exception burdens *all* women for whom it is relevant—women who, in the judgment of their doctors, require an intact D & E because other procedures would place their health at risk.[ ] It makes no sense to conclude that this facial challenge fails because respondents have not shown that a health exception is necessary for a large fraction of second-trimester abortions, including those for which a health exception is unnecessary: The very purpose of a health *exception* is to protect women in *exceptional* cases.

B

If there is anything at all redemptive to be said of today's opinion, it is that the Court is not willing to foreclose entirely a constitutional challenge to the Act. "The Act is open," the Court states, "to a proper as-applied challenge in a discrete case."[ ] But the Court offers no clue on what a "proper" lawsuit might look like.[ ] Nor does the Court explain why the injunctions ordered by the District Courts should not remain in place, trimmed only to exclude instances in which another procedure would safeguard a woman's health at least equally well. Surely the Court cannot mean that no suit may be brought until a woman's health is immediately jeopardized by the ban on intact D & E. A woman "suffering from medical complications,"[ ] needs access to the medical procedure at once and cannot wait for the judicial process to unfold.[ ]

* * *

IV

As the Court wrote in *Casey*, "overruling *Roe*'s central holding would not only reach an unjustifiable result under principles of *stare decisis*, but would seriously weaken the Court's capacity to exercise the judicial power and to function as the Supreme Court of a Nation dedicated to the rule of law." * * *

Though today's opinion does not go so far as to discard *Roe* or *Casey*, the Court, differently composed than it was when we last considered a restrictive abortion regulation, is hardly faithful to our earlier invocations of "the rule of law" and the "principles of *stare decisis*." Congress imposed a ban despite our clear prior holdings that the State cannot proscribe an abortion procedure when its use is necessary to protect a woman's health.[ ] Although Congress' findings could not withstand the crucible of trial, the Court defers to the legislative override of our Constitution-based rulings.[ ] A decision so at odds with our jurisprudence should not have staying power.

In sum, the notion that the Partial–Birth Abortion Ban Act furthers any legitimate governmental interest is, quite simply, irrational. The Court's defense of the statute provides no saving explanation. In candor, the Act, and the Court's defense of it, cannot be understood as anything other than an effort to chip away at a right declared again and again by this Court—and with increasing comprehension of its centrality to women's lives.[ ] When "a statute burdens constitutional rights and all that can be said on its behalf is that it is the vehicle that legislators have chosen for expressing their hostility to those rights, the burden is undue."[ ]

For the reasons stated, I dissent from the Court's disposition and would affirm the judgments before us for review.

Notes and Questions

1.   Does *Casey* really affirm *Roe*? Did the holding of *Roe* survive *Casey*? Does *Gonzales v. Carhart* really affirm and apply *Casey*? Does the holding of *Casey* survive *Gonzales v. Carhart*? How would you articulate the current Constitutional standard with regard to what kinds of legislative restrictions on abortion are permissible?

2.   How, exactly, is a court to apply the Supreme Court's "undue burden" test? Does *Gonzales v. Carhart* provide any insight into what constitutes an

"undue burden" or a "substantial obstacle" in the path of a woman seeking an abortion? In finding whether a state law "has the purpose or effect of placing a substantial obstacle in the path of a woman seeking an abortion of a nonviable fetus," is the Court really proposing a two-part (purpose and effect) analysis?

How is a court expected to divine the purpose of such an act? From the terms of the law? From formal legislative statements? Where did the Court look to determine the purpose of the Partial Birth Abortion Ban Act in *Gonzales v. Carhart*? Are you convinced by the Court's analysis? Is Congress (or any state legislature) likely to promulgate an enacting clause declaring that their purpose is to unduly burden those who seek to abort nonviable fetuses? Of course, we know that a state law has the effect of establishing an "undue burden" when it puts a "substantial obstacle" in the path of a woman seeking to abort a nonviable fetus, but how much does that advance the inquiry? Is an obstacle substantial because it imposes a serious limitation on any identifiable woman, or because it affects a large number of women, or because it affects a large percentage of the cases in which women would seek abortions? How does Does *Gonzales v. Carhart* answer these questions?

Unlike in *Roe v. Wade*, in which the Court dealt with virtually absolute bans on abortion, in *Casey* the Court faced several narrow regulations on abortion that had been promulgated by the Pennsylvania legislature, and it thus was required to apply its test to a series of articulated restrictions. These included the requirement that particular state-mandated information be provided to the pregnant woman before the abortion is performed, the requirement that the information be provided by a physician, a 24 hour waiting period between the receipt of the information and the pregnant woman's formal consent to the abortion (and thus a "two-step" procedure), the requirement that a minor get parental consent (with a judicial bypass procedure to avoid that requirement in some cases), and various state reporting requirements, none of which were found to constitute "undue burdens," at least in Pennsylvania on the evidence presented to the Court in 1992. On the other hand, the Court did find that a spousal notification requirement constituted an undue burden (as did any reporting requirement related to that notification requirement), and the Court struck that down.

3. Between 1973 and 1992 many state legislatures had attempted to impose the most restrictive abortion laws short of a complete ban. Since 1992, few have gone beyond what is clearly permitted in *Casey*, although legislatures have tested the limits of *Casey* by promulgating partial birth abortion bans and new forms of funding restrictions. Why have the state legislatures become comparatively restrained? Will they remain so after *Carhart*?

Since *Casey* pro-choice advocates have also gone on the offensive in some state legislatures. Instead of merely opposing new restrictions on abortion, in some states advocates are supporting legislation that would make some procedures more easily available. For example, some state legislatures have passed legislation that requires hospital emergency rooms to have emergency contraception available for women who have been sexually assaulted.

In those few cases where state legislatures went far beyond what Pennsylvania did in *Casey*, the courts have had no trouble striking down the statutes by applying the "undue burden" test. See, e.g. Sojourner T v. Edwards, 974 F.2d 27 (5th Cir.1992), cert. denied, 507 U.S. 972, 113 S.Ct. 1414, 122 L.Ed.2d 785 (1993)(statute would have outlawed all abortions except to remove a dead fetus, to save the life of the pregnant woman, or, if performed in the first trimester only, if the pregnancy was a result of rape or incest); Women's Med. Prof. Corp. v.

Voinovich, 911 F.Supp. 1051 (S.D.Ohio 1995) (preliminary injunction against statute that would, inter alia, ban all postviability abortions, even if the mother's life were at stake). Would the results in these cases be the same after *Carhart*?

4.   What were the relevant differences between the partial birth abortion ban that was rejected in *Stenberg* and the one that was accepted in *Gonzales v. Carhart*? Was it the legislative findings that saved the federal statute? The more precise definition of the banned procedure? The scienter requirement? The fact that D & E abortions are still permitted? Some combination of these? Was the change in the Court's approach to partial birth abortion legislation the result of the form of the challenge, the language of the statute, or, perhaps, the replacement of Justice O'Connor by Justice Alito?

5.   The Court did not formally address the question of whether Congress had authority to promulgate the Partial Birth Abortion Ban of 2003 because that issue was neither raised nor argued. Congress found its authority in its power to regulate commerce among the states. Is that an adequate basis? Is there any other source of authority that could justify this Act of Congress? As a matter of policy, is it more appropriate for abortion restrictions to be enacted on a state by state basis (as had generally been the case before Congress passed this ban), or by Congress? Why?

6.   Although *Gonzales v. Carhart* rejected a facial attack on this federal statute, it left open the possibility that an "as applied" attack on the statute might be successful under the right circumstances. What are those circumstances? If you were to mount a judicial challenge to the Partial Birth Abortion Act of 2003 after *Gonzales v. Carhart,* who would be your ideal plaintiff? If you were defending such a challenge, whom would you like to see as the opposing party?

As a matter of Constitutional jurisprudence, should an issue like this be resolved in a facial challenge, or an "as applied" challenge, to the statute? Justice Kennedy pointed out that the Court had applied different standards with regard to facial Constitutional challenges to restrictions on abortions over the past few decades, and he indicated that there was no need for the Court to finally resolve the issue of when such a facial challenge would be appropriate. Justice Ginsburg was concerned about the difficulty that would be faced by anyone attempting the "as applied" challenge left open by the majority:

> The Court's allowance only of an "as-applied challenge in a discrete case,"[ ] jeopardizes women's health and places doctors in an untenable position. Even if courts were able to carve-out exceptions through piecemeal litigation for "discrete and well-defined instances,"[ ] women whose circumstances have not been anticipated by prior litigation could well be left unprotected. In treating those women, physicians would risk criminal prosecution, conviction, and imprisonment if they exercise their best judgment as to the safest medical procedure for their patients. The Court is thus gravely mistaken to conclude that narrow as-applied challenges are "the proper manner to protect the health of the woman."[ ]

7.   *Consent and Notification Requirements.* There remain, of course, other kinds of regulation with uncertain Constitutional status, too. It is now clear that it does not violate the United States Constitution for minors to be required to obtain the consent of a parent to an abortion, as long as the state permits a court (or, perhaps, an appropriate administrative agency) to dispense with that requirement under some circumstances. The Supreme Court has never determined if a two-parent consent requirement (with a proper judicial bypass provision) would pass Constitutional muster, however. See Barnes v. Mississippi, 992 F.2d 1335

(5th Cir.1993), cert. denied, 510 U.S. 976, 114 S.Ct. 468, 126 L.Ed.2d 419 (1993)(upholding two-parent consent requirement because involvement of both parents will increase "reflection and deliberation" on the process, and if one parent denies consent the other will be able to go to court in support of the child) and S.H. v. D.H., 796 N.E.2d 1243 (Ind.App.2003)(family court judge cannot require consent of both parents before an abortion is performed, even if the divorced parents have joint custody). The Supreme Court has suggested that a state requirement of mere parental notification (rather than consent) requires a judicial bypass, and lower courts have generally assumed that it does. Ohio v. Akron Ctr. for Reproductive Health, 497 U.S. 502, 110 S.Ct. 2972, 111 L.Ed.2d 405 (1990). One state supreme court has found that a parental notification requirement violates the state constitution's equal protection clause when it is imposed only on those who seek abortions, not on pregnant children making other, equally medically risky, reproductive decisions. Planned Parenthood of Central New Jersey v. Farmer, 165 N.J. 609, 762 A.2d 620 (2000).

It is not entirely clear what Constitutional standard a court must apply in a "bypass" case. Is the court required to waive consent or notification (1) if it finds that the minor is sufficiently mature that she should be able to make the decision herself, or (2) if it finds that if she seeks consent from (or notifies) her parents she will be subject to abuse, or (3) if it finds that it is in her best interest to have the abortion, or (4) if it finds that it is in her best interest not to be required to notify, or get consent from, her parent, or some combination of all of these? See Lambert v. Wicklund, 520 U.S. 292, 297, 117 S.Ct. 1169, 137 L.Ed.2d 464 (1997) (per curiam).

If the statute does include a substantively Constitutional bypass provision, what kind of procedural conditions may be placed on a bypass case? May the petitioner be required to prove her case by clear and convincing evidence? Is she entitled to counsel? Is she required to have a special guardian appointed for purposes of the litigation? Can the state require an expedited hearing? Can it allow the court to refuse an expedited hearing? Can it require the petition be filed within a very short time after the commencement of the pregnancy? Can it limit appeals by those who unsuccessfully seek judicial bypass?

The debate for and against consent and notification requirements reveals an even deeper debate about the current role of the family in contemporary life. While most agree that a teenager's abortion should be a decision made in consultation with her parents, that belief rests upon several assumptions. First, it assumes that the family dynamics are such that the daughter's disclosure will not trigger domestic violence or other forms of family abuse. Second, it assumes that the daughter lives within a traditional nuclear family, or can readily reach her biological parents. Finally, and most critically, it assumes that parents will act in the daughter's best interest. Some of these assumptions may, sadly, be based upon an idealized view of contemporary family life. While many children are brought up in healthy families, as Justice Kennard of the California Supreme Court has pointed out, "[n]ot every pregnant adolescent has parents out of the comforting and idyllic world of Norman Rockwell." American Academy of Pediatrics v. Lungren, 51 Cal.Rptr.2d 201, 224, 912 P.2d 1148, 1171 (1996) (Kennard, J., dissenting).

Those who support consent and notification statutes offer many stories of girls who had abortions secretly and now regret not discussing it with their parents. Indeed, those stories seem to have influenced Justice Kennedy's opinion in *Gonzales v. Carhart*. Those who oppose these statutes offer stories about girls who committed suicide rather than go through the notification procedures. Is this anecdotal evidence offered by both sides of much value? Could respectable research data on these issues be developed? Why do you think it has not been developed in any reliable way? Does it seem ironic that under a consent or notification statute a court could declare a pregnant minor to be too immature to proceed without parental consultation, with the result that she will become a mother?

Whatever may be the uncertain status of the details surrounding parental consent and notification, *Casey* established that spousal consent and spousal notification requirements are unconstitutional. See Jane L. v. Bangerter, 61 F.3d 1493 (10th Cir.1995) (rejecting notification done by someone other than the pregnant woman); Planned Parenthood of Southern Arizona, Inc. v. Woods, 982 F.Supp. 1369, 1380 (D.Ariz.1997) (rejecting statute that did not require spousal consent but provided for civil liability for physician providing abortion without that consent).

8. *Regulation of Medical Procedures.* As a general matter, until Gonzales v. Carhart, courts had been reluctant to uphold statutory limitations on abortion procedures. Since 2007, it has been clear that such restrictions can be constitutional, at least when they do not impose an undue burden on the woman seeking an abortion. In Gonzales v. Carhart, counsel for the government agreed that outlawing the classic D & E abortion would constitute an "undue burden," and thus would be unconstitutional. Should counsel have made that concession? After all, D & E abortions are very similar to the outlawed partial-birth abortions; some may even consider them more offensive because they require dismembering a fetus before removing it from the uterus. Might a future facial attack on a statute that bars all D & E abortions be successful?

One state supreme court has determined that a requirement that second trimester abortions be performed in a hospital violated the state constitution, which was read to be more protective of abortion rights than the United States Constitution. See Planned Parenthood of Middle Tennessee v. Sundquist, 38 S.W.3d 1 (Tenn.2000). But see Greenville Women's Clinic v. Bryant, 222 F.3d 157 (4th Cir.2000)(upholding rigid South Carolina licensing requirements for facilities where abortions are performed). Courts have had little trouble with a requirement that only physicians, not physicians' assistants or others, perform abortions, because the authority granted with professional licenses is a matter state law. See Armstrong v. Mazurek, 906 F.Supp. 561 (D.Mont.1995). Such licensing requirements are seen as ways of protecting the pregnant woman, not imposing a burden on her decision to have an abortion.

9. *Two-trip Requirements.* When a state imposes a waiting period between the time the pregnant woman is provided the information that is to be the basis of her informed consent to an abortion and the medical procedure itself, it may, de facto, be requiring that the pregnant woman make two trips to the medical facility where the abortion is to be performed. In *Casey* the Court announced that a 24-hour waiting period did not constitute an unconstitutional undue burden. For an interesting and controversial econometric argument that some kinds of waiting periods reduce the chance of suicide, and thus are valuable for women who are subject to them, see Jonathan Klick, Mandatory Waiting Periods for Abortions and Female Mental Health, 16 Health Matrix 183 (2006). The Tennessee Supreme Court determined that imposing what amounts to a three day waiting period violated the state constitution's protected right of privacy. See Planned Parenthood of Middle Tennessee v. Sundquist, 38 S.W.3d 1 (Tenn.2000).

10. *Other Informed Consent Requirements.* In *Casey* the Court upheld a statute that requires that a state-approved packet of material be given to the pregnant woman as a part of the informed consent process, and that the consent process be obtained by the physician, not by anyone else. The only requirement *Casey* appears to put on the distributed material is that it contain information that is true. In early 1996 a couple of epidemiological studies arguably suggested a very weak relationship between having an abortion and the subsequent risk of developing breast cancer and the severity of that cancer. Subsequent reports cast doubt on this relationship. See P.A. Newcomb, B. E. Storer, M. P. Longnecker et al., Pregnancy Termination in Relation to Risk of Breast Cancer, 275 JAMA 283 (1996). May states require that physicians inform potential abortion patients that there is a correlation between abortion and the risk of breast cancer? May states require that patients be provided the information about this correlation even if they do not require that patients be told of the different, but significantly higher, risks of ordinary pregnancy? Could the state require that a woman attend a short course on fetal development as a condition of having an abortion? See a graphic movie dealing with that same subject? Talk to other women who have had abortions? Speak with adoptive couples?

11. Could a state ban abortions for certain purposes? Pennsylvania considered outlawing abortion for gender selection; could they legally do so? Could the state outlaw abortion if it is used as a primary method of birth control? As a method for controlling the genetic makeup of a child? If it could do so legally, how would it do so as a practical matter?

12. Some believe that the ultimate disappearance of abortion practice will be the result of the fact that medical schools and residency programs are discontinuing training in abortion techniques because offering that training is not worth the political cost. Should all Obstetrics and Gynecology training programs include, at the very least, some exposure to the abortion process, or may a medical school decide that it will not provide that training because it finds the practice of abortion morally unacceptable? Should students who find such practice abhorrent be able to opt out of that training? Are there Constitutional implications to the removal of abortion from the medical school curriculum at a state university, or from the list of procedures done at a teaching hospital? See Barbara Gottlieb, Sounding Board, 332 JAMA 532 (1995).

13. Neighboring states often have very different laws regulating abortion, and women from one state may go to another state to take advantage of what they consider a favorable law. May a state prohibit a woman from crossing a state line to obtain an abortion that would be illegal in the first state? In 1996 a New York jury convicted a woman of "interfering with the custody of a minor," a felony, for taking a 13–year-old pregnant girl from Pennsylvania (which requires parental consent) to New York (which does not) to obtain an abortion. See David Stout, Guilty Verdict for Enabling Girl to Have An Abortion, *New York Times*, Oct. 31, 1996, A–8.

14. There may be some basic value issues upon which the pro-choice and pro-life partisans agree. While pro-choice supporters argue that an abortion should be among the choices of a pregnant woman, no one views an abortion as a happy event. Both sides would be pleased if society reached a point where there were no need for abortions. Similarly, while some pro-life supporters believe that every fetus is entitled to be born alive, many recognize that there are some times when the mother's interest does trump that of the fetus—when the mother's life is at stake, for example, and, perhaps, when the pregnancy is a result of rape or incest—and many recognize that the medical condition of the fetus is a relevant

consideration. Very few people oppose early abortions of anencephalic fetuses, for example, or early abortions of other fetuses who are certain to be stillborn or to die within the first few minutes of birth. Both sides may also support expanded state funding for prenatal care and post-natal care, each of which may make abortion a less attractive alternative to pregnant women. Is there a common ground that could give rise to some kind of generally acceptable state policy on abortion, at least in some states? If pro-choice partisans and pro-life partisans were to sit with you and enumerate their common concerns, would there be some basic issues and basic principles upon which they would agree?

15. *The Freedom of Access to Clinic Entrances Act of 1994 and Abortion Protests.* In the 1990s, the focus of the challenge to abortion practices was moving from the courts and the legislatures to medical clinics that provided abortion services. Often those clinics were the subject of protests, prayer vigils, or other demonstrations, and in a few cases violence resulted. Some employees of the clinics feared for their safety, and some were also concerned that patients coming to the clinics were being harassed and intimidated by those outside. Those participating in the demonstrations argued that they were doing nothing more than exercising their first amendment rights, and that they were doing their best to make the exercise of those rights effective by dissuading patients from having abortions. In response to some particularly egregious incidents of violence perpetrated against a few abortion clinics, Congress passed the Freedom of Access to Clinic Entrances Act of 1994 ("FACE"), which provides:

> Whoever (1) by force or threat of force or by physical obstruction, intentionally injures, intimidates or interferes with or attempts to injure, intimidate or interfere with any person because that person is or has been, or in order to intimidate such person or any other person or any class of persons from, obtaining or providing reproductive health services; * * * (3) intentionally damages or destroys the property of a facility, or attempts to do so, because such facility provides reproductive health services * * * shall be guilty of a crime and fined or imprisoned.

18 U.S.C.A. § 248(a). The statute provides longer prison terms and larger fines for repeat offenders and shorter prison terms and smaller fines for offenses "involving exclusively a nonviolent physical intrusion." 18 U.S.C.A. § 248(b). The term "reproductive health services" is expansively defined to include "medical, surgical, counseling or referral services * * * including services relating to * * * the termination of a pregnancy" whether those services are provided "in a hospital, clinic, physician's office, or other facility." 18 U.S.C.A. § 248(e)(5). In addition to its criminal sanctions, the Act provides for civil enforcement by the United States Attorney General and the attorneys general of the states, and for civil damages of $5,000 per violation in lieu of actual damages, at the election of the plaintiff. 18 U.S.C.A. § 248(c)(1)(B).

This Act is not the only weapon provided to those who are concerned about the effects of demonstrations around clinics that perform abortions. Earlier in 1994 the United States Supreme Court declared that RICO could be applied against those who violate laws to blockade the clinics, and that created the possibility of substantial civil damage awards against organizations and individuals that encourage or participate in illegal conduct to limit the access of women to the clinics. National Organization for Women, Inc. v. Scheidler, 510 U.S. 249, 114 S.Ct. 798, 127 L.Ed.2d 99 (1994). Both the Freedom of Access to Clinic Entrances Act and RICO were implicated in early 1999 when an Oregon federal court jury returned a verdict in excess of $107 million against twelve individuals, the American Coalition of Life Activists and the Advocates for Life Ministries, for maintaining a web site that threatened those who performed abortions. See Sam

Howe Verhook, Creators of Anti–Abortion Web Site Told to Pay Millions, New York Times, February 3, 1999.

Trial courts have also issued injunctions limiting abortion protesters where judges thought that was necessary to protect the rights of clinic patients. In Schenck v. Pro–Choice Network, 519 U.S. 357, 117 S.Ct. 855, 137 L.Ed.2d 1 (1997) the Supreme Court upheld an injunction which created a 15–foot protected "bubble zone" around the doorways and driveways of a clinic offering abortion services, and it also upheld a limit on the number of people who could "counsel" a woman entering the clinic. The Court determined, further, that those trying to dissuade a patient from having an abortion could be required to desist when the patient asked them to do so, although the Court found that a moveable bubble zone that followed the patient as she entered the clinic would violate the free speech rights of pro-life protesters. In Hill v. Colorado, 530 U.S. 703, 120 S.Ct. 2480, 147 L.Ed.2d 597 (2000), the Supreme Court upheld a Colorado statute that prohibited any person within 100 feet of a health care facility's entrance door from knowingly coming within 8 feet of another person, without the consent of that person, to pass a "leaflet [or] handbill, to displa[y] a sign to, or [e]ngage in oral protest, education or counseling with that person * * *."

16.   There has been a great deal of writing about abortion law. Some recent and provocative articles include an econometrics approach to abortion, Jonathan Klick, The Current State of Abortion Law and Reproductive Rights: Econometric Analysis of U.S. Abortion Policy: A Critical Review, 31 Fordham Urb. L.J. 751 (2004), and a more thorough analysis of the relationship between the role of women in society and reproductive rights, Reva Siegel, Sex Equality Arguments for Reproductive Rights: Their Critical Basis and Evolving Constitutional Expression, 56 Emory L.J. 815 (2007). For a state-by-state account of the status of state law in the event of the reversal of Roe v. Wade, see Paul Linton, The Legal Status of Abortion in the States if Roe v. Wade is Overruled, 23 Issues L. & Med. 3 (2007). For a broad ranging symposium on this issue, see Symposium—If Roe Were Overruled: Abortion and the Constitution in a Post–Roe World, 51 St. Louis U. L. J. 611 (2007). For a comparative approach, see Timothy Stoltzfus Jost, Rights of Embryos and Foetuses in Private Law, 50 Am. J. Comp. L. 633 (2002).

B. ASSISTED REPRODUCTIVE TECHNOLOGIES (ART)

UNIFORM PARENTAGE ACT

(1973).

* * *

§ 5. [Artificial Insemination.]

(a) If, under the supervision of a licensed physician and with the consent of her husband, a wife is inseminated artificially with semen donated by a man not her husband, the husband is treated in law as if he were the natural father of a child thereby conceived. The husband's consent must be in writing and signed by him and his wife. The physician shall certify their signatures and the date of the insemination, and file the husband's consent with the [State Department of Health], where it shall be kept confidential and in a sealed file. However, the physician's failure to do so does not affect the father and child relationship. All papers and records pertaining to the insemination, whether part of the permanent record of a court or of a file held by the supervising physician or elsewhere, are subject to inspection only upon an order of the court for good cause shown.

(b) The donor of semen provided to a licensed physician for use in artificial insemination of a married woman other than the donor's wife is treated in law as if he were not the natural father of a child thereby conceived.

* * *

§ 23. [Birth Records.]

(a) Upon order of a court of this State or upon request of a court of another state, the [registrar of births] shall prepare [an amended birth registration] [a new certificate of birth] consistent with the findings of the court [and shall substitute the new certificate for the original certificate of birth].

(b) The fact that the father and child relationship was declared after the child's birth shall not be ascertainable from the [amended birth registration] [new certificate] but the actual place and date of birth shall be shown.

(c) The evidence upon which the [amended birth registration] [new certificate] was made and the original birth certificate shall be kept in a sealed and confidential file and be subject to inspection only upon consent of the court and all interested persons, or in exceptional cases only upon an order of the court for good cause shown.

UNIFORM PARENTAGE ACT

(2000, as amended in 2002).

* * *

§ 102. DEFINITIONS.

(4) "Assisted reproduction" means a method of causing pregnancy other than sexual intercourse. The term includes:

(A) intrauterine insemination;

(B) donation of eggs;

(C) donation of embryos;

(D) in-vitro fertilization and transfer of embryos; and

(E) intracytoplasmic sperm injection.

* * *

(8) "Donor" means an individual who produces eggs or sperm used for assisted reproduction, whether or not for consideration. The term does not include:

(A) a husband who provides sperm, or a wife who provides eggs, to be used for assisted reproduction by the wife;

(B) a woman who gives birth to a child by means of assisted reproduction [, except as otherwise provided in [Article] 8]; or

(C) a parent under Article 7 [or an intended parent under Article 8].

* * *

§ 201. ESTABLISHMENT OF PARENT–CHILD RELATIONSHIP.

(a) The mother-child relationship is established between a woman and a child by:

(1) the woman's having given birth to the child [, except as otherwise provided in [Article] 8, concerning gestational surrogacy];

(2) an adjudication of the woman's maternity; [or]

(3) adoption of the child by the woman * * *

(b) The father-child relationship is established between a man and a child by:

(1) an unrebutted presumption of the man's paternity of the child * * *;

(2) an effective acknowledgment of paternity by the man * * *;

(3) an adjudication of the man's paternity;

(4) adoption of the child by the man; [or]

(5) the man's having consented to assisted reproduction by his wife under [this Act] which resulted in the birth of the child * * *.

ARTICLE 7—CHILD OF ASSISTED REPRODUCTION

§ 701. SCOPE OF ARTICLE.

This [article] does not apply to the birth of a child conceived by means of sexual intercourse[, or as the result of a gestational agreement as provided in [Article] 8]. [For a discussion of section 8, see below]

§ 702. PARENTAL STATUS OF DONOR.

A donor is not a parent of a child conceived by means of assisted reproduction.

§ 703. PATERNITY OF CHILD OF ASSISTED REPRODUCTION.

A man who provides sperm for, or consents to, assisted reproduction by his wife as provided in Section 704, is a parent of a resulting child.

§ 704. CONSENT TO ASSISTED REPRODUCTION.

(a) Consent by a woman, and a man who intends to be a parent of a child born to the woman by assisted reproduction must be in a record signed by the woman and the man. This requirement does not apply to a donor.

(b) Failure by a man to sign a consent required by subsection (a), before or after birth of the child, does not preclude a finding of paternity if the woman and the man, during the first two years of the child's life, resided together in the same household with the child and openly held out the child as their own.

* * *

§ 706. EFFECT OF DISSOLUTION OF MARRIAGE OR WITHDRAWAL OF CONSENT.

(a) If a marriage is dissolved before placement of eggs, sperm, or embryos, the former spouse is not a parent of the resulting child unless the former spouse consented in a record that if assisted reproduction were to occur after a divorce, the former spouse would be a parent of the child.

(b) The consent of a former spouse to assisted reproduction may be withdrawn by that individual in a record at any time before placement of eggs, sperm, or embryos. An individual who withdraws consent under this section is not a parent of the resulting child.

§ 707. PARENTAL STATUS OF DECEASED SPOUSE.

If an individual who consented in a record to be a parent by assisted reproduction dies before placement of eggs, sperm, or embryos, the deceased individual is not a parent of the resulting child unless the deceased [individual] consented in a record that if assisted reproduction were to occur after death, the deceased individual would be a parent of the child.

IN THE INTEREST OF K.M.H.

Supreme Court of Kansas, 2007.
285 Kan. 53, 169 P.3d 1025.

BEIER, J.: This appeal from a consolidated child in need of care (CINC) case and a paternity action arises out of an artificial insemination leading to the birth of twins K.M.H. and K.C.H. We are called upon to decide the existence and extent of the parental rights of the known sperm donor, who alleges he had an agreement with the children's mother to act as the twins' father.

The twins' mother filed a CINC petition to establish that the donor had no parental rights under Kansas law. The donor sued for determination of his paternity. The district court sustained the mother's motion to dismiss, ruling that [the Kansas AI statute] was controlling and constitutional. That statute provides:

"The donor of semen provided to a licensed physician for use in artificial insemination of a woman other than the donor's wife is treated in law as if he were not the birth father of a child thereby conceived, unless agreed to in writing by the donor and the woman." K.S.A. 38–1114(f).

Factual and Procedural Background

* * * The mother, S.H., is an unmarried female lawyer who wanted to become a parent through artificial insemination from a known donor. She was a friend of the donor, D.H., an unmarried male nonlawyer, who agreed to provide sperm for the insemination. Both S.H. and D.H. are Kansas residents, and their oral arrangements for the donation occurred in Kansas, but S.H. underwent two inseminations with D.H.'s sperm in Missouri. [After the second, she became pregnant and ultimately gave birth to twins.]

* * *

There was no formal written contract between S.H. and D.H. concerning the donation of sperm, the artificial insemination, or the expectations of the parties with regard to D.H.'s parental rights or lack thereof.

* * *

The district judge ruled that Kansas law governed, that [the Kansas AI statute] was constitutional and applicable * * *. The [trial court judge concluded] as a matter of law that D.H. had no legal rights or responsibilities regarding K.M.H. and K.C.H.

Issues on Appeal

* * * We * * * address six issues: (1) Did the district judge err in ruling that Kansas law would govern? (2) Did the district judge err in holding [the Kansas AI statute] constitutional under the Equal Protection and Due Process Clauses of the Kansas and the federal Constitutions? (3) Did the district judge err in interpreting and applying the "provided to a licensed physician" language of [the Kansas AI statute]? (4) Did the district judge err in determining that the CINC petition did not satisfy the requirement of a writing in [the Kansas AI statute]? (5) Did [the Kansas AI statute] grant D.H. parental rights? and (6) Does equity demand reversal of the district court?

* * *

Choice of Law

* * *

Various factors are relevant to a choice-of-law determination, including the procedural or substantive nature of the question involved, the residence of the parties involved, and the interest of the State in having its law applied. [ ] As long as Kansas has " 'significant contact or [a] significant aggregation of contacts' ... to ensure that the choice of Kansas law is not arbitrary or unfair,' constitutional limits are not violated."

* * *

* * * Here, the parties are Kansas residents. Whatever agreement that existed between the parties was arrived at in Kansas, where they exchanged promises supported by consideration, and D.H. literally delivered on his promise by giving his sperm to S.H. The twins were born in Kansas and reside in Kansas. The only fact tying any of the participants to Missouri is the location of the clinic where the insemination was performed.

Under these circumstances, we hold that Kansas law applies and that significant contacts and a significant aggregation of contacts with Kansas make application of our law to the parties' claims not only appropriate but also constitutional. * * *

Constitutionality of [the Kansas AI statute]

In his brief, D.H. makes a general allegation that [the Kansas AI statute] offends the [equal protection and due process clauses of the] Constitution. [At oral argument D.H.] acknowledged that he no longer challenges the statute as unconstitutional on its face; rather, he argues it cannot be constitutionally applied to him, as a known sperm donor who alleges he had an oral agreement with the twins' mother that granted him parental rights. * * *

* * *

Given the relative newness of the medical procedure of artificial insemination, and thus the newness of [the Kansas AI statute's] attempt to regulate the relationships arising from it, it is not surprising that the issue raised by D.H. is one of first impression, not only in Kansas but nationally. We therefore begin our discussion of the constitutionality of the statute by surveying the landscape of various states' laws governing the rights of sperm donors for artificial insemination. This landscape and its ongoing evolution provide helpful context for our analysis of [the Kansas AI statute].

The majority of states that have enacted statutes concerning artificial insemination state that the husband of a married woman bears all rights and obligations of paternity as to any child conceived by artificial insemination, whether the sperm used was his own or a donor's.[ ]

The 1973 Uniform Parentage Act* * * provided the model for many of the state artificial insemination statutes * * *. [The court then quoted section 5 of the 1973 Uniform Parentage Act, which is printed above].

The wording of this original Act and statutes that imitated it did not address the determination of a sperm donor's paternity when an *unmarried* woman conceived a child through artificial insemination. The earliest case to address this particular question arose in a state that had not yet adopted any statute regarding the effects of the procedure.

In that case, * * * [t]he New Jersey court relied upon a common-law presumption of paternity to award visitation rights to the donor as the "natural father" of the "illegitimate child." Had the mother and the donor been married and conceived the child through artificial insemination, the court said, the donor would have been considered the child's father. Given the evidence that the parties had intended to parent the child together, the court believed the same result should follow, despite the absence of wedding vows.[]

Certain states other than New Jersey either anticipated the need for their original statutes to govern the relationship of a sperm donor to the child of an unmarried recipient as well as a married recipient or modified their original uniform Act-patterned statutes to remove the word "married" from the § 5 (b) language. This meant these states' statutes contained complete bars to paternity for any sperm donor not married to the recipient, regardless of whether the recipient was married to someone else and regardless of whether the donor was known or anonymous. An example of such a provision reads: "The donor of semen provided to a licensed physician for use in artificial insemination of a woman other than the donor's wife is treated in law as if he were not the natural father of a child thereby conceived." See, e.g., Cal. Fam. Code § 7613(b) (West 2004)[ ].

Four cases interpreting one of these types of statutes covering both married and unmarried recipients and establishing an absolute bar to donor paternity were decided before a 2000 amendment to the uniform Act made it applicable to unmarried as well as married recipients of donor sperm.[ ]

The first of the four arose in California in 1986. In that case, *Jhordan C. v. Mary K.*, 179 Cal.App.3d 386, 224 Cal.Rptr. 530 (1986), a donor provided sperm to one of two unmarried women who had decided to raise a child together.

* * *

Because the parties had no doctor involved in the donation or insemination and thus the sperm was never "provided to a licensed physician," the court ruled that the case before it fell outside the statute. It therefore affirmed the lower court's recognition of the donor's paternity. * * *

The second case, *In Interest of R.C.*, 775 P.2d 27 (Colo.1989), arose in Colorado in 1989. In that case, the district court had refused to admit proffered evidence of an agreement that the donor would act as a father based on relevance * * *.

The Colorado Supreme Court reversed the district court * * *. It explicitly rejected the idea that an unmarried recipient lost the protection of the statute "merely because she knows the donor." * * *

The next case, *McIntyre v. Crouch*, 98 Ore. App. 462, 780 P.2d 239 (1989), *cert. denied* 495 U.S. 905, 110 S. Ct. 1924, 109 L. Ed. 2d 288 (1990), involved an unmarried woman who artificially inseminated herself with a known donor's semen. The donor sought recognition of his paternity, and both he and the woman sought summary judgment. The Oregon artificial insemination statute read:

> "If the donor of semen used in artificial insemination is not the mother's husband: (1) Such donor shall have no right, obligation or interest with respect to a child born as a result of the artificial insemination; and (2) A child born as a result of the artificial insemination shall have no right, obligation or interest with respect to the donor." Ore. Rev. Stat. § 109.239 (1977).

The donor challenged this statute under equal protection and due process principles.

* * *

[Applying a strict scrutiny standard], the Oregon court ruled that the statute before it drew an acceptable "classification of unmarried males and unmarried females ... based on biological differences.... Only a male could contribute the sperm to accomplish conception; only a female could conceive and bear the child."[ ] Further, the classification was rationally related to the purposes of the statute, which were: (1) to allow married couples to have children, even though the husband was infertile, impotent, or ill; (2) to allow an unmarried woman to conceive and bear a child without sexual intercourse; (3) to resolve potential disputes about parental rights and responsibilities: that is, (a) the mother's husband, if he consents, is father of the child, and (b) an unmarried mother is free from any claims by the donor of parental rights; (4) to encourage men to donate semen by protecting them against any claims by the mother or the child; and (5) to legitimate the child and give it rights against the mother's husband, if he consented to the insemination.[ ] Thus the statute did not offend equal protection either on its face or as applied.

The court also rebuffed the donor's due process challenge to the statute on its face[ ]. However, the donor also argued that the statute violated due process under the federal and state Constitutions as applied to him, a known donor who had an agreement with the mother to share the rights and responsibilities of parenthood. The court agreed the statute would violate the Due Process Clause of the Fourteenth Amendment as applied to the donor *if* such an agreement was proved, [depending primarily on the United States

Supreme Court decision in *Lehr v. Robertson,* 463 U.S. 248, 261, 77 L. Ed. 2d 614, 103 S. Ct. 2985 (1983), an adoption case which held that the due process clause protects the rights of those "unwed fathers" who are committed to raising their children].[ ]

* * *

The last of the four cases, *C.O. v. W.S.*, 64 Ohio Misc.2d 9, 639 N.E.2d 523 (1994), also concluded, as the *McIntyre* court did, that a statute purporting to be an absolute bar to paternity of sperm donors, while constitutional in the absence of an agreement to the contrary, could be unconstitutional as applied when the donor can establish that an agreement to share parenting existed between him and the unmarried woman who was the recipient of the sperm.[ ]

* * *

Since the Uniform Act was amended in 2000 to state simply, "A donor is not a parent of a child conceived by means of assisted reproduction," two of our sister states have decided three additional cases addressing statutes with identical or substantively indistinguishable provisions governing sperm donors and unmarried recipients.[ ] Two of these cases [were decided on technical standing grounds]. * * *

The third case, [*Steven S. v. Deborah D.*, 127 Cal.App.4th 319, 25 Cal.Rptr.3d 482 (2005)], from California, involved an unmarried woman and a known sperm donor who tried artificial insemination; when that resulted in a miscarriage, they attempted to conceive through sexual intercourse, also without success. Finally, a second artificial insemination attempt resulted in conception. The donor initially was very involved with the pregnancy and the child, and he filed a paternity action when the child was 3 years old.

The district court noted that California's statute presented a bar to paternity for unmarried sperm donors, but ruled in favor of the donor based on equitable estoppel. The donor was known; he had engaged in sexual intercourse with the unwed mother; and she had acknowledged him as the child's father and had allowed him to participate in the pregnancy and celebrate the birth of the child. The California Court of Appeals reversed, holding that the "words of [the California statute] are clear" and that, under such facts, "[t]here can be no paternity claim" because of the statute's absolute bar [on parentage of a sperm donor in the case of an unmarried recipient].

* * *

Where does our Kansas statute fit into this landscape and its ongoing evolution?

In 1985, Kansas became one of the states that adopted portions of the Uniform Parentage Act of 1973 regarding presumptions of paternity, but it did not adopt any provision relating to artificial insemination.[ ]

In 1994, Kansas amended its statute to incorporate the 1973 Uniform Act's § 5(b) * * *.[ ] It did not differentiate between known and unknown or anonymous donors, but it did make two notable changes in the uniform language.

As discussed above, although the 1973 Uniform Act governed the paternity of children born only to married women as a result of artificial insemination with donor sperm, the version adopted by Kansas omitted the word "married."[ ] This drafting decision demonstrates the legislature's intent that the bar to donor paternity apply regardless of whether the recipient was married or unmarried.

The other alteration in the 1973 Uniform Act's language is directly at issue here. The Kansas Legislature provided that a sperm donor and recipient could choose to opt out of the donor paternity bar by written agreement.[ ] * * *

This second drafting decision is critical and sets this case apart from all precedent. Our statute's allowance for a written agreement to grant a sperm donor parental rights and responsibilities means that, although we may concur with the [Oregon and Ohio] courts in their constitutional analyses of absolute-bar statutes, we need not arrive at the same result.[The Kansas AI statute] includes exactly the sort of escape clause the Oregon and Ohio courts found lacking-and unconstitutional-in their statutes.

Ultimately, in view of the requirement that we accept as true D.H.'s evidence supporting existence of an oral agreement, we are faced with a very precise question: Does our statute's requirement that any opt-out agreement between an unmarried mother and a known sperm donor be "in writing" result in an equal protection or due process violation? * * *

Equal Protection

[The Kansas AI statute] draws a gender-based line between a necessarily female sperm recipient and a necessarily male sperm donor for an artificial insemination. By operation of the statute, the female is a potential parent or actual parent under all circumstances; by operation of the same statute, the male will never be a potential parent or actual parent unless there is a written agreement to that effect with the female. [T]he male's ability to insist on father status effectively disappears once he donates sperm. Until that point, he can unilaterally refuse to participate unless a written agreement on his terms exists. After donation, the male cannot force the fatherhood issue. The female can unilaterally decide if and when to use the donation for artificial insemination and can unilaterally deny any wish of the male for parental rights by refusing to enter into a written agreement.

The guiding principle of equal protection analysis is that similarly situated individuals should be treated alike. * * * In order to pass muster under the federal and state equal protection provisions, a classification that treats otherwise similarly situated individuals differently based solely on the individuals' genders must substantially further a legitimate legislative purpose; the government's objective must be important, and the classification substantially related to achievement of it.[ ]

Given the biological differences between females and males and the immutable role those differences play in conceiving and bearing a child, regardless of whether conception is achieved through sexual intercourse or artificial insemination, we are skeptical that S.H. and D.H. are truly similarly situated. However, assuming for purposes of argument that they are, we perceive several legitimate legislative purposes or important governmental objectives underlying [the Kansas AI statute].

[The Kansas AI statute] envisions that both married and unmarried women may become parents without engaging in sexual intercourse, either because of personal choice or because a husband or partner is infertile, impotent, or ill. It encourages men who are able and willing to donate sperm to such women by protecting the men from later unwanted claims for support from the mothers or the children. It protects women recipients as well, preventing potential claims of donors to parental rights and responsibilities, in the absence of an agreement. Its requirement that any such agreement be in writing enhances predictability, clarity, and enforceability. Although the timing of entry into a written agreement is not set out explicitly, the design of the statute implicitly encourages early resolution of the elemental question of whether a donor will have parental rights. Effectively, the parties must decide whether they will enter into a written agreement before any donation is made, while there is still balanced bargaining power on both sides of the parenting equation.

In our view, the statute's gender classification substantially furthers and is thus substantially related to these legitimate legislative purposes and important governmental objectives[The Kansas AI statute] establishes the clear default positions of parties to artificial insemination. If these parties desire an arrangement different from the statutory norm, they are free to provide for it, as long as they do so in writing. * * *

Due Process

* * *

We simply are not persuaded that the requirement of a writing transforms what is an otherwise constitutional statute into one that violates D.H.'s substantive due process rights. Although we agree * * * that one goal of the Kansas Parentage Act as a whole is to encourage fathers to voluntarily acknowledge paternity and child support obligations, the obvious impact of the plain language of this particular provision in the Act is to prevent the creation of parental status where it is not desired or expected. To a certain extent, D.H. * * * evidently misunderstand[s] the statute's mechanism. It ensures no *attachment* of parental rights to sperm donors in the absence of a written agreement to the contrary; it does not *cut off* rights that have already arisen and attached.

* * *

We also reject the argument from D.H. * * * that the statute inevitably makes the female the sole arbiter of whether a male can be a father to a child his sperm helps to conceive. This may be true, as we discussed above, once a donation is made, a recipient who becomes pregnant through artificial insemination using that donation can refuse to enter into an agreement to provide for donor paternity. This does not make the requirement of written agreement unconstitutional. Indeed, it is consistent with United States Supreme Court precedent making even a married pregnant woman the sole arbiter, regardless of her husband's wishes, of whether she continues a pregnancy to term. * * *

All of this being said, we cannot close our discussion of the constitutionality of [the Kansas AI statute] without observing that all that is constitutional is not necessarily wise. We are mindful of, and moved by, the Center's advocacy for public policy to maximize the chance of the availability of two parents-and two parents' resources-to Kansas children. We are also aware of continued evolution in regulation of artificial insemination in this and other countries. In particular, Britain and The Netherlands now ban anonymous sperm donations, near-perfect analogs to donations from known donors who will have no role beyond facilitating artificial insemination. These shifts formally recognize the understandable desires of at least some children conceived through artificial insemination to know the males from whom they have received half of their genes. The Human Fertilisation and Embryology Authority Act of 1990, as amended by Disclosure of Donor Information, Regulations 2004 No. 1511 (requiring, effective April 2005, British donors' identities to be made available to donor-conceived children when children become 18); Netherlands Embryos Bill, Article 3 Dutch Ministry of Health, Welfare, and Sport (2004) www.minvws.nl/en (effective June 2004, child born using donated sperm have right to obtain information about biological father at age 16). As one such child recently wrote,

"[t]hose of us created with donated sperm won't stay bubbly babies forever. We're all going to grow into adults, and form opinions about the decision to bring us into the world in a way that deprives us of the basic right to know where we came from, what our history is and who both our parents are."

[ ] We sympathize. However, weighing of the interests of all involved in these procedures as well as the public policies that are furthered by favoring one or another in certain circumstances, is the charge of the Kansas Legislature, not of this court.

"Provided to a Licensed Physician"

D.H.'s next argument on appeal is that the district judge erred in applying [the Kansas AI statute] to him because his sperm was not "provided to a licensed physician," as required by the statute. Instead, it was provided to S.H., who, in turn, provided it to the medical personnel who performed the insemination. [The court rejected this argument.]

* * *

"Unless Agreed to in Writing"

Assuming arguendo the constitutionality and applicability of [the Kansas AI statute], D.H. next argues that the statute's requirement of a written agreement should be deemed satisfied by the CINC petition filed by S.H. or by the CINC petition and his paternity petition, read together. [The court rejected the argument that the pleading in the case constituted the written agreement that the sperm source would be the father.]

* * *

Equity

* * * D.H. asserts that the district court must be reversed because S.H. has "unclean hands." In essence, he argues that he, a nonlawyer, was tricked by lawyer S.H., who failed to inform him of the statute and failed to explain how the absence of independent legal advice or a written agreement could affect his legal rights. He asserts that he asked S.H. about whether he needed a lawyer or whether they should put their arrangement in writing and was told neither was necessary. This behavior, he alleges, may have constituted a violation of S.H.'s ethical duties as a licensed lawyer.

* * *

Generally speaking, mere ignorance of the law is no excuse for failing to abide by it.[ ] There may be a case in the future in which a donor can prove that the existence of [the Kansas AI statute] was concealed, or that he was fraudulently induced *not* to obtain independent legal advice or *not* to enter into a written agreement to ensure creation and preservation of his parental rights to a child conceived through artificial insemination. This is not such a case.

Affirmed.

CAPLINGER, J., dissenting: I respectfully disagree with the majority's analysis of the constitutionality of [the Kansas AI statute] as applied to D.H. I would hold the statute unconstitutional as applied to D.H. for the reason that it violates his fundamental right to parent his children without due process of law.

* * *

Requirement that donor take affirmative action to protect his parental rights

In concluding that the opt-out provision in [the Kansas AI statute] satisfies due process requirements, the majority states that D.H.'s "own *inaction* before donating his sperm" left him unable to meet the statute's requirements of a written agreement.[ ] Therein lies the constitutional problem with the statute. Fundamental rights must be actively waived, rather than passively lost due to inaction.

Initially, before analyzing this issue, I would note that the terminology employed by the majority, i.e., that D.H. failed to "opt out" of the statute, is a misnomer. In effect, the statute requires a known sperm donor, regardless of any agreement or understanding the donor may have as to his role in parenting a child conceived from his sperm, to *opt in* to parenthood or forever waive his right to parent.

* * *

Effect of "ignorance of the law" on an individual's fundamental right to parent

Nor can I agree with the majority's conclusion that D.H.'s ignorance of the statute's writing requirement has no effect on the statute's application.

* * *

I would urge the majority to consider the *complete* rationale of *Lehr*: "When an unwed father demonstrates a full commitment to the responsibilities of parenthood by 'com[ing] forward to participate in the rearing of his child,' his interest in personal contact with his child acquires substantial protection under the Due Process Clause."[ ]

That is the scenario with which this court is faced. A putative father has come forward to participate in the rearing of his children, emotionally and financially; consequently, his interest in doing so is entitled to full protection under the Due Process Clause. Instead of being given this protection and an opportunity to prove that he intended to actively parent his children, D.H. has been subjected to the workings of a statute of which he was unaware, that required him to "opt in" to fatherhood before ever donating his sperm, or be forever barred from parenting his children.

* * * Because the rights to parent are fundamental, those rights may be waived only through an intentional, free, and meaningful choice. Here, the record indicates D.H. was not even aware of [the Kansas AI statute], much less its requirement that he must enter into a written agreement formalizing his intent to parent his child before he provided his sperm to S.H.

* * *

The requirement of a "writing" under [the Kansas statute]

It is interesting to note that in considering whether the [the Kansas AI statute] writing requirement may be met by considering S.H.'s averments in her pleadings, the majority references Lewis Carroll's "looking glass."[ ]While I agree with the majority that we cannot interpret the pleadings filed by S.H. (in which she referred to D.H. as the "father" of her children at least 56 times) as the "writing" contemplated by [the Kansas AI statute], I would find that S.H.'s inconsistent pleadings and actions are evidence to be considered by the district court in determining whether the parties agreed that D.H. would play an active role in the twins' life.

* * *

Thus, I would remand for the district court to consider all evidence relevant to the existence of an agreement between the parties, including S.H.'s inconsistent allegations regarding D.H.'s responsibilities, her consistent reference to D.H. as the "father" of her children, and her failure to rely upon the statutory presumption in her initial petition.

As a final note, I agree that this court should not place fathers in an "Alice and Wonderland" scenario where the rules of the "chess game" are constantly changing and Kansas children are sometimes left without two supportive parents. And yet, it seems to me that rather than Lewis Carroll's looking glass, we are looking at this case through a "funny mirror" at the local carnival. It is apparent that D.H. seeks to be a loving and supportive parent to the two children he has biologically fathered-two children who have no other putative father. And yet, by operation of a statute of which D.H. was unaware, his rights to parent these children were cut off before the children were conceived with the use of his sperm. This is a result we should not abide for D.H. or for his children absent the protections of due process.

* * *

HILL, J., dissenting: I must respectfully join with Judge Caplinger in her dissent. I too agree that as applied in this case, [the Kansas AI statute] is unconstitutional when applied to a known donor.

But I raise my hand and ask a different question. Who speaks for the children in these proceedings? As applied by the majority in this case, this generative statute of frauds slices away half of their heritage. A man who was once considered a "putative father" in the initial child in need of care proceeding is now branded a mere "semen donor." The majority offers the children sympathy. But is this in their best interests? The trial court never got to the point of deciding the best interests of the children because it was convinced that such a consideration was barred by the operation of [the Kansas AI statute] to a known donor.

None of the elaborate and meticulous safeguards our Kansas laws afford parents *and children* in proceedings before our courts when confronted with questions of parentage have been extended to these children. * * *

I agree with the Ohio Court of Common Pleas when it said:

"A father's voluntary assumption of fiscal responsibility for his child should be endorsed as a socially responsible action. A statute which absolutely extinguishes a father's efforts to assert the rights and responsibility of being a father, in a case with such facts as those *sub judice,* runs contrary to due process safeguards.[ ]"

I think the same can be said about our statute.

Notes and Questions

1. What is the difference between the approach taken by the 1973 Uniform Parentage Act and the approach taken by the 2002 Act? How are they different from the Kansas statute that was the subject of the discussion in *K.M.H.?* In what kinds of cases would the application of the different Acts yield different parents? Are there children who would have no fathers under the 1973 Act or the Kansas statute but who would have a father under the new version of the Uniform Parentage Act?

2. While the 2002 version of the Uniform Parentage Act applies in every case of assisted conception, it has not been adopted by very many states. On the other hand, the 1973 version, parts of which have been adopted in a large number of states, applies only if the woman who is inseminated is a wife (i.e., is married), if she proceeds with the consent of her husband and the procedure is carried out under the supervision of a licensed physician. If any of these conditions is not met, the statute is inapplicable and the common law will define the rights and interests of all of the parties. See Marriage of Witbeck–Wildhagen, 281 Ill.App.3d 502, 217 Ill.Dec. 329, 667 N.E.2d 122 (1996) (husband did not consent to wife's insemination; statute did not apply). As the *K.M.H.* case suggests, some common law cases have treated the source of the sperm to be the father, with all of the rights (including visitation) and obligations (including child support) that come with such a designation; others have not.

3. In addition to the moral arguments that are made against artificial insemination by a husband, there are four additional arguments against the moral and social propriety of artificial insemination by a donor (AID) without a relationship with the woman inseminated. First, some believe that it constitutes adultery. Second, the uncertainty of the screening of the sperm source in AID can provide for uncertainty in the health of the child, and the anonymity of the sperm source can impose upon the woman or her child unforeseen emotional consequences. Third, there is a worry that the availability of AID will reshape and dilute family structure, replacing the nuclear family with unusual and inappropriate combina-

tions of adults and children. Finally, there is an argument that AID is inappropriate because if there is no limit on the number of times one man may donate sperm there may be a genetically unacceptably large number of "test tube" children who unknowingly have the same genetic father. This may lead to the dilution of the genetic pool of some communities. Do any of these arguments provide a good reason to prohibit the practice, or to regulate it?

4. If we reject genetic essentialism (i.e., that the source of the genetic contribution is the parent), where should we look to decide if a sperm source ought to be the legal father of the child? Should we look to the intent of the parties? Should we look to the best interest of the child, as the dissent in *K.M.H.* suggests? Is it always in the interest of a child to have as many support-paying parents as possible?

5. Should those who object to a finding of fatherhood be estopped from raising that claim when there has been a public holding-out of the claimant as the father? Can such an estoppel argument be used by each side? What is the relationship between the argument based in estoppel, which has become more popular as a way to establish parenthood over the past few years, and the statutory and Constitutional arguments?

6. Should a prospective mother (and, ultimately, the child) know the identity of the sperm source? What legal difference does it make? An anonymous (or, at least, unknown) sperm source will have a more difficult time establishing fatherhood rights than one who is known or identifiable, and that may encourage prospective mothers to choose unknown sperm sources. That, in turn, may encourage women seeking artificial insemination to seek the help of cryobanks, which are now commonly run as medical institutions with medical control over the processing of the sperm. In order to maintain control over the attributes of their child, though, those women who seek anonymous donors may still want to know something about those donors.

Sperm banks provide profiles of their various donors, and some issue catalogs of these profiles allowing their consumers to choose the profile that seems most appropriate. One "donor catalog" provides information on ethnicity, hair color and texture, eye color, height, weight, blood type, skin tone, years of education, and occupation (or major in college). Some catalogs provide information on teeth, the presence of freckles, the location of dimples, and the donor's favorite movies and songs. Some provide brief health histories of the donor's family members. Short (2–page) profiles, and longer (10–page) descriptions are available on all donors, and audio and video tapes, pictures, and other information may be available for some. In addition to relevant health information, what kind of information, if any, about the sperm source ought to be provided to the woman who is going to be inseminated?

7. As the *K.M.H.* case points out, the American legal preference for unknown or anonymous donors is not reflected elsewhere in the world, and, especially in Europe, the trend is toward a legal requirement that the source be made known to the child when the child becomes an adult. Which approach is better—the American preference for anonymity, or the preference elsewhere for release of this information? In the United States over the past few years there has been an increase in the number of "directed donations" of sperm—i.e., donations made by identifiable persons (fathers?) for use by identified mothers. Is that a healthy trend?

At the very least, should a child be informed that he or she was the product of ART, and that there may be a gamete source other than the parents? The American Society of Reproductive Medicine announced in 2004 that they recommended that parents provide such information. They concluded:

1.   While ultimately the choice of recipient parents, disclosure to offspring of the use of donor gametes is encouraged.

2.   Parties should agree in advance on how and when ART programs and sperm banks will release donor information to the recipients.

3.   Programs and sperm banks should gather and store medical and genetic information concerning donors.

4.   Counseling and informed consent about disclosure are essential for the donor and recipients.

5.   Programs and sperm banks should expect inquiries from donor offspring and consider developing a written policy to respond to these inquiries.

Ethics Committee of the American Society for Reproductive Medicine, Informing Offspring of Their Conception by Gamete Donation, 81 Fertilization and Sterilization 527 (2004).

8.   Should a determination of who will be inseminated be left to physicians who perform this procedure? May physicians doing artificial insemination reject a request for artificial insemination from a potential recipient because that recipient is unmarried (and with no partner), psychologically immature, homosexual, welfare dependent, has a history of serious genetic disorder, is HIV positive, is under 18 years old, has a criminal record, or there is evidence of past child abuse, drug abuse or alcohol abuse, or a history of genetic disorder. Twenty years ago, such rejections were commonplace, Office of Technology Assessment, Artificial Insemination Practice in the United States (1988), and they may be at some clinics today. Does the determination by these physicians not to inseminate the poor or those with criminal records harken back to the era of *Buck v. Bell* and *Skinner v. Oklahoma,* when there was a presumption that wealth and criminal proclivity were inheritable, or do such screening processes merely suggest that the physicians, who can choose whom they will make parents, are determining which of the proposed patients are likely to be the best parents? Should a physician ever be required to perform artificial insemination in a case where she believes that the woman being inseminated is not capable of the physical, mental, financial or emotional obligations of motherhood?

If there is to be gatekeeping for infertility services, who should be the gatekeeper? In Europe, that is a role largely undertaken by the government, while in the United States it is still left to private clinics. For a good discussion of this issue, see Richard Storrow, The Bioethics of Prospective Parenthood: In Pursuit of the Proper Standard for Gatekeeping in Infertility Clinics, 28 Cardozo L. Rev. 2283 (2007).

9.   The ability to freeze and preserve sperm gives rise to the possibility that the father of a child conceived through artificial insemination could have died years before that child's birth. The Social Security Administration faced this issue in a number of cases where claimants have sought survivor's benefits from fathers who had died before they were born (or even conceived). Their eligibility depends on whether they are recognized as heirs by the states where they reside. In some states a child may be an heir to a father who died pre-conception; in some states a child may not be. The Uniform Status of Children of Assisted Conception Act explicitly provided that one who died before implantation of his or her genetic contribution was not a parent of the "resulting child." The 2002 version of the

Uniform Parentage Act, on the other hand, provides that an insemination of a woman by a man's sperm after his death does not render him a parent unless he "consented" to this in writing. See Khabbaz v. Commissioner, Social Security Administration, 155 N.H. 798, 930 A.2d 1180 (2007) (New Hampshire answers certified question from the federal court that a child cannot inherit from a father who died before the child's conception) and Woodward v. Commissioner, 435 Mass. 536, 760 N.E.2d 257 (2002)(child of "posthumous reproduction" may be an heir of a father who consented to the reproduction and agreed to provide support).

10. What is the tort liability that arises out of the provision of inadequate sperm for purposes of artificial insemination? Might the physician or the sperm bank be liable in negligence for inadequately screening the count, health and motility of the sperm? What is the standard of care for screening sperm? How would you find out? In any case, might the doctor or the sperm bank be liable without negligence (on a products liability theory) for the provision of defective sperm?

Of course, the physician and the physician's staff could also be liable in negligence for failing to carry out properly the procedure or failing to adequately inform and counsel the woman to be inseminated about the risks, benefits and alternatives of the procedure.

Might there be a contract action against the physician or the sperm bank who deals commercially in the sale of sperm? If the sperm is sold to the woman who is to be inseminated, is it sold with any implied warranty—perhaps a warranty of fitness for a particular purpose—under the Uniform Commercial Code?

Could the sperm source himself be liable for providing defective sperm? What if the sperm source knew that his semen carried some venereal disease or that he had some unmanifested or concealed genetic defect? Would he be liable as a manufacturer of a product? In negligence? For fraud? On some other theory?

JOHNSON v. CALVERT

Supreme Court of California, 1993.
5 Cal.4th 84, 19 Cal.Rptr.2d 494, 851 P.2d 776.

PANELLI, J.:

* * *

Mark and Crispina Calvert are a married couple who desired to have a child. Crispina was forced to undergo a hysterectomy in 1984. Her ovaries remained capable of producing eggs, however, and the couple eventually considered surrogacy. In 1989 Anna Johnson heard about Crispina's plight from a coworker and offered to serve as a surrogate for the Calverts.

On January 15, 1990, Mark, Crispina, and Anna signed a contract providing that an embryo created by the sperm of Mark and the egg of Crispina would be implanted in Anna and the child born would be taken into Mark and Crispina's home "as their child." Anna agreed she would relinquish "all parental rights" to the child in favor of Mark and Crispina. In return, Mark and Crispina would pay Anna $10,000 in a series of installments, the last to be paid six weeks after the child's birth. Mark and Crispina were also to pay for a $200,000 life insurance policy on Anna's life.

The zygote was implanted on January 19, 1990. Less than a month later, an ultrasound test confirmed Anna was pregnant.

Unfortunately, relations deteriorated between the two sides. Mark learned that Anna had not disclosed she had suffered several stillbirths and miscarriages. Anna felt Mark and Crispina did not do enough to obtain the required insurance policy. She also felt abandoned during an onset of premature labor in June.

In July 1990, Anna sent Mark and Crispina a letter demanding the balance of the payments due her or else she would refuse to give up the child. The following month, Mark and Crispina responded with a lawsuit, seeking a declaration they were the legal parents of the unborn child. Anna filed her own action to be declared the mother of the child, and the two cases were eventually consolidated. The parties agreed to an independent guardian ad litem for the purposes of the suit.

The child was born on September 19, 1990, and blood samples were obtained from both Anna and the child for analysis. The blood test results excluded Anna as the genetic mother. The parties agreed to a court order providing that the child would remain with Mark and Crispina on a temporary basis with visits by Anna.

DISCUSSION

Determining Maternity Under the Uniform Parentage Act [of 1973]

* * * [W]e are left with the undisputed evidence that Anna, not Crispina, gave birth to the child and that Crispina, not Anna, is genetically related to him. Both women thus have adduced evidence of a mother and child relationship as contemplated by the [Uniform Parentage] Act [1973].[ ] Yet for any child California law recognizes only one natural mother, despite advances in reproductive technology rendering a different outcome biologically possible.

We decline to accept the contention of amicus curiae * * * that we should find the child has two mothers. Even though rising divorce rates have made multiple parent arrangements common in our society, we see no compelling reason to recognize such a situation here. The Calverts are the genetic and intending parents of their son and have provided him, by all accounts, with a stable, intact, and nurturing home. To recognize parental rights in a third party with whom the Calvert family has had little contact since shortly after the child's birth would diminish Crispina's role as mother.

We see no clear legislative preference in [the statutory law] as between blood testing evidence and proof of having given birth.

* * *

Because two women each have presented acceptable proof of maternity, we do not believe this case can be decided without enquiring into the parties' intentions as manifested in the surrogacy agreement. Mark and Crispina are a couple who desired to have a child of their own genes but are physically unable to do so without the help of reproductive technology. They affirmatively intended the birth of the child, and took the steps necessary to effect in vitro fertilization. But for their acted-on intention, the child would not exist. Anna agreed to facilitate the procreation of Mark's and Crispina's child. The parties' aim was to bring Mark's and Crispina's child into the world, not for Mark and Crispina to donate a zygote to Anna. Crispina from the outset intended to be the child's mother. Although the gestative function Anna performed was necessary to bring about the child's birth, it is safe to say that Anna would not have been given the opportunity to gestate or deliver the child had she, prior to implantation of the zygote, manifested her own intent to be the child's mother. No reason appears why Anna's later change of heart should vitiate the determination that Crispina is the child's natural mother.

We conclude that although the Act recognizes both genetic consanguinity and giving birth as means of establishing a mother and child relationship, when the two means do not coincide in one woman, she who intended to procreate the child—that is, she who intended to bring about the birth of a child that she intended to raise as her own—is the natural mother under California law.[5]

* * *

Anna urges that surrogacy contracts violate several social policies. Relying on her contention that she is the child's legal, natural mother, she cites the public policy embodied in [the] Penal Code[ ], prohibiting the payment for consent to adoption of a child. She argues further that the policies underlying the adoption laws of this state are violated by the surrogacy contract because it in effect constitutes a prebirth waiver of her parental rights.

We disagree. Gestational surrogacy differs in crucial respects from adoption and so is not subject to the adoption statutes. The parties voluntarily agreed to participate in in vitro fertilization and related medical procedures before the child was conceived; at the time when Anna entered into the contract, therefore, she was not vulnerable to financial inducements to part with her own expected offspring. As discussed above, Anna was not the genetic mother of the child. The payments to Anna under the contract were meant to compensate her for her services in gestating the fetus and undergoing labor, rather than for giving up "parental" rights to the child. Payments were due both during the pregnancy and after the child's birth.

* * *

Finally, Anna and some commentators have expressed concern that surrogacy contracts tend to exploit or dehumanize women, especially women of lower economic status. Anna's objections center around the psychological harm she asserts may result from the gestator's relinquishing the child to whom she has given birth. Some have also cautioned that the practice of

---

5. Thus, under our analysis, in a true "egg donation" situation, where a woman gestates and gives birth to a child formed from the egg of another woman with the intent to raise the child as her own, the birth mother is the natural mother under California law.

The dissent would decide parentage based on the best interests of the child. Such an approach raises the repugnant specter of governmental interference in matters implicating our most fundamental notions of privacy, and confuses concepts of parentage and custody. Logically, the determination of parentage must precede, and should not be dictated by, eventual custody decisions. The implicit assumption of the dissent is that a recognition of the genetic intending mother as the natural mother may sometimes harm the child. This assumption overlooks California's dependency laws, which are designed to protect all children irrespective of the manner of birth or conception. Moreover, the best interests standard poorly serves the child in the present situation: it fosters instability during litigation and, if applied to recognize the gestator as the natural mother, results in a split of custody between the natural father and the gestator, an outcome not likely to benefit the child. Further, it may be argued that, by voluntarily contracting away any rights to the child, the gestator has, in effect, conceded the best interests of the child are not with her.

surrogacy may encourage society to view children as commodities, subject to trade at their parents' will.

We are unpersuaded that gestational surrogacy arrangements are so likely to cause the untoward results Anna cites as to demand their invalidation on public policy grounds. Although common sense suggests that women of lesser means serve as surrogate mothers more often than do wealthy women, there has been no proof that surrogacy contracts exploit poor women to any greater degree than economic necessity in general exploits them by inducing them to accept lower-paid or otherwise undesirable employment. We are likewise unpersuaded by the claim that surrogacy will foster the attitude that children are mere commodities; no evidence is offered to support it.

The argument that a woman cannot knowingly and intelligently agree to gestate and deliver a baby for intending parents carries overtones of the reasoning that for centuries prevented women from attaining equal economic rights and professional status under the law. To resurrect this view is both to foreclose a personal and economic choice on the part of the surrogate mother, and to deny intending parents what may be their only means of procreating a child of their own genes.

* * *

The judgment of the Court of Appeal is affirmed.

[ARABIAN, J., concurred with the majority's Uniform Parentage Act analysis, but would leave the issue of whether surrogacy contracts could be consistent with public policy to the legislature.]

KENNARD, J., dissenting.

When a woman who wants to have a child provides her fertilized ovum to another woman who carries it through pregnancy and gives birth to a child, who is the child's legal mother? Unlike the majority, I do not agree that the determinative consideration should be the intent to have the child that originated with the woman who contributed the ovum. In my view, the woman who provided the fertilized ovum and the woman who gave birth to the child both have substantial claims to legal motherhood. Pregnancy entails a unique commitment, both psychological and emotional, to an unborn child. No less substantial, however, is the contribution of the woman from whose egg the child developed and without whose desire the child would not exist.

For each child, California law accords the legal rights and responsibilities of parenthood to only one "natural mother." When, as here, the female reproductive role is divided between two women, California law requires courts to make a decision as to which woman is the child's natural mother, but provides no standards by which to make that decision. The majority's resort to "intent" to break the "tie" between the genetic and gestational mothers is unsupported by statute, and, in the absence of appropriate protections in the law to guard against abuse of surrogacy arrangements, it is ill-advised. To determine who is the legal mother of a child born of a gestational surrogacy arrangement, I would apply the standard most protective of child welfare—the best interests of the child.

Notes and Questions

1. The gestating mother and the commissioning parents developed palpable animosity for each other in *Johnson v. Calvert*. In this case, Johnson argued that the Calverts failed to pay her adequately or treat her with respect. On the other hand, the Calverts argued that Johnson, who admitted to welfare fraud during the course of the pregnancy, was trying to extort money from them. To add a bit of complexity to this baffling case, Johnson also claimed that she was, in part, Native American, and thus subject to provisions of the Indian Child Welfare Act, which preempts state law and requires placement consistent with principles of tribal law.

Is the fact that the commissioning parents and gestating woman may develop such a deep-seated mutual hatred a reason to forbid these contracts absolutely, or a reason to regulate them?

Most of the arguments against surrogacy fall into three categories—those related to the contracting parties; those related to the child; and those related to the effect of the process on society as a whole.

The first argument generally advanced against surrogacy is that it exploits women who are willing to give or rent their bodies as vessels to carry other people's children. Could the inducement of payment for pregnancy cause a woman to consent to something that otherwise would be an unthinkable intrusion upon her body? Will the development of commercial surrogacy lead to a class of poor women who will become child bearers for wealthy women who do not want to spend the time or energy on pregnancy? Is it likely that the fact that there is a relationship between ethnicity and the distribution of wealth in this society mean that we will develop separate childbearing races and child-raising races? For an interesting discussion of American women who "outsource" pregnancy to women in India, where the service is available far cheaper than it is in the United States, see Judith Warner, Outsourced Wombs (Domestic Disturbances), New York Times, January 3, 2008.

Feminists are divided on this issue. Some are deeply offended by the overt use of the woman's body that is the whole goal of a surrogacy arrangement; others believe it is merely misguided paternalism that leads courts (and others) to conclude that women are incapable of deciding for themselves whether they should enter surrogacy contracts. Some economists argue that making surrogacy contracts unenforceable will merely lower the amount that is paid to surrogates. Thus, they suggest, making surrogacy contracts unenforceable is just another in a long history of allegedly protectionist regulations that restrict what a woman may choose to do with her body.

Some argue that surrogacy contracts ought to be prohibited or discouraged because they advance only the best interests of the contracting parties, not the best interest of the child. Normally in a custody dispute between those with claims as parents, the court will look to the best interest of the child in determining the appropriate placement. Enforcing a surrogacy contract is necessarily inconsistent with this principle. In addition, some believe that children who find out that they were carried by a surrogate will be injured by that discovery, and others argue that surrogacy contracts render children instruments for the use of parents, not ends in themselves, and that this is necessarily harmful for children.

Finally, some believe that the fabric of society as a whole is weakened by surrogacy arrangements, at least commercial ones. As Justice Wilentz points out in *Baby M,* there are some things that money cannot buy. How, exactly, could he define this class of things? Why might he conclude that surrogacy is one of them?

Perhaps a surrogacy contract, which is a contract to put one's body to work for the benefit of another, is nothing more than a form of slavery. Since the Thirteenth Amendment we have prohibited contracts for slavery, even if the contracting parties are all competent adults who are acting voluntarily. One argument for the Thirteenth Amendment is that in addition to whatever it offers those who might be or become slaves, society as a whole is better off if the status of "slave" is impossible for everyone. Are all people in this society—including those who would never participate in a surrogacy contract in any way—better off if the society simply eliminates surrogacy?

3. In her dissenting opinion in Johnson v. Calvert, Justice Kennard depended very heavily upon the surrogacy provisions of the Uniform Status of Children of Assisted Conception Act, which allowed states to choose between two options with regard to surrogacy: alternative A (which permitted but heavily regulated surrogacy contracts, and which was adopted by one state) and alternative B (which prohibited those contracts, and which also was adopted in one state). Although this Uniform Act provided the starting point for discussions on the propriety of state recognition and regulation of surrogacy contracts, the paucity of states that adopted it suggests that it was not very well received.

4. In McDonald v. McDonald, 196 A.D.2d 7, 608 N.Y.S.2d 477 (1994), another "true 'egg donation'" case, the New York Supreme Court, Appellate Division, determined that a woman who gestated a child produced through the fertilization of another woman's ovum with her husband's sperm was to be considered the mother of the child that resulted. The New York court depended heavily on the reasoning of *Johnson v. Calvert.* On the other hand, the Court of Common Pleas of Ohio rejected the *Johnson* reasoning in an uncontested case initiated to determine who was to be listed as the mother on the birth certificate in the case of gestational surrogacy. In Belsito v. Clark, 67 Ohio Misc.2d 54, 644 N.E.2d 760 (1994), the court determined that parentage was to be determined by genetic contribution, not by the intent-to-procreate of the parties to the original surrogacy agreement. The court found *Johnson* unpersuasive "for the following three important reasons: (1) the difficulty in applying the *Johnson* intent test; (2) public policy; and (3) *Johnson's* failure to recognize and emphasize the genetic provider's right to consent to procreation and to surrender potential parental rights."

This issue has also arisen in the context of the child custody portion of a divorce case. In Doe v. Doe, 244 Conn. 403, 710 A.2d 1297 (1998), the child was born as a result of artificial insemination of a surrogate mother with the sperm of the husband. The child (fourteen at the time of the divorce) was raised by husband and wife, but the child bore no genetic relationship to the wife. Should the wife be entitled to parental rights upon divorce? Should the court consider the case like any other custody dispute between biological parents, or should the court treat the case like one between the father and a legal stranger to the child? Should the court apply the best interest test in either case?

Would it make a difference if the mother had actually carried the child to term? In In re C.K.G., 173 S.W.3d 714 (Tenn.2005), the father's sperm was used to fertilize a donor's ovum *in vitro* and the resulting preembryo was placed in the uterus of the father's partner (to whom he was not married), intending that she should be the mother. When the couple split up, the woman sought custody and child support. The father responded that she had no genetic relationship with the child and no marital relationship with the father, and that there was no basis for declaring her to be a parent. The Supreme Court of Tennessee found that she was the mother because (1) that was the original intent of the parties, (2) she gave birth to the child in question, and (3) the case did not involve any dispute between the person who provided the ovum and the gestator. How would you weight these three factors? Should any one of them be enough by itself? What would be the result if the Tennessee rule were applied to *McDonald*, *Belsito* or *Doe v. Doe*?

5.   While legal pundits were creating ultimate assisted conception hypotheticals in which the sperm from one person was joined with the ovum of a second and implanted in the womb of a third to be raised by a fourth and fifth, the real case arose in California in Buzzanca v. Buzzanca, 61 Cal.App.4th 1410, 72 Cal.Rptr.2d 280 (1998):

> Jaycee was born because Luanne and John Buzzanca agreed to have an embryo genetically unrelated to either of them implanted in a woman—a surrogate—who would carry and give birth to the child for them. After the fertilization, implantation and pregnancy, Luanne and John split up, and the question of who are Jaycee's lawful parents came before the trial court.

> Luanne claimed that she and her erstwhile husband were the lawful parents, but John disclaimed any responsibility, financial or otherwise. The woman who gave birth also appeared in the case to make it clear that she made no claim to the child.

> The trial court then reached an extraordinary conclusion: Jaycee had no lawful parents. First, the woman who gave birth to Jaycee was not the mother; the court had—astonishingly—already accepted a stipulation that neither she nor her husband were the "biological" parents. Second, Luanne was not the mother. According to the trial court, she could not be the mother because she had neither contributed the egg nor given birth. And John could not be the father, because, not having contributed the sperm, he had no biological relationship with the child. We disagree. Let us get right to the point: Jaycee never would have been born had not Luanne and John both agreed to have a fertilized egg implanted in a surrogate.

> The trial judge erred because he assumed that legal motherhood, under the relevant California statutes, could only be established in one of two ways, either by giving birth or by contributing an egg. He failed to consider the substantial and well-settled body of law holding that there are times when fatherhood can be established by conduct apart from giving birth or being genetically related to a child. The typical example is when an infertile husband consents to allowing his wife to be artificially inseminated. * * *

> The same rule which makes a husband the lawful father of a child born because of his consent to artificial insemination should be applied here—by the same parity of reasoning that guided our Supreme Court in the first surrogacy case, Johnson v. Calvert[ ]—to both husband and wife. Just as a husband is deemed to be the lawful father of a child unrelated to him when his wife gives birth after artificial insemination, so should a husband and wife be deemed the lawful parents of a child after a surrogate bears a biologically unrelated child on their behalf. In each instance, a child is procreated because a medical procedure was initiated and consented to by intended parents. The only difference is that in this case—unlike artificial insemination—there is no reason to distinguish between husband and wife. We therefore must reverse the trial court's judgment and direct that a new judgment be entered, declaring that both Luanne and John are the lawful parents of Jaycee.

6. The technology for facilitating reproduction is of special interest to single men and women, and single sex couples. The use of a surrogate is the only way that a single man could expect to have a child to whom he would be genetically related. Similarly, the use of artificial insemination may be an especially attractive way for a single woman, or a lesbian couple, to have a child. While the law has put no formal restriction on the availability of reproductive techniques, some physicians and hospitals are reluctant to provide the full range of infertility services to single people or non-traditional families. Local and state statutes restricting discrimination on the basis of sexual preference may provide avenues of relief for those gay and lesbian potential parents who are denied reproductive services. *Eisenstadt v. Baird,* 405 U.S. 438, 92 S.Ct. 1029, 31 L.Ed.2d 349 (1972), which threw out a statute forbidding single people access to contraceptives under some circumstances in which they were available to married people, might suggest that the equal protection clause of the Fourteenth Amendment would also protect single people who are denied access to infertility treatment provided to married people by state hospitals and other state facilities. Might their arguments, and the arguments of gays and lesbians who seek parenthood, be bolstered by the decision in Lawrence v. Texas, 539 U.S. 558, 123 S.Ct. 2472, 156 L.Ed.2d 508 (2003), which determined that the Texas sodomy law was unconstitutional?

In *Johnson v. Calvert*, all of the justices agreed that the child could not have two mothers. Is this conclusion a justifiable one? In fact, many states now have no trouble recognizing two mothers or two fathers as the parents of a child. Sometimes this change has come about through common law, sometimes by statute, and sometime by practice (e.g., a state bureau of vital statistics could just change the "father" and "mother" lines on the birth certificate to "parent 1" and "parent 2," as some states have). States have not been willing to go beyond recognizing two parents—at most, of any gender—per child. Does that make sense? If a child can have two mothers, why not two mothers and a father? Why not birth certificate lines for "parent 1," "parent 2," and "parent 3"?

The rules for the formation of families vary from state to state, and what is permitted in some states is inconsistent with fundamental state policy in others. In addition, the parentage law of one state may be inconsistent with the parentage law of another. This can create particularly difficult problems when the courts of one state are asked to give full faith and credit, as is required by the Constitution, to the parentage and custody determinations of another state. This issue arose in Miller–Jenkins v. Miller–Jenkins, 180 Vt. 441, 912 A.2d 951 (2006), where Lisa and Janet, a lesbian couple from Virginia, traveled to Vermont to enter a civil union permitted under Vermont law, but not recognized by Virginia law.

After establishing their civil union, Lisa and Janet decided to start a family, and together they chose an anonymous sperm donor. Lisa became pregnant by artificial insemination and gave birth to a child in Virginia, and a few months later Lisa, Janet and their child moved to Vermont. After a year in Vermont, Lisa and Janet decided to separate. Lisa and her child moved back to Virginia, and Lisa filed an action to dissolve the civil union in the Vermont family court. That court found that both Lisa and Janet were parents of the child, and gave Lisa primary custody while Janet was given very substantial visitation rights. Lisa objected and filed an action in Virginia seeking a new parentage determination.

The Vermont court held Lisa in contempt for failing to allow Janet's visitation, and, the following week, the Virginia court entered an order finding that Lisa was the only mother of the child, and that Janet had no parentage rights. The Virginia court determined that Janet's rights were established through Vermont's civil union law, which were void under Virginia law. Lisa argued that the Virginia court did not have to give full faith and credit to the Vermont family court order because of the language of the Federal Defense of Marriage Act (DOMA), 28 U.S.C. section 1783(C), which reads:

> No state, territory or possession of the United States, or Indian tribe, shall be required to give effect to any public act, record or judicial proceeding of any other state, territory, possession, or tribe respecting a relationship between persons of the same sex that is treated as a marriage under the laws of such other State, territory, possession, or tribe, or a right or claim arising from such a relationship.

That argument was rejected by the Vermont court, which upheld the family court ruling. The Virginia Court of Appeals ultimately agreed with the position taken by the Vermont court, Miller–Jenkins v. Miller–Jenkins, 49 Va.App. 88, 637 S.E.2d 330 (2006), and, in an unreported opinion, the Virginia court subsequently granted an order allowing Janet to register the Vermont order in Virginia, and thus to enforce it there. The case was pending in the Virginia Supreme Court as this book went to press.

Was the Court of Appeals result the right outcome? Does DOMA attempt to permit what the full faith and credit clause prohibits? If Lisa had decided to go to court in Virginia rather than Vermont when she first sought to be declared the sole parent of the child, would the result have been different? Would the Vermont court have been required by the full faith and credit clause to register and enforce the Virginia decision on parentage?

Although there remains a great variance among states, many now formally recognize parental rights of same-sex partners. See, e.g., Elisa B. v. Superior Court, 37 Cal.4th 108, 33 Cal.Rptr.3d 46, 117 P.3d 660 (2005) and C.E.W. v. D.E.W., 845 A.2d 1146 (Me.2004).

Chapter 15

LIFE AND DEATH DECISIONS

I. INTRODUCTION

Over the last several years the law has been invoked regularly by physicians and other health care providers concerned about the ethical, legal, and medical propriety of discontinuing what is now generally referred to as "life sustaining treatment." A number of questions taken to the courts and legislatures arguably are outside the competence of the law. For example, consider what might constitute a "terminal illness," a concept that some have considered relevant in bioethical decision making. While there surely is a medical element to a determination that a patient is "terminally ill," reflection upon the suggestion that there could be a lab test for this condition indicates that it is more than that. Classifying a patient as "terminally ill" depends on a combination of the patient's medical condition and the social, ethical, and legal consequences of the classification. If such a classification triggers a provision in a living will or a durable power of attorney, or if it allows a physician to participate in an assisted suicide, for example, it might be treated differently than if it triggers the patient's relocation from one room to another within a hospital.

If a determination of terminal illness is not solely a medical decision, but rather a hybrid medical, ethical, social, political, and legal determination, where is the locus of appropriate decision making? Should the decision be made by health care professionals alone? By a patient and his family? By a hospital committee? By some external committee? By a court appointed guardian? By the court itself? By the state legislature? By Congress? Should the decision be based upon principles and rules that emerge from medicine, ethics, religion, litigation, or legislative social policy making? Finally, what substantive principles ought to govern the decision-maker?

The difficulties in allocating decision-making authority and developing appropriate substantive principles are not limited to the "terminal illness" classification. They extend to such defining terms as "irreversible coma," "life-sustaining treatment," "death prolonging," "maintenance medical care," "extraordinary means," "heroic efforts," "intractable pain," "suffering," "persistent vegetative state," and even breathing and feeding. For almost every question that arises within the bioethics sphere, we must make two determinations: (1) who should be authorized to resolve the problem, and (2) what substantive principles should apply. Thus, the questions become ones of process (who will decide and how) and substance (what principles must form the basis of a recognized decision). As one might expect, the substantive questions are often hidden in apparently procedural inquiries.

As issues of bioethics have come before the courts over the past few decades, the courts have looked both to the traditions of the common law and the traditions of ethics and medicine to discover principles for decisionmaking. In turn, judicial decisions have often formed the basis for new ethical and medical approaches. In fact, the debate over appropriate ethical policy in determining when life-sustaining treatment should be initiated or discontinued, and over whether physicians should be permitted to aid in the death of a patient, now involve lawyers as much as bioethics scholars, and the public debates on these issues have centered on the judicial resolution of cases as much as on any other source of formal principles, as the celebrated debate on the Schiavo case (see page 758, below) demonstrated. The law is not merely looking to ethics for potential methods of analysis, it is supplanting (some would say usurping) ethics in debate on these issues.

The law is not developed only through rationally justified and formally articulated judicial opinions. The law also comes out of political compromises in legislative action and public perceptions of well-publicized bioethical cases. Congress's decision to fund kidney dialysis through an expansion of the Medicare program for all those who need it, for example, had a substantial effect on determining who would live and who would die. Although it is hard to find a scholar of bioethics who supports Dr. Kevorkian's euthanasia procedures, he is largely responsible for starting the current active public debate on physician assisted death. Infants have names, and cry, and can be cuddled, while fetuses do none of these things; not surprisingly, we are willing to spend a great deal more to treat seriously ill newborns than we are to provide prenatal care.

Finally, the increasingly overtly political nature of some questions—such as whether physicians may assist in their patients' deaths—has brought formerly nonpolitical, personal questions into the political sphere. As a matter of social policy, is this society spending too much to extend the life of the very ill? In 1985, Governor Lamm of Colorado was considered outrageous when he suggested that the elderly may have an obligation to die; today the social consequences of health care decisions have become a matter of real concern to those who realize that all of a family's assets easily could be consumed by a final illness. Additionally, there is real controversy over whether there is any truth to the public perception that medical resources are being used (much less, wasted) to prolong the dying process.

The starting point for caselaw concerning end-of-life treatment decisionmaking is generally the law of informed consent, which is discussed above in chapter 3. The law of informed consent is bolstered by state administrative regulations (often from the state health department or its equivalent), state statutes (for example, patients' rights provisions in some states), state constitutional provisions (including the sometimes state-protected right of privacy), federal regulations (like those governing research involving human subjects), federal statutes, and the United States Constitution. A second starting point often has appeared in cases involving persons who are incapacitated and cannot make decisions for themselves. In such cases, the courts have often referenced the traditional law of guardianship in which the state assumes a parens patriae role to protect the incompetent person. These two starting points stream together in the cases you will be reading, at times finding reconciliation and at times finding conflict.

Because of the significance of medical decisions that will result in death, those decisions are more likely than other medical decisions to be litigated. As a result, general health care decision making principles frequently have been developed in these end-of-life cases, and then generalized to other, arguably easier, cases. Thus, this chapter will address "life and death decisions," but the principles that arise out of it are principles that apply to other health care decisions, too. In the *Cruzan* and *Glucksberg* cases, which you will be reading in this chapter, the United States Supreme Court was called upon to apply the Constitution to end-of-life care, but the principles it established in those cases have ramifications throughout the health care system.

In reading this chapter, consider what role individuals, families, hospitals, health care professionals, courts, legislatures, and others ought to play in dealing with the ethical, medical, legal, social and political questions that often arise out of our new found technical ability to maintain life. As you review the way courts and others have considered individual cases, attempt to distill reasoned principles from their judgments. Is your analysis a procedural or substantive one? Who ought to be involved in the decision making at each point? What principles are relevant to your analysis at each point?

II. THE UNITED STATES CONSTITUTION AND THE "RIGHT TO DIE"

CRUZAN v. DIRECTOR, MISSOURI DEPARTMENT OF HEALTH

Supreme Court of the United States, 1990.
497 U.S. 261, 110 S.Ct. 2841, 111 L.Ed.2d 224.

CHIEF JUSTICE REHNQUIST delivered the opinion of the Court.

Petitioner Nancy Beth Cruzan was rendered incompetent as a result of severe injuries sustained during an automobile accident. Co-petitioners Lester and Joyce Cruzan, Nancy's parents and co-guardians, sought a court order directing the withdrawal of their daughter's artificial feeding and hydration equipment after it became apparent that she had virtually no chance of recovering her cognitive faculties. The Supreme Court of Missouri held that because there was no clear and convincing evidence of Nancy's desire to have life-sustaining treatment withdrawn under such circumstances, her parents lacked authority to effectuate such a request. We granted certiorari and now affirm.

On the night of January 11, 1983, Nancy Cruzan lost control of her car as she traveled down Elm Road in Jasper County, Missouri. The vehicle overturned, and Cruzan was discovered lying face down in a ditch without detectable respiratory or cardiac function. Paramedics were able to restore her breathing and heartbeat at the accident site, and she was transported to a hospital in an unconscious state. An attending neurosurgeon diagnosed her as having sustained probable cerebral contusions compounded by significant anoxia (lack of oxygen). The Missouri trial court in this case found that permanent brain damage generally results after 6 minutes in an anoxic state; it was estimated that Cruzan was deprived of oxygen from 12 to 14 minutes. She remained in a coma for approximately three weeks and then progressed to an unconscious state in which she was able to orally ingest some nutrition. In order to ease feeding and further the recovery, surgeons implanted a gastrostomy feeding and hydration tube in Cruzan with the consent of her then husband. Subsequent rehabilitative efforts proved unavailing. She now lies in a Missouri state hospital in what is commonly referred to as a persistent vegetative state: generally, a condition in which a person exhibits motor reflexes but evinces no indications of significant cognitive function. The State of Missouri is bearing the cost of her care.

After it had become apparent that Nancy Cruzan had virtually no chance of regaining her mental faculties her parents asked hospital employees to terminate the artificial nutrition and hydration procedures. All agree that such a removal would cause her death. The employees refused to honor the request without court approval. The parents then sought and received authorization from the state trial court for termination. The court found that a person in Nancy's condition had a fundamental right under the State and Federal Constitutions to refuse or direct the withdrawal of "death prolonging procedures." The court also found that Nancy's "expressed thoughts at age twenty-five in somewhat serious conversation with a housemate friend that if sick or injured she would not wish to continue her life unless she could live at least halfway normally suggests that given her present condition she would not wish to continue on with her nutrition and hydration."

The Supreme Court of Missouri reversed by a divided vote. * * *

We granted certiorari to consider the question of whether Cruzan has a right under the United States Constitution which would require the hospital to withdraw life-sustaining treatment from her under these circumstances.

* * *

State courts have available to them for decision a number of sources—state constitutions, statutes, and common law—which are not available to us. In this Court, the question is simply and starkly whether the United States Constitution prohibits Missouri from choosing the rule of decision which it did. This is the first case in which we have been squarely presented with the issue of whether the United States Constitution grants what is in common parlance referred to as a "right to die."

* * *

The Fourteenth Amendment provides that no State shall "deprive any person of life, liberty, or property, without due process of law." The principle that a competent person has a constitutionally protected liberty interest in refusing unwanted medical treatment may be inferred from our prior decisions. * * *

But determining that a person has a "liberty interest" under the Due Process Clause does not end the inquiry;[7] "whether respondent's constitution-

---

7. Although many state courts have held that a right to refuse treatment is encom-   passed by a generalized constitutional right of privacy, we have never so held. We believe this

al rights have been violated must be determined by balancing his liberty interests against the relevant state interests." [ ]

Petitioners insist that under the general holdings of our cases, the forced administration of life-sustaining medical treatment, and even of artificially-delivered food and water essential to life, would implicate a competent person's liberty interest. Although we think the logic of the cases discussed above would embrace such a liberty interest, the dramatic consequences involved in refusal of such treatment would inform the inquiry as to whether the deprivation of that interest is constitutionally permissible. But for purposes of this case, we assume that the United States Constitution would grant a competent person a constitutionally protected right to refuse lifesaving hydration and nutrition.

Petitioners go on to assert that an incompetent person should possess the same right in this respect as is possessed by a competent person. * * *

The difficulty with petitioners' claim is that in a sense it begs the question: an incompetent person is not able to make an informed and voluntary choice to exercise a hypothetical right to refuse treatment or any other right. Such a "right" must be exercised for her, if at all, by some sort of surrogate. Here, Missouri has in effect recognized that under certain circumstances a surrogate may act for the patient in electing to have hydration and nutrition withdrawn in such a way as to cause death, but it has established a procedural safeguard to assure that the action of the surrogate conforms as best it may to the wishes expressed by the patient while competent. Missouri requires that evidence of the incompetent's wishes as to the withdrawal of treatment be proved by clear and convincing evidence. The question, then, is whether the United States Constitution forbids the establishment of this procedural requirement by the State. We hold that it does not.

Whether or not Missouri's clear and convincing evidence requirement comports with the United States Constitution depends in part on what interests the State may properly seek to protect in this situation. Missouri relies on its interest in the protection and preservation of human life, and there can be no gainsaying this interest. As a general matter, the States—indeed, all civilized nations—demonstrate their commitment to life by treating homicide as serious crime. Moreover, the majority of States in this country have laws imposing criminal penalties on one who assists another to commit suicide. We do not think a State is required to remain neutral in the face of an informed and voluntary decision by a physically-able adult to starve to death.

But in the context presented here, a State has more particular interests at stake. The choice between life and death is a deeply personal decision of obvious and overwhelming finality. We believe Missouri may legitimately seek to safeguard the personal element of this choice through the imposition of heightened evidentiary requirements. It cannot be disputed that the Due Process Clause protects an interest in life as well as an interest in refusing life-sustaining medical treatment. Not all incompetent patients will have loved ones available to serve as surrogate decisionmakers. * * * A State is entitled to guard against potential abuses in such situations. Similarly, a State is

issue is more properly analyzed in terms of a Fourteenth Amendment liberty interest. See   *Bowers v. Hardwick,* 478 U.S. 186, 194–195 (1986).

entitled to consider that a judicial proceeding to make a determination regarding an incompetent's wishes may very well not be an adversarial one, with the added guarantee of accurate factfinding that the adversary process brings with it. [ ] Finally, we think a State may properly decline to make judgments about the "quality" of life that a particular individual may enjoy, and simply assert an unqualified interest in the preservation of human life to be weighed against the constitutionally protected interests of the individual.

In our view, Missouri has permissibly sought to advance these interests through the adoption of a "clear and convincing" standard of proof to govern such proceedings.

* * *

We think it self-evident that the interests at stake in the instant proceedings are more substantial, both on an individual and societal level, than those involved in a run-of-the-mine civil dispute. But not only does the standard of proof reflect the importance of a particular adjudication, it also serves as "a societal judgment about how the risk of error should be distributed between the litigants." [ ] The more stringent the burden of proof a party must bear, the more that party bears the risk of an erroneous decision. We believe that Missouri may permissibly place an increased risk of an erroneous decision on those seeking to terminate an incompetent individual's life-sustaining treatment. An erroneous decision not to terminate results in a maintenance of the status quo; the possibility of subsequent developments such as advancements in medical science, the discovery of new evidence regarding the patient's intent, changes in the law, or simply the unexpected death of the patient despite the administration of life-sustaining treatment, at least create the potential that a wrong decision will eventually be corrected or its impact mitigated. An erroneous decision to withdraw life-sustaining treatment, however, is not susceptible of correction.

* * *

In sum, we conclude that a State may apply a clear and convincing evidence standard in proceedings where a guardian seeks to discontinue nutrition and hydration of a person diagnosed to be in a persistent vegetative state. * * *

The Supreme Court of Missouri held that in this case the testimony adduced at trial did not amount to clear and convincing proof of the patient's desire to have hydration and nutrition withdrawn. * * * The testimony adduced at trial consisted primarily of Nancy Cruzan's statements made to a housemate about a year before her accident that she would not want to live should she face life as a "vegetable," and other observations to the same effect. The observations did not deal in terms with withdrawal of medical treatment or of hydration and nutrition. We cannot say that the Supreme Court of Missouri committed constitutional error in reaching the conclusion that it did.

* * *

JUSTICE O'CONNOR, concurring.

I agree that a protected liberty interest in refusing unwanted medical treatment may be inferred from our prior decisions, and that the refusal of artificially delivered food and water is encompassed within that liberty interest. I write separately to clarify why I believe this to be so.

As the Court notes, the liberty interest in refusing medical treatment flows from decisions involving the State's invasions into the body. Because our notions of liberty are inextricably entwined with our idea of physical freedom and self-determination, the Court has often deemed state incursions into the body repugnant to the interests protected by the Due Process Clause. [ ] The State's imposition of medical treatment on an unwilling competent adult necessarily involves some form of restraint and intrusion. A seriously ill or dying patient whose wishes are not honored may feel a captive of the machinery required for life-sustaining measures or other medical interventions. Such forced treatment may burden that individual's liberty interests as much as any state coercion. [ ]

The State's artificial provision of nutrition and hydration implicates identical concerns. Artificial feeding cannot readily be distinguished from other forms of medical treatment. * * * Whether or not the techniques used to pass food and water into the patient's alimentary tract are termed "medical treatment," it is clear they all involve some degree of intrusion and restraint. Feeding a patient by means of a nasogastric tube requires a physician to pass a long flexible tube through the patient's nose, throat and esophagus and into the stomach. Because of the discomfort such a tube causes, "[m]any patients need to be restrained forcibly and their hands put into large mittens to prevent them from removing the tube." * * * A gastrostomy tube (as was used to provide food and water to Nancy Cruzan), or jejunostomy tube must be surgically implanted into the stomach or small intestine. * * * Requiring a competent adult to endure such procedures against her will burdens the patient's liberty, dignity, and freedom to determine the course of her own treatment. Accordingly, the liberty guaranteed by the Due Process Clause must protect, if it protects anything, an individual's deeply personal decision to reject medical treatment, including the artificial delivery of food and water.

I also write separately to emphasize that the Court does not today decide the issue whether a State must also give effect to the decisions of a surrogate decisionmaker. In my view, such a duty may well be constitutionally required to protect the patient's liberty interest in refusing medical treatment. Few individuals provide explicit oral or written instructions regarding their intent to refuse medical treatment should they become incompetent. States which decline to consider any evidence other than such instructions may frequently fail to honor a patient's intent. Such failures might be avoided if the State considered an equally probative source of evidence: the patient's appointment of a proxy to make health care decisions on her behalf.

* * *

Today's decision, holding only that the Constitution permits a State to require clear and convincing evidence of Nancy Cruzan's desire to have artificial hydration and nutrition withdrawn, does not preclude a future determination that the Constitution requires the States to implement the decisions of a patient's duly appointed surrogate. Nor does it prevent States from developing other approaches for protecting an incompetent individual's liberty interest in refusing medical treatment. * * * Today we decide only that one State's practice does not violate the Constitution; the more challenging task of crafting appropriate procedures for safeguarding incompetents' liberty interests is entrusted to the "laboratory" of the States, in the first instance.

JUSTICE SCALIA, concurring.

* * *

While I agree with the Court's analysis today, and therefore join in its opinion, I would have preferred that we announce, clearly and promptly, that the federal courts have no business in this field; that American law has always accorded the State the power to prevent, by force if necessary, suicide— including suicide by refusing to take appropriate measures necessary to preserve one's life; that the point at which life becomes "worthless," and the point at which the means necessary to preserve it become "extraordinary" or "inappropriate," are neither set forth in the Constitution nor known to the nine Justices of this Court any better than they are known to nine people picked at random from the Kansas City telephone directory; and hence, that even when it *is* demonstrated by clear and convincing evidence that a patient no longer wishes certain measures to be taken to preserve her life, it is up to the citizens of Missouri to decide, through their elected representatives, whether that wish will be honored. It is quite impossible (because the Constitution says nothing about the matter) that those citizens will decide upon a line less lawful than the one we would choose; and it is unlikely (because we know no more about "life-and-death" than they do) that they will decide upon a line less reasonable.

The text of the Due Process Clause does not protect individuals against deprivations of liberty *simpliciter.* It protects them against deprivations of liberty "without due process of law." To determine that such a deprivation would not occur if Nancy Cruzan were forced to take nourishment against her will, it is unnecessary to reopen the historically recurrent debate over whether "due process" includes substantive restrictions. [ ] It is at least true that no "substantive due process" claim can be maintained unless the claimant demonstrates that the State has deprived him of a right historically and traditionally protected against State interference. [ ] That cannot possibly be established here.

* * * "[T]here is no significant support for the claim that a right to suicide is so rooted in our tradition that it may be deemed 'fundamental' or 'implicit in the concept of ordered liberty.' "[ ]

Petitioners rely on three distinctions to separate Nancy Cruzan's case from ordinary suicide: (1) that she is permanently incapacitated and in pain; (2) that she would bring on her death not by any affirmative act but by merely declining treatment that provides nourishment; and (3) that preventing her from effectuating her presumed wish to die requires violation of her bodily integrity. None of these suffices.

[Scalia points out (1) that pain and incapacity have never constituted legal defenses to a charge of suicide, (2) that the distinction between "action" and "inaction" is logically and legally meaningless, and (3) that preventing suicide often (or always) requires the violation of bodily integrity, and it begs the question of whether the refusal of treatment is itself suicide.]

* * *

Are there, then, no reasonable and humane limits that ought not to be exceeded in requiring an individual to preserve his own life? There obviously are, but they are not set forth in the Due Process Clause. What assures us that those limits will not be exceeded is the same constitutional guarantee that is the source of most of our protection—what protects us, for example, from being assessed a tax of 100% of our income above the subsistence level, from being forbidden to drive cars, or from being required to send our children to school for 10 hours a day, none of which horribles is categorically prohibited by the Constitution. Our salvation is the Equal Protection Clause, which requires the democratic majority to accept for themselves and their loved ones what they impose on you and me. This Court need not, and has no authority to, inject itself into every field of human activity where irrationality and oppression may theoretically occur, and if it tries to do so it will destroy itself.

JUSTICE BRENNAN, with whom JUSTICE MARSHALL and JUSTICE BLACKMUN join, dissenting.

* * *

Today the Court, while tentatively accepting that there is some degree of constitutionally protected liberty interest in avoiding unwanted medical treatment, including life-sustaining medical treatment such as artificial nutrition and hydration, affirms the decision of the Missouri Supreme Court. The majority opinion, as I read it, would affirm that decision on the ground that a State may require "clear and convincing" evidence of Nancy Cruzan's prior decision to forgo life-sustaining treatment under circumstances such as hers in order to ensure that her actual wishes are honored. Because I believe that Nancy Cruzan has a fundamental right to be free of unwanted artificial nutrition and hydration, which right is not outweighed by any interests of the State, and because I find that the improperly biased procedural obstacles imposed by the Missouri Supreme Court impermissibly burden that right, I respectfully dissent. Nancy Cruzan is entitled to choose to die with dignity.

* * *

The right to be free from unwanted medical attention is a right to evaluate the potential benefit of treatment and its possible consequences according to one's own values and to make a personal decision whether to subject oneself to the intrusion. For a patient like Nancy Cruzan, the sole benefit of medical treatment is being kept metabolically alive. Neither artificial nutrition nor any other form of medical treatment available today can cure or in any way ameliorate her condition. Irreversibly vegetative patients are devoid of thought, emotion and sensation; they are permanently and completely unconscious. As the President's Commission concluded in approving the withdrawal of life support equipment from irreversibly vegetative patients:

> "[T]reatment ordinarily aims to benefit a patient through preserving life, relieving pain and suffering, protecting against disability, and returning maximally effective functioning. If a prognosis of permanent unconsciousness is correct, however, continued treatment cannot confer such benefits. Pain and suffering are absent, as are joy, satisfaction, and

pleasure. Disability is total and no return to an even minimal level of social or human functioning is possible." [ ]

There are also affirmative reasons why someone like Nancy might choose to forgo artificial nutrition and hydration under these circumstances. Dying is personal. And it is profound. For many, the thought of an ignoble end, steeped in decay, is abhorrent. A quiet, proud death, bodily integrity intact, is a matter of extreme consequence. "In certain, thankfully rare, circumstances the burden of maintaining the corporeal existence degrades the very humanity it was meant to serve." * * *

Such conditions are, for many, humiliating to contemplate, as is visiting a prolonged and anguished vigil on one's parents, spouse, and children. A long, drawn-out death can have a debilitating effect on family members. [ ] For some, the idea of being remembered in their persistent vegetative states rather than as they were before their illness or accident may be very disturbing.

* * *

The only state interest asserted here is a general interest in the preservation of life. But the State has no legitimate general interest in someone's life, completely abstracted from the interest of the person living that life, that could outweigh the person's choice to avoid medical treatment. * * * [T]he State's general interest in life must accede to Nancy Cruzan's particularized and intense interest in self-determination in her choice of medical treatment. There is simply nothing legitimately within the State's purview to be gained by superseding her decision.

* * *

As the majority recognizes Missouri has a *parens patriae* interest in providing Nancy Cruzan, now incompetent, with as accurate as possible a determination of how she would exercise her rights under these circumstances. * * *

Accuracy, therefore, must be our touchstone. Missouri may constitutionally impose only those procedural requirements that serve to enhance the accuracy of a determination of Nancy Cruzan's wishes or are at least consistent with an accurate determination. The Missouri "safeguard" that the Court upholds today does not meet that standard. The determination needed in this context is whether the incompetent person would choose to live in a persistent vegetative state on life-support or to avoid this medical treatment. Missouri's rule of decision imposes a markedly asymmetrical evidentiary burden. Only evidence of specific statements of treatment choice made by the patient when competent is admissible to support a finding that the patient, now in a persistent vegetative state, would wish to avoid further medical treatment. Moreover, this evidence must be clear and convincing. No proof is required to support a finding that the incompetent person would wish to continue treatment.

Even more than its heightened evidentiary standard, the Missouri court's categorical exclusion of relevant evidence dispenses with any semblance of accurate factfinding. The court adverted to no evidence supporting its decision, but held that no clear and convincing, inherently reliable evidence had been presented to show that Nancy would want to avoid further treatment. * * * The court did not specifically define what kind of evidence it would consider clear and convincing, but its general discussion suggests that only a living will or equivalently formal directive from the patient when competent would meet this standard.

* * *

Finally, I cannot agree with the majority that where it is not possible to determine what choice an incompetent patient would make, a State's role as *parens patriae* permits the State automatically to make that choice itself. [ ] Under fair rules of evidence, it is improbable that a court could not determine what the patient's choice would be. Under the rule of decision adopted by Missouri and upheld today by this Court, such occasions might be numerous. But in neither case does it follow that it is constitutionally acceptable for the State invariably to assume the role of deciding for the patient. A State's legitimate interest in safeguarding a patient's choice cannot be furthered by simply appropriating it.

* * *

JUSTICE STEVENS, dissenting.

* * *

Choices about death touch the core of liberty. Our duty, and the concomitant freedom, to come to terms with the conditions of our own mortality are undoubtedly "so rooted in the traditions and conscience of our people as to be ranked as fundamental," [ ] and indeed are essential incidents of the unalienable rights to life and liberty endowed us by our Creator. [ ]

The more precise constitutional significance of death is difficult to describe; not much may be said with confidence about death unless it is said from faith, and that alone is reason enough to protect the freedom to conform choices about death to individual conscience. We may also, however, justly assume that death is not life's simple opposite, or its necessary terminus, but rather its completion. Our ethical tradition has long regarded an appreciation of mortality as essential to understanding life's significance. It may, in fact, be impossible to live for anything without being prepared to die for something. * * *

These considerations cast into stark relief the injustice, and unconstitutionality, of Missouri's treatment of Nancy Beth Cruzan. Nancy Cruzan's death, when it comes, cannot be an historic act of heroism; it will inevitably be the consequence of her tragic accident. But Nancy Cruzan's interest in life, no less than that of any other person, includes an interest in how she will be thought of after her death by those whose opinions mattered to her. There can be no doubt that her life made her dear to her family, and to others. How she dies will affect how that life is remembered. The trial court's order authorizing Nancy's parents to cease their daughter's treatment would have permitted the family that cares for Nancy to bring to a close her tragedy and her death. Missouri's objection to that order subordinates Nancy's body, her family, and the lasting significance of her life to the State's own interests. The decision we review thereby interferes with constitutional interests of the highest order.

To be constitutionally permissible, Missouri's intrusion upon these fundamental liberties must, at a minimum, bear a reasonable relationship to a legitimate state end. [ ] Missouri asserts that its policy is related to a state interest in the protection of life. In my view, however, it is an effort to define life, rather than to protect it, that is the heart of Missouri's policy.

* * *

Life, particularly human life, is not commonly thought of as a merely physiological condition or function. Its sanctity is often thought to derive from the impossibility of any such reduction. When people speak of life, they often mean to describe the experiences that comprise a person's history, as when it is said that somebody "led a good life."[20] They may also mean to refer to the practical manifestation of the human spirit, a meaning captured by the familiar observation that somebody "added life" to an assembly. If there is a shared thread among the various opinions on this subject, it may be that life is an activity which is at once the matrix for and an integration of a person's interests. In any event, absent some theological abstraction, the idea of life is not conceived separately from the idea of a living person. Yet, it is by precisely such a separation that Missouri asserts an interest in Nancy Cruzan's life in opposition to Nancy Cruzan's own interests.

* * *

Only because Missouri has arrogated to itself the power to define life, and only because the Court permits this usurpation, are Nancy Cruzan's life and liberty put into disquieting conflict. If Nancy Cruzan's life were defined by reference to her own interests, so that her life expired when her biological existence ceased serving *any* of her own interests, then her constitutionally protected interest in freedom from unwanted treatment would not come into conflict with her constitutionally protected interest in life. Conversely, if there were *any* evidence that Nancy Cruzan herself defined life to encompass every form of biological persistence by a human being, so that the continuation of treatment would serve Nancy's own liberty, then once again there would be no conflict between life and liberty. The opposition of life and liberty in this case are thus not the result of Nancy Cruzan's tragic accident, but are instead the artificial consequence of Missouri's effort, and this Court's willingness, to abstract Nancy Cruzan's life from Nancy Cruzan's person.

* * *

The Cruzan family's continuing concern provides a concrete reminder that Nancy Cruzan's interests did not disappear with her vitality or her consciousness. However commendable may be the State's interest in human life, it cannot pursue that interest by appropriating Nancy Cruzan's life as a symbol for its own purposes. Lives do not exist in abstraction from persons, and to pretend otherwise is not to honor but to desecrate the State's responsibility for protecting life. A State that seeks to demonstrate its commitment to life may do so by aiding those who are actively struggling for life and health. In this endeavor, unfortunately, no State can lack for

---

20. It is this sense of the word that explains its use to describe a biography: for example, Boswell's Life of Johnson or Beveridge's The Life of John Marshall. The reader of a book so titled would be surprised to find that it contained a compilation of biological data.

opportunities: there can be no need to make an example of tragic cases like that of Nancy Cruzan.

Notes and Questions

1. Subsequent to this judgment the Missouri trial court heard additional evidence, provided by Nancy Cruzan's friends and colleagues, that she had made explicit and unambiguous statements that demonstrated, clearly and convincingly, that she would not want continued the treatment that she was receiving. Without opposition from the Attorney General of Missouri, the trial court authorized Ms. Cruzan's guardians to terminate her nutrition and hydration.

2. There are many ethical approaches to health care decisionmaking. The approach that has most influenced judicial decisionmaking is one that relies on the identification and application of particular principles, often called the "principlist approach." Tom Beauchamp and James Childress, Principles of Biomedical Ethics (5th ed. 2001). There are three primary substantive principles that operate here: autonomy, beneficence, and social justice. Autonomy and beneficence have been the principles most often relied upon in caselaw, which has largely ignored questions of cost (and allocation and rationing) that implicate social justice. The principle of autonomy declares that each person is in control of his own person, including his body and mind. This principle, in its purest form, presumes that no other person or social institution ought to overrule a person's choice, whether or not that choice is "right" from an external perspective. Essentially, it is a libertarian principle. The principle of beneficence declares that what is best for each person should be done. The principle incorporates both the negative obligation of nonmaleficence ("primum non nocere"—"first of all, do no harm"—the foundation of the Hippocratic Oath) and the positive obligation to do that which is good. Thus, a physician is obliged to provide the highest quality of medical care for her patients. Similarly, a physician ought to treat a seriously ill newborn, or incapacited adult child, in a way that best serves that patient, whatever she may think her patient "wants" and no matter what the parents of the patient may desire.

When a person does not desire what others determine to be in her best interests, the principles of autonomy and beneficence conflict. For example, if we consider the continued life of a healthy person to be in that person's interest, the values of autonomy and beneficence conflict when a healthy competent adult decides to take his own life. You can see that there can be serious conflict over what is in any individual's self interest and that values other than autonomy and beneficence will come into play in some of these cases. Did the Cruzan opinions address autonomy and beneficence? Did they imply any other values?

3. Does the Opinion of the Court recognize a constitutional right to die? Many authoritative sources presumed that the opinion did recognize a constitutionally protected liberty interest in a competent person to refuse unwanted medical treatment. Indeed, the syllabus prepared for the Court says just that, and the case was hailed by the New York Times as the first to recognize a right to die. On the other hand, the Chief Justice's language does not support such a conclusion. While the majority agrees that "[t]he principle that a competent person has a constitutionally protected liberty interest in refusing unwanted medical treatment *may* be inferred from our prior decisions," (emphasis added) the Court never makes the inference itself. In fact, the opinion says explicitly that "*for purposes of this case,* we assume that the United States Constitution would grant a competent person a constitutionally protected right to refuse life saving nutrition and hydration." (emphasis added)

Why is this assumption limited to the "purposes of this case"? Does the Court question (1) whether there is a constitutionally protected liberty interest in refusing unwanted medical treatment, (2) whether the right extends to life sustaining treatment, or (3) whether it covers hydration and nutrition?

It must have been difficult for the Chief Justice to craft an opinion that would be joined by a majority of the court. Justice Scalia clearly does not believe that there is any constitutional right implicated. If the Chief Justice were to formally recognize a constitutional right, he might have lost Justice Scalia's signature—and thus lost an opportunity for there to be any majority opinion.

The dissents filed in this case are long and obviously heartfelt. Do the dissenters, all of whom would recognize a constitutionally protected right to die, and Justice O'Connor, who would also do so, create a majority in support of this constitutional position?

4. The majority opinion permits a state to limit its consideration to those wishes previously expressed by the patient and to ignore the decisions of another person acting on behalf of the patient. In fact, the Court explicitly does not address the question of whether a state must defer to an appropriately nominated surrogate acting on behalf of the patient. On the other hand, the dissenting justices would recognize the decisions of a surrogate under appropriate circumstances, and Justice O'Connor suggests that the duty to give effect to those decisions "may well be constitutionally required." What is the constitutional status of surrogate decisionmaking after *Cruzan*?

5. Note that none of the opinions refers to the "right of privacy," a term which has caused the Court such tremendous grief in the abortion context. The Chief Justice analyzes this issue in the more general terms of a fourteenth amendment liberty interest, and none of the counsel argued the case in terms of the right to privacy. Apparently the Court just did not wish to entangle itself any further with the "P" word.

6. Seven years after *Cruzan* was decided, the Supreme Court again considered end-of-life medical decision making in Washington v. Glucksberg, below at page 773, which addressed the Constitutional status of physician assisted death. Chief Justice Rehnquist, writing for the Court, announced that "We have * * * assumed, and strongly suggested, that the Due Process Clause protects the traditional right to refuse unwanted lifesaving medical treatment." Is that an accurate description of the holding in *Cruzan*? A few pages later, in the same opinion, Chief Justice Rehnquist describes the *Cruzan* case slightly differently: "[A]lthough Cruzan is often described as a 'right to die' case [], we were, in fact, more precise: we assumed that the Constitution granted competent persons a 'constitutionally protected right to refuse lifesaving hydration and nutrition.' "Is that a more accurate account of what the Court decided in *Cruzan*?

Justice O'Connor, concurring in *Glucksberg*, says that "there is no need to address the question whether suffering patients have a constitutionally cognizable interest in obtaining relief from the suffering that they may experience in the last days of their lives." This issue, according to Justice O'Connor, was decided by *Cruzan*. Is she right? Justice Stevens also commented on the *Cruzan* case in the course of his concurring opinion in *Glucksberg*. He explained that "Cruzan did give recognition * * * to the more specific interest in making decisions about how to confront an imminent death. * * * Cruzan makes it clear that some individuals who no longer have the option of deciding whether to live or to die because they are already on the threshold of death have a constitutionally protected interest [in deciding how they will die] that may outweigh the State's interest in preserving life at all costs." Is this an accurate description of *Cruzan*? If the Justices who participated in both the *Cruzan* and *Glucksberg* cases cannot agree on just what the case really means, how can your health law teacher expect you to do so?

7. Constitutional arguments are not limited to those who want to forgo treatment; they can be asserted by seriously ill patients who want access to treatment, too. In Abigail Alliance v. von Eschenbach, 495 F.3d 695 (D.C. Cir. 2007) the D.C. Circuit, en banc, addressed the argument that a terminally ill patient had a Constitutional right to access drugs that had not yet been approved by the FDA. The Abigail Alliance, named for a 21–year-old student who died of cancer after being denied drugs in the earliest stages of testing, argued that *Cruzan* and *Glucksberg* paved the way for the recognition of a Constitutional right to access these not-yet-approved treatments, at least when those treatments provided the only hope of survival for the patient. The Court found, 8–2, that there was no such right, reversing the decision of the original three judge panel, Abigail Alliance v. von Eschenbach, 445 F.3d 470 (D.C. Cir. 2006), in part because of the longstanding tradition of governmental drug safety efforts in our legal system. The majority and the spirited dissenters disagreed about the way to articulate the right that Abigail Alliance sought to have recognized in this case. Was the right asserted the right "to access experimental and unproven drugs," as the majority suggested, or the right to "try to save one's life," as the dissent argued? As you have seen in *Cruzan*, and as you will recognize in *Glucksberg*, below, the due process arguments often depend upon the precise articulation of the right sought to be protected. Do you think the *Cruzan* case provides support for the position that an otherwise terminally ill cancer patient has access to drugs that have not yet been found to be effective through the government's required administrative process? From a Constitutional perspective, is the argument that a patient is entitled to forgo treatment any different from the argument that a patient is entitled to have access to treatment? Similar issues were at stake in the litigation over access to marijuana for medical purposes.

8. Except for a glancing reference by Justice Stevens in his dissent, the opinions do not consider the cost of providing care to Nancy Cruzan. Should the cost be relevant? Should the Constitutional right (to liberty or to life) vary depending on who bears the cost? See Harris v. McRae, 448 U.S. 297, 100 S.Ct. 2671, 65 L.Ed.2d 784 (1980), concerning federal funding for abortions. Would your analysis of this case be any different if the costs were being paid by an insurance company, by Ms. Cruzan's parents, or by community fund raising in Nancy Cruzan's neighborhood, rather than by the state of Missouri? Should the one who pays the bills get to participate in the health care decision making?

Judge Blackmar's dissent to the Missouri Supreme Court's opinion in *Cruzan* addresses the inconsistency of requiring some patients to be kept alive, at great expense, while the state is unable (or unwilling) to provide adequate care to others. He points out:

> The absolutist position is also infirm because the state does not stand prepared to finance the preservation of life, without regard to the cost, in very many cases. In this particular case the state has Nancy in its possession, and is litigating its right to keep her. Yet, several years ago, a respected judge needed extraordinary treatment which the hospital in which he was a patient was not willing to furnish without a huge advance deposit and the state apparently had no desire to help out. Many people die because of the

unavailability of heroic medical treatment. It simply cannot be said that the state's interest in preserving and prolonging life is absolute.

760 S.W.2d at 429. Judge Blackmar also points out, in a footnote, that "an absolutist would undoubtedly be offended by an inquiry as to whether the state, by prolonging Nancy's life at its own expense, is disabling itself from [providing] needed treatment to others who do not have such dire prognosis." 760 S.W.2d at 429 n. 4.

9. The result of the *Cruzan* case (confirmed in *Glucksberg*) is that most law regarding health care decision making has continued to be established on a state by state basis; there seems to be very little, if any, United States Constitutional limit on what states may do. *Cruzan* may have deflected the "right to die" debate to the political decisionmaking process in the same way that several abortion decisions have done. See Chapter 14, above.

10. The decision of the United States Supreme Court to opt out of providing much Constitutional guidance to the states may allow a crazy quilt of state laws to persist such that a patient who would have a "right to die" that could be exercised by his family in California or New Jersey would not have that right (or would not have a right that could be exercised by his family) in Missouri, Michigan or New York. Indeed, the conditions and extent of, and the restrictions and exceptions to, any "right to die" might be different in each state. State policies will thus require different results in factually identical cases. Is there anything wrong with this?

What would happen if Nancy Cruzan's family had decided to move her to the Yale Medical Center "because of the more favorable medical facilities" there? Could they have moved her from Missouri to Connecticut, where removal of the gastrostomy clearly would be legally permitted, just for the purpose of removing the gastrostomy? If they could not, then Nancy Cruzan could have become a prisoner of a state that rejects her family's values—values that have been incorporated into official state policies in other jurisdictions. If they could move her, however, Missouri would have allowed the family to undercut the important policy objectives of the state law and imperil the very life the law was designed to protect. Would it violate any criminal statute to move someone across state lines for the purpose of avoiding the laws governing termination of life support in the first state? Could a state make such an action a crime?

In early 1991 the father and guardian of Christine Busalacchi sought to have his daughter moved from Missouri to Minnesota for medical consultation with a nationally known neurologist who had consulted on several leading cases that resulted in the withdrawal of life-sustaining treatment. Ms. Busalacchi, who had been living in the same nursing home that had housed Nancy Cruzan, was arguably in a persistent vegetative state. The state of Missouri sought (and obtained) an order forbidding the move because of the fear that her father wanted only to find some place where his daughter could die. A divided Missouri Court of Appeals determined that the trial court was required to commence a new hearing on whether the move could be justified by other medical objectives. In deciding the case, the majority made it clear that "* * * we will not permit [the] guardian to forum shop in an effort to control whether Christine lives or dies." The dissent argued that "Minnesota is not a medical or ethical wasteland * * *. There is a parochial arrogance in suggesting, as the state does, that only in Missouri can Christine's medical, physical, and legal well being be protected and only here will her best interests be considered." Matter of Busalacchi, 1991 WL 26851 (Mo.App. 1991), transferred to Mo. Sup. Ct. Ultimately, the State decided not to pursue the case, and Busalacchi died in Missouri. See also Mack v. Mack, 329 Md. 188, 618

A.2d 744 (1993) (Maryland Court denies full faith and credit to Florida judgment appointing the Florida-resident wife of a Maryland patient in persistent vegetative state as guardian so that patient could be removed to Florida, where life sustaining treatment could be withdrawn.)

11.   Missouri is not the only state to adopt the strict standard approved by the majority and decried by the dissenters. At the least, that standard has also been adopted in New York and Michigan. See In re Westchester County Medical Center on Behalf of O'Connor, 72 N.Y.2d 517, 534 N.Y.S.2d 886, 531 N.E.2d 607 (1988) and In re Martin, 450 Mich. 204, 538 N.W.2d 399 (1995). Arguably, the same standard has also been adopted in California, Conservatorship of Wendland, 26 Cal.4th 519, 110 Cal.Rptr.2d 412, 28 P.3d 151 (2001), in at least one particular circumstance of a patient in a minimally conscious state.

12.   There is much to discuss about the health care decisionmaking issues in *Cruzan*, and the rest of this chapter is devoted to that inquiry. The September/October 1990 Hastings Center Report includes an excellent symposium on all aspects of the *Cruzan* case. The symposium includes an article written by counsel for the Cruzans, one by Christine Busalacchi's father, and several by leading bioethics scholars.

III. PATIENTS DECIDING FOR THEMSELVES

Problem: The Christian Scientist in the Emergency Room

Shortly after Ms. Elizabeth Boroff was hit by a drunk driver who went through a red light and directly into her Volkswagen bus, she found herself being attended by paramedics and loaded into an ambulance for a trip to the Big County General Hospital emergency room. Although she was briefly unconscious at the scene of the accident, and although she suffered a very substantial blood loss, several broken bones and a partially crushed skull, she had regained consciousness by her arrival at the hospital. The doctors explained to her that her life was at risk and that she needed a blood transfusion and brain surgery immediately. She explained that she was a Christian Scientist, that she believed in the healing power of prayer, that she rejected medical care, and that she wished to be discharged immediately so that she could consult a Christian Science healer.

A quick conference of emergency room staff revealed a consensus that failure to relieve the pressure caused by her intracranial bleed would result in loss of consciousness within a few hours, and, possibly, her death. When this information was provided to her she remained unmoved. The hospital staff asked her to identify her next of kin, and she explained that she was a widow with no living relatives except for her seven minor children, ages 1 through 9. Further inquiries revealed that she was the sole support for these children, that she had no life insurance, that she had an elementary school education, and that she had been employed as a clerk since her husband, a self-employed maintenance man, was himself killed in an automobile accident a year ago. Uncertain of what to do, the emergency room staff called you, the hospital legal counsel, for advice. What advice should you give? Should they discharge Ms. Boroff, as she requests? Should you commence a legal action to keep her in the hospital and institute treatment? If you were to file a legal action, what relief would you seek, and what would be the substantive basis of your claim?

A. THE GENERAL RULE

BOUVIA v. SUPERIOR COURT

California Court of Appeal, Second District, 1986.
179 Cal.App.3d 1127, 225 Cal.Rptr. 297.

BEACH, ASSOCIATE JUSTICE.

Petitioner, Elizabeth Bouvia, a patient in a public hospital, seeks the removal from her body of a nasogastric tube inserted and maintained against her will and without her consent by physicians who so placed it for the purpose of keeping her alive through involuntary forced feeding.

* * *

Petitioner is a 28–year–old woman. Since birth she has been afflicted with and suffered from severe cerebral palsy. She is quadriplegic. She is now a patient at a public hospital maintained by one of the real parties in interest, the County of Los Angeles. Other parties are physicians, nurses and the medical and support staff employed by the County of Los Angeles. Petitioner's physical handicaps of palsy and quadriplegia have progressed to the point where she is completely bedridden. Except for a few fingers of one hand and some slight head and facial movements, she is immobile. She is physically helpless and wholly unable to care for herself. * * * She suffers also from degenerative and severely crippling arthritis. She is in continual pain. * * *

She is intelligent, very mentally competent. She earned a college degree. She was married but her husband has left her. She suffered a miscarriage. She lived with her parents until her father told her that they could no longer care for her. She has stayed intermittently with friends and at public facilities. A search for a permanent place to live where she might receive the constant care which she needs has been unsuccessful. She is without financial means to support herself and, therefore, must accept public assistance for medical and other care.

She has on several occasions expressed the desire to die. In 1983 she sought the right to be cared for in a public hospital in Riverside County while she intentionally "starved herself to death." A court in that county denied her judicial assistance to accomplish that goal. * * * Thereafter, friends took her to several different facilities, both public and private, arriving finally at her present location. Efforts by * * * social workers to find her an apartment of her own with publicly paid live-in help or regular visiting nurses to care for her, or some other suitable facility have proved fruitless.

Petitioner must be spoon fed in order to eat. Her present medical and dietary staff have determined that she is not consuming a sufficient amount of nutrients. Petitioner stops eating when she feels she cannot orally swallow more, without nausea and vomiting. As she cannot now retain solids, she is fed soft liquid-like food. Because of her previously announced resolve to starve herself, the medical staff feared her weight loss might reach a life-threatening level. Her weight since admission to real parties' facility seems to hover between 65 and 70 pounds. Accordingly, they inserted the subject tube against her will and contrary to her express written instructions.*

---

* Her instructions were dictated to her lawyers, written by them and signed by her by means of her making a feeble "x" on the paper with a pen which she held in her mouth.

Petitioner's counsel argue that her weight loss was not such as to be life threatening and therefore the tube is unnecessary. However, the trial court found to the contrary as a matter of fact, a finding which we must accept. Nonetheless, the point is immaterial, for, as we will explain, a patient has the right to refuse any medical treatment or medical service, even when such treatment is labeled "furnishing nourishment and hydration." This right exists even if its exercise creates a "life threatening condition."

THE RIGHT TO REFUSE MEDICAL TREATMENT

"[A] person of adult years and in sound mind has the right, in the exercise of control over his own body, to determine whether or not to submit to lawful medical treatment." [ ] It follows that such a patient has the right to refuse *any* medical treatment, even that which may save or prolong her life. [ ]

* * *

A recent Presidential Commission for the Study of Ethical Problems in Medicine and Biomedical and Behavioral Research concluded in part: "The voluntary choice of a competent and informed patient should determine whether or not life-sustaining therapy will be undertaken, just as such choices provide the basis for other decisions about medical treatment. Health care institutions and professionals should try to enhance patients' abilities to make decisions on their own behalf and to promote understanding of the available treatment options * * *. Health care professionals serve patients best by maintaining a presumption in favor of sustaining life, while recognizing that competent patients are entitled to choose to forgo any treatments, including those that sustain life."

* * *

The American Hospital Association Policy and Statement of Patients' Choices of Treatment Options, approved by the American Hospital Association in February of 1985 discusses the value of a collaborative relationship between the patient and the physician and states in pertinent part: "Whenever possible, however, the authority to determine the course of treatment, if any, should rest with the patient" and "the right to choose treatment includes the right to refuse a specific treatment *or all treatment* * * *."

* * *

Significant also is the statement adopted on March 15, 1986, by the Council on Ethical and Judicial Affairs of the American Medical Association. It is entitled "Withholding or Withdrawing Life Prolonging Medical Treatment." In pertinent part, it declares: "The social commitment of the physician is to sustain life and relieve suffering. Where the performance of one duty conflicts with the other, the choice of the patient, or his family or legal representative if the patient is incompetent to act in his own behalf, should prevail."

* * *

It is indisputable that petitioner is mentally competent. She is not comatose. She is quite intelligent, alert and understands the risks involved.

THE CLAIMED EXCEPTIONS TO THE PATIENT'S RIGHT TO CHOOSE ARE INAPPLICABLE

* * * The real parties in interest, a county hospital, its physicians and administrators, urge that the interests of the State should prevail over the rights of Elizabeth Bouvia to refuse treatment. Advanced by real parties under this argument are the State's interests in (1) preserving life, (2) preventing suicide, (3) protecting innocent third parties, and (4) maintaining the ethical standards of the medical profession, including the right of physicians to effectively render necessary and appropriate medical service and to refuse treatment to an uncooperative and disruptive patient. Included, whether as part of the above or as separate and additional arguments, are what real parties assert as distinctive facts not present in other cases, i.e., (1) petitioner is a patient in a public facility, thereby making the State a party to the result of her conduct, (2) she is not comatose, nor incurably, nor terminally ill, nor in a vegetative state, all conditions which have justified the termination of life-support system in other instances, (3) she has asked for medical treatment, therefore, she cannot accept a part of it while cutting off the part that would be effective, and (4) she is, in truth, trying to starve herself to death and the State will not be a party to a suicide.

* * *

At bench the trial court concluded that with sufficient feeding petitioner could live an additional 15 to 20 years; therefore, the preservation of petitioner's life for that period outweighed her right to decide. In so holding the trial court mistakenly attached undue importance to the *amount of time* possibly available to petitioner, and failed to give equal weight and consideration for the *quality* of that life; an equal, if not more significant, consideration.

All decisions permitting cessation of medical treatment or life-support procedures to some degree hastened the arrival of death. In part, at least, this was permitted because the quality of life during the time remaining in those cases had been terribly diminished. In Elizabeth Bouvia's view, the quality of her life has been diminished to the point of hopelessness, uselessness, unenjoyability and frustration. She, as the patient, lying helplessly in bed, unable to care for herself, may consider her existence meaningless. She cannot be faulted for so concluding. If her right to choose may not be exercised because there remains to her, in the opinion of a court, a physician or some committee, a certain arbitrary number of years, months, or days, her right will have lost its value and meaning.

Who shall say what the minimum amount of available life must be? Does it matter if it be 15 to 20 years, 15 to 20 months, or 15 to 20 days, if such life has been physically destroyed and its quality, dignity and purpose gone? As in all matters lines must be drawn at some point, somewhere, but that decision must ultimately belong to the one whose life is in issue.

Here Elizabeth Bouvia's decision to forgo medical treatment or life-support through a mechanical means belongs to her. It is not a medical decision for her physicians to make. Neither is it a legal question whose soundness is to be resolved by lawyers or judges. It is not a conditional right subject to approval by ethics committees or courts of law. It is a moral and philosophical decision that, being a competent adult, is hers alone.

* * *

Here, if force fed, petitioner faces 15 to 20 years of a painful existence, endurable only by the constant administrations of morphine. Her condition is irreversible. There is no cure for her palsy or arthritis. Petitioner would have to be fed, cleaned, turned, bedded, toileted by others for 15 to 20 years! Although alert, bright, sensitive, perhaps even brave and feisty, she must lie immobile, unable to exist except through physical acts of others. Her mind and spirit may be free to take great flights but she herself is imprisoned and must lie physically helpless subject to the ignominy, embarrassment, humiliation and dehumanizing aspects created by her helplessness. We do not believe it is the policy of this State that all and every life must be preserved against the will of the sufferer. It is incongruous, if not monstrous, for medical practitioners to assert their right to preserve a life that someone else must live, or, more accurately, endure, for "15 to 20 years." We cannot conceive it to be the policy of this State to inflict such an ordeal upon anyone.

* * * Being competent she has the right to live out the remainder of her natural life in dignity and peace. It is precisely the aim and purpose of the many decisions upholding the withdrawal of life-support systems to accord and provide as large a measure of dignity, respect and comfort as possible to every patient for the remainder of his days, whatever be their number. This goal is not to hasten death, though its earlier arrival may be an expected and understood likelihood.

* * *

Moreover, the trial court seriously erred by basing its decision on the "motives" behind Elizabeth Bouvia's decision to exercise her rights. If a right exists, it matters not what "motivates" its exercise. We find nothing in the law to suggest the right to refuse medical treatment may be exercised only if the patient's *motives* meet someone else's approval. It certainly is not illegal or immoral to prefer a natural, albeit sooner, death than a drugged life attached to a mechanical device.

* * *

We do not purport to establish what will constitute proper medical practice in all other cases or even other aspects of the care to be provided petitioner. We hold only that her right to refuse medical treatment even of the life-sustaining variety, entitles her to the immediate removal of the nasogastric tube that has been involuntarily inserted into her body. The hospital and medical staff are still free to perform a substantial, if not the greater part of their duty, i.e., that of trying to alleviate Bouvia's pain and suffering.

Petitioner is without means to go to a private hospital and, apparently, real parties' hospital as a public facility was required to accept her. Having done so it may not deny her relief from pain and suffering merely because she has chosen to exercise her fundamental right to protect what little privacy remains to her.

Personal dignity is a part of one's right of privacy. * * *

Notes and Questions

1.   The *Bouvia* court depended, in large part, upon Bartling v. Superior Court, 163 Cal.App.3d 186, 209 Cal.Rptr. 220 (1984), the first case to confirm a competent patient's right to make decisions to forgo life sustaining treatment. Mr. Bartling was a competent adult suffering from depression (the original reason for his hospitalization), a tumor on his lung, and emphysema. He had a living will, a separate declaration asking that treatment be discontinued, and a durable power of attorney appointing his wife to make his health care decisions. He and his wife continuously asked that the ventilator that was preserving his life be removed, and he, his wife and his daughter all executed documents releasing the hospital from any liability claims arising out of honoring Mr. Bartling's request. Still, the hospital, which was a Christian hospital established and operated on pro-life principles, opposed allowing Mr. Bartling to die on ethical grounds. The California Court of Appeal found that the trial court should have granted Mr. Bartling's request for an injunction against the hospital, concluding that, "if the right to patient self-determination as to his own medical treatment means anything at all, it must be paramount to the interests of the patient's hospital and doctors. The right of a competent adult to refuse medical treatment is a constitutionally guaranteed right which must not be abridged."

2.   Do you agree that the hospital had an obligation to accept Ms. Bouvia and provide her with medical relief from her pain and suffering, even though the physicians and hospital found her conduct immoral and her request an abuse of the medical profession? Is the obligation anything more than to provide adequate end-of-life care, even when the patient refuses a particular course of treatment? Cf. Brophy v. New England Sinai Hospital, Inc., 398 Mass. 417, 497 N.E.2d 626 (1986), where the Massachusetts Supreme Judicial Court found that a patient in a persistent vegetative state could, through his family, deny consent to feeding through a gastric tube, but that the hospital need not remove or clamp the tube if it found it to be contrary to the ethical dictates of the medical profession. The *Brophy* decision required that the family move the patient to another medical institution more receptive to his apparent desires for his feeding tube to be removed. The New Jersey Supreme Court took a middle ground In re Jobes, 108 N.J. 394, 529 A.2d 434, 450 (1987):

> The trial court held that the nursing home could refuse to participate in the withdrawal of the j-tube by keeping Mrs. Jobes connected to it until she is transferred out of that facility. Under the circumstances of this case, we disagree, and we reverse that portion of the trial court's order.

> Mrs. Jobes' family had no reason to believe that they were surrendering the right to choose among medical alternatives when they placed her in the nursing home. [ ] The nursing home apparently did not inform Mrs. Jobes' family about its policy toward artificial feeding until May of 1985 when they requested that the j-tube be withdrawn. In fact there is no indication that this policy has ever been formalized. Under these circumstances Mrs. Jobes and her family were entitled to rely on the nursing home's willingness to defer to their choice among courses of medical treatment. * * *

> We do not decide the case in which a nursing home gave notice of its policy not to participate in the withdrawal or withholding of artificial feeding at the time of a patient's admission. Thus, we do not hold that such a policy is never enforceable. But we are confident in this case that it would be wrong to allow the nursing home to discharge Mrs. Jobes. The evidence indicates that at this point it would be extremely difficult, perhaps impossible, to find another facility that would accept Mrs. Jobes as a patient. Therefore, to allow

the nursing home to discharge Mrs. Jobes if her family does not consent to continued artificial feeding would essentially frustrate Mrs. Jobes' right of self-determination.

Some state statutes governing end-of-life decisionmaking include specific provisions for situations in which health care professionals or facilities object to the decisions of patients (or their surrogates). See, e.g., Uniform Health–Care Decisions Act, below. The option to inform patients in advance of particular policies and then seek transfer is the most common compromise. See generally George Annas, Transferring the Ethical Hot Potato, 17 Hastings Ctr. Rep. 20 (1987) (explaining how patients' rights are threatened by legal decisions that allow medical institutions to discharge "patients who do not accept everything they offer"). Many states also have enacted statutes allowing such conscience-based actions by health care professionals in particular contexts, such as abortion and assisted suicide. For a thorough discussion of this issue in the context of the pharmacist's obligation to dispense some controversial kinds of contraceptive medication, see chapter 14. For a discussion of the employment issues that could arise out of a decision by a health care professional to refrain from providing legal but morally objectionable care, see Chapter 8. Might such a decision also constitute abandonment? See chapter 3.

These conflicts raise serious moral and ethical issues. See discussion in Martha Swartz, "Conscience Clauses" or "Unconscionable Clauses": Personal Believes versus Professional Responsibilities, 6 Yale J. Health Pol'y L. & Ethics 269 (2006); Rebecca Dresser, Professionals, Conformity, and Conscience, 35 Hastings Ctr. Rep. 6 (2005); Edmund Pellegrino, The Physician's Conscience, Conscience Clauses, and Religious Belief: A Catholic Perspective, 30 Fordham U. Urban L. J. 221 (2002). Furthermore, especially when extended to account for health care facilities, these moral and religious conflicts can raise serious public policy and access concerns. See, Brietta Clark, When Free Exercise Exemptions Undermine Religious Liberty and the Liberty of Conscience: A Case Study of the Catholic Hospital Conflict, 82 Or. L. Rev. 625 (2003); Kathleen Boozang, Deciding the Fate of Religious Hospitals in the Emerging Health Care Market, 31 Hous. L. Rev. 1429 (1995).

3. If we take seriously the *Bouvia* suggestion that hospitals have an obligation to provide comfort to patients who choose to forgo treatment and thus die, do physicians have an obligation to inform patients of the various ways of dying that are available to them, and the consequences of choosing any one of them? Consider Margaret Battin, The Least Worst Death, 13 Hastings Ctr. Rep. 13–16 (April 1983):

> In the face of irreversible, terminal illness, a patient may wish to die sooner but "naturally," without artificial prolongation of any kind. By doing so, the patient may believe he is choosing a death that is, as a contributor to the *New England Journal of Medicine* has put it, "comfortable, decent, and peaceful". "[N]atural death," the patient may assume, means a death that is easier than a medically prolonged one.

> [H]e may assume that it will allow time for reviewing life and saying farewell to family and loved ones, for last rites or final words, for passing on hopes, wisdom, confessions, and blessings to the next generation. These ideas are of course heavily stereotyped * * * : Even the very term "natural" may have stereotyped connotations for the patient: something close to nature, uncontrived, and appropriate. As a result of these notions, the patient often takes "natural death" to be a painless, conscious, dignified, culminative slipping-away.

Now consider what sorts of death actually occur under the rubric of "natural death." A patient suffers a cardiac arrest and is not resuscitated. Result: sudden unconsciousness, without pain, and death within a number of seconds. Or a patient has an infection that is not treated. Result: * * * fever, delirium, rigor or shaking, and lightheadedness; death usually takes one or two days, depending on the organism involved.

* * *

What the patient who rejects active euthanasia or assisted suicide may realistically hope for is this: the least worst death among those that could naturally occur. Not all unavoidable surrenders need involve rout: in the face of inevitable death, the physician becomes strategist, the deviser of plans for how to meet death most favorably.

* * *

To recognize the patient's right to autonomous choice in matters concerning the treatment of his own body, the physician must provide information about all the legal options open to him, not just information sufficient to choose between accepting or rejecting a single proposed procedure.

* * *

In the current enthusiasm for "natural death" it is not patient autonomy that dismays physicians. What does dismay them is the way in which respect for patient autonomy can lead to cruel results. The cure for that dismay lies in the realization that the physician can contribute to the *genuine* honoring of the patient's autonomy and rights, assuring him of "natural death" in the way in which the patient understands it, and still remain within the confines of good medical practice and the law.

4. After the California Supreme Court confirmed Ms. Bouvia's right to choose to die, she changed her mind and decided to accept the medical care necessary to treat her pain and to keep her alive. She appeared on television (on "60 minutes") in 1998, when she expressed the hope that she would die soon. Why would someone seek judicial confirmation of a "right to die" and then not act upon it? Does it indicate that people waver on this issue? Does it suggest that knowing that one has the choice–when it becomes necessary–contributes to that person's well being? Are those who seek a judicially confirmed "right to die" really seeking control over their destiny, not their death? Ironically, the existence of a right to die may be the reason that some people choose to live. For a discussion of related issues, see L.M. Cohen, M.J. Germain and D.M. Poppel, Practical Considerations in Dialysis Withdrawal: "To Have That Option is a Blessing," 289 JAMA 2113 (2002).

5. The court describes the quality of Elizabeth Bouvia's life in startling terms. Does the court describe her life as useless, meaningless, and embarrassing solely because that was her view of her own life, or does the court agree that this must be the case? *Bouvia* is viewed by disabilities rights advocates as a case which denigrated the value of the lives of persons who were dependent and disabled and in which a disabled person was driven to desperate measures for lack of the support she needed to live to her fullest capacity. See, e.g., Paul K. Longmore, Elizabeth Bouvia, Assisted Suicide and Social Prejudice, 3 Issues L. & Med. 141 (1987). See also, Alicia Ouellette, Disability and the End of Life, 85 Or. L. Rev. 123 (2006). The disabilities rights movement has become a key player in controversies over end-of-life decisionmaking.

6. Is it surprising that the fundamental principle that competent adults can make all of their own health care decisions has made it into the statutes of only a very few states? For an exception to this general rule, see N.M. Stat. Ann. Section 24–7A–2. Especially after the concern shown for this issue in *Bouvia*, one might expect more legislatures to have confirmed this right. Have they failed to do so because the law is so clear that legislative confirmation is unnecessary, or because there is a real dispute about the substance of the principle?

7. It is not always easy to determine the wishes of a competent patient. In order to express a wish, the patient must be fully informed, but the very information that is most useful to a patient in deciding whether to forgo life-sustaining medical treatment may not be available, or the health care providers may not realize that it is relevant to the patient making the decision. One recent study set out to determine what kind of information is significant to patients making decisions about the removal of life-sustaining medical care:

> The provision of care at the end of life should honor patients' preferences. If these preferences are to be honored, they must first be understood. Our results suggest than an understanding of patients' preferences depends on an assessment of [1] how they view the burden of treatment [2] in relation to their possible outcomes and [3] their likelihood. The possibility of functional or cognitive impairment has a particularly important role in patients' preferences and thus merits explicit consideration in advance care planning.

Terri R. Fried et al., Understanding the Treatment Preferences of Seriously Ill Patients, 346 N. Eng. J. Med. 1061 (2002). What information would be relevant to you in making decisions about end-of-life care? Do you think that this study was correct in determining the significance of possible functional or cognitive impairments? For an interesting approach to this issue, see D.E. Meier & R.S. Morrison, Autonomy Reconsidered, 346 NEJM 1087 (2002). For evaluations of these issues within particular medical specialties, A.K. Simonds, Ethics and Decision Making in End Stage Lung Disease, 58 Thorax 272 (2003) and C.O. Granai, What Matters Matter?, 102 Obstetrics & Gynecology 393 (2003).

B. COUNTERVAILING STATE INTERESTS IN PROTECTING COMPETENT PATIENTS WHO REJECT LIFE SUSTAINING TREATMENT

The right to choose to forgo life-sustaining treatment is not absolute, even for competent adults. In Superintendent of Belchertown State School v. Saikewicz, 373 Mass. 728, 370 N.E.2d 417 (1977), the Massachusetts Supreme Judicial Court first identified the four "countervailing State interests" that could overcome a patient's choice: (1) preservation of life; (2) protection of the interests of innocent third parties; (3) prevention of suicide; and (4) maintenance of the ethical integrity of the medical profession.

Saikewicz involved an incompetent, mentally retarded patient. Those four interests have also been reiterated in subsequent cases involving competent patients—including *Bouvia*—but they have never been found to be sufficient to overcome the choice of a *competent* patient. You will see states' interests discussed in almost every case in this chapter.

In *Saikewicz* the Massachusetts Supreme Judicial Court explored the significance of these four state interests and their limitations:

> It is clear that the most significant of the asserted State interests is that of the preservation of human life. Recognition of such an interest,

however, does not necessarily resolve the problem where the affliction or disease clearly indicates that life will end soon, and inevitably be extinguished. The interest of the State in prolonging a life must be reconciled with the interest of an individual to reject the traumatic cost of that prolongation. There is a substantial distinction in the State's insistence that human life be saved where the affliction is curable, as opposed to the State interest where, as here, the issue is not whether but when, for how long, and at what cost to the individual that life may be briefly extended. Even if we assume that the State has an additional interest in seeing to it that individual decisions on the prolongation of life do not in any way tend to "cheapen" the value which is placed on the concept of living, we believe it is not inconsistent to recognize a right to decline medical treatment in a situation of incurable illness. The constitutional right to privacy, as we conceive it, is an expression of the sanctity of individual free choice and self-determination as fundamental constituents of life. The value of life as so perceived is lessened not by a decision to refuse treatment, but by the failure to allow a competent human being the right of a choice.

A second interest of considerable magnitude, which the State may have some interest in asserting, is that of protecting third parties, particularly minor children, from the emotional and financial damage which may occur as a result of the decision of a competent adult to refuse life-saving or life-prolonging treatment. Thus, even when the State's interest in preserving an individual's life was not sufficient, by itself, to outweigh the individual's interest in the exercise of free choice, the possible impact on minor children would be a factor which might have a critical effect on the outcome of the balancing process.

* * *

The last State interest requiring discussion* is that of the maintenance of the ethical integrity of the medical profession as well as allowing hospitals the full opportunity to care for people under their control. The force and impact of this interest is lessened by the prevailing medical ethical standards. Prevailing medical ethical practice does not, without exception, demand that all efforts toward life prolongation be made in all circumstances. Rather, the prevailing ethical practice seems to be to recognize that the dying are more often in need of comfort than treatment. Recognition of the right to refuse necessary treatment in appropriate circumstances is consistent with existing medical mores; such a doctrine does not threaten either the integrity of the medical profession, the proper role of hospitals in caring for such patients or the State's interest in protecting the same. It is not necessary to deny a right of self-

---

* The interest in protecting against suicide seems to require little if any discussion. In the case of the competent adult's refusing medical treatment such an act does not necessarily constitute suicide since (1) in refusing treatment the patient may not have the specific intent to die, and (2) even if he did, to the extent that the cause of death was from natural causes, the patient did not set the death producing agent in motion with the intent of causing his own death. Furthermore, the underlying State interest in this area lies in the prevention of irrational self-destruction. What we consider here is a competent, rational decision to refuse treatment when death is inevitable, and the treatment offers no hope of cure or preservation of life. There is no connection between the conduct here in issue and any State concern to prevent suicide.

determination to a patient in order to recognize the interest of doctors, hospitals, and medical personnel in attendance on the patient. Also, if the doctrines of informed consent and right of privacy have as their foundations in the right to bodily integrity, and control of one's own fate, then those rights are superior to the institutional considerations. 370 N.E.2d at 425–427.

In fact, these four interests raise issues beyond those discussed in Saikewicz:

(1) If the value of the preservation of life is the very question faced by the court in right-to-die cases, does it make sense to define it, *a priori,* as a value that is countervailing to the patient's desire to discontinue treatment?

The nature of the state's interest in the preservation of life was discussed in the *Cruzan* case, in which it was the only interest advanced by the state of Missouri. The Chief Justice said that "a state may properly decline to make judgments about the 'quality' of life that a particular individual may enjoy, and simply assert an unqualified interest in the preservation of human life to be weighed against the constitutionally protected interests of the individual." Not surprisingly, the dissenters viewed the state's interest in the preservation of life very differently. Justice Stevens objected to Missouri's policy of "equating [Cruzan's] life with the biological persistence of her bodily functions." He pointed out that, "[l]ife, particularly human life, is not commonly thought of as a merely physiological condition or function. Its sanctity is often thought to derive from the impossibility of any such reduction. When people speak of life, they often mean to describe the experiences that comprise a person's history. * * * " Justice Brennan was especially offended by the notion that the generalized state interest in life could overcome the liberty interest to forgo life-sustaining treatment. One's rights, he argued, may not be sacrificed just to make society feel good:

> If Missouri were correct that its interests outweigh Nancy's interests in avoiding medical procedures as long as she is free of pain and physical discomfort, [ ] it is not apparent why a state could not choose to remove one of her kidneys without consent on the ground that society would be better off if the recipient of that kidney were saved from renal poisoning * * *, patches of her skin could also be removed to provide grafts for burn victims, and scrapings of bone marrow to provide grafts for someone with leukemia. * * * Indeed, why could the state not perform medical experiments on her body, experiments that might save countless lives, and would cause her no greater burden than she already bears by being fed through her gastrostomy tube? This would be too brave a new world for me and, I submit, for our constitution.

497 U.S. 261, 312–14 n. 13, 110 S.Ct. 2841, 2869–70 n. 13, 111 L.Ed.2d 224. Chief Justice Rehnquist states in *Glucksberg,* below, that *Cruzan* had decided that states may choose to act to protect the sanctity of all life, independent of any inquiry into quality of life, and independent of the value of that life to the one living it.

(2) Does the protection of the interests of innocent third parties have any meaning if courts are not willing to force people to stop pursuing their own interests and to serve some undefined communal goal? Is it merely a make-weight argument in a society as individualistic as ours? On the other hand,

might children, for example, have a claim on the lives of their parents? Under what circumstances would such a claim be strongest?

(3) Although *Glucksberg* confirmed that a state could make assisting suicide a crime, committing suicide is no longer a crime in any state. Is there still a consensus behind Justice Nolan's position, dissenting in Brophy v. New England Sinai Hosp., 398 Mass. 417, 497 N.E.2d 626, 640 (1986), that "suicide is direct self-destruction and is intrinsically evil. No set of circumstances can make it moral * * *."

(4) Finally, there is no longer any reason to believe that the ethics of the medical profession do not permit discontinuation of medical treatment to a competent patient who refuses it. See AMA Ethical Opinion 2.20, Withholding or Withdrawing a Life–Prolonging Medical Treatment. Even if there were, though, should the protection of the "ethical integrity of the medical profession" overcome an otherwise proper decision to forgo some form of treatment? If all other analyses point to allowing a patient to deny consent to some form of treatment, in what cases, if any, should the medical profession be able to require the treatment in the interest of its own self-defined integrity?

Are there special circumstances in which the interest of the patient ought not to be recognized or the interest of the state is especially important? Can the state require a criminal defendant to submit to medical treatment to make him competent to stand trial? See Sell v. U.S., 539 U.S. 166, 123 S.Ct. 2174, 156 L.Ed.2d 197 (2003), holding that forced medication may violate Due Process rights. Does the national interest allow the military to require its soldiers to undergo life saving (or other) medical care so that they can be returned to the front? Can a prisoner refuse kidney dialysis that is necessary to save his life unless the prison administration moves him from a medium to minimum security prison? See Commissioner of Correction v. Myers, 379 Mass. 255, 399 N.E.2d 452 (1979) (interest in "orderly prison administration" outweighs any privacy right of the prisoner to refuse dialysis unless he were moved to another site); People ex rel. Illinois Department of Corrections v. Millard, 335 Ill.App.3d 1066, 270 Ill.Dec. 407, 782 N.E.2d 966 (2003) (force feeding of prisoner allowed). For a general discussion of several court's approaches to balancing a patient's right to refuse treatment with these countervailing state interests, see Alan Meisel & Kathy L. Cerminara, The Right to Die, 3rd ed. (2004).

Note: State Law Bases for a "Right to Die"

The strength of any of these countervailing interests depends upon the strength of the patient's right to choose to forgo treatment. That, in turn, may depend upon the source of that right. Although some courts have found that right in the United States Constitution, *Cruzan's* interpretation of the Fourteenth Amendment has encouraged state courts to look for other bases for this right, too. Some courts find this right in state common law, state statutes, or state constitutions.

The vast majority of state courts recognizing a right to refuse life-sustaining treatment have found that right in state common law, usually in the law of informed consent. As the Chief Justice recognized in *Cruzan,* "the informed consent doctrine has become firmly entrenched in American tort law * * * the logical corollary of the doctrine of informed consent is that the patient generally possesses the right not to consent, that is, to refuse treatment. * * * '' Once a court finds a common law right, it is not necessary to determine whether the right is also conferred by statute or by the U.S. or state constitution. See, e.g., In re Storar, 52 N.Y.2d 363, 438 N.Y.S.2d 266, 420 N.E.2d 64 (1981). Some courts, however, bolster their common law basis for a "right to die" with references to the state and federal constitutions. See In the Matter of Tavel, 661 A.2d 1061 (Del.1995). While the New Jersey court initially recognized a constitutional "right to die" in In re Quinlan, 70 N.J. 10, 355 A.2d 647, 664 (1976), it later recognized that the constitutional determination was unnecessary and retrenched: "While the right of privacy might apply in a case such as this, we need not decide that since the right to decline medical treatment is, in any event, embraced within the common law right to self determination." In re Conroy, 98 N.J. 321, 486 A.2d 1209, 1223 (1985).

Some courts have found the right to refuse life-sustaining treatment in state statutes. Generally, courts that rely on a statutory "right to die" also find a consistent common law right. See, e.g., McConnell v. Beverly Enterprises–Connecticut, 209 Conn. 692, 553 A.2d 596, 601–602 (1989). The Illinois Supreme Court, for example, explicitly rejected state and federal constitutional justifications for a "right to die" because of the existence of both state common law and state statutory remedies. In re Estate of Longeway, 133 Ill.2d 33, 139 Ill.Dec. 780, 549 N.E.2d 292, 297 (1989).

Several state courts have found the "right to die" in their state constitutions. A decision based on the state constitution may be the strongest kind of support such a right can ever find, because it is not subject to review by the United States Supreme Court (absent an improbable argument that a state created right would itself violate the United States Constitution) and it is not subject to change by the state legislature (except through the generally cumbersome state constitutional amendment process). Relevant state constitutional provisions take different forms. For example, the Florida Constitution provides that "[e]very natural person has the right to be let alone and free from governmental intrusion into his private life except as otherwise provided herein. * * * " Fla. Const., art. 1, section 23. The Arizona Constitution provides that "[n]o person shall be disturbed in his private affairs or his home invaded, without authority of law." Arizona Const., art. 2, section 8. Both of these constitutional provisions have given rise to state court recognized rights to forgo life-sustaining treatment. See In re Guardianship of Barry, 445 So.2d 365 (Fla.App.1984) and Rasmussen v. Fleming, 154 Ariz. 207, 741 P.2d 674 (1987). See also DeGrella v. Elston, 858 S.W.2d 698 (Ky.1993) and Lenz v. L.E. Phillips Career Dev. Ctr., 167 Wis.2d 53, 482 N.W.2d 60 (Wis. 1992). The California Court of Appeal also found that such a right for competent patients could be found in the California Constitution. See *Bouvia, supra*.

IV. DECIDING FOR THE PATIENT

It is very difficult to serve the underlying goal of autonomy, if that goal is defined as personal choice, in patients without decisional capacity. One way to serve this principle is through the application of the doctrine of substituted judgment. Under this doctrine, a person, committee, or institution attempts to determine what the patient would do if the patient had decisional capacity. It may be possible to review the values of a formerly competent patient to determine whether that patient would choose to undergo or forgo proposed medical care. This can be done through a thoughtful analysis of the patient's values during life or through review of formal statements made by the patient when the patient had capacity. The most relevant considerations may be statements made by the patient about the proposed treatment itself. Indeed, such statements may provide the only *Constitutionally* relevant information about an incompetent patient's wishes after *Cruzan.*

Of course, there is no way to know with certainty what the patient would do under those circumstances. Some have argued that the doctrine of substituted judgment is too speculative to be applied reliably and that there is simply no way to protect the autonomy of a patient without decisional capacity. Where there is no possible method for establishing what the autonomous patient would do, bioethicists (and increasingly, courts) move to the second principle of bioethical decisionmaking, beneficence. In these circumstances, the alternative to serving autonomy is serving beneficence, and the alternative to the doctrine of substituted judgment is the doctrine of the "best interest" of the patient. As we shall see, the more difficult it becomes to decide what the patient would do if that patient had decisional capacity, the more likely it is that the court will apply the principle of beneficence rather than the principle of autonomy.

A. A STATUTORY FRAMEWORK FOR HEALTH CARE DECISION MAKING: ADVANCE DIRECTIVES AND SURROGATE DECISIONMAKERS

UNIFORM HEALTH–CARE DECISIONS ACT

1993

SECTION 1. DEFINITIONS. In this [Act]:

(1) "Advance health-care directive" means an individual instruction or a power of attorney for health care.

(2) "Agent" means an individual designated in a power of attorney for health care to make a health-care decision for the individual granting the power.

(3) "Capacity" means an individual's ability to understand the significant benefits, risks, and alternatives to proposed health care and to make and communicate a health-care decision.

(4) "Guardian" means a judicially appointed guardian or conservator having authority to make a health-care decision for an individual.

(5) "Health care" means any care, treatment, service, or procedure to maintain, diagnose, or otherwise affect an individual's physical or mental condition.

(6) "Health-care decision" means a decision made by an individual or the individual's agent, guardian, or surrogate, regarding the individual's health care, including:

(i) selection and discharge of health-care providers and institutions;

(ii) approval or disapproval of diagnostic tests, surgical procedures, programs of medication, and orders not to resuscitate; and

(iii) directions to provide, withhold, or withdraw artificial nutrition and hydration and all other forms of health care.

* * *

(9) "Individual instruction" means an individual's direction concerning a health-care decision for the individual.

* * *

(12) "Power of attorney for health care" means the designation of an agent to make health-care decisions for the individual granting the power.

* * *

(16) "Supervising health-care provider" means the primary physician or, if there is no primary physician or the primary physician is not reasonably available, the health-care provider who has undertaken primary responsibility for an individual's health care.

(17) "Surrogate" means an individual, other than a patient's agent or guardian, authorized under this [Act] to make a health-care decision for the patient.

SECTION 2. ADVANCE HEALTH–CARE DIRECTIVES.

(a) An adult or emancipated minor may give an individual instruction. The instruction may be oral or written. The instruction may be limited to take effect only if a specified condition arises.

(b) An adult or emancipated minor may execute a power of attorney for health care, which may authorize the agent to make any health-care decision the principal could have made while having capacity. The power must be in writing and signed by the principal. The power remains in effect notwithstanding the principal's later incapacity and may include individual instructions. * * *

(c) Unless otherwise specified in a power of attorney for health care, the authority of an agent becomes effective only upon a determination that the principal lacks capacity, and ceases to be effective upon a determination that the principal has recovered capacity.

(d) Unless otherwise specified in a written advance health-care directive, a determination that an individual lacks or has recovered capacity, or that another condition exists that affects an individual instruction or the authority of an agent, must be made by the primary physician.

(e) An agent shall make a health-care decision in accordance with the principal's individual instructions, if any, and other wishes to the extent known to the agent. Otherwise, the agent shall make the decision in accordance with the agent's determination of the principal's best interest. In determining the principal's best interest, the agent shall consider the principal's personal values to the extent known to the agent.

(f) A health-care decision made by an agent for a principal is effective without judicial approval.

(g) A written advance health-care directive may include the individual's nomination of a guardian of the person.

(h) An advance health-care directive is valid for purposes of this [Act] if it complies with this [Act], regardless of when or where executed or communicated.

SECTION 3. REVOCATION OF ADVANCE HEALTH–CARE DIRECTIVE.

(a) An individual may revoke the designation of an agent only by a signed writing or by personally informing the supervising health-care provider.

(b) An individual may revoke all or part of an advance health-care directive, other than the designation of an agent, at any time and in any manner that communicates an intent to revoke.

(c) A health-care provider, agent, guardian, or surrogate who is informed of a revocation shall promptly communicate the fact of the revocation to the supervising health-care provider and to any health-care institution at which the patient is receiving care.

(d) A decree of annulment, divorce, dissolution of marriage, or legal separation revokes a previous designation of a spouse as agent unless otherwise specified in the decree or in a power of attorney for health care.

(e) An advance health-care directive that conflicts with an earlier advance health-care directive revokes the earlier directive to the extent of the conflict.

SECTION 4. OPTIONAL FORM. The following form may, but need not, be used to create an advance health-care directive. The other sections of this [Act] govern the effect of this or any other writing used to create an advance health-care directive. An individual may complete or modify all or any part of the following form:

ADVANCE HEALTH–CARE DIRECTIVE

Explanation

You have the right to give instructions about your own health care. You also have the right to name someone else to make health-care decisions for you. This form lets you do either or both of these things. It also lets you express your wishes regarding donation of organs and the designation of your primary physician. If you use this form, you may complete or modify all or any part of it. You are free to use a different form.

Part 1 of this form is a power of attorney for health care. Part 1 lets you name another individual as agent to make health-care decisions for you if you become incapable of making your own decisions or if you want someone else to make those decisions for you now even though you are still capable. You may also name an alternate agent to act for you if your first choice is not willing, able, or reasonably available to make decisions for you. Unless related to you, your agent may not be an owner, operator, or employee of [a residential long-term health-care institution] at which you are receiving care.

Unless the form you sign limits the authority of your agent, your agent may make all health-care decisions for you. This form has a place for you to limit the authority of your agent. You need not limit the authority of your agent if you wish to rely on your agent for all health-care decisions that may have to be made. * * *

Part 2 of this form lets you give specific instructions about any aspect of your health care. Choices are provided for you to express your wishes regarding the provision, withholding, or withdrawal of treatment to keep you alive, including the provision of artificial nutrition and hydration, as well as the provision of pain relief. Space is also provided for you to add to the choices you have made or for you to write out any additional wishes.

* * *

You have the right to revoke this advance health-care directive or replace this form at any time.

PART 1

POWER OF ATTORNEY FOR HEALTH CARE

(1) DESIGNATION OF AGENT: I designate the following individual as my agent to make health-care decisions for me:

* * *

OPTIONAL: If I revoke my agent's authority or if my agent is not willing, able, or reasonably available to make a health-care decision for me, I designate as my first alternate agent:

* * *

(2) AGENT'S AUTHORITY: My agent is authorized to make all health-care decisions for me, including decisions to provide, withhold, or withdraw artificial nutrition and hydration and all other forms of health care to keep me alive, except as I state here:

* * *

(3) WHEN AGENT'S AUTHORITY BECOMES EFFECTIVE: My agent's authority becomes effective when my primary physician determines that I am unable to make my own health-care decisions unless I mark the following box. If I mark this box [___], my agent's authority to make health-care decisions for me takes effect immediately.

(4) AGENT'S OBLIGATION: My agent shall make health-care decisions for me in accordance with this power of attorney for health care, any instructions I give in Part 2 of this form, and my other wishes to the extent known to my agent. To the extent my wishes are unknown, my agent shall make health-care decisions for me in accordance with what my agent determines to be in my best interest. In determining my best interest, my agent shall consider my personal values to the extent known to my agent.

(5) NOMINATION OF GUARDIAN: If a guardian of my person needs to be appointed for me by a court, I nominate the agent designated in this form. If that agent is not willing, able, or reasonably available to act as guardian, I nominate the alternate agents whom I have named, in the order designated.

PART 2

INSTRUCTIONS FOR HEALTH CARE

If you are satisfied to allow your agent to determine what is best for you in making end-of-life decisions, you need not fill out this part of the form. If you do fill out this part of the form, you may strike any wording you do not want.

(6) END–OF–LIFE DECISIONS: I direct that my health-care providers and others involved in my care provide, withhold, or withdraw treatment in accordance with the choice I have marked below:

[___] (a) Choice Not To Prolong Life

I do not want my life to be prolonged if (i) I have an incurable and irreversible condition that will result in my death within a relatively short time, (ii) I become unconscious and, to a reasonable degree of medical certainty, I will not regain consciousness, or (iii) the likely risks and burdens of treatment would outweigh the expected benefits, OR

[___] (b) Choice To Prolong Life

I want my life to be prolonged as long as possible within the limits of generally accepted health-care standards.

(7) ARTIFICIAL NUTRITION AND HYDRATION: Artificial nutrition and hydration must be provided, withheld, or withdrawn in accordance with the choice I have made in paragraph (6) unless I mark the following box. If I mark this box [___], artificial nutrition and hydration must be provided regardless of my condition and regardless of the choice I have made in paragraph (6).

(8) RELIEF FROM PAIN: Except as I state in the following space, I direct that treatment for alleviation of pain or discomfort be provided at all times, even if it hastens my death:

* * *

(9) OTHER WISHES: (If you do not agree with any of the optional choices above and wish to write your own, or if you wish to add to the instructions you have given above, you may do so here.) I direct that:

* * *

[Part III, dealing with organ donation, and Part IV, dealing with the appointment of a primary physician, are omitted.]

SECTION 5. DECISIONS BY SURROGATE.

(a) A surrogate may make a health-care decision for a patient who is an adult or emancipated minor if the patient has been determined by the primary physician to lack capacity and no agent or guardian has been appointed or the agent or guardian is not reasonably available.

(b) An adult or emancipated minor may designate any individual to act as surrogate by personally informing the supervising health-care provider. In the absence of a designation, or if the designee is not reasonably available, any member of the following classes of the patient's family who is reasonably available, in descending order of priority, may act as surrogate:

(1) the spouse, unless legally separated;

(2) an adult child;

(3) a parent; or

(4) an adult brother or sister.

(c) If none of the individuals eligible to act as surrogate under subsection (b) is reasonably available, an adult who has exhibited special care and concern for the patient, who is familiar with the patient's personal values, and who is reasonably available may act as surrogate.

(d) A surrogate shall communicate his or her assumption of authority as promptly as practicable to the members of the patient's family specified in subsection (b) who can be readily contacted.

(e) If more than one member of a class assumes authority to act as surrogate, and they do not agree on a health-care decision and the supervising health-care provider is so informed, the supervising health-care provider shall comply with the decision of a majority of the members of that class who have communicated their views to the provider. If the class is evenly divided concerning the health-care decision and the supervising health-care provider is so informed, that class and all individuals having lower priority are disqualified from making the decision.

(f) A surrogate shall make a health-care decision in accordance with the patient's individual instructions, if any, and other wishes to the extent known to the surrogate. Otherwise, the surrogate shall make the decision in accordance with the surrogate's determination of the patient's best interest. In determining the patient's best interest, the surrogate shall consider the patient's personal values to the extent known to the surrogate.

(g) A health-care decision made by a surrogate for a patient is effective without judicial approval.

(h) An individual at any time may disqualify another, including a member of the individual's family, from acting as the individual's surrogate by a signed writing or by personally informing the supervising health-care provider of the disqualification.

* * *

SECTION 7. OBLIGATIONS OF HEALTH–CARE PROVIDER.

(a) Before implementing a health-care decision made for a patient, a supervising health-care provider, if possible, shall promptly communicate to the patient the decision made and the identity of the person making the decision.

(b) A supervising health-care provider who knows of the existence of an advance health-care directive, a revocation of an advance health-care directive, or a designation or disqualification of a surrogate, shall promptly record its existence in the patient's health-care record and, if it is in writing, shall request a copy and if one is furnished shall arrange for its maintenance in the health-care record.

(c) A primary physician who makes or is informed of a determination that a patient lacks or has recovered capacity, or that another condition exists which affects an individual instruction or the authority of an agent, guardian, or surrogate, shall promptly record the determination in the patient's health-care record and communicate the determination to the patient, if possible, and to any person then authorized to make health-care decisions for the patient.

(d) Except as provided in subsections (e) and (f), a health-care provider or institution providing care to a patient shall:

(1) comply with an individual instruction of the patient and with a reasonable interpretation of that instruction made by a person then authorized to make health-care decisions for the patient; and

(2) comply with a health-care decision for the patient made by a person then authorized to make health-care decisions for the patient to the same extent as if the decision had been made by the patient while having capacity.

(e) A health-care provider may decline to comply with an individual instruction or health-care decision for reasons of conscience. A health-care institution may decline to comply with an individual instruction or health-care decision if the instruction or decision is contrary to a policy of the institution which is expressly based on reasons of conscience and if the policy was timely communicated to the patient or to a person then authorized to make health-care decisions for the patient.

(f) A health-care provider or institution may decline to comply with an individual instruction or health-care decision that requires medically ineffective health care or health care contrary to generally accepted health-care standards applicable to the health-care provider or institution.

(g) A health-care provider or institution that declines to comply with an individual instruction or health-care decision shall:

(1) promptly so inform the patient, if possible, and any person then authorized to make health-care decisions for the patient;

(2) provide continuing care to the patient until a transfer can be effected; and

(3) unless the patient or person then authorized to make health-care decisions for the patient refuses assistance, immediately make all reasonable efforts to assist in the transfer of the patient to another health-care provider or institution that is willing to comply with the instruction or decision.

(h) A health-care provider or institution may not require or prohibit the execution or revocation of an advance health-care directive as a condition for providing health care.

* * *

SECTION 11. CAPACITY.

(a) This [Act] does not affect the right of an individual to make health-care decisions while having capacity to do so.

(b) An individual is presumed to have capacity to make a health-care decision, to give or revoke an advance health-care directive, and to designate or disqualify a surrogate.

* * *

SECTION 14. JUDICIAL RELIEF. On petition of a patient, the patient's agent, guardian, or surrogate, a health-care provider or institution involved with the patient's care, or an individual described in Section 5(b) or (c), the [appropriate] court may enjoin or direct a health-care decision or order other equitable relief. A proceeding under this section is governed by [here insert appropriate reference to the rules of procedure or statutory provisions governing expedited proceedings and proceedings affecting incapacitated persons].

* * *

Note on Advance Directives and Surrogate Consent Laws

The History of Advance Directives: The Rise of Living Wills. Nearly two decades before the Uniform Health–Care Decisions Act was proposed, many people first became concerned about the potential abuses of powerful new forms of life-sustaining medical treatment. Frightened by the "treatment" provided to Karen Quinlan, whose life was sustained by a ventilator but who was given no chance of regaining consciousness, people began to search for a way to avoid a similar fate. Within two years of the first press reports of the *Quinlan* case, several states had adopted statutes that formally recognized certain forms of written statements requesting that some kinds of medical care be discontinued. These statutes, generally referred to as "living will" statutes, "right to die" legislation, or "natural death" acts, provided a political outlet for the frustration that accompanied the empathy for Ms. Quinlan.

The statutes, which still provide the governing law in many jurisdictions, differ in several respects. In some states living wills may be executed by any person, at any time (and in some states they may be executed on behalf of minors), while in other states they require a waiting period, and may not be executed during a terminal illness. In most states they are of indefinite duration, although in some states they expire after a determined number of years. Some statutes address only the terminally ill, others include those in "irreversible coma" or persistent vegetative state, and still others provide for different conditions to trigger the substantive provisions of the document. In many states, living wills are not effective while the patient is pregnant. Some states require the formalities of a will for the living will to be recognized by statute, while other states require different formalities. The statutes generally relieve physicians and other health care providers of any civil or criminal liability if they properly follow the requirements of the statute and implement the desires expressed in a legally executed living will. Some of the statutes also require that any physician who cannot, in good conscience, carry out those provisions, transfer the patient to a physician who can. The statutes also provide that carrying out the provisions of a properly executed living will does not constitute suicide for insurance purposes. It is hard to know whether the absence of litigation over the terms of living wills means that these documents are working well or not at all.

Some living will statutes do not apply to those in persistent vegetative state, irreversible coma, or any other medical condition that may not be considered "terminal." These statutes would be of no assistance to people in the position of Nancy Cruzan. Is there a reason to limit legislation to terminal conditions, or should such statutes be extended to other conditions, like persistent vegetative state, where there is broad social consensus that patients should have the right to forgo life-sustaining treatment?

Many living will statutes specifically exclude "the performance of any procedure to provide nutrition or hydration" from the definition of death-prolonging procedures, and thus do not extend any statutory protection to those who remove nutrition or hydration from a patient. For the most famous example, see Vernon's Ann.Mo.Stat. § 459.010(3). After the United States Supreme Court decision in *Cruzan,* are such exceptions legally meaningful? Are they Constitutional? In *Cruzan*, The Chief Justice reviewed those state cases that have treated nutrition and hydration just like any other form of medical care, apparently with approval. In her concurring opinion, Justice O'Connor cited AMA Ethical Opinion 2.20, Withholding or Withdrawing a Life–Prolonging Medical Treatment, to support her proposition that "artificial feeding cannot readily be distinguished from other forms of medical treatment." In his dissent, Justice Brennan states without reservation: "No material distinction can be drawn between the treatment to which Nancy Cruzan continues to be subject—artificial nutrition and hydration— and any other medical treatment." For a fuller discussion of the legal position of the withdrawal of nutrition and hydration, see pages 754–757, below. For an example of judicial avoidance of the apparent consequences of a nutrition and hydration exception to a living will statute, see McConnell v. Beverly Enterprises– Connecticut, 209 Conn. 692, 553 A.2d 596 (1989). See also In re Guardianship of Browning, 568 So.2d 4 (Fla.1990).

The Next Step: Durable Powers of Attorney for Health Care. Another means of identifying who should speak for the patient when the patient is incompetent is to allow the patient to designate a spokesperson during the patient's period of competence. This may be accomplished through the patient's execution of a durable power of attorney.

Powers of attorney have been available over the past several centuries to allow for financial transactions to be consummated by agents of a principal. A power of attorney may be executed by any competent person. It provides that the agent designated shall have the right to act on behalf of the principal for purposes that are described and limited in the document itself. Thus, a principal may give an agent a power of attorney to enter into a particular contract, a particular kind of contract, or all contracts. The power may be limited by time, by geographic area, or in any other way. It may be granted to any person, who, upon appoint- ment, becomes the agent and "attorney-in-fact" for the principal. At common law, a power of attorney expired upon the "incapacity" of the principal. This was necessary to assure that the principal could maintain adequate authority over his agent. As long as a power of attorney expired upon the incapacity of the principal, the power of attorney had no value in making medical decisions. After all, a competent patient could decide for himself; there was no reason for him to delegate authority to an agent.

In the mid 1970s it became clear that the value of the power of attorney could be increased if it could extend beyond the incapacity of the principal. For example, as an increasing number of very elderly people depended upon their children and others to handle their financial affairs, it became important that there be some device by which they could delegate their authority to these agents. For such principals it was most important that the authority remain with their agents when they did become incapacitated. The Uniform Probate Code was amended to provide for a durable power of attorney; that is, a power of attorney that would remain in effect (or even become effective) upon the incapacity of the principal if the document clearly stated that. There is no reported opinion formally holding that the authority of a durable power of attorney executed under the Uniform Probate Code extends to health care decision-making. The President's Commis- sion assumed, without any discussion, that it could be used for this purpose. See President's Commission, Deciding to Forego Life–Sustaining Treatment, 145–149 (1983). The vast majority of states have now adopted statutes that formally authorize the execution of durable powers of attorney for health care decisions.

Some state statutes now allow an agent authorized by a durable power of attorney to make health care decisions for a principal even if the principal has capacity—as long as that is the explicit desire of the principal. Why should an agent make a decision for a principal *with* capacity? Doesn't that undermine the principle of autonomy? One purpose of such a provision is to give health care providers a surrogate decisionmaker to turn to in the case of a patient with capacity that is highly variable. Some argue that, in such cases, health care providers ought to be able to depend upon the consent of a patient-designated surrogate without doing a full competency analysis each time a health care decision is to be made. Of course, the decision of the surrogate can always be overruled by the patient herself if she has capacity.

The legal significance of a durable power of attorney for health care is defined by each state's durable power statute. In her concurring opinion in *Cruzan*, Justice O'Connor suggests that there may also be Constitutional significance to a properly executed durable power of attorney:

> I also write separately to emphasize that the Court does not today decide the issue whether a state must also give effect to the decisions of a surrogate decision-maker. In my view, such a duty may well be Constitutionally required to protect the patient's liberty interest in refusing medical treatment.

497 U.S. at 289, 110 S.Ct. at 2857. She commends those several states that have recognized "the practical wisdom of such a procedure by enacting durable power of attorney statutes" and she suggests that a written appointment of a proxy "may be a valuable additional safeguard of the patient's interest in directing his medical care." In the final paragraph of her opinion she points out that "[t]oday's decision * * * does not preclude a future determination that the Constitution requires the states to implement the decisions of a patient's duly appointed surrogate."

For an interesting account of how to make durable powers of attorney more effective for health care purposes from the perspective of a lawyer specializing in estate planning, see G. Witherspoon, What I Learned from *Schiavo*, 37 Hastings Ctr. Rep. (6) 17 (2007). The *Schiavo* case is discussed in detail below.

The Development of the Uniform Health–Care Decisions Act. The Uniform Health–Care Decisions Act (UHCDA), which you have just read, was designed to replace the Uniform Rights of the Terminally Ill Act, state durable powers acts and parts of the Uniform Anatomical Gifts Act. It was approved by the National Conference of Commissioners on Uniform State Laws in 1993 and by the American Bar Association House of Delegates in 1994. The UHCDA substantially alters the form and utility of living wills and durable powers, and it provides a method of making health care decisions for incompetent patients who do not have advance directives. As of early 2008, some version of the uniform act was adopted in Alabama, Alaska, Delaware, Hawaii, Maine, Mississippi, New Mexico and Wyoming. The California statute governing health care decisions is also largely based on the UHCDA.

The UHCDA takes a comprehensive approach by placing the living will (which is retitled the "individual instruction"), the durable power of attorney (now called the "power of attorney for health care"), a family consent law, and some provisions concerning organ donation together in one statute. Further, the statute integrates the current living will and durable power (and statement of desire to donate organs) into a single document. The UHCDA provides a statutory form, but it also explicitly declares that the form is not a mandatory one, and that individuals may draft their own form that includes only some of the kinds of instructions permitted in the unified form.

The new "individual instruction" can apply to virtually any health care decision, not just the end of life decisions to which living wills are typically applicable. Further, "health care decision" is defined very broadly.

The uniform act also makes the execution of the unified document very easy. It has no witness requirement, and it does not require that the document be notarized. The drafters of the proposed act concluded that the formalities often associated with living wills and durable powers served to discourage their execution more than to deter fraud.

The residual decisionmaking portion of the act is very much like the family consent statutes that have now been adopted in a majority of states and this section of the act applies only if there is no applicable individual instruction or appointed agent. While it provides for a common family hierarchy of decisionmakers for decisionally incapacitated patients, it also provides that the family can be trumped by an "orally designated surrogate," who may be appointed by a patient informing her "supervising physician" that the surrogate is entitled to make health care decisions on her behalf. Thus, patients can effectively orally appoint decisionmaking agents who previously could only be appointed in a writing signed pursuant to a rigorous process. In the same manner a patient may orally *disqualify* someone who otherwise would be entitled to make decisions on her behalf. If you do not want your brother making health care decisions for you, you need only tell your supervising physician. Thus, in essence, any health care decision will be made by the first available in this hierarchy:

(1) the patient, if the patient has decisional capacity,

(2) the patient, through an individual instruction,

(3) an agent appointed by the patient in a written power of attorney for health care, unless a court has given this authority explicitly to a guardian,

(4) a guardian appointed by the court,

(5) a surrogate appointed orally by the patient,

(6) a surrogate selected from the list of family members and others who can make health care decisions on behalf of the patient.

The drafters of the UHCDA make it clear in their comments that one purpose of the statute is to assure that these intimate health care decisions remain within the realm of the patient, the patient's family and close friends, and the health care providers, and that others not be permitted to disrupt that process. The court would very rarely have a role in any decisionmaking under this statute, and outsiders (including outside organizations) who do not think a patient is adequately protected have no standing to seek judicial intervention. See Protection and Advocacy System, Inc. v. Presbyterian Healthcare Services, 128 N.M. 73, 989 P.2d 890 (1999).

The UHCDA explicitly provides that the decisionmaker (whether an agent, guardian or surrogate) should make a decision based on the principle of substituted judgment (i.e., on the basis of what the patient would choose, if that patient were competent) rather than the best interest principle. If it is impossible to apply the substituted judgment principle, the statute would apply the best interests principle.

The UHCDA includes the normal raft of recordkeeping provisions, limitations on the reach of the criminal law, assurances regarding the insurance rights of those who execute the documents, and restrictions on the liability of those who act under the statute in good faith. A provision for $500 in liquidated damages in actions for breach of the act may not encourage litigation when the statute is ignored, but the provision for attorney's fees in those cases might provide an incentive for lawyers to bring those cases. The act applies only to adults.

Should your state adopt the UHCDA? If you were advising your state legislature on this issue, what portions of the uniform act would you suggest be changed? How would you change those portions?

The Values History and the "Five Wishes" Form. Because it is almost impossible to predict exactly what kinds of medical care one might need and what kind of medical condition one will suffer, some courts and scholars have suggested that the most helpful kind of advance directive would be one that deals generally with the interests and values of the patient and which encourages every competent person to discuss with prospective agents and surrogates the values that are likely to be significant in subsequent decisionmaking over medical treatment.

One particularly good device for encouraging such discussion (and for recording the results) is the "Values History Form," which asks prospective patients about their general values, their medical values, their relationships with family members, friends, and health care providers, their wishes in particular cases and a host of other issues likely to become relevant if they become incompetent and health care decisions must be made on their behalf. While such a values history has no formal legal significance, and while some may be put off by such questions as "What makes you laugh?" and "What makes you cry?," there is no doubt that the existence of such a document would be of great value to a substitute decisionmaker and to any court called upon to confirm that substitute's decision. See Joan McIver Gibson, Reflecting on Values, 51 Ohio St.L.J. 451 (1990).

In addition, over the past few years the "Five Wishes" document, a simple and easy to use advance directive that is (arguably) legally effective under the laws of most states, has become popular. The Five Wishes document "lets your family and doctors know:

1. Which person you want to make health care decisions for you when you can't make them,

2. The kind of medical treatment you want or don't want,

3. How comfortable you want to be,

4. How you want people to treat you,

5. What you want your loved ones to know."

It was developed by Aging with Dignity, and the form is available through www. agingwithdignity.org (visited December 1, 2007).

Family Consent Laws. Over the past century it became standard medical practice to seek consent to any medical procedure from close family members of an incompetent patient. There is no common law authority for this practice; it is an example of medical practice (and good common sense) being subtly absorbed by the law. The President's Commission suggests five reasons for this deference to family members:

(1) The family is generally most concerned about the good of the patient.

(2) The family will also usually be most knowledgeable about the patient's goals, preferences, and values.

(3) The family deserves recognition as an important social unit that ought to be treated, within limits, as a responsible decisionmaker in matters that intimately affect its members.

(4) Especially in a society in which many other traditional forms of community have eroded, participation in a family is often an important dimension of personal fulfillment.

(5) Since a protected sphere of privacy and autonomy is required for the flourishing of this interpersonal union, institutions and the state should be reluctant to intrude, particularly regarding matters that are personal and on which there is a wide range of opinion in society.

President's Commission, Deciding to Forego Life–Sustaining Treatment, 127 (1983). It is difficult to determine whether the resort to close relatives to give consent is merely a procedural device to discover what the patient, if competent, would choose, or whether it is based in an independent substantive doctrine. Although it seems essentially procedural—the family is most likely to know what the patient would choose—many courts are willing to accept the decisions of family members even when there is little support for the position that these family members are actually choosing what the patient would choose. Of course, the assumptions about family relationships are quite optimistic. Consulting with family members also neutralizes potential malpractice plaintiffs; this factor probably accounts for part of the longstanding popularity of this decisionmaking process.

Over the past decade most states have enacted "family consent laws" that authorize statutorily designated family members to make health care decisions for their relatives in circumscribed situations. These statutes often apply to a wide range of health care decisions (including, in most cases, decisions to forgo life sustaining treatment), although sometimes they apply only when there has been a physician's certification of the patient's inability to make the health care decision and sometimes they are limited to particular kinds of treatment (e.g., cardiopulmonary resuscitation). In addition, "family consent laws" often provide immunity from liability for family members and physicians acting in good faith, and judicial authority to resolve disputes about the authority of the family members under the statutes. The definition of "family member" and the position of each family member in the hierarchy varies from state to state. In some states those in a long term spouse-like relationship with the patient are included in the list of family members who can make decisions for the incompetent patient; in some states they are not. Some lists include a residuary class of anyone who knows the values, interest and wishes of the patient; some states list the physician as the residuary decisionmaker; some provide for no residuary decisionmaker. Some states give a general guardian top priority; some states do not. Some states allow the statutory surrogate to make any health care decisions, some states put some kinds of decisions (like discontinuing nutrition and hydration) off limits. Section 5 of the UHCDA provides a good example of a family consent law. Are there other classes of decisionmakers you would add to that hierarchy?

Physicians' orders regarding end-of-life care. By custom, health care institutions and health care workers caring for patients rely on orders given by the health care professional responsible for the patient's treatment. Recognizing this custom, some patient advocates argue that the best way to protect a patient's interests at the end of life is to incorporate the patient's health care decisions into a physician's order. One particularly thoughtful way of doing this is to incorporate those decisions into a Physician Order for Life Sustaining Treatment (POLST). POLST forms (called "scope of treatment" orders in some cases, and Medical Orders—"MOLST"—in New York) may include information about a patient's decisions with regard to resuscitation orders, the extent of appropriate medical intervention, the use of antibiotics and other pharmaceuticals, the provision of nutrition and hydration, the desired place of treatment (home, hospital or nursing home), the identity of the authorized health care decision maker, and other relevant issues likely to arise in each case.

POLST forms are generally entered in the patient's medical record after the physician has discussed all of the relevant issues with the patient, the patient's family, the agent or surrogate authorized to make health care decisions, and others. The POLST form may include a summary of the values and goals of the patient that form the basis of the order, and the nature of the discussions that gave rise to the order. The patient or the patient's decision maker may be asked to countersign the order, so it is clear that it represents the agreed view of the patient and the provider. In order to assure that these forms are not lost in the patient's chart, they are often printed on distinctively colored (usually bright pink or bright green) paper. Such orders can be recognized by state law (as they are in a few states), or by institutional or community policy.

The process of entering a POLST requires useful discussion among all of the relevant parties, and it provides a way of integrating a patient's advance directive and the physician's order. It does not trump a legally authorized advance directive, but it may make it easier for succeeding health care providers to be aware of advance directives made earlier by the patient, and it eliminates a provider's concern over the obligation to carry out an advance directive that appears to be inconsistent with an order of a physician. For a full account of the use of the POLST, see www.polst.org, last visited Dec. 1, 2007. See also, Susan Hickman, et al., Hope for the Future: Achieving the Original Intent of Advance Directives, 35 Hastings Ctr. Rep. (6) Supp. 26–30 (2005), and S.J. Baumrucker, Physician Orders for Scope of Treatment: An Idea Whose Time Has Come, 21 Am. J. Hospice & Palliative Care 247–248 (2004).

Religious objections to some provisions of advance directives. Some religious denominations have principled objections to facilitating certain decisions that might be made in advance directives. These objections are reflected in a range of state statutes because they are products of political compromise. For example, as this note suggests, many states limit the applicability of advance directives when the patient is pregnant or when the patient wishes to reject nutrition or hydration. These limitations are consistent with the tenets of particular religious groups (although there are other reasons for them as well). Advance directive laws without these explicit limitations often include other "conscience" provisions which serve to relieve health care institutions and individual providers from taking actions which violate their own values. See section 7(e) of the Uniform Health–Care Decisions Act, above.

The Patient Self–Determination Act and Advance Directives. The Patient Self–Determination Act became law as a part of the Federal Omnibus Budget Reconciliation Act of 1990, and it was designed to increase the role that advance directives—both living wills and durable powers of attorney—play in medical decisionmaking. The statute applies to hospitals, skilled nursing facilities, home health agencies, hospice programs, and HMOs that receive Medicaid or Medicare funding. It requires each of those covered by the Act to provide each patient with written information concerning:

(i) an individual's rights under State law (whether statutory or as recognized by the courts of the State) to make decisions concerning * * * medical care, including the right to accept or refuse medical or surgical treatment and the right to formulate advance directives * * * and

(ii) the written policies of the provider or organization respecting the implementation of such rights.

42 U.S.C.A. § 1395cc(a)(1)(f)(1)(A). In addition, those covered must document in each patient's record whether that patient has signed an advance directive, assure that the state law is followed in the institution, and provide for education of both the staff and the public concerning living wills and durable powers of attorney.

A few states have also taken action to increase the utility of advance directives. For example, a couple of states have central registries of advance directives, and a handful of states provide for drivers' licenses to show if a patient has an advance directive. At least one statute requires managed health care providers to discuss advance directives with their patients/enrollees.

B.   DECIDING FOR INCOMPETENT PATIENTS IN THE ABSENCE OF A STATUTE

IN RE CONROY

Supreme Court of New Jersey, 1985.
98 N.J. 321, 486 A.2d 1209.

SCHREIBER, JUSTICE.

* * * [W]e hold that life-sustaining treatment may be withheld or withdrawn from an incompetent patient when it is clear that the particular patient would have refused the treatment under the circumstances involved. The standard we are enunciating is a subjective one, consistent with the notion that the right that we are seeking to effectuate is a very personal right to control one's own life. The question is not what a reasonable or average person would have chosen to do under the circumstances but what the particular patient would have done if able to choose for himself.

* * *

We * * * hold that life-sustaining treatment may also be withheld or withdrawn from a patient in Claire Conroy's situation [i.e., a patient who was competent but is now incompetent] if either of two "best interests" tests—a limited-objective or a pure-objective test—is satisfied.

Under the limited-objective test, life-sustaining treatment may be withheld or withdrawn from a patient in Claire Conroy's situation when there is some trustworthy evidence that the patient would have refused the treatment, and the decision-maker is satisfied that it is clear that the burdens of the patient's continued life with the treatment outweigh the benefits of that life for him. By this we mean that the patient is suffering, and will continue to suffer throughout the expected duration of his life, unavoidable pain, and that the net burdens of his prolonged life (the pain and suffering of his life with the treatment less the amount and duration of pain that the patient would likely experience if the treatment were withdrawn) markedly outweigh any physical pleasure, emotional enjoyment, or intellectual satisfaction that the patient may still be able to derive from life. This limited-objective standard permits the termination of treatment for a patient who had not unequivocally expressed his desires before becoming incompetent, when it is clear that the treatment in question would merely prolong the patient's suffering.

* * *

This limited-objective test also requires some trustworthy evidence that the patient would have wanted the treatment terminated. This evidence could take any one or more of the various forms appropriate to prove the patient's intent under the subjective test. Evidence that, taken as a whole, would be too vague, casual, or remote to constitute the clear proof of the patient's subjective intent that is necessary to satisfy the subjective test—for example, informally expressed reactions to other people's medical conditions and treatment—might be sufficient to satisfy this prong of the limited-objective test.

In the absence of trustworthy evidence, or indeed any evidence at all, that the patient would have declined the treatment, life-sustaining treatment may still be withheld or withdrawn from a formerly competent person like Claire Conroy if a third, pure-objective test is satisfied. Under that test, as under the limited-objective test, the net burdens of the patient's life with the treatment should clearly and markedly outweigh the benefits that the patient derives from life. Further, the recurring, unavoidable and severe pain of the patient's life with the treatment should be such that the effect of administering life-sustaining treatment would be inhumane. Subjective evidence that the patient would not have wanted the treatment is not necessary under this pure-objective standard. Nevertheless, even in the context of severe pain, life-sustaining treatment should not be withdrawn from an incompetent patient who had previously expressed a wish to be kept alive in spite of any pain that he might experience.

* * * [W]e expressly decline to authorize decision-making based on assessments of the personal worth or social utility of another's life, or the value of that life to others.

* * *

We are aware that it will frequently be difficult to conclude that the evidence is sufficient to justify termination of treatment under either of the "best interests" tests that we have described. Often, it is unclear whether and to what extent a patient such as Claire Conroy is capable of, or is in fact, experiencing pain. Similarly, medical experts are often unable to determine with any degree of certainty the extent of a nonverbal person's intellectual functioning or the depth of his emotional life. When the evidence is insufficient to satisfy either the limited-objective or pure-objective standard, however, we cannot justify the termination of life-sustaining treatment as clearly furthering the best interests of a patient like Ms. Conroy.

* * * When evidence of a person's wishes or physical or mental condition is equivocal, it is best to err, if at all, in favor of preserving life. * * *

Notes and Questions

1. *The Martin Case, the Conroy Classifications, and the Principle of Autonomy.* The most substantial criticism of the "subjective", "limited-objective" and "pure objective" classifications is provided in In re Martin, 450 Mich. 204, 538 N.W.2d 399 (1995):

Rather than choose between the best interest standard and the substituted judgment standard, the New Jersey Supreme Court attempted to synthesize these two standards by creating an hierarchical decision-making continuum. [ ]. The starting point on the continuum is anchored by a purely subjective analysis, an approach that requires more definitive evidence of what the patient would choose than the substituted judgment standard. The other end of the continuum is anchored by a purely objective analysis, which is, in essence, a best interest standard.

We find that a purely subjective analysis is the most appropriate standard to apply under the circumstances of this case. The pure subjective standard allows the surrogate to withhold life-sustaining treatment from an incompetent patient "when it is clear that the particular patient would have refused the treatment under the circumstances involved." [ ]. Given that the right the surrogate is seeking to effectuate is the incompetent patient's right to control his own life, "the question is not what a reasonable or average person would have chosen to do under the circumstances but what the particular patient would have done if able to chose for himself."

The subjective and objective standards involve conceptually different bases for allowing he surrogate to make treatment decisions. The subjective standard is based on a patient's right to self-determination, while the objective standard is grounded in the state's parens patriae power. [ ]. An objective, best interest, standard cannot be grounded in the common-law right of informed consent because the right and the decision-making standard inherently conflict.

* * *

Any move from a purely subjective standard to an analysis that encompasses objective criteria is grounded in the state's parens patriae power, not in the common-law right of informed consent or self-determination. Thus, while the clearly expressed wishes of a patient, while competent, should be honored regardless of the patient's condition, we find nothing that prevents the state from grounding any objective analysis on a threshold requirement of pain, terminal illness, foreseeable death, a persistent vegetative state, or affliction of a similar genre.

Martin, 538 N.W.2d at 407–408. Do you agree that only the decision to apply the subjective standard (and not the decision to apply the two objective standards) can be justified by the principles behind the doctrine of informed consent? Is the application of any form of objective test (whether it be termed "substituted judgment" or "best interest") a *per se* violation of the principle of autonomy, as *Martin* suggests? If this is true, what is the justification for the application of the theory of substituted judgment? See Rebecca Dresser & John Robertson, Quality of Life and Non–Treatment Decisions for Incompetent Patients, a Critique of the Orthodox Approach, 17 L. Med. & Health Care 234 (1989). See also Rebecca Dresser, Life, Death and Incompetent Patients: Conceptual Infirmities and Hidden Values in the Law, 28 Ariz.L.Rev. 378 (1986).

2. *The Conroy Standard and Patients in Persistent Vegetative State.* Despite its rejection in the *Martin* case, the *Conroy* case has been extremely influential. Even the New Jersey courts have been reluctant to apply it when the patient is in persistent vegetative state, though. Persistent vegetative state describes a condition where a patient is physically alive but "functioning entirely in terms of its internal controls;" where "there is no behavioral evidence of either self-awareness or awareness of the surroundings* * *." In re Jobes, 108 N.J. 394, 529 A.2d 434, 438 (1987). As the New Jersey Supreme Court pointed out in a companion case,

While a benefits-burdens analysis is difficult with marginally cognitive patients like Claire Conroy, it is essentially impossible with patients in a persistent vegetative state. By definition such patients, like Ms. Peter, do not experience any of the benefits or burdens that the *Conroy* balancing tests are intended or able to appraise. Therefore, we hold that these tests should not be applied to patients in the persistent vegetative state.

In re Peter, 108 N.J. 365, 529 A.2d 419, 424–425 (1987). Essentially, the court found that there were no measurable benefits or burdens of continuing life in the case of a patient with persistent vegetative state. There could be no pain, happiness, sadness, sense of dignity, sense of hope, or, really, any meaningful sense of the current desires of a patient who is in persistent vegetative state, and thus no way to balance any such burdens and benefits.

Does it make any sense to treat a patient in a persistent vegetative state any differently from another incompetent patient? Should this make it easier or harder to remove life-sustaining medical care? What position does the Uniform Health–Care Decisions Act take with respect to patients in a persistent vegetative state? Are they treated any differently from patients who are not in that condition?

3. *Distinguishing Between Active and Passive Conduct, and Between Withholding and Withdrawing Life–Sustaining Medical Care.* These anachronistic distinctions have not found a safe harbor in the law, just as they have been increasingly recognized as meaningless in ethics. The *Conroy* opinion considered each of these distinctions, and summarized the ethical and legal literature and the reasons for rejecting the distinctions. As to the distinction between active and passive conduct, the *Conroy* court announced:

We emphasize that in making decisions whether to administer life-sustaining treatment to patients such as Claire Conroy, the primary focus should be the patient's desires and experience of pain and enjoyment—not the type of treatment involved. Thus, we reject the distinction that some have made between actively hastening death by terminating treatment and passively allowing a person to die of a disease as one of limited use in a legal analysis of such a decision-making situation.

Characterizing conduct as active or passive is often an elusive notion, even outside the context of medical decision-making * * *. The distinction is particularly nebulous, however, in the context of decisions whether to withhold or withdraw life-sustaining treatment. In a case like that of Claire Conroy, for example, would a physician who discontinued nasogastric feeding be actively causing her death by removing her primary source of nutrients; or would he merely be omitting to continue the artificial form of treatment, thus passively allowing her medical condition, which includes her inability to swallow, to take its natural course? [ ] The ambiguity inherent in this distinction is further heightened when one performs an act within an over-all plan of non-intervention, such as when a doctor writes an order not to resuscitate a patient. * * *

For a similar reason, we also reject any distinction between withholding and withdrawing life-sustaining treatment. Some commentators have suggested that discontinuing life-sustaining treatment once it has been commenced is morally more problematic than merely failing to begin the treatment. Discontinuing life-sustaining treatment, to some, is an "active" taking of life, as opposed to the more "passive" act of omitting the treatment in the first instance.

This distinction is more psychologically compelling than logically sound. As mentioned above, the line between active and passive conduct in the context of medical decisions is far too nebulous to constitute a principled basis for decisionmaking. Whether necessary treatment is withheld at the outset or withdrawn later on, the consequence—the patient's death—is the same. Moreover, from a policy standpoint, it might well be unwise to forbid persons from discontinuing a treatment under circumstances in which the treatment could permissibly be withheld. Such a rule could discourage families and doctors from even attempting certain types of care and could thereby force them into hasty and premature decisions to allow a patient to die. [ ]

486 A.2d at 1233–1234.

4. *Distinguishing Ordinary and Extraordinary Treatment*. As to the distinction between ordinary and extraordinary treatment, *Conroy* pointed out:

We also find unpersuasive the distinction relied upon by some courts, commentators, and theologians between "ordinary" treatment, which they would always require, and "extraordinary" treatment, which they deem optional. * * * The terms "ordinary" and "extraordinary" have assumed too many conflicting meanings to remain useful. To draw a line on this basis for determining whether treatment should be given leads to a semantical milieu that does not advance the analysis.

The distinction between ordinary and extraordinary treatment is frequently phrased as one between common and unusual, or simple and complex, treatment [ ]; "extraordinary" treatment also has been equated with elaborate, artificial, heroic, aggressive, expensive, or highly involved or invasive forms of medical intervention [ ]. Depending on the definitions applied, a particular treatment for a given patient may be considered both ordinary and extraordinary. [ ] Further, since the common/unusual and simple/complex distinctions among medical treatments "exist on continuums with no precise dividing line," [ ] and the continuum is constantly shifting due to progress in medical care, disagreement will often exist about whether a particular treatment is ordinary or extraordinary. In addition, the competent patient generally could refuse even ordinary treatment; therefore, an incompetent patient theoretically should also be able to make such a choice when the surrogate decision-making is effectuating the patient's subjective intent. In such cases, the ordinary/extraordinary distinction is irrelevant except insofar as the particular patient would have made the distinction.

The ordinary/extraordinary distinction has also been discussed in terms of the benefits and burdens of treatment for the patient. If the benefits of the treatment outweigh the burdens it imposes on the patient, it is characterized as ordinary and therefore ethically required; if not, it is characterized as extraordinary and therefore optional. [ ] This formulation is extremely fact-sensitive and would lead to different classifications of the same treatment in different situations.

* * * Moreover, while the analysis may be useful in weighing the implications of the specific treatment for the patient, essentially it merely restates the question: whether the burdens of a treatment so clearly outweigh its benefits to the patient that continued treatment would be inhumane.

468 A.2d at 1234–1235. See also Brophy v. New England Sinai Hosp., Inc., 398 Mass. 417, 497 N.E.2d 626 (1986) ("while we believe that the distinction between extraordinary and ordinary care is a factor to be considered, the use of such a distinction as the sole, or major, factor of decision tends * * * to create a distinction without meaning.")

5. *The Special Status of Nutrition and Hydration*. The issue of withdrawing nutrition and hydration has become an especially contentious one. Medical sources generally recognize the irrelevancy of distinguishing between nutrition and hydration and other forms of medical treatment. The Council on Ethical and Judicial Affairs of the American Medical Association has determined that "[l]ife-sustaining treatment may include, but is not limited to, * * * artificial nutrition or hydration." Opinion 2.20 (2006-2007 ed.). Generally, courts also have concluded that

the termination of nutrition and hydration is no different from the termination of other forms of mechanical support. For example, *Conroy* suggested:

> Some commentators, * * * have made yet [another] distinction, between the termination of artificial feedings and the termination of other forms of life-sustaining medical treatment. * * * According to the Appellate Division:
>
> > If, as here, the patient is not comatose and does not face imminent and inevitable death, nourishment accomplishes the substantial benefit of sustaining life until the illness takes its natural course. Under such circumstances nourishment always will be an essential element of ordinary care which physicians are ethically obligated to provide. [ ]
>
> Certainly, feeding has an emotional significance. As infants we could breathe without assistance, but we were dependent on others for our lifeline of nourishment. Even more, feeding is an expression of nurturing and caring, certainly for infants and children, and in many cases for adults as well.
>
> Once one enters the realm of complex, high-technology medical care, it is hard to shed the "emotional symbolism" of food. * * * Analytically, artificial feeding by means of a nasogastric tube or intravenous infusion can be seen as equivalent to artificial breathing by means of a respirator. Both prolong life through mechanical means when the body is no longer able to perform a vital bodily function on its own.
>
> Furthermore, while nasogastric feeding and other medical procedures to ensure nutrition and hydration are usually well tolerated, they are not free from risks or burdens; they have complications that are sometimes serious and distressing to the patient.
>
> * * *
>
> Finally, dehydration may well not be distressing or painful to a dying patient. For patients who are unable to sense hunger and thirst, withholding of feeding devices such as nasogastric tubes may not result in more pain than the termination of any other medical treatment. * * * Thus, it cannot be assumed that it will always be beneficial for an incompetent patient to receive artificial feeding or harmful for him not to receive it. * * *
>
> Under the analysis articulated above, withdrawal or withholding of artificial feeding, like any other medical treatment, would be permissible if there is sufficient proof to satisfy the subjective, limited-objective, or pure-objective test. A competent patient has the right to decline any medical treatment, including artificial feeding, and should retain that right when and if he becomes incompetent. In addition, in the case of an incompetent patient who has given little or no trustworthy indication of an intent to decline treatment and for whom it becomes necessary to engage in balancing under the limited-objective or pure-objective test, the pain and invasiveness of an artificial feeding device, and the pain of withdrawing that device, should be treated just like the results of administering or withholding any other medical treatment.

98 N.J. 321, 486 A.2d 1209, 1235–1237.

See also Gray v. Romeo, 697 F.Supp. 580 (D.R.I.1988) ("Although an emotional symbolism attaches itself to artificial feeding, there is no legal difference between a mechanical device that allows a person to breathe artificially and a mechanical device that allows a person nourishment. If a person has right to decline a respirator, then a person has the equal right to decline a gastrostomy tube."); Brophy v. New England Sinai Hosp., Inc., 398 Mass. 417, 497 N.E.2d 626 (1986); Corbett v. D'Alessandro, 487 So.2d 368 (Fla.App.1986) ("we see no reason to differentiate between the multitude of artificial devices that may be available to prolong the moment of death."); Bouvia v. Superior Court, 179 Cal.App.3d 1127, 225 Cal.Rptr. 297 (1986).

In McConnell v. Beverly Enterprises–Connecticut, 209 Conn. 692, 553 A.2d 596 (1989), the court authorized the withdrawal of feeding by a gastrostomy tube despite a statute that appeared to say that under such circumstances "nutrition and hydration must be provided." The court reasoned that the nutrition and hydration that was implicated in the statute was that provided by "a spoon or a straw," and that feeding by gastrostomy tube was no different than any other mechanical or electronic medical intervention.

In 1990, at least, a majority of the Supreme Court (the four dissenters and concurring Justice O'Connor in *Cruzan*) viewed nutrition and hydration as another form of medical care. As Justice O'Connor pointed out, "artificial feeding cannot readily be distinguished from other forms of medical treatment. Whether or not the techniques used to pass food and water into the patient's alimentary tract are termed 'medical treatment,' it is clear they all involve some degree of intrusion and restraint." She concluded that "the liberty guaranteed by the due process clause must protect, if it protects anything, an individual's deeply personal decision to reject medical treatment, including the artificial delivery of food and water."

In his dissent, Justice Brennan reached the same conclusion, vividly describing the medical processes involved:

> The artificial delivery of nutrition and hydration is undoubtedly medical treatment. The technique to which Nancy Cruzan is subject—artificial feeding through a gastrostomy tube—involves a tube implanted surgically into her stomach through incisions in her abdominal wall. It may obstruct the intestinal tract, erode and pierce the stomach wall, or cause leakage of the stomach's contents into the abdominal cavity. [ ] The tube can cause pneumonia from reflux of the stomach's contents into the lung. [ ] Typically, and in this case, commercially prepared formulas are used, rather than fresh food. [ ] The type of formula and method of administration must be experimented with to avoid gastrointestinal problems. [ ] The patient must be monitored daily by medical personnel as to weight, fluid intake and fluid output; blood tests must be done weekly.

> Artificial delivery of food and water is regarded as medical treatment by the medical profession and the federal government. * * * The federal government permits the cost of the medical devices and formulas used in enteral feeding to be reimbursed under Medicare. [ ] The formulas are regulated by the Federal Drug Administration as "medical foods," [ ] and the feeding tubes are regulated as medical devices [ ].

497 U.S. at 306–308, 110 S.Ct. at 2866–67.

To many, nutrition and hydration remain symbols of the bonds between human beings; the care we provide to the ones we love includes, at the very least, food and water. For others, the provision of artificial nutrition and hydration has religious and moral significance. Consider the following document from the Vatican:

CONGREGATION FOR THE DOCTRINE OF THE FAITH
RESPONSES TO CERTAIN QUESTIONS
OF THE UNITED STATES CONFERENCE OF CATHOLIC BISHOPS
CONCERNING ARTIFICIAL NUTRITION AND HYDRATION

First question: *Is the administration of food and water (whether by natural or artificial means) to a patient in a "vegetative state" morally obligatory* *except when they cannot be assimilated by the patient's body or cannot be administered to the patient without causing significant physical discomfort?*

Response: Yes. The administration of food and water even by artificial means is, in principle, an ordinary and proportionate means of preserving life. It is therefore obligatory to the extent to which, and for as long as, it is shown to accomplish its proper finality, which is the hydration and nourishment of the patient. In this way suffering and death by starvation and dehydration are prevented.

Second question: When nutrition and hydration are being supplied by artificial means to a patient in a "permanent vegetative state", may they be discontinued when competent physicians judge with moral certainty that the patient will never recover consciousness?

Response: No. A patient in a "permanent vegetative state" is a person with fundamental human dignity and must, therefore, receive ordinary and proportionate care which includes, in principle, the administration of water and food even by artificial means.

The Supreme Pontiff Benedict XVI, at the Audience granted to the undersigned Cardinal Prefect of the Congregation for the Doctrine of the Faith, approved these Responses, adopted in the Ordinary Session of the Congregation, and ordered their publication. August 1, 2007.

For interpretations of the content and application of this statement within the Roman Catholic tradition, see John Hardt & Kevin O'Rourke, Nutrition and Hydration: The [Congregation for the Doctrine of Faith], In Perspective, 88 Health Progress 1 (2007), arguing, inter alia, that Catholic Canon Law requires that the statement be interpreted strictly as it restricts rights; that the form of the statement has less force than other vehicles for establishing directives; and that the use of the term "in principle" indicates that there are exceptions. In particular, in contrast to earlier statements on nutrition and hydration, this statement is specifically confined to circumstances of confirmed diagnosis of PVS and addresses only nutrition and hydration and not other medical interventions. See also Daniel Sulmasy, Preserving Life? The Vatican and PVS, 134 Commonweal (No.21) 16 (Dec. 7, 2007). Vatican commentary on this statement evidences a particular concern about "persistent vegetative state," calling it a prognosis rather than a diagnosis. Available at http://www.vatican.va/roman_curia/congregations/cfaith/documents/rc_con_cfaith_doc_20070801_nota-commento_en.html .

The CDF statement is meant to guide Catholic health care providers. As such, it does illustrate situations in which health care providers may have moral or religious conflicts with patients and families over particular medical treatment decisions.

C. DISPUTES AMONG FAMILY MEMBERS ACTING AS DECISION MAKERS

For the months leading up to her death in 2005, people all over the country were riveted by the very public discussion of Terri Schiavo, whose case vividly raised the issue of how a dispute between family members with regard to the tube feeding of a patient in persistent vegetative state ought to be resolved. Although that case was heard by several state and federal courts (and addressed by both the Florida legislature and the United States Congress) in 2003 and 2004, the first substantive appeal was decided, and the facts were carefully laid out, in 2001:

GUARDIANSHIP OF SCHIAVO

Court of Appeal of Florida, Second District, 2001.
780 So.2d 176.

ALTENBERND, JUDGE.

Robert and Mary Schindler, the parents of Theresa Marie Schiavo, appeal the trial court's order authorizing the discontinuance of artificial life support to their adult daughter. Michael Schiavo, Theresa's husband and guardian, petitioned the trial court in May 1998 for entry of this order. We have carefully reviewed the record. The trial court made a difficult decision after considering all of the evidence and the applicable law. We conclude that the trial court's decision is supported by competent, substantial evidence and that it correctly applies the law. Accordingly, we affirm the decision.

Theresa Marie Schindler was born on December 3, 1963, and lived with or near her parents in Pennsylvania until she married Michael Schiavo on November 10, 1984. Michael and Theresa moved to Florida in 1986. They were happily married and both were employed. They had no children.

On February 25, 1990, their lives changed. Theresa, age 27, suffered a cardiac arrest as a result of a potassium imbalance. Michael called 911, and Theresa was rushed to the hospital. She never regained consciousness.

Since 1990, Theresa has lived in nursing homes with constant care. She is fed and hydrated by tubes. The staff changes her diapers regularly. She has had numerous health problems, but none have been life threatening.

The evidence is overwhelming that Theresa is in a permanent or persistent vegetative state. It is important to understand that a persistent vegetative state is not simply a coma. She is not asleep. She has cycles of apparent wakefulness and apparent sleep without any cognition or awareness. As she breathes, she often makes moaning sounds. Theresa has severe contractures of her hands, elbows, knees, and feet.

Over the span of this last decade, Theresa's brain has deteriorated because of the lack of oxygen it suffered at the time of the heart attack. By mid–1996, the CAT scans of her brain showed a severely abnormal structure. At this point, much of her cerebral cortex is simply gone and has been replaced by cerebral spinal fluid. Medicine cannot cure this condition. Unless an act of God, a true miracle, were to recreate her brain, Theresa will always remain in an unconscious, reflexive state, totally dependent upon others to feed her and care for her most private needs. She could remain in this state for many years.

Theresa has been blessed with loving parents and a loving husband. Many patients in this condition would have been abandoned by friends and family within the first year. Michael has continued to care for her and to visit her all these years. He has never divorced her. He has become a professional respiratory therapist and works in a nearby hospital. As a guardian, he has always attempted to provide optimum treatment for his wife. He has been a diligent watch guard of Theresa's care, never hesitating to annoy the nursing staff in order to assure that she receives the proper treatment.

Theresa's parents have continued to love her and visit her often. No one questions the sincerity of their prayers for the divine miracle that now is Theresa's only hope to regain any level of normal existence. No one questions that they have filed this appeal out of love for their daughter.

This lawsuit is affected by an earlier lawsuit. In the early 1990's, Michael Schiavo, as Theresa's guardian, filed a medical malpractice lawsuit. That case resulted in a sizable award of money for Theresa. This fund remains sufficient to care for Theresa for many years. If she were to die today, her husband would inherit the money under the laws of intestacy. If Michael eventually divorced Theresa in order to have a more normal family life, the fund remaining at the end of Theresa's life would presumably go to her parents.

Since the resolution of the malpractice lawsuit, both Michael and the Schindlers have become suspicious that the other party is assessing Theresa's wishes based upon their own monetary self-interest. The trial court discounted this concern, and we see no evidence in this record that either Michael or the Schindlers seek monetary gain from their actions. Michael and the Schindlers simply cannot agree on what decision Theresa would make today if she were able to assess her own condition and make her own decision.

There has been discussion among the parties that the money remaining when Theresa dies should be given to a suitable charity as a lasting memorial. If anything is undeniable in this case, it is that Theresa would never wish for this money to drive a wedge between the people she loves. We have no jurisdiction over the disposition of this money, but hopefully these parties will consider Theresa's desires and her memory when a decision about the money is ultimately required.

This is a case to authorize the termination of life-prolonging procedures * * *.

First, the Schindlers maintain that the trial court was required to appoint a guardian ad litem for this proceeding because Michael stands to inherit under the laws of intestacy. When a living will or other advance directive does not exist, it stands to reason that the surrogate decision-maker will be a person who is close to the patient and thereby likely to inherit from the patient. [ ] Thus, the fact that a surrogate decision-maker may ultimately inherit from the patient should not automatically compel the appointment of a guardian. On the other hand, there may be occasions when an inheritance could be a reason to question a surrogate's ability to make an objective decision.

In this case, however, Michael Schiavo has not been allowed to make a decision to disconnect life-support. The Schindlers have not been allowed to make a decision to maintain life-support. Each party in this case, absent their disagreement, might have been a suitable surrogate decision-maker for Theresa. Because Michael Schiavo and the Schindlers could not agree on the proper decision and the inheritance issue created the appearance of conflict, Michael Schiavo, as the guardian of Theresa, invoked the trial court's jurisdiction to allow the trial court to serve as the surrogate decision-maker.

[As this court said some years ago,]

We emphasize, * * * that courts are always open to adjudicate legitimate questions pertaining to the written or oral instructions. First, the surrogate or proxy may choose to present the question to the court for resolution. Second, interested parties may challenge the decision of the proxy or surrogate. [ ]

In this case, Michael Schiavo used the first approach. Under these circumstances, the two parties, as adversaries, present their evidence to the trial court. The trial court determines whether the evidence is sufficient to allow it to make the decision for the ward to discontinue life support. In this context, the trial court essentially serves as the ward's guardian. Although we do not rule out the occasional need for a guardian in this type of proceeding, a guardian ad litem would tend to duplicate the function of the judge, would add little of value to this process, and might cause the process to be influenced by hearsay or matters outside the record. Accordingly, we affirm the trial court's discretionary decision in this case to proceed without a guardian ad litem.

Second, the Schindlers argue that the trial court should not have heard evidence from Beverly Tyler, the executive director of Georgia Health Decisions. Al though it is doubtful that this issue is preserved for appeal, we have reviewed the issue as if it were. Ms. Tyler has studied American values, opinions, and attitudes about the decision to discontinue life-support systems. As a result, she has some special expertise concerning the words and expressions that Americans often use in discussing these difficult issues. She also has knowledge about trends within American attitudes on this subject.

We have considerable doubt that Ms. Tyler's testimony provided much in the way of relevant evidence. She testified about some social science surveys. Apparently most people, even those who favor initial life-supporting medical treatment, indicate that they would not wish this treatment to continue indefinitely once their medical condition presented no reasonable basis for a cure. There is some risk that a trial judge could rely upon this type of survey evidence to make a "best interests" decision for the ward. In this case, however, we are convinced that the trial judge did not give undue weight to this evidence and that the court made a proper surrogate decision rather than a best interests decision.

Finally, the Schindlers argue that the testimony, which was conflicting, was insufficient to support the trial court's decision by clear and convincing evidence. We have reviewed that testimony and conclude that the trial court had sufficient evidence to make this decision. The clear and convincing standard of proof, while very high, permits a decision in the face of inconsistent or conflicting evidence. [ ]

[As we have] stated:

In making this difficult decision, a surrogate decisionmaker should err on the side of life. . . . In cases of doubt, we must assume that a patient would choose to defend life in exercising his or her right of privacy. [ ]

We reconfirm today that a court's default position must favor life.

The testimony in this case establishes that Theresa was very young and very healthy when this tragedy struck. Like many young people without children, she had not prepared a will, much less a living will. She had been raised in the Catholic faith, but did not regularly attend mass or have a religious advisor who could assist the court in weighing her religious attitudes about life-support methods. Her statements to her friends and family about the dying process were few and they were oral. Nevertheless, those statements, along with other evidence about Theresa, gave the trial court a sufficient basis to make this decision for her.

In the final analysis, the difficult question that faced the trial court was whether Theresa Marie Schindler Schiavo, not after a few weeks in a coma, but after ten years in a persistent vegetative state that has robbed her of most of her cerebrum and all but the most instinctive of neurological functions, with no hope of a medical cure but with sufficient money and strength of body to live indefinitely, would choose to continue the constant nursing care and the supporting tubes in hopes that a miracle would somehow recreate her missing brain tissue, or whether she would wish to permit a natural death process to take its course and for her family members and loved ones to be free to continue their lives. After due consideration, we conclude that the trial judge had clear and convincing evidence to answer this question as he did.

Affirmed.

Note on the Legal and Political History of the Schiavo Case

The story of the Schiavo case runs through thirteen years and all three branches of government in Florida. As Chief Judge Altenbernd points out, it is a sad story of uncertainty, mistrust, hope, understanding (and misunderstanding) and politics. It is difficult to disentangle Schiavo the person (a shy animal lover and a quiet, kind young woman) from Schiavo the cause (on both sides of the issue).

The case returned to the Court of Appeals twice in 2001, and in the second of those the court determined that the trial court was required to have an evidentiary hearing on the Schindlers' motion seeking relief from the original judgment on the grounds that there were new treatments available for Terri. The remand included an instruction that each party be allowed to present two physician expert witnesses to support its position, and that the trial court appoint a fifth. These physicians were to be given access to all of Terri's medical records, including "high-quality brain scans." On remand, all of the experts agreed that there was "extensive permanent damage to her brain," and the only debate was "whether she has a small amount of living tissue in her cerebral cortex, or whether she has no living tissue in her cerebral cortex." *Guardianship of Schiavo (Schiavo IV)*, 851 So.2d 182 (Fla.App.2003). The court's appointed expert agreed with Michael's experts, and the trial court denied the Schindler's motion to reopen. The Court of Appeals affirmed *Schiavo IV* in an opinion again written by Judge Altenbernd. The difficulty of the decision–and the propriety of having the substantive decision made by the judge, applying the principle of substituted judgment–were again clearly articulated:

> The judges on this panel are called upon to make a collective, objective decision concerning a question of law. Each of us, however, has our own family, our own loved ones, our own children. From our review of the videotapes of Mrs. Schiavo, despite the irrefutable evidence that her cerebral cortex has sustained the most severe of irreparable injuries, we understand why a parent who had raised and nurtured a child from conception would hold out hope that some level of cognitive function remained. If Mrs. Schiavo were our own daughter, we could not but hold to such a faith.

But in the end, this case is not about the aspirations that loving parents have for their children. It is about Theresa Schiavo's right to make her own decision, independent of her parents and independent of her husband. In circumstances such as these, when families cannot agree, the law has opened the doors of the circuit courts to permit trial judges to serve as surrogates or proxies to make decisions about life-prolonging procedures. It is the trial judge's duty not to make the decision that the judge would make for himself or herself or for a loved one. Instead, the trial judge must make a decision that the clear and convincing evidence shows the ward would have made for herself. It is a thankless task, and one to be undertaken with care, objectivity, and a cautious legal standard designed to promote the value of life. But it is also a necessary function if all people are to be entitled to a personalized decision about life-prolonging procedures independent of the subjective and conflicting assessments of their friends and relatives. It may be unfortunate that when families cannot agree, the best forum we can offer for this private, personal decision is a public courtroom and the best decision-maker we can provide is a judge with no prior knowledge of the ward, but the law currently provides no better solution that adequately protects the interests of promoting the value of life. We have previously affirmed the guardianship court's decision in this regard, and we now affirm the denial of a motion for relief from that judgment.

851 So.2d at 187. The court remanded to the trial court "solely for the purpose of entering a new order scheduling the removal of the nutrition and hydration tube." On remand, the trial court set October 15, 2003, for the removal of the tube. By this time, several Right to Life and disability advocacy groups had enlisted Florida Governor Jeb Bush to help them find some way to save Terri's life, and Right to Die groups were organizing to oppose them. On October 15 the feeding tube was removed, and Terri was expected to die within the next two weeks.

An advocacy group also sought relief in the federal court, where it filed a petition for a temporary restraining order requiring the continuation of Terri's feeding until it could do a full investigation of alleged abuse and neglect against Terri. The federal court refused to be drawn into the controversy, and, after denying the order, the judge declared:

This case offers a vivid opportunity for the public, whose collective will ultimately decides such matters, to contemplate the confounding issues associated with degenerative illness and catastrophic disability and thereafter, by a means consistent with government in a republic, to direct their representatives to legislate in accord with their concerted desires, if in a conflict with the present state of the law.

Advocacy Center for Persons With Disabilities v. Schiavo, 8:03–CV–2167–T–23EAJ (M.D.Fla. 2003). Wasting no time, those advocating for continued feeding took the case to the floor of the state legislature on the very afternoon that the federal court decision was rendered, and the legislature was urged by the Governor to overturn the decision of the Florida Court of Appeals. Almost immediately (but with more than the normal wailing and gnashing of teeth) the Florida legislature passed, and the Governor signed, what became known as "Terri's Law." While the accuracy of titles of legislative acts named for individuals is often open to question, this was truly Terri's law; her case is the only one to which it could ever apply. The statute provided that:

The Governor shall have the authority to issue a one-time stay to prevent the withholding of nutrition and hydration from a patient if, as of October 15, 2003:

(a) That patient has no written advance directive;

(b) The court has found that the patient is in persistent vegetative state;

(c) That patient has had nutrition and hydration withheld; and

(d) A member of that patient's family has challenged the withholding of nutrition and hydration.

2003 Fl. Laws ch. 418. The statute provided that the Governor's authority would expire 15 days after the passage of the Act, and that upon the granting of such a stay the court would appoint a guardian ad litem for the patient "to make a recommendation to the Governor and the court."

The Governor issued the "one-time stay" immediately, and the court appointed Professor Jay Wolfson to be the guardian ad litem. Almost as quickly, Michael began challenging the constitutionality of Terri's law on the grounds that it violated the privacy provisions of the Florida constitution and the principles of separation of powers (because it amounted to a legislative reversal of a particular judicial decision). Professor Wolfson submitted his report in December of 2003, and he supported Michael's position that the tube be removed. In a separate action, the trial court also determined that Terri's Law was presumptively unconstitutional.

The Court of Appeals (and the Florida Supreme Court) ultimately considered the Governor's request that he be allowed to do a further investigation as a part of the case challenging the Constitutionality of Terri's law. The Governor wanted to ask Michael why he did not inform the trial court of Terri's wish to avoid extraordinary care when it awarded her $700,000 for her future medical care in her original malpractice case. Governor Bush also expressed concern that Michael, who was then living with a woman with whom he had two children, might not have Terri's best interest at heart. The Florida Supreme Court upheld the trial court's determination that Terri's law was unconstitutional.

Over the last few years of this litigation, Terri Schiavo's feeding tube was removed three times as a result of orders of the trial court. The first two times it was removed it was subsequently replaced. It was removed for the third and final time on March 18, 2005. There was an immediate reaction in Congress, which rushed to pass a bill to authorize federal court review of the *Schiavo* case. This private bill, aimed only at this one case, was approved by the Congress on Palm Sunday, 2005, and signed by the President almost immediately. Subsequently, the federal district court denied preliminary relief (i.e., an order to replace the feeding tube) under the federal statute because it was unlikely that the petitioners would be successful at trial, and the district court was quickly affirmed, 2–1, by a panel of the Eleventh Circuit, and then by that court en banc. The United States Supreme Court refused to review this decision.

Terri Schiavo died on March 31, 2005. For detailed chronology of the dispute, see Kathy Cerminara & Kenneth Goodman, Schiavo Case Resources, Key Events in the Case of Theresa Marie Schiavo (2006), http:// www.miami.edu/ethics2/schiavo/timeline.htm (outlining the events of this case, including the numerous judicial opinions generated).

Problem: Not Quite Persistent Vegetative State

When unhelmeted 57-year-old Tad Gonzales ran his motorcycle into a bridge support post on an interstate highway, he was revived at the scene and rushed to Big Central Hospital. There he underwent several hours of emergency surgery designed to preserve his life and repair the very substantial head injuries he sustained. A few days after the surgery, he began to regain consciousness, and a week later he was able to be removed from the ventilator which was supporting his breathing, although he still needs ventilator assistance from time to time. During his first two weeks in the hospital, Tad showed little improvement. He was not in a coma, but he was only occasionally responsive, and he demonstrated no awareness of Ralph, his partner of twenty-two years, or his two brothers and his parents, even though Tad had always shared a close relationship with all of them.

After two weeks, Big City Hospital transferred Tad to Commercial Affiliated Nursing Home, where he began receiving physical and occupational therapy. After a year of care there, he has shown little improvement. He still does not seem to recognize Ralph, who visits daily, or anyone else. He is able to sit up and his eyes sometimes seem to be following images on a screen. He grunts when he is hungry or uncomfortable. He cannot eat or drink, and he is fed through a feeding tube in his abdomen. He cannot control his bowels or bladder. He has regularly suffered from urinary tract infections and asthma during his nursing home stay, although his need for the ventilator is becoming rarer. On a few, increasingly rare, occasions, his heart stopped beating, but he was resuscitated immediately. Doctors believe that there is little chance of substantial improvement in his condition (although, in the words of one doctor, "Who knows? Anything can happen.") Tad's doctors estimate that his life expectancy could be another twenty years or more.

Tad's doctor and Ralph have developed a good working relationship, and the doctor has called upon Ralph to approve any change in Tad's treatment regimen even though Tad never signed any kind of advance directive. Ralph has now informed the doctor that he believes that Tad would want the use of the feeding tube (and the occasional use of the ventilator) discontinued, and that he would not want to be resuscitated (i.e., he would want to be DNR). When the doctor challenged him on this, Ralph respectfully ordered the doctor to terminate feeding, and to note that Tad was not to be mechanically ventilated or resuscitated. Ralph explained that he had spoken with Tad often about "this kind of thing," and that Tad had said that the indignity of being fed, or wearing diapers, or being bed-bound, was not worth the value of life to him. In particular, Ralph remembers Tad describing one of their friends, another motorcyclist who became a quadriplegic and suffered some intellectual impairment after an accident, as "better off dead." Tad and Ralph promised each other that neither would ever let that happen to the other. Tad's parents and one of his brothers agree that there is no doubt that Tad would want all treatment terminated under these circumstances. Tad's other brother disagrees. As he has articulated it, "How can we know what he would want? He could never have imagined himself in this situation, and we shouldn't read anything in to what he said about other people. Maybe he thought those other people could feel more pain than he can."

Tad's doctor has approached you, the hospital counsel, to ask you what she should do. Should she discontinue feeding? The use of the ventilator? Should the hospital pursue an action in court? What position should the hospital take if Ralph, or Tad's dissenting brother, pursue an action in court? How should that action be resolved?

D.   LETTING THE DOCTOR DECIDE: FUTILE TREATMENT

Problems: Futile or Not?

Two cases involving disputes over patient care have come to you as counsel for the hospital.

The Wanglie Case

Helen Wanglie, an 87–year-old retired school teacher, tripped on a rug in her home and fractured her hip. One month later, after surgery in one hospital, she was transferred to County Medical Center, where her doctors determined she needed assistance in breathing and placed her on a ventilator. Three months later she was transferred to yet another hospital to see if she could be weaned from her ventilator. While there, she suffered cardiac arrest and was resuscitated, but only after she suffered severe and irreversible brain damage that put her in a persistent vegetative state. She was moved back to County Medical Center, where she is maintained on a ventilator and fed through a gastrostomy tube. Mrs. Wanglie remained in a persistent vegetative state for several months before her physicians determined that the continuation of high-tech medical intervention was inappropriate. In essence, the doctors have determined that the care Mrs. Wanglie was receiving was no longer among the reasonable medical alternatives for a person in her condition.

Mrs. Wanglie's husband and her two children disagree. As Mrs. Wanglie's husband points out, "Only He who gave life has the right to take life." He also points out, "I am a prolifer. I take the position that human life is sacred." He and the children agree that Mrs. Wanglie would want treatment continued, even if the doctors believed that there were no chance of recovery. This is, as the family points out, a determination based on the patient's values, and there is no reason to defer to the doctors' collective ethical judgment.

The physicians and the hospital have searched in vain for some other healthcare facility that would be willing to take Mrs. Wanglie and continue to provide her care. None has come forward. Frustrated by what they considered the continued inappropriate use of medicine, the health care providers–the doctors and nurses–have asked whether they can discontinue treatment. Should the hospital seek a court order appointing a conservator to replace Mr. Wanglie to make healthcare decisions for Mrs. Wanglie so that her treatment can be discontinued? Should that order be granted? Is there any other legal remedy available to the hospital?

The Nighthorse Case

Emile Nighthorse is a 77–year-old man who has been hospitalized on and off over the past year. He suffers from serious kidney disease, congestive heart failure, severe headaches and increasingly severe dementia. His current hospitalization, which commenced two weeks ago, has resulted in him being supplied with kidney dialysis, which will, it appears, have to continue indefinitely, and a ventilator, which probably will be removed in a few weeks. He does not really understand his condition (or where he is), and he is cranky and abusive with the nurses, whom he believes to be torturing him. A psychiatrist does not believe there is any way to treat his mental condition without extremely heavy sedation. His prognosis is poor; his dementia will surely get worse, and his multi-system failure makes it likely that he will not live more than a few months. It is unlikely he will ever be discharged from the hospital.

Mr. Nighthorse never talked about his condition with anyone, and he has had a strained relationship with his wife of 50 years, who lives with him but rarely comes to the hospital to see him. He has two children who live in another city, and they both claim to have a relatively distant relationship with their father. Until his dementia became too severe, he spent most of his time at the Order of Eagles Aerie playing whist, and his long time whist partner, Ben Bitts, has been with Mr. Nighthorse constantly from the moment he entered the hospital. Whenever Mr.

Nighthorse is asked a question about his care, he turns to Ben and asks him what "they" should do.

Ben has asked the physician responsible for Mr. Nighthorse's care to discontinue the dialysis and the ventilator, and to begin antibiotics. There is no medical reason to use antibiotics, but Ben argues that he is absolutely sure that Mr. Nighthorse would want them anyway—he always wanted antibiotics when he was sick, even when his doctors told him that such drugs would be worthless. Ben says that he never really talked with Emile about what should be done under these circumstances, but that they had played whist together so long (almost 20 years) that he figures that he knows what Mr. Nighthorse would want. Mrs. Nighthorse has told the doctor to do whatever Ben wants to do; she doesn't care. The two children have not returned to town. When contacted by phone, they both insist that everything should be done to save their father, but neither is willing to come to the hospital.

Mr. Nighthorse's primary physician has asked you—the hospital legal counsel—what he should do. What should you tell him?

————————

In analyzing these problems, you may wish to consider two sources that might be helpful to health care decision makers. The first is hospital policy. Over the last decade many institutions have adopted futility policies, and the one printed below is a particularly short and elegant one. The second is state statute. In 2003 Texas became the first state to formally address the maintenance of futile medical care through statute. The statutory sections reprinted here were added to the Advance Directive statute already in place in Texas.

FROEDTERT HOSPITAL—MEDICAL COLLEGE OF WISCONSIN, FUTILITY POLICY

(revised 2007).

* * *

If, in the well-grounded judgment of the attending physician and a staff physician consultant, life-sustaining medical treatment would be futile, the attending physician may write an order withholding or withdrawing the treatment after notifying the patient (or other responsible individual if the patient lacks decision-making capacity). Appropriate palliative care measures should be instituted. A life-sustaining medical intervention should be considered "futile" if it cannot be expected to restore or maintain vital organ function or to achieve the expressed goals of the patient when decisional.

Life-sustaining medical treatment includes cardiopulmonary resuscitation, mechanical ventilation, artificial nutrition and hydration, blood products, renal dialysis, vasopressors, or any other treatment that prolongs dying.

Consultation with Palliative Medicine, Social Services, and Chaplaincy, as appropriate, is strongly encouraged. If there are remaining questions, the physician should consult the Ethics Committee. If the patient (or surrogate) disagrees, the attending physician should consider whether transfer to another attending physician, or another health care facility willing to accept the patient, is feasible. If transfer to a physician or facility willing to accept the patient is not feasible, further life-sustaining medical treatment may be withdrawn.

The attending physician must inform the Office of the Senior Vice President for Medical Affairs verbally when this policy is invoked and document the notice in the patient's medical record.

TEX. HEALTH & SAFETY CODE § 166.046 § 166.052; § 166.053 [THE TEXAS FUTILITY STATUTE]

§ 166.046—Procedure if Not Effectuating a Directive or Treatment Decision

(a) If an attending physician refuses to honor a patient's advance directive or a health care or treatment decision made by or on behalf of a patient, the physician's refusal shall be reviewed by an ethics or medical committee. The attending physician may not be a member of that committee. The patient shall be given life-sustaining treatment during the review.

(b) The patient or the person responsible for the health care decisions of the individual who has made the decision regarding the directive or treatment decision:

(1) may be given a written description of the ethics or medical committee review process and any other policies and procedures related to this section adopted by the health care facility;

(2) shall be informed of the committee review process not less than 48 hours before the meeting called to discuss the patient's directive, unless the time period is waived by mutual agreement;

(3) at the time of being so informed, shall be provided:

(A) a copy of the appropriate statement [describing this process]; and

(B) a copy of the registry list of health care providers and referral groups that have volunteered their readiness to consider accepting transfer or to assist in locating a provider willing to accept transfer * * *; and

(4) is entitled to:

(A) attend the meeting; and

(B) receive a written explanation of the decision reached during the review process.

(c) The written explanation * * * must be included in the patient's medical record.

(d) If the attending physician, the patient, or the person responsible for the health care decisions of the individual does not agree with the decision reached during the review process under Subsection (b), the physician shall make a reasonable effort to transfer the patient to a physician who is willing to comply with the directive. If the patient is a patient in a health care facility, the facility's personnel shall assist the physician in arranging the patient's transfer to:

(1) another physician;

(2) an alternative care setting within that facility; or

(3) another facility.

(e) If the patient or the person responsible for the health care decisions of the patient is requesting life-sustaining treatment that the attending physician has decided and the review process has affirmed is inappropriate treatment, the patient shall be given available life-sustaining treatment pending transfer * * *. The patient is responsible for any costs incurred in transferring the patient to another facility. The physician and the health care facility are not obligated to provide life-sustaining treatment after the 10th day after the written decision required under Subsection (b) is provided to the patient or the person responsible for the health care decisions of the patient unless ordered to do so under Subsection (g).

(e–1) If during a previous admission to a facility a patient's attending physician and the review process * * * have determined that life-sustaining treatment is inappropriate, and the patient is readmitted to the same facility within six months from the date of the decision reached during the review process conducted upon the previous admission, Subsections (b) through (e) need not be followed if the patient's attending physician and a consulting physician who is a member of the ethics or medical committee of the facility document on the patient's readmission that the patient's condition either has not improved or has deteriorated since the review process was conducted.

(f) Life-sustaining treatment under this section may not be entered in the patient's medical record as medically unnecessary treatment until the time period provided under Subsection (e) has expired.

(g) At the request of the patient or the person responsible for the health care decisions of the patient, the appropriate district or county court shall extend the time period provided under Subsection (e) only if the court finds, by a preponderance of the evidence, that there is a reasonable expectation that a physician or health care facility that will honor the patient's directive will be found if the time extension is granted.

(h) * * * This section does not apply to hospice services provided by a home and community support services agency * * *.

* * *

§ 166.052—Statements Explaining Patient's Right to Transfer

(a) In cases in which the attending physician refuses to honor an advance directive or treatment decision requesting the provision of life-sustaining treatment, the statement required * * * shall be in substantially the following form:

> You have been given this information because you have requested life-sustaining treatment,* which the attending physician believes is not

---

* "Life-sustaining treatment" means treatment that, based on reasonable medical judg- ment, sustains the life of a patient and without which the patient will die. The term includes

appropriate. This information is being provided to help you understand state law, your rights, and the resources available to you in such circumstances. It outlines the process for resolving disagreements about treatment among patients, families, and physicians. It is based upon [this section].

When There Is A Disagreement About Medical Treatment: The Physician Recommends Against Life–Sustaining Treatment That You Wish To Continue

When an attending physician refuses to comply with an advance directive or other request for life-sustaining treatment because of the physician's judgment that the treatment would be inappropriate, the case will be reviewed by an ethics or medical committee. Life-sustaining treatment will be provided through the review.

You will receive notification of this review at least 48 hours before a meeting of the committee related to your case. You are entitled to attend the meeting. With your agreement, the meeting may be held sooner than 48 hours, if possible.

You are entitled to receive a written explanation of the decision reached during the review process.

If after this review process both the attending physician and the ethics or medical committee conclude that life-sustaining treatment is inappropriate and yet you continue to request such treatment, then the following procedure will occur:

1. The physician, with the help of the health care facility, will assist you in trying to find a physician and facility willing to provide the requested treatment.

2. You are being given a list of health care providers and referral groups that have volunteered their readiness to consider accepting transfer, or to assist in locating a provider willing to accept transfer* * *. You may wish to contact providers or referral groups on the list or others of your choice to get help in arranging a transfer.

3. The patient will continue to be given life-sustaining treatment until he or she can be transferred to a willing provider for up to 10 days from the time you were given the committee's written decision that life-sustaining treatment is not appropriate.

4. If a transfer can be arranged, the patient will be responsible for the costs of the transfer.

5. If a provider cannot be found willing to give the requested treatment within 10 days, life-sustaining treatment may be withdrawn unless a court of law has granted an extension.

6. You may ask the appropriate district or county court to extend the 10–day period if the court finds that there is a reasonable expectation

---

both life-sustaining medications and artificial life support, such as mechanical breathing machines, kidney dialysis treatment, and artificial nutrition and hydration. The term does not include the administration of pain management medication or the performance of a medical procedure considered to be necessary to provide comfort care, or any other medical care provided to alleviate a patient's pain.

that a physician or health care facility willing to provide life-sustaining treatment will be found if the extension is granted.

* * *

(c) An attending physician or health care facility may, if it chooses, include any additional information concerning the physician's or facility's policy, perspective, experience, or review procedure.

§ 166.053—Registry to Assist Transfers

(a) The Texas Health Care Information Council shall maintain a registry listing the identity of and contact information for health care providers and referral groups * * * that have voluntarily notified the council they may consider accepting or may assist in locating a provider willing to accept transfer of a patient under [this statute].

(b) The listing of a provider or referral group in the registry described in this section does not obligate the provider or group to accept transfer of or provide services to any particular patient.

* * *

Notes and Questions on Futility

1.   When is requested care truly "futile"? Under the Froedtert Hospital Policy, how is futility defined? Who has the authority to make that decision? Under the Texas statute, how is futility defined? Who has the final authority to make that decision? How would you define futility? Whom would you allow to be the final arbiter of whether a proposed treatment is futile? For a review of existing hospital policies, see Sandra H. Johnson, et al., Legal and Institutional Policy Responses to Medical Futility, 30 J. Health & Hosp. L. 1 (1997), concluding that most hospital futility policies failed to identify the final authoritative decisionmaker.

2.   The term, futility, is subject to a variety of interpretations. Treatment is *scientifically futile* (or *medically futile*) when it cannot achieve the medical result that is expected by the patient (or by the family) making the request. As a general matter, scientifically futile treatment need not be offered or provided to a patient. A seriously ill cancer patient need not be provided with laetrile, a useless drug that has been popularized by those who would prey upon desperate patients and their families, even if that treatment is requested. A child with a viral illness need not be prescribed an antibiotic, even if the child's parents request one, because, as a matter of science, the antibiotic will not be effective in treating that illness. Doctors need not do a CAT scan on a patient with a cold, even if that is what the patient wants, because there is no reason to believe that there will be any connection between what can be discovered on the scan and the appropriate treatment of the cold. As a general matter healthcare providers, who are trained in the science of medicine, are entitled to determine which treatments are scientifically futile.

A harder question arises when a patient requests treatment that is not scientifically futile, but that is, in the opinion of the health care provider, *ethically futile*. Treatment is ethically futile if it will not serve the underlying interests of the patient. For example, some providers believe that it is ethically futile to keep a patient's body aerated and nourished when that patient is in persistent vegetative state. These healthcare providers believe that it is beyond the scope of medicine to sustain mere corporeal existence. Some healthcare providers believe that it would be ethically futile to engage in CPR under circumstances in which the most that can be accomplished through that intervention would be to prolong the patient's life by a few hours. Families may disagree with physicians over what constitutes ethically futile treatment. Is there any reason to adopt the provider's perspective, rather than the family's, as the ethically "correct" one? In the *Wanglie* case, for example, the family viewed the continued treatment as effective (in keeping the patient alive) while the healthcare providers viewed the treatment as ineffective (in serving any of the goals of medicine).

The Council on Ethical and Judicial Affairs of the AMA has determined that:

> [p]hysicians are not ethically obliged to deliver care that, in their best professional judgment, will not have a reasonable chance of benefiting their patients. Patients should not be given treatments simply because they demand them. Denials of treatment should be justified by reliance on openly stated ethical principles and acceptable standards of care, * * * not on the concept of "futility," which cannot be meaningfully defined.

Council on Ethical and Judicial Affairs, American Medical Association, Current Opinion 2.035, *Futility,* Code of Medical Ethics. Is the Council's position a convincing one, or is it merely a device to transfer the authority to make ethically charged decisions from patients to physicians? Do you think that futility can be meaningfully defined? For a detailed discussion of this point, and the argument that the solution is something like the Texas statute, see Patrick Moore, An End-of-Life Quandry in Need of a Statutory Response: When Patients Demand Life-Sustaining Treatment That Physicians Are Unwilling to Provide, 48 B.C.L.Rev. 433 (2007).

3. Do you think that there ought to be an appeal allowed to an ethics committee after a physician decides that treatment would be futile? Why do you think the statute mandates the availability of such an appeal, while the policy leaves the decision in the hands of the physician (in consultation with another physician)? How should a physician (or a court) deal with a request for futile medical care?

4. How would the policy and the statute that appear here have affected the Wanglie or Nighthorse cases if they had been in effect when those cases arose? How should those cases be handled in the absence of a law like the Texas statute or an institutional policy? Would you recommend that your hospital adopt the Froedtert Policy?

5. Under the Froedtert Policy, what process must be followed by a hospital whose administrators wish to discontinue allegedly futile treatment? How would you explain the hospital policy to a patient of that patient's family member? What potential litigation might arise from the application of this policy?

6. Under the Texas statute, what process must be followed? You might prepare a flow chart including all of the steps required by the statute. Do these requirements seem reasonable? Is ten days enough to find an alternative placement for one who is about to have futile treatment removed? While the statute requires the creation of a registry of those who are willing to assist in the transfer of patients whose treatment has been found to be futile, at the beginning of 2008 the registry included three lawyers willing to take on these cases, only one doctor, and the Texas Right to Life organizations. See http://www.dshs.state.tx.us/THCIC/Registry.shtm (visited on December 15, 2007). Why are there so few physicians willing to assist patients under these circumstances? Litigation has arisen out of

the application of the Texas statute in the case of an infant, Sun Hudson, whose mother did not want to discontinue treatment that physicians believed to be futile, and in the case of Spiro Nikolouzos, who had been transferred once after ventilator support was found to be futile, and whose family then sought more time to arrange for a second transfer after the new facility reached the same conclusion. Both cases were decided on procedural grounds largely unrelated to the substantive provisions of the statute, but each ultimately recognized the authority of the health care provider to make futility determinations. See Hudson v. Texas Children's Hosp., 177 S.W.3d 232 (Tex. Ct. App. 2005) and Nikolouzos v. St. Luke's Episcopal Hosp., 162 S.W.3d 678 (Tex. Ct. App. 2005).

7.   Some states with statutes modeled on the Uniform Health–Care Decisions Act also have statutory provisions that provide that physicians need not provide futile care. Recall that section 7(f) of that UHCDA provides that "A health-care provider or institution may decline to comply with an individual instruction or health-care decision that requires medically ineffective health care or health care contrary to generally accepted health-care standards applicable to the health-care provider or institution." See also Md. Code Ann., Health–Gen. section 5–611 and Va. Code Ann. section 54.1–2990. The Texas statute differs from these earlier statutes by providing an authoritative and conclusive endpoint for disputes. Thaddeus Pope, Medical Futility Statutes: No Safe Harbor to Unilaterally Refuse Life-sustaining Treatment, 51 Tenn. L. Rev. 1 (2007), arguing in part that the failure to provide conclusive procedures diminishes the utility of earlier statutes. See also *In re Baby K*, 16 F.3d 590 (4th Cir. 1994), in which physicians claimed that the Virginia statute authorized their decision to refuse to repeatedly resuscitate an anencephalic infant.

8.   How are autonomy and patients' choices honored if they are recognized only when a patient wants to refuse treatment, and not when they want to continue treatment? Were *Conroy* and other cases in which patients were allowed to forgo treatment while in persistent vegetative state really a subterfuge for a standard that says that it is inappropriate to provide medical treatment (i.e., it is futile) to extend life in those circumstances?

9.   There is a great deal of good writing on the proper legal approach to arguably futile treatment. For a good account of the fundamental issues at stake, see Lawrence Schneiderman & Nancy Jecker, Wrong Medicine (1995) and S. Rubin, When Doctors Say No: The Battleground of Medical Futility (1998). See also Jerry Menikoff, Demanded Medical Care, 30 Ariz. St. L. J. 1091 (1998), Judith Daar, Medical Futility and Implications for Physician Autonomy, 21 Am. J. L. & Med. 221 (1995), Paul Sorum, Limiting Cardiopulmonary Resuscitation, 57 Alb. L. Rev. 617 (1994), Daniel Callahan, Medical Futility, Medical Necessity: The Problem–Without–A–Name, Hastings Center Rep. 30 (July–August 1991). For a useful account of issues related to physicians' willingness to accept decisions to continue futile care, see M. Fetters et al., Conflict Resolution at the End of Life, 29 Critical Care Med. 921 (2001).

10.   The July–August 1991 issue of the Hastings Center Report contains several good articles on the *Wanglie* case, including a summary of the medical facts prepared by her neurologist. The description of the Wanglie case here is derived from Robert Schwartz, Autonomy, Futility and the Limits of Medicine, 2 Camb. Q. Healthcare Ethics 159, 160–61 (1992). The case on which the first problem was based, Conservatorship of Wanglie, No. PX–91–283 (Minn., Hennepin County Dist.Ct., 1993), is unreported. The second problem is entirely hypothetical.

V. PHYSICIAN ASSISTED DEATH

A. THE CONSTITUTIONAL FRAMEWORK

WASHINGTON v. GLUCKSBERG

Supreme Court of the United States, 1997.
521 U.S. 702, 117 S.Ct. 2258, 138 L.Ed.2d 772.

REHNQUIST, C. J., delivered the opinion of the Court, in which O'CONNOR, SCALIA, KENNEDY, and THOMAS, JJ., joined. O'CONNOR, J., filed a concurring opinion, in which GINSBURG and BREYER, JJ., joined in part. STEVENS, J., SOUTER, J., GINSBURG, J., and BREYER, J., filed opinions concurring in the judgment.

CHIEF JUSTICE REHNQUIST delivered the opinion of the Court.

The question presented in this case is whether Washington's prohibition against "causing" or "aiding" a suicide offends the Fourteenth Amendment to the United States Constitution. We hold that it does not.

* * *

The plaintiffs assert [ ] "the existence of a liberty interest protected by the Fourteenth Amendment which extends to a personal choice by a mentally competent, terminally ill adult to commit physician-assisted suicide." [ ] Relying primarily on Planned Parenthood v. Casey, [ ] and Cruzan v. Director, Missouri Dept. of Health, [ ] the District Court agreed, [ ] and concluded that Washington's assisted-suicide ban is unconstitutional because it "places an undue burden on the exercise of [that] constitutionally protected liberty interest." [ ] The District Court also decided that the Washington statute violated the Equal Protection Clause's requirement that " 'all persons similarly situated . . . be treated alike.' "[ ]

A panel of the Court of Appeals for the Ninth Circuit reversed, emphasizing that "in the two hundred and five years of our existence no constitutional right to aid in killing oneself has ever been asserted and upheld by a court of final jurisdiction." [ ] The Ninth Circuit reheard the case en banc, reversed the panel's decision, and affirmed the District Court. [ ] Like the District Court, the en banc Court of Appeals emphasized our Casey and Cruzan decisions. [ ] The court also discussed what it described as "historical" and "current societal attitudes" toward suicide and assisted suicide, [ ] and concluded that "the Constitution encompasses a due process liberty interest in controlling the time and manner of one's death—that there is, in short, a constitutionally-recognized 'right to die.' "[ ] After "weighing and then balancing" this interest against Washington's various interests, the court held that the State's assisted-suicide ban was unconstitutional "as applied to terminally ill competent [ ] adults who wish to hasten their deaths with medication prescribed by their physicians." [ ] We granted certiorari [ ] and now reverse.

I

We begin, as we do in all due-process cases, by examining our Nation's history, legal traditions, and practices. [ ] In almost every State—indeed, in almost every western democracy—it is a crime to assist a suicide. The States' assisted-suicide bans are not innovations. Rather, they are longstanding expressions of the States' commitment to the protection and preservation of all human life. [ ] Indeed, opposition to and condemnation of suicide—and, therefore, of assisting suicide—are consistent and enduring themes of our philosophical, legal, and cultural heritages. [ ]

More specifically, for over 700 years, the Anglo—American common-law tradition has punished or otherwise disapproved of both suicide and assisting suicide. * * * [The Chief Justice then reviews the common law of England and the American colonies and states with regards to suicide, from the 13th century to the present.]

* * *

Attitudes toward suicide itself have changed since [the 13th Century prohibitions on suicide] * * * but our laws have consistently condemned, and continue to prohibit, assisting suicide. Despite changes in medical technology and notwithstanding an increased emphasis on the importance of end-of-life decisionmaking, we have not retreated from this prohibition. Against this backdrop of history, tradition, and practice, we now turn to respondents' constitutional claim.

II

The Due Process Clause guarantees more than fair process, and the "liberty" it protects includes more than the absence of physical restraint. [ ] The Clause also provides heightened protection against government interference with certain fundamental rights and liberty interests. [ ] In a long line of cases, we have held that, in addition to the specific freedoms protected by the Bill of Rights, the "liberty" specially protected by the Due Process Clause includes the rights to marry, [ ]; to have children, [ ]; to direct the education and upbringing of one's children, [ ]; to marital privacy, [ ]; to use contraception, [ ]; to bodily integrity, [ ] and to abortion, [ ]. We have also assumed, and strongly suggested, that the Due Process Clause protects the traditional right to refuse unwanted lifesaving medical treatment. [ ]

But we "have always been reluctant to expand the concept of substantive due process because guideposts for responsible decisionmaking in this unchartered area are scarce and open-ended." [ ] By extending constitutional protection to an asserted right or liberty interest, we, to a great extent, place the matter outside the arena of public debate and legislative action. We must therefore "exercise the utmost care whenever we are asked to break new ground in this field" [ ] lest the liberty protected by the Due Process Clause be subtly transformed into the policy preferences of the members of this Court [ ].

Our established method of substantive-due-process analysis has two primary features: First, we have regularly observed that the Due Process Clause specially protects those fundamental rights and liberties which are, objectively, "deeply rooted in this Nation's history and tradition" [ ] and "implicit in the concept of ordered liberty," such that "neither liberty nor justice would exist if they were sacrificed" [ ]. Second, we have required in substantive-due-process cases a "careful description" of the asserted fundamental liberty interest. [ ] Cruzan, *supra*, at 277–278. Our Nation's history, legal traditions, and practices thus provide the crucial "guideposts for responsible decision-making" [ ] that direct and restrain our exposition of the Due Process Clause. As we stated recently in Flores, the Fourteenth Amendment "forbids the government to infringe ... 'fundamental' liberty interests at all, no matter what process is provided, unless the infringement is narrowly tailored to serve a compelling state interest." [ ]

* * *

Turning to the claim at issue here, the Court of Appeals stated that "properly analyzed, the first issue to be resolved is whether there is a liberty interest in determining the time and manner of one's death" [ ] or, in other words, "is there a right to die?" [ ]. Similarly, respondents assert a "liberty to choose how to die" and a right to "control of one's final days," [ ] and describe the asserted liberty as "the right to choose a humane, dignified death" [ ] and "the liberty to shape death" [ ]. As noted above, we have a tradition of carefully formulating the interest at stake in substantive-due-process cases. For example, although Cruzan is often described as a "right to die" case [ ] we were, in fact, more precise: we assumed that the Constitution granted competent persons a "constitutionally protected right to refuse life-saving hydration and nutrition." [ ] The Washington statute at issue in this case prohibits "aiding another person to attempt suicide," [ ] and, thus, the question before us is whether the "liberty" specially protected by the Due Process Clause includes a right to commit suicide which itself includes a right to assistance in doing so.

* * * With this "careful description" of respondents' claim in mind, we turn to Casey and Cruzan.

[The Chief Justice next discusses the Cruzan case, where, he says,] "we assumed that the United States Constitution would grant a competent person a constitutionally protected right to refuse lifesaving hydration and nutrition."

* * *

The right assumed in Cruzan, however, was not simply deduced from abstract concepts of personal autonomy. Given the common-law rule that forced medication was a battery, and the long legal tradition protecting the decision to refuse unwanted medical treatment, our assumption was entirely consistent with this Nation's history and constitutional traditions. The decision to commit suicide with the assistance of another may be just as personal and profound as the decision to refuse unwanted medical treatment, but it has never enjoyed similar legal protection. Indeed, the two acts are widely and reasonably regarded as quite distinct. [ ] In Cruzan itself, we recognized that most States outlawed assisted suicide?and even more do today—and we certainly gave no intimation that the right to refuse unwanted medical treatment could be somehow transmuted into a right to assistance in committing suicide. [ ]

Respondents also rely on Casey. There, the Court's opinion concluded that "the essential holding of Roe v. Wade should be retained and once again reaffirmed." [ ] We held, first, that a woman has a right, before her fetus is viable, to an abortion "without undue interference from the State"; second, that States may restrict post-viability abortions, so long as exceptions are made to protect a woman's life and health; and third, that the State has legitimate interests throughout a pregnancy in protecting the health of the woman and the life of the unborn child. [ ] In reaching this conclusion, the opinion discussed in some detail this Court's substantive-due-process tradition of interpreting the Due Process Clause to protect certain fundamental rights and "personal decisions relating to marriage, procreation, contraception, family relationships, child rearing, and education," and noted that many of those rights and liberties "involve the most intimate and personal choices a person may make in a lifetime." [ ]

* * *

That many of the rights and liberties protected by the Due Process Clause sound in personal autonomy does not warrant the sweeping conclusion that any and all important, intimate, and personal decisions are so protected, [ ] and Casey did not suggest otherwise.

The history of the law's treatment of assisted suicide in this country has been and continues to be one of the rejection of nearly all efforts to permit it. That being the case, our decisions lead us to conclude that the asserted "right" to assistance in committing suicide is not a fundamental liberty interest protected by the Due Process Clause. The Constitution also requires, however, that Washington's assisted-suicide ban be rationally related to legitimate government interests. [ ] This requirement is unquestionably met here. As the court below recognized, [ ] Washington's assisted-suicide ban implicates a number of state interests. [ ]

First, Washington has an "unqualified interest in the preservation of human life."

* * *

Relatedly, all admit that suicide is a serious public-health problem, especially among persons in otherwise vulnerable groups. [ ] The State has an interest in preventing suicide, and in studying, identifying, and treating its causes. [ ]

* * *

The State also has an interest in protecting the integrity and ethics of the medical profession. * * * [T]he American Medical Association, like many other medical and physicians' groups, has concluded that "physician-assisted suicide is fundamentally incompatible with the physician's role as healer." [ ] And physician-assisted suicide could, it is argued, undermine the trust that is essential to the doctor-patient relationship by blurring the time-honored line between healing and harming. [ ]

Next, the State has an interest in protecting vulnerable groups—including the poor, the elderly, and disabled persons—from abuse, neglect, and mistakes. * * * [One respected state task force] warned that "legalizing physician-assisted suicide would pose profound risks to many individuals who are ill and vulnerable.... The risk of harm is greatest for the many individuals in our society whose autonomy and well-being are already compromised by poverty, lack of access to good medical care, advanced age, or membership in a stigmatized social group." [ ] If physician-assisted suicide were permitted, many might resort to it to spare their families the substantial financial burden of end-of-life health-care costs.

* * * The State's assisted-suicide ban reflects and reinforces its policy that the lives of terminally ill, disabled, and elderly people must be no less valued than the lives of the young and healthy, and that a seriously disabled person's suicidal impulses should be interpreted and treated the same way as anyone else's. [ ]

Finally, the State may fear that permitting assisted suicide will start it down the path to voluntary and perhaps even involuntary euthanasia. * * * [Justice Rehnquist then discussed how this fear could arise out of the practice in the Nertherlands.]

We need not weigh exactly the relative strengths of these various interests. They are unquestionably important and legitimate, and Washington's ban on assisted suicide is at least reasonably related to their promotion and protection. We therefore hold that [ ] [the Washington ban on assisting suicide] does not violate the Fourteenth Amendment, either on its face or "as applied to competent, terminally ill adults who wish to hasten their deaths by obtaining medication prescribed by their doctors."* [ ]

* * *

Throughout the Nation, Americans are engaged in an earnest and profound debate about the morality, legality, and practicality of physician-assisted suicide. Our holding permits this debate to continue, as it should in a democratic society. The decision of the en banc Court of Appeals is reversed, and the case is remanded for further proceedings consistent with this opinion.

It is so ordered.

JUSTICE O'CONNOR, concurring [in both Glucksberg and Vacco].*

Death will be different for each of us. For many, the last days will be spent in physical pain and perhaps the despair that accompanies physical deterioration and a loss of control of basic bodily and mental functions. Some will seek medication to alleviate that pain and other symptoms.

The Court frames the issue in this case as whether the Due Process Clause of the Constitution protects a "right to commit suicide which itself includes a right to assistance in doing so," [ ] and concludes that our Nation's history, legal traditions, and practices do not support the existence of such a right. I join the Court's opinions because I agree that there is no generalized right to "commit suicide." But respondents urge us to address the narrower

---

* Justice Stevens states that "the Court does conceive of respondents' claim as a facial challenge—addressing not the application of the statute to a particular set of plaintiffs before it, but the constitutionality of the statute's categorical prohibition...." [ ] We emphasize that we today reject the Court of Appeals' specific holding that the statute is unconstitutional "as applied" to a particular class. [ ] Justice Stevens agrees with this holding, [ ] but would not "foreclose the possibility that an individual plaintiff seeking to hasten her death, or a doctor whose assistance was sought, could prevail in a more particularized challenge," ibid.

Our opinion does not absolutely foreclose such a claim. However, given our holding that the Due Process Clause of the Fourteenth Amendment does not provide heightened protection to the asserted liberty interest in ending one's life with a physician's assistance, such a claim would have to be quite different from the ones advanced by respondents here.

* Justice Ginsburg concurs in the Court's judgments substantially for the reasons stated in this opinion. Justice Breyer joins this opinion except insofar as it joins the opinions of the Court.

question whether a mentally competent person who is experiencing great suffering has a constitutionally cognizable interest in controlling the circumstances of his or her imminent death. I see no need to reach that question in the context of the facial challenges to the New York and Washington laws at issue here. [ ] The parties and amici agree that in these States a patient who is suffering from a terminal illness and who is experiencing great pain has no legal barriers to obtaining medication, from qualified physicians, to alleviate that suffering, even to the point of causing unconsciousness and hastening death. [ ] In this light, even assuming that we would recognize such an interest, I agree that the State's interests in protecting those who are not truly competent or facing imminent death, or those whose decisions to hasten death would not truly be voluntary, are sufficiently weighty to justify a prohibition against physician-assisted suicide. [ ]

Every one of us at some point may be affected by our own or a family member's terminal illness. There is no reason to think the democratic process will not strike the proper balance between the interests of terminally ill, mentally competent individuals who would seek to end their suffering and the State's interests in protecting those who might seek to end life mistakenly or under pressure. As the Court recognizes, States are presently undertaking extensive and serious evaluation of physician-assisted suicide and other related issues. [ ] In such circumstances, "the . . . challenging task of crafting appropriate procedures for safeguarding . . . liberty interests is entrusted to the 'laboratory' of the States . . . in the first instance." [ ]

In sum, there is no need to address the question whether suffering patients have a constitutionally cognizable interest in obtaining relief from the suffering that they may experience in the last days of their lives. There is no dispute that dying patients in Washington and New York can obtain palliative care, even when doing so would hasten their deaths. The difficulty in defining terminal illness and the risk that a dying patient's request for assistance in ending his or her life might not be truly voluntary justifies the prohibitions on assisted suicide we uphold here.

JUSTICE STEVENS, concurring in the judgments [in both Glucksberg and Vacco].

The Court ends its opinion with the important observation that our holding today is fully consistent with a continuation of the vigorous debate about the "morality, legality, and practicality of physician-assisted suicide" in a democratic society. [ ] I write separately to make it clear that there is also room for further debate about the limits that the Constitution places on the power of the States to punish the practice.

I

The morality, legality, and practicality of capital punishment have been the subject of debate for many years. In 1976, this Court upheld the constitutionality of the practice in cases coming to us from Georgia, Florida, and Texas. In those cases we concluded that a State does have the power to place a lesser value on some lives than on others; there is no absolute requirement that a State treat all human life as having an equal right to preservation. Because the state legislatures had sufficiently narrowed the category of lives that the State could terminate, and had enacted special procedures to ensure that the defendant belonged in that limited category, we concluded that the statutes were not unconstitutional on their face. In later cases coming to us from each of those States, however, we found that some applications of the statutes were unconstitutional.

Today, the Court decides that Washington's statute prohibiting assisted suicide is not invalid "on its face," that is to say, in all or most cases in which it might be applied. That holding, however, does not foreclose the possibility that some applications of the statute might well be invalid.

* * *

History and tradition provide ample support for refusing to recognize an open-ended constitutional right to commit suicide. Much more than the State's paternalistic interest in protecting the individual from the irrevocable consequences of an ill-advised decision motivated by temporary concerns is at stake. There is truth in John Donne's observation that "No man is an island." The State has an interest in preserving and fostering the benefits that every human being may provide to the community—a community that thrives on the exchange of ideas, expressions of affection, shared memories and humorous incidents as well as on the material contributions that its members create and support. The value to others of a person's life is far too precious to allow the individual to claim a constitutional entitlement to complete autonomy in making a decision to end that life. Thus, I fully agree with the Court that the "liberty" protected by the Due Process Clause does not include a categorical "right to commit suicide which itself includes a right to assistance in doing so." [ ]

But just as our conclusion that capital punishment is not always unconstitutional did not preclude later decisions holding that it is sometimes impermissibly cruel, so is it equally clear that a decision upholding a general statutory prohibition of assisted suicide does not mean that every possible application of the statute would be valid. A State, like Washington, that has authorized the death penalty and thereby has concluded that the sanctity of human life does not require that it always be preserved, must acknowledge that there are situations in which an interest in hastening death is legitimate. Indeed, not only is that interest sometimes legitimate, I am also convinced that there are times when it is entitled to constitutional protection.

II

In Cruzan [ ] the Court assumed that the interest in liberty protected by the Fourteenth Amendment encompassed the right of a terminally ill patient to direct the withdrawal of life-sustaining treatment. As the Court correctly observes today, that assumption "was not simply deduced from abstract concepts of personal autonomy." [ ] Instead, it was supported by the common-law tradition protecting the individual's general right to refuse unwanted medical treatment. [ ] We have recognized, however, that this common-law right to refuse treatment is neither absolute nor always sufficiently weighty to overcome valid countervailing state interests. * * *

Cruzan, however, was not the normal case. Given the irreversible nature of her illness and the progressive character of her suffering, Nancy Cruzan's interest in refusing medical care was incidental to her more basic interest in controlling the manner and timing of her death. In finding that her best interests would be served by cutting off the nourishment that kept her alive, the trial court did more than simply vindicate Cruzan's interest in refusing medical treatment; the court, in essence, authorized affirmative conduct that would hasten her death. When this Court reviewed the case and upheld Missouri's requirement that there be clear and convincing evidence establishing Nancy Cruzan's intent to have life-sustaining nourishment withdrawn, it made two important assumptions: (1) that there was a "liberty interest" in refusing unwanted treatment protected by the Due Process Clause; and (2) that this liberty interest did not "end the inquiry" because it might be outweighed by relevant state interests. [ ] I agree with both of those assumptions, but I insist that the source of Nancy Cruzan's right to refuse treatment was not just a common-law rule. Rather, this right is an aspect of a far broader and more basic concept of freedom that is even older than the common law. This freedom embraces, not merely a person's right to refuse a particular kind of unwanted treatment, but also her interest in dignity, and in determining the character of the memories that will survive long after her death. In recognizing that the State's interests did not outweigh Nancy Cruzan's liberty interest in refusing medical treatment, Cruzan rested not simply on the common-law right to refuse medical treatment, but—at least implicitly—on the even more fundamental right to make this "deeply personal decision," [ ].

* * *

While I agree with the Court that Cruzan does not decide the issue presented by these cases, Cruzan did give recognition, not just to vague, unbridled notions of autonomy, but to the more specific interest in making decisions about how to confront an imminent death. Although there is no absolute right to physician-assisted suicide, Cruzan makes it clear that some individuals who no longer have the option of deciding whether to live or to die because they are already on the threshold of death have a constitutionally protected interest that may outweigh the State's interest in preserving life at all costs. The liberty interest at stake in a case like this differs from, and is stronger than, both the common-law right to refuse medical treatment and the unbridled interest in deciding whether to live or die. It is an interest in deciding how, rather than whether, a critical threshold shall be crossed.

III

The state interests supporting a general rule banning the practice of physician-assisted suicide do not have the same force in all cases. First and foremost of these interests is the " 'unqualified interest in the preservation of human life' "[ ].

* * *. Although as a general matter the State's interest in the contributions each person may make to society outweighs the person's interest in ending her life, this interest does not have the same force for a terminally ill patient faced not with the choice of whether to live, only of how to die. * * *

Similarly, the State's legitimate interests in preventing suicide, protecting the vulnerable from coercion and abuse, and preventing euthanasia are less significant in this context. I agree that the State has a compelling interest in preventing persons from committing suicide because of depression, or coercion by third parties. But the State's legitimate interest in preventing abuse does not apply to an individual who is not victimized by abuse, who is not suffering from depression, and who makes a rational and voluntary decision to seek assistance in dying.

* * *

The final major interest asserted by the State is its interest in preserving the traditional integrity of the medical profession. The fear is that a rule permitting physicians to assist in suicide is inconsistent with the perception that they serve their patients solely as healers. But for some patients, it would be a physician's refusal to dispense medication to ease their suffering and make their death tolerable and dignified that would be inconsistent with the healing role * * * .

* * * I do not * * * foreclose the possibility that an individual plaintiff seeking to hasten her death, or a doctor whose assistance was sought, could prevail in a more particularized challenge. Future cases will determine whether such a challenge may succeed.

IV

* * *

There may be little distinction between the intent of a terminally-ill patient who decides to remove her life-support and one who seeks the assistance of a doctor in ending her life; in both situations, the patient is seeking to hasten a certain, impending death. The doctor's intent might also be the same in prescribing lethal medication as it is in terminating life support. * * *

Thus, although the differences the majority notes in causation and intent between terminating life-support and assisting in suicide support the Court's rejection of the respondents' facial challenge, these distinctions may be inapplicable to particular terminally ill patients and their doctors. Our holding today in Vacco v. Quill that the Equal Protection Clause is not violated by New York's classification, just like our holding in Washington v. Glucksberg that the Washington statute is not invalid on its face, does not foreclose the possibility that some applications of the New York statute may impose an intolerable intrusion on the patient's freedom.

There remains room for vigorous debate about the outcome of particular cases that are not necessarily resolved by the opinions announced today. How such cases may be decided will depend on their specific facts. In my judgment, however, it is clear that the so-called "unqualified interest in the preservation of human life," [ ] is not itself sufficient to outweigh the interest in liberty that may justify the only possible means of preserving a dying patient's dignity and alleviating her intolerable suffering.

JUSTICE SOUTER, concurring in the judgment.

* * *

When the physicians claim that the Washington law deprives them of a right falling within the scope of liberty that the Fourteenth Amendment guarantees against denial without due process of law, they are not claiming some sort of procedural defect in the process through which the statute has been enacted or is administered. Their claim, rather, is that the State has no substantively adequate justification for barring the assistance sought by the patient and sought to be offered by the physician. Thus, we are dealing with a claim to one of those rights sometimes described as rights of substantive due process and sometimes as unenumerated rights, in view of the breadth and indeterminacy of the "due process" serving as the claim's textual basis. The doctors accordingly arouse the skepticism of those who find the Due Process Clause an unduly vague or oxymoronic warrant for judicial review of substantive state law, just as they also invoke two centuries of American constitutional practice in recognizing unenumerated, substantive limits on governmental action. * * *

* * *

[Justice Souter explained that he was adopting Justice Harlan's approach to the Constitutional evaluation and protection of unenumerated rights under the Due Process Clause, as articulated in his dissent in Poe v. Ullman.] My understanding of unenumerated rights in the wake of the Poe dissent and subsequent cases avoids the absolutist failing of many older cases without embracing the opposite pole of equating reasonableness with past practice described at a very specific level. [ ] That understanding begins with a concept of "ordered liberty," [ ] comprising a continuum of rights to be free from "arbitrary impositions and purposeless restraints" [ ].

* * *

This approach calls for a court to assess the relative "weights" or dignities of the contending interests, and to this extent the judicial method is familiar to the common law. Common law method is subject, however, to two important constraints in the hands of a court engaged in substantive due process review. First, such a court is bound to confine the values that it recognizes to those truly deserving constitutional stature, either to those expressed in constitutional text, or those exemplified by "the traditions from which [the Nation] developed," or revealed by contrast with "the traditions from which it broke." [ ]

The second constraint, again, simply reflects the fact that constitutional review, not judicial lawmaking, is a court's business here. The weighing or valuing of contending interests in this sphere is only the first step, forming the basis for determining whether the statute in question falls inside or outside the zone of what is reasonable in the way it resolves the conflict between the interests of state and individual.

* * *

The State has put forward several interests to justify the Washington law as applied to physicians treating terminally ill patients, even those competent to make responsible choices: protecting life generally [ ] discouraging suicide even if knowing and voluntary [ ] and protecting terminally ill patients from involuntary suicide and euthanasia, both voluntary and nonvoluntary [ ].

It is not necessary to discuss the exact strengths of the first two claims of justification in the present circumstances, for the third is dispositive for me. * * * [Justice Souter then explained why the Washington state legislature, on the basis of information now available, could have reasonably decided that a statute forbidding assisting suicide might protect terminally ill patients.]

* * *

The Court should accordingly stay its hand to allow reasonable legislative consideration. While I do not decide for all time that respondents' claim should not be recognized, I acknowledge the legislative institutional competence as the better one to deal with that claim at this time.

JUSTICE BREYER, concurring in the judgments [in both Glucksberg and Vacco].

I believe that Justice O'Connor's views, which I share, have greater legal significance than the Court's opinion suggests. I join her separate opinion, except insofar as it joins the majority. * * *

I agree with the Court in Vacco v. Quill [ ] that the articulated state interests justify the distinction drawn between physician assisted suicide and withdrawal of life-support. I also agree with the Court that the critical question in both of the cases before us is whether "the 'liberty' specially protected by the Due Process Clause includes a right" of the sort that the respondents assert. [ ] I do not agree, however, with the Court's formulation of that claimed "liberty" interest. The Court describes it as a "right to commit suicide with another's assistance." [ ] But I would not reject the respondents' claim without considering a different formulation, for which our legal tradition may provide greater support. That formulation would use words roughly like a "right to die with dignity." But irrespective of the exact words used, at its core would lie personal control over the manner of death, professional medical assistance, and the avoidance of unnecessary and severe physical suffering—combined.

* * *

I do not believe, however, that this Court need or now should decide whether or a not * * * [a right to die with dignity] is "fundamental." That is because, in my view, the avoidance of severe physical pain (connected with death) would have to comprise an essential part of any successful claim and because * * * the laws before us do not force a dying person to undergo that kind of pain. [ ] Rather, the laws of New York and of Washington do not prohibit doctors from providing patients with drugs sufficient to control pain despite the risk that those drugs themselves will kill. [ ] And under these circumstances the laws of New York and Washington would overcome any remaining significant interests and would be justified, regardless.

* * *

Were the legal circumstances different—for example, were state law to prevent the provision of palliative care, including the administration of drugs as needed to avoid pain at the end of life—then the law's impact upon serious and otherwise unavoidable physical pain (and accompanying death) would be more directly at issue. And as JUSTICE O'CONNOR suggests, the Court might have to revisit its conclusions in these cases.

* * *

VACCO v. QUILL

Supreme Court of the United States, 1997.
521 U.S. 793, 117 S.Ct. 2293, 138 L.Ed.2d 834.

CHIEF JUSTICE REHNQUIST delivered the opinion of the Court.

In New York, as in most States, it is a crime to aid another to commit or attempt suicide, but patients may refuse even lifesaving medical treatment. The question presented by this case is whether New York's prohibition on assisting suicide therefore violates the Equal Protection Clause of the Fourteenth Amendment. We hold that it does not.

* * * Respondents, and three gravely ill patients who have since died, sued the State's Attorney General in the United States District Court. They urged that because New York permits a competent person to refuse life-sustaining medical treatment, and because the refusal of such treatment is "essentially the same thing" as physician-assisted suicide, New York's assisted-suicide ban violates the Equal Protection Clause. [ ]

The District Court disagreed * * *.

The Court of Appeals for the Second Circuit reversed. [ ] The court determined that, despite the assisted-suicide ban's apparent general applicability, "New York law does not treat equally all competent persons who are in the final stages of fatal illness and wish to hasten their deaths," because "those in the final stages of terminal illness who are on life-support systems are allowed to hasten their deaths by directing the removal of such systems; but those who are similarly situated, except for the previous attachment of life-sustaining equipment, are not allowed to hasten death by self-administering prescribed drugs." [ ] The Court of Appeals then examined whether this supposed unequal treatment was rationally related to any legitimate state interests, and concluded that "to the extent that [New York's statutes] prohibit a physician from prescribing medications to be self-administered by a mentally competent, terminally-ill person in the final stages of his terminal illness, they are not rationally related to any legitimate state interest." [ ] We granted certiorari [ ] and now reverse.

The Equal Protection Clause commands that no State shall "deny to any person within its jurisdiction the equal protection of the laws." This provision creates no substantive rights. [ ] Instead, it embodies a general rule that States must treat like cases alike but may treat unlike cases accordingly. [ ] If a legislative classification or distinction "neither burdens a fundamental right nor targets a suspect class, we will uphold [it] so long as it bears a rational relation to some legitimate end." [ ]

New York's statutes outlawing assisting suicide affect and address matters of profound significance to all New Yorkers alike. They neither infringe fundamental rights nor involve suspect classifications. [ ] These laws are therefore entitled to a "strong presumption of validity." [ ]

On their faces, neither New York's ban on assisting suicide nor its statutes permitting patients to refuse medical treatment treat anyone differently than anyone else or draw any distinctions between persons. Everyone, regardless of physical condition, is entitled, if competent, to refuse unwanted lifesaving medical treatment; no one is permitted to assist a suicide. Generally speaking, laws that apply evenhandedly to all "unquestionably comply" with the Equal Protection Clause. [ ]

The Court of Appeals, however, concluded that some terminally ill people—those who are on life-support systems—are treated differently than those who are not, in that the former may "hasten death" by ending treatment, but the latter may not "hasten death" through physician-assisted suicide. [ ] This conclusion depends on the submission that ending or refusing lifesaving medical treatment "is nothing more nor less than assisted suicide." [ ] Unlike the Court of Appeals, we think the distinction between assisting suicide and withdrawing life-sustaining treatment, a distinction widely recognized and endorsed in the medical profession and in our legal traditions, is both important and logical; it is certainly rational. [ ]

The distinction comports with fundamental legal principles of causation and intent. First, when a patient refuses life-sustaining medical treatment, he dies from an underlying fatal disease or pathology; but if a patient ingests lethal medication prescribed by a physician, he is killed by that medication. [ ]

Furthermore, a physician who withdraws, or honors a patient's refusal to begin, life-sustaining medical treatment purposefully intends, or may so intend, only to respect his patient's wishes and "to cease doing useless and futile or degrading things to the patient when [the patient] no longer stands to benefit from them." [ ] The same is true when a doctor provides aggressive palliative care; in some cases, painkilling drugs may hasten a patient's death, but the physician's purpose and intent is, or may be, only to ease his patient's pain. A doctor who assists a suicide, however, "must, necessarily and indubitably, intend primarily that the patient be made dead." [ ] Similarly, a patient who commits suicide with a doctor's aid necessarily has the specific intent to end his or her own life, while a patient who refuses or discontinues treatment might not. [ ]

The law has long used actors' intent or purpose to distinguish between two acts that may have the same result. [ ] Put differently, the law distinguishes actions taken "because of" a given end from actions taken "in spite of" their unintended but foreseen consequences. [ ]

Given these general principles, it is not surprising that many courts, including New York courts, have carefully distinguished refusing life-sustaining treatment from suicide. * * *

Similarly, the overwhelming majority of state legislatures have drawn a clear line between assisting suicide and withdrawing or permitting the refusal of unwanted lifesaving medical treatment by prohibiting the former and permitting the latter. [ ] And "nearly all states expressly disapprove of suicide and assisted suicide either in statutes dealing with durable powers of attorney in health-care situations, or in 'living will' statutes." [ ] Thus, even as the States move to protect and promote patients' dignity at the end of life, they remain opposed to physician-assisted suicide.

* * *

This Court has also recognized, at least implicitly, the distinction between letting a patient die and making that patient die. In Cruzan [ ] we concluded that "the principle that a competent person has a constitutionally protected liberty interest in refusing unwanted medical treatment may be inferred from our prior decisions," and we assumed the existence of such a right for purposes of that case [ ]. But our assumption of a right to refuse treatment was grounded not, as the Court of Appeals supposed, on the proposition that patients have a general and abstract "right to hasten death," [ ] but on well established, traditional rights to bodily integrity and freedom from unwanted touching [ ]. In fact, we observed that "the majority of States in this country have laws imposing criminal penalties on one who assists another to commit suicide." [ ] Cruzan therefore provides no support for the notion that refusing life-sustaining medical treatment is "nothing more nor less than suicide."

For all these reasons, we disagree with respondents' claim that the distinction between refusing lifesaving medical treatment and assisted suicide is "arbitrary" and "irrational."[11] Granted, in some cases, the line between the two may not be clear, but certainty is not required, even were it possible. Logic and contemporary practice support New York's judgment that the two acts are different, and New York may therefore, consistent with the Constitution, treat them differently. By permitting everyone to refuse unwanted medical treatment while prohibiting anyone from assisting a suicide, New York law follows a longstanding and rational distinction.

New York's reasons for recognizing and acting on this distinction— including prohibiting intentional killing and preserving life; preventing suicide; maintaining physicians' role as their patients' healers; protecting vulnerable people from indifference, prejudice, and psychological and financial pressure to end their lives; and avoiding a possible slide towards euthanasia— are discussed in greater detail in our opinion in Glucksberg, ante. These valid and important public interests easily satisfy the constitutional requirement that a legislative classification bear a rational relation to some legitimate end.

The judgment of the Court of Appeals is reversed.

* * *

JUSTICE SOUTER, concurring in the judgment.

Even though I do not conclude that assisted suicide is a fundamental right entitled to recognition at this time, I accord the claims raised by the patients and physicians in this case and Washington v. Glucksberg a high degree of importance, requiring a commensurate justification. [ ] The reasons that lead me to conclude in Glucksberg that the prohibition on assisted suicide is not arbitrary under the due process standard also support the distinction between assistance to suicide, which is banned, and practices such as termination of artificial life support and death-hastening pain medication, which are permitted. I accordingly concur in the judgment of the Court.

* * *

11. Respondents also argue that the State irrationally distinguishes between physician-assisted suicide and "terminal sedation," a process respondents characterize as "inducing barbiturate coma and then starving the person to death." [ ] Petitioners insist, however, that " 'although proponents of physician-assisted suicide and euthanasia contend that terminal sedation is covert physician-assisted suicide or euthanasia, the concept of sedating pharmacotherapy is based on informed consent and the principle of double effect.' "[ ] Just as a State may prohibit assisting suicide while permitting patients to refuse unwanted lifesaving treatment, it may permit palliative care related to that refusal, which may have the foreseen but unintended "double effect" of hastening the patient's death. [ ]

Notes and Questions

1. The Ninth Circuit's *en banc* decision and an extraordinarily diverse and thoughtful set of opinions in *Glucksberg* can be found at Compassion in Dying v. Washington, 79 F.3d 790 (9th Cir.1996). The en banc court reversed a 2–1 decision of the original panel, which also included an impassioned opinion on each side of the issue. See 49 F.3d 586 (9th Cir.1995). The meticulously organized district court opinion in the *Compassion in Dying* case is reported at 850 F.Supp. 1454 (W.D.Wash.1994). The Second Circuit's opinion in Quill v. Vacco can be found at 80 F.3d 716 (2d Cir.1996).

2. These cases generated many highly emotional responses. Although the Supreme Court's unanimous decision brought a semblance of propriety back to the discussion of these issues, supporters and opponents of physician assisted death continue to attack the arguments of their opponents—and, as in the case of the abortion debate—they continue to attack their opponents, too. Some of the commentary on the Ninth Circuit opinions was especially personal. Judge Reinhardt (who wrote the primary decision finding the Washington law to be unconstitutional) was roundly criticized for his ACLU connections, which, some said, made it impossible for him to fairly decide the case. On the other hand, Judge Noonan (who would have upheld the statute for the first panel) had been criticized for his right-to-life connections which, others argued, made it impossible for *him* to be impartial. Should judges recuse themselves from cases involving these difficult and controversial bioethics issues if they have deeply held personal beliefs about the underlying practice—here physician assisted death? Does it make a difference if they were members (or officers, or high ranking employees) of organizations which have taken explicit positions on the underlying issues? On the particular case in litigation? Should they recuse themselves if the issue is one on which the religion to which they subscribe has taken a formal position? Should Catholic judges recuse themselves from abortion and physician assisted death cases? Should judges who belong to the United Church of Christ (which has been strongly pro-choice for decades) recuse themselves from abortion cases? Should the member of a congregation whose rabbi helped organize a voting rights march recuse himself from all voting rights cases? Is their obligation any different from the obligation of a judge who is a dedicated ACLU (or American Family Association, or Republican Party) member and who confronts a case upon which the ACLU (or the American Family Association, or the Republican Party) has taken a firm position?

3. Judge Calabresi concurred in the Second Circuit decision in the *Quill* case, but on entirely different grounds. Depending on the theory of statutory construction that he had explained fifteen years earlier in his text, A Common Law for the Age of Statutes (1982), he concluded that the history of the New York manslaughter statute suggested that there was no reason to believe that its framers ever intended it to apply to cases of competent terminally ill patients seeking aid in dying from physicians. Still, as he pointed out, "neither *Cruzan*, nor *Casey*, nor the language of our Constitution, nor our constitutional tradition clearly makes these laws invalid."

So, what should the court do with a "highly suspect" but "not clearly invalid" statute that may no longer serves the purposes for which it was originally promulgated? The answer, according to Judge Calabresi, is the "constitutional remand."

I contend that when a law is neither plainly unconstitutional * * * nor plainly constitutional, the courts ought not to decide the ultimate validity of that law without current and clearly expressed statements by the people or their elected officials of the state involved. It is my further contention, that, absent such statements, the courts have frequently struck down such laws, while leaving open the possibility of reconsideration if appropriate statements were subsequently made.

Thus, Judge Calabresi finds the New York statute unconstitutional, but he "takes no position" on whether verbatim identical statutes would be constitutional "were New York to reenact them while articulating the reasons for the distinctions it makes* * *." Is this a reasonable way to deal with ancient statutes effectively criminalizing physician assisted death? Is this argument still available to those challenging state statutes that forbid assisting suicide?

4. Why has physician assisted death engendered such passion over the last three decades? Daniel Callahan has a suggestion:

> The power of medicine to extend life under poor circumstances is now widely and increasingly feared. The combined powers of a quasi-religious tradition of respect for individual life and a secular tradition of relentless medical progress creates a bias toward aggressive, often unremitting treatment that appears unstoppable.

> How is control to be gained? For many the answer seems obvious and unavoidable: active euthanasia and assisted suicide.

19 Hastings Ctr. Rep., Special Supplement, 4 (1989). Dr. Callahan goes on to suggest that those who strongly oppose euthanasia, as he does, ought to focus on "dampening * * * the push for medical progress, a return to older traditions of caring as an alternative to curing, and a willingness to accept decline and death as part of the human conditions (not a notable feature of American medicine)." Is he right? It used to be that people were afraid that if they went to the hospital they would die there. Now people are afraid that if they go to the hospital they will be kept alive there. Is it this fear that gives rise to our current interest in euthanasia?

5. For many years, nothing did more to keep the spotlight on physician assisted death than the consistent—and consistently high profile—actions of Dr. Jack Kevorkian. Dr. Kevorkian employed a "suicide machine" that allowed patients—sometimes young and still relatively healthy patients—to end their lives. Dr. Kevorkian chose Michigan for his practice because assisted suicide *per se* was not a crime in Michigan. On the other hand, an early Michigan case, People v. Roberts, 211 Mich. 187, 178 N.W. 690 (1920), had determined that assisting suicide could constitute murder. In that case a husband pleaded guilty to murder after he placed a poisonous mixture next to his wife, who was suffering from multiple sclerosis, was in excruciating pain, and had begged her husband to help her end her misery. The Michigan court determined that murder by poison, a form of first degree murder, was the proper charge.

Over a decade, Dr. Kevorkian faced several homicide charges arising out of his actions. In 1990 prosecutors indicted Dr. Kevorkian on homicide charges, which were subsequently dismissed. As a direct result of Kevorkian's activities, in 1992 the Michigan legislature enacted a statute to criminalize assistance to suicide, which rendered one criminally liable if one "provide[d] the physical means by which the other person attempt[ed] or commit[ted] suicide" or participated in the physical act of the suicide. Mich. Comp. Laws Ann. § 752–1027. The statute contained an expiration date to give the state the opportunity to work out this issue without the sense of thoughtless urgency that prevailed in 1992.

As soon as the new assistance to suicide statute became law, several terminally ill patients and some health care providers brought a declaratory judgment action seeking to have the new statute declared void because it violated due process, because it passed the legislature in a bill that did not have "a single object," because the purpose of the bill changed during the course of its consideration in the Michigan legislature, and because it was inadequately titled, all in violation of the Michigan constitution. Ultimately, the trial court found the statute unconstitutional. Charges brought against Dr. Kevorkian under the statute were dismissed.

In 1994 a divided Michigan Supreme Court issued a brief *per curiam* memorandum opinion and a series of separate opinions dealing with the various issues raised by appeals by Kervorkian and his allies with regard to the status of physician assisted death in Michigan. The court decided that (1) there was no technical problem in the form of the bill passed by the legislature (by unanimous vote), (2) a criminal statute penalizing assisted suicide does not violate the United States Constitution (5–2 vote), (3) *People v. Roberts* should be overruled; merely intentionally providing the means for another to commit suicide does not, as a general matter, constitute murder (5–2 vote) and (4) whether there was sufficient evidence to prosecute Dr. Kevorkian for murder should be reconsidered by the trial court (4–3 vote). See People v. Kevorkian, 447 Mich. 436, 527 N.W.2d 714 (1994) for the lengthy, thoughtful and heartfelt opinions on all sides of all of these issues.

Another prosecution for murder ended in a jury verdict of acquittal for Dr. Kevorkian. In 1996, after the Michigan statute had expired, he was charged with violation of the Michigan common law crime of assisting suicide, and, once again, he was aquitted.

Finally, in 1999, Dr. Kevorkian was convicted of second-degree murder after a very short trial in which he represented himself. While past cases had involved Dr. Kevorkian's use of a suicide machine which was actually operated by his client (patient? victim?), in this case he injected a lethal drug directly into Thomas Youk, a 52–year-old man suffering from amyotrophic lateral sclerosis (Lou Gehrig's disease) who had been totally disabled by his disease, was choking on his saliva, and was able to move only his thumb and forefinger on one hand. Dr. Kevorkian filmed the entire process, which was then shown to a national audience on "60 Minutes," the CBS news show, in November, 1998. Dr. Keviorkian was originally charged with first-degree murder and assisted suicide. The trial judge ruled that evidence of Mr. Youk's suffering, which would be provided by the testimony of his family members, would be relevant and admissible on the assisted suicide charge, but not on the murder charge. The prosecutor decided to drop the assisted suicide charge to keep out that kind of evidence, which had played so well in Dr. Kevorkian's earlier trials. The jury apparently found no premeditation, making the second degree murder conviction the most serious available. Dr. Kevorkian was also found guilty of delivery of a controlled substance.

Leading supporters of euthanasia were outraged by the conviction. The executive director of the Hemlock Society said, "To call it murder is barbaric. It highlights the necessity to change the law over the country * * * so that a compassionate physician can help a suffering patient die." One leader of a disability group expressed satisfaction that this "serial killer" of the disabled had finally been brought to justice. For an account of the trial, see Pam Belluck, Dr. Kevorkian is a Murderer, The Jury Finds, New York Times, March 27, 1999, at A–1. Dr. Kevorkian was sentenced to 10–to–25 years in prison, and he was released on June 1, 2007, after serving over eight years. As a condition of his release, he promised not to engage in any conduct that would break the law, but he said he would continue to be a strong advocate for physician assisted death.

6. Physician assisted death may constitute murder, manslaughter, some other form of homicide, or no crime at all, depending on the state statute and the nature of the physician's act. While most states criminalize assisting suicide, it is not always easy to determine what conduct is prohibited by those statutes. Consider one representative statute:

> Every person who deliberately aids, or advises, or encourages another to commit suicide, is guilty of a felony.

Cal. Pen. Code § 401.

Would this statute apply to a physician who clamps a feeding tube? To a physician who withholds antibiotics? To a physician who prescribes morphine to a patient in persistent pain, and provides enough tablets to take a lethal dose? To a physician who prescribes that same morphine and tells the patient what would constitute a lethal dose? To those who publish instructions on how to commit suicide for the use of those who are terminally ill or in excruciating pain? To those who make generally available information about how to commit suicide at home? See McCollum v. CBS, Inc., 202 Cal.App.3d 989, 249 Cal.Rptr. 187 (1988), rejecting application of the statute to those who play rock music with lyrics that suggest that suicide is acceptable.

7. Might women, specifically, be put at risk in a society that permits physician assisted death? That argument is made by Susan Wolf, who regularly has argued that women's requests should be better respected by the health care system and that requests to remove life sustaining treatment should be heeded.

> As I have argued, there is a strong right to be free of unwanted bodily invasion. Indeed, for women, a long history of being harmed specifically through unwanted bodily invasion such as rape presents particularly compelling reasons for honoring a woman's refusal of invasion and effort to maintain bodily intactness. When it comes to the question of whether women's suicides should be aided, however, or whether women should be actively killed, there is no right to command physician assistance, the dangers of permitting assistance are immense, and the history of women's subordination cuts the other way. Women have historically been seen as fit objects for bodily invasion, self-sacrifice, and death at the hands of others. The task before us is to challenge all three.

> Certainly some women, including some feminists, will see this problem differently. That may be especially true of women who feel in control of their lives, are less subject to subordination by age or race or wealth, and seek yet another option to add to their many. I am not arguing that women should lose control of their lives and selves. Instead, I am arguing that when women request to be put to death or ask help in taking their own lives, they become part of a broader social dynamic of which we have properly learned to be extremely wary. These are fatal practices. We can no longer ignore questions of gender or insights of feminist argument.

Susan Wolf, Gender, Feminism and Death: Physician Assisted Suicide and Euthanasia, in S. Wolf, Feminism and Bioethics: Beyond Reproduction 308 (1996). For an account of Professor Wolf's thoughtful approach to death and dying, see Daniel Bergner, Death in the Family, New York Times Magazine (December 2, 2007), reporting that 72% of the 75 individuals assisted by Kervorkian were women. But see data on Oregon's experience, below.

8. Organized medical groups generally oppose any medical participation in euthanasia or assisted death. See AMA Council on Ethical and Judicial Affairs, Code of Medical Ethics, Current Opinion 2.21, Euthanasia, and Opinion 2.211, Physician–Assisted Suicide (2006–2007 ed.). Is this because it is morally reprehensible, or because it is too morally complicated?

> A strict proscription against aiding in death may betray a limited conceptual framework that seeks the safety of ironclad rules and principles to protect the physician from the true complexity of individual cases. Patients seeking comfort in their dying should not be held hostage to our inability or unwillingness to be responsible for knowing right from wrong in each specific situation.

Christine Cassel & Diane Meier, Morals and Moralism in the Debate Over Euthanasia and Assisted Suicide, 323 NEJM 750, 751 (1990).

9. In a footnote in *Vacco*, Justice Rehnquist raises the issue of the legal status of "terminal sedation," which is sometimes described as "palliative sedation" because it is employed to provide palliation both in patients who are quickly approaching death and in those who are suffering but not yet otherwise terminal. Patients whose suffering cannot be ameliorated in any other way can be sedated with enough medication so that they are put into a medication-induced coma. This sedation may be accompanied by the withdrawal of other forms of treatment, including artificial nutrition and hydration. This withdrawal may (and, with the withdrawal of nutrition and hydration, will) lead to the patient's death. Justice Rehnquist suggests that terminal sedation, which has not given rise to the ethical objections that have come with physician assisted death, is distinguishable from an affirmative act intended to bring about death, applying the principle of "double effect." Do you agree? Under *Vacco*, whether terminal sedation is treated like the withdrawal of life sustaining treatment or like an affirmative act causing death makes all the legal difference. As an ethical and legal matter, should terminal sedation be treated like the withdrawal of treatment or like physician assisted death? See J.A. Rietjens et al., Terminal Sedation and Euthanasia: A Comparison of Clinical Practices, 166 Archives Internal Med. 749 (2006). T. Morita et al., Terminal Sedation for Existential Distress, 17 Am. J. Hospital Palliation 189 (2000). For an early medical description of the process, see R.E. Enck, Drug–Induced Terminal Sedation for Symptom Control, 8 Am. J. Hosp. Palliative Care 3 (1991).

10. Litigation seeking a right to physician assisted death under state constitutional law has also failed thus far. In Krischer v. McIver, 697 So.2d 97 (Fla.1997), a terminally ill AIDS patient and his physician sought an injunction against the prosecution of the physician for assisting in his patient's suicide. The Florida Supreme Court rejected a claim that the privacy provision of the Florida Constitution included the right to have a physician assist in one's suicide. The Court announced that a properly drawn statute authorizing physician-assisted suicide would be constitutionally permissible, but that principles of separation of powers left the decision about whether it should be made legal to the legislature. The Chief Justice filed a vigorous dissent, arguing that, " * * *the right of privacy attaches with unusual force at the death bed. * * * What possible interest does society have in saving life when there is nothing of life to save but a final convulsion of agony? The state has no business in this arena." 697 So.2d at 111.

For another unsuccessful state constitutional challenge to a state law prohibiting physician assisted suicide, see Sampson v. State, 31 P.3d 88 (Alaska 2001).

B. LEGISLATION TO SUPPORT PHYSICIAN ASSISTED DEATH— "DEATH WITH DIGNITY" INITIATIVES

The debate over the proper role of physicians in assisting their patients in death has been carried on through the legislative and citizen initiative processes as well as through litigation. "Death with Dignity" initiatives were narrowly defeated in California in 1991 and in Washington in 1992. However, Oregon's "Death with Dignity" initiative was approved by voters in the November 1994 election, and it thus became part of the statute law of Oregon.

THE OREGON DEATH WITH DIGNITY ACT

Or.Rev.Stat. §§ 127.800–.897.

127.800. Definitions.

The following words and phrases, whenever used in ORS 127.800 to 127.897, have the following meanings:

(1) "Adult" means an individual who is 18 years of age or older.

(2) "Attending physician" means the physician who has primary responsibility for the care of the patient and treatment of the patient's terminal disease.

(3) "Capable" means that in the opinion of a court or in the opinion of the patient's attending physician or consulting physician, psychiatrist or psychologist, a patient has the ability to make and communicate health care decisions to health care providers, including communication through persons familiar with the patient's manner of communicating if those persons are available.

(4) "Consulting physician" means a physician who is qualified by specialty or experience to make a professional diagnosis and prognosis regarding the patient's disease.

(5) "Counseling" means one or more consultations as necessary between a state licensed psychiatrist or psychologist and a patient for the purpose of determining that the patient is capable and not suffering from a psychiatric or psychological disorder or depression causing impaired judgment.

(6) "Health care provider" means a person licensed, certified or otherwise authorized or permitted by the law of this state to administer health care or dispense medication in the ordinary course of business or practice of a profession, and includes a health care facility.

(7) "Informed decision" means a decision by a qualified patient, to request and obtain a prescription to end his or her life in a humane and dignified manner, that is based on an appreciation of the relevant facts and after being fully informed by the attending physician of:

(a) His or her medical diagnosis;

(b) His or her prognosis;

(c) The potential risks associated with taking the medication to be prescribed;

(d) The probable result of taking the medication to be prescribed; and

(e) The feasible alternatives, including, but not limited to, comfort care, hospice care and pain control.

(8) "Medically confirmed" means the medical opinion of the attending physician has been confirmed by a consulting physician who has examined the patient and the patient's relevant medical records.

(9) "Patient" means a person who is under the care of a physician.

(10) "Physician" means a doctor of medicine or osteopathy licensed to practice medicine by the Board of Medical Examiners for the State of Oregon.

(11) "Qualified patient" means a capable adult who is a resident of Oregon and has satisfied the requirements of ORS 127.800 to 127.897 in order to obtain a prescription for medication to end his or her life in a humane and dignified manner.

(12) "Terminal disease" means an incurable and irreversible disease that has been medically confirmed and will, within reasonable medical judgment, produce death within six months.

127.805. Who may initiate a written request for medication.

(1) An adult who is capable, is a resident of Oregon, and has been determined by the attending physician and consulting physician to be suffering from a terminal disease, and who has voluntarily expressed his or her wish to die, may make a written request for medication for the purpose of ending his or her life in a humane and dignified manner in accordance with ORS 127.800 to 127.897.

(2) No person shall qualify under the provisions of ORS 127.800 to 127.897 solely because of age or disability.

127.810. Form of the written request.

(1) A valid request for medication under ORS 127.800 to 127.897 shall be in substantially the form described in ORS 127.897, signed and dated by the patient and witnessed by at least two individuals who, in the presence of the patient, attest that to the best of their knowledge and belief the patient is capable, acting voluntarily, and is not being coerced to sign the request.

(2) One of the witnesses shall be a person who is not:

(a) A relative of the patient by blood, marriage or adoption;

(b) A person who at the time the request is signed would be entitled to any portion of the estate of the qualified patient upon death under any will or by operation of law; or

(c) An owner, operator or employee of a health care facility where the qualified patient is receiving medical treatment or is a resident.

(3) The patient's attending physician at the time the request is signed shall not be a witness.

(4) If the patient is a patient in a long term care facility at the time the written request is made, one of the witnesses shall be an individual designated by the facility and having the qualifications specified by the Department of Human Services by rule.

127.815. Attending physician responsibilities.

(1) The attending physician shall:

(a) Make the initial determination of whether a patient has a terminal disease, is capable, and has made the request voluntarily;

(b) Request that the patient demonstrate Oregon residency pursuant to ORS 127.860;

(c) To ensure that the patient is making an informed decision, inform the patient of:

(A) His or her medical diagnosis;

(B) His or her prognosis;

(C) The potential risks associated with taking the medication to be prescribed;

(D) The probable result of taking the medication to be prescribed; and

(E) The feasible alternatives, including, but not limited to, comfort care, hospice care and pain control;

(d) Refer the patient to a consulting physician for medical confirmation of the diagnosis, and for a determination that the patient is capable and acting voluntarily;

(e) Refer the patient for counseling if appropriate pursuant to ORS 127.825;

(f) Recommend that the patient notify next of kin;

(g) Counsel the patient about the importance of having another person present when the patient takes the medication prescribed pursuant to ORS 127.800 to 127.897 and of not taking the medication in a public place;

(h) Inform the patient that he or she has an opportunity to rescind the request at any time and in any manner, and offer the patient an opportunity to rescind at the end of the 15 day waiting period pursuant to ORS 127.840;

(i) Verify, immediately prior to writing the prescription for medication under ORS 127.800 to 127.897, that the patient is making an informed decision;

(j) Fulfill the medical record documentation requirements of ORS 127.855;

(k) Ensure that all appropriate steps are carried out in accordance with ORS 127.800 to 127.897 prior to writing a prescription for medication to enable a qualified patient to end his or her life in a humane and dignified manner; and

(A) Dispense medications directly* * *or [(B) through a pharmacist].

(2) Notwithstanding any other provision of law, the attending physician may sign the patient's death certificate.

127.820. Consulting physician confirmation.

Before a patient is qualified under ORS 127.800 to 127.897, a consulting physician shall examine the patient and his or her relevant medical records and confirm, in writing, the attending physician's diagnosis that the patient is suffering from a terminal disease, and verify that the patient is capable, is acting voluntarily and has made an informed decision.

127.825. Counseling referral.

If in the opinion of the attending physician or the consulting physician a patient may be suffering from a psychiatric or psychological disorder or depression causing impaired judgment, either physician shall refer the patient for counseling. No medication to end a patient's life in a humane and dignified manner shall be prescribed until the person performing the counseling determines that the patient is not suffering from a psychiatric or psychological disorder or depression causing impaired judgment.

127.830. Informed decision.

No person shall receive a prescription for medication to end his or her life in a humane and dignified manner unless he or she has made an informed decision as defined in ORS 127.800 (7). Immediately prior to writing a prescription for medication under ORS 127.800 to 127.897, the attending physician shall verify that the patient is making an informed decision.

127.835. Family notification.

The attending physician shall recommend that the patient notify the next of kin of his or her request for medication pursuant to ORS 127.800 to 127.897. A patient who declines or is unable to notify next of kin shall not have his or her request denied for that reason.

127.840. Written and oral requests.

In order to receive a prescription for medication to end his or her life in a humane and dignified manner, a qualified patient shall have made an oral request and a written request, and reiterate the oral request to his or her attending physician no less than fifteen (15) days after making the initial oral request. At the time the qualified patient makes his or her second oral request, the attending physician shall offer the patient an opportunity to rescind the request.

127.845. Right to rescind request.

A patient may rescind his or her request at any time and in any manner without regard to his or her mental state. No prescription for medication under ORS 127.800 to 127.897 may be written without the attending physician offering the qualified patient an opportunity to rescind the request.

127.850. Waiting periods.

No less than fifteen (15) days shall elapse between the patient's initial oral request and the writing of a prescription under ORS 127.800 to 127.897. No less than 48 hours shall elapse between the patient's written request and the writing of a prescription under ORS 127.800 to 127.897.

* * *

127.860. Residency requirement.

Only requests made by Oregon residents under ORS 127.800 to 127.897 shall be granted. Factors demonstrating Oregon residency include but are not limited to [being licensed to drive, registering to vote, owning property, and paying taxes in Oregon.]

* * *

127.880. Construction of Act.

Nothing in ORS 127.800 to 127.897 shall be construed to authorize a physician or any other person to end a patient's life by lethal injection, mercy killing or active euthanasia. Actions taken in accordance with ORS 127.800 to 127.897 shall not, for any purpose, constitute suicide, assisted suicide, mercy killing or homicide, under the law.

* * *

127.897. Form of the request.

A request for a medication as authorized by ORS 127.800 to 127.897 shall be in substantially the following form:

REQUEST FOR MEDICATION TO END MY LIFE
IN A HUMANE AND DIGNIFIED MANNER

I, _____, am an adult of sound mind.

I am suffering from _____, which my attending physician has determined is a terminal disease and which has been medically confirmed by a consulting physician.

I have been fully informed of my diagnosis, prognosis, the nature of medication to be prescribed and potential associated risks, the expected result, and the feasible alternatives, including comfort care, hospice care and pain control.

I request that my attending physician prescribe medication that will end my life in a humane and dignified manner.

INITIAL ONE:

_____ I have informed my family of my decision and taken their opinions into consideration.

_____ I have decided not to inform my family of my decision.

_____ I have no family to inform of my decision.

I understand that I have the right to rescind this request at any time.

I understand the full import of this request and I expect to die when I take the medication to be prescribed. I further understand that although most deaths occur within three hours, my death may take longer and my physician has counseled me about this possibility.

I make this request voluntarily and without reservation, and I accept full moral responsibility for my actions.

[Signature line; witness lines]

* * *

Early in 1999 the Oregon Department of Health issued its first annual report, which collected data on those who received lethal prescriptions under the Act during its first year of operation. Each year for eight years the Oregon Department of Health issued a comprehensive annual report describing activity under the Death with Dignity Act. Starting with the report for the ninth year of the operation of the statute, reflecting activity in 2006 and released in 2007, the Department of Health made available a brief summary of activity under the statute and other charts and tables. All of the annual reports, and the summaries (starting in 2007), are available at http://www.oregon.gov/ DHS/ph/pas/ar-index.shtml. The Summary released in 2007 provides some detail on the first nine years of operation under the statute, with a focus on activity over the most recent year.

OREGON DEPARTMENT OF HUMAN SERVICES, SUMMARY OF OREGON'S DEATH WITH DIGNITY ACT—2006

(released March 2007).

Under Oregon's Death with Dignity Act (DWDA), terminally-ill adult Oregonians are allowed to obtain and use prescriptions from their physicians for self-administered, lethal medications. The Oregon Public Health Division is required by the Act to collect information on compliance and to issue an annual report. The key findings from 2006 are listed below. * * *

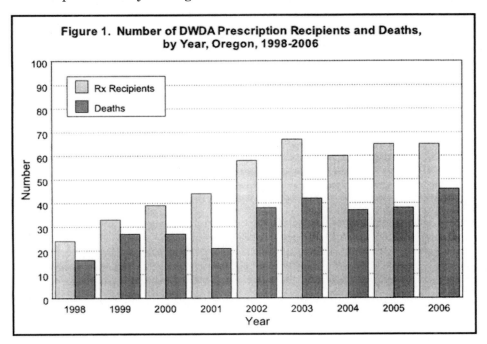

Figure 1. Number of DWDA Prescription Recipients and Deaths, by Year, Oregon, 1998-2006

• During 2006, 65 prescriptions for lethal medications under the provisions of the DWDA were written [ ]. Of these, 35 patients took the medications, 19 died of their underlying disease, and 11 were alive at the end of 2006. In addition, 11 patients with earlier prescriptions died from taking the medications, resulting in a total of 46 DWDA deaths during 2006. This corresponds to an estimated 14.7 DWDA deaths per 10,000 total deaths.

• Forty physicians wrote the 65 prescriptions (range 1–7).

• Since the law was passed in 1997, 292 patients have died under the terms of the law.

• As in prior years, participants were more likely to have cancer (87%), and have more formal education (41% had at least a baccalaureate degree) than other Oregonians who died. Patients who died in 2006 were slightly older (median age 74 years) than in previous years (median age 69 years).

• Most patients died at home (93%); and were enrolled in hospice care (76%), although the number enrolled in hospice was less than in previous years (87%).

• All patients, except one, had some form of health insurance: 64% had private insurance and 33% had Medicare or Medicaid.

• Complications were reported in four patients during 2006; they all regurgitated some of the medication.

• As in previous years, the most frequently mentioned end-of-life concerns were: loss of autonomy (96%), decreasing ability to participate in activities that made life enjoyable (96%), and loss of dignity (76%). During 2006, more participants were concerned about inadequate pain control (48%) than in previous years (22%).

• During 2006, 10 referrals were made to the Board of Medical Examiners (BME) for incorrectly completed reporting forms. The BME found no violations of "good faith compliance" with the Act and did not sanction any physicians for "unprofessional conduct" regarding the Act.

Notes and Questions

1. The Oregon Death with Dignity Act also provides that no contract or statute can affect a person's request for physician assisted suicide, and that no insurance policy can be conditioned upon, or affected by, a patient's decision to choose (or reject) physician assisted suicide. The measure includes a section providing immunity for those who follow the requirements of the statute, and imposing liability on those who violate it.

2. As the Summary published in 2007 indicates, most Oregonians who have sought physician assisted death have done so because of their fear of losing control of their lives (and the concomitant suffering that would follow), not because of physical pain. In 2006, twice as many patients listed loss of autonomy as a reason for seeking physician assisted death as listed inadequate pain control. An excerpt from Oregon's Second Annual Report, published in 2000, explains this:

Responses from both physician and family interviews indicate that patient's decisions to request PAS were motivated by multiple interrelated concerns.

Physical suffering was discussed by several families as a cause of loss of autonomy, inability to participate in activities that made life enjoyable, or a "non-existent" quality of life. For example, "She would have stuck it out through the pain if she thought she'd get better ... [but she believed that] when quality of life has no meaning, it's no use hanging around." For another participant, a feeling of being trapped because of ALS contributed to concern about loss of autonomy. Family members frequently commented on loss of control of bodily functions when discussing loss of autonomy. Those reporting patient concern about being a burden on friends and family also reported concern about loss of autonomy and control of bodily functions. Reasons for requesting a prescription were sometimes so interrelated they were difficult to categorize. According to one family member being asked to distinguish reasons for the patient's decision, "It was everything; it was nothing; [he was suffering terribly]."

Difficulty categorizing and differences in interpreting the nature of the concerns made physician and family member responses hard to compare quantitatively. Nonetheless, family interviews corroborate physician reports from both years that patients are greatly concerned about issues of autonomy and control. In addition, responses of both physicians and family consistently pointed to patient concerns about quality of life and the wish to have a means of controlling the end of life should it become unbearable. As one family member said, "She always thought that if something was terminal, she would [want to] control the end ... It was not the dying that she dreaded, it was getting to that death."

* * *

Oregonians choosing physician-assisted suicide appeared to want control over how they died. One woman had purchased poison over a decade before her participation, when her cancer was first diagnosed, so that she would never be without the means of controlling the end of her life should it become unbearable. Like many others who participated, she was described as "determined" to have this control. Another woman was described as a "gutsy woman" who was "... determined in her lifetime, and determined about [physician-assisted suicide]." Family members expressed profound grief at losing a loved one. However, mixed with this grief was great respect for the patient's determination and choice to use physician-assisted suicide. As one husband said about his wife of almost 50 years, "She was my only girl; I didn't want to lose her ... but she wanted to do this."

Could the expressed concerns have been relieved by better medical and nursing care? Should these individuals have toughed it out, or did they choose the better course for themselves? For their families? Are those who do take advantage of the statute brave? Cowardly?

3.   The Oregon initiative was immediately challenged for a wide range of reasons. Some argued that it discriminated against the disabled, for example, by coercing them into choosing physician assisted death, and others argued it discriminated against the disabled because those with physical disabilities making it impossible to take oral medications would not be able to use the statute. The United States District Court in Oregon issued a preliminary injunction against enforcing the initiative shortly after its passage and issued a permanent injunction several months later. Ultimately, the Ninth Circuit reversed the District Court, finding that those challenging the Oregon initiative had no standing to raise the issue in federal court. Lee v. Oregon, 107 F.3d 1382 (9th Cir.1997).

4.   The federal government has not ignored physician assisted death, either. Even before the Oregon statute became effective, Congress passed the Assisted Suicide Prevention Restriction Act of 1997, which outlaws the use of federal money to aid physician assisted death, directly or indirectly.

Shortly after the Oregon Death with Dignity Act became effective, some suggested that any physician who prescribed a lethal drug under that statute would be prescribing that drug without a "legitimate medical purpose," and thus would be acting inconsistently with the federal Controlled Substances Act (CSA). A physician's violation of the Act could lead to both the loss of prescribing authority and criminal indictment. In June of 1998, after the matter had been pending for some time, the United States Department of Justice published a report concluding that use of controlled substances under the Oregon statute would satisfy the "legitimate medical purpose" requirement of the federal Act. See discussion of the CSA in Chapter 1.

Members of the House and Senate then introduced the Lethal Drug Abuse Prevention Act of 1998, which would have expanded the authority of the Drug Enforcement Agency to investigate lethal use of controlled substances, which could not be used with the *intent* of causing death. Supporters of physician assisted death joined many of their staunchest opponents and mainstream medical organizations (including the AMA) to oppose the bill because, they said, it would be likely to chill physicians from providing adequate pain relief at the end of life. Although the bill failed, it was resurrected in slightly milder form in 2000 as the Pain Relief Promotion Act ("PRPA"), which included a well publicized section announcing that the provision of medication with the intent to manage pain (and not the intent to cause death) was protected. The 2000 version of the bill also provided for the education of health care professionals on issues related to pain management, and it was supported by the AMA (but opposed by the ABA, the American Cancer Society and most groups advocating for improved pain management). Although the stated purpose of PRPA was to promote adequate pain relief practices, its effect would be (and, some say, its real purpose was) to render it impossible for physicians in Oregon to carry out the provisions of the Death With Dignity Act. PRPA died when Congress adjourned in late 2000, and there have not been serious attempts to undermine the Oregon statute through federal legislation since that time.

In 2001, however, the Attorney General, John Ashcroft, issued an interpretive rule that reversed the 1998 Department of Justice position on the issue of the application of the CSA and implemented an enforcement action. Within a day of the announcement of this change in the federal position, Oregon sought relief from the Attorney General's decision in the federal court. A private action seeking an injunction against the Ashcroft position was filed shortly thereafter on behalf of an Oregon oncologist. The District Court immediately restrained the United States from enforcing the new interpretation of the CSA, and in 2006 the Supreme Court determined that the Attorney General's interpretive rule was beyond the scope of his authority and was improperly promulgated. Gonzales v. Oregon, 546 U.S. 243, 126 S.Ct. 904, 163 L.Ed.2d 748 (2006). The Court left open the possibility that the Attorney General could properly promulgate a substantive rule that would bar the operation of the Oregon Death with Dignity Act, and that Congress could amend the Controlled Substances Act to achieve this end.

5.   The Oregon statute has been amended, but the changes are not substantial. The legislature added the definition of "capable," added some new language designed to encourage patients to discuss the matter with their families, and provided some factors to be considered in determining residency. The amendments

also made clear the broad extent of the institutional conscience exception to the statute, which permits health care institutions to limit physicians from engaging in assisted death on their premises or in their organizations, and it changed the written consent form to assure that patients recognize that death will probably, but not always, take place about three hours after taking the medication.

6. Emboldened by the success in Oregon, many groups have sought state statutes that would accomplish what Oregon's Measure 16 did. A measure similar to the Oregon statute was very narrowly defeated at the polls in Maine in 2000. In part as a result of the narrow defeat of the Maine measure, during the next legislative session both supporters and opponents of physician assisted death joined to support a number of bills improving the quality of end-of-life care in that state. The question of physician assisted death itself has not moved off the legislative radar screen, though. In 2002 the Hawai'i House of Representatives passed an Oregon-like bill that came within a couple of votes of passing the Senate. In 2007 the California legislature gave serious consideration to a bill that would have provided for physician assisted death, and advocates in that state expect the issue to arise again over the next few years. Finally, in 2008 advocates for physician assisted death in Washington hope to make that the second state to use the initiative process to provide for such a law. Former Washington Governor Booth Gardner, who suffers from Parkinson's disease, has become a leading advocate for an Oregon-like statute, and he is committed to campaign for it. For the story of Governor Gardner's "last campaign" from the perspective of someone who opposes physician assisted death, see Daniel Bergner, Death in the Family, New York Times Magazine (December 2, 2007). For a wonderful account of the meaning of euthanasia and suicide in our society and others, and a description of how these arguments are likely to be discussed in the future, see Margaret Battin, Ending Life: Ethics and the Way We Die (2005).

7. Is there some common ground available to those, on the one hand, who believe that permitting physician assisted death is necessary for patients to be properly treated at the end of life, and those, on the other hand, who believe that physician assisted death must be outlawed for patients to be properly treated? Both groups agree that pain is often inadequately treated at the end of life, in part because physicians fear legal action for homicide (if pain relief results in the death of the patient) or distribution of drugs (if the condition of a patient requires a larger dose of narcotic medication than is standard). As Oregon's Fifth Annual Report described this in 2003:

> The availability of [Physician Assisted Suicide, "PAS"] may have led to efforts to improve end-of-life care through other modalities. While it may be common for patients with a terminal illness to consider PAS, a request for PAS can be an opportunity for a medical provider to explore with patients their fears and wishes around end-of-life care, and to make patients aware of other options. Often once the provider has addressed patients' concerns, they may choose not to pursue PAS. The availability of PAS as an option in Oregon also may have spurred Oregon doctors to address other end-of life care options more effectively. In one study Oregon physicians reported that, since the passage of the Death with Dignity Act in 1994, they had made efforts to improve their knowledge of the use of pain medications in the terminally ill, to improve their recognition of psychiatric disorders such as depression, and to refer patients more frequently to hospice.

Is there a way to achieve this end without allowing for physician assisted death? In some states advocates on both sides of the physician assisted death issue have joined together to support intractable pain relief statutes, which are designed to protect health care providers who deliver adequate pain relief from adverse licensing and criminal actions. These statutes generally provide that a health care provider will not be liable in a state disciplinary proceeding or a criminal action for the aggressive prescription of pain medication as long as the use of that medication is in accord with accepted guidelines for pain management. Several states have promulgated intractable pain relief acts, and several more are considering them. For a model "Pain Relief Act," see 24 J.L., Med. & Ethics 317 (1996). See also, Ann Alpers, Criminal Act or Palliative Care? Prosecutions Involving the Care of the Dying, 26 J. L. Med. & Ethics 308 (1998), identifying factors that create a risk of prosecution. For a series of articles on the relationship between pain relief and physician assisted death, with the conclusion that we ought to create a system that provides excellent palliative care in every case and allows for physician assisted death in the rare cases in which it is necessary, see Timothy Quill & Margaret Battin, eds., Physician–Assisted Dying: the Right to Excellent End-of-Life Care and Patient Choice (2004). See also, Kathleen Foley, The Case Against Assisted Suicide: For the Right to End of Life Care (2002), written by a leading palliative care physician.

8.   Federal and state policy may conflict on one kind of palliative care—the use of marijuana. Some cancer patients, patients with glaucoma, AIDS patients, patients with multiple sclerosis, those with migraine headaches and others find that they can obtain relief from some of the symptoms of the disease–or from some of the side effects of the treatments for the disease–through the use of marijuana. In particular, some cancer patients find that marijuana helps them overcome the nausea that follows the use of many chemotherapeutic agents. While several states have now legalized the use of marijuana under such circumstances, the manufacture and distribution of marijuana is still a felony under the Federal Controlled Substances Act (CSA). In 2001, the Supreme Court determined that there was no medical necessity defense available to those who manufactured or distributed marijuana to patients in violation of the Federal law. United States v. Oakland Cannabis Buyers' Cooperative, 532 U.S. 483, 121 S.Ct. 1711, 149 L.Ed.2d 722 (2001). Four years later the Supreme Court confirmed that the CSA marijuana prohibition fell within Congress's commerce power. Gonzales v. Raich, 545 U.S. 1, 125 S.Ct. 2195, 162 L.Ed.2d 1 (2005).

9.   The public interest in this issue is not limited to the United States. Physician assisted death has been tolerated in the Netherlands, as a legal matter, since 1969, and it was formally legalized by the parliament in 2001 in cases of intractable suffering (not just pain), where the patient has been informed of all of the alternative treatments available, has consulted two physicians, and has followed other requirements established by the national medical association. Belgium recently joined the Netherlands in legalizing physician assisted death through the legislative process, and the practice is now officially tolerated under some circumstances in Switzerland. The Constitutional Court of Colombia has approved legislation that provides for physician assisted death, and there has been an active debate over the propriety of permitting physician assisted death in France, Venezuela and Australia. In fact, Australia's Northern Territory's parliament passed The Rights of the Terminally Ill Act (1995), which permitted what some have called "voluntary euthanasia" under some circumstances; however, the national parliament effectively overturned that territorial statute. For a brief description of the current state of the law in other countries, see Alan Meisel & Kathy Cerminara, The Right to Die (3d ed. 2005).

The European Court of Human Rights considered a challenge to the laws of the United Kingdom that outlawed physician assisted death in Pretty v. United

Kingdom, 35 Eur. H. R. Rep 1 (2002). Applying analysis similar, in many respects, to that in *Glucksberg* and *Vacco*, the Court found that the United Kingdom had the authority to enforce its law.

Problem: Drafting Legislation

You are the nonpolitical legislative counsel to a state legislature. Currently that state has a statute prohibiting assisting suicide. You have been asked by several members of the legislature to draft bills relating to physician assisted death. One member has asked you to draft a bill that would outlaw all physician assisted death, under all circumstances. A second member wants you to draft a bill that would put as few limitations on physician assisted death as is possible; this libertarian member believes that the decision should be left to individual doctors and patients. Another member has asked you to draft a statute that would protect health care providers from potential liability for participating in physician assisted deaths, and would give providers an option to avoid participating in physician assisted deaths if they chose not to do so. Yet another member has asked you to draft a statute that would prohibit managed care organizations from directly or indirectly giving any incentives to their members to choose physician assisted deaths. Finally, one long time incumbent has asked you to draft a consensus statute—one with enough political support across the spectrum that it has a reasonable chance of passing.

How would you go about drafting these statutes? How would they be different? What facts (about the legal landscape in this state, about the politics of the current officeholders, about the religious backgrounds of those within the state, about other issues) would you want to have before you started drafting these statutes?

Chapter 16

PUBLIC HEALTH

I. INTRODUCTION

BARRY LEVY, TWENTY–FIRST CENTURY CHALLENGES FOR LAW AND PUBLIC HEALTH (1999)

32 Ind. L. Rev. 1149.

PUBLIC HEALTH

I am often asked, "What is public health?" I respond by describing typical daily activities that have been impacted by public health to make our lives safer and more healthful: drinking clean (and often, fluoridated) water, eating more nutritious meals (even with "Nutrition Facts" printed on packages of processed foods), driving safer and less polluting cars, regularly exercising, working in safer and more healthful workplaces, and, for many of us, having access to high quality, comprehensive health care, including preventive clinical services. All of this, and more, is the result of public health. Public health has accounted for about twenty-five of the thirty years of increased life expectancy in the United States since the turn of the century. Most people take all of this for granted—unless there is an outbreak of disease, an increase in the occurrence of some disease or injury, an outbreak of domestic or community violence, or a natural disaster.

When public health is most successful, public health activities—in public health practice, education, research, policy development and implementation, and administration and finance—are all almost invisible.

As stated in a landmark report of the Institute of Medicine in 1988, public health is "what we, as a society, do collectively to assure the conditions in which people can be healthy." It takes a society to practice public health—not just public health professionals. * * *

THE LAW

Laws concerning public health, at the national, state, and local level, are designed primarily to protect and promote health, and, at the same time, to ensure the rights of individuals. In various situations, different laws take precedence. Public health legal powers derive from the United States Constitution and the state constitutions. Many states have reasonably well-defined codes of public health that provide a basis for public health practice. Many state and local health officers are not fully aware of all the public health powers that they have—powers that can enable them to take necessary actions. For example, in a city in Massachusetts recently, the public health council realized existing laws enabled it to take actions to support a needle exchange program to prevent transmission of HIV and other pathogens. Many public health laws are enacted and enforced under the state's police powers— something that can cut both ways. Many of us public health professionals do not see ourselves as police officers; indeed when we come across as police officers, we may be undermining the public trust that is so essential for our work.

A prominent textbook on public health [Douglas Scutchfield and C. William Keck, Principles of Public Health Practice (1997)] outlines eight areas of public health law:

1. *Environmental Health Laws.*—These deal with food, workplace safety, wastewater disposal, and air pollution. Issues often arise concerning right of entry and compensation—not only compensation to victims who may have been harmed, but also compensation to those whose property may have been taken as a result of public health measures.

2. *Laws and Regulations on Reporting (Surveillance) of Disease and Injury.*—These enable public health workers to track disease, to identify disease outbreaks, to identify disturbing disease and injury trends, and to provide the basis for intervention to control disease and injury. Many of these laws and regulations transcend an individual's or a patient's right to privacy. Even though physicians are mandated to report specific diseases and injuries of public health importance, most do not; much disease and injury reporting rests on reporting from state laboratories or other sources of data.

3. *Laws Pertaining to Vital Statistics.*—Birth and death records provide an important basis for much public health work, despite frequent inaccuracies, especially in the cause of death recorded on death certificates.

4. *Disease and Injury Control.*—These laws often focus on prevention of disease and injury at the community level. Many policies and programs on such issues as tobacco and alcohol control—like preventing teenagers from drinking and smoking—pertain to this area of public health law.

5. *Involuntary Testing.*—These laws provide a basis to determine disease prevalence, such as prevalence of HIV/AIDS in a given community, and to identify those who need treatment or restriction from work. In many jurisdictions, food handlers are tested on a regular basis to determine if they have certain infections that might be spread through food preparation.

6. *Contact Tracing.*—Voluntary in nature, contact tracing has proven to be a very effective and efficient way of controlling diseases, such as tuberculosis and sexually transmitted diseases. It played an important role in the worldwide eradication of smallpox.

7. *Immunization and Mandatory Treatment.*—The book *How Can I Help?* [ ] describes a dramatic episode in India during the smallpox eradication campaign: An international immunization team invaded a household in the middle of the night to forcibly vaccinate a family against their will. This episode raises many interesting legal, sociocultural, and public health questions. In the United States and many other countries, laws that mandate certain immunizations exempt people who have religious objections to immu-

nizations. We need also recognize that even safe and efficacious immunizations can be fatal to some people who receive them. Approximately one in a million people who receive polio vaccine may actually contract and die from polio.

8. *Personal Restrictions.*—Public health authorities have the right to restrict a person carrying salmonella bacteria from working as a food handler. In the past, public health workers often quarantined people who had contagious diseases of public health significance, such as tuberculosis, before effective drugs were available. Quarantine is a form of isolation; while we believe that we are well beyond the age of quarantine, some people believe that we will need to quarantine in the future those infected with resistant infectious agents that pose public health threats. While quarantine is seldom used in the United States today, Cuba has quarantined (isolated from the rest of society) people infected with HIV.

Notes

1. Which of these eight areas of Public Health Law have contributed most substantially to the health of the American public? While most public health officials have pointed to the first—environmental health policies—each of the others has made a substantial contribution to public health over the past century. Most public health activities—like restricting an infected person from working as a food handler—will fit in two, three, or more of these categories.

2. What makes an issue a "public health" issue? Is the quality of the gene pool a public health issue? The widespread use of alternative medicines? Tobacco? Gun violence? Domestic violence? What difference does it make whether an issue is characterized as a public health issue? Are we more likely to defer to governmental decisions, and more likely to accept governmental intrusions on individual liberties, where the public health is involved?

3. Another approach to public health law is provided by Lawrence Gostin, who defines public health law as "the study of the legal powers and duties of the state to assure the conditions for people to be healthy (e.g., to identify prevent and ameliorate risks to health in the population) and the limitations on the power of the state to constrain the autonomy, privacy, liberty, proprietary, or other legally protected interests of individuals for the protection or promotion of community health." Professor Gostin goes on to suggest "five essential characteristics of public health law:"

Government: Public health activities are a special responsibility of the government

Populations: Public health focuses on the health of populations.

Relationships: Public health addresses the relationship between the state and the population (or between the state and individuals who place themselves or the community at risk).

Services: Public health deals with the provision of population-based services grounded on the scientific methodologies of public health (e.g., biostatistics and epidemiology).

Coercion: Public health authorities possess the power to coerce individuals and businesses for the protection of the community, rather than relying on a near universal ethic of voluntarism.

Lawrence Gostin, Public Health Law: Power, Duty Restraint (2000), at 4.

4. In the article excerpted above, Dr. Levy also quotes Article 25 of the Universal Declaration of Human Rights:

> Everyone has a right to a standard of living adequate for the health and well-being of [oneself] and [one's] family, including food, clothing, housing and medical care and necessary social services, and the right to security in the event of unemployment, sickness, disability, widowhood, old age or other lack of livelihood in circumstances beyond one's control.

Is this a principle of public health?

5. Lawrence Gostin's public health textbook, supra note 3, provides an exceptional account of the breadth of public health law, and an excellent bibliography as well. Other good general sources include Joel Teitelbaum and Sara Wilensky, Essentials of Public Health and Policy (2007) and Ken Wing, The Law and the Public's Health (6th ed. 2003). See also Lawrence Gostin, Scott Burris and Zita Lazzarini, The Law and the Public's Health: A Study of Infectious Disease Law in the United States, 99 Colum. L. Rev. 59 (1999). For interesting historical and constitutional approach to these issues, see Wendy Parmet, From Slaughter–House to Lochner: The Rise and Fall of the Cosnstitutionalization of Public Health, 40 Am. J. Leg. Hist. 476 (1996).

Problem: Obesity as a Public Health Issue

As a legislator in your state, you have become very concerned about obesity in the population, and you are worried about the long range consequences of this condition on the vitality of the public. In particular, you have become concerned about the proliferation of fast food sites that offer primarily economical but very high fat foods. You are also disturbed by the relatively unhealthy foods available at public schools, many of which have contracts with beverage companies to run their vending machines and snack bars, and by the disappearance of mandatory physical education requirements at the high school level. There is also an indication that a comparatively sedentary lifestyle that includes watching television and playing video games contributes to what some have called the "epidemic" of obesity.

Is the problem of obesity a "public health" problem, or simply a problem for some individuals? Is it a matter or personal responsibility that should be unrelated to the obligations of the law? Would it make any difference if you classified obesity as a "public health" problem? What legal responses might be available to the state legislature to address this problem? Are there ways to use school law, tax law, criminal law, tort law, food and drug law, or general public health regulatory law to address this problem? What are the legal, political and social consequences of doing so? Are there civil liberties interests of the obese that are at stake in using the law in this way?

Do you feel the same way about tobacco or school violence or "extreme sports" as public health problems?

II. THE CONSTITUTIONAL FOUNDATION OF PUBLIC HEALTH LAW

JACOBSON v. MASSACHUSETTS

Supreme Court of the United States, 1905.
197 U.S. 11, 25 S.Ct. 358, 49 L.Ed. 643.

[The Revised Laws of that Commonwealth, c. 75, § 137, provide that "the board of health of a city or town if, in its opinion, it is necessary for the public health or safety shall require and enforce the vaccination and revaccination of all the inhabitants thereof and shall provide them with the means of free vaccination. Whoever, being over twenty-one years of age and not under guardianship, refuses or neglects to comply with such requirement shall forfeit five dollars."

* * *

Proceeding under the above statutes, the Board of Health of the city of Cambridge, Massachusetts, on the twenty-seventh day of February, 1902, adopted the following regulation: "Whereas, smallpox has been prevalent to some extent in the city of Cambridge and still continues to increase; and whereas, it is necessary for the speedy extermination of the disease, that all persons not protected by vaccination should be vaccinated; and whereas, in the opinion of the board, the public health and safety require the vaccination or revaccination of all the inhabitants of Cambridge; be it ordered, that all the inhabitants of the city who have not been successfully vaccinated since March, 1, 1897, be vaccinated or revaccinated."] [Ed. Note: This description is reprinted from the syllabus of the Court.]

MR. JUSTICE HARLAN, after making the foregoing statement, delivered the opinion of the court.

We pass without extended discussion the suggestion that the particular section of the statute of Massachusetts now in question [ ] is in derogation of rights secured by the Preamble of the Constitution of the United States. Although that Preamble indicates the general purposes for which the people ordained and established the Constitution, it has never been regarded as the source of any substantive power conferred on the Government of the United States or on any of its Departments. Such powers embrace only those expressly granted in the body of the Constitution and such as may be implied from those so granted. Although, therefore, one of the declared objects of the Constitution was to secure the blessings of liberty to all under the sovereign jurisdiction and authority of the United States, no power can be exerted to that end by the United States unless, apart from the Preamble, it be found in some express delegation of power or in some power to be properly implied therefrom. [ ]

We also pass without discussion the suggestion that the above section of the statute is opposed to the spirit of the Constitution. * * * We have no need in this case to go beyond the plain, obvious meaning of the words in those provisions of the Constitution which, it is contended, must control our decision.

What, according to the judgment of the state court, is the scope and effect of the statute? What results were intended to be accomplished by it? These questions must be answered.

* * *

The authority of the State to enact this statute is to be referred to what is commonly called the police power—a power which the State did not surrender when becoming a member of the Union under the Constitution. Although this court has refrained from any attempt to define the limits of that power, yet it has distinctly recognized the authority of a State to enact quarantine laws and "health laws of every description;" indeed, all laws that relate to matters completely within its territory and which do not by their necessary operation affect the people of other States. According to settled principles the police power of a State must be held to embrace, at least, such reasonable regulations established directly by legislative enactment as will protect the public health and the public safety. [ ]. It is equally true that the State may invest local bodies called into existence for purposes of local administration with authority in some appropriate way to safeguard the public health and the public safety. The mode or manner in which those results are to be accomplished is within the discretion of the State, subject, of course, so far as Federal power is concerned, only to the condition that no rule prescribed by a State, nor any regulation adopted by a local governmental agency acting under the sanction of state legislation, shall contravene the Constitution of the United States or infringe any right granted or secured by that instrument. * * *

We come, then, to inquire whether any right given, or secured by the Constitution, is invaded by the statute as interpreted by the state court. The defendant insists that his liberty is invaded when the State subjects him to fine or imprisonment for neglecting or refusing to submit to vaccination; that a compulsory vaccination law is unreasonable, arbitrary and oppressive, and, therefore, hostile to the inherent right of every freeman to care for his own body and health in such way as to him seems best; and that the execution of such a law against one who objects to vaccination, no matter for what reason, is nothing short of an assault upon his person. But the liberty secured by the Constitution of the United States to every person within its jurisdiction does not import an absolute right in each person to be, at all times and in all circumstances, wholly freed from restraint. There are manifold restraints to which every person is necessarily subject for the common good. On any other basis organized society could not exist with safety to its members. Society based on the rule that each one is a law unto himself would soon be confronted with disorder and anarchy. Real liberty for all could not exist under the operation of a principle which recognizes the right of each individual person to use his own, whether in respect of his person or his property, regardless of the injury that may be done to others. * * * The good and welfare of the Commonwealth, of which the legislature is primarily the judge, is the basis on which the police power rests in Massachusetts[ ].

Applying these principles to the present case, it is to be observed that the legislature of Massachusetts required the inhabitants of a city or town to be vaccinated only when, in the opinion of the Board of Health, that was necessary for the public health or the public safety. The authority to determine for all what ought to be done in such an emergency must have been lodged somewhere or in some body; and surely it was appropriate for the legislature to refer that question, in the first instance, to a Board of Health, composed of persons residing in the locality affected and appointed, presumably, because of their fitness to determine such questions. To invest such a body with authority over such matters was not an unusual nor an unreasonable or arbitrary requirement. Upon the principle of self-defense, of paramount necessity, a community has the right to protect itself against an epidemic of disease which threatens the safety of its members. * * * Smallpox being prevalent and increasing at Cambridge, the court would usurp the functions of another branch of government if it adjudged, as matter of law, that the mode adopted under the sanction of the State, to protect the people at large, was arbitrary and not justified by the necessities of the case. We say necessities of the case, because it might be that an acknowledged power of a local community to protect itself against an epidemic threatening the safety of all, might be exercised in particular circumstances and in reference to particular persons in such an arbitrary, unreasonable manner, or might go so far beyond what was reasonably required for the safety of the public, as to authorize or compel the courts to interfere for the protection of such persons. * * * There is, of course, a sphere within which the individual may assert the supremacy of his own will and rightfully dispute the authority of any human government, especially of any free government existing under a written constitution, to interfere with the exercise of that will. But it is equally true that in every well-ordered society charged with the duty of conserving the safety of its members the rights of the individual in respect of his liberty may at times, under the pressure of great dangers, be subjected to such restraint, to be enforced by reasonable regulations, as the safety of the general public may demand.

* * *

Looking at the propositions embodied in the defendant's rejected offers of proof it is clear that they are more formidable by their number than by their inherent value. Those offers in the main seem to have had no purpose except to state the general theory of those of the medical profession who attach little or no value to vaccination as a means of preventing the spread of smallpox or who think that vaccination causes other diseases of the body. What everybody knows the court must know, and therefore the state court judicially knew, as this court knows, that an opposite theory accords with the common belief and is maintained by high medical authority. We must assume that when the statute in question was passed, the legislature of Massachusetts was not unaware of these opposing theories, and was compelled, of necessity, to choose between them. It was not compelled to commit a matter involving the public health and safety to the final decision of a court or jury. It is no part of the function of a court or a jury to determine which one of two modes was likely to be the most effective for the protection of the public against disease. That was for the legislative department to determine in the light of all the information it had or could obtain. * * * Upon what sound principles as to the relations existing between the different departments of government can the court review this action of the legislature? If there is any such power in the judiciary to review legislative action in respect of a matter affecting the general welfare, it can only be when that which the legislature has done comes within the rule that if a statute purporting to have been enacted to protect the public health, the public morals or the public safety, has no real or substantial relation to those objects, or is, beyond all question, a plain, palpable invasion of rights secured by the fundamental law, it is the duty of the courts to so adjudge, and thereby give effect to the Constitution. [ ]

Whatever may be thought of the expediency of this statute, it cannot be affirmed to be, beyond question, in palpable conflict with the Constitution. Nor, in view of the methods employed to stamp out the disease of smallpox, can anyone confidently assert that the means prescribed by the State to that end has no real or substantial relation to the protection of the public health and the public safety. Such an assertion would not be consistent with the experience of this and other countries whose authorities have dealt with the disease of smallpox. [The Court then summarizes the history of vaccination in Europe and America.]

* * *

Since then vaccination, as a means of protecting a community against smallpox, finds strong support in the experience of this and other countries, no court, much less a jury, is justified in disregarding the action of the legislature simply because in its or their opinion that particular method was— perhaps or possibly—not the best either for children or adults.

* * *

We are not prepared to hold that a minority, residing or remaining in any city or town where smallpox is prevalent, and enjoying the general protection afforded by an organized local government, may thus defy the will of its constituted authorities, acting in good faith for all, under the legislative sanction of the State [by refusing to be vaccinated]. If such be the privilege of a minority then a like privilege would belong to each individual of the community, and the spectacle would be presented of the welfare and safety of an entire population being subordinated to the notions of a single individual who chooses to remain a part of that population. * * * The safety and the health of the people of Massachusetts are, in the first instance, for that Commonwealth to guard and protect. They are matters that do not ordinarily concern the National Government. So far as they can be reached by any government, they depend, primarily, upon such action as the State in its wisdom may take; and we do not perceive that this legislation has invaded by right secured by the Federal Constitution.

Before closing this opinion we deem it appropriate, in order to prevent misapprehension as to our views, to observe * * * that the police power of a State * * * may be exerted in such circumstances or by regulations so arbitrary and oppressive in particular cases as to justify the interference of the courts to prevent wrong and oppression. Extreme cases can be readily suggested. Ordinarily such cases are not safe guides in the administration of the law. It is easy, for instance, to suppose the case of an adult who is embraced by the mere words of the act, but yet to subject whom to vaccination in a particular condition of his health or body, would be cruel and inhuman in the last degree. We are not to be understood as holding that the statute was intended to be applied to such a case, or, if it was so intended, that the judiciary would not be competent to interfere and protect the health and life of the individual concerned.

MR. JUSTICE BREWER and MR. JUSTICE PECKHAM dissent [without opinion].

Notes and Questions

1.   This oft-cited case established the foundation for public health regulation that came during the ensuing century. While it plainly recognizes the authority of the state to exercise its police powers by imposing public health restrictions on willing and unwilling citizens (and others), it does leave some questions open. It provides that the legislature (or others, with powers properly delegated from the legislature) may make judgments on scientific questions relating to public health. However, the state may not act "by regulations so arbitrary and oppressive in particular cases as to justify the interference of the courts to prevent wrong and oppression." When will the state cross this line? The Court says that, "Extreme Cases can readily be suggested," but it doesn't actually suggest them. Can you identify these cases?

2.   The Jacobson case was not the first vaccination case to be litigated in the federal courts. In Wong Wai v. Williamson, 103 F. 1 (N.D.Cal.1900) the Circuit Court faced an action by Wong Wai, "a subject of the emperor of China, residing in the city and county of San Francisco," seeking to enjoin the city from enforcing a resolution of the board of health that prohibited Chinese residents from traveling outside of the city without proof that they had been inoculated with the "Haffkine Prophylactic," which was thought to provide immunization against bubonic plague. The resolution applied only to those of Chinese extraction, although there was no evidence that they were any more likely than other to be subject to the plague. The Circuit Court recognized the public health authority of the city, but also recognized that there were limits to the exercise of this police power.

> The conditions of a great city frequently present unexpected emergencies affecting the public health, comfort, and convenience. Under such circumstances, officers charged with the duties pertaining to this department of the municipal government should be clothed with sufficient authority to deal with the conditions in a prompt and effective manner. Measures of this character, having a uniform operation, and reasonably adapted to the purpose of protecting the health and preserving the welfare of the inhabitants of a city, are constantly upheld by the courts as valid acts of legislation, however inconvenient they may prove to be, and a wide discretion has also been sanctioned in their execution. But when the municipal authority has neglected to provide suitable rules and regulations upon the subject, and the officers are left to adopt such methods as they may deem proper for the occasion, their acts are open to judicial review, and may be examined in every detail to determine whether individual rights have been respected in accordance with constitutional requirements.

* * *

In the light of these well-established principles [that provide that public health measures must have an appropriate relationship with the ends they seek to serve], the action of the defendants as described in the bill of complaint cannot be justified. They are not based upon any established distinction in the conditions that are supposed to attend this plague, or the persons exposed to its contagion, but they are boldly directed against the Asiatic or Mongolian race as a class, without regard to the previous condition, habits, exposure to disease, or residence of the individual; and the only justification offered for this discrimination was a suggestion made by counsel for the defendants in the course of the argument, that this particular race is more liable to the plague than any other. No evidence has, however, been offered to support this claim, and it is not known to be a fact. This explanation must therefore be dismissed as unsatisfactory.

103 F. at 12–15. The Court went on to find that the actions of the board of health violated not only "the express provisions of the constitution of the United States, in several particulars, but also of the express provisions of our several treaties with China and of the statutes of the United States." 13 F. at 23.

3.   The Court suggests that it may be improper to apply the Massachusetts statute and the Cambridge order to an adult whose health would be placed at risk by vaccination, even though the only exception in the statute is for children whose health would be at risk. Could an adult with some legitimate health concerns about vaccination forgo it? Would this be a matter to be determined by the Board of Health, or by the courts?

4.   In a long historical footnote, the Court traces the history of vaccination from the "first compulsory act" in England in 1853. In fact, as early as 1827 the city of Boston required vaccination for school attendance, and in 1855 the Massachusetts became the first state with required childhood vaccination laws associated with school attendance. The laws were fairly common by the end of the nineteenth century, but, for political and other reasons, they were not regularly enforced. Some were limited to application when there was a public health threat in the community, and some courts recognized religious defenses to the obligation to be vaccinated. See Rhea v. Board of Education, 41 N.D. 449, 171 N.W. 103 (1919). Today all states provide for exemptions when the vaccination would threaten the health of the child, all but two allow for religious exemption (although the nature of those exemptions varies from state to state), and just under half the states allow for an exemption on "moral" or other grounds. Are states Constitutionally required to have religious exemptions? If a state has a religious exemption, should that legislation also permit a "moral" exemption?

The immunizations children must have to be enrolled in school is a matter of state law, but, as a general matter, states adopt the Centers for Disease Control (CDC) list recommended by the Advisory Committee on Immunization Practices. In order to keep some kinds of federal funding, the states now must make an effort to enforce their own immunization laws. This issue is not entirely a scientific one, though, and vaccine manufacturers do lobby state legislatures to have their own products included on the mandatory list. See Note: The HPV Vaccine and Public Health Law, below.

5.   While the health value of continued required immunization is now well established, those who fear government conspiracies have often had special concerns about vaccinations. It is unclear just why this has become a political issue as well as a public health issue, but it is not hard to find those who oppose vaccination with missionary zeal. The CDC, the World Health Organization, and other organizations have joined together to refute several myths about vaccination that sometimes scare parents into seeking exemptions. For a full list of the most common arguments against vaccination and the refutation of each, see the CDC's pamphlet designed for primary care providers, 6 Common Misconceptions about Vaccinations and How to Respond to Them,

http://www.cdc.gov/nip/publications/6mishome.htm. For an excellent account of this issue, and the basis for much of these notes, see James Hodge Jr., School Vaccination Requirements: Legal and Social Perspectives, 27 NCSL State Legislative Report, No. 14 (August 2002). For a an excellent overview of the issue and a clever proposal to finesse the opposition to immunization while respecting individuals' liberties, see Ross Silverman, *No More Kidding Around: Restructuring Childhood Immunization Exceptions in Insure Public Health Protection*, 12 Ann. Health L. 277 (2003).

6. Of course, there are side effects to some vaccination, and some are very serious. While we are all safer if everyone is vaccinated, the safest possible course of action is to assure that everyone else's child is vaccinated, and yet not have your own child vaccinated. If everyone else is immunized, there is no chance you will be subject to the disease, whether or not you are immunized. Is it an altruistic decision to decide against seeking an exemption from a required immunization law? Is there any way to avoid this version of the prisoner's dilemma without eliminating all exemptions?

7. Compensation for injuries that arise out of immunization is specifically addressed in the National Vaccine Injury Compensation Program, 42 U.S.C. sections 300aa–10 through 34. This statute may be unique in providing that attorneys must inform potential plaintiffs in vaccine injury cases of the existence of the law and the remedy it provides:

> It shall be the ethical obligation of any attorney who is consulted by an individual with respect to a vaccine-related injury or death to advise such individual that compensation may be available under the program for such injury or death.

42 U.S.C. section 300aa–10(b). For a history of the liability litigation-induced vaccine shortages that gave rise to this no-fault compensation scheme and its predecessors, see Elizabeth Scott, *The National Childhood Vaccine Injury Act Turns Fifteen*, 56 Food & Drug L.J. 351 (2001).

8. How does the Jacobson case affect other kinds of public health regulation? Does it place limits on the efforts of states to limit pollution? Maintain vital statistics? Do involuntary disease testing? Engage in contact tracing? Impose mandatory treatment, quarantine, or isolation? Do genetic screening?

Problem: Opting Out of Childhood Immunization

You are the legal counsel to the school district in Gadsden, Alabama. The Code of Alabama § 16–30–1 requires certain immunizations as a condition of school attendance. Exemptions to this provision are found in the following section:

§ 16–30–3. Exemptions

The provisions of this chapter shall not apply if:

(1) In the absence of an epidemic or immediate threat thereof, the parent or guardian of the child shall object thereto in writing on grounds that such immunization or testing conflicts with his religious tenets and practices; or

(2) Certification by a competent medical authority providing individual exemption from the required immunization or testing is presented the admissions officer of the school.

First grader Miranda Black's parents, who resent the heavy burden of government, have decided that they will not submit to any immunization requirement. They reason that Miranda should not have to shoulder the public health value of immunization by risking the side effects of the immunizations. Her doctor will not provide the "certification" that the school authorities want because there is no medical reason for her to avoid immunization, and thus her parents have submitted to the school authorities a statement that "compulsory immunization violates our Christian view that the government cannot make us do anything." School health officials are concerned because there were four cases of whooping cough in Gadsden during the last year—up from two the year before, and one the year before that. They attribute the increase to the increasing number of people who have obtained exemptions. The school officials have asked you how they should react to the request that Miranda be exempt.

Note: The HPV Vaccine and Public Health Law

The Human Papillomavirus (HPV), which is the most common sexually transmitted disease, is the major cause of cervical cancer and an important cause of genital warts. It is implicated in over 99% of cervical cancer cases in the United States. One in four women have evidence of the HPV, and the rate is considerably higher for African–American, Hispanic and poor women. The virus is transmitted primarily through sexual intercourse, although it might be communicated through other forms of sexual conduct, like oral sex, as well. There are dozens of strains of the virus, and many (but not all) carry the risk of disease. HPV usually does not manifest itself in identifiable symptoms early on; the resulting cancer and genital warts may not manifest themselves until years after the original infection.

In 2006 Gardasil, a drug that will immunize uninfected women (and men), was approved for use in the United States. While it is effective against only some of the strains of HPV, it is effective against the strains most likely to cause cervical cancer or genital warts. For the immunization to be effective, there must be three injections at appropriate time intervals during a six month period. In addition, it is effective only against subsequent exposure to HPV; it does not provide any benefit for those who already are infected with HPV. The three-immunization Gardasil regimen is effective for at least five years, although whether it will provide life long protection, or whether a booster will be necessary, has yet to be determined (because it has only been the subject of clinical testing over that five year period). Each immunization costs about $120, and thus the series costs $360. Merck, which manufactures Gardasil, has been engaged in marketing the drug before a competitor appears on the scene. GlaxoSmithKline has developed such a potential competitor, Cervarix, but it has not yet been approved by the FDA.

The Advisory Committee on Immunization Practices recommends vaccination of girls at age 11 or 12, before they are likely to be sexually active and when they are very likely to be HPV-free. It also recommends that girls and women up to age 26 be vaccinated if they have not been before. Most insurance companies cover HPV immunization, but many of the girls and women in the target group do not have coverage through private insurance or any government program. A few states have promulgated insurance mandates requiring this immunization be covered, and there are some other government programs that cover this immunization for those under 21. In some states public health agencies will provide the immunizations to those who request them.

Some school districts have considered adding HPV to the list of conditions for which enrolled students must be immunized, primarily as a result of the Advisory Committee's recommendation. As of January 2008 Virginia was the only state that had passed an enrollment mandate statute, which, with many broadly defined opt-out provisions, is scheduled to require sixth graders to be immunized by October of 2008. The issue became particularly politicized in Texas, where Merck lobbied in 2006 and 2007 to have the state require the immunization. In 2007 Governor Perry issued an executive order requiring the immunization for school enrollment and providing state funds, through other established programs, to pay for the immunization of girls and women under 21. There was a strong and angry public reaction to the promulgation of the executive order, and a backlash to the immunization developed out of what some claimed was Merck's profit-driven decision to lobby on behalf of a Gardasil immunization. Ultimately, Merck stopped its lobbying on this issue, but the legislature overturned the Governor's executive order by statute that he allowed to become law without his signature.

The arguments in favor of some kind of mandatory immunization are very powerful. A vaccination with few and relatively insignificant side effects will end cervical cancer and eliminate most cases of genital warts if it is administered before girls become sexually active. The development of a vaccine against a form of cancer is a truly remarkable scientific achievement; many believe it ought to be mandated for every girl and financed for everyone who cannot otherwise pay for it.

On the other hand, some parent groups and some religious organizations oppose any HPV immunization mandate. First, they argue that long term health risks of the vaccine are unknown, and that it is too expensive to mandate without more information. This is especially true, they argue, when a competitor like Cervarix is about to come to market and, potentially, lower the price of the immunization. Some believe that in creating the immunization requirement the government would be doing nothing more than conspiring with the drug companies to increase their profits. Perhaps the most significant opposition comes from those who are concerned that Gardasil would remove one of the costs of sexual intercourse and thus increase the possibility that young girls would participate in such immoral activity. Finally, many who oppose an immunization requirement believe that the issue should be left to the parents of the girls to be immunized. This essentially libertarian objection to any immunization requirement is based on the notion that we are freer and better off with less government control of our lives.

What is the appropriate policy for local school districts? For state government? For the federal government? Should HPV immunization be a requirement for attending school? Should it otherwise be required by law? Should the government be involved in funding these immunizations? For everyone, or just for those who cannot otherwise afford it? What opt-out provisions should be available to those parents who do not want their daughters to be immunized? Should the requirement of immunization be extended to boys as well as girls?

Most of the facts described here come from Kaiser Family Foundation, Fact Sheet—HPV Vaccine: Implementation and Financing Policy in the U.S. (February 2008), available (with a number of other extremely valuable public health fact sheets) at http://www.kff.org. An excellent survey of the arguments is available in Pauline Self, The HPV Vaccination: Necessary or Evil, 19 Hastings Women's L.J. 149 (2008). See also R. Skov, Examining Mandatory HPV Vaccination for All School–Aged Children, 62 Food Drug L.J. 805 (2007).

III. FORCED TREATMENT, ISOLATION AND QUARANTINE

One public health technique that has been employed since contagion was understood (and, perhaps paradoxically, before) is separating those who may be contagious from those who are to be protected. Those who are ill are generally said to be "isolated" from others, while those who have been exposed, but have not yet become ill (and who may never become ill) are said to be put in "quarantine" for the incubation period of the relevant disease. These techniques—which require a direct and severe limitation on the liberty of people who have violated no law—have been used to protect the community from a wide range of diseases, from plague to smallpox. Until the beginning of the twentieth century most quarantine was implemented through orders given by public health officials under statutes that gave them authority to act whenever they decided that the public health required it. Very little process, if any, was given to those very few patients who were quarantined or isolated, and the quarantine or isolation—which could be in the patient's house, in a hospital or in another institution of some sort—lasted until the one locked up was no longer a public health threat. In many states, the only way one quarantined or isolated could seek judicial relief was through a petition for a writ of habeas corpus.

While statutes authorizing quarantine and isolation were rarely invoked since the due process revolution of forty years ago, in states where the issue arose courts grafted Constitutional due process requirements on to the broad statutory grants of authority given public health agencies. In the 1980s a few states modernized and updated their quarantine statutes out of a concern that they would eventually be invoked to address the issue of HIV and AIDS, although, fortunately, they were never used for that purpose in the United States. Over the past decade the increase in drug resistant strains of tuberculosis has given rise to a new round of state revisions of quarantine and isolation statutes. One example of the new generation of statutes, enacted in 2000, follows.

TUBERCULOSIS CONTROL UNITS

Ohio Code §§ 339.80–89 (2008).

* * *

§ 339.80. Investigation of reported cases

When a county or district tuberculosis control unit receives a report * * * of a confirmed or suspected case of tuberculosis, the unit shall conduct an investigation that includes personal contact with the individual with tuberculosis. The investigation shall commence not later than three working days after the unit receives the report.

§ 339.81. Confidentiality of information, data, reports

Any information, data, and reports with respect to a case of tuberculosis that are furnished to, or procured by, a county or district tuberculosis control unit or the department of health shall be confidential and used only for statistical, scientific, and medical research for the purpose of controlling tuberculosis in this state. No physician, hospital, or other entity furnishing information, data, or reports pursuant to this chapter shall by reason of such furnishing be deemed to have violated any confidential relationship, be held to answer for willful betrayal of a professional confidence, or be held liable in damages to any person.

§ 339.82. Responsibilities of individual with active or communicable tuberculosis

Except as provided [in the section on spiritual treatment, below], all of the following apply to individuals with tuberculosis:

(A) (1) An individual who has been diagnosed as having active tuberculosis shall complete the entire tuberculosis treatment regimen prescribed for the individual by a physician. The regimen prescribed shall include a course of antituberculosis medication, recommendations for management of tuberculosis, and instructions for following contagion precautions to prevent the spread of tuberculosis.

(2) If an individual fails to take prescribed antituberculosis medication in accordance with division (A)(1) of this section, the county or district tuberculosis control unit shall establish a procedure under which the individual is required to be witnessed ingesting the antituberculosis medication by individuals designated by the unit. The individual shall take the medication in accordance with the procedure.

(B) An individual with communicable tuberculosis who is not hospitalized or otherwise confined shall not attend any public gathering or be in any public place that the county or district tuberculosis control unit determines cannot be maintained in a manner adequate to protect others from the spread of the disease. An individual with communicable tuberculosis who cannot be maintained outside of a hospital in a manner adequate to protect others from the spread of the disease shall submit to hospitalization and remain hospitalized.

(C) An individual with active tuberculosis who intends to travel or relocate shall notify the county or district tuberculosis control unit. The unit shall notify the Ohio department of health when an individual with active tuberculosis relocates. The department shall notify the tuberculosis control unit of the tuberculosis control district to which the individual intends to travel or relocate or the appropriate public health authority of the state to which the individual intends to travel or relocate.

§ 339.83. Notice to individual not in compliance

When a county or district tuberculosis control unit becomes aware that an individual with active or communicable tuberculosis is not in compliance with [this section], the unit shall inform the individual that [the law] requires compliance and that the unit may issue an * * * compelling the individual to comply.

§ 339.84. Order compelling compliance

If an individual fails to comply with [this Act], the county or district tuberculosis control unit may issue an order compelling the individual to comply.

§ 339.85. Injunction against violation of order

If an individual fails to comply with an order * * *, the county or district tuberculosis control unit may apply to the probate court of the appropriate county for an injunction prohibiting the individual from continuing to violate the unit's order. If the tuberculosis control unit believes that an individual's failure to comply with its order involves an immediate danger to the public health, the unit may request that the court issue an injunction without granting the individual an opportunity for a prior hearing or that the court hold an expedited hearing on the matter.

§ 339.86. Court order for detention of noncomplying individual

(A) If an individual fails to comply with an injunction issued * * *, the county or district tuberculosis control unit may request that the probate court of the appropriate county issue an order under which the unit is granted the authority to detain the individual in a hospital or other place to be examined or treated for tuberculosis. In the request, the unit shall provide the following information:

(1) The name of the individual;

(2) The purpose of making the request for detention;

(3) An individualized assessment that contains a description of the circumstances and behavior of the individual that constitutes the basis for making the request;

(4) A recommendation for the length of time that the individual should be detained;

(5) A recommendation of a hospital or other place to be used for the detention.

(B) The court may issue an order for detention for an initial period of not more than one hundred eighty days. At the end of the initial period of detention, the court shall review the case and may extend the order for subsequent periods of not more than ninety days. At the end of each subsequent period of detention, the court shall review the case. When the court receives satisfactory evidence that the individual subject to the order no longer has active tuberculosis, the court shall terminate the order for detention.

(C) An individual who has been detained under this section may provide the tuberculosis control unit with the names, addresses, and telephone numbers of relatives and friends to be notified of the detention, and the unit shall notify all or a reasonable number of those individuals. An individual who has been detained shall not be subject to forcible administration of antituberculosis medication. The individual may, at any time, submit a request to the tuberculosis control unit to be released from detention.

During any proceeding pertaining to an individual's detention or proposed detention, the individual has the right to be represented by counsel. If the individual is indigent, the individual may apply for court-appointed counsel. The court may appoint counsel for the individual if it determines that the individual is indigent.

§ 339.87. Emergency detention order

(A) When a tuberculosis control unit has reasonable grounds to believe that an individual who has, or is suspected of having, active tuberculosis poses a substantial danger to the health of other individuals, the tuberculosis control unit may issue an emergency detention order directing a sheriff or other law enforcement officer to remove the individual to a hospital or other place to be examined and treated for tuberculosis.

(B) Not later than the end of the third business day after detention of an individual under division (A) of this section, the tuberculosis control unit shall apply to the probate court of the county from which the individual was removed for a detention order * * *.

§ 339.88. Expenses of detention

The expenses incurred for detention * * * shall be paid by the individual detained or if the individual is indigent, by the board of county commissioners of the county from which the individual was removed. * * *

§ 339.89. Spiritual treatment in lieu of medical treatment

[The preceding sections] do not require a person to undergo testing, medical treatment, or detention in a hospital or other place for treatment if the person, or, in the case of a child, the child's parents, rely exclusively on spiritual treatment through prayer, in lieu of medical treatment, in accordance with a recognized, religious method of healing. The person may be quarantined or otherwise safely isolated in the home or another place that is suitable to the health of the person and has been approved by the tuberculosis control unit as a place that provides appropriate protection to other persons and the community.

Notes and Questions

1. Does the Ohio law properly balance the public health interest of the community and the personal civil liberties of those who might have tuberculosis? Is the statute legally sound? Is it medically sound—i.e., is it likely to actually lead to the delivery of appropriate medical care to those who have tuberculosis but refuse treatment? Might the prospect of the application of the statute drive some potential patients underground? What would be the public health consequences if that were to happen?

2. What procedures are Constitutionally required before a person with a communicable disease can be forced to accept treatment, or be isolated or quarantined? Would the processes be different for those who are merely required to undergo treatment, those who are isolated in their own homes, those who are quarantined in a hospital, and those who are locked up in a jail for the criminal offense of failing to comply with a public health order? For each attribute of the quarantine and isolation process listed below, apply the Mathews v. Eldridge, 424 U.S. 319, 96 S.Ct. 893, 47 L.Ed.2d 18 (1976), balancing test and evaluate (1) the importance of the individual's interest (here, in being free of unwanted treatment, isolation or quarantine), (2) the risk that there will be an erroneous determination unless the additional procedure is afforded, and (3) the public interest in forgoing that procedure (including the interest in quick and efficient resolution of the matter).

3. What kind of notice should be required before an order of isolation or quarantine is issued? Given the liberty interest that is at stake, is it ever appropriate to issue an order of isolation or quarantine without giving the respondent an opportunity to appear? Given the public health interest that is at stake, is it necessary to notify the respondent before an order is issued? Is it always necessary to have a pre-isolation or pre-quarantine hearing, or is a hearing shortly after the order is implemented sufficient?

If a hearing is required before a person is isolated or quarantined, what rights must be afforded the respondent at such a hearing? Must it be before a judge, or may a public health officer issue the order? Is the respondent entitled to counsel? Is the state obliged to provide counsel if the respondent cannot afford to hire one? Is the respondent entitled to present evidence? Must she be able to subpoena witnesses? If she needs expert medical testimony (that she poses no public health danger, for example) but she is indigent, must the state pay for her expert witness? May the respondent be required to testify against herself?

Who bears what burden of proof at the hearing? If the state initially bears the burden of proof, must it prove each element necessary to obtain an order by a preponderance of the evidence (this is a civil case, after all), by clear and convincing evidence (this might be analogous to a civil commitment proceeding, where this standard is required under Addington v. Texas, 441 U.S. 418, 99 S.Ct. 1804, 60 L.Ed.2d 323 (1979)), or beyond a reasonable doubt (this does result in a loss of liberty, much like a criminal case)? After the state meets its initial burden, may the burden be shifted to the respondent to show that he is no longer subject to isolation or quarantine before he can be released?

Must there be an opportunity for appeal? Must a patient who, after being in quarantine, suddenly is willing to comply with a treatment regimen, be able to seek review of his isolation or quarantine? Must the state regularly prove that continuing quarantine and isolation is appropriate? Should isolation and quarantine orders automatically expire after a certain amount of time? How long? How often should there be review of those who have been isolated or quarantined?

Must the medical and legal proceedings be kept confidential? As a matter of common law? Under the HIPAA privacy regulations? Does this mean that the hearing must be closed to the public and the record sealed? Can the information still be used for purposes of contact tracing—i.e. to find others who may have contacted the disease from the respondent? For particular other purposes? What are they?

Different states give a very wide range of different answers to almost all of these questions. Because quarantine and isolation are so infrequently imposed, there has been little litigation to determine the process that are Constitutionally required. Of course, the United States Constitution is not the only source of process in these cases. Process will also be determined by state constitutions, which may impose greater procedural requirements than the United States Constitution, state statutes, and state rules (including rules of procedure and rules of evidence). For a good account of the underlying social issue, see Sheila Rothman, Living in the Shadow of Death: Tuberculosis and the Social Experience of Illness in American History (1994). See also Felice Batlan, Law in the Time of Cholera: Disease, State Power, and Quarantines of the Past and Future, 80 Temp. L. Rev. 53 (2007), Rosemary Reilly, Combating the Tuberculosis Epidemic: The Legality of Coercive Treatment Measures, 27 Colum. J. L. & Soc. Prob. 101 (1993), and Lawrence Gostin, The Resurgent Tuberculosis Epidemic in the Era of AIDS, 54 Md. L. Rev. 1 (1995).

4.　Since 9/11 there has been a substantially increased fear of the public health calamity that could be a consequence of bioterrorism. Most states have passed legislation that allows for the declaration of a health emergency and the provision of special emergency powers following such an event. There are two model acts that have formed the basis of much of this state legislation, the Turning Point Public Health Statute Modernization National Collaborative's

Model State Public Health Act, and the Model State Emergency Health Powers Act.

In the time of a national public health emergency brought on by bioterrorism, should the law permit the state to take extraordinary actions to quarantine and isolate its citizens, limit the individual process that each one would be due before such quarantine or isolation is accomplished, seize and operate private health facilities and supplies, require vaccination and forcibly require treatment? If such government authority is appropriate, what limitations ought to be placed on it? In any case, does it make sense for these emergency processes to be implemented on a state by state basis? Does practical public health policy suggest that this should be an issue for the federal government rather than the state? Does the Constitution provide the federal government any authority over public health issues like this, or, as a matter of law, must it be left to the states?

There is a great deal that has been written about bioterrorism and its legal consequences. A wonderful debate over the role for the government in such an emergency, and the fear the government could generate (and has generated, some believe) over such an eventuality, see Lawrence O. Gostin, The Model State Emergency Health Powers Act: Public Health and Civil Liberties in a Time of Terrorism, 13 Health Matrix 3 (2003), and George J. Annas, Blinded by Bioterrorism: Public Health and Liberty in the 21st Century, 13 Health Matrix 33 (2003). For a strong critique of the influential Model State Emergency Public Health Act, see Ken Wing, Policy Choices and Model Acts: Preparing for the Next Public Health Emergency, 13 Health Matrix 71 (2003), Wendy Parmet, Quarantine Redux: Bioterrorism, AIDS and the Curtailment of Individual Liberty in the Name of Public Health, 13 Health Matrix 85 (2003), and David Reich, Modernizing Local Responses to Public Health Emergencies: Bioterrorism, Epidemics and the Model State Emergency Health Powers Act, 19 J. Contemp. Health L. & Pol. 379 (2003). For another view, see Lori L. Buchsbaum, The U.S. Public Health Response to Bioterrorism: Need for a Stronger Legislative Approach, 7 Mich. St. J. Med. & Law 1 (2007). For an international approach, see David Fidler, Public Health and International Law: Bioterrorism, Public Health and International Law, 3 Chi. J. Int. L. 7 (2002).

Problem: Public Health Law, Immigration Law and Infectious Disease

You are a public health official who has been appointed as chief of a tuberculosis control unit in one county in Ohio. You have learned that Cristina Gonzalez, a ten year old child who lives with her parents, is now being treated for an active and highly communicable form of tuberculosis. Because there is no other apparent source of the disease, the child's pediatrician has reported that she believes that the child may have contracted the disease from her uncle, Jesus Chavez, who recently moved in with Cristina's family after leaving an area with a particularly high rate of tuberculosis infection. Cristina told the pediatrician that her uncle had a very heavy cough and that he sometimes had some trouble breathing when he walked up the stairs.

Cristina's parents have told you that Mr. Chavez does not have proper immigration documents, and that he is very frightened about meeting with any authorities. He once sought treatment at the local public hospital, where he was denied care and treated very rudely; he would never go back, under any circumstances. The Gonzalezes also told you that any attempt to find Mr. Chavez in the Gonzalez home would force him to move to another relative's house, and that he would not agree to any treatment that is imposed by the authorities. The

Gonzalezes have suggested to the public health authorities that they should not worry about the case, because Mr. Chavez is planning to move back to Honduras in the next few months anyway.

What can you do under the Ohio statute? What should you do?

*

Index

References are to Pages

825

†